FIFTH EDITION

ENVIRONMENTAL ETHICS

Readings in Theory and Application

LOUIS P. POJMAN
Late of the United States Military Academy, West Point

PAUL POJMAN
Towson University

WADSWORTH
CENGAGE Learning™

Australia • Brazil • Japan • Korea • Mexico • Singapore • Spain • United Kingdom • United States

WADSWORTH
CENGAGE Learning™

Environmental Ethics:
Readings in Theory and Application,
Fifth Edition
Louis P. Pojman, Paul Pojman

Philosophy Editor: Worth Hawes

Assistant Editor: Barbara Hillaker

Editorial Assistant: Patrick Stockstill

Technology Project Manager: Julie Aguilar

Marketing Manager: Christina Shea

Marketing Assistant: Mary Anne Payumo

Marketing Communications Manager:
  Stacey Purviance

Creative Director: Rob Hugel

Executive Art Director: Maria Epes

Print Buyer: Nora Massuda

Permissions Editor: Bob Kauser

Production Service: Ruth Cottrell

Text Designer: Lisa Henry

Copy Editor: Ruth Cottrell

Cover Designer: Yvo Riezebos Design/
  Hatty Lee

Cover Image: Hite Marina, Lake Powell,
  Utah/Getty Images

Compositor: International Typesetting
  and Composition

For product information and technology assistance, contact us at
Cengage Learning Customer & Sales Support, 1-800-354-9706
For permission to use material from this text or product,
submit all requests online at **cengage.com/permissions**
Further permissions questions can be emailed to
permissionrequest@cengage.com

Library of Congress Control Number: 2007923271

ISBN-13: 978-0-495-09503-3

ISBN-10: 0-495-09503-6

Wadsworth
10 Davis Drive
Belmont, CA 94002-3098
USA

Cengage Learning is a leading provider of customized learning solutions with office locations around the globe, including Singapore, the United Kingdom, Australia, Mexico, Brazil, and Japan. Locate your local office at: **international.cengage.com/region**

Cengage Learning products are represented in Canada by Nelson Education, Ltd.

For your course and learning solutions, visit **academic.cengage.com**

Purchase any of our products at your local college store or at our preferred online store **www.ichapters.com**

Printed in Canada
3 4 5 6 7 11 10 09

In Memory of Louis Pojman

CONTENTS

14 From Dysfunctional to Sustainable Society 701

LOUIS PAUL POJMAN, my father, died on October 15, 2005, of liver cancer. My father was the single greatest influence on my life in regard to philosophy and environmental thinking and living. I was thus honored when he asked me to continue this anthology. He was at the cutting edge of his generation in regard to environmental thinking, and it is thus no accident that this book was one of the first environmental philosophy textbooks published. He was an avid hiker, rode his bike to work (even in the rain and snow), kept the heat and air conditioning down or off, and was a vegetarian. He saw environmentalism as a natural outcome of enlightened thinking and one of the most important challenges for philosophers today. That is, green consciousness is the natural response of reason, of the entire tradition of Western philosophy, to living in the twenty-first century's industrialized culture. Over his desk, as he wrote and edited this and many other books and articles, was Gandhi's quotation: "Live simply so others may simply live." This text, with its attempt at balanced perspectives, is an outgrowth of his passion that the world could become a better place through reason. At the very least, it isn't going to become a better place any other way.

Environmental philosophy is a peculiar field in that it is grounded in the oldest academic tradition (philosophy), as well as one of the youngest (environmental thinking). To make matters more difficult, environmental thinking is spread out over fields as diverse as biology, economics, chemistry, geology, and political theory to name a few. This text is divided into two sections, "Theory" (Part One) and "Practice" (Part Two). It would be simple if the theory section contained topics that were independent of time and place, concerns of universal importance to all peoples. In pure ethics, indeed, this is what theory might mean. Inasmuch as this is a text in applied ethics, however, even the theory has ground in practice. Thus, although our moral questions about, for instance, other animals, can be asked theoretically (Do they have consciousness? Are they worthy of moral treatment and rights? etc.), there is also the immediate practical question of "Should we eat them?" or "Should we mass slaughter them in factory farms?" Nonetheless, the question of animal rights is more of a theoretical question than, say, the issues of genetically modified foods or environmental racism—issues clearly grounded in human practice.

I see the theory side as those issues that change slowly, debates that may develop over time with new ideas but not new facts. On the practice side, the issues change with new developments, with new facts. A cataclysmic drop in human population (due to war, mass famine, or disease, etc.) would make irrelevant Garret Hardin's "Lifeboat Ethics," but the remaining humans would still have to consider their relationship to nature. It is no surprise then that it is the practice side that must be updated more frequently, and indeed significant changes have been made in this section of the book. I have removed eleven articles and added twelve since the fourth edition, with most of the changes in fields that are changing rapidly.

Two articles on Kant and environmental ethics have been added in the theory section of the book. The first, by Martin Schönfeld, looks at the relevance of Kant's Categorical Imperative to the critical concept of sustainability. The second, by Holly Wilson, re-examines Kant's infamous distinction between humans and animals, arguing that Kant is much friendlier to a green ethics than is normally supposed. In the first chapter, Karen Warren's article, "The Power and Promise of Ecological Feminism," offers a previously lacking ecofeminist perspective.

In the practice section, several articles had become out of date (for instance the ones on population and climate change), and growing areas of the field needed to be more adequately represented (food ethics and environmental justice). The chapters have thus been re-structured to reflect these needed changes, with some articles being removed and ten articles added.

Chapter 7 is now called "Population and Consumption" to reflect the current understanding that population and consumption should be examined in relation to one another. A recent article, "The State of Consumption Today," has replaced an outdated article on China's baby budget.

Chapter 8 has been renamed "Food Ethics," with added articles on genetically modified foods as well as on the environmental impact of meat eating.

Chapter 10, "Pesticides," now includes an article on the role of DDT in combating malaria (an earlier article on the Alar scare was removed, being somewhat dated).

Chapter 11 has been renamed "Climate Change," and all the articles are new. This is perhaps the fastest changing field in environmental policy. The first article examines the current situation and is fact orientated, whereas the second article is a comprehensive philosophical examination by Stephan Gardiner of the ethical issues facing us in regard to climate change.

Chapter 13 has been renamed "Environmental Justice." Robert Bullard's seminal article, "Overcoming Racism in Environmental Decision Making," is included, and Laura Westra's article, "Environmental Risks," has been moved to this chapter.

Chapter 14 has been expanded to include Michael Martin's analysis of ecosabotage, in "Ecosabotage and Civil Disobedience."

Many of the introductions to sections, chapters, and individual articles have also been updated.

I wish to thank the reviewers who made suggestions for this edition: Daniel W. Conway, Penn State University; Karánn Curland, Austin College; Mark Sheldon, Northwestern University; Kenneth Shockley, SUNY at Buffalo; and Kevin Sweeney, University of Tampa.

Of course I wish to thank Louis Pojman. Also Trudy Pojman and the Wadsworth editors, Worth Hawes and Barbara Hillaker, who have guided me through this process, and Ruth Cottrell who did the copyediting and handled the production. I especially wish to thank Evelyn Wright for both her support and her help, especially with the chapters on climate change and economics. I also wish to thank numerous students for their inspiration, insight, conversations, and suggestions.

Paul Pojman
Towson University, 2006

ENVIRONMENTAL ETHICS
Readings in Theory and Application

ENVIRONMENTAL ETHICS, as presented in this text, concerns our religions, our economies, our politics, our future on this planet, and our health. It includes problems of race, class, gender, and globalization. It is not separate from our conception of what it means to be human, of our relationship to nature and technology. It is an interdisciplinary field that is of vital concern to us all. This introduction aims to do two things: first, place environmental thinking within an historical context, and second, to review the following book.

Human beings have lived on Earth for about 100,000 years, a very short time in relation to the age of the universe (15 billion years) or even to the life of our planet (4.6 billion years). Humans started domesticating animals and growing crops about 10,000 years ago. If we compacted the history of Earth into a movie lasting 1 year, running 146 years per second, life would not appear until March, multicellular organisms not until November, dinosaurs not until December 13 (lasting until the 26th), mammals not until December 15, *Homo sapiens* (our species) not until 11 minutes to midnight on December 25, and civilization not until 1 minute to midnight on December 31. Yet in a very short time, since the Industrial Revolution began 250 years ago—humans, a mere .000002% of Earth's life—have become capable of seriously altering the entire biosphere.

With the Industrial Revolution, a vast acceleration of forest cutting, mining, land development, and fishing began. Industrialized societies saw forests disappearing to fuel the factories, mass migrations of people moving to cities to work in factories, and clouds of pollution hanging over the cities. Many voices lamented this, including most notably Henry David Thoreau (who published *Walden* in 1848), and John Muir (who started the Sierra Club in 1892). Their concerns were echoed in poetry and novels, by unionizers and workplace reformers, as well as by other disparate thinkers and movements. Further complicating matters was the increasing exploitation of newly colonized or conquered societies. The environment was turned into a site of economic competition between the various industrialized nations, continuing up through the twentieth century.

The early twentieth century saw the industrialized nations in the midst of war and economic depression, leaving little time for ideas of environmental awareness. It is notable that the folk singer Woody Guthrie, arguably one of the most passionate voices for social reform the United States has ever heard, saw the environment simply as a source of economics. Dam up the rivers, cut down the forests, just give people jobs.

Post World War II, with the economy in the United Sates booming, people finally had a chance to examine where hundreds of years of unrestrained economic development had left us. Aldo Leopold published *A Sand County Almanac* in 1949, arguing for the need to extend our ethical sensibilities beyond the human to include nature. Then in 1962, Rachel Carson's book *Silent Spring,* documenting the poisoning of the environment with DDT, achieved national attention. DDT was banned and the environmental movement was in a sense born.

Since the early 1960s the environmental movement has changed the world. It is arguably one of the most successful social movements in human history. Of course some may argue that this success has been harmful to humans (especially to economic development), and others may argue that the success is too little too late, but nonetheless it has changed the consciousness and the laws in those places where it has taken root. Our children are being taught recycling in schools, environmental science and studies programs abound at colleges and universities, numerous state and federal governmental agencies have been formed, organic food is available in grocery stores (going from nonexistent, to small time, to one of the most profitable sectors of the food industry), and thousands of laws regulate pollution and development. Undeveloped land cannot be developed without an environmental impact study. Endangered species are protected under law, factories and power plants are regulated, streams are sampled, new chemicals are tested, and in every sector of human interaction with the environment there has been at least discussion if not legislation. No one, not even polluting businesses or apparently anti-environment politicians, can get away without paying lip service to environmentalism. Today who can say, "I don't care about the environment"? The line has to be, "We really do care about the environment—but our plan is safe," whether the statement is true or not. Now, some may feel that all this is great, but it is not nearly enough, and they may be correct. But, considering the environmental movement is only about 50 years old, we have come a long way.

In this work we consider readings in both environmental theory and practice. In Part One, "Theory," we focus on the causes of our environmental problems.

Chapter 1 is introductory, looking at the historical roots of our environmental crisis and our attempts to philosophically ground environmental thought.

Next, in Chapter 2 we examine rival theories on the locus of intrinsic value, especially in regard to the wider animal kingdom. What makes something valuable or morally considerable? Is it being human or rationally self-conscious, as Kant and most Western "anthropocentric" philosophers have held, or is it *sentience,* the ability to have experiences and, specifically, to suffer? What are our duties to animals, who are sentient, but (for the most part) not rationally self-conscious?

In Chapter 3 we go beyond rationality and sentience and inquire whether nature itself has intrinsic value. Do we need a broader environmental ethic that incorporates nature as a good in itself? Several theories are treated here: biocentric ethics, ecocentric ethics, and deep ecology.

In Chapter 4 we examine the value of endangered species, the wilderness, and natural objects and consider the moral, aesthetic, and institutional implications of these objects (e.g., granting trees and ecosystems legal rights).

In Chapter 5 we go beyond Western horizons and view environmental ethics through non-Western eyes and theories. Our readings present viewpoints from India, Ceylon, the Arab world, and Nigeria.

In Chapter 6 we take up the difficult philosophical issue of responsibility to future generations. Do we have responsibilities to those not yet born, and, if so, on what basis? Most moral theory holds that obligations hold only toward concrete individuals, so how can we have duties to nonexistent entities?

In Part Two, "Practice," we turn to practical concerns. First we discuss population and consumption in Chapter 7. The industrialized parts of the world tend to have a far lower population growth rate than the less industrialized sections, but they also consume and pollute at far higher rates. Clearly there are limits to how many people the planet can hold, but what that number is, and what we should do about it, are controversial. Similarly, there are clear limits to consumption, and clearly the industrialized world is already consuming at rates that are unsustainable. Furthermore, countries like China and India (the two most populous countries, although with radically different birthrates) are increasing their industrialization and consumption.

In Chapter 8, we look at food. What are the responsibilities of the wealthy to feed the poor, even if the poor are having children at rates that appear to be unsustainable? Are genetically modified foods the answer to world food shortages, or are they tools for corporations to control world food supply and ultimately dangerous for humans and our environment? Does eating mass-produced meat place an undue burden on the environment?

In Chapters 9, 10, and 11 we look at pollution (focusing on pesticides and air) and especially climate change, arguably one of the hottest topics this year.

In Chapter 12 we examine the relationship between economics and the environment. Can the entire panoply of our value assessments be reduced to economic cost–benefit analysis? Is the classical free-market view of economics an adequate guide for protecting the environment? Or, do we need a new more socialist or nature-centered approach?

In Chapter 13 we consider the issue of environmental justice, including the relations of rich nations to poor ones and the relevance of this difference to environmental concerns.

In the last chapter, we look at some practical ways we can work to maintain a sustainable, ecologically responsible society. For instance, what should we do about the powerful tool of advertising, which helps fuel the consumer society, a society that is environmentally harmful? Should we de-emphasize automobile transport and instead support mass transport and bicycle use? How can we get beyond a throwaway, nationalistic society to a recycling, sustainable global society?

This text is necessarily limited; the field is enormous. And this text represents only one part of environmental philosophy: learning. The thinking and speaking are up to us.

We are discussing no small matter, but how we ought to live.

SOCRATES *in Plato's Republic*

WHAT IS IT TO BE a moral person? What is the nature of morality, and why do we need it? What is the good, and how will I know it? Are moral principles absolute or simply relative to social groups or individual decision? Is it in my interest to be moral? Is it sometimes in my best interest to act immorally? What is the relationship between morality and religion? What is the relationship between morality and law? What is the relationship between morality and etiquette?

These are some of the questions that we will be examining in this chapter. We want to know how we should live.

The terms *moral* and *ethics* come from Latin and Greek, respectively (*mores* and *ethos*), deriving their meaning from the idea of custom. Although philosophers sometimes distinguish these terms—*morality* referring to the customs, principles, and practices of a people or culture, and *ethics* referring to the whole domain of morality and moral philosophy—I shall use them interchangeably in this book, using the context to make any differences clear.

Moral philosophy refers to the systematic endeavor to understand moral concepts and justify moral principles and theories. It undertakes to analyze such concepts as "right," "wrong," "permissible," "ought," "good," and "evil" in their moral contexts. Moral philosophy seeks to establish principles of right behavior that may serve as action guides for individuals and groups. It investigates which values and virtues are paramount to the worthwhile life or society. It builds and scrutinizes arguments in ethical theories, and it seeks to discover valid principles (e.g., "Never kill innocent human beings") and the relationship between those principles (e.g., "Does saving a life in some situations constitute a valid reason for breaking a promise?").

MORALITY AS COMPARED WITH OTHER NORMATIVE SUBJECTS

Moral precepts are concerned with norms—not with what is but with what *ought* to be. How should I live my life? What is the right thing to do in this situation? Should one always tell the truth? Do I have a duty to report a student whom I have seen cheating in class or a co-worker whom I have seen stealing office supplies? Should I tell my friend that his spouse is having an affair? Ought a woman ever to have an abortion? Should we permit the cloning of human beings? Morality has a distinct action guiding or *normative* aspect,[1] an aspect it shares with other practical institutions, such as religion, law, and etiquette.

Moral behavior, as defined by a given religion, is often held to be essential to the practice of that religion. But neither the practices nor precepts of morality should be identified with religion. The practice of morality need not be motivated by religious considerations. And moral precepts need not be grounded in revelation or divine authority—as religious teachings invariably are. The most salient characteristic of ethics—by which I mean both philosophical morality (or morality, as I will simply refer to it) and moral philosophy—is that it is grounded in reason and human experience.

To use a spatial metaphor, secular ethics is horizontal, omitting a vertical or transcendental dimension. Religious ethics has a vertical dimension, being grounded in revelation or divine authority, though generally using reason to supplement or complement revelation. These two differing orientations will often generate different moral principles and standards of evaluation, but they need not. Some versions of religious ethics that posit God's revelation of the moral law in nature or conscience hold that reason can discover what is right or wrong even apart from divine revelation.

Morality is also closely related to law, and some people equate the two practices. Many laws are instituted to promote well-being (i.e., resolve conflicts of interest and/or promote social harmony), just as morality does, but ethics may judge that some laws are immoral without denying that they are valid laws. For example, laws may permit slavery or irrelevant discrimination against people on the basis of race or sex. An antiabortion advocate may believe that the laws permitting abortion are immoral.

In the television series *Ethics in America* (PBS, 1989), James Neal, a trial lawyer, was asked what he would do if he discovered that his client had committed a murder for which another man had been convicted and would soon be executed. Mr. Neal said that he had a legal obligation to keep this information confidential and that if he divulged it, he would be disbarred. It is arguable that he has a moral obligation that overrides his legal obligation and that demands he take action to protect the innocent man from being executed.

Furthermore, there are some aspects of morality that are not covered by law. For example, it is generally agreed that lying is usually immoral, but there is no general law against it (except under special conditions, such as in cases of perjury or falsifying income tax returns). Sometimes college newspapers publish advertisements for "research assistance," where it is known in advance that the companies will aid and abet plagiarism. The publishing of such research paper ads is legal, but it is doubtful whether it is morally correct. In 1963, 39 people in Queens, New York, watched from their apartments for some forty-five minutes as a man beat and stabbed to death a woman, Kitty Genovese, and did nothing to intervene, not even call the police. These people broke no law, but they were very likely morally culpable for not calling the police.

There is one other major difference between law and morality. In 1351, King Edward of England promulgated a law against treason that made it a crime merely to think homicidal thoughts about the king. But, alas, the law could not be enforced, for no tribunal can search the heart and fathom the intentions of the mind. It is true that *intention*, such as malice aforethought, plays a role in the legal process in determining the legal character of the act, once the act has been committed. But preemptive punishment for people presumed to have bad intentions is illegal. If malicious intentions (called in law *mens rea*) were criminally illegal, would we not all deserve imprisonment? Even if it were possible to detect intentions, when should the punishment be administered? As soon as the subject has the intention? But how do we know that he will not change his mind? Furthermore, is there not a continuum between imagining some harm to X, wishing a harm to X, desiring a harm to X, and intending a harm to X?

Although it is impractical to have laws against bad intentions, these intentions are still bad, still morally wrong. Suppose I plan to push Uncle Charlie off a 1000-foot cliff when we next hike together in order to inherit his wealth but never have a chance to do it (e.g., Uncle Charlie breaks his leg and forswears hiking). Although I have not committed a crime, I have committed a moral wrong. Law generally aims at setting an important but minimal framework in a society of plural values.

Finally, law differs from morality in that there are physical and financial sanctions (e.g., imprisonment and fines) enforcing the law but only the sanctions of conscience and reputation enforcing morality.

Morality also differs from etiquette, which concerns form and style rather than the essence of social existence. Etiquette determines what is polite behavior rather than what is right behavior in a deeper sense. It represents society's decisions about how we are to dress, greet one another, eat, celebrate festivals, dispose of the dead, express gratitude and appreciation, and, in general carry out social transactions. Whether we greet each other with a handshake, a bow, a hug, or a kiss on the cheek will differ in different social systems; none of these rituals has any moral superiority. People in England hold their forks in their left hands when they eat, whereas people in other countries hold them in their right hands or in whichever hand a person feels like holding them; people in India typically eat without forks at all, using their right hands for conveying food from their plates to their mouths.

At the same time, it can be immoral to disregard or flout etiquette. Whether to shake hands when greeting a person for the first time or put one's hands together and forward as one bows, as people in India do, is a matter of cultural decision; but once the custom is adopted, the practice takes on the importance of a moral rule, subsumed under the wider principle of Show Respect to People. Similarly, there is no moral necessity of wearing clothes, but many cultures have adopted the custom partly for warmth and partly out of social control of sexuality. But there is nothing wrong with nudists who decide to live together naked in nudist colonies. But, it may well be the case that people running nude in classrooms, stores, and along the road would constitute offensive, or morally insensitive, behavior. Recently, there was a scandal on the beaches of South India where American tourists swam in bikinis, shocking the more modest Indians. There was nothing immoral in itself about wearing bikinis, but given the cultural context, the Americans, in willfully violating etiquette, were guilty of moral impropriety.

Law, etiquette, and religion are all important institutions, but each has limitations. The limitation of the law is that you can't have a law against every social malady nor can you enforce every desirable rule. The limitation of etiquette is that it doesn't get to the heart of what is of vital importance for personal and social existence. Whether or not one eats with one's fingers pales in significance compared with the importance of being honest or trustworthy or just. Etiquette is a cultural invention, but morality claims to be a discovery.

TABLE 1 The Relationship Between Ethics, Religion, Etiquette, and Law

Subject	Normative Disjuncts	Sanctions
Ethics	Right, wrong, or permissible—as defined by conscience or reason	Conscience; Praise and blame; Reputation
Religion	Right, wrong (sin), or permissible—as defined by religious authority	Conscience: Eternal; Reward and punishment caused by a supernatural agent or force
Law	Legal and illegal—as defined by a judicial body	Punishments determined by the legislative body
Etiquette	Proper and improper—as defined by culture	Social disapprobation and approbation

The limitation of the religious injunction is that it rests on authority, and we are not always sure of or in agreement about the credentials of the authority, nor on how the authority would rule in ambiguous or new cases. Since religion is not founded on reason but on revelation, you cannot use reason to convince someone who does not share your religious views that your view is the right one. I hasten to add that, when moral differences are caused by fundamental moral principles, it is unlikely that philosophical reasoning will settle the matter. Often, however, our moral differences turn out to be rooted in worldviews, not moral principles. For example, whether or not you believe in killing animals may hinge on your metaphysical view on animals and humans. If you do not believe animals experience pain, you probably have little reason not to eat them.

Table 1 may characterize the relationship between ethics, religion, etiquette, and law.

In summary, morality distinguishes itself from law and etiquette by going deeper into the essence of rational existence. It distinguishes itself from religion in that it seeks reasons, rather than authority, to justify its principles. The central purpose of moral philosophy is to secure valid principles of conduct and values that can be instrumental in guiding human actions and producing good character. As such, it is the most important activity known to humans, because it has to do with how we are to live.

NOTE

1. The term *normative* means seeking to make certain types of behavior a norm or a standard in society. *Webster's Collegiate Dictionary* defines it as "of, relating or conforming to, or prescribing norms or standards."

STUDY QUESTIONS

1. Illustrate the difference between ethics, law, religion, and etiquette. How are these concepts related? Do you think any one of law, religion, or etiquette is more important than morality in guiding human action? Explain your answer.
2. Based on what you know now, do you think that environmental concerns force us to radically revise our understanding of morality, to merely extend it, or neither?

✑ FOR FURTHER READING

Frankena, William. *Ethics* (Englewood Cliffs, NJ: Prentice-Hall, 1973).

Kagan, Shelly. *Normative Ethics* (Boulder, CO: Westview Press, 1997).

Mackie, J. L. *Ethics: Inventing Right and Wrong* (New York: Penguin, 1977).

Pojman, Louis. *Ethics: Discovering Right and Wrong*, 3rd ed. (Belmont, CA: Wadsworth, 1989).

Pojman, Louis, ed., *Ethical Theory*, 4th ed. (Belmont, CA: Wadsworth, 2002).

Rachels, James. *Elements of Moral Philosophy* (New York: McGraw-Hill, 1993).

Singer, Peter. *The Expanding Circle: Ethics and Sociobiology* (Oxford: Oxford University Press, 1983).

Taylor, Richard. *Good and Evil* (Buffalo, NY: Prometheus, 1970).

Williams, Bernard. *Morality* (New York: Harper, 1972).

Wilson, James Q. *The Moral Sense* (New York: Free Press, 1993).

Theory

C H A P T E R   O N E

Perspectives

IN 1967 LYNN WHITE, professor of history at the University of California at Los Angeles, wrote an article contending that our current ecological crisis was primarily due to "the orthodox Christian arrogance towards nature." This arrogance, he argued, was rooted in a domineering, anthropocentric attitude that could be traced back to Genesis (reprinted as our first reading), especially Chapter 1:28, "God blessed [Adam and Eve], saying to them, 'Be fruitful and multiply, fill the earth and conquer it. Be masters of [*dominate*] the fish of the sea, the birds of the heaven and all living animals on earth.'" The Hebrew word for 'have dominion' or 'be masters of' in Genesis 1:26, 28 is the verb *rada*. It is linked with man's being made in the image of God. Just as God has dominion over the whole universe, including man, so man has god-like dominion over the natural world. White contrasted the pagan panpsychicism (i.e., seeing spirits in natural objects) with the anthropocentricism of Christianity. In the pagan worldview, animals, trees, and streams are seen as endowed with the sacred, so it is evil to harm them without good cause and after going through proper rituals. Sometimes forgiveness is asked from the animal. In the Christian worldview, according to White, "Man shares, in great measure, God's transcendence of nature.... By destroying pagan animism, Christianity made it possible to exploit nature in a mood of indifference to the feelings of natural objects."

At the end of his article, White, himself a Christian, recommended that Christians follow the medieval monk St. Francis of Assisi (1181–1226), who preached to the birds and fellowshipped with the foxes, whose view of "nature and man rested on a unique sort of panpsychicism of all things animate and inanimate, designed for the glorification of their transcendent Creator." By embracing this more holistic and symbiotic view of the relation of humanity to nature, we might be better armed to save our world.

Some Christians were awakened by his essay and resolved to take more notice of a theology of nature. Others, like Patrick Dobel in our fourth reading, agreed that there was much insight in White's analysis but that the biblical picture was not as crudely domineering as White claimed. Human beings were to serve as *stewards* of Earth, which was God's gift for our careful use. Still others, like sociologist Lewis

Moncrief in our third reading, argued that White's analysis was too simple and that a complex web of forces—including democracy, technology, urbanization, and an aggressive attitude toward nature—accounted for the ecological mess in which we now find ourselves. Karen Warren examines the possibility of ecofeminism providing an alternative, nonoppressive, ethic toward nature. Finally, Martin Schönfeld argues that environmental ethics is in need of better philosophical grounding, and that inasmuch as sustainability is a goal of environmental thinking, such grounding can be found in Kant's Categorical Imperative.

At this point let us pause to consider the central questions that are raised in this theoretical part of our work.

1. What is the correct attitude toward nature? Should we regard nature as spiritually empowered? As inherently valuable or only instrumentally valuable? As god indwelt or as simply a wild force to be subdued?

2. How can we *know* which attitude is the correct one? Suppose we conclude that it were better for us all if almost everyone believed in animism (the view that spirits indwell natural objects), but concluded that animism was in fact false? Should we try to get ourselves to believe something we have no evidence for simply to save ourselves and nature? What if we discover that the best way to save the environment is to draw up a new myth or invent a new religion (or change the one we believe in order to get the same result). Should we do it?

3. Can an anthropocentric philosophy, which values only humans, ever be sufficient to save the environment? Is enlightened self-interest adequate to resolve our environmental needs?

4. What is our obligation to animals, especially higher animals? Should we be as concerned about their welfare as about human welfare? Do animals have rights—not to be unnecessarily harmed, experimented on, hunted, or eaten?

5. What is our obligation for preserving other species? Is there a sacred holism that suffers as species are forever destroyed? Is there a hierarchy of being that is preserved in the variety of species?

6. What is our obligation to future and distant people with regard to the environment? Do future people have rights so that we must be frugal (and even sacrifice) with regard to natural resources and prevent large-scale pollution? Or is the notion of rights an unwarranted moral view? Or do we at most have duties to the succeeding generation—to leave it enough resources to live on?

These are some of the central questions that we will examine in this part of this work. We will represent divergent points of view with the *best* arguments available. Your own position cannot be secure until you have critically considered all sides of an issue. And unless you have undermined the best case your opponent can make, you can never be sure it has been defeated. Philosophy is the quest for truth and the best position that reason can arrive at. Use your reason. The world needs your judgment!

We turn now to our first reading from the Book of Genesis in the Hebrew Bible (Old Testament), followed by Lynn White's important essay on the historical roots of our ecological crisis.

1   Genesis 1–3

According to ancient Hebrew tradition, Moses (ca. 1450 BCE) wrote this account of the creation of the heavens, Earth, and all that dwells therein. While scholars dispute the authorship and date, they agree that it is a very old account and sets forth the Hebrew-Christian view of a divine Creator who creates the world as good and man and woman in his own image. Scholars often refer to the two accounts of the creation as the E and J accounts, since in the first God is referred to as Elohim and in the second as Yahweh (or Jehovah). These chapters form the basis for the Western religious view of the relationship of humanity to nature.

1. THE CREATION AND THE FALL

The First (E) Account of the Creation. 1. [1]In the beginning God created the heavens and the earth. [2]Now the earth was a formless void, there was darkness over the deep, and God's spirit hovered over the water.

[3]God said, "Let there be light," and there was light. [4]God saw that light was good, and God divided light from darkness. [5]God called light "day," and darkness he called "night." Evening came and morning came: the first day.

[6]God said, "Let there be a vault in the waters to divide the waters in two." And so it was. [7]God made the vault, and it divided the waters above the vault from the waters under the vault. [8]God called the vault "heaven." Evening came and morning came: the second day.

[9]God said, "Let the waters under heaven come together into a single mass, and let dry land appear." And so it was. [10]God called the dry land "earth" and the mass of waters "seas," and God saw that it was good.

[11]God said, "Let the earth produce vegetation: seed-bearing plants, and fruit trees bearing fruit with their seed inside, on the earth." And so it was. [12]The earth produced vegetation: plants bearing seed in their several kinds, and trees bearing fruit with their seed inside in their several kinds. God saw that it was good. [13]Evening came and morning came: the third day.

[14]God said, "Let there be lights in the vault of heaven to divide day from night, and let them indicate festivals, days and years. [15]Let them be lights in the vault of heaven to shine on the earth." And so it was. [16]God made the two great lights: the greater light to govern the day, the smaller light to govern the night, and the stars. [17]God set them in the vault of heaven to shine on the earth, [18]to govern the day and the night and to divide light from darkness. God saw that it was good. [19]Evening came and morning came: the fourth day.

[20]God said, "Let the waters teem with living creatures, and let birds fly above the earth within the vault of heaven." And so it was. [21]God created great sea-serpents and every kind of living creature with which the waters teem, and every kind of winged creature. God saw that it was good. [22]God blessed them, saying, "Be fruitful and multiply, and fill the waters of the seas; and let the birds multiply upon the earth." [23]Evening came and morning came: the fifth day.

[24]God said, "Let the earth produce every kind of living creature: cattle, reptiles, and every kind of wild beast." And so it was. [25]God made every kind of wild beast, every kind of cattle, and every kind of land reptile. God saw that it was good.

[26]God said, "Let us make man in our own image, in the likeness of ourselves, and let them be masters of the fish of the sea, the birds of heaven, the cattle, all the wild beasts and all the reptiles that crawl upon the earth."

[27]God created man in the image of himself, in the image of God he created him, male and female he created them.

[28]God blessed them, saying to them, "Be fruitful, multiply, fill the earth and conquer it. Be masters of the fish of the sea, the birds of heaven and all living animals on the earth." [29]God said, "See, I give you all the seed-bearing plants that are upon the whole earth, and all the trees with seed-bearing fruit; this shall be your food. [30]To all wild beasts, all birds of heaven and all living reptiles on the earth I give all the foliage of plants for food." And so it was. [31]God saw all he had made, and indeed it was very good. Evening came and morning came: the sixth day....

The Second (J) Account of the Creation: Paradise
⁵At the time when Yahweh God made earth and heaven there was as yet no wild bush on the earth nor had any wild plant yet sprung up, for Yahweh God had not sent rain on the earth, nor was there any man to till the soil. ⁶However, a flood was rising from the earth and watering all the surface of the soil. ⁷Yahweh God fashioned man of dust from the soil. Then he breathed into his nostrils a breath of life, and thus man became a living being.

⁸Yahweh God planted a garden in Eden which is in the east, and there he put the man he had fashioned. ⁹Yahweh God caused to spring up from the soil every kind of tree, enticing to look at and good to eat, with the tree of life and the tree of the knowledge of good and evil in the middle of the garden. ¹⁰A river flowed from Eden to water the garden, and from there it divided to make four streams. ¹¹The first is named the Pishon, and this encircles the whole land of Havilah where there is gold. ¹²The gold of this land is pure; bdellium and onyx stone are found there. ¹³The second river is named the Gihon, and this encircles the whole land of Cush. ¹⁴The third river is named the Tigris, and this flows to the east of Ashur. The fourth river is the Euphrates. ¹⁵Yahweh God took the man and settled him in the garden of Eden to cultivate and take care of it. ¹⁶Then Yahweh God gave the man this admonition, "You may eat indeed of all the trees in the garden. ¹⁷Nevertheless of the tree of the knowledge of good and evil you are not to eat, for on the day you eat of it you shall most surely die."

¹⁸Yahweh God said, "It is not good that the man should be alone. I will make him a helpmate." ¹⁹So from the soil Yahweh God fashioned all the wild beasts and all the birds of heaven. These he brought to the man to see what he would call them; each one was to bear the name the man would give it. ²⁰The man gave names to all the cattle, all the birds of heaven and all the wild beasts. But no helpmate suitable for man was found for him. ²¹So Yahweh God made the man fall into a deep sleep. And while he slept, he took one of his ribs and enclosed it in flesh. ²²Yahweh God built the rib he had taken from the man into a woman, and brought her to the man. ²³The man exclaimed: "This at last is bone from my bones, and flesh from my flesh! This is to be called woman, for this was taken from man." ²⁴This is why a man leaves his father and mother and joins himself to his wife, and they become one body.

²⁵Now both of them were naked, the man and his wife, but they felt no shame in front of each other.

The Fall. 3. ¹The serpent was the most subtle of all the wild beasts that Yahweh God had made. It asked the woman, "Did God really say you were not to eat from any of the trees in the garden?" ²The woman answered the serpent, "We may eat the fruit of the trees in the garden. ³But of the fruit of the tree in the middle of the garden God said, 'You must not eat it, nor touch it, under pain of death.'" ⁴Then the serpent said to the woman, "No! you will not die! ⁵God knows in fact that on the day you eat it your eyes will be opened and you will be like gods, knowing good and evil." ⁶The woman saw that the tree was good to eat and pleasing to the eye, and that it was desirable for the knowledge that it could give. So she took some of its fruit and ate it. She gave some also to her husband who was with her, and he ate it. ⁷Then the eyes of both of them were opened and they realized that they were naked. So they sewed fig leaves together to make themselves loincloths.

⁸The man and his wife heard the sound of Yahweh God walking in the garden in the cool of the day, and they hid from Yahweh God among the trees of the garden. ⁹But Yahweh God called to the man. "Where are you?" he asked. ¹⁰"I heard the sound of you in the garden," he replied. "I was afraid because I was naked, so I hid." ¹¹"Who told you that you were naked?" he asked. "Have you been eating of the tree I forbade you to eat?" ¹²The man replied, "It was the woman you put with me; she gave me the fruit, and I ate it." ¹³Then Yahweh God asked the woman, "What is this you have done?" The woman replied, "The serpent tempted me and I ate."

¹⁴Then Yahweh God said to the serpent, "Because you have done this, Be accursed beyond all cattle, all wild beasts. You shall crawl on your belly and eat dust every day of your life. ¹⁵I will make you enemies of each other: you and the woman, your offspring and

her offspring. It will crush your head and you will strike its heel."

¹⁶To the woman he said: "I will multiply your pains in childbearing, you shall give birth to your children in pain. Your yearning shall be for your husband, yet he will lord it over you."

¹⁷To the man he said, "Because you listened to the voice of your wife and ate from the tree of which I had forbidden you to eat, Accursed be the soil because of you. With suffering shall you get your food from it every day of your life. ¹⁸It shall yield you brambles and thistles, and you shall eat wild plants. ¹⁹With sweat on your brow shall you eat your bread, until you return to the soil, as you were taken from it. For dust you are and to dust you shall return."

²⁰The man named his wife "Eve" because she was the mother of all those who live. ²¹Yahweh God made clothes out of skins for the man and his wife, and they put them on. ²²Then Yahweh God said, "See, the man has become like one of us, with his knowledge of good and evil. He must not be allowed to stretch his hand out next and pick from the tree of life also, and eat some and live for ever." ²³So Yahweh God expelled him from the garden of Eden, to till the soil from which he had been taken. ²⁴He banished the man, and in front of the garden of Eden he posted the cherubs, and the flame of a flashing sword, to guard the way to the tree of life.

NOTE

1. See James Barr, "Man and Nature: The Ecological Controversy and the Old Testament." Bulletin of the John Rylands Library, 1972.

STUDY QUESTIONS

1. What is the proper relationship between humanity and nature according to the Genesis account? Go over Genesis 1:26–29. Then compare it with Chapter 2:15. Do you see a different message in the two accounts?

2. The Hebrew word for 'have dominion' or 'be masters of' in Genesis 1:26, 28 is the verb *rada*. It is linked with man's being made in the image of God. Just as God has dominion over the whole universe, including man, so man has god-like dominion over the natural world. The words "have dominion" are used of the physical treading or trampling down of the wine-press; and the verb *kaba*, "subdue," means "stamp down." It is elsewhere used for the military subjugation of conquered territory and clearly implies reliance on force. This powerful expression of man's attitude toward the rest of nature suggests that he sees himself in a position of absolute command.¹ How literally should we take these commands?

3. For a more explicit statement on the high value of human beings, consider Psalm 8. Does it confirm the picture of human dominance conveyed in the Genesis account?

2   The Historical Roots of Our Ecological Crisis

LYNN WHITE

Lynn White (1907–1987), internationally known medieval scholar, taught history at Princeton University, Stanford University, and the University of California at Los Angeles.

White set forth the thesis that the roots of our ecological crisis lie in our Judeo-Christian idea that humanity is to *dominate* nature. By seeing nature as alien, as a mere resource to be exploited, we have wreaked havoc on Earth and are reaping the consequences. Either a new

This article, which has become a classic, appeared originally in *Science*, Vol. 155, pp. 1203–1207 (10 March 1967). Copyright 1967 by the American Association for the Advancement of Science. Reprinted by permission.

religion or a revision of our old one is called for to get us out of this mess. He suggests the Italian medieval saint St. Francis of Assisi (1182–1226) as a proper example of a suitable attitude toward nature.

A conversation with Aldous Huxley not infrequently put one at the receiving end of an unforgettable monologue. About a year before his lamented death he was discoursing on a favorite topic: Man's unnatural treatment of nature and its sad results. To illustrate his point he told how, during the previous summer, he had returned to a little valley in England where he had spent many happy months as a child. Once it had been composed of delightful grassy glades; now it was becoming overgrown with unsightly brush because the rabbits that formerly kept such growth under control had largely succumbed to a disease, myxomatosis, that was deliberately introduced by the local farmers to reduce the rabbits' destruction of crops. Being something of a Philistine, I could be silent no longer, even in the interests of great rhetoric. I interrupted to point out that the rabbit itself had been brought as a domestic animal to England in 1176, presumably to improve the protein diet of the peasantry.

All forms of life modify their contexts. The most spectacular and benign instance is doubtless the coral polyp. By serving its own ends, it has created a vast undersea world favorable to thousands of other kinds of animals and plants. Ever since man became a numerous species he has affected his environment notably. The hypothesis that his fire-drive method of hunting created the world's great grasslands and helped to exterminate the monster mammals of the Pleistocene from much of the globe is plausible, if not proved. For 6 millennia at least, the banks of the lower Nile have been a human artifact rather than the swampy African jungle which nature, apart from man, would have made it. The Aswan Dam, flooding 5000 square miles, is only the latest stage in a long process. In many regions terracing or irrigation, overgrazing, the cutting of forests by Romans to build ships to fight Carthaginians or by Crusaders to solve the logistics problems of their expeditions, have profoundly changed some ecologies. Observation that the French landscape falls into two basic types, the open fields of the north and the *bocage* of the south and west, inspired Marc Bloch to undertake his classic study of medieval agricultural methods. Quite unintentionally, changes in human ways often affect nonhuman nature. It has been noted, for example, that the advent of the automobile eliminated huge flocks of sparrows that once fed on the horse manure littering every street.

The history of ecologic change is still so rudimentary that we know little about what really happened, or what the results were. The extinction of the European aurochs as late as 1627 would seem to have been a simple case of overenthusiastic hunting. On more intricate matters it often is impossible to find solid information. For a thousand years or more the Frisians and Hollanders have been pushing back the North Sea, and the process is culminating in our own time in the reclamation of the Zuider Zee. What, if any, species of animals, birds, fish, shore life, or plants have died out in the process? In their epic combat with Neptune, have the Netherlanders overlooked ecological values in such a way that the quality of human life in the Netherlands has suffered? I cannot discover that the questions have ever been asked, much less answered.

People, then, have often been a dynamic element in their own environment, but in the present state of historical scholarship we usually do not know exactly when, where, or with what effects man-induced changes came. As we enter the last third of the 20th century, however, concern for the problem of ecological backlash is mounting feverishly. Natural science, conceived as the effort to understand the nature of things, had flourished in several eras and among several peoples. Similarly there had been an age-old accumulation of technological skills, sometimes growing rapidly, sometimes slowly. But it was not until about four generations ago that Western Europe and North America arranged a marriage between science and technology, a union of the theoretical and the empirical approaches to our natural environment. The emergence in widespread practice of the Baconian creed that scientific knowledge means technological power over nature can scarcely be dated before about 1850, save in the chemical industries, where it is anticipated in the 18th century. Its acceptance as a normal pattern of action may mark the greatest event in human history since the invention of agriculture, and perhaps in nonhuman terrestrial history as well.

Almost at once the new situation forced the crystallization of the novel concept of ecology; indeed, the word *ecology* first appeared in the English language in 1873. Today, less than a century later, the impact of our race upon the environment has so increased in force that it has changed in essence. When the first cannons were fired, in the early 14th century, they affected ecology by sending workers scrambling to the forests and mountains for more potash, sulfur, iron ore, and charcoal, with some resulting erosion and deforestation. Hydrogen bombs are of a different order: a war fought with them might alter the genetics of all life on this planet. By 1285 London had a smog problem arising from the burning of soft coal, but our present combustion of fossil fuels threatens to change the chemistry of the globe's atmosphere as a whole, with consequences which we are only beginning to guess. With the population explosion, the carcinoma of planless urbanism, the now geological deposits of sewage and garbage, surely no creature other than man has ever managed to foul its nest in such short order.

There are many calls to action, but specific proposals, however worthy as individual items, seem too partial, palliative, negative: ban the bomb, tear down the billboards, give the Hindus contraceptives and tell them to eat their sacred cows. The simplest solution to any suspect change is, of course, to stop it, or, better yet, to revert to a romanticized past: make those ugly gasoline stations look like Anne Hathaway's cottage or (in the Far West) like ghost-town saloons. The "wilderness area" mentality invariably advocates deep-freezing an ecology, whether San Gimignano or the High Sierra, as it was before the first Kleenex was dropped. But neither atavism nor prettification will cope with the ecologic crisis of our time.

What shall we do? No one yet knows. Unless we think about fundamentals, our specific measures may produce new backlashes more serious than those they are designed to remedy.

As a beginning we should try to clarify our thinking by looking, in some historical depth, at the presuppositions that underlie modern technology and science. Science was traditionally aristocratic, speculative, intellectual in intent; technology was lower-class, empirical, action-oriented. The quite sudden fusion of these two, towards the middle of the 19th century, is surely related to the slightly prior and contemporary democratic revolutions which, by reducing social barriers, tended to assert a functional unity of brain and hand. Our ecologic crisis is the product of an emerging, entirely novel, democratic culture. The issue is whether a democratized world can survive its own implications. Presumably we cannot, unless we rethink our axioms.

THE WESTERN TRADITIONS OF TECHNOLOGY AND SCIENCE

One thing is so certain that it seems stupid to verbalize it: both modern technology and modern science are distinctively *Occidental*. Our technology has absorbed elements from all over the world, notably from China; yet everywhere today, whether in Japan or in Nigeria, successful technology is Western. Our science is the heir to all the sciences of the past, especially perhaps to the work of the great Islamic scientists of the Middle Ages, who so often outdid the ancient Greeks in skill and perspicacity: al-Rā z-ī in medicine, for example; or ibn-al-Haytham in optics; or Omar Khayyám in mathematics. Indeed, not a few works of such geniuses seem to have vanished in the original Arabic and to survive only in medieval Latin translations that helped to lay the foundations for later Western developments. Today, around the globe, all significant science is Western in style and method, whatever the pigmentation or language of the scientists.

A second pair of facts is less well recognized because they result from quite recent historical scholarship. The leadership of the West, both in technology and in science, is far older than the so-called Scientific Revolution of the 17th century or the so-called Industrial Revolution of the 18th century. These terms are in fact outmoded and obscure the true nature of what they try to describe—significant stages in two long and separate developments. By A.D. 1000 at the latest—and perhaps, feebly, as much as 200 years earlier—the West began to apply water power to industrial processes other than milling grain. This was followed in the late 12th century by the harnessing of wind power. From simple beginnings, but with remarkable consistency of style, the West rapidly expanded its skills in the development of power machinery, labor-saving devices, and automation. Those who doubt should contemplate that most monumental achievement in the history of automation: the weight-driven mechanical clock, which appeared in two forms in the early 14th century. Not in craftsmanship but in basic technological capacity, the Latin West of the later Middle Ages far outstripped its elaborate, sophisticated, and esthetically magnificent sister cultures, Byzantium and Islam. In 1444 a great Greek ecclesiastic, Bessarion, who had gone to Italy, wrote a letter to a prince in Greece. He is amazed by the superiority of Western ships, arms, textiles, glass. But above all he is astonished by the spectacle of waterwheels sawing timbers and pumping the bellows to blast furnaces. Clearly, he had seen nothing of the sort in the Near East.

By the end of the 15th century the technological superiority of Europe was such that its small, mutually hostile nations could spill out over all the rest of the world, conquering, looting, and colonizing. The symbol of this technological superiority is the fact that Portugal, one of the weakest states of the Occident, was able to become, and to remain for a century, mistress of the East Indies. And we must remember that the technology of Vasco da Gama and Albuquerque was built by pure empiricism, drawing remarkably little support or inspiration from science.

In the present-day vernacular of understanding, modern science is supposed to have begun in 1543, when both Copernicus and Vesalius published their great works. It is no derogation of their accomplishments, however, to point out that such structures as the *Fabrica* and the *De revolutionibus* do not appear overnight. The distinctive Western tradition of science, in fact, began in the late 11th century with a massive movement of translation of Arabic and Greek scientific works into Latin. A few notable books—Theophrastus, for example—escaped the West's avid new appetite for science, but within less than 200 years, effectively the entire corpus of Greek and Muslim science was available in Latin, and was being eagerly read and criticized in the new European universities. Out of criticism arose new observation, speculation, and increasing distrust of ancient authorities. By the late 13th century Europe had seized global scientific leadership from the faltering hands of Islam. It would be as absurd to deny the profound originality of Newton, Galileo, or Copernicus as to deny that of the 14th century scholastic scientists like Buridan or Oresme on whose work they built. Before the 11th century, science scarcely existed in the Latin West, even in Roman times. From the 11th century onward, the scientific sector of Occidental culture has increased in a steady crescendo.

Since both our technological and our scientific movements got their start, acquired their character, and achieved world dominance in the Middle Ages, it would seem that we cannot understand their nature or their present impact upon ecology without examining fundamental medieval assumptions and developments.

MEDIEVAL VIEW OF MAN AND NATURE

Until recently, agriculture has been the chief occupation even in "advanced" societies; hence, any change in methods of tillage has much importance. Early plows, drawn by two oxen, did not normally turn the sod but merely scratched it. Thus, cross-plowing was needed and fields tended to be squarish. In the fairly light soils and semi-arid climates of the Near East and Mediterranean, this worked well. But such a plow was inappropriate to the wet climate and often sticky soils of northern Europe. By the latter part of the 7th century after Christ, however, following obscure beginnings, certain northern peasants were using an entirely new kind of plow, equipped with a vertical knife to cut the line of the furrow, a horizontal share to slice under the sod, and a moldboard to turn it over. The friction of this plow with the soil was so great that it normally required not two but eight oxen. It attacked the land with such violence that cross-plowing was not needed, and fields tended to be shaped in long strips.

In the days of the scratch-plow, fields were distributed generally in units capable of supporting a single family. Subsistence farming was the presupposition. But no peasant owned eight oxen: to use the new and more efficient plow, peasants pooled their oxen to form large plow-teams, originally receiving (it would appear) plowed strips in proportion to their contribution. Thus, distribution of land was based no longer on the needs of a family but, rather, on the capacity of a power machine to till the earth. Man's relation to the soil was profoundly changed. Formerly man had been part of nature; now he was the exploiter of nature. Nowhere else in the world did farmers develop any analogous agricultural implement. Is it coincidence that modern technology, with its ruthlessness toward nature, has so largely been produced by descendants of these peasants of northern Europe?

This same exploitive attitude appears slightly before A.D. 830 in Western illustrated calendars. In older calendars the months were shown as passive personifications. The new Frankish calendars, which set the style for the Middle Ages, are very different: they show men coercing the world around them—plowing, harvesting, chopping trees, butchering pigs. Man and nature are two things, and man is master.

These novelties seem to be in harmony with larger intellectual patterns. What people do about their ecology depends on what they think about themselves in relation to things around them. Human ecology is deeply conditioned by beliefs about our nature and destiny—that is, by religion. To Western eyes this is very evident in, say, India or Ceylon. It is equally true of ourselves and of our medieval ancestors.

The victory of Christianity over paganism was the greatest psychic revolution in the history of our culture. It has become fashionable today to say that, for better or worse, we live in "the post-Christian age." Certainly the forms of our thinking and language have largely ceased to be Christian, but to my eye the substance often remains amazingly akin to that of the past. Our daily habits of action, for example, are dominated by an implicit faith in perpetual progress which was unknown either to Greco-Roman antiquity or to the Orient. It is rooted in, and is indefensible apart from, Judeo-Christian teleology. The fact that Communists share it merely helps to show what can be demonstrated on many other grounds: that Marxism, like Islam, is a Judeo-Christian heresy. We continue today to live, as we have lived for about 1700 years, very largely in a context of Christian axioms.

What did Christianity tell people about their relations with the environment?

While many of the world's mythologies provide stories of creation, Greco-Roman mythology was singularly incoherent in this respect. Like Aristotle, the intellectuals of the ancient West denied that the visible world had had a beginning. Indeed, the idea of a beginning was impossible in the framework of their cyclical notion of time. In sharp contrast, Christianity inherited from Judaism not only a concept of time as non-repetitive and linear but also a striking story of creation. By gradual stages a loving and all-powerful God had created light and darkness, the heavenly bodies, and earth and all its plants, animals, birds, and fishes. Finally, God had created Adam and, as an after thought, Eve to keep man from being lonely. Man named all the animals, thus establishing his dominance over them. God planned all of this explicitly for man's benefit and rule: no item in the physical creation had any purpose save to serve man's purposes. And, although man's body is made of clay, he is not simply part of nature: he is made in God's image.

Especially in its Western form, Christianity is the most anthropocentric religion the world has seen. As early as the 2nd century both Tertullian and St. Irenaeus of Lyons were insisting that when God shaped Adam he was foreshadowing the image of the incarnate Christ, the Second Adam. Man shares, in great measure, God's transcendence of nature. Christianity, in absolute contrast to ancient paganism and Asia's religions (except, perhaps, Zoroastrianism), not only established a dualism of man and nature but also insisted that it is God's will that man exploit nature for his proper ends.

At the level of the common people this worked out in an interesting way. In Antiquity every tree, every spring, every stream, every hill had its own *genius loci*, its guardian spirit. These spirits were accessible to men, but were very unlike men; centaurs, fauns, and mermaids show their ambivalence. Before one cut a tree, mined a mountain, or dammed a brook, it was important to placate the spirit in charge of that particular situation, and to keep it placated. By destroying pagan animism, Christianity made it possible to exploit nature in a mood of indifference to the feelings of natural objects.

It is often said that for animism the Church substituted the cult of saints. True; but the cult of saints is functionally quite different from animism. The saint is not *in* natural objects; he may have special shrines, but his citizenship is in heaven. Moreover, a saint is entirely a man; he can be approached in human terms. In addition to saints, Christianity of course also had angels and demons inherited from Judaism and perhaps, at one remove, from Zoroastrianism. But these were all as mobile as the saints themselves. The spirits *in* natural objects, which formerly had protected nature from man, evaporated. Man's effective monopoly on spirit in this world was confirmed, and the old inhibitions to the exploitation of nature crumbled.

When one speaks in such sweeping terms, a note of caution is in order. Christianity is a complex faith, and its consequences differ in differing contexts. What I have said may well apply to the medieval West, where in fact technology made spectacular advances. But the Greek East, a highly civilized realm of equal Christian devotion, seems to have produced no marked technological innovation after the late 7th century, when Greek fire was invented. The key to the contrast may perhaps be found in a difference in the tonality of piety and thought which students of comparative theology find between the Greek and the Latin Churches. The Greeks believed that sin was intellectual blindness, and that salvation was found in illumination, orthodoxy—that is, clear thinking. The Latins, on the other hand, felt that sin was moral evil, and that salvation was to be found in

right conduct. Eastern theology has been intellectualist. Western theology has been voluntarist. The Greek saint contemplates; the Western saint acts. The implications of Christianity for the conquest of nature would emerge more easily in the Western atmosphere.

The Christian dogma of creation, which is found in the first clause of all the Creeds, has another meaning for our comprehension of today's ecologic crisis. By revelation, God had given man the Bible, the Book of Scripture. But since God had made nature, nature also must reveal the divine mentality. The religious study of nature for the better understanding of God was known as natural theology. In the early Church, and always in the Greek East, nature was conceived primarily as a symbolic system through which God speaks to men: the ant is a sermon to sluggards; rising flames are the symbol of the soul's aspiration. This view of nature was essentially artistic rather than scientific. While Byzantium preserved and copied great numbers of ancient Greek scientific texts, science as we conceive it could scarcely flourish in such an ambiance.

However, in the Latin West by the early 13th century natural theology was following a very different bent. It was ceasing to be the decoding of the physical symbols of God's communication with man and was becoming the effort to understand God's mind by discovering how his creation operates. The rainbow was no longer simply a symbol of hope first sent to Noah after the Deluge: Robert Grosseteste, Friar Roger Bacon, and Theodoric of Freiberg produced startlingly sophisticated work on the optics of the rainbow, but they did it as a venture in religious understanding. From the 13th century onward, up to and including Leibnitz and Newton, every major scientist, in effect, explained his motivations in religious terms. Indeed if Galileo had not been so expert an amateur theologian he would have got into far less trouble: the professionals resented his intrusion. And Newton seems to have regarded himself more as a theologian than as a scientist. It was not until the late 18th century that the hypothesis of God became unnecessary to many scientists.

It is often hard for the historian to judge, when men explain why they are doing what they want to do, whether they are offering real reasons or merely culturally acceptable reasons. The consistency with which scientists during the long formative centuries of Western science said that the task and the reward of the scientist was "to think God's thoughts after him" leads one to believe that this was their real motivation. If so, then modern Western science was cast in a matrix of Christian theology. The dynamism of religious devotion, shaped by the Judeo-Christian dogma of creation, gave it impetus.

AN ALTERNATIVE CHRISTIAN VIEW

We would seem to be headed toward conclusions unpalatable to many Christians. Since both *science* and *technology* are blessed words in our contemporary vocabulary, some may be happy at the notions, first, that, viewed historically, modern science is an extrapolation of natural theology and, second, that modern technology is at least partly to be explained as an Occidental, voluntarist realization of the Christian dogma of man's transcendence of and rightful mastery over nature. But, as we now recognize, somewhat over a century ago science and technology—hitherto quite separate activities—joined to give mankind powers which, to judge by many of the ecologic effects, are out of control. If so, Christianity bears a huge burden of guilt.

I personally doubt that disastrous ecologic backlash can be avoided simply by applying to our problems more science and more technology. Our science and technology have grown out of Christian attitudes toward man's relation to nature which are almost universally held not only by Christians and neo-Christians but also by those who fondly regard themselves as post-Christians. Despite Copernicus, all the cosmos rotates around our little globe. Despite Darwin, we are *not*, in our hearts, part of the natural process. We are superior to nature, contemptuous of it, willing to use it for our slightest whim. The newly elected Governor of California, like myself a churchman but less troubled than I, spoke for the Christian tradition when he said (as is alleged), "when you've seen one redwood tree, you've seen them all." To a Christian a tree can be no more than a physical fact. The whole concept of the sacred grove is alien to Christianity and to the ethos of the West. For nearly 2 millennia Christian missionaries have been chopping down sacred groves, which are idolatrous because they assume spirit in nature.

What we do about ecology depends on our ideas of the man–nature relationship. More science and more technology are not going to get us out of the present ecologic crisis until we find a new religion, or rethink our old one. The beatniks, who are the basic revolutionaries of our time, show a sound instinct in their affinity for Zen Buddhism, which conceives of the man–nature relationship as very nearly the mirror image of the Christian view. Zen, however, is as deeply conditioned by Asian history as Christianity is by the experience of the West, and I am dubious of its viability among us.

Possibly we should ponder the greatest radical in Christian history since Christ: St. Francis of Assisi. The prime miracle of St. Francis is the fact that he did not end at the stake, as many of his left-wing followers did. He was so clearly heretical that a General of the Franciscan Order, St. Bonaventura, a great and perceptive Christian, tried to suppress the early accounts of Franciscanism. The key to an understanding of Francis is his belief in the virtue of humility—not merely for the individual but for man as a species. Francis tried to depose man from his monarchy over creation and set up a democracy of all God's creatures. With him the ant is no longer simply a homily for the lazy, flames a sign of the thrust of the soul toward union with God; now they are Brother Ant and Sister Fire, praising the Creator in their own ways as Brother Man does in his.

Later commentators have said that Francis preached to the birds as a rebuke to men who would not listen. The records do not read so: he urged the little birds to praise God, and in spiritual ecstasy they flapped their wings and chirped rejoicing. Legends of saints, especially the Irish saints, had long told of their dealings with animals but always, I believe, to show their human dominance over creatures. With Francis it is different. The land around Gubbio in the Apennines was being ravaged by a fierce wolf. St. Francis, says the legend, talked to the wolf and persuaded him of the error of his ways. The wolf repented, died in the odor of sanctity, and was buried in consecrated ground.

What Sir Steven Runciman calls the Franciscan doctrine of the "animal soul" was quickly stamped out. Quite possibly it was in part inspired, consciously or unconsciously, by the belief in reincarnation held by the Cathar heretics who at that time teemed in Italy and southern France, and who presumably had got it originally from India. It is significant that at just the same moment, about 1200, traces of metempsychosis are found also in western Judaism, in the Provençal *Cabbala*. But Francis held neither to transmigration of souls nor to pantheism. His view of nature and of man rested on a unique sort of pan-psychism of all things animate and inanimate, designed for the glorification of their transcendent Creator, who, in the ultimate gesture of cosmic humility, assumed flesh, lay helpless in a manger, and hung dying on a scaffold.

I am not suggesting that many contemporary Americans who are concerned about our ecologic crisis will be either able or willing to counsel with wolves or exhort birds. However, the present increasing disruption of the global environment is the product of a dynamic technology and science which were originating in the Western medieval world against which St. Francis was rebelling in so original a way. Their growth cannot be understood historically apart from distinctive attitudes toward nature which are deeply grounded in Christian dogma. The fact that most people do not think of these attitudes as Christian is irrelevant. No new set of basic values has been accepted in our society to displace those of Christianity. Hence we shall continue to have a worsening ecologic crisis until we reject the Christian axiom that nature has no reason for existence save to serve man.

The greatest spiritual revolutionary in Western history, St. Francis, proposed what he thought was an alternative Christian view of nature and man's relation to it: he tried to substitute the idea of the equality of all creatures, including man, for the idea of man's limitless rule of creation. He failed. Both our present science and our present technology are so tinctured with orthodox Christian arrogance toward nature that no solution for our ecologic crisis can be expected from them alone. Since the roots of our trouble are so largely religious, the remedy must also be essentially religious, whether we call it that or not. We must rethink and refeel our nature and destiny. The profoundly religious, but heretical, sense of the primitive Franciscans for the spiritual autonomy of all parts of nature may point a direction. I propose Francis as a patron saint for ecologists.

🐾 STUDY QUESTIONS

1. Do you agree with White's assessment that it is our Judeo-Christian dominance model that has led to our ecological crisis? Go back over Genesis 1–3 and compare it with White's analysis. Is his account a correct interpretation of the text?

2. What is the appeal of St. Francis? Here is part of St. Francis's "Canticle of Brother Sun."*

Praised be You, my Lord, with all your creatures,
Especially Sir Brother Sun,
Who is the day and through whom You give us light.
Praised be you, my Lord, through Sister Moon and
the stars,
In heaven You formed them clear and precious and
beautiful.
Praised be you, my Lord, through Brother Wind,

And through the air, cloudy and serene, and every
kind of weather
Through which You give sustenance to Your
creatures.
Praised be You, my Lord, through Sister Water,
Which is very useful and humble and precious and
chaste.
Praised be You, my Lord, through our Sister Mother
Earth,
Who sustains us and governs us.
And who produces varied fruits with colored flowers
and herbs.

What environmental attitude does St. Francis's poem embody? Is it helpful? Is it true? Explain your judgment.

---

*FROM: The Canticle of Brother Sun, *translated by R. J. Armstrong and I. Brady (New York: Paulist Press, 1982).*

3   The Cultural Basis of Our Environmental Crisis

LEWIS W. MONCRIEF

Lewis W. Moncrief is a sociologist who taught for many years in the Department of Park and Recreation Resources at Michigan State University.

In this reply to Lynn White's article, Moncrief argues that White's analysis misses the essential point that human beings have been altering the environment from their beginning. He asks, "If our environmental crisis is a 'religious problem,' why are other parts of the world experiencing the same environmental problems that we are so well acquainted with in the Western world?" A more plausible account of the causes of our crisis is complex and has to do with the nature of capitalism, technology, democratization, urbanization, and individualism.

One hundred years ago at almost any location in the United States, potable water was no farther away than the closest brook or stream. Today there are hardly any streams in the United States, except in a few high mountainous reaches, that can safely satisfy human thirst without chemical treatment. An oft-mentioned satisfaction in the lives of urbanites in an earlier era was a leisurely stroll in late afternoon to get a breath of fresh air in a neighborhood park or along a quiet street. Today in many of our major metropolitan areas it is difficult to find a quiet, peaceful place to take a leisurely stroll and sometimes impossible to get a breath of fresh air. These contrasts point up the dramatic changes that have occurred in the quality of our environment.

It is not my intent in this article, however, to document the existence of an environmental crisis but rather to discuss the cultural basis for such a crisis. Particular attention will be given to the institutional structures as expressions of our culture.

SOCIAL ORGANIZATION

In her book entitled *Social Institutions*, J. O. Hertzler classified all social institutions into nine functional categories: (i) economic and industrial, (ii) matrimonial and domestic, (iii) political, (iv) religious, (v) ethical, (vi) educational, (vii) communications, (viii) esthetic, and (ix) health. Institutions exist to carry on each of these functions in all cultures, regardless of their location or relative complexity. Thus, it is not surprising that one of the analytical criteria used by anthropologists in the study of various cultures is the comparison and contrast of the various social institutions as to form and relative importance.

A number of attempts have been made to explain attitudes and behavior that are commonly associated with one institutional function as the result of influence from a presumably independent institutional factor. The classic example of such an analysis is *The Protestant Ethic and the Spirit of Capitalism* by Max Weber. In this significant work Weber attributes much of the economic and industrial growth in Western Europe and North America to capitalism, which, he argued, was an economic form that developed as a result of the religious teachings of Calvin, particularly spiritual determinism.

Social scientists have been particularly active in attempting to assess the influence of religious teaching and practice and of economic

This reply to Lynn White's article was published in *Science*, Vol. 170, pp. 508–512 (30 October 1970) by the American Association for the Advancement of Science. Reprinted by permission. Notes deleted.

motivation on other institutional forms and behavior and on each other. In this connection, L. White suggested that the exploitative attitude that has prompted much of the environmental crisis in Western Europe and North America is a result of the teachings of the Judeo-Christian tradition, which conceives of man as superior to all other creation and of everything else as created for his use and enjoyment. He goes on to contend that the only way to reduce the ecologic crisis which we are now facing is to "reject the Christian axiom that nature has no reason for existence save to serve man." As with other ideas that appear to be new and novel, Professor White's observations have begun to be widely circulated and accepted in scholarly circles, as witness the article by religious writer E. B. Fiske in the *New York Times* earlier this year. In this article, note is taken of the fact that several prominent theologians and theological groups have accepted this basic premise that Judeo-Christian doctrine regarding man's relation to the rest of creation is at the root of the West's environmental crisis. I would suggest that the wide acceptance of such a simplistic explanation is at this point based more on fad than on fact.

Certainly, no fault can be found with White's statement that "Human ecology is deeply conditioned by beliefs about our nature and destiny—that is, by religion." However, to argue that it is the primary conditioner of human behavior toward the environment is much more than the data that he cites to support this proposition will bear. For example, White himself notes very early in his article that there is evidence for the idea that man has been dramatically altering his environment since antiquity. If this be true, and there is evidence that it is, then this mediates against the idea that the Judeo-Christian religion uniquely predisposes cultures within which it thrives to exploit their natural resources with indiscretion. White's own examples weaken his argument considerably. He points out that human intervention in the periodic flooding of the Nile River basin and the fire-drive method of hunting by prehistoric man have both probably wrought significant "unnatural" changes in man's environment. The absence of Judeo-Christian influence in these cases is obvious.

It seems tenable to affirm that the role played by religion in man-to-man and man-to-environment relationships is one of establishing a very broad system of allowable beliefs and behavior and of articulating and invoking a system of social and spiritual rewards for those who conform and of negative sanctions for individuals or groups who approach or cross the pale of the religiously unacceptable. In other words, it defines the ball park in which the game is played, and, by the very nature of the park, some types of games cannot be played. However, the kind of game that ultimately evolves is not itself defined by the ball park. For example, where animism is practiced, it is not likely that the believers will indiscriminately destroy objects of nature because such activity would incur the danger of spiritual and social sanctions. However, the fact that another culture does not associate spiritual beings with natural objects does not mean that such a culture will invariably ruthlessly exploit its resources. It simply means that there are fewer social and psychological constraints against such action.

In the remainder of this article, I present an alternative set of hypotheses based on cultural variables which, it seems to me, are more plausible and more defensible as an explanation of the environmental crisis that is now confronting us.

No culture has been able to completely screen out the egocentric tendencies of human beings. There also exists in all cultures a status hierarchy of positions and values, with certain groups partially or totally excluded from access to these normatively desirable goals. Historically, the differences in most cultures between the "rich" and the "poor" have been great. The many very poor have often produced the wealth of the few who controlled the means of production. There may have been no alternative where scarcity of supply and unsatiated demand were economic reality. Still, the desire for a "better life" is universal; that is, the desire for higher status positions and the achievement of culturally defined desirable goals is common to all societies.

THE EXPERIENCE IN THE WESTERN WORLD

In the West two significant revolutions that occurred in the 18th and 19th centuries completely redirected its political, social, and economic destiny. These two types of revolutions were unique to the West until very recently. The French revolution marked the beginnings of widespread democratization. In specific terms, this revolution involved a redistribution of the means of production and a reallocation of the natural and human resources that are an integral part of the production process. In effect new channels of social mobility were created, which theoretically made more wealth accessible to more people. Even though the revolution was partially perpetrated in the guise of overthrowing the control of presumably Christian institutions and of destroying the influence of God over the minds of men, still it would be superficial to argue that Christianity did not influence this revolution. After all, biblical teaching is one of the strongest of all pronouncements concerning human dignity and individual worth.

At about the same time but over a more extended period, another kind of revolution was taking place, primarily in England. As White points out very well, this phenomenon, which began with a number of technological innovations, eventually consummated a marriage with natural science and began to take on the character that it has retained until today. With this revolution the productive capacity of each worker was amplified by several times his potential prior to the revolution. It also became feasible to produce goods that were not previously producible on a commercial scale.

Later, with the integration of the democratic and technological ideals, the increased wealth began to be distributed more equitably among the population. In addition, as the capital to land ratio increased in the production process and the demand grew for labor to work in the factories, large populations from the agrarian hinterlands began to concentrate in the emerging industrial cities. The stage was set for the development of the conditions that now exist in the Western world.

With growing affluence for an increasingly large segment of the population, there generally develops an increased demand for goods and services. The usual by-product of this affluence is waste from both the production and consumption processes. The disposal of that waste is further complicated by the high concentration of heavy waste producers in urban areas. Under these conditions the maxim that "Dilution is the solution to pollution" does not withstand the test of time, because the volume of such wastes is greater than the system can absorb and purify through natural means. With increasing population, increasing production, increasing urban concentrations, and increasing real median incomes for well over a hundred years, it is not surprising that our environment has taken a terrible beating in absorbing our filth and refuse.

THE AMERICAN SITUATION

The North American colonies of England and France were quick to pick up the technical and social innovations that were taking place in their motherlands. Thus, it is not surprising that the inclination to develop an industrial and manufacturing base is observable rather early in the colonies. A strong trend toward democratization also evidenced itself very early in the struggle for nationhood. In fact, Thistlewaite notes the significance of the concept of democracy as embodied in French thought to the framers of constitutional government in the colonies.

From the time of the dissolution of the Roman Empire, resource ownership in the Western world was vested primarily with the monarchy or the Roman Catholic Church, which in turn bestowed control of the land resources on vassals who pledged fealty to the sovereign. Very slowly the concept of private ownership developed during the Middle Ages in Europe, until it finally developed into the fee simple concept.

In America, however, national policy from the outset was designed to convey ownership of the land and other natural resources into the hands of the citizenry. Thomas Jefferson was perhaps more influential in crystallizing this philosophy in the new nation than anyone else. It was his conviction that an agrarian society made up of small landowners would furnish the most stable foundation for building the nation. This concept has received support up to the present and, against growing economic pressures in recent years, through government programs that have encouraged the conventional family farm. This point is clearly relevant to the subject of this article because it explains how the natural resources of the nation came to be controlled not by a few aristocrats but by many citizens. It explains how decisions that ultimately degrade the environment are made not only by corporation boards and city engineers but by millions of owners of our natural resources. This is democracy exemplified!

CHALLENGE OF THE FRONTIER

Perhaps the most significant interpretation of American history has been Frederick Jackson Turner's much criticized thesis that the western frontier was the prime force in shaping our societies. In his own words,

> If one would understand why we are today one nation, rather than a collection of isolated states, he must study this economic and social consolidation of the country.... The effect of the Indian frontier as a consolidating agent in our history is important.

He further postulated that the nation experienced a series of frontier challenges that moved across the continent in waves. These included the explorers' and traders' frontier, the Indian frontier, the cattle frontier, and three distinct agrarian frontiers. His thesis can be extended to interpret the expansionist period of our history in Panama, in Cuba, and in the Philippines as a need for a continued frontier challenge.

Turner's insights furnish a starting point for suggesting a second variable in analyzing the cultural basis of the United States' environmental crisis. As the nation began to expand westward, the settlers faced many obstacles, including a primitive transportation system, hostile Indians, and the absence of physical and social security. To many frontiersmen, particularly small farmers, many of the natural resources that are now highly valued were originally perceived more as obstacles

than as assets. Forests needed to be cleared to permit farming. Marshes needed to be drained. Rivers needed to be controlled. Wildlife often represented a competitive threat in addition to being a source of food. Sod was considered a nuisance—to be burned, plowed, or otherwise destroyed to permit "desirable" use of the land.

Undoubtedly, part of this attitude was the product of perceiving these resources as inexhaustible. After all, if a section of timber was put to the torch to clear it for farming, it made little difference because there was still plenty to be had very easily. It is no coincidence that the "First Conservation Movement" began to develop about 1890. At that point settlement of the frontier was almost complete. With the passing of the frontier era of American history, it began to dawn on people that our resources were indeed exhaustible. This realization ushered in a new philosophy of our national government toward natural resources management under the guidance of Theodore Roosevelt and Gifford Pinchot. Samuel Hays has characterized this movement as the appearance of a new "Gospel of Efficiency" in the management and utilization of our natural resources.

THE PRESENT AMERICAN SCENE

America is the archetype of what happens when democracy, technology, urbanization, capitalistic mission, and antagonism (or apathy) toward natural environment are blended together. The present situation is characterized by three dominant features that mediate against quick solution to this impending crisis: (i) an absence of personal moral direction concerning our treatment of our natural resources, (ii) an inability on the part of our social institutions to make adjustments to this stress, and (iii) an abiding faith in technology.

The first characteristic is the absence of personal moral direction. There is moral disparity when a corporation executive can receive a prison sentence for embezzlement but be congratulated for increasing profits by ignoring pollution abatement laws. That the absolute cost to society of the second act may be infinitely greater than the first is often not even considered.

The moral principle that we are to treat others as we would want to be treated seems as appropriate a guide as it ever has been. The rarity of such teaching and the even more uncommon instance of its being practiced help to explain how one municipality can, without scruple, dump its effluent into a stream even though it may do irreparable damage to the resource and add tremendously to the cost incurred by downstream municipalities that use the same water. Such attitudes are not restricted to any one culture. There appears to be an almost universal tendency to maximize self-interests and a widespread willingness to shift production costs to society to promote individual ends.

Undoubtedly, much of this behavior is the result of ignorance. If our accounting systems were more efficient in computing the cost of such irresponsibility both to the present generation and to those who will inherit the environment we are creating, steps would undoubtedly be taken to enforce compliance with measures designed to conserve resources and protect the environment. And perhaps if the total costs were known, we might optimistically speculate that more voluntary compliance would result.

A second characteristic of our current situation involves institutional inadequacies. It has been said that "what belongs to everyone belongs to no one." The maxim seems particularly appropriate to the problem we are discussing. So much of our environment is so apparently abundant that it is considered a free commodity. Air and water are particularly good examples. Great liberties have been permitted in the use and abuse of these resources for at least two reasons. First, these resources have typically been considered of less economic value than other natural resources except when conditions of extreme scarcity impose limiting factors. Second, the right of use is more difficult to establish for resources that are not associated with a fixed location.

Government, as the institution representing the corporate interests of all its citizens, has responded to date with dozens of legislative acts and numerous court decisions which give it authority to regulate the use of natural resources. However, the decisiveness to act has thus far been generally lacking. This indecisiveness cannot be understood without noting that the simplistic models that depict the conflict as that of a few powerful special interests versus "The People" are altogether inadequate. A very large proportion of the total citizenry is implicated in environmental degradation; the responsibility ranges from that of the board and executives of a utility company who might wish to thermally pollute a river with impunity to that of the average citizen who votes against a bond issue to improve the efficiency of a municipal sanitation system in order to keep his taxes from being raised. The magnitude of irresponsibility among individuals and institutions might be characterized as failing along a continuum from highly irresponsible to indirectly responsible. With such a broad base of interests being threatened with every change in resource policy direction, it is not surprising, although regrettable, that government has been so indecisive.

A third characteristic of the present American scene is an abiding faith in technology. It is very evident that the idea that technology can overcome almost any problem is widespread in Western society. This optimism exists in the face of strong evidence that much of man's technology, when misused, has produced harmful results, particularly in the long run. The reasoning goes something like this: "After all, we have gone to the moon. All we need to do is allocate enough money and brainpower and we can solve any problem."

It is both interesting and alarming that many people view technology almost as something beyond human control. Rickover put it this way:

> It troubles me that we are so easily pressured by purveyors of technology into permitting so called "progress" to alter our lives without attempting to control it—as if technology were an irrepressible force of nature to which we must meekly submit.

He goes on to add:

> It is important to maintain a humanistic attitude toward technology; to recognize clearly that since it is the product of human effort, technology can have no legitimate purpose but to serve man—man in general, not merely some men: future generations, not merely those who currently wish to gain advantage for themselves: man in the totality

of his humanity, encompassing all his manifold interests and needs, not merely some one particular concern of his. When viewed humanistically, technology is seen not as an end in itself but a means to an end, the end being determined by man himself in accordance with the laws prevailing in his society.

In short, it is one thing to appreciate the value of technology; it is something else entirely to view it as our environmental savior—which will save us in spite of ourselves.

CONCLUSION

The forces of democracy, technology, urbanization, increasing individual wealth, and an aggressive attitude toward nature seem to be directly related to the environmental crisis now being confronted in the Western world. The Judeo-Christian tradition has probably influenced the character of each of these forces: However, to isolate religious tradition as a cultural component and to contend that it is the "historical root of our ecological crisis" is a bold affirmation for which there is little historical or scientific support.

To assert that the primary cultural condition that has created our environmental crisis is Judeo-Christian teaching avoids several hard questions. For example: Is there less tendency for those who control the resources of non-Christian cultures to live in extravagant affluence with attendant high levels of waste and inefficient consumption? If non-Judeo Christian cultures had the same levels of economic productivity, urbanization, and high average household incomes, is there evidence to indicate that these cultures would not exploit or disregard nature as our culture does?

If our environmental crisis is a "religious problem," why are other parts of the world experiencing in various degrees the same environmental problems that we are so well acquainted with in the Western world? It is readily observable that the science and technology that developed on a large scale first in the West have been adopted elsewhere. Judeo-Christian tradition has not been adopted as a predecessor to science and technology on a

comparable scale. Thus, all White can defensibly argue is that the West developed modern science and technology *first*. This says nothing about the origin or existence of a particular ethic toward our environment.

In essence, White has proposed this simple model:

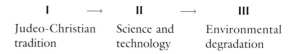

I	→	II	→	III
Judeo-Christian tradition		Science and technology		Environmental degradation

I have suggested here that, at best, Judeo-Christian teaching has had only an indirect effect on the treatment of our environment. The model could be characterized as follows:

I	→	II	→	III	→	IV
Judeo-Christian tradition		1. Capitalism (with the attendant development of science and technology) 2. Democratization		1. Urbanization 2. Increased wealth 3. Increased population 4. Individual resource ownership		Environmental degradation

Even here, the link between Judeo-Christian tradition and the proposed dependent variables certainly have the least empirical support. One need only look at the veritable mountain of criticism of Weber's conclusions in *The Protestant Ethic and the Spirit of Capitalism* to sense the tenuous nature of this link. The second and third phases of this model are common to many parts of the world. Phase I is not.

Jean Mayer, the eminent food scientist, gave an appropriate conclusion about the cultural basis for our environmental crisis:

> It might be bad in China with 700 million poor people but 700 million rich Chinese would wreck China in no time.... It is the rich who wreck the environment ... occupy much more space, consume more of each natural resource, disturb ecology more, litter the landscape ... and create more pollution.

1. What is Moncrief's view of our environmental crisis?
2. What does Moncrief think about White's position? Do you agree with his critique of White's position?
3. Can you imagine how White might reply to Moncrief?

4 The Judeo-Christian Stewardship Attitude to Nature

PATRICK DOBEL

Patrick Dobel is associate professor and director of the Graduate School of Public Affairs at the University of Washington in Seattle.

Dobel disagrees with White's thesis that the Christian attitude toward nature is one of arrogance and dominance ("limitless rule of creation"). He argues that the Judeo-Christian attitude is an ethics of stewardship and that humility toward God regarding nature, not arrogance, is enjoined by our religious heritage.

Browsing in a local bookstore recently, I took down several of the more general books from the "Ecology" shelf. Scanning the tables of contents and indexes of 13 books, I discovered that nine of them made reference to "Christianity," "the Bible" or the "Judeo-Christian tradition." Examining their contents more closely, I found that seven of these books blamed specific Christian or Bible-based values as significant "causes" of the ecology crisis.

Over half these books referenced an article by Lynn White, Jr., titled "The Historical Roots of Our Ecologic Crisis" (*Science*, March 10, 1967). In this short, undocumented and simplistic article White argues that the root of the entire problem lies in "the Christian maxim that nature has no reason for existence save to serve man." From the Christians' penchant for cutting down sacred Druidic groves to the development of "modern science from natural theology," Christianity, White argues, laid the foundations of Western "arrogance towards nature" and "limitless rule of creation."

Almost all similar statements are indebted to White; they even cite the same examples: grief over the destruction of the sacred groves; respect for Saint Francis of Assisi. Although few of the authors have read anything about him except that he talked to birds, they have raised poor Francis to the rank of first "ecological saint," while conveniently ignoring his myriad admonitions about asceticism and communal ownership of property.

DOMINION OVER THE EARTH

The ecological indictment of Christianity boils down to two somewhat contradictory assertions: that the postulated transcendence and domination of humanity over nature encourages thoughtless exploitation of the earth and that the otherworldly orientation of Christianity encourages contempt and disregard for the earth. In documenting the first indictment authors often cite Genesis 1:26: "Let us make man in our image, after our likeness; and let them have dominion over the fish of the

sea, and over the birds of the air, and over the cattle, and over every creeping thing that creeps upon
the earth." Some also quote Genesis 1:28: "Be
fruitful and multiply, and fill the earth and subdue
it; and have dominion over the fish of the sea and
over the birds of the air and over every living thing
that moves upon the earth."

These texts lead to the conclusion that the
Bible emphasizes the absolute superiority of
humanity over the rest of creation. And this relation must be primarily one of antagonism and
alienation, for "cursed is the ground because of
you; in toil you shall eat of it all the days of
your life.... In the sweat of your face you shall
eat bread" (Gen. 3:17).

Thus Christianity separates both humanity
and God from the earth and destroys the inherent
sacredness of the earth. This alienation is coupled
with humanity's innate superiority over nature
and the divine mandate to exploit nature limit-
lessly for human ends—a mandate that is carried
out in the context of antagonism and an expectation that the earth must be treated harshly to gain
the yield of human survival. Together these
notions have shaped Western culture's spoliation
of the earth.

In bringing the second indictment, critics
point out that Christianity's otherworldly preoccupation also contributes to human abuse of
the environment. Christians are instructed to
"kill everything in you that belongs only to
the earthly life" and to "let your thoughts be
on heavenly things, not on the things that are
on the earth" (Col. 3:2–5). The emphasis is
upon awaiting "a new heaven and a new earth
in which righteousness dwells" (II Pet. 3:13).
In some ways this stress undercuts the mandates
of superiority and rule since it implies that
humanity rules nothing but a fallen and con-
temptible orb. If the contempt, however, is
tied to an antagonistic human domination and
the need of people to discipline their unruly
bodies through work, it can provide an ethical
framework to support the thoughtless and arrogant exploitation which is part of the ecology
crisis. The thesis linking Calvinism with the
rise of industrialization reflects this ambivalent
world-hating but smug and exploitative
attitude.

The critics see modern science and technology along with notions of unbridled progress
and exploitation emerging from this Judeo-
Christian matrix. They conclude that Christianity must accept most of the "blame" for the
unique "Western" perspectives which have led
to the present state of affairs. This "blame"
somehow rings false when the ecologists extend
the link to the later implications of a secularized
technology and a liberal view of human
progress.

LOOKING FOR THE ROOTS

The attempt to discover historical roots is a dubious business at best, and in this case it borders on
the ludicrous. Christianity's ecological critics
consistently underestimate the economic, social
and political influences on modern science and
economy; their approach makes for good
polemics but bad history. Their thesis lacks a
careful historical analysis of the intellectual and
practical attitudes toward the earth and its use
in the consciously Christian Middle Ages. They
disregard the earth-centered ideals of the Christian Renaissance and its concern with the delicate
limitations of the Great Chain of Being, and they
pay little attention to the emergence of a peculiarly non-Christian deism and theism which
defined God in the 17th and 18th centuries to
accommodate a newly secularized nature and
new developments in science and trade. These
critics neglect to mention the specifically Christian prohibitions which often made religion a detriment to economic and scientific development.

They also ignore the rise of the secularized
nation-state from the decay of "Christendom";
yet these new government regimes provided
much of the impetus to maximize the exploitation
of resources and the discovery of new lands. Most
of the operative "roots" of the present crisis are to
be found in the far more secularized and non-
Christian world of nationalism, science and liberalism in the 16th through the 19th centuries.

Given the unsoundness of the theory that
blames Christianity for the environmental crisis,
it is surprising that it has gained such remarkable
currency. In light of this fact there are two
distinct tasks which confront the Christian

community. First, this thesis should be addressed in some detail, not only to show its flaws but to discover what ideas and practices the tradition can contribute to a concrete ecological program. Second, we must use the vast ethical and conceptual resources of the Judeo-Christian tradition to develop a God-centered ecological ethic which accounts for the sacredness of the earth without losing sight of human worth and justice. In addressing myself to this second task, I will try to develop appropriate responses to the following questions through textual exegesis of the Bible: What is the ethical status of the earth as an entity in creation? What is the proper relation of humanity to the earth and its resources?

Ecological critics have nostalgically lamented the decline of "nature worship" and have spoken wistfully of the need to import "Eastern" concepts of pantheism or quietist respect for the "equality of all life." Even some of the most secularized ecologists are calling for a rediscovery of the "sacredness" of nature.

Although it is hard to discover the enduring sacredness of anything in a totally secularized world, we must keep several points in mind about these calls. First, all cultures, regardless of religion, have abused or destroyed large areas of the world either because of economic or population pressures or from simple ignorance. Second, the ethical consequences of the new nature worship, neopantheism and the militant assertion of the equality of all creaturehood pose grave problems for establishing any prior claims of worth or inherent dignity for human beings. The more undifferentiated God and the world become, the harder it is to define individual humans as worthwhile with specific claims to social justice and care. Third, a sort of mindless ecological imperative based upon such notions is ultimately reactionary and anti-human, as well as anti-Christian. There are fundamental ethical differences between plants and animals and between animals and human beings. To resort simplistically to militantly pro-earth and antiprogress positions misses the vital Christian and humanistic point that our sojourn upon the earth is not yet completed and that we must continue to work unflaggingly toward social justice and the well-being of all people.

The unique contribution a Christian ecology can make to the earth is the assertion that we can insist on a reasonable harmony with our world without abandoning our commitment to social justice for all members of our unique and self-consciously alienated species. We can love and respect our environment without obliterating all ethical and technological distinctions, and without denying the demand that we cautiously but steadily use the earth for the benefit of all humanity.

The first question to address is the status of the earth and its resources. A different way of putting this is "Who owns the earth?" The answer of the entire Judeo-Christian tradition is clear: God. "In the beginning God created the heavens and the earth" (Gen. 1:3). In direct ethical terms God created the earth, and in distributive-justice terms it belongs to him: "The earth is the Lord's and the fullness thereof" (Ps. 24:1). As an act of pure love he created a world and he "founded the earth to endure" (Ps. 119:90–91).

What kind of world did God create? The answer has two dimensions: the physical or descriptive and the ethical. As a product of nature the world was created as a law-bound entity. The laws are derivative of God's will for all creation as "maintained by your rulings" (Ps. 119:90–91). Things coexist in intricate and regulated harmony—the basic postulate of science, mythology and reason. Although we have a world of laws, it is also a world of bounty and harmony. For it had been promised that "while the earth remains, seedtime and harvest shall not cease" (Gen. 8:22). It was arranged "in wisdom" so that in the balance of nature, "All creatures depend upon you to feed them . . . you provide the food with a generous hand." God's presence ultimately "holds all things in unity" (Col. 1:16–20) and constantly "renews" the world (Ps. 104:24–30). This world abounds in life and is held together in a seamless web maintained by God-willed laws.

In ethical terms, God saw that the world was "very good" (Gen. 1:31). In love and freedom he created the world and valued it as good. All the creatures of the world also share in this goodness (I Tim. 4:4). This does not mean that the world is "good for" some purpose or simply has utilitarian value to humanity. The world, in its bounty and multiplicity of life, is independently good and ought to be respected as such.

As an independent good, the earth possesses an autonomous status as an ethical and covenanted entity. In Genesis 9:8–17, God directly includes the earth and all the animals as participants in the covenant. He urges the animals to "be fruitful and multiply." Earlier in Genesis 1:30, he takes care specifically to grant the plant life of the earth to the creatures who possess "breath of life." In the great covenant with Noah and all humanity, he expressly includes all other creatures and the earth.

> And God said, "This is a sign of the covenant which I make between *me and you and every living creature* that is with you, for all future generations: I set my bow in the sky, and it shall be a sign of the *covenant between* me and the earth" [emphasis added].

The prophets, Isaiah especially, constantly address the earth and describe its independent travail. Paul describes the turmoil and travail of the earth as a midwife of all creation and redemption (Rom. 8:18–22). The earth must be regarded as an autonomous ethical entity bound not just by the restraints of physical law but also by respect for its inherent goodness and the covenanted limitations placed upon our sojourn. Perhaps we must think seriously of defining a category of "sins against the earth."

The proper relation between humanity and the bountiful earth is more complex. One fact is of outstanding moral relevance: the earth does not belong to humanity; it belongs to God. Jeremiah summarizes it quite succinctly: "I by my great power and outstretched arm made the earth, land and animals that are on the earth. And I can give them to whom I please" (Jer. 27:5). For an ecological ethic this fact cannot be ignored. The resources and environment of the earth are not ours in any sovereign or unlimited sense; they belong to someone else.

A TRUST FOR FUTURE GENERATIONS

Humanity's relation to the earth is dominated by the next fact: God "bestows" the earth upon all of humanity (Ps. 115:16). This gift does not,

however, grant sovereign control. The prophets constantly remind us that God is still the "king" and the ruler/owner to whom the earth reverts. No one generation of people possesses the earth. The earth was made "to endure" and was given for all future generations. Consequently the texts constantly reaffirm that the gift comes under covenanted conditions, and that the covenant is "forever." The Bible is permeated with a careful concern for preserving the "land" and the "earth" as an "allotted heritage" (Ps. 2:7–12).

This point is central to the Judeo-Christian response to the world. The world is given to all. Its heritage is something of enduring value designed to benefit all future generations. Those who receive such a gift and benefit from it are duty-bound to conserve the resources and pass them on for future generations to enjoy. An "earth of abundance" (Judg. 18:10) provides for humanity's needs and survival (Gen. 1:26–28, 9:2–5). But the injunction "obey the covenant" (I Chron. 16:14–18) accompanies the gift.

There are some fairly clear principles that direct our covenanted responsibilities toward the earth. Each generation exists only as "sojourner" or "pilgrim." We hold the resources and the earth as a "trust" for future generations. Our covenanted relations to the earth—and for that matter, to all human beings—must be predicated upon the recognition and acceptance of the limits of reality. For there is a "limit upon all perfection" (Ps. 119:96), and we must discover and respect the limits upon ourselves, our use of resources, our consumption, our treatment of others and the environment with its delicate ecosystems. Abiding by the covenant means abiding by the laws of nature, both scientific and moral. In ecological terms the balance of nature embodies God's careful plan that the earth and its bounty shall provide for the needs and survival of all humanity of all generations.

The combined emphases upon God's ownership, our trusteeship and the limits of life call for an attitude of humility and care in dealing with the world. Only "the humble shall have the land for their own to enjoy untroubled peace"

(Ps. 37:11). Knowledge of limits, especially of the intricacy of the ecosystems, makes humility and care a much more natural response. The transgression of limits usually brings either unknown or clearly dangerous consequences and ought to influence all actions with a singular sense of caution. Humility and respect do not mean simple awe, or withdrawal from all attempts to use or improve the bounty we are given. At the very least, they lead to the loss of arrogant ignorance which leads us to pursue policies in contradiction to the clear limits and laws of nature and particular ecosystems.

THE STEWARDSHIP IMPERATIVE

The New Testament distills these notions and adds a strong activist imperative with its account of stewardship. This activist element is a vital alternative to some of the more extreme ethical positions in reactionary ecological ethics. The parable of the good steward in Luke 12:41–48 and the parable of the talents in Matthew 25:14–30 summarize the concept. The preservation of what is given "in trust" demands a recognition of the owner's dictates for the resources. We must know the limits and laws of the world in order to use them wisely. Our actions must be guided, in part, by concerns for future generations. Above all, we must never knowingly exhaust or ruin what has been given to us. If doing so is absolutely necessary to sustain life, then equity demands that we must leave some equally accessible and beneficial legacy to replace what has been exhausted.

But there is more involved in being a "faithful and wise steward." Even the most conservative banker is obliged to improve the stock for the benefit of the heirs. The parable of the talents makes it abundantly clear that we who are entrusted with his property will be called to account for our obligation to improve the earth. The stewardship imperative assumes that the moral and ecological constraints are respected, and it adds the obligation to distribute the benefits justly. The steward must "give them their portion of the food at the proper time." Mistreating his charges, gorging himself on the resources in excess consumption, and not caring for the resources will all cause the stewards to be "cut off." True stewardship requires both respect for the trusteeship and covenanted imperatives and an active effort to improve the land for the future and to use it in a manner to benefit others. Ethical proportionality applies to all those responsible for the earth, for "when a man has had a great deal given to him on trust, even more will be expected of him" (Luke 12:48–49).

AN INFORMED HUMILITY

The lessons are clear. Any ecological ethic which takes into account both God and humanity and does not reduce both to some extension of undifferentiated nature must begin with a rejection of the unbridled sovereignty of humanity over the earth. In this rejection is the recognition that all work upon the earth must be informed by a clear understanding of and respect for the earth as an autonomous and valuable entity and the laws of nature on which the bounty of the earth depends.

These are necessary but by no means sufficient within the Judeo-Christian tradition. For the earth, while it possesses its own moral autonomy, is not God and must not be confused as such. Our own relation to it must be predicated upon a careful understanding that earth and its resources are for any generation a restricted gift held in trust for future generations. We must never lose sight of the fact that a just and informed humility provides the framework for a working relationship with the earth.

Much more work remains to be done on the "ethics of stewardship"; I have merely suggested a few ethical considerations: the obligation not to exhaust nonrenewable resources, the imperative to provide accessible replacements, the necessity to improve our heritage modestly and carefully, the greater responsibility of the advantaged to improve that which exists and to share, and the obligation to refrain from excessive consumption and waste. "Each of you has received a special gift, so like good stewards responsible for all the different gifts of God, put yourselves at the service of others" (I Pet. 4:10–11).

🐾 STUDY QUESTIONS

1. Compare Dobel's account with White's critique. Which account do you think is closer to the truth? Explain your answer.
2. If human beings do not own Earth, what is our role, according to Dobel? Do you agree? Explain your answer.

3. If one does not accept a theistic version of creation, does the stewardship model make any sense? A steward is one who manages the household affairs of another person. If there is no God, Earth is not God's household. But then whose is it? To whom are we stewards?

5   The Power and the Promise of Ecological Feminism

KAREN J. WARREN

Karen Warren is the editor of several books and the author of numerous articles in environmental philosophy. She is professor of philosophy at Macalester College. In this reading she examines the connections between the domination of nature and the domination of woman, suggesting that ecofeminism, a feminist ethic of nature, holds great promise for developing humanity on both accounts.

Ecological feminism is the position that there are important connections—historical, symbolic, theoretical—between the domination of women and the domination of nonhuman nature. I argue that because the conceptual connections between the dual dominations of women and nature are located in an oppressive patriarchal conceptual framework characterized by a logic of domination, (1) the logic of traditional feminism requires the expansion of feminism to include ecological feminism and (2) ecological feminism provides a framework for developing a distinctively feminist environmental ethic. I conclude that any feminist theory and any environmental ethic which fails to take seriously the interconnected dominations of women and nature is simply inadequate.

INTRODUCTION

Ecological feminism (ecofeminism) has begun to receive a fair amount of attention lately as an alternative feminism and environmental ethic.[1] Since Francoise d'Eaubonne introduced the term *eco-feminisme* in 1974 to bring attention to women's potential for bringing about an ecological revolution[2] the term has been used in a variety of ways. As I use the term in this paper, ecological feminism is the position that there are important connections—historical, experiential, symbolic, theoretical—between the domination of women and the domination of nature, an understanding of which is crucial to both feminism and environmental ethics. I argue that the promise and power of ecological feminism is that *it provides a distinctive framework both for reconceiving feminism and for developing an environmental ethic which takes seriously connections between the domination of women and the domination of nature.* I do so by discussing the nature of a feminist ethic and the ways in which ecofeminism provides a feminist and environmental ethic. I conclude that any feminist theory *and* any environmental ethic which fails to take seriously the twin and interconnected dominations of women and nature is at best incomplete and at worst simply inadequate.

Reprinted by permission of the publisher from *Environmental Ethics*, v. 12, Summer 1990.

FEMINISM, ECOLOGICAL FEMINISM, AND CONCEPTUAL FRAMEWORKS

Whatever else it is, feminism is at least the movement to end sexist oppression. It involves the elimination of any and all factors that contribute to the continued and systematic domination or subordination of women. While feminists disagree about the nature of and solutions to the subordination of women, all feminists agree that sexist oppression exists, is wrong, and must be abolished.

A "feminist issue" is any issue that contributes in some way to understanding the oppression of women. Equal rights, comparable pay for comparable work, and food production are feminist issues wherever and whenever an understanding of them contributes to an understanding of the continued exploitation or subjugation of women. Carrying water and searching for firewood are feminist issues wherever and whenever women's primary responsibility for these tasks contributes to their lack of full participation in decision making, income producing, or high status positions engaged in by men. What counts as a feminist issue, then, depends largely on context, particularly the historical and material conditions of women's lives.

Environmental degradation and exploitation are feminist issues because an understanding of them contributes to an understanding of the oppression of women. In India, for example, both deforestation and reforestation through the introduction of a monoculture species tree (e.g., eucalyptus) intended for commercial production are feminist issues because the loss of indigenous forests and multiple species of trees has drastically affected rural Indian women's ability to maintain a subsistence household. Indigenous forests provide a variety of trees for food, fuel, fodder, household utensils, dyes, medicines, and income-generating uses, while monoculture-species forests do not.[3] Although I do not argue for this claim here, a look at the global impact of environmental degradation on women's lives suggests important respects in which environmental degradation is a feminist issue.

Feminist philosophers claim that some of the most important feminist issues are *conceptual* ones: these issues concern how one conceptualizes such mainstay philosophical notions as reason and rationality, ethics, and what it is to be human. Ecofeminists extend this feminist philosophical concern to nature. They argue that, ultimately, some of the most important connections between the domination of women and the domination of nature are conceptual. To see this, consider the nature of conceptual frameworks.

A *conceptual framework* is a set of *basic* beliefs, values, attitudes, and assumptions which shape and reflect how one views oneself and one's world. It is a socially constructed lens through which we perceive ourselves and others. It is affected by such factors as gender, race, class, age, affectional orientation, nationality, and religious background.

Some conceptual frameworks are oppressive. An *oppressive conceptual framework* is one that explains, justifies, and maintains relationships of domination and subordination. When an oppressive conceptual framework is *patriarchal*, it explains, justifies, and maintains the subordination of women by men.

I have argued elsewhere that there are three significant features of oppressive conceptual frameworks: (1) value-hierarchical thinking, i.e., "up-down" thinking which places higher value, status, or prestige on what is "up" rather than on what is "down"; (2) value dualisms, i.e., disjunctive pairs in which the disjuncts are seen as oppositional (rather than as complementary) and exclusive (rather than as inclusive), and which place higher value (status, prestige) on one disjunct rather than the other (e.g., dualisms which give higher value or status to that which has historically been identified as "mind," "reason," and "male" than to that which has historically been identified as "body," "emotion," and "female"); and (3) logic of domination, i.e., a structure of argumentation which leads to a justification of subordination.[4]

The third feature of oppressive conceptual frameworks is the most significant. A logic of domination is not *just* a logical structure. It also involves a substantive value system, since an ethical premise is needed to permit or sanction the "just" subordination of that which is subordinate. This justification typically is given on grounds of some alleged characteristic (e.g., rationality) which the dominant (e.g., men) have and the subordinate (e.g., women) lack.

Contrary to what many feminists and ecofeminists have said or suggested, there may be nothing *inherently* problematic about "hierarchical thinking" or even "value-hierarchical thinking" in contexts other than contexts of oppression. Hierarchical thinking is important in daily living for classifying data, comparing information, and organizing material. Taxonomies (e.g., plant taxonomies) and biological nomenclature seem to require *some* form of "hierarchical thinking." Even "value-hierarchical thinking" may be quite acceptable in certain contexts. (The same may be said of "value dualisms" in non-oppressive contexts.) For example, suppose it is true that what is unique about humans is our conscious capacity to radically reshape our social environments (or "societies"), as Murray Bookchin suggests.[5] Then one could truthfully say that humans are better equipped to radically reshape their environments than are rocks or plants—a "value-hierarchical" way of speaking.

The problem is not simply *that* value-hierarchical thinking and value dualisms are used, but *the way* in which each has been used *in oppressive conceptual frameworks* to establish inferiority and to justify subordination.[6] It is the logic of domination, *coupled with* value-hierarchical thinking and value dualisms, which "justifies" subordination. What is explanatorily basic, then, about the nature of oppressive conceptual frameworks is the logic of domination.

For ecofeminism, that a logic of domination is explanatorily basic is important for at least three reasons. First, without a logic of domination, a description of similarities and differences would be just that—a description of similarities and differences. Consider the claim, "Humans are different from plants and rocks in that humans can (and plants and rocks cannot) consciously and radically reshape the communities in which they live; humans are similar to plants and rocks in that they are both members of an ecological

community." Even if humans are "better" than plants and rocks with respect to the conscious ability of humans to radically transform communities, one does not *thereby* get any *morally* relevant distinction between humans and nonhumans, or an argument for the domination of plants and rocks by humans. To get *those* conclusions one needs to add at least two powerful assumptions, viz., (A2) and (A4) in argument A below:

(A1) Humans do, and plants and rocks do not, have the capacity to consciously and radically change the community in which they live.

(A2) Whatever has the capacity to consciously and radically change the community in which it lives is morally superior to whatever lacks this capacity.

(A3) Thus, humans are morally superior to plants and rocks.

(A4) For any X and Y, if X is morally superior to Y, then X is morally justified in subordinating Y.

(A5) Thus, humans are morally justified in subordinating plants and rocks.

Without the two assumptions that *humans are morally superior* to (at least some) nonhumans, (A2), and that *superiority justifies subordination*, (A4), all one has is some difference between humans and some nonhumans. This is true *even if* that difference is given in terms of superiority. Thus, it is the logic of domination, (A4), which is the bottom line in ecofeminist discussions of oppression.

Second, ecofeminists argue that, at least in Western societies, the oppressive conceptual framework which sanctions the twin dominations of women and nature is a patriarchal one characterized by all three features of an oppressive conceptual framework. Many ecofeminists claim that, historically, within at least the dominant Western culture, a patriarchal conceptual framework has sanctioned the following argument B:

(B1) Women are identified with nature and the realm of the physical; men are identified with the "human" and the realm of the mental.

(B2) Whatever is identified with nature and the realm of the physical is inferior to ("below") whatever is identified with the "human" and the realm of the mental; or, conversely, the latter is superior to ("above") the former.

(B3) Thus, women are inferior to ("below") men; or, conversely, men are superior to ("above") women.

(B4) For any X and Y, if X is superior to Y, then X is justified in subordinating Y.

(B5) Thus, men are justified in subordinating women.

If sound, argument B establishes *patriarchy*, i.e., the conclusion given at (B5) that the systematic domination of women by men is justified. But according to ecofeminists, (B5) is justified by just those three features of an oppressive conceptual framework identified earlier: value-hierarchical thinking, the assumption at (B2); value dualisms, the assumed dualism of the mental and the physical at (B1) and the assumed inferiority of the physical vis-à-vis the mental at (B2); and a logic of domination, the assumption at (B4), the same as the previous premise (A4). Hence, according to ecofeminists, insofar as an oppressive patriarchal conceptual framework has functioned historically (within at least dominant Western culture) to sanction the twin dominations of women and nature (argument B), both argument B and the patriarchal conceptual framework, from whence it comes, ought to be rejected.

Of course, the preceeding does not identify which premises of B are false. What is the status of premises (B1) and (B2)? Most, if not all, feminists claim that (B1), and many ecofeminists claim that (B2), have been assumed or asserted within the dominant Western philosophical and intellectual tradition.[7] As such, these feminists assert, as a matter of historical fact, that the dominant Western philosophical tradition has assumed the truth of (B1) and (B2). Ecofeminists, however, either deny (B2) or do not affirm (B2). Furthermore, because some ecofeminists are anxious to deny any ahistorical identification of women with nature, some ecofeminists deny (B1) when (B1) is used to support anything

other than a strictly historical claim about what has been asserted or assumed to be true within patriarchal culture—e.g., when (B1) is used to assert that women properly are identified with the realm of nature and the physical.[8] Thus, from an ecofeminist perspective, (B1) and (B2) are properly viewed as problematic though historically sanctioned claims: they are problematic precisely because of the way they have functioned historically in a patriarchal conceptual framework and culture to sanction the dominations of women and nature.

What *all* ecofeminists agree about, then, is the way in which *the logic of domination* has functioned historically within patriarchy to sustain and justify the twin dominations of women and nature.[9] Since *all* feminists (and not just ecofeminists) oppose patriarchy, the conclusion given at (B5), all feminists (including ecofeminists) must oppose at least the logic of domination, premise (B4), on which argument B rests— whatever the truth-value status of (B1) and (B2) *outside of* a patriarchal context.

That *all* feminists must oppose the logic of domination shows the breadth and depth of the ecofeminist critique of B: it is a critique not only of the three assumptions on which this argument for the domination of women and nature rests, viz., the assumptions at (B1), (B2), and (B4); it is also a critique of patriarchal conceptual frameworks generally, i.e., of those oppressive conceptual frameworks which put men "up" and women "down," allege some way in which women are morally inferior to men, and use that alleged difference to justify the subordination of women by men. Therefore, ecofeminism is necessary to *any* feminist critique of patriarchy, and, hence, necessary to feminism (a point I discuss again later).

Third, ecofeminism clarifies why the logic of domination, and any conceptual framework which gives rise to it, must be abolished in order both to make possible a meaningful notion of difference which does not breed domination and to prevent feminism from becoming a "support" movement based primarily on shared experiences. In contemporary society, there is no one "woman's voice," no *woman* (or *human*) *simpliciter*: every woman (or human) is a woman (or human) of some race, class, age, affectional orientation, marital status, regional or national background, and so forth. Because there are no "monolithic experiences" that all women share, feminism must be a "solidarity movement" based on shared beliefs and interests rather than a "unity in sameness" movement based on shared experiences and shared victimization.[10] In the words of Maria Lugones, "Unity—not to be confused with solidarity—is understood as conceptually tied to domination."[11]

Ecofeminists insist that the sort of logic of domination used to justify the domination of humans by gender, racial or ethnic, or class status is also used to justify the domination of nature. Because eliminating a logic of domination is part of a feminist critique—whether a critique of patriarchy, white supremacist culture, or imperialism—ecofeminists insist that *naturism* is properly viewed as an integral part of any feminist solidarity movement to end sexist oppression and the logic of domination which conceptually grounds it.

ECOFEMINISM RECONCEIVES FEMINISM

The discussion so far has focused on some of the oppressive conceptual features of patriarchy. As I use the phrase, the "logic of traditional feminism" refers to the location of the conceptual roots of sexist oppression, at least in Western societies, in an oppressive patriarchal conceptual framework characterized by a logic of domination. Insofar as other systems of oppression (e.g., racism, classism, ageism, heterosexism) are also conceptually maintained by a logic of domination, appeal to the logic of traditional feminism ultimately locates the basic conceptual interconnections among *all* systems of oppression in the logic of domination. It thereby explains at a *conceptual* level why the eradication of sexist oppression requires the eradication of the other forms of oppression.[12] It is by clarifying this conceptual connection between systems of oppression that a movement to end sexist oppression—traditionally the special turf of feminist theory and practice—leads to a reconceiving of feminism as *a movement to end all forms of oppression*.

Suppose one agrees that the logic of traditional feminism requires the expansion of feminism to include other social systems of domination (e.g., racism and classism). What warrants the inclusion of nature in these "social systems of domination"? Why must the logic of traditional feminism include the abolition of "naturism" (i.e., the domination or oppression of nonhuman nature) among the "isms" feminism must confront? The conceptual justification for expanding feminism to include ecofeminism is twofold. One basis has already been suggested: by showing that the conceptual connections between the dual dominations of women and nature are located in an oppressive and, at least in Western societies, patriarchal conceptual framework characterized by a logic of domination, ecofeminism explains how and why feminism, conceived as a movement to end sexist oppression, must be expanded and reconceived as also a movement to end naturism." This is made explicit by the following argument C:

(C1) Feminism is a movement to end sexism.
(C2) But Sexism is conceptually linked with naturism (through an oppressive conceptual framework characterized by a logic of domination).
(C3) Thus, Feminism is (also) a movement to end naturism.

Because, ultimately, these connections between sexism and naturism are conceptual—embedded in an oppressive conceptual framework—the logic of traditional feminism leads to the embracement of ecological feminism.[13]

The other justification for reconceiving feminism to include ecofeminism has to do with the concepts of gender and nature. Just as conceptions of gender are socially constructed, so are conceptions of nature. Of course, the claim that women and nature are social constructions does not require anyone to deny that there are actual humans and actual trees, rivers, and plants. It simply implies that *how* women and nature are conceived is a matter of historical and social reality. These conceptions vary cross-culturally and by historical time period. As a result, any discussion of the "oppression or domination of nature" involves reference to historically specific forms of social domination of nonhuman nature by humans, just as discussion of the "domination of women" refers to historically specific forms of social domination of women by men. Although I do not argue for it here, an ecofeminist defense of the historical connections between the dominations of women and of nature, claims (B1) and (B2) in argument B, involves showing that within patriarchy the feminization of nature and the naturalization of women have been crucial to the historically successful subordinations of both.[14]

If ecofeminism promises to reconceive traditional feminism in ways which include naturism as a legitimate feminist issue, does ecofeminism also promise to reconceive environmental ethics in ways which are feminist? I think so. This is the subject of the remainder of the paper.

CLIMBING FROM ECOFEMINISM TO ENVIRONMENTAL ETHICS

Many feminists and some environmental ethicists have begun to explore the use of first-person narrative as a way of raising philosophically germane issues in ethics often lost or underplayed in mainstream philosophical ethics. Why is this so? What is it about narrative which makes it a significant resource for theory and practice in feminism and environmental ethics? Even if appeal to first-person narrative is a helpful literary device for describing ineffable experience or a legitimate social science methodology for documenting personal and social history, how is first-person narrative a valuable vehicle of argumentation for ethical decision making and theory building? One fruitful way to begin answering these questions is to ask them of a particular first-person narrative.

Consider the following first-person narrative about rock climbing:

> For my very first rock climbing experience, I chose a somewhat private spot, away from other climbers and on-lookers. After studying "the chimney," I focused all my energy on making it to the top. I climbed with intense determination, using whatever strength and skills I had to accomplish this challenging feat. By midway I was exhausted and anxious. I couldn't see what to do next—where

to put my hands or feet. Growing increasingly more weary as I clung somewhat desperately to the rock, I made a move. It didn't work. I fell. There I was, dangling midair above the rocky ground below, frightened but terribly relieved that the belay rope had held me. I knew I was safe. I took a look up at the climb that remained. I was determined to make it to the top. With renewed confidence and concentration, I finished the climb to the top.

On my second day of climbing, I rappelled down about 200 feet from the top of the Palisades at Lake Superior to just a few feet above the water level. I could see no one—not my belayer, not the other climbers, no one. I unhooked slowly from the rappel rope and took a deep cleansing breath. I looked all around me—really looked—and listened. I heard a cacophony of voices—birds, trickles of water on the rock before me, waves lapping against the rocks below. I closed my eyes and began to feel the rock with my hands—the cracks and crannies, the raised lichen and mosses, the almost imperceptible nubs that might provide a resting place for my fingers and toes when I began to climb. At that moment I was bathed in serenity. I began to talk to the rock in an almost inaudible, child-like way, as if the rock were my friend. I felt an overwhelming sense of gratitude for what it offered me—a chance to know myself and the rock differently, to appreciate unforeseen miracles like the tiny flowers growing in the even tinier cracks in the rock's surface, and to come to know a sense of *being in relationship* with the natural environment. It felt as if the rock and I were silent conversational partners in a longstanding friendship. I realized then that I had come to care about this cliff which was so different from me, so unmovable and invincible, independent and seemingly indifferent to my presence. I wanted to be with the rock as I climbed. Gone was the determination to conquer the rock, to forcefully impose my will on it; I wanted simply to work respectfully with the rock as I climbed. And as I climbed, that is what I felt. I felt myself *caring* for this rock and feeling thankful that climbing provided the opportunity for me to know it and myself in this new way.

There are at least four reasons why use of such a first-person narrative is important to feminism and environmental ethics. First, such a narrative gives voice to a felt sensitivity often lacking in traditional analytical ethical discourse, viz., a sensitivity to conceiving of oneself as fundamentally "in relationship with" others, including the nonhuman environment. It is a modality which *takes relationships themselves seriously*. It thereby stands in contrast to a strictly reductionist modality that takes relationships seriously only or primarily because of the nature of the *relators* or parties to those relationships (e.g., relators conceived as moral agents, right holders, interest carriers, or sentient beings). In the rock-climbing narrative above, it is the climber's relationship with the rock she climbs which takes on special significance—which is itself a locus of value—in addition to whatever moral status or moral considerability she or the rock or any other parties to the relationship may also have.[15]

Second, such a first-person narrative gives expression to a variety of ethical attitudes and behaviors often overlooked or underplayed in mainstream Western ethics, e.g., the difference in attitudes and behaviors toward a rock when one is "making it to the top" and when one thinks of oneself as "friends with" or "caring about" the rock one climbs.[16] These different attitudes and behaviors suggest an ethically germane contrast between two different types of relationship humans or climbers may have toward a rock: an imposed conqueror-type relationship, and an emergent caring-type relationship. This contrast grows out of, and is faithful to, felt, lived experience.

The difference between conquering and caring attitudes and behaviors in relation to the natural environment provides a third reason why the use of first-person narrative is important to feminism and environmental ethics: it provides a way of conceiving of ethics and ethical meaning as *emerging out of* particular situations moral agents find themselves in, rather than as being *imposed on* those situations (e.g., as a derivation or instantiation of some predetermined abstract principle or rule). This emergent feature of narrative centralizes the importance of *voice*. When a multiplicity of cross-cultural *voices* are centralized, narrative is able to give expression to a range of attitudes, values, beliefs, and behaviors which may be overlooked or silenced by imposed ethical meaning and theory. As a reflection of and on felt, lived experiences, the use of narrative in ethics provides a stance from which ethical discourse can be held accountable to the historical, material, and social realities in which moral subjects find themselves.

Lastly, and for our purposes perhaps most importantly, the use of narrative has argumentative significance. Jim Cheney calls attention to this feature of narrative when he claims, "To contextualize ethical deliberation is, in some sense, to provide a narrative or story, from which the solution to the ethical dilemma emerges as the fitting conclusion."[17] Narrative has argumentative force by suggesting *what counts* as an appropriate conclusion to an ethical situation. One ethical conclusion suggested by the climbing narrative is that what counts as a proper ethical attitude toward mountains and rocks is an attitude of respect and care (whatever that turns out to be or involve), not one of domination and conquest.

In an essay entitled "In and Out of Harm's Way: Arrogance and Love," feminist philosopher Marilyn Frye distinguishes between "arrogant" and "loving" perception as one way of getting at this difference in the ethical attitudes of care and conquest.[18] Frye writes:

> The loving eye is a contrary of the arrogant eye.
>
> The loving eye knows the independence of the other. It is the eye of a seer who knows that nature is indifferent. It is the eye of one who knows that to know the seen, one must consult something other than one's own will and interests and fears and imagination. One must look at the thing. One must look and listen and check and question.
>
> The loving eye is one that pays a certain sort of attention. This attention can require a discipline but *not* a self-denial. The discipline is one of self-knowledge, knowledge of the scope and boundary of the self.... In particular, it is a matter of being able to tell one's own interests from those of others and of knowing where one's self leaves off and another begins....
>
> The loving eye does not make the object of perception into something edible, does not try to assimilate it, does not reduce it to the size of the seer's desire, fear and imagination, and hence does not have to simplify. It knows the complexity of the other as something which will forever present new things to be known. The science of the loving eye would favor The Complexity Theory

of Truth [in contrast to The Simplicity Theory of Truth] and presuppose The Endless Interestingness of the Universe.[19]

According to Frye, the loving eye is not an invasive, coercive eye which annexes others to itself, but one which "knows the complexity of the other as something which will forever present new things to be known."

When one climbs a rock as a conqueror, one climbs with an arrogant eye. When one climbs with a loving eye, one constantly "must look and listen and check and question." One recognizes the rock as something very different, something perhaps totally indifferent to one's own presence, and finds in that difference joyous occasion for celebration. One knows "the boundary of the self," where the self—the "I," the climber—leaves off and the rock begins. There is no fusion of two into one, but a complement of two entities *acknowledged* as separate, different, independent, yet *in relationship;* they are in relationship *if only* because the loving eye is perceiving it, responding to it, noticing it, attending to it.

An ecofeminist perspective about both women and nature involves this shift in attitude from "arrogant perception" to "loving perception" of the nonhuman world. Arrogant perception of nonhumans by humans presupposes and maintains *sameness* in such a way that it expands the moral community to those beings who are thought to resemble (be like, similar to, or the same as) humans in some morally significant way. Any environmental movement or ethic based on arrogant perception builds a moral hierarchy of beings and assumes some common denominator of moral considerability in virtue of which like beings deserve similar treatment or moral consideration and unlike beings do not. Such environmental ethics are or generate a "unity in sameness." In contrast, "loving perception" presupposes and maintains *difference*—a distinction between the self and other, between human and at least some nonhumans—in such a way that perception of the other as other *is* an expression of love for one who/which is recognized at the outset as independent, dissimilar, different. As Maria Lugones says, in loving perception, "Love is seen not as fusion and erasure of difference but as incompatible

with them."[20] "Unity in sameness" alone is *an erasure of difference.*

"Loving perception" of the nonhuman natural world is an attempt to understand what it means *for humans* to care about the nonhuman world, a world *acknowledged* as being independent, different, perhaps even indifferent to humans. Humans *are* different from rocks in important ways, even if they are also both members of some ecological community. A moral community based on loving perception of oneself *in relationship with* a rock, or with the natural environment as a whole, is one which acknowledges and respects difference, whatever "sameness" also exists.[21] The limits of loving perception are determined only by the limits of one's (e.g., a person's, a community's) ability to respond lovingly (or with appropriate care, trust, or friendship)—whether it is to other humans or to the nonhuman world and elements of it.[22]

If what I have said so far is correct, then there are very different ways to climb a mountain and *how* one climbs it and *how* one narrates the experience of climbing it matter ethically. If one climbs with "arrogant perception," with an attitude of "conquer and control," one keeps intact the very sorts of thinking that characterize a logic of domination and an oppressive conceptual framework. Since the oppressive conceptual framework which sanctions the domination of nature is a patriarchal one, one also thereby keeps intact, even if unwittingly, a patriarchal conceptual framework. Because the dismantling of patriarchal conceptual frameworks is a feminist issue, *how* one climbs a mountain and *how* one narrates—or tells the story—about the experience of climbing also are *feminist issues*. In this way, ecofeminism makes visible why, at a conceptual level, environmental ethics is a feminist issue. I turn now to a consideration of ecofeminism as a distinctively feminist and environmental ethic.

ECOFEMINISM AS A FEMINIST AND ENVIRONMENTAL ETHIC

A feminist ethic involves a twofold commitment to critique male bias in ethics wherever it occurs, and to develop ethics which are not male-biased. Sometimes this involves articulation of values (e.g., values of care, appropriate trust, kinship, friendship) often lost or underplayed in main-stream ethics.[23] Sometimes it involves engaging in theory building by pioneering in new directions or by revamping old theories in gender sensitive ways. What makes the critiques of old theories or conceptualizations of new ones "feminist" is that they emerge out of sex-gender analyses and reflect whatever those analyses reveal about gendered experience and gendered social reality.

As I conceive feminist ethics in the pre-feminist present, it rejects attempts to conceive of ethical theory in terms of necessary and sufficient conditions, because it assumes that there is no essence (in the sense of some transhistorical, universal, absolute abstraction) of feminist ethics. While attempts to formulate joint necessary and sufficient conditions of a feminist ethic are unfruitful, nonetheless, there are some necessary conditions, what I prefer to call "boundary conditions," of a feminist ethic. These boundary conditions clarify some of the minimal conditions of a feminist ethic without suggesting that feminist ethics has some ahistorical essence. They are like the boundaries of a quilt or collage. They delimit the territory of the piece without dictating what the interior, the design, the actual pattern of the piece looks like. Because the actual design of the quilt emerges from the multiplicity of voices of women in a cross-cultural context, the design will change over time. It is not something static.

What are some of the boundary conditions of a feminist ethic? First, nothing can become part of a feminist ethic—can be part of the quilt—that promotes sexism, racism, classism, or any other "isms" of social domination. Of course, people may disagree about what counts as a sexist act, racist attitude, classist behavior. What counts as sexism, racism, or classism may vary cross-culturally. Still, because a feminist ethic aims at eliminating sexism and sexist bias, and (as I have already shown) sexism is intimately connected in conceptualization and in practice to racism, classism, and naturism, a feminist ethic must be anti-sexist, anti-racist, anti-classist, anti-naturist and opposed to any "ism" which presupposes or advances a logic of domination.

Second, a feminist ethic is a *contextualist* ethic. A contextualist ethic is one which sees

ethical discourse and practice as emerging from the voices of people located in different historical circumstances. A contextualist ethic is properly viewed as a *collage* or *mosaic,* a *tapestry* of voices that emerges out of felt experiences. Like any collage or mosaic, the point is not to have *one picture* based on a unity of voices, but a *pattern* which emerges out of the very different voices of people located in different circumstances. When a contextualist ethic is *feminist,* it gives central place to the voices of women.

Third, since a feminist ethic gives central significance to the diversity of women's voices, a feminist ethic must be structurally pluralistic rather than unitary or reductionistic It rejects the assumption that there is "one voice" in terms of which ethical values, beliefs, attitudes, and conduct can be assessed.

Fourth, a feminist ethic reconceives ethical theory as theory in process which will change over time. Like all theory, a feminist ethic is based on some generalizations.[24] Nevertheless, the generalizations associated with it are themselves a pattern of voices within which the different voices emerging out of concrete and alternative descriptions of ethical situations have meaning. The coherence of a feminist theory so conceived is given within a historical and conceptual context, i.e., within a set of historical, socio-economic circumstances (including circumstances of race, class, age, and affectional orientation) and within a set of basic beliefs, values, attitudes, and assumptions about the world.

Fifth, because a feminist ethic is contextualist, structurally pluralistic, and "in-process," one way to evaluate the claims of a feminist ethic is in terms of their *inclusiveness:* those claims (voices, patterns of voices) are morally and epistemologically favored (preferred, better, less partial, less biased) which are more inclusive of the felt experiences and perspectives of oppressed persons. The condition of inclusiveness requires and ensures that the diverse voices of women (as oppressed persons) will be given legitimacy in ethical theory building. It thereby helps to minimize empirical bias, e.g., bias rising from faulty or false generalizations based on stereotyping, too small a sample size, or a skewed sample. It does so by ensuring that any generalizations which are made about ethics and ethical decision making include—indeed cohere with—the patterned voices of women.[25]

Sixth, a feminist ethic makes no attempt to provide an "objective" point of view, since it assumes that in contemporary culture there really is no such point of view. As such, it does not claim to be "unbiased" in the sense of "value-neutral" or "objective." However, it does assume that whatever bias it has as an ethic centralizing the voices of oppressed persons is a *better bias*—"better" because it is more inclusive and therefore less partial—than those which exclude those voices.[26]

Seventh, a feminist ethic provides a central place for values typically unnoticed, underplayed, or misrepresented in traditional ethics, e.g., values of care, love, friendship, and appropriate trust.[27] Again, it need not do this at the exclusion of considerations of rights, rules, or utility. There may be many contexts in which talk of rights or of utility is useful or appropriate. For instance, in contracts or property relationships, talk of rights may be useful and appropriate. In deciding what is cost-effective or advantageous to the most people, talk of utility may be useful and appropriate. In a feminist *qua* contextualist ethic, whether or not such talk is useful or appropriate depends on the context; *other values* (e.g., values of care, trust, friendship) are *not* viewed as reducible to or captured solely in terms of such talk.[28]

Eighth, a feminist ethic also involves a reconception of what it is to be human and what it is for humans to engage in ethical decision making, since it rejects as either meaningless or currently untenable any gender-free or gender-neutral description of humans, ethics, and ethical decision making. It thereby rejects what Alison Jaggar calls "abstract individualism," i.e., the position that it is possible to identify a human essence or human nature that exists independently of any particular historical context.[29] Humans and human moral conduct are properly understood essentially (and not merely accidentally) in terms of networks or webs of historical and concrete relationships.

All the props are now in place for seeing how ecofeminism provides the framework for a distinctively feminist and environmental ethic. It is a feminism that critiques male bias wherever it occurs in ethics (including environmental ethics) and aims at providing an ethic (including an environmental ethic) which is not male biased—and it does so in a way that satisfies the preliminary boundary conditions of a feminist ethic.

First, ecofeminism is quintessentially anti-naturist. Its anti-naturism consists in the rejection of any way of thinking about or acting toward nonhuman nature that reflects a logic, values, or attitude of domination. Its anti-naturist, anti-sexist, anti-racist, anti-classist (and so forth, for all other "isms" of social domination) stance forms the outer boundary of the quilt: nothing gets on the quilt which is naturist, sexist, racist, classist, and so forth.

Second, ecofeminism is a contextualist ethic. It involves a shift *from* a conception of ethics as primarily a matter of rights, rules, or principles predetermined and applied in specific cases to entities viewed as competitors in the contest of moral standing, *to* a conception of ethics as growing out of what Jim Cheney calls "defining relationships," i.e., relationships conceived in some sense as defining who one is.[30] As a contextualist ethic, it is not that rights, or rules, or principles are *not* relevant or important. Clearly they are in certain contexts and for certain purposes.[31] It is just that what *makes* them relevant or important is that those to whom they apply are entities in *relationship with* others.

Ecofeminism also involves an ethical shift *from* granting moral consideration to nonhumans *exclusively* on the grounds of some similarity they share with humans (e.g., rationality, interests, moral agency, sentiency, right-holder status) *to* "a highly contextual account to see clearly what a human being is and what the nonhuman world might be, morally speaking, *for* human beings."[32] For an ecofeminist, *how* a moral agent is in relationship to another becomes of central significance, not simply *that* a moral agent is a moral agent or is bound by rights, duties, virtue, or utility to act in a certain way.

Third, ecofeminism is structurally pluralistic in that it presupposes and maintains difference—difference among humans as well as between humans and at least some elements of nonhuman nature. Thus, while ecofeminism denies the "nature/culture" split, it affirms that humans are both members of an ecological community (in some respects) and different from it (in other respects). Ecofeminism's attention to relationships and community is not, therefore, an erasure of difference but a respectful acknowledgement of it.

Fourth, ecofeminism reconceives theory as theory in process. It focuses on patterns of meaning which emerge, for instance, from the storytelling and first-person narratives of women (and others) who deplore the twin dominations of women and nature. The use of narrative is one way to ensure that the content of the ethic—the pattern of the quilt—may/will change over time, as the historical and material realities of women's lives change and as more is learned about women-nature connections and the destruction of the nonhuman world.[33]

Fifth, ecofeminism is inclusivist. It emerges from the voices of women who experience the harmful domination of nature and the way that domination is tied to their domination as women. It emerges from listening to the voices of indigenous peoples such as Native Americans who have been dislocated from their land and have witnessed the attendant undermining of such values as appropriate reciprocity, sharing, and kinship that characterize traditional Indian culture. It emerges from listening to voices of those who, like Nathan Hare, critique traditional approaches to environmental ethics as white and bourgeois, and as failing to address issues of "black ecology" and the "ecology" of the inner city and urban spaces.[34] It also emerges out of the voices of Chipko women who see the destruction of "earth, soil, and water" as intimately connected with their own inability to survive economically.[35] With its emphasis on inclusivity and difference, ecofeminism provides a framework for recognizing that what counts as ecology and what counts as appropriate conduct toward both human and nonhuman environments is largely a matter of context.

Sixth, as a feminism, ecofeminism makes no attempt to provide an "objective" point of view. It is a social ecology. It recognizes the twin dominations of women and nature as social

problems rooted both in very concrete, historical, socioeconomic circumstances and in oppressive patriarchal conceptual frameworks which maintain and sanction these circumstances.

Seventh, ecofeminism makes a central place for values of care, love, friendship, trust, and appropriate reciprocity—values that presuppose that our relationships to others are central to our understanding of who we are.[36] It thereby gives voice to the sensitivity that in climbing a mountain, one is doing something in relationship with an "other," an "other" whom one can come to care about and treat respectfully.

Lastly, an ecofeminist ethic involves a reconception of what it means to be human, and in what human ethical behavior consists. Ecofeminism denies abstract individualism. Humans are who we are in large part by virtue of the historical and social contexts and the relationships we are in, including our relationships with nonhuman nature. Relationships are not something extrinsic to who we are, not an "add on" feature of human nature; they play an essential role in shaping what it is to be human. Relationships of humans to the nonhuman environment are, in part, constitutive of what it is to be a human.

By making visible the interconnections among the dominations of women and nature, ecofeminism shows that both are feminist issues and that explicit acknowledgement of both is vital to any responsible environmental ethic. Feminism *must* embrace ecological feminism if it is to end the domination of women because the domination of women is tied conceptually and historically to the domination of nature.

A responsible environmental ethic also *must* embrace feminism. Otherwise, even the seemingly most revolutionary, liberational, and holistic ecological ethic will fail to take seriously the interconnected dominations of nature and women that are so much a part of the historical legacy and conceptual framework that sanctions the exploitation of nonhuman nature. Failure to make visible these interconnected, twin dominations results in an inaccurate account of how it is that nature has been and continues to be dominated and exploited and produces an environmental ethic that lacks the depth necessary to be truly *inclusive* of the realities of persons who at least in dominant Western culture have been intimately tied with that exploitation, viz., women. Whatever else can be said in favor of such holistic ethics, a failure to make visible ecofeminist insights into the common denominators of the twin oppressions of women and nature is to perpetuate, rather than overcome, the source of that oppression.

This last point deserves further attention. It may be objected that as long as the end result is "the same"—the development of an environmental ethic which does not emerge out of or reinforce an oppressive conceptual framework—it does not matter whether that ethic (or the ethic endorsed in getting there) is feminist or not. Hence, it simply is *not* the case that any adequate environmental ethic must be feminist. My argument, in contrast, has been that it *does* matter, and for three important reasons. First, there is the scholarly issue of accurately representing historical reality, and that, ecofeminists claim, requires acknowledging the historical feminization of nature and naturalization of women as part of the exploitation of nature. Second, I have shown that the conceptual connections between the domination of women and the domination of nature are located in an oppressive and, at least in Western societies, patriarchal conceptual framework characterized by a logic of domination. Thus, I have shown that failure to notice the nature of this connection leaves at best an incomplete, inaccurate, and partial account of what is required of a conceptually adequate environmental ethic. An ethic which *does not* acknowledge this is simply *not* the same as one that does, whatever else the similarities between them. Third, the claim that, in contemporary culture, one can have an adequate environmental ethic which is *not* feminist assumes that, in contemporary culture, the label *feminist* does not add anything crucial to the nature or description of environmental ethics. I have shown that at least in contemporary culture this is false, for the word *feminist* currently helps to clarify just *how* the domination of nature is conceptually linked to patriarchy and, hence, how the liberation of nature, is conceptually linked to the termination of patriarchy. Thus, because it has critical bite in contemporary culture, it serves as an important reminder that in contemporary sex-gendered, raced, classed, and naturist culture, an unlabeled position functions as a privileged and "unmarked" position. That is, without the addition of the word *feminist*, one presents environmental ethics as if it has no bias, including male-gender bias, which is just what ecofeminists deny: failure to notice the connections between the twin oppressions of women and nature *is* male-gender bias.

One of the goals of feminism is the eradication of all oppressive sex-gender (and related race, class, age, affectional preference) categories and the creation of a world in which *difference does not breed domination*—say, the world of 4001. If in 4001 an "adequate environmental ethic" is a "feminist environmental ethic," the word *feminist* may then be redundant and unnecessary. However, this is *not* 4001, and in terms of the current historical and conceptual reality the dominations of nature and of women are intimately connected. Failure to notice or make visible that connection in 1990 perpetuates the mistaken (and privileged) view that "environmental ethics" is *not* a feminist issue, and that *feminist* adds nothing to environmental ethics.[37]

CONCLUSION

I have argued in this paper that ecofeminism provides a framework for a distinctively feminist and environmental ethic. Ecofeminism grows out of the felt and theorized about connections between the domination of women and the domination of nature. As a contextualist ethic, ecofeminism refocuses environmental ethics on what nature might mean, morally speaking, *for* humans, and on how the relational attitudes of humans to others—humans as well as nonhumans—sculpt both what it is to be human and the nature and ground of human responsibilities to the nonhuman environment. Part of what this refocusing does is to take seriously the voices of women and other oppressed persons in the construction of that ethic.

A Sioux elder once told me a story about his son. He sent his seven-year-old son to live with the child's grandparents on a Sioux reservation so that he could "learn the Indian ways." Part of what the grandparents taught the son was how to hunt the four leggeds of the forest. As I heard the story, the boy was taught, "to shoot your four-legged brother in his hind area, slowing it down but not killing it. Then, take the four legged's head in your hands, and look into his eyes. The eyes are where all the suffering is. Look into your brother's eyes and feel his pain. Then, take your knife and cut the four-legged under his chin, here, on his neck, so that he dies quickly. And as you do, ask your brother, the four-legged, for forgiveness for what you do. Offer also a prayer of thanks to your four-legged kin for offering his body to you just now, when you need food to eat and clothing to wear. And promise the four-legged that you will put yourself back into the earth when you die, to become nourishment for the earth, and for the sister flowers, and for the brother deer. It is appropriate that you should offer this blessing for the four-legged and, in due time, reciprocate in turn with your body in this way, as the four-legged gives life to you for your survival." As I reflect upon that story, I am struck by the power of the environmental ethic that grows out of and takes seriously narrative, context, and such values and relational attitudes as care, loving perception, and appropriate reciprocity, and doing what is appropriate in a given situation—however that notion of appropriateness eventually gets filled out. I am also struck by what one is able to see, once one begins to explore some of the historical and conceptual connections between the dominations of women and of nature. A *re-conceiving* and *re-visioning* of both feminism and environmental ethics, is, I think, the power and promise of ecofeminism.

NOTES

1. Explicit ecological feminist literature includes works from a variety of scholarly perspectives and sources. Some of these works are Leonie Caldecott and Stephanie Leland, eds., *Reclaim the Earth: Women Speak Out for Life on Earth* (London: The Women's Press, 1983); Jim Cheney, "Eco-Feminism and Deep Ecology," *Environmental Ethics* 9 (1987): 115–45; Andrée Collard with Joyce Contrucci, *Rape of the Wild: Man's Violence against Animals and the Earth* (Bloomington: Indiana University Press, 1988); Katherine Davies, "Historical Associations: Women and the Natural World," *Women & Environments* 9, no. 2 (Spring 1987): 4–6; Sharon Doubiago, "Deeper than Deep Ecology: Men Must Become Feminists," in *The New Catalyst Quarterly,* no 10. (Winter 1987/88): 10–11; Brian Easlea, *Science and Sexual Oppression: Patriarchy's Confrontation with Women and Nature* (London: Weidenfeld & Nicholson, 1981); Elizabeth Dodson Gray, *Green Paradise Lost* (Wellesley, Mass.: Roundtable Press, 1979): Susan Griffin, *Women and Nature: The Roaring Inside Her* (San Francisco: Harper and Row, 1978); Joan L. Griscom, "On Healing the Nature/History Split in Feminist Thought," in *Heresies #13: Feminism and Ecology* 4 no. 1(1981): 4–9; Ynestra King, "The Ecology of Feminism and the Feminism of Ecology," in *Healing Our Wounds: The Power of Ecological Feminism,* ed. Judith Plant (Boston: New Society Publishers, 1989), pp. 18–28; "The Eco-feminist Imperative," in *Reclaim the Earth,* ed. Caldecott and Leland (London: The Women's Press, 1983), pp. 12–16, "Feminism and the Revolt of Nature," in *Heresies # 13: Feminism and Ecology* 4, no. 1 (1981): 12–16, and "What is Ecofeminism?" *The Nation,* 12 December 1987; Marti Kheel, "Animal Liberation Is A Feminist Issue," *The New Catalyst Quarterly,* no. 10 (Winter 1987–88): 8–9; Carolyn Merchant, *The Death of Nature: Women, Ecology and the Scientific Revolution* (San Francisco: Harper and Row, 1980); Patrick Murphy, ed., "Feminism, Ecology, and the Future of the Humanities," special issue of *Studies in the Humanities* 15, no. 2 (December 1988); Abby Peterson and Carolyn Merchant, "Peace with the Earth: Women and the Environmental Movement in Sweden," *Women's Studies International Forum* 9, no. 5–6 (1986): 465–79; Judith Plant, "Searching for Common Ground: Ecofeminism and Bioregionalism," in *The New Catalyst Quarterly,* no. 10 (Winter 1987/88):

6–7; Judith Plant,ed., *Healing Our Wounds: The Power of Ecological Feminism* (Boston: New Society Publishers, 1989); Val Plumwood, "Ecofeminism: An Overview and Discussion of Positions and Arguments," *Australasian Journal of Philosophy*, Supplement to vol. 64 (June 1986): 120–37; Rosemary Radford Ruether, *New Woman/New Earth: Sexist Ideologies & Human Liberation* (New York: Seabury Press, 1975); Kirkpatrick Sale, "Ecofeminism—A New Perspective," *The Nation*, 26 September 1987): 302–05; Ariel Kay Salleh, "Deeper than Deep Ecology: The Eco-Feminist Connection," *Environmental Ethics* 6 (1984): 339–45, and "Epistemology and the Metaphors of Production: An Eco-Feminist Reading of Critical Theory," in *Studies in the Humanities* 15 (1988): 130–39; Vandana Shiva, *Staying Alive: Women, Ecology and Development* (London: Zed Books, 1988); Charlene Spretnak, "Ecofeminism: Our Roots and Flowering," *The Elmswood Newsletter*, Winter Solstice 1988; Karen J. Warren, "Feminism and Ecology: Making Connections," *Environmental Ethics* 9 (1987): 3–21; "Toward an Ecofeminist Ethic," *Studies in the Humanities* 15 (1988): 140–156; Miriam Wyman, "Explorations of Eco-feminism," *Women & Environments* (Spring 1987): 6–7; Iris Young, "'Feminism and Ecology' and 'Women and Life on Earth: Eco-Feminism in the 80's'," *Environmental Ethics* 5 (1983): 173–80; Michael Zimmerman, "Feminism, Deep Ecology, and Environmental Ethics," *Environmental Ethics* 9 (1987): 21–44.

2. Francoise d'Eaubonne, *Le Feminisme ou la Mort* (Paris: Pierre Horay, 1974), pp. 213–52.

3. I discuss this in my paper, "Toward An Ecofeminist Ethic."

4. The account offered here is a revision of the account given earlier in my paper "Feminism and Ecology: Making Connections." I have changed the account to be about "oppressive" rather than strictly "patriarchal" conceptual frameworks in order to leave open the possibility that there may be some patriarchal conceptual frameworks (e.g., in non-Western cultures) which are *not* properly characterized as based on value dualisms.

5. Murray Bookshin, "Social Ecology versus 'Deep Ecology'," in *Green Perspectives: Newsletter of the Green Program Project*, no. 4–5 (Summer 1987): 9.

6. It may be that in contemporary Western society, which is so thoroughly structured by categories of gender, race, class, age, and affectional orientation, that there simply is no meaningful notion of "value-hierarchical thinking" which does not function in an oppressive context. For purposes of this paper, I leave that question open.

7. Many feminists who argue for the historical point that claims (B1) and (B2) have been asserted or assumed to be true within the dominant Western philosophical tradition do so by discussion of that tradition's conceptions of reason, rationality, and science. For a sampling of the sorts of claims made within that context, see "Reason, Rationality, and Gender," ed. Nancy Tuana and Karen J. Warren, a special issue of the American Philosophical Association's *Newsletter on Feminism and Philosophy* 88, no. 2 (March 1989): 17–71. Ecofeminists who claim that (B2) has been assumed to be true within the dominant Western philosophical tradition include: Gray, *Green Paradise Lost;* Griffin, *Woman and Nature: The Roaring Inside Her;* Merchant, *The Death of Nature;* Ruether, *New Woman/New Earth.* For a discussion of some of these ecofeminist historical accounts, see Plumwood, "Ecofeminism." While I agree that the historical connections between the domination of women and the domination of nature is a crucial one, I do not argue for that claim here.

8. Ecofeminists who deny (B1) when (B1) is offered as anything other than a true, descriptive, historical claim about patriarchal culture often do so on grounds that an objectionable sort of biological determinism, or at least harmful female sex-gender stereotypes, underlie (B1). For a discussion of this "split" among those ecofeminists ("nature feminists") who assert and those ecofeminists ("social feminists") who deny (B1) as anything other than a true historical claim about how women are described in patriarchal culture, see Griscom, "On Healing the Nature/History Split."

9. I make no attempt here to defend the historically sanctioned truth of these premises.

10. See, e.g., Bell Hooks, *Feminist Theory: From Margin to Center* (Boston: South End Press, 1984), pp. 51–52.

11. Maria Lugones, "Playfulness, 'World-Travelling,' and Loving Perception," *Hypatia* 2, no. 2 (Summer 1987): 3.

12. At an *experiential* level, some women are "women of color," poor, old, lesbian, Jewish, and physically challenged. Thus, if feminism is going to liberate these women, it also needs to end the racism, classism, heterosexism, anti-Semitism, and discrimination against the handicapped that is constitutive of their oppression as black, or Latina, or poor, or older, or lesbian, or Jewish, or physically challenged women.

13. This same sort of reasoning shows that feminism is also a movement to end racism, classism, ageism, heterosexism and other "isms," which are based in oppressive conceptual frameworks characterized by a logic of domination. However, there is an important caveat: ecofeminism is *not* compatible with all feminisms and all environmentalisms. For a discussion of this point, see my article, "Feminism and Ecology: Making Connections. What it *is* compatible with is the minimal condition characterization of feminism as a movement to end sexism that is accepted by all contemporary feminisms (liberal, traditional Marxist, radical, socialist, Blacks and non-Western).

14. See, e.g., Gray, *Green Paradise Lost;* Griffin, *Women and Nature;* Merchant, *The Death of Nature;* and Ruether, *New Woman/New Earth.*

15. Suppose, as I think is the case, that a necessary condition for the existence of a moral relationship is that at least one party to the relationship is a moral being (leaving open for our purposes what counts as a "moral being"). If this is so, then the Mona Lisa cannot properly be said to have or stand in a moral relationship with the wall on which she hangs, and a wolf cannot have or properly be said to have or stand in a moral relationship with a moose. Such a necessary-condition account leaves open the question whether *both* parties to the relationship must be moral beings. My point here is simply that however one resolves *that* question, recognition of the relationships themselves as a locus of value is a recognition of a source of value that is different from and not reducible to the values of the "moral beings" in those relationships.

16. It is interesting to note that the image of being friends with the Earth is one which cytogeneticist Barbara McClintock uses when she describes the importance of having "a feeling for the organism," "listening to the material [in this case the corn plant]," in one's work as a scientist. See Evelyn Fox Keller, "Women, Science, and Popular Mythology," in *Machina Ex Dea: Feminist Perspectives on Technology,* ed. Joan Rothschild (New York: Pergamon Press, 1983), and Evelyn Fox Keller, *A Feeling For the Organism: The Life and Work of Barbara McClintock* (San Francisco: W. H. Freeman, 1983).

17. Cheney, "Eco-Feminism and Deep Ecology," 144.

18. Marilyn Frye, "In and Out of Harm's Way: Arrogance and Love," *The Politics of Reality* (Trumansburg, New York: The Crossing Press, 1983), pp. 66–72.

19. Ibid., pp. 75–76.

20. Maria Lugones, "Playfulness," p. 3.

21. Cheney makes a similar point in "Eco-Feminism and Deep Ecology," p. 140.

22. Ibid., p. 138.

23. This account of a feminist ethic draws on my paper "Toward an Ecofeminist Ethic."

24. Marilyn Frye makes this point in her illuminating paper, "The Possibility of Feminist Theory," read at the American Philosophical Association Central Division Meetings in Chicago, 29 April–1 May 1986. My discussion of feminist theory is inspired largely by that paper and by Kathryn Addelson's paper "Moral Revolution," in *Women and Values: Reading in Recent Feminist Philosophy,* ed. Marilyn Pearsall (Belmont, Calif.: Wadsworth Publishing Co., 1986) pp. 291–309.

25. Notice that the standard of inclusiveness does not exclude the voices of men. It is just that those voices must cohere with the voices of women.

26. For a more in-depth discussion of the notions of impartiality and bias, see my paper, "Critical Thinking and Feminism," *Informal Logic* 10, no. 1 (Winter 1988): 31–44.

27. The burgeoning literature on these values is noteworthy. See, e.g., Carol Gilligan, *In a Different Voice: Psychological Theories and Women's Development* (Cambridge: Harvard University Press, 1982); *Mapping the Moral Domain: A Contribution of Women's Thinking to Psychological Theory and Education,* ed. Carol Gilligan, Janie Victoria Ward, and Jill McLean Taylor, with Betty Bardige (Cambridge: Harvard University Press, 1988); Nel Noddings, *Caring: A Feminine Approach to Ethics and Moral Education* (Berkeley: University of California Press, 1984); Maria Lugones and Elizabeth V. Spelman, "Have We Got a Theory for You! Feminist Theory, Cultural Imperialism, and the Women's Voice," *Women's Studies International Forum* 6 (1983): 573–81; Maria Lugones,

"Playfulness"; Annette C. Baier, "What Do Women Want In A Moral Theory?" *Nous* 19 (1985): 53–63.

28. Jim Cheney would claim that our fundamental relationships to one another as moral agents are not as moral agents to rights holders, and that whatever rights a person properly may be said to have are relationally defined rights, not rights possessed by atomistic individuals conceived as Robinson Crusoes who do not exist essentially in relation to others. On this view, even right talk itself is properly conceived as growing out of a relational ethic, not vice versa.

29. Alison Jaggar, *Feminist Politics and Human Nature* (Totowa, N.J.: Rowman and Allanheld, 1980), pp. 42–44.

30. Henry West has pointed out that the expression "defining relations" is ambiguous. According to West, "the "defining" as Cheney uses it is an adjective, not a principle—it is not that ethics defines relationships; it is that ethics grows out of conceiving of the relationships that one is in as defining what the individual is."

31. For example, in relationships involving contracts or promises, those relationships might be correctly described as that of moral agent to rights holders. In relationships involving mere property, those relationships might be correctly described as that of moral agent to objects having only instrumental value, "relationships of instrumentality." In comments on an earlier draft of this paper, West suggested that possessive individualism, for instance, might be recast in such a way that an individual is defined by his or her property relationships.

32. Cheney, "Eco-Feminism and Deep Ecology," p. 144.

33. One might object that such permission for change opens the door for environmental exploitation. This is not the case. An ecofeminist ethic is anti-naturist. Hence, the unjust domination and exploitation of nature is a "boundary condition" of the ethic; no such actions are sanctioned or justified on ecofeminist grounds. What it *does* leave open is some leeway about what counts as domination and exploitation. This, I think, is a strength of the ethic, not a weakness, since it acknowledges that *that* issue cannot be resolved in any practical way in the abstract, independent of a historical and social context.

34. Nathan Hare, "Black Ecology," in *Environmental Ethics*, ed. K. S. Shrader-Frechette (Pacific Grove, Calif.: Boxwood Press, 1981), pp. 229–36.

35. For an ecofeminist discussion of the Chipko movement, see my "Toward an Ecofeminist Ethic," and Shiva's *Staying Alive*.

36. See Cheney, "Eco-Feminism and Deep Ecology," p. 122.

37. I offer the same sort of reply to critics of ecofeminism such as Warwick Fox who suggest that for the sort of ecofeminism I defend, the word *feminist* does not add anything significant to environmental ethics and, consequently, that an ecofeminist like myself might as well call herself a deep ecologist. He asks: "Why doesn't she just call it [i.e., Warren's vision of a transformative feminism] deep ecology? Why specifically attach the label *feminist* to it . . . ?"(Warwick Fox, "The Deep Ecology-Ecofeminism Debate and Its Parallels," *Environmental Ethics* 11, no. 1 [1989]: 14, n. 22). Whatever the important similarities between deep ecology and ecofeminism (or, specifically, my version of ecofeminism)—and, indeed, there are many—it is precisely my point here that the word *feminist* does add something significant to the conception of environmental ethics, and that any environmental ethic (including deep ecology) that fails to make explicit the different kinds of interconnections among the domination of nature and the domination of women will be, from a feminist (and ecofeminist) perspective such as mine, inadequate.

🐾 STUDY QUESTIONS

1. What are the central connections between feminism and environmental ethics?

2. What does Warren mean by the 'logic of domination'?

3. In the section "Ecofeminism as a Feminist and Environmental Ethics," Warren offers eight criteria for a feminist ethic. Discuss two of them.

4. In the same section as Question 3, Warren gives eight characteristics of an ecofeminist ethics. Discuss two of them.

6   The Green Kant: Environmental Dynamics and Sustainable Policies*

MARTIN SCHÖNFELD

Martin Schönfeld is a professor of philosophy at the University of South Florida and the author of numerous works on Kant. Here he argues that the idea of sustainability in environmental ethics is derivable from, and thus can be grounded in, Kant's Categorical Imperative (CI). Various formulations of the CI exist, but in part it equates moral actions with actions that one can rationally will to occur universally. Any activity that leads to environmental destruction—that is, any nonsustainable way of living—thus violates the CI.

In environmental ethics, Immanuel Kant's ideas have not yet received much attention, but they turn out to be of fundamental importance for making sense of sustainable development. Today, sustainability is recognized as the core principle of international environmental policy, and the dangerous trends of population growth in under-developed countries, resource depletion, and climate change underscore the need for the sustainable management of biospherical resources, for the sake of everyone.

At the same time, we do not quite know yet what "sustainability" is supposed to mean. The United Nations uses a definition based on a report by the Brundtland Commission (1987): Development is sustainable when it meets the needs of the present without compromising the ability of future generations to meet theirs. This definition is simple enough and politically clear-cut. Sustainable development concerns the right treatment of the environment; its goal is to meet present and future needs, and it points to the obligation to work for intergenerational well-being. But it is not clear how this concept ties to philosophy. How is sustainability supposed to integrate in the range of ethical theories? What is the ground for its moral force? Which thinker accounts for sustainable behavior patterns best? I argue that sustainability is grounded in Kantian

ethics. To prove this, I must show how sustainable environmental policies relate to Kant's main moral idea, the Categorical Imperative. Several consequences will follow from such a proof. First, sustainability will gain a rational and naturalistic meaning, next to its pragmatic dimension. Second, environmental policy will anchor its core principle in a deeper philosophical framework. And finally, Kant's ideas will help to unify environmental ethics and mainstream moral philosophy.

The Categorical Imperative challenges the belief that natural facts and moral values are logically disconnected. Over the form of universalizable practices, Kant shows a way of closing this gap, of grounding sustainable morals in material patterns, and of bridging value and nature. This makes him appear rather green. But the case for a "Green Kant" faces several obstacles. Although his ideas are basic to ethics (consider the Universal Declaration of Human Rights), they have remained quite problematic and controversial in environmental ethics. This tension needs to be reduced first, and it can be done by a historical reminder—by showing how Kantian influences have actually been good for the rise of environmental ethics as a field of study (part 1). Kant's ideas have been an inspiration to the formulation of ecological and biocentric approaches.

This article was commissioned for this anthology and appears in the 5th edition for the first time.

*The author thanks Paul T. Pojman for helpful clarifications and comments on an earlier draft of this essay and wishes to acknowledge his indebtedness to the late Louis P. Pojman, especially to his "Kant's Perpetual Peace and World Government," Tehran Kant Congress, 20–22 November 2004.

Another problem for an ecological interpretation of Kant is that such readings may seem arbitrary. After all, it is one thing to explicate ideas of a philosopher consistently, and it is an altogether different matter to lift some statements out of context and misuse them for new goals. Thus it must be shown that the case for the Green Kant is based on the texts and their backgrounds. Any interpretation involves creativity, and an ecological reconstruction of Kant is no exception. But I argue that such a reading is faithful to the works and sensitive to their circumstances. This interpretation requires looking at where Kant was coming from and what he was driving at (part 2). It matters that his first book, *Living Forces*, praises Leibniz's take on Aristotle's organic potentials. It also matters that his career ended with praising Spinoza's notion of a self-realizing, active nature (*natura naturans*), equating it with the human mind, integrating idealism and realism (1802; the last page of his last book, the *Opus Postumum*). Deep ecology would not have come about without Spinoza's influence, and the environmental and life sciences have fleshed out Aristotle's concept of organic potentials with a vast amount of information. As soon as we look at Kant in context—adding his early, critical, and final works together—an ecological reading becomes inescapable and the case for the Green Kant is compelling.

Unfortunately, there is still a third obstacle that needs to be cleared away before we can make sense of the Categorical Imperative as the naturalistic blueprint of sustainable activities. The problem is that different disciplines work with disconnected aspects of Kant's philosophy. The humanities discuss the old, critical Kant as a tough-minded ethicist, and they dismiss the young, precritical Kant as a flaky naturalist suffering from a hyperactive imagination. In a way, the natural sciences do the opposite—his early, precritical advances now inform the Standard Model, whereas his old, critical insights don't seem to matter much. Although Kant's tale is told differently in the humanities and the sciences, combining the stories gives us pointers (part 3). In this integration, naturalism is essential to morals. This interpretation allows us to understand the meaning of sustainable development in precisely the terms of the Categorical Imperative. Kant's lesson, apparently, is that

environments and ethics do have something in common after all, and the solution to the problem of fact-value distinctions turns out to be that rational value mirrors empirical fact (part 4).

1. KANT'S IDEAS IN ETHICS AND ENVIRONMENTAL ETHICS

In ethics, Kant is known for the Categorical Imperative as a blueprint for moral action. One of its key elements is absolute respect for humankind. He applied this respect to persons and societies, predicted the fall of colonialism and the rise of a global village of free countries, and in 1795 proposed an autonomous world jury for settling international conflicts. After World War I, Kant's proposal became a reality when the League of Nations came into being. The League adopted the First Geneva Convention as a rulebook for fighting wars and as the first blueprint of global legislation (1925). After World War II, the League of Nations was rebuilt as the United Nations (1945). The fifty million war dead (mostly civilians), the horrors of the concentration camps, and the failure of the perpetrators were reminders that Kant had a point. Apparently there is no good way around the imperative of respecting humanity because the alternative—the inhumanity of fascism—led to self-defeating outcomes. In consequence, the United Nations adopted the Universal Declaration of Human Rights (1948)—another international rulebook about how to treat people in principle. More recently (2002), the United Nations created, against the resistance of the United States, the International Criminal Court as a way of bringing war criminals to justice. In the Geneva Conventions, the Universal Declaration of Human Rights, and the International Criminal Court, Kant's Categorical Imperative is now a political reality on the planet.

In environmental ethics, however, Kant's insistence on acting according to human worth has sparked critique. Clearly, human rights are a good thing, but don't animals have a worth of their own, too? And if so, wouldn't they be right-holders, too, to whom we owe a few basic moral obligations? Some environmental ethicists, such as Christina Hoff and Tom Regan, criticize

Kant's humanism as a dogmatically anthropocentric perspective, at unfair expense to animals.[1] Regan made a case for animal rights that was as categorical as Kant's humanistic case was. The similarity of styles prompted others, not without irony, to call Regan a "Kantian."[2] But such similarities aside, animal ethicists feel let down by Kant. He believed that duties were owed to humans only, that cruelty to animals was wrong because it was dehumanizing, and that animal rights, as such, did not really exist. Some of his contemporaries, such as Johanna Unzer and Jeremy Bentham, saw that animal misery points to sentience and rights. Kant's humanism is a letdown by comparison.

Kant is notorious for insisting on respect for humans while disrespecting animals. But is this his position? Did he disconnect humans and animals? Answering these questions needs a systematic parsing of his statements on animals, which is not the focus of this essay.[3] But what we can show here is that his anthropocentric preference has little to do with the usual dualism of humans and nature. Instead this anthropocentrism integrates a normative ranking of progressively emerging conscious beings in an evolutionary cosmic framework (parts 2 and 3).

Kant's hierarchy of values, with human interests overriding nonhuman interests, is part of his natural philosophy, which takes environments, the world, and the cosmos as a coherent whole. This whole is in time. The universe moves to stages of ever higher complexity. This view of a self-organizing natural evolution, from the Big Bang to initial chaos to present structure, is now part of the Standard Model in the sciences.[4] Kant shared this view (then still metaphysics) with other philosophers, such as Aristotle, Spinoza, and Leibniz. The influence of Kantian ideas on environmental ethics is more extensive than it appears at first sight. Paul Taylor, who pioneered biocentrism, relied on Kantian ideas for deducing the value of life.[5] Although it sounds paradoxical that a biocentric thinker such as Taylor took his cue from an anthropocentric thinker such as Kant, this is what happened, and Taylor was not alone in that. Another and earlier pioneer of biocentrism, Albert Schweitzer, had already set a precedent in taking his cue for the articulation of the "reverence for life" from a Kantian (Arthur Schopenhauer).[6] Aldo Leopold, the founder of the land ethic, claimed an ethical sequence from human rights to nonhuman rights to land rights. The expansion of rights from some to all is an old Kantian legacy: the vision of a collective and naturally possible evolution toward an enlightened, practical reason.

Thus it turns out that Kant's ideas not only are important in ethics but also have been quite influential, in subtle ways, on the historical development of environmental ethics, as the leanings of the biocentric pioneers show. It also turns out that the objections by animal ethicists deserve a new look. Regardless of whether these objections are valid, two facts are clear. First, Kant's ideas on animals are part of a bigger picture—a set of ideas on nature—and this picture of nature's coherence and evolution is perfectly realistic. Second, even if we grant that animals deserve moral consideration, environmental policy, for better or worse, will operate with a non-egalitarian, hierarchical approach. Egalitarian approaches, by which animals and humans are equal right-holders, generate problems in legislation and do not work in policy. Hence Kant is arguably more useful for environmental ethics than egalitarian animal ethicists would have us believe.

2. INTRODUCING KANT

But who was Kant really? Where was he coming from—what was his real background? And what was he driving at—what were his goals? He was born in 1724 and died in 1804, and he lived for most of his life in a Baltic harbor town that was then at the eastern edge of Germany and is now at the western edge of Russia. Judged by the influence of his ideas, he belongs in the same league as Confucius or Aristotle. His philosophy completed the Age of Reason, a period in the seventeenth and eighteenth centuries (ca. 1680–1781). This period was also known as the Age of Enlightenment (*Aufklärung*), an age of progress in the sciences, with innovators such as Euler (math), Leibniz (calculus, information theory, dynamics), and Newton (calculus, mechanics, physics). The Age of Enlightenment contributed to a huge cultural leap forward in the modern understanding of nature.

Kant reacted to the work of predecessors and peers. His background matters because his work is characterized by efforts to combine known data into a system, a natural philosophy, or a 'theory of everything' (1745–1770/1786–1802). In these combinations, he often struck gold. The elements of his world-system have turned out to be quite realistic in light of what is known today about biospherical and astrophysical environments (see part 3). In hindsight, we can say that when Kant was making claims on nature's structure, he apparently knew what he was talking about.

However, in the 1780s, his most famous period, Kant changed his focus. He suspended the metaphysical project of figuring out how natural environments are put together. Instead, he now proposed systematic theories about epistemology, ethics, and aesthetics. His first work in this decade was the *Critique of Pure Reason* (1781). Its publication led to the turn from Early Modern Thought to the Age of Modernity (1781–1945). An examination of the book shows what he was driving at. The *Critique* is a roadmap of cognition and a blueprint for progress. It contributed to the theories of knowledge and to cognitive psychology, and it amounted to a critical analysis of metaphysics. Old-style philosophers, by and large, did not like it. Older metaphysicians were upset by Kant's charge that metaphysics was weak on method. At that time, metaphysics (or what is the same, ontology) involved three fields. Rational theology was the study of ultimate meaning; rational cosmology was the study of natural order; and rational psychology was the study of the mind. This setup did not impress Kant. He argued that ontology is a "random groping" and "worst of all, a groping among mere concepts," a boring "battlefield of endless controversies" (1781 A viii/B xv). The evolution of ontology into science would first require that metaphysicians face up to the fact that their three fields possessed too few hard facts and involved too much arbitrary speculation.

Kant called ontology dogmatic and targeted the School Philosophy, which was inspired by Spinoza and Leibniz and explained by Wolff.

The School Philosophy was big on metaphysics. Kant's critique made such an impression that the conceptual systems advanced by its thinkers were quickly appearing to be old-fashioned, misguided, and essentially flawed. But this impression made philosophy swing too far to the other extreme. Thinking about natural order and the human mind was left to the scientists, and thinking about ultimate meaning was left to the theologians. Philosophers became skeptics who retreated to safer grounds, narrowing their focus on logic, language, and other second-order investigations. The impressions that School philosophers had been on the wrong track, and that conceptual investigations of meaning, nature, and rationality were doomed, conflict with the fact that the old-style metaphysicians had been rather successful. Their contributions were fertile and spawned the development of whole new academic disciplines. The School Philosophy created aesthetics as a discipline in the humanities (Baumgarten), and its insights had grassroots influences on social economics, strategic studies, and evolutionary theory.

A central concern of the metaphysicians targeted by Kant in his critical period was the idea of environmental design (not to be confused with what creationists call 'intelligent design'). Dazzled by the revolutionary scientific breakthroughs of their own age, the School philosophers were optimistic that a final theory was just around the corner and that everything that happens has a reason. Nature, so these metaphysicians said, is set up in perfectly lawful and orderly ways. Moreover, nature is not just a big machine or a giant clock, as French and English thinkers saw it. Spinoza, Leibniz, and the School philosophers looked at it as a self-organizing dynamic matrix. Nature is well designed, and whereas the ultimate root of this design may well have a divine cause, the design was harmoniously pre-established at nature's birth. The big machine runs on its own. What is more, it is evolving by its intrinsic, natural, and integral processes. Nature is not static, matter is not only inert but also energetic, and the whole cosmic setup is accessible to the mind. The German world "concept" (*Begriff*) comes from the School Philosophy, and so does our modern conception of the world, nature, and environment as an interactive network (*nexus rerum*).

Kant's critique on the network-metaphysics of the School Philosophy was constructive. He tried integrating the dogma of Eastern Enlightenment with the doubt of Scottish Enlightenment. The *Critique* (2nd edition 1787 B i) starts with the need to do science. The prefaces (1781 A/1787 B) are long complaints that metaphysics is not yet on the new level. As soon as we think about ultimate structures, patterns, or the matrix, contradictory data entangle us in dialectic conflicts. The book ends with an encouragement to do ontology anyway. Per definition, we must grant that "metaphysics is the full and complete development of human reason" (A 850/B 878). And if this is true, we need to work on getting it right and make headway. The reason is pragmatic—developing ontology into science serves "the supreme end, the happiness of all humankind" (A 851/B 879). Kant's final advice is about the big questions, of what we can know, what we should do, and what we may hope. Everybody can try to answer them, but anybody working on them must deal with them coherently or systematically. Different approaches are good for scientific progress, and although some prefer to be dogmatic Wolffs, others prefer to be skeptical Humes. Either way, the point of Kant's critique (B i/B 884) is that in conflicts truth always emerges along a middle way. This path of reason is a critical line between the opposites of dogma and doubt (A 856/B 884)—along this path, metaphysical hopes or speculative ontology will generate the Standard Model. Apparently this productive conflict, evolutionary interplay, and dialectic is the hallmark of reality.

After his death in 1804, his friends chose one of his ideas for his grave marker. He had first suggested it at the end of his evolutionary cosmology, *General Natural History* (1755), and reformulated it later, in one sentence, at the end of the *Critique of Practical Reason* (1788):

> Two things fill the mind with ever new and increasing admiration and respect, the more often and longer one reflects on them: starry sky, above me; and moral law, within me.[7]

His friends thought that this saying captures what Kant's philosophy is all about. When we look around and wonder what it all may mean, we are confronted with two facts. When looking outside and up, we see a well-ordered, self-regulating natural whole—the starry sky. And when looking inside ourselves, we find conscience, reason, and heart—the moral law. On the one hand, nothing could be more different from what is outside and what is inside: natural facts here, and moral values there; the environment here, and ethics there. Throughout his life, Kant thought about starry skies and moral laws and wondered about their relationship. In his critical works, this relationship appears to be one of opposites (and to some extent, this is just what facts and values are). In his naturalistic and metaphysical works, however, this relationship entails a nexus: Facts inform values, and values create facts. Kant was indebted to Spinoza and Leibniz, and he believed he may have found a naturalistic solution to the puzzle of Hume's fact-value distinction. In a Kantian way of looking at things, environments and ethics are deeply and rationally linked.

3. STARRY SKY, MORAL LAW— INTEGRATING THE SCIENTIFIC AND PHILOSOPHICAL KANT

Whereas the humanities deal with the critical works of Kant's famous philosophical period, the precritical works (1745–1766) are now more relevant to natural and environmental science. Kant worked initially as a metaphysician, and as an old man, he returned to these topics. These metaphysical efforts concern the attempt to construct a comprehensive philosophy of nature. Typically, Kant used data from others to construct larger and more sweeping arguments. In retrospect, many of these hypotheses and speculations have turned out to anticipate elements of the Standard Model. Christians had difficulties with his work. His first teacher, the Lutheran Pietist Martin Knutzen, flunked him out of college (1748) for a book on living forces or momenergy (p. 1749). There, Kant suggested that nature develops organically, organizes itself on the basis of its own forces, and weaves spacetime grids. The radiation of force and the grid of spacetime interact. Although radiation weaves the grid, the grid orders radiation (1749 § 10). Kant's insight in *Living Forces* is now judged in physics as the first formulation of the law of free field radiation.[8]

When Kant returned to college to write his master's thesis, a "meditation on fire" (1754), he suggested that light shines depending on how you see it and can be both wave and particle at the same time (1755a § 7). Next he anonymously published a book on evolutionary cosmology (1755b). His claims there were later substantiated in solar dynamics and stellar evolution. Today scientists judge this book, *General Natural History*, as "the essence of modern models."[9] The praised 'essence' is his model of systems formation and environmental fate (Kant's so-called Nebular Hypothesis). Sixty years ago, the astrophysicist C. F. v. Weizsäcker, who learned from the quantum mechanic pioneer Max Born, built a new theory of nebular turbulences to explain the origin of the Sun and the Earth. He based his theory on Kant's model and credited Born for pointing him to the worth of Kant's scientific insights for quantum methods.[10] The point of a "direct path from Kant to quantum theory" is now made by J. D. Barrow at Cambridge.[11] Stephen Hawking, in Newton's chair at Cambridge, sharpened it into a broad dismissal of all post-Kantian philosophy as "a comedown"; to him, Kant wrote the last philosophy in top scientific form.[12]

In the eighteenth century, philosophical realism about natural structures was not necessarily an advantage for philosophers. Christian professors found out that Kant was the author of the anonymous book on evolutionary cosmology and turned down his application for a job (1756). Meanwhile he defended his PhD thesis on the power-grid of material environments. There he argued that ultimate elements are dynamic powerpoints, radiating outward, which create material structure as energetic 'activity bubbles' (1756 § 7). Today, physicists work with similar models. In string theory, for instance, such Kantian powerpoint-bubbles are called Calabi-Yau spaces.

Kant's conception of nature evokes an evolving, interactive, and coherent environment, whose structure is shaped by energetic interplays. This concept is relevant for climate studies. Because nature apparently has a general form, it may not be coincidental that the precritical metaphysics contains meteorological discoveries. In the 1750s, Kant identified the causal seesaw of coastal winds, explaining how they blow in opposite directions at sunrise and sundown; he traced the direction of trade winds back to Earth's axial rotation, and he discovered how the monsoons work. As we have said, such advances were liabilities in his day, and the fact that he came up with such ideas did not further his career (he worked as an adjunct until his late forties, and his first full-time job offer was for a professorship in poetry, which he turned down).

Christian professors did not like to hear philosophers talk about self-regulating natural orders and dynamic systems. The problem for Christians was that God's word is not God's world. God is an active creator; nature is a passive creation. And whereas God is good and rational, nature is evil and absurd. Kant's naturalistic approach contradicted this theological view and was not politically correct; basically, he was flirting with heresy. His approach was typical of the Eurasian Enlightenment and shared by a range of thinkers (e.g., Laozi, Confucius, Spinoza, Leibniz, Wolff, and Bilfinger). Before he qualified for a real job, he had to submit to self-critique. In 1770, he recanted his holistic claims of dialectical power grids and gained full-time employment.

Today we have an advantage because science has caught up with Kant's ideas, and what used to sound obscure is now concrete information. Still, the view that natural environments are self-generating and share dynamic structure, and that mind, culture, and value are evolutionary products, remains problematic in the humanities. Kant's epitaph, the reflection of starry sky and moral law, is a troubling idea. But according to the friends who selected this idea from Kant's writings for his tombstone, it is this nexus between outside and inside, this mirror of starry sky and moral law, which describes the essence of Kant's work. The idea of a fundamental resonance of inner and outer ways sounds Asian. Suggesting a joint vector of natural evolution and moral cultivation seems to be something a Taoist might say. This is not a coincidence. Historically, Kant was first influenced by Leibniz, Wolff, and Bilfinger, three philosophers who defended Chinese metaphysics. The environmental mirror of starry sky and moral law is an Eastern idea that informed Kant's teachers, and Kant expanded it into a magnificent vision. Philosophically, this requires us to rethink Kant's views and to reexamine the traditional separation of facts and values.

Enlightenment thinkers inspired by the East conceived of reality in evolutionary terms. The starry sky is the historical product of a very long chain of processes in the network of nature. Over time, nature unfolded or organized itself from uniform, simple, and chaotic stages toward systems of ever increasing diversity, complexity, and order. The moral law is also a historical product of a very long chain of processes in the network of life. Over time, life developed itself from primitive organisms toward ever more complexly evolved intelligences. At a certain level of animal evolution, social communities and thus the need for regulated cooperation emerged. Social interplay spawned more differentiations and eventually the need for lawful organization. Over time, values emerge as moral ideas, which can, do, and should become ever more rational. In the Enlightenment view of reality—shared by Confucius, Wolff, and Kant—nature is subject to evolution (Kant calls it *Auswicklung der Natur* or nature's "outwrapping"), and culture is subject to progress. The vision of a natural evolution and the hope for civil progression were quite typical of the Enlightenment philosophers. Kant's starry sky and moral law (Wolff's natural macrocosm and cultural microcosm) are outcomes of an environmental design that generates structure over time. Natural order and moral law both emerge and develop along a shared vector of rational evolution.

The Enlightenment thinkers who inspired Kant suspected that consciousness is not just a human feature. For Leibniz, nonhuman creatures were not mindless machines (as Descartes had thought) but simple organic spirits instead. Mind, in this perspective, is integral to nature. Recent scientific discoveries of culture among animals, and fairness-rules in primate societies, indicate that animal minds are sufficiently complex to generate notions of value on their own. Apparently value, in the animal sense of the Golden Rule or fair play, is indeed an evolutionary product of nature and thus arises from facts after all. And it seems that this result makes sense only if we are willing to conceive of nature in the Kantian sense stated: as an evolving, interactive, and holistic environmental network, a dynamic progression of spatial systems over time, from the uniform to the differentiated, from the simple to the complex, organized in energetic interplays. Cosmic, organic, and cultural environments emerge in space over time. When viewed as moving through spacetime, these types of environments display additions in information and structure. For Kant, this increase is an upward evolution that is fully natural and points to a final good. Natural events, in this view, are material reflections of a steady development toward perfect value.

In the world philosophy of the twenty-first century, this enlightened perspective about natural evolution, organic growth, and a joint vector of factual and normative processes is controversial. For East Asian, Eurasian, and East European intellectuals, this view is traditional and congenial. For French, English, and other Atlantic intellectuals, this view seems counterintuitive and weird. As a result, English thinkers, such as G. E. Moore, have tended to judge holistic attempts at bridging the fact-value distinction as instances of the "naturalistic fallacy," whereas Chinese thinkers, such as S. C. Chen, have tended to judge dualistic attempts at keeping the fact-value distinction as the "fallacy of bifurcating nature." In their naturalistic orientation, Spinoza, Leibniz, Wolff, and Kant were more Eurasian than Western. If we are willing to look at environmental dynamics in their somewhat unfamiliar way, the Categorical Imperative will come into view as the rational form and natural pattern of sustainable development.

4. THE KANTIAN BLUEPRINT OF SUSTAINABLE DEVELOPMENT

Garret Hardin envisioned the biosphere as an ocean and likened humankind to a crew in a boat. When one rocks the boat, there is the risk of toppling over, capsizing, and drowning in the ocean. The human boat is now rocking in self-made climate pulses. The question of maintaining balance in the biosphere points to two prior assumptions. First, let's assume freedom of action, and second, let's value future action. Neither of these stipulations is necessarily given in real life. Some persons may be too weak or too ill to stop the rocking; not everyone has freedom of action. Others may have the power to change things but do not care; not everyone values future action. But freedom of action and valuing future action are still realistic assumptions: Most people have some choice: most people want a tomorrow, and often we can do something about lowering risks.

Now imagine how this environmental dynamic can be functionally ruled or how the human boat can stay afloat on the planetary ocean. The strategy to stay afloat concerns the logic of role models. We can say that an action is rationally defensible if others can imitate it without such imitation producing a situation precluding future action. Suppose one sits in a boat, rocks it, and turns it over. Now imagine everybody following suit in all boats: All boats woul turn over, and there would be no more boats to capsize. Then no one could follow the first model anymore; the collective rocking caused collective capsizing, which caused the end of rocking. Universalizing the action caused a structure that made the action impossible.

This is Kant's litmus test on whether a plan qualifies as morally sound or as a bad idea. In real life, the litmus test applies to cases such as truth-telling. Suppose someone decides to tell the truth from now on, and imagine everyone following suit. Now all people would tell the truth, and that's that. Collective honesty does not make honesty impossible. Open-ended, progressive universalizability is the hallmark of morally correct action.

The breakdown of universalizability is consequently Kant's hallmark of immoral actions. Consider lying. If someone decided to lie systematically all the time, and others replicated this decision as if it were a natural law or a principle of legislation, then data exchange would collapse and communication would break down—the natural precondition for the freedom to lie in the first place. As a rule, an action is wrong if its replication entails the end of replication.

We can find counterexamples to Kant's litmus test of moral essences. During World War II, Nazi soldiers and police searched for Jews to arrest and murder. Some people hid Jewish neighbors and misled the inquiring killers. Such lies saved lives, whereas truth-telling in that situation would have made the speakers accessories to murder. The exception qualifies Kant's rule, but (and this is why the Categorical Imperative does suggest a real pattern) the exception does not *negate* the rule. First, lying to inquiring murderers can be accounted for within the general assumptions of Kant's theory. The universalizability-rule determines plain actions on a level playing field, when all else is equal. The exception, lying to inquiring murderers, concerns compound actions on a slanted field, when things are not really that equal (after all, the questioner intends to commit a crime), and when choices are not only about right and wrong but also about lesser and greater evils (lying tied to life-saving; honesty tied to homicide). Second, what matters for moral blueprints is the predictable fate of trendlines. Kant's litmus test of moral essences concerns the likely, ultimate outcomes of implemented rules. The eventual results of universalized actions chart trajectories of dynamic effects cascading in space and over time. Such trajectories are statistically meaningful. Actions failing the test (such as lying) consequently map a trend, but the very nature of trendlines is fuzzy—lying is mostly wrong and rarely right.

For Kant, an action is good if it works as a model others can follow. The universalizability of respect for humanity is a determining feature of rational moral practices. Rational moral practices, seen in their replication in space and over time, mirror the natural form of evolutionary replication. Some processes in nature are fertile, spawning more of the same, until they rise to a steady state that may remain stable unless they are destroyed by outside events, but not by internal faults. Other processes, such as grass fires, are inherently unstable and eliminate themselves. Morally sound actions, so Kant said, mirror fertile processes; immoral actions mirror self-terminating processes. The giveaway feature of any flawed policy is its self-destructive nature.

Kant's Categorical Imperative involves several interconnected elements. Its content is respect for human beings. Its form is the universalizability of moral action. Respecting humanity and universalizable activities are necessary conditions of any cultural evolution. In *Groundwork for the Metaphysics of Morals* (1785), Kant describes these key elements. The first formulation of the Categorical Imperative turns on the universalizability test:

> So act as if the idea of your action were to evolve by your will to a *general natural law.* (4:421.18–20)

That is to say, the categorical order of morally sound action is that the plan of action involved in your doing can be naturally copied by others and be used as if it were a legal principle. The potential of a rule to evolve into a general and naturally self-sustaining schema of action is what makes the action right. Crossing sustainable yield thresholds of natural resources cannot be rationally willed as a general natural law simply because it is illogical and self-terminating. To understand this schema it is important to look at practices as dynamic networks within larger environmental structures, and to see how both the dynamic networks of intentional activity and their social and material frameworks are pulsing through time. The Categorical Imperative does not make any sense as long as we think of environments as static, and as long as we disconnect individual choices from their collective impacts. But as soon as we are willing to entertain the idea that natural environments, just as human activity networks, vary over time, this first and formal aspect of the Categorical Imperative emerges as the blueprint of sustainability.

The second formulation of the Categorical Imperative turns on respect for humankind:

> Act so that you use humankind, as much in your own person as in the person of every other, at all times simultaneously as purpose and never just as tool. (4:429.10–12)

The form of sustainable patterns is linked to the content of humanism. In a sense, respect for persons is the very heart of the Categorical Imperative. It is worth considering how naturalistic this heart actually is. By respecting a person as a person (and acting accordingly), the normative activity of the subject is intended as a mirror of the physical state of the object. That is to say, respecting persons simply means to be obligated by their natural constitution. The natural constitution of people is that they grow up to be independent and autonomous (and that when they become old, they can look back on a life lived in independence and autonomy). Autonomy matters in time—as the future of kids, the present of adults, and the past of the old. Given this core potential of human autonomy and its realization in time, slavery is not a natural goal-state of humans. Freedom is. Respecting persons means to treat them as they are, as potentials in time. Thus treating a person as a thing is to mistake a potentially autonomous subject for an inert object; it is not only morally wrong but also a cognitive mistake, a rational error. Values reflect the facts.

Morality, in Kant's humanistic model, concerns all people, at all times, and not just one's self. By default, the universalizability condition points from present states to future states. Morality does not discount against the future. On the contrary, sustainable behavior patterns concern offspring and are guided by the predictable resource needs of all those who can be expected to be born. Respect for humankind is consequently also the respect for future generations. Although the wait for an apocalypse and the hope for rapture define Christian fundamentalism, the moral imperative to care for future generations, and the duty of evolution, are the essence of Kant's secular humanism.

Both sustainable form and humanistic content consequently point to future generations, and the third and last formulation of the Categorical Imperative turns on this futuristic orientation:

> Act in harmony with maxims of any legislative member for a possible realm of ends. (4:439.1–3)

Now the form of sustainable behavior and the content of respectful humanity combine into a natural algorithm of moral order. The possible realm of ends, the ultimate goal of action, is a natural probability. It is not real in the current environmental situation, but it is in the cards. People presently acting in this sustainable humanistic order will naturally, inexorably bring it about. For Kant, this goal meant the continued civil progression toward a rationally interactive network. Everyone in this realm of ends or kingdom of purposes is an autonomous player, a powerpoint, as it were, who affects the network. Everyone counts. Sustainable development thus emerges in this reading as a three-sided figure with a sustainable face, a humane face, and a future face. The three faces, or formulations, of the Categorical Imperative jointly constitute sustainability. This is the blueprint. It is naturalistic in that moral behavior is a dialectic mirror of natural fields, but it is also naturalistic in another sense, by involving a certain inexorable harshness. Although we are free to do what we want, statistically, collectively, and structurally, we do not have a choice. Either we realize Kant's blueprint over sustainable management of our resources and climate—or we don't. In the first case, humankind will soar to greater heights of civilization and insight. In the second case, we will earn a Darwin Award: game over.

NOTES

1. Christina Hoff, "Kant's Invidious Humanism," *Environmental Ethics* 5 (1983): 63–70; Tom Regan, *The Case for Animal Rights* (University of California PressBerkeley/Los Angeles: 1983), 174–194.

2. E.g., Claire Rasmussen, "Tom Regan's *Defending Animal Rights* (2001)," *Law and Politics Book Review* 15 (2005): 1030–1033.

3. For such a careful scholarly analysis, which qualifies the typical objections by animal ethicists, see Holly Wilson, "Kant's Treatment of Animals," in this anthology.

4. The term Standard Model is taken from physics. After the qualification of classical mechanics by general relativity and quantum physics, scientists had a problem. General relativity works for making sense of very large things, quantum physics works for making sense of very small things, but the core assumptions of either theory differ. General relativity evokes a perfectly predictable nature, which is unaffected by observers. Quantum physics evokes an imperfectly predictable nature, which is affected by observers. Both very small and very large things are part of nature, and the fact that two mutually contradictory tools were required for studying one and the same nature was a theoretical headache for much of the last century. Today, scientists have found ways to bridge both approaches; the result of combining tools has been the emergence of quantum cosmology (a field made famous by R. Penrose, S. Hawking, and others). Scientists don't have all the answers and continue to disagree, but a coherent picture of ultimate cosmic environments has now come into view, partly by formal advances and partly by empirical findings (e.g., with the Hubble telescope). Now there exists an overall conception of how nature as such has come about, how it is set up, and how it will go on. This is the Standard Model. Efforts at combining the Standard Model of the universe with hypotheses about the structure of matter and the relations among forces are seen by many scientists as hopeful steps toward a systematic "theory of everything."

5. Paul Taylor, *Respect for Nature: A Theory of Environmental Ethics* (Princeton: Princeton University Press, 1986), 27–32. See also p. 198 note.

6. Albert Schweitzer, *Kulturphilosophie* (Bern: Paul Haupt, 1923); see the influential section "The Ethic of Reverence for Life," in Schweitzer, *Cultural Philosophy II: Civilization and Ethics* (vol. 2 of *Kulturphilosophie*), tr. John Nash (London: Black, 1929), 79–91. See also Arthur Schopenhauer, *The World as Will and Representation*, tr. E. F. J. Payne (New York: Dover, 1969), vol. 1, "Preface to the First Edition (1818)," p. xv; "Preface to the Second Edition (1844)," p. xxiii.

7. The epitaph is tough to translate. "Mind" is really *Gemüt*, which means also courage, character, or beautiful spirit. "Sky" is really *Himmel*, a term as ambivalent as Latin *caelum* and Chinese *tian*; English translators traditionally prefer their Christian word "heaven." "Law" is originally *Gesetz*, which literally means the setting-down of fixed information or the setup of how

anything works. All Kant translations are from the Academy Edition: Immanuel Kant, *Gesammelte Schriften* edited by the Akademie der Wissenschaften (Berlin: Reimer; later De Gruyter, 1910ff.), 29 volumes. For the original, see *ibid.* vol. 5, p. 161, lines 33–36, and compare with vol. 1, pp. 366–368.

8. John D. Barrow, *The Universe That Discovered Itself* (Oxford: Oxford University Press, 2000), 85–86. Barrow notes (p. 209): "The fact that we experience three dimensions of space is intimately connected to the laws of Nature that exist in those three dimensions. This connection was first recognized by Immanuel Kant ... he claimed that the ubiquity of the inverse-square law in Nature was the reason for space possessing three spatial dimensions. Kepler also appreciated the connection between spatial geometry and the inverse-square law of light intensity falloff, pointing out the differences expected in two- and three-dimensional spaces. (Today we would turn this argument around and say that three dimensions lead to inverse-square laws for basic force fields)." In *The Constants of Nature* (New York: Pantheon, 2002), p. 204–205, Barrow comments on Kant's *Living Forces* § 10: "Kant's insight showed for the first time that there is a connection between the number of dimensions of space and the forms of the laws of Nature and the constants of Nature that live within them. Kant went on to speculate about some of the ... aspects of extra dimensions, and saw that it might be possible to study the properties of these hypothetical spaces by mathematical means.... His speculation was correct. During the nineteenth century mathematicians 'discovered' other geometries which described lines and shapes on curved surfaces. It was lucky they did. It ensured that Einstein had this 'pure' mathematics available for use when he developed his new theory of gravitation, the general theory of relativity, between 1905 and 1915."

9. Peter Coles, ed., *Routledge Companion to the New Cosmology* (London/New York: Routledge 2001), 240.

10. Carl Friedrich von Weizsäcker, "Immanuel Kant," in Weizsäcker, *Grosse Physiker* (Munich: DTV, 2002), 181–203.

11. J. D. Barrow, *The Universe that Discovered Itself, loc. cit.*, 154.

12. Stephen Hawking, *The Theory of Everything* (Los Angeles: New Millennium, 2003), 166.

STUDY QUESTIONS

1. Kant believes his Categorical Imperative can and should serve as the foundation for ethics and political theory. Discuss and criticize.

2. How important is the idea of sustainability to environmental ethics? Are there concepts more central than this one?

3. How can the idea of sustainability in environmental policy be grounded in Kant's Categorical Imperative? What other arguments are there for sustainable environmental policies?

FOR FURTHER READING

Armstrong, Susan, and Richard Botzler, eds. *Environmental Ethics*. New York: McGraw-Hill, 1993.

Attfield, Robin. *The Ethics of Environmental Concern*. New York: Columbia University Press, 1983.

Barbour, Ian G., ed. *Western Man and Environmental Ethics*. Menlo Park, CA: Addison-Wesley, 1973.

Bratton, Susan Power. "Christian Ecotheology and the Old Testament." *Environmental Ethics* 6, 1984.

———. "The Original Desert Solitaire: Early Christian Monasticism and Wilderness." *Environmental Ethics*, 10, 1988.

DesJardins, Joseph. *Environmental Ethics*. Belmont, CA: Wadsworth, 2001.

Glacken, Clarence J. *Traces on the Rhodian Shore: Nature and Culture in Western Thought from Ancient Times to the End of the Eighteenth Century*. Berkeley: University of California Press, 1967.

Gruen, Lori, and Dale Jamieson, eds. *Reflecting on Nature*. New York: Oxford University Press, 1994.

Hargrove, Eugene. *Foundations of Environmental Ethics*. Englewood Cliffs, NJ: Prentice Hall, 1989.

Mathews, Freya. *The Ecological Self.* London: Routledge, 1991.

Nash, Roderick. *The Rights of Nature.* Madison: University of Wisconsin Press, 1989.

Norton, Bryan. *Towards Unity Among Environmentalists.* New York: Oxford University Press, 1991.

Passmore, John. *Man's Responsibility for Nature.* New York: Scribner, 1974.

Rolston, Holmes, III. *Philosophy Gone Wild: Essays in Environmental Ethics.* Buffalo, NY: Prometheus Press, 1986.

———. *Environmental Ethics.* Philadelphia: Temple University Press, 1988.

Shrader-Frechette, Kristin. *Environmental Ethics.* Pacific Grove, CA: Boxwood Press, 1981.

Sterba, James P., ed. *Earth Ethics.* Upper Saddle River, NJ: Prentice Hall, 1995.

Taylor, Paul. *Respect for Nature.* Princeton, NJ: Princeton University Press, 1986.

VanDeVeer, Donald, and Christine Pierce, eds. *The Environmental Ethics and Policy Book.* Belmont, CA: Wadsworth, 2001.

Wenz, Peter. *Environmental Justice.* Albany, NY: SUNY Press, 1988.

Westra, Laura. *An Environmental Proposal for Ethics: The Principle of Integrity.* Lanham, MD: Rowman & Littlefield, 1994.

Wilkerson, Loren, ed. *Earthkeeping in the '90s: Stewardship of Creation.* Grand Rapids, MI: Eerdmans, 1991.

Animal Rights

WHAT SORT OF BEINGS are deserving of moral regard? Only human beings or
nonhuman animals as well? How ought we to treat animals? Do they have moral
rights? Is their suffering to be equated with human suffering? Should experimentation on animals cease? Should large-scale commercial ("factory") farms be abolished
because they tend to cause animals great suffering? Do we have a moral duty to
become vegetarians? What exactly is the moral status of animals?

In 1975 a book that opened with the following words appeared: "This book is
about the tyranny of human over nonhuman animals. This tyranny has caused and
today is still causing an amount of pain and suffering that can only be compared
with that which resulted from the centuries of tyranny by white humans over black
humans." Thus, Peter Singer began his epoch-making *Animal Liberation*, which
launched the modern animal rights movement.

Before the 1970s, vegetarianism was restricted to Hindus, Buddhists, and small
numbers of other people with relevant moral or spiritual convictions. Today hundreds
of millions more are vegetarians. Exact numbers are, of course, hard to locate, but various polls indicate that 20 to 30% of the people in the United States lean toward vegetarianism (that is, they look for vegetarian food on restaurant menus or at least
generally prefer it). The number of strict vegetarians is probably around 5%. We
will look later (see Chapter 8, Food Ethics) at other reasons for vegetarianism, focusing in this chapter on animal rights issues.

There are two separate defenses of the moral status (or rights) of animals: the
utilitarian[1] and the deontological arguments. Peter Singer is the main representative
of the utilitarian argument. Utilitarians follow Jeremy Bentham in asserting that what
makes beings morally considerable is not reason but *sentience*. All sentient creatures
have the ability to suffer and, as such, have interests. The frustration of those interests
leads to suffering. Utilitarianism seeks to maximize the satisfaction of interests
whether they be those of humans or animals. In some cases, human interests will
make special claims on us; for example, humans but not mice or pigs will need
schools and books. But if a pig and a child are in pain and you only have one pain
reliever, you may have a moral dilemma as to who should receive the pain reliever.
Utilitarians will generally allow some animal experimentation; for example, if experimenting on chimpanzees promises to help us find a cure for AIDS, it's probably

justified, but a utilitarian animal liberationist like Singer would also be willing to experiment on retarded children if it maximized utility.

The second type of defense of animal rights is the deontological *rights* position, of which Tom Regan is the foremost proponent. The equal-rights position on animal rights contends that the same essential psychological properties—desires, memory, intelligence, and so on—link all animals and the human animal and thereby give us equal intrinsic value upon which equal rights are founded. These rights are inalienable and cannot be forfeited. Contrary to Singer's position, we have no right to experiment on chimpanzees in order to maximize the satisfaction of interests—that's exploitation. Animals like people are "ends in themselves," persons, so that utility is not sufficient to override these rights. Regan is thus more radical than Singer. He calls not for reform but for the total dissolution of commercial animal farming, the total elimination of hunting and trapping, and the total abolition of animal experiments. Just as we would condemn a scientist who took children and performed dangerous experiments on them for the good of others, so we must condemn the institutions that use coercion on animals.

Both utilitarian and deontological animal rights proponents have been attacked on their own ground. R. G. Frey, for example, has argued that utilitarianism does not justify the sweeping indictments or proposals that Singer advocates. He says that because of the greater complexity of the human psyche and its social system, utility will be maximized by exploiting animals. What is needed is an amelioration of existing large-scale farms and safeguards in animal experimentation to ensure against unnecessary suffering.

In our readings, Mary Anne Warren attacks Regan's deontological position for failing to see important differences between human beings and even higher animals, especially our ability to reason. Warren—who agrees that we do have duties to be kind to animals, not to kill them without good reason, and to do what we can to make their lives enjoyable—points out that Regan's notion of inherent value is obscure.

We begin our readings with Kant's view that because animals are not self-conscious rational agents capable of forming the moral law, they are not directly morally considerable, followed by Holly Wilson. She examines Kant's argument over animal egalitarianism (whether all animals are equal).

NOTE

1. *Utilitarianism* is the view that the morally right act is the one that maximizes utility. It aims at producing the best overall consequences. *Deontological* ethics holds that certain features in the moral act itself have intrinsic value regardless of the consequences. It is wrong to kill innocent people even to procure good consequences. Some utilitarians deny animals have rights but argue that we should seek to procure their welfare.

7 Rational Beings Alone Have Moral Worth

IMMANUEL KANT

Immanuel Kant (1724–1804) was born into a deeply pietistic Lutheran family in Königsberg, Germany, and was a professor of philosophy at the University of Königsberg. He is a premier philosopher in the Western tradition, setting forth major works in

The first section is from Kant's *Foundations of the Metaphysics of Morals* (1873), trans. T. K. Abbott. The second section is from Kant's *Lectures on Ethics*, Trans. Louis Infield (New York: Harper & Row, 1963).

metaphysics, philosophy of religion, ethics, epistemology, political theory, and philosophy of science.

Here, Kant first argues that rational beings are ends-in-themselves and must never be used as mere means. Only they have intrinsic moral worth. Animals are not persons because they are not rational, self-conscious beings capable of grasping the moral law. Since they are not part of the kingdom of moral legislators, we who are members of that "kingdom" do not owe them anything. But we should be kind to them since that will help develop good character in us and help us treat our fellow human beings with greater consideration. That is, our duties to animals are simply indirect duties to other human beings. See the next reading for further interpretation.

I. SECOND FORMULATION OF THE CATEGORICAL IMPERATIVE: HUMANITY AS AN END IN ITSELF

The will is conceived as a faculty of determining oneself to action in *accordance with the conception of certain laws*. And such a faculty can be found only in rational beings. Now that which serves the will as the objective ground of its self-determination is the *end*, and if this is assigned by reason alone, it must hold for all rational beings. On the other hand, that which merely contains the ground of possibility of the action of which the effect is the end, this is called the *means*. The subjective ground of the desire is the *spring*, the objective ground of the volition is the *motive*; hence the distinction between subjective ends which rest on springs, and objective ends which depend on motives valid for every rational being. Practical principles are *formal* when they abstract from all subjective ends; they are *material* when they assume these, and therefore particular springs of action. The ends which a rational being proposes to himself at pleasure as *effects* of his actions (material ends) are all only relative, for it is only their relation to the particular desires of the subject that gives them their worth, which therefore cannot furnish principles universal and necessary for all rational beings and for every volition, that is to say practical laws. Hence all these relative ends can give rise only to hypothetical imperatives.

Supposing, however, that there were something *whose existence* has *in itself* an absolute worth, something which, being *an end in itself,*

could be a source of definite laws, then in this and this alone would lie the source of a possible categorical imperative, *i.e.* a practical law.

Now I say: man and generally any rational being *exists* as an end in himself, *not merely as a means* to be arbitrarily used by this or that will, but in all his actions, whether they concern himself or other rational beings, must be always regarded at the same time as an end. All objects of the inclinations have only a conditional worth; for if the inclinations and the wants founded on them did not exist, then their object would be without value. But the inclinations themselves being sources of want are so far from having an absolute worth for which they should be desired, that, on the contrary, it must be the universal wish of every rational being to be wholly free from them. Thus the worth of any object which is *to be acquired* by our action is always conditional. Beings whose existence depends not on our will but on nature's, have nevertheless, if they are nonrational beings, only a relative value as means, and are therefore called *things;* rational beings, on the contrary, are called *persons,* because their very nature points them out as ends in themselves, that is as something which must not be used merely as means, and so far therefore restricts freedom of action (and is an object of respect). These, therefore, are not merely subjective ends whose existence has a worth *for us* as an effect of our action, but *objective ends,* that is things whose existence is an end in itself: an end moreover for which no other can be substituted, which they should subserve *merely* as means, for otherwise nothing whatever would possess *absolute worth;* but if all worth were conditioned and therefore contingent, then there would be no supreme practical principle of reason whatever.

If then there is a supreme practical principle or, in respect of the human will, a categorical imperative, it must be one which, being drawn from the conception of that which is necessarily an end for everyone because it is an *end in itself,* constitutes an *objective* principle of will, and can therefore serve as a universal practical law. The foundation of this principle is: *rational nature exists as an end in itself.* Man necessarily conceives his own existence as being so: so far then this is a *subjective* principle of human actions. But every other rational being regards its existence similarly, just on the same rational principle that holds for me: so that it is at the same time an objective principle, from which as a supreme practical law all laws of the will must be capable of being deduced. Accordingly the practical imperative will be as follows: *So act as to treat humanity, whether in thine own person or in that of any other, in every case as an end-withal, never as means only.* We will now inquire whether this can be practically carried out.

II.

Baumgarten speaks of duties towards beings which are beneath us and beings which are above us. But so far as animals are concerned, we have no direct duties. Animals are not self-conscious and are there merely as a means to an end. That end is man. We can ask, "Why do animals exist?" But to ask, "Why does man exist?" is a meaningless question. *Our duties towards animals are merely indirect duties towards humanity.* Animal nature has analogies to human nature, and by doing our duties to animals in respect of manifestations of human nature, we indirectly do our duty towards humanity. Thus, if a dog has served his master long and faithfully, his service, on the analogy of human service, deserves reward, and when the dog has grown too old to serve, his master ought to keep him until he dies. Such action helps to support us in our duties towards human beings, where they are bounden

duties. If then any acts of animals are analogous to human acts and spring from the same principles, we have duties towards the animals because thus we cultivate the corresponding duties towards human beings. If a man shoots his dog because the animal is no longer capable of service, he does not fail in his duty to the dog, for the dog cannot judge, but his *act is inhuman and damages in himself that humanity which it is his duty to show towards mankind.* If he is not to stifle his human feelings, he must practise kindness towards animals, for he who is cruel to animals becomes hard also in his dealing with men. We can judge the heart of a man by his treatment of animals. Hogarth depicts this in his engravings. He shows how cruelty grows and develops. He shows the child's cruelty to animals, pinch the tail of a dog or a cat; he then depicts the grown man in his cart running over a child; and lastly, the culmination of cruelty in murder. He thus brings home to us in a terrible fashion the rewards of cruelty, and this should be an impressive lesson to children. The more we come in contact with animals and observe their behaviour, the more we love them, for we see how great is their care for their young. It is then difficult for us to be cruel in thought even to a wolf. Leibnitz used a tiny worm for purposes of observation, and then carefully replaced it with its leaf on the tree so that it should not come to harm through any act of his. He would have been sorry—a natural feeling for a humane man—to destroy such a creature for no reason. Tender feelings towards dumb animals develop humane feelings towards mankind. In England butchers and doctors do not sit on a jury because they are accustomed to the sight of death and hardened. Vivisectionists, who use living animals for their experiments, certainly act cruelly, although their aim is praiseworthy, and they can justify their cruelty, since animals must be regarded as man's instruments; but any such cruelty for sport cannot be justified. A master who turns out his ass or his dog because the animal can no longer earn its keep manifests a small mind. The Greeks' ideas in this respect were highminded, as can be seen from the fable of the ass and the bell of ingratitude. Our duties towards animals, then, are indirect duties towards mankind.

STUDY QUESTIONS

1. According to Kant, do animals have rights? What capacity do they lack that deprives them of rights?

2. Why should we be kind to animals? Do you agree with Kant? How would an opponent respond to Kant's arguments?

8   The Green Kant: Kant's Treatment of Animals

HOLLY L. WILSON

Holly Wilson is the author of *Kant's Pragmatic Anthropology.* Here she argues that the central reason Kant gave animals lower moral status is that raising the status of animals would diminish the status of humans. She further points out that Kant is thus naturally able to address the problem of animal egalitarianism, and that Kant should no longer be seen as in opposition to environmental thinking.

Some environmental theorists want to give animals rights and in so doing raise their moral status. None of these theorists seem at all concerned that this move may lower the moral status of human beings. It is simply assumed that human status will remain unaffected when the status of some or all animals is raised. Kant, on the other hand, was very concerned about maintaining the moral status and dignity of human beings, and for him that meant that animals cannot have rights and must be conceived of as being "mere means" to the end of humanity. It is important to note that he did not mean that they have the same status as things when he says "mere means"; but they also do not have the same status as human beings because they are not ends-in-themselves. Kant spent a lot of time distinguishing between humans and animals ontologically, and in doing so it appears that he did not want human status to decline to that of animals. For him, human dignity depended on human beings distancing themselves from their animality.

Although Kant is criticized for holding that animals are "mere means," none of the interpreters understand correctly what he meant by "mere means" or why he thought that characterization is important. I will show that Kant, by using teleological judgment, does not mean that

animals have no moral status and are no more than things. I will also show that his use of teleological judgment has a lot to offer environmental philosophy. I will hold that his position on humans is able to deal with some of the problems environmental philosophers are struggling with, while sidestepping the problems these philosophers ascribe to Kant. Kant's views on animals are consistent with green concerns and are more positive than is usually assumed.

KANT'S VIEWS ON ANIMALS

Kant holds that animals have souls because they move. This is already an ontological distinction between things and animals. In a *Metaphysics* lecture note Kant writes,

Animals are not mere machines or just matter, for they do have souls, and they do so because everything in nature is either inanimate or animate. When, e.g., we see a mote on a paper, we look to see whether it moves. If it doesn't we'll take it as inanimate matter but as soon as it moves, we'll look to see whether it does so voluntarily. If we see *that* in the mote, we'll see that it is *animate,* an animal. So an animal is animated matter, for life is the power to determine oneself from an inner principle. Matter as such lacks an inner principle of spontaneity of motion while all matter that is animate has it, as an object of inner sense. Thus: all matter that lives is alive because of a principle of life.... And to the extent it is animated, to that extent it is besouled.[1]

Animals, in contrast to matter, have an inner principle that gives rise to spontaneous movement. Here is a clear and significant difference between things and animals. Such a distinction gives rise to the presumption that animals should be treated differently from things. Yet, at the same time, having a soul does not mean that an animal is an end-in-itself. To further determine the nature of animals, we turn to the *Critique of Teleological Judgment* where Kant makes the distinction between organized beings and things.

Our teleological judgment recognizes that there is a distinction between organized beings and artifacts and other natural realities. Kant holds that organized beings (living beings) have intrinsic purposiveness.[2] By this he means that we judge the inner organization of an organized being to be constituted by parts (organs), which are means to the ends of the organism and also means to each other's ends. There is a kind of organization that one does not find in a watch, for example. The inner organs of the organized being are mutually means and ends for each other, whereas this is not the case in a watch.[3] In a body the blood is the means of distributing oxygen to the brain; the brain is the means for keeping the blood supplied with nutrients (through eating, for instance). In a watch, one part may make the other part move, but that part is not the productive cause of the other part. The watch does not produce other watches, nor does it produce new parts when old ones malfunction. Even a tree is an organized being for Kant, and hence differs from things. The tree produces itself (maintains itself), reproduces, and its parts are teleological wholes in their own right insofar as a branch can be taken from a tree and grafted onto another tree.[4] Organized beings have formative forces [*Bildungstrieb*]; things do not.[5] Organized beings have intrinsic purposiveness; things do not. Again we find an important distinction between animals and plants, and things.

The distinction extends even further. Kant contrasts natural things like rivers and mountains with organized beings. Here too we find a significant difference between natural objects. Organized beings do not have only intrinsic purposiveness; they are also things for which other things can be extrinsically purposive.[6] Kant writes that the sandy soil "enabled extensive spruce forests to establish themselves, for which unreasonable destruction we often blame our ancestors."[7] The sandy soil was extrinsically purposive for the forests, but the forests were not extrinsically purposive for the soil. When we make such purposive judgments it is with regard to beings that are themselves intrinsically purposive. Hence, animals and plants are intrinsically purposive and things for which other things are extrinsically purposive.[8] We make such judgments whenever we characterize an ecosystem as something in which organized beings find a "habitat." That habitat is purposive for the organized being, and that organized being may well be purposive for other organized beings, but the spotted owl is not purposive for the natural objects like dirt or stones or any other objects in the ecosystem.

Hence, organized beings (animals and plants) have another distinction from things. They can be beings for which other things are purposive, which means that they are ends for the sake of which means exist. That they are intrinsically purposive already means that they are ends for which the means of their parts exist, but we can go even further and now say they are ends for which other things and beings exist. Things don't have this kind of distinction.

There is a qualified sense in which one can say that animals have inherent worth, according to Kant, because they are intrinsically and extrinsically purposive. With respect to human beings as natural beings, we are no different from other organized beings in terms of intrinsic and extrinsic purposiveness. We too are intrinsically purposive, we too may be beings for which other beings and things are purposive, and we too may well be means to another organized being's ends (especially for the ends of bacteria and viruses). Several times Kant exclaims that there is no reason why a human being needs to exist as far as ecosystems are concerned.[9] As natural beings we too have the qualified sense of inherent worth, but as natural animals we certainly are not ends-in-ourselves according to Kant. In this limited sense we are no better than animals. However, he makes an argument that it is only as "beings under moral laws" that we have a status of being ends-in-ourselves.[10] Because animals are not capable of 'being under moral laws,' they do not have this same status. In this human beings distinguish themselves from animals.

There is an additional way in which animals distinguish themselves from things and also may be compared to human beings. Namely, animals have a will [*Willkür*]. A will, Kant writes in the *Critique of Pure Reason*, "is purely *animal (arbitrium brutum)*, which cannot be determined save through sensuous impulses, that is, pathologically."[11] These wills are not determined by the concept of a law but rather by forces that are impelled from outside.[12] For instance, a lion may well choose between this zebra and that antelope in the hunt, and hence it exhibits freedom of choice (*arbitrium brutum*). Yet, the lion does not have the freedom not to hunt. It is heteronomously impelled by the presentation of the prey and reacts compelled by its instincts. The prey triggers the impulse to pursue and kill and hence the motive of the pursuit is heteronomous. The lion does not have the autonomy to choose not to be a predator, and hence it does not have a free will (*Wille*), only the freedom of choice (*Willkür*). Animals, as distinct from human beings, do not have the capacity to resist their inclinations (instincts or impulses) based on the concept of a law (for instance, a maxim that would say "refrain from killing animals"). In contrast, a human being may well choose to be a vegetarian based on the concept that killing animals is wrong. Human beings then have the possibility of autonomous action based on the free will (*Wille*).[13] As a result, human beings can act contrary to sensuously determined carnivorous inclinations. Kant assumes animals are driven by instincts rather than by concepts of laws and in this way, animals, though like human beings, are different from human beings.

KANT'S VIEWS ON HUMAN BEINGS

There is another way in which animals differ from human beings. Human beings are capable of the idea of "I." The fact, Kant claims,

> that man can have the idea "I" raises him infinitely above all other beings living on earth. By this he is a person; and by virtue of his unity of consciousness through all the changes he may undergo, he is one and the same person.[14]

Animals are indeed conscious, have presentations,[15] and also reflect,[16] but they are not self-conscious and do not have an "I." As a student from Kant's anthropology class notes, "If a horse could grasp the idea of I, then I would dismount and regard it as my society."[17] If animals don't have an "I," then they are not our equals.

Kant does a curious thing at this point in the *Anthropology*. Right after the preceding quote he goes on to say that a human being is "altogether different in rank and dignity from things, such as irrational animals, which we can dispose of as we please." First of all, he makes it a point to say that animals are things [*Sachen*], and from this he concludes that they do not have the same rank and dignity that human beings have. He emphasizes that we may dispose of animals as we please, just like we may dispose of things as we please. But why is it so important for him now (1798) to equate animals and things after he has made it so clear that animals are not things in his earlier writings? Systematically and ontologically, Kant has established a distinction between things and animals, but now he equates them and claims we may treat them the same way. Is this a considered position, or is there another reason why Kant is taking pains to distance animals from human beings?

I think we can find a clue to unravel this mystery within Kant's essay *The Speculative Beginning of Human History* (1786). Kant acknowledges he is writing a speculative flight of fancy about the beginnings of human freedom and the departure from animality. It is about the first appearance of reason in the human species. In the experience of reason, human beings are raised "beyond any community with animals."[18] A human being

(Adam) views himself for the first time as the "true end of nature" because "nothing living on earth can compete with him." He says to the sheep,

> 'the pelt you bear was given to you by nature not for yourself, but for me'; the first time he took that pelt off the sheep and put it on himself (Gen. 3:21); at that same time he saw within himself a privilege by virtue of which his nature surpassed that of all animals, which he now no longer regarded as his fellows in creation, but as subject to his will as means and tools for achieving his own chosen objectives.[19]

This story of using a sheepskin is not about how we ought to relate to animals but rather about how we can indeed use animals as mere means, because we are superior in our ability to compete with animals. It is an account of how human beings, through skills, are able to use animals as means toward human's arbitrarily chosen ends. Kant is right: In the struggle for survival, human beings have clearly outperformed other animals. Our success means that nonhuman animals are no longer our equals, our fellows, or our society.

Yet this experience entails even more. Human beings draw the conclusion that they are not only the last end of nature (*letzter Zweck*), but that they, unlike animals, are ends-in-themselves (*Endzweck*) and that no fellow human being ought to be used "merely as a means to any other end." In other words, human beings are "the equal of all rational beings." Kant ties the moment of recognition of our human dignity to the moment we are able to recognize our ability to use animals as mere means.[20] This association of the two insights is exactly what he is doing in the *Anthropology*. Our dignity as humans is in part determined by our ability to distance ourselves from animals, by using them as means to our ends. This distancing is not just from animals, but also from our own animality because we no longer identify with animal society. The very capacity to turn animals into mere means is one way in which we distance ourselves from our own animality. Is it possible to come to this recognition without having to see animals are mere means? Could we have come to this recognition of our dignity with the use of tools?

Kant seems to think that before we used reason we were animals and that our society was with other animals. Thus, the earliest use of reason required our distancing ourselves not only from other animals but also from our own animality. That distancing doesn't seem to be something we could accomplish just by becoming aware of the possibility of using tools because we are not like tools. We are like animals. For Kant we are animals that have the capacity for reason (*animal rationabilis*).[21] One use of reason is found in our technical predisposition, that is, our capacity for skills that are capable of manipulating things "in any way whatsoever."[22] It is because of this predisposition that we are capable of turning animals into "mere means." We have the capacity to develop skills for survival nonspecific ends, or, as Kant puts it in the *Critique of Teleological Judgment*, for arbitrary ends.[23] Kant goes on to say that the culture of skill is "not adequate to assist the will in the determination and selection of its purposes...."[24] Nothing about our technical predisposition and technical skills specifies only worthy ends, and hence there is nothing about these skills that would keep us from turning animals into mere means.

But our technical predisposition is only one of reason's expressions. We also have a pragmatic predisposition and a moral predisposition. These two present necessary ends for reason. The pragmatic predisposition is expressed in the skill of prudence, which aims at our happiness, a necessary end. Prudence is the capacity we have for using other human beings as means to our own ends. The moral predisposition is expressed in our capacity for limiting and refusing specific technical and pragmatic ends for moral reasons.[25] Treating animals as mere means may well have a detrimental effect on our happiness, and we may hence put a limit on how we relate to animals. Many people love animals, become friends with them, and as a result treat them very well, sometimes even like children, because it brings them happiness to do so. This treatment is the result of our pragmatic predisposition, because we are limiting our use of animals in order to allow them to bring us happiness. Some people refuse to eat animals because they are saddened by the way animals are farm-raised and slaughtered.

This refusal too is a result of our pragmatic predisposition. Others want to protect animals from cruelty because they believe that animals are like us (feel pain and pleasure) and that it is ethically wrong to cause them suffering. This protection is possible using moral reasoning. Still others want to limit our ability to treat animals as mere means by even stronger measures. They want to accord animals rights to ensure their safety and well-being. They do not want our limits to be based on internal measures, mere subjective feelings for animals (as in the pragmatic predisposition), or even benevolence and good will (as in the moral predisposition). They want external coercive juridical forces to come to the aid of animals. They believe that granting animal rights would ensure to a greater extent the well-being of animals and that it would raise the status of animals to that of humans because we would no longer be able to treat animals as mere means.

CAN ANIMALS HAVE RIGHTS?

For Kant, a lot would be at stake if we did move toward according animals rights. First of all, it would entail that we could never use animals, even as we use human beings, because we could never gain their informed consent. According to the third formulation of the categorical imperative we may never treat the humanity in ourselves or in others as means only. This formulation means we may never use human beings as means only. Yet we use people all the time, and our pragmatic predisposition is precisely for that purpose. Kant says in the *Lectures on Ethics,* "A person can, indeed, serve as a means for others, by his work, for example, but in such a way that he does not cease to exist as a person and an end."[26] The reason we can use others without turning them into mere means is because we have the other's consent or free choice.[27] I use students as students, and they use me as a professor. What makes it morally permissible to use another human being is the informed consent she gives ahead of time, which is why students register for their classes themselves and I give out a syllabus at the start of every semester. They are consenting to take the class, and I am giving them the information they

need to make an informed decision about whether to permit me to evaluate them. It is impossible to gain the informed consent from animals, however, because we would need to convey information regarding the means used and the possible consequences, and we would need to procure a sure sign of their consent. Such a rigorous requirement would make it impossible for me to take my cat to the vet. She doesn't consent to being in the cat carrier, in the car, at the vet's, and she certainly doesn't consent to the vaccine shots. Having to gain animals' informed consent can be a hindrance to helping them as well as making it impossible to treat them as means. Clearly, by treating animals as "mere means" Kant means *inter alia* that we do not have to gain their consent to use them or take care of them, although, for the most part, it is preferable to treat a pet in a way it wants to be treated whenever possible.

This position, however, raises the marginal case of humans for whom we also cannot gain informed consent (children, the mentally handicapped, and those who are comatose). If we include these marginal cases as persons, why can we not also include animals, or at least animals that exhibit some rationality? Why should animals who exhibit some form of rationality be denied moral personhood while human beings not exhibiting rationality are accorded moral personhood? Kant's answer would be that it is not important for each member of the human species to exhibit all features of rationality; it is enough that the species exhibits all forms. That view is implicit in his formulation of the human species as the *animal rationabilis,* rather than the rational animal.[28] Human beings are the animals who have the capacity for reason. Each human being, as a member of the species, has the potential for rationality even if she never exhibits it. This potential entails that we must still treat humans who do not exhibit rationality as ends-in-themselves. When it is impossible to gain their consent, it does not inhibit our ability to help them.

What is crucial here is that Kant does not want to isolate an individual human being and evaluate whether that particular individual has the capacity for reason. His position is that human nature is intrinsically communal, and hence the capacity for reason is something we share as a species rather than as individuals. Human beings are defined as the animals capable of developing reason (*animal rationabilis*), so that whether any one individual human being does or does not exhibit reason will not affect one's status and nature. Our natural predispositions, which define human nature for Kant, relate us to all other members of the human species.[29] Hence, to treat any one human being as less than an end-in-herself is already to call into question the status of all other human beings. Nonetheless, Kant's definition of human nature as *animal rationabilis* does not exclude other animals as being "like human beings" in that they exhibit "reason-like" capacities.

So, what about those cases in which animals exhibit primitive forms of rationality? Shouldn't they be granted moral personhood? How would Kant deal with animals who are very much like us? That animals are like us is relevant to moral consideration of them. In the very same section, "Of Duties to Animals and Spirits" in the *Lectures on Ethics,* where Kant grants us permission to use animals as mere means, he also claims we have indirect duties with regard to dogs that serve us and wolves that, like us, care for their young.[30] First, he makes it clear that they are like us (analogues of us), and then he claims that our mistreatment of them (animals like us) would result in diminishing our humanity. The duty is then only indirect because it is contingent upon whether our humanity is furthered or diminished. We have a direct duty to our own humanity, but Kant is equally convinced that our treatment of animals matters because they are like us. By implication one could draw the conclusion that the more like us they are, the more consideration they deserve. This conclusion makes Kantian sense of the problem of marginal cases. Animals who exhibit rudimentary rationality certainly deserve more consideration than flies, because they are more like us. Kant's position also solves the obvious problem with animal egalitarianism, which outrageously implies that all animate beings deserve equal consideration. The less like human beings an animate being is, the less it deserves consideration. The more like us they are, the more consideration they deserve. And Kant does not have to be taken as implying that animals are like us only insofar as they exhibit

reasonlike capacities. Dogs are like us in that they exhibit loyalty. Wolves are like us in that they care for their young. Thus animals can be like us in many different ways, not only in that they can suffer pain and pleasure or have capacities for reason.

Kant is also right to give human beings only indirect duties to nonhuman animals because they do not have moral rationality. They are not capable of acting on the conception of a law. They do exhibit cooperation and social behaviors, but these traits appear to be a result of survival mechanisms and conditioned inclinations and not a result of acting on the concept of treating animality as an end and never as a means only. Their behaviors do exhibit order and uniformity, but this display is due to the natural organization in their instincts and to socialized learned behavior, not due to considered reflection on whether every chimp could act on that maxim. Human beings exhibit order and character only when they submit their maxims to the moral law. Humans are held to higher standards morally because there are ontological differences between human beings and animals. We have the capacity for technical and pragmatic reason, and we need morality to limit these ends to morally permissible and worthy ends.

What about the position that would say, 'granted, animals cannot give informed consent, develop character, and act on the conception of the law, but that is just the case with children'? We have the authority to make children do what is in their own best interest, while according them rights not to be mistreated. Why not treat animals the same way? But are there no ontological differences between animals and children? Children have the potential to develop reason. Should this not inform their treatment? Children should be raised rather than trained. They need to be taught in a way that develops their free will. They need to be given alternatives and to be encouraged to evaluate consequences for their actions. Eventually, they also need to be encouraged to deliberate and reflect on possible actions and on the reasons and motives for those actions. Animals, on the other hand, should be trained. They can be trained to associate reward and punishment with certain behaviors. We cannot reason with them and encourage them to choose between alternative behaviors. Would we be blurring the distinction between children and animals if we were to treat animals like children?

The blurring of the distinction between human beings and nonhuman animals is already occurring in evolutionary psychology, evolutionary ethics, and behaviorism. Human behavior is being understood on the animal model of behaviors. Focus is being put on behavior rather than action. More concern is attached to explaining and controlling behavior than developing ways to teach and instill the importance of making choices and taking responsibility for those choices. A Kantian ought to be concerned about this, and I think Kant would be were he here today.

Clearly humans need to be treated differently from animals because they are different, and animals need to be treated differently from humans. Animals should not be treated as things, but they should also not be treated as humans. The locus of our treatment of animals should be ethical rather than juridical. Cruelty to animals should be against the law, not only because it harms animals but also because it harms our humanity and makes us more likely to be cruel to humans. We can and are able to treat animals humanely without giving animals rights. We ought not to treat animal nature as an end-in-itself, as Christine Korsgaard proposes, however, because animal nature is pursued by animals heteronomously, pathologically, and reactively. To treat animal nature as an end-in-itself would mean having to cooperate in the ends that animal nature pursues, and that would make our actions heteronomously motivated.

IN CONCLUSION

Human beings, for Kant, are under moral laws and animals are not. We find ourselves obligated not by the needs of animals but by the moral law. Animals do not find themselves obligated by the moral law nor by us and hence they cannot directly obligate us. Nevertheless, animals, in their vulnerabilities and needs, present reasons for taking them into consideration and reasons for refraining from harming them. Insofar as I have a maxim of benevolence toward human beings who have needs, and I can see those same needs

in animals, then out of care for the humanity in myself, I can feel obligated to care about animals, but always by virtue of my concern for the state of my own humanity. Kant is asking us to value the best in ourselves, our humanity, and out of that to find motivation for caring for animals. When we do so it solves the problem of the apparent conflict between doing what is good for us and doing what is good for animals. Taking care of animals and not being cruel to them is good for us. Finding our care for animals in our care for our humanity does not preclude legislating against cruel or arbitrary treatment of animals, but rather gives us reason to legislate against such treatment. We can do this without considering animals to be ends-in-themselves, and thereby lowering the worth of human beings and blurring the ontological and moral lines between human life and animal life.

For Kant, animals, like human beings, are organic beings and do have a sense of inherent worth insofar as they are intrinsically and extrinsically purposive. Animals can be ends for which our actions are means, and we treat them as ends when we treat animals kindly, with benevolence, and when we refrain from harming them and their habitats. What is at stake for Kant is the motive for not treating animals cruelly. Animal rights theorists want people to be coercively motivated to keep them from treating animals cruelly by giving animals rights. If animals have a right not to be treated cruelly, then human beings can be punished if they do treat them cruelly. Kant wants us to be motivated out of respect for our own humanity to keep us from treating animals cruelly, because he knows that our dignity as human beings is always at stake in our treatment of animals. Kant holds that we preserve our moral and inherent dignity by treating animals kindly because in so doing we take our humanity as an end-in-itself since animals are like us. It would be like treating our own humanity as a mere means if we were to be arbitrarily cruel to animals like us. Kant wants us not only to treat animals well but also to learn to respect our own humanity and dignity. And for that we have to distinguish between animals and humans.

NOTES

1. Immanuel Kant, *Metaphysik L1,* in KGS 28:275 (1776), translation by Martin Schönfeld.
2. Immanuel Kant, KU, KGS V:372-76; pp. 251–56.
3. Immanuel Kant, KU, KGS V:373; p. 252.
4. Immanuel Kant, KU, KGS V:371; pp. 249–250.
5. Immanuel Kant, KU, KGS V:374; p. 253.
6. Immanuel Kant, KU, KGS V:367–68; p. 245.
7. Immanuel Kant, Ibid.
8. Immanuel Kant, KU, KGS V:369; p. 246.
9. Immanuel Kant, KU, KGS V:369; p. 247; KU, KGS V:378; p. 258.
10. Immanuel Kant, KU, KGS 435; p. 323.
11. Immanuel Kant, *Critique of Pure Reason* [A802/B830].
12. Immanuel Kant, LoE, KGS 27:344; p. 125. Friedländer, KGS 25 (2,1):577.
13. Immanuel Kant, GR, KGS IV:412; p. 23.
14. Immanuel Kant, Anth, KGS VII:127; p. 9.
15. Immanuel Kant, KU, KGS V:464n; p. 356n.
16. Immanuel Kant, First Intro, KGS, XX:211; p. 400.
17. Immanuel Kant, Menschenkunde, KGS 25(2): 859.
18. Immanuel Kant, Mut, KGS VIII:114; p. 52.
19. Immanuel Kant, Mut, KGS VIII:114; p. 52–3.
20. Immanuel Kant, Ibid.
21. Immanuel Kant, Anth, KGS VII:321; p. 183.
22. Immanuel Kant, Anth, KGS VII:323; p. 184.
23. Immanuel Kant, KU, KGS V:430; p. 317.
24. Immanuel Kant, KU, KGS V:432; p. 319.
25. Immanuel Kant, Anth, KGS VII:323–24; p. 185.
26. Immanuel Kant, LoE, KGS 27:343; p. 124.
27. Immanuel Kant, LoE, KGS 27:384; p. 155.
28. Immanuel Kant, Anth, KGS VI:321; p. 183.
29. Holly L. Wilson, *Kant's Pragmatic Anthropology,* Chapter 3.
30. Immanuel Kant, LoE, KGS 27:459; p. 212.

STUDY QUESTIONS

1. According to Kant, what are the differences among humans, nonhuman animals, and plants?
2. What does it mean to treat an entity as an 'end-in-itself'? What is it problematic to treat animals this way?
3. Animal egalitarianism claims that all animals deserve equal moral consideration. Discuss this view and Kant's account of why this is wrong.

BIBLIOGRAPHY

Citations from Immanuel Kant are from, *Kant's Gesammelte Schriften,* edited by the Königlich Preußische [now Deutsche] Akademie der Wissenschaft, vols. 1–29 (Berlin: G. Reimer [now de Gruyter],1902-)[KGS].

Immanuel Kant, *Kritik der Urteilskraft,* in KGS V; *Critique of Judgment,* trans. by Werner S. Pluhar (Indianapolis: Hackett Publishing Co., 1987) [KU].

Immanuel Kant, Erste Einleitung in die Kritik der Urteilskraft, in KGS XX; First Introduction to the Critique of Judgment, in *Critique of Judgment,* trans. by Werner S. Pluhar (Indianapolis: Hackett Publishing Co., 1987) [First Intro].

Immanuel Kant, *Critique of Pure Reason,* trans. by Normen Kemp Smith (New York: St. Martin's Press, 1965) [A/B].

Immanuel Kant, *Lectures on Ethics,* in KGS, 27, trans. by Peter Heath (Cambridge: Cambridge University Press, 1997) [LoE].

Immanuel Kant, *Grundlegung zur Metaphysik der Sitten,* in KGS IV; *Grounding for the Metaphysics of Morals,* trans. by James W. Ellington (Indianapolis: Hackett Publishing Co., Inc., 1981) [GR].

Immanuel Kant, *Anthropologie im pragmatischer Hinsicht,* in KGS, VII; *Anthropology from a Pragmatic Point of View,* trans. by Mary Gregor (The Hague: Maritinus Nijhoff, 1974).

Immanuel Kant, *Menschenkunde,* in KGS, XXV(2) [Menschenkunde].

Immanuel Kant, "Muthmaßlicher Anfang der Menschengeschichte" in KGS VIII; "Speculative Beginning of Human History" in *Perpetual Peace and other Essays on Politics, History, and Morals,* trans. by Ted Humphrey (Indianapolis: Hackett Publishing Co., 1983) [Mut].

Christine M. Korsgaard, "Fellow Creatures: Kantian Ethics and Our Duties to Animals" in *The Tanner Lectures on Human Values,* Volume 25/26, ed. by Grethe B. Peterson. Salt Lake City: Utah University Press, 2004.

Holly L. Wilson, *Kant's Pragmatic Anthropology: Its Origin, Meaning, and Critical Significance* (New York: State University of New York Press, 2006).

9   A Utilitarian Defense of Animal Liberation

PETER SINGER

Peter Singer, professor of philosophy at Princeton University, was included in *Time* magazine's 2005 list of the world's most influential people. His book *Animal Liberation* (1975), from which the following selection is taken, is the most influential book written on the subject, having in a sense started the animal rights movement. Singer argues that animal liberation today is analogous to racial and gender justice in the past. Just as people once thought it incredible that women or blacks should be treated as equal to white men, so now speciesists mock the idea that all animals should be given equal consideration. Singer defines *speciesism* (a term devised by Richard Ryder) as the prejudice (unjustified bias) that favors one's own species over every other. What equalizes all sentient beings is our ability to suffer. In that, we and animals are equal and deserving equal consideration of interests. Singer's argument is a utilitarian one, having as its goal the maximization of interest satisfaction.

In recent years a number of oppressed groups have campaigned vigorously for equality. The classic instance is the Black Liberation movement, which demands an end to the prejudice and discrimination that has made blacks second-class citizens. The immediate appeal of the black liberation movement and its initial, if limited, success made it a model for other oppressed groups to follow. We became familiar with liberation movements for Spanish-Americans, gay people, and a variety of other minorities. When a majority group—women—began their campaign, some thought we had come to the end of the road. Discrimination on the basis of sex, it has been said, is the last universally accepted form of discrimination, practiced without secrecy or pretense even in those liberal circles that have long prided themselves on their freedom from prejudice against racial minorities.

One should always be wary of talking of "the last remaining form of discrimination." If we have learnt anything from the liberation movements, we should have learnt how difficult it is to be aware of latent prejudice in our attitudes to particular groups until this prejudice is forcefully pointed out.

A liberation movement demands an expansion of our moral horizons and an extension or reinterpretation of the basic moral principle of equality. Practices that were previously regarded as natural and inevitable come to be seen as the result of an unjustifiable prejudice. Who can say with confidence that all his or her attitudes and practices are beyond criticism? If we wish to avoid being numbered amongst the oppressors, we must be prepared to re-think even our most fundamental attitudes. We need to consider them from the point of view of those most disadvantaged by our attitudes, and the practices that follow from these attitudes. If we can make this unaccustomed mental switch we may discover a pattern in our attitudes and practices that consistently operates so as to benefit one group—usually the one to which we ourselves belong—at the expense of another. In this way we may come to see that there is a case for a new liberation movement. My aim is to advocate that we make this mental switch in respect of our attitudes and practices towards a very large group of beings: members of species other than our own—or, as we popularly though misleadingly call them, animals. In other words, I am urging that we extend to

Reprinted from *Animal Rights and Human Obligations* (Englewood Cliffs, NJ: Prentice-Hall, 1976) by permission of Peter Singer.

other species the basic principle of equality that most of us recognize should be extended to all members of our own species.

All this may sound a little far-fetched, more like a parody of other liberation movements than a serious objective. In fact, in the past the idea of "The Rights of Animals" really has been used to parody the case for women's rights. When Mary Wollstonecroft, a forerunner of later feminists, published her *Vindication of the Rights of Women* in 1792, her ideas were widely regarded as absurd, and they were satirized in an anonymous publication entitled *A Vindication of the Rights of Brutes.* The author of this satire (actually Thomas Taylor, a distinguished Cambridge philosopher) tried to refute Wollstonecroft's reasonings by showing that they could be carried one stage further. If sound when applied to women, why should the arguments not be applied to dogs, cats, and horses? They seemed to hold equally well for these "brutes"; yet to hold that brutes had rights was manifestly absurd; therefore the reasoning by which this conclusion had been reached must be unsound, and if unsound when applied to brutes, it must also be unsound when applied to women, since the very same arguments had been used in each case.

One way in which we might reply to this argument is by saying that the case for equality between men and women cannot validly be extended to nonhuman animals. Women have a right to vote, for instance, because they are just as capable of making rational decisions as men are; dogs, on the other hand, are incapable of understanding the significance of voting, so they cannot have the right to vote. There are many other obvious ways in which men and women resemble each other closely, while humans and other animals differ greatly. So, it might be said, men and women are similar beings, and should have equal rights, while humans and nonhumans are different and should not have equal rights.

The thought behind this reply to Taylor's analogy is correct up to a point, but it does not go far enough. There *are* important differences between humans and other animals, and these differences must give rise to *some* differences in the rights that each have. Recognizing this

obvious fact, however, is no barrier to the case for extending the basic principle of equality to nonhuman animals. The differences that exist between men and women are equally undeniable, and the supporters of Women's Liberation are aware that these differences may give rise to different rights. Many feminists hold that women have the right to an abortion on request. It does not follow that since these same people are campaigning for equality between men and women they must support the right of men to have abortions too. Since a man cannot have an abortion, it is meaningless to talk of his right to have one. Since a pig can't vote, it is meaningless to talk of its right to vote. There is no reason why either Women's Liberation or Animal Liberation should get involved in such nonsense. The extension of the basic principle of equality from one group to another does not imply that we must treat both groups in exactly the same way, or grant exactly the same rights to both groups. Whether we should do so will depend on the nature of the members of the two groups. The basic principle of equality, I shall argue, is equality of consideration; and equal consideration for different beings may lead to different treatment and different rights.

So there is a different way of replying to Taylor's attempt to parody Wollstonecroft's arguments, a way which does not deny the differences between humans and nonhumans, but goes more deeply into the question of equality, and concludes by finding nothing absurd in the idea that the basic principle of equality applies to so called "brutes." I believe that we reach this conclusion if we examine the basis on which our opposition to discrimination on grounds of race or sex ultimately rests. We will then see that we would be on shaky ground if we were to demand equality for blacks, women, and other groups of oppressed humans while denying equal consideration to nonhumans.

When we say that all human beings, whatever their race, creed or sex, are equal, what is it that we are asserting? Those who wish to defend a hierarchical, inegalitarian society have often pointed out that by whatever test we choose, it simply is not true that all humans are equal.

Like it or not, we must face the fact that humans come in different shapes and sizes; they come with differing moral capacities, differing intellectual abilities, differing amounts of benevolent feeling and sensitivity to the needs of others, differing abilities to communicate effectively, and differing capacities to experience pleasure and pain. In short, if the demand for equality were based on the actual equality of all human beings, we would have to stop demanding equality. It would be an unjustifiable demand.

Still, one might cling to the view that the demand for equality among human beings is based on the actual equality of the different races and sexes. Although humans differ as individuals in various ways, there are no differences between the races and sexes *as such*. From the mere fact that a person is black, or a woman, we cannot infer anything else about that person. This, it may be said, is what is wrong with racism and sexism. The white racist claims that whites are superior to blacks, but this is false—although there are differences between individuals, some blacks are superior to some whites in all of the capacities and abilities that could conceivably be relevant. The opponent of sexism would say the same: a person's sex is no guide to his or her abilities, and this is why it is unjustifiable to discriminate on the basis of sex.

This is a possible line of objection to racial and sexual discrimination. It is not, however, the way that someone really concerned about equality would choose, because taking this line could, in some circumstances, force one to accept a most inegalitarian society. The fact that humans differ as individuals, rather than as races or sexes, is a valid reply to someone who defends a hierarchical society like, say, South Africa, in which all whites are superior in status to all blacks. The existence of individual variations that cut across the lines of race or sex, however, provides us with no defence at all against a more sophisticated opponent of equality, one who proposes that, say, the interests of those with I.Q. ratings above 100 be preferred to the interests of those with I.Q.s below 100. Would a hierarchical society of this sort really be so much better than one based on race or sex? I think not. But if we tie the moral principle of equality to the factual equality of the different races or sexes, taken as a whole, our opposition to racism and sexism does not provide us with any basis for objecting to this kind of inegalitarianism.

There is a second important reason why we ought not to base our opposition to racism and sexism on any kind of factual equality, even the limited kind which asserts that variations in capacities and abilities are spread evenly between the different races and sexes: we can have no absolute guarantee that these abilities and capacities really are distributed evenly, without regard to race or sex, among human beings. So far as actual abilities are concerned, there do seem to be certain measurable differences between both races and sexes. These differences do not, of course, appear in each case, but only when averages are taken. More important still, we do not yet know how much of these differences is really due to the different genetic endowments of the various races and sexes, and how much is due to environmental differences that are the result of past and continuing discrimination. Perhaps all of the important differences will eventually prove to be environmental rather than genetic. Anyone opposed to racism and sexism will certainly hope that this will be so, for it will make the task of ending discrimination a lot easier; nevertheless it would be dangerous to rest the case against racism and sexism on the belief that all significant differences are environmental in origin. The opponent of, say, racism who takes this line will be unable to avoid conceding that if differences in ability did after all prove to have some generic connection with race, racism would in some way be defensible.

It would be folly for the opponent of racism to stake his whole case on a dogmatic commitment to one particular outcome of a difficult scientific issue which is still a long way from being settled. While attempts to prove that differences in certain selected abilities between races and sexes are primarily genetic in origin have certainly not been conclusive, the same must be said of attempts to prove that these differences are largely the result of environment. At this stage of the investigation we cannot be certain which view is correct, however much we may hope it is the latter.

Fortunately, there is no need to pin the case for equality to one particular outcome of this scientific investigation. The appropriate response to those who claim to have found evidence of genetically based differences in ability between the races or sexes is not to stick to the belief that the genetic explanation must be wrong, whatever evidence to the contrary may turn up: instead we should make it quite clear that the claim to equality does not depend on intelligence, moral capacity, physical strength, or similar matters of fact. Equality is a moral ideal, not a simple assertion of fact. There is no logically compelling reason for assuming that a factual difference in ability between two people justifies any *difference in the amount of consideration we give to satisfying their needs and interests*. The principle of the equality of human beings is not a description of an alleged actual equality among humans: it is a prescription of how we should treat humans.

Jeremy Bentham incorporated the essential basis of moral equality into his utilitarian system of ethics in the formula: "Each to count for one and none for more than one." In other words, the interests of every being affected by an action are to be taken into account and given the same weight as the like interests of any other being. A later utilitarian, Henry Sidgwick, put the point in this way: "The good of any one individual is of no more importance, from the point of view (if I may say so) of the Universe, than the good of any other."[1] More recently, the leading figures in contemporary moral philosophy have shown a great deal of agreement in specifying as a fundamental presupposition of their moral theories some similar requirement which operates so as to give everyone's interests equal consideration—although they cannot agree on how this requirement is best formulated.[2]

It is an implication of this principle of equality that our concern for others ought not to depend on what they are like, or what abilities they possess—although precisely what this concern requires us to do may vary according to the characteristics of those affected by what we do. It is on this basis that the case against racism and the case against sexism must both ultimately rest; and it is in accordance with this principle that speciesism is also to be condemned. If possessing a higher degree of intelligence does not entitle one human to use another for his own ends, how can it entitle humans to exploit nonhumans?

Many philosophers have proposed the principle of equal consideration of interests, in some form or other, as a basic moral principle; but, as we shall see in more detail shortly, not many of them have recognized that this principle applies to members of other species as well as to our own. Bentham was one of the few who did realize this. In a forward-looking passage, written at a time when black slaves in British dominions were still being treated much as we now treat nonhuman animals, Bentham wrote:

> The day *may* come when the rest of the animal creation may acquire those rights which never could have been witholden from them but by the hand of tyranny. The French have already discovered that the blackness of the skin is no reason why a human being should be abandoned without redress to the caprice of a tormentor. It may one day come to be recognized that the number of the legs, the villosity of the skin, or the termination of the *os sacrum*, are reasons equally insufficient for abandoning a sensitive being to the same fate. What else is it that should trace the insuperable line? Is it the faculty of reason, or perhaps the faculty of discourse? But a full grown horse or dog is beyond comparison a more rational, as well as a more conversable animal, than an infant of a day, or a week, or even a month, old. But suppose they were otherwise, what would it avail? The question is not, Can they reason? nor Can they *talk*? but, *Can they suffer?*[3]

In this passage Bentham points to the capacity for suffering as the vital characteristic that gives a being the *right* to equal consideration. The capacity for suffering—or more strictly, for suffering and/or enjoyment or happiness—is not just another characteristic like the capacity for language, or for higher mathematics. Bentham is not saying that those who try to mark the "insuperable line" that determines whether the interests of a being should be considered happen to have selected the wrong characteristic. The capacity for suffering and enjoying things is a prerequisite for having interests at all, a condition that must be satisfied before we can speak of interests in any meaningful way. It would be nonsense to say that it was not in the interests of a stone to be kicked along the road by a schoolboy. A stone does not have interests because it cannot suffer. Nothing that we can do to it could possibly make any difference to its welfare. A mouse, on the other hand, does have an interest in not being tormented, because it will suffer if it is.

If a being suffers, there can be no moral justification for refusing to take that suffering into consideration. No matter what the nature of the being, the principle of equality requires that its suffering be counted equally with the like suffering—in so far as rough comparisons can be made—of any other being. If a being is not capable of suffering, or of experiencing enjoyment or happiness, there is nothing to be taken into account. This is why the limit of sentience (using the term as a convenient, if not strictly accurate, shorthand for the capacity to suffer or experience enjoyment or happiness) is the only defensible boundary of concern for the interests of others. To mark this boundary by some characteristic like intelligence or rationality would be to mark it in an arbitrary way. Why not choose some other characteristic, like skin color?

The racist violates the principle of equality by giving greater weight to the interests of members of his own race, when there is a clash between their interests and the interests of those of another race. Similarly the speciesist allows the interests of his own species to override the greater interests of members of other species.[4] The pattern is the same in each case. Most human beings are speciesists. I shall now very briefly describe some of the practices that show this.

For the great majority of human beings, especially in urban, industrialized societies, the most direct form of contact with members of other species is at mealtimes: we eat them. In doing so we treat them purely as means to our ends. We regard their life and well-being as subordinate to our taste for a particular kind of dish. I say "taste" deliberately—this is purely a matter of pleasing our palate. There can be no defence of eating flesh in terms of satisfying nutritional needs, since it has been established beyond doubt that we could satisfy our need for protein and other essential nutrients far more efficiently with a diet that replaced animal flesh by soy beans, or products derived from soy beans, and other high-protein vegetable products.[5]

It is not merely the act of killing that indicates what we are ready to do to other species in order to gratify our tastes. The suffering we inflict on the animals while they are alive is perhaps an even clearer indication of our speciesism than the fact that we are prepared to kill them. In order to have meat on the table at a price that people can afford, our society tolerates methods of meat production that confine sentient animals in cramped, unsuitable conditions for the entire durations of their lives. Animals are treated like machines that convert fodder into flesh, and any innovation that results in a higher "conversion ratio" is liable to be adopted. As one authority on the subject has said, "cruelty is acknowledged only when profitability ceases."[6] . . .

Since, as I have said, none of these practices cater for anything more than our pleasures of taste, our practice of rearing and killing other animals in order to eat them is a clear instance of the sacrifice of the most important interests of other beings in order to satisfy trivial interests of our own. To avoid speciesism we must stop this practice, and each of us has a moral obligation to cease supporting the practice. Our custom is all the support that the meat-industry needs. The decision to cease giving it that support may be difficult, but it is no more difficult than it would have been for a white Southerner to go against the traditions of his society and free his slaves: if we do not change our dietary habits, how can we censure those slaveholders who would not change their own way of living?

The same form of discrimination may be observed in the widespread practice of experimenting on other species in order to see if certain substances are safe for human beings, or to test some psychological theory about the effect of severe punishment on learning, or to try out various new compounds just in case something turns up. . . .

In the past, argument about vivisection has often missed this point, because it has been put in absolutist terms: Would the abolitionist be prepared to let thousands die if they could be saved by experimenting on a single animal? The way to reply to this purely hypothetical question is to pose another: *Would the experimenter be prepared to perform his experiment on an orphaned human infant, if that were the only way to save many lives?* (I say "orphan" to avoid the complication of parental feelings, although in doing so I am being overfair to the experimenter, since the non-human subjects of experiments are not orphans.) If the experimenter is not prepared to use an orphaned human infant, then his readiness to use nonhumans is simple discrimination, since adult apes, cats, mice and other mammals are more aware of what is happening to them, more self-directing and, so far as we can tell, at least as sensitive to pain, as any human infant. There seems to be no relevant characteristic that human infants possess that adult mammals do not have to the same or a higher degree. (Some-one might try to argue that what makes it wrong to experiment on a human infant is that the infant will, in time and if left alone, develop into more than the nonhuman, but one would then, to be consistent, have to oppose abortion, since the fetus has the same potential as the infant—indeed, even contraception and absti-nence might be wrong on this ground, since the egg and sperm, considered jointly, also have the same potential. In any case, this argument still gives us no reason for selecting a nonhuman, rather than a human with severe and irreversible brain damage, as the subject for our experiments.)

The experimenter, then, shows a bias in favor of his own species whenever he carries out an experiment on a nonhuman for a purpose that he would not think justified him in using a human being at an equal or lower level of sen-tience, awareness, ability to be self-directing, etc. No one familiar with the kind of results yielded by most experiments on animals can have the slightest doubt that if this bias were eliminated the number of experiments performed would be a minute fraction of the number per-formed today.

Experimenting on animals, and eating their flesh, are perhaps the two major forms of spe-ciesism in our society. By comparison, the third and last form of speciesism is so minor as to be insignificant, but it is perhaps of some

special interest to those for whom this article was written. I am referring to speciesism in con-temporary philosophy.

Philosophy ought to question the basic assumptions of the age. Thinking through, criti-cally and carefully, what most people take for granted is, I believe, the chief task of philosophy, and it is this task that makes philosophy a worth-while activity. Regrettably, philosophy does not always live up to its historic role. Philosophers are human beings and they are subject to all the preconceptions of the society to which they belong. Sometimes they succeed in breaking free of the prevailing ideology: more often they become its most sophisticated defenders. So, in this case, philosophy as practiced in the univer-sities today does not challenge anyone's precon-ceptions about our relations with other species. By their writings, those philosophers who tackle problems that touch upon the issue reveal that they make the same unquestioned assumptions as most other humans, and what they say tends to confirm the reader in his or her comfortable speciesist habits.

I could illustrate this claim by referring to the writings of philosophers in various fields—for instance, the attempts that have been made by those interested in rights to draw the boundary of the sphere of rights so that it runs parallel to the biological boundaries of the species *homo sapiens,* including infants and even mental defec-tives, but excluding those other beings of equal or greater capacity who are so useful to us at mealtimes and in our laboratories. I think it would be a more appropriate conclusion to this article, however, if I concentrated on the problem with which we have been centrally concerned, the problem of equality.

It is significant that the problem of *equality,* in moral and political philosophy, is invariably formulated in terms of human equality. The effect of this is that the question of the equality of other animals does not confront the philoso-pher, or student, as an issue itself—and this is already an indication of the failure of philosophy to challenge accepted beliefs. Still, philosophers have found it difficult to discuss the issue of human equality without raising, in a paragraph or two, the question of the status of other animals. The reason for this, which should be apparent from what I have said already, is that if humans are to be regarded as equal to one another, we need some sense of "equal" that does not require any actual, descriptive equality of capacities, talents or other qualities. If equality is to be related to any actual characteristics of humans, these characteristics must be some lowest common denominator, pitched so low that no human lacks them—but then the philosopher comes up against the catch that any such set of characteristics which covers *all* humans will not be possessed *only by humans.* In other words, it turns out that in the only sense in which we can truly say, as an assertion of fact, that all humans are equal, at least some members of other species are also equal—equal, that is, to each other and to humans. If, on the other hand, we regard the statement "All humans are equal" in some non-factual way, perhaps as a prescription, then, as I have already argued, it is even more difficult to exclude nonhumans from the sphere of equality.

This result is not what the egalitarian philosopher originally intended to assert. Instead of accepting the radical outcome to which their own reasonings naturally point, however, most philosophers try to reconcile their beliefs in human equality and animal inequality by arguments that can only be described as devious.

As a first example, I take William Frankena's well-known article "The Concept of Social Justice." Frankena opposes the idea of basing justice on merit, because he sees that this could lead to highly inegalitarian results. Instead he proposes the principle that

> ...all men are to be treated as equals, not because they are equal, in any respect, but *simply because they are human.* They are human because they have *emotions* and *desires,* and are able to *think,* and hence are capable of enjoying a good life in a sense in which other animals are not.[7]

But what is this capacity to enjoy the good life which all humans have, but no other animals? Other animals have emotions and desires, and appear to be capable of enjoying a good life. We may doubt that they can think—although the behavior of some apes, dolphins and even dogs suggests that some of them can—but what is the relevance of thinking? Frankena goes on to admit that by "the good life" he means "not so much the morally good life as the happy or satisfactory life," so thought would appear to be unnecessary for enjoying the good life; in fact to emphasize the need for thought would make difficulties for the egalitarian since only some people are capable of leading intellectually satisfying lives, or morally good lives. This makes it difficult to see what Frankena's principle of equality has to do with simply being *human.* Surely every sentient being is capable of leading a life that is happier or less miserable than some alternative life, and hence has a claim to be taken into account. In this respect the distinction between humans and non-humans is not a sharp division, but rather a continuum along which we move gradually, and with overlaps between the species, from simple capacities for enjoyment and satisfaction, or pain and suffering, to more complex ones.

Faced with a situation in which they see a need for some basis for the moral gulf that is commonly thought to separate humans and animals, but finding no concrete difference that will do the job without undermining the equality of humans, philosophers tend to waffle. They resort to high-sounding phrases like "the intrinsic dignity of the human individual";[8] they talk of the "intrinsic worth of all men" as if men (humans?) had some worth that other beings did not,[9] or they say that humans, and only humans, are "ends in themselves," while "everything other than a person can only have value for a person."[10]

This idea of a distinctive human dignity and worth has a long history; it can be traced back directly to the Renaissance humanists, for instance to Pico della Mirandola's *Oration on the Dignity of Man.* Pico and other humanists based their estimate of human dignity on the idea that man possessed the central, pivotal position in the "Great Chain of Being" that led from the lowliest forms of matter to God himself; this view of the universe, in turn, goes back to both classical and Judeo-Christian doctrines. Contemporary philosophers have cast off these metaphysical and religious shackles and freely invoke the dignity of mankind without needing to justify the idea at all. Why should we not attribute "intrinsic dignity" or "intrinsic worth" to ourselves? Fellow-humans are unlikely to reject the accolades we so generously bestow on them, and those to whom we deny the honor are unable to object. Indeed, when one thinks only of humans, it can be very liberal, very progressive, to talk of the dignity of all human beings. In so doing, we implicitly condemn slavery, racism, and other violations of human rights. We admit that we ourselves are in some fundamental sense on a par with the poorest, most ignorant members of our own species. It is only when we think of humans as no more than a small subgroup of all the beings that inhabit our planet that we may realize that in elevating our own species we are at the same time lowering the relative status of all other species.

The truth is that the appeal to the intrinsic dignity of human beings appears to solve the egalitarian's problems only as long as it goes unchallenged. Once we ask *why* it should be that all humans—including infants, mental defectives, psychopaths, Hitler, Stalin and the rest—have some kind of dignity or worth that no elephant, pig, or chimpanzee can ever achieve, we see that this question is as difficult to answer as our original request for some relevant fact that justifies the inequality of humans and other animals. In fact, these two questions are really one: talk of intrinsic dignity or moral worth only takes the problem back one step, because any satisfactory defence of the claim that all and only humans have intrinsic dignity would need to refer to some relevant capacities or characteristics that all and only humans possess. Philosophers frequently introduce ideas of dignity, respect and worth at the point at which other reasons appear to be lacking, but this is hardly good enough. Fine phrases are the last resource of those who have run out of arguments.

In case there are those who still think it may be possible to find some relevant characteristic that distinguishes all humans from all members of other species, I shall refer again, before I conclude, to the existence of some humans who quite clearly are below the level of awareness, self-consciousness, intelligence, and sentience, of many nonhumans. I am thinking of humans with severe and irreparable brain damage, and also of infant humans. To avoid the complication of the relevance of a being's potential, however, I shall henceforth concentrate on permanently retarded humans.

Philosophers who set out to find a characteristic that will distinguish humans from other animals rarely take the course of abandoning these groups of humans by lumping them in with the other animals. It is easy to see why they do not. To take this line without re-thinking our attitudes to other animals would entail that we have the right to perform painful experiments on retarded humans for trivial reasons; similarly it would follow that we had the right to rear and kill these humans for food. To most philosophers these consequences are as unacceptable as the view that we should stop treating nonhumans in this way.

Of course, when discussing the problem of equality it is possible to ignore the problem of mental defectives, or brush it aside as if somehow insignificant.[11] This is the easiest way out. What else remains? My final example of speciesism in contemporary philosophy has been selected to show what happens when a writer is prepared to face the question of human equality and animal equality without ignoring the existence of mental defectives, and without resorting to obscurantist mumbo-jumbo. Stanley Benn's clear and honest article "Egalitarianism and Equal Consideration of Interests"[12] fits this description.

Benn, after noting the usual "evident human inequalities" argues, correctly I think, for equality of consideration as the only possible basis for egalitarianism. Yet Benn, like other writers, is thinking only of "equal consideration of human interests." Benn is quite open in his defence of this restriction of equal consideration:

> ...not to possess human shape *is* a disqualifying condition. However faithful or intelligent a dog may be, it would be a monstrous sentimentality to attribute to him interests that could be weighed in an equal balance with those of human beings...if, for instance, one had to decide between feeding a hungry baby or a hungry dog, anyone who chose the dog would generally be reckoned morally defective, unable to recognize a fundamental inequality of claims.
>
> This is what distinguishes our attitude to animals from our attitude to imbeciles. It would be

odd to say that we ought to respect equally the dignity or personality of the imbecile and of the rational man...but there is nothing odd about saying that we should respect their interests equally, that is, that we should give to the interests of each the same serious consideration as claims to considerations necessary for some standard of well-being that we can recognize and endorse.

Benn's statement of the basis of the consideration we should have for imbeciles seems to me correct, but why should there be any fundamental inequality of claims between a dog and a human imbecile? Benn sees that if equal consideration depended on rationality, no reason could be given against using imbeciles for research purposes, as we now use dogs and guinea pigs. This will not do: "But of course we do distinguish imbeciles from animals in this regard," he says. That the common distinction is justifiable is something Benn does not question; his problem is how it is to be justified. The answer he gives is this:

> ...we respect the interests of men and give them priority over dogs not *insofar* as they are rational, but because rationality is the human norm. We say it is *unfair* to exploit the deficiencies of the imbecile who falls short of the norm, just as it would be unfair, and not just ordinarily dishonest, to steal from a blind man. If we do not think in this way about dogs, it is because we do not see the irrationality of the dog as a deficiency or a handicap, but as normal for the species. The characteristics, therefore, that distinguish the normal man from the normal dog make it intelligible for us to talk of other men having interests and capacities, and therefore claims, of precisely the same kind as we make on our own behalf. But although these characteristics may provide the point of the distinction between men and other species, they are *not* in fact the qualifying conditions for membership, or the distinguishing criteria of the class of morally considerable persons; *and this is precisely because a man does not become a member of a different species, with its own standards of normality, by reason of not possessing these characteristics.*

The final sentence of this passage gives the argument away. An imbecile, Benn concedes, may have no characteristics superior to those of a dog; nevertheless this does not make the imbecile a member of "a different species" as the dog is.

Therefore it would be "unfair" to use the imbecile for medical research as we use the dog. But why? That the imbecile is not rational is just the way things have worked out, and the same is true of the dog—neither is any more responsible for their mental level. If it is unfair to take advantage of an isolated defect, why is it fair to take advantage of a more general limitation? I find it hard to see anything in this argument except a defence of preferring the interests of members of our own species because they are members of our own species. To those who think there might be more to it, I suggest the following mental exercise. Assume that it has been proven that there is a difference in the average, or normal, intelligence quotient for two different races, say whites and blacks. Then substitute the term "white" for every occurrence of "men" and "black" for every occurrence of "dog" in the passage quoted; and substitute "high I.Q." for "rationality" and when Benn talks of "imbeciles" replace this term by "dumb whites"—that is, whites who fall well below the normal white I.Q. score. Finally, change "species" to "race." Now re-read the passage. It has become a defence of a rigid, no-exceptions division between whites and blacks, based on I.Q. scores, *not withstanding an admitted overlap* between whites and blacks in this respect. The revised passage is, of course, outrageous, and this is not only because we have made fictitious assumptions in our substitutions. The point is that in the original passage Benn was defending a rigid division in the amount of consideration due to members of different species, despite admitted cases of overlap. If the original did not, at first reading strike us as being as outrageous as the revised version does, this is largely because although we are not racists ourselves, most of us are speciesists. Like the other articles, Benn's stands as a warning of the ease with which the best minds can fall victim to a prevailing ideology.

NOTES

1. *The Methods of Ethics* (7th Ed.), p. 382.
2. For example, R. M. Hare, *Freedom and Reason* (Oxford, 1963) and J. Rawls, *A Theory of Justice* (Harvard, 1972). For a brief account of the essential agreement on this issue between these and other positions, see R. M. Hare, "Rules of War

and Moral Reasoning," *Philosophy and Public Affairs,* vol. 1, no. 2 (1972).

3. *Introduction to the Principles of Morals and Legislation,* ch. XVII.

4. I owe the term "speciesism" to Richard Ryder.

5. In order to produce 1 lb. of protein in the form of beef or veal, we must feed 21 lbs. of protein to the animal. Other forms of livestock are slightly less inefficient, but the average ratio in the U.S. is still 1:8. It has been estimated that the amount of protein lost to humans in this way is equivalent to 90% of the annual world protein deficit. For a brief account, see Frances Moore Lappé, *Diet for a Small Planet* (Friends of The Earth/Ballantine-New York, 1971), pp. 4–11.

6. Ruth Harrison, *Animal Machines* (Stuart, London, 1964). For an account of farming conditions, see

my *Animal Liberation* (New York Review Company, 1975).

7. R. Brandt (ed.), *Social Justice* (Prentice-Hall, Englewood Cliffs, 1962), p. 19.

8. Frankena, *Op. cit.,* p. 23.

9. H. A. Bedau, "Egalitarianism and the Idea of Equality" in *Nomos IX: Equality,* ed. J. R. Pennock and J. W. Chapman, New York, 1967.

10. G. Vlastos, "Justice and Equality" in Brandt, *Social Justice,* p. 48.

11. For example, Bernard Williams, "The Idea of Equality," in *Philosophy, Politics and Society* (second series), ed. P. Laslett and W. Runciman (Blackwell, Oxford, 1962), p. 118; J. Rawls, *A Theory of Justice,* pp. 509–10.

12. *Nomos IX: Equality;* the passages quoted are on p. 62ff.

✎ STUDY QUESTIONS

1. According to Singer, what is the relationship between civil rights movements and the animal rights movement?

2. What is s*peciesism*? Why is it bad, according to Singer? Do you agree?

3. Are all humans equal, according to Singer? In what way are all sentient beings equal?

4. How does Singer apply the notion of equal consideration of interests?

10 The Radical Egalitarian Case for Animal Rights

TOM REGAN

Professor of philosophy at North Carolina State University and a leading animal rights advocate in the United States, Tom Regan is the author of several articles and books on moral philosophy, including *The Case for Animal Rights* (1983).

Regan disagrees with Singer's utilitarian program for animal liberation, for he rejects utilitarianism as lacking a notion of intrinsic worth. Regan's position is that animals and humans all have equal intrinsic value on which their right to life and concern are based. Regan is revolutionary. He calls for not reform but the total abolition of the use of animals in science, the total dissolution of the commercial animal agriculture system, and the total elimination of commercial and sport hunting and trapping. "The fundamental wrong is the system that allows us to view animals as our resources. . . . Lab animals are not our tasters; we are not their kings."

From *In Defense of Animals,* ed. Peter Singer (Oxford: Basil Blackwell, 1985). Reprinted by permission of Blackwell Publishers.

I regard myself as an advocate of animal rights—as a part of the animal rights movement. That movement, as I conceive it, is committed to a number of goals, including:

1. the total abolition of the use of animals in science
2. the total dissolution of commercial animal agriculture
3. and the total elimination of commercial and sport hunting and trapping.

There are, I know, people who profess to believe in animal rights who do not avow these goals. Factory farming they say, is wrong—violates animals' rights—but traditional animal agriculture is all right. Toxicity tests of cosmetics on animals violate their rights; but not important medical research—cancer research, for example. The clubbing of baby seals is abhorrent; but not the harvesting of adult seals. I used to think I understood this reasoning. Not any more. You don't change unjust institutions by tidying them up.

What's wrong—what's fundamentally wrong—with the way animals are treated isn't the details that vary from case to case. It's the whole system. The forlornness of the veal calf is pathetic—heart wrenching; the pulsing pain of the chimp with electrodes planted deep in her brain is repulsive; the slow, torturous death of the raccoon caught in the leg hold trap, agonizing. But what is fundamentally wrong isn't the pain, isn't the suffering, isn't the deprivation. These compound what's wrong. Sometimes—often—they make it much worse. But they are not the fundamental wrong.

The fundamental wrong is the system that allows us to view animals as our resources, here for us—to be eaten, or surgically manipulated, or put in our cross hairs for sport or money. Once we accept this view of animals—as our resources—the rest is as predictable as it is regrettable. Why worry about their loneliness, their pain, their death? Since animals exist for us, here to benefit us in one way or another, what harms them really doesn't matter—or matters only if it starts to bother us, makes us feel a trifle uneasy when we eat our veal scampi, for example. So, yes, let us get veal calves out of solitary confinement, give them more space, a little straw, a few companions. But let us keep our veal scampi.

But a little straw, more space, and a few companions don't eliminate—don't even touch—the fundamental wrong, the wrong that attaches to our viewing and treating these animals as our resources. A veal calf killed to be eaten after living in close confinement is viewed and treated in this way: but so, too, is another who is raised (as they say) "more humanely." To right the fundamental wrong of our treatment of farm animals requires more than making rearing methods "more human"—requires something quite different—requires the *total dissolution of commercial animal agriculture.*

How we do this—whether we do this, or as in the case of animals in science, whether and how we abolish their use—these are to a large extent political questions. People must change their beliefs before they change their habits. Enough people, especially those elected to public office, must believe in change—must want it—before we will have laws that protect the rights of animals. This process of change is very complicated, very demanding, very exhausting, calling for the efforts of many hands—in education, publicity, political organization and activity, down to the licking of envelopes and stamps. As a trained and practicing philosopher the sort of contribution I can make is limited, but I like to think, important. The currency of philosophy is ideas—their meaning and rational foundation—not the nuts and bolts of the legislative process say, or the mechanics of community organization. That's what I have been exploring over the past ten years or so in my essays and talks and, more recently, in my book, *The Case for Animal Rights.*[1] I believe the major conclusions I reach in that book are true because they are supported by the weight of the *best arguments.* I believe the idea of animal rights has reason, not just emotion, on its side.

In the space I have at my disposal here I can only sketch, in the barest outlines, some of the main features of the book. Its main themes—and we should not be surprised by this—involve asking and answering deep foundational moral questions, questions about what morality is, how it should be understood, what is the best moral theory all considered. I hope I can convey something of the shape I think this theory is. The attempt to do this will be—to use a word a friendly critic once used to describe my work—cerebral. In fact I was told by this person that my work is "too cerebral." But this is misleading. My feelings about how animals sometimes are treated are just as deep and just as strong as those of my more volatile compatriots. Philosophers do—to use the jargon of the day—have a right side to their brains. If it's the left side we contribute or mainly should—that's because what talents we have reside there.

How to proceed? We begin by asking how the moral status of animals has been understood by thinkers who deny that animals have rights. Then we test the mettle of their ideas by seeing how well they stand up under the heat of fair criticism. If we start our thinking in this way we soon find that some people believe that we have no duties directly to animals—that we owe nothing *to them*—that we can do nothing that *wrongs them*. Rather, we can do wrong acts that involve animals, and so we have duties regarding them, though none to them. Such views may be called indirect duty views. By way of illustration:

Suppose your neighbor kicks your dog. Then your neighbor has done something wrong. But not to your dog. The wrong that has been done is a wrong to you. After all, it is wrong to upset people, and your neighbor's kicking your dog upsets you. So you are the one who is wronged, not your dog. Or again: by kicking your dog your neighbor damages your property. And since it is wrong to damage another person's property, your neighbor has done something wrong—to you, of course, not to your dog. Your neighbor no more wrongs your dog than your car would be wronged if the windshield were smashed. Your neighbor's duties involving your dog are indirect duties to you. More generally, all of our duties regarding animals are indirect duties to one another—to humanity.

How could someone try to justify such a view? One could say that your dog doesn't feel anything and so isn't hurt by your neighbor's kick, doesn't care about the pain since none is felt, is as unaware of anything as your windshield.

Someone could say this but no rational person will since, among other considerations, such a view will commit one who holds it to the position that no human being feels pain either—that human beings also don't care about what happens to them. A second possibility is that though both humans and your dog are hurt when kicked, it is only human pain that matters. But, again, no rational person can believe this. Pain is pain wheresoever it occurs. If your neighbor's causing you pain is wrong because of the pain that is caused, we cannot rationally ignore or dismiss the moral relevance of the pain your dog feels.

Philosophers who hold indirect duty views—and many still do—have come to understand that they must avoid the two defects just noted—avoid, that is, both the view that animals don't feel anything as well as the idea that only human pain can be morally relevant. Among such thinkers the sort of view now favored is one or another form of what is called *contractarianism*.

Here, very crudely, is the root idea: morality consists of a set of rules that individuals voluntarily agree to abide by—as we do when we sign a contract (hence the name: contractarianism). Those who understand and accept the terms of the contract are covered directly—have rights created by, and recognized and protected in, the contract. And these contractors can also have protection spelled out for others who, though they lack the ability to understand morality and so cannot sign the contract themselves, are loved or cherished by those who can. Thus young children, for example, are unable to sign and lack rights. But they are protected by the contract nonetheless because of the sentimental interests of others, most notably their parents. So we have, then, duties involving these children, duties regarding them, but no duties to them. Our duties in their case are indirect duties to other human beings, usually their parents.

As for animals, since they cannot understand the contract, they obviously cannot sign; and since they cannot sign; they have no rights. Like children, however, some animals are the objects of the sentimental interest of others. You, for example, love your dog...or cat. So these animals—those enough people care about: companion animals, whales, baby seals, the American bald eagle—these animals, though they lack rights themselves, will be protected because of the sentimental interests of people. I have, then, according to contractarianism, no duty directly to your dog or any other animal, not even the duty not to cause them pain or suffering; my duty not to hurt them is a duty I have to those people who care about what happens to them. As for other animals, where no or little sentimental interest is present—farm animals, for example, or laboratory rats—what duties we have grow weaker and weaker, perhaps to the vanishing point. The pain and death they endure, though real, are not wrong if no one cares about them.

Contractarianism could be a hard view to refute when it comes to the moral status of animals if it was an adequate theoretical approach to the moral status of human beings. It is not adequate in this latter respect, however, which makes the question of its adequacy in the former—regarding animals—utterly moot. For consider: morality, according to the (crude) contractarian position before us, consists of rules people agree to abide by. What people? Well, enough to make a difference—enough, that is, so that collectively they have the power to enforce the rules that are drawn up in the contract. That is very well and good for the signatories—but not so good for anyone who is not asked to sign. And there is nothing in contractarianism of the sort we are discussing that guarantees or requires that everyone will have a chance to participate equitably in framing the rules of morality. The result is that this approach to ethics could sanction the most blatant forms of social, economic, moral, and political injustice, ranging from a repressive caste system to systematic racial or sexual discrimination. Might, on this theory, does make right. Let those who are the victims of injustice suffer as they will. It matters not so long as no one else—no contractor, or too few of them—cares about it. Such a theory takes one's moral breath away...as if, for example, there is nothing wrong with apartheid in South Africa if too few white South Africans are upset by it. A theory with so little to recommend it at the level of the ethics of our treatment of our fellow humans cannot have anything more to recommend it when it

comes to the ethics of how we treat our fellow animals.

The version of contractarianism just examined is, as I have noted, a crude variety, and in fairness to those of a contractarian persuasion it must be noted that much more refined, subtle, and ingenious varieties are possible. For example, John Rawls, in his *A Theory of Justice*, sets forth a version of contractarianism that forces the contractors to ignore the accidental features of being a human being—for example, whether one is white or black, male or female, a genius or of modest intellect. Only by ignoring such features, Rawls believes, can we insure that the principles of justice contractors would agree upon are not based on bias or prejudice. Despite the improvement a view such as Rawls's shows over the cruder forms of contractarianism, it remains deficient: it systematically denies that we have direct duties to those human beings who do not have a sense of justice—young children, for instance, and many mentally retarded humans. And yet it seems reasonably certain that, were we to torture a young child or a retarded elder, we would be doing something that wrongs them, not something that is wrong if (and only if) other humans with a sense of justice are upset. And since this is true in the case of these humans, we cannot rationally deny the same in the case of animals.

Indirect duty views, then, including the best among them, fail to command our rational assent. Whatever ethical theory we rationally should accept, therefore, it must at least recognize that we have some duties directly to animals, just as we have some duties directly to each other. The next two theories I'll sketch attempt to meet this requirement.

The first I call the *cruelty-kindness* view. Simply stated, this view says that we have a direct duty to be kind to animals and a direct duty not to be cruel to them. Despite the familiar, reassuring ring of these ideas, I do not believe this view offers an adequate theory. To make this clearer, consider kindness. A kind person acts from a certain kind of motive—compassion or concern, for example. And that is a virtue. But there is no guarantee that a kind act is a right act. If I am a generous racist, for example, I will be inclined to act kindly toward members of my own own race, favoring their interests above others. My kindness would be real and, so far as it goes, good. But I trust it is too obvious to require comment that my kind acts may not be above moral reproach—may, in fact, be positively wrong because rooted in injustice. So kindness, not withstanding its status as a virtue to be encouraged, simply will not cancel the weight of a theory of right action.

Cruelty fares no better. People or their acts are cruel if they display either a lack of sympathy for or, worse, the presence of enjoyment in, seeing another suffer. Cruelty in all its guises *is* a bad thing—*is* a tragic human failing. But just as a person's being motivated by kindness does not guarantee that they do what is right, so the absence of cruelty does not assure that they avoid doing what is wrong. Many people who perform abortions, for example, are not cruel, sadistic people. But that fact about their character and motivation does not settle the terribly difficult question about the morality of abortion. The case is no different when we examine the ethics of our treatment of animals. So, yes, let us be for kindness and against cruelty. But let us not suppose that being for the one and against the other answers questions about moral right and wrong.

Some people think the theory we are looking for is *utilitarianism.* A utilitarian accepts two moral principles. The first is a principle of *equality: everyone's interests count, and similar interests must be counted as having similar weight or importance.* White or black, male or female, American or Iranian, human or animal: everyone's pain or frustration matter and matter equally with the like pain or frustration of anyone else. The second principle a utilitarian accepts is the principle of *utility: do that act that will bring about the best balance of satisfaction over frustration for everyone affected by the outcome.*

As a utilitarian, then, here is how I am to approach the task of deciding what I morally ought to do: I must ask who will be affected if I choose to do one thing rather than another, how much each individual will be affected, and where the best results are most likely to lie—which option, in other words, is most likely to bring about the best results, the best balance of satisfaction over frustration. That option, whatever it may

be, is the one I ought to choose. That is where my moral duty lies.

The great appeal of utilitarianism rests with its uncompromising *egalitarianism:* everyone's interests count and count equally with the like interests of everyone else. The kind of odious discrimination some forms of contractarianism can justify—discrimination based on race or sex, for example—seems disallowed in principle by utilitarianism, as is speciesism—systematic discrimination based on species membership.

The sort of equality we find in utilitarianism, however, is not the sort an advocate of animal or human rights should have in mind. Utilitarianism has no room for the *equal moral rights of different individuals because it has no room for their equal inherent value or worth.* What has value for the utilitarian is the satisfaction of an individual's interests, not the individual whose interests they are. A universe in which you satisfy your desire for water, food, and warmth, is, other things being equal, better than a universe in which these desires are frustrated. And the same is true in the case of an animal with similar desires. But neither you nor the animal have any value in your own right. *Only your feelings do.*

Here is an analogy to help make the philosophical point clearer: a cup contains different liquids—sometimes sweet, sometimes bitter, sometimes a mix of the two. What has value are the liquids: the sweeter the better, the bitter the worse. The cup—the container—has no value. It's what goes into it, not what they go into, that has value. For the utilitarian, you and I are like the cup; we have no value as individuals and thus no equal value. What has value is what goes into us, what we serve as receptacles for; our feelings of satisfaction have positive value, our feelings of frustration have negative value.

Serious problems arise for utilitarianism when we remind ourselves that it enjoins us to bring about the best consequences. What does this mean? It doesn't mean the best consequences for me alone, or for my family or friends, or any other person taken individually. No, what we must do is, roughly, as follows: we must add up—somehow!—the separate satisfactions and frustrations of everyone likely to be affected by our choice, the satisfactions in one column, the frustrations in the other. We must total each column for each of the opinions before us. That is what it means to say the theory is aggregative. And then we must choose that option which is most likely to bring about the best balance of totaled satisfactions over totaled frustrations. Whatever act would lead to this outcome is the one we morally ought to perform—is where our moral duty lies. And that act quite clearly might not be the same one that would bring about the best results for me personally, or my family or friends, or a lab animal. The best aggregated consequences for everyone concerned are not necessarily the best for each individual.

That utilitarianism is an aggregative theory—that different individuals' satisfactions or frustrations are added, or summed, or totaled—is the key objection to this theory. My Aunt Bea is old, inactive, a cranky, sour person, though not physically ill. She prefers to go on living. She is also rather rich. I could make a fortune if I could get my hands on her money, money she intends to give me in any event, after she dies, but which she refuses to give me now. In order to avoid a huge tax bite, I plan to donate a handsome sum of my profits to a local children's hospital. Many, many children will benefit from my generosity, and much joy will be brought to their parents, relatives, and friends. If I don't get the money rather soon, all these ambitions will come to naught. The once-in-a-lifetime-opportunity to make a real killing will be gone. Why, then, not really kill my Aunt Bea? Oh, of course I *might* get caught. But I'm no fool and, besides, her doctor can be counted on to cooperate (he has an eye for the same investment and I happen to know a good deal about his shady past). The deed can be done . . . professionally, shall we say. There is *very* little chance of getting caught. And as for my conscience being guilt ridden, I am a resourceful sort of fellow and will take more than sufficient comfort—as I lie on the beach at Acapulco—in contemplating the joy and health I have brought to so many others.

Suppose Aunt Bea is killed and the rest of the story comes out as told. Would I have done anything wrong? Anything immoral? One would have thought that I had. But not according to utilitarianism. Since what I did brought about the best balance of totaled satisfaction over frustration for all those affected by the outcome, what I did was not wrong. Indeed, in killing Aunt Bea the physician and I did what duty required.

This same kind of argument can be repeated in all sorts of cases, illustrating time after time, how the utilitarian's position leads to results that impartial people find morally callous. It is wrong to kill my Aunt Bea in the name of bringing about the best results for others. A good end does not justify an evil means. Any adequate moral theory will have to explain why this is so. Utilitarianism fails in this respect and so cannot be the theory we seek.

What to do? Where to begin anew? The place to begin, I think, is with the utilitarian's view of the value of the individual—or, rather, lack of value. In its place suppose we consider that you and I, for example, do have value as individuals—what we'll call *inherent value.* To say we have such value is to say that we are something more than, something different from, mere receptacles. Moreover, to insure that we do not pave the way for such injustices as slavery or sexual discrimination, we must believe that all who have inherent value have it equally, regardless of their sex, race, religion, birthplace, and so on. Similarly to be discarded as irrelevant are one's talents or skills, intelligence and wealth, personality or pathology, whether one is loved and admired—or despised and loathed. The genius and the retarded child, the prince and the pauper, the brain surgeon and the fruit vendor, Mother Theresa and the most unscrupulous used car salesman—all have inherent value, all possess it *equally,* and *all have an equal right to be treated with respect,* to be treated in ways that do not reduce them to the status of things, as if they exist as resources for others. My value as an individual is independent of my usefulness to you. Yours is not dependent on your usefulness to me. For either of us to treat the other in ways that fail to show respect for the other's independent value is to act immorally—is to violate the individual's rights.

Some of the rational virtues of this view— what I call the rights view—should be evident.

Unlike (crude) contractarianism, for example, the rights view *in principle* denies the moral tolerability of any and all forms of racial, sexual, or social discrimination; and unlike utilitarianism, this view *in principle* denies that we can justify good results by using evil means that violate an individual's rights—denies, for example, that it could be moral to kill my Aunt Bea to harvest beneficial consequences for others. That would be to sanction the disrespectful treatment of the individual in the name of the social good, something the rights view will not—categorically will not—ever allow.

The rights view—or so I believe—is rationally the most satisfactory moral theory. It surpasses all other theories in the degree to which it illuminates and explains the foundation of our duties to one another—the domain of human morality. On this score, it has the best reasons, the best arguments, on its side. Of course, if it were possible to show that only human beings are included within its scope, then a person like myself, who believes in animal rights, would be obliged to look elsewhere than to the rights view.

But attempts to limit its scope to humans only can be shown to be rationally defective. Animals, it is true, lack many of the abilities humans possess. They can't read, do higher mathematics, build a bookcase, or make *baba ghanoush*. Neither can many human beings, however, and yet we don't say—and shouldn't say—that they (these humans) therefore have less inherent value, less of a right to be treated with respect, than do others. It is the similarities between those human beings who most clearly, most noncontroversially have such value—the people reading this, for example—it is our similarities, not our differences, that matter most. And the really crucial, the basic similarity is simply this; *we are each of us the experiencing subject of a life, each of us a conscious creature having an individual welfare that has importance to us whatever our usefulness to others*. We want and prefer things; believe and feel things; recall and expect things. And all these dimensions of our life, including our pleasure and pain, our enjoyment and suffering, our satisfaction and frustration, our continued existence or our untimely death—all make a difference to the quality of our life as lived, as experienced by us as individuals. As the same is true of those animals who concern us (those who are eaten and trapped, for example), they, too, must be viewed as the experiencing subjects of a life with inherent value of their own.

There are some who resist the idea that animals have inherent value. "Only humans have such value," they profess. How might this narrow view be defended? Shall we say that only humans have the requisite intelligence, or autonomy, or reason? But there are many, many humans who will fail to meet these standards and yet who are reasonably viewed as having value above and beyond their usefulness to others. Shall we claim that only humans belong to the right species—the species *Homo sapiens*? But this is blatant speciesism. Will it be said, then, that all—and only—humans have immortal souls? Then our opponents more than have their work cut out for them. I am myself not ill-disposed to there being immortal souls. Personally, I profoundly hope I have one. But I would not want to rest my position on a controversial, ethical issue on the even more controversial question about who or what has an immortal soul. That is to dig one's hole deeper, not climb out. Rationally, it is better to resolve moral issues without making more controversial assumptions than are needed. The question of who has inherent value is such a question, one that is more rationally resolved without the introduction of the idea of immortal souls than by its use.

Well, perhaps some will say that animals have some inherent value, only *less* than we do. Once again, however, attempts to defend this view can be shown to lack rational justification. What could be the basis of our having more inherent value than animals? Will it be their lack of reason, or autonomy, or intellect? Only if we are willing to make the same judgment in the case of humans who are similarly deficient. But it is not true that such humans—the retarded child, for example, or the mentally deranged—have less inherent value than you or I. Neither, then, can we rationally sustain the view that animals like them in being the experiencing subjects of a life have less inherent value. *All who have inherent value have it equally, whether they be human animals or not.*

Inherent value, then, belongs equally to those who are the experiencing subjects of a life. Whether it belongs to others—to rocks and rivers, trees and glaciers, for example—we do not know. And may never know. But neither do we need to know, if we are to make the case for animal rights. We do not need to know how many people, for example, are eligible to vote in the next presidential election before we can know whether I am. Similarly, we do not need to know *how many* individuals have inherent value before we can know that some do. When it comes to the case for animal rights, then what we need to know is whether the animals who, in our culture are routinely eaten, hunted, and used in our laboratories, for example, are like us in being subjects of a life. And we *do* know this. We do *know* that many—literally, billions and billions—of these animals are subjects of a life in the sense explained and so have inherent value if we do. And since, in order to have the best theory of our duties to one another, we must recognize our equal inherent value, as individuals, *reason*—not sentiment, not emotion—*reason compels us to recognize the equal inherent value of these animals.* And, with this, their equal right to be treated with respect.

That, *very* roughly, is the shape and feel of the case for animal rights. Most of the details of the supporting argument are missing. They are to be found in the book I alluded to earlier. Here, the details go begging and I must in closing, limit myself to four final points.

The first is how the theory that underlies the case for animal rights shows that the animal rights movement is a part of, not antagonistic to, the human rights movement. The theory that rationally grounds the rights of animals also grounds the rights of humans. Thus are those involved in the animal rights movement partners in the struggle to secure respect for human rights—the rights of women, for example, or minorities and workers. The animal rights movement is cut from the same moral cloth as these.

Second, having set out the broad outlines of the rights view, I can now say why its *implications for farming and science,* for example, are both clear and uncompromising. In the case of using animals in science, the rights view is categorically abolitionist. *Lab animals are not our tasters; we are not their kings.* Because these animals are treated—routinely, systematically—as if their value is reducible to their usefulness to others, they are routinely systematically treated with a lack of respect, and thus their rights routinely, systematically violated. This is just as true when they are used in trivial, duplicative, unnecessary or unwise research as it is when they are used in studies that hold out real promise of human benefits. We can't justify harming or killing a human being (my Aunt Bea, for example) just for these sorts of reasons. Neither can we do so even in the case of so lowly a creature as a laboratory rat. It is not just refinement or reduction that are called for, not just larger, cleaner cages, not just more generous use of anesthetic or the elimination of multiple surgery, not just tidying up the system. It is replacement—completely. The best we can do when it comes to using animals in science is—not to use them. That is where our duty lies, according to the rights view.

As for commercial animal agriculture, the rights view takes a similar abolitionist position. The fundamental moral wrong here is not that animals are kept in stressful close confinement, or in isolation, or that they have their pain and suffering, their needs and preferences ignored or discounted. *All* these *are* wrong, of course, but they are not the fundamental wrong. They are symptoms and effects of the deeper, systematic wrong that allows these animals to be viewed and treated as lacking independent value, as resources for us—as, indeed, a renewable resource. Giving farm animals more space, more natural environments, more companions does not right the fundamental wrong, any more than giving lab animals more anesthesia or bigger, cleaner cages would right the fundamental wrong in their case. Nothing less than the total dissolution of commercial animal agriculture will do this, just as, for similar reasons I won't develop at length here, morality requires nothing less than the total elimination of commercial and sport hunting and trapping. The rights view's implications, then, as I have said, are clear—and are uncompromising.

My last two points are about philosophy—my profession. It is most obviously, no substitute for political action. The words I have written here and in other places by themselves don't change a thing. It is what we do with the thoughts the words express—our acts, our deeds—that change things. All that philosophy can do, and all I have attempted, is to offer a vision of what our deeds could aim at. And the why. But not the how.

Finally, I am reminded of my thoughtful critic, the one I mentioned earlier, who chastised me for being "too cerebral." Well, cerebral I have been: indirect duty views, utilitarianism, contractarianism—hardly the stuff deep passions are made of. I am also reminded, however, of the image another friend once set before me—the image of the ballerina as expressive of disciplined passion. Long hours of sweat and toil, of loneliness and practice, of doubt and fatigue; that is the discipline of her craft. But the passion is there, too: the fierce drive to excel, to speak through her body, to do it right, to pierce our minds. That is the image of philosophy I would leave with you; not "too cerebral," but *disciplined passion.* Of the discipline, enough has been seen. As for the passion:

There are times, and these are not infrequent, when tears come to my eyes when I see, or read, or hear of the wretched plight of animals in the hands of humans. Their pain, their suffering, their loneliness, their innocence, their death. Anger. Rage. Pity. Sorrow. Disgust. The whole creation groans under the weight of the evil we humans visit upon these mute, powerless creatures. It *is* our heart, not just our head, that calls for an end, that demands of us that we overcome, for them, the habits and forces behind their systematic oppression. All great movements, it is written, go through three stages: ridicule, discussion, adoption. It is the realization of this third stage—adoption—that demands both our passion and our discipline, our heart and our head. *The fate of animals is in our hands. God grant we are equal to the task.*

NOTE

1. Tom Regan, *The Case for Animal Rights* (Berkeley: University of California Press, 1983).

✤ STUDY QUESTIONS

1. How is Regan's position on animal rights different from Singer's? Explain.
2. What are Regan's reasons for granting animals equal moral rights?
3. Does Regan allow for experimentation on animals? If we have to test a dangerous AIDS vaccine, on whom should we test it?

11   A Critique of Regan's Animal Rights Theory

MARY ANNE WARREN

The author of several articles in moral philosophy, Mary Anne Warren teaches philosophy at San Francisco State University.

Warren reconstructs Regan's argument for animal rights and criticizes it for depending on the obscure notion of inherent value. She then argues that all rational human beings are equally part of the moral community since we can reason with each other about our behavior, whereas we cannot so reason with an animal. She puts forth a "weak animal rights theory," which asserts that we ought not to be cruel to animals or kill them without good reason.

Reprinted from *Between the Species*, Vol. 2, no. 4 (Fall 1987) by permission.

Tom Regan has produced what is perhaps the definitive defense of the view that the basic moral rights of at least some non-human animals are in no way inferior to our own. In *The Case for Animal Rights,* he argues that all normal mammals over a year of age have the same basic moral rights.[1] Non-human mammals have essentially the same right not to be harmed or killed as we do. I shall call this "the strong animal rights position," although it is weaker than the claims made by some animal liberationists in that it ascribes rights to only some sentient animals.[2]

I will argue that Regan's case for the strong animal rights position is unpersuasive and that this position entails consequences which a reasonable person cannot accept. I do not deny that some non-human animals have moral rights; indeed, I would extend the scope of the rights claim to include all sentient animals, that is, all those capable of having experiences, including experiences of pleasure or satisfaction and pain, suffering, or frustration.[3] However, I do not think that the moral rights of most non-human animals are identical in strength to those of persons.[4] The rights of most non-human animals may be overridden in circumstances which would not justify overriding the rights of persons. There are, for instance, compelling realities which sometimes require that we kill animals for reasons which could not justify the killing of persons. I will call this view "the weak animal rights" position, even though it ascribes rights to a wider range of animals than does the strong animal rights position.

I will begin by summarizing Regan's case for the strong animal rights position and noting two problems with it. Next, I will explore some consequences of the strong animal rights position which I think are unacceptable. Finally, I will outline the case for the weak animal rights position.

REGAN'S CASE

Regan's argument moves through three stages. First, he argues that normal, mature mammals are not only sentient but have other mental capacities as well. These include the capacities for emotion, memory, belief, desire, the use of general concepts, intentional action, a sense of the future, and some degree of self-awareness. Creatures with such capacities are said to be subjects-of-a-life. They are not only alive in the biological sense but have a psychological identity over time and an existence which can go better or worse for them. Thus, they can be harmed or benefited. These are plausible claims, and well defended. One of the strongest parts of the book is the rebuttal of philosophers, such as R. G. Frey, who object to the application of such mentalistic terms to creatures that do not use a human-style language.[5] The second and third stages of the argument are more problematic.

In the second stage, Regan argues that subjects-of-a-life have inherent value. His concept of inherent value grows out of his opposition to utilitarianism. Utilitarian moral theory, he says, treats individuals as "mere receptacles" for morally significant value, in that harm to one individual may be justified by the production of a greater net benefit to other individuals. In opposition to this, he holds that subjects-of-a-life have a value independent of both the value they may place upon their lives or experiences and the value others may place upon them.

Inherent value, Regan argues, does not come in degrees. To hold that some individuals have more inherent value than others is to adopt a "perfectionist" theory, i.e., one which assigns different moral worth to individuals according to how well they are thought to exemplify some virtue(s), such as intelligence or moral autonomy. Perfectionist theories have been used, at least since the time of Aristotle, to rationalize such injustices as slavery and male domination, as well as the unrestrained exploitation of animals. Regan argues that if we reject these injustices, then we must also reject perfectionism and conclude that all subjects-of-a-life have equal inherent value. Moral agents have no more inherent value than moral patients, i.e., subjects-of-a-life who are not morally responsible for their actions.

In the third phase of the argument, Regan uses the thesis of equal inherent value to derive strong moral rights for all subjects-of-a-life. This thesis underlies the Respect Principle, which forbids us to treat beings who have inherent value as mere receptacles, i.e., mere means to the production of the greatest overall good. This principle, in turn, underlies the Harm Principle, which says that we have a direct *prima facie* duty not to harm beings who have inherent value. Together, these principles give rise to moral rights. Rights are defined as valid claims, claims to certain goods and against certain beings, i.e., moral agents. Moral rights generate duties not only to refrain from inflicting harm upon beings with inherent value but also to come to their aid when they are threatened by other moral agents. Rights are not absolute but may be overridden in certain circumstances. Just what these circumstances are we will consider later. But first, let's look at some difficulties in the theory as thus far presented.

THE MYSTERY OF INHERENT VALUE

Inherent value is a key concept in Regan's theory. It is the bridge between the plausible claim that all normal, mature mammals—human or otherwise—are subjects-of-a-life and the more debatable claim that they all have basic moral rights of the same strength. But it is a highly obscure concept, and its obscurity makes it ill-suited to play this crucial role.

Inherent value is defined almost entirely in negative terms. It is not dependent upon the value which either the inherently valuable individual or anyone else may place upon that individual's life or experiences. It is not (necessarily) a function of sentience or any other mental capacity, because, Regan says, some entities which are not sentient (e.g., trees, rivers, or rocks) may, nevertheless, have inherent value (p. 246). It cannot attach to anything other than an individual; species, ecosystems, and the like cannot have inherent value.

These are some of the things which inherent value is not. But what is it? Unfortunately, we are not told. Inherent value appears as a mysterious non-natural property which we must take on faith. Regan says that it is a *postulate* that subjects-of-a-life have inherent value, a postulate justified by the fact that it avoids certain absurdities which he thinks follow from a purely utilitarian theory (p. 247). But why is it a postulate that *subjects-of-a-life* have inherent value? If the inherent value of a being is completely independent of

the value that it or anyone else places upon its experiences, then why does the fact that it has certain sorts of experiences constitute evidence that it has inherent value? If the reason is that subjects-of-a-life have an existence which can go better or worse for them, then why isn't the appropriate conclusion that all sentient beings have inherent value, since they would all seem to meet that condition? Sentient but mentally unsophisticated beings may have a less extensive range of possible satisfactions and frustrations, but why should it follow that they have—or may have—no inherent value at all?

In the absence of a positive account of inherent value, it is also difficult to grasp the connection between being inherently valuable and having moral rights. Intuitively, it seems that value is one thing, and rights are another. It does not seem incoherent to say that some things (e.g., mountains, rivers, redwood trees) are inherently valuable and yet are not the sorts of things which can have moral rights. Nor does it seem incoherent to ascribe inherent value to some things which are not individuals, e.g., plant or animal species, though it may well be incoherent to ascribe moral rights to such things.

In short, the concept of inherent value seems to create at least as many problems as it solves. If inherent value is based on some natural property, then why not try to identify that property and explain its moral significance, without appealing to inherent value? And if it is not based on any natural property, then why should we believe in it? That it may enable us to avoid some of the problems faced by the utilitarian is not a sufficient reason, if it creates other problems which are just as serious.

IS THERE A SHARP LINE?

Perhaps the most serious problems are those that arise when we try to apply the strong animal rights position to animals other than normal, mature mammals. Regan's theory requires us to divide all living things into two categories: those which have the same inherent value and the same basic moral rights that we do, and those which have no inherent value and presumably no moral rights.

But wherever we try to draw the line, such a sharp division is implausible.

It would surely be arbitrary to draw such a sharp line between normal, mature mammals and all other living things. Some birds (e.g., crows, magpies, parrots, mynahs) appear to be just as mentally sophisticated as most mammals and thus are equally strong candidates for inclusion under the subject-of-a-life criterion. Regan is not in fact advocating that we draw the line here. His claim is only that normal mature mammals are clear cases, while other cases are less clear. Yet, on his theory, there must be such a sharp line *somewhere,* since there are no degrees of inherent value. But why should we believe that there is a sharp line between creatures that are subjects-of-a-life and creatures that are not? Isn't it more likely that "subjecthood" comes in degrees, that some creatures have only a little self-awareness, and only a little capacity to anticipate the future, while some have a little more, and some a good deal more?

Should we, for instance, regard fish, amphibians, and reptiles as subjects-of-a-life? A simple yes-or-no answer seems inadequate. On the one hand, some of their behavior is difficult to explain without the assumption that they have sensations, beliefs, desires, emotions, and memories; on the other hand, they do not seem to exhibit very much self-awareness or very much conscious anticipation of future events. Do they have enough mental sophistication to count as subjects-of-a-life? Exactly how much is enough?

It is still more unclear what we should say about insects, spiders, octopi, and other invertebrate animals which have brains and sensory organs but whose minds (if they have minds) are even more alien to us than those of fish or reptiles. Such creatures are probably sentient. Some people doubt that they can feel pain, since they lack certain neurological structures which are crucial to the processing of pain impulses in vertebrate animals. But this argument is inconclusive, since their nervous systems might process pain in ways different from ours. When injured, they sometimes act as if they are in pain. On evolutionary grounds, it seems unlikely that highly mobile creatures with complex sensory systems would not have developed a capacity for pain (and pleasure), since such a capacity has obvious survival value. It must, however, be admitted that we do not *know* whether spiders can feel pain (or something very like it), let alone whether they have emotions, memories, beliefs, desires, self-awareness, or a sense of the future.

Even more mysterious are the mental capacities (if any) of mobile microfauna. The brisk and efficient way that paramecia move about in their incessant search for food *might* indicate some kind of sentience, in spite of their lack of eyes, ears, brains, and other organs associated with sentience in more complex organisms. It is conceivable—though not very probable—that they, too, are subjects-of-a-life.

The existence of a few unclear cases need not pose a serious problem for a moral theory, but in this case, the unclear cases constitute most of those with which an adequate theory of animal rights would need to deal. The subject-of-a-life criterion can provide us with little or no moral guidance in our interactions with the vast majority of animals. That might be acceptable if it could be supplemented with additional principles which would provide such guidance. However, the radical dualism of the theory precludes supplementing it in this way. We are forced to say that either a spider has the same right to life as you and I do, or it has no right to life whatever—and that only the gods know which of these alternatives is true.

Regan's suggestion for dealing with such unclear cases is to apply the "benefit of the doubt" principle. That is, when dealing with beings that may or may not be subjects-of-a-life, we should act as if they are.[6] But if we try to apply this principle to the entire range of doubtful cases, we will find ourselves with moral obligations which we cannot possibly fulfill. In many climates, it is virtually impossible to live without swatting mosquitoes and exterminating cockroaches, and not all of us can afford to hire someone to sweep the path before we walk, in order to make sure that we do not step on ants. Thus, we are still faced with the daunting task of drawing a sharp line somewhere on the continuum of life forms—this time, a line demarcating the limits of the benefit of the doubt principle.

The weak animal rights theory provides a more plausible way of dealing with this range of cases, in that it allows the rights of animals of different kinds to vary in strength....

WHY ARE ANIMAL RIGHTS WEAKER THAN HUMAN RIGHTS?

How can we justify regarding the rights of persons as generally stronger than those of sentient beings which are not persons? There are a plethora of bad justifications, based on religious premises or false or unprovable claims about the differences between human and non-human nature. But there is one difference which has a clear moral relevance: people are at least sometimes capable of being moved to action or inaction by the force of reasoned argument. Rationality rests upon other mental capacities, notably those which Regan cites as criteria for being a subject-of-a-life. We share these capacities with many other animals But it is not just because we are subjects-of-a-life that we are both able and morally compelled to recognize one another as beings with equal basic moral rights. It is also because we are able to "listen to reason" in order to settle our conflicts and cooperate in shared projects. This capacity, unlike the others, may require something like a human language.

Why is rationality morally relevant? It does not make us "better" than other animals or more "perfect." It does not even automatically make us more intelligent. (Bad reasoning reduces our effective intelligence rather than increasing it.) But it is morally relevant insofar as it provides greater possibilities for cooperation and for the nonviolent resolution of problems. It also makes us more dangerous than non-rational beings can ever be. Because we are potentially more dangerous and less predictable than wolves, we need an articulated system of morality to regulate our conduct. Any human morality, to be workable in the long run, must recognize the equal moral status of all persons, whether through the postulate of equal basic moral rights or in some other way. The recognition of the moral equality of other persons is the price we must each pay for their recognition of our moral equality. Without this mutual recognition of moral equality, human society can exist only in a state of chronic and bitter conflict. The war between the sexes will persist so long as there is sexism and male domination; racial conflict will never be eliminated so long as there are racist laws and practices. But, to the extent that we achieve a mutual recognition of equality, we can hope to live together, perhaps as peacefully as wolves, achieving (in part) through explicit moral principles what they do not seem to need explicit moral principles to achieve.

Why not extend this recognition of moral equality to other creatures, even though they cannot do the same for us? The answer is that we cannot. Because we cannot reason with most non-human animals, we cannot always solve the problems which they may cause without harming them—although we are always obligated to try. We cannot negotiate a treaty with the feral cats and foxes, requiring them to stop preying on endangered native species in return for suitable concessions on our part.

> If rats invade our houses . . . we cannot reason with them, hoping to persuade them of the injustice they do us. We can only attempt to get rid of them.[7]

Aristotle was not wrong in claiming that the capacity to alter one's behavior on the basis of reasoned argument is relevant to the full moral status which he accorded to free men. Of course, he was wrong in his other premise, that women and slaves by nature cannot reason well enough to function as autonomous moral agents. Had that premise been true, so would his conclusion that women and slaves are not quite the moral equals of free men. In the case of most non-human animals, the corresponding premise is true. If, on the other hand, there are animals with whom we can learn to reason, then we are obligated to do this and to regard them as our moral equals.

Thus, to distinguish between the rights of persons and those of most other animals on the grounds that only people can alter their behavior on the basis of reasoned argument does not commit us to a perfectionist theory of the sort Aristotle endorsed. There is no excuse for refusing to recognize the moral equality of some people on the grounds that we don't regard them as quite as rational as we are, since it is perfectly clear that most people can reason well enough to determine how to act so as to respect the basic rights of others (if they choose to), and that is enough for moral equality.

But what about people who are clearly not rational? It is often argued that sophisticated mental capacities such as rationality cannot be essential for the possession of equal basic moral rights, since nearly everyone agrees that human infants and mentally incompetent persons have such rights, even though they may lack those sophisticated mental capacities. But this argument is inconclusive, because there are powerful practical and emotional reasons for protecting non-rational human beings, reasons which are absent in the case of most non-human animals. Infancy and mental incompetence are human conditions which all of us either have experienced or are likely to experience at some time. We also protect babies and mentally incompetent people because we care for them. We don't normally care for animals in the same way, and when we do—e.g., in the case of much-loved pets—we may regard them as having special rights by virtue of their relationship to us. We protect them not only for their sake but also for our own, lest we be hurt by harm done to them. Regan holds that such "side-effects" are irrelevant to moral rights, and perhaps they are. But in ordinary usage, there is no sharp line between moral rights and those moral protections which are not rights. The extension of strong moral protections to infants and the mentally impaired in no way proves that non-human animals have the same basic moral rights as people.

WHY SPEAK OF "ANIMAL RIGHTS" AT ALL?

If, as I have argued, reality precludes our treating all animals as our moral equals, then why should we still ascribe rights to them? Everyone agrees that animals are entitled to some protection against human abuse, but why speak of animal *rights* if we are not prepared to accept most animals as our moral equals? The weak animal rights position may seem an unstable compromise between the bold claim that animals have the same basic moral rights that we do and the more common view that animals have no rights at all.

It is probably impossible to either prove or disprove the thesis that animals have moral rights by producing an analysis of the concept of a moral right and checking to see if some or all animals satisfy the conditions for having rights. The concept of a moral right is complex, and it is not clear which of its strands are essential. Paradigm rights holders, i.e., mature and mentally competent persons, are *both* rational and morally autonomous beings and sentient subjects-of-a-life. Opponents of animal rights claim that rationality and moral autonomy are essential for the possession of rights, while defenders of animal rights claim that they are not. The ordinary concept of a moral right is probably not precise enough to enable us to determine who is right on purely definitional grounds.

If logical analysis will not answer the question of whether animals have moral rights, practical considerations may, nevertheless incline us to say that they do. The most plausible alternative to the view that animals have moral rights is that, while they do not have *rights,* we are, nevertheless, obligated not to be cruel to them. Regan argues persuasively that the injunction to avoid being cruel to animals is inadequate to express our obligations towards animals, because it focuses on the mental states of those who cause animal suffering, rather than on the harm done to the animals themselves (p. 158). Cruelty is inflicting pain or suffering and either taking pleasure in that pain or suffering or being more or less indifferent to it. Thus, to express the demand for the decent treatment of animals in terms of the rejection of cruelty is to invite the too easy response that those who subject animals to suffering are not being cruel because they regret the suffering they cause but sincerely believe that what they do is justified. The injunction to avoid cruelty is also inadequate in that it does not preclude the killing of animals—for any reason, however trivial—so long as it is done relatively painlessly.

The inadequacy of the anti-cruelty view provides one practical reason for speaking of animal rights. Another practical reason is that this is an age in which nearly all significant moral claims tend to be expressed in terms of rights. Thus, the denial that animals have rights, however carefully qualified, is likely to be taken to mean that we may do whatever we like to them, provided that we do not violate any human rights. In such a context, speaking of the rights of animals may be the only way to persuade many people to take seriously protests against the abuse of animals.

Why not extend this line of argument and speak of the rights of trees, mountains, oceans, or anything else which we may wish to see protected from destruction? Some environmentalists have not hesitated to speak in this way, and, given the importance of protecting such elements of the natural world, they cannot be blamed for using this rhetorical device. But, I would argue that moral rights can meaningfully be ascribed only to entities which have some capacity for sentience. This is because moral rights are protections designed to protect rights holders from harms or to provide them with benefits which matter *to them*. Only beings capable of sentience can be harmed or benefited in ways which matter to them, for only such beings can like or dislike what happens to them or prefer some conditions to others. Thus, sentient animals, unlike mountains, rivers, or species, are at least logically possible candidates for moral rights. This fact together with the need to end current abuses of animals—e.g., in scientific research . . .—provides a plausible case for speaking of animal rights.

CONCLUSION

I have argued that Regan's case for ascribing strong moral rights to all normal, mature mammals is unpersuasive because (1) it rests upon the obscure concept of inherent value, which is defined only in negative terms, and (2) it seems to preclude any plausible answer to questions about the moral status of the vast majority of sentient animals. . . .

The weak animal rights theory asserts that (1) any creature whose natural mode of life includes the pursuit of certain satisfactions has the right not to be forced to exist without the opportunity to pursue those satisfactions; (2) that any creature which is capable of pain, suffering, or frustration has the right that such experiences not be deliberately inflicted upon it without some compelling reason; and (3) that no sentient being should be killed without good reason. However, moral rights are not an all-or-nothing affair. The strength of the reasons required to override the rights of a non-human organism varies, depending upon—among other things—the probability that it is sentient and (if it is clearly sentient) its probable degree of mental sophistication. . . .

NOTES

1. Tom Regan, *The Case for Animal Rights* (Berkeley, University of California Press, 1983). All page references are to this edition.
2. For instance, Peter Singer, although he does not like to speak of rights, includes all sentient beings under the protection of his basic utilitarian principle of equal respect for like interests. (*Animal Liberation* [New York: Avon Books, 1975], p. 3.)
3. The capacity for sentience like all of the mental capacities mentioned in what follows is a disposition. Dispositions do not disappear whenever they are not currently manifested. Thus, sleeping or temporarily unconscious persons or non-human animals are still sentient in the relevant sense (i.e., still capable of sentience), so long as they still have the neurological mechanisms necessary for the occurrence of experiences.
4. It is possible, perhaps probable that some non-human animals—such as cetaceans and anthropoid apes—should be regarded as persons. If so, then the weak animal rights position holds that these animals have the same basic moral rights as human persons.
5. See R. G. Frey, *Interests and Rights: The Case Against Animals* (Oxford: Oxford University Press, 1980).
6. See, for instance, p. 319, where Regan appeals to the benefit of the doubt principle when dealing with infanticide and late-term abortion.
7. Bonnie Steinbock, "Speciesism and the Idea of Equality," *Philosophy* 53 (1978):253.

🐝 STUDY QUESTIONS

1. Examine Warren's critique of Regan's position. What is her main criticism? How strong is her criticism?
2. What is the basis for granting human beings moral rights that we do not grant animals? Do you agree with her arguments?
3. What is the weak animal rights position? What is Warren's argument for it?

12   Against Zoos

DALE JAMIESON

Dale Jamieson is professor of environmental studies and philosophy at New York University.

In this controversial essay, which has been greeted with some hostility, Jamieson first details a brief history of public uses of animals up until the time of our present zoological parks. He inquires whether there is any justification for zoos, examining four possible reasons for them: amusement, education, scientific research, and preserving species. While these have some merit, it is not sufficient to justify zoos, which deprive animals of their freedom and a chance to develop their potential. No doubt this is impossible and/or impractical now, but should we not aim at more humane treatment of animals, including the abolition or lessening of violence?

ZOOS AND THEIR HISTORY

We can start with a rough-and-ready definition of zoos: they are public parks which display animals, primarily for the purposes of recreation or education. Although large collections of animals were maintained in antiquity, they were not zoos in this sense. Typically these ancient collections were not exhibited in public parks, or they were maintained for purposes other than recreation or education.

The Romans, for example, kept animals in order to have living fodder for the games. Their enthusiasm for the games was so great that even the first tigers brought to Rome, gifts to Caesar Augustus from an Indian ruler, wound up in the arena. The emperor Trajan staged 123 consecutive days of games in order to celebrate his conquest of Dacia. Eleven thousand animals were slaughtered, including lions, tigers, elephants, rhinoceroses, hippopotami, giraffes, bulls, stags, crocodiles and serpents. The games were popular in all parts of the Empire. Nearly every city had an arena and a collection of animals to stock it. In fifth-century France there were twenty-six such arenas, and they continued to thrive until at least the eighth century.

In antiquity rulers also kept large collections of animals as a sign of their power, which they would demonstrate on occasion by destroying their entire collections. This happened as late as 1719 when Elector Augustus II of Dresden personally slaughtered his entire menagerie, which included tigers, lions, bulls, bears and boars.

The first modern zoos were founded in Vienna, Madrid and Paris in the eighteenth century and in London and Berlin in the nineteenth. The first American zoos were established in Philadelphia and Cincinnati in the 1870s. Today in the United States alone there are hundreds of

Reprinted from Dale Jamieson, "Against Zoos," *In Defense of Animals*, ed. Peter Singer (Oxford: Basil Blackwell, 1985). Reprinted by permission of the author.

zoos, and they are visited by millions of people every year. They range from roadside menageries run by hucksters, to elaborate zoological parks staffed by trained scientists.

The Roman games no longer exist, though bullfights and rodeos follow in their tradition. Nowadays the power of our leaders is amply demonstrated by their command of nuclear weapons. Yet we still have zoos. Why?

ANIMALS AND LIBERTY

Before we consider the reasons that are usually given for the survival of zoos, we should see that there is a moral presumption against keeping wild animals in captivity. What this involves, after all, is taking animals out of their native habitats, transporting them great distances and keeping them in alien environments in which their liberty is severely restricted. It is surely true that in being taken from the wild and confined in zoos, animals are deprived of a great many goods. For the most part they are prevented from gathering their own food, developing their own social orders and generally behaving in ways that are natural to them. These activities all require significantly more liberty than most animals are permitted in zoos. If we are justified in keeping animals in zoos, it must be because there are some important benefits that can be obtained only by doing so.

This conclusion is not the property of some particular moral theory; it follows from most reasonable moral theories. Either we have duties to animals or we do not. If we do have duties to animals, surely they include respecting those interests which are most important to them, so long as this does not conflict with other, more stringent duties that we may have. Since an interest in not being taken from the wild and kept confined is very important for most animals, it follows that if everything else is equal, we should respect this interest.

Suppose, on the other hand, that we do not have duties to animals. There are two further possibilities: either we have duties to people that sometimes concern animals, or what we do to animals is utterly without moral import. The latter view is quite implausible, and I shall not consider it further. People who have held the former view, that we have duties to people that concern animals, have sometimes thought that such duties arise because we can "judge the heart of a man by his treatment of animals," as Kant remarked in "Duties to Animals." It is for this reason that he condemns the man who shoots a faithful dog who has become too old to serve. If we accept Kant's premise, it is surely plausible to say that someone who, for no good reason, removes wild animals from their natural habitats and denies them liberty is someone whose heart deserves to be judged harshly. If this is so, then even if we believe that we do not have duties to animals but only duties concerning them, we may still hold that there is a presumption against keeping wild animals in captivity. If this presumption is to be overcome, it must be shown that there are important benefits that can be obtained only by keeping animals in zoos.

ARGUMENTS FOR ZOOS

What might some of these important benefits be? Four are commonly cited: amusement, education, opportunities for scientific research and help in preserving species.

Amusement was certainly an important reason for the establishment of the early zoos, and it remains an important function of contemporary zoos as well. Most people visit zoos in order to be entertained, and any zoo that wishes to remain financially sound must cater to this desire. Even highly regarded zoos, like the San Diego Zoo, have their share of dancing bears and trained birds of prey. But although providing amusement for people is viewed by the general public as a very important function of zoos, it is hard to see how providing such amusement could possibly justify keeping wild animals in captivity.

Most curators and administrators reject the idea that the primary purpose of zoos is to provide entertainment. Indeed, many agree that the pleasure we take in viewing wild animals is not in itself a good enough reason to keep them in captivity. Some curators see baby elephant walks, for example, as a necessary evil, or defend such amusements because of their role in educating people, especially children, about animals. It is sometimes said that people must be interested in what they are seeing if they are to be educated about it, and entertainments keep people interested, thus making education possible.

This brings us to a second reason for having zoos: their role in education. This reason has been cited as long as zoos have existed. For example, in 1898 the New York Zoological Society resolved to take "measures to inform the public of the great decrease in animal life, to stimulate sentiment in favor of better protection, and to cooperate with other scientific bodies...[in] efforts calculated to secure the perpetual preservation of our higher vertebrates." Despite the pious platitudes that are often uttered about the educational efforts of zoos, however, there is little evidence that zoos are very successful in educating people about animals. Stephen Kellert's paper "Zoological Parks in American Society," delivered at the annual meeting of the American Association of Zoological Parks and Aquariums in 1979, indicates that zoo-goers are much less knowledgeable about animals than backpackers, hunters, fishermen and others who claim an interest in animals, and only slightly more knowledgeable than those who claim no interest in animals at all. Even more disturbing, zoo-goers express the usual prejudices about animals; 73 per cent say they dislike rattlesnakes, 52 per cent vultures and only 4 per cent elephants. One reason why some zoos have not done a better job in educating people is that many of them make no real effort at education. In the case of others the problem is an apathetic and unappreciative public.

Edward G. Ludwig's study of the zoo in Buffalo, New York, in the *International Journal for the Study of Animal Problems* for 1981, revealed a surprising amount of dissatisfaction on the part of young, scientifically inclined zoo employees. Much of this dissatisfaction stemmed from the almost complete indifference of the public to the zoo's educational efforts. Ludwig's study indicated that most animals are viewed only briefly as people move quickly past cages. The typical zoo-goer stops only to watch baby animals or those who are begging, feeding or making

sounds. Ludwig reported that the most common expressions used to describe animals are "cute," "funny-looking," "lazy," "dirty," "weird" and "strange."

Of course, it is undeniable that some education occurs in some zoos. But this very fact raises other issues. What is it that we want people to learn from visiting zoos? Facts about the physiology and behaviour of various animals? Attitudes towards the survival of endangered species? Compassion for the fate of all animals? To what degree does education require keeping wild animals in captivity? Couldn't most of the educational benefits of zoos be obtained by presenting films, slides, lectures and so forth? Indeed, couldn't most of the important educational objectives better be achieved by exhibiting empty cages with explanations of why they are empty?

A third reason for having zoos is that they support scientific research. This, too, is a benefit that was pointed out long ago. Sir Humphrey Davy, one of the founders of the Zoological Society of London, wrote in 1825: "It would become Britain to offer another, and a very different series of exhibitions to the population of her metropolis; namely, animals brought from every part of the globe to be applied either to some useful purpose, or as objects of scientific research—not of vulgar admiration!" Zoos support scientific research in at least three ways: they fund field research by scientists not affiliated with zoos; they employ other scientists as members of zoo staffs; and they make otherwise inaccessible animals available for study.

The first point we should note is that very few zoos support any real scientific research. Fewer still have staff scientists with full-time research appointments. Among those that do, it is common for their scientists to study animals in the wild rather than those in zoo collections. Much of this research, as well as other field research that is supported by zoos, could just as well be funded in a different way—say, by a government agency. The question of whether there should be zoos does not turn on the funding for field research which zoos currently provide. The significance of the research that is actually conducted in zoos is a more important consideration.

Research that is conducted in zoos can be divided into two categories: studies in behaviour and studies in anatomy and pathology.

Behavioural research conducted on zoo animals is very controversial. Some have argued that nothing can be learned by studying animals that are kept in the unnatural conditions that obtain in most zoos. Others have argued that captive animals are more interesting research subjects than are wild animals: since captive animals are free from predation, they exhibit a wider range of physical and behavioural traits than animals in the wild, thus permitting researchers to view the full range of their genetic possibilities. Both of these positions are surely extreme. Conditions in some zoos are natural enough to permit some interesting research possibilities. But the claim that captive animals are more interesting research subjects than those in the wild is not very plausible. Environments trigger behaviours. No doubt a predation-free environment triggers behaviours different from those of an animal's natural habitat, but there is no reason to believe that better, fuller or more accurate data can be obtained in predation-free environments than in natural habitats.

Studies in anatomy and pathology are the most common forms of zoo research. Such research has three main purposes: to improve zoo conditions so that captive animals will live longer, be happier and breed more frequently; to contribute to human health by providing animal models for human ailments; and to increase our knowledge of wild animals for its own sake.

The first of these aims is surely laudable, if we concede that there should be zoos in the first place. But the fact that zoo research contributes to improving conditions in zoos is not a reason for having them. If there were no zoos, there would be no need to improve them.

The second aim, to contribute to human health by providing animal models for human ailments, appears to justify zoos to some extent, but in practice this consideration is not as important as one might think. There are very severe constraints on the experiments that may be conducted on zoo animals. In an article entitled "A Search for Animal Models at Zoos," published in *ILAR News* in 1982, Richard Montali and Mitchell Bush drew the following conclusion:

> Despite the great potential of a zoo as a resource for models, there are many limitations and, of necessity, some restrictions for use. There is little opportunity to conduct overly manipulative or invasive research procedures—probably less than would be allowed in clinical research trials involving human beings. Many of the species are difficult to work with or are difficult to breed, so that the numbers of animals available for study are limited. In fact, it is safe to say that over the past years, humans have served more as "animal models" for zoo species than is true of the reverse.

Whether for this reason or others, much of what has been done in using zoo animals as models for humans seems redundant or trivial. For example, the article cited above reports that zoo animals provide good models for studying lead toxicity in humans, since it is common for zoo animals to develop lead poisoning from chewing paint and inhaling polluted city air. There are available for study plenty of humans who suffer from lead poisoning for the same reasons. That zoos make available some additional non-human subjects for this kind of research seems at best unimportant and at worst deplorable.

Finally, there is the goal of obtaining knowledge about animals for its own sake. Knowledge is certainly something which is good and, everything being equal, we should encourage people to seek it for its own sake. But everything is not equal in this case. There is a moral presumption against keeping animals in captivity. This presumption can be overcome only by demonstrating that there are important benefits that must be obtained in this way if they are to be obtained at all. It is clear that this is not the case with knowledge for its own sake. There are other channels for our intellectual curiosity, ones that do not exact such a high moral price. Although our quest for knowledge for its own sake is important, it is not important enough to overcome the moral presumption against keeping animals in captivity.

In assessing the significance of research as a reason for having zoos, it is important to remember that very few zoos do any research at all. Whatever benefits result from zoo research could just as well be obtained by having a few zoos instead of the hundreds which now exist. The most this argument could establish is that we are justified in having a few very good zoos. It does not provide a defence of the vast majority of zoos which now exist.

A fourth reason for having zoos is that they preserve species that would otherwise become extinct. As the destruction of habitat accelerates and as breeding programmes become increasingly successful, this rationale for zoos gains in popularity. There is some reason for questioning the commitment of zoos to preservation: it can be argued that they continue to remove more animals from the wild than they return. Still, zoo breeding programmes have had some notable successes: without them the Père David Deer, the Mongolian Wild Horse and the European Bison would all now be extinct. Recently, however, some problems have begun to be noticed.

A 1979 study by Katherine Ralls, Kristin Brugger and Jonathan Ballou, which was reported in *Science,* convincingly argues that lack of genetic diversity among captive animals is a serious problem for zoo breeding programmes. In some species the infant mortality rate among inbred animals is six or seven times that among non-inbred animals. In other species the infant mortality rate among inbred animals is 100 per cent. What is most disturbing is that zoo curators have been largely unaware of the problems caused by inbreeding because adequate breeding and health records have not been kept. It is hard to believe that zoos are serious about their role in preserving endangered species when all too often they do not take even this minimal step.

In addition to these problems, the lack of genetic diversity among captive animals also means that surviving members of endangered species have traits very different from their conspecifics in the wild. This should make us wonder what is really being preserved in zoos. Are captive Mongolian Wild Horses really Mongolian Wild Horses in any but the thinnest biological sense?

There is another problem with zoo breeding programmes: they create many unwanted animals. In some species (lions, tigers and zebras, for example) a few males can service an entire herd. Extra males are unnecessary to the programme and are a financial burden. Some of these animals are sold and wind up in the hands of individuals and institutions which lack proper facilities. Others are shot and killed by Great White Hunters in private hunting camps. In order to avoid these problems, some zoos have been considering proposals to "recycle" excess animals: a euphemism for killing them and feeding their bodies to other zoo animals. Many people are surprised when they hear of zoos killing animals. They should not be. Zoos have limited capacities. They want to maintain diverse collections. This can be done only by careful management of their "stock."

Even if breeding programmes were run in the best possible way, there are limits to what can be done to save endangered species. For many large mammals a breeding herd of at least a hundred animals, half of them born in captivity, is required if they are to survive in zoos. As of 1971 only eight mammal species satisfied these conditions. Paul and Anne Ehrlich estimate in their book *Extinction* that under the best possible conditions American zoos could preserve only about a hundred species of mammals—and only at a very high price: maintaining a breeding herd of herbivores costs between $75,000 and $250,000 per year.

There are further questions one might ask about preserving endangered species in zoos. Is it really better to confine a few hapless Mountain Gorillas in a zoo than to permit the species to become extinct? To most environmentalists the answer is obvious: the species must be preserved at all costs. But this smacks of sacrificing the lower-case gorilla for the upper-case Gorilla. In doing this, aren't we using animals as mere vehicles for their genes? Aren't we preserving genetic material at the expense of the animals themselves? If it is true that we are inevitably moving towards a world in which Mountain Gorillas can survive only in zoos, then we must ask whether it is really better for them to live in artificial environments of our design than not to be born at all.

Even if all of these difficulties are overlooked, the importance of preserving endangered species does not provide much support for the existing system of zoos. Most zoos do very little breeding or breed only species which are not endangered. Many of the major breeding programmes are run in special facilities which have been established for that purpose. They are often located in remote places, far from the attention of zoo-goers. (For example, the Bronx Zoo operates its Rare Animal Survival Center on St Catherine's Island off the coast of Georgia, and the National Zoo runs its Conservation and Research Center in the Shenandoah Valley of Virginia.) If our main concern is to do what we can to preserve endangered species, we should support such large-scale breeding centres rather than conventional zoos, most of which have neither the staff nor the facilities to run successful breeding programmes.

The four reasons for having zoos which I have surveyed carry some weight. But different reasons provide support for different kinds of zoos. Preservation and perhaps research are better carried out in large-scale animal preserves, but these provide few opportunities for amusement and education. Amusement and perhaps education are better provided in urban zoos, but they offer few opportunities for research and preservation. Moreover, whatever benefits are obtained from any kind of zoo must confront the moral presumption against keeping wild animals in captivity. Which way do the scales tip? There are two further considerations which, in my view, tip the scales against zoos.

First, captivity does not just deny animals liberty but is often detrimental to them in other respects as well. The history of chimpanzees in the zoos of Europe and America is a good example.

Chimpanzees first entered the zoo world in about 1640 when a Dutch prince, Frederick Henry of Nassau, obtained one for his castle menagerie. The chimpanzee didn't last very long. In 1835 the London Zoo obtained its first chimpanzee; he died immediately. Another was obtained in 1845; she lived six months. All through the nineteenth and early twentieth centuries zoos obtained chimpanzees who promptly died within nine months. It wasn't until the 1930s that it was discovered that chimpanzees are extremely vulnerable to human respiratory diseases, and that special steps must be taken to protect them. But for nearly a century zoos removed them from the wild and subjected them to almost certain death. Problems remain today. When chimpanzees are taken from the wild the usual procedure is to shoot the mother and kidnap the child. The rule of thumb among trappers is that ten chimpanzees die for every one that is delivered alive to the United States or Europe. On arrival many of these animals are confined under abysmal conditions.

Chimpanzees are not the only animals to suffer in zoos. In 1974 Peter Batten, former director of the San Jose Zoological Gardens, undertook an exhaustive study of two hundred American zoos. In his book *Living Trophies* he documented large numbers of neurotic, overweight animals kept in cramped, cold cells and fed unpalatable synthetic food. Many had deformed feet and appendages caused by unsuitable floor surfaces. Almost every zoo studied had excessive mortality rates, resulting from preventable factors ranging from vandalism to inadequate husbandry practices. Battan's conclusion was: "The majority of American zoos are badly run, their direction incompetent, and animal husbandry inept and in some cases nonexistent."

Many of these same conditions and others are documented in *Pathology of Zoo Animals,* a review of necropsies conducted by Lynn Griner over the last fourteen years at the San Diego Zoo. This zoo may well be the best in the country, and its staff is clearly well-trained and well-intentioned. Yet this study documents widespread malnutrition among zoo animals; high mortality rates from the use of anaesthetics and tranquillizers; serious injuries and deaths sustained in transport; and frequent occurrences of cannibalism, infanticide and fighting almost certainly caused by overcrowded conditions. Although the zoo has learned from its mistakes, it is still unable to keep many wild animals in captivity without killing or injuring them, directly or indirectly. If this is true of the San Diego Zoo, it is certainly true, to an even greater extent, at most other zoos.

The second consideration is more difficult to articulate but is, to my mind, even more important. Zoos teach us a false sense of our place in the natural order. The means of confinement mark a difference between humans and animals. They are there at our pleasure, to be used for our purposes. Morality and perhaps our very survival require that we learn to live as one species among many rather than as one species over many. To do this, we must forget what we learn at zoos. Because what zoos teach us is false and dangerous, both humans and animals will be better off when they are abolished.

STUDY QUESTIONS

1. Examine the four reasons for zoos. Can you improve on them? Examine Jamieson's reasons for rejecting them as sufficient to justify zoos. Do you agree with him? Are zoos immoral?
2. Can Jamieson's arguments against zoos be applied to owning pets? Why or why not?
3. How would Jamieson (or you) respond to the objection that since we have duties toward animal welfare, we ought to protect weaker animals from their predators, so that zoos could help play a role in promoting their welfare? And just as we want to eliminate gratuitous violence by humans, should we not work to eliminate it in animals—perhaps developing meat substitutes for them, as well as human carnivores?

FOR FURTHER READING

Finsen, Lawrence, and Susan Finsen, *The Animal Rights Movement in America*. New York: Twayne Publishers, 1994.

Frey, R. G. *Rights, Killing, and Suffering*. Oxford: Basil Blackwell, 1983.

Midgley, Mary. *Animals and Why They Matter*. London: Routledge, 1983.

Rachels, James. *Created from Animals: The Moral Implications of Darwinism*. Oxford: Oxford University Press, 1990.

Regan, Tom. *The Case for Animal Rights*. Berkeley: University of California, 1983. The most comprehensive philosophical treatise in favor of animal rights.

Regan, Tom, and Peter Singer, eds. *Animal Rights and Human Obligations*. Englewood Cliffs, NJ: Prentice-Hall, 1976.

Robbins, John. *Diet for a New America: How Your Food Choices Affect Your Health, Happiness, and the Future of Life on Earth*. Walpole, NH: Stillpoint, 1987. A strong case for vegetarianism.

Rohr, Janelle, ed. *Animal Rights: Opposing Viewpoints*. San Diego: Greenhaven Press, 1989.

Sapontzis, S. F. *Morals, Reason, and Animals*. Philadelphia: Temple University Press, 1987.

Singer, Peter. *Animal Liberation*, 2d ed. New York: New York Review of Books, 1990.

Philosophical Theories of Nature, Biocentric Ethics, Ecocentric Ethics, and Deep Ecology

IN THIS CHAPTER, we consider the wide-ranging debates over why humans should value nature. There are three general reasons for humans to value nature. First, nature can be valued simply as a source of economics. We derive our food, water, air, clothing, building materials, etc., from nature. We mine its ores, cut its trees, harvest its fish, and develop its land. We value it for the material products it provides. Second, we value nature as a source not just of economic resource but also of aesthetics. Forests, streams, and mountains are beautiful and uplifting. Nature is seen as pure, uncorrupted by humans, a place of moral and spiritual rejuvenation. As with the first, we here value nature for what nature offers us. Even though we are valuing nature in a less exploitative way, some still argue we need to go further. Thus the third way is to value nature simply for nature's sake, not for what nature offers us. That is, nature has intrinsic value. Many nature-centered spiritual systems indeed hold this view (for instance, some varieties of Pagans and Wiccans). Many people with green leanings are sympathetic to this position, but as we shall see, it is hard to defend intellectually. At the same time, its pull is strong, and one of the central challenges to environmental thinking is whether to base an environmental ethic on human needs or upon nature itself.

We begin with Holmes Rolston's defense of the thesis that nature has intrinsic and objective value. Nature is good in itself or has a good, so even if there were no sentient beings, it would still have a good. Rolston argues that not only sentient beings but biological systems, too, have intrinsic value. But not everything in nature has objective value. It occurs only where there is positive creativity. Next Ned Hettinger comments on and critically develops Rolston's theory, pointing out its strengths and weaknesses. John Stuart Mill takes a very different position, contending that Nature is wild and destructive and that it ought to be "corrected" by moral beings.

The objectivist position takes as its principal watershed the work of Albert Schweitzer. It was Schweitzer's *Civilization and Ethics* in 1923 that launched the project of extending the range of value to include all of life. He called this position "Reverence for Life." Every living thing (every "will-to-live") in nature is endowed with something sacred or intrinsically valuable and should be respected as such:

> Just as in my own will-to-live there is a yearning for more life . . . so the same obtains in all the will-to-live around me, equally whether it can express itself to my comprehension or whether it remains unvoiced.
>
> Ethics consists in this, that I experience the necessity of practicing the same reverence for life toward all will-to-live, as toward my own.

Although Reverence for Life bears a resemblance to older Eastern views about the sanctity of all of life, especially in Hinduism and Buddhism, the chief proponents of that view usually tie their doctrines to reincarnation and the transmigration of souls. No such implications are present in Schweitzer's doctrine.

Schweitzer's thought has been a point of departure for biocentric ethics (i.e., life-centered ethics), represented by his seminal work, along with Paul Taylor's and Kenneth Goodpaster's essays, as well as deep ecology. Paul Taylor develops Schweitzer's seminal idea. Whereas Schweitzer is not always clear about whether he regards all life-forms as equal—and he sometimes writes as though the will-to-live is embodied in the idea of pleasure and its denial in the idea of pain—Taylor is clearer, self-consciously egalitarian, and separates inherent value from the idea of hedonism (pleasure and pain). For Taylor, all living beings—from amoebas to humans—are of equal inherent value. Each living individual has a goal (what the Greeks called a *telos*), and to have a goal implies a will or desire to attain it. One's goal is one's good, so all living things are inherently good. Kant's notion "end-in-itself," which he applied only to rational beings, is radically expanded by Taylor to cover all living things.

Kenneth Goodpaster offers a careful, nonegalitarian argument for the claim that possessing a life makes one morally considerable. Richard Watson's and Murray Bookchin's articles consider and attack these sorts of arguments.

Let us turn to ecocentric ethics. Like biocentric theories, ecocentrism also imputes intrinsic value to nature, but whereas biocentric ethics is *individualistic*, ecocentric ethics is *holistic*. It views the biosphere as a totality, including species, populations, land, and ecosystems. The primary source of the modern ecocentric movement is Aldo Leopold's (1887–1948) book *Sand County Almanac* (1949); Leopold, a Wisconsin forest ranger and, later, professor of game management at the University of Wisconsin, attempted to produce a new paradigm through which to evaluate our conduct. Rather than seeing the environment as merely a resource for human beings, we should view it as the center of value. It is primarily the biotic community that is valuable, and this should guide our moral sensitivities. "A thing is right when it tends to preserve the integrity, stability, and beauty of the biotic community. It is wrong when it tends otherwise." So humans must change their role from conqueror of the land-community to plain member and citizen of it. We must extend our social conscience from people to ecosystems to the land.

Brilliant though he was, Leopold was not a philosopher and did not develop the implications of his position. Baird Callicott, a disciple of Leopold, attempts to draw out the full picture of the land ethic. Callicott locates the historic sources of Leopold's thought in David Hume, Adam Smith, and Charles Darwin. Hume and Smith made sympathy the basis of moral action, from which altruistic feelings arise. Darwin held that the primeval moral affections centered on the tribe, rather than its individual members. Leopold, according to Callicott, simply extended this idea to the biotic community. To quote Leopold, "The land ethic simply enlarges the boundaries of the community to include soils, waters, plants, and animals, or collectively: the land.... It implies respect for ... fellow members and also respect for the community as such."

Callicott holds that intrinsic value is neither purely subjective nor objective but arises when beings like us, with a certain nature, respond to nature. Some philosophers, such as Tom Regan, H. J. McCloskey, and L. W. Sumner, have interpreted Leopold as being antihuman, holding that the biocentric community is the only thing that matters. Sumner calls this "dangerous nonsense" and Regan "environmental fascism." Callicott holds that a more charitable (and accurate) interpretation is to view the land ethic as an extension of our moral consciousness, not canceling out our obligations to other human beings but putting them in a wider ecological context.

Bill Throop and Ned Hettinger try to refocus ecocentrism, emphasizing the notion of wildness rather than ecological stability, and Michael Nelson explores the debate on the idea of wilderness, illuminating the key issues. Roger Paden ends this section with a comparison of two kinds of preservationist ethics.

Now we turn to the most radical of the main environmental theories, deep ecology, first set forth by the Norwegian philosopher Arne Naess and elaborated by Bill Devall and George Sessions. Drawing on Eastern thought, especially Vedantic Hinduism and Buddhism, deep ecology holds that all of us—humans, nonhumans, and biotic communities—are intrinsically related to one another. Underlying all is an essential unity of being so that, in some sense, no one can realize his, her, or its deepest potential without everyone realizing it. Deep ecology is egalitarian in that everyone and everything is equally valuable as part of the whole. This transpersonal ecology calls on us to go beyond class, gender, and species and find our deepest fulfillment in harmony with nature. In its eightfold path (see Devall and Sessions's article), deep ecology calls for the promotion and greater protection of biodiversity and a reduction of human population. We must also learn to live more simply. It's motto is "Simple in Means, Rich in Ends," signifying an antimaterialist perspective.

Next, Richard Watson criticizes many of the above ecophilosophies for being antianthropocentric—that is, for opposing the place of human beings at the center of things. Murray Bookchin offers a Marxist and anarchist critique of deep ecology, opposing it to social ecology. John Rodman defends the idea that ecological sensibility, an attitude that recognizes intrinsic value, is the appropriate attitude toward nature. Finally, James Sterba attempts to reconcile anthropocentric and nonanthropocentric ethics.

We turn to our first set of readings on intrinsic value.

DOES NATURE HAVE INTRINSIC VALUE?

13 Naturalizing Values: Organisms and Species

HOLMES ROLSTON, III

Holmes Rolston, III is professor of philosophy at Colorado State University. He is the author of numerous works on environmental ethics, including *Philosophy Gone Wild: Essays in Environmental Ethics* (1986) and *Environmental Ethics: Duties to and Values in the Natural World* (1988).

In this essay, Rolston examines the fact/value problem as it applies to nature. He argues that values are objective in nature, and that just as philosophers are naturalizing ethics, epistemology, and metaphysics, they should naturalize values.

In an age of naturalism, philosophers seem as yet unable to naturalize values. They are naturalizing ethics, epistemology, and metaphysics. They have connected human ethical behavior to Darwinian reciprocity, kin selection, genetic fitness, and so on. They analyze human capacities for epistemology with care to notice how our human perceptions, our sense organs, have an evolutionary history. Our mind and its cognitive capacities are pragmatic ways of functioning in the world. They interpret ideologies and metaphysical views as means of coping, worldviews that enable humans in their societies to cohere and to out compete other societies. Ethics, epistemology, and metaphysics are survival tools, whatever else they may also become.

But philosophers are slow to naturalize axiology. If they do, they try to demonstrate the biological roots of human values. They show that our values root in our biological needs—for food, shelter, security, resources, self-defense, offspring, stability, and status in our societies. Beyond that, philosophers do not naturalize values in any deeper sense. They cannot disconnect nature from humans so that anything else in nature can have any intrinsic value on its own. That is disconcerting. Nature comes to have value only when humans take it up into their experience. This, they may think, is a naturalized account of value; but, I shall argue here, such analysis has not yet come within reach of a biologically based account of values. Somewhat curiously, the more obvious kind of naturalizing—showing that our values are framed by our evolutionary embodiment in the world—blinds us to the deeper kind of naturalizing—recognizing an evolutionary world in which values, some of which we share, are pervasively embodied in the nonhuman world.

The debate is complex and multi-leveled. We touch the nerve of it here by focusing on value as this is present in living organisms and their species lines. Let's start by looking over the shoulders of some recent scientists and their discoveries.

1. DRAGONFLIES, LEAF STOMATA, BACTERIAL CLOCKS, AND GENOMES

Studies of dragonflies in the Carboniferous show that their wings "are proving to be spectacular examples of microengineering" giving them "the agile, versatile flight necessary to catch prey in flight." They are "adapted for high-performance flight" (Wootton et al., 1998). "To execute these aerobatic maneuvers, the insects come equipped with highly engineered wings that automatically change their flight shape in response to airflow, putting the designers of the latest jet fighters to shame" (Vogel, 1998). Dragonflies have to change their wing shape in flight without benefit of muscles (as in birds and bats), so they use a flexible aerofoil with veins that enables the wing surface to twist in direct response to aerodynamic loading when suddenly changing directions or shifting from upstroke to downstroke. A hind-wing base mechanism is especially impressive in the way it mixes flexibility and rigidity. "The 'smart' wing-base mechanism is best interpreted as an elegant means of maintaining downstroke efficiency in the presence of these adaptations to improve upstroke usefulness" (Wootton et al., 1998).

Botanists report studies in what they call "a plant's dilemma." Plants need to photosynthesize to gain energy from the sun, which requires access to carbon dioxide in the atmosphere. They also need to conserve water, vital to their metabolism, and access to atmosphere which evaporates water. This forces a trade-off in leaves between too much and too little exposure to atmosphere. The problem is solved by stomata on the undersides of leaves, which can open and close, letting in or shutting out the air. "The stomatal aperture is controlled by osmotic adjustment in the surrounding cells. In a sophisticated regulatory mechanism, light, the carbon dioxide required for photosynthesis, and the water status of the plant are integrated to regulate stomatal aperture for optimization of the plant's growth and performance" (Grill and Ziegler, 1998). The details of such "plant strategies" vary in different species but are quite complex, integrating multiple environmental and metabolic variables—water availability, drought, heat, cold, sunlight, water stress, and energy needs in the plant—for sophisticated solutions to the plant's dilemma.

Even the cyanobacteria, blue-green algae, which are relatively primitive single-celled organisms, can track day and night with molecular clocks built with a genetic oscillator rather similar to those in more advanced organisms. Discovering this, Marcia Barinaga says, "Keeping track of day-night cycles is apparently so essential, perhaps because it helps organisms prepare for the special physiological needs they will have at various times during the daily cycle, that clocks seem to have arisen multiple times, recreating the same design each time" (1998).

Reporting a June 1998 conference on "Molecular Strategies in Evolution," geneticists have found so many examples of "how the genome readies itself for evolution" that they are making a "paradigm shift." Abandoning the idea that genetic mutation is entirely blind and random, and that genetic errors are suppressed to minimize change, geneticists are impressed with the innovative, creative capacities in the genome. These "new findings are persuading them that the most successful genomes may be those that have evolved to be able to change quickly and substantially if necessary" (Pennisi, 1998). Genes do this by using transposons—gene segments, mobile elements—that they can use rapidly to alter DNA and the resulting protein structures and metabolisms in time of stress. "Chance favors the prepared genome," says Lynn Caporale, a biotechnology geneticist. James Shapiro, a bacterial geneticist at the University of Chicago, comments: "The capability of cells has gone far beyond what we had imagined." "Cells engineer their own genomes" (quoted in Pennisi, 1998).

The genome in vertebrates, for example, has evolved quite successful capacities to resist diseases. Transposons turn out to be especially useful in the acquired immune system, which is not present in invertebrates, but which was discovered and elaborated in vertebrates. "The immune system is a wonderful example of how a mobile piece of DNA can have an astounding impact on evolution," says David Schatz of Yale University (quoted in Pennisi, 1998). Innate immunity, which is present in vertebrates, is coded in the genes and "remembers" what has happened in the organism's evolutionary past. But acquired immunity "remembers" what has come along during the organism's biographical past. An organism gets the disease; then its body remembers, forms antigens, and does not get the disease a second time.

One has to use language with care; we should guard against overly cognitive language. But scientists do have to describe what is going on; and there is a kind of acquired learning in immunity, mechanical though the system also is. Immunologists use a term here that philosophers will find revealing. When stem cells from the bone marrow mature in the thymus (T cells), this is called "thymic education" (Abbas et al., 1991, p. 169). Once such an educated T cell meets an alien microbe, it not only triggers defenses, it triggers a memory. What immunologists call "memory cells" are made; these are both long-lived and reproduce themselves, so that acquired immunity can continue for decades, even a lifetime. The body can remember what sorts of organisms it has met before and be ready for their return. From a philosophical perspective, we may wish to be circumspect about "memory" cells, as we are about "remembering"; and yet the vocabulary is widespread in immunology and seems equally legitimate, say, to the use of "memory" in computer science. Additionally, in organisms—as it is not in computers—this is vital to life. Such capacity is much smarter than mere genetics; the body has defensive capacities far in excess of anything that could have been coded for in the genes.

The immune system has a complex task. A host of metabolically and structurally different cells have to be choreographed in organic unity. Further, invader cells, myriads of kinds of them, and insider cells gone wrong in many different ways—all these must be seen and eliminated. This has to be done at microscopic and molecular ranges with careful regulation, which involves complement molecules that work in a cascade reaction—15–20 different molecules, and 10 or more inhibitors, a total of some 30–40 molecules. Such a cascade might seem overly complex, but it is really a sophisticated form of regulation; there are amplification circuits and stabilizing loops, shut-down provisions and backup pathways. This is, of course, a causal system, but it is more than that; the system is protecting an organismic self.

Complement can be quite destructive and that is a good thing when it provides immunity for the organism, but it is also a bad thing if it goes out of control. So complement requires tight, fail-safe regulation. Immunologists use here the language of a fine-tuned mechanism: "Because of these regulatory mechanisms, a delicate balance of activation and inhibition of the complement cascades is achieved which prevents damage to autologous [self] cells and tissues but promotes the effective destruction of foreign organisms" (Abbas et al., 1991, p. 268). "The consequences of complement activation are so significant and potentially dangerous that the system must be very carefully regulated" (Tizard, 1992, p. 200). Some threats and achievements here seem to be "significant," "dangerous," "effective," and "damaging"; something vital is at stake.

Can you see that philosophers, looking over the shoulders of these scientists with their descriptions of what is going on, have some value questions to ask? The immune system is a sophisticated means of preserving biological identity at a high level of idiographic organismic diversity. All this is going on spontaneously, autonomously, without any animal awareness, much less any humans thinking about it.

There is praise for those dragonfly wings in the Carboniferous, coming from the scientists who study them. What is a philosopher to say? "Well, those are interesting wings to the scientists who study them, but they were of no value to the dragonflies." That seems implausible. Perhaps one can go part way and say: "Well, those wings did have value to the individual dragonflies who owned them. Instrumentally, the dragonflies found them useful. But a dragonfly is incapable of intrinsically valuing anything. Much less do these wings represent anything of value to the species line. Similar engineering features persist, Wootton and his associates add, in present-day dragonflies, living 320 million years later than the fossil dragonflies they studied in Argentina. That does sound like something that has been useful for quite a long time. Could that be of value to the species line?

The repeated discovery of molecular clocks in those cyanobacteria is important in fulfilling the organisms' "needs," and that seems pretty much fact of the matter. After that, do we want to insist that nevertheless this has no "value" to these organisms or their species lines, who have several times discovered how these internal clocks, similarly "designed," increase their adapted fit?

Studying those immune systems, a cell biologist finds something "wonderful." But, you will insist, this is only "wonderful" when cell biologists get there to wonder about it. Perhaps nothing is "astounding" until a human being comes around to be astounded. We do not think that the genomes are astounded. Still, the biological achievements are there long before we get let in on them. Set aside the wonder. In the objective facts—leaf stomata, genome evolution, bacterial clocks—is there anything there of value?

2. ANTHROPIC VALUERS AND THEIR VALUES

Most philosophers insist there is not. Values in nature are always "anthropocentric," human-centered, or at least "anthropogenic" (generated by humans). Bryan G. Norton concludes: "Moralists among environmental ethicists have erred in looking for a value in living things that is *independent* of human valuing. They have therefore forgotten a most elementary point about valuing anything. Valuing always occurs from the viewpoint of a conscious valuer.... Only the humans are valuing agents" (1991, p. 251). Norton, of course, believes in an objective world that he is anxious to conserve. Walking along a beach, he values, for example, the sand dollars *(Mellita quinquiesperforata)* he finds there. He has respect for life (1991, pp. 3–13). He chose a sand dollar to picture on the cover of his book. Such encounters make him a better person, give him an enlarged sense of his place in the world, and increase his wonder over the world he lives in. So he celebrates "the character-building transformative value of interactions with nature" (1987, pp. 10–11). He gets a lot of good out of respecting sand dollars.

But Norton does not want any epistemological "foundationalism" or "metaphysical realism," as though humans (whether scientists or philosophers) could actually know anything out there in nature independently of ourselves, much less that there are values intrinsic to some of these nonhuman organisms out there. There is no getting out of our epistemological bondage, no getting past "interactions"; it is naive for humans to claim to know objective value in sand dollars. Norton regrets that I, when I claim to know more than "interactions," have fallen into the "devastating legacy" of "outmoded" Cartesian dualism, "a bewitchment of ossified language" (1992, pp. 216–218, p. 224).

J. Baird Callicott, equally zealous for the conservation of nature, is equally clear about our unique human value-ability. All intrinsic value attached to nature is "grounded in human feelings" but is "projected" onto the natural objects that "excites" the value. "Intrinsic value ultimately depends upon human valuers." "Value depends upon human sentiments" (1984, p. 305). We humans can and ought *place* such value on natural things, at times, but there is no value already *in place* before we come. Intrinsic value is our construct, interactively with nature, but not something discovered which was there before we came. "There can be no value apart from an evaluator,... all value is as it were in the eye of the beholder [and]... therefore, is humanly dependent" (1989, p. 26). Such value is "anthropogenic" (1992, p. 132).

> The *source* of all value is human consciousness, but it by no means follows that the *locus* of all value is consciousness itself.... An intrinsically valuable thing on this reading is valuable *for* its own sake, *for* itself, but it is not valuable *in* itself, that is, completely independently of any consciousness, since no value can, in principle,... be altogether independent of a valuing consciousness.... Value is, as it were, projected onto natural objects or events by the subjective feelings of observers. If all consciousness were annihilated at a stroke, there would be no good and evil, no beauty and ugliness, no right and wrong; only impassive phenomena would remain. (1989, pp. 133–134, 147)

What that means, of course, is that the dragonfly wings were no "good" to them, or at least of no "value" to them. Though insects, sand dollars, bacteria, and plants may engineer their own genomes, there is nothing valuable about any of these activities, much less right or beautiful. Take our evaluating consciousness away, and there remain only impassive phenomena.

These philosophers have to conclude so because according to classical value theory only humans produce value; wild nature is intrinsically valueless. That seems to be a metaphysical claim in Callicott. We can know what is there without us: impassive phenomena; we can know what is not there: intrinsic value. Or if not so ontological, this is at least an epistemological claim, as with Norton: we are unable to know what is there without us. All we can know is that some things in nature, before we get there, have the potential to be evaluated by humans. We know this because if and when we humans appear, we may incline, sometimes, to value nature in noninstrumental ways, as when we project intrinsic value onto sequoia trees while hiking through the forest, or have transformative experiences encountering sand dollars on a beach.

The best we can do is to give a dispositional twist to value. To say that *n* is valuable means that *n* (some object in *n*ature) is able to be valued, if and when human valuers, *H*'s (some *H*umans), come along, although *n* has these properties whether or not humans arrive. The object plays its necessary part, though this is not sufficient without the subject. Nature contains "a range of *potential* values in nature actualizable upon interaction with consciousness" (Callicott, 1992, p. 129). By this account there is no actual value ownership autonomous to the dragonflies, bacteria, plants, or genome lines—none at least that we can know about. When cellular biologists arrive with their wonder and resolve to admire and perhaps also to conserve these things, there is value ignition. Intrinsic value in the realized sense emerges relationally with the appearance of the subject-generator. This is something like opening the door of a refrigerator, when things previously in the dark light up. But axiologically speaking, nature is always in the dark—unless and until humans come.

Perhaps you can begin to see why I am disconcerted that philosophers can be so naturalistic

one moment and so separatist the next. Naturalists wish to claim that we humans are not metaphysically different from the rest of nature, whether in substance or process. Human activities and those in wild nature are equally natural. Humans are completely natural in their physiologies and in their evolutionary histories. We are a part of nature and not apart from nature. Still, they still practice value apartheid. They resolutely find humans quite axiologically different, with this unique valuing capacity. That does set us apart from the rest of nature.

At the same time that they set us humans apart so surely, they may also find us so epistemologically ignorant that we cannot really know what we might share with the nonhuman lives we encounter. In these values that arise when we interact with nature we are unable to discover anything more than these values that arise within us, based on some potential nature has for us. But humans are sealed off from making any further claims about the objective world. This too is value apartheid.

The anthropogenic view values nature only in association with human participation. This leaves us with an uneasy concern that, however generously we may come to care for some nonhuman others, since it is only *we* who can place value anywhere, since it is only our own values that we can attend to or know about, humans really do remain at the center of concern. Their concern is central to having any value at all. Their concern is all that matters, and it is not always going to be easy to get up concern for animals, plants, species, or ecosystems that really don't matter in themselves, not at least so far as anybody knows.

We are likely to be concerned only if they matter to and for us, and that is going to place humans right back at the center. Nature is actually valuable only when it pleases us, as well as serves us. That seems to be the ultimate truth, even though we penultimately have placed intrinsic value on nature, and take our pleasure enjoying these natural things for what they are in themselves. Without us there is no such pleasure taken in anything. What is value-able, able to value things, is people; nature is able to be valued only if there are such able people there to do such valuing. Nature is not value-able—able to generate values—on its own, nor do plants and animals have any such value-ability.

3. SENTIENT VALUERS AND THEIR VALUES

Peter Singer offers a more expansive account. It is not just humans but the higher animals that can value. We have to move from an anthropocentric to a "sentiocentric" view. Or, better, from an anthropogenic to a "sentiogenic" view. (Please pardon the nonce words). Animals can value on their own, provided that they have preferences that can be satisfied or frustrated. A mother free-tailed bat, a mammal like ourselves, can, using sonar, wend her way out of Bracken Cave, in Texas, in total darkness, catch 500–1000 insects each hour on the wing, and return to find and nurse her own young. That gives evidence of bat-valuing; she values the insects and the pup.

Now, it seems absurd to say that there are no valuers until humans arrive. There is no better evidence of nonhuman values and valuers than spontaneous wildlife, born free and on its own. Animals hunt and howl; find shelter; seek out their habitats and mates; care for their young; flee from threats; grow hungry, thirsty, hot, tired, excited, sleepy. They suffer injury and lick their wounds. Here we are quite convinced that value is nonanthropogenic, to say nothing of anthropocentric.

These wild animals defend their own lives because they have a good of their own. There is somebody there behind the fur or feathers. Our gaze is returned by an animal that itself has a concerned outlook. Here is value right before our eyes, right behind those eyes. Animals are valuable, able to value things in their world. But we may still want to say that value exists only where a subject has an object of interest. Callicott modifies his position and says that value is not always "anthropogenic"; it may sometimes be "vertebragenic, since nonhuman animals, all vertebrates at the very least, are conscious and therefore may be said, in the widest sense of the term, to value things" (1992, pp. 132, 138).[1]

Well, that's a help, since at least the fellow vertebrates share in our ability to value things.

They value things instrumentally, no doubt, since they seek other animals, plants, and insects for food. They value water to drink, dens for shelter, and so on.

Do they value anything intrinsically? Callicott does not address this question, but perhaps he would say (and I would agree) that a vertebrate animal values its own life intrinsically. The deer defends its life as a good of its own. Such life is valued without further contributory reference, even if wolves in turn make use of deer for food. Perhaps the mother wolf can value her young intrinsically, since she puts herself at risk to bear young. Perhaps, unawares, she values the ongoing species line.

Nevertheless, for both Singer and Callicott, when we run out of psychological experience, value is over. Callicott's vertebragenic value still leaves most of the world valueless, since the vertebrates are only about 4 percent of the described species. Indeed, since the numbers of individuals in vertebrate species is typically much lower than the numbers of individuals in invertebrate or plant species, real valuers form only some minuscule fraction of the living organisms on Earth. Nearly everything on Earth is still quite valueless, unless and until these humans come along and place intrinsic value there. As Callicott insists, until humans do this, "there simply is no inherent or intrinsic value in nature" (1989, p. 160). Singer is more generous than Callicott to the invertebrates. Still he claims that we must stop "somewhere between a shrimp and an oyster" (1990, p. 174). Beyond that, he insists, "there is nothing to be taken into account" (1990, p. 8). With Singer, too, most of the biological world has yet to be taken into account.

Moving any further is impossible on a sentience-based theory. Value, like a tickle or remorse, must be felt to be there. Its *esse* is *percipi*. Nonsensed value is nonsense. Only beings with "insides" to them have value. There is no unexperienced value, no value without an experiencing valuer. According to the classical paradigm, so long dominant that to Norton and Callicott it seems elementary, there is no value without an experiencing valuer, just as there are no thoughts without a thinker, no percepts without a perceiver, no deeds without a doer, no targets without an aimer. Valuing is felt preferring by human choosers. Extending this paradigm, sentient animals may also value. Nothing else.

But the problem with the "no value without a valuer" axiom is that it is too subjectivist; it looks for some center of value located in a subjective self. And we nowhere wish to deny that such valuers are sufficient for value. But that is not the whole account of value. Perhaps there can be no doing science without a scientist, no religion without a believer, no tickle without somebody tickled. But there can be law without a lawgiver, history without a historian; there is biology without biologists, physics without physicists, creativity without creators, achievement without conscious achievers—and value without experiencing valuers.

A sentient valuer is not necessary for value. Another way is for there to be a value-generating system able to generate value, such as a plant or a genome. If you like, that is another meaning of value-er; any x is a valuer if x is value-able, able to produce values.

No, comes the protest, naturalizing value has to be kept close in to our human embodiment. We simply do not have the cognitive capacities to know all this about other valuers out there. Metaphysics, epistemology, and ethics can and ought to be naturalized, but that does not mean there are any metaphysicians, epistemologists, or ethicists among the dragonflies, the bacteria, or the plants; we only mean that when humans do these activities, they do so using their naturally evolved capacities. Similarly with axiology, which can and ought to be naturalized, that is interpreted in terms of our naturally evolved capacities. But there are no philosophical axiologists in wild nature, any more than there are metaphysicians, epistemologists, or ethicists.

Maybe we can extend feelings into the higher animals, because evolution does teach their kinship with us. So vertebragenic axiology is a possibility. We can and ought to defer to animals who are close enough kin to us to share some of our cognitive and perceptual abilities. Beyond that, value is over.

Social philosophers are likely to be quite sure about this, and quite uncomfortable with the idea of natural values apart from human persons in their society. Milton Rokeach defines a value this way: "I consider a value to be a type of belief, centrally located within one's belief system, about how one ought or ought not to behave, or about some end-state of existence worth or not worth obtaining." These belief systems are culturally constructed and transmitted; they are personally endorsed, enjoyed, and critiqued. Values have to be thought about, chosen from among options, persistently held, and to satisfy felt preferences (Rokeach, 1968, p. 124). If so, ipso facto, there are none in mere organisms which have no such capacities. So much for the dragonflies and their wings, sand dollars, plants with their leaf stomata, bacteria with their clocks, and those genomes getting ready for evolution.

4. ORGANISMS AND THEIR BIOCENTRIC VALUES

Maybe the problem is that we have let ourselves get imprisoned in our own felt experiences. There is an epistemological problem, but look at it another way. We do have blinders on, psychological and philosophical blinders, that leave us unable to detect anything but experientially based valuers and their felt values. So we are unable to accept a biologically based value account that is otherwise staring us in the face. Let's take another look at organisms and their biocentric values, focusing on plants, to make sure we are not hoping for minimal neural experience.

A plant is not an experiencing subject, but neither is it an inanimate object, like a stone. Nor is it a geomorphological process, like a river. Plants are quite alive. Plants, like all other organisms, are self-actualizing. Plants are unified entities of the botanical though not of the zoological kind; that is, they are not unitary organisms highly integrated with centered neural control, but they are modular organisms, with a meristem that can repeatedly and indefinitely produce new vegetative modules, additional stem nodes, and leaves when there is available space and resources, as well as new reproductive modules, fruits, and seeds.

Plants repair injuries and move water, nutrients, and photosynthate from cell to cell;

they store sugars; they make tannin and other toxins and regulate their levels in defense against grazers; they make nectars and emit pheromones to influence the behavior of pollinating insects and the responses of other plants; they emit alle-lopathic agents to suppress invaders; they make thorns, trap insects, and so on. They can reject genetically incompatible grafts. They have engineered those remarkable stomata.

A plant is a spontaneous, self-maintaining system, sustaining and reproducing itself, executing its program, making a way through the world, checking against performance by means of responsive capacities with which to measure success. Something more than merely physical causes, even when less than sentience, is operating within every organism. There is *information* superintending the causes; without it the organism would collapse into a sand heap. The information is used to preserve the plant identity. This information is recorded in the genes, and such information, unlike matter and energy, can be created and destroyed. That is what worries environmentalists about extinction, for example. In such information lies the secret of life.

Values are like color, the traditionalists say. Both arise in interaction. Trees are no more valuable than they are green on their own. This account seems plausible if one is asking about certain kinds of values, such as the fall colors we enjoy. But consider rather the information that makes photosynthesis possible. Photosynthesis is rather more objective than greenness. What is good for a tree (nitrogen, carbon dioxide, water) is observer-independent. But is not the good of the tree (whether it is injured or healthy) equally observer-independent? The tree's coping based on DNA coding is quite objective (even if, no doubt, there is some observer construction in the theories and instruments by which all this is known). The sequoia tree has, after all, been there two thousand years, whether or not any green-experiencing humans were around. *Sequoia sempervirens,* the species line, has been around several million years, with each of its individual sequoia trees defending a good of their kind.

The tree is value-able ("able-to-value") itself. If we cannot say this, then we will have to ask, as an open question, "Well, the tree has a good of its own, but is there anything of value to it?" "This tree was injured when the elk rubbed its velvet off its antlers, and the tannin secreted there is killing the invading bacteria. But is this valuable to the tree?" Botanists say that the tree is irritable in the biological sense; it responds with the repair of injury. Such capacities can be "vital." These are observations of value in nature with just as much certainty as they are biological facts; that is what they are: facts about value relationships in nature.

We are really quite certain that organisms use their resources, and one is overinstructed in philosophy who denies that such resources are of value to organisms instrumentally. But then, why is the tree not defending its own life just as much fact of the matter as its use of nitrogen and photosynthesis to do so?

But nothing "matters" to a tree; a plant is without minimally sentient awareness—so Callicott, Norton, and Singer protest. By contrast, things do matter to a vertebrate. True, things do not matter *to* trees; still, a great deal matters *for* them. We ask, of a failing tree, What's the matter *with* that tree? If it is lacking sunshine and soil nutrients, and we arrange for these, we say, The tree is benefiting from them; and *benefit* is—everywhere else we encounter it—a value word. Every organism has a *good-of-its-kind*; it defends its own kind as a *good kind*. In this sense, the genome is a set of conservation molecules. To say that the plant has a good of its own seems the plain fact of the matter. The flexible wings did "matter" to the Carboniferous dragonflies. Being prepared for rapid evolution under stress does "matter" to species lines. Biologists regularly speak of the "selective value" or "adaptive value" of genetic variations (Ayala, 1982, p. 88; Tamarin, 1996, p. 558). Plant activities have "survival value," such as the seeds they disperse or the thorns they make.

Natural selection picks out whatever traits an organism has that are valuable to it, relative to its survival. When natural selection has been at work gathering these traits into an organism, that organism is able to value on the basis of those traits. It is a valuing organism, even if the organism is not a sentient valuer, much less a vertebrate, much less a human evaluator. And those traits, though picked out by natural selection, are innate in the organism. It is difficult to dissociate the idea of value from natural selection.

Any sentigenic, psychogenic, vertebragenic, or anthropogenic theory of value has got to argue away all such natural selection as not dealing with "real" value at all, but mere function. Those arguments are, in the end, more likely to be stipulations than real arguments. If you stipulate that valuing must be felt valuing, that there must be some subject of a life, then trees are not able to value, their leaves and thorns are no good to them, and that is so by your definition. But we wish to examine whether that definition, faced with the facts of biology, is plausible. The sentientist definition covers correctly but narrowly certain kinds of higher animal valuing—namely, that done by humans and their vertebrate relatives—and omits all the rest.

5. SMART GENES, INTELLIGENT SPECIES

These organisms are found in species lines, and next we must evaluate species lines and the genetic creativity that makes speciation possible. As noticed earlier, contemporary geneticists are insisting that thinking of this process as being entirely "blind" misperceives it.[2] Genes have substantial solution-generating capacities. Though not deliberated in the conscious sense, the process is cognitive, somewhat like computers, which, likewise witout felt experience, can run problem-solving programs. For these genes in organisms, much is vital, as nothing is in a computer. The genome, getting ready to evolve, has a vast array of sophisticated enzymes to cut, splice, digest, rearrange, mutate, reiterate, edit, correct, translocate, invert, and truncate particular gene sequences. There is much redundancy (multiple and variant copies of a gene in multigene families) that shields the species from accidental loss of a beneficial gene, provides flexibility—both overlapping backup and unique detail—on which these enzymes can work.

John H. Campbell, a molecular geneticist, writes, "Cells are richly provided with special enzymes to tamper with DNA structure," enzymes that biologists are extracting and using

for genetic engineering. But this "engineering" is already going on in spontaneous nature:

> Gene-processing enzymes also engineer comparable changes in genes in vivo....We have discovered enzymes and enzyme pathways for almost every conceivable change in the structure of genes. The scope for self-engineering of multigene families seems to be limited only by the ingenuity of control systems for regulating these pathways. (1983, pp. 408–409)

These pathways may have "governors" that are "extraordinarily sophisticated." "Self-governed genes are 'smart' machines in the current vernacular sense. Smart genes suggest smart cells and smart evolution. It is the promise of radically new genetic and evolutionary principles that are motivating today's study..." (1983, pp. 410, 414).

In a study of whether species as historical lines can be considered "intelligent," Jonathan Schull concludes:

> Plant and animal species are information-processing entities of such complexity, integration, and adaptive competence that it may be scientifically fruitful to consider them intelligent....Plant and animal species process information via multiple nested levels of variation and selection in a manner that is surprisingly similar to what must go on in intelligent animals. As biological entities, and as processors of information, plant and animal species are no less complicated than, say, monkeys. Their adaptive achievements (the brilliant design and exquisite production of biological organisms) are no less impressive, and certainly rival those of the animal and electronic systems to which the term "intelligence" is routinely (and perhaps validly) applied today. (1990, p. 63)

Analogies with artificial intelligence in computers are particularly striking. Such cognitive processing is not conscious, but that does not mean it is not intelligent, where there are clever means of problem solving in a phyletic lineage. Schull continues:

> Gene pools in evolving populations acquire, store, transmit, transform, and use vast amounts of fitness-relative information....The information-processing capacities of these massively parallel distributed processing systems surpasses that of even the most sophisticated man-made

systems. . . . It seems likely that an evolving species is a better simulation of "real" intelligence than even the best computer program likely to be produced by cognitive scientists for many years. (1990, pp. 64, 74)

The result, according to David S. Thaler, is "the evolution of genetic intelligence" (1994). So it seems that if we recognize that there are smart computers, we must also recognize that there are even smarter genes. Smarter, and more vital.

Leslie E. Orgel, summarizing the origin of life on Earth, says "Life emerged only after self-reproducing molecules appeared. . . . Such molecules yielded a biology based on ribonucleic acids. The RNA system then invented proteins. As the RNA system evolved, proteins became the main workers in cells, and DNA became the prime repository of genetic information." "The emergence of catalytic RNA was a crucial early step" (1994, p. 4). That is interesting, because here is "a crucial early step" among Callicott's mere "impassive phenomena."

Not only does such problem solving take place early on, and continuously thereafter, but the genes, over the millennia, get better at it. Past achievements are recapitulated in the present, with variations; and these results get tested today and then folded into the future. Christopher Wills concludes,

There is an accumulated wisdom of the genes that actually makes them better at evolving (and sometimes makes them better at not evolving) than were the genes of our distant ancestors. . . . This wisdom consists both of the ways that genes have become organized in the course of evolution and the ways in which the factors that change the genes have actually become better at their task. (1989, pp. 6–8)

At least we seem to be getting better and better impassive phenomena.

Donald J. Cram, accepting the Nobel prize for his work deciphering how complex and unique biological molecules recognize each other and interlock, concludes: "Few scientists acquainted with the chemistry of biological systems at the molecular level can avoid being inspired. Evolution has produced chemical compounds that are exquisitely organized to accomplish the most complicated and delicate of tasks." Organic chemists can hardly "dream of designing and synthesizing" such "marvels" (1988, p. 760). Marvels they may be, but not until we get there, Norton must say, and experience their "transformative value."

Talk of a genetic "strategy" has become commonplace among biologists, not thereby implying consciousness, but strongly suggesting a problem-solving skill. A marine snail has evolved a "strategy for rapid immobilization of prey" and can "capture prey with remarkable efficiency and speed" (Teriau et al., 1998). Well, maybe "strategy" is a metaphor, but what the facts that underlie the metaphor still force is the question whether these snails "know how" to capture the fish they catch. And this is only one instance of information pervasively present as needed for an organism's competence in its ecological niche. All biology is cybernetic; the information storage in DNA, the know-how for life, is the principal difference between biology and chemistry or physics.

Is a philosopher still going to insist: Well, all this inventiveness, strategy, remarkable efficiency, wisdom of the genes, exquisite organization to accomplish delicate tasks, and crucial discoveries in evolution to the contrary, there is nothing of value here? Maybe it is time to face up to a crisis?

6. AN EPISTEMIC CRISIS? AN AXIOLOGICAL CRISIS?

The cell biologists, we were saying, have been finding something "wonderful" in genome strategies, but it did seem that this was only "wonderful" when cell biologists got there to wonder about it. Or at least that nothing was "astounding" until a human being came around to be astounded. We do not think that the genomes have a sense of wonder or are astounded. Still, the biological achievements are there long before we get let in on them. Facing up to these facts, which are quite as certain as that we humans are valuers in the world, it can seem "astounding" arrogance to say that, in our ignorance of these events, before we arrived there was nothing of value there.

No, my critics will reply. Rolston has not yet faced up to his epistemological naiveté; he persists in his ontological realism, unaware of how contemporary philosophy has made any scientific knowing of any objective nature out there impossible, much less any realism about natural values. Rolston needs to get his Cartesian epistemology and metaphysics naturalized. He will have to realize how scientists are exporting human experiences and overlaying nature with them when they set up these frameworks of understanding. We need to recognize the metaphors we are projecting onto nature—not so much to strip them all away and see nature without metaphor, as to realize that all of our knowing of nature is metaphorical. That will take care of his plant "dilemmas," of things that "matter" to plants, of genome "engineering," and dragonfly "strategies." Whatever values Rolston is finding in nature are being projected there by these metaphors. He is not naturalizing values at all.

I agree that sometimes we do need to strip off the metaphors that scientists may use. When the comet Shoemaker-Levy crashed into Jupiter in July 1994, astronomers watched with interest; some of them even got ecstatic about the size of the explosive impact. Was this event of any value, or disvalue? Let us grant that nothing matters to Jupiter, nothing matters on Jupiter. The swirls in the planetary winds were disrupted by this outside comet crashing in, but the fierce winds soon mixed up the debris and the flow patterns, after about a month, returned to their pre-impact formations, the effect of the gigantic impact fading. A headline in *Science* put it this way: "A Giant Licks Its Wounds" (Kerr, 1994). John Horgan in *Scientific American* noted that scientists were interested in watching "how bruises left by Shoemaker-Levy disperse" (Horgan, 1994). "Wounds" and "bruises" are only journalistic metaphor, even in science journals, when applied to Jupiter. The excited scientists were observing impassive phenomena.

But what do we say when a wolf, injured in a territorial fight, licks its wounds and limps from a bruised leg? Is that still journalistic metaphor? Or that the elk, rubbing the velvet off its antlers, has "bruised" the tree, and that the tannin is secreted to protect this "injury"? Hard-nosed

functionalists can no doubt strip away ideas such as "getting ready," "being prepared," also words such as "engineer" and "information," if such words require conscious deliberation. But even after this stripping down, there remains something here that demands value language. Maybe you can sanitize the language if you have strong enough detergent. But you well may be washing out something important that is going on. In a Darwinian world, where survival is ever at stake, the question of value has a way of dirtying up the cleanest humanistic value theory.

We philosophers may protest that we know how to use words with precision, and scientists can be rather careless with them. That is what has dirtied up otherwise perfectly good value theory. Though unsophisticated biologists have used "value" regarding plants, careful analysis will put that kind of "value" in scare quotes. This so-called value is not a value, really, not one of interest to philosophers because it is not a value with interest in itself. Even if we found such interest-taking value, as we do in the higher animals, we humans would still have to evaluate any such animal values before we knew whether any "real" values were present.

True, the female wolf takes an interest in the deer she slays and the pups she feeds. So one can say, biologically speaking, that she values the deer and her pups. But we do not yet know whether there is any "philosophical" value here. There could in fact be disvalue—a big bad killer wolf, rearing more such killers in the world. Jack the Ripper was a good killer, good of his kind, but a very bad person in the world. We humans have to evaluate what is going on out there, before we can say whether there is any positive value there.

Otherwise we will commit the naturalistic fallacy. We find what biologically *is* in nature and conclude that something valuable is there, something which we may say we *ought* to protect. Considered as normative organismic systems organisms might have goods of their kind and still they might be bad kinds taken for what they are in themselves, or considered in the roles they play. There is a radical gap between finding that these organisms and species have goods of their kinds and in concluding, in a philosophical worldview, that these are good kinds. The gap is between finding animals and plants that have values defended on their own, a biological description, and finding that these animals and plants have intrinsic value worthy of philosophical consideration, which ought to be preserved. That latter step requires philosophical analysis past any biological description.

Man is the measure of things, said Protagoras. Humans are the measurers, the valuers of things, even when we measure what they are in themselves. So humans are the only evaluators who can reflect about what is going on at this global scale, who can deliberate about what they ought to do conserving it. When humans do this, they must set up the scales; and humans are the measurers of things. Animals, organisms, species, ecosystems, Earth cannot teach us how to do this evaluating. Perhaps not, but still they can and do display what it is that is to be evaluated. The axiological scales we construct do not constitute the value any more than the scientific scales we erect create what we thereby measure.

What are we evaluating? Among much else, we are appraising organisms in species lines with their adaptive fits. In this evaluation, we do consider our options, and adopt attitudes toward nature with conscious reflection (such as whether we choose and why to save endangered species) that may result in the values we humans choose. But in the biological world which we have under consideration, such capacities drop out. The plants and animals are not so capable. But that does not mean that value disappears, only that it shifts to the biological level.

An organism cannot survive without situated environmental fitness. There organisms do mostly unconsciously (and sometimes consciously) defend their lives and their kinds. Might they be bad kinds? The cautious philosophical critic will say that, even though an organism evolves to have a situated environmental fitness, not all such situations are necessarily good arrangements; some can be clumsy or bad. They could involve bad organisms in bad evolutionary patterns—perhaps those efficient and venomous snails, destroying those fish, or dragonflies so efficient in flight that they devastate their prey and upset previously stable ecosystems. Perhaps, at times. But with rare exceptions, organisms are well adapted to the niches they fill, and remain so as the co-evolutionary process goes on. By natural selection their ecosystemic roles must mesh with the kinds of goods to which they are genetically programmed. At least we ought to put the burden of proof on a human evaluator to say why any natural kind is a bad kind and ought not to call forth admiring respect.

The world is a field of the contest of values. We can hardly deny that, even if we suppose that those are bad snails killing those fish, or that pest insects come along, eat plant leaves, and capture the stored energy that plants would have otherwise used to preserve their own good kinds. When we recognize how the ecosystem is a perpetual contest of goods in dialectic and exchange, it will become difficult to say that all or even any of the organisms in it are bad kinds, ill-situated in their niches. The misfits are extinct, or soon will be. Rather it seems that many of them, maybe even all of them, will have to be respected for the skills and achievements by which they survive over the millennia. At least we will have to recognize the possibility of intrinsic value in nature, and it will seem arrogant to retreat into a human-centered environmental ethics. This is true no matter how much the anti-foundationalists and the anti-realists protest that we humans cannot know enough about what these animals and plants are like in themselves to escape our own blinders.

Does it not rather seem that when we are describing what benefits the dragonflies or the snails, the plants with their leaf stomata, or the bacteria with their clocks, such value is pretty much fact of the matter. If we refuse to recognize such values as objectively there, have we committed some fallacy? Rather, the danger is the other way round. We commit the subjectivist fallacy if we think all values lie in subjective experience, and, worse still, the anthropocentrist fallacy if we think all values lie in human options and preferences. These plants and animals do not make man the measure of things at all.

Humans are not so much lighting up value in a merely potentially valuable world, as they are psychologically joining ongoing planetary natural history in which there is value wherever there is positive creativity. While such creativity can be present in subjects with their interests and preferences, it can also be present objectively in living organisms with their lives defended, and in species that defend an identity over time, and in systems that are self-organizing and that project storied achievements. The valuing human subject in an otherwise valueless world is an insufficient premise for the experienced conclusions of those who value natural history.

Conversion to a biological and geological view seems truer to world experience and more logically compelling. This too is a perspective, but ecologically better informed; we know our place on a home planet, which is not only our home but that for five or ten million other species. From this more objective viewpoint, there is something subjective, something philosophically naive, and even something hazardous in a time of ecological crisis, about living in a reference frame where one species takes itself as absolute and values every thing else in nature relative to its potential to produce value for itself.

NOTES

1. Callicott recognized this possibility from the start, despite his insistence that humans project all the value present in nature (1989, p. 26).

2. See further analysis and sources in Rolston, 1999, pp. 23–37.

REFERENCES

Abbas, Abul K., Andrew H. Lichtman, and Jordan S. Pober. 1991. *Cellular and Molecular Immunology*. Philadelphia: W. B. Saunders.

Ayala, Francisco J. 1982. *Population and Evolutionary Genetics: A Primer*. Menlo Park, CA: Benjamin/Cummings.

Barinaga, Marcia. 1998. "New Timepiece Has a Familiar Ring," *Science* 281 (4 September): 1429–1431.

Callicott, J. Baird. 1984. "Non-anthropocentric Value Theory and Environmental Ethics," *American Philosophical Quarterly* 21:299–309.

———1989. *In Defense of the Land Ethic*. Albany, NY: State University of New York Press.

——— 1992. "Rolston on Intrinsic Value: A Deconstruction," *Environmental Ethics* 14:129–143.

Campbell, John H. 1983. "Evolving Concepts of Multigene Families," *Isozymes: Current Topics in Biological and Medical Research, Volume 10: Genetics and Evolution*, 401–417.

Cram, Donald J. 1988. "The Design of Molecular Hosts, Guests, and Their Complexes," *Science* 240 (6 May): 760–767.

Grill, Erwin, and Hubert Ziegler. 1998. "A Plant's Dilemma," *Science* 282 (9 October):252–254.

Horgan, John. 1994. "By Jove!" *Scientific American* 271 (no. 4, October):16–20.

Kerr, Richard A. 1994. "A Giant Licks Its Wounds," *Science* 266 (7 October): 31.

Norton, Bryan G. 1987. *Why Preserve Natural Variety?* Princeton, NJ: Princeton University Press.

——— 1991. *Toward Unity Among Environmentalists*. New York: Oxford University Press.

——— 1992. "Epistemology and Environmental Values," *The Monist* 75:208–226.

Orgel, Leslie E. 1994. "The Origin of Life on the Earth," *Scientific American* 271 (no. 4, October): 76–83 and abstract p. 4.

Pennisi, Elizabeth. 1998. "How the Genome Readies Itself for Evolution," *Science* 281 (21 August): 1131–1134.

Rokeach, Milton. 1968. *Beliefs, Attitudes, and Values*. San Francisco: Jossey-Bass.

Rolston, Holmes, III. 1999. *Genes, Genesis, and God*. New York: Cambridge University Press.

Schull, Jonathan. 1990. "Are Species Intelligent?" *Behavioral and Brain Sciences* 13:63–75.

Singer, Peter. 1990. *Animal Liberation*, 2nd ed. New York: New York Review Book.

Tamarin, Robert H. 1996. *Principles of Genetics*, 5th ed. Dubuque, IA: William C. Brown.

Teriau, Heinrich, et al. 1998. "Strategy for Rapid Immobilization of Prey by a Fish-hunting Marine Snail," *Nature* 381 (9 May): 148–151.

Thaler, David S. 1994. "The Evolution of Genetic Intelligence," *Science* 264 (8 April):224–225.

Tizard, Ian R. 1992. *Immunology: An Introduction*, 3rd ed. Fort Worth, TX: Saunders College Publishing.

Vogel, Gretchen. 1998. "Insect Wings Point to Early Sophistication," *Science* 282 (23 October):599–601.

Wills, Christopher. 1989. *The Wisdom of the Genes: New Pathways in Evolution.* New York: Basic Books.

Wootton, R. J., J. Kuikalová, D. J. S. Newman, and J. Muzón. 1998. "Smart Engineering in the Mid-Carboniferous: How Well Could Palaeozoic Dragonflies Fly?" *Science* 282 (23 October): 749–751.

✏ STUDY QUESTIONS

1. What does Rolston mean by *naturalizing value?* How does he make a case for this thesis?
2. What is Rolston's objection to subjectivism in values, the idea that all values arise by sentient beings' valuing objects? In another place he calls this the refrigerator-light theory of values. The refrigerator light does not come on until someone opens the door. Similarly, the subjectivist says that values only come into existence when humans or conscious valuers value states of affairs.
3. Discuss the arguments for and against the thesis that nature has objective value—that is, it has value whether or not conscious beings value nature.

14   Comments on Holmes Rolston's "Naturalizing Values"

NED HETTINGER

Ned Hettinger is professor of philosophy at the College of Charleston and the author of several works in environmental ethics.

Holmes Rolston has been forcefully defending the value of nature for over twenty-five years. He does so again here today with his characteristic mix of deep biological and philosophical insight. It is a pleasure to help us think about the ideas and arguments of this most able philosophical defender of nature.

Professor Rolston has argued that much natural value is nonanthropocentric; that is, that nature is valuable independently of its use to humans. Humans valuing nature as an end and not simply as a means is an example of such nonanthropocentric value. For instance, people who value the existence of the Arctic National Wildlife Refuge—even though they have no intentions of ever visiting it—value the Refuge for reasons other than its utility to them. Such noninstrumental valuing of nature, though not anthropocentric, is nonetheless *anthropogenic.* Rolston argues that much natural value is also not generated by humans and that it is not dependent on humans in any way. Nature's usefulness to nonhuman sentient animals clearly illustrates these human-independent values. Deer are instrumentally valuable to wolves, whether or not these animals benefit humans or are noninstrumentally valued by them.

Sentient animals may also demonstrate another of Rolston's claims: that there is nonanthropogenic *intrinsic value* in nature. I don't know whether a mother wolf can intrinsically value her young as Rolston suggests; wolves may not have the cognitive equipment such judgments of value about others may require. Nevertheless, wolves would seem to value the experience of pleasure in their lives, immediately and for itself. The presence of such intrinsic

"A Response to Holmes Rolston, III," © 1998 Ned Hettinger, was first delivered at the North American Society for Social Philosophy in Washington, DC, in December 1998, and it appeared in a previous edition of this work for the first time. It is reprinted by permission of the author.

valuing in nonhuman nature has nothing to do with human utility or valuing.

Rolston's defense of natural value independent of humans goes well beyond the existence of instrumental value for *sentient* animals or their possible intrinsic valuings. Rolston argues that instrumental value permeates the biological world. The dragonfly's wings are useful to it, and sunlight, carbon dioxide, and water are instrumentally valuable for plants, even though these organisms do not take a conscious interest in what benefits them. I think Rolston is right that only a philosopher in the grip of a theory would deny that there are instrumental goods for all living beings, including insentient ones. Rolston suggests that biological descriptions about what is good for organisms are factual statements about values in the natural world. Here, he suggests, there is no gap between facts and values. Biological description alone, however, will not allow us to conclude that water is good for plants in a way that oil is not also good for machines. As Rolston knows, we need an argument to show that what is good for machines is only good because machines are useful to humans, while living beings have goods of their own that do not require such further contributory reference.

Rolston also argues that human-independent natural value exists in species and ecosystems, because they too are the beneficiaries of instrumental value. Particular genes are good or bad for species and certain species are beneficial or destructive for self-organizing natural systems. Rolston avoids the potentially problematic position that value is everywhere in nature, theorizing instead that value is present wherever there is positive creativity. Thus, nothing matters on Jupiter; which is to say, I think, that there is no value there, because there is not enough "positive creativity" in the processes of that planet. Rolston has said similar things about the lack of value of clouds and dust devils here on Earth. But he has also suggested that some *abiotic* features of the earth are remarkable, valuable achievements that ought to call forth our admiring respect. Work remains in explaining why, for example, building roads to the top of fourteen-thousand-foot mountains destroys value in these geological marvels, while nothing humans could do to Jupiter would destroy any value there.

Rolston is known for his defense of "objective" value in nature, and we again get such a defense today. By "objective value," I mean value that is not dependent on a valuing subject. Rolston rejects the psychological account of value that allows value only where there are mental states. Value on this subjectivist view is conscious valuing. Rolston points out that instrumental goods for insentient organisms are clear examples of nonpsychological, objective values in nature. Insentient organisms are not subjects; they have no experiential life and thus do not consciously value anything; yet much is good or bad for them. Such biological goods strongly support objectivism about value.

Interestingly, when Rolston finds value in nature, he tends to posit some valuing of that value. He suggests, for example, that because water is good for trees, trees value water, though they obviously do not do so consciously or psychologically. Thus, Rolston rejects that value requires a *conscious* valuer, but he clings to the idea that value requires a valuer of some sort. I suggest he drop this second connection as well. Once we reject a mental state theory of value, we'd do better to drop the assumed necessary connection between value and valuing entirely. Claiming that insentient organisms are valuing entities stretches our concept of valuing in a way that is not helpful, nor needed. That something is good for a being does not imply that the being values it. A suicidal person may not value food, but the food is nonetheless good for her. A vegetarian-fed cat may have a vitamin deficiency but not value the supplements she needs. Why think a tree needs to value water in order for water to be good for it?

Rolston argues for both objective instrumental and objective intrinsic value in nature. The pleasures of sentient animals mentioned above demonstrate only *subjective* intrinsic value or intrinsic *valuing* in nature, not objective intrinsic value. On one standard view of the relation between instrumental and intrinsic values, we can infer the existence of intrinsic goods from the instrumental goods of insentient organisms. If instrumental goods are good only insofar as they are a means to some other good, and if we rule out an endless series or loop of instrumental values (as some pragmatists would allow), then objective instrumental goods for insentient organisms entail the existence of objective intrinsic goods. If water is instrumentally good for trees without further contributory reference, then the flourishing of trees must be good-in-itself.

The question remains, however, whether we humans should value such goods and additionally whether we have obligations to morally consider them. That some being has a good of its own or that some entity is flourishing does not automatically mean we should value that good or flourishing. That bureaucracies are flourishing does not require us to approve of this situation, and, as Rolston suggests, the happiness of Jack the Ripper is not a good we ought to value. I agree with Rolston, however, that the burden is very much on those who suggest that the goods of natural organisms, species, and ecosystems are *bad* goods of this sort. Unless there is some consideration to the contrary, that something is flourishing or has a good of its own presents a prima facie reason for valuing it. There remains, however, the further question about our obligation to promote some acknowledged good. Some theories of right action do not connect obligation with promotion of the good. Some account is needed as to why we humans ought to preserve, protect, and restore these goods in nonhuman nature. Here and elsewhere, Rolston's compelling descriptions of the remarkable characteristics of natural organisms and systems and the story he tells about humans' place in nature goes a long way to providing such an account.

One of the most intuitively powerful arguments Rolston presents for nonanthropogenic value in nature is that it is arrogant to think that for hundreds of millions of years flourishing nature on Earth was actually valueless and then became valuable when humans arrived to bestow value on it. If all value depends on conscious human valuing, Rolston suggests we would not be able to say that the earth in the age of the early dragonflies was of any *actual* value. And this is something that most of us want to say. However, those who think all value is a function of valuing subjects argue that they can say this. Even if humans are the source of

all value that does not preclude humans from assigning value to a world where they do not exist. Subjectivists argue that because humans are here now and intrinsically value those earlier epochs, we can truthfully say that the world of the dragonflies was valuable back then. There is no requirement that the valued thing be contemporaneous with the valuer.

Still, a subjectivist's account of value might seem committed to the view that a world in which valuers never exist is one in which the flourishing earth is *never* valued and thus lacks actual value. To use Rolston's analogy, the refrigerator door in such a world will never be opened, and thus the light of value will never shine on the flourishing earth in that world. However, an ideal observer version of subjectivism about value seems able to handle this problem. If what is of value is what ideal observers would value, and if we assume that such ideal valuers would find the flourishing nonhuman earth valuable, then the actual value of the earth is guaranteed even if humans or other real valuers never arrive on the scene. On this version of subjectivism, the possibility of such idealized valuers is sufficient to actualize value. Thus, I think a version of subjectivism can avoid this problem Rolston has identified.

Finally, I'd like to consider Rolston's suggestion that there is "something hazardous in a time of ecological crisis" about theories of natural value that do no find values in nature but rather in the human response to nature. Is it important for environmental policy that our theory of nature's value be nonanthropocentric and nonanthropogenic? Although anthropocentric values are of crucial importance in environmental policy, I believe it is dangerous to limit our defense of nature to arguments based on its usefulness to us. This is especially true if what one wants to defend is a wild, autonomous nature. Humans often find a technologically enhanced and controlled nature of most use to them.

I am much less confident that it makes a pragmatic difference whether we view nature's noninstrumental value as objective or as the result of human intrinsic valuing. Is our defense of nature more powerful, compelling, and effective if nature is seen to have intrinsic value on its own, rather than having intrinsic value bestowed on it by humans who value it for its own sake? One worry is that a subjectivist account of nature's value would be open to the charge that we are foisting an idiosyncratic value onto those who don't appreciate nature in this way. But wouldn't the objectivist defender of nature be open to a similar charge that she wants us to act to protect values whose existence others don't acknowledge? I do think that a certain conception of the objective value of nature would allow for a response to a liberal critic of environmental policies that is not available to subjectivists. For the liberal, liberty-limiting laws are only justifiable when they prevent harm to others or unjust treatment of them. If we conceive of nature as having its own good that we can harm and as a valuable other that we must treat justly, then laws and policies that protect nature will pass the liberal's test for justifiable constraints on human liberty. A subjectivist who claims that we ought to value nature for its own sake will not be able to make the case that those whose actions disregard such values are harming nonhuman others, treating them unjustly, and thus that they may be justifiably constrained from such acts by society.

STUDY QUESTIONS

1. Does Hettinger completely agree with Rolston on the objective value of nature? If not, where does he differ?
2. How, according to Hettinger, could a subjectivist respond to Rolston's theory? A subjectivist on values holds that without conscious valuers, no values exist.
3. What is the difference between value that is anthropocentric and value that is anthropogenic?

Give an example of an anthropogenic value that is not anthropocentric.
4. Explain why Hettinger thinks that a certain account of nature's value as objective can provide a response to a liberal critic of environmental laws that is not possible on a subjectivist account of nature's value. Do you think he is right?

15   Nature

JOHN STUART MILL

John Stuart Mill (1806–1873), one of the most important British philosophers of the nineteenth century, was born in London and educated by his father, James Mill, a first-rate philosopher in his own right, learning Greek at the age of three and Latin at the age of eight. By the time he was fourteen he had received a thorough classic education at home. He began work as a clerk for the East India Company at the age of seventeen and eventually became a director of the company. Influenced by the work of Jeremy Bentham (1748–1832), he embraced utilitarianism and ardently worked for social reform.

When he was twenty-five, Mill became close friends with Harriet Taylor, a married woman. Their mutual devotion and intimacy, though apparently Platonic, caused a scandal in a society where the only approved intimacies between the opposite sexes were familial, either as married couples or brother and sister. After Harriet's husband died, Mill married her in 1851. Harriet's ideas changed Mill's, and Mill regarded her as the most profound mind he had ever known. He claims that much of the credit for his work *On Liberty* (1859) goes to her. His arguments in *The Subjection of Women* (1861) show her influence.

From John Stuart Mill, *Three Essays on Religion*. New York: H. Holt, 1874.

Mill was a prolific writer. His *A System of Logic* (1848) is one of the most original works on inductive logic ever written. His *Utilitarianism* (1861) is the classic work on the topic.

Mill was elected to Parliament in 1865. A man with an independent and penetrating mind, he fought for woman's suffrage, the rights of blacks in Jamaica, Irish land reform, the retention of capital punishment, and weighted votes for the better informed over the less educated ("It is not useful, but hurtful, that the constitution of the country should declare ignorance to be entitled to as much political power as knowledge").

Our first selection is his essay "Nature" in which Mill first explains that the term *Nature* is ambiguous and used to mean three different things: (1) the aggregate of objects and processes in the universe; (2) that which is not artificial; and (3) that which ought to be the case, the ethical sense (what is sometimes referred to as "Natural Law"). Mill argues that this third sense is not a valid sense of the word at all. Mill then goes on to criticize those who would emulate Nature or see it as the proper model for moral action. He argues that given any crime that humans commit—murder, stealing, harming sentient beings—Nature commits it in far greater amounts and with impunity. As Tennyson was to write later,

> From scraped cliff and quarried stone
> She cries "A thousand types are gone:
> I care for nothing, all shall go....
>
> Who trusted God was love indeed
> And love Creation's final law—
> Tho[ugh] Nature, red in tooth and claw
> With ravine, shriek'd against his creed—

So we should not copy Nature or imitate her but correct and improve her.

Nature, Natural, and the group of words derived from them, or allied to them in etymology, have at all times filled a great place in the thoughts and taken a strong hold on the feelings of mankind. That they should have done so is not surprising, when we consider what the words, in their primitive and most obvious signification, represent; but it is unfortunate that a set of terms which play so great a part in moral and metaphysical speculation, should have acquired many meanings different from the primary one, yet sufficiently allied to it to admit of confusion. The words have thus become entangled in so many foreign associations, mostly of a very powerful and tenacious character, that they have come to excite, and to be the symbols of, feelings which their original meaning will by no means justify; and which have made them one of the most copious sources of false taste, false philosophy, false morality, and even bad law....

As the nature of any given thing is the aggregate of its powers and properties, so Nature in the abstract is the aggregate of the powers and properties of all things. Nature means the sum of all phenomena, together with the causes which produce them; including not only all that happens, but all that is capable of happening; the unused capabilities of causes being as much a part of the idea of Nature, as those which take effect. Since all phenomena which have been sufficiently examined are found to take place with regularity, each having certain fixed conditions, positive and negative, on the occurrence of which it invariably happens; mankind have been able to ascertain, either by direct observation or by reasoning processes grounded on it, the conditions of the occurrence of many phenomena; and the progress of science mainly consists in ascertaining those conditions. When discovered they can be expressed in general propositions, which are called laws of the particular phenomenon, and also, more generally, Laws of Nature. Thus, the truth that all material objects tend towards one another with a force directly as their masses and inversely as the square of their distance, is a law of Nature. The proposition that air and food are necessary to animal life, if it be as we have good reason to believe, true without exception, is also a law of nature, though the phenomenon of which it is the law is special, and not, like gravitation, universal.

Nature, then, in this its simplest acceptation, is a collective name for all facts, actual and possible: or (to speak more accurately) a name for the mode, partly known to us and partly unknown, in which all things take place. For the word suggests, not so much the multitudinous detail of the phenomena, as the conception which might be formed of their manner of existence as a mental whole, by a mind possessing a complete knowledge of them: to which conception it is the aim of science to raise itself, by successive steps of generalization from experience.

Such, then, is a correct definition of the word Nature. But this definition corresponds only to one of the senses of that ambiguous term. It is evidently inapplicable to some of the modes in which the word is familiarly employed. For example, it entirely conflicts with the common form of speech by which Nature is opposed to Art, and natural to artificial. For in the sense of the word Nature which has just been defined, and which is the true scientific sense, Art is as much Nature as anything else; and everything which is artificial is natural—Art has no independent powers of its own: Art is but the employment of the powers of Nature for an end. Phenomena produced by human agency, no less than those which as far as we are concerned are spontaneous, depend on the properties of the elementary forces, or of the elementary substances and their compounds. The united powers of the whole human race could not create a new property of matter in general, or of any one of its species. We can only take advantage for our purposes of the properties which we find. A ship floats by the same laws of specific gravity and equilibrium, as a tree uprooted by the wind and blown into the water. The corn which men raise for food, grows and produces its grain by the same laws of vegetation by which the wild rose and the mountain strawberry bring forth their flowers and fruit. A house stands and holds together by the natural properties, the weight and cohesion of the materials which compose it: a steam engine works by the natural expansive force of steam, exerting a pressure upon one part of a system of arrangements, which pressure, by the mechanical properties of the lever, is transferred from that to another part where it raises the weight or removes the obstacle brought into connexion with it. In these and all other artificial operations the office of man is, as has often been remarked, a very limited one; it consists in moving things into certain places. We move objects, and by doing this, bring some things into contact which were separate, or separate others which were in contact: and by this simple change of place, natural forces previously dormant are called into action, and produce the desired effect. Even the volition which designs, the intelligence which contrives, and the muscular force which executes these movements, are themselves powers of Nature.

It thus appears that we must recognize at least two principal meanings in the word Nature. In one sense, it means all the powers existing in either the outer or the inner world and everything which takes place by means of those powers. In another sense, it means, not everything which happens, but only what takes place without the agency, or without the voluntary and intentional agency, of man. This distinction is far from exhausting the ambiguities of the word; but it is the key to most of those on which important consequences depend.

Such, then, being the two principal senses of the word Nature; in which of these is it taken, or is it taken in either, when the word and its derivatives are used to convey ideas of commendation, approval, and even moral obligation?

It has conveyed such ideas in all ages. *Naturam sequi* was the fundamental principle of morals in many of the most admired schools of philosophy. Among the ancients, especially in the declining period of ancient intellect and thought, it was the test to which all ethical doctrines were brought. The Stoics and the Epicureans, however irreconcilable in the rest of their systems, agreed in holding themselves bound to prove that their respective maxims of conduct were the dictates of nature. Under their influence the Roman jurists, when attempting to systematize jurisprudence, placed in the front of their exposition a certain *Jus Naturale*, "quod natura," as Justinian declares in the Institutes, "omnia animalia docuit": and as the modern systematic writers not only on law but on moral philosophy, have generally taken the Roman jurists for their models, treatises on the so-called Law of Nature have abounded; and references to this Law as a supreme rule and ultimate standard have pervaded literature. The writers on International Law have done more than any others to give currency to this style of ethical speculation; inasmuch as having no positive law to write about, and yet being anxious to invest the most approved opinions respecting international morality with as much as they could of the authority of law, they endeavoured to find such an authority in Nature's imaginary code. The Christian theology during the period of its greatest ascendancy, opposed some, though not a complete, hindrance to the modes of thought which erected Nature into the criterion of morals, inasmuch as, according to the creed of most denominations of Christians (though assuredly not of Christ) man is by nature wicked. But this very doctrine, by the reaction which it provoked, has made the deistical moralists almost unanimous in proclaiming the divinity of Nature, and setting up its fancied dictates as an authoritative rule of action. A reference to that supposed standard is the predominant ingredient in the vein of thought and feeling which was opened by Rousseau, and which has infiltrated itself most widely into the modern mind, not excepting that portion of it which calls itself Christian. The doctrines of Christianity have in every age been largely accommodated to the philosophy which happened to be prevalent, and the Christianity of our day has borrowed a considerable part of its colour and flavour from sentimental deism. At the present time it cannot be said that Nature, or any other standard, is applied as it was wont to be, to deduce rules of action with juridical precision, and with an attempt to make its application co-extensive with all human agency. The people of this generation do not commonly apply principles with any such studious exactness, nor own such binding allegiance to any standard, but live in a kind of confusion of many standards; a condition not propitious to the formation of steady moral convictions, but convenient enough to those whose moral opinions sit lightly on them, since it gives them a much wider range of arguments for defending the doctrine of the

moment. But though perhaps no one could now be found who like the institutional writers of former times, adopts the so-called Law of Nature as the foundation of ethics, and endeavours consistently to reason from it, the word and its cognates must still be counted among those which carry great weight in moral argumentation. That any mode of thinking, feeling, or acting is "according to nature" is usually accepted as a strong argument for its goodness. If it can be said with any plausibility that "nature enjoins" anything, the propriety of obeying the injunction is by most people considered to be made out: and conversely, the imputation of being contrary to nature, is thought to bar the door against any pretension on the part of the thing so designated, to be tolerated or excused; and the word unnatural has not ceased to be one of the most vituperative epithets in the language. . . .

Is it necessary to recognize in these forms of speech, another distinct meaning of the word Nature? Or can they be connected, by any rational bond of union, with either of the two meanings already treated of? At first it may seem that we have no option but to admit another ambiguity in the term. All inquiries are either into what is, or into what ought to be: science and history belonging to the first division, art, morals and politics to the second. But the two senses of the word Nature first pointed out, agree in referring only to what is. In the first meaning, Nature is a collective name for everything which is. In the second, it is a name for everything which is of itself, without voluntary human intervention. But the employment of the word Nature as a term of ethics seems to disclose a third meaning, in which Nature does not stand for what is, but for what ought to be; or for the rule or standard of what ought to be. A little consideration, however, will show that this is not a case of ambiguity; there is not here a third sense of the word. Those who set up Nature as a standard of action do not intend a merely verbal proposition; they do not mean that the standard, whatever it be, should be *called* Nature; they think they are giving some information as to what the standard of action really is. Those who say that we ought to act according to Nature do not mean the mere identical proposition that we ought to do what we ought to do. They think that the word Nature affords some external criterion of what we should do; and if they lay down as a rule for what ought to be, a word which in its proper signification denotes what is, they do so because they have a notion, either clearly or confusedly, that what is, constitutes the rule and standard of what ought to be.

The examination of this notion is the object of the present Essay. It is proposed to inquire into the truth of the doctrines which make Nature a test of right and wrong, good and evil, or which in any mode or degree attach merit or approval to following, imitating, or obeying Nature. To this inquiry the foregoing discussion respecting the meaning of terms, was an indispensable introduction. Language is as it were the atmosphere of philosophical investigation, which must be made transparent before anything can be seen through it in the true figure and position. In the present case it is necessary to guard against a further ambiguity, which though abundantly obvious, has sometimes misled even sagacious minds, and of which it is well to take distinct note before proceeding further. No word is more commonly associated with the word Nature, than Law; and this last word has distinctly two meanings, in one of which it denotes some definite portion of what is, in the other, of what ought to be. We speak of the law of gravitation, the three laws of motion, the law of definite proportions in chemical combination, the vital laws of organized beings. All these are portions of what is. We also speak of the criminal law, the civil law, the law of honour, the law of veracity, the law of justice; all of which are portions of what ought to be, or of somebody's suppositions, feelings, or commands respecting what ought to be. The first kind of laws, such as the laws of motion, and of gravitation, are neither more nor less than the observed uniformities in the occurrence of phenomena: partly uniformities of antecedence and sequence, partly of concomitance. These are what, in science, and even in ordinary parlance, are meant by laws of nature. Laws in the other sense are the laws of the land, the law of nations, or moral laws; among which, as already noticed, is dragged in, by jurists and publicists, something which they think proper to call the Law of Nature. Of the liability of these two meanings of the word to be confounded there can be no better example than the first chapter of Montesquieu; where he remarks, that the material world has its laws, the inferior animals have their laws, and man has his laws; and calls attention to the much greater strictness with which the first two sets of laws are observed, than the last; as if it were an inconsistency, and a paradox, that things always are what they are, but men not always what they ought to be.... The conception which the ethical use of the word Nature implies, of a close relation if not absolute identity between what is and what ought to be, certainly derives part of its hold on the mind from the custom of designating what is, by the expression "laws of nature," while the same word Law is also used, and even more familiarly and emphatically, to express what ought to be.

When it is asserted, or implied, that Nature, or the laws of Nature, should be conformed to, is the Nature which is meant, Nature in the first sense of the term, meaning all which is—the powers and properties of all things? But in this signification, there is no need of a recommendation to act according to nature, since it is what nobody can possibly help doing, and equally whether he acts well or ill. There is no mode of acting which is not conformable to Nature in this sense of the term, and all modes of acting are so in exactly the same degree. Every action is the exertion of some natural power, and its effects of all sorts are so many phenomena of nature, produced by the powers and properties of some of the objects of nature, in exact obedience to some law or laws of nature. When I voluntarily use my organs to take in food, the act, and its consequences, take place according to laws of nature: if instead of food I swallow poison, the case is exactly the same. To bid people conform to the laws of nature when they have no power but what the laws of nature give them—when it is a physical impossibility for them to do the smallest thing otherwise than through some law of nature, is an absurdity. The thing they need to be told is, what particular law of nature they should make use of in a particular case. When, for example, a person is crossing a river by a narrow bridge to which there is no parapet, he will do well to regulate his proceedings by the laws of equilibrium in moving bodies, instead of conforming only to the law of gravitation, and falling into the river.

Yet, idle as it is to exhort people to do what they cannot avoid doing, and absurd as it is to prescribe as a rule of right conduct what agrees exactly as well with wrong; nevertheless a rational rule of conduct *may* be constructed out of the relation which it ought to bear to the laws of nature in this widest acceptation of the term. Man necessarily obeys the laws of nature, or in other words the properties of things, but he does not necessarily *guide* himself by them. . . . Though we cannot emancipate ourselves from the laws of nature as a whole, we can escape from any particular law of nature, if we are able to withdraw ourselves from the circumstances in which it acts. Though we can do nothing except through laws of nature, we can use one law to counteract another. According to Bacon's maxim, we can obey nature in such a manner as to command it. Every alteration of circumstances alters more or less the laws of nature under which we act; and by every choice which we make either of ends or of means, we place ourselves to a greater or less extent under one set of laws of nature instead of another. If, therefore, the useless precept to follow nature were changed into a precept to study nature; to know and take heed of the properties of the things we have to deal with, so far as these properties are capable of forwarding or obstructing any given purpose; we should have arrived at the first principle of all intelligent action, or rather at the definition of intelligent action itself. And a confused notion of this true principle, is, I doubt not, in the minds of many of those who set up the unmeaning doctrine which superficially resembles it. They perceive that the essential difference between wise and foolish conduct consists in attending, or not attending, to the particular laws of nature on which some important result depends. And they think, that a person who attends to a law of nature in order to shape his conduct by it, may be said to obey it, while a person who practically disregards it, and acts as if no such law existed, may be said to disobey it: the

circumstance being overlooked, that what is thus called disobedience to a law of nature is obedience to some other or perhaps to the very law itself. For example, a person who goes into a powder magazine either not knowing, or carelessly omitting to think of, the explosive force of gunpowder, is likely to do some act which will cause him to be blown to atoms in obedience to the very law which he has disregarded.

. . . But the maxim of obedience to Nature, or conformity to Nature, is held up not as a simply prudential but as an ethical maxim; and by those who talk of *jus naturæ,* even as a law, fit to be administered by tribunals and enforced by sanctions. Right action, must mean something more and other than merely intelligent action: yet no precept beyond this last, can be connected with the word Nature in the wider and more philosophical of its acceptations. We must try it therefore in the other sense, that in which Nature stands distinguished from Art, and denotes, not the whole course of the phenomena which come under our observation, but only their spontaneous course. . . .

. . . If the artificial is not better than the natural, to what end are all the arts of life? To dig, to plough, to build, to wear clothes, are direct infringements of the injunction to follow nature.

Accordingly it would be said by every one, even of those most under the influence of the feelings which prompt the injunction, that to apply it to such cases as those just spoken of, would be to push it too far. Everybody professes to approve and admire many great triumphs of Art over Nature: the junction by bridges of shores which Nature had made separate, the draining of Nature's marshes, the excavation of her wells, the dragging to light of what she has buried at immense depths in the earth; the turning away of her thunderbolts by lightning rods, of her inundations by embankments, of her ocean by breakwaters. But to commend these and similar feats, is to acknowledge that the ways of Nature are to be conquered, not obeyed. . . .

. . . No one, indeed, asserts it to be the intention of the Creator that the spontaneous order of the creation should not be altered, or even that it should not be altered in any new way. But there still exists a vague notion that though it is very proper to control this or the other natural phenomenon, the general scheme of nature is a model for us to imitate: that with more or less liberty in details, we should on the whole be guided by the spirit and general conception of nature's own ways: that they are God's work, and as such perfect; that man cannot rival their unapproachable excellence, and can best show his skill and piety by attempting, in however imperfect a way, to reproduce their likeness; and that if not the whole, yet some particular parts of the spontaneous order of nature, selected according to the speaker's predilections, are in a peculiar sense, manifestations of the Creator's will....

If this notion of imitating the ways of Providence as manifested in Nature, is seldom expressed plainly and downrightly as a maxim of general application, it also is seldom directly contradicted. Those who find it on their path, prefer to turn the obstacle rather than to attack it, being often themselves not free from the feeling, and in any case afraid of incurring the charge of impiety by saying anything which might be held to disparage the works of the Creator's power. They therefore, for the most part, rather endeavour to show, that they have as much right to the religious argument as their opponents, and that if the course they recommend seems to conflict with some part of the ways of Providence, there is some other part with which it agrees better than what is contended for on the other side. In this mode of dealing with the great *à priori* fallacies, the progress of improvement clears away particular errors while the causes of errors are still left standing, and very little weakened by each conflict: yet by a long series of such partial victories precedents are accumulated, to which an appeal may be made against these powerful pre-possessions, and which afford a growing hope that the misplaced feeling, after having so often learnt to recede, may some day be compelled to an unconditional surrender. For however offensive the proposition may appear to many religious persons, they should be willing to look in the face the undeniable fact, that the order of nature, in so far as unmodified by man, is such as no being, whose attributes are justice and benevolence, would have made, with the intention that his rational creatures should follow it as an example. If made wholly by such a Being, and not partly by beings of very different qualities, it could only be as a designedly imperfect work, which man, in his limited sphere, is to exercise justice and benevolence in amending.

[MILL CONSIDERS THE THESIS THAT WE OUGHT TO IMITATE NATURE]

The best persons have always held it to be the essence of religion, that the paramount duty of man upon earth is to amend himself: but all except monkish quietists have annexed to this in their inmost minds (though seldom willing to enunciate the obligation with the same clearness) the additional religious duty of amending the world, and not solely the human part of it but the material; the order of physical nature.

In considering this subject it is necessary to divest ourselves of certain preconceptions which may justly be called natural prejudices, being grounded on feelings which, in themselves natural and inevitable, intrude into matters with which they ought to have no concern. One of these feelings is the astonishment, rising into awe, which is inspired (even independently of all religious sentiment) by any of the greater natural phenomena. A hurricane; a mountain precipice; the desert; the ocean, either agitated or at rest; the solar system, and the great cosmic forces which hold it together; the boundless firmament, and to an educated mind any single star; excite feelings which make all human enterprises and powers appear so insignificant, that to a mind thus occupied it seems insufferable presumption in so puny a creature as man to look critically on things so far above him, or dare to measure himself against the grandeur of the universe. But a little interrogation of our own consciousness will suffice to convince us, that what makes these phenomena so impressive is simply their vastness. The enormous extension in space and time, or the enormous power they exemplify, constitutes their sublimity; a feeling in all cases, more allied to terror than to any moral emotion. And though the vast scale of these phenomena may well excite wonder, and sets at defiance all idea of rivalry, the feeling it inspires is of a totally different character from admiration of excellence. Those in whom awe produces admiration may be æsthetically developed, but they are morally uncultivated. It is one of the endowments of the imaginative part of our mental nature that conceptions of greatness and power, vividly realized, produce a feeling which though in its higher degrees closely bordering on pain, we prefer to most of what are accounted pleasures. But we are quite equally capable of experiencing this feeling towards maleficent power; and we never experience it so strongly towards most of the powers of the universe, as when we have most present to our consciousness a vivid sense of their capacity of inflicting evil. Because these natural powers have what we cannot imitate, enormous might, and overawe us by that one attribute, it would be a great error to infer that their other attributes are such as we ought to emulate, or that we should be justified in using our small powers after the example which Nature sets us with her vast forces.

For, how stands the fact? That next to the greatness of these cosmic forces, the quality which most forcibly strikes every one who does not avert his eyes from it, is their perfect and absolute recklessness. They go straight to their end, without regarding what or whom they crush on the road. Optimists, in their attempts to prove that "whatever is, is right," are obliged to maintain, not that Nature ever turns one step from her path to avoid trampling us into destruction, but that it would be very unreasonable in us to expect that she should. Pope's "Shall gravitation cease when you go by?" may be a just rebuke to anyone who should be so silly as to expect common human morality from nature. But if the question were between two men, instead of between a man and a natural phenomenon, that triumphant apostrophe would be thought a rare piece of impudence. A man who should persist in hurling stones or firing cannon when another man "goes by," and having killed him should urge a similar plea in exculpation, would very deservedly be found guilty of murder.

In sober truth, nearly all the things for which men are hanged or imprisoned for doing to one another, are nature's every day performances.

Killing, the most criminal act recognized by human laws, Nature does once to every being that lives; and in a large proportion of cases, after protracted tortures such as only the greatest monsters of whom we read of ever purposely inflicted on their living fellow-creatures. If, by an arbitrary reservation, we refuse to account anything murder but what abridges a certain term supposed to be allotted to human life, nature also does this to all but a small percentage of lives, and does it in all the modes, violent or insidious, in which the worst human beings take the lives of one another. Nature impales men, breaks them as if on the wheel, casts them to be devoured by wild beasts, burns them to death, crushes them with stones like the first christian martyr, starves them with hunger, freezes them with cold, poisons them by the quick or slow venom of her exhalations, and has hundreds of other hideous deaths in reserve, such as the ingenious cruelty of a Nabis or a Domitian never surpassed. All this, Nature does with the most supercilious disregard both of mercy and of justice, emptying her shafts upon the best and noblest indifferently with the meanest and worst; upon those who are engaged in the highest and worthiest enterprises, and often as the direct consequence of the noblest acts; and it might almost be imagined as a punishment for them. She mows down those on whose existence hangs the well-being of a whole people, perhaps the prospects of the human race for generations to come, with as little compunction as those whose death is a relief to themselves, or a blessing to those under their noxious influence. Such are Nature's dealings with life. Even when she does not intend to kill, she inflicts the same tortures in apparent wantonness. In the clumsy provision which she has made for that perpetual renewal of animal life, rendered necessary by the prompt termination she puts to it in every individual instance, no human being ever comes into the world but another human being is literally stretched on the rack for hours or days, not unfrequently issuing in death. Next to taking life (equal to it according to a high authority) is taking the means by which we live; and Nature does this too on the largest scale and with the most callous indifference. A single hurricane destroys the hopes of a season; a flight of locusts, or an inundation, desolates a district; a trifling chemical change in an edible root, starves a million of people. The waves of the sea, like banditti seize and appropriate the wealth of the rich and the little all of the poor with the same accompaniments of stripping, wounding, and killing as their human antitypes. Everything in short, which the worst men commit either against life or property is perpetrated on a larger scale by natural agents. Nature has Noyades* more fatal than those of Carrier; her explosions of fire damp are as destructive as human artillery; her plague and cholera far surpass the poison cups of the Borgias. Even the love of "order" which is thought to be a following of the ways of Nature, is in fact a contradiction of them. All which people are accus-

*Carrier was a French revolutionary who executed large numbers of prisoners by drowning in 1794. The practice is referred to as Noyades. [Ed.]

tomed to deprecate as "disorder" and its consequences, is precisely a counterpart of Nature's ways. Anarchy and the Reign of Terror are overmatched in injustice, ruin, and death, by a hurricane and a pestilence.

But, it is said, all these things are for wise and good ends. On this I must first remark that whether they are so or not, is altogether beside the point. Supposing it true that contrary to appearances these horrors when perpetrated by Nature, promote good ends, still as no one believes that good ends would be promoted by our following the example, the course of Nature cannot be a proper model for us to imitate. Either it is right that we should kill because nature kills; torture because nature tortures; ruin and devastate because nature does the like; or we ought not to consider at all what nature does, but what it is good to do. If there is such a thing as a *reductio ad absurdum*, this surely amounts to one. . . .

❧ STUDY QUESTIONS

1. Do you agree with Mill's assessment that the term *Nature* is ambiguous? What are the three meanings he gives? Do you agree with his analysis?
2. Is Mill correct in his analysis of Natural Law? Should we follow Nature and imitate her ways?
3. Mill says we should correct Nature, not imitate her. How would we go about improving or correcting Nature?
4. Compare Mill's views with Rolston's and others who would preserve the wilderness intact.

BIOCENTRIC ETHICS

16 Reverence for Life

ALBERT SCHWEITZER

Albert Schweitzer (1875–1965) was born in Kaiserberg, Germany, and educated at Strasbourg in Alsace. He was an extraordinarily versatile genius: a concert organist, a musicologist, a theologian, a missionary, a philosopher, and a physician who dedicated his life to the amelioration of suffering and the promotion of life. He built and served in a hospital in Lambarene in French Equatorial Africa (now Gabon). His most famous writings are *The Quest for the Historical Jesus* (1906), *Out of My Life and Thought* (1933), and *Civilization and Ethics* (1923) from which the present selection is taken.

Reprinted from *Civilization and Ethics*, trans. A. Naish (London: Black, 1923).

Schweitzer describes his theory of Reverence for Life—the idea that all of life is sacred and that we must live accordingly, treating each living being as an inherently valuable "will-to-live." He was awarded the Nobel Peace Prize in 1952.

Schweitzer relates how the phrase "Reverence for Life" came to him one day in 1915 while on a river journey to assist a missionary's sick wife.

> At sunset of the third day, near the village of Igendja, we moved along an island in the middle of the wide river. On a sandbank to our left, four hippopotamuses and their young plodded along in our same direction. Just then, in my great tiredness and discouragement, the phrase "Reverence for Life" struck me like a flash. As far as I knew, it was a phrase I had never heard nor ever read. I realized at once that it carried within itself the solution to the problem that had been torturing me. Now I knew a system of values which concerns itself only with our relationship to other people is incomplete and therefore lacking in power for good. Only by means of reverence for life can we establish a spiritual and humane relationship with both people and all living creatures within our reach. Only in this fashion can we avoid harming others, and, within the limits of our capacity, go to their aid whenever they need us.

The following passage is a fuller description of his views. He begins by citing the French philosopher René Descartes (1596–1650) and contrasting that theory of knowledge, which begins with an abstract, isolated self, with the deeper self-awareness that comes from our understanding that all living things ("will-to-lives") are sacred and interdependent.

Descartes tells us that philosophizing is based on the judgment: "I think therefore I am." From this meagre and arbitrarily selected beginning it is inevitable that it should wander into the path of the abstract. It does not find the entrance to the ethical realm, and remains held fast in a dead view of the world and of life. True philosophy must commence with the most immediate and comprehensive facts of consciousness. And this may be formulated as follows: "I am life which wills to live, and I exist in the midst of life which wills to live." This is no mere excogitated subtlety. Day after day and hour after hour I proceed on my way invested in it. In every moment of reflection it forces itself on me anew. A living world- and life-view, informing all the facts of life, gushes forth from it continually, as from an eternal spring. A mystically ethical oneness with existence grows forth from it unceasingly.

Just as in my own will-to-live there is a yearning for more life, and for that mysterious exaltation of the will-to-live which is called pleasure, and terror in face of annihilation and that injury to the will-to-live which is called pain; so the same obtains in all the will-to-live around me, equally whether it can express itself to my comprehension or whether it remains unvoiced.

Ethics thus consists in this, that I experience the necessity of practising the same reverence for life toward all will-to-live, as toward my own. Therein I have already the needed fundamental principle of morality. It is *good* to maintain and cherish life; it is *evil* to destroy and to check life.

As a matter of fact, everything which in the usual ethical valuation of inter-human relations is looked upon as good can be traced back to the material and spiritual maintenance or enhancement of human life and to the effort to raise it to its highest level of value. And contrariwise everything in human relations which is considered as evil, is in the final analysis found to be material or spiritual destruction or checking of human life and slackening of the effort to raise it to its highest value. Individual concepts of good and evil which are widely divergent and apparently unconnected fit into one another like pieces which belong together, the moment they are comprehended and their essential nature is grasped in this general notion.

The fundamental principle of morality which we seek as a necessity for thought is not, however, a matter only of arranging and deepening current views of good and evil, but also of expanding and extending these. A man is really ethical only when he obeys the constraint laid on him to help all life which he is able to succour, and when he goes out of his way to avoid injuring anything living. He does not ask how far this or that life deserves sympathy as valuable in itself, nor how far it is capable of feeling. To him life as such is sacred. He shatters no ice crystal that sparkles in the sun, tears no leaf from its tree, breaks off no flower, and is careful not to crush any insect as he walks. If he works by lamplight on a summer evening, he prefers to keep the window shut and to breathe stifling air, rather than to see insect after insect fall on his table with singed and sinking wings.

If he goes out into the street after a rainstorm and sees a worm which has strayed there, he reflects that it will certainly dry up in the sunshine, if it does not quickly regain the damp soil into which it can creep, and so he helps it back from the deadly paving stones into the lush grass. Should he pass by an insect which has fallen into a pool, he spares the time to reach it a leaf or stalk on which it may clamber and save itself.

He is not afraid of being laughed at as sentimental. It is indeed the fate of every truth to be an object of ridicule when it is first acclaimed. It was once considered foolish to suppose that coloured men were really human beings and ought to be treated as such. What was once foolishness has now become a recognized truth. Today it is considered as exaggeration to proclaim constant respect for every form of life as being the serious demand of a rational ethic. But the time is coming when people will be amazed that the human race was so long before it recognized that thoughtless injury to life is incompatible with real ethics. Ethics is in its unqualified form extended responsibility with regard to everything that has life.

The general idea of ethics as a partaking of the mental atmosphere of reverence for life is not perhaps attractive. But it is the only complete notion possible. Mere sympathy is too narrow a concept to serve as the intellectual expression of the ethical element. It denotes, indeed, only a sharing of the suffering of the will-to-live. But

to be ethical is to share the whole experience of all the circumstances and aspirations of the will-to-live, to live with it in its pleasures, in its yearnings, in its struggles toward perfection.

Love is a more inclusive term, since it signifies fellowship in suffering, in joy, and in effort. But it describes the ethical element only as it were by a simile, however natural and profound that simile may be. It places the solidarity created by ethics in analogy to that which nature has caused to come into being in a more or less superficial physical manner, and with a view to the fulfillment of their destiny, between two sexually attracted existences, or between these and their offspring.

Thought must strive to find a formula for the essential nature of the ethical. In so doing it is led to characterize ethics as self-devotion for the sake of life, motived by reverence for life. Although the phrase "reverence for life" may perhaps sound a trifle unreal, yet that which it denotes is something which never lets go its hold of the man in whose thought it has once found a place. Sympathy, love, and, in general, all enthusiastic feeling of real value are summed up in it. It works with restless vitality on the mental nature in which it has found a footing and flings this into the restless activity of a responsibility which never ceases and stops nowhere. Reverence for life drives a man on as the whirling thrashing screw forces a ship through the water.

The ethic of reverence for life, arising as it does out of an inward necessity, is not dependent on the question as to how far or how little it is capable of development into a satisfactory view of life. It does not need to prove that the action of ethical men, as directed to maintaining, enhancing and exalting life, has any significance for the total course of the world-process. Nor is it disturbed by the consideration that the preservation and enhancement of life which it practises are of almost no account at all beside the mighty destruction of life which takes place every moment as the result of natural forces. Determined as it is to act, it is yet able to ignore all the problems raised as to the result of its action. The fact that in the man who has become ethical a will informed by reverence for life and self-sacrifice for the sake of life exists in the world, is itself significant for the world.

The universal will-to-live experiences itself in my personal will-to-live otherwise than it does in other phenomena. For here it enters on an individualization, which, so far as I am able to gather in trying to view it from the outside, struggles only to live itself out, and not at all to become one with will-to-live external to itself. The world is indeed the grisly drama of will-to-live at variance with itself. One existence survives at the expense of another of which it yet knows nothing. But in me the will-to-live has become cognizant of the existence of other will-to-live. There is in it a yearning for unity with itself, a longing to become universal.

Why is it that the will-to-live has this experience only in myself? Is it a result of my having become capable of reflection about the totality of existence? Whither will the evolution lead which has thus begun in me?

There is no answer to these questions. It remains a painful enigma how I am to live by the rule of reverence for life in a world ruled by creative will which is at the same time destructive will, and by destructive will which is also creative.

I can do no other than hold on to the fact that the will-to-live appears in me as will-to-live which aims at becoming one with other will-to-live. This fact is the light which shines for me in the darkness. My ignorance regarding the real nature of the objective world no longer troubles me. I am set free from the world. I have been cast by my reverence for life into a state of unrest foreign to the world. By this, too, I am placed in a state of beatitude which the world cannot give. If in the happiness induced by our independence of the world I and another afford each other mutual help in understanding and in forgiveness, when otherwise will would harass other will, then the will-to-live is no longer at variance with itself. If I rescue an insect from a pool of water, then life has given itself for life, and again the self-contradiction of the will-to-live has been removed. Whenever my life has given itself out in any way for other life, my eternal will-to-live experiences union with the eternal, since all life is one. I possess a cordial which secures me from dying of thirst in the desert of life.

Therefore I recognize it as the destiny of my existence to be obedient to the higher revelation of the will-to-live which I find in myself. I choose as my activity the removal of the self-contradiction of the will-to-live, as far as the influence of my own existence extends. Knowing as I do the one thing needful, I am content to offer no opinion about the enigma of the objective world and my own being.

Thought becomes religious when it thinks itself out to the end. The ethic of reverence for life is the ethic of Jesus brought to philosophical expression, extended into cosmical form, and conceived as intellectually necessary.

The surmising and longing of all deeply religious personalities is comprehended and contained in the ethic of reverence for life. This, however, does not build up a world-view as a completed system, but resigns itself to leave the cathedral perforce incomplete. It is only able to finish the choir. Yet in this true piety celebrates a living and continuous divine service....

The ethic of reverence for life also proves its own truth by the way in which it comprehends and includes the most various forms of the ethical impulse. No ethical system has yet proved capable of presenting the effort to attain self-perfection, in which man works on his own being without any action directed externally, on the one hand, and the activist ethic on the other hand, in connection and interrelation. The ethic of reverence for life accomplishes this, and in such a way that it does not merely solve an academic problem, but brings with it a real deepening of ethical insight.

Ethics is in fact reverence for the will-to-live both within and without my own personality. The immediate product of reverence for the will-to-live which I find in myself is the profound life-affirmation of resignation. I comprehend my will-to-live not only as something which lives itself out in fortunate moments of success, but also as something which is conscious of itself and its own experiences. If I do not allow this experiencing of myself to be dissipated by heedless lack of reflection, but, on the contrary, deliberately pause in it as one who feels its real value, I am rewarded by a disclosure of the secret of spiritual independence. I become a partaker in an unguessed-at freedom amid the destinies of life. At moments when I should otherwise have thought myself to be overwhelmed and crushed, I feel myself uplifted in a state of inexpressible joy, astounding to myself, in which I am conscious of freedom from the world and experience a clarifying of my whole view of life. Resignation is the vestibule through which we pass in entering the palace of ethics. Only he who experiences inner freedom from external events in profound surrender to his own will-to-live is capable of the profound and permanent surrender of himself for the sake of other life.

As I struggle for freedom from the external occurrences of life in reverence for my own will-to-live, so also do I wrestle for freedom from myself. I practise the higher independence not only with regard to that which happens to me personally, but also in respect to the way in which I behave towards the world.

As the result of reverence for my own existence I force myself to be sincere with myself. Anything that I acquire by acting contrary to my convictions is bought too dearly. I am afraid of wounding my will-to-live with poisoned spears by disloyalty to my own personality.

That Kant places sincerity toward oneself in the very centre of his ethical system is a witness to the profoundity of his own ethical perception. But he is unable to grasp the connection between self-sincerity and activist ethics because in his search for the essential nature of the ethical he never gets as far as the idea of reverence for life.

In actual practice the ethic of self-sincerity passes over unconsciously into that of self-sacrifice for others. Sincerity toward myself forces me to acts which appear so much like self-sacrifice that the current ethic derives them from this latter impulse.

Why do I forgive my fellow-man? The current ethic says that it is because I sympathize with him. It presents men as impossibly good when they forgive, and allows them to practise a kind of forgiveness which is really humiliating to the person forgiven. Thus it turns forgiveness into a sort of sweetened triumph of self-sacrifice.

The ethic of reverence for life clears away these obscure and misty notions. All forebearance and forgiveness is for it an act to which it is compelled by sincerity towards itself. I am obliged to exercise unlimited forgiveness because, if I did not forgive, I should be untrue to myself, in that I should thus act as if I were not guilty in the same way as the other has been guilty with regard to me. I must forgive the lies directed against myself, because my own life has been so many times blotted by lies; I must forgive the lovelessness, the hatred, the slander, the fraud, the arrogance which I encounter, since I myself have so often lacked love, hated, slandered, defrauded, and been arrogant. I must forgive without noise or fuss. In general I do not forgive, I do not even get as far as being merely just. And this also is no exaggeration, but a necessary extension and refinement of our usual ethic.

We have to conduct the fight against the evil element which exists in man, not by judging others, but only by judging ourselves. The conflict with our own nature, and sincerity towards ourselves, are the instruments with which we work on others. We move silently into the midst of the struggle for that profound spiritual independence which grows from reverence for our own life. True power makes no noise. It is there, and it produces its effect. True ethic begins where the use of words stops.

The most essential element of activist ethics, even if it does appear as surrender, is thus a product of the impulse to sincerity towards oneself, and in that is contained its real value. The whole ethic of independence from the world only runs as a clear stream when it issues from this source. I am not gentle, peaceable, patient and friendly from a kindly disposition towards others, but because I thus secure the most profound independence. There is an indissoluble connection between the reverence for life with which I face my own existence, and that in which I relate myself to others in acts of self sacrifice.

It is because the current ethic possesses no fundamental principle of morality that it plunges immediately into the discussion of various conflicting opinions in the ethical realm. The ethic of reverence for life is in no hurry to do this. It takes its own time to think out its fundamental moral principle on all sites. Then, complete in itself, it takes up its own position with regard to these conflicts.

Ethics has to come to an understanding with three opponents; with lack of thought, with egoistic independence, and with the community.

Of the first of these, ethics has not usually taken sufficient account, because it never comes to any open conflict between the two. But, unnoticed, this opponent is constantly on the offensive.

Ethics can take possession of an extensive tract without encountering the troops of egoism. A man can do a great deal of good without being obliged to sacrifice his own interests or desires. Even if he does lose a little bit of his own life in so doing, it is such an insignificant fragment that he misses it no more than he would a single hair or a tiny scale of skin.

To a very large extent the attainment of inner freedom from the world, loyalty to one's own being, existence in distinction from the world, even self-sacrifice for the sake of other life, is only a matter of concentrating attention on this relation. We miss so much of it because we do not keep steadfastly to the point. We do not place ourselves directly under the pressure of the inner impulse to ethical existence. Steam spurts out in all directions from a leaky boiler. The losses of energy on every site are so great in the current ethic because it has at its command no single fundamental moral principle which can act on its thought. It cannot make its boiler steam-tight, nay, it does not even thoroughly inspect it. But reverence for life, which is always present to thought, informs and penetrates, continually and in every direction, a man's observation, reflection and decisions. He can as little resist this process as water can hinder the dyestuff dropped into it from tinting it. The struggle with lack of thought is a conscious process and is always going on.

How does the ethic of reverence for life stand in the conflicts which arise between the inner impulse to self-sacrifice and necessary self-maintenance?

I also am subject to the variance with itself of the will-to-live. My existence is in conflict at a thousand points with that of others. The necessity is laid upon me of destroying and injuring life. If I walk along a lonely road my foot brings annihilation and pain on the tiny beings which people it. In order to maintain my own existence I am obliged to protect it from the existences which would harm it. I become a persecutor of the little mouse which inhabits my dwelling, a destroyer of the insect which desires to breed there, no less than a wholesale murderer of the bacteria which may endanger my life. I can only secure nourishment for myself by destroying animals and plants. My own good fortune is built on the injuries and hardships of my fellowmen.

How is ethics to exist at all amid the gruesome necessities to which I am a slave because the will-to-live is at variance with itself?

The current ethic seeks for a compromise. It tries to lay down rules as to how much of my own existence and of my own happiness I must give up, and how much I may continue to hold at the expense of the existence and happiness of other life. In so deciding it creates an experimental and relative ethic. That which is actually not ethical at all, but is a hotch-potch of non-ethical necessity and of real ethics, gives itself out as genuinely ethical and normative. Thus a monstrous confusion arises, and thereby a constantly increasing obscuration of the notion of the ethical element.

The ethic of reverence for life recognizes no such thing as a relative ethic. The maintenance and enhancement of life are the only things it counts as being good in themselves. All destruction of and injury to life, from whatever circumstances they may result, are reckoned by it as evil. It does not give place to ready-made accommodations of ethics and necessity which are too eager to occupy the ground. The absolute ethic of reverence makes its own agreements with the individual from moment to moment, agreements always fresh and always original and basic. It does not relieve him of the conflict, but rather forces him to decide for himself in each case how far he can remain ethical and how far he must submit himself to the necessity of destroying and harming life and thus become guilty. Man does not make ethical progress by assimilating instruction with regard to accommodations between the ethical and the necessary, but only by hearing ever more clearly the voice of the ethical element, by being ever more under the control of his own yearning to maintain and to enhance life, and by becoming ever more obstinate in his opposition to the necessity of destroying and injuring life.

In ethical conflicts it is only subjective decisions that a man has to face. No one else can determine for him where lies the utmost limit of the possibility of continuing to maintain and cherish life. He alone has to judge by allowing himself to be led by a sense of responsibility for other lives raised to the highest degree possible. We must never let this sense become dulled and blunted. In effect, however, we are doing so, if we are content to find the conflicts becoming continually more insoluble. The good conscience is an invention of the devil.

What does reverence for life teach us about the relations of man and the non-human animals?

Whenever I injure life of any kind I must be quite clear as to whether this is necessary or not. I ought never to pass the limits of the unavoidable, even in apparently insignificant cases. The countryman who has mowed down a thousand blossoms in his meadow as fodder for his cows should take care that on the way home he does not, in wanton pastime, switch off the head of a single flower growing on the edge of the road, for in so doing he injures life without being forced to do so by necessity.

Those who test operations or drugs on animals, or who inoculate them with diseases so that they may be able to help human beings by means of the results thus obtained, ought never to rest satisfied with the general idea that their dreadful doings are performed in pursuit of a worthy aim. It is their duty to ponder in every separate case whether it is really and truly necessary thus to sacrifice an animal for humanity. They ought to be filled with anxious care to alleviate as much as possible the pain which they cause. How many outrages are committed in this way in scientific institutions where narcotics are often omitted to save time and trouble! How many also when animals are made to suffer agonizing tortures, only in order to demonstrate to students scientific truths which are perfectly well known. The very fact that the animal, as a victim of research, has in his pain rendered such services to suffering men, has itself created a new and unique relation of solidarity between him and ourselves. The result is that a fresh obligation is laid on each of us to do as much good as we possibly can to all creatures in all sorts of circumstances. When I help an insect out of his troubles all that I do is to attempt to remove some of the guilt contracted through these crimes against animals.

Wherever any animal is forced into the service of man, the sufferings which it has to bear on that account are the concern of every one of us. No one ought to permit, in so far as he can prevent it, pain or suffering for which he will not take the responsibility. No one ought to rest at ease in the thought that in so doing he would mix himself up in affairs which are not his business. Let no one shirk the burden of his responsibility. When there is so much maltreatment of animals, when the cries of thirsting creatures go up unnoticed from the railway trucks, when there is so much roughness in our slaughterhouses, when in our kitchens so many animals suffer horrible deaths from unskillful hands, when animals endure unheard-of-agonies from heartless men, or are delivered to the dreadful play of children, then we are all guilty and must bear the blame.

We are afraid of shocking or offending by showing too plainly how deeply we are moved by the sufferings which man causes to the non-human creatures. We tend to reflect that others are more "rational" than we are, and would consider that which so disturbs us as customary and as a matter of course. And then, suddenly, they let fall some expression which shows us that they, too, are not really satisfied with the situation. Strangers to us hitherto, they are now quite near our own position. The masks, in which we had each concealed ourselves from the other, fall off. We now know that neither of us can cut ourselves free from the horrible necessity which plays ceaselessly around us. What a wonderful thing it is thus to get to know each other!

The ethic of reverence for life forbids any of us to deduce from the silence of our contemporaries that they, or in their case we, have ceased to feel what as thinking men we all cannot but feel. It prompts us to keep a mutual watch in this atmosphere of suffering and endurance, and to speak and act without panic according to the responsibility which we feel. It inspires us to join in a search for opportunities to afford help of some kind or other to the animals, to make up for the great amount of misery which they endure at our hands, and thus to escape for a moment from the inconceivable horrors of existence.

But the ethic of reverence for life also places us in a position of fearful responsibility with regard to our relations to other men.

We find, again, that it offers us no teaching about the bounds of legitimate self-maintenance; it calls us again to come to a separate understanding with the ethic of self-sacrifice in each individual case. According to the sense of responsibility which is my personal experience so I must decide what part of my life, my possessions, my rights, my happiness, my time or my rest, I ought to give up, and what part I ought to keep back.

Regarding the question of property, the ethic of reverence for life is outspokenly individualist in the sense that goods earned or inherited are to be placed at the disposition of the community, not according to any standards whatever laid down by society, but according to the absolutely free decision of the individual. It places all its hopes on the enhancement of the feeling of responsibility in man. It defines possessions as the property of the community, of which the individual is sovereign steward. One serves society by conducting a business from which a certain number of employees draw their means of sustenance; another, by giving away his property in order to help his fellow-men. Each one will decide on his own course somewhere between these two extreme cases according to the sense of responsibility which is determined for him by the particular circumstances of his own life. No one is to judge others. It is a question of individual responsibility; each is to value his possessions as

instruments with which he is to work. It makes no difference whether the work is done by keeping and increasing, or by giving up, the property. Possessions must belong to the community in the most various ways, if they are to be used to the best advantage in its service.

Those who have very little that they can call their own are in most danger of becoming purely egoistic. A deep truth lies in the parable of Jesus, which makes the servant who had received the least the least faithful of all.

The ethic of reverence for life does not even allow me to possess my own rights absolutely. It does not allow me to rest in the thought that I, as the more capable, advance at the expense of the less capable. It presents to me as a problem what human law and opinion allow as a matter of course. It prompts me to think of others and to ponder whether I can really allow myself the intrinsic right of plucking all the fruits which my hand is physically able to reach. And then it may occur that following my regard for the existence of others, I do what appears as foolishness to the generality of men. It may, indeed, prove itself to have been actually foolishness so far as my renunciation for the sake of others has really no useful effect. Yet all the same I was right in doing as I did. Reverence for life is the supreme motive. That which it commands has its own meaning, even if it seems foolish or useless. Indeed, we all really seek in one another for that sort of foolishness which shows that we are impelled by the higher responsibility. It is only as we become less rational in the ordinary sense of the word that the ethical disposition works out in us and solves problems previously insoluble.

✎ STUDY QUESTIONS

1. What is Schweitzer's theory of reverence for life? Does it value life itself or a special feature of life?
2. Is Schweitzer an egalitarian? Are all forms of life of equal worth?
3. What does Schweitzer mean in the second paragraph of this selection where he says that the

"mysterious exaltation of the will-to-live" is "called pleasure" and "injury to the will-to-live" "pain"? Is this a form of hedonism?
4. Compare Schweitzer's position with Taylor's essay, which follows, as well as with the Hindu and Buddhist views in Chapter 5.

17 Biocentric Egalitarianism

PAUL TAYLOR

Paul Taylor is professor emeritus of philosophy at Brooklyn College, City University of New York, and the author of several works in ethics, including *Respect for Nature* (1986), in which the ideas in the following essay are developed.

Taylor develops Schweitzer's life-centered system of environmental ethics. He argues that each living individual has a "teleological center of life," which pursues its own good in its own way, and possesses equal inherent worth. Human beings are no more intrinsically valuable than any other living thing but should see themselves as equal members of Earth's community.

I. HUMAN-CENTERED AND LIFE-CENTERED SYSTEMS OF ENVIRONMENTAL ETHICS

In this paper I show how the taking of a certain ultimate moral attitude toward nature, which I call "respect for nature," has a central place in the foundations of a life-centered system of environmental ethics. I hold that a set of moral norms (both standards of character and rules of conduct) governing human treatment of the natural world is a rationally grounded set if and only if, first, commitment to those norms is a practical entailment of adopting the attitude of respect for nature as an ultimate moral attitude, and second, the adopting of that attitude on the part of all rational agents can itself be justified. When the basic characteristics of the attitude of respect for nature are made clear, it will be seen that a life-centered system of environmental ethics need not be holistic or organicist in its conception of the kinds of entities that are deemed the appropriate objects of moral concern and consideration. Nor does such a system require that the concepts of ecological homeostasis, equilibrium, and integrity provide us with normative principles from which could be derived (with the addition of factual knowledge) our obligations with regard to natural ecosystems. The "balance of nature" is not itself a moral norm, however important may be the role it plays in our general outlook on the natural world that underlies the attitude of respect for nature. I argue that finally it is the good (well-being, welfare) of individual organisms, considered as entities having inherent worth, that determines our moral relations with the Earth's wild communities of life.

In designating the theory to be set forth as life-centered, I intend to contrast it with all anthropocentric views. According to the latter, human actions affecting the natural environment and its nonhuman inhabitants are right (or wrong) by either of two criteria: they have consequences which are favorable (or unfavorable) to human well-being, or they are consistent (or inconsistent) with the system of norms that protect and implement human rights. From this human-centered standpoint it is to humans and only to humans that all duties are ultimately owed. We may have responsibilities *with regard* to the natural ecosystems and biotic communities of our planet, but these responsibilities are in every case based on the contingent fact that our treatment of those ecosystems and communities of life can further the realization of human values and/or human rights. We have no obligation to promote or protect the good of nonhuman living things, independently of this contingent fact.

A life-centered system of environmental ethics is opposed to human-centered ones precisely on this point. From the perspective of a

Reprinted from *Environmental Ethics*, Vol. 3 (Fall 1981) by permission.

life-centered theory, we have prima facie moral obligations that are owed to wild plants and animals themselves as members of the Earth's biotic community. We are morally bound (other things being equal) to protect or promote their good for *their* sake. Our duties to respect the integrity of natural ecosystems, to preserve endangered species, and to avoid environmental pollution stem from the fact that these are ways in which we can help make it possible for wild species populations to achieve and maintain a healthy existence in a natural state. Such obligations are due those living things out of recognition of their inherent worth. They are entirely additional to and independent of the obligations we owe to our fellow humans. Although many of the actions that fulfill one set of obligations will also fulfill the other, two different grounds of obligation are involved. Their well-being, as well as human well-being, is something to be realized *as an end in itself.*

If we were to accept a life-centered theory of environmental ethics, a profound reordering of our moral universe would take place. We would begin to look at the whole of the Earth's biosphere in a new light. Our duties with respect to the "world" of nature would be seen as making prima facie claims upon us to be balanced against our duties with respect to the "world" of human civilization. We could no longer simply take the human point of view and consider the effects of our actions exclusively from the perspective of our own good.

II. THE GOOD OF A BEING AND THE CONCEPT OF INHERENT WORTH

What would justify acceptance of a life-centered system of ethical principles? In order to answer this it is first necessary to make clear the fundamental moral attitude that underlies and makes intelligible the commitment to live by such a system. It is then necessary to examine the considerations that would justify any rational agent's adopting that moral attitude.

Two concepts are essential to the taking of a moral attitude of the sort in question. A being

which does not "have" these concepts, that is, which is unable to grasp their meaning and conditions of applicability, cannot be said to have the attitude as part of its moral outlook. These concepts are, first, that of the good (well-being, welfare) of a living thing, and second, the idea of an entity possessing inherent worth. I examine each concept in turn.

1. Every organism, species population, and community of life has a good of its own which moral agents can intentionally further or damage by their actions. To say that an entity has a good of its own is simply to say that, without reference to any *other* entity, it can be benefited or harmed. One can act in its overall interest or contrary to its overall interest, and environmental conditions can be good for it (advantageous to it) or bad for it (disadvantageous to it). What is good for an entity is what "does it good" in the sense of enhancing or preserving its life and well-being. What is bad for an entity is something that is detrimental to its life and well-being.[1]

We can think of the good of an individual nonhuman organism as consisting in the full development of its biological powers. Its good is realized to the extent that it is strong and healthy. It possesses whatever capacities it needs for successfully coping with its environment and so preserving its existence throughout the various stages of the normal life cycle of its species. The good of a population or community of such individuals consists in the population or community maintaining itself from generation to generation as a coherent system of genetically and ecologically related organisms whose average good is at an optimum level for the given environment. Mere *average good* means that the degree of realization of the good of *individual organisms* in the population or community is, on average, greater than would be the case under any other ecologically functioning order of interrelations (among those species populations in the given ecosystem).

The idea of a being having a good of its own, as I understand it, does not entail that the being must have interests or take an interest in what affects its life for better or for worse. We can act in a being's interest or contrary to its interest without its being interested in what we are doing to it in the sense of wanting or not wanting us to do it. It may, indeed, be wholly unaware that favorable and unfavorable events are taking place in its life. I take it that trees, for example, have no knowledge or desires or feelings. Yet it is undoubtedly the case that trees can be harmed or benefited by our actions. We can crush their roots by running a bulldozer too close to them. We can see to it that they get adequate nourishment and moisture by fertilizing and watering the soil around them. Thus we can help or hinder them in the realization of their good. It is the good of trees themselves that is thereby affected. We can similarly act so as to further the good of an entire tree population of a certain species (say, all the redwood trees in a California valley) or the good of a whole community of plant life in a given wilderness area, just as we can do harm to such a population or community.

When construed in this way, the concept of a being's good is not coextensive with sentience or the capacity for feeling pain. William Frankena has argued for a general theory of environmental ethics in which the ground of a creature's being worthy of moral consideration is its sentience. I have offered some criticisms of this view elsewhere, but the full refutation of such a position, it seems to me, finally depends on the positive reasons for accepting a life-centered theory of the kind I am defending in this essay.[2]

It should be noted further that I am leaving open the question of whether machines—in particular, those which are not only goal-directed, but also self-regulating—can properly be said to have a good of their own.[3] Since I am concerned only with human treatment of wild organisms, species populations, and communities of life as they occur in our planet's natural ecosystems, it is to those entities alone that the concept "having a good of its own" will here be applied. I am not denying that other living things, whose genetic origin and environmental conditions have been produced, controlled, and manipulated by humans for human ends, do have a good of their own in the same sense as do wild plants and animals. It is not my purpose in this essay, however, to set out or defend the principles that should guide our conduct with regard to their good. It is only insofar as their production

and use by humans have good or ill effects upon natural ecosystems and their wild inhabitants that the ethics of respect for nature comes into play.

2. The second concept essential to the moral attitude of respect for nature is the idea of inherent worth. We take that attitude toward wild living things (individuals, species populations, or whole biotic communities) when and only when we regard them as entities possessing inherent worth. Indeed, it is only because they are conceived in this way that moral agents can think of themselves as having validly binding duties, obligations, and responsibilities that are *owed* to them as their *due*. I am not at this juncture arguing why they *should* be so regarded; I consider it at length below. But so regarding them is a presupposition of our taking the attitude of respect toward them and accordingly understanding ourselves as bearing certain moral relations to them. This can be shown as follows:

What does it mean to regard an entity that has a good of its own as possessing inherent worth? Two general principles are involved: the principle of moral consideration and the principle of intrinsic value.

According to the principle of moral consideration, wild living things are deserving of the concern and consideration of all moral agents simply in virtue of their being members of the Earth's community of life. From the moral point of view their good must be taken into account whenever it is affected for better or worse by the conduct of rational agents. This holds no matter what species the creature belongs to. The good of each is to be accorded some value and so acknowledged as having some weight in the deliberations of all rational agents. Of course, it may be necessary for such agents to act in ways contrary to the good of this or that particular organism or group of organisms in order to further the good of others, including the good of humans. But the principle of moral consideration prescribes that, with respect to each being an entity having its own good, every individual is deserving of consideration.

The principle of intrinsic value states that, regardless of what kind of entity it is in other respects, if it is a member of the Earth's community of life, the realization of its good is something *intrinsically* valuable. This means that its good is prima facie worthy of being preserved or promoted as an end in itself and for the sake of the entity whose good it is. Insofar as we regard any organism, species population, or life community as an entity having inherent worth, we believe that it must never be treated as if it were a mere object or thing whose entire value lies in being instrumental to the good of some other entity. The well-being of each is judged to have value in and of itself.

Combining these two principles, we can now define what it means for a living thing or group of living things to possess inherent worth. To say that it possesses inherent worth is to say that its good is deserving of the concern and consideration of all moral agents, and that the realization of its good has intrinsic value, to be pursued as an end in itself and for the sake of the entity whose good it is.

The duties owed to wild organisms, species populations, and communities of life in the Earth's natural ecosystems are grounded on their inherent worth. When rational, autonomous agents regard such entities as possessing inherent worth, they place intrinsic value on the realization of their good and so hold themselves responsible for performing actions that will have this effect and for refraining from actions having the contrary effect.

III. THE ATTITUDE OF RESPECT FOR NATURE

Why should moral agents regard wild living things in the natural world as possessing inherent worth? To answer this question we must first take into account the fact that, when rational, autonomous agents subscribe to the principles of moral consideration and intrinsic value and so conceive of wild living things as having that kind of worth, such agents are *adopting a certain ultimate moral attitude toward the natural world*. This is the attitude I call "respect for nature." It parallels the attitude of respect for persons in human ethics. When we adopt the attitude of respect for persons as the proper (fitting, appropriate) attitude to take toward all persons as persons, we consider the fulfillment of the basic interests of each

individual to have intrinsic value. We thereby make a moral commitment to live a certain kind of life in relation to other persons. We place ourselves under the direction of a system of standards and rules that we consider validly binding on all moral agents as such.[4]

Similarly, when we adopt the attitude of respect for nature as an ultimate moral attitude we make a commitment to live by certain normative principles. These principles constitute the rules of conduct and standards of character that are to govern our treatment of the natural world. This is, first, an *ultimate* commitment because it is not derived from any higher norm. The attitude of respect for nature is not grounded on some other, more general, or more fundamental attitude. It sets the total framework for our responsibilities toward the natural world. It can be justified, as I show below, but its justification cannot consist in referring to a more general attitude or a more basic normative principle.

Second, the commitment is a *moral* one because it is understood to be a disinterested matter of principle. It is this feature that distinguishes the attitude of respect for nature from the set of feelings and dispositions that comprise the love of nature. The latter stems from one's personal interest in and response to the natural world. Like the affectionate feelings we have toward certain individual human beings, one's love of nature is nothing more than the particular way one feels about the natural environment and its wild inhabitants. And just as our love for an individual person differs from our respect for all persons as such (whether we happen to love them or not), so love of nature differs from respect for nature. Respect for nature is an attitude we believe all moral agents ought to have simply as moral agents, regardless of whether or not they also love nature. Indeed, we have not truly taken the attitude of respect for nature ourselves unless we believe this. To put it in a Kantian way, to adopt the attitude of respect for nature is to take a stance that one wills it to be a universal law for all rational beings. It is to hold that stance categorically, as being validly applicable to every moral agent without exception, irrespective of whatever personal feelings toward nature such an agent might have or might lack.

Although the attitude of respect for nature is in this sense a disinterested and universalizable attitude, anyone who does adopt it has certain steady, more or less permanent dispositions. These dispositions, which are themselves to be considered disinterested and universalizable, comprise three interlocking sets: dispositions to seek certain ends, dispositions to carry on one's practical reasoning and deliberation in a certain way, and dispositions to have certain feelings. We may accordingly analyze the attitude of respect for nature into the following components. (a) The disposition to aim at, and to take steps to bring about, as final and disinterested ends, the promoting and protecting of the good of organisms, species populations, and life communities in natural ecosystems. (These ends are "final" in not being pursued as means to further ends. They are "disinterested" in being independent of the self-interest of the agent.) (b) The disposition to consider actions that tend to realize those ends to be prima facie obligatory *because* they have that tendency. (c) The disposition to experience positive and negative feelings toward states of affairs in the world *because* they are favorable or unfavorable to the good of organisms, species populations, and life communities in natural ecosystems.

The logical connection between the attitude of respect for nature and the duties of a life-centered system of environmental ethics can now be made clear. Insofar as one sincerely takes that attitude and so has the three sets of dispositions, one will at the same time be disposed to comply with certain rules of duty (such as nonmaleficence and noninterference) and with standards of character (such as fairness and benevolence) that determine the obligations and virtues of moral agents with regard to the Earth's wild living things. We can say that the actions one performs and the character traits one develops in fulfilling these moral requirements are the way one *expresses* or *embodies* the attitude in one's conduct and character. In his famous essay, "Justice as Fairness," John Rawls describes the rules of the duties of human morality (such as fidelity, gratitude, honesty, and justice) as "forms of conduct in which recognition of others as persons is manifested."[5] I hold that the rules of duty governing our treatment of the natural world and its inhabitants are forms of conduct in which the attitude of respect for nature is manifested.

IV. THE JUSTIFIABILITY OF THE ATTITUDE OF RESPECT FOR NATURE

I return to the question posed earlier, which has not yet been answered: why *should* moral agents regard wild living things as possessing inherent worth? I now argue that the only way we can answer this question is by showing how adopting the attitude of respect for nature is justified for all moral agents. Let us suppose that we were able to establish that there are good reasons for adopting the attitude, reasons which are intersubjectively valid for every rational agent. If there are such reasons, they would justify anyone's having the three sets of dispositions mentioned above as constituting what it means to have the attitude. Since these include the disposition to promote or protect the good of wild living things as a disinterested and ultimate end, as well as the disposition to perform actions for the reason that they tend to realize that end, we see that such dispositions commit a person to the principles of moral consideration and intrinsic value. To be disposed to further, as an end in itself, the good of any entity in nature just because it is that kind of entity, is to be disposed to give consideration to *every* such entity and to place intrinsic value on the realization of its good. Insofar as we subscribe to these two principles we regard living things as possessing inherent worth. Subscribing to the principle is what it *means* to so regard them. To justify the attitude of respect for nature, then, is to justify commitment to these principles and thereby to justify regarding wild creatures as possessing inherent worth.

We must keep in mind that inherent worth is not some mysterious sort of objective property belonging to living things that can be discovered by empirical observation or scientific investigation. To ascribe inherent worth to an entity is not to describe it by citing some feature discernible by sense perception or inferable by inductive reasoning. Nor is there a logically necessary connection between the concept of a being having a good of its own and the concept of inherent worth. We do not contradict ourselves by asserting that an entity that has a good of its own lacks inherent worth. In order to show that such an entity "has" inherent worth we must give good reasons for ascribing that kind of value to it (placing that kind of value upon it, conceiving of it to be valuable in that way). Although it is humans (persons, valuers) who must do the valuing, for the ethics of respect for nature, the value so ascribed is not a human value. That is to say, it is not a value derived from considerations regarding human well-being or human rights. It is a value that is ascribed to nonhuman animals and plants themselves, independently of their relationship to what humans judge to be conducive to their own good.

Whatever reasons, then, justify our taking the attitude of respect for nature as defined above are also reasons that show why we *should* regard the living things of the natural world as possessing inherent worth. We saw earlier that, since the attitude is an ultimate one, it cannot be derived from a more fundamental attitude nor shown to be a special case of a more general one. On what sort of grounds, then, can it be established?

The attitude we take toward living things in the natural world depends on the way we look at them, on what kind of beings we conceive them to be, and on how we understand the relations we bear to them. Underlying and supporting our attitude is a certain *belief system* that constitutes a particular world view or outlook on nature and the place of human life in it. To give good reasons for adopting the attitude of respect for nature, then, we must first articulate the belief system which underlies and supports that attitude. If it appears that the belief system is internally coherent and well-ordered, and if, as far as we can now tell, it is consistent with all known scientific truths relevant to our knowledge of the object of the attitude (which in this case includes the whole set of the Earth's natural ecosystems and their communities of life), then there remains the task of indicating why scientifically informed and rational thinkers with a developed capacity of reality awareness can find it acceptable as a way of conceiving of the natural world and

our place in it. To the extent we can do this we provide at least a reasonable argument for accepting the belief system and the ultimate moral attitude it supports.

I do not hold that such a belief system can be *proven* to be true, either inductively or deductively. As we shall see, not all of its components can be stated in the form of empirically verifiable propositions. Nor is its internal order governed by purely logical relationships. But the system as a whole, I contend, constitutes a coherent, unified, and rationally acceptable "picture" or "map" of a total world. By examining each of its main components and seeing how they fit together, we obtain a scientifically informed and well-ordered conception of nature and the place of humans in it.

This belief system underlying the attitude of respect for nature I call (for want of a better name) "the biocentric outlook on nature." Since it is not wholly analyzable into empirically confirmable assertions, it should not be thought of as simply a compendium of the biological sciences concerning our planet's ecosystems. It might best be described as a philosophical world view, to distinguish it from a scientific theory or explanatory system. However, one of its major tenets is the great lesson we have learned from the science of ecology: the interdependence of all living things in an organically unified order whose balance and stability are necessary conditions for the realization of the good of its constituent biotic communities.

Before turning to an account of the main components of the biocentric outlook, it is convenient here to set forth the overall structure of my theory of environmental ethics as it has now emerged. The ethics of respect for nature is made up of three basic elements: a belief system, an ultimate moral attitude, and a set of rules of duty and standards of character. These elements are connected with each other in the following manner. The belief system provides a certain outlook on nature which supports and makes intelligible an autonomous agent's adopting, as an ultimate moral attitude, the attitude of respect for nature. It supports and makes intelligible the attitude in the sense that, when an autonomous agent understands its moral relations to the natural world in terms of this outlook, it recognizes the attitude of respect to be the only *suitable* or *fitting* attitude to take toward all wild forms of life in the Earth's biosphere. Living things are now viewed as *the appropriate objects of the attitude of respect* and are accordingly regarded as entities possessing inherent worth. One then places intrinsic value on the promotion and protection of their good. As a consequence of this, one makes a moral commitment to abide by a set of rules of duty and to fulfill (as far as one can by one's own efforts) certain standards of good character. Given one's adoption of the attitude of respect, one makes that moral commitment because one considers those rules and standards to be validly binding on all moral agents. They are seen as embodying forms of conduct and character structures in which the attitude of respect for nature is manifested.

This three-part complex which internally orders the ethics of respect for nature is symmetrical with a theory of human ethics grounded on respect for persons. Such a theory includes, first, a conception of oneself and others as persons, that is, as centers of autonomous choice. Second, there is the attitude of respect for persons as persons. When this is adopted as an ultimate moral attitude it involves the disposition to treat every person as having inherent worth or "human dignity." Every human being, just in virtue of her or his humanity, is understood to be worthy of moral consideration, and intrinsic value is placed on the autonomy and well-being of each. This is what Kant meant by conceiving of persons as ends in themselves. Third, there is an ethical system of duties which are acknowledged to be owed by everyone to everyone. These duties are forms of conduct in which public recognition is given to each individual's inherent worth as a person.

This structural framework for a theory of human ethics is meant to leave open the issue of consequentialism (utilitarianism) versus non-consequentialism (deontology). That issue concerns the particular kind of system of rules defining the duties of moral agents toward persons. Similarly, I am leaving open in this paper the question of what particular kind of system of rules defines our duties with respect to the natural world.

V. THE BIOCENTRIC OUTLOOK ON NATURE

The biocentric outlook on nature has four main components. (1) Humans are thought of as members of the Earth's community of life, holding that membership on the same terms as apply to all the nonhuman members. (2) The Earth's natural ecosystems as a totality are seen as a complex web of interconnected elements, with the sound biological functioning of each being dependent on the sound biological functioning of the others. (This is the component referred to above as the great lesson that the science of ecology has taught us.) (3) Each individual organism is conceived of as a teleological center of life, pursuing its own good in its own way. (4) Whether we are concerned with standards of merit or with the concept of inherent worth, the claim that humans by their very nature are superior to other species is a groundless claim and, in the light of elements (1), (2), and (3) above, must be rejected as nothing more than an irrational bias in our own favor.

The conjunction of these four ideas constitutes the biocentric outlook on nature. In the remainder of this paper I give a brief account of the first three components, followed by a more detailed analysis of the fourth. I then conclude by indicating how this outlook provides a way of justifying the attitude of respect for nature.

VI. HUMANS AS MEMBERS OF THE EARTH'S COMMUNITY OF LIFE

We share with other species a common relationship to the Earth. In accepting the biocentric outlook we take the fact of our being an animal species to be a fundamental feature of our existence. We consider it an essential aspect of "the human condition." We do not deny the differences between ourselves and other species, but we keep in the forefront of our consciousness the fact that in relation to our planet's natural ecosystems we are but one species population among many. Thus we acknowledge our origin in the very same evolutionary process that gave rise to all other species and we recognize ourselves to be confronted with similar environmental challenges to those that confront them. The laws of genetics, of natural selection, and of adaptation apply equally to all of us as biological creatures. In this light we consider ourselves as one with them, not set apart from them. We, as well as they, must face certain basic conditions of existence that impose requirements on us for our survival and well-being. Each animal and plant is like us in having a good of its own. Although our human good (what is of true value in human life, including the exercise of individual autonomy in choosing our own particular value systems) is not like the good of a nonhuman animal or plant, it can no more be realized than their good can without the biological necessities for survival and physical health.

When we look at ourselves from the evolutionary point of view, we see that not only are we very recent arrivals on Earth, but that our emergence as a new species on the planet was originally an event of no particular importance to the entire scheme of things. The Earth was teeming with life long before we appeared. Putting the point metaphorically, we are relative newcomers, entering a home that has been the residence of others for hundreds of millions of years, a home that must now be shared by all of us together.

The comparative brevity of human life on Earth may be vividly depicted by imagining the geological time scale in spatial terms. Suppose we start with algae, which have been around for at least 600 million years. (The earliest protozoa actually predated this by several *billion* years.) If the time that algae have been here were represented by the length of a football field (300 feet), then the period during which sharks have been swimming in the world's oceans and spiders have been spinning their webs would occupy three quarters of the length of the field; reptiles would show up at about the center of the field; mammals would cover the last third of the field; hominids (mammals of the family *Hominidae*) the last two feet; and the species *Homo sapiens* the last six inches.

Whether this newcomer is able to survive as long as other species remains to be seen. But there is surely something presumptuous about the way humans look down on the "lower" animals, especially those that have become extinct. We consider the dinosaurs, for example, to be biological failures, though they existed on our planet for 65 million years. One writer has made the point with beautiful simplicity:

> We sometimes speak of the dinosaurs as failures; there will be time enough for that judgment when we have lasted even for one tenth as long.... [6]

The possibility of the extinction of the human species, a possibility which starkly confronts us in the contemporary world, makes us aware of another respect in which we should not consider ourselves privileged beings in relation to other species. This is the fact that the well-being of humans is dependent upon the ecological soundness and health of many plant and animal communities, while their soundness and health does not in the least depend upon human well-being. Indeed, from their standpoint the very existence of humans is quite unnecessary. Every last man, woman, and child would disappear from the face of the Earth without any significant detrimental consequence for the good of wild animals and plants. On the contrary, many of them would be greatly benefited. The destruction of their habitats by human "developments" would cease. The poisoning and polluting of their environment would come to an end. The Earth's land, air, and water would no longer be subject to the degradation they are now undergoing as the result of large-scale technology and uncontrolled population growth. Life communities in natural ecosystems would gradually return to their former healthy state. Tropical rain forests, for example, would again be able to make their full contribution to a life-sustaining atmosphere for the whole planet. The rivers, lakes, and oceans of the world would (perhaps) eventually become clean again. Spilled oil, plastic trash, and even radioactive waste might finally, after many centuries, cease doing their terrible work. Ecosystems would return to their proper balance, suffering only the disruptions of natural events such as volcanic eruptions and glaciation. From these the community of life could recover, as it has so often done in the past. But the ecological disasters now perpetrated on it by humans—disasters from which it might never recover— these it would no longer have to endure.

If, then, the total, final, absolute extermination of our species (by our own hands?) should take place and if we should not carry all the others with us into oblivion, not only would the Earth's community of life continue to exist, but in all probability its well-being would be enhanced. Our presence, in short, is not needed. If we were to take the standpoint of the community and give voice to its true interest, the ending of our six-inch epoch would most likely be greeted with a hearty "Good riddance!"

VII. THE NATURAL WORLD AS AN ORGANIC SYSTEM

To accept the biocentric outlook and regard ourselves and our place in the world from its perspective is to see the whole natural order of the Earth's biosphere as a complex but unified web of interconnected organisms, objects, and events. The ecological relationships between any community of living things and their environment form an organic whole of functionally interdependent parts. Each ecosystem is a small universe itself in which the interactions of its various species populations comprise an intricately woven network of cause-effect relations. Such dynamic but at the same time relatively stable structures as food chains, predator-prey relations, and plant succession in a forest are self-regulating, energy-recycling mechanisms that preserve the equilibrium of the whole.

As far as the well-being of wild animals and plants is concerned, this ecological equilibrium must not be destroyed. The same holds true of the well-being of humans. When one views the realm of nature from the perspective of the biocentric outlook, one never forgets that in the long run the integrity of the entire biosphere of our planet is essential to the realization of the good of its constituent communities of life, both human and nonhuman.

Although the importance of this idea cannot be overemphasized, it is by now so familiar and so widely acknowledged that I shall not further elaborate on it here. However, I do wish to point out that this "holistic" view of the Earth's ecological systems does not itself constitute a moral norm. It is a factual aspect of biological reality, to be understood as a set of causal connections in ordinary empirical terms. Its significance for humans is the same as its significance for nonhumans, namely, in setting basic conditions for the realization of the good of living things. Its ethical implications for our treatment of the natural environment lie entirely in the fact that our *knowledge* of these causal connections is an essential *means* to fulfilling the aims we set for ourselves in adopting the attitude of respect for nature. In addition, its theoretical implications for the ethics of respect for nature lie in the fact that it (along with the other elements of the biocentric outlook) makes the adopting of that attitude a rational and intelligible thing to do.

VIII. INDIVIDUAL ORGANISMS AS TELEOLOGICAL CENTERS OF LIFE

As our knowledge of living things increases, as we come to a deeper understanding of their life cycles, their interactions with other organisms, and the manifold ways in which they adjust to the environment, we become more fully aware of how each of them is carrying out its biological functions according to the laws of its species-specific nature. But besides this, our increasing knowledge and understanding also develop in us a sharpened awareness of the uniqueness of each individual organism. Scientists who have made careful studies of particular plants and animals, whether in the field or in laboratories, have often acquired a knowledge of their subjects as identifiable individuals. Close observation over extended periods of time has led them to an appreciation of the unique "personalities" of their subjects. Sometimes a scientist may come to take a special interest in a particular animal or plant, all the while remaining strictly objective in the gathering and recording of data. Nonscientists may likewise experience this development of interest when, as amateur naturalists, they make accurate observations over sustained periods of close acquaintance with an individual organism. As one becomes more and more familiar with the organism and its behavior, one becomes fully sensitive to the particular way it is living out its life cycle. One may become fascinated by it and even experience some involvement with its good and bad fortunes (that is, with the occurrence of environmental conditions favorable or unfavorable to the realization of its good). The organism comes to mean something to one as a unique, irreplaceable individual. The final culmination of this process is the achievement of a genuine understanding of its point of view and, with that understanding, an ability to "take" that point of view. *Conceiving of it as a center of life, one is able to look at the world from its perspective.*

This development from objective knowledge to the recognition of individuality, and from the recognition of individuality to full awareness of an organism's standpoint, is a process of heightening our consciousness of what it means to be an individual living thing. We grasp the particularity of the organism as a teleological center of life, striving to preserve itself and to realize its own good in its own unique way.

It is to be noted that we need not be falsely anthropomorphizing when we conceive of individual plants and animals in this manner. Understanding them as teleological centers of life does not necessitate "reading into" them human characteristics. We need not, for example, consider them to have consciousness. Some of them may be aware of the world around them and others may not. Nor need we deny that different kinds and levels of awareness are exemplified when consciousness in some form is present. But conscious or not, all are equally teleological centers of life in the sense that each is a unified system of goal-oriented activities directed toward their preservation and well-being.

When considered from an ethical point of view, a teleological center of life is an entity whose "world" can be viewed from the perspective of *its* life. In looking at the world from that perspective we recognize objects and events occurring in its life as being beneficent, maleficent, or indifferent. The first are occurrences which increase its powers to preserve its existence and realize its good. The second decrease or destroy those powers. The third have neither of these effects on the entity. With regard to our human role as moral agents, we can conceive of a teleological center of life as a being whose standpoint we can take in making judgments about what events in the world are good or evil, desirable or undesirable. In making those judgments it is what promotes or protects the being's own good, not what benefits moral agents themselves, that sets the standard of evaluation. Such judgments can be made about anything that happens to the entity which is favorable or unfavorable in relation to its good. As we pointed out earlier, the entity itself need not have any (conscious) *interest* in what is happening to it for such judgments to be meaningful and true.

It is precisely judgments of this sort that we are disposed to make when we take the attitude of respect for nature. In adopting that attitude those judgments are given weight as reasons for action in our practical deliberation. They become morally relevant facts in the guidance of our conduct.

IX. THE DENIAL OF HUMAN SUPERIORITY

The fourth component of the biocentric outlook on nature is the single most important idea in establishing the justifiability of the attitude of respect for nature. Its central role is due to the special relationship it bears to the first three components of the outlook. This relationship will be brought out after the concept of human superiority is examined and analyzed.[7]

In what sense are humans alleged to be superior to other animals? We are different from them in having certain capacities that they lack. But why should these capacities be a mark of superiority? From what point of view are they judged to be signs of superiority and what sense of superiority is meant? After all, various nonhuman species have capacities that humans lack. There is the speed of a cheetah, the vision of an eagle, the agility of a monkey. Why should not these be taken as signs of *their* superiority over humans?

One answer that comes immediately to mind is that these capacities are not as *valuable* as the human capacities that are claimed to make us superior. Such uniquely human characteristics as rational thought, aesthetic creativity, autonomy and self-determination, and moral freedom, it might be held, have a higher value than the capacities found in other species. Yet we must ask: valuable to whom, and on what grounds?

The human characteristics mentioned are all valuable to humans. They are essential to the preservation and enrichment of our civilization and culture. Clearly it is from the human standpoint that they are being judged to be desirable and good. It is not difficult here to recognize a begging of the question. Humans are claiming human superiority from a strictly human point of view, that is, from a point of view in which the good of humans is taken as the standard of judgment. All we need to do is look at the capacities of nonhuman animals (or plants, for that matter) from the standpoint of *their* good to find a contrary judgment of superiority. The speed of the cheetah, for example, is a sign of its superiority to humans when considered from the standpoint of the good of its species. If it were as slow a runner as a human, it would not be able to survive. And so for all the other abilities of nonhumans which further their good but which are lacking in humans. In each case the claim to human superiority would be rejected from a nonhuman standpoint.

When superiority assertions are interpreted in this way, they are based on judgments of *merit*. To judge the merits of a person or an organism one must apply grading or ranking standards to it. (As I show below, this distinguishes judgments of merit from judgments of inherent worth.) Empirical investigation then determines whether it has the "good-making properties" (merits) in virtue of which it fulfills the standards being applied. In the case of humans, merits may be either moral or nonmoral. We can judge one person to be better than (superior to) another from the moral point of view by applying certain standards to their character and conduct. Similarly, we can appeal to nonmoral criteria in judging someone to be an excellent piano player, a fair cook, a poor tennis player, and so on. Different social purposes and roles are implicit in the making of such judgments, providing the frame of

reference for the choice of standards by which the nonmoral merits of people are determined. Ultimately such purposes and roles stem from a society's way of life as a whole. Now a society's way of life may be thought of as the cultural form given to the realization of human values. Whether moral or nonmoral standards are being applied, then, all judgments of people's merits finally depend on human values. All are made from an exclusively human standpoint.

The question that naturally arises at this juncture is: why should standards that are based on human values be assumed to be the only valid criteria of merit and hence the only true signs of superiority? This question is especially pressing when humans are being judged superior in merit to nonhumans. It is true that a human being may be a better mathematician than a monkey, but the monkey may be a better tree climber than a human being. If we humans value mathematics more than tree climbing, that is because our conception of civilized life makes the development of mathematical ability more desirable than the ability to climb trees. But is it not unreasonable to judge nonhumans by the values of human civilization, rather than by values connected with what it is for a member of *that* species to live a good life? If all living things have a good of their own, it at least makes sense to judge the merits of nonhumans by standards derived from *their* good. To use only standards based on human values is already to commit oneself to holding that humans are superior to nonhumans, which is the point in question.

A further logical flaw arises in connection with the widely held conviction that humans are *morally* superior beings because they possess, while others lack, the capacities of a moral agent (free will, accountability, deliberation, judgment, practical reason). This view rests on a conceptual confusion. As far as moral standards are concerned, only beings that have the capacities of a moral agent can properly be judged to be *either* moral (morally good) *or* immoral (morally deficient). Moral standards are simply not applicable to beings that lack such capacities. Animals and plants cannot therefore be said to be morally inferior in merit to humans. Since the only beings that can have moral merits *or be deficient in such merits* are moral agents, it is conceptually incoherent to judge humans as superior to nonhumans on the ground that humans have moral capacities while nonhumans don't.

Up to this point I have been interpreting the claim that humans are superior to other living things as a grading or ranking judgment regarding their comparative merits. There is, however, another way of understanding the idea of human superiority. According to this interpretation, humans are superior to nonhumans not as regards their merits but as regards their inherent worth. Thus the claim of human superiority is to be understood as asserting that all humans, simply in virtue of their humanity, have *a greater inherent worth* than other living things.

The inherent worth of an entity does not depend on its merits.[8] To consider something as possessing inherent worth, we have seen, is to place intrinsic value on the realization of its good. This is done regardless of whatever particular merits it might have or might lack, as judged by a set of grading or ranking standards. In human affairs, we are all familiar with the principle that one's worth as a person does not vary with one's merits or lack of merits. The same can hold true of animals and plants. To regard such entities as possessing inherent worth entails disregarding their merits and deficiencies, whether they are being judged from a human standpoint or from the standpoint of their own species.

The idea of one entity having more merit than another, and so being superior to it in merit, makes perfectly good sense. Merit is a grading or ranking concept, and judgments of comparative merit are based on the different degrees to which things satisfy a given standard. But what can it mean to talk about one thing being superior to another in inherent worth? In order to get at what is being asserted in such a claim it is helpful first to look at the social origin of the concept of degrees of inherent worth.

The idea that humans can possess different degrees of inherent worth originated in societies having rigid class structures. Before the rise of modern democracies with their egalitarian outlook, one's membership in a hereditary class determined one's social status. People in the upper classes were looked up to, while those in the lower classes were looked down upon. In such a society one's social superiors and social inferiors were clearly defined and easily recognized.

Two aspects of these class-structured societies are especially relevant to the idea of degrees of inherent worth. First, those born into the upper classes were deemed more worthy of respect than those born into the lower orders. Second, the superior worth of upper class people had nothing to do with their merits nor did the inferior worth of those in the lower classes rest on their lack of merits. One's superiority or inferiority entirely derived from a social position one was born into. The modern concept of a meritocracy simply did not apply. One could not advance into a higher class by any sort of moral or nonmoral achievement. Similarly, an aristocrat held his title and all the privileges that went with it just because he was the eldest son of a titled nobleman. Unlike the bestowing of knighthood in contemporary Great Britain, one did not earn membership in the nobility by meritorious conduct.

We who live in modern democracies no longer believe in such hereditary social distinctions. Indeed, we would wholeheartedly condemn them on moral grounds as being fundamentally unjust. We have come to think of class systems as a paradigm of social injustice, it being a central principle of the democratic way of life that among humans there are no superiors and no inferiors. Thus we have rejected the whole conceptual framework in which people are judged to have different degrees of inherent worth. That idea is incompatible with our notion of human equality based on the doctrine that all humans, simply in virtue of their humanity, have the same inherent worth. (The belief in universal human rights is one form that this egalitarianism takes.)

The vast majority of people in modern democracies, however, do not maintain an egalitarian outlook when it comes to comparing human beings with other living things. Most people consider our own species to be superior to all other species and this superiority is understood to be a matter of inherent worth, not merit. There may exist thoroughly vicious and depraved humans who lack all merit. Yet because they are human they are thought to belong to a higher class of entities than any plant or animal. That one is born into the species *Homo sapiens* entitles one to have lordship over those who are one's inferiors, namely, those born into other species. The parallel with hereditary social classes is very close. Implicit in this view is a hierarchical conception of nature according to which an organism has a position of superiority or inferiority in the Earth's community of life simply on the basis of its genetic background. The "lower" orders of life are looked down upon and it is considered perfectly proper that they serve the interests of those belonging to the highest order, namely humans. The intrinsic value we place on the well-being of our fellow humans reflects our recognition of their rightful position as our equals. No such intrinsic value is to be placed on the good of other animals, unless we choose to do so out of fondness or affection for them. But their well-being imposes no moral requirement on us. In this respect there is an absolute difference in moral status between ourselves and them.

This is the structure of concepts and beliefs that people are committed to insofar as they regard humans to be superior in inherent worth to all other species. I now wish to argue that this structure of concepts and beliefs is completely groundless. If we accept the first three components of the biocentric outlook and from that perspective look at the major philosophical traditions which have supported that structure, we find it to be at bottom nothing more than the expression of an irrational bias in our own favor. The philosophical traditions themselves rest on very questionable assumptions or else simply beg the question. I briefly consider three of the main traditions to substantiate the point. These are classical Greek humanism, Cartesian dualism, and the Judeo-Christian concept of the Great Chain of Being.

The inherent superiority of humans over other species was implicit in the Greek definition of man as a rational animal. Our animal nature was identified with "brute" desires that need the order and restraint of reason to rule them (just as reason is the special virtue of those who rule in the ideal state). Rationality was then seen to be the key to our superiority over animals. It enables us to live on a higher plane and endows

us with a nobility and worth that other creatures lack. This familiar way of comparing humans with other species is deeply ingrained in our Western philosophical outlook. The point to consider here is that this view does not actually provide an argument *for* human superiority but rather makes explicit the framework of thought that is implicitly used by those who think of humans as inherently superior to nonhumans. The Greeks who held that humans, in virtue of their rational capacities, have a kind of worth greater than that of any nonrational being, never looked at rationality as but one capacity of living things among many others. But when we consider rationality from the standpoint of the first three elements of the ecological outlook, we see that its value lies in its importance for *human* life. Other creatures achieve their species-specific good without the need of rationality, although they often make use of capacities that humans lack. So the humanistic outlook of classical Greek thought does not give us a neutral (non-question-begging) ground on which to construct a scale of degrees of inherent worth possessed by different species of living things.

The second tradition, centering on the Cartesian dualism of soul and body, also fails to justify the claim to human superiority. That superiority is supposed to derive from the fact that we have souls while animals do not. Animals are mere automata and lack the divine element that makes us spiritual beings. I won't go into the now familiar criticisms of this two-substance view. I only add the point that, even if humans are composed of an immaterial, un-extended soul and a material, extended body, this in itself is not a reason to deem them of greater worth than entities that are only bodies. Why is a soul substance a thing that adds value to its possessor? Unless some theological reasoning is offered here (which many, including myself, would find unacceptable on epistemological grounds), no logical connection is evident. An immaterial something which thinks is better than a material something which does not think only if thinking itself has value, either intrinsically or instrumentally. Now it is intrinsically valuable to humans alone, who value it as an end in itself, and it is instrumentally valuable to those who benefit from it, namely humans.

For animals that neither enjoy thinking for its own sake nor need it for living the kind of life for which they are best adapted, it has no value. Even if "thinking" is broadened to include all forms of consciousness, there are still many living things that can do without it and yet live what is for their species a good life. The anthropocentricity underlying the claim to human superiority runs throughout Cartesian dualism.

A third major source of the idea of human superiority is the Judeo-Christian concept of the Great Chain of Being. Humans are superior to animals and plants because their Creator has given them a higher place on the chain. It begins with God at the top, and then moves to the angels, who are lower than God but higher than humans, then to humans, positioned between the angels and the beasts (partaking of the nature of both), and then on down to the lower levels occupied by nonhuman animals, plants, and finally inanimate objects. Humans, being "made in God's image," are inherently superior to animals and plants by virtue of their being closer (in their essential nature) to God.

The metaphysical and epistemological difficulties with this conception of a hierarchy of entities are, in my mind, insuperable. Without entering into this matter here, I only point out that if we are unwilling to accept the metaphysics of traditional Judaism and Christianity, we are again left without good reasons for holding to the claim of inherent human superiority.

The foregoing considerations (and others like them) leave us with but one ground for the assertion that a human being, regardless of merit, is a higher kind of entity than any other living thing. This is the mere fact of the genetic makeup of the species *Homo sapiens*. But this is surely irrational and arbitrary. Why should the arrangement of genes of a certain type be a mark of superior value, especially when this fact about an organism is taken by itself, unrelated to any other aspect of its life? We might just as well refer to any other genetic makeup as a ground of superior value. Clearly we are confronted here with a wholly arbitrary claim that can only be explained as an irrational bias in our own favor.

That the claim is nothing more than a deep-seated prejudice is brought home to us when we look at our relation to other species in the light of the first three elements of the biocentric outlook. Those elements taken conjointly give us a certain overall view of the natural world and of the place of humans in it. When we take this view we come to understand other living things, their environmental conditions, and their ecological relationships in such a way as to awake in us a deep sense of our kinship with them as fellow members of the Earth's community of life. Humans and nonhumans alike are viewed together as integral parts of one unified whole in which all living things are functionally interrelated. Finally, when our awareness focuses on the individual lives of plants and animals, each is seen to share with us the characteristic of being a teleological center of life striving to realize its own good in its own unique way.

As this entire belief system becomes part of the conceptual framework through which we understand and perceive the world, we come to see ourselves as bearing a certain moral relation to nonhuman forms of life. Our ethical role in nature takes on a new significance. We begin to look at other species as we look at ourselves, seeing them as beings which have a good they are striving to realize just as we have a good we are striving to realize. We accordingly develop the disposition to view the world from the standpoint of their good as well as from the standpoint of our own good. Now if the groundlessness of the claim that humans are inherently superior to other species were brought clearly before our minds, we would not remain intellectually neutral toward that claim but would reject it as being fundamentally at variance with our total world outlook. In the absence of any good reasons for holding it, the assertion of human superiority would then appear simply as the expression of an irrational and self-serving prejudice that favors one particular species over several million others.

Rejecting the notion of human superiority entails its positive counterpart: the doctrine of species impartially. One who accepts that doctrine regards all living things as possessing inherent worth—the *same* inherent worth, since no one species has been shown to be either "higher" or "lower" than any other. Now we saw earlier that, insofar as one thinks of a living thing as possessing inherent worth, one considers it to be the appropriate object of the attitude of respect and believes that attitude to be the only fitting or suitable one for all moral agents to take toward it.

Here, then, is the key to understanding how the attitude of respect is rooted in the biocentric outlook on nature. The basic connection is made through the denial of human superiority. Once we reject the claim that humans are superior either in merit or in worth to other living things, we are ready to adopt the attitude of respect. The denial of human superiority is itself the result of taking the perspective on nature built into the first three elements of the biocentric outlook.

Now the first three elements of the biocentric outlook, it seems clear, would be found acceptable to any rational and scientifically informed thinker who is fully "open" to the reality of the lives of nonhuman organisms. Without denying our distinctively human characteristics, such a thinker can acknowledge the fundamental respects in which we are members of the Earth's community of life and in which the biological conditions necessary for the realization of our human values are inextricably linked with the whole system of nature. In addition, the conception of individual living things as teleological centers of life simply articulates how a scientifically informed thinker comes to understand them as the result of increasingly careful and detailed observations. Thus, the biocentric outlook recommends itself as an acceptable system of concepts and beliefs to anyone who is clear-minded, unbiased, and factually enlightened, and who has a developed capacity of reality awareness with regard to the lives of individual organisms. This, I submit, is as good a reason for making the moral commitment involved in adopting the attitude of respect for nature as any theory of environmental ethics could possibly have.

X. MORAL RIGHTS AND THE MATTER OF COMPETING CLAIMS

I have not asserted anywhere in the foregoing account that animals or plants have moral rights. This omission was deliberate. I do not think that the reference class of the concept, bearer of moral rights, should be extended to include nonhuman living things. My reasons for taking this position, however, go beyond the scope of this paper. I believe I have been able to accomplish many of the same ends which those who ascribe rights to animals or plants wish to accomplish. There is no reason, moreover, why plants and animals, including whole species populations and life communities, cannot be accorded *legal* rights under my theory. To grant them legal protection could be interpreted as giving them legal entitlement to be protected, and this, in fact, would be a means by which a society that subscribed to the ethics of respect for nature could give public recognition to their inherent worth.

There remains the problem of competing claims, even when wild plants and animals are not thought of as bearers of moral rights. If we accept the biocentric outlook and accordingly adopt the attitude of respect for nature as our ultimate moral attitude, how do we resolve conflicts that arise from our respect for persons in the domain of human ethics and our respect for nature in the domain of environmental ethics? This is a question that cannot be adequately dealt with here. My main purpose in this paper has been to try to establish a base point from which we can start working toward a solution to the problem. I have shown why we cannot just begin with an initial presumption in favor of the interests of our own species. It is after all within our power as moral beings to place limits on human population and technology with the deliberate intention of sharing the Earth's bounty with other species. That such sharing is an ideal difficult to realize even in an approximate way does not take away its claim to our deepest moral commitment.

NOTES

1. The conceptual links between an entity *having* a good, something being good *for* it, and events doing good to it are examined by G. H. Von Wright in *The Varieties of Goodness* (New York: Humanities Press, 1963), chaps. 3 and 5.
2. See W. K. Frankena, "Ethics and the Environment," in K. E. Goodpaster and K. M. Sayre, eds. *Ethics and Problems of the 21st Century* (Notre Dame: University of Notre Dame Press, 1979),

pp. 3–20. I critically examine Frankena's views in "Frankena on Environmental Ethics," *Monist,* forthcoming.

3. In the light of considerations set forth in Daniel Dennett's *Brain Storms: Philosophical Essays on Mind and Psychology* (Montgomery, Vermont: Bradford Books, 1978), it is advisable to leave this question unsettled at this time. When machines are developed that function in the way our brains do, we may well come to deem them proper subjects of moral consideration.

4. I have analyzed the nature of this commitment of human ethics in "On Taking the Moral Point of View," *Midwest Studies in Philosophy,* vol. 3, *Studies in Ethical Theory* (1978), pp. 35–61.

5. John Rawls, "Justice as Fairness," *Philosophical Review* 67 (1958): 183.

6. Stephen R. L. Clark, *The Moral Status of Animals* (Oxford: Clarendon Press, 1977), p. 112.

7. My criticisms of the dogma of human superiority gain independent support from a carefully reasoned essay by R. and V. Routley showing the many logical weaknesses in arguments for human-centered theories of environmental ethics. R. and V. Routley, "Against the Inevitability of Human Chauvinism," in K. E. Goodpaster and K. M. Sayre, eds., *Ethics and Problems of the 21st Century* (Notre Dame: University of Notre Dame Press, 1979), pp. 36–59.

8. For this way of distinguishing between merit and inherent worth, I am indebted to Gregory Vlastos, "Justice and Equality," in R. Brandt, ed., *Social Justice* (Englewood Cliffs, NJ: Prentice-Hall 1962), pp. 31–72.

STUDY QUESTIONS

1. Taylor leaves the matter of resolving conflicting claims between humans and nonhumans open in this article. But in his book he lists five principles: self-defense, proportionality, minimum harm, distributive justice, and restitutive justice (restoring ill-gotten gains). The basic needs of humans and nonhumans are to be decided impartially (distributive justice), but the basic needs of nonhumans should override the nonbasic needs of humans. Work out implications of these principles.

2. Is Taylor's biocentrism workable? How would it apply to our relationship with viruses, bacteria, ringworms, parasites, and the predatory animals? Would the basic needs of the two weeds or worms override the needs of one human?

3. Is the notion of objective intrinsic value clear? Is it true? Do we value certain things (e.g., life) because they are intrinsically good, or are they intrinsically good because we value them?

4. What does Taylor say about the relationship between *having a good* and having *inherent worth* or being good? Can something have a good, an interest, without *being* good?

18   On Being Morally Considerable

KENNETH GOODPASTER

Kenneth Goodpaster (b. 1944) has taught philosophy at the University of Notre Dame and Harvard University Business School and now teaches at the University of St. Thomas in St. Paul, Minnesota. He is the author or editor of several works in ethics.

Beginning with an insight from the ecologist Aldo Leopold that moral rightness involves preserving the "integrity, stability, and beauty of the biotic community," Goodpaster argues for an ethic centered in life itself. He argues against both anthropocentric ethics and ethics based on sentience, pointing out that trees and plants have needs and interests. Unlike Albert Schweitzer and Paul Taylor, Goodpaster's version of biocentric ethics is not egalitarian. Possessing a life makes one morally considerable, not of equal moral worth with human beings.

Reprinted from "On Being Morally Considerable," *Journal of Philosophy* (1978) by permission. Slightly edited.

A thing is right when it tends to preserve the integrity, stability and beauty of the biotic community. It is wrong when it tends otherwise.

ALDO LEOPOLD

What follows is a preliminary inquiry into a question which needs more elaborate treatment than an essay can provide. The question can be and has been addressed in different rhetorical formats, but perhaps G. J. Warnock's formulation of it[1] is the best to start with:

> Let us consider the question to whom principles of morality apply from, so to speak, the other end— from the standpoint not of the agent, but of the "patient." What, we may ask here, is the condition of moral *relevance*? What is the condition of having a claim to be *considered*, by rational agents to whom moral principles apply? (148)

In terminology of R. M. Hare (or even Kant), the same question might be put thus: In universalizing our putative moral maxims, what is the scope of the variable over which universalization is to range? A more legalistic idiom, employed recently by Christopher D. Stone,[2] might ask: What are the requirements for "having standing" in the moral sphere? However the question gets formulated, the thrust is in the direction of necessary and sufficient conditions on X in

1. For all *A, X* deserves moral consideration from *A* where *A* ranges over rational moral agents and moral "consideration" is construed broadly to include the most basic forms of practical respect (and so is not restricted to "possession of rights" by *X*). . . .

I

Modern moral philosophy has taken ethical egoism as its principal foil for developing what can fairly be called a *humanistic* perspective on value and obligation. That is, both Kantian and Humean approaches to ethics tend to view the philosophical challenge as that of providing an epistemological and motivational generalization of an agent's natural self-interested concern. Because of this preoccupation with moral "take-off," however, too little critical thought has been

devoted to the flight and its destination. One result might be a certain feeling of impotence in the minds of many moral philosophers when faced with the sorts of issues mentioned earlier, issues that question the breadth of the moral enterprise more than its departure point. To be sure, questions of conservation, preservation of the environment, and technology assessment *can* be approached simply as application questions, e.g., "How shall we evaluate the alternatives available to us instrumentally in relation to humanistic satisfactions?" But there is something distressingly uncritical in this way of framing such issues— distressingly uncritical in the way that deciding foreign policy solely in terms of "the national interest" is uncritical. Or at least, so I think.

It seems to me that we should not only wonder about, but actually follow "the road not taken into the wood." Neither rationality nor the capacity to experience pleasure and pain seem to me necessary (even though they may be sufficient) conditions for moral considerability. And only our hedonistic and concentric forms of ethical reflection keep us from acknowledging this fact. Nothing short of the condition of *being alive* seems to me to be a plausible and nonarbitrary criterion. What is more, this criterion, if taken seriously, could admit of application to entities and systems of entities heretofore unimagined as claimants on our moral attention (such as the biosystem itself). Some may be inclined to take such implications as a *reductio* of the move "beyond humanism." I am beginning to be persuaded, however, that such implications may provide both a meaningful ethical vision and the hope of a more adequate action guide for the long-term future. Paradigms are crucial components in knowledge—but they can conceal as much as they reveal. Our paradigms of moral considerability are individual persons and their joys and sorrows. I want to venture the belief that the universe of moral consideration is more complex than these paradigms allow.

II

My strategy, now that my cards are on the table, will be to spell out a few rules of the game (in this section) and then to examine the "hands" of several respected philosophers whose arguments seem to count against casting the moral net as widely as I am inclined to. . . . In the concluding section . . . , I will discuss several objections and touch on further questions needing attention.

The first . . . distinctions that must be kept clear in addressing our question [have] already been alluded to. It is that between moral *rights* and moral *considerability*. My inclination is to construe the notion of rights as more specific than that of considerability, largely to avoid what seem to be unnecessary complications over the requirements for something's being an appropriate "bearer of rights." The concept of rights is used in wider and narrower senses, of course. Some authors (indeed, one whom we shall consider later in this paper) use it as roughly synonymous with Warnock's notion of "moral relevance." Others believe that being a bearer of rights involves the satisfaction of much more demanding requirements. The sentiments of John Passmore[3] are probably typical of this narrower view:

> The idea of "rights" is simply not applicable to what is non-human. . . . It is one thing to say that it is wrong to treat animals cruelly, quite another to say that animals have rights (116/7).

I doubt whether it is so clear that the class of rights-bearers is or ought to be restricted to human beings, but I propose to suspend this question entirely by framing the discussion in terms of the notion of moral considerability (following Warnock), except in contexts where there is reason to think the widest sense of "rights" is at work. Whether beings who deserve moral consideration in themselves, not simply by reason of their utility to human beings, also possess moral *rights* in some narrow sense is a question which will, therefore, remain open here—and it is a question the answer to which need not be determined in advance.

A second distinction is that between what might be called a *criterion of moral considerability* and a *criterion of moral significance*. The former represents the central quarry here, while the latter, which might easily get confused with the former, aims at governing *comparative* judgments of moral "weight" in cases of conflict. Whether a tree, say, deserves any moral consideration is a question that must be kept separate from the question of whether trees deserve more or less consideration than dogs, or dogs than human persons. We should not expect that the criterion for having "moral standing" at all will be the same as the criterion for adjudicating competing claims to priority among beings that merit that standing. . . .

III

Let us begin with Warnock's own answer to the question, now that the question has been clarified somewhat. In setting out his answer, Warnock argues (in my view, persuasively) against two more restrictive candidates. The first, what might be called the *Kantian principle*, amounts to little more than a reflection of the requirements of moral *agency* onto those of moral considerability:

2. For X to deserve moral consideration from A, X must be a rational human person.

Observing that such a criterion of considerability eliminates children and mentally handicapped adults, among others, Warnock dismisses it as intolerably narrow.

The second candidate, actually a more generous variant of the first, sets the limits of moral considerability by disjoining "potentiality":

3. For all A, X deserves moral consideration from A if and only if X is a rational human person or is a potential rational human person.

Warnock's reply to this suggestion is also persuasive. Infants and imbeciles are no doubt potentially rational, but this does not appear to be the reason why we should not maltreat them. And we would not say that an imbecile reasonably judged to be incurable would thereby reasonably be taken to have no moral claims (151). In short, it seems arbitrary to draw the boundary of moral *considerability* around rational human beings (actual or potential), however plausible it might be to draw the boundary of moral *responsibility* there.

Warnock then settles upon his own solution. The basis of moral claims, he says, may be put as follows:

> ...just as liability to be judged as a moral agent follows from one's general capability of alleviating, by moral action, the ills of the predicament, and is for that reason confined to rational beings, so the condition of being a proper "beneficiary" of moral action is the capability of *suffering* the ills of the predicament—and for that reason is not confined to rational beings, nor even to potential members of that class (151).

The criterion of moral considerability then, is located in the *capacity to suffer:*

4. For all *A*, *X* deserves moral consideration from *A* if and only if *X* is capable of suffering pain (or experiencing enjoyment).

And the defense involves appeal to what Warnock considers to be (analytically) the *object* of the moral enterprise: amelioration of "the predicament."

Now two issues arise immediately in the wake of this sort of appeal. The first has to do with Warnock's own over-all strategy in the context of the quoted passage. Earlier on in his book, he insists that the appropriate analysis of the concept of morality will lead us to an "object" whose pursuit provides the framework for ethics. But the "object" seems to be more restrictive:

> ...the general object of moral evaluation must be to contribute in some respects, by way of the actions of rational beings, to the amelioration of the human predicament—that is, of the conditions in which *these* rational beings, humans, actually find themselves (16; emphasis in the original).

It appears that, by the time moral considerability comes up later in the book, Warnock has changed his mind about the object of morality by enlarging the "predicament" to include nonhumans.

The second issue turns on the question of analysis itself. As I suggested earlier, it is difficult to keep conceptual and substantive questions apart in the present context. We can, of course, stipulatively *define* "morality" as both having an object and having the object of mitigating suffering. But, in the absence of more argument, such definition is itself in need of a warrant. Twentieth-century preoccupation with the naturalistic or definist fallacy should have taught us at least this much.

Neither of these two observations shows that Warnock's suggested criterion is wrong, of course. But they do, I think, put us in a rather more demanding mood. And the mood is aggravated when we look to two other writers on the subject who appear to hold similar views.

W. K. Frankena, in a recent paper,[4] joins forces:

> Like Warnock, I believe that there are right and wrong ways to treat infants, animals, imbeciles, and idiots even if or even though (as the case may be) they are not persons or human beings—just because they are capable of pleasure and suffering, and not just because their lives happen to have some value to or for those who clearly are persons or human beings.

And Peter Singer[5] writes:

> If a being is not capable of suffering, or of experiencing enjoyment or happiness, there is nothing to be taken into account. This is why the limit of sentience (using the term as a convenient, if not strictly accurate, shorthand for the capacity to suffer or experience enjoyment or happiness) is the only defensible boundary of concern for the interests of others (154).

I say that the mood is aggravated because, although I acknowledge and even applaud the conviction expressed by these philosophers that the capacity to suffer (or perhaps better, *sentience*) is sufficient for moral considerability, I fail to understand their reasons for thinking such a criterion necessary. To be sure, there are hints at reasons in each case. Warnock implies that nonsentient beings could not be proper "beneficiaries" of moral action. Singer seems to think that beyond sentience "there is nothing to take into account." And Frankena suggests that nonsentient beings simply do not provide us with moral reasons for respecting them unless it be potentiality for sentience.[6] Yet it is so clear that there *is* something to take into account, something that is not merely "potential sentience" and which surely does qualify beings as beneficiaries and capable of harm—namely, *life*—that the hints provided seem to me to fall short of good reasons.

Biologically, it appears that sentience is an adaptive characteristic of living organisms that provides them with a better capacity to anticipate, and so avoid, threats to life. This at least suggests, though of course it does not prove, that the capacities to suffer and to enjoy are ancillary to something more important rather than tickets to considerability in their own right. In the words of one perceptive scientific observer:

> If we view pleasure as rooted in our sensory physiology, it is not difficult to see that our neurophysiological equipment must have evolved via variation and selective retention in such a way as to record a positive signal to adaptationally satisfactory conditions and a negative signal to adaptationally unsatisfactory conditions....The pleasure signal is only an evolutionarily derived indicator, not the goal itself. It is the applause which signals a job well done, but not the actual completion of the job.[7]

Nor is it absurd to imagine that evolution might have resulted (indeed might still result?) in beings whose capacities to maintain, protect, and advance their lives did not depend upon mechanisms of pain and pleasure at all.

So far, then, we can see that the search for a criterion of moral considerability takes one quickly and plausibly beyond humanism. But there is a tendency, exhibited in the remarks of Warnock, Frankena, and Singer, to draw up the wagons around the notion of sentience. I have suggested that there is reason to go further and not very much in the way of argument not to. But perhaps there is a stronger and more explicit case that can be made for sentience. I think there is, in a way, and I propose to discuss it in detail in the section that follows.

IV

Joel Feinberg offers (51) what may be the clearest and most explicit case for a restrictive criterion on moral considerability (restrictive with respect to life)....[8]

[In] Feinberg's discussion...we discover the clearest line of argument in favor of something like sentience, an argument which was only hinted at in the remarks of Warnock, Frankena, and Singer.

The central thesis defended by Feinberg is that a being cannot intelligibly be said to possess moral rights (read: deserve moral consideration) unless that being satisfies the "interest principle," and that only the subclass of humans and higher animals among living beings satisfies this principle:

> ...the sorts of beings who can have rights are precisely those who have (or can have) interests. I have come to this tentative conclusion for two reasons: (1) because a right holder must be capable of being represented and it is impossible to represent a being that has no interests, and (2) because a right holder must be capable of being a beneficiary in his own person, and a being without interests is a being that is incapable of being harmed or benefited, having no good or "sake" of its own (51).

Implicit in this passage are the following two arguments, interpreted in terms of moral considerability:

(A1) Only beings who can be represented can deserve moral consideration.

Only beings who have (or can have) interests can be represented.

Therefore, only beings who have (or can have) interests can deserve moral consideration.

(A2) Only beings capable of being beneficiaries can deserve moral consideration.

Only beings who have (or can have) interests are capable of being beneficiaries.

Therefore, only beings who have (or can have) interests can deserve moral consideration.

I suspect that these two arguments are at work between the lines in Warnock, Frenkena, and Singer, though of course one can never be sure. In any case, I propose to consider them as the best defense of the sentience criterion in recent literature.

I am prepared to grant, with some reservations, the first premises in each of these obviously valid arguments. The second premises, though, are *both* importantly equivocal. To claim that only beings who have (or can have) interests can be represented might mean that "mere things" cannot be represented because they have nothing to represent, no "interests" as opposed to "usefulness" to defend or protect. Similarly, to claim that only beings who have (or can have) interests are capable of being beneficiaries might mean that "mere things" are incapable of being benefited or harmed—they have no "well-being" to be sought or acknowledged by rational moral agents. So construed, Feinberg seems to be right; but he also seems to be committed to allowing any *living* thing the status of moral considerability. For as he himself admits, even plants

> ...are not "mere things"; they are vital objects with inherited biological propensities determining their natural growth. Moreover we do say that certain conditions are "good" or "bad" for plants, thereby suggesting that plants, unlike rocks, are capable of having a "good" (51).

But Feinberg pretty clearly wants to draw the nets tighter than this—and he does so by interpreting the notion of "interests" in the two second premises more narrowly. The contrast term he favors is not "mere things" but "mindless creatures." And he makes this move by insisting that "interests" logically presuppose *desires* or *wants* or *aims,* the equipment for which is not possessed by plants (nor, we might add, by many animals or even some humans?).

But why should we accept this shift in strength of the criterion? In doing so, we clearly abandon one sense in which living organisms like plants do have interests that can be represented. There is no absurdity in imagining the representation of the needs of a tree for sun and water in the face of a proposal to cut it down or pave its immediate radius for a parking lot. We might of course, on reflection, decide to go ahead and cut it down or do the paving, but there is hardly an intelligibility problem about representing the tree's interest in our deciding not to. In the face of their obvious tendencies

to maintain and heal themselves, it is very difficult to reject the idea of interests on the part of trees (and plants generally) in remaining alive.[9]

Nor will it do to suggest, as Feinberg does, that the needs (interests) of living things like trees are not really their own but implicitly *ours:* "Plants may need things in order to discharge their functions, but their functions are assigned by human interests, not their own" (54). As if it were human interests that assigned to trees the tasks of growth or maintenance! The interests at stake are clearly those of the living things themselves, not simply those of the owners or users or other human persons involved. Indeed, there is a suggestion in this passage that, to be capable of being represented, an organism must *matter* to human beings somehow—a suggestion whose implications for human rights (disenfranchisement) let alone the rights of animals (inconsistently for Feinberg, I think) are grim.

The truth seems to be that the "interests" that nonsentient beings share with sentient beings (over and against "mere things") are far more plausible as criteria of *considerability* than the "interests" that sentient beings share (over and against "mindless creatures"). This is not to say that interests construed in the latter way are morally irrelevant—for they may play a role as criteria of moral *significance*—but it is to say that psychological or hedonic capacities seem unnecessarily sophisticated when it comes to locating the minimal conditions for something's deserving to be valued for its own sake. Surprisingly, Feinberg's own reflections on "mere things" appear to support this very point:

> ...mere things have no conative life: no conscious wishes, desires, and hopes; or urges and impulses; or unconscious drives, aims, and goals; or latent tendencies, direction of growth, and natural fulfillments. Interests must be compounded somehow out of conations; hence mere things have no interests (49).

Together with the acknowledgment, quoted earlier, that plants, for example, are not "mere things," such observations seem to undermine the interest principle in its more restrictive form. I conclude, with appropriate caution, that the interest principle either grows to fit what we might call a "life principle" or requires an arbitrary stipulation of psychological capacities (for desires, wants, etc.) which are neither warranted by (A1) and (A2) nor independently plausible.

V

Thus far, I have examined the views of four philosophers on the necessity of sentience or interests (narrowly conceived) as a condition on moral considerability. I have maintained that these views are not plausibly supported, when they are supported at all, because of a reluctance to acknowledge in nonsentient living beings the presence of independent needs, capacities for benefit and harm, etc. I should like, briefly, to reflect on a more general level about the roots of this reluctance before proceeding to a consideration of objections against the "life" criterion which I have been defending. In the course of this reflection, we might gain some insight into the sources of our collective hesitation in viewing environmental ethics in a "nonchauvinistic" way.

When we consider the reluctance to go beyond sentience in the context of moral consideration—and look for both explanations and justifications—two thoughts come to mind. The first is that, given the connection between beneficence (or nonmaleficence) and morality, it is natural that limits on moral considerability will come directly from limits on the range of beneficiaries (or "maleficiaries"). This is implicit in Warnock and explicit in Feinberg. The second thought is that, if one's conception of the good is *hedonistic* in character, one's conception of a beneficiary will quite naturally be restricted to beings who are capable of pleasure and pain. If pleasure or satisfaction is the only ultimate gift we have to give, morally, then it is to be expected that only those equipped to receive such a gift will enter into our moral deliberation. And if pain or dissatisfaction is the only ultimate harm we can cause, then it is to be expected that only those equipped for it will deserve our consideration. There seems, therefore, to be a noncontingent connection between a hedonistic or quasi-hedonistic theory of value and a response to the moral-considerability question which favors sentience or interest possession (narrowly conceived).

One must, of course, avoid drawing too strong a conclusion about this connection. It does not

follow from the fact that hedonism leads naturally to the sentience criterion either that it entails that criterion or that one who holds that criterion must be a hedonist in his theory of value. For one might be a hedonist with respect to the good and yet think that moral consideration was, on other grounds, restricted to a subclass of the beings capable of enjoyment or pain. And one might hold to the sentience criterion for considerability while denying that pleasure, for example, was the only intrinsically good thing in the life of a human (or nonhuman) being. So hedonism about value and the sentience criterion of moral considerability are not logically equivalent. Nor does either entail the other. But there is some sense, I think, in which they mutually support each other—both in terms of "rendering plausible" and in terms of "helping to explain." As Derek Parfit is fond of putting it, "there are no entailments, but then there seldom are in moral reasoning."[10]

Let me hazard the hypothesis, then, that there is a nonaccidental affinity between a person's or a society's conception of value and its conception of moral considerability. More specifically, there is an affinity between hedonism or some variation on hedonism and a predilection for the sentience criterion of considerability or some variation on it. The implications one might draw from this are many. In the context of a quest for a richer moral framework to deal with a new awareness of the environment, one might be led to expect significant resistance from a hedonistic society unless one forced one's imperatives into an instrumental form. One might also be led to an appreciation of how technology aimed at largely hedonistic goals could gradually "harden the hearts" of a civilization to the biotic community in which it lives—at least until crisis or upheaval raised some questions.

VI

Let us now turn to several objections that might be thought to render a "life principle" of moral considerability untenable quite independently of the adequacy or inadequacy of the sentience or interest principle.

(O1) A principle of moral respect or consideration for life in all its forms is mere Schweitzerian romanticism, even if it does not involve, as it probably does, the projection of mental or psychological categories beyond their responsible boundaries into the realms of plants, insects, and microbes.

(R1) This objection misses the central thrust of my discussion, which is *not* that the sentience criterion is necessary, but applicable to all life forms—rather the point is that the possession of sentience is not necessary for moral considerability. Schweitzer himself may have held the former view—and so have been "romantic"—but this is beside the point.

(O2) To suggest seriously that moral considerability is coextensive with life is to suggest that conscious, feeling beings have no more central role in the moral life than vegetables, which is downright absurd—if not perverse.

(R2) This objection misses the central thrust of my discussion as well, for a different reason. It is consistent with acknowledging the moral considerability of all life forms to go on to point out differences of moral significance among these life forms. And as far as perversion is concerned, history will perhaps be a better judge of our civilization's treatment of animals and the living environment on that score.

(O3) Consideration of life can serve as a criterion only to the degree that life itself can be given a precise definition; and it can't.

(R3) I fail to see why a criterion of moral considerability must be strictly decidable in order to be tenable. Surely rationality, potential rationality, sentience, and the capacity for or possession of interests fare no better here. Moreover, there do seem to be empirically respectable accounts of the nature of living beings available which are not intolerably vague or open-textured:

> The typifying mark of a living system . . . appears to be its persistent state of low entropy, sustained by metabolic processes for accumulating energy, and maintained in equilibrium with its environment by homeostatic feedback processes.[11]

Granting the need for certain further qualifications, a definition such as this strikes me as not only plausible in its own right, but ethically illuminating, since it suggests that the core of moral concern lies in respect for self-sustaining organization and integration in the face of pressures toward high entropy.

(O4) If life, as understood in the previous response, is really taken as the key to moral considerability, then it is possible that larger systems besides our ordinarily understood "linear" extrapolations from human beings (e.g., animals, plants, etc.) might satisfy the conditions, such as the biosystem as a whole. This surely would be a *reductio* of the life principle.

(R4) At best, it would be a *reductio* of the life principle in this form or without qualification. But it seems to be that such (perhaps surprising) implications, if true, should be taken seriously. There is some evidence that the biosystem as a whole exhibits behavior approximating to the definition sketched above,[12] and I see no reason to deny it moral considerability on that account. Why should the universe of moral considerability map neatly onto our medium-sized framework of organisms?

(O5) There are severe epistemological problems about imputing interests, benefits, harms, etc. to nonsentient beings. What is it for a tree to have needs?

(R5) I am not convinced that the epistemological problems are more severe in this context than they would be in numerous others which the objector would probably not find problematic. Christopher Stone has put this point nicely:

> I am sure I can judge with more certainty and meaningfulness whether and when my lawn wants (needs) water than the Attorney General can judge whether and when the United States wants (needs) to take an appeal from an adverse judgment by a lower court. The lawn tells me that it wants water by a certain dryness of the blades and soil—immediately obvious to the touch—the appearance of bald spots, yellowing, and a lack of springiness after being walked on; how does "the United States" communicate to the Attorney General? (24).[13]

We make decisions in the interests of others or on behalf of others every day—"others" whose wants are far less verifiable than those of most living creatures.

(O6) Whatever the force of the previous objections, the clearest and most decisive refutation of the principle of respect for life is that one cannot *live* according to it, nor is there any indication in nature that we were intended to. We must eat, experiment to gain knowledge, protect ourselves from predation (macroscopic and microscopic), and in general deal with the overwhelming complexities of the moral life while remaining psychologically intact. To take seriously the criterion of considerability being defended, all these things must be seen as somehow morally wrong.

(R6) This objection, if it is not met by implication in (R2), can be met, I think, by recalling the distinction made earlier between regulative and operative moral consideration. It seems to me that there clearly are limits to the operational character of respect for living things. We must eat, and usually this involves killing (though not always). We must have knowledge, and sometimes this involves experimentation with living things and killing (though not always). We must protect ourselves from predation and disease, and sometimes this involves killing (though not always). The regulative character of the moral consideration due to all living things asks, as far as I can see, for sensitivity and awareness, not for suicide (psychic or otherwise). But it is not vacuous, in that it does provide a *ceteris paribus* encouragement in the direction of nutritional, scientific, and medical practices of a genuinely life-respecting sort.

As for the implicit claim, in the objection, that since nature doesn't respect life, we needn't, there are two rejoinders. The first is that the premise is not so clearly true. Gratuitous killing in nature is rare indeed. The second, and more important, response is that the issue at hand has to do with the appropriate moral demands to be made on rational moral agents, not on beings who are not rational moral agents. Besides, this objection would tell equally against *any* criterion of moral considerability so far as I can see, if the suggestion is that nature is amoral.

NOTES

1. *The Object of Morality* (New York: Methuen, 1971); parenthetical page references to Warnock will be to this book.

2. Stone, *Should Trees Have Standing?* (Los Altos: William Kaufmann, 1974).

3. Passmore, *Man's Responsibility for Nature* (New York: Scribners, 1974).

4. "Ethics and the Environment" in K. Goodpaster and K. Sayre, eds., *Ethics and Problems of the 21st Century* (Notre Dame University Press, 1978).

5. "All Animals Are Equal," in Tom Regan and Peter Singer, *Animal Rights and Human Obligations* (Englewood Cliffs, NJ: Prentice-Hall, 1976), p. 316.

6. "I can see no reason, from the moral point of view, why we should respect something that is alive but has no conscious sentiency and so can experience no pleasure or pain, joy or suffering, unless perhaps it is potentially a consciously sentient being, as in the case of a fetus. Why, if leaves and trees have no capacity to feel pleasure or to suffer, should I tear no leaf from a tree? Why should I respect its location any more than that of a stone in my driveway, if no benefit or harm comes to any person or sentient being by my moving it?" ("Ethics and the Environment").

7. Mark W. Lipsey, "Value Science and Developing Society," paper delivered to the Society for Religion in Higher Education, Institute on Society, Technology and Values (July 15–Aug. 4, 1973).

8. Joel Feinberg, "The Rights of Animals and Unborn Generations" in Blackstone, ed., *Philosophy and Environmental Crisis.*

9. See Albert Szent-Gyorgyi, *The Living State* (New York: Academic Press, 1972), esp. ch. vi, "Vegetable Defense Systems."

10. "Later Selves and Moral Principles," in A. Montefiori, ed. *Philosophy and Personal Relations* (Boston: Routledge & Kegan Paul, 1973), p. 147.

11. K. M. Sayre, *Cybernetics and the Philosophy of Mind* (New York: Humanities, 1976), p. 91.

12. See J. Lovelock and S. Epton, "In Quest for Gaia," *The New Scientist* LXV, 935 (Feb. 6, 1975).

13. Stone, op. cit. p. 24.

✺ STUDY QUESTIONS

1. Compare Goodpaster's version of biocentric ethics with Schweitzer's and Taylor's versions. What are the similarities and differences? Which has the stronger case?

2. According to Goodpaster, what does modern moral philosophy take as its main obstacle in developing a *humanistic* perspective on value and obligation? How does this fact affect modern ethics?

3. What does Goodpaster mean by "moral considerability"?

4. What are Goodpaster's objections to those like Feinberg and Singer who would make *sentience* the necessary condition for moral considerability?

5. What is Goodpaster's definition of "interests"? Do you agree that all living things have needs and interests? Is this morally significant?

ECOCENTRIC ETHICS

19   Ecocentrism: The Land Ethic

ALDO LEOPOLD

Aldo Leopold (1887–1947) worked for the U.S. Forest Service before becoming the first professor of Wildlife Management at the University of Wisconsin. He is considered the father of "The Land Ethic." His main work is *Sand County Almanac* (1947) from which our selection is taken.

Leopold was distressed at the degradation of the environment, and argued that we must begin to realize our symbiotic relationship to Earth so that we value "the land" or biotic community for its own sake. We must come to see ourselves, not as conquerors of the land but rather, as plain members and citizens of the biotic community.

When god-like Odysseus returned from the wars in Troy, he hanged all on one rope a dozen slave-girls of his household whom he suspected of misbehavior during his absence.

This hanging involved no question of propriety. The girls were property. The disposal of property was then, as now, a matter of expediency, not of right and wrong.

Concepts of right and wrong were not lacking from Odysseus' Greece: witness the fidelity of his wife through the long years before at last his black-prowed galleys clove the wine-dark seas for home. The ethical structure of that day covered wives, but had not yet been extended to human chattels. During the three thousand years which have since elapsed, ethical criteria have been extended to many fields of conduct, with corresponding shrinkages in those judged by expediency only.

THE ETHICAL SEQUENCE

This extension of ethics, so far studied only by philosophers, is actually a process in ecological evolution. Its sequences may be described in ecological as well as in philosophical terms. An ethic, ecologically, is a limitation on freedom of action in the struggle for existence. An ethic, philosophically, is a differentiation of social from anti-social conduct. These are two definitions of one thing. The thing has its origin in the tendency of interdependent individuals or groups to evolve modes of cooperation. The ecologist calls these symbioses. Politics and economics are advanced symbioses in which the original free-for-all competition has been replaced, in part, by cooperative mechanisms with an ethical content.

The complexity of cooperative mechanisms has increased with population density, and with the efficiency of tools. It was simpler, for example, to define the anti-social uses of sticks and stones in the days of the mastodons than of bullets and billboards in the age of motors.

The first ethics dealt with the relation between individuals; the Mosaic Decalogue is an example. Later accretions dealt with the relation between the individual and society. The Golden Rule tries to integrate the individual to society; democracy to integrate social organization to the individual.

There is as yet no ethic dealing with man's relation to land and to the animals and plants which grow upon it. Land, like Odysseus' slave-girls, is still property. The land-relation is still strictly economic, entailing privileges but not obligations.

The extension of ethics to this third element in human environment is, if I read the evidence correctly, an evolutionary possibility and an ecological necessity. It is the third step in a sequence. The first two have already been taken. Individual thinkers since the days of Ezekiel and Isaiah have asserted that the despoliation of land is not only inexpedient but wrong. Society, however, has not yet affirmed their belief. I regard the present conservation movement as the embryo of such an affirmation.

An ethic may be regarded as a mode of guidance for meeting ecological situations so new or intricate, or involving such deferred reactions, that the path of social expediency is not discernible to the average individual. Animal instincts are modes of guidance for the individual in meeting such situations. Ethics are possibly a kind of community instinct in-the-making.

THE COMMUNITY CONCEPT

All ethics so far evolved rest upon a single premise: that the individual is a member of a community of interdependent parts. His instincts prompt him to compete for his place in the community, but his ethics prompt him also to cooperate (perhaps in order that there may be a place to compete for).

The land ethic simply enlarges the boundaries of the community to include soils, waters, plants, and animals, or collectively: the land.

This sounds simple: do we not already sing our love for and obligation to the land of the free and the home of the brave? Yes, but just what and whom do we love? Certainly not the soil, which we are sending helter-skelter downriver. Certainly not the waters, which we assume have no function except to turn turbines, float barges, and carry off sewage. Certainly not the plants, of which we exterminate whole communities without batting an eye. Certainly not the animals, of which we have already extirpated many of the largest and most beautiful species. A land ethic of course cannot prevent the alteration, management, and use of these "resources," but it does affirm their right to continued existence, and, at least in spots, their continued existence in a natural state.

In short, a land ethic changes the role of *Homo sapiens* from conqueror of the land-community to plain member and citizen of it. It implies respect for his fellow-members, and also respect for the community as such.

In human history, we have learned (I hope) that the conqueror role is eventually self-defeating. Why? Because it is implicit in such a role that the conqueror knows, *ex cathedra,* just what makes the community clock tick, and just what and who is valuable, and what and who is worthless, in community life. It always turns out that he knows neither, and this is why his conquests eventually defeat themselves.

In the biotic community, a parallel situation exists. Abraham knew exactly what the Land was for: it was to drip milk and honey into Abraham's mouth. At the present moment, the assurance with which we regard this assumption is inverse to the degree of our education.

The ordinary citizen today assumes that science knows what makes the community clock tick; the scientist is equally sure that he does not. He knows that the biotic mechanism is so complex that its workings may never be fully understood.

That man is, in fact, only a member of a biotic team is shown by an ecological interpretation of history. Many historical events, hitherto explained solely in terms of human enterprise, were actually biotic interactions between people and land. The characteristics of the land determined the facts quite as potently as the characteristics of the men who lived on it.

Consider, for example, the settlement of the Mississippi valley. In the years following the Revolution, three groups were contending for its control: the native Indian, the French and English traders, and the American settlers. Historians wonder what would have happened if the English at Detroit had thrown a little more weight into the Indian side of those tipsy scales which decided the outcome of the colonial migration into the cane-lands of Kentucky. It is time now to ponder the fact that the cane-lands, when subjected to the particular mixture of forces represented by the cow, plow, fire, and ax of the pioneer, became bluegrass. What if the plant succession inherent in this dark and bloody ground had, under the impact of these forces, given us some worthless sedge, shrub, or weed? Would Boone and Kenton have held out? Would there have been any overflow into Ohio, Indiana, Illinois, and Missouri? Any Louisiana Purchase? Any transcontinental union of new states? Any Civil War?

Kentucky was one sentence in the drama of history. We are commonly told what the human actors in this drama tried to do, but we are seldom told that their success, or the lack of it, hung in large degree on the reaction of particular soils to the impact of the particular forces exerted by their occupancy. In the case of Kentucky, we do not even know where the bluegrass came from—whether it is a native species, or a stowaway from Europe.

Contrast the cane-lands with what hindsight tells us about the Southwest, where the pioneers were equally brave, resourceful, and persevering. The impact of occupancy here brought no bluegrass, or other plant fitted to withstand the bumps and buffetings of hard use. This region, when grazed by livestock, reverted through a sense of more and more worthless grasses, shrubs, and weeds to a condition of unstable equilibrium. Each recession of plant types bred erosion; each increment to erosion bred a further recession of plants. The result today is a progressive and mutual deterioration, not only of plants and soils, but of the animal community subsisting thereon. The early settlers did not expect this: on the ciénegas of New Mexico some even cut ditches to hasten it. So subtle has been its

progress that few residents of the region are aware of it. It is quite invisible to the tourist who finds this wrecked landscape colorful and charming (as indeed it is, but it bears scant resemblance to what it was in 1848).

This same landscape was "developed" once before, but with quite different results. The Pueblo Indians settled the Southwest in pre-Columbian times, but they happened *not* to be equipped with range livestock. Their civilization expired, but not because their land expired.

In India, regions devoid of any sod-forming grass have been settled, apparently without wrecking the land, by the simple expedient of carrying the grass to the cow, rather than vice versa. (Was this the result of some deep wisdom, or was it just good luck? I do not know.)

In short, the plant succession steered the course of history; the pioneer simply demonstrated, for good or ill, what successions inhered in the land. Is history taught in this spirit? It will be, once the concept of land as a community really penetrates our intellectual life.

THE ECOLOGICAL CONSCIENCE

Conservation is a state of harmony between men and land. Despite nearly a century of propaganda, conservation still proceeds at a snail's pace; progress still consists largely of letterhead pieties and convention oratory. On the back forty we still slip two steps backward for each forward stride.

The usual answer to this dilemma is "more conservation education." No one will debate this, but is it certain that only the *volume* of education needs stepping up? Is something lacking in the *content* as well?

It is difficult to give a fair summary of its content in brief form, but, as I understand it, the content is substantially this: obey the law, vote right, join some organizations, and practice what conservation is profitable on your own land; the government will do the rest.

Is not this formula too easy to accomplish anything worthwhile? It defines no right or wrong, assigns no obligation, calls for no sacrifice, implies no change in the current philosophy of values. In respect of land-use, it urges only enlightened self-interest. Just how far will such education take us? An example will perhaps yield a partial answer.

By 1930 it had become clear to all except the ecologically blind that southwestern Wisconsin's topsoil was slipping seaward. In 1933 the farmers were told that if they would adopt certain remedial practices for five years, the public would donate CCC labor to install them, plus the necessary machinery and materials. The offer was widely accepted, but the practices were widely forgotten when the five-year contract period was up. The farmers continued only those practices that yielded an immediate and visible economic gain for themselves.

This led to the idea that maybe farmers would learn more quickly if they themselves wrote the rules. Accordingly the Wisconsin Legislature in 1937 passed the Soil Conservation District Law. This said to farmers, in effect: *We, the public, will furnish you free technical service and loan you specialized machinery, if you will write your own rules for land-use. Each county may write its own rules, and these will have the force of law.* Nearly all the counties promptly organized to accept the proffered help, but after a decade of operation, *no county has yet written a single rule.* There has been visible progress in such practices as strip-cropping, pasture renovation, and soil liming, but none in fencing woodlots against grazing, and none in excluding plow and cow from steep slopes. The farmers, in short, have selected those remedial practices which were profitable anyhow, and ignored those which were profitable to the community, but not clearly profitable to themselves.

When one asks why no rules have been written, one is told that the community is not yet ready to support them; education must precede rules. But the education actually in progress makes no mention of obligations to land over and above those dictated by self-interest. The net result is that we have more education but less soil, fewer healthy woods, and as many floods as in 1937.

The puzzling aspect of such situations is that the existence of obligations over and above self-interest is taken for granted in such rural community enterprises as the betterment of roads, schools, churches, and baseball teams. Their existence is not taken for granted, nor as yet seriously discussed, in bettering the behavior of the water that falls on the land, or in the preserving of the beauty or diversity of the farm landscape. Land-use ethics are still governed wholly by economic self-interest, just as social ethics were a century ago.

To sum up: we asked the farmer to do what he conveniently could to save his soil, and he has done just that, and only that. The farmer who clears the woods off a 75 per cent slope, turns his cows into the clearing, and dumps its rainfall, rocks, and soil into the community creek, is still (if otherwise decent) a respected member of society. If he puts lime on his fields and plants his crops on contour, he is still entitled to all the privileges and emoluments of his Soil Conservation District. The District is a beautiful piece of social machinery, but it is coughing along on two cylinders because we have been too timid, and too anxious for quick success, to tell the farmer the true magnitude of his obligations. Obligations have no meaning without conscience, and the problem we face is the extension of the social conscience from people to land.

No important change in ethics was ever accomplished without an internal change in our intellectual emphasis, loyalties, affections, and convictions. The proof that conservation has not yet touched these foundations of conduct lies in the fact that philosophy and religion have not yet heard of it. In our attempt to make conservation easy, we have made it trivial.

SUBSTITUTES FOR A LAND ETHIC

When the logic of history hungers for bread and we hand out a stone, we are at pains to explain how much the stone resembles bread. I now describe some of the stones which serve in lieu of a land ethic.

One basic weakness in a conservation system based wholly on economic motives is that most members of the land community have no economic value. Wildflowers and songbirds are examples. Of the 22,000 higher plants and animals native to Wisconsin, it is doubtful whether more than 5 per cent can be sold, fed, eaten, or otherwise put to economic use. Yet these creatures are members of the biotic community, and if (as I believe) its stability depends on its integrity, they are entitled to continuance.

When one of these non-economic categories is threatened, and if we happen to love it, we invent subterfuges to give it economic importance. At the beginning of the century songbirds were supposed to be disappearing. Ornithologists jumped to the rescue with some distinctly shaky evidence to the effect that insects would eat us up if birds failed to control them. The evidence had to be economic in order to be valid.

It is painful to read these circumlocutions today. We have no land ethic yet, but we have at least drawn nearer the point of admitting that birds should continue as a matter of biotic right, regardless of the presence or absence of economic advantage to us.

A parallel situation exists in respect of predatory mammals, raptorial birds, and fish-eating birds. Time was when biologists somewhat overworked the evidence that these creatures preserve the health of game by killing weaklings, or that they control rodents for the farmer, or that they prey only on "worthless" species. Here again, the evidence had to be economic in order to be valid. It is only in recent years that we hear the more honest argument that predators are members of the community, and that no special interest has the right to exterminate them for the sake of a benefit, real or fancied, to itself. Unfortunately this enlightened view is still in the talk stage. In the field the extermination of predators goes merrily on: witness the impending erasure of the timber wolf by fiat of Congress, the Conservation Bureaus, and many state legislatures.

Some species of trees have been "read out of the party" by economics-minded foresters because they grow too slowly, or have too low a sale value to pay as timber crops: white cedar, tamarack, cypress, beech, and hemlock are examples. In Europe, where forestry is ecologically more advanced, the non-commercial tree species are recognized as members of the native forest community, to be preserved as such, within reason. Moreover some (like beech) have been found to have a valuable function in building up soil fertility. The interdependence of the forest and its constituent tree species, ground flora, and fauna is taken for granted.

Lack of economic value is sometimes a character not only of species or groups, but of entire biotic communities: marshes, bogs, dunes, and "deserts" are examples. Our formula in such cases is to relegate their conservation to government as refuges, monuments, or parks. The difficulty is that these communities are usually interspersed with more valuable private lands; the government cannot possibly own or control such scattered parcels. The net effect is that we have relegated some of them to ultimate extinction over large areas. If the private owner were ecologically minded, he would be proud to be the custodian of a reasonable proportion of such areas, which add diversity and beauty to his farm and to his community.

In some instances, the assumed lack of profit in these "waste" areas has proved to be wrong, but only after most of them had been done away with. The present scramble to reflood muskrat marshes is a case in point.

There is a clear tendency in American conservation to relegate to government all necessary jobs that private landowners fail to perform. Government ownership, operation, subsidy, or regulation is now widely prevalent in forestry, range management, soil and watershed management, park and wilderness conservation, fisheries management, and migratory bird management, with more to come. Most of this growth in governmental conservation is proper and logical, some of it is inevitable. That I imply no disapproval of it is implicit in the fact that I have spent most of my life working for it. Nevertheless the question arises: What is the ultimate magnitude of the enterprise? Will the tax base carry its eventual ramifications? At what point will governmental conservation, like the mastodon, become handicapped by its own dimensions? The answer, if there is any, seems to be in a land ethic, or some other force which assigns more obligation to the private landowner.

Industrial landowners and users, especially lumbermen and stockmen, are inclined to wail long and loudly about the extension of government ownership and regulation to land, but (with notable exceptions) they show little disposition to develop the only visible alternative: the voluntary practice of conservation on their own lands.

When the private landowner is asked to perform some unprofitable act for the good of the community, he today assents only with outstretched palm. If the act costs him cash this is fair and proper, but when it costs only forethought, open-mindedness, or time, the issue is at least debatable. The overwhelming growth of land-uses subsidies in recent years must be ascribed, in large part, to the government's own agencies for conservation education: the land bureaus, the agricultural colleges, and the extension services. As far as I can detect, no ethical obligation toward land is taught in these institutions.

To sum up: a system of conservation based solely on economic self-interest is hopelessly lopsided. It tends to ignore, and thus eventually to eliminate, many elements in the land community that lack commercial value, but that are (as far as we know) essential to its healthy functioning. It assumes, falsely, I think, that the economic parts of the biotic clock will function without the uneconomic parts. It tends to relegate to government many functions eventually too large, too complex, or too widely dispersed to be performed by government.

An ethical obligation on the part of the private owner is the only visible remedy for these situations.

THE LAND PYRAMID

An ethic to supplement and guide the economic relation to land presupposes the existence of some mental image of land as a biotic mechanism. We can be ethical only in relation to something we can see, feel, understand, love, or otherwise have faith in.

The image commonly employed in conservation education is "the balance of nature." For reasons too lengthy to detail here, this figure of speech fails to describe accurately what little we know about the land mechanism. A much truer image is the one employed in ecology: the biotic pyramid. I shall first sketch the pyramid as a symbol of land, and later develop some of its implications in terms of land-use.

Plants absorb energy from the sun. This energy flows through a circuit called the biota, which may be represented by a pyramid consisting of layers. The bottom layer is the soil. A plant layer rests on the soil, an insect layer on the plants, a bird and rodent layer on the insects, and so on up through various animal groups to the apex layer, which consists of the larger carnivores.

The species of a layer are alike not in where they came from, or in what they look like, but rather in what they eat. Each successive layer depends on those below it for food and often for other services, and each in turn furnishes food and services to those above. Proceeding upward, each successive layer decreases in numerical abundance. Thus, for every carnivore there are hundreds of his prey, thousands of their prey, millions of insects, uncountable plants. The pyramidal form of the system reflects this numerical progression from apex to base. Man shares an intermediate layer with the bears, raccoons, and squirrels which eat both meat and vegetables.

The lines of dependency for food and other services are called food chains. Thus soil-oak-deer-Indian is a chain that has now been largely converted to soil-corn-cow-farmer. Each species, including ourselves, is a link in many chains. The deer eats a hundred plants other than oak, and the cow a hundred plants other than corn. Both, then, are links in a hundred chains. The pyramid is a tangle of chains so complex as to seem disorderly, yet the stability of the system proves it to be a highly organized structure. Its functioning depends on the cooperation and competition of its diverse parts.

In the beginning, the pyramid of life was low and squat; the food chains short and simple. Evolution has added layer after layer, link after link. Man is one of thousands of accretions to the height and complexity of the pyramid. Science has given us many doubts, but it has given us at least one certainty: the trend of evolution is to elaborate and diversify the biota.

Land, then, is not merely soil; it is a fountain of energy flowing through a circuit of soils, plants, and animals. Food chains are the living channels which conduct energy upward; death and decay return it to the soil. The circuit is not closed; some energy is dissipated in decay, some is added by absorption from the air, some is stored in soils, peats, and long-lived forests; but it is a sustained circuit, like a slowly augmented revolving fund of life. There is always a net loss by downhill wash, but this is normally small and offset by the decay of rocks. It is deposited in the ocean and, in the course of geological time, raised to form new lands and new pyramids.

The velocity and character of the upward flow of energy depend on the complex structure of the plant and animal community, much as the upward flow of sap in a tree depends on its complex cellular organization. Without this complexity, normal circulation would presumably not occur. Structure means the characteristic numbers, as well as the characteristic kinds and functions, of the component species. This interdependence between the complex structure of the land and its smooth functioning as an energy unit is one of its basic attributes.

When a change occurs in one part of the circuit, many other parts must adjust themselves to it. Change does not necessarily obstruct or divert the flow of energy; evolution is a long series of self-induced changes, the net result of which has been to elaborate the flow mechanism and to lengthen the circuit. Evolutionary changes, however, are usually slow and local. Man's invention of tools has enabled him to make changes of unprecedented violence, rapidity, and scope.

One change is in the composition of floras and faunas. The larger predators are lopped off the apex of the pyramid; food chains, for the first time in history, become shorter rather than longer. Domesticated species from other lands are substituted for wild ones, and wild ones are moved to new habitats. In this world-wide pooling of faunas and floras, some species get out of bounds as pests and diseases, others are extinguished. Such effects are seldom intended or foreseen; they represent unpredicted and often untraceable readjustments in the structure. Agricultural science is largely a race between the emergence of new pests and the emergence of new techniques for their control.

Another change touches the flow of energy through plants and animals and its return to the soil. Fertility is the ability of soil to receive, store, and release energy. Agriculture, by

overdrafts on the soil, or by too radical a substitution of domestic for native species in the superstructure, may derange the channels of flow or deplete storage. Soils depleted of their storage, or of the organic matter which anchors it, wash away faster than they form. This is erosion.

Waters, like soil, are part of the energy circuit. Industry, by polluting waters or obstructing them with dams, may exclude the plants and animals necessary to keep energy in circulation.

Transportation brings about another basic change: the plants or animals grown in one region are now consumed and returned to the soil in another. Transportation taps the energy stored in rocks, and in the air, and uses it elsewhere; thus we fertilize the garden with nitrogen gleaned by the guano birds from the fishes of seas on the other side of the Equator. Thus the formerly localized and self-contained circuits are pooled on a world-wide scale.

The process of altering the pyramid for human occupation releases stored energy, and this often gives rise, during the pioneering period, to a deceptive exuberance of plant and animal life, both wild and tame. These releases of biotic capital tend to becloud or postpone the penalties of violence.

This thumbnail sketch of land as an energy circuit conveys three basic ideas:

1. That land is not merely soil.
2. That the native plants and animals kept the energy circuit open; others may or may not.
3. That man-made changes are of a different order than evolutionary changes, and have effects more comprehensive than is intended or foreseen.

These ideas, collectively, raise two basic issues: Can the land adjust itself to the new order? Can the desired alterations be accomplished with less violence?

Biotas seem to differ in their capacity to sustain violent conversion. Western Europe, for example, carries a far different pyramid than Caesar found there. Some large animals are lost; swampy forests have become meadows or plowland; many new plants and animals are introduced, some of which escape as pests; the remaining natives are greatly changed in distribution and abundance. Yet the soil is still there and, with the help of imported nutrients, still fertile; and waters flow normally; the new structure seems to function and to persist. There is no visible stoppage or derangement of the circuit.

Western Europe, then, has a resistant biota. Its inner processes are tough, elastic, resistant to strain. No matter how violent the alterations, the pyramid, so far, has developed some new *modus vivendi* which preserves its habitability for man, and for most of the other natives.

Japan seems to present another instance of radical conversion without disorganization.

Most other civilized regions, and some as yet barely touched by civilization, display various stages of disorganization, varying from initial symptoms to advanced wastage. In Asia Minor and North Africa diagnosis is confused by climatic changes, which may have been either the cause or the effect of advanced wastage. In the United States the degree of disorganization varies locally; it is worst in the Southwest, the Ozarks, and parts of the South, and least in New England and the Northwest. Better land-uses may still arrest it in the less advanced regions. In parts of Mexico, South America, South Africa, and Australia a violent and accelerating wastage is in progress, but I cannot assess the prospects.

This almost world-wide display of disorganization in the land seems to be similar to disease in an animal, except that it never culminates in complete disorganization or death. The land recovers, but at some reduced level of complexity, and with a reduced carrying capacity for people, plants, and animals. Many biotas currently regarded as "lands of opportunity" are in fact already subsisting on exploitative agriculture, i.e. they have already exceeded their sustained carrying capacity. Most of South America is overpopulated in this sense.

In arid regions we attempt to offset the process of wastage by reclamation, but it is only too evident that the prospective longevity of reclamation projects is often short. In our own West, the best of them may not last a century.

The combined evidence of history and ecology seems to support one general deduction: the less violent the man-made changes, the greater the probability of successful readjustment

in the pyramid. Violence, in turn, varies with human population density; a dense population requires a more violent conversion. In this respect, North America has a better chance for permanence than Europe, if she can contrive to limit her density.

This deduction runs counter to our current philosophy, which assumes that because a small increase in density enriched human life, that an indefinite increase will enrich it indefinitely. Ecology knows of no density relationship that holds for indefinitely wide limits. All gains from density are subject to a law of diminishing returns.

Whatever may be the equation for men and land, it is improbable that we as yet know all its terms. Recent discoveries in mineral and vitamin nutrition reveal unsuspected dependencies in the up-circuit: incredibly minute quantities of certain substances determine the value of soils to plants, of plants to animals. What of the down-circuit? What of the vanishing species, the preservation of which we now regard as an esthetic luxury? They helped build the soil; in what unsuspected ways may they be essential to its maintenance? Professor Weaver proposes that we use prairie flowers to refloculate the wasting soils of the dust bowl; who knows for what purpose cranes and condors, otters and grizzlies may some day be used?

LAND HEALTH AND THE A-B CLEAVAGE

A land ethic, then, reflects the existence of an ecological conscience, and this in turn reflects a conviction of individual responsibility for the health of the land. Health is the capacity of the land for self-renewal. Conservation is our effort to understand and preserve this capacity.

Conservationists are notorious for their dissensions. Superficially these seem to add up to mere confusion, but a more careful scrutiny reveals a single plane of cleavage common to many specialized fields. In each field one group (A) regards the land as soil, and its function as commodity-production; another group (B) regards the land as a biota, and its function as something broader. How much broader is admittedly in a state of doubt and confusion.

In my own field, forestry, group A is quite content to grow trees like cabbages, with cellulose as the basic forest commodity. It feels no inhibition against violence; its ideology is agronomic. Group B, on the other hand, sees forestry as fundamentally different from agronomy because it employs natural species, and manages a natural environment rather than creating an artificial one. Group B prefers natural reproduction on principle. It worries on biotic as well as economic grounds about the loss of species like chestnut, and the threatened loss of the white pines. It worries about a whole series of secondary forest functions: wildlife, recreation, watersheds, wilderness areas. To my mind, Group B feels the stirrings of an ecological conscience.

In the wildlife field, a parallel cleavage exists. For Group A the basic commodities are sport and meat; the yardsticks of production are ciphers of take in pheasants and trout. Artificial propagation is acceptable as a permanent as well as a temporary recourse—if its unit costs permit. Group B, on the other hand, worries about a whole series of biotic side-issues. What is the cost in predators of producing a game crop? Should we have further recourse to exotics? How can management restore the shrinking species, like prairie grouse, already hopeless as shootable game? How can management restore the threatened rarities, like trumpeter swan and whooping crane? Can management principles be extended to wildflowers? Here again it is clear to me that we have the same A-B cleavage as in forestry.

In the larger field of agriculture I am less competent to speak, but there seem to be somewhat parallel cleavages. Scientific agriculture was actively developing before ecology was born, hence a slower penetration of ecological concepts might be expected. Moreover the farmer, by the very nature of his techniques, must modify the biota more radically than the forester or the wildlife manager. Nevertheless, there are many discontents in agriculture which seem to add up to a new vision of "biotic farming."

Perhaps the most important of these is the new evidence that poundage or tonnage is no measure of the food-value of farm crops; the products of fertile soil may be qualitatively as

well as quantitatively superior. We can bolster poundage from depleted soils by pouring on imported fertility, but we are not necessarily bolstering food-value. The possible ultimate ramifications of this idea are so immense that I must leave their exposition to abler pens.

The discontent that labels itself "organic farming," while bearing some of the earmarks of a cult, is nevertheless biotic in its direction, particularly in its insistence on the importance of soil flora and fauna.

The ecological fundamentals of agriculture are just as poorly known to the public as in other fields of land-use. For example, few educated people realize that the marvelous advances in technique made during recent decades are improvements in the pump, rather than the well. Acre for acre, they have barely sufficed to offset the sinking level of fertility.

In all of these cleavages, we see repeated the same basic paradoxes: man the conqueror *versus* man the biotic citizen; science the sharpener of his sword *versus* science the searchlight on his universe; land the slave and servant *versus* land the collective organism. Robinson's injunction to Tristram may well be applied, at this juncture, to *Homo sapiens* as a species in geological time:

> Whether you will or not
> You are a King, Tristram, for you are one
> Of the time-tested few that leave the world,
> When they are gone, not the same place it was.
> Mark what you leave.

THE OUTLOOK

It is inconceivable to me that an ethical relation to land can exist without love, respect, and admiration for land, and a high regard for its value. By value, I of course mean something far broader than mere economic value; I mean value in the philosophical sense.

Perhaps the most serious obstacle impeding the evolution of a land ethic is the fact that our educational and economic system is headed away from, rather than toward, an intense consciousness of land. Your true modern is separated from the land by many middlemen, and by innumerable physical gadgets. He has no vital relation to it; to him it is the space between cities on which crops grow. Turn him loose for a day on the land, and if the spot does not happen to be a golf links or a "scenic" area, he is bored stiff. If crops could be raised by hydroponics instead of farming, it would suit him very well. Synthetic substitutes for wood, leather, wool, and other natural land products suit him better than the originals. In short, land is something he has "outgrown."

Almost equally serious as an obstacle to a land ethic is the attitude of the farmer for whom the land is still an adversary, or a taskmaster that keeps him in slavery. Theoretically, the mechanization of farming ought to cut the farmer's chains, but whether it really does is debatable.

One of the requisites for an ecological comprehension of land is an understanding of ecology, and this is by no means co-extensive with "education"; in fact, much higher education seems deliberately to avoid ecological concepts. An understanding of ecology does not necessarily originate in courses bearing ecological labels; it is quite as likely to be labeled geography, botany, agronomy, history, or economics. This is as it should be, but whatever the label, ecological training is scarce.

The case for a land ethic would appear hopeless but for the minority which is in obvious revolt against these "modern" trends.

The "key-log" which must be moved to release the evolutionary process for an ethic is simply this: quit thinking about decent land-use as solely an economic problem. Examine each question in terms of what is ethically and esthetically right, as well as what is economically expedient. A thing is right when it tends to preserve the integrity, stability, and beauty of the biotic community. It is wrong when it tends otherwise.

It of course goes without saying that economic feasibility limits the tether of what can or cannot be done for land. It always has and it always will. The fallacy the economic determinists have tied around our collective neck, and which we now need to cast off, is the belief that economics determines *all* land-use. This is simply not true. An innumerable host of actions and attitudes, comprising perhaps the bulk of all land relations, is determined by the land-users' tastes and predilections, rather than by his purse. The bulk of all land relations hinges on investments of time, forethought, skill, and faith rather than on investments of cash. As a land-user thinketh, so is he.

I have purposely presented the land ethic as a product of social evolution because nothing so important as an ethic is ever "written." Only the most superficial student of history supposes that Moses "wrote" the Decalogue; it evolved in the minds of a thinking community, and Moses wrote a tentative summary of it for a "seminar." I say tentative because evolution never stops.

The evolution of a land ethic is an intellectual as well as emotional process. Conservation is paved with good intentions which prove to be futile, or even dangerous, because they are devoid of critical understanding either of the land, or of economic land-use. I think it is a truism that as the ethical frontier advances from the individual to the community, its intellectual content increases.

The mechanism of operation is the same for any ethic: social approbation for right actions, social disapproval for wrong actions.

By and large, our present problem is one of attitudes and implements. We are remodeling the Alhambra with a steamshovel, and we are proud of our yardage. We shall hardly relinquish the shovel, which after all has many good points, but we are in need of gentler and more objective criteria for its successful use.

STUDY QUESTIONS

1. Does Leopold make a case for the intrinsic value of the biotic community, or does he only assume this?
2. Analyze Leopold's view of humans and of biotic communities. How do we resolve conflicts between their claims and needs? Which are more important, ecosystems or individuals?
3. Critically discuss the strengths and weaknesses of Leopold's position.
4. Leopold makes two fundamental claims of the American conservation movement. What are they? Has American environmentalism moved in the direction that Leopold advocated?

20   The Conceptual Foundations of the Land Ethic

J. BAIRD CALLICOTT

J. Baird Callicott (b. 1941) is professor of philosophy and natural resources at the University of North Texas and the author of several works in environmental philosophy, including *In Defense of the Land Ethic* (1989) from which this essay is taken.

Callicott develops the philosophical implications of Leopold's land ethic. He shows how it is rooted in the eighteenth-century Scottish Sentimentalist School of David Hume and Adam Smith, who said that ethics is based in natural sympathy or sentiments. Leopold, adding a Darwinian dimension to these thoughts, extended the notion of natural sentiments to ecosystems as the locus of value. Callicott argues that Leopold is not claiming that we should sacrifice basic human needs to the environment, but rather that we should see ourselves as members of a wider ecological community.

The two great cultural advances of the past century were the Darwinian theory and the development of geology.... Just as important, however, as the origin of plants, animals, and soil is the question of how they operate as a community. That task has fallen to the new science of ecology, which is daily uncovering a web of interdependencies so intricate as to amaze—were he here—even Darwin himself, who, of all men, should have least cause to tremble before the veil.

ALDO LEOPOLD, FRAGMENT 6B16,
NO. 36, LEOPOLD PAPERS,
UNIVERSITY OF WISCONSIN–
MADISON ARCHIVES

I

As Wallace Stegner observes, *A Sand County Almanac* is considered "almost a holy book in conservation circles," and Aldo Leopold a prophet, "an American Isaiah." And as Curt Meine points out, "The Land Ethic" is the climactic essay of *Sand County,* "the upshot of 'The Upshot.'" One might, therefore, fairly say that the

recommendation and justification of moral obligations on the part of people to nature is what the prophetic *A Sand County Almanac* is all about.

But, with few exceptions, "The Land Ethic" has not been favorably received by contemporary academic philosophers. Most have ignored it. Of those who have not, most have been either nonplussed or hostile. Distinguished Australian philosopher John Passmore dismissed it out of hand, in the first book-length academic discussion of the new philosophical subdiscipline called "environmental ethics." In a more recent and more deliberate discussion, the equally distinguished Australian philosopher H. J. McCloskey patronized Aldo Leopold and saddled "The Land Ethic" with various far-fetched "interpretations." He concludes that "there is a real problem in attributing a coherent meaning to Leopold's statements, one that exhibits his land ethic as representing a major advance in ethics rather than a retrogression to a morality of a kind held by various primitive peoples." Echoing McCloskey, English philosopher Robin Attfield went out of his way to impugn the philosophical respectability of "The Land Ethic." And Canadian philosopher L. W. Sumner has called it "dangerous nonsense."

Among those philosophers more favorably disposed, "The Land Ethic" has usually been simply quoted, as if it were little more than a noble, but naive, moral plea, altogether lacking a supporting theoretical framework—that is, foundational principles and premises which lead, by compelling argument, to ethical precepts.

The professional neglect, confusion, and (in some cases) contempt for "The Land Ethic" may, in my judgment, be attributed to three things: (1) Leopold's extremely condensed prose style in which an entire conceptual complex may be conveyed in a few sentences, or even in a phrase or two; (2) his departure from the assumptions and paradigms of contemporary philosophical ethics; and (3) the unsettling practical implications to which a land ethic appears to lead. "The Land Ethic," in short, is, from a philosophical point of view, abbreviated, unfamiliar, and radical.

Here I first examine and elaborate the compactly expressed abstract elements of the land ethic and expose the "logic" which binds them into a proper, but revolutionary, moral theory. I then discuss the controversial features of the land ethic and defend them against actual and potential criticism. I hope to show that the land ethic cannot be ignored as merely the groundless emotive exhortations of a moonstruck conservationist or dismissed as entailing wildly untoward practical consequences. It poses, rather, a serious intellectual challenge to business-as-usual moral philosophy.

II

"The Land Ethic" opens with a charming and poetic evocation of Homer's Greece, the point of which is to suggest that today land is just as routinely and remorselessly enslaved as human beings then were. A panoramic glance backward to our most distant cultural origins, Leopold suggests, reveals a slow but steady moral development over three millennia. More of our relationships and activities ("fields of conduct") have fallen under the aegis of moral principles ("ethical criteria") as civilization has grown and matured. If moral growth and development continue, as not only a synoptic review of history, but recent past experience suggest that it will, future

generations will censure today's casual and universal environmental bondage as today we censure the casual and universal human bondage of three thousand years ago.

A cynically inclined critic might scoff at Leopold's sanguine portrayal of human history. Slavery survived as an institution in the "civilized" West, more particularly in the morally self-congratulatory United States, until a mere generation before Leopold's own birth. And Western history from imperial Athens and Rome to the Spanish Inquisition and the Third Reich has been a disgraceful series of wars, persecutions, tyrannies, pogroms, and other atrocities.

The history of moral practice, however, is not identical with the history of moral consciousness. Morality is not descriptive; it is prescriptive or normative. In light of this distinction, it is clear that today, despite rising rates of violent crime in the United States and institutional abuses of human rights in Iran, Chile, Ethiopia, Guatemala, South Africa, and many other places, and despite persistent organized social injustice and oppression in still others, moral consciousness is expanding more rapidly now than ever before. Civil rights, human rights, women's liberation, children's liberation, animal liberation, and so forth, all indicate, as expressions of newly emergent moral ideals, that ethical consciousness (as distinct from practice) has if anything recently accelerated—thus confirming Leopold's historical observation.

III

Leopold next points out that "this extension of ethics, so far studied only by philosophers"—and therefore, the implication is clear, not very satisfactorily studied "is actually a process in ecological evolution" (p. 202). What Leopold is saying here, simply, is that we may understand the history of ethics, fancifully alluded to by means of the Odysseus vignette, in biological as well as philosophical terms. From a biological point of view, an ethic is "a limitation on freedom of action in the struggle for existence" (p. 202). . . .

Let me put the problem in perspective. How, . . . did ethics originate and, once in existence, grow in scope and complexity?

The oldest answer in living human memory is theological. God (or the gods) imposes morality on people. And God (or the gods) sanctions it. A most vivid and graphic example of this kind of account occurs in the Bible when Moses goes up on Mount Sinai to receive the Ten Commandments directly from God. That text also clearly illustrates the divine sanctions (plagues, pestilences, droughts, military defeats, and so forth) for moral disobedience. Ongoing revelation of the divine will, of course, as handily and as simply explains subsequent moral growth and development.

Western philosophy, on the other hand, is almost unanimous in the opinion that the origin of ethics in human experience has somehow to do with human reason. Reason figures centrally and pivotally in the "social contract theory" of the origin and nature of morals in all its ancient, modern, and contemporary expressions from Protagoras, to Hobbes, to Rawls. Reason is the wellspring of virtue, according to both Plato and Aristotle, and of categorical imperatives, according to Kant. In short, the weight of Western philosophy inclines to the view that we are moral beings because we are rational beings. The ongoing sophistication of reason and the progressive illumination it sheds upon the good and the right explain "the ethical sequence," the historical growth and development of morality, noticed by Leopold.

An evolutionary natural historian, however, cannot be satisfied with either of these general accounts of the origin and development of ethics. The idea that God gave morals to man is ruled out in principle—as any supernatural explanation of a natural phenomenon is ruled out in principle in natural science. And while morality might *in principle* be a function of human reason (as, say, mathematical calculation clearly is), to suppose that it is so *in fact* would be to put the cart before the horse. Reason appears to be a delicate, variable, and recently emerged faculty. It cannot, under any circumstances, be supposed to have evolved in the absence of complex linguistic capabilities which depend, in turn, for their evolution upon a highly developed social matrix. But we cannot have become social beings unless we assumed limitations on freedom of action in the struggle for existence. Hence we must have become ethical before we became rational.

Darwin, probably in consequence of reflections somewhat like these, turned to a minority tradition of modern philosophy for a moral psychology consistent with and useful to a general evolutionary account of ethical phenomena. A century earlier, Scottish philosophers David Hume and Adam Smith had argued that ethics rest upon feelings or "sentiments"—which, to be sure, may be both amplified and informed by reason. And since in the animal kingdom feelings or sentiments are arguably far more common or widespread than reason, they would be a far more likely starting point for an evolutionary account of the origin and growth of ethics.

Darwin's account, to which Leopold unmistakably (if elliptically) alludes in "The Land Ethic," begins with the parental and filial affections common, perhaps, to all mammals. Bonds of affection and sympathy between parents and offspring permitted the formation of small, closely knit social groups, Darwin argued. Should the parental and familial affections bonding family members chance to extend to less closely related individuals, that would permit an enlargement of the family group. And should the newly extended community more successfully defend itself and/or more efficiently provision itself, the inclusive fitness of its members severally would be increased, Darwin reasoned. Thus the more diffuse familial affections, which Darwin (echoing Hume and Smith) calls the "social sentiments" would be spread throughout a population.

Morality, properly speaking—that is, morality as opposed to mere altruistic instinct—requires, in Darwin's terms, "intellectual powers" sufficient to recall the past and imagine the future, "the power of language" sufficient to express "common opinion," and "habituation" to patterns of behavior deemed, by common opinion, to be socially acceptable and beneficial. Even so, ethics proper, in Darwin's account, remains firmly rooted in moral feelings or social sentiments which were—no less than physical faculties, he expressly avers—naturally selected, by the advantages for survival and especially for successful reproduction, afforded by society.

The protosociobiological perspective on ethical phenomena, to which Leopold as a natural historian was heir, leads him to a generalization which is remarkably explicit in his condensed and often merely resonant rendering of Darwin's more deliberate and extended paradigm: Since "the thing [ethics] has its origin in the tendency of interdependent individuals or groups to evolve modes of co-operation, . . . all ethics so far evolved rest upon a single premise: that the individual is a member of a community of interdependent parts" (pp. 202–3).

Hence, we may expect to find that the scope and specific content of ethics will reflect both the perceived boundaries and actual structure or organization of a cooperative community or society. *Ethics and society or community are correlative.* This single, simple principle constitutes a powerful tool for the analysis of moral natural history, for the anticipation of future moral development (including, ultimately, the land ethic), and for systematically deriving the specific precepts, the prescriptions and proscriptions, of an emergent and culturally unprecedented ethic like a land or environmental ethic.

IV

Anthropological studies of ethics reveal that in fact the boundaries of the moral community are generally coextensive with the perceived boundaries of society. And the peculiar (and, from the urbane point of view, sometimes inverted) representation of virtue and vice in tribal society—the virtue, for example, of sharing to the point of personal destitution and the vice of privacy and private property—reflects and fosters the life way of tribal peoples. Darwin, in his leisurely, anecdotal discussion, paints a vivid picture of the intensity, peculiarity, and sharp circumscription of "savage" mores: "A savage will risk his life to save that of a member of the same community, but will be wholly indifferent about a stranger." As Darwin portrays them, tribespeople are at once paragons of virtue "within the limits of the same tribe" and enthusiastic thieves, manslaughterers, and torturers without.

For purposes of more effective defense against common enemies, or because of increased population density, or in response to innovations in subsistence methods and technologies, or for some mix of these or other forces, human societies have grown in extent or scope and changed in form or structure. Nations—like the Iroquois nation or the Sioux nation—came into being upon the merger of previously separate and mutually hostile tribes. Animals and plants were domesticated and erstwhile hunter-gatherers became herders and farmers. Permanent habitations were established. Trade, craft, and (later) industry flourished. With each change in society came corresponding and correlative changes in ethics. The moral community expanded to become co-extensive with the newly drawn boundaries of societies and the representation of virtue and vice, right and wrong, good and evil, changed to accommodate, foster, and preserve the economic and institutional organization of emergent social orders.

Today we are witnessing the painful birth of a human supercommunity, global in scope. Modern transportation and communication technologies, international economic interdependencies, international economic entities, and nuclear arms have brought into being a "global village." It has not yet become fully formed and it is at tension—a very dangerous tension—with its predecessor, the nation-state. Its eventual institutional structure, a global federalism or whatever it may turn out to be, is at this point completely unpredictable. Interestingly, however, a corresponding global human ethic—the "human rights" ethic, as it is popularly called—has been more definitely articulated.

Most educated people today pay lip service at least to the ethical precept that all members of the human species, regardless of race, creed, or national origin, are endowed with certain fundamental rights which it is wrong not to respect. According to the evolutionary scenario set out by Darwin, the contemporary moral ideal of human rights is a response to a perception—however vague and indefinite—that mankind worldwide is united into one society, one community, however indeterminate or yet institutionally unorganized. As Darwin presciently wrote:

As man advances in civilization, and small tribes are united into larger communities, the simplest reason would tell each individual that he ought to extend his social instincts and sympathies to all the members of the same nation, though personally unknown to him. This point being once reached, there is only an artificial barrier to prevent his sympathies extending to the men of all nations and races. If, indeed, such men are separated from him by great differences of appearance or habits, experience unfortunately shows us how long it is, before we look at them as our fellow-creatures.

According to Leopold, the next step in this sequence beyond the still incomplete ethic of universal humanity, a step that is clearly discernible on the horizon, is the land ethic. The "community concept" has, so far, propelled the development of ethics from the savage clan to the family of man. "The land ethic simply enlarges the boundary of the community to include soils, water, plants, and animals, or collectively: the land" (p. 204).

As the foreword to *Sand County* makes plain, the overarching thematic principle of the book is the inculcation of the idea—through narrative description, discursive exposition, abstractive generalization, and occasional preachment— "that land is a community" (viii). The community concept is "the basic concept of ecology" (viii). Once land is popularly perceived as a biotic community—as it is professionally perceived in ecology—a correlative land ethic will emerge in the collective cultural consciousness.

V

Although anticipated as far back as the mid-eighteenth century—in the notion of an "economy of nature"—the concept of the biotic community was more fully and deliberately developed as a working model or paradigm for ecology by Charles Elton in the 1920s. The natural world is organized as an intricate corporate society in which plants and animals occupy "niches," or as Elton alternatively called them, "roles" or "professions," in the economy of nature. As in a feudal community, little or no socioeconomic mobility (upward or otherwise) exists in the biotic community. One is born to one's trade.

Human society, Leopold argues, is founded, in large part, upon mutual security and economic interdependency and preserved only by limitations on freedom of action in the struggle for existence—that is, by ethical constraints. Since the biotic community exhibits, as modern ecology reveals, an analogous structure, it too can be preserved, given the newly amplified impact of "mechanized man," only by analogous limitations on freedom of action—that is, by a land ethic (viii). A land ethic, furthermore, is not only "an ecological necessity," but an "evolutionary possibility" because a moral response to the natural environment—Darwin's social sympathies, sentiments, and instincts translated and codified into a body of principles and precepts— would be automatically triggered in human beings by ecology's social representation of nature (p. 203).

Therefore, the key to the emergence of a land ethic is, simply, universal ecological literacy.

VI

The land ethic rests upon three scientific cornerstones: (1) evolutionary and (2) ecological biology set in a background of (3) Copernican astronomy. Evolutionary theory provides the conceptual link between ethics and social organization and development. It provides a sense of "kinship with fellow-creatures" as well, "fellow-voyagers" with us in the "odyssey of evolution" (p. 109). It establishes a diachronic link between people and nonhuman nature.

Ecological theory provides a synchronic link—the community concept—a sense of social integration of human and nonhuman nature. Human beings, plants, animals, soils, and waters are "all interlocked in one humming community of cooperations and competitions, one biota." The simplest reason, to paraphrase Darwin, should, therefore, tell each individual that he or she ought to extend his or her social instincts and sympathies to all the members of the biotic community though different from him or her in appearance or habits.

And although Leopold never directly mentions it in *A Sand County Almanac,* the Copernican perspective, the perception of the earth as "a small planet" in an immense and utterly hostile universe beyond, contributes, perhaps subconsciously, but nevertheless very powerfully, to our sense of kinship, community, and interdependence with fellow denizens of the earth household. It scales the earth down to something like a cozy island paradise in a desert ocean.

Here in outline, then, are the conceptual and logical foundations of the land ethic: Its conceptual elements are a Copernican cosmology, a Darwinian protosociobiological natural history of ethics, Darwinian ties of kinship among all forms of life on earth, and an Eltonian model of the structure of biocenoses all overlaid on a Humean–Smithian moral psychology. Its logic is that natural selection has endowed human beings with an affective moral response to perceived bonds of kinship and community membership and identity; that today the natural environment, the land, is represented as a community, the biotic community; and that, therefore, an environmental or land ethic is both possible—the biopsychological and cognitive conditions are in place—and necessary, since human beings collectively have acquired the power to destroy the integrity, diversity, and stability of the environing and supporting economy of nature. In the remainder of this essay I discuss special features and problems of the land ethic germane to moral philosophy.

The most salient feature of Leopold's land ethic is its provision of what Kenneth Goodpaster has carefully called "moral considerability" for the biotic community per se, not just for fellow members of the biotic community.

> In short, a land ethic changes the role of *Homo sapiens* from conqueror of the land-community to plain member and citizen of it. It implies respect for his fellow-members, *and also respect for the community as such.* (p. 204, emphasis added)

The land ethic, thus, has a holistic as well as an individualistic cast.

Indeed, as "The Land Ethic" develops, the focus of moral concern shifts gradually away from plants, animals, soils, and waters severally to the biotic community collectively. Toward the middle, in the subsection called "Substitutes for a Land Ethic," Leopold invokes the "biotic rights" of *species*—as the context indicates—of wildflowers, songbirds, and predators. In "The

Out-look," the climactic section of "The Land Ethic," nonhuman natural entities, first appearing as fellow members, then considered in profile as species, are not so much as mentioned in what might be called the "summary moral maxim" of the land ethic: "A thing is right when it tends to preserve the integrity, stability, and beauty of the biotic community. It is wrong when it tends otherwise" (pp. 224–25).

By this measure of right and wrong, not only would it be wrong for a farmer, in the interest of higher profits, to clear the woods off a 75 percent slope, turn his cows into the clearing and dump its rainfall, rocks, and soil into the community creek, it would also be wrong for the federal fish and wildlife agency, in the interest of individual animal welfare, to permit populations of deer, rabbits, feral burros, or whatever to increase unchecked and thus to threaten the integrity, stability, and beauty of the biotic communities of which they are members. The land ethic not only provides moral considerability for the biotic community per se, but ethical consideration of its individual members is preempted by concern for the preservation of the integrity, stability, and beauty of the biotic community. The land ethic, thus, not only has a holistic aspect; it is holistic with a vengeance.

The holism of the land ethic, more than any other feature, sets it apart from the predominant paradigm of modern moral philosophy. It is, therefore, the feature of the land ethic which requires the most patient theoretical analysis and the most sensitive practical interpretation.

VII

As Kenneth Goodpaster pointed out, mainstream modern ethical philosophy has taken egoism as its point of departure and reached a wider circle of moral entitlement by a process of generalization: I am sure that *I*, the enveloped ego, am intrinsically or inherently valuable and thus that *my* interests ought to be considered, taken into account, by "others" when their actions may substantively affect *me*. My own claim to moral consideration, according to the conventional wisdom, ultimately rests upon a psychological capacity—rationality or sentiency were the classical candidates of Kant and Bentham, respectively—which is arguably valuable in itself and which thus qualifies *me* for moral standing. However, then I am forced grudgingly to grant the same moral consideration I demand from others, on this basis, to those others who can also claim to possess the same general psychological characteristic.

A criterion of moral value and consideration is thus identified. Goodpaster convincingly argues that mainstream moral theory is based, when all the learned dust has settled, on this simple paradigm of ethical justification and logic exemplified by the Benthamic and Kantian prototypes. If the criterion of moral values and consideration is pitched low enough—as it is in Bentham's criterion of sentiency—a wide variety of animals are admitted to moral entitlement. If the criterion of moral value and consideration is pushed lower still—as it is in Albert Schweitzer's reverence-for-life ethic—all minimally conative things (plants as well as animals) would be extended moral considerability. The contemporary animal liberation/rights, and reverence-for-life/life-principle ethics are, at bottom, simply direct applications of the modern classical paradigm of moral argument. But this standard modern model of ethical theory provides no possibility whatever for the moral consideration of wholes—of threatened population of animals and plants, or of endemic, rare, or endangered species, or of biotic communities, or most expansively, of the biosphere in its totality—since wholes per se have no psychological experience of any kind. Because mainstream modern moral theory has been "psychocentric," it has been radically and intractably individualistic or "atomistic" in its fundamental theoretical orientation.

Hume, Smith, and Darwin diverged from the prevailing theoretical model by recognizing that altruism is as fundamental and autochthonous in human nature as is egoism. According to their analysis, moral value is not identified with a natural quality objectively present in morally considerable beings—as reason and/or sentiency is objectively present in people and/or animals—it is, as it were, projected by valuing subjects.

Hume and Darwin, furthermore, recognize inborn moral sentiments which have society as such as their natural object. Hume insists that "we must renounce the theory which accounts

for every moral sentiment by the principle of self-love. We must adopt a more *publick affection* and allow that the *interests of society* are not, *even on their own account,* entirely indifferent to us." And Darwin, somewhat ironically (since "Darwinian evolution" very often means natural selection operating exclusively with respect to individuals), sometimes writes as if morality had no other object than the commonweal, the welfare of the community as a corporate entity:

> We have now seen that actions are regarded by savages, and were probably so regarded by primeval man, as good or bad, solely as they obviously affect the welfare of the tribe,—not that of the species, nor that of the individual member of the tribe. This conclusion agrees well with the belief that the so called moral sense is aboriginally derived from social instincts, for both relate at first exclusively to the community.

Theoretically then, the biotic community owns what Leopold, in the lead paragraph of "The Outlook," calls "value in the philosophical sense"—that is, direct moral considerability—because it is a newly discovered proper object of a specially evolved "publick affection" or "moral sense" which all psychologically normal human beings have inherited from a long line of ancestral social primates (p. 223).

VIII

In the land ethic, as in all earlier stages of social–ethical evolution, there exists a tension between the good of the community as a whole and the "rights" of its individual members considered severally. . . .

In any case, the conceptual foundations of the land ethic provide a well-informed, self-consistent theoretical basis for including both fellow members of the biotic community and the biotic community itself (considered as a corporate entity) within the purview of morals. The preemptive emphasis, however, on the welfare of the community as a whole, in Leopold's articulation of the land ethic, while certainly consistent with its Humean–Darwinian theoretical foundations, is not determined by them alone. The overriding holism of the land ethic results, rather, more from the way our moral sensibilities are informed by ecology.

IX

Ecological thought, historically, has tended to be holistic in outlook. Ecology is the study of the relationships of organisms to one another and to the elemental environment. These relationships bind the *relata*—plants, animals, soils, and waters—into a seamless fabric. The ontological primacy of objects and the ontological subordination of relationships characteristic of classical Western science is, in fact, reversed in ecology. Ecological relationships determine the nature of organisms rather than the other way around. A species is what it is because it has adapted to a niche in the ecosystem. The whole, the system itself, thus, literally and quite straightforwardly shapes and forms its component species.

Antedating Charles Elton's community model of ecology was F. E. Clements and S. A. Forbes's organism model. Plants and animals, soils and waters, according to this paradigm, are integrated into one superorganism. Species are, as it were, its organs; specimens its cells. Although Elton's community paradigm (later modified, as we shall see, by Arthur Tansley's ecosystem idea) is the principal and morally fertile ecological concept of "The Land Ethic," the more radically holistic superorganism paradigm of Clements and Forbes resonates in "The Land Ethic" as an audible overtone. In the peroration of "Land Health and the A-B Cleavage," for example, which immediately precedes "The Outlook," Leopold insists that

> in all these cleavages, we see repeated the same basic paradoxes: man the conqueror *versus* man the biotic citizen; science the sharpener of his sword *versus* science the searchlight on his universe; land the slave and servant *versus* land the collective organism. (p. 223)

And on more than one occasion Leopold, in the latter quarter of "The Land Ethic," talks about the "health" and "disease" of the land—terms which are at once descriptive and normative and which, taken literally, characterize only organisms proper.

In an early essay, "Some Fundamentals of Conservation in the Southwest," Leopold speculatively flirted with the intensely holistic superorganism model of the environment as a paradigm pregnant with moral implications....

Had Leopold retained this overall theoretical approach in "The Land Ethic," the land ethic would doubtless have enjoyed more critical attention from philosophers. The moral foundations of a land or, as he might then have called it, "earth" ethic would rest upon the hypothesis that the Earth is alive and ensouled—possessing inherent psychological characteristics, logically parallel to reason and sentiency. This notion of a conative whole earth could plausibly have served as a general criterion of intrinsic worth and moral considerability, in the familiar format of mainstream moral thought.

Part of the reason, therefore, that "The Land Ethic" emphasizes more and more the integrity, stability, and beauty of the environment as a whole, and less and less the biotic right of individual plants and animals to life, liberty, and the pursuit of happiness, is that the superorganism ecological paradigm invites one, much more than does the community paradigm, to hypostatize, to reify the whole, and to subordinate its individual members.

In any case, as we see, rereading "The Land Ethic" in light of "Some Fundamentals," the whole Earth organism image of nature is vestigially present in Leopold's later thinking. Leopold may have abandoned the "earth ethic" because ecology had abandoned the organism analogy in favor of the community analogy as a working theoretical paradigm. And the community model was more suitably given moral implications by the social/sentimental ethical natural history of Hume and Darwin.

Meanwhile, the biotic community ecological paradigm itself had acquired, by the late thirties and forties, a more holistic cast of its own. In 1935 British ecologist Arthur Tansley pointed out that from the perspective of physics the "currency" of the "economy of nature" is energy. Tansley suggested that Elton's qualitative and descriptive food chains, food webs, trophic niches, and biosocial professions could be quantitatively expressed by means of a thermodynamic flow model. It is Tansley's state-of-the-art thermodynamic paradigm of the environment that Leopold explicitly sets out as a "mental image of land" in relation to which "we can be ethical" (p. 214). And it is the ecosystemic model of land which informs the cardinal practical precepts of the land ethic.

"The Land Pyramid" is the pivotal section of "The Land Ethic"—the section which effects a complete transition from concern for "fellow-members" to the "community as such." It is also its longest and most technical section. A description of the "ecosystem" (Tansley's deliberately nonmetaphorical term) begins with the sun. Solar energy "flows through a circuit called the biota" (p. 215). It enters the biota through the leaves of green plants and courses through plant-eating animals, and then on to omnivores and carnivores. At last the tiny fraction of solar energy converted to biomass by green plants remaining in the corpse of a predator, animal feces, plant detritus, or other dead organic material is garnered by decomposers—worms, fungi, and bacteria. They recycle the participating elements and degrade into entropic equilibrium any remaining energy. According to this paradigm

> land, then, is not merely soil; it is a fountain of energy flowing through a circuit of soils, plants, and animals. Food chains are the living channels which conduct energy upward; death and decay return it to the soil. The circuit is not closed;... but it is a sustained circuit, like a slowly augmented revolving fund of life. (p. 216)

In this exceedingly abstract (albeit poetically expressed) model of nature, process precedes substance and energy is more fundamental than matter. Individual plants and animals become less autonomous beings than ephemeral structures in a patterned flux of energy. According to Yale biophysicist Harold Morowitz,

> viewed from the point of view of modern [ecology], each living thing... is a dissipative structure, that is it does not endure in and of itself but only as a result of the continual flow of energy in the system. An example might be instructive. Consider a vortex in a stream of flowing water. The vortex is a structure made of an ever-changing group of water molecules. It does not exist as an entity in the classical Western sense; it exists only because of the flow of water through the stream. In the same sense, the structures out of which biological entities are made are transient, unstable entities with constantly changing molecules,

dependent on a constant flow of energy from food in order to maintain form and structure.... From this point of view the reality of individuals is problematic because they do not exist per se but only as local perturbations in this universal flow.

Though less bluntly stated and made more palatable by the unfailing charm of his prose, Leopold's proffered mental image of land is just as expansive, systemic, and distanced as Morowitz's. The maintenance of "the complex structure of the land and its smooth functioning as an energy unit" emerges in "The Land Pyramid" as the *summum bonum* of the land ethic (p. 216).

X

From this good Leopold derives several practical principles slightly less general, and therefore more substantive, than the summary moral maxim of the land ethic distilled in "The Outlook." "The trend of evolution [not its "goal," since evolution is ateleological] is to elaborate and diversify the biota" (p. 216). Hence, among our cardinal duties is the duty to preserve what species we can, especially those at the apex of the pyramid—the top carnivores. "In the beginning, the pyramid of life was low and squat; the food chains short and simple. Evolution has added layer after layer, link after link" (pp. 215–16). Human activities today, especially those like systematic deforestation in the tropics, resulting in abrupt massive extinctions of species, are in effect "devolutionary;" they flatten the biotic pyramid; they choke off some of the channels and gorge others (those which terminate in our own species).

The land ethic does not enshrine the ecological status quo and devalue the dynamic dimension of nature. Leopold explains that "evolution is a long series of self-induced changes, the net result of which has been to elaborate the flow mechanism and to lengthen the circuit. Evolutionary changes, however, are usually slow and local. Man's invention of tools has enabled him to make changes of unprecedented violence, rapidity, and scope" (pp. 216–17). "Natural" species extinction, that is, species extinction in the normal course of evolution, occurs when a species is replaced by competitive exclusion or evolves into another form. Normally speciation outpaces extinction. Mankind inherited a richer, more diverse world than had ever existed before in the 3.5 billion-year odyssey of life on Earth. What is wrong with anthropogenic species extirpation and extinction is the *rate* at which it is occurring and the *result:* biological impoverishment instead of enrichment.

Leopold goes on here to condemn, in terms of its impact on the eco-system, "the world-wide pooling of faunas and floras," that is, the indiscriminate introduction of exotic and domestic species and the dislocation of native and endemic species, mining the soil for its stored biotic energy, leading ultimately to diminished fertility and to erosion; and polluting and damming water courses (p. 217).

According to the land ethic, therefore: Thou shalt not extirpate or render species extinct; thou shalt exercise great caution in introducing exotic and domestic species into local exosystems, in exacting energy from the soil and releasing it into the biota, and in damming or polluting water courses; and thou shalt be especially solicitous of predatory birds and mammals. Here in brief are the express moral precepts of the land ethic. They are all explicitly informed—not to say derived—from the energy circuit model of the environment.

XI

The living channels—food chains—through which energy courses are composed of individual plants and animals. A central, stark fact lies at the heart of ecological processes: Energy, the currency of the economy nature, passes from one organism to another, not from hand to hand, like coined money, but, so to speak, from stomach to stomach. Eating *and being eaten,* living *and dying* are what make the biotic community hum.

The precepts of the land ethic, like those of all previous accretions, reflect and reinforce the structure of the community to which it is correlative. Trophic asymmetries constitute the kernel of the biotic community. It seems unjust, unfair. But that is how the economy of nature is organized (and has been for thousands of millions of years). The land ethic, thus, affirms as good, and strives to preserve, the very inequities in nature whose social counterparts in human communities are condemned as bad and would be eradicated by familiar social ethics, especially by the more recent Christian and secular egalitarian exemplars. A "right to life" for individual members is not consistent with the structure of the biotic community and hence is not mandated by the land ethic. This disparity between the land ethic and its more familiar social precedents contributes to the apparent devaluation of individual members of the biotic community and augments and reinforces the tendency of the land ethic, driven by the systemic vision of ecology, toward a more holistic or community-per-se orientation.

Of the few moral philosophers who have given the land ethic a moment's serious thought, most have regarded it with horror because of its emphasis on the good of the community and its deemphasis on the welfare of individual members of the community. Not only are other sentient creatures members of the biotic community and subordinate to its integrity, beauty, and stability; so are *we*. Thus, if it is not only morally permissible, from the point of view of the land ethic, but morally required, that members of certain species be abandoned to predation and other vicissitudes of wild life or even deliberately culled (as in the case of alert and sentient whitetail deer) for the sake of the integrity, stability, and beauty of the biotic community, how can we consistently exempt ourselves from a similar draconian regime? We too are only "plain members and citizens" of the biotic community. And our global population is growing unchecked. According to William Aiken, from the point of view of the land ethic, therefore, "massive human diebacks would be good. It is our duty to cause them. It is our species' duty, relative to the whole, to eliminate 90 percent of our numbers." Thus, according to Tom Regan, the land ethic is a clear case of "environmental fascism."

Of course Leopold never intended the land ethic to have either inhumane or antihumanitarian implications or consequences. But whether he intended them or not, a logically consistent deduction from the theoretical premises of the land ethic might force such untoward conclusions. And given their magnitude and monstrosity, these derivations would constitute a *reductio ad absurdum* of the whole land ethic enterprise and entrench and reinforce our current human chauvinism and moral alienation from nature. If this is what membership in the biotic community entails, then all but the most radical misanthropes would surely want to opt out.

XII

The land ethic, happily, implies neither inhumane nor inhuman consequences. That some philosophers think it must follows more from their own theoretical presuppositions than from the theoretical elements of the land ethic itself. Conventional modern ethical theory rests moral entitlement, as I earlier pointed out, on a criterion or qualification. If a candidate meets the criterion—rationality or sentiency are the most commonly posited—he, she, or it is entitled to equal moral standing with others who possess the same qualification in equal degree. Hence, reasoning in this philosophically orthodox way, and forcing Leopold's theory to conform: if human beings are, with other animals, plants, soils, and waters, equally members of the biotic community, and if community membership is the criterion of equal moral consideration, then not only do animals, plants, soils, and waters have equal (highly attenuated) "rights," but human beings are equally subject to the same subordination of individual welfare and rights in respect to the good of the community as a whole.

But the land ethic, as I have been at pains to point out, is heir to a line of moral analysis different from that institutionalized in contemporary moral philosophy. From the biosocial evolutionary analysis of ethics upon which Leopold builds the land ethic, it (the land ethic) neither replaces nor overrides previous accretions. Prior moral sensibilities and obligations attendant upon and correlative to prior strata of social involvement remain operative and preemptive.

Being citizens of the United States, or the United Kingdom, or the Soviet Union, or

Venezuela, or some other nation-state, and therefore having national obligations and patriotic duties, does not mean that we are not also members of smaller communities or social groups—cities or townships, neighborhoods, and families—or that we are relieved of the peculiar moral responsibilities attendant upon and correlative to these memberships as well. Similarly, our recognition of the biotic community and our immersion in it does not imply that we do not also remain members of the human community—the "family of man" or "global village"—or that we are relieved of the attendant and correlative moral responsibilities of that membership, among them to respect universal human rights and uphold the principles of individual human worth and dignity. The biosocial development of morality does not grow in extent like an expanding balloon, leaving no trace of its previous boundaries, so much like the circumference of a tree. Each emergent, and larger, social unit is layered over the more primitive, and intimate, ones.

Moreover, as a general rule, the duties correlative to the inner social circles to which we belong eclipse those correlative to the rings farther from the heartwood when conflicts arise. Consider our moral revulsion when zealous ideological nationalists encourage children to turn their parents in to the authorities if their parents dissent from the political or economic doctrines of the ruling party. A zealous environmentalist who advocated visiting war, famine, or pestilence on human populations (those existing somewhere else, of course) in the name of the integrity, beauty, and stability of the biotic community would be similarly perverse. Family obligations in general come before nationalistic duties and humanitarian obligations in general come before environmental duties. The land ethic, therefore, is not draconian or fascist. It does not cancel human morality. The land ethic may, however, as with any new accretion, demand choices which affect, in turn, the demands of the more interior social–ethical circles. Taxes and the military draft may conflict with family-level obligations. While the land ethic, certainly, does not cancel human morality, neither does it leave it unaffected.

Nor is the land ethic inhumane. Nonhuman fellow members of the biotic community have no "human rights," because they are not, by definition, members of the human community. As fellow members of the biotic community, however, they deserve respect.

How exactly to express or manifest respect, while at the same time abandoning our fellow members of the biotic community to their several fates or even actively consuming them for our own needs (and wants), or deliberately making them casualties of wildlife management for ecological integrity, is a difficult and delicate question.

Fortunately, American Indian and other traditional patterns of human–nature interaction provide rich and detailed models. Algonkian woodland peoples, for instance, represented animals, plants, birds, waters, and minerals as other-than-human persons engaged in reciprocal, mutually beneficial socioeconomic intercourse with human beings. Tokens of payment, together with expressions of apology, were routinely offered to the beings whom it was necessary for these Indians to exploit. Care not to waste the usable parts and care in the disposal of unusable animal and plant remains were also an aspect of the respectful, albeit necessarily consumptive, Algonquian relationship with fellow members of the land community. As I have more fully argued elsewhere, the Algonquian portrayal of human–nature relationships is, indeed, although certainly different in specifics, identical in abstract form to that recommended by Leopold in the land ethic.... Is the land ethic prudential or deontological? Is the land ethic, in other words, a matter of enlightened (collective, human) self-interest, or does it genuinely admit nonhuman natural entities and nature as a whole to true moral standing?

The conceptual foundations of the land ethic, as I have here set them out, and much of Leopold's hortatory rhetoric, would certainly indicate that the land ethic is deontological (or duty oriented) rather than prudential. In the section significantly titled "The Ecological Conscience," Leopold complains that the then-current conservation philosophy is inadequate because "it defines no right or wrong, assigns no obligation, calls for no sacrifice, implies no change in the current philosophy of values. In respect of land-use, it urges *only* enlightened self-interest" (pp. 207–8, emphasis added). Clearly, Leopold himself thinks that the land ethic goes beyond prudence. In this section he disparages mere "self-interest" two more times, and concludes that "obligations have no meaning without conscience, and the problem we face is the extension of the social conscience from people to land" (p. 209).

In the next section, "Substitutes for a Land Ethic," he mentions rights twice—the "biotic right" of birds to continuance and the absence of a right on the part of human special interest to exterminate predators.

Finally, the first sentences of "The Outlook" read: "It is inconceivable to me that an ethical relation to land can exist without love, respect, and admiration for land, and a high regard for its value. By value, I of course mean something far broader than mere economic value; I mean value in the philosophical sense" (p. 223). By "value in the philosophical sense," Leopold can only mean what philosophers more technically call "intrinsic value" or "inherent worth." Something that has intrinsic value or inherent worth is valuable in and of itself, not because of what it can do for us. "Obligation," "sacrifice," "a conscience," "respect," the ascription of rights, and intrinsic value—all of these are consistently opposed to self-interest and seem to indicate decisively that the land ethic is of the deontological type.

Some philosophers, however, have seen it differently. Scott Lehmann, for example, writes,

> Although Leopold claims for communities of plants and animals a "right to continued existence," his argument is homocentric, appealing to the human stake in preservation. Basically it is an argument from enlightened self-interest, where the self in question is not an individual human being but humanity—present and future—as a whole.

Lehmann's claim has some merits, even though it flies in the face of Leopold's express commitments. Leopold does frequently lapse into the language of (collective, long-range, human) self-interest. Early on, for example, he remarks, "in human history, we have learned (I hope) that the conqueror role is eventually *self*-defeating" (p. 204, emphasis added). And later, of the 95 percent of Wisconsin species which cannot be "sold, fed, eaten, or otherwise put to economic use," Leopold reminds us that "these creatures are members of the biotic community, and if (as I believe) its stability depends on its integrity, they are entitled to continuance" (p. 210). The implication is clear: the economic 5 percent cannot survive if a significant portion of the uneconomic 95 percent are extirpated; nor may *we,* it goes without saying, survive without these "resources."

Leopold, in fact, seems to be consciously aware of this moral paradox. Consistent with the biosocial foundations of his theory, he expresses it in sociobiological terms:

> An ethic may be regarded as a mode of guidance for meeting ecological situations so new or intricate, or involving such deferred reactions, that the path of social expediency is not discernible to the average individual. Animal instincts are modes of guidance for the individual in meeting such situations. Ethics are possibly a kind of community instinct in-the-making. (p. 203)

From an objective, descriptive sociobiological point of view, ethics evolve because they contribute to the inclusive fitness of their carriers (or, more reductively still, to the multiplication of their carriers' genes); they are expedient. However, the path to self-interest (or to the self-interest of the selfish gene) is not discernible to the participating individuals (nor, certainly, to their genes). Hence, ethics are grounded in instinctive feeling—love, sympathy, respect—not in self-conscious calculating intelligence. Somewhat like the paradox of hedonism—the notion that one cannot achieve happiness if one directly pursues happiness per se and not other things—one can only secure self-interest by putting the interests of others on a par with one's own (in this case long-range collective human self-interest and the interest of other forms of life and of the biotic community per se).

So, is the land ethic deontological or prudential, after all? It is both—self-consistently both—depending upon one's point of view. From the inside, from the lived, felt point of view of the community member with evolved moral sensibilities, it is deontological. It involves an affective–cognitive posture of genuine love, respect, admiration, obligation, self-sacrifice, conscience, duty, and the ascription of intrinsic value and biotic rights. From the outside, from the objective and analytic scientific point of view, it is prudential. "There is no other way for land to survive the impact of mechanized man,"nor, therefore, for mechanized man to survive his own impact upon the land (p. viii).

🐝 STUDY QUESTIONS

1. What are the three reasons for the professional neglect, confusion, and neglect of Leopold's "land ethics," according to Callicott?
2. How is the land ethic different from classical and mainstream modern ethical philosophy, such as Kant's and Bentham's systems? Note Goodpaster's criticisms on which Callicott draws.
3. Is Callicott successful in arguing for the natural basis of value in the interaction between valuers (humans) and the environment? Can you see any problems with this view?
4. Leopold wrote "A thing is right when it tends to preserve the integrity, stability, and beauty of the biotic community. It is wrong when it tends otherwise." This passage has been interpreted by some to mean that humans should be sacrificed if they interfere with the good of the biotic community. Callicott tries to modify this statement, removing the misanthropic implications. Go over his defense. Has Callicott strengthened or weakened Leopold's land ethic by modifying it as he does?

21   Refocusing Ecocentrism: De-emphasizing Stability and Defending Wildness

NED HETTINGER AND BILL THROOP*

Ned Hettinger is a professor of philosophy at the College of Charleston in Charleston, South Carolina. Bill Throop is a professor of philosophy and environmental studies at Green Mountain College in Poultney, Vermont.

Traditional ecocentric ethics relies on an ecology that emphasizes the stability and integrity of ecosystems. Numerous ecologists now focus on natural systems that are less clearly characterized by these properties. Hettinger and Throop use the elimination and restoration of wolves in Yellowstone to illustrate troubles for traditional ecocentric ethics caused by ecological models emphasizing instability in natural systems. They identify several other problems for a stability-integrity based ecocentrism as well. They also show how an ecocentric ethic can avoid these difficulties by emphasizing the value of the wildness of natural systems, and they defend wildness value from a rising tide of criticisms.

There are some who can live without wild things, and some who cannot.... Like winds and sunsets. Wild things were taken for granted until progress began to do away with them. Now we face the question whether a still higher "standard of living" is worth its cost in things natural, wild and free.... These wild things, I admit, had little human value until mechanization assured us of a good breakfast, and until science disclosed the drama of where they come from and how they live. The whole conflict thus boils down to a question of degree. We of the minority see a law of diminishing returns in progress; our opponents do not.

—ALDO LEOPOLD[1]

I. INTRODUCTION

At the beginning of the century, the howl of wolves still haunted Yellowstone National Park. But wolves were considered "varmints" and were poisoned, trapped, and shot as part of an official government policy of predator extermination that succeeded in eradicating wolves from Yellowstone by 1940. Today, most environmentalists believe that the extermination of the wolf was wrong and that its recent restoration was right.

Several widely held rationales for these judgments are rooted in ecocentric ethics. An ecocentric ethic treats natural systems as intrinsically valuable and/or morally considerable. This ethic is holistic in that it bases moral concern primarily on features of natural systems rather than on the individuals in them. Traditionally, ecocentric ethics has relied heavily on "holistic" ecological theory to provide its empirical foundation. It has evaluated human impacts on the environment primarily in terms of their effect on the integrity, stability, and balance of ecosystems.

Many have argued, for example, that without wolves the Yellowstone ecosystem was incomplete. Wolves were in Yellowstone long before

Reprinted from *Environmental Ethics* (Spring 1999) by permission of William Throop and Ned Hettinger.

*The authors thank Baird Callicott, Gary Comstock, Todd Grantham, Carl Whitney, two referees for *Environmental Ethics,* Wayne Ouderkirk and Brian K. Steverson, and especially Holmes Rolston, III, for stimulating comments and criticisms. We also benefited from discussing these ideas with audiences at Baylor University and Texas A&M University and at meetings of the Society for Conservation Biology and the International Society for Environmental Ethics.

modern settlement of the area, and they are integral to the identity of that ecosystem. Holmes Rolston, III says that Yellowstone is the "largest, nearest intact ecosystem in the temperate zone of earth"[2] and suggests that the wolf was one of the few missing components. Wolf biologist David Mech supports wolf reintroduction by arguing that "one of the mandates of the national parks is to preserve complete natural systems. Somehow Yellowstone was shorted. For more than sixty years it has preserved an incomplete system."[3] On this view, returning the wolf helps restore Yellowstone's integrity by making it whole again.

Many also support returning the wolves in order to restore the balance and stability of the Yellowstone ecosystem.[4] Wolf predation helps to control ungulate populations. Absent a major predator with which they coevolved, the elk population in Yellowstone increased dramatically. Vast herds of elk confined year round in this hunting sanctuary have eaten so much of the aspen and willow that these species are not regenerating. The decline in aspens and willows led to the decline of the beaver, a keystone species in maintaining riparian areas and park hydrology. On these grounds, Alston Chase, among others, argues that the balance of the Yellowstone ecosystem was upset by the restriction of the range of the ungulate population, by fire suppression, and by human eradication of wolves and other predators. Restoring the wolf is perceived to be an important step in allowing the Yellowstone equilibrium to return.

The idea that integrity and stability fundamentally characterize natural systems is far from uncontroversial. According to numerous ecologists, disturbance, disequilibria, and chaotic dynamics characterize many natural systems at a variety of scales.[5] Ecosystems are frequently interpreted by these ecologists as historically contingent, transient associations, rather than as persisting, integrated communities. Although many ecologists continue to find stable dimensions of some ecosystems, the presence of instability is trouble for traditional ecocentric ethics. It is risky to advocate preserving the integrity of natural systems when such integrity may not exist, and it is questionable to criticize humans for causing instability in what may already be unstable natural systems.

In this article, we assess the implications of instability models in ecological theory for ecocentric ethics. We use the elimination and restoration of wolves in Yellowstone to illustrate troubles for traditional ecocentric ethics caused by ecological models emphasizing instability in natural systems. We identify several other problems for a stability-integrity based ecocentrism as well. We show how an ecocentric ethic can avoid these difficulties by emphasizing the value of wildness in natural systems and we defend wildness value from a rising tide of criticisms. We do not attempt a full-fledged justification of ecocentrism; in particular, we do not defend ecocentrism against individualistic or anthropocentric environmental ethics.

II. THE ECOLOGY OF STABILITY AND TRADITIONAL ECOCENTRISM

The ecological theories on which traditional ecocentric ethics are based, theories we call collectively the "ecology of stability," were developed by Frederic Clements and Eugene Odum, among others. They tended to view natural systems as integrated, stable wholes that are either at, or moving toward, mature equilibrium states. The terms *equilibrium, balance, stability,* and *integrity* often go unexplained in traditional ecocentric ethics. Kristin Shrader-Frechette and Earl McCoy have identified over twenty different uses of *stability* and *equilibrium* in ecology.[6] Central among these are the following uses.

A system is in equilibrium if the various forces acting on it are sufficiently balanced that the system is constant and orderly with respect to those features under consideration; thus *balance* and *equilibrium* are closely related. A balance or equilibrium can be either static or dynamic: equilibrium is displayed both by a constancy in tree species in a mature forest ecosystem and by a regular oscillation in a predator-prey system. A system is stable (1) if it is relatively constant over time, (2) if it resists alteration (i.e., it is not fragile), (3) if upon being disturbed it has a strong tendency to return to its predisturbance state (i.e., it is resilient), or (4) if it moves toward some end point ("matures"), despite differences in starting points ("trajectory stability").[7] Whether a system is in equilibrium and/or stable depends on the features under consideration and the scale at which the system is described. Vernal pools that exist for perhaps a dozen weeks each year and then dry up are ephemeral on a time scale of months but constant if the scale is years.

Integrity is also used in a variety of senses. The general idea is that the elements of the ecosystem are blended into a unified whole. This idea is commonly associated with the view that ecosystems come in fixed packages of species whose coordinated functioning creates a unified community. A system which has integrity is characterized by a high degree of integration of its parts. Complex patterns of interdependency weave the parts into a well-integrated unit.

In the ecology of stability, natural systems do undergo some changes, such as fluctuations in the populations of predators and prey, but usually such changes are regular and predictable (as in the cycling of predator and prey according to the Lotka-Volterra equations). Disturbances are considered atypical, and when they occur, ecosystems resist upset. When a natural system is disturbed, it typically returns to its pre-disturbance state or trajectory. Successional ecosystems will move through a predictable series of stages to their mature climax states. In these end states, biotic and abiotic elements of the ecosystems are in balance and the system has "as large and diverse an organic structure" as is possible given available energy and environmental limitations.[8] According to this paradigm, the loss of a species, such as the wolf, upsets the balance and often results in a decline in ecosystem stability, for species diversity in an ecosystem is thought to be proportional to its stability. Thus, ecosystem integrity, stability, and diversity are seen to be closely interrelated phenomena.

This conception of natural systems provides a powerful and seemingly objective basis for determining when ecosystems have been damaged or their value diminished.[9] Integrity, stability, and balance are properties that have widespread and powerful normative appeal. In an ecocentric ethic that emphasizes these properties, our duties to natural systems seem to arise from the nature of ecosystems themselves, rather than from human preferences concerning natural systems. An ecosystem missing a top predator is not simply one that environmentalists do not like; it is a damaged ecosystem. Ignoring this damage betrays ecological ignorance. Ecological science thus appears to underwrite environmental ethics and environmentalist policies. Further, because nature tends towards these states absent human intervention, the ethic based on this normative ecological paradigm warrants preserving ecosystems intact, limiting human impacts, and restoring nature after human degradation.

Advocates of ecocentric ethics frequently appeal to the basic notions of the ecology of stability. Aldo Leopold's often quoted summary maxim—"A thing is right when it tends to preserve the integrity, stability, and beauty of the biotic community; it is wrong when it tends otherwise"—relies on these ideas.[10] Many, such as J. Baird Callicott, have taken Leopold's views as the basis for their environmental ethic.[11] In articulating his ecocentrism, Holmes Rolston puts considerable evaluative weight on the integrity and stability of biotic communities: "A biotic community is a dynamic web of interacting parts in which lives are supported and defended, where there is integrity (integration of the members) and health (niches and resources for the flourishing of species), stability and historical development (dependable regeneration, resilience, and evolution)....[12] Although Rolston's ecocentrism relies on a number of values that systemically make nature valuable (such as diversity, complexity, creativity, and a tendency to produce increasingly valuable "ecological achievements"), ecosystem integrity and stability are central among them.[13]

III. THE ECOLOGY OF INSTABILITY

An ethic based on the integrity, stability, and balance of natural systems ill accords with some trends in ecology.[14] The more radical proponents of what we call the "ecology of instability" argue that disturbance is the norm for many ecosystems and that natural systems typically do not tend toward mature, stable, integrated states.[15] On a broad scale, climatic changes show little pattern, and they ensure that over the long term, natural systems remain in flux. On a smaller scale, fires,

storms, droughts, shifts in the chemical composi-
tions of soils, chance invasions of new species,
and a wealth of other factors continually alter
the structures of natural systems in ways that do
not create repeating patterns of return to the
same equilibrium states.[16]

Many empirical studies show that populations
fluctuate irregularly.[17] Simple predator/prey
models in which numbers of predators and prey
oscillate predictably over time ignore the myriad
of factors that affect population size. Major population explosions and declines are inherent features of numerous natural systems. Some
ecologists suggest that many interacting populations are chaotic systems, in the mathematical
sense of *chaos*.[18] Although these systems are
fully deterministic, accurate predictions about
them are impossible because tiny (and thus hard
to measure) differences in initial conditions can
produce drastically different results. Furthermore,
ecologists no longer assume a tight correlation
between stability and diversity. There is evidence
that an intermediate level of disturbance can
increase diversity.[19] Also, some stable ecosystems
are not very diverse, such as east coast U.S. salt
marsh grass ecosystems where *Spartina alterni-
flora* grows in vast stands that are simple in species
composition but quite stable.

With flux taken to be the norm on a variety
of levels, it becomes more difficult to interpret
natural systems as well-integrated, persisting
wholes, much like organisms. Ecosystem integrity
becomes problematic when species relationships
are opportunistic. Noting that co-occurrence of
species is determined by abiotic factors as much
as by species interactions and that typical interactions between species involve competition, predation, parasitism, and disease, one well-known
conservation biologist claims that "the idea that
species live in integrated communities is a
myth."[20] Evidence suggests that species groupings are historically contingent and are not fixed
packages that come and go as units.[21] Insofar as
species associations are transient, individualistic,
biotic assemblages, we must begin to question
the ideas that ecosystems are supposed to have
certain species, that without all of its species an
ecosystem is "incomplete," and that exotic species do not belong.

Indeed, the very notion of an ecosystem has
become suspect in some quarters. A number
of ecologists now investigate the dynamics of
"patches" of land, giving up on the idea of
homogenous ecosystems. Others retain the
notion of an ecosystem, but drop the organismic
assumptions often associated with it. We follow
the latter course, recognizing that without these
assumptions, what counts as an ecosystem
depends on our purposes as well as on the empirical facts.

One intriguing response to these worries has
been advanced by J. Baird Callicott.[22] Callicott
points out that, like biotic communities, human
communities are neither stable nor typological—
that is, they change over time and do not come
and go as units. Human communities are also
composed of individualistic, self-promoting, and
competitive individuals. Callicott concludes that
biotic communities are no less integrated and
no harder to demarcate than are human communities, and thus that if human communities
are sufficiently coherent to generate obligations
to them, then so are biotic communities.

One problem with this argument is that
human communities are held together by shared
purpose and meaning. That people see themselves as part of a human community is essential
to its unity. Self-seeking individualism, predatory
competition, and parasitism, unchecked by community spirit and identity, tear apart human communities. Sprawl development characterized by
vacant strip malls, big-box stores adjacent to diseased local merchants, and aggressive automobile
traffic hardly constitutes a community that generates preservationist obligations. Callicott's analogy ignores the fact that the shared purpose
and meaning that bind together changing, self-
seeking individuals into human communities are
lacking in biotic communities.[23]

Callicott also suggests that the Leopoldian
response to the ecology of instability should be
to modify Leopold's dictum to say: "A thing is
right when it tends to disturb the biotic community only at normal spatial and temporal scales. It
is wrong when it tends otherwise."[24] This
implausibly suggests that it is morally permissible
to intentionally extirpate other species so long as
we do so at rates comparable to normal extinction

frequencies in evolutionary history. It also has the unfortunate consequence that extensive restoration projects are impermissible insofar as they disturb nature at nonnormal scales. Callicott has not quieted the worries about ecocentric ethics generated by the ecology of instability.

We want to stress that there are important ways in which many natural systems display significant degrees of integrity and stability in various respects. Ecosystems are certainly not mere jumbles of self-sufficient individuals. No one denies the existence of causal connections between individuals in ecosystems or dependencies between species. Species adapt to each other, to disturbances, and to changing environments. Sometimes these adaptations can make ecosystems more resistant (and persistent), as when a keystone tree species on hurricane-prone barrier islands evolves a thicker trunk and begins to hug the ground. Selective pressures also put a brake on species self-aggrandizement, for example, by working against predator species that drive their prey to extinction and parasites that destroy their hosts. Many dimensions of natural systems clearly persist on human time scales.

The ecology of instability is far from achieving the status of a dominant paradigm. There continues to be ongoing fruitful work on stability at larger scales and in systems where the disturbance interval is long relative to recovery time.[25] Some recent experimental research supports the claim that increases in diversity produce increases in stability.[26] Additionally, ongoing research in group selection (i.e., natural selection operating on higher levels of organization than the individual), including selection at the community level, may provide support for ecosystem stability and integrity of certain sorts.[27]

Some respected ecologists even suggest that the emphasis on disturbance, instability, and chaos is as much a function of sociological factors, such as the novelty of research on disequilibrium, as it is of new data in ecology.[28] Ecologists are exploring a variety of fruitful metaphors drawn from other sciences and society at large. The success of population biology and of chaos theory outside ecology, as well as our culture's increasing individualism, provide resources for plausible sociological explanations of the popularity of the metaphors and models informing contemporary ecology. Nonetheless, these models have also proved to be empirically fruitful.

Although it would be unreasonable to reject wholesale the ecology of stability, the dangers of basing an environmental ethic on that ecology are significant. An ecocentrism that emphasizes preserving the stability and integrity in ecosystems would seem to leave those ecosystems which lack significant stability or integrity largely unprotected. If an ecocentric ethic is based on valuing stability and integrity, would it not follow, implausibly, that less stable and integrated ecosystems were less valuable and thus less worthy of protection? Michael Soulé thinks it positively dangerous to emphasize the equilibrial, self-regulating, stability producing tendencies of ecosystems.[29] If nature is so stable, it ought to be able to handle human disturbance. If it can, it seems we ought to be protecting the more fragile ecosystems rather than the more stable ones. Moreover, what about the different kinds of stability? Would ecosystems that lacked resilience, but had constancy, such as tundra ecosystems, be subject to more or less protection than those that are resilient, but less constant, such as fire-prone chaparral? Would more tightly integrated biotic communities (e.g., ecosystems with keystone species) take precedence over looser species assemblages? Such questions indicate how developments in ecology muddy the waters for all ecocentrism that emphasizes stability and integrity and leave it with a range of unpalatable implications. Leopold's dictum that what is right is what "preserves the integrity, stability and beauty of the biotic community" seems all too vulnerable to the charge that we may be obligating ourselves to preserve something that frequently does not exist.

In particular, consider the implications of viewing the case of the Yellowstone wolves through the lens of the ecology of instability. It is no longer clear that ecocentrists can justify the claims that elimination of wolves from Yellowstone damaged the ecosystem and that their restoration is desirable. Perhaps those who hunted and poisoned the wolves did not disrupt any significant stability and integrity of the system. They may have merely changed the system, much like other phenomena might change it (e.g., an ice age, disease, etc.); now it is governed by a different set of dynamics.

Of course, it may be that characteristics of the Yellowstone ecosystem relevant to wolves can be most fruitfully explained by stability models. But what if, in relevant respects, Yellowstone is better interpreted using instability models? Suppose that elk populations would fluctuate dramatically and irregularly with or without wolves and that such fluctuations had a variety of unpredictable impacts on animals dependent on elk forage. Do we want our obligations to Yellowstone to depend on how stable or unstable, integrated or loosely organized it is? We think not. We may, of course, decide that we should restore wolves to Yellowstone for other reasons, perhaps because we enjoy seeing wolves and want our children to be able to experience them. But then we have abandoned an ecocentric ethic, and this, we believe, is premature.

IV. WILDNESS AND ECOCENTRISM

We think that advocates of ecocentric ethics should shift the emphasis away from integrity and stability toward other intrinsically valuable features of natural systems, such as diversity, complexity, creativity, beauty, fecundity, and wildness. For reasons we outline below, we think that the value of wildness plays a central role in this nexus of values. Emphasizing wildness provides the most promising general strategy for defending ecocentric ethics. Others have suggested that the wildness of some natural systems gives us a strong reason for valuing them intrinsically.[30] We support this claim by showing how wildness value is in reflective equilibrium with many considered judgments, by showing how a focus on wildness avoids a number of problems with traditional ecocentrism, and by defending the value of the wild from a host of criticisms.

The term *wild* has a variety of meanings, many of which are not relevant to our defense of ecocentrism. For example, by *wild* we do not mean "chaotic," "fierce," or "uncontrollable." As we use the term, something is wild in a certain respect to the extent that it is *not humanized* in that respect. An entity is humanized in the degree to which it is influenced, altered, or controlled by humans. While one person walking through the woods does little to diminish its wildness, leaving garbage, culling deer, or clear cutting do diminish wildness, although in different degrees. Do we tend to value wildness so defined?

Numerous examples from ordinary life suggest that people do value wildness in a variety of contexts. For instance, admiration of a person's attractive features is likely to diminish when it is learned that they were produced by elective plastic surgery. People prefer the birth of a child without the use of drugs or a Caesarean section, and they do so not just because the former may be more conducive to health. Picking raspberries discovered in a local ravine is preferable to procuring the store-bought commercial variety (and not just because of the beauty of the setting). Our appreciation of catching cutthroat trout in an isolated and rugged mountain valley is reduced by reports that the Department of Fish and Game stocked the stream the previous week. Imagine how visitors to Yellowstone would feel about Old Faithful if they thought that the National Park Service put soap into the geyser to regulate and enhance its eruptions. In each example, people value more highly what is less subject to human alteration or control than a more humanized variant of the same phenomenon. The value differential may result from several features of these cases, but central among them is the difference in wildness. Notice that if we focus on different aspects of these situations, the judgment of wildness changes: the mountain stream may be wild in many respects, even if its fish are not. Although we value wildness in many things, an ecocentric ethic will focus on the value of the wildness of natural systems.

In addition to such specific judgments, there are powerful and widespread general intuitions that support the value of the nonhumanized. People rightfully value the existence of a realm not significantly under human control—the weather, the seasons, the mountains, and the seas. This is one reason why the idea of humans as planetary managers is so objectionable to many.[31] Consider a world in which human beings determine when it rains, when spring comes, how the tides run, and where mountains rise. The surprise and awe we feel at the workings of spontaneous nature would be replaced by appraisal of the decisions of these managers. Our wonder at the mystery of these phenomena would not survive such management. People value being a part of a world not of their own making. Valuing the wild acknowledges that limits to human mastery and domination of the world are imperative.

Humans also need to be able to confront, honor, and celebrate the "other."[32] In an increasingly secular society, "Nature" takes on the role of the other. Humans need to be able to feel small in comparison with something nonhuman which is of great value. Confronting the other helps humans to cultivate a proper sense of humility. Many people find the other powerfully in parts of nature that do not bend to our will and where the nonhuman carries on in relative autonomy, unfolding on its own.

With dramatic humanization of the planet, wildness becomes especially significant. In general, when something of value becomes rare, that value increases. Today, the spontaneous workings of nature are becoming increasingly rare. Reportedly, humans appropriate between twenty and forty percent of the photosynthetic energy produced by terrestrial plants.[33] Humans now rival the major geologic forces in our propensity to move around soil and rock.[34] Human population, now approaching six billion, is projected to increase by fifty percent by the middle of the next century. Leaving out Antarctica, there are now 100 humans for every square mile of the land surface of the Earth.[35] Almost everyone knows a special natural area that has been "developed" and is now gone. The increasing importance of biotechnology further manifests our domestication, artificialization, and humanization of nature. Wildness is threatened on a variety of fronts, and the passions that fuel many environmental disputes can often be explained by this rapid loss of the wild and the consequent increase in the value of what remains.

By positing wildness as a significant value-enhancing property, we account for a wide range of intuitions. Of course, the nature that we value in virtue of its wildness is also valuable because it is complex, creative, fecund, diverse, beautiful, and so on. Why focus on wildness,

rather than on biodiversity, as is currently fashionable (or on some other characteristic)? We believe that the emphasis on wildness is justified by the transformative and intensifying roles it plays in this nexus of values. These roles suggest that wildness is a kind of "root" value, that is, a significant source of these other values.

Wildness is transformative in that it can combine with a property that has neutral or even negative value and turn the whole into a positive value. For example, wildness helps to transform biodiversity into the powerful value it is in today's environmental debates. Biodiversity is not by itself valuable. If it were, we could add value to ecosystems by integrating large numbers of genetically engineered organisms into them. But doing so seems unacceptable. It is *wild* biodiversity that people wish to protect. Wildness transforms biodiversity into a significant value-bearing property. The presence or absence of wildness frequently transforms our evaluation of things; a beautiful sunset is diminished in value when it is caused by pollution. Wildness also intensifies the value of properties that are already valuable.[36] For example, wildness often significantly enhances the value of beauty. As Eugene Hargrove argues, "our aesthetic admiration and appreciation for natural beauty is an appreciation of the achievement of complex form that is entirely unplanned. It is in fact because it is unplanned and independent of human involvement that the achievement is so amazing, wonderful, and delightful."[37]

An ecocentrism that emphasizes wildness value also puts a brake on alleged human improvements of nature through anthropogenic production of the properties in virtue of which we value nature. A stability and integrity based ecocentrism would have to judge human activity that enhanced ecosystem stability or integrity as value increasing. A highly humanized ecosystem could be more stable, integrated, and diverse than a natural ecosystem that it replaced. For example, an engineered beach with breakwaters and keystone exotics that held the sand might be more stable, integrated, and diverse than the naturally eroding beach it replaced. Only an ecocentrism that puts its central focus on wildness value can prevent the unpalatable conclusion that such human manipulation of nature would, if successful, increase intrinsic value.

While we argue that it is now reasonable to strongly value wildness, it was not always reasonable to do so. The value of wildness varies with context. For example, clearing an old-growth forest in the late twentieth century has very different value implications from doing so ten thousand years ago. In early periods of human history, wildness was ubiquitous and threatening. Controlling a small patch of land was a significant achievement for humanity and had significant value in itself. In contrast, wildness had little or no value in itself: there was simply too much of it relative to humanized environments. This contextualization of the value of wildness fits well with the "holistic" insight that the seriousness of environmental threats depends on what else is taking place on the planet. Humans extirpating the wolf from the Yellowstone region in the first part of this century had a vastly different impact on wildness value than did comparable prehistoric anthropogenic extinctions.

The value of wildness depends not only on the larger historical context, but also on the kind of object it characterizes. For example, a vegetable garden gone wild is less valuable than one under the gardener's control because of the purposes implicit in the description "vegetable garden." We do not here undertake the difficult task of providing a theory of the appropriate contexts and object descriptions for evaluating wildness. One may worry that contexts could be gerrymandered or objects artificially described so that implausible appraisals of wildness result. For example, wildness on the Earth is of great value given its relative rarity, but if the context is the solar system with its abundance of wildness, we might reach a different conclusion. In most cases people can recognize such clearly inappropriate contextualizations or descriptions, but it is often difficult to specify how they do so. This difficulty applies to almost any theory of value, as the contextualization of value is pervasive.

In arguing that ecocentrism should emphasize wildness value, we are not suggesting that wildness is always an overriding value or that highly wild ecosystems are always more valuable than less wild places. Wild things can have value-subtracting qualities that are more weighty than wildness value. Both anthropocentric values and nonanthropocentric values may trump wildness values in some situations. For example, to protect biodiversity, we might put out a fluke lightning-lit fire in order to protect the biodiversity of an island packed with endemic plants. Moreover, a somewhat wilder, but much less biodiverse landscape (e.g., Antarctica) is not necessarily of greater intrinsic value than a somewhat less wild, but much more biodiverse landscape (e.g., the Amazon rain forest). A full theory of wildness value would include some priority principles indicating when wildness value will trump other goods. We cannot provide such thorough guidance here, though we do suggest that as the planet becomes more humanized, wildness value will increasingly trump other values.

Some may worry that an environmental ethic that emphasizes wildness value abandons ecocentrism in favor of an instrumental anthropocentrism because it apparently appeals to human pleasure at contemplating wildness. But this worry confuses what is being valued with the valuing itself (or with a by-product of the valuing). Valuing nature for its wildness is not valuing wild nature for the pleasure it brings us, anymore than valuing a friend is simply valuing the pleasure one derives from the friendship. Pleasure may be a sign of value without being its source.

We are not maintaining that the value of wildness inheres in natural systems themselves independent of consciousness of them. We remain neutral on the issue of whether wildness value is objective in this sense or is a function of a valuing subject. We also remain neutral about what kind of a value wildness is. Some may think that wildness value is an aesthetic or religious value rather than a moral value. As long as the presence of aesthetic or religious value can obligate us in significant ways, we need not decide whether wildness value is aesthetic, religious, or moral (or some combination of these).

V. OBJECTIONS AND RESPONSES

Wildness has come under increasing criticism. One concern is that intuitions about the value of wildness are idiosyncratic. Many people do not seem to value wildness, but instead fear it or profess dislike for things not under human control.[38] David Orr identifies a trend he calls "biophobia" and claims that the more "we dwell in and among our own creations," the more we become "uncomfortable with nature lying beyond our direct control."[39]

We are not suggesting that everyone will immediately assent to the claim that wildness is valuable. Rather, we claim that valuing wildness is a rational and reflective response to the current situation on the planet.[40] We grant that it is not the only rational response. No doubt, the valuing of wildness springs from and reflects certain cultural traditions.[41] In this respect, it is no different from many other values that orient ethics and policy, such as the value of human equality or freedom of political speech. Even if the valuing of wildness originated in Western culture, wildness value can have much wider significance. After all, the notion of human rights arose from movements in Western thought, but it is now believed to have universal validity. We believe that, for a wide range of people, increased education about the massive humanization of the Earth will lead to greater recognition of the value of wildness.

Furthermore, many people value wildness without understanding their evaluations in these terms. Wildness comes in degrees and often people value things in virtue of lesser degrees of wildness. People value gardening, bird watching, golfing, dinner on the porch, or walks in the park, partially because these activities put them in touch with nonhuman nature. Even the ranchers who opposed the restoration of wolves into Yellowstone seem to love the outdoor lives they have chosen in part because it involves an encounter with the relatively nonhumanized.

An increasingly frequent objection to "wilderness environmentalism" is that by privileging big wilderness areas, it ignores the value of more local, humanized landscapes.[42] Our position avoids this objection by valuing some natural systems, such as pasture and parks, for their intermediate degrees of wildness. It would be a mistake to equate wildness with wilderness, though wilderness is an important manifestation of wildness and would be strongly protected by the proposed ecocentrism. A related concern is that a focus on wildland preservation ignores the central importance of finding a way for humans to live in nature without destroying it.[43] We too believe that turning human societies toward a sustainable use of nature is crucial. An ecocentric ethic that emphasizes wildness value does suggest that we should diminish our impacts on nature, and this is one aspect of sustainability. But clearly other values, including anthropocentric ones, are needed to fully guide humans to a more sustainable relationship with the Earth. We believe, however, that without an emphasis on wildness value, sustainability will all too likely result in human domination of the Earth.[44]

Embracing degrees of wildness also allows for a response to the objection that there is no wild nature left to value. Recent work in ecology, anthropology, and environmental history points to long-standing and sustained human impact on the planet. On the basis of such research, J. Baird Callicott (among others) has attacked the idea of wilderness, claiming that "in 1492, Antarctica was the only true wilderness land mass on the planet"—that is, the only place "undominated by the works of man."[45] If we add to this large-scale early human influence the impact of more numerous and technologically powerful modern humans, then valuing the wildness of natural systems may appear to be a will-o'-the-wisp.

We have noted that relatively less humanized places carry significant wildness value. It may be arbitrary to make fine discriminations in degrees of wildness, but that should not obscure obvious distinctions. The following environments are ordered in clearly increasing degrees of wildness: an air conditioned building, a parking lot with weeds sprouting up, a garden, a tree farm, a national park, a wilderness area. Even extensively humanized places like backyards, gardens, or New York's Central Park carry important wildness value in the right context and when contrasted with more humanized places.

This objection also fails to account for ways in which humanization "washes out" of natural systems. Early human influence on a system is dampened by intervening epochs with little impact. A system can recapture previous levels of wildness as human influence diminishes. Intuitively, Dartmoor in England and the Western Adirondacks in the U.S. (both areas once stripped of their tree-cover by humans) are examples of high degrees of wildness returning after significant human impact.

Some charge that emphasizing the value of wildness dichotomizes humans and nature and ignores the Darwinian insight that humans, like any species, are a part of nature and are not separate from it.[46] Many are inclined to view humans, especially native peoples, as "biotic citizens" who are members of the natural communities they alter, just as beavers are members of the natural communities they radically alter. We do not deny that humans are part of nature in important senses of this phrase. To a significant extent, humans are the result of and are embedded in natural processes. Certain dimensions of human life are properly understood and valued as manifestations of wild nature. Allowing our bodies to reflect the impacts of sun, wind, and aging is to partake in wildness. Acting on instinct is letting the spontaneous processes of nature unfold within us. We value the wild in humans as well as in nonhuman nature.[47] Of course, we do not always value wildness in humans, just as we do not always value wildness in ecosystems. Much depends on competing values and the context. It is obviously appropriate for humans to civilize themselves and civilization clearly has enhanced human value. Nonetheless, we agree with Thoreau when he says, "I would not have every man nor every part of a man cultivated, any more than I would have every acre of earth cultivated."[48]

Although humans are a part of nature in the above senses (and others), there are important reasons to distinguish human activity from the activity of wild nature.[49] Human transformations of the land are different in evaluatively relevant ways from transformations imposed by nonhuman species or processes. For example, only human activities are fully morally assessable. Also, human activities can affect nature on a scale and speed much greater than the activities of other individual species. Rolston has identified important differences in the methods and speed by which humans transfer and use information.[50] Little in nonhuman nature approaches the deeply layered intentional, cultural, social, economic, and technological dimensions of much human activity.

As a group, humans have become too powerful and too populous to be simply "plain members and citizens" of biotic communities. Given the intense human domination of the planet, the metaphor of the biotic citizen is as likely to mislead as it is to help. It suggests that modern humans should be fully assimilated into natural systems, but doing so would have a disastrous effect on many ecosystems. For an environmental ethic to interpret the human presence in, and influence on, natural systems as not different in evaluatively relevant ways from that of any other species or natural phenomenon is to carry a valid Darwinian insight to absurd lengths.

VI. RESTORATION, WOLVES, AND THE WILD

Appealing to the value of wildness provides strong reasons to believe that it was wrong to extirpate wolves from Yellowstone. Eliminating wolves involved significant human alteration of the processes that characterized that system. In the context of the twentieth century, this loss of wildness in Yellowstone carried with it significant loss of value. Nonetheless, we cannot directly infer from the loss of wild value in Yellowstone that wildness counts in favor of restoration of wolves, for reintroducing wolves involves significant additional human alteration and management of Yellowstone, and it is hard to see how such a reintroduction can be sanctioned by the value of wildness. Indeed, intuitions about the positive value of restoration result in another objection to wildness value. As Robin Attfield puts the point, "How can anything be restored by human agency the essence of which is to be independent of human agency?"[51] Restoration is a contentious environmental issue. Some philosophers disparage restorations as fakes or artifacts.[52] Other philosophers stress our obligations to restore nature and suggest that certain types of restoration can increase value significantly.[53] We believe that an ecocentric ethic that emphasizes the value of wildness has the virtue of maintaining and explaining this ambivalent attitude.

Although restoration typically fails to increase wildness in the short run, it can speed recovery of wildness by helping humanization wash out of natural systems.

Notice that a stability-integrity ecocentrism must be quite sanguine about restoration (at least in theory). If an ecosystem's stability or integrity is restored, no loss has occurred. In contrast, restoration designed to enhance wildness value wears its limitations on its sleeve. Not only will the additional human activity involved in restoration tend to detract from wildness value, but restoring the original system's wildness will not be possible in one respect: human activity will forever remain part of the causal chain leading to that ecosystem. Nevertheless, wildness value can count in favor of restoration projects. By returning the system to what it would have been had humans not altered it, restoration can help diminish human influence.

A number of factors affect the speed and extent of "washout." In general, the greater the human influence on a system, the longer it will take for the humanization to wash out. For example, previous levels of wildness will return more quickly to a selectively cut forest than to a clear-cut forest. Temporal distance from the humanization also affects washout. The mere fact that it has been at least six hundred years since humans removed the trees from Dartmoor makes that landscape significantly wilder than it would be had the deforestation occurred fifty years ago. Complete washout of human influence can occur rapidly. A volcanic eruption that destroys a humanized landscape and covers it with a thick layer of lava would seem to return the full wildness of the landscape almost instantaneously. The land becomes very much like what it would have been whether or not it had been humanized. Such transformations suggest that washout is also a function of the extent to which a system instantiates a pattern it would have displayed absent some relatively recent humanization. A fourth factor affecting washout is the extent to which natural processes rework an humanized area, whether or not the result instantiates what it would have been absent humanization. For example, Dartmoor has recovered more of its lost wildness

than has the cliffs of Mount Rushmore because natural processes have been more successful in changing the humanized state.

We think that restoring wolves to Yellowstone is a case in which additional human activity can help humanization washout of a natural system. The human involvement in the restoration does initially subtract from wildness in important respects: humans transporting wolves from Canada into the park, attaching radio collars to the animals, and then tracking their movements involves additional and significant human activity in natural systems and it alters natural systems as they are currently constituted. Yellowstone would become wilder sooner if wolves returned without human assistance. Still, we believe this additional human activity will eventually decrease the degree to which Yellowstone is a humanized environment. By putting wolves back, we diminish the overall impact of humans on Yellowstone, much the way picking up litter in a forest diminishes the human impact on the forest or removing a dam reduces the human impact on a river—despite involving additional human activity. Contrast wolf restoration with introducing snow leopards into Yellowstone. Wildness value counts significantly in favor of wolf restoration rather than snow leopard introduction because wolves and not snow leopards would have been in Yellowstone today. An ecocentrism based on stability would have no reason to support putting back the native species rather than a functionally equivalent exotic.

VII. CONCLUSION

We have argued that an ecocentric ethic that emphasizes the value of wildness of natural systems has a number of virtues in comparison with traditional ecocentrism. Most important, it avoids the ecologically and philosophically troubling assumptions that natural systems worthy of protection are integrated and stable. Moreover, by focusing on wildness, ecocentrism can avoid the counterintuitive result that humans can improve ecosystems' value by increasing their integrity, stability, biodiversity, and so on. An ecocentrism that emphasizes wildness allows for a more ambivalent assessment of restoration than the overly sanguine approach resulting from traditional ecocentrism.

We have shown how focusing ecocentrism on the wildness of natural systems can explain a wide range of intuitions, including beliefs about our obligations to preserve and restore natural systems like Yellowstone. We have also shown how common objections to emphasizing wildness can be avoided. It seems unwise to ground ecocentrism in general theories, such as the ecology of stability or the ecology of instability, when nature displays so much variation and complexity. Powerful intuitions about the value of wildness that are accepted by many people can provide that grounding. Other values can also play important roles in a fully developed ecocentric ethic, though, if we are right, their roles will usually depend on wildness.

NOTES

1. Aldo Leopold, *A Sand County Almanac* (New York: Oxford University Press, 1949), p. ix.

2. Holmes Rolston, III, "Biology and Philosophy in Yellowstone," *Biology and Philosophy* 5 (1990): 242.

3. David Mech, "Returning the Wolf to Yellowstone," in Robert Keiter and Mark Boyce, eds., *The Greater Yellowstone Ecosystem* (New Haven: Yale University Press, 1991), p. 309.

4. The following account comes from Alston Chase, *Playing God in Yellowstone* (San Diego: Harcourt Brace Jovanovich, 1987), pp. 19–30, 382.

5. For an overview of this emphasis in ecology, see Donald Worster, "The Ecology of Order and Chaos," *Environmental History Review* (1990): 1–18.

6. K. S. Shrader-Frechette and E. D. McCoy, *Method in Ecology* (New York: Cambridge University Press, 1993), pp. 65–67.

7. Compare Gordon Orians, "Diversity, Stability and Maturity in Natural Ecosystems," W. H. van Dobben and R. H. Lowe-McConnell, eds., *Unifying Concepts in Ecology* (The Hague: Dr. W. Junk B. V. Publishers, 1975), pp. 139–50.

8. See Worster, "The Ecology of Order," p. 41, quoting Odum.

9. A number of U.S. environmental laws use concepts like balance and stability to define the goals they set for public policy. See Mark Sagoff, "Fact and Value in Ecological Science," *Environmental Ethics* 7 (1985): 101.

10. Leopold, *Sand County Almanac,* p. 240.

11. J. Baird Callicott, *In Defense of the Land Ethic* (Albany: State University of New York Press, 1989).

12. Holmes Rolston, III, *Conserving Natural Value* (New York: Columbia University Press, 1994), p. 78.

13. In arguing that the most important natural value is the "systemic value" of ecosystems, that is, their ability to create value, Rolston says: "the stability, integrity, and beauty of biotic communities is what is most fundamentally to be conserved" (ibid., p. 177). Rolston is well aware of ecologists' ambivalence toward ecosystem stability and integrity. He ties his discussion of ecosystem stability to a discussion of historical change. At one point, he calls the notion that ecosystems tend toward equilibrium "a half-truth."

14. For one development of this argument, see Kristin Shrader-Frechette, "Ecological Theories and Ethical Imperatives," in William Shea and Beat Sitter, eds., *Scientists and Their Responsibility* (Canton, Mass.: Watson Publishing International, 1989).

15. See Daniel Botkin, *Discordant Harmonies* (New York: Oxford University Press, 1990). In "Nonequilibrium Determinants of Biological Community Structure," *American Scientist* 82 (1994): 427, Seth Reice contends that "equilibrium is an unusual state for natural ecosystems.... the normal state of communities and ecosystems is to be recovering from the last disturbance. Natural systems are so frequently disturbed that equilibrium is rarely achieved."

16. See the articles in S. T. A. Pickett and P. S. White, eds., *The Ecology of Natural Disturbance and Patch Dynamics* (Orlando: Academic Press, 1985), for examples of research in this area.

17. Botkin, *Discordant Harmonies,* chap. 3.

18. Ibid. For research documenting chaotic behavior of populations independent of perturbations, see Alan Hastings and Kevin Higgins, "Persistence of Transients in Spatially Structured Ecological Models," *Science* 263 (1994): 1133–36.

19. See Reice, "Nonequilibrium Determinants," p. 428.

20. Michael Soulé, "The Social Siege of Nature," in Michael Soulé and Gary Lease, eds., *Reinventing Nature?* (Washington, D.C.: Island Press, 1995), p. 143.

21. "Looking at the fossil record of the last 50,000 years," David Jablonski says, "the most important message...is that ecological communities do not respond as units to environmental change....

Species are highly individualistic in their behavior, so that few, if any, modern terrestrial communities existed in their present form 10,000 years ago." See Jablonski's "Extinction: A Paleontological Perspective," *Science* 253 (1991): 756. In a similar vein, Michael Soulé suggests that historical "studies are undermining typological concepts of community composition, structure, dynamics, and organization by showing that existing species once constituted quite different groupings or 'communities.'" See Soulé's "The Onslaught of Alien Species, and Other Challenges in the Coming Decades," *Conservation Biology* 4 (1990): 234.

22. J. Baird Callicott, "Do Deconstructive Ecology and Sociobiology Undermine Leopold's Land Ethic?" *Environmental Ethics* 18 (1996): 353–72.

23. This fact does not show that there are no biotic communities, for properties essential to human community may not be necessary for biotic ones. Perhaps some communities need not be intentional ones. Or perhaps humans can see themselves as parts of biotic communities and provide the requisite intentionality. In any case, Callicott's insightful analogy between human and biotic communities is insufficient to make the case that biotic communities are robust enough to engender moral obligations to them.

24. Callicott, "Deconstructive Ecology," p. 372.

25. See Stuart Pimm, *The Balance of Nature?* (Chicago: University of Chicago Press, 1991) and Monica G. Turner et al., "A Revised Concept of Landscape Equilibrium: Disturbance and Stability on Scaled Landscapes," *Landscape Ecology* 8 (1993): 213–27. Frank Golley's informative *A History of the Ecosystem Concept in Ecology* (New Haven: Yale University Press, 1994) traces the development of ecosystem ecology and responds to some of the important challenges to it.

26. See Elizabeth Culotta, "Exploring Biodiversity's Benefits," *Science* 273 (1996): 1045–46.

27. Charles Goodnight, "Experimental Studies of Community Evolution I: The Response at the Community Level," *Evolution* 44 (1990): 1614–24.

28. David Ehrenfeld calls this emphasis a "fad." See "Ecosystem Health and Ecological Theories," in Robert Costanza, Bryan Norton, and Benjamin Haskell, eds., *Ecosystem Health* (Washington, D.C.: Island Press, 1992), p. 140. For another suggestion that the focus on instability is due to sociological factors, see P. Koetsier et al., "Rejecting Equilibrium Theory—A Cautionary Note," *Bulletin of the Ecology Society of America* 71 (1990): 229–30.

29. See Soulé, "The Social Siege of Nature," p. 160.

30. Although a number of philosophers have appealed to wildness and the related notion of naturalness, there is no uniform agreement on its meaning or justification. See Robert Elliot, "Extinction, Restoration, Naturalness," *Environmental Ethics* 16 (1994): 135–44, and "Faking Nature," *Inquiry* 25 (1982): 81–93; Eric Katz, "The Big Lie; The Human Restoration of Nature," *Research in Philosophy and Technology* 12 (1992): 231–41, and "The Call of the Wild," *Environmental Ethics* 14 (1992): 265–73; and Holmes Rolston, III, *Environmental Ethics* (Philadelphia: Temple University Press, 1988), pp. 32–44, and *Conserving Natural Value*, pp. 1–9, 12–16, 72–73, 102, 184–92, 197–202, 223–28. Some philosophers interpret *integrity* in a way that seems to include wildness. See Laura Westra, *An Environmental Proposal for Ethics: The Principle of Integrity* (Lanham, Md.: Rowman & Littlefield, 1994). Mark Woods, "Rethinking Wilderness" (Ph.D. diss., Ann Arbor, Michigan, 1997), chap. 6, draws useful distinctions between kinds of wildness.

31. For a powerful treatment or this topic, see Rolston, *Conserving Natural Value*, pp. 223–28.

32. Tom Birch discusses wildness as "otherness" in "The Incarceration of Wildness: Wilderness Areas as Prisons," *Environmental Ethics* 12 (1990): 3–26.

33. See Edward O. Wilson, *The Diversity of Life* (Cambridge: The Belknap Press of Harvard University Press, 1992), p. 272.

34. Richard Monastersky, "Earthmovers: Humans Take Their Place Alongside Wind, Water, and Ice," *Science News* 146 (1994): 432.

35. Donald Worster, "The Nature We Have Lost," in *The Wealth of Nature* (New York: Oxford University Press, 1993), p. 6.

36. According to Robert Elliot, "Extinction, Restoration, Naturalness," p. 138, "intensification of value occurs when the co-instantiation of value-adding properties yields more value than the sum of the values of the properties would if they were instantiated singly."

37. Eugene Hargrove, "The Paradox of Humanity: Two Views of Biodiversity and Landscapes," in Ke Chung Kim and Robert D. Weaver, eds., *Biodiversity and Landscapes* (Cambridge: Cambridge University Press, 1994), p. 183.

38. We thank Baird Callicott for forcefully drawing our attention to this criticism.

39. David Off, *Earth in Mind: On Education, Environment and the Human Prospect* (Washington, D.C.: Island Press, 1994), p. 131.

40. We presume that one's warranted value judgments may be some distance from one's initial judgments, as in ideal observer accounts of value. See Tom Carson, *The Status of Morality* (Boston: D. Reidel Publishing, 1984).

41. For the charge that wildness value is ethnocentric, see Ramachandra Guha, "Radical American Environmentalism and Wilderness Preservation: A Third World Critique," *Environmental Ethics* 11 (1989): 71–83.

42. See, for example, Anthony Weston, *Back to Earth* (Philadelphia: Temple University Press, 1994), pp. 130–32.

43. See William Cronon's "The Trouble with Wilderness," in William Cronon, ed., *Uncommon Ground: Toward Reinventing Nature* (New York: W. W. Norton & Company, 1995), p. 85.

44. Both Guha and Cronon worry that "wilderness environmentalism" results in native peoples being forced off their land to create wilderness areas. By distinguishing between wildness and wilderness, by recognizing wildness in humans, by valuing intermediate degrees of wildness, and by allowing that anthropocentric concerns—as well as ecocentric ones—play a large role in sustainability, we believe that we have significantly diminished the potential that wildness value could be used to justify such activities.

45. J. Baird Callicott, "The Wilderness Idea Revisited: The Sustainable Development Alternative," *Environmental Professional* 13 (1991): 241.

46. Ibid., p. 240.

47. For a discussion of how wildness in humans can be valuable, see Bill Throop, "Humans and the Value of the Wild," *Human Ecology Review* 3 (1996): 3–7.

48. Henry David Thoreau, "Walking," from *The Natural History Essays*. Reprinted in Susan Armstrong and Richard Botzler, eds., *Environmental Ethics: Divergence and Convergence* (New York: McGraw-Hill. 1993), p. 114.

49. In "The Paradox of Humanity," Eugene Hargrove points out the need for a more sophisticated view of the human/nature relationship than the simplistic views that either humans are, or are not, a part of nature.

50. Holmes Rolston, III, "The Wilderness Idea Reaffirmed," *The Environmental Professional* 13 (1991): 370–71.

51. Robin Attfield, "Rehabilitating Nature and Making Nature Habitable," in Robin Attfield and Andrew Belsey, eds., *Philosophy and the Natural Environment* (New York: Cambridge University Press, 1994), p. 45.

52. See Elliot's "Faking Nature" and Katz's "The Big Lie."

53. See, for example, Richard Sylvan's "Mucking with Nature," in Sylvan, *Against the Main Stream*. Discussion Papers in Environmental Philosophy, no. 21 (Canberra: Research School of Social Sciences, Australian National University, 1994).

✂ STUDY QUESTIONS

1. What do Throop and Hettinger mean by the ecology of stability? Contrast this with the ecology of instability. Explain why they want to de-emphasize stability as a foundation for ecocentrism (and explain what this means). Do you think this is important to do?

2. What do Throop and Hettinger mean by "wildness value"? Give some examples. What reasons do they give for thinking wildness is an important environmental value? What advantages do they see in emphasizing the value of wildness in natural systems rather than the value of biodiversity or integrity?

3. What are some objections to the idea that natural systems should be valued because of their wildness? How do Throop and Hettinger respond to these objections? Are their responses successful?

4. Do you think wildness is an important environmental value? Why, or why not?

5. Why is it difficult to justify restoring natural systems as a way to increase their wildness? According to Throop and Hettinger, how is this possible?

6. Here is a question for ecocentrists like Throop and Hettinger who value wildness.

   Suppose God creates an aesthetically superior ecosystem—a combination of the Grand Canyon, Yellowstone, and Yosemite—something even more spectacular and stable—but it would not be wild because God would be guiding it. Would it be any less wonderful for not being "wild"? After all, until recent times many people believed Nature was God's handiwork.

   Well, suppose in the year 2500 we have the technology to do what God did in the above story. Would it be any less valuable?

22 The Great New Wilderness Debate: An Overview

MICHAEL NELSON

Michael Nelson is a professor of philosophy at the University of Wisconsin at Sevens Point and a leading environmental thinker. He is (with Baird Callicott) the editor of *The Great New Wilderness Debate* (1998). He is preparing a second volume of this work. In this essay Nelson sets forth the charges that the received concept *wilderness* is an inadequate, confused notion. He then considers the responses to these charges by environmentalists like Gary Snyder, Dave Foreman, David Rothenberg, and others, concluding that whereas no solution to the debate is apparent, the debate is salutary in that it is helping to clarify the issues surrounding the conception.

The anthology, *The Great New Wilderness Debate* (TGNWD) that I edited in 1998 with Baird Callicott is an attempt to represent the essence of a debate that began in academia in the early 1990s: a debate over the concept of wilderness—a concept that is "alleged to be ethnocentric, androcentric, phallagocentric, unscientific, unphilosophic, impolitic, outmoded, even genocidal."[1] A list of such dreadful assertions, of course, depends on evidence that there is a concept of wilderness that has been historically molded, a concept which in turn serves as a model for our current and collective idea of wilderness—a concept that we refer to as the "received view of wilderness."

We assert, then, that the concept of wilderness is a social construct. Hence, we deny the realism of the concept—that "wilderness" has an existence beyond that which we socially create for it—and that it is this social construct that is flawed. The idea of a social construction of wilderness is often a difficult notion to embrace from within a culture where the idea is generally agreed upon, but it is far easier to glimpse when we see how it is that others from distinct cultural backgrounds construe wilderness (or completely fail to construe it in the first place). As Nepalese scholar Pramod Parajuli points out,

> I cannot bifurcate "nature" from "culture" or the "domesticated" from the "wild." It seems to me that mainstream notions of wild and wilderness are primarily a product of the industrial economy and Cartesian reality.[2]

We contend that this received view portrays wilderness as the highest manifestation of that which is considered natural, as that which sits in starkest contrast with that which is human or the product of human agency. This view crystallized over the first part of the 20th century, when the early wilderness battles in the United States were fought. It then appropriately found its way into the single most important piece of wilderness legislation in the world, the U.S. Wilderness Act of 1964, where wilderness is defined (both conceptually and legally): "... in contrast to those areas where man and his own works dominate the landscape, ... an area where the earth and its community of life are untrammeled by man, where man himself is a visitor who does not remain" (Public Law 88-577). In all fairness, this definition is not absolutely human exclusive: "Dominate" is not the same as "present," "untrammeled" is not the same as "untouched," and "does not remain" is not the same as "is not allowed" or "has never been." But wilderness certainly does not have to be human exclusive to be set up in opposition to humans. Let us consider the criticisms of this received view of wilderness in groupings.

FROM ETHNOCENTRIC TO GENOCIDAL TO IMPOLITIC

"Wilderness," unlike many of the words for the things within a wilderness area, is not readily translatable into a wide variety of languages. This linguistic lack forms, in part, the first critique of the received view—that it is ethnocentric (emanating from one culture and inappropriately applied to other cultures). I am told that there is no word for "wilderness" in Japanese, Chinese, or even many European languages. It is an English word that we find, obviously enough, in English-speaking places such as Britain, the United States, and Australia. Interestingly, however, it does not seem to be a word that we find in the languages of the aboriginal inhabitants of those lands. In fact, it has been ridiculed by American Indians such as Chief Luther Standing Bear, who writes,

> Only to the white man was nature a "wilderness" and only to him was the land "infested" with "wild" animals and "savage" people. To us it was tame.... Not until the hairy man from the east came and with brutal frenzy heaped injustices upon us...was it "wild" for us, [did] the "Wild West" begin."[3]

Likewise, Australian aborigines claim that they have no word or concept for wilderness, and I have no reason to doubt them.[4] Hence, to the extent that we universalize a concept to all cultures that seems to be particular to one or a few, we are being ethnocentric.

But the ethnocentrism of "wilderness" is far more insidious than that. It has been suggested that reference to the lands of Australia and North America as wilderness has allowed for, enforced, and justified the historic eradication of American and Australian first peoples on the basis that these were essentially *terra nullis*, empty lands, devoid of humans, open for immediate occupancy. Of course they were not empty. But the die was already cast, the landscape already socially constructed as "wilderness." The testament to the power of the idea of wilderness came when these European settlers were faced with the choice of rethinking "wilderness," or at least the (mis)application of the idea in these contexts or forcing the idea to fit by categorizing the human occupants of the land as nonhuman wildlife. The sport hunting of Australian aborigines and the common North American frontier slogan, "the only good Indian is a dead Indian," indicate the choice often made. The idea of wilderness, among other things to be sure, served as a tool for genocide in these cases. And perhaps it still does.

A number of examples of the importation of the North American concept of wilderness correlate with the removal of tribal peoples from their homeland: from the African Ik of the Kidepo Valley in Uganda, to the Juwesi San of the Kalahari Bushmen in Namibia, to the various wilderness sanctuaries in India. After all, the *U.S. Wilderness Act of 1964* asserts that wilderness is land "without permanent improvements *or human habitation*" (Public Law 88-577, emphasis added).

ANDROCENTRISM AND PHALLAGOCENTRISM

It has been alleged that the perpetuation of the received view of wilderness is a perpetuation of male-centeredness, the idea that wilderness is macho. The early American framers of this received view clearly thought so. Theodore Roosevelt considered wilderness adventures as a means to shape and sharpen our American character—to keep us rugged and manly: Wilderness promoted a lacking "vigorous manliness." Bob Marshall saw wilderness adventure as providing Williams James's "moral equivalent to war." And Northwoods nature writer Sigurd Olson imagined wilderness travel as "the virile, masculine type of experience men need today." Some have asserted that the received view of wilderness, and any importation of it, still carries with it this objectionable type of androcentrism. As Marvin Henberg phrases the objection,

> Theodore Roosevelt, for instance, thought of the wilds as a proving ground for virility, male camaraderie, and the honing of a warrior caste. Such a view is less than palatable in these decades of deep ecology and ecofeminism. Why virility and aggressiveness over placidity and nurture?[5]

UNSCIENTIFIC, UNPHILOSOPHIC, OUTMODED

It has been suggested that the wilderness idea presents a problem for restoration ecologists. The received view evolved in an era when pre-European-contact American Indian and Australian aboriginie populations and impacts were thought to be minimal to nonexistent. Although the population numbers and the amount and extent of their impact are hotly debated, we do know that past inhabitants of North America, for instance, were active managers of their landscapes and that the so-called wilderness experienced by the new Euro-Americans was often the result of a combination of pathogenic-induced population decimation and a European preconception of, and lack of familiarity with, the North American landscape. But the goal of wilderness management, set by the incredibly influential Leopold Report of 1963, is often taken to be the preservation, or restoration, of landscapes to "the condition that prevailed when the area was first visited by the white man." Hence, the "wilderness" state of North America was in many ways *artificial*— the product of profound, direct and indirect human intervention, and, therefore, by definition, not wilderness at all. We are here, then, brought up short by the paradoxical requirement that to fulfill our restoration mandate we must first of all ignore pre-European impact and, secondly, that we must actively manage (trammel) the landscapes that are supposed to remain untrammeled in order to restore them.

The received view of wilderness is also alleged to be informed by the now outmoded climax community model of nature, the idea that without any significant impact by humans, nature remains in a steady state. Rear-looking attempts to recreate a certain state (pre-European in the United States, for example) perpetuate this now outmoded ecological paradigm, a paradigm currently replaced by a disturbance model. Of course it is easy to understand why this is so: The ideal of wilderness preservation developed at the same time as the ecological modeling of nature went from the Clementsian superorganismic model of nature to an Eltonian economic model of nature to a Tanslian ecosystemic model of nature. All these models, however different, perpetuate the idea of nature as moving toward an integration and maturation if left alone by humans. The way to properly tend nature, given an interest in doing so, was to leave nature alone. However, the current disturbance model of ecology—a model that prompts in many ways the critique of wilderness—asserts that various scales of disturbance and discord are the normal background "harmony" in nature. This ecological model sheds a fundamentally different light on our received view of wilderness and hence on our ideas about wilderness preservation. It is sometimes suggested that our contemporary received view of wilderness is therefore ecologically outmoded.

Finally, it is alleged that characterizing wilderness in opposition to humans and their works also perpetuates the false dualism between humans and nature. And, if values are attached to those ends of the spectrum (wilderness = good, human by default = bad), then we also invoke a false value dualism, the result of which is the condemnation of human interactions, even ecological restoration, because it is perpetuated by humans. Again, our philosophical assumptions lead us to troubling scientific and management assumptions. Wilderness proponent Dave Foreman admits this human separateness when he says, "Many kinds of wilderness foes especially bristle at this barring of human habitation. I believe this lack of long-lasting settlement is key to wil-der-ness [self-willed land]."[6]

Indeed they do bristle. In fact, this "unpeopling" of the landscape may be that which most upsets those outside of the United States. Brazilian professor Antonio Carlos Diegues recently wrote that

> A North American model…which dichotomizes "people" and "parks" has spread rapidly throughout the world. Because this approach has been adopted rather uncritically by the countries of the Third World, its effects have been devastating for the traditional populations.[7]

Another Third-World scholar comments that

> For a majority of people who eke out their livelihoods from nature's economy, the widely held ideas that nature can be preserved in wilderness and that wilderness is what is untouched by humans are simply untenable.[8]

This dualism also presents problems for environmental ethics. I continue to be disturbed by what has now become an explicit attempt by some environmental thinkers to separate humans from nature, to say that we are not just different in degree from the nonhuman world but different in kind. Although I can only speculate on the origins of such affirmation, and although I am unsure of the scientific soundness of a human/nature dualism, my main concern as an ethicist is with the moral implications of such a split.[9]

I adhere to the Land Ethic of Aldo Leopold as not only the most reasonable starting point for the development of an environmental ethic but also as a helpful field guide to understanding the very essence of human ethical obligations and the nature of ethical entailment in the abstract. According to this line of thought, a shared sense of social community is an absolute necessity for a prompting of our moral sentiments and the resulting ethical obligation that those sentiments provoke. The lack of this social inclusion results in the inability to extend directly our moral sentiments, and hence ethical inclusion, to those outside of this realm. For example, the intentional dehumanization of those against whom we would go to war makes it much easier to pull a trigger or drop a bomb because they become viewed as separate or "others," no longer members of either our human social or human ethical community. On the other hand, it is the recognition of similarity and social membership that has driven such ethically inclusive

movements as civil rights, women's suffrage, and animal liberation. Given an historical assessment of our ethical development, I am fearful of any attempt at making a human/nature dichotomy, of making nature "other." I do not believe that we are ethically well served by it. In fact, I think that such divisiveness threatens the environmental ethical progress we have made. In short, if Aldo Leopold is correct, if an appropriate moral relationship between humans and the nonhuman world depends on our seeing ourselves as *part* of an inclusive biotic community, then anything that severs that community, that serves to conceptually separate humans from nature, stands forever in the way of a satisfactory environmental ethic.

However, in the Western concept of wilderness, and to the degree that this concept has been imported elsewhere, it seems to me that there is a strong attempt to envision wilderness as the epitome of that which is natural, employing natural to mean that which is not a product of human agency or that which is apart from humans.

Many of the reactions to the big Boundary Waters Canoe Area Wilderness blowdown in Northern Minnesota in 1999 serve as a nice example. The blowdown itself was viewed by many as a natural process and not threatening to the wilderness quality of the area because it was not the product of human agency, whereas the move to clear portages and camp sites by utilizing chain saws met with heated resistance in some quarters.[10]

Admittedly I have only glossed over the critiques offered against the received view of wilderness. Each of these deserves far more attention than I have given it here. Next I will gloss over a taxonomy of responses to the critique presented by traditional wilderness defenders. Essentially there are four types of responses to the critique for the received view of wilderness (RVW).

DENY THE EXISTENCE OF THE RVW—AT LEAST THE "RECEIVED" PART

First, there are those who have denied the "received" part of the expression—the claim that wilderness is a social construct—and have asserted instead a philosophy of realism with regard to wilderness. "Naturalness exists out there," "wilderness areas are for real," says Dave Foreman." Nature as seen from the Kitkit-dizze is no 'social construction' " asserts nature poet Gary Snyder. Some wilderness defenders deny the significance of the name "wilderness," claiming that because what the word refers to has an existence apart from humans—including human linguistics—and that the name is merely a benign placeholder for the thing to which it refers: a rose smelling as sweet by any other name as it were. The names of common plants and animals (fern, fox, or fawn) might indeed be innocuous and unproblematic English references for things that actually exist in the world. But "wilderness" is not one of these words. It is no mere benign descriptor. The feminist movement has made us keenly aware that names can frame, color, allow for, or sanction certain types of uses and abuses. Words like "babe," "chick," and even "lady" are rightly rejected by feminists as inappropriate labels for women because of the unacceptable social constructs that accompany them ("babes" and "chicks" are sexual objects; "ladies" are inherently delicate models of virtue). "Wilderness" clearly comes with baggage as well. For Colonial Puritans it carried a negative value; it was the house of the devil, whereas its opposite, humans and human intervention, was good. Wilderness was therefore to be transformed and civilized; such work was viewed as Godly. At the turn of the twentieth century neo-Calvinists flipped the value of nature; nature was now the handiwork of God and therefore good. Humans, at the opposite end of the spectrum, were assigned the opposite value— bad, or unworthy.[11] The human/nature dualism and changing value associations are part of the meaning of wilderness. In the early and mid-1900s the movement to preserve areas of wilderness was motivated primarily by the preservation of recreational opportunities; wilderness had a purely anthropocentric and instrumental value. More recently, of course, wilderness areas have come to be seen as set-asides for threatened species, standards of land health, and scientific study areas; the value of wilderness has become more nonanthropocentric, with gestures toward intrinsic value made by some. We have clearly socially

construed and reconstrued "wilderness" over the years. So, if "wilderness" is socially constructed, we need to think carefully about what connotations and history we inevitably evoke when we use the term. We need to ask whether those associations can be disentangled from the term.

There is also a bizarre metaphysical confusion lurking here. Gary Snyder assumes that to assert that a concept is a social construction is at the same time to deny the existence of that to which the concept is applied. Along these same lines, I have personally observed far more than one person attempt to dismiss the idea of wilderness as a social contruction by saying something to the effect that, "I bet if we dropped you social constructivists in the middle of the Bob Marshall wilderness area with no supplies you wouldn't think it was unreal." Snyder's remedy for social constructivism is somewhat similar: "I'd say take these dubious professors out for a walk, show them a bit of the passing ecosystem show, and maybe get them to help clean up a creek."[12] I will not comment on the inappropriately brash and completely mistaken assumption that those who engage in such conceptual analysis do not care for or act to protect various places in nature, however socially construed. The shared assumption here, of course, is that no one with direct experiences of the places we call wilderness could deny the existence of it, or fail to value it for its own sake. The reply is obvious. Merely because one asserts that "wilderness" is a social construct does not mean that one denies the existence of the places that the term is applied to. The feminist assertion that "babe," "chick," and "lady" are merely socially constructed does not deny the existence of those whom we so label.

ADMIT AN RVW—"IT'S JUST THAT WE HAVE IT WRONG"

As noted above, Dave Foreman often defends a wilderness realism and denies the existence of the received/social constructivist possibility of wilderness. At least sometimes he does. In a recent essay he seems to admit the historical (or social) construction of wilderness but argues that we have gone beyond this outdated view and that we have redefined or reconstructed wilderness. "This Real Wilderness Idea," Foreman asserts, "is very different from The Received Wilderness Idea invented and then lambasted by Baird Callicott, Bill Cronon and other Deconstructionists."[13] Currently wilderness is valued because of its importance for such things as the preservation of biological diversity, scientific study, and measures of land health, as well as for recreational values, according to Foreman. In other words, we have matured, and our maturation has come with an enriched valuation of wilderness, a new received view. Fair enough. Foreman may be right. He certainly is to some degree. But his very own rendition of the history of his wilderness idea is still a social construction. He just asserts we can and have transcended more narrowly conceived instrumental values, whereas Callicott and Cronon seem to argue that we have not, and perhaps cannot, go beyond them.

ADMIT THE RVW—DENY THE CRITIQUES

Some have admitted, at least provisionally, the existence of the received view of wilderness but have attempted to get around the critiques, usually by simply rejecting them outright.

For example, although I am not aware of any direct attempt to do this, one could just reject the claim that the received view is so much male-centered *machismo*. One could either attempt to do so by simply denying the evidence—the impact of the words and ideas of Theodore Roosevelt, Bob Marshall, and Sigurd Olson on the received view—or by denying the persistence of this attitude, arguing that it is no longer present in our views of wilderness—that it has been replaced.

Some have dealt directly with the charge of ethnocentrism. Although again I am not aware of anyone directly denying or somehow explaining away the terrible outcomes of importing North American-style wilderness to Africa and India, Dave Foreman has alleged that folks such as Ramachandra Guha, who offer a Third-World critique of the received view, "are suffering from Third World jingoism." Foreman asserts that "wilderness is a victim of chronic anti-Americanism"

and is, in his own words, "racist."[14] Foreman, David Orr, Holmes Rolston, Gary Snyder, Tom Vale, and others have also attempted to minimize—or at least have asserted that the wilderness critique has inappropriately maximized—the impact that pre-European North Americans had on the North American landscape in an attempt to avoid the charge of ethnocentrism. In a recent review to *TGNWD*, environmental philosopher David Rothenberg even went so far as to claim "that the notion of wilderness has supporters all over the world" and therefore that "wilderness has a place in the environmental philosophies of all cultures," even though, as he admits, "many cultures do not have a word for wilderness, [but] when they think about what it means, they know what to do with it."[15]

Many have asserted, without much argument unfortunately, that wilderness does *not* perpetuate the human/nature dualism. However, they have gone on to discuss wilderness in exactly those terms: as "self-willed" land, meaning "apart from humans"; "the arena of evolution," implying a strange notion that evolution is somehow corrupted or nonexistent outside of wilderness areas in the human-dominated areas; embracing the idea that humans and human actions are the corrupting influences on wilderness by continually casting the discussions in these very terms. "At some point, land quits being mostly dominated by humans; at some other point, land begins to be controlled primarily by the forces of Nature. There is a wide gray area in between, where human and natural forces both have some sway. After natural forces become dominant, the land is self-willed."[16]

I will admit that the one place where I see some of the best and most heartening responses to the critique of wilderness is in the area of scientific assumptions. Wilderness defenders—from Reed Noss to Michael Soulé to Dave Foreman at times—very nicely dynamize the scientific assumptions of wilderness. They have really attempted to take into account the most modern ecological paradigms of change in their reconceptualization of wilderness. They have, for the most part, even rid themselves of the metaphors of climax community models and the rhetoric of pristine and untouched wilderness.

GUILT BY ASSOCIATION, NAME CALLING, RAW ASSERTIONS, DAMNING ANALOGIES

The last attempt to respond to the critique deserves little attention here. Essentially it amounts to name calling. Wilderness critics are called "wilderness foes," "anticonservationists," "antinature intellectuals," "faddish philosophers who will soon be forgotten," "high-paid intellectual types . . . trying to knock Nature, knock the people who value Nature, and still come out smelling smart and progressive." Also, disturbing analogies have been drawn: "the high end of the wise-use movement," playing into the bureaucrats' hands," just another part of the overall "war against nature." For example, the philosopher Socrates once asserted that he could learn nothing from nature; Callicott and Nelson are philosophers; therefore, they must believe that as well. Although these responses are interesting (even somewhat entertaining) in that they demonstrate the power of ideas and conceptual analysis (the power of philosophy), they are not arguments; they are merely emotive and vituperative diatribes.

PROPOSED SOLUTIONS AND CONCLUSION

Thus far we seem to have two possible solutions.

The first is to jettison the word "wilderness" and all the baggage it carries. Many formerly called "zoos" are now often referred to by such titles as "animal sanctuaries" because it was thought that the word "zoo" was inevitably associated with connotations that zookeepers wanted to do without—venues for animal gawking, for human entertainment, the value of which was wholly anthropocentric—whereas the term "animal sanctuary" contained a very different connotation and value structure. An animal sanctuary is first and foremost for the animals, where animal gawking may be allowed, but only if it is compatible with the primary value. Likewise, Baird Callicott has proposed that the term "wilderness" is inevitably and of necessity coupled with unattractive and inappropriate baggage and should therefore be replaced by the term "biodiversity

reserve."[17] This solution seems to suggest that the term and concept "wilderness" is too far gone—that it cannot be rethought.

Others have asserted that the concept of wilderness can be rethought, can be salvaged, and that we can therefore still utilize the term. In fact, they argue that we are already moving beyond the received view, already reconceptualizing it.[18]

Of course, given the dynamism of the human imagination, and given the fact that we have historically construed and reconstrued wilderness, it seems perfectly reasonable to think that such a rethinking is possible. Perhaps the salvation for wilderness lies somehow, then, in the human mind.

THE IMPORTANCE OF CONCEPTUAL ANALYSIS

So, "What's next?" I am often asked. To be honest, I am not sure. I am not sure that jumping ahead to "What's next?" is not tantamount to "draining the bath water before the baby is bathed" (to mutilate a metaphor). That is to say, one might argue that the debate needs to brew a bit longer before the "What's next?" question can be properly addressed. That being said, I would like to offer some very rough and very preliminary comments on what might happen next. Please note that my intellectual timidity here is dictated not by an unwillingness to say something substantive but rather by an honest assessment of an incomplete discussion.

First of all, I am struck and surprised by the amount, persistence, and level of response that has been generated by the critique of the concept of wilderness. In short, it has been hot and heavy. Certainly, conceptual analysis is provocative![19] This debate proves it. However, the benefit of conceptual analysis has not yet been made lucid enough.

I think we need to more clearly articulate the nature of the criticism of the concept of wilderness; to explain the character and attributes of conceptual analysis; to show why conceptual analysis is important, even crucial, and how it is the wilderness proponents' ally; and hopefully to begin to bridge some of the gaps that seem to have appeared between those wilderness advocates engaging in the conceptual analysis of wilderness and those wilderness advocates who see such an analysis as not only a threat but also a heresy.

For example, I am concerned about many of the responses to this debate that I have thus far encountered. David Orr's attempt to lump responsible criticisms of the concept of wilderness by those such as Cronon and Callicott with the nearly delusional rantings against wilderness by Marilynne Robinson is irresponsible.[20] Dave Foreman's and Gary Snyder's matching of environmentalists who engage in the analysis of concepts such as wilderness with the perversely named Wise-Use movement as all part of the same antinature, antiwilderness conspiracy, or as merely different fronts on "the war against nature," is simply wrongheaded.

Although I am not withdrawing the criticisms of the received view of wilderness that have been leveled elsewhere, I do think that the critics have sometimes failed to make it clear why conceptual analysis is warranted, why it is not a threat, and how it might serve the wilderness advocate.

In short, I think the fruits of this debate over the concept of wilderness will help us clarify our thinking and make us better prepared to defend the concept against the true enemies of wilderness areas—those who wish to do away with places referred to as "wilderness." Yes, the critique is claiming that the emperor has no clothes (or at least that the emperor's clothes don't fit), but its proponents are exposing the emperor for the sake of reclothing him or, in other words, for the emperor's own good. The real enemy of wilderness is not only exposing the emperor but also attempting to depose him as well.

Some have argued that there is nothing wrong with the concept of wilderness or the arguments for wilderness preservation, but these are people who already consider themselves advocates of wilderness. If there is one thing students of philosophy learn early on it is that the strength of an argument is not to be measured by how persuasive it is to those who already tend to agree with the argument's conclusion, but rather on what sort of force it has against dissenters, those who disagree with the conclusions. *And the dissenters are not persuaded.* Wouldn't it be wonderful to have an argument that swayed some of these dissenters (or at least some of the fence-sitters)? The hope in this debate seems to me to lie in recognition of the power and benefit of, and a commitment to, conceptual analysis. We desperately need to recognize the conceptual shortcomings of our current received view of wilderness and to forge better definitions and conceptualizations of wilderness. Only in this manner can we present a more unified and carefully thought out front against those who would attempt to undo that which so many of our environmentally minded ancestors accomplished.

NOTES

1. Callicott and Nelson, eds., *The Great New Wilderness Debate (TGNWD)* (Athens, GA: University of Georgia Press, 1998), p. 2.
2. From "How Can Four Trees Make a Jungle?" in David Rothenberg and Marta Ulvaeus, eds., *The World and the Wild: Expanding Wilderness Conservation Beyond Its American Roots* (Tucson: University of Arizona Press, 2001), p. 5.
3. From "Indian Wisdom" in *TGNWD*, p. 201.
4. See Fabienne Bayet's essay "Overturning the Doctrine: Indigenous People and Wilderness—Being Aboriginal in the Environmental Movement," in *TGNWD*.
5. From "Wilderness, Myth, and American Character," in *TGNWD*, p. 504.
6. "The Real Wilderness Idea," in David N. Col, et al., eds., *Wilderness Science in a Time of Change, Vol. 1,* USDA, USFS, Rocky Mountain Research Station, Proceedings RMRS-P-15-Vol-1, September, 2000, p. 34.
7. "Recycled Rain Forest Myths," in *The World and the Wild*, p. 157.
8. Ibid., p. 13.
9. Consider, for example, the attempt to replace "integrity and stability" as a worthy aim of ecosystem management with "wildness" as found in "Refocusing Ecocentrism: De-emphasizing Stability and Defending Wildness" by Ned Hettinger and Bill Throop, *Environmental Ethics* Spring 1999 (21:1), pp. 3–21. The authors define "wildness" by stating that "something is wild in a certain respect to the extent that it is *not humanized* in that respect" (p. 12, emphasis in the original).

10. Evidence of a popular expression of a predisturbance ecological model came by way of a very common expression that the BWCA was now ruined.

11. The most dramatic representation of this is the difference between Calvinist minister Daniel Muir and his nuturalist son John Muir. Both separated humans from nature but assigned opposing values to the ends of the spectrum. For Daniel, turning the wilderness into the agricultural land was to do God's handiwork, whereas for John leaving certain instances of nature untouched was to protect God's handiwork.

12. "Nature as Seen from the Kitkitdizze Is No 'Social Construction'," *Wild Earth*, Winter 1996/97, p. 9.

13. "The Real Wilderness Idea," p. 33.

14. In *TGNWD*, p. 399.

15. In *Environmental Ethics,* Summer 2000 (22:2), p. 202. Indeed, many of the Third-World voices in Rothenberg's own anthology, *The World and the Wild,* are very clear about what the first world can do with its idea of wilderness.

16. Foreman, "The Real Wilderness Idea," p. 34.

17. "Should Wilderness Areas Become Biodiversity Reserves?," *TGNWD*, pp. 585–94.

18. See, for instance, Mark Woods, *Rethinking Wilderness,* forthcoming from Broadview Press.

19. In fact, one of the critics of the received view of wilderness has even received a death threat over this debate.

20. "The Not-So-Great Wilderness Debate . . . Continued," *Wild Earth*, Summer 1999, pp. 74–80.

STUDY QUESTIONS

1. Why do you think that Nelson thinks the concept "wilderness" is a social construction? How does he respond to charges that labeling the concept is tantamount to a denial of that which we name "wilderness"? How significant is Nelson's critique here? Isn't every word and concept a social construction in that, as language, it arises out of social existence?

2. Examine the definition of "wilderness" embodied in the *U.S. Wilderness Act of 1964* (mentioned at the beginning of this essay as embodying the "received view of wilderness"—RVW): "in contrast to those areas where man and his own works dominate the landscape, . . . an area where the earth and its community of life are untrammeled by man, where man himself is a visitor who does not remain." Evaluate this definition. Is it a good one? Why don't Nelson and other critics accept it as sufficient for a working definition?

3. Discuss the criticisms of the received view of wilderness (RVW) and Nelson's responses to them. With whom do you agree more—the critics or the proponents of RVW?

23 Two Kinds of Preservationist Ethics*

ROGER PADEN

Roger Paden is a professor of philosophy at George Mason University and the author of several essays in environmental ethics and on philosophy and urban planning. In this essay he distinguishes two main types of environmental theories—the anthropocentric and the biocentric—and shows how they are both based on a type of interest utilitarianism. Paden argues that a better distinction is that between two different preservationist policies: *product* and *process* policies. He goes on to contrast these policies and to show how Aldo Leopold's formula is ambiguous regarding this distinction. Finally, Paden criticizes interest-based environmental theories, arguing that because nature does not have goals, it cannot have interests. He recommends that we replace interest-based theories with aesthetic ones.

Published by permission of Roger Paden. Copyright © 2003 Roger Paden.
*I would like to thank Gary Varner for his careful and helpful criticisms of an earlier version of this essay.

Debates within the field of environmental ethics have been decisively shaped by two related distinctions. The first is a distinction between two supposedly radically dissimilar and opposing ethical positions, the traditional Western "anthropocentric" ethic and a new environmentalist "biocentric ethic." Although these ethics are generally considered to be polar opposites, in fact, I believe, both often make use of the same moral theory, namely, preference or "interest" utilitarianism.[1] According to the interpretation of this theory, most common among anthropocentrists, the only thing that has "intrinsic" value is the satisfaction of human interests. Other things may have instrumental value to the degree that they are useful in helping to satisfy those interests, but the only "final goods," to use Aristotle's phrase, are those satisfactions. A biocentric theory, on the other hand, typically holds that the satisfaction of the interests of nonhumans, such as animals and, perhaps, plants, is also intrinsically valuable, is also a final good. On this view, actions that result in the satisfaction of those interests are also morally commendable, *ceteris paribus,* independently of their effect on human interest satisfaction.

This distinction gives rise to another distinction between two kinds of positions concerned with the protection of the environment. One position, "conservationism," seeks to protect the environment in order to guarantee the long-term availability for humans of scarce natural resources. As the goal of this policy is to maximize total (present and future) human interest-satisfaction, conservationism is taken to be based on traditional anthropocentric concerns. The other position, "preservationism," is usually thought to be based on the newer biocentric ethic because it holds that nature must be protected and preserved in a pristine state "for its own sake" in order to guard its interests, independently of any potential instrumental value that protection may have in satisfying human interests.[2]

Given these distinctions, two general approaches to environmental protection follow. Environmental ethicists have typically taken the articulation and defense of one or the other of these positions to be the central task of their field. However, I believe that these neat distinctions will not withstand careful investigation. Moreover, I think that they obscure the moral foundations of our duties to natural entities and may prevent us from fully grasping and acting on those duties. In part, these distinctions are misleading because they obscure another distinction, one between two types of preservationist policies. I believe that an understanding of that distinction is essential to the development and defense of any truly adequate preservationist position.

I

Unless we have a clear idea of what we mean by the term "nature," any claim that we have a direct duty to nature to protect it will be open to multiple and perhaps conflicting interpretations. In our society, as I will outline below, "nature" generally has been understood in two ways. These two interpretations of nature, I believe, can be associated with two radically different approaches to environmental preservation. Unfortunately, these two interpretations and the approaches to environmental preservation that they support entail opposing kinds of policies. Let us look at two important examples.

In 1973, Congress passed the first Endangered Species Act. Arguably, this act, together with its successors, has done more to preserve wilderness areas than any other law. Oddly enough, however, the original purpose of the act was not to protect wilderness areas, but to protect endangered species, by protecting individual members of those species from hunters, developers, and polluting industries. However, as the law was written, it not only forbid the direct killing of those animals but also required the preservation of their "critical habitats." As the Supreme Court interpreted this law, this must be done "without exception" and at "whatever cost." Unfortunately, as the act was written and later amended, it contained several loopholes, such as the possibility of administrative review of controversial applications. In these reviews, economic considerations would be allowed to play a significant role, possibly resulting in reduced protection. Nevertheless, endangered species legislation still provides significant protection to the environment, and is a paradigm example of this type of preservationist policy.[3]

In 1964 the U.S. Park Service adopted a controversial fire management policy that best exemplifies another kind of preservationist program. This policy, recognizing that naturally occurring forest fires play an important role in maintaining a viable ecosystem, forbids Park Service employees from fighting naturally occurring forest fires unless the fires threaten famous landmarks or tourist areas. Instead, these fires were to be left to burn themselves out.[4] This policy clearly represents a different kind of preservation policy, one that seeks not to preserve specific species or other parts of nature, but instead to isolate nature from human interference or, in the words of the policy itself, to "neutralize the unnatural influences of man, thus permitting the natural environment to be maintained essentially by nature."[5]

These two examples represent two vastly different approaches to environmental preservation. The Endangered Species Act is a paradigm example of what I will call a "product preservation policy." It tries to preserve specific parts or products of nature, in this case specific endangered species. It assumes that our direct duty to nature is a duty to protect those products. On the other hand, the Park Service's fire management policy is a paradigm example of what I will call a "process preservation policy." It does not seek to protect specific parts of nature, but instead requires us to preserve natural systems—the dynamic processes of nature. Obviously, these two general kinds of policies differ in several ways.

First, these policies entail contradictory programs. Product preservation policies, such as those aimed at the preservation of species, as recent attempts to preserve the California condor have demonstrated, will often require humans to interfere with ongoing natural processes. For example, to prevent an extinction, people might have to manipulate an endangered species' habitat by controlling predators and diseases or by ensuring an adequate food supply. As a result, the adoption of such a policy would probably require a high level of intervention in natural systems. Moreover, it is important to understand

that such a policy would require these interventions even if the extinctions could be traced to natural causes.[6] In these cases, policies that aim at the preservation of species would require people to halt or control the natural developmental processes that are the cause of the extinctions. Because these policies are based on the assumption that all species have intrinsic value and, therefore, deserve to be preserved, they cannot, in principle, distinguish between extinctions based on their causes. On the other hand, the Park Service's fire management policy, if taken to its logical conclusion, would forbid such interference, even if interference were necessary to preserve valuable parts of nature, for on this view, it is essential to preserve intrinsically valuable natural processes. As a result, it is probable that, if the environmental movement continues to influence federal legislation, these two kinds of policies will come increasingly into conflict. While process preservation policies would require us, with some exceptions, to let naturally occurring, but destructive, processes continue without interference, even if this threatens intrinsically valuable natural products, product preservation policies would require us to protect those products, even if doing so necessitated the creation of largely "artificial" environments.

Second, these two kinds of policies are based on two different ideas of nature. Product preservation policies assume that nature consists of a collection of discrete parts or products, each with its own interests that, *ceteris paribus,* should be satisfied. Process preservation policies, on the other hand, assume that nature is a dynamic system. Unfortunately, these two conceptions are often confused in environmentalist declarations. For example, when Aldo Leopold declares that we must protect the "integrity, stability, and beauty" of the "biotic community,"[7] it is unclear what he intends us to do. Leopold's principle, that is to say, cannot support a consistent preservation policy because it inconsistently requires us to protect both the "stability" and the "integrity" of ecosystems. To see that this principle is inconsistent, it is necessary to understand its fundamental terms. "Stability," I believe, simply implies a lack of change.[8] A thing is stable if its internal structure remains the same and if its constituent parts do not change. For example, a society is stable if it maintains an unchanging institutional structure and as long as the nature of its members does not undergo any radical changes as one generation replaces another. "Integrity," however, has an entirely different meaning. People have integrity, I believe, if they are not easily influenced by outside events; for example, if they do not allow considerations of temporary political gain to alter their fundamental principles. Indeed, integrity can even lead people to change, as when a more complex understanding of moral principles leads a person to abandon a previously held policy position. Thus, a person has integrity to the degree that he or she is self-determining. Similarly, a natural system could be said to possess integrity to the degree that it is self-determining, that is, to the degree to which it is free from significant human interference. Because Leopold's principle is cast in terms of these two very different terms, it entails inconsistent duties. If we have a duty to protect the stability of a biotic community, we would, on occasion, have to intervene in the biotic community. However, if we have a duty to respect that community's integrity, we would have to refrain from interfering with that community.

The fundamental reason that Leopold's principle is ambiguous, however, is not because he failed to appreciate the distinction between stability and integrity, but rather because he held an ambiguous conception of the "biotic community." In using that phrase, no doubt, Leopold wanted to draw our attention to the similarities between the biotic and human "communities." Perhaps the best way to explain the source of Leopold's problem is to point out that human communities can be understood on two different models. While "libertarians" understand human communities to consist of essentially independent, intrinsically valuable persons, "communitarians" understand them in terms of developing traditions. Unfortunately Leopold, in effect, adopted both these views, despite the fact that they are incompatible. When stressing stability, Leopold adopted the libertarian model which emphasizes the intrinsic value of the parts, but when stressing integrity, he adopted the

communitarian model, which emphasizes the importance of the whole. Thus, implicit in Leopold's principle are two contradictory conceptions of nature. One conception is essentially individualistic, in which nature is thought of as a set of relatively independent parts. The other is essentially holistic, in which nature is thought of as a dynamic whole. Unfortunately, from these differing conceptions, different programs follow.

II

Product and process preservation approaches to environmental preservation can be distinguished on practical and conceptual grounds, but they *must* also be distinguished on moral grounds. These two approaches can only be defended through appeals to fundamentally different kinds of moral arguments. Unfortunately, this has not been generally recognized.

The reason for this is that environmental ethics has been dominated by a particular moral paradigm which understands value solely in terms of the satisfaction of interests. Work in environmental ethics typically falls within the utilitarian tradition of moral philosophy, broadly construed.[9] In particular, most justifications of preservationist policies have been constructed within this paradigm. There is nothing necessarily wrong with this, if what is to be justified is a product preservation policy—at least in those cases in which the product in question can conceivably have some kind of interest. If natural products do have interests, then it might be possible to justify a product preservation policy within this paradigm.

However, justifications of process preservation policies could only be constructed within this paradigm, if it is plausible to attribute interests to natural processes or natural wholes—for example, to ecosystems. Of course, many environmentalists have claimed—citing as evidence the striking stability and resilience of ecosystems, especially their ability to maintain a dynamic equilibrium—that ecosystems are goal-directed.[10] Moreover, because there is a conceptual connection between being goal-directed and having interests, such that to be directed at a goal is to have an interest, many environmentalists have argued that if nature is goal-directed, it must have morally significant interests.[11] I would argue, however, that nature is not goal-directed and, therefore, that it can have no interests. If this is true, then it would be impossible to justify process preservation policies by appealing to the interests of nature.

If a thing is to be said to have a goal, it must not only pursue that goal through a variety of flexible, but persistent, behaviors but also engage in those behaviors *because* they will lead to that goal. That is, a system is goal-directed only if its actions tend to bring about a goal *and* its actions occur *because* they tend to bring about that goal.[12] It is clear that animals and plants qualify as goal-directed according to this definition. As a result, it may be possible to attribute morally significant interests to them. Given this definition, it might even be possible to attribute morally significant interests to some robots and sophisticated guided missiles. However, even given this definition, it is not possible to attribute morally significant interests to ecosystems. The fact that ecosystems can maintain complex dynamic equilibriums does not, as many environmental ethicists believe, show that they are goal-directed. This is the case because stability is not the "goal" of ecosystems; it is instead a "by-product" of the goal-directed behavior of their constituent organisms.[13]

To illustrate this point, a direct analogy could be drawn between ecosystems and economies. Although the people participating in an economy are goal-directed and, therefore, have interests, this does not imply that the economy is goal-directed. This is the case despite the fact that the economy, through a variety of mechanisms, maintains a dynamic equilibrium. The economy does not aim at equilibrium, nor does it have an interest in maintaining equilibrium. Therefore, although various political actions may affect the economy, and possibly hurt the interests of the people participating in it, no such action can negatively affect the interests of the economy itself, as it has none. Similarly, with ecosystems. Because ecosystems are not goal-directed, they have no interests. If this is the case, however, it is a mistake to attribute interests to them.

If ecosystems have no interests, then we can have no obligation to protect their interests. However, if this is true, the moral justification of product preservation policies, which can be based on appeals to the interests of those products, must be very different from the moral justification of process preservation policies, which cannot be based on an appeal to the interests of those processes. While product preservation policies can be based on principles requiring the equal protection of interests, process preservation policies must be based on wholly different considerations.

III

The realization that there are two distinct kinds of preservationist positions indicates that the simple division of "ethics" into traditional anthropocentric and modern biocentric ethics may be mistaken. Indeed, recognition of the unique character of process preservation policies puts that distinction in a new light: Anthropocentrism and biocentrism, as they are usually conceived, actually differ very little. Both are typically constructed within a moral paradigm that understands morality to be a matter of the satisfaction of interests. They disagree only on the range of entities that can be said to have interests. Thus, whereas conservationism seeks to maximize only human interests, product preservationism seeks to include nonhuman interests into the moral calculus. However, if process preservation policies can be morally justified on biocentric grounds and if my argument that ecosystems do not have interests is correct, then that paradigm is, at the very least, incomplete. Given my arguments, therefore, it might seem to be a good idea for environmental ethicists to abandon the project of developing teleological accounts of nature in order to explore the possibility of developing a new moral paradigm that could better justify process preservation policies.[14] Such work, however, would face two immediate problems.

The first problem is conceptual. Process preservation policies entail that a distinction can be drawn between natural processes and artificial processes ("human interference"). In practice this distinction is relatively easy to make. In theory, however, it is open to the objection that human beings are merely another part of nature. If so, then this distinction is clearly a spurious one; the residue, it might be thought, of an older "dualistic" anthropocentric metaphysics that in other contexts preservationists have rejected. Still, it might be possible to maintain this distinction without reverting to a dualistic metaphysics. Indeed, one way to maintain this distinction has already been suggested in this paper: We are beings with interests and goals, while nature is not.[15]

The second problem is more "practical." If process preservation policies cannot be justified within the paradigm that has dominated environmental ethics, then it would seem that a new moral paradigm, a new ethic, must be developed. This would, however, in all probability be an impossible task, for, as John Passmore has put it, "an ethic . . . is not the sort of thing one can simply decide to have; 'needing an ethic' is not the least like 'needing a new coat.' A 'new ethic' will arise out of existing attitudes or not at all."[16] Luckily, as several environmental ethicists, most notably perhaps, Sagoff[17] and Hargrove,[18] have pointed out, there is no need to develop a "new" ethic, for a close examination of Western—and particularly American—attitudes toward nature will reveal an existing, but often overlooked, ethic sufficient to ground preservationist policies.

This older ethic is based on a variety of "attitudes" or judgments about nature, such as that nature is beautiful, or intensely interesting, or connected with or essential to our humanity. Unfortunately, modern philosophers, who, like Passmore, have adopted the interest-satisfaction model of morality, have tended either to ignore these attitudes, believing them to be irrelevant to moral theory, or they have understood them in terms of that model. For example, they have understood the moral significance of the statement that something is beautiful to be that it is "aesthetically satisfying." They have tended, that is to say, to cash out the moral value of a beautiful object in terms of its ability to satisfy an aesthetic interest. It then follows that our duty to preserve beautiful objects is, in fact, a duty to ourselves to maximize the satisfaction of our aesthetic interests. Given this view, together with the fact that our desires for aesthetic experiences are typically relatively weak, it follows that it will be difficult to justify any process preservation policy on these grounds. It is for this reason, in fact, that I believe, that some environmentalists

have been driven to attribute strong countervailing interests to nature. However, a better approach, one more in line with our moral intuitions, would be to resist the reduction of beauty to interest-satisfaction and to argue that we have a direct duty to protect beautiful things simply because they are beautiful. This duty is not only independent of any duty we might have to ensure future interest-satisfaction; it is also, at least arguably, more important.[19]

Modern philosophers typically feel uncomfortable with these kinds of claims. We are not used to dealing with such "thick" moral concepts, and we lack a developed theory within which they can be deployed. Therefore, we are worried about the proper response to their inevitable conflict. Finally, that those philosophers who adopt this view often also seem to adopt forms of intuitionism and relativism worries us even more.[20] But, given the problems with the attempt to attribute interests to nature, if a process preservation policy is to be defended on biocentric grounds, it may, in the end, be better to defend it through an appeal to such thick moral concepts as beauty.

Beyond the discomfort engendered by the use of these thick concepts, two objections have been raised to this kind of defense of preservation policies. First, it has been argued that, as it is human beings who judge things to be beautiful, beauty must itself be anthropocentric, and anthropocentrism fails to do justice to the intrinsic value of nature. This, however, is misleading. Although judging something to be beautiful, like believing something to be important, is a subjective—perhaps uniquely human, as Kant pointed out, such judgments, like all beliefs, have objective content. We claim that nature is beautiful, understanding ourselves to be making an objective claim. The beauty is *for* us, but it is *in* nature. Our duty to preserve nature is a duty to it, based on the fact that it is beautiful. It is not a duty to our subjective experience, although that experience may inform us of our duty.

Second, it might be objected that, because our ability to recognize, appreciate, and respond to beauty is so fragile, beauty is not a strong foundation for preservationist policies. It is, of course, true that we will be motivated to protect nature's beauty only if we recognize that beauty, and that our ability to recognize beauty depends on our subjective, perhaps socially determined, constitution. Moreover, it might be added that we are becoming, seemingly, a society of people who do not respond (as a society) to beauty nor value it. As noted above, our aesthetic interests—and, therefore, our aesthetic motivations—are notoriously weak. Because of these factors, it might be argued, it is imperative that we develop preservationist arguments based on some other ground, such as the assumption that nature has interests.

This argument, however, rests on a confusion between the justification of a moral claim and our motivation to act morally, and it will lead us to give bad reasons for good policies. Even worse, such an argument will be counterproductive, partly because, as I have argued, it will be impossible to sustain the claim that nature has morally significant interests. More importantly, such an argument will be counterproductive because it will tend to undercut all arguments for the preservation of nature, such as Leopold's appeal to natural beauty, that are grounded in its aesthetic value. This is so for the following reason. A good case can be made, I believe, for the claim that our increasing social inability to respond to beauty is, at least in part, a consequence of our rigid adherence to the interest-satisfaction paradigm of morality. If this is the case, then our dependence on that paradigm may be self-fulfilling, in that it may ultimately diminish our ability to respond to arguments based on thick moral concepts and, thereby, undercut all preservationist policies.

The adoption of an aesthetically grounded approach to preservationism would allow us to dispense with the simple distinction between anthropocentric and biocentric ethics, as it relieves us of the burden of discovering and evaluating interests "centered" in ourselves or nature. As a result, we would not have to pretend that nature is intrinsically valuable solely because it has interests, nor would we have to pretend that beauty is valuable solely because it satisfies our interests in having aesthetic experiences. Giving up this view would be liberating. It would allow us to abandon the attempt to reconstruct a teleological conception of nature. It would allow us to adopt a more plausible explanation of the value of beauty. Most importantly, it would help us overcome the idea that the relationship between humans and nature is necessarily antagonistic that lies implicit in the distinction between anthropocentrism and biocentrism. Abandoning this distinction would not only lead to a healthy reexamination of our relations to nature but also might allow us to fully understand the foundation of our duties to nature.

NOTES

1. In what follows, I will focus my remarks on those biocentric philosophers who use this moral theory. Some biocentrists do not use this theory, but instead appeal to "the rights of nature," e.g., see Roderick Nash, *The Rights of Nature: A History of Environmental Ethics* (Madison: University of Wisconsin Press, 1989). I believe that my criticisms would also apply to them, but I will not develop that line here.

2. For a more detailed discussion of the history of conservationism and preservationism in U.S. history, see my "Wilderness Management" forthcoming in *Environmental Rights in Conflict,* Joseph Pappin, ed., Temple University Press.

3. For an excellent history of this legislation, see, Nash, *The Rights of Nature,* pp. 174–78.

4. USDA, *Final Report on Fire Management Policy, May 5, 1989* (Washington, DC: U.S. Government Printing Office, 1989), p.2.

5. A. S. Leopold, et al., "Resource Management Policy," in National Park Service, *Compilation of Administrative Policies for the National Parks and National Monuments of Scientific Significance (Natural Area Category)*, rev. ed. (Washington, DC: U.S. Government Printing Office, 1970), p. 106, quoted in Eugene Hargrove, *Foundations of Environmental Ethics* (Englewood Cliffs, NJ: Prentice-Hall, 1989), pp. 139–40.

6. Indeed, section 1533 of the Endangered Species Act explicitly protects all endangered species, no matter the cause of their endangerment.

7. Aldo Leopold, *A Sand County Almanac: With Essays on Conservation from Round River* (New York: Ballantine Books, 1968), p. 262.

8. For example, see Bryan Norton, "Agricultural Development and Environmental Policy: The Conceptual Issues," *Agriculture and Human Values* 2 (1985), 62–63, for a discussion of the meaning of "stability" as it applies to environmental issues.

9. Of course, many environmentalists, unlike some utilitarians, believe that animals and plants have interests.

10. For example, see J. E. Lovelock, *Gaia: A New Look at Life on Earth* (Oxford: Oxford University Press, 1979), or Holmes Rolston, *Environmental Ethics: Duties to and Values in the Natural World* (Philadelphia: Temple University Press, 1988).

11. Harley Cahen, "Against the Moral Considerability of Ecosystems," *Environmental Ethics* 10 (1988): 195–216.

12. Larry Wright, "Explanation and Teleology," *Philosophy of Science* 19 (1972): 211–23.

13. Cahen, "Against the Moral Considerability of Nature."

14. Another possibility, of course, would be to develop purely anthropocentric arguments for process preservation policies. An example of this kind of argument can be found in Bryan Norton, *Why Preserve Natural Variety?* (Princeton, NJ: Princeton University Press, 1987). Of course, one problem with these kinds of arguments is that they are not "biocentric," that is, they do not support our intuition that nature is valuable in itself. This may not be a serious problem, however.

15. Of course, to draw a distinction between humans and nature in this way undercuts any claim that nature is morally significant *because* it has interests. In any case, however, more work would have to be done on this issue to show the moral significance of this distinction.

16. John Passmore, *Man's Responsibility for Nature: Ecological Problems and Western Traditions*, 2nd ed. (London: Duckworth, 1980), p. 56.

17. Mark Sagoff, *The Economy of the Earth* (Cambridge: Cambridge University Press, 1988), pp. 124–145.

18. Hargrove, *Foundations*, pp. 77–136.

19. See Sagoff, *The Economy of the Earth*, pp. 101–106, for such an argument.

20. For examples of this tendency toward intuitionism, see Hargrove, *Foundations*, pp. 1–13, and Sagoff, *Economy of the Earth*, pp. 146–170.

STUDY QUESTIONS

1. Examine Paden's distinction between two kinds of environmental ethics. What do they have in common? What is Paden's suggestion for a better distinction?

2. What are Paden's two kinds of preservationist policies? How are they based on different ideas of nature?

3. Explain Paden's criticism of Leopold's Land Ethic formula. Is he correct? Why, or why not?

4. Why are interest-based environmental theories inadequate? What does Paden suggest we put in their place?

DEEP ECOLOGY

24   The Shallow and the Deep, Long-Range Ecological Movement

ARNE NAESS

Arne Naess (b. 1912) was for many years the head of the philosophy department of the University of Oslo, Norway, and the founder of the modern theory of deep ecology.

"Deep ecology" (or "ecosophy" = ecological wisdom) is a movement calling for a deeper questioning and a deeper set of answers to our environmental concerns. Specifically,

Reprinted from *Inquiry* 16 (Spring 1973) by permission.

it calls into question some of the major assumptions about consumerism and materialism, challenging us to live more simply. Its motto is "Simple in Means, Rich in Ends." It seeks self-realization through oneness with all things. The following is Naess's now classic summary of his lecture at the 3rd World Future Research Conference, Bucharest, September 3, 1972. Naess included the following abstract:

Ecologically responsible policies are concerned only in part with pollution and resource depletion. There are deeper concerns which touch upon principles of diversity, complexity, autonomy, decentralization, symbiosis, egalitarianism, and classlessness.

The emergence of ecologists from their former relative obscurity marks a turning-point in our scientific communities. But their message is twisted and misused. A shallow, but presently rather powerful movement, and a deep, but less influential movement, compete for our attention. I shall make an effort to characterize the two.

1. The Shallow Ecology movement: Fight against pollution and resource depletion. Central objective: the health and affluence of people in the developed countries.

2. The Deep Ecology movement: (1) Rejection of the man-in-environment image in favour of the *relational, total-field image.* Organisms as knots in the biospherical net or field of intrinsic relations. An intrinsic relation between two things *A* and *B* is such that the relation belongs to the definitions or basic constitutions of *A* and *B*, so that without the relation, *A* and *B* are no longer the same things. The total-field model dissolves not only the man-in-environment concept, but every compact thing-in-milieu concept—except when talking at a superficial or preliminary level of communication.

(2) *Biospherical egalitarianism*—in principle. The "in principle" clause is inserted because any realistic praxis necessitates some killing, exploitation, and suppression. The ecological field-worker acquires a deep-seated respect, or even veneration, for ways and forms of life. He reaches an understanding from within, a kind of understanding that others reserve for fellow men and for a narrow section of ways and forms of life. To the ecological field-worker, *the equal right to live and blossom* is an intuitively clear and obvious value axiom. Its restriction to humans is an anthropocentrism with detrimental effects upon the life quality of humans themselves. This quality depends in part upon the deep pleasure and satisfaction we receive from close partnership with other forms of life. The attempt to ignore our dependence and to establish a master–slave role has contributed to the alienation of man from himself.

Ecological egalitarianism implies the reinterpretation of the future-research variable, "level of crowding," so that *general* mammalian crowding and loss of life-equality is taken seriously, not only human crowding. (Research on the high requirements of free space of certain mammals has, incidentally, suggested that theorists of human urbanism have largely underestimated human life-space requirements. Behavioural crowding symptoms [neuroses, aggressiveness, loss of traditions ...] are largely the same among mammals.)

(3) *Principles of diversity and symbiosis.* Diversity enhances the potentialities of survival, the chances of new modes of life, the richness of forms. And the so-called struggle of life, and survival of the fittest, should be interpreted in the sense of ability to coexist and cooperate in complex relationships, rather than ability to kill, exploit, and suppress. "Live and let live" is a more powerful ecological principle than "Either you or me."

The latter tends to reduce the multiplicity of kinds of forms of life, and also to create destruction within the communities of the same species. Ecologically inspired attitudes therefore favour diversity of human ways of life, of cultures, of occupations, of economies. They support the fight against economic and cultural, as much as military, invasion and domination, and they are opposed to the annihilation of seals and whales as much as to that of human tribes or cultures.

(4) *Anti-class posture.* Diversity of human ways of life is in part due to (intended or unintended) exploitation and suppression on the part of certain groups. The exploiter lives differently from the exploited, but both are adversely affected in their potentialities of self-realization. The principle of diversity does not cover differences due merely to certain attitudes or behaviours forcibly blocked or restrained. The principles of ecological egalitarianism and of symbiosis support the same anti-class posture. The ecological attitude favours the extension of all three principles to any group conflicts, including those of today between developing and developed nations. The three principles also favour extreme caution towards any over-all plans for the future, except those consistent with wide and widening classless diversity.

(5) Fight against *pollution and resource depletion.* In this fight ecologists have found powerful supporters, but sometimes to the detriment of their total stand. This happens when attention is focused on pollution and resource depletion rather than on the other points, or when projects are implemented which reduce pollution but increase evils of the other kinds. Thus, if prices of life necessities increase because of the installation of anti-pollution devices, class differences increase too. An ethics of responsibility implies that ecologists do not serve the shallow, but the deep ecological movement. That is, not only point (5), but all seven points must be considered together.

Ecologists are irreplaceable informants in any society, whatever their political contour. If well organized, they have the power to reject jobs in which they submit themselves to institutions or to planners with limited ecological perspectives. As it is now, ecologists sometimes serve masters who deliberately ignore the wider perspectives.

(6) *Complexity, not complication.* The theory of ecosystems contains an important distinction between what is complicated without any Gestalt or unifying principles—we may think of finding our way through a chaotic city—and what is complex. A multiplicity of more or less lawful, interacting factors may operate together to form a unity, a system. We make a shoe or use a map or integrate a variety of activities into a workaday pattern. Organisms, ways of life, and interactions in the biosphere in general, exhibit complexity of such an astoundingly high level as to colour the general outlook of ecologists. Such complexity makes thinking in terms of vast systems inevitable. It also makes for a keen, steady perception of the profound *human ignorance* of biospherical relationships and therefore of the effect of disturbances.

Applied to humans, the complexity-not-complication principle favours division of labour, *not fragmentation of labour.* It favours integrated actions in which the whole person is active, not mere reactions. It favours complex economies, an integrated variety of means of living. (Combinations of industrial and agricultural activity, of intellectual and manual work, of specialized and non-specialized occupations, of urban and non-urban activity, of work in city and recreation in nature with recreation in city and work in nature . . .)

It favours soft technique and "soft future-research," less prognosis, more clarification of possibilities. More sensitivity towards continuity and live traditions, and—most importantly—towards our state of ignorance.

The implementation of ecologically responsible policies requires in this century an exponential growth of technical skill and invention—but in new directions, directions which today are not consistently and liberally supported by the research policy organs of our nation-states.

(7) *Local autonomy and decentralization.* The vulnerability of a form of life is roughly proportional to the weight of influences from afar, from outside the local region in which that form has obtained an ecological equilibrium. This lends support to our efforts to strengthen local self-government and material and mental self-sufficiency. But these efforts presuppose an impetus towards decentralization. Pollution problems, including those of thermal pollution and recirculation of materials, also lead us in this direction, because increased local autonomy, if we are able to keep other factors constant, reduces energy consumption. (Compare an approximately self-sufficient locality with one

requiring the importation of foodstuff, materials for house construction, fuel and skilled labour from other continents. The former may use only five per cent of the energy used by the latter.) Local autonomy is strengthened by a reduction in the number of links in the hierarchical chains of decision. (For example, a chain consisting of local board, municipal council, highest sub-national decision-maker, a state-wide institution in a state federation, a federal national government institution, a coalition of nations, and of institutions, e.g. E.E.C.* top levels, and a global institution, can be reduced to one made up of local board, nation-wide institution, and global institution.) Even if a decision follows majority rules at each step, many local interests may be dropped along the line, if it is too long.

Summing up, then, it should, first of all, be borne in mind that the norms and tendencies of the Deep Ecology movement are not derived from ecology by logic or induction. Ecological knowledge and the life-style of the ecological field-worker have *suggested, inspired, and fortified* the perspectives of the Deep Ecology movement. Many of the formulations in the above seven-point survey are rather vague generalizations, only tenable if made more precise in certain directions. But all over the world the inspiration from ecology has shown remarkable convergencies. The survey does not pretend to be more than one of the possible condensed codifications of these convergencies.

Secondly, it should be fully appreciated that the significant tenets of the Deep Ecology movement are clearly and forcefully *normative*. They express a value priority system only in part based on results (or lack of results, cf. point [6]) of scientific research. Today, ecologists try to influence policy-making bodies largely through threats, through predictions concerning pollutants and resource depletion, knowing that policy-makers accept at least certain minimum *norms* concerning health and just distribution. But it is clear that there is a vast number of people in all countries, and even a considerable number of people in power, who accept as valid the wider norms and values characteristic of the Deep Ecology movement. There are political potentials in this movement which should not be overlooked and which have little to do with pollution and resource depletion. In plotting possible futures, the norms should be freely used and elaborated.

Thirdly, in so far as ecology movements deserve our attention, they are *ecophilosophical* rather than ecological. Ecology is *limited* science which makes *use* of scientific methods. Philosophy is the most general forum of debate on fundamentals, descriptive as well as prescriptive, and political philosophy is one of its subsections. By an *ecosophy* I mean a philosophy of ecological harmony or equilibrium. A philosophy as a kind of *sofia* wisdom, is openly normative, it contains *both* norms, rules, postulates, value priority announcements *and* hypotheses concerning the state of affairs in our universe. Wisdom is policy wisdom, prescription, not only scientific description and prediction.

The details of an ecosophy will show many variations due to significant differences concerning not only "facts" of pollution, resources, population, etc., but also value priorities. Today, however, the seven points listed provide one unified framework for ecosophical systems.

In general system theory, systems are mostly conceived in terms of causally or functionally interacting or interrelated items. An ecosophy, however, is more like a system of the kind constructed by Aristotle or Spinoza. It is expressed verbally as a set of sentences with a variety of functions, descriptive and prescriptive. The basic relation is that between subsets of premises and subsets of conclusions, that is, the relation of derivability.

The relevant notions of derivability may be classed according to rigour, with logical and mathematical deductions topping the list, but also according to how much is implicitly taken for granted. An exposition of an ecosophy must necessarily be only moderately precise considering the vast scope of relevant ecological and normative (social, political, ethical) material. At the

---

*E.E.C. stands for European Economic Community.

moment, ecosophy might profitably use models of systems, rough approximations of global systematizations. It is the global character, not preciseness in detail, which distinguishes an ecosophy. It articulates and integrates the efforts of an ideal ecological team, a team comprising not only scientists from an extreme variety of disciplines, but also students of politics and active policy-makers.

Under the name of *ecologism,* various deviations from the deep movement have been championed—primarily with a one-sided stress on pollution and resource depletion, but also with a neglect of the great differences between under- and over-developed countries in favour of a vague global approach. The global approach is essential, but regional differences must largely determine policies in the coming years.

✦ STUDY QUESTIONS

1. Is *deep ecology* a good name for Naess's theory? Does it incorporate positive value unwarrantedly? If not, what should it be called?
2. Are the seven principles of the deep ecology movement good ones? Examine each one, compare them with the corresponding principles of shallow ecology, and comment on their validity.
3. Compare Naess's deep ecology with biocentrism and ecocentrism.

25   Ecosophy T: Deep Versus Shallow Ecology

ARNE NAESS

In this 1985 essay, Naess develops the philosophical implications of deep ecology, which he calls "Ecosophy." He calls his version of ecosophy "Ecosophy T." Naess develops his theory of wider self-realization through identifying one's Self with individuals, species, ecosystems, and landscapes.

THE SHALLOW AND THE DEEP ECOLOGICAL MOVEMENT

In the 1960s two convergent trends made headway: a deep ecological concern, and a concern for saving deep cultural diversity. These may be put under the general heading "deep ecology" if we view human ecology as a genuine part of general ecology. For each species of living beings there is a corresponding ecology. In what follows I adopt this terminology which I introduced in 1973 (Naess 1973).

The term *deep* is supposed to suggest explication of fundamental presuppositions of valuation as well as of facts and hypotheses. Deep ecology,

therefore, transcends the limit of any particular science of today, including systems theory and scientific ecology. *Deepness of normative and descriptive premises questioned* characterize the movement. . . .

Deep ecological argumentation questions both the left-hand and the right-hand slogans. But tentative conclusions are in terms of the latter.

The shallow ecological argument carries today much heavier weight in political life than the deep. It is therefore often necessary for tactical reasons to hide our deeper attitudes and argue strictly homocentrically. This colors the indispensible publication, *World Conservation Strategy.*[1]

Reprinted by permission from Arne Naess, "Identification as a Source of Deep Ecological Attitudes" in Michael Tobias, ed. *Deep Ecology* (Santa Monica, CA: IMT Productions, 1985). Notes renumbered.

As an academic philosopher raised within analytic traditions it has been natural for me to pose the questions: How can departments of philosophy, our establishment of professionals, be made interested in the matter? What are the philosophical problems explicitly and implicitly raised or answered in the deep ecological movement? Can they be formulated so to be of academic interest?

My answer is that the movement is rich in philosophical implications. There has however, been only moderately eager response in philosophical institutions.

The deep ecological movement is furthered by people and groups with much in common. Roughly speaking, what they have in common concerns ways of experiencing nature and diversity of cultures. Furthermore, many share priorities of life style, such as those of "voluntary simplicity." They wish to live "lightly" in nature. There are of course differences, but until now the conflicts of philosophically relevant opinion and of recommended policies have, to a surprisingly small degree, disturbed the growth of the movement.

In what follows I introduce some sections of a philosophy inspired by the deep ecological movement. Some people in the movement feel at home with that philosophy or at least approximately such a philosophy, others feel that they, at one or more points, clearly have different value priorities, attitudes or opinions. To avoid unfruitful polemics, I call my philosophy "Ecosophy T," using the character *T* just to emphasize that other people in the movement would, if motivated to formulate their world view and general value priorities, arrive at different ecosophies: Ecosophy "A," "B," ..., "T," ..., "Z."

By an "ecosophy" I here mean a philosophy inspired by the deep ecological movement. The ending *-sophy* stresses that what we modestly try to realize is wisdom rather than science or information. A philosophy, as articulated wisdom, has to be a synthesis of theory and practice. It must not shun concrete policy recommendations but has to base them on fundamental priorities of value and basic views concerning the development of our societies.[2]

Which societies? The movement started in the richest industrial societies, and the words used by its academic supporters inevitably reflect the cultural provinciality of those societies. The way I am going to say things perhaps reflects a bias in favor of analytic philosophy intimately related to social science, including academic psychology. It shows itself in my acceptance in Ecosophy T of the theory of thinking in terms of "gestalts." But this provinciality and narrowness of training does not imply criticism of contributions in terms of trends or traditions of wisdom with which I am not at home, and it does not imply an underestimation of the immense value of what artists in many countries have contributed to the movement.

SELECTED ECOSOPHICAL TOPICS

The themes of Ecosophy T which will be introduced are the following:

> The narrow self (ego) and the comprehensive Self (written with capital *S*)
>
> Self-realization as the realization of the comprehensive Self, not the cultivation of the ego
>
> The process of identification as the basic tool of widening the self and as a natural consequence of increased maturity
>
> Strong identification with the whole of nature in its diversity and interdependence of parts as a source of active participation in the deep ecological movement
>
> Identification as a source of belief in intrinsic values. The question of "objective" validity.[3]

SELF-REALIZATION, YES, BUT WHICH SELF?

When asked about *where* their self, their "I," or their ego is, some people place it in the neighborhood of the *larynx*. When thinking, we can sometimes perceive movement in that area. Others find it near their eyes. Many tend to feel that their ego, somehow, is inside their body, or identical with the whole of it, or with its functioning. Some call their ego spiritual, or immaterial and not within space. This has interesting consequences. A Bedouin in Yemen would not have an ego nearer the equator than a whale-hunting eskimo. "Nearer" implies space.

William James (1890: Chapter 10) offers an excellent introduction to the problems concerning the constitution and the limits of the self.

> The Empirical Self of each of us is all that he is tempted to call by the name of *me*. But it is clear that between what a man calls *me* and what he simply calls *mine* the line is difficult to draw. We feel and act about certain things that are ours very much as we feel and act about ourselves. Our fame, our children, the work of our hands, may be as dear to us as our bodies are, and arouse the same feelings and the same acts of reprisal if attacked. And our bodies, themselves, are they simply ours, or are they *us*?
>
> The body is the innermost part of *the material Self* in each of us; and certain parts of the body seem more intimately ours than the rest. The clothes come next.... Next, our immediate family is a part of ourselves. Our father and mother, our wife and babes, are bone of our bone and flesh of our flesh. When they die, a part of our very selves is gone. If they do anything wrong, it is our shame. If they are insulted, our anger flashes forth as readily as if we stood in their place. Our *home* comes next. Its scenes are part of our life; its aspects awaken the tenderest feelings of affection.

One of his conclusions is of importance to the concepts of self-realization: "We see then that we are dealing with a fluctuating material. The same object being sometimes treated as a part of me, at other times is simply mine, and then again as if I had nothing to do with it all."

If the term *self-realization* is applied, it should be kept in mind that "I," "me," "ego," and "self" have shifting denotations. Nothing is evident and indisputable. Even *that* we are is debatable if we make the question dependent upon answering *what* we are.

One of the central terms in Indian philosophy is *ātman*. Until this century it was mostly translated with "spirit," but it is now generally recognized that "self" is more appropriate. It is a term with similar connotations and ambiguities as those of "self"—analyzed by William James and other Western philosophers and psychologists. Gandhi represented a *maha-ātman,* a *mahatma,* a great (and certainly very wide) self.

As a term for a kind of metaphysical maximum self we find *ātman* in *The Bhagavadgita*.

Verse 29 of Chapter 6 is characteristic of the truly great *ātman*. The Sanskrit of this verse is not overwhelmingly difficult and deserves quotation ahead of translations.

> sarvabhūtastham ātmānam
> sarvabhutāni cā'tmani
> Itsate yogayuktātmā
> sarvatra samadarśanah

Radhakrishnan: "He whose self is harmonized by yoga seeth the Self abiding in all beings and all beings in Self; everywhere he sees the same."

Eliot Deutsch: "He whose self is disciplined by yoga sees the Self abiding in all beings and all beings in the Self; he sees the same in all beings."

Juan Mascaró: "He sees himself in the heart of all beings and he sees all beings in his heart. This is the vision of the Yogi of harmony, a vision which is ever one."

Gandhi: "The man equipped with *yoga* looks on all with an impartial eye, seeing *Atman* in all beings and all beings in *Atman*."

Self-realization in its absolute maximum is, as I see it, the mature experience of oneness in diversity as depicted in the above verse. The minimum is the self-realization by more or less consistent egotism—by the narrowest experience of what constitutes one's self and a maximum of alienation. As empirical beings we dwell somewhere in between, but increased maturity involves increase of the wideness of the self.

The self-realization maximum should not necessarily be conceived as a mystical or meditational state. "By meditation some perceive the Self in the self by the self; others by the path of knowledge and still others by the path of works (*karma-yoga*)" [*Gita*: Chapter 13, verse 24]. Gandhi was a *karma-yogi*, realizing himself through social and political action.

The terms *mystical union* and *mysticism* are avoided here for three reasons: First, strong mystical traditions stress the dissolution of individual selves into a nondiversified supreme whole. Both from cultural and ecological points of view diversity and individuality are essential. Second, there is a strong terminological trend within scientific communities to associate mysticism with vagueness and confusion.[4] Third, mystics tend to agree that mystical consciousness is rarely sustained under normal, everyday conditions. But strong, wide identification *can* color experience under such conditions.

Gandhi was only marginally concerned with "nature." In his *ashram* poisonous snakes were permitted to live inside and outside human dwellings. Anti-poison medicines were frowned upon. Gandhi insisted that trust awakens trust, and that snakes have the same right to live and blossom as the humans (Naess, 1974).

THE PROCESS OF IDENTIFICATION

How do we develop a wider self? What kind of process makes it possible? One way of answering these questions: There is a process of ever-widening identification and ever-narrowing alienation which widens the self. The self is as comprehensive as the totality of our identifications. Or, more succinctly: Our Self is that with which we identify. The question then reads: How do we widen identifications?

Identification is a spontaneous, non-rational, but not irrational, process through which *the interest or interests of another being are reacted to as our own interest or interests.* The emotional tone of gratification or frustration is a consequence carried over from the other to oneself: joy elicits joy, sorrow sorrow. Intense identification obliterates the experience of a distinction between *ego* and *alter,* between me and the sufferer. But only momentarily or intermittently: If my fellow being tries to vomit, I do not, or at least not persistently, try to vomit. I recognize that we are different individuals.

The term *identification, in the sense used here,* is rather technical, but there are today scarcely any alternatives. "Solidarity"' and a corresponding adjective in German, "solidarisch," and the corresponding words in Scandinavian languages are very common and useful. But genuine and spontaneous solidarity with others already presupposes a process of identification. Without identification, no solidarity. Thus, the latter term cannot quite replace the former.

The same holds true of empathy and sympathy. It is a necessary, but not sufficient, condition of empathy and sympathy that one "sees" or experiences something similar or identical with oneself.[5]

A high level of identification does not eliminate conflicts of interest: Our vital interests, if we are not plants, imply killing at least some other living beings. A culture of hunters, where identification with hunted animals reaches a remarkably high level, does not prohibit killing for food. But a great variety of ceremonies and rituals have the function to express the gravity of the alienating incident and restore the identification.

Identification with individuals, species, ecosystems and landscapes results in difficult problems of priority. What should be the relation of ecosystem ethics to other parts of general ethics?

There are no definite limits to the broadness and intensity of identification. Mammals and birds sometimes show remarkable, often rather touching, intraspecies and cross-species identification. Konrad Lorenz tells of how one of his bird friends tried to seduce him, trying to push him into its little home. This presupposes a deep identification between bird and man (but also an alarming mistake of size). In certain forms of mysticism, there is an experience of identification with every life form, using this term in a wide sense. Within the deep ecological movement, poetical and philosophical expressions of such experiences are not uncommon. In the shallow ecological movement, intense and wide identification is described and explained psychologically. In the deep movement this philosophy is at least taken seriously: reality consists of wholes which we cut down rather than of isolated items which we put together. In other words: there is not, strictly speaking, a primordial causal process of identification, but one of largely unconscious alienation which is overcome in experiences of identity. To some "environmental" philosophers such thoughts seem to be irrational, even "rubbish."[6] This is, as far as I can judge, due to a too narrow conception of irrationality.

The opposite of *identification* is *alienation,* if we use these ambiguous terms in one of their basic meanings.[7]

The alienated son does perhaps what is required of a son toward his parents, but as performance of moral duties and as a burden, not spontaneously, out of joy. If one loves and respects oneself, identification will be positive, and, in what follows, the term covers this case. Self-hatred or dislike of certain of one's traits induces hatred and dislike of the beings with which one identifies.

Identification is not limited to beings which can reciprocate: Any animal, plant, mountain, ocean may induce such processes. In poetry this is articulated most impressively, but ordinary language testifies to its power as a universal human trait.

Through identification, higher level unity is experienced: from identifying with "one's nearest," higher unities are created through circles of friends, local communities, tribes, compatriots, races, humanity, life, and, ultimately, as articulated by religious and philosophic leaders, unity with the supreme whole, the "world" in a broader and deeper sense than the usual. I prefer a terminology such that the largest units are not said to comprise life *and* "the not living." One may broaden the sense of "living" so that any natural whole, however large, is a living whole.

This way of thinking and feeling at its maximum corresponds to that of the enlightened, or yogi, who sees "the same," the ātman, and who is not alienated from anything.

The process of identification is sometimes expressed in terms of loss of self and gain of Self through "self-less" action. Each new sort of identification corresponds to a widening of the self, and strengthens the urge to further widening, furthering Self-seeking. This urge is in the system of Spinoza called *conatus in suo esse perseverare,* striving to persevere in oneself or one's being (*in se, in suo esse*). It is not a mere urge to survive, but to increase the level of *acting out* (ex) *one's own nature or essence,* and is not different from the urge toward higher levels of "freedom" (*libertas*). Under favorable circumstances, this involves wide identification.

In Western social science, self-realization is the term most often used for the competitive development of a person's talents and the pursuit of an individual's specific interests (Maslow and

others). A conflict is foreseen between giving self-realization high priority and cultivation of social bonds, friends, family, nation, nature. Such unfortunate notions have narrow concepts of self as a point of departure. They go together with the egoism-altruism distinction. Altruism is, according to this, a moral quality developed through suppression of selfishness, through sacrifice of one's "own" interests in favor of those of others. Thus, alienation is taken to be the normal state. Identification precludes sacrifice, but not devotion. The moral of self-sacrifice presupposes immaturity. Its relative importance is clear, in so far as we all are more or less immature.

WIDENESS AND DEPTH OF IDENTIFICATION AS A CONSEQUENCE OF INCREASED MATURITY

Against the belief in fundamental ego-alter conflict, the psychology and philosophy of the (comprehensive) Self insist that the gradual maturing of a person *inevitably* widens and deepens the self through the process of identification. There is no need for altruism toward those with whom we identify. The pursuit of self-realization conceived as actualization and development of the Self takes care of what altruism is supposed to accomplish. Thus, the distinction egoism-altruism is transcended.

The notion of maturing has to do with getting out what is latent in the nature of a being. Some learning is presupposed, but thinking of present conditions of competition in industrial, economic growth societies, specialized learning may inhibit the process of maturing. A competitive cult of talents does not favor Self-realization. As a consequence of the imperfect conditions for maturing as persons, there is much pessimism or disbelief in relation to the widening of the Self, and more stress on developing altruism and moral pressure.

The conditions under which the self is widened are experienced as positive and are basically joyful. The constant exposure to life in the poorest countries through television and other media contributes to the spread of the voluntary simplicity movement (Elgin, 1981). But people laugh: What does it help the hungry that you renounce the luxuries of your own country? But identification makes the efforts of simplicity joyful and there is not a feeling of moral compulsion. The widening of the self implies widening perspectives, deepening experiences, and reaching higher levels of activeness (in Spinoza's sense, not as just being busy). Joy and activeness make the appeal to Self-realization stronger than appeal to altruism. The state of alienation is not joyful, and is often connected with feelings of being threatened and narrowed. The "rights" of other living beings are felt to threaten our "own" interests.

The close connection between trends of alienation and putting duty and altruism as a highest value is exemplified in the philosophy of Kant. Acting morally, we should not abstain from maltreating animals because of their sufferings, but because of its bad effect on us. Animals were to Kant, essentially, so different from human beings, that he felt we should not have any moral obligations toward them. Their unnecessary sufferings are morally indifferent and norms of altruism do not apply in our relations to them. When we decide ethically to be kind to them, it should be because of the favorable effect of kindness of us—a strange doctrine.

Suffering is perhaps the most potent source of identification. Only special social conditions are able to make people inhibit their normal spontaneous reaction toward suffering. If we alleviate suffering because of a spontaneous urge to do so, Kant would be willing to call the act "beautiful," but not moral. And his greatest admiration was, as we all know, for stars and the moral imperative, not spontaneous goodness. The history of cruelty inflicted in the name of morals has convinced me that increase of identification might achieve what moralizing cannot: beautiful actions.

RELEVANCE OF THE ABOVE FOR DEEP ECOLOGY

This perhaps rather lengthy philosophical discourse serves as a preliminary for the understanding of two things: first, the powerful indignation of Rachel Carson and others who, with great courage and stubborn determination, challenged authorities in the early 1960s, and triggered the international ecological movement. Second, the radical shift (see Sahlins, 1972) toward more positive appreciation of nonindustrial cultures and minorities—also in the 1960s, and expressing itself in efforts to "save" such cultures and in a new social anthropology.

The second movement reflects identification with threatened cultures. Both reactions were made possible by doubt that the industrial societies are as uniquely progressive as they usually had been supposed to be. Former haughtiness gave way to humility or at least willingness to look for deep changes both socially and in relation to nature.

Ecological information about the intimate dependency of humanity upon decent behavior toward the natural environment offered a much needed rational and economic justification for processes of identification which many people already had more or less completed. Their relative high degree of identification with animals, plants, landscapes, were seen to correspond to *factual relations* between themselves and nature. "Not man apart" was transformed from a romantic norm to a statement of fact. The distinction between man and environment, as applied within the shallow ecological movement, was seen to be illusory. Your Self crosses the boundaries.

When it was made known that the penguins of the Antarctic might die out because of the effects of DDT upon the toughness of their eggs, there was a widespread, *spontaneous* reaction of indignation and sorrow. People who never see penguins and who would never think of such animals as "useful" in any way, insisted that they had a right to live and flourish, and that it was our obligation not to interfere. But we must admit that even the mere appearance of penguins makes intense identification easy.

Thus, ecology helped many to know more *about themselves*. We are living beings. Penguins are too. We are all expressions of life. The fateful dependencies and interrelations which were brought to light, thanks to ecologists, made it easier for people to admit and even to cultivate their deep concern for nature, and to express their latent hostility toward the excesses of the economic growth of societies.

LIVING BEINGS HAVE INTRINSIC VALUE AND A RIGHT TO LIVE AND FLOURISH

How can these attitudes be talked about? What are the most helpful conceptualizations and slogans?

One important attitude might be thus expressed: "Every living being has a *right* to live." One way of answering the question is to insist upon the value in themselves, the autotelic value, of every living being. This opposes the notion that one may be justified in treating any living being as just a means to an end. It also generalizes the rightly famous dictum of Kant "never use a person solely as a means." Identification tells me: if *I* have a right to live, *you* have the same right.

Insofar as we consider ourselves and our family and friends to have an intrinsic value, the widening identification inevitably leads to the attribution of intrinsic value to others. The metaphysical maximum will then involve the attribution of intrinsic value to all living beings. The right to live is only a different way of expressing this evaluation.

THE END OF THE WHY'S

But why has *any* living being autotelic value? Faced with the ever returning question of "why?," we have to stop somewhere. Here is a place where we well might stop. We shall admit that the value in itself is something shown in intuition. We attribute intrinsic value to ourselves and our nearest, and the validity of further identification can be contested, and *is* contested by many. The negation may, however, also be attacked through series of "whys?" Ultimately, we are in the same human predicament of having to start somewhere, at least for the moment. We must stop somewhere and treat where we then stand as a foundation.

The use of "Every living being has a value in itself" as a fundamental norm or principle does not rule out other fundamentals. On the contrary, the normal situation will be one in which several, in part conflicting, fundamental norms are relevant. And some consequences of fundamental norms *seem* compatible, but in fact are not.

The designation "fundamental" does not need to mean more than "not based on something deeper," which in practice often is indistinguishable from "not derived logically from deeper premises." It must be considered a rare case, if some body is able to stick to one and only one fundamental norm. (I have made an attempt to work with a *model* with only one, Self-realization, in Ecosophy T.)

THE RIGHT TO LIVE IS ONE AND THE SAME, BUT VITAL INTERESTS OF OUR NEAREST HAVE PRIORITY OF DEFENSE

Under symbiotic conditions, there are rules which manifest two important factors operating when interests are conflicting: vitalness and nearness. The more vital interest has priority over the less vital. The nearer has priority over the more remote—in space, time, culture, species. Nearness derives its priority from our special responsibilities, obligations and insights.

The terms used in these rules are of course vague and ambiguous. But even so, the rules point toward ways of thinking and acting which do not leave us quite helpless in the many inevitable conflicts of norms. The vast increase of consequences for life in general, which industrialization and the population explosion have brought about, necessitates new guidelines.

Examples: The use of threatened species for food or clothing (fur) may be more or less vital for certain poor, nonindustrial, human communities. For the less poor, such use is clearly ecologically irresponsible. Considering the fabulous possibilities open to the richest industrial societies, it is their responsibility to assist the poor communities in such a way that undue exploitation of threatened species, populations, and ecosystems is avoided.

It may be of vital interest to a family of poisonous snakes to remain in a small area where small children play, but it is also of vital interest to children and parents that there are no accidents. The priority rule of nearness makes it justifiable for the parents to remove the snakes. But the priority of vital interest of snakes is important when deciding where to establish the playgrounds.

The importance of nearness is, to a large degree, dependent upon vital interests of communities rather than individuals. The obligations with the family keep the family together, the obligations within a nation keep it from disintegration. But if the nonvital interests of a nation, or a species, conflict with the vital interests of another nation, or of other species, the rules give priority to the "alien nation" or "alien species."

How these conflicts may be straightened out is of course much too large a subject to be treated even cursorily in this connection. What is said only points toward the existence of rules of some help. (For further discussion, see Naess [1979].)

INTRINSIC VALUES

The term "objectivism" may have undesirable associations, but value pronouncements within the deep ecological movement imply what in philosophy is often termed "value objectivism" as opposed to value subjectivism, for instance, "the emotive theory of value." At the time of Nietzsche there was in Europe a profound movement toward separation of value as a genuine aspect of reality on a par with scientific, "factual" descriptions. Value tended to be conceived as something projected by man into a completely value-neutral reality. The *Tractatus Philosophico-Logicus* of the early Wittgenstein expresses a well-known variant of this attitude. It represents a unique trend of *alienation of value* if we compare this attitude with those of cultures other than our technological-industrial society.

The professional philosophical debate on value objectivism, which in different senses—according to different versions, posits positive and negative values independent of value for human subjects—is of course very intricate. Here I shall only point out some kinds of statements within the deep

ecological movement which imply value objectivism in the sense of intrinsic value:

> Animals have value in themselves, not only as resources for humans.
>
> Animals have a right to live even if of no use to humans.
>
> We have no right to destroy the natural features of this planet.
>
> Nature does not belong to man.
>
> Nature is worth defending, whatever the fate of humans.
>
> A wilderness area has a value independent of whether humans have access to it.

In these statements, something *A* is said to have a value independent of whether *A* has a value for something else, *B*. The value of *A* must therefore be said to have a value inherent in *A*. *A* has *intrinsic value*. This does not imply that *A* has value *for B*. Thus *A* may have, and usually does have, both intrinsic and extrinsic value.

Subjectivistic arguments tend to take for granted that a subject is somehow implied. There "must be" somebody who performs the valuation process. For this subject, something may have value.

The burden of proof lies with the subjectivists insofar as naive attitudes lack the clear-cut separation of value from reality and the conception of value as something projected by man into reality or the neutral facts by a subject.

The most promising way of defending intrinsic values today is, in my view, to take gestalt thinking seriously. "Objects" will then be defined in terms of gestalts, rather than in terms of heaps of things with external relations and dominated by forces. This undermines the subject-object dualism essential for value subjectivism.

OUTLOOK FOR THE FUTURE

What is the outlook for growth of ecological, relevant identification and of policies in harmony with a high level of identification?

A major nuclear war will involve a setback of tremendous dimensions. Words need not be wasted in support of that conclusion. But continued militarization is a threat: It means further domination of technology and centralization.

Continued population growth makes benevolent policies still more difficult to pursue than they already are. Poor people in megacities do not have the opportunity to meet nature, and shortsighted policies which favor increasing the number of poor are destructive. Even a small population growth in rich nations is scarcely less destructive.

The economic policy of growth (as conceived today in the richest nations of all times) is increasingly destructive. It does not *prevent* growth of identification but makes it politically powerless. This reminds us of the possibility of significant *growth* of identification in the near future.

The increasing destruction plus increasing information about the destruction is apt to elicit strong feelings of sorrow, despair, desperate actions and tireless efforts to save what is left. With the forecast that more than a million species will die out before the year 2000 and most cultures be done away with, identification may grow rapidly among a minority.

At the present about 10% to 15% of the populace of some European countries are in favor of strong policies in harmony with the attitudes of identification. But this percentage may increase without major changes of policies. So far as I can see, the most probable course of events is continued devastation of conditions of life on this planet, combined with a powerless upsurge of sorrow and lamentation.

What actually happens is often wildly "improbable," and perhaps the strong anthropocentric arguments and wise recommendations of *World Conservation Strategy* (1980) will, after all, make a significant effect.

NOTES

1. Commissioned by The United Nations Environmental Programme (UNEP) which worked together with the World Wildlife Fund (WWF). Published 1980. Copies available through IUNC, 1196 Gland, Switzerland. In India: Department of Environment.

2. This aim implies a synthesis of views developed in the different branches of philosophy—ontology, epistemology, logic, methodology, theory of value, ethics, philosophy of history, and politics. As a philosopher the deep ecologist is a "generalist."

3. For comprehensive treatment of Ecosophy T, see Naess (1981, Chapter 7).

4. See Passmore (1980). For a reasonable, unemotional approach to "mysticism," see Stahl (1975).

5. For deeper study more distinctions have to be taken into account. See, for instance, Scheler (1954) and Mercer (1972).

6. See, for instance, the chapter "Removing the Rubbish" in Passmore (1980).

7. The diverse uses of the term *alienation (Entfremdung)* have an interesting and complicated history from the time of Rousseau. Rousseau himself offers interesting observations of how social conditions through the process of alienation make *amour de soi* change into *amour propre*. I would say: How the process of maturing is hindered and self-love hardens into egotism instead of softening and widening into Self-realization.

✑ REFERENCES

Elgin, Duane. 1981. *Voluntary Simplicity*. New York: William Morrow.

James, William. 1890. *The Principles of Psychology*. New York , Chapter 10: The Consciousness of Self.

Mercer, Philip. 1972. *Sympathy and Ethics*. Oxford: The Clarendon Press. Discusses forms of identification.

Naess, Arne. 1973. "The Shadow and the Deep, Long-Range Ecology Movement," *Inquiry* 16:(95–100).

———. 1974. *Gandhi and Group Conflict*. 1981, Oslo: Universitetsforlaget.

———. 1979. "Self-realization in Mixed Communities of Humans, Bears, Sheep and Wolves," *Inquiry*, Vol. 22 (pp. 231–241).

———. 1981. *Ekologi, samhälle och livsstil. Utkast til en ekosofi*. Stockholm: LTs förlag.

Passmore, John. 1980. *Man's Responsibility for Nature*. 2nd ed., London: Duckworth.

Sahlins, Marshall. 1972. *Stone Age Economics*. Chicago: Aldine.

Scheler, Max. 1954. *The Nature of Sympathy*. London: Routledge & Keegan Paul.

✎ STUDY QUESTIONS

1. What does Naess mean by *Ecosophy*? What does the ending *-sophy* refer to?
2. What are the basic tenets of Ecosophy T?
3. What does Naess mean by *Self-realization*? Analyze the quotations from Radhakrishnan, Eliot Deutsch, Juan Mascaró, and Gandhi. What do they tell us about Self-realization?
4. How do we develop a wider Self?
5. Explain Naess's idea of *identification*. Is it mystical? How can we identify with "individuals, species, ecosystems, and landscapes"?
6. What is Naess saying about *value objectivism*? Critically discuss this issue.

26 Deep Ecology

BILL DEVALL AND GEORGE SESSIONS

Bill Devall teaches in the sociology department at Humboldt State University in Arcata, California, and George Sessions teaches philosophy at Sierra College in Rocklin, California. Together they have authored *Deep Ecology: Living as if Nature Mattered* (1985) from which the present selection is taken.

This essay sets forth a more recent version of deep ecology than Naess's 1972 summary version, linking it to Zen Buddhism, Taoism, Native American rituals, and Christianity. They contrast deep ecology with the dominant worldview and set forth the eight principles of deep ecology.

The term *deep ecology* was coined by Arne Naess in his 1973 article, "The Shallow and the Deep, Long-Range Ecology Movements." Naess was attempting to describe the deeper, more spiritual approach to Nature exemplified in the writings of Aldo Leopold and Rachel Carson. He thought that this deeper approach resulted from a more sensitive openness to ourselves and nonhuman life around us. The essence of deep ecology is to keep asking more searching questions about human life, society, and Nature as in the Western philosophical tradition of Socrates. As examples of this deep questioning, Naess points out "that we ask why and how, where others do not. For instance, ecology as a science does not ask what kind of a society would be the best for maintaining a particular ecosystem—that is considered a question for value theory, for politics, for ethics." Thus deep ecology goes beyond the so-called factual scientific level to the level of self and Earth wisdom.

Deep ecology goes beyond a limited piecemeal shallow approach to environmental problems and attempts to articulate a comprehensive religious and philosophical worldview. The foundations of deep ecology are the basic intuitions and experiencing of ourselves and Nature which comprise ecological consciousness. Certain outlooks on politics and public policy flow naturally from this consciousness. And in the context of this book, we discuss the minority tradition as the type of community most conducive both to cultivating ecological consciousness and to asking the basic questions of values and ethics addressed in these pages.

Many of these questions are perennial philosophical and religious questions faced by humans in all cultures over the ages. What does it mean to be a unique human individual? How can the individual self maintain and increase its uniqueness while also being an inseparable aspect of the whole system wherein there are no sharp breaks

Reprinted from *Deep Ecology: Living as if Nature Mattered* (Salt Lake City: Peregrine Smith Book (1985), by permission. Footnotes deleted.

between self and the *other*? An ecological perspective, in this deeper sense, results in what Theodore Roszak calls "an awakening of wholes greater than the sum of their parts. In spirit, the discipline is contemplative and therapeutic."

Ecological consciousness and deep ecology are in sharp contrast with the dominant worldview of technocratic–industrial societies which regard humans as isolated and fundamentally separate from the rest of Nature, as superior to, and in charge of, the rest of creation. But the view of humans as separate and superior to the rest of Nature is only part of larger cultural patterns. For thousands of years, Western culture has become increasingly obsessed with the idea of *dominance:* with dominance of humans over non-human Nature, masculine over the feminine, wealthy and powerful over the poor, with the dominance of the West over non-Western cultures. Deep ecological consciousness allows us to see through these erroneous and dangerous illusions.

For deep ecology, the study of our place in the Earth household includes the study of ourselves as part of the organic whole. Going beyond a narrowly materialist scientific understanding of reality, the spiritual and the material aspects of reality fuse together. While the leading intellectuals of the dominant worldview have tended to view religion as "just superstition," and have looked upon ancient spiritual practice and enlightenment, such as found in Zen Buddhism, as essentially subjective, the search for deep ecological consciousness is the search for a more objective consciousness and state of being through an active deep questioning and meditative process and way of life.

Many people have asked these deeper questions and cultivated ecological consciousness within the context of different spiritual traditions—Christianity, Taoism, Buddhism, and Native American rituals, for example. While differing greatly in other regards, many in these traditions agree with the basic principles of deep ecology.

Warwick Fox, an Australian philosopher, has succinctly expressed the central intuition of deep ecology: "It is the idea that we can make no firm ontological divide in the field of existence: That there is no bifurcation in reality between the human and the non-human realms...to the extent that we perceive boundaries, we fall short of deep ecological consciousness."

From this most basic insight or characteristic of deep ecological consciousness, Arne Naess has developed two *ultimate norms* or intuitions which are themselves not derivable from other principles or intuitions. They are arrived at by the deep questioning process and reveal the importance of moving to the philosophical and religious level of wisdom. They cannot be validated, of course, by the methodology of modern science based on its usual mechanistic assumptions and its very narrow definition of data. These ultimate norms are *self-realization* and *biocentric equality.*

I. SELF-REALIZATION

In keeping with the spiritual traditions of many of the world's religions, the deep ecology norm of self-realization goes beyond the modern Western *self* which is defined as an isolated ego striving primarily for hedonistic gratification or for a narrow sense of individual salvation in this life or the next. This socially programmed sense of the narrow self or social self dislocates us, and leaves us prey to whatever fad or fashion is prevalent in our society or social reference group. We are thus robbed of beginning the search for our unique spiritual/biological personhood. Spiritual growth, or unfolding, begins when we cease to understand or see ourselves as isolated and narrow competing egos and begin to identify with other humans from our family and friends to, eventually, our species. But the deep ecology sense of self requires a further maturity and growth, an identification which goes beyond humanity to include the nonhuman world. We must see beyond our narrow contemporary cultural assumptions and values, and the conventional wisdom of our time and place, and this is best achieved by the meditative deep questioning process. Only in this way can we hope to attain full mature personhood and uniqueness.

A nurturing nondominating society can help in the "real work" of becoming a whole person.

The "real work" can be summarized symbolically as the realization of "self-in-Self" where "Self" stands for organic wholeness. This process of the full unfolding of the self can also be summarized by the phrase, "No one is saved until we are all saved," where the phrase "one" includes not only me, an individual human, but all humans, whales, grizzly bears, whole rain forest ecosystems, mountains and rivers, the tiniest microbes in the soil, and so on.

II. BIOCENTRIC EQUALITY

The intuition of biocentric equality is that all things in the biosphere have an equal right to live and blossom and to reach their own individual forms of unfolding and self-realization within the larger Self-realization. This basic intuition is that all organisms and entities in the ecosphere, as parts of the interrelated whole, are equal in intrinsic worth. Naess suggests that biocentric equality as an intuition is true in principle, although in the process of living, all species use each other as food, shelter, etc. Mutual predation is a biological fact of life, and many of the world's religions have struggled with the spiritual implications of this. Some animal liberationists who attempt to side-step this problem by advocating vegetarianism are forced to say that the entire plant kingdom including rain forests have no right to their own existence. This evasion flies in the face of the basic intuition of equality. Aldo Leopold expressed this intuition when he said humans are "plain citizens" of the biotic community, not lord and master over all other species.

Biocentric equality is intimately related to the all-inclusive Self-realization in the sense that if we harm the rest of Nature then we are harming ourselves. There are no boundaries and everything is interrelated. But insofar as we perceive things as individual organisms or entities, the insight draws us to respect all human and nonhuman individuals in their own right as parts of the whole without feeling the need to set up hierarchies of species with humans at the top.

The practical implications of this intuition or norm suggest that we should live with minimum rather than maximum impact on other species and on the Earth in general. Thus we see another aspect of our guiding principle: "simple in means, rich in ends."

A fuller discussion of the biocentric norm as it unfolds itself in practice begins with the realization that we, as individual humans, and as communities of humans, have vital needs which go beyond such basics as food, water, and shelter to include love, play, creative expression, intimate relationships with a particular landscape (or Nature taken in its entirety) as well as intimate relationships with other humans, and the vital need for spiritual growth, for becoming a mature human being.

Our vital material needs are probably more simple than many realize. In technocratic-industrial societies there is overwhelming propaganda and advertising which encourages false needs and destructive desires designed to foster increased production and consumption of goods. Most of this actually diverts us from facing reality in an objective way and from beginning the "real work" of spiritual growth and maturity.

Many people who do not see themselves as supporters of deep ecology nevertheless recognize an overriding vital human need for a healthy and high-quality natural environment for humans, if not for all life, with minimum intrusion of toxic waste, nuclear radiation from human enterprises, minimum acid rain and smog, and enough free flowing wilderness so humans can get in touch with their sources, the natural rhythms and the flow of time and place.

Drawing from the minority tradition and from the wisdom of many who have offered the insight of interconnectedness, we recognize that deep ecologists can offer suggestions for gaining maturity and encouraging the processes of harmony with Nature, but that there is no grand solution which is guaranteed to save us from ourselves.

The ultimate norms of deep ecology suggest a view of the nature of reality and our place as an individual (many in the one) in the larger scheme of things. They cannot be fully grasped intellectually but are ultimately experiential. We encourage readers to consider our further discussion of the psychological, social and ecological implications of these norms in later chapters.

FIGURE 1

Dominant Worldview	Deep Ecology
Dominance over Nature	Harmony with Nature
Natural environment as resource for humans	All nature has intrinsic worth/biospecies equality
Material/economic growth for growing human population	Elegantly simple material needs (material goals serving the larger goal of self-realization)
Belief in ample resource reserves	Earth "supplies" limited
High technological progress and solutions	Appropriate technology; nondominating science
Consumerism	Doing with enough/recycling
National/centralized community	Minority tradition/bioregion

As a brief summary of our position thus far, Figure 1 summarizes the contrast between the dominant worldview and deep ecology.

III. BASIC PRINCIPLES OF DEEP ECOLOGY

In April 1984, during the advent of spring and John Muir's birthday, George Sessions and Arne Naess summarized fifteen years of thinking on the principles of deep ecology while camping in Death Valley, California. In this great and special place, they articulated these principles in a literal, somewhat neutral way, hoping that they would be understood and accepted by persons coming from different philosophical and religious positions.

Readers are encouraged to elaborate their own versions of deep ecology, clarify key concepts and think through the consequences of acting from these principles.

Basic Principles

1. The well-being and flourishing of human and nonhuman Life on Earth have value in themselves (synonyms: intrinsic value, inherent value). These values are independent of the usefulness of the nonhuman world for human purposes.
2. Richness and diversity of life forms contribute to the realization of these values and are also values in themselves.

3. Humans have no right to reduce this richness and diversity except to satisfy *vital* needs.
4. The flourishing of human life and cultures is compatible with a substantial decrease of the human population. The flourishing of nonhuman life requires such a decrease.
5. Present human interference with the nonhuman world is excessive, and the situation is rapidly worsening.
6. Policies must therefore be changed. These policies affect basic economic, technological, and ideological structures. The resulting state of affairs will be deeply different from the present.
7. The ideological change is mainly that of appreciating *life quality* (dwelling in situations of inherent value) rather than adhering to an increasingly higher standard of living. There will be a profound awareness of the difference between big and great.
8. Those who subscribe to the foregoing points have an obligation directly or indirectly to try to implement the necessary changes.

Naess and Sessions Provide Comments on the Basic Principles

RE (1). This formulation refers to the biosphere, or more accurately, to the ecosphere as a whole. This includes individuals, species, populations, habitat, as well as human and nonhuman cultures. From our current knowledge of all-pervasive intimate relationships, this implies a fundamental deep concern and respect. Ecological processes of the planet should, on the whole, remain intact. "The world environment should remain 'natural'" (Gary Snyder).

The term "life" is used here in a more comprehensive nontechnical way to refer also to what biologists classify as "nonliving"; rivers (watersheds), landscapes, ecosystems. For supporters of deep ecology, slogans such as "Let the river live" illustrate this broader usage so common in most cultures.

Inherent value as used in (1) is common in deep ecology literature ("The presence of inherent value in a natural object is independent of any awareness, interest, or appreciation of it by a conscious being.")

RE (2). More technically, this is a formulation concerning diversity and complexity. From an ecological standpoint, complexity and symbiosis are conditions for maximizing diversity. So-called simple, lower, or primitive species of plants and animals contribute essentially to the richness and diversity of life. They have value in themselves and are not merely steps toward the so-called higher or rational life forms. The second principle presupposes that life itself, as a process over evolutionary time, implies an increase of diversity and richness. The refusal to acknowledge that some life forms have greater or lesser intrinsic value than others (see points 1 and 2) runs counter to the formulations of some ecological philosophers and New Age writers.

Complexity, as referred to here, is different from complication. Urban life may be more complicated than life in a natural setting without being more complex in the sense of multifaceted quality.

RE (3). The term "vital need" is left deliberately vague to allow for considerable latitude in judgment. Differences in climate and related factors, together with differences in the structures of societies as they now exist, need to be considered (for some Eskimos, snowmobiles are necessary today to satisfy vital needs).

People in the materially richest countries cannot be expected to reduce their excessive interference with the nonhuman world to a moderate level overnight. The stabilization and reduction of the human population will take time. Interim strategies need to be developed. But this in no way excuses the present complacency—the extreme seriousness of our current situation must first be realized. But the longer we wait the more drastic will be the measures needed. Until deep changes are made, substantial decreases in richness and diversity are liable to occur: the rate of extinction of species will be ten to one hundred times greater than any other period of earth history.

RE (4). The United Nations Fund for Population Activities in their State of World Population Report (1984) said that high human population growth rates (over 2.0 percent annum) in many developing countries "were diminishing the quality of life for many millions of people." During the decade 1974–1984, the world population grew by nearly 800 million—more than the size of India. "And we will be adding about one Bangladesh (population 93 million) per annum between now and the year 2000."

The report noted that "The growth rate of the human population has declined for the first time in human history. But at the same time, the number of people being added to the human population is bigger than at any time in history because the population base is larger."

Most of the nations in the developing world (including India and China) have as their official government policy the goal of reducing the rate of human population increase, but there are debates over the types of measures to take (contraception, abortion, etc.) consistent with human rights and feasibility.

The report concludes that if all governments set specific population targets as public policy to help alleviate poverty and advance the quality of life, the current situation could be improved.

As many ecologists have pointed out, it is also absolutely crucial to curb population growth in the so-called developed (i.e., overdeveloped) industrial societies. Given the tremendous rate of consumption and waste production of individuals in these societies, they represent a much greater threat and impact on the biosphere per capita than individuals in Second and Third World countries.

RE (5). This formulation is mild. For a realistic assessment of the situation, see the unabbreviated version of the I.U.C.N.'s *World Conservation Strategy*. There are other works to be highly recommended, such as Gerald Barney's *Global 2000 Report to the President of the United States*.

The slogan of "noninterference" does not imply that humans should not modify some ecosystems as do other species. Humans have modified the earth and will probably continue to do so. At issue is the nature and extent of such interference.

The fight to preserve and extend areas of wilderness or near-wilderness should continue and should focus on the general ecological functions of these areas (one such function: large wilderness areas are required in the biosphere to allow for continued evolutionary speciation of animals and plants). Most present designated wilderness areas and game preserves are not large enough to allow for such speciation.

RE (6). Economic growth as conceived and implemented today by the industrial states is incompatible with (1)–(5). There is only a faint resemblance between ideal sustainable forms of economic growth and present policies of the industrial societies. And "sustainable" still means "sustainable in relation to humans."

Present ideology tends to value things because they are scarce and because they have a commodity value. There is prestige in vast consumption and waste (to mention only several relevant factors).

Whereas "self-determination," "local community," and "think globally, act locally," will remain key terms in the ecology of human societies, nevertheless the implementation of deep changes requires increasingly global action—action across borders.

Governments in Third World countries (with the exception of Costa Rica and a few others) are uninterested in deep ecological issues. When the governments of industrial societies try to promote ecological measures through Third World governments, practically nothing is accomplished (e.g., with problems of desertification). Given this situation, support for global action through nongovernmental international organizations becomes increasingly important. Many of these organizations are able to act globally "from grassroots to grassroots," thus avoiding negative governmental interference.

Cultural diversity today requires advanced technology, that is, techniques that advance the basic goals of each culture. So-called soft, intermediate, and alternative technologies are steps in this direction.

RE (7). Some economists criticize the term "quality of life" because it is supposed to be vague. But on closer inspection, what they consider to be vague is actually the nonquantitative nature of the term. One cannot quantify adequately what is important for the quality of life as discussed here, and there is no need to do so.

RE (8). There is ample room for different opinions about priorities: what should be done first, what next? What is most urgent? What is clearly necessary as opposed to what is highly desirable but not absolutely pressing?

STUDY QUESTIONS

1. Analyze the eight principles of deep ecology. What problems, if any, do you find with them? Do you accept the first principle that natural objects have inherent value? What things do you think have inherent value and why?

2. What are the implications of Principle 4? If people do not voluntarily curb their population, how would a deep ecologist solve this problem?

3. Is deep ecology workable? Why, or why not?

27   A Critique of Anti-Anthropocentric Ethics

RICHARD WATSON

Richard Watson is professor of philosophy at Washington University in St. Louis and the author of several works in philosophy. Here is his abstract:

Arne Naess, John Rodman, George Sessions, and others designated herein as ecosophers, propose an egalitarian anti-anthropocentric bio-centrism as a basis for a new environmental ethic. I outline their "hands-off-nature" position and show it to be based on setting man apart. The ecosophic position is thus neither egalitarian nor fully biocentric. A fully egalitarian biocentric ethic would place no more restrictions on the behavior of human beings than on the behavior of any other animals. Uncontrolled human behavior might lead to the destruction of the environment and thus to the extinction of human beings. I thus conclude that human interest in survival is the best ground on which to argue for an ecological balance which is good both for human beings and for the whole biological community.

Anthropocentric is defined specifically as the position "that considers man as the central fact, or final aim, of the universe" and generally "conceiv[es] of everything in the universe in terms of human values."[1] In the literature of environmental ethics, anti-anthropocentric biocentrism is the position that human needs, goals, and desires should not be taken as privileged or overriding in considering the needs, desires, interests, and goals of all members of all biological species taken together, and in general that the Earth as a whole should not be interpreted or managed from a human standpoint. According to this position, birds, trees, and the land itself considered as the biosphere have a right to be and to live out their individual and species' potentials, and that members of the human species have no right to

disturb, perturb, or destroy the ecological balance of the planet.

An often quoted statement of this right of natural objects to continue to be as they are found to be occurs in John Rodman's "The Liberation of Nature?":

> To affirm that "natural objects" have "rights" is symbolically to affirm that ALL NATURAL ENTITIES (INCLUDING HUMANS) HAVE INTRINSIC WORTH SIMPLY BY VIRTUE OF BEING AND BEING WHAT THEY ARE.[2]

In "On the Nature and Possibility of an Environmental Ethic," Tom Regan follows an implication of this view by presenting a "preservation principle":

> By the "preservation principle" I mean a principle of nondestruction, noninterference, and, generally, nonmeddling. By characterizing this in terms of a principle, moreover, I am emphasizing that preservation (letting-be) be regarded as a moral imperative.[3]

Support for this hands-off-nature approach is provided by George Sessions in his "Spinoza, Perennial Philosophy, and Deep Ecology," where, among other things, he describes how Aldo Leopold moved from a position considering humans as stewards or managers of nature to one considering humans as "plain members" of the total biotic community.[4] As Leopold himself puts it:

> A thing is right when it tends to preserve the integrity, stability, and beauty of the biotic community. It is wrong when it tends otherwise.[5]

According to Sessions, Leopold reached this position in part as a result of his dawning

Reprinted from *Environmental Ethics*, Vol. 5 (Fall 1983) by permission. Notes edited.

realization that ecological communities are internally integrated and highly complex. He saw how human activities have disrupted many ecological communities and was himself involved in some unsuccessful attempts to manage communities of animals in the wild. These failures led Leopold to conclude that "the biotic mechanism is so complex that its workings may never be fully understood."[6]

Like many other environmentalists, Sessions associates Leopold's position with Barry Commoner's first law of ecology: "Everything is connected to everything else,"[7] according to which "any major man-made change in a natural system is likely to be *detrimental* to that system." This view, which considers all environmental managers who try to alter the environment to be suffering from scientific hubris, leads to an almost biblical statement of nescience. In this connection, Sessions quotes the ecologist Frank Egler as saying that "Nature is not only more complex than we think, but it is more complex than we can ever think." The attitude of humble acquiescence to the ways of nature which follows from this view, Sessions says, is summed up in Commoner's third law, "Nature knows best."

The position is presented at length by G. Tyler Miller, in another quotation cited by Sessions:

One of the purposes of this Book [*Replenish the Earth*] is to show the bankruptcy of the term "spaceship earth." . . . This is an upside-down view of reality and is yet another manifestation of our arrogance toward nature. . . . Our task is not to learn how to pilot spaceship earth. It is not to learn how—as Teilhard de Chardin would have it—"to seize the tiller of the world": Our task is to give up our fantasies of omnipotence. In other words, *we must stop trying to steer* [my italics]. The solution to our present dilemma does not lie in attempting to extend our technical and managerial skills into every sphere of existence. Thus, *from a human standpoint our environmental crisis is the result* of our arrogance towards nature [Miller's italics]. Somehow we must tune our senses again to the beat of existence, sensing in nature fundamental rhythms we can trust even though we may never fully understand them. We must learn anew that it is we who belong to earth and not the earth to us.

Thus rediscovery of our finitude is fundamental to any genuinely human future.[8]

Sessions, at least, is not naive about some of the problems that arise from these pronouncements. He says that if an environmental ethic is to be derived from ecological principles and concepts, this raises

the old problem of attempting to derive moral principles and imperatives from supposedly empirical fact (the "is-ought problem"). The attempt to justify ecosystem ethics on conventional utilitarian or "rights and obligations" grounds presents formidable obstacles. And, so far, little headway has been made in finding other acceptable grounds for an ecosystem ethics other than a growing intuitive ecological awareness that *it is right*.[9]

The anti-anthropocentric biocentrists have sought a metaphysical foundation for a holistic environmental ethic in Spinoza. The clearest statement of this appears in Arne Naess's "Spinoza and Ecology." Naess expands from Spinoza in sixteen points, several of which are crucial to my discussion of anti-anthropocentric biocentrism:

1. The nature conceived by field ecologists is not the passive, dead, value-neutral nature of mechanistic science, but akin to the *Deus sive Natura* of Spinoza. All-inclusive, creative (as *natura naturans*), infinitely diverse, and alive in the broad sense of pan-psychism, but also manifesting a structure, the so-called laws of nature. There are always causes to be found, but extremely complex and difficult to unearth. Nature with a capital N is intuitively conceived as perfect in a sense that Spinoza and out-door ecologists have more or less in common: it is not narrowly moral, utilitarian, or aesthetic perfection. Nature is perfect "in itself."

Perfection can only mean completeness of some sort when applied in general, and not to specifically human achievements. . . .

2. . . . The two aspects of Nature, those of extension and thought (better: non-extension), are both complete aspects of one single reality, and *perfection characterizes both*. . . .

3. . . . As an *absolutely* all-embracing reality, Nature has no purpose, aim, or goal. . . .

4. There is no established moral world-order. Human justice is not a law of nature. There are,

on the other hand, no natural laws limiting the endeavour to extend the realm of justice as conceived in a society of free human beings....

5. Good and evil must be defined in relation to beings for which something is good or evil, useful or detrimental. The terms are meaningless when not thus related....

6. Every thing is connected with every other....Intimate interconnectedness in the sense of internal rather than external relations characterizes ecological ontology....

9. If one insists upon using the term "rights," every being may be said to have the right to do what is in its power. It is "right" to express its own nature as clearly and extensively as natural conditions permit.

That right which they [the animals] have in relation to us, we have in relation to them (*Ethics,* Part IV, first scholium to proposition 37).

That rights are a part of a separate moral world order is fiction.

Field ecologists tend to accept a general "right to live and blossom." Humans have no special right to kill and injure. Nature does not belong to them.[10]

Spinoza has also been cited for the general position that the ultimate goal, good, and joy of human beings is understanding which amounts to contemplation of Nature. In "Spinoza and Jeffers on Man in Nature," Sessions says:

> Spinoza's purpose in philosophizing, then, is to break free from the bonds of desire and ignorance which captivate and frustrate most men, thus standing in the way of what real happiness is available to them, and to attain a higher Self which is aligned with a *correct* [my italics] understanding of God/Nature.[11]

The position, however, is not restricted to Spinoza, for, as Sessions notes elsewhere, the best-known statement of this view is probably found in Aldous Huxley's *Perennial Philosophy:*

> Happiness and moral progress depend, it is [mistakenly] thought [today], on bigger and better gadgets and a higher standard of living....In all the historic formulations of the Perennial Philosophy it is axiomatic that the end of human life is contemplation, or the direct and intuitive

awareness of God; that action is the means to that end; that a society is good to the extent that it renders contemplation possible for its members.[12]

A difficult question that arises for advocates of this position is whether or not humans can be activists. For example, near-total passivism seems to be suggested by Michael Zimmerman in his approving summation of what he takes to be Heidegger's admonition to the Western World:

> Only Western man's thinking has ended up by viewing the world as a storehouse of raw material for the enhancement of man's Power....[A] new kind of thinking must...pass beyond the subjectivistic thinking of philosophy-science-technology....Heidegger indicates that the new way must "let beings be," i.e., it must let them manifest themselves in their own presence and worth, and not merely as objects for the all-powerful Subject.[13]

On the other hand, Naess is an activist; he and others think that civil disobedience is appropriate to thwart human "misuse" of the environment. And although Naess stresses what he calls the "biospherical egalitarianism" of all biological species on earth," he says in "Environmental Ethics and Spinoza":

> Animals cannot be citizens [i.e., members of a human moral community]. But animals may, as far as I can understand, be members of *life communities* on a par with babies, lunatics, and others who do not cooperate as citizens but are cared for in part for their own good.

This is consistent with Naess's Spinozistic approach, but the more general implication of the species egalitarian approach seems to be inactivism.

In summary, advocates of anti-anthropocentric biocentrism such as Sessions speak of the Judeo-Christian-Platonic-Aristotelian tradition as leading to

> an extreme subjectivist anthropocentrism in which the whole of non-human nature is viewed as a resource for man. By way of a long and convoluted intellectual history, we have managed to subvert completely the organic ecological world view of the hunter and gatherer.

Sessions goes on to deplore "the demise of pantheism and the desacralization of Nature." He then makes a statement highly typical of anti-anthropomorphic biocentrists:

> Part of the genius of Bacon and Descartes was to realize, contrary to the conservatism of the Church authorities, that a new science was needed to consummate the goal of Judeo-Christian-Platonic-Aristotelian domination of nature. The Enlightenment retained the Christian idea of man's perpetual progress (now defined as increasing scientific-technological control and mastery over nature), thus setting the stage for, and passing its unbridled optimism on to, its twentieth-century successors, Marxism and American pragmatism. The floodgates had been opened. The Pythagorean theory of the cosmos and the whole idea of a meaningful perennial philosophy were swept away in a deluge of secularism, the fragmentation of knowledge, pronouncements that God was dead and the universe and life of man meaningless, industrialization, the quest for material happiness, and the consequent destruction of the environment. The emphasis was no longer upon either *God* or *Nature*, but *Man*.

Sessions by no means advocates or thinks possible a simple return to pre-Socratic religion or pantheism. But what, on the basis of ecological principles and concepts, is the underlying motif or guiding ideal today for "a correct understanding of God/Nature"? According to Naess, the proper position is an *ecosophy* defined as "a philosophy of ecological harmony or equilibrium." Thus, while deploring the Greek contribution to the present desacralization of nature, these ecosophers do acknowledge the Stoic and Epicurean contributions to the philosophy of balance, harmony, and equilibrium. They present a holistic vision of the Earth circling in dynamic ecological equilibrium as the preferred and proper contemplative object of right-thinking environmental man.

In pursuing a statement of anti-anthropomorphic biocentrism, then, I have exposed five principles of the movement:

1. The needs, desires, interests, and goals of humans are not privileged.
2. The human species should not change the ecology of the planet.
3. The world ecological system is too complex for human beings ever to understand.
4. The ultimate goal, good, and joy of humankind is contemplative understanding of Nature.
5. Nature is a holistic system of parts (of which man is merely one among many equals) all of which are internally interrelated in dynamic, harmonious, ecological equilibrium.

The moral imperative derived from this "ecosophy" is that human beings do not have the right to, and should not, alter the equilibrium.

II

I do not intend to challenge the controversial naturalistic assumption that some such environmental ethic can be derived from ecological principles and concepts. Whatever the logical problems of deriving value from fact, it is not (and probably never has been) a practical problem for large numbers of people who base their moral convictions on factual premises.

Nevertheless, it must be obvious to most careful readers that the general position characterized in section 1 suffers from serious internal contradictions. I think they are so serious that the position must be abandoned. In what follows I detail the problems that arise in the system, and then offer an alternative to the call for developing a new ecosophic ethic.

To go immediately to the heart of the matter, I take anti-anthropocentrism more seriously than do any of the ecosophers I have quoted or read. If man is a part of nature, if he is a "plain citizen," if he is just one nonprivileged member of a "biospherical egalitarianism," then the human species should be treated in no way different from any other species. However, the entire tone of the position outlined in section 1 is to set man apart from nature and above all other living species. Naess says that nonhuman animals should be "cared for in part for their own good." Sessions says that humans should curb their technological enthusiasms to preserve ecological equilibrium. Rodman says flatly that man should let nature be.

Now, the posing of man against nature in any way is anthropocentric. Man is a part of nature.

Human ways—human culture—and human actions are as natural as are the ways in which any other species of animals behaves. But if we view the state of nature or Nature as being natural, undisturbed, and unperturbed only when human beings are *not* present, or only when human beings are curbing their natural behavior, then we are assuming that human beings are apart from, separate from, different from, removed from, or above nature. It is obvious that the ecosophy described above is based on this position of setting man apart from or above nature. (Do I mean even "sordid" and "perverted" human behavior? Yes, that is natural, too.)

To avoid this separation of man from nature, this special treatment of human beings as other than nature, we must stress that man's works (yes, including H-bombs and gas chambers) are as natural as those of bower birds and beavers.

But civilized man wreaks havoc on the environment. We disrupt the ecology of the planet, cause the extinction of myriad other species of living things, and even alter the climate of the Earth. Should we not attempt to curb our behavior to avoid these results? Indeed we should as a matter of prudence if we want to preserve our habitat and guarantee the survival of our species. But this is anthropocentric thinking.

Only if we are thinking anthropocentrically will we set the human species apart as *the* species that is to be thwarted in its natural behavior. Anti-anthropocentric biocentrists suggest that other species are to be allowed to manifest themselves naturally. They are to be allowed to live out their evolutionary potential in interaction with one another. But man is different. Man is *too* powerful, *too* destructive of the environment and other species, *too* successful in reproducing, and so on. What a phenomenon is man! Man is so wonderfully bad that he is not to be allowed to live out his evolutionary potential in egalitarian interaction with all other species.

Why not? The only reason is anthropocentric. We are not treating man as a plain member of the biotic community. We are not treating the human species as an equal among other species. We think of man as being better than other animals, or worse, as the case may be, because man is so powerful.

One reason we think this is that we think in terms of an anthropocentric moral community. All other species are viewed as morally neutral; their behavior is neither good nor bad. But we evaluate human behavior morally. And this sets man apart. If we are to treat man as a part of nature on egalitarian terms with other species, then man's behavior must be treated as morally neutral, too. It is absurd, of course, to suggest the opposite alternative, that we evaluate the behavior of nonhuman animals morally.

Bluntly, if we think there is nothing morally wrong with one species taking over the habitat of another and eventually causing the extinction of the dispossessed species—as has happened millions of times in the history of the Earth—then we should not think that there is anything morally or ecosophically wrong with the human species dispossessing and causing the extinction of other species.

Man's nature, his role, his forte, his glory and ambition has been to propagate and thrive at the expense of many other species and to the disruption—or, neutrally, to the change—of the planet's ecology. I do not want to engage in speculation about the religion of preliterate peoples, or in debates about the interpretation of documented non-Judeo-Christian-Platonic-Aristotelian religions. I am skeptical, however, of the panegyrics about pantheism and harmonious integration with sacred Nature. But these speculations do not matter. The fact is that for about 50,000 years human beings (*Homo sapiens*) have been advancing like wildfire (to use an inflammatory metaphor) to occupy more and more of the planet. A peak of low-energy technology was reached about 35,000 years ago at which time man wiped out many species of large animals. About 10,000 years ago man domesticated plants and animals and started changing the face of the Earth with grazing, farming, deforestation, and desertification. About 200 years ago man started burning fossil fuels with results that will probably change the climate of the planet (at least temporarily) and that have already resulted in the extinction of many species of living things that perhaps might otherwise have survived. In 1945 man entered an atomic age and we now have the ability to desertify large portions of the

Earth and perhaps to cause the extinction of most of the higher forms of life.

Human beings do alter things. They cause the extinction of many species, and they change the Earth's ecology. This is what humans do. This is their destiny. If they destroy many other species and themselves in the process, they do no more than has been done by many another species. The human species should be allowed—if any species can be said to have a right—to live out its evolutionary potential, to its own destruction if that is the end result. It is nature's way.

This is not a popular view. But most alternative anti-anthropocentric biocentric arguments for preserving nature are self-contradictory. Man is a part of nature. The only way man will survive is if he uses his brains to save himself. One reason why we should curb human behavior that is destructive of other species and the environment is because in the end it is destructive of the human species as well.

I hope it is human nature to survive because we are smart. But those who appeal for a new ethic or religion or ecosophy based on an intuitive belief that they know what is right not only for other people, but also for the planet as a whole, exhibit the hubris that they themselves say got us in such a mess in the first place. If the ecosphere is so complicated that we may never understand its workings, how is it that so many ecosophers are so sure that they know what is right for us to do now? Beyond the issue of man's right to do whatever he can according to the power-makes-right ecosophic ethic outlined by Naess, we may simply be wrong about what is "good" for the planet. Large numbers of species have been wiped out before, e.g., at the time the dinosaurs became extinct. Perhaps wiping out and renewal is just the way things go. Of course, a lot of genetic material is lost, but presumably all the species that ever existed came out of the same primordial soup, and could again. In situations where genetic material was limited, as in the Galapagos Islands or Australia, evolutionary radiation filled the niches. Even on the basis of our present knowledge about evolution and ecology, we have little ground to worry about the proliferation of life on Earth even if man manages to wipe out most of the species now living. Such a clearing out might be just the thing to allow for variety and diversity. And why is it that we harp about genetic banks today anyway? For one thing, we are worried that disease might wipe out our domesticated grain crops. Then where would *man* be?

Another obvious anthropocentric element in ecosophic thinking is the predilection for ecological communities of great internal variety and complexity. But the barren limestone plateaus that surround the Mediterranean now are just as much in ecological balance as were the forests that grew there before man cut them down. And "dead" Lake Erie is just as much in ecological balance with the life on the land that surrounds it as it was in pre-Columbian times. The notion of a climax situation in ecology is a human invention, based on anthropocentric ideas of variety, completion, wholeness, and balance. A preference for equilibrium rather than change, for forests over deserts, for complexity and variety over simplicity and monoculture, all of these are matters of human economics and aesthetics. What *would* it be, after all, to think like a mountain as Aldo Leopold is said to have recommended? It would be anthropocentric because mountains do not think, but also because mountains are imagined to be thinking about which human interests in their preservation or development they prefer. The anthropocentrism of ecosophers is most obvious in their pronouncements about what is normal and natural. Perhaps it is not natural to remain in equilibrium, to be in ecological balance.

As far as that goes, most of the universe is apparently dead—or at least inanimate—anyway. And as far as we know, the movement of things is toward entropy. By simplifying things, man is on the side of the universe.

And as for making a mess of things, destroying things, disrupting and breaking down things, the best information we have about the origin of the universe is that it is the result of an explosion. If we are going to derive an ethic from our knowledge of nature, is it wrong to suggest that high-technology man might be doing the right thing? Naess does try to meet this objection with his tenth principle:

10 There is nothing in human nature or essence, according to Spinoza, which can *only* manifest or express itself through injury to others. That is, the striving for expression of one's nature does not inevitably imply an attitude of hostile domination over other beings, human or non-human. Violence, in the sense of violent activity, is not the same as violence as injury to others.[14]

But "injury" is a human moral concept. There is no injury to others in neutral nature. Naess and Spinoza are still bound by Judeo-Christian-Platonic-Aristotelian notions of human goodness. But to call for curbing man is like trying to make vegetarians of pet cats.

I have often been puzzled about why so many environmental philosophers insist on harking to Spinoza as a ground for environmental ethics. It is perfectly plain as Curley and Lloyd point out that Spinoza's moral views are humanistic. They show how difficult it is to reconcile Spinoza's sense of freedom as the recognition of necessity with any notion of autonomy of self that is required to make moral imperatives or morality itself meaningful. That is, to recognize and accept what one is determined to do—even if this recognition and acceptance were not itself determined—is not the same as choosing between two equally possible (undetermined) courses of action. Moral action depends on free choice among undetermined alternatives.

III

There are anthropocentric foundations in most environmental and ecosophical literature. In particular, most ecosophers say outright or openly imply that human individuals and the human species would be better off if we were required to live in ecological balance with nature. Few ecosophers really think that man is just one part of nature among others. Man is privileged—or cursed—at least by having a moral sensibility that as far as we can tell no other entities have. But it is pretty clear (as I argue in "Self-Consciousness and the Rights of Nonhuman Animals and Nature") that on this planet at least only human beings are (so far) full members of a moral community. We ought to be kinder to nonhuman animals, but I do not think that this is because they have any intrinsic rights. As far as that goes, human beings have no intrinsic rights either (as Naess and Spinoza agree). We have to earn our rights as cooperating citizens in a moral community.

Because, unlike many ecosophers, I do not believe that we can return to religion, or that given what we know about the world today we can believe in pantheism or panpsychism, I think it is a mistake to strive for a new environmental ethic based on religious or mystical grounds. And I trust that I have demonstrated both how difficult it is to be fully biocentric, and also how the results of anti-anthropocentric biocentrism go far beyond the limits that ecosophers have drawn. Ecosophers obviously want to avoid the direct implications of treating the human species in the egalitarian and hands-off way they say other species should be treated. It is nice that human survival is compatible with the preservation of a rich planetary ecology, but I think it is a mistake to try to cover up the fact that human survival and the good life for man is some part of what we are interested in. There is very good reason for thinking ecologically, and for encouraging human beings to act in such a way as to preserve a rich and balanced planetary ecology: human survival depends on it.

NOTES

1. *Webster's New World Dictionary,* 2nd ed. (Cleveland, Ohio: William Collins and World Publishing Co., 1976), p. 59.
2. John Rodman, "The Liberation of Nature?" *Inquiry* 20 (1977): 108 (quoted with emphasis in capitals by George Sessions in *Ecophilosophy III*, p. 5a).
3. Tom Regan, "The Nature and Possibility of an Environmental Ethic," *Environmental Ethics* 3 (1981): 31–32.
4. George Sessions, "Spinoza, Perennial Philosophy, and Deep Ecology," unpublished, p. 15.
5. Aldo Leopold, *A Sand County Almanac* (Oxford: Oxford University Press, 1966), p. 240 (quoted by George Sessions in "Spinoza, Perennial Philosophy, and Deep Ecology," unpublished, p. 15).
6. Ibid.
7. Barry Commoner, *The Closing Circle: Nature, Man, and Technology* (New York: Alfred A. Knopf, 1971), p. 33 (quoted by George Sessions in "Panpsychism versus Modern Materialism:

Some Implications for an Ecological Ethics," unpublished, p. 35).

8. G. Tyler Miller, *Replenish the Earth* (Belmont, Calif.: Wadsworth, 1972), p. 53 (quoted by George Sessions in "Shallow and Deep Ecology: A Review of the Philosophical Literature," unpublished, pp. 44–45).

9. George Sessions, "Shallow and Deep Ecology: A Review of the Philosophical Literature," unpublished, p. 16.

10. Arne Naess, "Spinoza and Ecology," in Sigfried Hessing, ed., *Speculum Spinozanum 1677–1977* (London: Routledge & Kegan Paul, 1977), pp. 419–21.

11. George Sessions, "Spinoza and Jeffers on Man and Nature," *Inquiry* 20 (1977): 494–95.

12. Aldous Huxley, *Perennial Philosophy* (New York: Harper's, 1945), pp. 159–60 (quoted by George Sessions in "Shallow and Deep Ecology: A Review of the Philosophical Literature," unpublished, p. 47).

13. Michael Zimmerman, "Technological Change and the End of Philosophy," unpublished, no page given (quoted by George Sessions in "Spinoza and Jeffers on Man and Nature," *Inquiry* 20 (1977): 489).

14. Arne Naess, "Spinoza and Ecology," in Sigfried Hessing, ed., *Speculum Spinozanum 1677–1977* (London: Routledge & Kegan Paul, 1977, p. 421).

STUDY QUESTIONS

1. What is *anthropocentrism* according to Watson? How does it differ from *biocentrism*?

2. Carefully compare Watson's criticism with the articles by Taylor, Leopold, Callicott, Naess, and Sessions. Which of these writers does he attack most directly? Do any escape his critique? Are his critical objections sound?

3. Is Watson's version of environmental anthropocentrism plausible? Explain your answer.

28   Social Ecology Versus Deep Ecology

MURRAY BOOKCHIN

Murray Bookchin has been a leading anarchist and utopian political theorist, especially regarding the philosophy of nature. He is the cofounder and director emeritus of the Institute for Social Ecology. His many books include *Toward an Ecological Society, The Ecology of Freedom*, and *The Philosophy of Social Ecology*.

Social ecology, which Bookchin develops in this essay, is an egalitarian system that has its roots in Marxist and anarchistic thought, though he disagrees with both at crucial points. Against Marx, Bookchin rejects economic determinism and the dictatorship of the proletariat. He rejects anarchist analysis that identifies the modern nation-state as the primary cause of social domination. Bookchin's primary attack is on social domination, and he shows how it is connected to ecology. In *The Ecology of Freedom*, he writes:

> The cultural, traditional and psychological systems of obedience and command are not merely the economic and political systems to which the terms *class* and *State* most appropriately refer. Accordingly, hierarchy and domination could easily continue to exist in a "classless" or "Stateless" society. I refer to the domination of the young by the old, of women by men, of one ethnic group by another, of "masses" by bureaucrats who profess to speak of "higher social interests," of countryside by town, and in a more subtle psychological sense, of body by mind, of spirit by a shallow instrumental rationality.

From: *Socialist Review*, Vol. 88, no. 3 (1988): 11–29. Reprinted with permission of the publisher.

Bookchin promotes an organic view of social theory, wherein the individual finds meaning only in community that he helps create and of which he is a creation. In this essay, Bookchin opposes social ecology to deep ecology.

BEYOND "ENVIRONMENTALISM"

The environmental movement has travelled a long way beyond those annual "Earth Day" festivals when millions of school kids were ritualistically mobilized to clean up streets and their parents were scolded by Arthur Godfrey, Barry Commoner, and Paul Ehrlich. The movement has gone beyond a naive belief that patchwork reforms and solemn vows by EPA bureaucrats will seriously arrest the insane pace at which we are tearing down the planet. This shopworn "Earth Day" approach toward "engineering" nature so that we can ravage the Earth with minimal effects on ourselves—an approach that I called "environmentalism"—has shown signs of giving way to a more searching and radical mentality. Today, the new word in vogue is "ecology"—be it "deep ecology," "human ecology," "biocentric ecology," "anti-humanist ecology," or, to use a term uniquely rich in meaning, "*social* ecology."

Happily, the new relevance of the word "ecology" reveals a growing dissatisfaction with attempts to use our vast ecological problems for cheaply spectacular and politically manipulative ends. Our forests disappear due to mindless cutting and increasing acid rain; the ozone layer thins out from widespread use of fluorocarbons; toxic dumps multiply all over the planet; highly dangerous, often radioactive pollutants enter into our air, water, and food chains. These innumerable hazards threaten the integrity of life itself, raising far more basic issues than can be resolved by "Earth Day" cleanups and faint-hearted changes in environmental laws.

For good reason, more and more people are trying to go beyond the vapid "environmentalism" of the early 1970s and toward an *ecological* approach: one that is rooted in an ecological philosophy, ethics, sensibility, image of nature, and, ultimately, an ecological movement that will transform our domineering market society into a nonhierarchical cooperative one that will

live in harmony with nature, because its members live in harmony with each other. They are beginning to sense that there is a tie-in between the way people deal with each other as social beings—men with women, old with young, rich with poor, white with people of color, first world with third, elites with "masses"—and the way they deal with nature.

The questions that now face us are: what do we really mean by an *ecological* approach? What is a *coherent* ecological philosophy, ethics, and movement? How can the answers to these questions and many others *fit together* so that they form a meaningful and creative whole? If we are not to repeat all the mistakes of the early seventies with their hoopla about "population control," their latent anti-feminism, elitism, arrogance, and ugly authoritarian tendencies, so we must honestly and seriously appraise the new tendencies that today go under the name of one or another form of "ecology."

TWO CONFLICTING TENDENCIES

Let us agree from the outset that the word "ecology" is no magic term that unlocks the real secret of our abuse of nature. It is a word that can be as easily abused, distorted, and tainted as words like "democracy" and "freedom." Nor does the word "ecology" put us all—whoever "we" may be—in the same boat against environmentalists who are simply trying to make a rotten society work by dressing it in green leaves and colorful flowers, while ignoring the deep-seated *roots* of our ecological problems.

It is time to face the fact that there are differences within the so-called "ecology movement" of the present time that are as serious as those between the "environmentalism" and "ecologism" of the early seventies. There are barely disguised racists, survivalists, macho Daniel Boones, and outright social reactionaries who use the word "ecology" to express their views, just as there are deeply concerned naturalists, communitarians, social radicals, and feminists who use the word "ecology" to express theirs.

The differences between these two tendencies in the so-called "ecology movement" consist not only in quarrels over theory, sensibility, and ethics. They have far-reaching *practical* and *political* consequences on the way we view nature, "humanity," and ecology. Most significantly, they concern how we propose to *change* society and by what *means*.

The greatest differences that are emerging within the so-called "ecology movement" of our day are between a vague, formless, often self-contradictory ideology called "deep ecology" and a socially oriented body of ideas best termed "social ecology." Deep ecology has parachuted into our midst quite recently from the Sunbelt's bizarre mix of Hollywood and Disneyland, spiced with homilies from Taoism, Buddhism, spiritualism, reborn Christianity, and, in some cases, eco-fascism. Social ecology, on the other hand, draws its inspiration from such radical decentralist thinkers as Peter Kropotkin, William Morris, and Paul Goodman, among many others who have challenged society's vast hierarchical, sexist, class-ruled, statist, and militaristic apparatus.

Bluntly speaking, deep ecology, despite all its social rhetoric, has no real sense that our ecological problems have their roots in society and in social problems. It preaches a gospel of a kind of "original sin" that accuses a vague species called "humanity"—as though people of color were equatable with whites, women with men, the third world with the first, the poor with the rich, and the exploited with their exploiters. This vague, undifferentiated humanity is seen as an ugly "anthropocentric" thing—presumably a malignant product of natural evolution—that is "overpopulating" the planet, "devouring" its resources, destroying its wildlife and the biosphere. It assumes that some vague domain called "nature" stands opposed to a constellation of non-natural things called "human beings," with their "technology," "minds," "society," and so on. Formulated largely by privileged white male academics, deep ecology has brought sincere naturalists like Paul Shepard into the same company with patently anti-humanist and macho mountain-men like David Foreman, who writes in *Earth First!*—a Tucson-based journal that styles itself as the voice of a wilderness-oriented movement of the same name—that "humanity" is a cancer in the world of life.

It is easy to forget that this same kind of crude eco-brutalism led Hitler to fashion theories of blood and soil that led to the transport of millions of people to murder camps like Auschwitz. The same eco-brutalism now reappears a half-century later among self-professed deep ecologists who believe that famines are nature's "population control" and immigration into the US should be restricted in order to preserve "our" ecological resources.

Simply Living, an Australian periodical, published this sort of eco-brutalism as part of a laudatory interview of David Foreman by Professor Bill Devall, co-author of *Deep Ecology,* the manifesto of the deep ecology movement. Foreman, who exuberantly ex-pressed his commitment to deep ecology, frankly informs Devall that

> When I tell people how the worst thing we could do in Ethiopia is to give aid—the best thing would be to just let nature seek its own balance, to let the people there just starve—they think this is monstrous.... Likewise, letting the USA be an overflow valve for problems in Latin America is not solving a thing. It's just putting more pressure on the resources we have in the USA.

One could reasonably ask what it means for "nature to seek its own balance" in a part of the world where agribusiness, colonialism, and exploitation have ravaged a once culturally and ecologically stable area like East Africa. And who is this all-American "our" that owns the "resources we have in the USA"? Is it the ordinary people who are driven by sheer need to cut timber, mine ores, operate nuclear power plants? Or are they the giant corporations that are not only wrecking the good old USA, but have produced the main problems in Latin America that are sending Indian folk across the Rio Grande? As an ex-Washington lobbyist and political huckster, David Foreman need not be expected to answer these subtle questions in a radical way. But what is truly surprising is the reaction—more precisely, the *lack* of any reaction—which marked Professor Devall's behavior. Indeed, the interview was notable for his almost reverential introduction and description of Foreman.

WHAT IS "DEEP ECOLOGY"?

Deep ecology is enough of a "black hole" of half-digested and ill-formed ideas that a man like Foreman can easily express utterly vicious notions and still sound like a fiery pro-ecology radical. The very words "deep ecology" clue us into the fact that we are not dealing with a body of clear ideas, but with an ideological toxic dump. Does it make sense, for example, to counterpose "deep ecology" with "superficial ecology" as though the word "ecology" were applicable to *everything* that involves environmental issues? Does it not completely degrade the rich meaning of the word "ecology" to append words like "shallow" and "deep" to it? Arne Naess, the pontiff of deep ecology—who, together with George Sessions and Bill Devall, inflicted this vocabulary upon us—has taken a pregnant word—ecology—and stripped it of any inner meaning and integrity by designating the most pedestrian environmentalists as "ecologists," albeit "shallow" ones, in contrast to their notion of "deep."

This is not an example of mere wordplay. It tells us something about the mindset that exists among these "deep" thinkers. To parody the word "shallow" and "deep ecology" is to show not only the absurdity of this terminology but to reveal the superficiality of its inventors. In fact, this kind of absurdity tells us more than we realize about the confusion Naess-Sessions-Devall, not to mention eco-brutalists like Foreman, have introduced into the current ecology movement. Indeed, this trio relies very heavily on the ease with which people forget the history of the ecology movement, the way in which the wheel is reinvented every few years by newly arrived individuals who, well-meaning as they may be, often accept a crude version of highly developed ideas that appeared earlier in a richer context and tradition of ideas. At worst, they shatter such contexts and traditions, picking out tasty pieces that become utterly distorted in a new, utterly alien framework. No regard is paid by such "deep thinkers" to the fact that *the new context in which an idea is placed may utterly change the meaning of the idea itself.* German "National Socialism" was militantly "anti-capitalist." But its "anti-capitalism" was placed in a strongly racist, imperialist, and seemingly "naturalist" context which extolled wilderness, a crude biologism, and anti-rationalism—features one finds in latent or explicit form in Sessions' and Devall's *Deep Ecology*.[1]

Neither Naess, Sessions, nor Devall have written a single line about decentralization, a nonhierarchical society, democracy, small-scale communities, local autonomy, mutual aid, communalism, and tolerance that was not already conceived in painstaking detail and brilliant contextualization by Peter Kropotkin a century ago. But what the boys from Ecotopia do is to totally recontextualize the framework of these ideas, bringing in personalities and notions that basically change their radical libertarian thrust. *Deep Ecology* mingles Woody Guthrie, a Communist Party centralist who no more believed in decentralization than Stalin, with Paul Goodman, an anarchist who would have been mortified to be placed in the same tradition with Guthrie. In philosophy, the book also intermingles Spinoza, a Jew in spirit if not in religious commitment, with Heidegger, a former member of the Nazi party in spirit as well as ideological affiliation—all in the name of a vague word called "process philosophy." Almost opportunistic in their use of catch words and what Orwell called "doublespeak," "process philosophy" makes it possible for Sessions-Devall to add Alfred North Whitehead to their list of ideological ancestors because he called his ideas "processual."

One could go on indefinitely describing this sloppy admixture of "ancestors," philosophical traditions, social pedigrees, and religions that often have nothing in common with each other and, properly conceived, are commonly in sharp opposition with each other. Thus, a reactionary like Thomas Malthus and the tradition he spawned is celebrated with the same enthusiasm in *Deep Ecology* as Henry Thoreau, a radical libertarian who fostered a highly humanistic tradition. Eclecticism would be too mild a word for this kind of hodge-podge, one that seems shrewdly calculated to embrace everyone under the rubric of deep ecology who is prepared to reduce ecology to a religion rather than a systematic and critical body of ideas. This kind of "ecological" thinking surfaces in an appendix to the Devall-Sessions book, called *Ecosophy T,* by Arne Naess, who regales us with flow diagrams and corporate-type tables of organization that have more in common with logical positivist forms of exposition (Naess, in fact, was an acolyte of this school of thought for years) than anything that could be truly called organic philosophy.

If we look beyond the spiritual eco-babble and examine the *context* in which demands like decentralization, small-scale communities, local autonomy, mutual aid, communalism, and tolerance are placed, the blurred images that Sessions and Devall create come into clearer focus. These demands are not intrinsically ecological or emancipatory. Few societies were more decentralized than European feudalism, which was structured around small-scale communities, mutual aid, and the communal use of land. Local autonomy was highly prized, and autarchy formed the economic key to feudal communities. Yet few societies were more hierarchical. The manorial economy of the Middle Ages placed a high premium on autarchy or "self-sufficiency" and spirituality. Yet oppression was often intolerable and the great mass of people who belonged to that society lived in utter subjugation by their "betters" and the nobility.

If "nature worship," with its bouquet of wood sprites, animistic fetishes, fertility rites and other such ceremonies, paves the way to an ecological sensibility and society, then it would be hard to understand how ancient Egypt, with its animal deities and all-presiding goddesses, managed to become one of the most hierarchical and oppressive societies in the ancient world. The Nile River, which provided the "life-giving" waters of the valley, was used in a highly ecological manner. Yet the entire society was structured around the oppression of millions of serfs by opulent nobles, such that one wonders how notions of spirituality can be given priority over the need for a critical evaluation of social structures.

Even if one grants the need for a new sensibility and outlook—a point that has been made repeatedly in the literature of social ecology—one can look behind even this limited context of deep ecology to a still broader context. The love affair of deep ecology with Malthusian doctrines, a spirituality that emphasizes self-effacement, a flirtation with a *super*naturalism that stands in flat contradiction to the refreshing naturalism that ecology has introduced into social theory, a crude positivism in the spirit of Naess—all work against a truly organic dialectic so needed to understand *development*. We shall see that all the bumper-sticker demands like decentralization, small-scale communities, local autonomy, mutual aid, communalism, tolerance, and even an avowed opposition to hierarchy, go awry when we place them in the larger context of anti-humanism and "biocentrism" that mark the authentic ideological infrastructure of deep ecology.

THE ART OF EVADING SOCIETY

The seeming ideological "tolerance" and pluralism which deep ecology celebrates has a sinister function of its own. It not only reduces richly nuanced ideas and conflicting traditions to their lowest common denominator; it legitimates extremely primitivistic and reactionary notions in the company of authentically radical contexts and traditions.

Deep ecology reduces people from social beings to a simple species—to zoological entities that are interchangeable with bears, bisons, deer, or, for that matter, fruit flies and microbes. The fact that people can consciously change themselves and society, indeed enhance that natural world in a free ecological society, is dismissed as "humanism." Deep ecology essentially ignores the social nature of humanity and the social origins of the ecological crises.

This "zoologization" of human beings and of society yields sinister results. The role of capitalism with its competitive "grow or die" market economy—an economy that would devour the biosphere whether there were 10 billion people on the planet or 10 million—is simply vaporized into a vapid spiritualism. Taoist and Buddhist pieties replace the need for social and economic analysis, and self-indulgent encounter groups replace the need for political organization and action. Above all, deep ecologists explain the destruction of human beings in terms of the same "natural laws" that are said to govern the population vicissitudes of lemmings. The fact that major reductions of populations would not diminish levels of production and the destruction of the biosphere in a capitalist economy totally eludes Devall, Sessions, and their followers.

In failing to emphasize the unique characteristics of human societies and to give full due to the self-reflective role of human consciousness, deep ecologists essentially evade the *social* roots of the ecological crisis. Deep ecology contains no history of the emergence of society out of nature, a crucial development that brings social theory into organic contact with ecological theory. It presents no explanation of—indeed, it reveals no interest in—the emergence of hierarchy out of society, of classes out of hierarchy, of the state out of classes—in short, the highly graded social as well as ideological developments which are at the roots of the ecological problem.

Instead, we not only lose sight of the social differences that fragment "humanity" into a host of human beings—men and women, ethnic groups, oppressors and oppressed—we lose sight of the individual self in an unending flow of eco-babble that preaches the "realization of self-in-Self where the 'Self' stands for organic wholeness." More of the same cosmic eco-babble appears when we are informed that the "phrase 'one' includes not only men, an individual human, but all humans, grizzly bears, whole rain forest ecosystems, mountains and rivers, the tiniest microbes in the soil, and so on."

ON SELFHOOD AND VIRUSES

Such flippant abstractions of human individuality are extremely dangerous. Historically, a "Self" that absorbs all real existential selves has been used from time immemorial to absorb individual uniqueness and freedom into a supreme "Individual" who heads the state, churches of various sorts, adoring congregations, and spellbound constituencies. The purpose is the same, no matter how much such a "Self" is dressed up in ecological, naturalistic, and "biocentric" attributes. The Paleolithic shaman, in reindeer skins and

horns, is the predecessor of the Pharaoh, the Buddha, and, in more recent times, of Hitler, Stalin, and Mussolini.

That the egotistical, greedy, and soloist bourgeois "self" has always been a repellent being goes without saying, and deep ecology as put forth by Devall and Sessions makes the most of it. But is there not a free, independently minded, ecologically concerned, idealistic self with a unique personality that can think of itself as different from "whales, grizzly bears, whole rain forest ecosystems (no less!), mountains and rivers, the tiniest microbes in the soil, and so on"? Is it not indispensable, in fact, for the individual self to disengage itself from a Pharonic "Self," discover its own capacities and uniqueness, and acquire a sense of personality, of self-control and self-direction—all traits indispensable for the achievement of *freedom*? Here, one can imagine Heidegger grimacing with satisfaction at the sight of this self-effacing and passive personality so yielding that it can easily be shaped, distorted, and manipulated by a new "ecological" state machinery with a supreme "Self" at its head. And this all in the name of a "biocentric equality" that is slowly reworked as it has been so often in history, into a social hierarchy. From Shaman to Monarch, from Priest or Priestess to Dictator, our warped social development has been marked by "nature worshippers" and their ritual Supreme Ones who produced unfinished individuals at best or deindividuated the "self-in-Self" at worst, often in the name of the "Great Connected Whole" (to use *exactly* the language of the Chinese ruling classes who kept their peasantry in abject servitude, as Leon E. Stover points out in his *The Cultural Ecology of Chinese Civilization*).

What makes this eco-babble especially dangerous today is that we are already living in a period of massive de-individuation. This is not because deep ecology or Taoism is making any serious in-roads into our own cultural ecology, but because the mass media, the commodity culture, and a market society are "reconnecting" us into an increasingly depersonalized "whole" whose essence is passivity and a chronic vulnerability to economic and political manipulation. It is not an excess of "selfhood" from which we are suffering, but rather the surrender of personality to the security and control of corporations, centralized government, and the military. If "selfhood" is identified with a grasping, "anthropocentric," and devouring personality, these traits are to be found not so much among ordinary people, who basically sense they have no control over their destinies, but among the giant corporations and state leaders who are not only plundering the planet, but also robbing from women, people of color, and the underprivileged. It is not deindividuation that the oppressed of the world require, but *re*individuation that will transform them into active agents in the task of remaking society and arresting the growing totalitarianism that threatens to homogenize us all into a Western version of the "Great Connected Whole."

We are also confronted with the delicious "and so on" that follows the "tiniest microbes in the soil" with which our deep ecologists identify the "Self." Taking their argument to its logical extreme, one might ask: why stop with the "tiniest microbes in the soil" and ignore the leprosy microbe, the viruses that give us smallpox, polio, and, more recently, AIDS? Are they, too, not part of "all organisms and entities in the eco-sphere-of the interrelated whole...equal in intrinsic worth...,"as Devall and Sessions remind us in their effluvium of eco-babble? Naess, Devall, and Sessions rescue themselves by introducing a number of highly debatable qualifiers:

> The slogan of "noninterference" does not imply that humans should not modify some ecosystems as do other species. Humans have modified the Earth and will probably continue to do so. At issue is the nature and extent of such interference.

One does not leave the muck of deep ecology without having mud all over one's feet. Exactly *who* is to decide the "nature" of human "interference" in nature and the "extent" to which it can be done? What are "some" of the ecosystems we can modify and which ones are not subject to human "interference"? Here, again, we encounter the key problem that deep ecology poses for serious, ecologically concerned people: the *social* bases of our ecological problems and the role of

the human species in the evolutionary scheme of things.

Implicit in deep ecology is the notion that a "Humanity" exists that accurses the natural world; that individual selfhood must be transformed into a cosmic "Selfhood" that essentially transcends the person and his or her uniqueness. Even nature is not spared from a kind of static, prepositional logic that is cultivated by the logical positivists. "Nature," in deep ecology and David Foreman's interpretation of it, becomes a kind of scenic view, a spectacle to be admired around the campfire. It is not viewed as an *evolutionary* development that is cumulative and *includes* the human species.

The problems deep ecology and biocentricity raise have not gone unnoticed in the more thoughtful press in England. During a discussion of "biocentric ethics" in *The New Scientist* 69 (1976), for example, Bernard Dixon observed that no "logical line can be drawn" between the conservation of whales, gentians, and flamingoes on the one hand and the extinction of pathogenic microbes like the smallpox virus. At which point David Ehrenfeld, in his *Arrogance of Humanism,*[2]—a work that is so selective and tendentious in its use of quotations that it should validly be renamed "The Arrogance of Ignorance"—cutely observes that the smallpox virus is "an endangered species." One wonders what to do about the AIDS virus if a vaccine or therapy should threaten its "survival"? Further, given the passion for perpetuating the "ecosystem" of every species, one wonders how smallpox and AIDS viruses should be preserved? In test tubes? Laboratory cultures? Or, to be truly "ecological" in their "native habitat," the human body? In which case, idealistic acolytes of deep ecology should be invited to offer their own bloodstreams in the interests of "biocentric equality." Certainly, "if nature should be permitted to take its course"—as Foreman advises for Ethiopians and Indian peasants—plagues, famines, suffering, wars, and perhaps even lethal asteroids of the kind that exterminated the great reptiles of the Mesozoic should not be kept from defacing the purity of "first nature" by the intervention of human ingenuity and—yes!—*technology*. With so much absurdity to unscramble, one can indeed get heady, almost dizzy, with a sense of polemical intoxication.

At root, the eclecticism which turns deep ecology into a goulash of notions and moods is insufferably reformist and surprisingly environmentalist—all its condemnations of "superficial ecology" aside. Are you, perhaps, a mild-mannered liberal? Then do not fear: Devall and Sessions give a patronizing nod to "reform legislation," "coalitions," "protests," the "women's movement" (this earns all of ten lines in their "Minority Tradition and Direct Action" essay), "working in the Christian tradition" "questioning technology" (a hammering remark, if there ever was one), "working in Green politics" (which faction, the "fundies" or the "realos"?). In short, everything can be expected in so "cosmic" a philosophy. Anything seems to pass through deep ecology's donut hole: anarchism at one extreme and eco-fascism at the other. Like the fast food emporiums that make up our culture, deep ecology is the fast food of quasi-radical environmentalists.

Despite its pretense of "radicality," deep ecology is more "New Age" and "Aquarian" than the environmentalist movements it denounces under those names. Indeed, the extent to which deep ecology accommodates itself to some of the worst features of the "dominant view" it professes to reject is seen with extraordinary clarity in one of its most fundamental and repeatedly asserted demands—namely, that the world's population must be drastically reduced, according to one of its devotees, to 500 million. If deep ecologists have even the faintest knowledge of the "population theorists" Devall and Sessions invoke with admiration—notably, Thomas Malthus, William Vogt, and Paul Ehrlich—then they would be obliged to add: by measures that are virtually eco-fascist. This specter clearly looms before us in Devall's and Sessions' sinister remark: "...the longer we wait [for population control], the more drastic will be the measures needed."

THE "DEEP" MALTHUSIANS

Devall and Sessions often write with smug assurance on issues they know virtually nothing about. This is most notably the case in the so-called "population debate," a debate that has raged for over two hundred years and more and involves explosive political and social issues that have pitted the most reactionary elements in English and American society against authentic radicals. In fact, the eco-babble which Devall and Sessions dump on us in only two paragraphs would require a full-sized volume of careful analysis to unravel.

Devall and Sessions hail Thomas Malthus (1766–1854) as a prophet whose warning "that human population growth would exponentially outstrip food production...was ignored by the rising tide of industrial/technological optimism." First of all, Thomas Malthus was not a prophet; he was an apologist for the misery that the Industrial Revolution was inflicting on the English peasantry and working classes. His utterly fallacious argument that population increases exponentially while food supplies increase arithmetically was not ignored by England's ruling classes; it was taken to heart and even incorporated into social Darwinism as an explanation of why oppression was a necessary feature of society and why the rich, the white imperialists, and the privileged were the "fittest" who were equipped to "survive"—needless to say, at the expense of the impoverished many. Written and directed in great part as an attack upon the liberatory vision of William Godwin, Malthus' mean-spirited *Essay on the Principle of Population* tried to demonstrate that hunger, poverty, disease, and premature death are *inevitable* precisely because population and food supply increase at different rates. Hence war, famines, and plagues (Malthus later added "moral restraint") were necessary to keep population down—needless to say, among the "lower orders of society," whom he singles out as the chief offenders of his inexorable population "laws."[3] Malthus, in effect, became the ideologue par excellence for the land-grabbing English nobility in its effort to dispossess the peasantry of their traditional common lands and for the English capitalists to work children, women, and men to death in the newly emergent "industrial/technological" factory system.

Malthusianism contributed in great part to that meanness of spirit that Charles Dickens captured in his famous novels, *Oliver Twist* and

Hard Times. The doctrine, its author, and its overstuffed wealthy beneficiaries were bitterly fought by the great English anarchist, William Godwin, the pioneering socialist, Robert Owen, and the emerging Chartist movement of English workers in the early 19th century. However, Malthusianism was naively picked up by Charles Darwin to explain his theory of "natural selection." It then became the bedrock theory for the new *social* Darwinism, so very much in vogue in the late nineteenth and early twentieth centuries, which saw society as a "jungle" in which only the "fit" (usually, the rich and white) could "survive" at the expense of the "unfit" (usually, the poor and people of color). Malthus, in effect, had provided an ideology that justified class domination, racism, the degradation of women, and, ultimately, British imperialism.

Malthusianism was not only revived in Hitler's Third Reich; it also reemerged in the late 1940s, following the discoveries of antibiotics to control infectious diseases. Riding on the tide of the new Pax Americana after World War II, William F. Vogt and a whole bouquet of neo-Malthusians were to challenge the use of the new antibiotic discoveries to control disease and prevent death—as usual, mainly in Asia, Africa, and Latin America. Again, a new "population debate" erupted, with the Rockefeller interests and large corporate sharks aligning themselves with the neo-Malthusians, and caring people of every sort aligning themselves with third world theorists like Josua de Castro, who wrote damning, highly informed critiques of this new version of misanthropy.

Zero Population Growth fanatics in the early seventies literally polluted the environmental movement with demands for a government bureau to "control" population, advancing the infamous "triage" ethic, according to which various "underdeveloped" countries would be granted or refused aid on the basis of their compliance to population control measures. In *Food First*, Francis Moore Lappe and Joseph Collins have done a superb job in showing how hunger has its origins not in "natural" shortages of food or population growth, but in social and cultural dislocations. (It is notable that Devall and Sessions do *not* list this excellent book in their bibliography.) The book has to be read to

understand the reactionary implications of deep ecology's demographic positions.

Demography is a highly ambiguous and ideologically charged social discipline that cannot be reduced to a mere numbers game in biological reproduction. Human beings are not fruit flies (the species which the neo-Malthusians love to cite). Their reproductive behavior is profoundly conditioned by cultural values, standards of living, social traditions, gender relations, religious beliefs, socio-political conflicts, and various socio-political expectations. Smash up a stable, precapitalist culture and throw its people off the land into city slums, and, due to demoralization, population may soar rather than decline. As Gandhi told the British, imperialism left India's wretched poor and homeless with little more in life than the immediate gratification provided by sex and an understandably numbed sense of personal, much less social, responsibility. Reduce women to mere reproductive factories and population rates will explode.

Conversely, provide people with decent lives, education, a sense of creative meaning in life, and, above all, expand the role of women in society—and population growth begins to stabilize and population rates even reverse their direction. Nothing more clearly reveals deep ecology's crude, often reactionary, and certainly superficial ideological framework—all its decentralist, anti-hierarchical, and "radical" rhetoric aside—than its suffocating "biological" treatment of the population issue and its inclusion of Malthus, Vogt, and Ehrlich in its firmament of prophets.

Not surprisingly, the *Earth First!* newsletter, whose editor professes to be an enthusiastic deep ecologist, carried an article titled "Population and AIDS" which advanced the obscene argument that AIDS is desirable as a means of population control. This was no spoof. It was earnestly argued and carefully reasoned in a Paleolithic sort of way. Not only will AIDS claim large numbers of lives, asserts the author (who hides under the pseudonym of "Miss Ann Thropy," a form of black humor that could also pass as an example of macho-male arrogance), but it "may cause a breakdown in technology (read: human food supply) and its export which could also decrease human population." These people feed on human disasters, suffering, and misery, preferably in third world countries where AIDS is by far a more monstrous problem than elsewhere.

We have little reason to doubt that this mentality is perfectly consistent with the "more drastic . . . measures" Devall and Sessions believe we will have to explore. Nor is it inconsistent with Malthus and Vogt that we should make no effort to find a cure for this disease which may do so much to depopulate the world. "Biocentric democracy," I assume, should call for nothing less than a "hands-off" policy on the AIDS virus and perhaps equally lethal pathogens that appear in the human species.

WHAT IS SOCIAL ECOLOGY?

Social ecology is neither "deep," "tall," "fat," nor "thick." It is *social*. It does not fall back on incantations, sutras, flow diagrams or spiritual vagaries. It is avowedly *rational*. It does not try to regale metaphorical forms of spiritual mechanism and crude biologism with Taoist, Buddhist, Christian, or shamanistic eco-babble. It is a coherent form of *naturalism* that looks to *evolution* and the *biosphere*, not to deities in the sky or under the earth for quasi-religious and supernaturalistic explanations of natural and social phenomena.

Philosophically, social ecology stems from a solid organismic tradition in Western philosophy, beginning with Heraclitus, the near-evolutionary dialectic of Aristotle and Hegel, and the critical approach of the famous Frankfurt School—particularly its devastating critique of logical positivism (which surfaces in Naess repeatedly) and the primitivistic mysticism of Heidegger (which pops up all over the place in deep ecology's literature).

Socially, it is revolutionary, not merely "radical." It critically unmasks the entire evolution of hierarchy in all its forms, including neo-Malthusian elitism, the eco-brutalism of David Foreman, the anti-humanism of David Ehrenfeld and "Miss Ann Thropy," and the latent racism, first-world arrogance, and Yuppie nihilism of postmodernistic spiritualism. It is noted in the profound eco-anarchistic analyses of Peter Kropotkin, the radical economic insights of Karl Marx, the emancipatory promise of the revolutionary Enlightenment as articulated by the great

encyclopedist, Denis Diderot, the *Enrages* of the French Revolution, the revolutionary feminist ideals of Louise Michel and Emma Goldman, the communitarian visions of Paul Goodman and E. A. Gutkind, and the various eco-revolutionary manifestoes of the early 1960s.

Politically, it is *green*—radically green. It takes its stand with the left-wing tendencies in the German Greens and extra-parliamentary street movements of European cities; with the American radical ecofeminist movement; with the demands for a new politics based on citizens' initiatives, neighborhood assemblies, and New England's tradition of town-meetings; with non-aligned anti-imperialist movements at home and abroad; with the struggle by people of color for complete freedom from the domination of privileged whites and from the superpowers.

Morally, it is *humanistic* in the high Renaissance meaning of the term, not the degraded meaning of "humanism" that has been imparted to the world by David Foreman, David Ehrenfeld, and a salad of academic deep ecologists. Humanism from its inception has meant a shift in vision from the skies to the earth, from superstition to reason, from deities to people—who are no less products of natural evolution than grizzly bears and whales. Social ecology accepts neither a "biocentricity" that essentially denies or degrades the uniqueness of human beings, human subjectivity, rationality, aesthetic sensibility, and the ethical potentiality of humanity, nor an "anthropocentricity" that confers on the privileged few the right to plunder the world of life, including human life. Indeed, it opposes "centricity" of *any* kind as a new word for hierarchy and domination—be it that of nature by a mystical "Man" or the domination of people by an equally mystical "Nature." It firmly denies that nature is a static, scenic view which Mountain Men like a Foreman survey from a peak in Nevada or a picture window that spoiled yuppies view from their ticky-tacky country homes. To social ecology, nature *is* natural *evolution*, not a cosmic arrangement of beings frozen in a moment of eternity to be abjectly revered, adored, and worshipped like Gods and Goddesses in a realm of "*super*nature." Natural evolution is nature in the very real sense that it is composed of atoms, molecules that have evolved into amino acids, proteins, unicellular organisms, genetic codes, invertebrates and vertebrates, amphibia, reptiles, mammals, primates, and human beings—all, in a cumulative thrust toward ever-greater complexity, ever-greater subjectivity, and finally, an ever-greater capacity for conceptual thought, symbolic communication, and self-consciousness.

This marvel we call "Nature" has produced a marvel we call homo sapiens—"thinking man"—and, more significantly for the development of society, "thinking woman," whose primeval domestic domain provided the arena for the origins of a caring society, human empathy, love, and idealistic commitment. The human species, in effect, is no less a product of natural evolution and differentiation than blue-green algae. To degrade the human species in the name of "anti-humanism," to deny people their uniqueness as thinking beings with an unprecedented gift for conceptual thought, is to deny the rich fecundity of natural evolution itself. To separate human beings and society from nature is to dualize and truncate nature itself, to diminish the meaning and thrust of natural evolution in the name of a "biocentricity" that spends more time disporting itself with mantras, deities, and supernature than with the realities of the biosphere and the role of society in ecological problems.

Accordingly, social ecology does not try to hide its critical and reconstructive thrust in metaphors. It calls "technological/industrial" society *capitalism*—a word which places the onus for our ecological problems on the *living* sources and *social* relationships that produce them, not on a cutesy "Third Wave" abstraction which buries these sources in technics, a technical "mentality," or perhaps the technicians who work on machines. It sees the domination of women not simply as a "spiritual" problem that can be resolved by rituals, incantations, and shamannesses, important as ritual may be in solidarizing women into a unique community of people, but in the long, highly graded, and subtly nuanced development of hierarchy, which long preceded the development of classes. Nor does it ignore class, ethnic differences, imperialism, and oppression by creating a grab-bag called "Humanity" that is placed in opposition to a mystified "Nature," divested of all development.

All of which brings us as social ecologists to an issue that seems to be totally alien to the crude concerns of deep ecology: natural evolution has conferred on human beings the capacity to form a "second" or cultural nature out of "first" or primeval nature. Natural evolution has not only provided humans with the *ability,* but also the *necessity* to be purposive interveners into "first nature," to consciously *change* "first nature" by means of a highly institutionalized form of community we call "society." It is not alien to natural evolution that a species called human beings have emerged over the billions of years who are capable of thinking in a sophisticated way. Nor is it alien for human beings to develop a highly sophisticated form of symbolic communication which a new kind of community—institutionalized, guided by thought rather than by instinct alone, and ever-changing—has emerged called "society."

Taken together, all of these human traits—intellectual, communicative, and social—have not only emerged from natural evolution and are inherently human; they can also be placed at the *service* of natural evolution to consciously increase biotic diversity, diminish suffering, foster the further evolution of new and ecologically valuable life-forms, reduce the impact of disastrous accidents or the harsh effects of mere change.

Whether this species, gifted by the creativity of natural evolution, can play the role of a nature rendered self-conscious or cut against the grain of natural evolution by simplifying the biosphere, polluting it, and undermining the cumulative results of organic evolution is above all a *social* problem. The primary question ecology faces today is whether an ecologically oriented society can be created out of the present anti-ecological one.

Unless there is a resolute attempt to fully anchor ecological dislocations in social dislocations; to challenge the vested corporate and political interests we should properly call *capitalism;* to analyze, explore, and attack hierarchy as a *reality,* not only as a sensibility; to recognize the material needs of the poor and of third world people; to function politically, and not simply as a religious cult; to give the human species and mind their due in natural evolution, rather than regard them as " in the biosphere; to examine economies as well as "souls," and freedom instead of scholastic arguments about the "rights" of pathogenic viruses—unless, in short, North American Greens and the ecology movement shift their focus toward a *social ecology* and let deep ecology sink into the pit it has created for us, the ecology movement will become another ugly wart on the skin of society.

What we must do, today, is return to *nature,* conceived in all its fecundity, richness of potentialities, and subjectivity—not to *super*nature with its shamans, priests, priestesses, and fanciful deities that are merely anthropomorphic extensions and distortions of the "Human" as all-embracing divinities. And what we must "enchant" is not only an abstract image of "Nature" *that often reflects our own systems of power, hierarchy, and domination*—but rather human beings, the human mind, the human spirit.

NOTES

1. Unless otherwise indicated, all future references and quotes come from Bills Devall and George Sessions, *Deep Ecology* (Layton, UT: Gibbs M. Smith, 1985), a book which has essentially become the bible of the "movement" that bears its name.
2. David Ehrenfeld, *The Arrogance of Humanism* (New York: The Modern Library, 1978) pp. 207–211.
3. Chapter Five of his *Essay,* which, for all its "concern" over the misery of the "lower classes," inveighs against the poor laws and argues that the "pressures of distress on this part of the community is an evil so deeply seated that no human ingenuity can reach it." Thomas Malthus, *On Population* (New York: The Modern Library), p. 34.

STUDY QUESTIONS

1. Examine Bookchin's attack on deep ecology. What are his reasons for opposing it? Are his epithets "eco-brutalism," eco-babble," and so forth, justified? Does Bookchin make a good case for rejecting deep ecology? Or are his attacks incomplete, rhetorical, and ad hominem?

2. What are Bookchin's major assumptions in this essay? Are they defended? Are they defensible?
3. What is *social ecology*? What are its main features? How well does Bookchin defend it?

29   Environmental Justice: Reconciling Anthropocentric and Nonanthropocentric Ethics

JAMES P. STERBA

James Sterba is professor of philosophy at the University of Notre Dame and president of the North American Society for Social Philosophy. His many books include *How to Make People Just, Morality in Practice, Feminist Philosophies,* and *Justice: Alternative Political Perspectives.*

Sterba has offered the following abstract:

This essay was written for the second edition of this book and appeared there in print for the first time.

A central debate, if not the most central debate, in contemporary environmental ethics is between those who defend anthropocentric ethics, which holds that humans are superior overall to the members of other species, and those who defend nonanthropocentric ethics, which holds that the members of all species are equal. In this essay, I propose to go some way toward resolving this debate by showing that, when the most morally defensible versions of each of these perspectives are laid out, they do not lead to different practical requirements. In this way, I hope to show how it is possible for defenders of anthropocentric and nonanthropocentric environmental ethics, despite their theoretical disagreement concerning whether humans are superior to members of other species, to agree on a common set of principles for achieving environmental justice.

NONANTHROPOCENTRIC ENVIRONMENTAL ETHICS

Consider first the nonanthropocentric perspective. In support of this perspective, it can be argued that we have no non-question-begging grounds for regarding the members of any living species as superior to the members of any other. It allows that the members of species differ in a myriad of ways but argues that these differences do not provide grounds for thinking that the members of any one species are superior to the members of any other. In particular, it denies that the differences between species provides grounds for thinking that humans are superior to the members of other species. Of course, the nonanthropocentric perspective recognizes that humans have distinctive traits that members of other species lack, like rationality and moral agency. It just points out that the members of nonhuman species also have distinctive traits that humans lack, like the homing ability of pigeons, the speed of the cheetah, and the ruminative ability of sheep and cattle.

Nor will it do to claim that the distinctive traits that humans have are more valuable than the distinctive traits that members of other species possess because there is no non-question-begging standpoint from which to justify that claim. From a human standpoint, rationality and moral agency are more valuable than any of the distinctive traits found in nonhuman species, since, as humans, we would not be better off if we were to trade in those traits for the distinctive traits found in nonhuman species. Yet the same holds true of nonhuman species. Generally, pigeons, cheetahs, sheep, and cattle would not be better off if they were to trade in their distinctive traits for the distinctive traits of other species.

Of course, the members of some species might be better off if they could retain the distinctive traits of their species while acquiring one or another of the distinctive traits possessed by some other species. For example, we humans might be better off if we could retain our distinctive traits while acquiring the ruminative ability of sheep and cattle. But many of the distinctive traits of species cannot be even imaginatively added to the members of other species without substantially altering the original species. For example, for the cheetah to acquire the distinctive traits possessed by humans, presumably it would have to be so transformed that its paws became something like hands to accommodate its humanlike mental capabilities, thereby losing its distinctive speed and ceasing to be a cheetah. So possessing distinctively human traits would not be good for the cheetah. And with the possible exception of our nearest evolutionary relatives, the same holds true for the members of other species; they would not be better off having distinctively human traits. Only in fairy tales and in the world of Disney can the members of nonhuman species enjoy a full array of distinctively human traits. So there would appear to be no non-question-begging perspective from which to judge that distinctively human traits are more valuable than the distinctive traits possessed by other species. Judged from a non-question-begging perspective, we would seemingly have to regard the members of all species as equals.

It might be useful at this point to make my argument even more explicit. Here is one way this could be done.

1. We should not aggress against any living being unless there are either self-evident or

non-question-begging reasons for doing so. (It would be difficult to reject this principle given the various analogous principles we accept, such as the principle of formal equality: Equals should be treated equally and unequals unequally.)

2. To treat humans as superior overall to other living beings is to aggress against them by sacrificing their basic needs to meet the nonbasic needs of humans. (Definition)

3. Therefore, we should not treat humans as superior overall to other living beings unless we have either self-evident or non-question-begging reasons for doing so. (From 1 and 2)

4. We do not have either self-evident or non-question-begging reasons for treating humans as superior overall to other living beings. (That we do not have any non-question-begging reasons for treating humans as superior overall to other living beings was established by the previous argument. That we do not have any self-evident reasons for doing so, I take it, is obvious.)

5. Therefore, we should not treat humans as superior overall to other living beings. (From 3 and 4)

6. Not to treat humans as superior overall to other living beings is to treat them as equal overall to other living beings. (Definition)

7. Therefore, we should treat humans as equal overall to other living beings. (From 5 and 6)

Nevertheless, I want to go on to claim that regarding the members of all species as equals still allows for human preference in the same way that regarding all humans as equals still allows for self preference. First of all, human preference can be justified on grounds of defense. Thus, we have a

Principle of human defense: Actions that defend oneself and other human beings against harmful aggression are permissible even when they necessitate killing or harming animals or plants.

This principle of human defense allows us to defend ourselves and other human beings from harmful aggression first against our persons and the persons of other humans beings that we are committed to or happen to care about and second against our justifiably held property and the justifiably held property of other human beings that we are committed to or happen to care about.

This principle is analogous to the principle of self-defense that applies in human ethics and permits actions in defense of oneself or other human beings against harmful human aggression. In the case of human aggression, however, it will sometimes be possible to effectively defend oneself and other human beings by first suffering the aggression and then securing adequate compensation later. Since in the case of nonhuman aggression this is unlikely to obtain, more harmful preventive actions such as killing a rabid dog or swatting a mosquito will be justified. There are simply more ways to effectively stop aggressive humans than there are to stop aggressive nonhumans.

Second, human preference can also be justified on grounds of preservation. Accordingly, we have a

Principle of human preservation: Actions that are necessary for meeting one's basic needs or the basic needs of other human beings are permissible even when they require aggressing against the basic needs of animals and plants.

Now needs, in general, if not satisfied, lead to lacks or deficiencies with respect to various standards. The basic needs of humans, if not satisfied, lead to lacks or deficiencies with respect to a standard of a decent life. The basic needs of animals and plants, if not satisfied, lead to lacks or deficiencies with respect to a standard of a healthy life. The means necessary for meeting the basic needs of humans can vary widely from society to society. By contrast, the means necessary for meeting the basic needs of particular species of animals and plants are more invariant.

In human ethics, there is no principle that is strictly analogous to this principle of human preservation. There is a principle of self-preservation in human ethics that permits actions that are necessary for meeting one's own basic needs or the basic needs of other people, even if this requires *failing to meet* (through an act of omission) the basic needs of still other people. For example, we can use our resources to feed ourselves and our family, even if this necessitates failing to meet the basic needs of people in third world countries. But, in general, we don't have a principle that allows us to *aggress against* (through an act of commission) the basic needs of some people in order to meet our own basic needs or the basic needs of other people to whom we are committed or happen to care about. Actually, the closest we come to permitting aggressing against the basic needs of other people in order to meet our own basic needs or the basic needs of people to whom we are committed or happen to care about is our acceptance of the outcome of life and death struggles in lifeboat cases, where no one has an antecedent right to the available resources. For example, if you had to fight off others in order to secure the last place in a lifeboat for yourself or for a member of your family, we might say that you justifiably aggressed against the basic needs of those whom you fought to meet your own basic needs or the basic needs of the member of your family.

Nevertheless, our survival requires a principle of preservation that permits aggressing against the basic needs of at least some other living things whenever this is necessary to meet our own basic needs or the basic needs of other human beings. Here there are two possibilities. The first is a principle of preservation that allows us to aggress against the basic needs of both humans and nonhumans whenever it would serve our own basic needs or the basic needs of other human beings. The second is the principle, given above, that allows us to aggress against the basic needs of only nonhumans whenever it would serve our own basic needs or the basic needs of other human beings. The first principle does not express any general preference for the members of the human species, and thus it permits even cannibalism provided that it serves to meet our own basic needs or the basic needs of other human beings. In contrast, the second principle does express a degree of preference for the members of the human species in cases where their basic needs are at stake. Happily, this degree of preference for our own species is still compatible with the equality of all species because favoring the members of one's own species to this extent is characteristic of the members of nearly all species with which we interact and is thereby

legitimated. The reason it is legitimated is that we would be required to sacrifice the basic needs of members of the human species only if the members of other species were making similar sacrifices for the sake of members of the human species. In addition, if we were to prefer consistently the basic needs of the members of other species whenever those needs conflicted with our own (or even if we do so half the time), given the characteristic behavior of the members of other species, we would soon be facing extinction, and, fortunately, we have no reason to think that we are morally required to bring about our own extinction. For these reasons, the degree of preference for our own species found in the principle of human preservation is justified, even if we were to adopt a nonanthropocentric perspective.

Nevertheless, preference for humans can go beyond bounds, and the bounds that are compatible with a nonanthropocentric perspective are expressed by the following:

> *Principle of disproportionality:* Actions that meet nonbasic or luxury needs of humans are prohibited when they aggress against the basic needs of animals and plants.

This principle is strictly analogous to the principle in human ethics mentioned previously that prohibits meeting some people's nonbasic or luxury needs by aggressing against the basic needs of other people.

Without a doubt, the adoption of such a principle with respect to nonhuman nature would significantly change the way we live our lives. Such a principle is required, however, if there is to be any substance to the claim that the members of all species are equal. We can no more consistently claim that the members of all species are equal and yet aggress against the basic needs of some animals or plants whenever this serves our own nonbasic or luxury needs than we can consistently claim that all humans are equal and aggress against the basic needs of some other human beings whenever this serves our nonbasic or luxury needs. Consequently, if species equality is to mean anything, it must be the case that the basic needs of the members of nonhuman species are protected against aggressive actions which only serve to meet the nonbasic needs of humans, as required by the principle of disproportionality.

So while a nonanthropocentric perspective allows for a degree of preference for the members of the human species, it also significantly limits that preference.

To see why these limits on preference for the members of the human species are all that is required for recognizing the equality of species, we need to understand the equality of species by analogy with the equality of humans. We need to see that just as we claim that humans are equal but treat them differently, so too we can claim that all species are equal but treat them differently. In human ethics, there are various interpretations given to human equality that allow for different treatment of humans. In ethical egoism, everyone is *equally at liberty* to pursue his or her own interests, but this allows us to always prefer ourselves to others, who are understood to be like opponents in a competitive game. In libertarianism, everyone has an *equal right to liberty,* but although this imposes some limits on the pursuit of self-interest, it is said to allow us to refrain from helping others in severe need. In welfare liberalism, everyone has an *equal right to welfare and opportunity,* but this need not commit us to providing everyone with exactly the same resources. In socialism, everyone has an *equal right* to self-development, and although this may commit us to providing everyone with the same resources, it still sanctions some degree of self-preference. So just as there are these various ways to interpret human equality that still allow us to treat humans differently, there are various ways that we can interpret species equality that allow us to treat species differently.

Now one might interpret species equality in a very strong sense, analogous to the interpretation of equality found in socialism. But the kind of species equality that I have defended is more akin to the equality found in welfare liberalism or in libertarianism than it is to the equality found in socialism. In brief, this form of equality requires that we not aggress against the basic needs of the members of other species for the sake of the nonbasic needs of the members of our own species (the principle of disproportionality), but it permits us to aggress against the basic needs of the members of other species for the sake of the basic needs of the members of our own species (the principle of human preservation) and also permits us to defend the basic and even the nonbasic needs of the members of our own species against harmful aggression by members of other species (the principle of human defense). In this way, I have argued that we can accept the claim of species equality, while avoiding imposing an unreasonable sacrifice on the members of our own species.

INDIVIDUALISM AND HOLISM

It might be objected here that I have not yet taken into account the conflict within a nonanthropocentric ethics between holists and individualists. According to holists, the good of a species or the good of an ecosystem or the good of the whole biotic community can trump the good of individual living things.[1] According to individualists, the good of each individual living thing must be respected.[2]

Now one might think that holists would require that we abandon my principle of human preservation. Yet consider. Assuming that people's basic needs are at stake, how could it be morally objectionable for them to try to meet those needs, even if this were to harm nonhuman individuals, or species, or whole ecosystems, or even, to some degree, the whole biotic community? Of course, we can *ask* people in such conflict cases not to meet their basic needs in order to prevent harm to nonhuman individuals or species, ecosystems or the whole biotic community. But if people's basic needs are at stake, we cannot reasonably demand that they make such a sacrifice. We could demand, of course, that people do all that they reasonably can to keep such conflicts from arising in the first place, for, just as in human ethics, many severe conflicts of interest can be avoided simply by doing what is morally required early on. Nevertheless, when people's basic needs are at stake, the individualist perspective seems incontrovertible. We cannot reasonably require people to be saints.

At the same time, when people's basic needs are not at stake, we would be justified in acting on holistic grounds to prevent serious harm to nonhuman individuals, or species, or ecosystems, or the whole biotic community. Obviously, it will be difficult to know when our interventions will have this effect, but when we can be reasonably sure that they will, such interventions (e.g., culling elk herds in wolf-free ranges or preserving the habitat of endangered species) would be morally permissible and maybe even morally required.[3] This shows that it is possible to agree with individualists when the basic needs of human beings are at stake and to agree with holists when they are not.

Yet this combination of individualism and holism appears to conflict with the equality of species by imposing greater sacrifices on the members of nonhuman species than it does on the members of the human species. Fortunately, appearances are deceiving here. Although the proposed resolution only justifies imposing holism when people's basic needs are not at stake, it does not justify imposing individualism at all. Rather it would simply permit individualism when people's basic needs *are* at stake. Of course, we could impose holism under all conditions. But given that this would, in effect, involve going to war against people who are simply striving to meet their own basic needs in the only way they can, as permitted by the principle of human preservation, intervention in such cases would not be justified. It would involve taking away the means of survival from people, even when these means are not required for one's own survival.

Nevertheless, this combination of individualism and holism may leave animal liberationists wondering about the further implications of this resolution for the treatment of animals. Obviously, a good deal of work has already been done on this topic. Initially, philosophers thought that humanism could be extended to include animal liberation and eventually environmental concern.[4] Then Baird Callicott argued that animal liberation and environmental concern were as opposed to each other as they were to humanism.[5] The resulting conflict Callicott called "a triangular affair." Agreeing with Callicott, Mark Sagoff contended that any attempt to link together animal liberation and environmental concern would lead to "a bad marriage and a

quick divorce."[6] Yet more recently, such philosophers as Mary Anne Warren have tended to play down the opposition between animal liberation and environmental concern, and even Callicott now thinks he can bring the two back together again.[7] There are good reasons for thinking that such a reconciliation is possible.

Right off, it would be good for the environment if people generally, especially people in the first world, adopted a more vegetarian diet of the sort that animal liberationists are recommending. This is because a good portion of livestock production today consumes grains that could be more effectively used for direct human consumption. For example, 90% of the protein, 99% of the carbohydrate, and 100% of the fiber value of grain is wasted by cycling it through livestock, and currently 64% of the U.S. grain crop is fed to livestock.[8] So by adopting a more vegetarian diet, people generally, and especially people in the first world, could significantly reduce the amount of farmland that has to be kept in production to feed the human population. This in turn could have beneficial effects on the whole biotic community by eliminating the amount of soil erosion and environmental pollutants that result from raising livestock. For example, it has been estimated that 85% of U.S. topsoil lost from cropland, pasture, range land, and forest land is directly associated with raising livestock.[9] So, in addition to preventing animal suffering, there are these additional reasons to favor a more vegetarian diet.

But even though a more vegetarian diet seems in order, it is not clear that the interests of farm animals would be well served if all of us became complete vegetarians. Sagoff assumes that in a completely vegetarian human world people would continue to feed farm animals as before.[10] But it is not clear that we would have any obligation to do so. Moreover, in a completely vegetarian human world, we would probably need about half of the grain we now feed livestock to meet people's nutritional needs, particularly in second and third world countries. There simply would not be enough grain to go around. And then there would be the need to conserve cropland for future generations. So in a completely vegetarian human world, it seems likely that the population of farm animals would be decimated, relegating many of the farm animals that remain to zoos. On this account, it would seem to be more in the interest of farm animals generally that they be maintained under healthy conditions, and hence not in the numbers sustainable only with factory farms, but then killed relatively painlessly and eaten, rather than that they not be maintained at all. So a completely vegetarian human world would not seem to serve the interest of farm animals.

Nor, it seems, would it be in the interest of wild species who no longer have their natural predators not to be hunted by humans. Of course, where possible, it may be preferable to reintroduce natural predators. But this may not always be possible because of the proximity of farm animals and human populations, and then if action is not taken to control the populations of wild species, disaster could result for the species and their environments. For example, deer, rabbits, squirrels, quails, and ducks reproduce rapidly, and in the absence of predators can quickly exceed the carrying capacity of their environments. So it may be in the interest of certain wild species and their environments that humans intervene periodically to maintain a balance. Of course, there will be many natural environments where it is in the interest of the environment and the wild animals that inhabit it to be simply left alone. But here too animal liberation and environmental concern would not be in conflict. For these reasons, animal liberationists would have little reason to object to the proposed combination of individualism and holism within a nonanthropocentric environmental ethics.

ANTHROPOCENTRIC ENVIRONMENTAL ETHICS

Suppose, however, we were to reject the central contention of the nonanthropocentric perspective and deny that the members of all species are equal. We might claim, for example, that humans are superior because they, through culture, "realize a greater range of values" than members of nonhuman species, or we might claim that humans are superior in virtue of their "unprecedented capacity to create ethical systems that impart worth to other life-forms."[11] Or we might offer some other grounds for human superiority. Suppose, then, we adopt this anthropocentric perspective. What follows?

First, we will still need a principle of human defense. However, there is no need to adopt a different principle of human defense from the principle favored by a nonanthropocentric perspective. Whether we judge humans to be equal or superior to the members of other species, we will still want a principle that allows us to defend ourselves and other human beings from harmful aggression, even when this necessitates killing or harming animals or plants.

Second, we will also need a principle of human preservation. But here too there is no need to adopt a different principle from the principle of human preservation favored by a nonanthropocentric perspective. Whether we judge humans to be equal or superior to the members of other species, we will still want a principle that permits actions that are necessary for meeting our own basic needs or the basic needs of other human beings, even when this requires aggressing against the basic needs of animals and plants.

The crucial question is whether we will need a different principle of disproportionality. If we judge humans to be superior to the members of other species, will we still have grounds for protecting the basic needs of animals and plants against aggressive action to meet the nonbasic or luxury needs of humans?

Here it is important to distinguish between two degrees of preference that we noted earlier. First, we could prefer the basic needs of animals and plants over the nonbasic or luxury needs of humans when to do otherwise would involve *aggressing against* (by an act of commission) the basic needs of animals and plants. Second, we could prefer the basic needs of animals and plants over the nonbasic or luxury needs of humans when to do otherwise would involve simply *failing to meet* (by an act of omission) the basic needs of animals and plants.

Now in human ethics when the basic needs of some people are in conflict with the nonbasic or luxury needs of others, the distinction between failing to meet and aggressing against basic needs seems to have little moral force. In such conflict cases, both ways of not meeting basic needs are objectionable.

In environmental ethics, however, whether we adopt an anthropocentric or a nonanthropocentric perspective, we would seem to have grounds for morally distinguishing between the two cases, favoring the basic needs of animals and plants when to do otherwise would involve *aggressing against* those needs in order to meet our own nonbasic or luxury needs, but not when it would involve simply *failing to meet* those needs in order to meet our own nonbasic or luxury needs. This degree of preference for the members of the human species would be compatible with the equality of species insofar as members of nonhuman species similarly fail to meet the basic needs of members of the human species where there is a conflict of interest.

Even so, this theoretical distinction would have little practical force since most of the ways that we have of preferring our own nonbasic needs over the basic needs of animals and plants actually involve aggressing against their basic needs to meet our own nonbasic or luxury needs rather than simply failing to meet their basic needs.

Yet even if most of the ways that we have of preferring our own nonbasic or luxury needs do involve aggressing against the basic needs of animals and plants, wouldn't human superiority provide grounds for preferring ourselves or other human beings in these ways? Or put another way, shouldn't human superiority have more theoretical and practical significance than I am allowing? Not, I claim, if we are looking for the most morally defensible position to take.

For consider: The claim that humans are superior to the members of other species, if it can be justified at all, is something like the claim that a person came in first in a race where others came in second, third, fourth, and so on. It would not imply that the members of other species are without intrinsic value. In fact, it would imply just the opposite—that the members of other species are also intrinsically valuable, although not as intrinsically valuable as humans, just as the claim that a person came in first in a race implies that the persons who came in second, third, fourth, and so on are also meritorious, although not as meritorious as the person who came in first.

This line of argument draws further support once we consider the fact that many animals and plants are superior to humans in one respect or another, for example, the sense of smell of the wolf, the acuity of sight of the eagle, the survivability of the cockroach, or the photosynthetic power of plants. So any claim of human superiority must allow for the recognition of excellences in nonhuman species, even for some excellences that are superior to their corresponding human excellences. In fact, it demands that recognition.

Moreover, if the claim of human superiority is to have any moral force, it must rest on non-question-begging grounds. Accordingly, we must be able to give a non-question-begging response to the nonanthropocentric argument for the equality of species. Yet for any such argument to be successful, it would have to recognize the intrinsic value of the members of nonhuman species. Even if it could be established that human beings have greater intrinsic value, we would still have to recognize that nonhuman nature has intrinsic value as well. So the relevant question is: How are we going to recognize the presumably lesser intrinsic value of nonhuman nature?

Now if human needs, even nonbasic or luxury ones, are always preferred to even the basic needs of the members of nonhuman species, we would not be giving any recognition to the intrinsic value of nonhuman nature. But what if we allowed the nonbasic or luxury needs of humans to trump the basic needs of nonhuman nature half the time, and half the time we allowed the basic needs of nonhuman nature to trump the nonbasic or luxury needs of humans. Would that be enough? Certainly, it would be a significant advance over what we are presently doing. For what we are presently doing is meeting the basic needs of nonhuman nature, at best, only when it serves our own needs or the needs of those we are committed to or happen to care about, and that does not recognize the intrinsic value of nonhuman nature at all. A fifty-fifty arrangement would be an advance indeed. But it would not be enough.

The reason why it would not be enough is that the claim that humans are superior to nonhuman nature no more supports the practice of aggressing against the basic needs of nonhuman nature to satisfy our own nonbasic or luxury needs than the claim that a person came in first in a race would support the practice of aggressing against the basic needs of those who came in second, third, fourth, and so on to satisfy the nonbasic or luxury needs of the person who came in first. A higher degree of merit does not translate into a right of domination, and to claim a right to aggress against the basic needs of nonhuman nature in order to meet our own nonbasic or luxury needs is clearly to claim a right of domination. All that our superiority as humans would justify is not meeting the basic needs of nonhuman nature when this conflicts with our nonbasic or luxury needs. What it does not justify is aggressing against the basic needs of nonhuman nature when this conflicts with our nonbasic or luxury needs.

OBJECTIVE AND SUBJECTIVE VALUE THEORY

Now it might be objected that my argument so far presupposes an objective theory of value that regards things as valuable because of the qualities they actually have rather than a subjective theory of value that regards things as valuable simply because humans happen to value them. However, I contend that when both these theories are defensibly formulated they will lead to the same practical requirements.

For consider: Suppose we begin with a subjective theory of value that regards things as valuable simply because humans value them. Of course, some things would be valued by humans instrumentally, others intrinsically, but, according to this theory, all things would have the value they have, if they have any value at all, simply because they are valued by humans either instrumentally or intrinsically.

One problem facing such a theory is why should we think that humans alone determine the value that things have? For example, why not say that things are valuable because the members of other species value them? Why not say

that grass is valuable because zebras value it, and that zebras are valuable because lions value them, and so on? Or why not say, assuming God exists, that things are valuable because God values them?

Nor would it do simply to claim that we authoritatively determine what is valuable for ourselves, that nonhuman species authoritatively determine what is valuable for themselves, and that God authoritatively determines what is valuable for the Godhead. For what others value should at least be relevant data when authoritatively determining what is valuable for ourselves.

Another problem for a subjective theory of value is that we probably would not want to say that just anything we happen to value determines what is valuable for ourselves. For surely we would want to say that at least some of the things that people value, especially people who are evil or deficient in certain ways, are not really valuable, even for them. Merely thinking that something is valuable doesn't make it so.

Suppose then we modified this subjective theory of value to deal with these problems. Let the theory claim that what is truly valuable for people is what they would value if they had all the relevant information (including, where it is relevant, the knowledge of what others would value) and reasoned correctly. Of course, there will be many occasions where we are unsure that ideal conditions have been realized, unsure, that is, that we have all the relevant information and have reasoned correctly. And even when we are sure that ideal conditions have been realized, we may not always be willing to act upon what we come to value due to weakness of will.

Nevertheless, when a subjective theory of value is formulated in this way, it will have the same practical requirements as an objective theory of value that is also defensibly formulated. For an objective theory of value holds that what is valuable is determined by the qualities things actually have. But in order for the qualities things actually have to be valuable in the sense of being capable of being valued, they must be accessible to us, at least under ideal conditions, that is, they must be the sort of qualities that we would value if we had all the relevant information and reasoned correctly. But this is just what is valuable according to our modified subjective theory of value. So once a subjective theory of value and an objective theory of value are defensibly formulated in the manner I propose, they will lead us to value the same things.

Now it is important to note here that with respect to some of the things we value intrinsically, such as animals and plants, our valuing them depends simply on our ability to discover the value that they actually have based on their qualities, whereas for other things that we value intrinsically, such as our aesthetic experiences and the objects that provided us with those experiences, the value that these things have depends significantly on the way we are constituted. So that if we were constituted differently, what we value aesthetically would be different as well. Of course, the same holds true for some of the things that we value morally. For example, we morally value not killing human beings because of the way we are constituted. Constituted as we are, killing is usually bad for any human that we would kill. But suppose we were constituted differently such that killing human beings was immensely pleasurable for those humans that we killed, following which they immediately sprang back to life asking us to kill them again. If human beings were constituted in this way, we would no longer morally value not killing. In fact, constituted in this new way, I think we would come to morally value *killing* and the relevant rule for us might be "Kill human beings as often as you can." But while such aesthetic and moral values are clearly dependent on the way we are constituted, they still are not anthropocentric in the sense that they imply human superiority. Such values can be recognized from both an anthropocentric and a nonanthropocentric perspective.

It might be objected, however, that while the intrinsic values of an environmental ethics need not be anthropocentric in the sense that they imply human superiority, these values must be anthropocentric in the sense that humans would reasonably come to hold them. This seems correct. However, appealing to this sense of anthropocentric, Eugene Hargrove has argued that not all living things would turn out to be intrinsically valuable as a nonanthropocentric environmental ethics maintains.[12] Hargrove cites as hypothetical

examples of living things that would not turn out to be intrinsically valuable the creatures in the films *Alien* and *Aliens*. What is distinctive about these creatures is that they require the deaths of many other living creatures, whomever they happen upon, to reproduce and survive as a species. Newly hatched, these creatures emerge from their eggs and immediately enter host organisms, which they keep alive and feed upon while they develop. When the creatures are fully developed, they explode out of the chest of their host organisms, killing their hosts with some fanfare. Hargrove suggests that if such creatures existed, we would not intrinsically value them because it would not be reasonable for us to do so.[13]

Following Paul Taylor, Hargrove assumes that to intrinsically value a creature is to recognize a negative duty not to destroy or harm that creature and a positive duty to protect it from being destroyed or harmed by others. Since Hargrove thinks that we would be loath to recognize any such duties with respect to such alien creatures, we would not consider them to be intrinsically valuable.

Surely it seems clear that we would seek to kill such alien creatures by whatever means are available to us, but why should that preclude our recognizing them as having intrinsic value any more than our seeking to kill any person who is engaged in lethal aggression against us would preclude our recognizing that person as having intrinsic value? To recognize something as having intrinsic value does not preclude destroying it to preserve other things that also have intrinsic value when there is good reason to do so. Furthermore, recognizing a prima facie negative duty not to destroy or harm something and a prima facie positive duty to protect it from being destroyed or harmed by others is perfectly consistent with recognizing an all-things-considered duty to destroy that thing when it is engaged in lethal aggression against us. Actually, all we are doing here is simply applying our principle of human defense, and, as I have argued earlier, there is no reason to think that the application of this principle would preclude our recognizing the intrinsic value of every living being.

Still another objection that might be raised to my reconciliationist argument is that my view is too individualistic, as evidenced by the fact that my principles of environmental justice refer to individual humans, plants, and animals, but not specifically to species or ecosystems. Now, I would certainly agree with Paul Taylor that all individual living beings as well as species populations can be benefited or harmed and have a good of their own and hence qualify as moral subjects.[14] But Taylor goes on to deny that species themselves are moral subjects with a good of their own because he regards "species" as a class name, and classes, he contends, have no good of their own.[15] Yet here I would disagree with Taylor because species are unlike abstract classes in that they evolve, split, bud off new species, become endangered, go extinct, and have interests distinct from the interests of their members.[16] For example, a particular species of deer, but not individual members of that species, can have an interest in being preyed upon. Hence, species can be benefited and harmed and have a good of their own and so should qualify on Taylor's view, as well as my own, as moral subjects. So too ecosystems should qualify as moral subjects since they can be benefited and harmed and have a good of their own, having features and interests not shared by their components.[17] Following Lawrence Johnson, we can go on to characterize moral subjects as living systems in a persistent state of low entropy sustained by metabolic processes for accumulating energy whose organic unity and self-identity is maintained in equilibrium by homeostatic feedback processes.[18] Thus, modifying my view in order to take into account species and ecosystems requires the following changes in my first three principles of environmental justice:

Principle of human defense: Actions that defend oneself and other human beings against harmful aggression are permissible even when they necessitate killing or harming individual animals or plants or even destroying whole species or ecosystems.

Principle of human preservation: Actions that are necessary for meeting one's basic needs or the basic needs of other human beings are permissible even when they require aggressing against the basic needs of individual animals and plants or even of whole species or ecosystems.

Principle of disproportionality: Actions that meet nonbasic or luxury needs of humans are prohibited when they aggress against the basic needs of individual animals and plants, or of whole species or ecosystems.

But while this modification is of theoretical interest since it allows that species and ecosystems as well as individuals count morally, it actually has little or no practical effect on the application of these principles. This is because, for the most part, the positive or negative impact the application of these principles would have on species and ecosystems is correspondingly reflected in the positive or negative impact the application of these principles would have on the individual members of those species or ecosystems. As a consequence, actions that are permitted or prohibited with respect to species and ecosystems according to the modified principles are already permitted or prohibited respectively through their correspondence with actions that are permitted or prohibited according to the unmodified principles.

However, this is not always the case. In fact, considerations about what benefits nonhuman species or subspecies as opposed to individuals of those species or subspecies have already figured in my previous argument. For example, I have argued for culling elk herds in wolf-free ranges, but this is primarily for the good of herds or species of elk and certainly not for the good of the particular elk who are being culled from those herds. I also have argued that it would be for the good of farm animals generally that they be maintained under healthy conditions and then killed relatively painlessly and eaten, rather than that they not be maintained at all. But clearly this is an argument about what would be good for existing flocks or herds, or species or subspecies of farm animals. It is not an argument about what would be good for the existing individual farm animals who would be killed relatively painlessly and eaten. Nevertheless, for the most part, because of the coincidence between the welfare of species and ecosystems and the welfare of individual members of those species and ecosystems, the two formulations of the first three principles turn out to be practically equivalent.

In sum, I have argued that whether we endorse an anthropocentric or a nonanthropocentric environmental ethics, we should favor a principle of human defense, a principle of human preservation, and a principle of disproportionality as I have interpreted them. In the past, failure to recognize the importance of a principle of human defense and a principle of human preservation has led philosophers to overestimate the amount of sacrifice required of humans.[19] By contrast, failure to recognize the importance of a principle of disproportionality has led philosophers to underestimate the amount of sacrifice required of humans.[20] I claim that taken together these three principles strike the right balance between concerns of human welfare and the welfare of nonhuman nature.

NOTES

1. Aldo Leopold's view is usually interpreted as holistic in this sense. Leopold wrote "A thing is right when it tends to preserve the integrity, stability and beauty of the biotic community. It is wrong when it tends otherwise." See his *A Sand County Almanac* (Oxford, 1949).
2. For a defender of this view, see Paul Taylor, *Respect for Nature.*
3. Where it is most likely to be morally required is where our negligent actions have caused the environmental problem in the first place.
4. Peter Singer's *Animal Liberation* (New York, 1975) inspired this view.
5. Baird Callicott, "Animal Liberation: A Triangular Affair," *Environmental Ethics* (1980): 311–328.
6. Mark Sagoff, "Animal Liberation and Environmental Ethics: Bad Marriage, Quick Divorce," *Osgood Hall Law Journal* (1984): 297–307.
7. Mary Anne Warren, "The Rights of the Nonhuman World," in *Environmental Philosophy*, edited by Robert Elliot and Arran Gare (London, 1983), 109–134; and Baird Callicott, *In Defense of the Land Ethic* (Albany, 1989), Chapter 3.
8. *Realities for the 90's* (Santa Cruz, 1991), 4.
9. Ibid., 5.
10. Sagoff, op. cit., 301–305.
11. Holmes Rolston, *Environmental Ethics* (Philadelphia, 1988), 66–68; Murray Bookchin, *The Ecology of Freedom* (Montreal, 1991), xxxvi.
12. Eugene Hargrove, "Weak Anthropocentric Intrinsic Value," in *After Earth Day*, edited by Max Oelschlaeger (Denton, 1992), 147ff.
13. Ibid., 151. Notice that there are at least two ways that X might intrinsically value Y. First, X might regard Y as good in itself for X or as an end in itself for X, by contrast with valuing Y instrumentally. Second, X might regard the good of Y as constraining the way that X can use Y. This second way of intrinsically valuing Y is the principal way we value human beings. It is the sense of value that Kantians are referring to when they claim that people should never be used as means only. Another way to put what I have been arguing is that we should extend this second way of intrinsically valuing to animals and plants.
14. Taylor, op. cit., 17, 68–71.
15. Ibid., 68–71.
16. One way to think about species are as ongoing genetic lineages sequentially embodied in different organisms. See Lawrence Johnson, *A Morally Deep World* (New York: Cambridge University Press, 1991), 156; Rolston op. cit., Chapter 4.
17. Ecosystems can be simple or complex, stable or unstable, and they can suffer total collapse.
18. *A Morally Deep World*, Chapter 6. Happily, this definition distinguishes moral subjects (living systems) from cars, refrigerators, etc. See also Lawrence Johnson, "Toward the Moral Considerability of Species and Ecosystems," *Environmental Ethics* 14 (1992).
19. For example, in "Animal Liberation: A Triangular Affair," Baird Callicott had defended Edward Abbey's assertion that he would sooner shoot a man than a snake.
20. For example, Eugene Hargrove argues that from a traditional wildlife perspective, the lives of individual specimens of quite plentiful nonhuman species count for almost nothing at all. See Chapter 4 of his *Foundations of Environmental Ethics* (Prentice Hall , 1989).

✥ STUDY QUESTIONS

1. Outline Sterba's argument for reconciling anthropocentric and nonanthropocentric ethics. First, examine his description of nonanthropocentric ethics. Next, examine his description of anthropocentric ethics. Is Sterba successful? What assumptions are necessary for his project?

2. Do you agree with Sterba that regarding members of all species as equals still allows for human preferences in the same way regarding humans as equals still allows for self-preference? What is Sterba's basis of equality? Discuss his theory of equality.

3. Consider Sterba's treatment of objective and subjective value. How does he seek to reconcile them? Is he successful?

4. At the end of his article, Sterba treats species as subjects that can be harmed or benefited just as individuals can be benefited. Do you agree? Explain your view.

✿ FOR FURTHER READING

Attfield, Robin. *The Ethics of Environmental Concern* (New York: Columbia University, 1983).

Callicott, Baird. *In Defense of the Land Ethic* (Buffalo, NY: SUNY Press, 1989).

Chase, Alston. *In a Dark Wood: The Fight over Forests and the Rising Tyranny of Ecology.* Boston: Houghton Mifflin, 1995.

———. *Playing God at Yellowstone Park.* Fort Worth, TX: 1987.

Devall, Bill. *Simple in Means, Rich in Ends: Practicing Deep Ecology.* Salt Lake City, UT: Peregrine Smith Books, 1985.

Devall, Bill, and George Sessions. *Deep Ecology: Living as if Nature Mattered.* Salt Lake City, UT: Peregrine Smith Books, 1985.

Ehrenfeld, David. *The Arrogance of Humanism.* New York: Oxford University Press: 1978.

Fox, Warwick. "Deep Ecology: A New Philosophy of Our Time." *The Ecologist* 14 (1984).

Goodpaster, Kenneth. "On Being Morally Considerable." *Journal of Philosophy* 75 (June 1978).

Guha, R. "Radical Environmentalism and Wilderness Preservation: A Third World Critique," *Environmental Ethics* VII reprinted in this volume as Reading 39.

Johnson, Lawrence. *A Morally Deep World.* New York: Cambridge University Press, 1991.

Leopold, Aldo. *A Sand County Almanac.* New York: Oxford University Press, 1949.

Lewis, Martin. *Green Delusions: An Environmentalist Critique of Radical Environmentalism.* Durham, NC: Duke University Press, 1992.

List, Peter C., ed. *Radical Environmentalism.* Belmont, CA: Wadsworth, 1993.

Naess, Arne. *Ecology, Community and Lifestyle,* ed. and trans. David Rothenberg. Cambridge: Cambridge University Press, 1989.

Rolston, Holmes, III. *Environmental Ethics: Duties to and Values in the Natural World.* Philadelphia: Temple University Press, 1987.

Sylvan, Richard. "A Critique of Deep Ecology." *Radical Philosophy* 40 (1985).

Taylor, Paul. *Respect for Nature.* Princeton, NJ: Princeton University Press, 1986.

Wenz, Peter. *Environmental Justice.* Buffalo, NY: SUNY Press, 1988.

Zimmerman, Michael, ed. *Environmental Philosophy: From Animal Rights to Radical Ecology.* Englewood Cliffs, NJ: Prentice-Hall, 1993.

Preservation of the Species, Nature, and Natural Objects

Biodiversity is our most valuable but least appreciated resource

EDWARD O. WILSON, *The Diversity of Life*

ACCORDING TO DONELLA MEADOWS, the author of our first reading in this chapter, the total number of species of life is somewhere between 10 million and 30 million, of which only 1.7 million are named and only a small fraction have been studied. Yet we are destroying these species at a record rate. Many types of plants and animals, like the California condor and the blue whale, are endangered. The majority of the unnamed and unstudied species reside in tropical rain forests in poor countries and are rapidly being destroyed for economic reasons. What should be done about this destruction?

Why should we be concerned with the preservation of species? Why is biodiversity so important that we must make sacrifices to preserve and enhance it? Who cares if the snail darter, a fish of no known use to humans, perishes in the process of building a dam that will develop the economy of the Tennessee Valley? Is biodiversity important in itself? Or do other species of plants and animals have only instrumental value, relative to human need? Do species have intrinsic value?

The philosopher Nicholas Rescher says they do: "When a species vanishes from nature, the world is thereby diminished. Species do not just have an instrumental value...they have a value in their own right—an intrinsic value." And one of the leading proponents of the land ethic, Baird Callicott, wrote, "[T]he preciousness of individual [animals]...is inversely proportional to the population of the species." "[T]he human population has become so disproportionate from the biological point of view that if one had to choose between a specimen of *Homo sapiens* and a specimen of a rare even if unattractive species, the choice would be moot."

Some land ethicists, like Callicott at one stage in his development, and many deep ecologists would hold that nature has intrinsic value, so ecosystems and species should be valued in their own right. Donella Meadows argues that three strong reasons should compel us to protect biodiversity: economic value in terms of new drugs and food products; environmental service (without the complex service of microorganisms and other species, life would stop); and genetic information (vast stores of knowledge are stored in the DNA structure of the living cells of these species). So we have two different kinds of motives: (1) self-interested concern for our survival and flourishing and (2) moral respect for something magnificent that we did not create and do not understand.

In our second reading, Lilly-Marlene Russow asks "Why Do Species Matter?" She argues that we normally ascribe rights to someone because he or she has interests, but species cannot suffer or have interests, since only individual objects can have interests. Since it doesn't make sense to attribute interests to species, it follows that they do not have rights, and so we cannot have obligations to them. She examines three arguments for species preservation and argues that they all fail. She concludes that individual animals can have aesthetic value, and this is the basis for our obligation to preserve animals of that sort.

Some parts of nature are undomesticated by human manipulation. Vast mountain ranges or rain forests may be visited by human beings without being significantly altered. Individual objects or forests like the California Redwood trees, the Grand Canyon, or Niagara Falls may be valued for their own sake, or, at least, for aesthetic reasons. The question raised by Holmes Rolston, III reemerges now: Do natural objects like redwood trees or Niagara Falls or the Grand Canyon have intrinsic value in such a way that they cannot be replaced by artificial surrogates—for example, plastic trees, man-made waterfalls, and Disneyland gorges?

In "What's Wrong with Plastic Trees?" Martin Krieger questions the preservationist thesis that we must preserve original natural objects. He challenges us to state precisely why artificial objects may not serve us as well as natural ones. We must not worship nature but examine the cost/benefits of preserving natural objects and "wildernesses" (a human designation) in relation to other economic and social needs.

In "Faking Nature," Robert Elliot considers the views of Krieger and other anti-preservationists who hold the "restoration thesis." The restoration thesis argues that a restored, artificial replica of natural objects would preserve their full aesthetic value. Elliot, while granting that the restoration thesis carries some weight, argues that it leaves out too much. Comparing natural objects to art, he maintains that fakes or replicas have less value than the original. Our understanding of the origins of these objects affects our evaluation of them, so something is lost in the replication process.

We usually seek to protect valuable objects that are threatened by human intervention. While our legal system covers such inanimate objects as corporations and states, it has not widely been extended to cover natural objects.

In our final reading in this section—"Should Trees Have Standing?"—Christopher Stone argues that from both anthropocentric and holistic perspectives, we should assign natural objects (rivers, oceans, trees, the atmosphere, and animals) legal rights. He points out that we already grant such inanimate objects as corporations and municipalities such rights, so why not extend the rights further, using the idea of "legal guardian" to cover these objects?

Stone agrees that the idea of granting natural objects legal standing will seem "unthinkable" to many, but he notes, quoting Darwin on the expanding circle of our moral sentiments, that at one time the idea of granting equal rights to women, blacks, and children was thought to be unthinkable. He asks us to consider the arguments on their merits.

30   Biodiversity: The Key to Saving Life on Earth

DONELLA H. MEADOWS

Donella Meadows is an adjunct professor of environmental and policy studies at Dartmouth College and the author of several works in environmental studies, including Limits to Growth. *In this essay, Meadows sets forth three reasons for preserving biodiversity: economic, environmental, and informational. She appeals both to our enlightened self-interest and wider moral sensitivity for nature and its phenomena in calling on us to leave nature alone so that biodiversity may not be threatened by us.*

The Ozone Hole and the greenhouse effect have entered our public vocabulary, but we have no catchy label for the third great environmental problem of the late 20th century. It's even more diffuse than depletion of the ozone layer or global warming, harder to grasp and summarize. The experts call it "the loss of biodiversity."

Biodiversity obviously has something to do with pandas, tigers and tropical forests. But preserving biodiversity is a much bigger job than protecting rain forests or charismatic megafauna. It's the job of protecting all life—microscopic creepy-crawlies as well as elephants and condors—and all life's habitats—tundra, prairie and swamp as well as forests.

Why care about tundra, swamp, blue beetles or little blue-stem grasses? Ecologists give three reasons, which boil down to simple self-interest on three levels of escalating importance.

- Biodiversity has both immediate and potential economic value. This is the argument most commonly put forward to defend biodiversity, because it's the one our culture is most ready to hear. It cites the importance of the industries most directly dependent upon nature—fisheries, forestry, tourism, recreation and the harvesting of wild foods, medicines, dyes, rubber and chemicals.

Some ecologists are so tired of this line of reasoning that they refer wearily to the "Madagascar periwinkle argument." That obscure plant yields the drugs vincristine and vinblastine, which have revolutionized the treatment of leukemia. About a third of all modern medicines have derived from molds and plants.

The potential for future discoveries is astounding. The total number of species of life is somewhere between 10 million and 30 million, only 1.7 million of which we have named, only a fraction of which we have tested for usefulness.

The economic value of biodiversity is very real, but ecologists hate the argument because it is both arrogant and trivial. It assumes that the Earth's millions of species are here to serve the economic purposes of just one species. And even if you buy that idea, it misses the larger and more valuable ways that nature serves us.

- Biodiversity performs environmental services beyond price. How would you like the job of pollinating trillions of apple blossoms some sunny afternoon in May? It's conceivable, maybe, that you could invent a machine to do it, but inconceivable that the machine could work as elegantly and cheaply as the honeybee, much less make honey on the side.

Suppose you were assigned to turn every bit of dead organic matter, from fallen leaves to urban garbage, into nutrients that feed new life. Even if you knew how, what would it cost?

Reprinted from *The Land Steward Letter* (Summer 1990) by permission.

A host of bacteria, molds, mites and worms do it for free. If they ever stopped, all life would stop. We would not last long if green plants stopped turning our exhaled carbon dioxide back into oxygen. Plants would not last long if a few genera of soil bacteria stopped turning nitrogen from the air into nitrate fertilizer.

Human reckoning cannot put a value on the services performed by the ecosystems of Earth. These services include the cleansing of air and water, flood control, drought prevention, pest control, temperature regulation and maintenance of the world's most valuable library—the genes of all living orgasms.

- Biodiversity contains the accumulated wisdom of nature and the key to its future. If you ever wanted to destroy a society, you would burn its libraries and kill its intellectuals. You would destroy its knowledge. Nature's knowledge is contained in the DNA within living cells. The variety of that genetic information is the driving engine of evolution, the immune system for life, the source of adaptability—not just the variety of species but also the variety of individuals within each species.

Individuals are never quite alike. Each is genetically unique mostly in subterranean ways that will only appear in future generations. We recognize that is true of human beings. Plant and animal breeders recognize it in dogs, cattle, wheat, roses, apples. The only reason they can bring forth bigger fruits or sweeter smells or disease resistance is that those traits are already present in the genes carried by some individuals.

The amount of information in a single cell is hard to comprehend. A simple one-celled bacterium can carry genes for 1,000 traits, a flowering plant for 400,000. Biologist E. O. Wilson says the information in the genes of an ordinary house mouse, if translated into printed letters, would fill all the 15 editions of the Encyclopedia Britannica that have been published since 1768.

The wealth of genetic information has been selected over billions of years to fit the ever-changing necessities of the planet. As Earth's atmosphere filled with oxygen, as land masses drifted apart, as humans invented agriculture and altered the land, there were lurking within individuals pieces of genetic code that allowed them to defend against or take advantage of the changes. These individuals were more fit for the new environment. They bred more successfully. The population began to take on their characteristics. New species came into being.

Biodiversity is the accumulation of all life's past adaptations, and it is the basis for all further adaptations (even those mediated by human gene-splicers).

That's why ecologists value biodiversity as one of Earth's great resources. It's why they take seriously the loss of even the most insignificant species; why they defend not only the preservation of species but the preservation of populations within species, and why they regard the rate of human-induced extinctions as an unparalleled catastrophe.

We don't know how many species we are eliminating, because we don't know how many species there are. It's a fair guess that, at the rate we're destroying habitat, we're pushing to extinction about one species every hour. That doesn't count the species whose populations are being reduced so greatly that diversity within the population is essentially gone. Earth has not seen a spasm of extinctions like this for 65 million years.

Biologists estimate that human beings usurp, directly or indirectly, about 40 percent of each year's total biological production. There is hardly a place on Earth where people do not log, pave, spray, drain, flood, graze, fish, plow, burn, drill, spill or dump. There is no life zone, with the possible exception of the deep ocean, that we are not degrading.

Besides "loss of diversity," biologists have another name for this problem—"biotic impoverishment." What is impoverished is not just biodiversity, it is also the human economy and human spirit.

Ecologist Paul Ehrlich describes biotic impoverishment this way: "Unless current trends are reversed, Americans will gradually be living in a nation that has fewer warblers and ducks and more starlings and herring gulls, fewer native wildflowers and more noxious weeds, fewer swallowtail butterflies and more cockroaches, smaller herds of elk and bigger herds of rats, less edible seafood, less productive croplands, less dependable supplies of pure fresh water, more desert wastes and dust storms, more frequent floods and more uncomfortable weather."

Biodiversity cannot be maintained by protecting a few species in a zoo, nor by preserving greenbelts or even national parks. To function properly nature needs more room than that. It can maintain itself, however, without human expense, without zookeepers, park rangers, foresters or gene banks. All it needs is to be left alone.

To provide their priceless pollination service, the honeybees ask only that we stop saturating the landscape with poisons, stop paving the meadows where bee-food grows and leave them enough honey to get through the winter.

To maintain our planet, our lives and our future potential, the other species have similar requests, all of which add up to: Control yourselves. Control your numbers. Control your greed. See yourselves as what you are, part of an interdependent biological community—the most intelligent part, though you don't often act that way.

So act that way, either out of a moral respect for something magnificent that you didn't create and do not understand, or out of a practical interest in your own survival.

STUDY QUESTIONS

1. What are Meadows's main reasons for protecting biodiversity? Do her conclusions follow from her specific reasons? Explain.
2. Why can't we simply preserve species in zoos and national parks?
3. Some species are quite harmful to humans, like the smallpox virus. Shouldn't we destroy these altogether?
4. The U.S. Endangered Species Act of 1973 protects hundreds of species, preventing activities that might further threaten these species. In December 1992, the Bush administration yielded to pressures from environmental groups and agreed to add 400 species to its list of endangered (and protected) species over the next four years, bringing the total to 750 protected species. Business groups complain that such acts hurt business and threaten jobs. Should species be protected if such protection causes unemployment and is bad for the economy?

31   Why Do Species Matter?

LILLY-MARLENE RUSSOW

Lilly-Marlene Russow teaches philosophy at Purdue University and is the author of several works in philosophy. In this essay, she first examines various test cases to show some of the complexities involved in any attempt to describe obligations to species. Next, she analyzes three arguments for obligations to protect endangered species and concludes that not only do they fail but that there is a conceptual confusion in any attempt to ascribe value to a species. Whatever duty we do have in this regard must rest on the "value—often aesthetic—of individual members of certain species."

Reprinted from *Environmental Ethics,* Vol. 3 (1981) by permission.

I. INTRODUCTION

Consider the following extension of the standard sort of objection to treating animals differently just because they are not humans: the fact that a being is or is not a member of species *S* is not a morally relevant fact, and does not justify treating that being differently from members of other species. If so, we cannot treat a bird differently *just* because it is a California condor rather than a turkey vulture. The problem, then, becomes one of determining what special obligations, if any, a person might have toward California condors, and what might account for those obligations in a way that is generally consistent with the condemnation of speciesism. Since it will turn out that the solution I offer does not admit of a direct and tidy proof, what follows comprises three sections which approach this issue from different directions. The resulting triangulation should serve as justification and motivation for the conclusion sketched in the final section.

II. SPECIES AND INDIVIDUALS

Much of the discussion in the general area of ethics and animals has dealt with the rights of animals, or obligations and duties toward individual animals. The first thing to note is that some, but not all, of the actions normally thought of as obligatory with respect to the protection of vanishing species can be recast as possible duties to individual members of that species. Thus, if it could be shown that we have a *prima facie duty* not to kill a sentient being, it would follow that it would be wrong, other things being equal, to kill a blue whale or a California condor. But it would be wrong for the same reason, and to the same degree, that it would be wrong to kill a turkey vulture or a pilot whale. Similarly, if it is wrong (something which I do not think can be shown) to deprive an individual animal of its natural habitat, it would be wrong, for the same reasons and to the same degree, to do that to a member of an endangered species. And so on. Thus, an appeal to our duties toward individual animals may provide some protection, but they do not justify the claim that we should treat members of a vanishing species with *more* care than members of other species.

More importantly, duties toward individual beings (or the rights of those individuals) will not always account for all the actions that people feel obligated to do for endangered species—e.g., bring into the world as many individuals of that species as possible, protect them from natural predation, or establish separate breeding colonies. In fact, the protection of a species might involve actions that are demonstrably contrary to the interests of some or all of the individual animals: this seems true in cases when we remove all the animals we can from their natural environment and raise them in zoos, or where we severely restrict the range of a species by hunting all those outside a certain area, as is done in Minnesota to protect the timber wolf. If such efforts are morally correct, our duties to preserve a species cannot be grounded in obligations that we have toward individual animals.

Nor will it be fruitful to treat our obligations to a species as duties toward, or as arising out of the rights of, a species thought of as some special superentity. It is simply not clear that we can make sense of talk about the interests of a species in the absence of beliefs, desires, purposeful action, etc. Since having interests is generally accepted as at least a necessary condition for having rights, and since many of the duties we have toward animals arise directly out of the animals' interests, arguments which show that animals have rights, or that we have duties towards them, will not apply to species. Since arguments which proceed from interests to rights or from interests to obligations make up a majority of the literature on ethics and animals, it is unlikely that these arguments will serve as a key to possible obligations toward species.

Having eliminated the possibility that our obligations toward species are somehow parallel to, or similar to, our obligation not to cause unwarranted pain to an animal, there seem to be only a few possibilities left. We may find that our duties toward species arise not out of the interests of the species, but are rooted in the general obligation to preserve things of value. Alternatively, our obligations to species may in fact be obligations to individuals (either members of the species or other individuals), but obligations that differ from the ones just discussed in that they are not determined simply by the interests of the individual.

III. SOME TEST CASES

If we are to find some intuitively acceptable foundation for claims about our obligations to protect species, we must start afresh. In order to get clear about what, precisely, we are looking for in this context, what obligations we might think we have toward species, what moral claims we are seeking a foundation for, I turn now to a description of some test cases. An examination of these cases illustrates why the object of our search is not something as straightforward as "Do whatever is possible or necessary to preserve the existence of the species"; a consideration of some of the differences between cases will guide our search for the nature of our obligations and the underlying reasons for those obligations.

Case 1. The snail darter is known to exist only in one part of one river. This stretch of river would be destroyed by the building of the Tellico dam. Defenders of the dam have successfully argued that the dam is nonetheless necessary for the economic development and well-being of the area's population. To my knowledge, no serious or large scale attempt has been made to breed large numbers of snail darters in captivity (for any reason other than research).

Case 2. The Pére David deer was first discovered by a Western naturalist in 1865, when Pére Armand David found herds of the deer in the Imperial Gardens in Peking: even at that time, they were only known to exist in captivity. Pére David brought several animals back to Europe, where they bred readily enough so that now there are healthy populations in several major zoos. There is no reasonable hope of reintroducing the Pére David deer to its natural habitat; indeed, it is not even definitely known what its natural habitat was.

Case 3. The red wolf (*Canis rufus*) formerly ranged over the southeastern and south-central United States. As with most wolves, they were threatened, and their range curtailed, by trapping, hunting, and the destruction of habitat. However,

a more immediate threat to the continued existence of the red wolf is that these changes extended the range of the more adaptable coyote, with whom the red wolf interbreeds very readily; as a result, there are very few "pure" red wolves left. An attempt has been made to capture some pure breeding stock and raise wolves on preserves.

Case 4. The Baltimore oriole and the Bullock's oriole were long recognized and classified as two separate species of birds. As a result of extensive interbreeding between the two species in areas where their ranges overlapped, the American Ornithologists' Union recently declared that there were no longer two separate species; both ex-species are now called "northern orioles."

Case 5. The Appaloosa is a breed of horse with a distinctively spotted coat; the Lewis and Clark expedition discovered that the breed was associated with the Nez Percé Indians. When the Nez Percé tribe was defeated by the U.S. Cavalry in 1877 and forced to move, their horses were scattered and interbred with other horses. The distinctive coat pattern was almost lost; not until the middle of the twentieth century was a concerted effort made to gather together the few remaining specimens and reestablish the breed.

Case 6. Many strains of laboratory rats are bred specifically for a certain type of research. Once the need for a particular variety ceases— once the type of research is completed—the rats are usually killed, with the result that the variety becomes extinct.

Case 7. It is commonly known that several diseases such as sleeping sickness, malaria, and human encephalitis are caused by one variety of mosquito but not by others. Much of the disease control in these cases is aimed at exterminating the disease carrying insect; most people do not find it morally wrong to wipe out the whole species.

Case 8. Suppose that zebras were threatened solely because they were hunted for their distinctive striped coats. Suppose, too, that we could remove this threat by selectively breeding zebras that are not striped, that look exactly like mules, although they are still pure zebras. Have we preserved all that we ought to have preserved?

What does an examination of these test cases reveal? First, that our concept of what a species *is* is not at all unambiguous; at least in part, what counts as a species is a matter of current fashions in taxonomy. Furthermore, it seems that it is not the sheer diversity or number of species that matters: if that were what is valued, moral preference would be given to taxonomic schemes that separated individuals into a larger number of species, a suggestion which seems absurd. The case of the orioles suggests that the decision as to whether to call these things one species or two is not a moral issue at all. Since we are not evidently concerned with the existence or diversity of species in *this* sense, there must be something more at issue than the simple question of whether we have today the same number of species represented as we had yesterday. Confusion sets in, however, when we try to specify another sense in which it is possible to speak of the "existence" of a species. This only serves to emphasize the basic murkiness of our intuitions about what the object of our concern really is.

This murkiness is further revealed by the fact that it is not at all obvious what we are trying to preserve in some of the test cases. Sometimes, as in the case of the Appaloosa or attempts to save a subspecies like the Arctic wolf or the Mexican wolf, it is not a whole species that is in question. But not all genetic subgroups are of interest—witness the case of the laboratory rat—and sometimes the preservation of the species at the cost of one of its externally obvious features (the stripes on a zebra) is not our only concern. This is not a minor puzzle which can be resolved by changing our question from "why do species matter?" to "why do species and/or subspecies matter?" It is rather a serious issue of what makes a group of animals "special" enough or "unique" enough to warrant concern. And of course, the test cases reveal that our intuitions are not always consistent: although the cases of the red wolf and the northern oriole are parallel in important respects, we are more uneasy about simply reclassifying the red wolf and allowing things to continue along their present path.

The final point to be established is that whatever moral weight is finally attached to the preservation of a species (or subspecies), it can be overridden. We apparently have no compunction

about wiping out a species of mosquito if the benefits gained by such action are sufficiently important, although many people were unconvinced by similar arguments in favor of the Tellico dam.

The lesson to be drawn from this section can be stated in a somewhat simplistic form: it is not simply the case that we can solve our problems by arguing that there is some value attached to the mere existence of a species. Our final analysis must take account of various features or properties of certain kinds or groups of animals, and it has to recognize that our concern is with the continued existence of individuals that may or may not have some distinctive characteristics.

IV. SOME TRADITIONAL ANSWERS

There are, of course, some standard replies to the question "Why do species matter?" or, more particularly, to the question "Why do we have at least a *prima facie* duty not to cause a species to become extinct, and in some cases, a duty to try actively to preserve species?" With some tolerance for borderline cases, these replies generally fall into three groups: (1) those that appeal to our role as "stewards" or "caretakers," (2) those that claim that species have some extrinsic value (I include in this group those that argue that the species is valuable as part of the ecosystem or as a link in the evolutionary scheme of things), and (3) those that appeal to some intrinsic or inherent value that is supposed to make a species worth preserving. In this section, with the help of the test cases just discussed, I indicate some serious flaws with each of these responses.

The first type of view has been put forward in the philosophical literature by Joel Feinberg, who states that our duty to preserve whole species may be more important than any rights had by individual animals. He argues, first, that this duty does not arise from a right or claim that can properly be attributed to the species as a whole (his reasons are much the same as the ones I cited in section 2 of this paper), and second, while we have some duty to unborn generations that directs us to preserve species, that duty is much weaker than the actual duty we have to preserve species. The fact that our actual duty extends beyond our duties to future generations is explained by the claim that we have duties of "stewardship" with respect to the world as a whole. Thus, Feinberg notes that his "inclination is to seek an explanation in terms of the requirements of our unique station as rational custodians of the planet we temporarily occupy."

The main objection to this appeal to our role as stewards or caretakers is that it begs the question. The job of a custodian is to protect that which is deserving of protection, that which has some value or worth. But the issue before us now is precisely *whether* species have value, and why. If we justify our obligations of stewardship by reference to the value of that which is cared for, we cannot also explain the value by pointing to the duties of stewardship.

The second type of argument is the one which establishes the value of a species by locating it in the "larger scheme of things." That is, one might try to argue that species matter because they contribute to, or form an essential part of, some other good. This line of defense has several variations.

The first version is completely anthropocentric: it is claimed that vanishing species are of concern to us because their difficulties serve as a warning that we have polluted or altered the environment in a way that is potentially dangerous or undesirable for us. Thus, the California condor whose eggshells are weakened due to the absorption of DDT indicates that something is wrong: presumably we are being affected in subtle ways by the absorption of DDT, and that is bad for us. Alternatively, diminishing numbers of game animals may signal overhunting which, if left unchecked, would leave the sportsman with fewer things to hunt. And, as we become more aware of the benefits that might be obtained from rare varieties of plants and animals (drugs, substitutes for other natural resources, tools for research), we may become reluctant to risk the disappearance of a species that might be of practical use to us in the future.

This line of argument does not carry us very far. In the case of a subspecies, most benefits could be derived from other varieties of the same species. More important, when faced with the loss of a unique variety or species, we may simply decide that, even taking into account the possibility of error, there is not enough reason to think that the species will ever be of use; we may take a calculated risk and decide that it is not worth it. Finally, the use of a species as a danger signal may apply to species whose decline is due to some subtle and unforeseen change in the environment, but will not justify concern for a species threatened by a known and foreseen event like the building of a dam.

Other attempts to ascribe extrinsic value to a species do not limit themselves to potential human and practical goods. Thus, it is often argued that each species occupies a unique niche in a rich and complex, but delicately balanced, ecosystem. By destroying a single species, we upset the balance of the whole system. On the assumption that the system as a whole should be preserved, the value of a species is determined, at least in part, by its contribution to the whole.

In assessing this argument, it is important to realize that such a justification (a) may lead to odd conclusions about some of the test cases, and (b) allows for changes which do not affect the system, or which result in the substitution of a richer, more complex system for one that is more primitive or less evolved. With regard to the first of these points, species that exist only in zoos would seem to have no special value. In terms of our test cases, the David deer does not exist as part of a system, but only in isolation. Similarly, the Appaloosa horse, a domesticated variety which is neither better suited nor worse than any other sort of horse, would not have any special value. In contrast, the whole cycle of mosquitoes, disease organisms adapted to these hosts, and other beings susceptible to those diseases is quite a complex and marvelous bit of systematic adaptation. Thus, it would seem to be wrong to wipe out the encephalitis-bearing mosquito.

With regard to the second point, we might consider changes effected by white settlers in previously isolated areas such as New Zealand and Australia. The introduction of new species has resulted in a whole new ecosystem, with many of the former indigenous species being replaced by introduced varieties. As long as the new system works, there seems to be no grounds for objections.

The third version of an appeal to extrinsic value is sometimes presented in Darwinian terms: species are important as links in the evolutionary chain. This will get us nowhere, however, because the extinction of one species, the replacement of one by another, is as much a part of evolution as is the development of a new species.

One should also consider a more general concern about all those versions of the argument which focus on the species' role in the natural order of things: all of these arguments presuppose that "the natural order of things" is, in itself, good. As William Blackstone pointed out, this is by no means obvious: "Unless one adheres dogmatically to a position of a 'reverence for all life,' the extinction of some species or forms of life may be seen as quite desirable. (This is parallel to the point often made by philosophers that not all 'customary' or 'natural' behavior is necessarily good.)" Unless we have some other way of ascribing value to a system, and to the animals which actually fulfill a certain function in that system (as opposed to possible replacements), the argument will not get off the ground.

Finally, then, the process of elimination leads us to the set of arguments which point to some *intrinsic value* that a species is supposed to have. The notion that species have an intrinsic value, if established, would allow us to defend much stronger claims about human obligations toward threatened species. Thus, if a species is intrinsically valuable, we should try to preserve it even when it no longer has a place in the natural ecosystem, or when it could be replaced by another species that would occupy the same niche. Most important, we should not ignore a species just because it serves no useful purpose.

Unsurprisingly, the stumbling block is what this intrinsic value might be grounded in. Without an explanation of that, we have no nonarbitrary way of deciding whether subspecies as well as species have intrinsic value or how much intrinsic value a species might have. The last question is meant to bring out issues that will arise in cases of

conflict of interests: is the intrinsic value of a species of mosquito sufficient to outweigh the benefits to be gained by eradicating the means of spreading a disease like encephalitis? Is the intrinsic value of the snail darter sufficient to outweigh the economic hardship that might be alleviated by the construction of a dam? In short, to say that something has intrinsic value does not tell us *how much* value it has, nor does it allow us to make the sorts of judgments that are often called for in considering the fate of an endangered species.

The attempt to sidestep the difficulties raised by subspecies by broadening the ascription of value to include subspecies opens a whole Pandora's box. It would follow that any genetic variation within a species that results in distinctive characteristics would need separate protection. In the case of forms developed through selective breeding, it is not clear whether we have a situation analogous to natural subspecies, or whether no special value is attached to different breeds.

In order to speak to either of these issues, and in order to lend plausibility to the whole enterprise, it would seem necessary to consider first the justification for ascribing value to whichever groups have such value. If intrinsic value does not spring from anything, if it becomes merely another way of saying that we should protect species, we are going around in circles, without explaining anything. Some further explanation is needed.

Some appeals to intrinsic value are grounded in the intuition that diversity itself is a virtue. If so, it would seem incumbent upon us to create new species wherever possible, even bizarre ones that would have no purpose other than to be different. Something other than diversity must therefore be valued.

The comparison that is often made between species and natural wonders, spectacular landscapes, or even works of art, suggests that species might have some aesthetic value. This seems to accord well with our naive intuitions, provided that *aesthetic value* is interpreted rather loosely; most of us believe that the world would be a poorer place for the loss of bald eagles in the same way that it would be poorer for the loss of the Grand Canyon or a great work of art. In all cases, the experience of seeing these things is an inherently worthwhile experience. And since diversity in some cases is a component in aesthetic appreciation, part of the previous intuition would be preserved. There is also room for degrees of selectivity and concern with superficial changes: the variety of rat that is allowed to become extinct may have no special aesthetic value, and a bird is neither more nor less aesthetically pleasing when we change its name.

There are some drawbacks to this line of argument: there are some species which, by no stretch of the imagination, are aesthetically significant. But aesthetic value can cover a surprising range of things: a tiger may be simply beautiful; a blue whale is awe-inspiring; a bird might be decorative; an Appaloosa is of interest because of its historical significance; and even a drab little plant may inspire admiration for the marvelous way it has been adapted to a special environment. Even so, there may be species such as the snail darter that simply have no aesthetic value. In these cases, lacking any alternative, we may be forced to the conclusion that such species are not worth preserving.

Seen from other angles, once again the appeal to the aesthetic value of species is illuminating. Things that have an aesthetic value may be compared and ranked in some cases, and commitment of resources made accordingly. We believe that diminishing the aesthetic value of a thing for mere economic benefits is immoral, but that aesthetic value is not absolute—that the fact that something has aesthetic value may be overridden by the fact that harming that thing, or destroying it, may result in some greater good. That is, someone who agrees to destroy a piece of Greek statuary for personal gain would be condemned as having done something immoral, but someone who is faced with a choice between saving his children and saving a "priceless" painting would be said to have skewed values if he chose to save the painting. Applying these observations to species, we can see that an appeal to aesthetic value would justify putting more effort into the preservation of one species than the preservation of another; indeed, just as we think that the doodling of a would-be artist may have no merit at all, we may think that the accidental and unfortunate mutation of a species is not worth preserving. Following the analogy, allowing a species to become extinct for *mere* economic gain might be seen as immoral, while the possibility remains open that other (human?) good might outweigh the goods achieved by the preservation of a species.

Although the appeal to aesthetic values has much to recommend it—even when we have taken account of the fact that it does not guarantee that all species matter—there seems to be a fundamental confusion that still affects the cogency of the whole argument and its application to the question of special obligations to endangered species, for if the value of a species is based on its aesthetic value, it is impossible to explain why an endangered species should be more valuable, or more worthy of preservation, than an unendangered species. The appeal to "rarity" will not help, if what we are talking about is species: each species is unique, no more or less rare than any other species: there is in each case one and only one species that we are talking about.

This problem of application seems to arise because the object of aesthetic appreciation, and hence of aesthetic value, has been misidentified, for it is not the case that we perceive, admire, and appreciate a *species*—species construed either as a group or set of similar animals or as a name that we attach to certain kinds of animals in virtue of some classification scheme. What we value is the existence of individuals with certain characteristics. If this is correct, then the whole attempt to explain why species matter by arguing that *they* have aesthetic value needs to be redirected. This is what I try to do in the final section of this paper.

V. VALUING THE INDIVIDUAL

What I propose is that the intuition behind the argument from aesthetic value is correct, but misdirected. The reasons that were given for the value of a species are, in fact, reasons for saying that an individual has value. We do not admire the grace and beauty of the species *Panthera tigris;* rather, we admire the grace and beauty of the individual Bengal tigers that we may encounter. What we value then is the existence of that individual and the existence (present or future) of individuals like that. The ways in which other individuals should be "like that" will depend on why we value that particular sort of individual: the stripes on a zebra do not matter if we value zebras primarily for the way they are adapted to a certain environment, their unique fitness for a certain sort of life. If, on the other hand, we value zebras because their stripes are aesthetically pleasing, the stripes do matter. Since our attitudes toward zebras probably include both of these features, it is not surprising to find that my hypothetical test case produces conflicting intuitions.

The shift of emphasis from species to individuals allows us to make sense of the stronger feelings we have about endangered species in two ways. First, the fact that there are very few members of a species—the fact that we rarely encounter one-itself increases the value of those encounters. I can see turkey vultures almost every day, and I can eat apples almost every day, but seeing a bald eagle or eating wild strawberries are experiences that are much less common, more delightful just for their rarity and unexpectedness. Even snail darters, which, if we encountered them every day would be drab and uninteresting, become more interesting just because we don't—or may not—see them everyday. Second, part of our interest in an individual carries over to a desire that there be future opportunities to see these things again (just as when, upon finding a new and beautiful work of art, I will wish to go back and see it again). In the case of animals, unlike works of art, I know that this animal will not live forever, but that other animals like this one will have similar aesthetic value. Thus, because I value possible future encounters, I will also want to do what is needed to ensure the possibility of such encounters—i.e., make sure that enough presently existing individuals of this type will be able to reproduce and survive. This is rather like the duty that we have to support and contribute to museums, or to other efforts to preserve works of art.

To sum up, then: individual animals can have, to a greater or lesser degree, aesthetic value: they are valued for their simple beauty, for their awesomeness, for their intriguing adaptations, for their rarity, and for many other reasons. We have moral obligations to protect things of aesthetic value, and to ensure (in an odd sense) their continued existence; thus we have a duty to protect individual animals (the duty may be weaker or stronger depending on the value of the individual), and to ensure that there will continue to be animals of this sort (this duty will also be weaker or stronger, depending on value).

I began this paper by suggesting that our obligations to vanishing species might appear inconsistent with a general condemnation of speciesism. My proposal is not inconsistent: we value and protect animals because of their aesthetic value, not because they are members of a given species.

🦎 STUDY QUESTIONS

1. Do you agree with Russow's rejection of inherent value in species?
2. Is Russow's argument for aesthetic value in individual animals of certain types just another version of anthropocentrism? We get pleasure from beholding certain animals. Does that mean that they are merely resources for our enjoyment?
3. The blue whale is an endangered species, which is valuable for its oil and meat. Supposing its immediate economic value outweighs its aesthetic value, would Russow's arguments conclude that no moral evil would be done in eliminating this species? What do you think?
4. Richard Routley asks the following question to those who see no intrinsic value in other species. Suppose human beings were about to die out. Nothing can be done to save our species. Would it be morally permissible to kill (painlessly, just in case that matters) all other life on Earth before we became extinct? Why, or why not?

32   What's Wrong with Plastic Trees?

MARTIN H. KRIEGER

Martin Krieger is a research planner in the Institute of Urban and Regional Development and a lecturer in the College of Environmental Design at the University of California, Berkeley.

In this essay, he argues that rationales for preserving rare natural environments are not independent issues but involve economic, societal, and political factors. Krieger has provided this abstract:

A tree's a tree. How many more [redwoods] do you need to look at? If you've seen one, you've seen them all. [Attributed to Ronald Reagan, then candidate for governor of California.]

A tree is a tree, and when you've seen one redwood, given your general knowledge about trees, you have a pretty good idea of the characteristics of a redwood. Yet most people believe that when you've seen one, you haven't seen them all. Why is this so? What implications does this have for public policy in a world where resources are not scarce, but do have to be manufactured; where choice is always present; and where the competition for resources is becoming clearer and keener? In this article I attempt to explore some of these issues, while trying to understand the reasons that are given, or might be given, for preserving certain natural environments.

THE ECOLOGY MOVEMENT

In the past few years, a movement concerned with the preservation and careful use of the natural environment in this country has grown substantially. This ecology movement, as I shall call it, is beginning to have genuine power in governmental decision-making and is becoming a link between certain government agencies and the publics to which they are responsible. The ecology movement should be distinguished from related movements concerned with the conservation and wise use of natural resources. The latter, ascendant in the United States during the first half of this century, were mostly concerned with making sure that natural resources and environments were used in a fashion that reflected their true worth to man. This resulted in a utilitarian conception of environments and in the adoption of means to partially preserve them—for example, cost–benefit analysis and policies of multiple use on federal lands.

The ecology movement is not necessarily committed to such policies. Noting the spoliation of the environment under the policies of the conservation movement, the ecology movement demands much greater concern about what is done to the environment, independently of how much it may cost. The ecology movement seeks to have man's environment valued in and of itself and thereby prevent its being traded off for the other benefits it offers to man.

It seems likely that the ecology movement will have to become more programmatic and responsive to compromise as it moves into more responsible and bureaucratic positions vis-à-vis governments and administrative agencies. As they now stand, the policies of the ecology movement may work against resource-conserving strategies designed to lead to the movement's desired ends in 20 or 30 years. Meier has said:

> The best hope, it seems now, is that the newly evolved ideologies will progress as social movements.

A number of the major tenets of the belief system may then be expected to lose their centrality and move to the periphery of collective attention. Believers may thereupon only "satisfice" with respect to these principles; they are ready to consider compromise.

What is needed is an approach midway between the preservationist and conservationist–utilitarian policies. It is necessary to find ways of preserving the opportunity for experiences in natural environments, while having, at the same time, some flexibility in the alternatives that the ecology movement could advocate.

A new approach is needed because of the success of economic arguments in the past. We are now more concerned about social equity and about finding arguments from economics for preserving "untouched" environments. Such environments have not been manipulated very much by mankind in the recent past (hundreds or thousands of years). Traditional resource economics has been concerned not as much with preservation as with deciding which intertemporal...use of natural resources over a period of years yields a maximum return to man, essentially independent of considerations of equity. If one believes that untouched environments are unlikely to have substitutes, then this economics is not very useful. In fact, a different orientation toward preservation has developed and is beginning to be applied in ways that will provide powerful arguments for preservation. At the same time, some ideas about how man experiences the environment are becoming better understood, and they suggest that the new economic approach will be in need of some modification, even if most of its assumptions are sound.

I first examine what is usually meant by natural environments and rarity; I will then examine some of the rationales for preservation. It is important to understand the character and the weak points of the usual arguments. I also suggest how our knowledge and sophistication about environments and our differential access to them are likely to lead to levers for policy changes that will effectively preserve the possibility of experiencing nature, yet offer alternatives in the management of natural resources.

One limitation of my analysis should be made clear. I have restricted my discussion to the nation-state, particularly to the United States. If it were possible to take a global view, then environmental questions would be best phrased in terms of the world's resources. If we want undisturbed natural areas, it might be best to develop some of them in other countries. But we do not live in a politically united world, and such a proposal is imperialistic at worst, and unrealistic at best. Global questions about the environment need to be considered, but they must be considered in terms of controls that can exist. If we are concerned about preserving natural environments, it seems clear that, for the moment, we will most likely have to preserve them in our own country.

THE AMERICAN FALLS: KEEPING IT NATURAL

For the last few thousand years, Niagara Falls has been receding. Water going over the Falls insinuates itself into crevices of the rock, freezes and expands in winter, and thereby causes cracks in the formation. The formation itself is a problem in that the hard rock on the surface covers a softer substratum. This weakness results not only in small amounts of erosion or small rockfalls, but also in very substantial ones when the substratum gives way. About 350,000 cubic yards (1 cubic yard equals 0.77 cubic meter) of talus lie at the base of the American Falls.

The various hydroelectric projects that have been constructed during the years have also affected the amount of water that flows over the Falls. It is now possible to alter the flow of water over the American Falls by a factor of 2 and, consequently, to diminish that of the Horseshoe (Canadian) Falls by about 10%.

As a result of these forces, the quality of the Falls—its grandeur, its height, its smoothness of flow—changes over the millennia and the months.

There is nothing pernicious about the changes wrought by nature; the problem is that Americans' image of the Falls does not change. Our ideal of a waterfall, an ideal formed by experiences with small, local waterfalls that seem perfect and by images created by artists and photographers, is not about to change without some effort.

When one visits the Falls today, he sees rocks and debris at the base, too much or too little water going over the edge, and imperfections in the flow of water. These sights are not likely to make anyone feel that he is seeing or experiencing the genuine Niagara Falls. The consequent effects of tourism, a multimillion-dollar-per-year industry, could be substantial.

At the instigation of local forces, the American Falls International Board has been formed under the auspices of the International Joint Commission of the United States and Canada. Some $5 to $6 million are being spent to investigate, by means of "dewatering" the Falls and building scale models, policies for intervention. That such efforts are commissioned suggests that we, as a nation, believe that it is proper and possible to do something about the future evolution of the Falls. A "Fallscape" committee, which is especially concerned with the visual quality of the Falls, has been formed. It suggests that three strategies, varying in degree of intervention, be considered.

1. The Falls can be converted into a monument. By means of strengthening the structure of the Falls, it is possible to prevent rockfalls. Also, excess rock from the base can be removed. Such a strategy might cost tens of millions of dollars, a large part of this cost being for the removal of talus.
2. The Falls could become an event. Some of the rocks at the base could be removed for convenience and esthetics, but the rockfalls themselves would not be hindered. Instead, instruments for predicting rockfalls could be installed. People might then come to the Falls at certain times, knowing that they would see an interesting and grand event, part of the cycle of nature, such as Old Faithful.
3. The Falls might be treated as a show. The "director" could control the amount of water flowing over the Falls, the size of the pool below, and the amount of debris, thereby producing a variety of spectacles. Not only could there be *son et lumière*, but it could take place on an orchestrated physical mass.

Which of these is the most nearly natural environment? Current practice, exemplified by the National Park Service's administration of natural areas, might suggest that the second procedure be followed and that the Falls not be "perfected." But would that be the famous Niagara Falls, the place where Marilyn Monroe met her fate in the movie *Niagara*? The answer to this question lies in the ways in which efforts at preservation are presented to the public. If the public is seeking a symbolic Falls, then the Falls has to be returned to its former state. If the public wants to see a natural phenomenon at work, then the Falls should be allowed to fall.

Paradoxically, the phenomena that the public thinks of as "natural" often require great artifice in their creation. The natural phenomenon of the Falls today has been created to a great extent by hydroelectric projects over the years. Esthetic appreciation of the Falls has been conditioned by the rather mundane considerations of routes of tourist excursions and views from hotel windows, as well as the efforts of artists.

I think that we can provide a smooth flow of water over the Falls and at the same time not be completely insensitive to natural processes if we adopt a procedure like that described in the third proposal. Niagara Falls is not a virgin territory, the skyscrapers and motels will not disappear. Therefore, an aggressive attitude toward the Falls seems appropriate. This does not imply heavy-handedness in intervention (the first proposal), but a willingness to touch the "sacred" for esthetic as well as utilitarian purposes.

The effort to analyze this fairly straightforward policy question is not trivial. Other questions concerning preservation have fuzzier boundaries, less clear costs (direct and indirect), and much more complicated political considerations. For these reasons it seems worthwhile to examine some of the concepts I use in this discussion.

NATURAL ENVIRONMENTS

What is considered a natural environment depends on the particular culture and society defining it. It might be possible to create for our culture and society a single definition that is usable (that is, the definition would mean the same thing to many people), but this, of course, says nothing about the applicability of such a definition to other cultures. However, I restrict my discussion to the development of the American idea of a natural environment.

The history of the idea of the wilderness is a good example of the development of one concept of natural environment. I follow Nash's discussion[1] in the following.

A wilderness may be viewed as a state of mind, as an attitude toward a collection of trees, other plants, animals, and the land on which they all exist. The idea that a wilderness exists as a product of an intellectual movement is important. A wilderness is not discovered in the sense that some man from a civilization looked upon a piece of territory for the first time. It is the meanings that we attach to such a piece of territory that convert it to a wilderness.

The Romantic appreciation of nature, with its associated enthusiasm for the "strange, remote, solitary and mysterious," converted territory that was a threatening wildland into a desirable area capable of producing an invigorating spirit of wilderness. The "appreciation of the wilderness in this form began in cities," for whose residents the wildland was a novelty. Because of the massive destruction of this territory for resources (primarily timber), city dwellers, whose livelihood did not depend on these resources and who were not familiar with the territory, called for the preservation of wildlands. At first, they did not try to keep the most easily accessible, and therefore most economically useful, lands from being exploited, but noted that Yellowstone and the Adirondacks were rare wonders and had no other utility. They did not think of these areas as wilderness, but as untouched lands. Eventually, a battle developed between conservationists and preservationists. The conservationists (Pinchot, for example) were concerned with the wise use of lands, with science and civilization and forestry; the preservationists (Muir, for example) based their argument on art and wilderness. This latter concept of wilderness is the significant one. The preservationists converted wildland into wilderness—a good that is indivisible and valuable in itself.

This capsule history suggests that the wilderness, as we think of it now, is the product of a political effort to give a special meaning to a biological system organized in a specific way. I suspect that this history is the appropriate model for the manner in which biological systems come to be designated as special.

But it might be said that natural environments can be defined in the way ecosystems are—in terms of complexity, energy and entropy flows, and so on. This is true, but only because of all the spadework that has gone into developing in the public a consensual picture of natural environments. What a society takes to be a natural environment is one.

Natural environments are likely to be named when there are unnatural environments and are likely to be noted only when they are outnumbered by these unnatural environments. The wildlands of the past, which were frightening, were plentiful and were not valued. The new wilderness, which is a source of revitalization, is rare and so valued that it needs to be preserved.

WHEN IS SOMETHING RARE?

Something is considered to be rare when there do not exist very many objects or events that are similar to it. It is clear that one object must be distinguishable from another in order to be declared rare, but the basis for this distinction is not clear.

One may take a realist's or an idealist's view of rarity. For the realist, an object is unique within a purview: given a certain boundary, there exists no other object like it. Certainly the Grand Canyon is unique within the United States. Perhaps Niagara Falls is also unique. But there are many other waterfalls throughout the world that are equally impressive, if not of identical dimensions.

For the idealist, a rare object is one that is archetypal: it is the most nearly typical of all the objects it represents, having the most nearly perfect form. We frequently preserve archetypal specimens in museums and botanical gardens. Natural areas often have these qualities.

A given object is not always rare. Rather, it is designated as rare at one time and may, at some other time, be considered common. How does this happen? Objects become rare when a large number of people change their attitudes toward them. This may come about in a number of ways, but it is necessary that the object in question be noticed and singled out. Perhaps one individual discovers it, or perhaps it is common to everyone's experience. Someone must convince the public that the object is something special. The publicist must develop in others the ability to differentiate one object from among a large number of others, as well as to value the characteristic that makes the particular object different. If he convinces a group of people influential in the society, people who are able to affect a much larger group's beliefs, then he will have succeeded in his task. Thus it may be important that some form of snob appeal be created for the special object.

In order to create the differentiations and the differential valuations of characteristics, information and knowledge are crucial. A physical object can be transformed into an instrument of beauty, pleasure, or pride, thereby developing sufficient characteristics to be called rare, only by means of changing the knowledge we have of it and of its relation to the rest of the world. In this sense, knowledge serves an important function in the creation of rare environments, very much as knowledge in society serves an important function in designating what should be considered natural resources.

Advertising is one means of changing states of knowledge—nor does such advertising have to be wholly sponsored by commercial interests. Picture post cards, for example, are quite effective:[2]

> ...a large number of quiet beauty spots which in consequence of the excellence of their photographs had become tourist centres....
>
> The essential was to "establish" a picture, e.g., the Tower [of London] with barges in the foreground. People came to look for the barges and in the end wouldn't have the Tower without barges. Much of the public was very conservative and though such things as high-rise building and general facade-washing had made them [the post card producers] rephotograph the whole of London recently, some people still insisted on the old sky-line, and grubby facades, and liked to believe certain new roads had never happened.

Similarly, the publicity given to prices paid at art auctions spurs the rise of these prices.

As a *result* of the social process of creating a rare object, the usual indicators of rarity become important. Economically, prices rise; physically, the locations of the rare objects become central, or at least highly significant spatially; and socially, rare objects and their possessors are associated with statuses that are valued and activities that are considered to be good.

ENVIRONMENTS CAN BE AND ARE CREATED

To recapitulate, objects are rare because men decide that they are and, through social action, convince others that they are. The rarity of an object is created through four mechanisms: designating the object as rare; differentiating it from other objects of the same species; establishing its significance; and determining its position in the context of society. The last two mechanisms are especially important, for the meaning that an environment has and its relation to other things in the society are crucial to its being considered rare. That a rare environment be irreproducible or of unchanging character is usually a necessary preliminary to our desire to preserve it. Technologies, which may involve physical processes or social organization and processes, determine how reproducible an object is, for we may make a copy of the original or we may transfer to another object the significance attached to the original. (Copying natural environments may be easier than copying artistic objects because the qualities of replicas and forgeries are not as well characterized in the case of the natural environment.) Insofar as we are incapable of doing either of these, we may desire to preserve the original environment.

In considering the clientele of rare environments, one finds that accessibility by means of transportation and communication is important. If there is no means of transportation to a rare environment then it is not likely that the public will care about that environment. An alternative to transportation is some form of communication, either verbal or pictorial, that simulates a feeling of being in the environment.

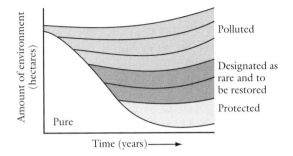

FIGURE 4.1 The Development of Rare Environments

I am concerned here with the history of environments that, at first, are not considered unique. However, a similar argument could be applied to environments regarded as unique (for example, the Grand Canyon), provided they were classed with those environments most like them. Figure 4.1 should aid in the explanation that follows.

For example, suppose that a particular kind of environment is plentiful and that, over a period of time, frequent use causes it to become polluted. (Note that pollution need not refer just to our conventional concepts of dirtying the environment, but to a wide variety of uncleanliness and stigma as well.) Because there is a substantial amount of that environment available, man's use of it will, at first, have little effect on his perception of its rarity. As time goes on, however, someone will notice that there used to be a great deal more of that particular environment available. Suddenly, the once vast quantities of that environment begin to look less plentiful. The environment seems more special as it becomes distinguishable from the polluted environments around it. At that point, it is likely that there will be a movement to designate some fraction of the remaining environment as rare and in need of protection. There will also be a movement to restore those parts of the environment that have already been polluted. People will intervene to convert the polluted environment to a simulation of the original one.[3]

REASONS FOR PRESERVATION

That something is rare does not imply that it must be preserved. The characteristics that distinguish it as rare must also be valued. Arguments in favor of preserving an object can be based on the fact that the object is a luxury, a necessity, or a merit.

We build temples or other monuments to our society (often by means of preservation) and believe that they represent important investments in social unity and coherence. If a forest symbolizes the frontier for a society and if that frontier is meaningful in the society's history, then there may be good reasons for preserving it. An object may also be preserved in order that it may be used in the future. Another reason, not often given but still true, for preserving things is that there is nothing else worth doing with them. For example, it may cost very little to preserve something that no one seems to have any particular reason for despoiling; therefore, we expend some small effort in trying to keep it untouched.

Natural environments are preserved for reasons of necessity also. Environments may provide ecological samples that will be useful to future generations. Recently, the long-lived bristlecone pine has helped to check radiocarbon dating and has thereby revised our knowledge of early Europe. It may be that the preservation of an environment is necessary for the preservation of an ecosystem and that our destruction of it will also destroy, as a product of a series of interactions, some highly valued aspects of our lives. Finally, it may be necessary to preserve environments in order that the economic development of the adjacent areas can proceed in a desired fashion.

Other reasons for preservation are based on merit: it may be felt by the society that it is good to preserve natural environments. It is good for people to be exposed to nature. Natural beauty is worth having, and the amenity resulting from preservation is important.

RARITY, UNIQUENESS, AND FORGERY: AN ARTISTIC INTERLUDE

The problems encountered in describing the qualities that make for "real" artistic experiences and genuine works of art are similar to those encountered in describing rare natural objects. The ideas of replica and forgery will serve to make the point.

Kubler[4] observes that, if one examines objects in a time sequence, he may decide that some are prime objects and the rest are replicas. Why should this be so? One may look at the properties of earlier objects and note that some of them serve as a source of later objects; however, since the future always has its sources in the present, any given object is a source. Therefore, one must distinguish important characteristics, perhaps arbitrarily, and say that they are seminal. Prime objects are the first to clearly and decisively exhibit important characteristics.

Why are there so few prime objects? By definition, prime objects exhibit characteristics in a clear and decisive way, and this must eliminate many other objects from the category; but why do artists not constantly create new objects, each so original that it would be prime? Not all artists are geniuses, it might be said. But this is just a restatement of the argument that most objects do not exhibit important characteristics in a clear, decisive manner. It might also be said that, if there are no followers, there will be no leaders, but this does not explain why some eras are filled with prime works and others are not.

Kubler suggests that invention, especially if too frequent, leads to chaos, which is frightening. Replication is calmer and leads only to dullness. Therefore, man would rather repair, replicate what he has done, than innovate and discard the past. We are, perhaps justifiably, afraid of what the prime objects of the future will be. We prefer natural environments to synthesized ones because we are familiar with techniques of managing the natural ones and know what the effects of such management are. Plastic trees are frightening.

What about those replicas of prime objects that are called forgeries? Something is a forgery if its provenance has been faked. Why should this bother us? If the forgery provides us with the same kind of experience we might have had with the original, except that we know it is a forgery, then we are snobbish to demand the original. But we do not like to be called snobs. Rather, we say that our opinion of the work, or the quality of our experience of it, depends on its context. History, social position, and ideology affect the way in which we experience the object. It may be

concluded that our appreciation of something is only partly a product of the thing itself.

Art replicas and forgeries exist in an historical framework. So do the prime and genuine objects. And so do natural environments.

CRITERIA FOR PRESERVATION

Whatever argument one uses for preservation, there must be some criteria for deciding what to preserve. Given that something is rare and is believed to be worth preserving, rarity itself, as well as economic, ecological, or socio-historical reasons, can be used to justify preservation. I consider each of these here.

There are many economic reasons for planned intervention to achieve preservation, and I discuss two of them: one concerns the application of cost–benefit analysis to preservation; the other concerns the argument that present value should be determined by future benefits.

The work of Krutilla is an ingenious application of economics; it rescues environments from current use by arguing for their future utility.[5] The crux of the argument follows.

Nature is irreproducible compared to the materials it provides. As Barnett and Morse have shown, there have been enough substitutions of natural materials to obviate the idea of a shortage of nature resources. It also seems likely that the value of nature and of experiences in nature will increase in the future, while the supply of natural environments will remain constant. Because it is comparatively easy to produce substitutes for the materials we get from natural environments, the cost of not exploiting an environment is small, compared to the cost of producing that environment. Finally, there is an option demand for environments: that is, there will be a demand, at a certain price, for that environment in the future. If a substantial fraction of the supply of the environment is destroyed now, it will be impossible to fill the demand in the future at a reasonable price. Therefore, we are willing to pay to preserve that option. The problem is not the intertemporal use of natural environments (as it is for natural resources), but the preservation of our options to use environments in the future, or at least the reduction of uncertainty about the availability of environments in the future....

Robinson has criticized Krutilla's argument from the following perspectives:[6] he suggests that the amenity valued so highly by Krutilla is not necessarily that valuable; that the experiences of nature are reproducible; that refraining from current use may be costly; and that the arguments for public intervention into such environments depend on the collective consumption aspects of these environments. That is, these environments benefit everyone, and, since people cannot be differentially charged for using them, the public must pay for these environments collectively, through government. It is well known that the users of rare environments tend to be that small fraction of the population who are better off socially and economically than the majority. However, a greater difficulty than any of these may be discerned.

It seems to me that the limitations of Krutilla's argument lie in his assumptions about how quickly spoiled environments can be restored (rate of reversion) and how great the supply of environments is. Krutilla *et al.* are sensitive to the possibility that the rate of reversion may well be amenable to technological intervention:

> Perhaps more significant, however, is the need to investigate more fully the presumption of asymmetric implications of technological progress for the value of attributes of the natural environment when used as intermediate goods, compared with their retention as assets supplying final consumption services. Irreproducibility, it might be argued, is not synonymous with irreplaceability. If reasonably good substitutes can be found, by reliance on product development, the argument for the presumption of differential effects of technological progress is weakened; or if not weakened, the value which is selected [for the reversion rate]...would not remain unaffected.

The supply of natural environments is affected by technology in that it can manipulate both biological processes and information and significance. The advertising that created rare environments can also create plentiful substitutes. The supply of special environments can be increased dramatically by highlighting (in ways not uncommon to those of differentiating among groups of equivalent

toothpastes) significant and rare parts of what are commonly thought to be uninteresting environments.

The accessibility of certain environments to population centers can be altered to create new rare environments. Also, environments that are especially rare, or are created to be especially rare, could be very far away, since people would be willing to pay more to see them. Thus it may be possible to satisfy a large variety of customers for rare environments. The following kind of situation might result.

1. Those individuals who demand "truly" natural environments could be encouraged to fly to some isolated location where a national park with such an environment is maintained; a substantial sum of money would be required of those who use such parks.
2. For those who find a rare environment in state parks or perhaps in small national parks, such parks could be made more accessible and could be developed more. In this way, a greater number of people could use them and the fee for using them would be less than the fee for using isolated areas.
3. Finally, for those who wish to have an environment that is just some trees, some woods, and some grass, there might be a very small park. Access would be very easy, and the rareness of such environments might well be enhanced beyond what is commonly thought possible by means of sophisticated methods of landscape gardening.

It seems to me that, as Krutilla suggests, the demand for rare environments is a learned one. It also seems likely that conscious public choice can manipulate this learning so that the environments which people learn to use and want reflect environments that are likely to be available at low cost. There is no lack of merit in natural environments, but this merit is not canonical.

THE VALUATION OF THE FUTURE

In any cost–benefit analysis that attempts to include future values, the rate at which the future is discounted is crucial to the analysis. (That is, a sum of money received today is worth more to us now than the same sum received in the future. To allow for this, one discounts, by a certain percent each year, these future payments.) Changes in discount rates can alter the feasibility of a given project. If different clientele's preferences for projects correspond to different discount rates at which these projects are feasible, then the choice of a particular discount rate would place the preferences of one group over another. Preservation yields benefits that come in the future. The rich have a low rate of discount compared to the poor (say, 5 percent as opposed to 10 or 20 percent) and would impute much higher present value to these future benefits than the poor would. Baumol suggests (though it is only a hunch) that:[7]

> . . . by and large, the future can be left to take care of itself. There is no need to lower artificially the social rate of discount in order to increase further the prospective wealth of future generations. . . . However, this does not mean that the future should in every respect be left at the mercy of the free market. . . . Investment in the preservation of such items then seems perfectly proper, but for this purpose the appropriate instrument would appear to be a set of selective subsidies rather than a low general discount rate that encourages indiscriminately all sorts of investment programs whether or not they are relevant.

Baumol is saying that the process of preserving environments may not always be fruitfully analyzed in terms of cost–benefit analyses; we are preserving things in very special cases, and each choice is not a utilitarian choice in any simple sense, but represents a balancing of all other costs to the society of having *no* preserved environments. Preservation often entails a gross change in policy, and utilitarian analyses cannot easily compare choices in which values may be drastically altered.

OTHER CRITERIA

We may decide to preserve things just because they are rare. In that case, we need to know which things are rarer than others. Leopold has tried to do this for a set of natural environments. He listed a large number of attributes for each

environment and then weighted each attribute as follows. For any single attribute, determine how many environments share that attribute and assign each of them a value of $1/N$ units, where N is the number of environments that share an attribute. Then add all the weights for the environments; the environment with the largest weight is the rarest. It is clear that, if an environment has attributes which are unique, it will get one unit of weight for each attribute and thus its total weight will just equal the number of attributes. If all of the environments are about the same, then each of them will have roughly the same weight, which will equal the number of attributes divided by the number of environments. The procedure is sensitive to how differentiated we wish to make our attributes and to the attributes we choose. It is straightforward and usable, as Leopold has shown.

It seems to me that there are two major difficulties in this approach. The first, and more important, is that the accessibility of environments to their clientele, which Leopold treats as one of his 34 attributes, needs to be further emphasized in deciding what to preserve. An environment that is quite rare but essentially inaccessible may not be as worthy of preservation as one that is fairly common but quite accessible. The other difficulty is that probably the quantity that should be used is the amount of information possessed by each environment—rather than taking $1/N$, one should take a function of its logarithm to the base 2.

An ecological argument is that environments which contribute to our stability and survival as an ecosystem should be preserved. It is quite difficult to define what survival means, however. If it means the continued existence of man in an environment quite similar to the one he lives in now, then survival is likely to become very difficult as we use part of our environment for the maintenance of life and as new technologies come to the fore. If survival means the maintenance of a healthy and rich culture, then ecology can only partially guide us in the choices, since technology has substantially changed the risk from catastrophe in the natural world. Our complex political and social organizations may serve to develop means for survival and stability sufficient to save man from the catastrophic tricks of his own technology.

If a taxonomy of environments were established, a few environments might stand out from all the rest. But what would be the criteria involved in such a taxonomy?

Another possibility is to search for relics of cultural, historical, and social significance to the nation. Such physical artifacts are preserved because the experiences they represent affect the nature of the present society. In this sense, forests are preserved to recall a frontier, and historic homes are preserved to recall the individuals who inhabited them. Of course the problem here is that there is no simple way of ordering the importance of relics and their referents. Perhaps a survey of a large number of people might enable one to assign priorities to these relics.

Finally, it might be suggested that preservation should only be used, or could sometimes be used, to serve the interests of social justice. Rather than preserving things for what they are or for the experiences they provide, we preserve them as monuments to people who deserve commemoration or as a means of redistributing wealth (when an environment is designated as rare, local values are affected). Rather than buy forests and preserve them, perhaps we should preserve slums and suitably reward their inhabitants.

All of these criteria are problematic. Whichever ones are chosen, priorities for intervention must still be developed.

PRIORITIES FOR PRESERVING THE ENVIRONMENT

Not every problem in environmental quality is urgent, nor does every undesirable condition that exists need to be improved. We need to classify environmental problems in order that we can choose from among the possible improvements.

1. There are conditions about which we must do something soon or we will lose a special thing. These conditions pertain especially to rare environments, environments we wish to preserve for their special beauty or their uniqueness. We

might allocate a fixed amount of money every year to such urgent problems. Niagara Falls might be one of these, and it might cost a fraction of a dollar per family to keep it in good repair. Wilderness and monument maintenance have direct costs of a few dollars per family per year.

2. There are situations in which conditions are poor, but fairly stable. In such situations, it might be possible to handle the problem in 10 years without too much loss. However, the losses to society resulting from the delayed improvement of these facilities need to be carefully computed. For example, the eutrophied Lake Erie might be such a project. There, society loses fishing and recreational facilities. It might cost $100 per family, locally, to clean up the lake. Perhaps our environmental dollar should be spent elsewhere.

3. There are also situations in which conditions are rapidly deteriorating and in which a small injection of environmental improvement and amelioration would cause dramatic changes in a trend. Smog control devices have probably raised the cost of driving by 2 or 3 percent, yet their contribution to the relative improvement of the environment in certain areas (for example, Los Angeles) has been substantial. Fifty dollars per car per year is the estimated current cost to the car owner.

4. There may be situations in which large infusions of money are needed to stop a change. These problems are especially irksome. Perhaps the best response to them would be to change the system of production sufficiently that we can avoid such costs in the future. The costs of such change, one-time costs we hope, may be much smaller than the long-term costs of the problems themselves, although this need not be the case. The development of cleaner industrial processes is a case in point.

This is not an all-inclusive or especially inventive classification of problems, but I have devised it to suggest that many of the "urgent" problems are not so urgent.

Rare environments pose special problems and may require an approach different from that required by other environments. A poor nation is unlikely to destroy very much of its special environments. It lacks the technical and economic power to do so. It may certainly perform minor miracles of destruction through a series of small decisions or in single, major projects. These latter are often done with the aid of rich countries.

The industrialized, but not wealthy, nations have wreaked havoc with their environments in their efforts to gain some degree of wealth. It is interesting that they are willing to caution the poor nations against such a course, even though it may be a very rapid way of developing. At the U.N. Conference on the Environment this year, the poor nations indicated their awareness of these problems and their desire to develop without such havoc.

The rich nations can afford to have environments that are rare and consciously preserved. These environments are comparable to the temples of old, in that these environments will be relics of *our* time, yet this is no criterion for deciding how much should be spent on "temple building." The amount of money needed is only a small proportion of a rich country's wealth (as opposed to the cost of churches in medieval times).

Politically, the situation is complicated. There are many small groups in this country for whom certain environments are highly significant. The problem for each group is to somehow get its piece of turf, preferably uncut, unrenewed, or untouched. It seems likely that the ultimate determinant of which environments are preserved will be a process of political trade-off, in which some environments are preserved for some groups and other environments for others. Natural environments are likely to be viewed in a continuum with a large number of other environments that are especially valued by some subgroup of the society. In this sense, environmental issues will become continuous with a number of other special interests and will no longer be seen as a part of a "whole earth" movement. The power of the intellectuals, in the media, and even in union bureaucracies, with their upper middle class preferences for nature, suggests that special interest groups who are advocates for the poor and working classes will have to be wary of their own staffs.

Projects might be ranked in importance on the basis of the net benefits they provide a particular group. Marglin has suggested a means by which income redistribution could be explicitly included in cost–benefit calculations for environmental programs. If one wishes to take efficiency into account, costs minus benefits could be minimized with a constraint relating to income redistribution. This is not a simple task, however, because pricing some commodities at zero dollars, seemingly the best way of attempting a redistribution of income, may not be politically desirable or feasible. As Clawson and Knetsch have pointed out, we have to be sure that in making some prices low we do not make others prohibitively high and thereby deny the persons who are to benefit access to the low-priced goods.[8] In any case, Marglin shows that the degree to which income is redistributed will depend on how the same amount of money might have been spent in alternative activities (marginal opportunity cost). This parallels Kneese and Bower's view that the level of pollution we tolerate, or is "optimal," is that at which the marginal benefits of increasing pollution are balanced by the marginal costs of abatement measures.[9]

In doing these cost–benefit calculations, one must consider the value of 10 years of clean lake (if we can clean up the lake now) versus 10 years of uneducated man (if we wait 10 years for a manpower training program). According to Freeman:[10]

> ... [the] equity characteristics of projects *within* broad classifications . . . will be roughly similar. If this surmise is correct, then the ranking of projects within these classes is not likely to be significantly affected by equity considerations. On the other hand, we would expect more marked differences in distribution patterns among classes of projects, e.g., rural recreation vs. urban air quality.

He goes on to point out that it is unlikely that such seemingly incommensurable kinds of projects will be compared with respect to equity. I suspect that it is still possible to affect specific groups in the design of a given project; furthermore, equity can be taken into consideration more concretely at this level. Careful disaggregation, in measuring effects and benefits, will be needed to ensure that minorities are properly represented.

AN ETHICAL QUESTION

I still feel quite uncomfortable with what I have said here. I have tried to show that the utilitarian and manipulative rationality inherited from the conservationist movement and currently embodied in economic analyses and modes of argument can be helpful in deciding questions of preservation and rarity. By manipulating attitudes, we have levers for intervening into what is ordinarily considered fixed and uncontrollable. But to what end?

Our ability to manipulate preferences and values tends to lead to systems that make no sense. For example, an electrical utility encourages its customers to use more electricity, and the customers proceed to do so. As a result, there are power shortages. Similarly, if we allocate resources now in order to preserve environments for future generations, their preferences for environments may be altered by this action, and there may be larger shortages.

I also fear that my own proposals might get out of hand. My purpose in proposing interventions is not to preserve man's opportunity to experience nature, although this is important, but to promote social justice. I believe that this concern should guide our attempts to manipulate, trade off, and control environments. A summum bonum of preserving trees has no place in an ethic of social justice. If I took this ethic seriously, I could not argue the relative merits of schemes to manipulate environments. I would argue that the ecology movement is wrong and would not answer its question about what we are going to do about the earth—I would be worried about what we are going to do about men.

CONCLUSION

With some ingenuity, a transformation of our attitudes toward preservation of the environment will take place fairly soon. We will recognize the symbolic and social meanings of environments, not just their economic utility; we will emphasize their historical significance as well as the future generations that will use them.

At the same time, we must realize that there are things we may not want to trade at all, except in the sense of letting someone else have his share of the environment also. As environments become more differentiated, smaller areas will probably be given greater significance, and it may be possible for more groups to have a share.

It is likely that we shall want to apply our technology to the creation of artificial environments. It may be possible to create environments that are evocative of other environments in other times and places. It is possible that, by manipulating memory through the rewriting of history, environments will come to have new meaning. Finally, we may want to create proxy environments by means of substitution and simulation. In order to create substitutes, we must endow new objects with significance by means of advertising and by social practice. Sophistication about differentiation will become very important for appreciating the substitute environments. We may simulate the environment by means of photographs, recordings, models, and perhaps even manipulations in the brain. What we experience in natural environments may actually be more controllable than we imagine. Artificial prairies and wildernesses have been created, and there is no reason to believe that these artificial environments need be unsatisfactory for those who experience them.

Rare environments are relative, can be created, are dependent on our knowledge, and are a function of policy, not only tradition. It seems likely that economic arguments will not be sufficient to preserve environments or to suggest how we can create new ones. Rather, conscious choice about what matters, and then a financial and social investment in an effort to create significant experiences and environments, will become a policy alternative available to us.

What's wrong with plastic trees? My guess is that there is very little wrong with them. Much more can be done with plastic trees and the like[11] to give most people the feeling that they are experiencing nature. We will have to realize that the way in which we experience nature is conditioned by our society—which more and more is seen to be receptive to responsible interventions.

Bentham, the father of utilitarianism, was very concerned about the uses of the dead to the living and suggested:[12]

> If a country gentleman have rows of trees leading to his dwelling, the auto-icons [embalmed bodies in an upright position] of his family might alternate with the trees: copal varnish would protect the face from the effects of rain—caoutchouc [rubber] the habiliments.

NOTES

1. R. Nash, *Wilderness and the American Mind* (Yale University Press, 1967).
2. A. Hamilton, *The Manchester Guardian*, 4 September 1971, p. 8.
3. This analysis is as useful for paintings in museums and stamps in collections as it is for trees in parks. Art museums are places where rare objects are preserved in order to enhance the quality of experience available to people. [Grana's discussions of museums make the analogy with rare natural environments stand out. The conflict between the didactic ("New York" style) and the pure ("Boston" style) approaches to museum organization reminds one of the conflict between recreationists and preservationists. These conflicts reflect, of course, much larger issues in mass society. See C. Grana, *Transaction* 4, 20 (April 1967).] Originally, they were developed to help artists by showing their works, thereby institutionalizing the artist's relationships with his patron-clients. Eventually, these galleries became sources of orthodoxy, thereby establishing what the acceptable forms of art were. [F. Haskell, in *International Encyclopedia of the Social Sciences*, D. Sills, Ed. (Macmillan, New York, 1968), vol. 5, p. 439.] The creation of museums and their continued development is not simply a product of the increased rareness of works of art, per se, for the rareness of a work of art is actually, in part, the result of museums. The stock of art must be viewed in terms of public and private consumption. If it is believed that the public ought to have access to art, then putting art in private collections uses it up, as far as the public is concerned. An ideology that encourages the development of means of public consumption of art—for example, building museums in order to be saved either after a life of sin (as in the case of the robber barons) or from taxes—rescues these objects from oblivion.

4. G. Kubler, *The Shape of Time* (Yale University Press, 1962).
5. J. Krutilla, *Amer. Econ. Rev.* 57, 777 (1967).
6. W. Robinson, *Land Econ.* 45, 453 (1969).
7. W. Baumol, *Amer. Econ. Rev.* 58, 788 (1968).
8. M. Clawson and J. Knetsch, *Economics of Outdoor Recreation* (Johns Hopkins Press, 1966).
9. A. Kneese and B. Bower, *Managing Water Quality: Economics, Technology and Institutions* (Johns Hopkins Press, 1972).
10. A. Freeman, III, in *Environmental Quality Analysis* (Johns Hopkins Press, 1972).
11. The introduction of artificial turf and trees has not been very smooth. Adaption to the artificial product and realization of the alternatives takes some time. In the case of turf, some controversy has arisen about its being safe for football players. The rejoinders of manufacturers suggest that players and coaches have to adapt playing styles and equipment to the new surfaces (see assorted pamphlets from Monsanto, the manufacturer of Astroturf). Similarly, the introduction of plastic trees in the center meridian of Jefferson Boulevard in Los Angeles has been greeted with much criticism. As set up, there is insufficient support for living plants on the boulevard, and the only alternative is concrete.
12. J. Bentham, *Auto-Icon, or the Uses of the Dead to the Living in Dictionary of National Biography*, L. Stephen and S. Lee, eds. (Oxford University Press, 1917), vol. 2, p. 268.

✎ STUDY QUESTIONS

1. What is the dispute between the conservationists (Pinchot) and preservationists (Muir), and how does Krieger try to resolve the dispute? What, if anything, does this have to do with Krieger's discussion of Niagara Falls?
2. Examine Krieger's discussion of "Natural Environments." Do you agree with him that "what a society takes to be a natural environment is one" and that "objects are rare because men decide that they are and, through social action, convince others that they are"? Explain your answer.
3. Explain the four mechanisms for creating rare objects. Does society create rarity the way it creates money or cars? Or does Krieger leave something out?—That there really are few of the

items available, like photographs from the 1850s, seven-foot humans, or condors?

4. Why are plastic trees frightening, according to Krieger? Does Krieger see anything really wrong with them? Explain your answer. Do you agree with him?

5. What does Krieger mean by proposing intervention into nature in order to promote social justice? (See especially the last paragraph before the conclusion and the conclusion itself.) Do you see any problems with his proposal for creating artificial or proxy environments? Explain your answer.

33   Faking Nature

ROBERT ELLIOT

Robert Elliot is senior lecturer in the philosophy department at the University of New England, Armidale, New South Wales. In this essay, Elliot considers the contention by those who would greatly alter nature that the artificial creation of something similar would preserve whatever aesthetic value that part of nature had in the first place. He calls this the "restoration thesis." Elliot compares natural areas, such as a wilderness, to works of art. He argues that just as knowing that the Vermeer painting you have is a replica lowers its value, so likewise knowing that the experience you are having is only a replica of the natural original lowers the value of that experience. "Origin is important as an integral part of the evaluation process."

I

Consider the following case. There is a proposal to mine beach sands for rutile. Large areas of dune are to be cleared of vegetation and the dunes themselves destroyed. It is agreed, by all parties concerned, that the dune area has value quite apart from a utilitarian one. It is agreed, in other words, that it would be a bad thing considered in itself for the dune area to be dramatically altered. Acknowledging this the mining company expresses its willingness, indeed its desire, to restore the dune area to its original condition after the minerals have been extracted. The company goes on to argue that any loss of value is merely temporary and that full value will in fact be restored. In other words they are claiming that the destruction of what has value is compensated for by the later creation (recreation) of something of equal value. I shall call this "the restoration thesis."

In the actual world many such proposals are made, not because of shared conservationist principles, but as a way of undermining the arguments of conservationists. Such proposals are in fact effective in defeating environmentalist protest. They are also notoriously ineffective in putting right, or indeed even seeming to put right, the particular wrong that has been done to the environment. The sandmining case is just one of a number of similar cases involving such things as open-cut mining, clear-felling of forests, river diversion, and highway construction. Across a range of such cases some concession is made by way of acknowledging the value of pieces of landscape, rivers, forests and so forth, and a suggestion is made that this value can be restored once the environmentally disruptive process has been completed.

Imagine, contrary to fact, that restoration projects are largely successful; that the environment is brought back to its original condition and that even a close inspection will fail to reveal that the area has been mined, clear-felled, or whatever. If this is so then there is temptation to think that one particular environmentalist

From: *Inquiry,* Vol. 25, no. 1 (Mar. 1982), pp. 81–93. Reprinted by permission. Footnotes deleted.

objection is defeated. The issue is by no means merely academic. I have already claimed that restoration promises do in fact carry weight against environmental arguments. Thus Mr. Doug Anthony, the Australian Deputy Prime Minister, saw fit to suggest that sand-mining on Fraser Island could be resumed once "the community becomes more informed and more enlightened as to what reclamation work is being carried out by mining companies...." Or consider how the protests of environmentalists might be deflected in the light of the following report of environmental engineering in the United States.

> ...about 2 km of creek 25 feet wide has been moved to accommodate a highway and in doing so engineers with the aid of landscape architects and biologists have rebuilt the creek to the same standard as before. Boulders, bends, irregularities and natural vegetation have all been designed into the new section. In addition, special log structures have been built to improve the habitat as part of a fish development program.

Not surprisingly the claim that revegetation, rehabilitation, and the like restore value has been strongly contested. J. G. Mosley reports that:

> The Fraser Island Environmental Inquiry Commissioners did in fact face up to the question of the relevance of successful rehabilitation to the decision on whether to ban exports (of beach sand minerals) and were quite unequivocal in saying that if the aim was to protect a natural area such success was irrelevant.... The Inquiry said: "...even if, contrary to the overwhelming weight of evidence before the Commission, successful rehabilitation of the flora after mining is found to be ecologically possible on all mined sites on the Island...the overall impression of a wild, uncultivated island refuge will be destroyed forever by mining."

I want to show both that there is a rational, coherent ethical system which supports decisive objections to the restoration thesis, and that that system is not lacking in normative appeal. The system I have in mind will make valuation depend, in part, on the presence of properties which cannot survive the disruption-restoration process. There is, however, one point that needs clarifying before discussion proceeds. Establishing that restoration projects, even if empirically successful, do not fully restore value does not by any means constitute a knockdown argument against some environmentally disruptive policy. The value that would be lost if such a policy were implemented may be just one value among many which conflict in this situation. Countervailing considerations may be decisive and the policy thereby shown to be the right one. If my argument turns out to be correct it will provide an extra, though by no means decisive, reason for adopting certain environmentalist policies. It will show that the resistance which environmentalists display in the face of restoration promises is not merely silly, or emotional, or irrational. This is important because so much of the debate assumes that settling the dispute about what is ecologically possible automatically settles the value question. The thrust of much of the discussion is that if restoration is shown to be possible, and economically feasible, then recalcitrant environmentalists are behaving irrationally, being merely obstinate or being selfish.

There are indeed familiar ethical systems which will serve to explain what is wrong with the restoration thesis in a certain range of cases. Thus preference utilitarianism will support objections to some restoration proposal if that proposal fails to maximally satisfy preferences. Likewise classical utilitarianism will lend support to a conservationist stance provided that the restoration proposal fails to maximize happiness and pleasure. However, in both cases the support offered is contingent upon the way in which the preferences and utilities line up. And it is simply not clear that they line up in such a way that the conservationist position is even usually vindicated. While appeal to utilitarian considerations might be strategically useful in certain cases they do not reflect the underlying motivation of the conservationists. The conservationists seem committed to an account of what has value which allows that restoration proposals fail to compensate for environmental destruction despite the fact that such proposals would maximize utility. What then is this distinct source of value which motivates and underpins the stance taken by, among others, the Commissioners of the Fraser Island Environmental Inquiry?

II

It is instructive to list some reasons that might be given in support of the claim that something of value would be lost if a certain bit of the environment were destroyed. It may be that the area supports a diversity of plant and animal life, it may be that it is the habitat of some endangered species, it may be that it contains striking rock formations or particularly fine specimens of mountain ash. If it is only considerations such as these that contribute to the area's value then perhaps opposition to the environmentally disruptive project would be irrational provided certain firm guarantees were available; for instance that the mining company or timber company would carry out the restoration and that it would be successful. Presumably there are steps that could be taken to ensure the continuance of species diversity and the continued existence of the endangered species. Some of the other requirements might prove harder to meet, but in some sense or other it is possible to recreate the rock formations and to plant mountain ash that will turn out to be particularly fine specimens. If value consists of the presence of objects of these various kinds, independently of what explains their presence, then the restoration thesis would seem to hold. The environmentalist needs to appeal to some feature which cannot be replicated as a source of some part of a natural area's value.

Putting the point thus indicates the direction the environmentalist could take. He might suggest that an area is valuable, partly, because it is a natural area, one that has not been modified by human hand, one that is undeveloped, unspoilt, or even unsullied. This suggestion is in accordance with much environmentalist rhetoric, and something like it at least must be at the basis of resistance to restoration proposals. One way of teasing out the suggestion and giving it a normative basis is to take over a notion from aesthetics. Thus we might claim that what the environmental engineers are proposing is that we accept a fake or a forgery instead of the real thing. If the claim can be made good then perhaps an adequate response to restoration proposals is to point out that they merely fake nature; that they offer us something less than was taken away. Certainly there is a weight of opinion to the effect that, in art at least, fakes lack a value possessed by the real thing.

One way in which this argument might be nipped in the bud is by claiming that it is bound to exploit an ultimately unworkable distinction between what is natural and what is not. Admittedly the distinction between the natural and the non-natural requires detailed working out. This is something I do not propose doing. However, I do think the distinction can be made good in a way sufficient to the present need. For present purposes I shall take it that "natural" means something like "unmodified by human activity." Obviously some areas will be more natural than others according to the degree to which they have been shaped by human hand. Indeed most rural landscapes will, on this view, count as non-natural to a very high degree. Nor do I intend the natural/non-natural distinction to exactly parallel some dependent moral evaluations; that is, I do not want to be taken as claiming that what is natural is good and what is non-natural is not. The distinction between natural and non-natural connects with valuation in a much more subtle way than that. This is something to which I shall presently return. My claim then is that restoration policies do not always fully restore value because part of the reason that we value bits of the environment is because they are natural to a high degree. It is time to consider some counter-arguments.

An environmental engineer might urge that the exact similarity which holds between the original and the perfectly restored environment leaves no room for a value discrimination between them. He may urge that if they are *exactly* alike, down to the minutest detail (and let us imagine for the sake of argument that this is a technological possibility), then they must be *equally* valuable. The suggestion is that value-discriminations depend on there being intrinsic differences between the states of affairs evaluated. This begs the question against the environmentalist, since it simply discounts the possibility that events temporally and spatially outside the immediate landscape in question can serve as the basis of some valuation of it. It discounts the possibility that the manner of the landscape's genesis, for example, has a legitimate role in determining its value. Here are some examples which suggest that an object's origins do affect its value and our valuations of it.

Imagine that I have a piece of sculpture in my garden which is too fragile to be moved at all. For some reason it would suit the local council to lay sewerage pipes just where the sculpture happens to be. The council engineer informs me of this and explains that my sculpture will have to go. However, I need not despair because he promises to replace it with an exactly similar artifact, one which, he assures me, not even the very best experts could tell was not the original. The example may be unlikely, but it does have some point. While I may concede that the replica would be better than nothing at all (and I may not even concede that), it is utterly improbable that I would accept it as full compensation for the original. Nor is my reluctance entirely explained by the monetary value of the original work. My reluctance springs from the fact that I value the original as an aesthetic object, as an object with a specific genesis and history.

Alternatively, imagine I have been promised a Vermeer for my birthday. The day arrives and I am given a painting which looks just like a Vermeer. I am understandably pleased. However, my pleasure does not last for long. I am told that the painting I am holding is not a Vermeer but instead an exact replica of one previously destroyed. Any attempt to allay my disappointment by insisting that there just is no difference between the replica and the original misses the mark completely. There is a difference and it is one which affects my perception, and consequent valuation, of the painting. The difference of course lies in the painting's genesis.

I shall offer one last example which perhaps bears even more closely on the environmental issue. I am given a rather beautiful, delicately constructed, object. It is something I treasure and admire, something in which I find considerable aesthetic value. Everything is fine until I discover certain facts about its origin. I discover that it is carved out of the bone of someone killed especially for that purpose. This discovery affects me deeply and I cease to value the object in the way that I once did. I regard it as in some sense

sullied, spoilt by the facts of its origin. The object itself has not changed but my perceptions of it have. I now know that it is not quite the kind of thing I thought it was, and that my prior valuation of it was mistaken. The discovery is like the discovery that a painting one believed to be an original is in fact a forgery. The discovery about the object's origin changes the valuation made of it, since it reveals that the object is not of the kind that I value.

What these examples suggest is that there is at least a prima facie case for partially explaining the value of objects in terms of their origins, in terms of the kinds of processes that brought them into being. It is easy to find evidence in the writings of people who have valued nature that things extrinsic to the present, immediate environment determine valuations of it. John Muir's remarks about Hetch Hetchy Valley are a case in point. Muir regarded the valley as a place where he could have direct contact with primeval nature; he valued it, not just because it was a place of great beauty, but because it was also a part of the world that had not been shaped by human hand. Muir's valuation was conditional upon certain facts about the valley's genesis; his valuation was of a, literally, natural object, of an object with a special kind of continuity with the past. The news that it was a carefully contrived elaborate *ecological* artifact would have transformed that valuation immediately and radically.

The appeal that many find in areas of wilderness, in natural forests and wild rivers depends very much on the naturalness of such places. There may be similarities between the experience one has when confronted with the multi-faceted complexity, the magnitude, the awesomeness of a very large city, and the experience one has walking through a rain forest. There may be similarities between the feeling one has listening to the roar of water over the spillway of a dam, and the feeling one has listening to a similar roar as a wild river tumbles down rapids. Despite the similarities there are also differences. We value the forest and river in part because they are representative of the world outside our dominion, because their existence is independent of us. We may value the city and the dam because of what they represent of human achievement. Pointing out the differences is not necessarily to denigrate either. However, there will be cases where we rightly judge that it is better to have the natural object than it is to have the artifact.

It is appropriate to return to a point mentioned earlier concerning the relationship between the natural and the valuable. It will not do to argue that what is natural is necessarily of value. The environmentalist can comfortably concede this point. He is not claiming that all natural phenomena have value in virtue of being natural. Sickness and disease are natural in a straightforward sense and are certainly not good. Natural phenomena such as fires, hurricanes, volcanic eruptions can totally alter landscapes and alter them for the worse. All of this can be conceded. What the environmentalist wants to claim is that, within certain constraints, the naturalness of a landscape is a reason for preserving it, a determinant of its value. Artificially transforming an utterly barren, ecologically bankrupt landscape into something richer and more subtle may be a good thing. That is a view quite compatible with the belief that replacing a rich natural environment with a rich artificial one is a bad thing. What the environmentalist insists on is that naturalness is one factor in determining the value of pieces of the environment. But that, as I have tried to suggest, is no news. The castle by the Scottish loch is a very different kind of object, value-wise, from the exact replica in the appropriately shaped environment of some Disneyland of the future. The barrenness of some Cycladic island would stand in a different, better perspective if it were not brought about by human intervention.

As I have glossed it, the environmentalist's complaint concerning restoration proposals is that nature is not replaceable without depreciation in one aspect of its value which has to do with its genesis, its history. Given this, an opponent might be tempted to argue that there is no longer any such thing as "natural" wilderness, since the preservation of those bits of it which remain is achievable only by deliberate policy. The idea is that by placing boundaries around national parks, by actively discouraging grazing, trail-biking and the like, by prohibiting sand-mining, we are turning the wilderness into an artifact, that in some negative or indirect way we are creating an environment. There is some truth in this suggestion. In fact we need to take notice of it if we do value wilderness, since positive policies *are* required to preserve it. But as an argument against my over-all claim it fails. What is significant about wilderness is its causal continuity with the past. This is something that is not destroyed by demarcating an area and declaring it a national park. There is a distinction between the "naturalness" of the wilderness itself and the means used to maintain and protect it. What remains within the park boundaries is, as it were, the real thing. The environmentalist may regret that such positive policy is required to preserve the wilderness against human, or even natural, assault. However, the regret does not follow from the belief that what remains is of depreciated value. There is a significant difference between preventing damage and repairing damage once it is done. That is the difference that leaves room for an argument in favour of a preservation policy over and above a restoration policy.

There is another important issue which needs highlighting. It might be thought that naturalness only matters in so far as it is perceived. In other words it might be thought that if the environmentalist engineer could perform the restoration quickly and secretly, then there would be no room for complaint. Of course, in one sense there would not be, since the knowledge which would motivate complaint would be missing. What this shows is that there can be loss of value without the loss being perceived. It allows room for valuations to be mistaken because of ignorance concerning relevant facts. Thus my Vermeer can be removed and secretly replaced with the perfect replica. I have lost something of value without knowing that I have. This is possible because it is not simply the states of mind engendered by looking at the painting, by gloatingly contemplating my possession of it, by giving myself over to aesthetic pleasure, and so on which explain why it has value. It has value because of the kind of thing that it is, and one thing that it is is a painting executed by a man with certain intentions, at a certain stage of his artistic development, living in a certain aesthetic *milieu*. Similarly, it is not just those things which make me feel the joy that wilderness makes me feel, that I value. That would be a reason for desiring such things, but that is a distinct consideration.

I value the forest because it is of a specific kind, because there is a certain kind of causal history which explains its existence. Of course I can be deceived into thinking that a piece of landscape has that kind of history, has developed in the appropriate way. The success of the deception does not elevate the restored landscape to the level of the original, no more than the success of the deception in the previous example confers on the fake the value of a real Vermeer. What has value in both cases are objects which are of the kind that I value, not merely objects which I think are of that kind. This point, it should be noted, is appropriate independently of views concerning the subjectivity or objectivity of value.

An example might bring the point home. Imagine that John is someone who values wilderness. John may find himself in one of the following situations:

1. He falls into the clutches of a utilitarian-minded super-technologist. John's captor has erected a rather incredible device which he calls an experience machine. Once the electrodes are attached and the right buttons pressed one can be brought to experience anything whatsoever. John is plugged into the machine, and since his captor knows full well John's love of wilderness, given an extended experience as of hiking through a spectacular wilderness. This is environmental engineering at its most extreme. Quite assuredly John is being short-changed. John wants there to be wilderness and he wants to experience it. He wants the world to be a certain way and he wants to have experiences of a certain kind; veridical.

2. John is abducted, blindfolded and taken to a simulated, plastic wilderness area. When the blindfold is removed John is thrilled by what he sees around him: the tall gums, the wattles, the lichen on the rocks. At least that is what he thinks is there. We know better: we know that John is deceived, that he is once again being short-changed. He has been presented with an environment which he thinks is of value but isn't. If he knew that the leaves through which the artificially generated breeze now stirred were synthetic he would be profoundly disappointed, perhaps even disgusted at what at best is a cruel joke.

3. John is taken to a place which was once devastated by strip-mining. The forest which had stood there for some thousands of years had been felled and the earth torn up, and the animals either killed or driven from their habitat. Times have changed, however, and the area has been restored. Trees of the species which grew there before the devastation grow there again, and the animal species have resumed. John knows nothing of this and thinks he is in pristine forest. Once again, he has been short-changed, presented with less than what he values most.

In the same way that the plastic trees may be thought a (minimal) improvement on the experience machine, so too the real trees are an improvement on the plastic ones. In fact in the third situation there is incomparably more of value than in the second, but there could be more. The forest, though real, is not genuinely what John wants it to be. If it were not the product of contrivance he would value it more. It is a product of contrivance. Even in the situation where the devastated area regenerates rather than is restored, it is possible to understand and sympathize with John's claim that the environment does not have the fullest possible value. Admittedly in this case there is not so much room for that claim, since the environment has regenerated of its own accord. Still the regenerated environment does not have the right kind of continuity with the forest that stood there initially; that continuity has been interfered with by the earlier devastation. (In actual fact the regenerated forest is likely to be perceivably quite different to the kind of thing originally there.)

III

I have argued that the causal genesis of forests, rivers, lakes, and so on is important in establishing their value. I have also tried to give an indication of why this is. In the course of my argument I drew various analogies, implicit rather than explicit, between faking art and faking nature. This should not be taken to suggest, however, that the concepts of aesthetic evaluation and judgment are to be carried straight over to evaluations of, and judgments about, the natural environment. Indeed there is good reason to believe that this cannot be done. For one thing an apparently integral part of aesthetic evaluation depends on viewing the aesthetic object as an intentional object, as an artifact, as something that is shaped by the purposes and designs of its author. Evaluating works of art involves explaining them, and judging them, in terms of their author's intentions; it involves placing them within the author's corpus of work; it involves locating them in some tradition and in some special *milieu*. Nature is not a work of art though works of art (in some suitably broad sense) may look very much like natural objects.

None of this is to deny that certain concepts which are frequently deployed in aesthetic evaluation cannot usefully and legitimately be deployed in evaluations of the environment. We admire the intricacy and delicacy of coloring in paintings as we might admire the intricate and delicate shadings in a eucalypt forest. We admire the solid grandeur of a building as we might admire the solidity and grandeur of a massive rock outcrop. And of course the ubiquitous notion of *the beautiful* has a purchase in environmental evaluations as it does in aesthetic evaluations. Even granted all this there are various arguments which might be developed to drive a wedge between the two kinds of evaluation, which would weaken the analogies between faking art and faking nature. One such argument turns on the claim that aesthetic evaluation has, as a central component, a judgmental factor, concerning the author's intentions and the like in the way that was sketched above. The idea is that nature, like works of art, may elicit any of a range of emotional responses in viewers. We may be awed by a mountain, soothed by the sound of water over rocks, excited by the power of a waterfall and so on. However, the judgmental element in aesthetic evaluation serves to differentiate it from environmental evaluation and serves to explain, or so the argument would go, exactly what it is about fakes and forgeries in art which discounts their value with respect to the original. The claim is that if there is no judgmental element in environmental evaluation, then there is no rational basis to preferring real to

faked nature when the latter is a good replica. The argument can, I think, be met.

Meeting the argument does not require arguing that responses to nature count as aesthetic responses. I agree that they are not. Nevertheless there are analogies which go beyond emotional content, and which may persuade us to take more seriously the claim that faked nature is inferior. It is important to make the point that only in fanciful situations dreamt up by philosophers are there no detectable differences between fakes and originals, both in the case of artifacts and in the case of natural objects. By taking a realistic example where there are discernible, and possibly discernible, differences between the fake and the real thing, it is possible to bring out the judgmental element in responses to, and evaluations of, the environment. Right now I may not be able to tell a real Vermeer from a Van Meegaran, though I might learn to do so. By the same token I might not be able to tell apart a naturally evolved stand of mountain ash from one which has been planted, but might later acquire the ability to make the requisite judgment. Perhaps an anecdote is appropriate here. There is a particular stand of mountain ash that I had long admired. The trees were straight and tall, of uniform stature, neither densely packed nor too open-spaced. I then discovered what would have been obvious to a more expert eye, namely that the stand of mountain ash had been planted to replace original forest which had been burnt out. This explained the uniformity in size, the density and so on: it also changed my attitude to that piece of landscape. The evaluation that I make now of the landscape is to a certain extent informed, the response is not merely emotive but cognitive as well. The evaluation is informed and directed by my beliefs about the forest, the type of forest it is, its condition as a member of that kind, its causal genesis and so on. What is more, the judgmental element affects the emotive one. Knowing that the forest is not a naturally evolved forest causes me to feel differently about it: it causes me to perceive the forest differently and to assign it less value than naturally evolved forests.

Val Routley has eloquently reminded us that people who value wilderness do not do so merely because they like to soak up pretty scenery. They see much more and value much more than this. What they do see, and what they value, is very much a function of the degree to which they understand the ecological mechanisms which maintain the landscape and which determine that it appears the way it does. Similarly, knowledge of art history, of painting techniques, and the like will inform aesthetic evaluations and alter aesthetic perceptions. Knowledge of this kind is capable of transforming a hitherto uninteresting landscape into one that is compelling. Holmes Rolston has discussed at length the way in which an understanding and appreciation of ecology generates new values. He does not claim that ecology reveals values previously unnoticed, but rather that the understanding of the complexity, diversity, and integration of the natural world which ecology affords us, opens up a new area of valuation. As the facts are uncovered, the values are generated. What the remarks of Routley and Rolston highlight is the judgmental factor which is present in environmental appraisal. Understanding and evaluation do go hand in hand; and the responses individuals have to forests, wild rivers, and the like are not merely raw, emotional responses.

IV

Not all forests are alike, not all rain forests are alike. There are countless possible discriminations that the informed observer may make. Comparative judgments between areas of the natural environment are possible with regard to ecological richness, stage of development, stability, peculiar local circumstance, and the like. Judgments of this kind will very often underlie hierarchical orderings of environments in terms of their intrinsic worth. Appeal to judgments of this kind will frequently strengthen the case for preserving some bit of the environment....

One reason that a faked forest is not just as good as a naturally evolved forest is that there is always the possibility that the trained eye will tell the difference. It takes some time to discriminate areas of Alpine plain which are naturally clear of snow gums from those that have been cleared. It takes some time to discriminate regrowth forest which has been logged from forest which has not been touched. These are discriminations which it is possible to make and which are made. Moreover, they are discriminations which affect valuations. The reasons why the "faked" forest counts for less, more often than not, than the real thing are similar to the reasons why faked works of art count for less than the real thing.

Origin is important as an integral part of the evaluation process. It is important because our beliefs about it determine the valuations we make. It is also important in that the discovery that something has an origin quite different to the origin we initially believe that it has can literally alter the way we perceive that thing. The point concerning the possibility of detecting fakes is important in that it stresses just how much detail must be written into the claim that environmental engineers can replicate nature. Even if environmental engineering could achieve such exactitude, there is, I suggest, no compelling reasons for accepting the restoration thesis. It is worth stressing though that, as a matter of strategy, environmentalists must argue the empirical inadequacy of restoration proposals. This is the strongest argument against restoration ploys, because it appeals to diverse value-frameworks, and because such proposals are promises to deliver a specific good. Showing that the good won't be delivered is thus a useful move to make.

🐛 STUDY QUESTIONS

1. Is Elliot correct about the analogy of nature with works of art? Does the fact that a wilderness has been replicated by human contrivance lessen the value of the replicated product?

2. Can you imagine a situation where a natural object is replicated and where its value is greater than the original? Explain your thinking here.

3. Eugene Hargrove relates the following: Due to effects of tourism, the famous ancient cave paintings at Lascaux in France were in danger of irreparable damage. So the authorities built a full-scale model of the cave nearby (*Foundations of Environmental Ethics* [Englewood Cliffs, NJ: Prentice Hall, 1989] p. 169). Hargrove argues that, while the aesthetic experience of the replicated cave is not as valuable as the original, nevertheless, "the knowledge that the original still exists enhances the experience afforded by the representation."

Hargrove then compares this with threatened damage to natural objects. An extremely beautiful passageway in Mammoth Cave, Kentucky, called Turner Avenue, was in danger of severe damage due to tourism, so the authorities photographed it, closed it off from aesthetic experiences, and allowed only the indirect aesthetic experience that comes from beholding the pictures. Hargrove argues, analogous to the first situation, that knowledge that the original still exists enhances the experience afforded by the representation.

Do you agree with this analysis? Does such knowledge that an artwork or a natural object still exists enhance the aesthetic experience? Explain.

34   Should Trees Have Standing? Toward Legal Rights for Natural Objects

CHRISTOPHER D. STONE

Christopher Stone is professor of law at the University of Southern California, Los Angeles, and the author of several works in law and environmental ethics, including *Should Trees Have Standing?* from which the present selection is taken.

Stone argues that a strong case can be made for the "unthinkable idea" of extending legal rights to natural objects. Building on the models of inanimate objects, such as trusts, corporations, nation-states, and municipalities, he proposes that we extend the notion of legal guardian for legal incompetents to cover these natural objects. Note the three main ways that natural objects are denied rights under common law and how Stone's proposal addresses these considerations.

INTRODUCTION: THE UNTHINKABLE

In *Descent of Man,* Darwin observes that the history of man's moral development has been a continual extension in the objects of his "social instincts and sympathies." Originally each man had regard only for himself and those of a very narrow circle about him; later, he came to regard more and more "not only the welfare, but the happiness of all his fellow-men"; then "his sympathies became more tender and widely diffused, extending to men of all races, to the imbecile, maimed, and other useless members of society, and finally to the lower animals...."

The history of the law suggests a parallel development. Perhaps there never was a pure Hobbesian state of nature, in which no "rights" existed except in the vacant sense of each man's "right to self-defense." But it is not unlikely that so far as the earliest "families" (including extended kinship groups and clans) were concerned, everyone outside the family was suspect, alien, rightless. And even within the family, persons we presently regard as the natural holders of at least some rights had none. Take, for

Reprinted from *Should Trees Have Standing? Toward Legal Rights for Natural Objects* (Los Altos, CA: William Kaufman, Inc., 1974), by permission. Notes deleted.

example, children. We know something of the early rights-status of children from the widespread practice of infanticide—especially of the deformed and female. (Senicide, as among the North American Indians, was the corresponding rightlessness of the aged.) Maine tells us that as late as the Patria Potestas of the Romans, the father had *jus vitae necisque*—the power of life and death— over his children. A fortiori, Maine writes, he had power of "uncontrolled corporal chastisement; he can modify their personal condition at pleasure; he can give a wife to his son; he can give his daughter in marriage; he can divorce his children of either sex; he can transfer them to another family by adoption; and he can sell them." The child was less than a person: an object, a thing.

The legal rights of children have long since been recognized in principle, and are still expanding in practice. Witness, just within recent time, *In re Gault*, guaranteeing basic constitutional protections to juvenile defendants, and the Voting Rights Act of 1970. We have been making persons of children although they were not, in law, always so. And we have done the same, albeit imperfectly some would say, with prisoners, aliens, women (especially of the married variety), the insane, Blacks, foetuses, and Indians.

Nor is it only matter in human form that has come to be recognized as the possessor of rights. The world of the lawyer is peopled with inanimate right-holders: trusts, corporations, joint ventures, municipalities, Subchapter R partnerships, and nation-states, to mention just a few. Ships, still referred to by courts in the feminine gender, have long had an independent jural life, often with striking consequences. We have become so accustomed to the idea of a corporation having "its" own rights, and being a "person" and "citizen" for so many statutory and constitutional purposes, that we forget how jarring the notion was to early jurists. "That invisible, intangible and artificial being, that mere legal entity" Chief Justice Marshall wrote of the corporation in *Bank of the United States v. Deveaux*—could a suit be brought in *its* name? Ten years later, in the *Dartmouth College* case, he was still refusing to let pass unnoticed the wonder of an entity "existing only in contemplation of law." Yet, long before Marshall worried

over the personifying of the modern corporation, the best medieval legal scholars had spent hundreds of years struggling with the notion of the legal nature of those great public "corporate bodies," the Church and the State. How could they exist in law, as entities transcending the living Pope and King? It was clear how a king could bind *himself*—on his honor—by a treaty. But when the king died, what was it that was burdened with the obligations of, and claimed the rights under, the treaty *his* tangible hand had signed? The medieval mind saw (what we have lost our capacity to see) how *unthinkable* it was, and worked out the most elaborate conceits and fallacies to serve as anthropomorphic flesh for the Universal Church and the Universal Empire.

It is this note of the *unthinkable* that I want to dwell upon for a moment. Throughout legal history, each successive extension of rights to some new entity has been, theretofore, a bit unthinkable. We are inclined to suppose the rightlessness of rightless "things" to be a decree of Nature, not a legal convention acting in support of some status quo. It is thus that we defer considering the choices involved in all their moral, social, and economic dimensions. And so the United States Supreme Court could straight-facedly tell us in *Dred Scott* that Blacks had been denied the rights of citizenship "as a subordinate and inferior class of beings, who had been subjugated by the dominant race...." In the nineteenth century, the highest court in California explained that Chinese had not the right to testify against white men in criminal matters because they were "a race of people whom nature has marked as inferior, and who are incapable of progress or intellectual development beyond a certain point...between whom and ourselves nature has placed an impassable difference." The popular conception of the Jew in the 13th Century contributed to a law which treated them as "men *ferae naturae*, protected by a quasi-forest law. Like the roe and the deer, they form an order apart." Recall, too, that it was not so long ago that the foetus was "like the roe and the deer." In an early suit attempting to establish a wrongful death action on behalf of a negligently killed foetus (now widely accepted practice), Holmes, then on the Massachusetts

Supreme Court, seems to have thought it simply inconceivable "that a man might owe a civil duty and incur a conditional prospective liability in tort to one not yet in being." The first woman in Wisconsin who thought she might have a right to practice law was told that she did not, in the following terms:

> The law of nature destines and qualifies the female sex for the bearing and nurture of the children of our race and for the custody of the homes of the world.... [A]ll life-long callings of women, inconsistent with these radical and sacred duties of their sex, as the profession of the law, are departures from the order of nature; and when voluntary, treason against it.... The peculiar qualities of womanhood, its gentle graces, its quick sensibility, its tender susceptibility, its purity, its delicacy, its emotional impulses, its subordination of hard reason to sympathetic feeling, are surely not qualifications for forensic strife. Nature has tempered woman as little for the juridical conflicts of the court room, as for the physical conflicts of the battle field....

The fact is, that each time there is a movement to confer rights onto some new "entity," the proposal is bound to sound odd or frightening or laughable. This is partly because until the rightless thing receives its rights, we cannot see it as anything but a *thing* for the use of "us"— those who are holding rights at the time. In this vein, what is striking about the Wisconsin case above is that the court, for all its talk about women, so clearly was never able to see women as they are (and might become). All it could see was the popular "idealized" version of *an object it needed*. Such is the way the slave South looked upon the Black. There is something of a seamless web involved: there will be resistance to giving the thing "rights" until it can be seen and valued for itself; yet, it is hard to see it and value it for itself until we can bring ourselves to give it "rights"—which is almost inevitably going to sound inconceivable to a large group of people.

The reason for this little discourse on the unthinkable, the reader must know by now, if only from the title of the paper. I am quite seriously proposing that we give legal rights to forests, oceans, rivers and other so-called "natural objects" in the environment—indeed, to the natural environment as a whole.

As strange as such a notion may sound, it is neither fanciful nor devoid of operational content. In fact, I do not think it would be a misdescription of recent developments in the law to say that we are already on the verge of assigning some such rights, although we have not faced up to what we are doing in those particular terms. We should do so now, and begin to explore the implications such a notion would hold.

TOWARD RIGHTS FOR THE ENVIRONMENT

Now, to say that the natural environment should have rights is not to say anything as silly as that no one should be allowed to cut down a tree. We say human beings have rights, but—at least as of the time of this writing—they can be executed. Corporations have rights, but they cannot plead the fifth amendment; *In re Gault* gave 15-year-olds certain rights in juvenile proceedings, but it did not give them the right to vote. Thus, to say that the environment should have rights is not to say that it should have every right we can imagine, or even the same body of rights as human beings have. Nor is it to say that everything in the environment should have the same rights as every other thing in the environment.

What the granting of rights does involve has two sides to it. The first involves what might be called the legal-operational aspects; the second, the psychic and socio-psychic aspects. I shall deal with these aspects in turn.

THE LEGAL-OPERATIONAL ASPECTS

What It Means to Be a Holder of Legal Rights

There is, so far as I know, no generally accepted standard for how one ought to use the term "legal rights." Let me indicate how I shall be using it in this piece.

First and most obviously, if the term is to have any content at all, an entity cannot be said to hold a legal right unless and until *some public authoritative body* is prepared to give *some amount of review* to actions that are colorably inconsistent with that "right." For example, if a student can be expelled from a university and cannot get any public official, even a judge or administrative agent at the lowest level, either (i) to require the university to justify its actions (if only to the extent of filling out an affidavit alleging that the expulsion "was not wholly arbitrary and capricious") or (ii) to compel the university to accord the student some procedural safeguards (a hearing, right to counsel, right to have notice of charges), then the minimum requirements for saying that the student has a legal right to his education do not exist.

But for a thing to be *a holder of legal rights,* something more is needed than that some authoritative body will review the actions and processes of those who threaten it. As I shall use the term, "holder of legal rights," each of three additional criteria must be satisfied. All three, one will observe, go towards making a thing *count* jurally—to have a legally recognized worth and dignity in its own right, and not merely to serve as a means to benefit "us" (whoever the contemporary group of rights-holders may be). They are, first, that the thing can institute legal actions *at its behest;* second, that in determining the granting of legal relief, the court must take *injury to it* into account; and, third, that relief must run to the *benefit of it....*

The Rightlessness of Natural Objects at Common Law

Consider, for example, the common law's posture toward the pollution of a stream. True, courts have always been able, in some circumstances, to issue orders that will stop the pollution.... But the stream itself is fundamentally rightless, with implications that deserve careful reconsideration.

The first sense in which the stream is not a rights-holder has to do with standing. The stream itself has none. So far as the common law is concerned, there is in general no way to challenge the polluter's actions save at the behest of a lower *riparian**—another human being—able to show an invasion of *his* rights. This conception of the riparian as the holder of the right to bring suit has more than theoretical interest. The lower riparians may simply not care about the pollution. They themselves may be polluting, and not wish to stir up legal waters. They may be economically dependent on their polluting neighbor. And, of course, when they discount the value of winning by the costs of bringing suit and the chances of success, the action may not seem worth undertaking. Consider, for example, that while the polluter might be injuring 100 downstream riparians $10,000 a year *in the aggregate,* each riparian separately might be suffering injury only to the extent of $100—possibly not enough for any one of them to want to press suit by himself, or even to go to the trouble and cost of securing co-plaintiffs to make it worth everyone's while. This hesitance will be especially likely when the potential plaintiffs consider the burdens the law puts in their way: proving, *e.g.,* specific damages, the "unreasonableness" of defendant's use of the water, the fact that practicable means of abatement exist, and overcoming difficulties raised by issues such as joint causality, right to pollute by prescription, and so forth. Even in states which, like California, sought to overcome these difficulties by empowering the attorney-general to sue for abatement of pollution in limited instances, the power has been sparingly invoked and, when invoked, narrowly construed by the courts.

The second sense in which the common law denies "rights" to natural objects has to do with the way in which the merits are decided in those cases in which someone is competent and willing to establish standing. At its more primitive levels, the system protected the "rights" of the property owning human with minimal weighing of any values: *"Cujus est solum, ejus est usque ad coelum et ad infernos."*† Today we have come more and more to make balances—but only such as will adjust the economic best interests of identifiable humans. For example, continuing with the case of streams, there are commentators who speak of a "general rule" that "a riparian owner is legally entitled to have the stream flow

---

*Riparian—related to living on the bank of a natural waterway.

†To whosoever the soil belongs, he owns also to the sky and to the depths.

by his land with its quality unimpaired" and observe that "an upper owner has, prima facie, no right to pollute the water." Such a doctrine, if strictly invoked, would protect the stream absolutely whenever a suit was brought; but obviously, to look around us, the law does not work that way. Almost everywhere there are doctrinal qualifications on riparian "rights" to an unpolluted stream. Although these rules vary from jurisdiction to jurisdiction, and upon whether one is suing for an equitable injunction or for damages, what they all have in common is some sort of balancing. Whether under language of "reasonable use," "reasonable methods of use," "balance of convenience" or "the public interest doctrine," what the courts are balancing, with varying degrees of directness, are the economic hardships on the upper riparian (or dependent community) of abating the pollution vis-à-vis the economic hardships of continued pollution on the lower riparians. What does not weigh in the balance is the damage to the stream, its fish and turtles and "lower" life. So long as the natural environment itself is rightless, these are not matters for judicial cognizance. Thus, we find the highest court of Pennsylvania refusing to stop a coal company from discharging polluted mine water into a tributary of the Lackawana River because a plaintiff's "grievance is for a mere personal inconvenience; and... mere private personal inconveniences... must yield to the necessities of a great public industry, which although in the hands of a private corporation, subserves a great public interest." The stream itself is lost sight of in "a quantitative compromise between *two* conflicting interests."

The third way in which the common law makes natural objects rightless has to do with who is regarded as the beneficiary of a favorable judgment. Here, too, it makes a considerable difference that it is not the natural object that counts in its own right. To illustrate this point, let me begin by observing that it makes perfectly good sense to speak of, and ascertain, the legal damage to a natural object, if only in the sense of "making it whole" with respect to the most obvious factors. The costs of making a forest whole, for example, would include the costs of reseeding, repairing watersheds, restocking wildlife—the sorts of costs

the Forest Service undergoes after a fire. Making a polluted stream whole would include the costs of restocking with fish, water-fowl, and other animal and vegetable life, dredging, washing out impurities, establishing natural and/or artificial aerating agents, and so forth. Now, what is important to note is that, under our present system, even if a plaintiff riparian wins a water pollution suit for damages, no money goes to the benefit of the stream itself to repair *its* damages. This omission has the further effect that, at most, the law confronts a polluter with what it takes to make the plaintiff riparians whole; this may be far less than the damages to the stream, but not so much as to force the polluter to desist. For example, it is easy to imagine a polluter whose activities damage a stream to the extent of $10,000 annually, although the aggregate damage to all the riparian plaintiffs who come into the suit is only $3000. If $3000 is less than the cost to the polluter of shutting down, or making the requisite technological changes, he might prefer to pay off the damages (*i.e.,* the legally cognizable damages) and continue to pollute the stream. Similarly, even if the jurisdiction issues an injunction at the plaintiffs' behest (rather than to order payment of damages), there is nothing to stop the plaintiffs from "selling out" the stream, *i.e.,* agreeing to dissolve or not enforce the injunction at some price (in the example above, somewhere between plaintiffs' damages—$3000—and defendant's next best economic alternative). Indeed, I take it this is exactly what Learned Hand had in mind in an opinion in which, after issuing an anti-pollution injunction, he suggests that the defendant "make its peace with the plaintiff as best it can." What is meant is a peace between *them*, and not amongst them and the river.

I ought to make clear at this point that the common law as it affects streams and rivers, which I have been using as an example so far, is not exactly the same as the law affecting other environmental objects. Indeed, one would be hard pressed to say that there was a "typical" environmental object, so far as its treatment at the hands of the law is concerned. There are some differences in the law applicable to all the various resources that are held in common: rivers, lakes, oceans, dunes, air, streams (surface and subterranean), beaches, and so forth. And there is an even greater difference as between these traditional communal resources on the one hand, and natural objects on traditionally private land, *e.g.,* the pond on the farmer's field, or the stand of trees on the suburbanite's lawn.

On the other hand, although there be these differences which would make it fatuous to generalize about a law of the natural environment, most of these differences simply underscore the points made in the instance of rivers and streams. None of the natural objects, whether held in common or situated on private land, has any of the three criteria of a rights-holder. They have no standing in their own right; their unique damages do not count in determining outcome; and they are not the beneficiaries of awards. In such fashion, these objects have traditionally been regarded by the common law, and even by all but the most recent legislation, as objects for man to conquer and master and use—in such a way as the law once looked upon "man's" relationships to African Negroes. Even where special measures have been taken to conserve them, as by seasons on game and limits on timber cutting, the dominant motive has been to conserve them *for us*—for the greatest good of the greatest number of human beings. Conservationists, so far as I am aware, are generally reluctant to maintain otherwise. As the name implies, they want to conserve and guarantee *our* consumption and *our* enjoyment of these other living things. In their own right, natural objects have counted for little, in law as in popular movements.

As I mentioned at the outset, however, the rightlessness of the natural environment can and should change; it already shows some signs of doing so.

Toward Having Standing in Its Own Right

It is not inevitable, nor is it wise, that natural objects should have no rights to seek redress in their own behalf. It is no answer to say that streams and forests cannot have standing because streams and forest cannot speak. Corporations cannot speak either; nor can states, estates, infants, incompetents, municipalities or universities. Lawyers speak for them, as they customarily do for the ordinary citizen with legal problems. One ought, I think, to handle the legal problems of natural objects as one does the problems of legal incompetents—human beings who have become vegetable. If a human being shows signs of becoming senile and has affairs that he is de jure incompetent to manage, those concerned with his well being make such a showing to the court, and someone is designated by the court with the authority to manage the incompetent's affairs. The guardian (or "conservator" or "committee"—the terminology varies) then represents the incompetent in his legal affairs. Courts make similar appointments when a corporation has become "incompetent"—they appoint a trustee in bankruptcy or reorganization to oversee its affairs and speak for it in court when that becomes necessary.

On a parity of reasoning, we should have a system in which, when a friend of a natural object perceives it to be endangered, he can apply to a court for the creation of a guardianship. Perhaps we already have the machinery to do so. California law, for example, defines an incompetent as "any person, whether insane or not, who by reason of old age, disease, weakness of mind, or other cause, is unable, unassisted, properly to manage and take care of himself or his property, and by reason thereof is likely to be deceived or imposed upon by artful or designing persons." Of course, to urge a court that an endangered river is "a person" under this provision will call for lawyers as bold and imaginative as those who convinced the Supreme Court that a railroad corporation was a "person" under the fourteenth amendment, a constitutional provision theretofore generally thought of as designed to secure the rights of freedmen....

The guardianship approach, however, is apt to raise...[the following objection]: a committee or guardian could not judge the needs of the river or forest in its charge; indeed, the very concept of "needs," it might be said, could be used here only in the most metaphorical way....

...Natural objects *can* communicate their wants (needs) to us, and in ways that are not terribly ambiguous. I am sure I can judge with more certainty and meaningfulness whether and when my lawn wants (needs) water, than the Attorney

General can judge whether and when the United States wants (needs) to take an appeal from an adverse judgment by a lower court. The lawn tells me that it wants water by a certain dryness of the blades and soil—immediately obvious to the touch—the appearance of bald spots, yellowing, and a lack of springiness after being walked on; how does "the United States" communicate to the Attorney General? For similar reasons, the guardian-attorney for a smog endangered stand of pines could venture with more confidence that his client wants the smog stopped, than the directors of a corporation can assert that "the corporation" wants dividends declared. We make decisions on behalf of, and in the purported interests of, others every day; these "others" are often creatures whose wants are far less verifiable, and even far more metaphysical in conception, than the wants of rivers, trees, and land....

The argument for "personifying" the environment, from the point of damage calculations, can best be demonstrated from the welfare economics position. Every well-working legal-economic system should be so structured as to confront each of us with the full costs that our activities are imposing on society. Ideally, a paper-mill, in deciding what to produce—and where, and by what methods—ought to be forced to take into account not only the lumber, acid and labor that its production "takes" from other uses in the society, but also what costs alternative production plans will impose on society through pollution. The legal system, through the law of contracts and the criminal law, for example, makes the mill confront the costs of the first group of demands. When, for example, the company's purchasing agent orders 1000 drums of acid from the Z Company, the Z Company can bind the mill to pay for them, and thereby reimburse the society for what the mill is removing from alternative uses.

Unfortunately, so far as the pollution costs are concerned, the allocative ideal begins to break down, because the traditional legal institutions have a more difficult time "catching" and confronting us with the full social costs of our activities. In the lakeside mill example, major riparian interests might bring an action, forcing a court to weigh *their* aggregate losses against the costs to the mill of installing the anti-pollution device.

But many other interests—and I am speaking for the moment of recognized homocentric interests—are too fragmented and perhaps "too remote" causally to warrant securing representation and pressing for recovery: the people who own summer homes and motels, the man who sells fishing tackle and bait, the man who rents rowboats. There is no reason not to allow the lake to prove damages to them as the prima facie measure of damages to it. *By doing so, we in effect make the natural object, through its guardian, a jural entity competent to gather up these fragmented and otherwise unrepresented damage claims, and press them before the court even where, for legal or practical reasons, they are not going to be pressed by traditional class action plaintiffs.* Indeed, one way—the homocentric way—to view what I am proposing so far, is to view the guardian of the natural object as the guardian of unborn generations, as well as of the otherwise unrepresented, but distantly injured, contemporary humans. By making the lake itself the focus of these damages, and "incorporating" it so to speak, the legal system can effectively take proof upon, and confront the mill with, a larger and more representative measure of the damages its pollution causes.

So far, I do not suppose that my economist friends (unremittent human chauvinists, every one of them!) will have any large quarrel in principle with the concept. Many will view it as a *trompe l'oeil* that comes down, at best, to effectuate the goals of the paragon class action, or the paragon water pollution control district. Where we are apt to part company is here—I propose going beyond gathering up the loose ends of what most people would presently recognize as economically valid damages. The guardian would urge before the court injuries not presently cognizable—the death of eagles and inedible crabs, the suffering of sea lions, the loss from the face of the earth of species of commercially valueless birds, the disappearance of a wilderness area. One might, of course, speak of the damages involved as "damages" to us humans, and indeed, the widespread growth of environmental groups shows that human beings do feel these losses. But they are not, at present, economically measurable losses: how can they have a monetary value for the guardian to prove in court?

The answer for me is simple. Wherever it carves out "property" rights, the legal system is engaged in the process of *creating* monetary worth. One's literary works would have minimal monetary value if anyone could copy them at will. Their economic value to the author is a product of the law of copyright; the person who copies a copyrighted book has to bear a cost to the copyright-holder because the law says he must. Similarly, it is through the law of torts that we have made a "right" of—and guaranteed an economically meaningful value to—privacy. (The value we place on gold—a yellow inanimate dirt—is not simply a function of supply and demand—wilderness areas are scarce and pretty too—but results from the actions of the legal systems of the world, which have institutionalized that value; they have even done a remarkable job of stabilizing the price.) I am proposing we do the same with eagles and wilderness areas as we do with copyrighted works, patented inventions, and privacy: *make* the violation of rights in them to be a cost by declaring the "pirating" of them to be the invasion of a property interest. If we do so, the net social costs the polluter would be confronted with would include not only the extended homocentric costs of his pollution (explained above) but also costs to the environment *per se.*

How, though, would these costs be calculated? When we protect an invention, we can at least speak of a fair market value for it, by reference to which damages can be computed. But the lost environmental "values" of which we are now speaking are by definition over and above those that the market is prepared to bid for: they are priceless.

One possible measure of damages, suggested earlier, would be the cost of making the environment whole, just as, when a man is injured in an automobile accident, we impose upon the responsible party the injured man's medical expenses. Comparable expenses to a polluted river would be the costs of dredging, restocking with fish, and so forth. It is on the basis of such costs as these, I assume, that we get the figure of $1 billion as the cost of saving Lake Erie. As an ideal, I think this is a good guide applicable in many environmental situations. It is by no means free from difficulties, however.

One problem with computing damages on the basis of making the environment whole is that, if understood most literally, it is tantamount to asking for a "freeze" on environmental quality, even at the costs (and there will be costs) of preserving "useless" objects. Such a "freeze" is not inconceivable to me as a general goal, especially considering that, even by the most immediately discernible homocentric interests, in so many areas we ought to be cleaning up and not merely preserving the environmental status quo. In fact, there is presently strong sentiment in the Congress for a total elimination of all river pollutants by 1985, notwithstanding that such a decision would impose quite large direct and indirect costs on us all. Here one is inclined to recall the instructions of Judge Hays, in remanding Consolidated Edison's Storm King application to the Federal Power Commission in *Scenic Hudson:*

> The Commission's renewed proceedings must include as a basic concern the preservation of natural beauty and of natural history shrines, keeping in mind that, in our affluent society, the cost of a project is only one of several factors to be considered.

Nevertheless, whatever the merits of such a goal in principle, there are many cases in which the social price tag of putting it into effect are going to seem too high to accept. Consider, for example, an oceanside nuclear generator that could produce low cost electricity for a million homes at a savings of $1 a year per home, spare us the air pollution that comes of burning fossil fuels, but which through a slight heating effect threatened to kill off a rare species of temperature-sensitive sea urchins; suppose further that technological improvements adequate to reduce the temperature to present environmental quality would expend the entire one million dollars in anticipated fuel savings. Are we prepared to tax ourselves $1,000,000 a year on behalf of the sea urchins? In comparable problems under the present law of damages, we work out practicable compromises by abandoning restoration costs and calling upon fair market value. For example, if an automobile is so severely damaged that the cost of bringing the car to its original state by repair is greater than the fair market value, we would allow the responsible tortfeasor to pay the fair market value only. Or if a human being suffers the loss of an arm (as we might conceive of the ocean having irreparably lost the sea urchins), we can fall back on the capitalization of reduced earning power (and pain and suffering) to measure the damages. But what is the fair market value of sea urchins? How can we capitalize their loss to the ocean, independent of any commercial value they may have to someone else?

One answer is that the problem can sometimes be sidestepped quite satisfactorily. In the sea urchin example, one compromise solution would be to impose on the nuclear generator the costs of making the ocean whole somewhere else, in some other way, *e.g.*, reestablishing a sea urchin colony elsewhere, or making a somehow comparable contribution. In the debate over the laying of the trans-Alaskan pipeline, the builders are apparently prepared to meet conservationists' objections halfway by re-establishing wildlife away from the pipeline, so far as is feasible.

But even if damage calculations have to be made, one ought to recognize that the measurement of damages is rarely a simple report of economic facts about "the market," whether we are valuing the loss of a foot, a foetus, or a work of fine art. Decisions of this sort are always hard, but not impossible. We have increasingly taken (human) pain and suffering into account in reckoning damages, not because we think we can ascertain them as objective "facts" about the universe, but because, even in view of all the room for disagreement, we come up with a better society by making rude estimates of them than by ignoring them. We can make such estimates in regard to environmental losses fully aware that what we are really doing is making implicit normative judgments (as with pain and suffering)—laying down rules as to what the society is going to "value" rather than reporting market evaluations. In making such normative estimates decision-makers would not go wrong if they estimated on the "high side," putting the burden of trimming the figure down on the immediate human interests present. All burdens of proof should reflect common experience; our experience in environmental matters has been a continual

discovery that our acts have caused more long-range damage than we were able to appreciate at the outset.

To what extent the decision-maker should factor in costs such as the pain and suffering of animals and other sentient natural objects, I cannot say; although I am prepared to do so in principle.

The Psychic and Socio-psychic Aspects

... The strongest case can be made from the perspective of human advantage for conferring rights on the environment. Scientists have been warning of the crises the earth and all humans on it face if we do not change our ways—radically—and these crises make the lost "recreational use" of rivers seem absolutely trivial. The earth's very atmosphere is threatened with frightening possibilities: absorption of sunlight, upon which the entire life cycle depends, may be diminished; the oceans may warm (increasing the "greenhouse effect" of the atmosphere), melting the polar ice caps, and destroying our great coastal cities; the portion of the atmosphere that shields us from dangerous radiation may be destroyed. Testifying before Congress, sea explorer Jacques Cousteau predicted that the oceans (to which we dreamily look to feed our booming populations) are headed toward their own death: "The cycle of life is intricately tied up with the cycle of water ... the water system has to remain alive if we are to remain alive on earth." We are depleting our energy and our food sources at a rate that takes little account of the needs even of humans now living.

These problems will not be solved easily; they very likely can be solved, if at all, only through a willingness to suspend the rate of increase in the standard of living (by present values) of the earth's "advanced" nations, and by stabilizing the total human population. For some of us this will involve forfeiting material comforts; for others it will involve abandoning the hope someday to obtain comforts long envied. For all of us it will involve giving up the right to have as many offspring as we might wish. Such a program is not impossible of realization, however. Many of our so called "material comforts" are not only in excess of, but are probably in opposition to, basic biological needs. Further, the "costs" to the advanced nations is not as large as would appear from Gross National Product figures. G.N.P. reflects social gain (of a sort) without discounting for the social *cost* of that gain, *e.g.,* the losses through depletion of resources, pollution, and so forth. As has well been shown, as societies become more and more "advanced," their real marginal gains become less and less for each additional dollar of G.N.P. Thus, to give up "human progress" would not be as costly as might appear on first blush.

Nonetheless, such far-reaching social changes are going to involve us in a serious reconsideration of our consciousness towards the environment. . . .

. . . A few years ago the pollution of streams was thought of only as a problem of smelly, unsightly, unpotable water, *i.e.,* to us. Now we are beginning to discover that pollution is a process that destroys wondrously subtle balances of life within the water, and as between the water and its banks. This heightened awareness enlarges our sense of the dangers to us. But it also enlarges our empathy. We are not only developing the scientific capacity, but we are cultivating the personal capacities *within us* to recognize more and more the ways in which nature—like the woman, the Black, the Indian and the Alien—is like us (and we will also become more able realistically to define, confront, live with and admire the ways in which we are all different).

The time may be on hand when these sentiments, and the early stirrings of the law, can be coalesced into a radical new theory or myth—felt as well as intellectualized—of man's relationships to the rest of nature. I do not mean "myth" in a demeaning sense of the term, but in the sense in which, at different times in history, our social "facts" and relationships have been comprehended and integrated by reference to the "myths" that we are co-signers of a social contract, that the Pope is God's agent, and that all men are created equal. Pantheism, Shinto and Tao all have myths to offer. But they are all, each in its own fashion, quaint, primitive and archaic. What is needed is a myth that can fit our growing body of knowledge of geophysics, biology and the cosmos. In this vein, I do not think it too remote that we may come to regard the Earth, as some have suggested, as one organism, of which Mankind is a functional

part—the mind, perhaps: different from the rest of nature, but different as a man's brain is from his lungs. . . .

> . . . As I see it, the Earth is only one organized "field" of activities—and so is the *human person*—but these activities take place at various levels, in different "spheres" of being and realms of consciousness. The lithosphere is not the biosphere, and the latter not the . . . ionosphere. The Earth is not *only* a material mass. Consciousness is not only "human"; it exists at animal and vegetable levels, and most likely must be latent, or operating in some form, in the molecule and the atom; and all these diverse and in a sense hierarchical modes of activity and consciousness should be seen integrated in and perhaps transcended by an all-encompassing and "eonic" planetary Consciousness.
>
> Mankind's function within the Earth-organism is to extract from the activities of all other operative systems within this organism the type of consciousness which we call "reflective" or "self"-consciousness—or, we may also say to *mentalize* and give meaning, value, and "name" to all that takes place anywhere within the Earth-field. . . .

As radical as such a consciousness may sound today, all the dominant changes we see about us point in its direction. Consider just the impact of space travel, of world-wide mass media, of increasing scientific discoveries about the interrelatedness of all life processes. Is it any wonder that the term "spaceship earth" has so captured the popular imagination? The problems we have to confront are increasingly the world-wide crises of a global organism: not pollution of a stream, but pollution of the atmosphere and of the ocean. Increasingly, the death that occupies each human's imagination is not his own, but that of the entire life cycle of the planet earth, to which each of us is as but a cell to a body.

To shift from such a lofty fancy as the planetarization of consciousness to the operation of our municipal legal system is to come down to earth hard. Before the forces that are at work, our highest court is but a frail and feeble—a distinctly human—institution. Yet, the Court may be at its best not in its work of handing down decrees, but at the very task that is called for: of summoning up from the human spirit the kindest and most generous and worthy ideas that abound there, giving them shape and reality and legitimacy. Witness the School Desegregation Cases which, more importantly than to integrate the schools (assuming they did), awakened us to moral needs which, when made visible, could not be denied. And so here, too, in the case of the environment, the Supreme Court may find itself in a position to award "rights" in a way that will contribute to a change in popular consciousness. It would be a modest move, to be sure, but one in furtherance of a large goal: the future of the planet as we know it.

How far we are from such a state of affairs, where the law treats "environmental objects" as holders of legal rights, I cannot say. But there is certainly intriguing language in one of Justice Black's last dissents, regarding the Texas Highway Department's plan to run a six-lane expressway through a San Antonio Park. Complaining of the Court's refusal to stay the plan, Black observed that "after today's decision, the people of San Antonio and the birds and animals that make their home in the park will share their quiet retreat with an ugly, smelly stream of traffic.... Trees, shrubs, and flowers will be mowed down." Elsewhere he speaks of the "burial of public parks," of segments of a highway which "devour parkland," and of the park's heartland. Was he, at the end of his great career, on the verge of saying— just saying—that "nature has 'rights' on its own account"? Would it be so hard to do?

✎ STUDY QUESTIONS

1. Is the analogy with extending the circle of moral considerability and rights (from white male adults to women, other races, children, etc.) a good way to view our extending rights to natural objects? Or are there relevant differences? Could the Right to Life Movement use Stone's analogy-argument to institute legislation to protect fetuses?

2. Is Stone's basic argument anthropocentric? That is, underneath the concerns for granting legal standing to natural objects is there really anything more than enlightened self-interest? Or is there something further? (See Garrett Hardin's "Tragedy of the Commons" [Reading 46] for a way that might reduce Stone's arguments to an antropocentric model.)

3. To which natural objects should we grant rights? If any, we'd probably choose objects traditionally valued by humans, such as the Mississippi River, the Giant Redwoods of California, and the Grand Canyon and Yellowstone National Parks, but how about deer, rats, weeds, ordinary trees, bacteria, lice, and termites? Would they get legal standing? Why, or why not?

4. Sum up the pluses and minuses of Stone's proposal. How would granting legal rights to natural objects be a good thing, and how could it lead to bad consequences?

✎ FOR FURTHER READING

Carlson, Alan. "Appreciation and the Natural Environment." *Journal of Aesthetics and Art* 37 (1979).

Hargrove, Eugene. *Foundations of Environmental Ethics.* Englewood Cliffs, NJ: Prentice-Hall, 1989.

Myers, Norman. *The Sinking Ark.* Oxford: Pergamon Press, 1980.

———. *The Primary Source: Tropical Forests and Our Future.* New York: Norton, 1984.

Nash, Roderick. *The Rights of Nature.* Madison: University of Wisconsin Press, 1989.

Norton, Bryan G. "Thoreau's Insect Analogies: Or Why Environmentalists Hate Mainstream Economists." *Environmental Ethics* 13:3 (1991).

———. *Why Preserve Natural Variety?* Princeton, NJ: Princeton University Press, 1987.

Shoumatoff, Alex. *The World Is Burning.* Boston: Little, Brown, 1990.

Stone, Christopher D. *Should Trees Have Standing?* Los Altos, CA: Kaufmann, 1974.

Thoreau, Henry David. "Walking." In *The Natural History Essays.* Salt Lake City: Peregrine Smith, 1980.

Wilson, Edward O. *The Diversity of Life.* Cambridge, MA: Harvard University Press, 1992.

———. *Biophilia.* Cambridge, MA: Harvard University Press, 1984.

Wolf, Edward. "Avoiding a Mass Extinction of Species." *State of the World 1988.* Washington, D.C.: Worldwatch Institute, 1988.

CHAPTER FIVE

Non-Western Voices

IN CHAPTER 13 on environmental justice we look at the impact of economic and environmental policies of the wealthy on the quality of life of the poor. In this section, we turn to environmental concepts developed outside of the Western intellectual tradition. Every culture has an implicit attitude toward nature. Environmental philosophy, as presented in this text, is a product of the very cultures, those that industrialized first, which are most responsible for its degradation. Whether materialism, capitalism, Christianity and the subsequent loss of premonotheistic earth-centered spiritualism, technological development, or simple greed cause our problems, it is a fact that many cultures (including those in the West) had built-in environmental ethics that were lacking in the industrialized Western cultures. For instance, Hindu and Buddhist cultures have thought deeply on animal rights issues for thousands of years, many Native Americans had a highly developed land ethic, and pre-Christian paganism in Europe saw the environment as something we were part of rather than in control of.

Our first three readings examine non-Western religious attitudes toward nature. We begin with O. P. Dwivedi's "*Satyagraha* for Conservation: A Hindu View," for a Hindu view of environmental philosophy. Dwivedi argues that religion can play a vital role in saving the environment. He explains the Hindu view of *satyagraha*, the persistent search of truth, with regard to the environment and shows how Hinduism has had a deep nonviolent (*ahimsa*) attitude toward animals, trees, and nature in general. He claims that non-Indian influences in India have negatively affected this philosophy, but that it is beginning to reassert itself.

In our second reading, "The Buddhist Attitude Towards Nature," Lily de Silva explains the Buddhist view of the environment. Buddhists emphasize escaping the suffering of existence, a gentle nonaggressive attitude toward nature, and compassion toward all living things. Buddhism provides a moral and spiritual antidote to the greed and exploitation by humans of nature.

In our third reading, "Islamic Environmental Ethics, Law, and Society," Mawil Y. Izzi Deen sets forth the Islamic view of environmental ethics as he finds it encoded in the Koran. Islam urges us to go beyond self-interest and see Earth as God's gift for satisfying our needs and for our enjoyment, not something to be exploited ruthlessly and spoiled. Deen offers some specific practices that aid in promoting a sustainable environmental policy.

Our last two readings consider more secular non-Western perspectives on environmental ethics. First, the Nigerian philosopher Segun Ogungbemi shows how a combination of ignorance, poverty, and poor leadership have combined with technological power to devastate much of the sub-Saharan African environment.

In our final reading, Ramachandra Guha criticizes Western movements like deep ecology as being irrelevant (and even harmful) for the third world because they fail to address two underlying causes of our global environmental crisis: overconsumption by the rich West and militarism.

35   *Satyagraha* for Conservation: A Hindu View

O. P. DWIVEDI

O. P. Dwivedi is chair and professor, Department of Political Studies, University of Guelph, Canada, and has served as World Health Organization consultant to the Department of Environment, India. He is the coauthor of *Hindu Religion and the Environmental Crisis.*

In this essay, Dwivedi argues that a profound environmental ethics, consisting in *satyagraha* (the persistent quest for truth) permeates Hinduism. Hinduism holds to a strong version of the equal sanctity of all life and for thousands of years practiced sustainable agriculture and nonviolence (*ahimsa*) toward animals and nature. Dwivedi argues that in the last hundreds of years *satyagraha* lost much of its effectiveness, but there are signs that it is reasserting itself.

The World Commission on Environment and Development acknowledged that to reconcile human affairs with natural laws "our cultural and spiritual heritages can reinforce our economic interests and survival imperatives." But until very recently, the role of our cultural and spiritual heritages in environmental protection and sustainable development was ignored by international bodies, national governments, policy planners, and even environmentalists. Many fear that bringing religion into the environmental movement will threaten objectivity, scientific investigation, professionalism, or democratic values. But none of these need be displaced in order to include the spiritual dimension in environmental protection. That dimension, if introduced in the process of environmental policy planning, administration, education, and law, could help create a self-consciously moral society which would put conservation and respect for God's creation first, and relegate individualism, materialism, and our modern desire to dominate nature in a subordinate place. Thus my plea for a definite role of religion in conservation and environmental protection.

From the perspective of many world religions, the abuse and exploitation of nature for immediate gain is unjust, immoral, and unethical. For example, in the ancient past, Hindus and Buddhists were careful to observe moral teachings regarding the treatment of nature. In their cultures, not only the common person but also

Reprinted from *Ethics of Environment*, ed. J. Ronald Engel and Joan Gibb Engel (London: Bellhaven Press, 1990), by permission of the author.

rulers and kings followed those ethical guidelines and tried to create an example for others. But now in the twentieth century, the materialistic orientation of the West has equally affected the cultures of the East. India, Sri Lanka, Thailand, and Japan have witnessed wanton exploitation of the environment by their own peoples, despite the strictures and injunctions inherent in their religions and cultures. Thus, no culture has remained immune from human irreverence towards nature. How can we change the attitude of human beings towards nature? Are religions the answer?

I believe that religion can evoke a kind of awareness in persons that is different from scientific or technological reasoning. Religion helps make human beings aware that there are limits to their control over the animate and inanimate world and that their arrogance and manipulative power over nature can backfire. Religion instills the recognition that human life cannot be measured by material possessions and that the ends of life go beyond conspicuous consumption.

As a matter of fact, religion can provide at least three fundamental mainstays to help human beings cope in a technological society. First, it defends the individual's existence against the depersonalizing effects of the technoindustrial process. Second, it forces the individual to recognize human fallibility and to combine realism with idealism. Third, while technology gives the individual the physical power to create or to destroy the world, religion gives the moral strength to grow in virtue by nurturing restraint, humility, and liberation from self-centredness. Directly and indirectly, religion can be a powerful source for environmental conservation and protection. Thus, we need a strategy for conservation that does not ignore the powerful influence of religions, but instead draws from all religious foundations and cultures.

World religions, each in their own way, offer a unique set of moral values and rules to guide human beings in their relationship with the environment. Religions also provide sanctions and offer stiffer penalties, such as fear of hell, for those who do not treat God's creation with respect. Although it is true that, in the recent past, religions have not been in the forefront of protecting the environment from human greed and exploitation, many are now willing to take up the challenge and help protect and conserve the environment. But their offer of help will remain purely rhetorical unless secular institutions, national governments, and international organizations are willing to acknowledge the role of religion in environmental study and education. And I believe that environmental education will remain incomplete until it includes cultural values and religious imperatives. For this, we require an ecumenical approach. While there are metaphysical, ethical, anthropological and social disagreements among world religions, a synthesis of the key concepts and precepts from each of them pertaining to conservation could become a foundation for a global environmental ethic. The world needs such an ethic.

THE RELIGION AND ENVIRONMENT DEBATE

In 1967, the historian, Lynn White, Jr., wrote an article in *Science* on the historical roots of the ecological crisis. According to White, what people do to their environment depends upon how they see themselves in relation to nature. White asserted that the exploitative view that has generated much of the environmental crisis, particularly in Europe and North America, is a result of the teachings of late medieval Latin Christianity, which conceived of humankind as superior to the rest of God's creation and everything else as created for human use and enjoyment. He suggested that the only way to address the ecological crisis was to reject the view that nature has no reason to exist except to serve humanity. White's proposition impelled scientists, theologians, and environmentalists to debate the bases of his argument that religion could be blamed for the ecological crisis.

In the course of this debate, examples from other cultures were cited to support the view that, even in countries where there is religious respect for nature, exploitation of the environment has been ruthless. Countries where Hinduism, Buddhism, Taoism and Shintoism have been practiced were cited to support the criticism of

Thomas Derr, among others, that "We are simply being gullible when we take at face value the advertisement for the ecological harmony of non-Western cultures." Derr goes on to say:

> even if Christian doctrine had produced technological culture and its environmental troubles, one would be at a loss to understand the absence of the same result in equally Christian Eastern Europe. And conversely, if ecological disaster is a particularly Christian habit, how can one explain the disasters non-Christian cultures have visited upon their environments? Primitive cultures, Oriental cultures, classical cultures—all show examples of human dominance over nature which has led to ecological catastrophe. Overgrazing, deforestation and similar errors of sufficient magnitude to destroy civilizations have been committed by Egyptians, Assyrians, Romans, North Africans, Persians, Indians, Aztecs, and even Buddhists, who are foolishly supposed by some Western admirers to be immune from this sort of thing.

This chapter challenges Derr's assertion with respect to the role of the Hindu religion in the ecological crisis. We need to understand how a Hindu's attitude to nature has been shaped by his religion's view of the cosmos and creation. Such an exposition is necessary to explain the traditional values and beliefs of Hindus and hence what role Hindu religion once played with respect to human treatment of the environment. At the same time, we need to know how it is that this religion, which taught harmony with and respect for nature, and which influenced other religions such as Jainism and Buddhism, has been in recent times unable to sustain a caring attitude towards nature. What are the features of the Hindu religion which strengthen human respect for God's creation, and how were these features repressed by the modern view of the natural environment and its resources?

THE SANCTITY OF LIFE IN HINDUISM

The principle of the sanctity of life is clearly ingrained in the Hindu religion. Only God has absolute sovereignty over all creatures, thus, human beings have no dominion over their own lives or non-human life. Consequently, humanity cannot act as a viceroy of God over the planet, nor assign degrees of relative worth to other species. The idea of the Divine Being as the one underlying power of unity is beautifully expressed in the Yajurveda:

> *The loving sage beholds that Being, hidden in*
>   *mystery,*
> *wherein the universe comes to have one home;*
> *Therein unites and therefrom emanates the whole;*
> *The Omnipresent One pervades souls and matter*
>   *like warp and woof in created beings.*

> (YAJURVEDA 32.8)

The sacredness of God's creation means no damage may be inflicted on other species without adequate justification. Therefore, all lives, human and nonhuman, are of equal value and all have the same right to existence. According to the Atharvaveda, the Earth is not for human beings alone, but for other creatures as well:

> *Born of Thee, on Thee move mortal creatures;*
> *Thou bearest them—the biped and the quadruped;*
> *Thine, O Earth, are the five races of men, for whom*
> *Surya (Sun), as he rises spreads with his rays*
>   *the light that is immortal.*

> (ATHARVAVEDA 12.1–15)

Srsti: God's Creation

Hindus contemplate divinity as the one in many and the many in one. This conceptualization resembles both monotheism and polytheism. Monotheism is the belief in a single divine Person. In monotheistic creeds that Person is God. Polytheism, on the other hand, believes in the many; and the concept of God is not monarchical. The Hindu concept of God resembles monotheism in that it portrays the divinity as one, and polytheism in that it contemplates the divinity as one in many. Although there are many gods, each one is the Supreme Being. This attitude we may call non-dualistic theism.

The earliest Sanskrit texts, the Veda and Upanishads, teach the non-dualism of the supreme power that existed before the creation. God as the efficient cause, and nature, *Prakrti*, as the material cause of the universe, are unconditionally accepted, as is their harmonious relationship. However, while these texts agree on the concept of non-dualistic theism, they differ in their theories regarding the creation of the universe. Why have different theories been elaborated in the Veda and the Upanishads? This is one of the most important and intriguing questions we can ask. A suitable reply is given in the Rigveda:

> He is one, but the wise call him by different names; such as Indra, Mitra, Varuna, Agni, Divya—one who pervaded all the luminous bodies, the source of light; Suparna—the protector and preserver of the universe; whose works are perfect; Matriswa—powerful like wind; Garutman—mighty by nature. (Rigveda 1.164.46)

The Hindu concept of creation can be presented in four categories. First is the Vedic theory, which is followed by further elaboration in Vedanta and Sankhya philosophies; the second is Upanishadic theory; the third is known as Puranic theory; and the fourth is enunciated in the great Hindu epics *Ramayana* and *Mahabharata*. Although the Puranic theory differs from the other three, a single thought flows between them. This unifying theory is well stated in the Rigveda:

> The Vedas and the universal laws of nature which control the universe and govern the cycles of creation and dissolution were made manifest by the All-knowing One. By His great power were produced the clouds and the vapors. After the production of the vapors, there intervened a period of darkness after which the Great Lord and Controller of the universe arranged the motions which produce days, nights, and other durations of time. The Great One then produced the sun, the moon, the earth, and all other regions as He did in previous cycles of creation. (Rigveda 10:190.1–3)

All the Hindu scriptures attest to the belief that the creation, maintenance, and annihilation of the cosmos is completely dependent on the Supreme will. In the *Gita*, Lord Krishna says to Arjuna: "Of all that is material and all that is spiritual in this world, know for certain that I am both its origin and dissolution" (*Gita* 7.6). And the Lord says: again "The whole cosmic order is under me. By my will it is manifested again and again and by my will, it is annihilated at the end" (*Gita* 9.8). Thus, for ancient Hindus,

both God and *Prakriti* (nature) was to be one and the same. While the *Prajapati* (as mentioned in Regveda) is the creator of sky, the earth, oceans, and all other species, he is also their protector and eventual destroyer. He is the only Lord of creation. Human beings have no special privilege or authority over other creatures; on the other hand, they have more obligations and duties.

Duties to Animals and Birds

The most important aspect of Hindu theology pertaining to treatment of animal life is the belief that the Supreme Being was himself incarnated in the form of various species. The Lord says: "This form is the source and indestructible seed of multifarious incarnations within the universe, and from the particle and portion of this form, different living entities, like demigods, animals, human beings and others, are created" (*Srimad-Bhagavata* Book I, Discourse III: 5). Among the various incarnations of God (numbering from ten to twenty-four depending upon the source of the text), He first incarnated Himself in the form of a fish, then a tortoise, a boar, and a dwarf. His fifth incarnation was as a man-lion. As Rama he was closely associated with monkeys, and as Krishna he was always surrounded by the cows. Thus, other species are accorded reverence.

Further, the Hindu belief in the cycle of birth and rebirth where a person may come back as an animal or a bird gives these species not only respect, but also reverence. This provides a solid foundation for the doctrine of *ahimsa—nonviolence* against animals and human beings alike. Hindus have a deep faith in the doctrine of nonviolence. Almost all the Hindu scriptures place strong emphasis on the notion that God's grace can be received by not killing his creatures or harming his creation: "God, Kesava, is pleased with a person who does not harm or destroy other non-speaking creatures or animals" (Visnupurana 3.8.15). To not eat meat in Hinduism is considered both an appropriate conduct and a duty. Yajnavalkya Smriti warns of hell-fire (*Ghora Naraka*) to those who are the killers of domesticated and protected animals: "The wicked person who kills animals which are protected has to live in hell-fire for the days equal to the number of hairs on the body of that animal" (*Yajnavalkyasmriti, Acaradhyayah,* v. 180). By the end of the Vedic and Upanishadic period, Buddhism and Jainism came into existence, and the protection of animals, birds and vegetation was further strengthened by the various kings practicing these religions. These religions, which arose in part as a protest against the orthodoxy and rituals of Hindu religion, continued its precepts for environmental protection. The Buddhist emperor, Ashoka (273–236 BCE), promoted through public proclamations the planting and preservation of flora and fauna. Pillar Edicts, erected at various public places, expressed his concerns about the welfare of creatures, plants and trees and prescribed various punishments for the killing of animals, including ants, squirrels, and rats.

Flora in Hindu Religion

As early as in the time of Regveda, tree worship was quite popular and universal. The tree symbolized the various attributes of God to the Regvedic seers. Regveda regarded plants as having divine powers, with one entire hymn devoted to their praise, chiefly with reference to their healing properties (Regveda 10.97). During the period of the great epics and Puranas, the Hindu respect for flora expanded further. Trees were considered as being animate and feeling happiness and sorrow. It is still popularly believed that every tree has a *Vriksadevata,* or "tree deity," who is worshipped with prayers and offerings of water, flowers, sweets, and encircled by sacred threads. Also, for Hindus, the planting of a tree is still a religious duty. Fifteen hundred years ago, the Matsya Purana described the proper ceremony for tree planting:

> Clean the soil first and water it. Decorate trees with garlands, burn the guggula perfume in front of them, and place one pitcher filled with water by the side of each tree. Offer prayer and oblation and then sprinkle holy water on trees. Recite hymns from the Regveda, Yajur and Sama and kindle fire. After such worship the actual plantation should be celebrated. He who plants even

one tree, goes directly to Heaven and obtains Moksha. (Matsya Purana 59.159)

The cutting of trees and destruction of flora were considered a sinful act. *Kautilya's Arthasastra* prescribed various punishments for destroying trees and plants:

> For cutting off the tender sprouts of fruit trees or shady trees in the parks near a city, a fine of six panas shall be imposed; for cutting off the minor branches of the same trees, twelve panas, and for cutting off the big branches, twenty four panas shall be levied. Cutting off the trunks of the same, shall be punished with the first amercement; and felling shall be punished with the middlemost amercement. (*Kautilya's Arthasastra* III 19:197)

The Hindu worship of trees and plants has been based partly on utility, but mostly on religious duty and mythology. Hindu ancestors considered it their duty to save trees; and in order to do that they attached to every tree a religious sanctity.

Pradushana: Pollution and Its Prevention in Hindu Scriptures

Hindu scriptures revealed a clear conception of the ecosystem. On this basis a discipline of environmental ethics developed which formulated codes of conduct (*dharma*) and defined humanity's relationship to nature. An important part of that conduct is maintaining proper sanitation. In the past, this was considered to be the duty of everyone and any default was a punishable offence. Hindu society did not even consider it proper to throw dirt on a public path. Kautilya wrote:

> The punishment of one-eighth of a pana should be awarded to those who throw dirt on the roads. For muddy water one-fourth Pana, if both are thrown the punishment should be double. If latrine is thrown or caused near a temple, well, or pond, sacred place, or government building, then the punishment should increase gradually by one pana in each case. For urine the punishment should be only half. (*Kautilya's Arthasastra* II 36:145)

Hindus considered cremation of dead bodies and maintaining the sanitation of the human habitat as essential acts. When, in about 200 BCE, Caraka wrote about *Vikrti* (pollution) and diseases, he mentioned air pollution specifically as a cause of many diseases.

> The polluted air is mixed with bad elements. The air is uncharacteristic of the season, full of moisture, stormy, hard to breathe, icy cool, hot and dry, harmful, roaring, coming at the same time from all directions, badsmelling, oily, full of dirt, sand, steam, creating diseases in the body and is considered polluted. (*Caraka Samhita, Vimanastanam* III 6:1)

Similarly, about water pollution, Caraka Samhita says:

> Water is considered polluted when it is excessively smelly, unnatural in color, taste and touch, slimy, not frequented by aquatic birds, aquatic life is reduced, and the appearance is unpleasing. (*Caraka Samhita, Vimanastanam* III 6:2)

Water is considered by Hindus as a powerful media of purification and also as a source of energy. Sometimes, just by the sprinkling of pure water in religious ceremonies, it is believed purity is achieved. That is why, in Regveda, prayer is offered to the deity of water: "The waters in the sky, the waters of rivers, and water in the well whose source is the ocean, may all these sacred waters protect me" (Regveda 7.49.2). The healing property and medicinal value of water has been universally accepted, provided it is pure and free from all pollution. When polluted water and pure water were the point of discussion among ancient Indian thinkers, they were aware of the reasons for the polluted water. Therefore Manu advised: "One should not cause urine, stool, cough in the water. Anything which is mixed with these unpious objects, blood and poison, should not be thrown into water" (*Manusmrti* IV: 56).

Still today, many rivers are considered sacred. Among these, the river Ganges is considered by Hindus as the most sacred and respectable. Disposal of human waste or other pollutants has been prohibited since time immemorial:

> One should not perform these 14 acts near the holy waters of the river Ganga: i.e., remove excrement, brushing and gargling, removing cerumen

from body, throwing hairs, dry garlands, playing in water, taking donations, performing sex, attachment with other sacred places, praising other holy places, washing clothes, throwing dirty clothes, thumping water and swimming. (*Pravascitta Tatva* 1.535)

Persons doing such unsocial activities and engaging in acts polluting the environment were cursed: "A person, who is engaged in killing creatures, polluting wells, and ponds, and tanks and destroying gardens, certainly goes to hell" (*Padmapurana, Bhoomikhanda* 96: 7–8).

EFFECTIVENESS OF HINDUISM IN CONSERVATION

The effectiveness of any religion in protecting the environment depends upon how much faith its believers have in its precepts and injunctions. It also depends upon how those precepts are transmitted and adapted in everyday social interactions. In the case of the Hindu religion, which is practised as *dharma*—way of life—many of its precepts became ingrained in the daily life and social institutions of the people. Three specific examples are given below to illustrate this point.

The Caste System and Sustainable Development

The Hindu religion is known for its elaborate caste system which divides individuals among four main castes and several hundred sub-castes. Over the centuries, the system degenerated into a very rigid, hereditarily determined, hierarchical, and oppressive social structure, particularly for the untouchables and lower castes. But the amazing phenomenon is that it lasted for so many millennia even with centuries of domination by Islamic and Christian cultures.

One explanation by the ecologist, Madhav Gadgil, and the anthropologist, Kailash Malhotra, is that the caste system, as continued until the early decades of the twentieth century, was actually based on an ancient concept of sustainable development which disciplined the society by partitioning the use of natural resources according to specific occupations (or castes);

and "created" the right social milieu in which sustainable patterns of resource use were encouraged to emerge. The caste system regulated the occupations that individuals could undertake. Thus, an "ecological space" was created in ancient Hindu society which helped to reduce competition among various people for limited natural resources. A system of "resource partitioning" emerged whereby the primary users of natural resources did not worry about encroachment from other castes. At the same time, these users also knew that if they depleted the natural resources in their own space, they would not survive economically or physically because no one would allow them to move on to other occupations. Religious injunctions also created the psychological environment whereby each caste or sub-caste respected the occupational boundaries of the others. In a sense, the Hindu caste system can be seen as a progenitor of the concept of sustainable development.

But the system started malfunctioning during the British Raj when demands for raw materials for their fast-growing industrial economy had to be met by commercial exploitation of India's natural resources. As traditional relationships between various castes started disappearing, competition and tension grew. The trend kept on accelerating in independent India, as each caste (or sub-caste) tried to discard its traditional role and seize eagerly any opportunity to land a job. When this happened, the ancient religious injunction for doing one's prescribed duty within a caste system could no longer be maintained; this caused the disappearance of the concept of "ecological space" among Hindus. There is no doubt that the caste system also degenerated within and became a source of oppression; nevertheless, from an ecological spacing view point, the caste system played a key role in preserving India's natural riches for centuries.

Bishnois: Defenders of the Environment

The Bishnois are a small community in Rajasthan, India, who practise a religion of environmental conservation. They believe that cutting a tree or killing an animal or bird is blasphemy. Their religion, an offshoot of Hinduism, was founded by Guru Maharaj Jambaji, who was born in 1450

CE in the Marwar area. When he was young he witnessed how, during a severe drought, people cut down trees to feed animals but when the drought continued, nothing was left to feed the animals, so they died. Jambaji thought that if trees are protected, animal life would be sustained, and his community would survive. He gave 29 injunctions and principal among them being a ban on the cutting of any green tree and killing of any animal or bird. About 300 years later, when the King of Jodhpur wanted to build a new palace, he sent his soldiers to the Bishnois area where trees were in abundance. Villagers protested, and when soldiers would not pay any attention to the protest, the Bishnois, led by a woman, hugged the trees to protect them with their bodies. As soldiers kept on killing villagers, more and more of the Bishnois came forward to honour the religious injunction of their Guru Maharaj Jambaji. The massacre continued until 363 persons were killed defending trees. When the king heard about this human sacrifice, he stopped the operation, and gave the Bishnois state protection for their belief.

Today, the Bishnois community continues to protect trees and animals with the same fervour. Their community is the best example of a true Hindu-based ritual defense of the environment in India, and their sacrifices became the inspiration for the Chipko movement of 1973.

The Chipko Movement

In March 1973, in the town of Gopeshwar in Chamoli district (Uttar Pradesh, India), villagers formed a human chain and hugged the earmarked trees to keep them from being felled for a nearby factory producing sports equipment. The same situation later occurred in another village when forest contractors wanted to cut trees under licence from the Government Department of Forests. Again, in 1974, women from the village of Reni, near Joshimath in the Himalayas, confronted the loggers by hugging trees and forced contractors to leave. Since then, the *Chipko Andolan* (the movement to hug trees) has grown as a grassroots ecodevelopment movement.

The genesis of the Chipko movement is not only in the ecological or economic background, but in religious belief. Villagers have noted how industrial and commercial demands have denuded their forests, how they cannot sustain their livelihood in a deforested area, and how floods continually play havoc with their small agricultural communities. The religious basis of the movement is evident in the fact that it is inspired and guided by women. Women have not only seen how their men would not mind destroying nature in order to get money while they had to walk miles in search of firewood, fodder and other grazing materials, but, being more religious, they also are more sensitive to injunctions such as *ahimsa*. In a sense, the Chipko movement is a kind of feminist movement to protect nature from the greed of men. In the Himalayan areas, the pivot of the family is the woman. It is the woman who worries most about nature and its conservation in order that its resources are available for her family's sustenance. On the other hand, men go away to distant places in search of jobs, leaving women and old people behind. These women also believe that each tree has a *Vriksadevata* (tree god) and that the deity *Van Devi* (the Goddess of forests) will protect their family welfare. They also believe that each green tree is an abode of the Almighty God *Hari*.

The Chipko movement has caught the attention of others in India. For example, in Karnataka state, the Appiko movement began in September 1983, when 163 men, women, and children hugged the trees and forced the lumberjacks to leave. That movement swiftly spread to the adjoining districts. These people are against the kind of commercial felling of trees which clears the vegetation in its entirety. They do recognize the firewood needs of urban people (mostly poor) and therefore do not want a total ban on felling. However, they are against indiscriminate clearing and would like to see a consultative process established so that local people are able to participate in timber management.

These three examples are illustrative of the practical impact of Hinduism on conservation and sustainable development. While the effectiveness of the caste system to act as a resource partitioning system is no longer viable, the examples of Bishnois and Chipko/Appiko are illustrative of the fact that when appeal to secular norms

fails, one can draw on the cultural and religious sources for "forest *satyagraha*." ("Satyagraha" means "insistence or persistence in search of truth." In this context, the term "forest satyagraha" means "persistence in search of truth pertaining to the rights of trees.")

LOSS OF RESPECT FOR NATURE

If such has been the tradition, philosophy, and ideology of Hindu religion, what then are the reasons behind the present state of environmental crisis? As we have seen, our ethical beliefs and religious values influence our behaviour towards others, including our relationship with all creatures and plant life. If, for some reason, these noble values become displaced by other beliefs which are either thrust upon the society or transplanted from another culture through invasion, then the faith of the masses in the earlier cultural tradition is shaken. As the foreign culture, language and system of administration slowly takes root and penetrates all levels of society, and as appropriate answers and leadership are not forthcoming from the religious leaders and Brahmans, it is only natural for the masses to become more inward-looking and self-centered. Under such circumstances, religious values which acted as sanctions against environmental destruction do not retain a high priority because people have to worry about their very survival and freedom; hence, respect for nature gets displaced by economic factors.

That, it seems, is what happened in India during the 700 years of foreign cultural domination. The ancient educational system which taught respect for nature and reasons for its preservation was no longer available. On the other hand, the imported culture was unable to replace the ancient Hindu religion; consequently, a conflict continued between the two value systems. The situation became more complex when, in addition to the Muslim culture, the British introduced Christianity and Western secular institutions and values. While it is too easy to blame these external forces for the change in attitudes of Hindus towards nature, nevertheless it is a fact that they greatly inhibited the religion from continuing to transmit ancient values which encourage respect and due regard for God's creation.

The Hindu religion teaches a renunciation of worldly goods, and preaches against materialism and consumerism. Such teachings could act as a great source of strength for Hindu societies in their struggle to achieve sustainable development. I detect in countries like India and Nepal a revival of respect for ancient cultural values. Such a revival need not turn into fundamentalism; instead it could be based on the lessons learned from environmental destruction in the West, and on the relevant precepts enshrined in the Hindu scriptures. That should not cause any damage to the secularism now practised in India. As a matter of fact, this could develop into a movement whereby spiritual guidance is made available to the secular system of governance and socioeconomic interaction.

HOPE FOR OUR COMMON FUTURE

Mahatma Gandhi warned that "nature had enough for everybody's need but not for everybody's greed." Gandhi was a great believer in drawing upon the rich variety of spiritual and cultural heritages of India. His *satyagraha* movements were the perfect example of how one could confront an unjust and uncaring though extremely superior power. Similarly, the Bishnois, Chipko, and Appiko people are engaged in a kind of "forest *satyagraha*" today. Their movements could easily be turned into a common front—"satyagraha for

the environment,"—to be used against the forces of big government and big business. This could include such other movements as *Mitti Bachao Abhiyan* (save the soil movement), *Van Mahotsava* (tree planting ceremony), *Chetna March* (public awareness march), *Kalpavriksha* (voluntary organization in Delhi for environmental conservation), and many others. The Hindu people are accustomed to suffering a great level of personal and physical hardships if such suffering is directed against unjust and uncaring forces. The minds of the Hindu people are slowly being awakened through the Chipko, Appiko, Bishnois, Chetna March, and other movements. *Satyagraha* for conservation could very well be a rallying point for the awakened spirit of Hinduism.

Hindu culture, in ancient and medieval times, provided a system of moral guidelines towards environmental preservation and conservation. Environmental ethics, as propounded by ancient Hindu scriptures and seers, was practised not only by common persons, but even by rulers and kings. They observed these fundamentals sometimes as religious duties, often as rules of administration or obligation for law and order, but either way these principles were properly knitted within the Hindu way of life. In Hindu culture, a human being is authorized to use natural resources, but has no divine power of control and dominion over nature and its elements. Hence, from the perspective of Hindu culture, abuse and exploitation of nature for selfish gain is unjust and sacrilegious. Against the continuation of such exploitation, the only viable strategy appears to be *satyagraha* for conservation.

🐾 STUDY QUESTIONS

1. What are the strengths and weaknesses of the Hindu doctrine of *satyagraha* toward nature? If, as Dwivedi suggests, the teachings of the world's religions could be brought together to develop an ecumenical, global environmental ethic, what would be the unique contribution of *satyagraha*?

2. Compare the Hindu view of sanctity of life with Schweitzer's Reverence for Life (Reading 16). How are they similar and different?

3. What does Dwivedi think about the caste system in Hinduism?

4. Compare the Bishnoi and Chipko movements in India to "tree huggers" in the United States and to other Western activist movements.

36   The Buddhist Attitude Towards Nature

LILY DE SILVA

Lily de Silva is professor of Buddhist studies at the University of Peradeniya, Sri Lanka. In this essay, she sets forth a Buddhist perspective on environmental ethics, arguing that Buddhism emphasizes simple, nonviolent, gentle living. In its doctrine of karma and rebirth (similar to Hinduism), it recognizes that all animals and humans are spiritual entities to be treated with loving kindness.

Buddhism strictly limits itself to the delineation of a way of life designed to eradicate human suffering. The Buddha refused to answer questions which did not directly or indirectly bear on the central problem of human suffering and its ending. Furthermore, environmental pollution is a problem of the modern age, unheard of and unsuspected during the time of the Buddha. Therefore it is difficult to find any specific discourse which deals with the topic we are interested in here. Nevertheless, as Buddhism is a full-fledged philosophy of life reflecting all aspects of experience, it is possible to find enough material in the Pali Canon to delineate the Buddhist attitude towards nature.

The word "nature" means everything in the world which is not organised and constructed by man. The Pali equivalents which come closest to "nature" are *loka* and *yathābhūta*. The former is usually translated as "world" while the latter literally means "things as they really are." The words *dhammatā* and *niyāma* are used in the Pali Canon to mean "natural law or way."

NATURE AS DYNAMIC

According to Buddhism changeability is one of the perennial principles of nature. Everything changes in nature and nothing remains static. This concept is expressed by the Pali term *anicca*. Everything formed is in a constant process of change (*sabbe sankhārā aniccā*). The world is therefore defined as that which disintegrates (*lujjati ti loko*); the world is so called because it is dynamic and kinetic, it is constantly in a process of undergoing change. In nature there are no static and stable "things"; there are only ever-changing, ever-moving processes....

MORALITY AND NATURE

The world passes through alternating cycles of evolution and dissolution, each of which endures for a long period of time. Though change is inherent in nature, Buddhism believes that natural processes are affected by the morals of man.... Buddhism believes that though change is a factor inherent in nature, man's moral deterioration accelerates the process of change and brings about changes which are adverse to human well being and happiness....

[S]everal suttas from the Pali Canon show that early Buddhism believes there to be a close relationship between human morality and the natural environment. This idea has been systematised in the theory of the five natural laws in the later commentaries. According to this theory, in the cosmos there are five natural laws or forces at work, namely *utuniyāma* (lit. "season-law"), *bijaniyāma* (lit. "seed-law"), *cittaniyāma*, *kammaniyāma* and *dhammaniyāma*. They can be translated as physical laws, biological laws, psychological laws, moral laws and causal laws, respectively. While the first four laws operate within their respective spheres, the last-mentioned law of causality operates *within* each of them as well as *among* them.

Reprinted from *The Buddhist Attitude Towards Nature*, ed. K. Sandell (Buddhist Publication Society, Sri Lanka, 1987). Notes deleted.

This means that the physical environment of any given area conditions the growth and development of its biological component, i.e., flora and fauna. These in turn influence the thought pattern of the people interacting with them. Modes of thinking determine moral standards. The opposite process of interaction is also possible. The morals of man influence not only the psychological make-up of the people but the biological and physical environment of the area as well. Thus the five laws demonstrate that man and nature are bound together in a reciprocal causal relationship with changes in one necessarily bringing about changes in the other.

The commentary on the *Cakkavattisīhanāda Sutta* goes on to explain the pattern of mutual interaction further. When mankind is demoralised through greed, famine is the natural outcome; when moral degeneration is due to ignorance, epidemic is the inevitable result; when hatred is the demoralising force, widespread violence is the ultimate outcome. If and when mankind realizes that large-scale devastation has taken place as a result of his moral degeneration, a change of heart takes place among the few surviving human beings. With gradual moral regeneration conditions improve through a long period of cause and effect and mankind again starts to enjoy gradually increasing prosperity and longer life. The world, including nature and mankind, stands or falls with the type of moral force at work. If immorality grips society, man and nature deteriorate; if morality reigns, the quality of human life and nature improves. Thus greed, hatred and delusion produce pollution within and without. Generosity, compassion and wisdom produce purity within and without. This is one reason the Buddha has pronounced that the world is led by the mind, *cittena niyata loko.* Thus man and nature, according to the ideas expressed in early Buddhism, are interdependent.

HUMAN USE OF NATURAL RESOURCES

For survival mankind has to depend on nature for his food, clothing, shelter, medicine and other requisites. For optimum benefits man has to understand nature so that he can utilise natural resources and live harmoniously with nature. By understanding the working of nature—for example, the seasonal rainfall pattern, methods of conserving water by irrigation, the soil types, the physical conditions required for growth of various food crops, etc.—man can learn to get better returns from his agricultural pursuits. But this learning has to be accompanied by moral restraint if he is to enjoy the benefits of natural resources for a long time. Man must learn to satisfy his needs and not feed his greeds. The resources of the world are not unlimited whereas man's greed knows neither limit nor satiation. Modern man in his unbridled voracious greed for pleasure and acquisition of wealth has exploited nature to the point of near impoverishment....

Buddhism tirelessly advocates the virtues of non-greed, non-hatred, and non-delusion in all human pursuits. Greed breeds sorrow and unhealthy consequences. Contentment (*santuṭṭhi*) is a much praised virtue in Buddhism. The man leading a simple life with few wants easily satisfied is upheld and appreciated as an exemplary character. Miserliness and wastefulness are equally deplored in Buddhism as two degenerative extremes. Wealth has only instrumental value; it is to be utilised for the satisfaction of man's needs. Hoarding is a senseless anti-social habit comparable to the attitude of the dog in the manger. The vast hoarding of wealth in some countries and the methodical destruction of large quantities of agricultural produce to keep the market prices from falling, while half the world is dying of hunger and starvation, is really a sad paradox of the present affluent age.

Buddhism commends frugality as a virtue in its own right. Once Ānanda explained to King Udena the thrifty economic use of robes by the monks in the following order. When new robes are received the old robes are used as coverlets, the old coverlets as mattress covers, the old mattress covers as rugs, the old rugs as dusters, and the old tattered dusters are kneaded with clay and used to repair cracked floors and walls. Thus nothing usable is wasted. Those who waste are derided as "wood-apple eaters." A man shakes the branch of a wood-apple tree and all the fruits, ripe as well as unripe, fall. The man would collect only what he wants and walk away leaving the rest to rot. Such a wasteful attitude is certainly deplored in Buddhism as not only anti-social but criminal. The excessive exploitation of nature as is done today would certainly be condemned by Buddhism in the strongest possible terms.

Buddhism advocates a gentle non-aggressive attitude towards nature. According to the *Sigālovāda Sutta* a householder should accumulate wealth as a bee collects pollen from a flower. The bee harms neither the fragrance nor the beauty of the flower, but gathers pollen to turn it into sweet honey. Similarly, man is expected to make legitimate use of nature so that he can rise above nature and realise his innate spiritual potential.

ATTITUDE TOWARDS ANIMAL AND PLANT LIFE

The well-known Five Precepts (*pañca sīla*) form the minimum code of ethics that every lay Buddhist is expected to adhere to. Its first precept involves abstention from injury to life. It is explained as the casting aside of all forms of weapons, being conscientious about depriving a living being of life. In its positive sense it means the cultivation of compassion and sympathy for all living beings. The Buddhist layman is expected to abstain from trading in meat too.

The Buddhist monk has to abide by an even stricter code of ethics than the layman. He has to abstain from practices which would involve even unintentional injury to living creatures. For instance, the Buddha promulgated the rule against going on a journey during the rainy season because of possible injury to worms and insects that come to the surface in wet weather. The same concern for non-violence prevents a monk from digging the ground. Once a monk who was a potter prior to ordination built for himself a clay hut and set it on fire to give it a fine finish. The Buddha strongly objected to this as so many living creatures would have been burnt in the process. The hut was broken down on the Buddha's instructions to prevent it from creating a bad precedent for later generations. The scrupulous non-violent attitude towards even the smallest living creatures prevents the monks from drinking unstrained water. It is no

doubt a sound hygienic habit, but what is noteworthy is the reason which prompts the practice, namely, sympathy for living creatures.

Buddhism also prescribes the practice of *mettā*, "loving-kindness" towards all creatures of all quarters without restriction. The *Karanīyamettā Sutta* enjoins the cultivation of loving-kindness towards all creatures, timid and steady, long and short, big and small, minute and great, visible and invisible, near and far, born and awaiting birth. All quarters are to be suffused with this loving attitude. Just as one's own life is precious to oneself, so is the life of the other precious to himself. Therefore a reverential attitude must be cultivated towards all forms of life. . . .

The understanding of karma and rebirth, too, prepares the Buddhist to adopt a sympathetic attitude towards animals. According to this belief it is possible for human beings to be reborn in subhuman states among animals. The *Kukkuravatika Sutta* can be cited as a canonical reference which substantiates this view. The Jātakas provide ample testimony to this view from commentarial literature. It is possible that our own close relatives have been reborn as animals. Therefore it is only right that we should treat animals with kindness and sympathy. The Buddhist notion of merit also engenders a gentle non-violent attitude towards living creatures. It is said that if one throws dish-washing water into a pool where there are insects and living creatures, intending that they feed on the tiny particles of food thus washed away, one accumulates merit even by such trivial generosity. According to the *Macchuddāna Jātaka* the Bodhisatta threw his leftover food into a river in order to feed the fish, and by the power of that merit he was saved from an impending disaster. Thus kindness to animals, be they big or small, is a source of merit—merit needed for human beings to improve their lot in the cycle of rebirths and to approach the final goal of Nibbāna.

Buddhism expresses a gentle non-violent attitude towards the vegetable kingdom as well. It is said that one should not even break the branch of a tree that has given one shelter. Plants are so helpful to us in providing us with all necessities of life that we are expected not to adopt a callous attitude towards them. The more strict monastic rules prevent monks from injuring plant life.

Prior to the rise of Buddhism people regarded natural phenomena such as mountains, forests, groves and trees with a sense of awe and reverence. They considered them as the abode of powerful non-human beings who could assist human beings at times of need. Though Buddhism gave man a far superior Triple Refuge (*tisaraṇa*) in the Buddha, Dhamma and Sangha, these places continued to enjoy public patronage at a popular level, as the acceptance of terrestrial non-human beings such as *devatās* and *yakkhas* did not violate the belief system of Buddhism. Therefore among the Buddhists there is a reverential attitude towards specially long-standing gigantic trees. They are called *vanaspati* in Pali, meaning "lords of the forests." As huge trees such as the ironwood, the sāla and the fig are also recognised as the Bodhi trees of former Buddhas, the deferential attitude towards trees is further strengthened. It is well known that the *ficus religiosa* is held as an object of great veneration in the Buddhist world today as the tree under which the Buddha attained Enlightenment.

The construction of parks and pleasure groves for public use is considered a great meritorious deed. Sakka the lord of gods is said to have reached this status as a result of social services such as the construction of parks, pleasure groves, ponds, wells and roads.

The open air, natural habitats and forest trees have a special fascination for the Eastern mind as symbols of spiritual freedom. The home life is regarded as a fetter (*sambādha*) that keeps man in bondage and misery. Renunciation is like the open air (*abbhokāsa*), nature unhampered by man's activity....The Buddha's constant advice to his disciples also was to resort to natural habitats such as forest groves and glades. There, undisturbed by human activity, they could zealously engage themselves in meditation.

ATTITUDE TOWARDS POLLUTION

...Cleanliness was highly commended by the Buddhists both in the person and in the environment. They were much concerned about keeping water clean, be it in the river, pond or well. These sources of water were for public use and each individual had to use them with proper public-spirited caution so that others after him could use them with the same degree of cleanliness. Rules regarding the cleanliness of green grass were prompted by ethical and aesthetic considerations. Moreover, grass is food for most animals and it is man's duty to refrain from polluting it by his activities.

Noise is today recognised as a serious personal and environmental pollutant troubling everyone to some extent....

The Buddha and his disciples revelled in the silent solitary natural habitats unencumbered by human activity. Even in the choice of monasteries the presence of undisturbed silence was an important quality they looked for. Silence invigorates those who are pure at heart and raises their efficiency for meditation. But silence overawes those who are impure with ignoble impulses of greed, hatred and delusion....

The psychological training of the monks is so advanced that they are expected to cultivate a taste not only for external silence, but for inner silence of speech, desire and thought as well. The subvocal speech, the inner chatter that goes on constantly within us in our waking life, is expected to be silenced through meditation. The sage who succeeds in quelling this inner speech completely is described as a *muni,* a silent one. His inner silence is maintained even when he speaks!...

NATURE AS BEAUTIFUL

The Buddha and his disciples regarded natural beauty as a source of great joy and aesthetic satisfaction. The saints who purged themselves of sensuous worldly pleasures responded to natural beauty with a detached sense of appreciation. The average poet looks at nature and derives inspiration mostly by the sentiments it evokes in his own heart; he becomes emotionally involved with nature. For instance, he may compare the sun's rays passing over the mountain tops to the blush on a sensitive face, he may see a tear in a dew drop, the lips of his beloved in a rose petal, etc. But the appreciation of the saint is quite different. He appreciates nature's beauty for its own sake, and derives joy unsullied by sensuous associations and self-projected ideas....

CONCLUSION

... In the present ecocrisis man has to look for radical solutions. "Pollution cannot be dealt with in the long term on a remedial or cosmetic basis or by tackling symptoms: all measures should deal with basic causes. These are determined largely by our values, priorities and choices." Man must reappraise his value system. The materialism that has guided his lifestyle has landed him in very severe problems. Buddhism teaches that mind is the forerunner of all things, mind is supreme. If one acts with an impure mind, i.e., a mind sullied with greed, hatred and delusion, suffering is the inevitable result. If one acts with a pure mind, i.e., with the opposite qualities of contentment, compassion and wisdom, happiness will follow like a shadow. Man has to understand that pollution in the environment has been caused because there has been psychological pollution within himself. If he wants a clean environment he has to adopt a lifestyle that springs from a moral and spiritual dimension.

Buddhism offers man a simple moderate lifestyle eschewing both extremes of self-deprivation and self-indulgence. Satisfaction of basic human necessities, reduction of wants to the minimum, frugality and contentment are its important characteristics. Each man has to order his life on moral principles, exercise self-control in the enjoyment of the senses, discharge his duties in his various social roles, and conduct himself with wisdom and self-awareness in all activities. It is only when each man adopts a simple moderate lifestyle that mankind as a whole will stop polluting the environment. This seems to be the only way of overcoming the present ecocrisis and the problem of alienation. With such a lifestyle, man will adopt a non-exploitative, non-aggressive, gentle attitude towards nature. He can then live in harmony with nature, utilising its resources for the satisfaction of his basic needs. The Buddhist admonition is to utilise nature in the same way as a bee collects pollen from the flower, neither polluting its beauty nor depleting its fragrance. Just as the bee manufactures honey out of pollen, so man should be able to find happiness and fulfilment in life without harming the natural world in which he lives.

ॐ STUDY QUESTIONS

1. Compare de Silva's Buddhist ethics with Dwivedi's Hindu perspective. How are they different or similar? Then compare each with Western views. Do you think we could help each other understand our responsibilities with regard to the environment? What would Western views' distinctive contributions be?

2. How does the Buddhist concern to become liberated from suffering influence its understanding of our duties to nature?

3. Do you agree that "modes of thinking determine moral standards"?

37   Islamic Environmental Ethics, Law, and Society

MAWIL Y. IZZI DEEN (SAMARRAI)

Mawil Y. Izzi Deen (Samarrai) is assistant professor, King Abdul Aziz University, Jeddah, consultant to the Saudi Arabian Center for Science and Technology, and co-author of *Islamic Principles for the Conservation of the Natural Environment*. Deen sets forth the Islamic

Reprinted from *Ethics of Environment*, ed. J. Ronald Engel and Joan Gibb Engel (London: Bellhaven Press, 1990). Notes deleted.

view that the foundation of environmental protection is found in the idea that God created the world and set human beings in it to enjoy and carefully use it. Ecological balance and sustainable care of nature are promoted by Islam.

Islamic environmental ethics, like all other forms of ethics in Islam, is based on clear-cut legal foundations which Muslims hold to be formulated by God. Thus, in Islam, an acceptance of what is legal and what is ethical has not involved the same processes as in cultures which base their laws on humanistic philosophies.

Muslim scholars have found it difficult to accept the term "Islamic Law," since "law" implies a rigidity and dryness alien to Islam. They prefer the Arabic word *Sharī'ah* (Shariah) which literally means the "source of water." The Shariah is the source of life in that it contains both legal rules and ethical principles. This is indicated by the division of the Shariah relevant to human action into the categories of: obligatory actions (*wājib*),—those which a Muslim is required to perform; devotional and ethical virtues (*mandūb*),—those actions a Muslim is encouraged to perform, the non-observance of which, however, incurs no liability; permissible actions (*mubāh*),—those in which a Muslim is given complete freedom of choice; abominable actions (*makrūh*),—those which are morally but not legally wrong; and prohibited actions (*haram*),—all those practices forbidden by Islam.

A complete separation into the two elements, law and ethics, is thus unnecessary in Islam. For a Muslim is obliged to obey whatever God has ordered, his philosophical questions having been answered before he became a follower of the faith.

THE FOUNDATION OF ENVIRONMENTAL PROTECTION

In Islam, the conservation of the environment is based on the principle that all the individual components of the environment were created by God, and that all living things were created with different functions, functions carefully measured and meticulously balanced by the Almighty Creator. Although the various components of the natural environment serve humanity as one of their functions, this does not imply that human use is the sole reason for their creation. The comments of the medieval Muslim scholar, Ibn Tamyah on those verses of the Holy Qur'ān which state that God created the various parts of the environment to serve humanity, are relevant here:

> In considering all these verses it must be remembered that Allah in His wisdom created these creatures for reasons other than serving man, for in these verses He only explains the benefits of these creatures [to man].

The legal and ethical reasons for protecting the environment can be summarized as follows: First, the environment is God's creation and to protect it is to preserve its values as a sign of the Creator. To assume that the environment's benefits to human beings are the sole reason for its protection may lead to environmental misuse or destruction.

Second, the component parts of nature are entities in continuous praise of their Creator. Humans may not be able to understand the form or nature of this praise, but the fact that the Qur'ān describes it is an additional reason for environmental preservation:

> The seven heavens and the earth and all that is therein praise Him, and there is not such a thing but hymneth his praise; but ye understand not their praise. Lo! He is ever Clement, Forgiving. (Sūrah 17:44)

Third, all the laws of nature are laws made by the Creator and based on the concept of the absolute continuity of existence. Although God may sometimes wish otherwise, what happens, happens according to the natural law of God (*sunnah*), and human beings must accept this as the will of the Creator. Attempts to break the law of God must be prevented. As the Qurān states:

> Hast thou not seen that unto Allah payeth adoration whosoever is in the heavens and whosoever is

in the earth, and the sun, and the moon, and the stars, and the hills, and the trees, and the beasts, and many of mankind. (Sūrah 22:18)

Fourth, the Qur'ān's acknowledgment that humankind is not the only community to live in this world—"There is not an animal in the earth, nor a flying creature flying on two wings, but they are peoples like unto you" (Sūrah 6:38)—means that while humans may currently have the upper hand over other "peoples," these other creatures are beings and, like us, are worthy of respect and protection. The Prophet Muhammad (peace be upon him) considered all living creatures worthy of protection (*hurmah*) and kind treatment. He was once asked whether there will be a reward from God for charity shown to animals. His reply was very explicit: "For [charity shown to] each creature which has a wet heart there is a reward." Ibn Hajar comments further upon this tradition, explaining that wetness is an indication of life (and so charity extends to all creatures), although human beings are more worthy of the charity if a choice must be made.

Fifth, Islamic environmental ethics is based on the concept that all human relationships are established on justice ('*adl*) and equity (*ihsān*): "Lo! Allah enjoineth justice and kindness" (Sūrah 16:90). The prophetic tradition limits benefits derived at the cost of animal suffering. The Prophet Muhammad instructed: "Verily Allah has prescribed equity (*ihsān*) in all things. Thus if you kill, kill well, and if you slaughter, slaughter well. Let each of you sharpen his blade and let him spare suffering to the animal he slaughters."

Sixth, the balance of the universe created by God must also be preserved. For "Everything with Him is measure" (Sūrah 13:8). Also, "There is not a thing but with Us are the stores thereof. And We send it not down save in appointed measure" (Sūrah 15:21).

Seventh, the environment is not in the service of the present generation alone. Rather, it is the gift of God to all ages, past, present and future. This can be understood from the general meaning of Sūrah 2:29: "He it is Who created for you all that is in the earth." The word "you" as used here refers to all persons with no limit as to time or place.

Finally, no other creature is able to perform the task of protecting the environment. God entrusted humans with the duty of viceregency, a duty so onerous and burdensome that no other creature would accept it: "Lo! We offered the trust unto the heavens and the earth and the hills, but they shrank from bearing it and were afraid of it. And man assumed it" (Sūrah 33:72).

THE COMPREHENSIVE NATURE OF ISLAMIC ETHICS

Islamic ethics is founded on two principles—human nature, and religious and legal grounds. The first principle, natural instinct (*fitrah*), was imprinted in the human soul by God at the time of creation (Sūrah 91:7–8). Having natural instinct, the ordinary individual can, at least to some extent, distinguish not only between good and bad, but also between these and that which is neutral, neither good nor bad. However, an ethical conscience is not a sufficient personal guide. Due to the complexities of life an ethical conscience alone cannot define the correct attitude to every problem. Moreover, a person does not live in a vacuum, but is affected by outside influences which may corrupt the ability to choose between good and evil. Outside influences include customs, personal interests, and prevailing concepts concerning one's surroundings.

The religious and legal grounds upon which Islamic ethics is founded were presented by the messengers of God. These messengers were possessed of a special nature, and since they were inspired by God, they were able to avoid the outside influences which may affect other individuals.

Legal instructions in Islam are not negative in the sense of forcing the conscience to obey. On the contrary, legal instructions have been revealed in such a way that the conscience approves and acknowledges them to be correct. Thus the law itself becomes a part of human conscience, thereby guaranteeing its application and its success.

An imported, alien law cannot work because, while it may be possible to make it legally binding, it cannot be made morally binding upon

Muslims. Muslims willingly pay the poor-tax (*zakāh*) because they know that if they fail to do so they will be both legally and ethically responsible. Managing to avoid the legal consequences of failure to pay what is due will not help them to avoid the ethical consequences, and they are aware of this. Although a Muslim poacher may be able to shoot elephants and avoid park game wardens, if a framework based on Islamic principles for the protection of the environment has been published, he knows that he will not be able to avoid the ever-watchful divine Warden. The Muslim knows that Islamic values are all based on what God loves and wants: "And when he turns away [from thee] his effort in the land is to make mischief therein and to destroy the crops and the cattle; and Allah loveth not mischief" (Sūrah 2:205).

When the Prophet Solomon and his army were about to destroy a nest of ants, one ant warned the rest of the colony of the coming destruction. When Solomon heard this he begged God for the wisdom to do the good thing which God wanted him to do. Solomon was obviously facing an environmental problem and needed an ethical decision; he begged God for guidance:

> Till, when they reached the Valley of the Ants, an ant exclaimed: O, ants! Enter your dwellings lest Solomon and his armies crush you, unperceiving.
>
> And [Solomon] smiled, laughing at her speech, and said: My Lord, arouse me to be thankful for Thy favor wherewith Thou hast favored me and my parents, and to do good that shall be pleasing unto Thee, and include me among [the number of] Thy righteous slaves. (Sūrah 27: 18–19)

Ethics in Islam is not based on a variety of separate scattered virtues, with each virtue, such as honesty or truth, standing isolated from others. Rather virtue in Islam is a part of a total, comprehensive way of life which serves to guide and control all human activity. Truthfulness is an ethical value, as are protecting life, conserving the environment, and sustaining its development within the confines of what God has ordered. When 'Āisha, the wife of the Prophet Muhammad, was asked about his ethics she replied: "His ethics are the whole Qur'ān." The Qur'ān does not contain separate scattered ethical values. Rather it contains the instructions for a complete way of life. There are political, social and economic principles side by side with instructions for the construction and preservation of the earth.

Islamic ethical values are based not on human reasoning, as Aristotle claimed values to be, nor on what society imposes on the individual, as Durkheim thought, nor on the interests of a certain class, as Marxists maintain. In each of these claims values are affected by circumstances. In Islam, ethical values are held to be based on an accurate scale which is unalterable as to time and place. Islam's values are those without which neither persons nor the natural environment can be sustained.

THE HUMAN–ENVIRONMENT RELATIONSHIP

As we have seen, within the Islamic faith, an individual's relationship with the environment is governed by certain moral precepts. These originate with God's creation of humans and the role they were given upon the Earth. Our universe, with all its diverse component elements was created by God and the human being is an essential part of His Measured and Balanced Creation. The role of humans, however, is not only to enjoy, use and benefit from their surroundings. They are expected to preserve, protect and promote their fellow creatures. The Prophet Muhammad (peace be upon him) said: "All creatures are God's dependents and the best among them is the one who is most useful to God's dependents." The Prophet of Islam looked upon himself as responsible for the trees and the animals and all natural elements. He also said: "The only reasons that God does not cause his punishment to pour over you are the elderly, the suckling babes, and the animals which graze upon your land." Muhammad prayed for rain when he was reminded that water was short, the trees suffering from drought, and animals dying. He begged for God's mercy to fall upon his creatures.

The relationship between human beings and their environment includes many features in addition to subjugation and utilization. Construction and development are primary but our relationship to nature also includes meditation, contemplation and enjoyment of its beauties. The most perfect Muslim was the Prophet Muhammad who was reported by Ibn 'Abbās to have enjoyed gazing at greenery and running water.

When reading verses about the Earth in the Holy Qur'ān, we find strong indications that the Earth was originally a place of peace and rest for humans:

> Is not He [best] Who made the earth a fixed abode, and placed rivers in the folds thereof, and placed firm hills therein, and hath set a barrier between the two seas? Is there any God beside Allah? Nay, but most of them know not! (Sūrah 27:61)

The Earth is important to the concept of interrelation. Human beings are made from two components of the Earth—dust and water.

> And Allah hath caused you to grow as a growth from the earth, And afterward He maketh you return thereto, and He will bring you forth again, a [new] forthbringing. And Allah hath made the earth a wide expanse for you. That ye may thread the valleyways thereof. (Sūrah 71:17–20)

The word "earth" (*arḍ*) is mentioned twice in this short quotation and in the Qur'ān the word occurs a total of 485 times, a simple measure of its importance.

The Earth is described as being subservient to humans: "He it is Who hath made the earth subservient unto you, so walk in the paths thereof and eat of His providence" (Sūrah 67:15). The Earth is also described as a receptacle: "Have we not made the earth a receptacle both for the living and the dead" (Sūrah 77: 25–26). Even more importantly, the Earth is considered by Islam to be a source of purity and a place for the worship of God. The Prophet Muhammad said: "The earth is made for me [and Muslims] as a prayer place (*masjid*) and as a purifier." This means that the Earth is to be used to cleanse oneself before prayer if water is unobtainable. Ibn 'Umar reported that the Prophet of Islam said: "God is beautiful and loved everything beautiful.

He is generous and loves generosity and is clean and loves cleanliness."

Thus it is not surprising that the Islamic position with regard to the environment is that humans must intervene in order to protect the Earth. They may not stand back while it is destroyed. "He brought you forth from the earth and hath made you husband it" (Sūrah 11:61). For, finally, the Earth is a source of blessedness. And the Prophet Muhammad said: "Some trees are blessed as the Muslim himself, especially palm."

THE SUSTAINABLE CARE OF NATURE

Islam permits the utilization of the natural environment but this utilization should not involve unnecessary destruction. Squandering is rejected by God: "O Children of Adam! Look to your adornment at every place of worship, and eat and drink, but be not prodigal. Lo! He loveth not the prodigals" (Sūrah 7:31). In this Qur'ānic passage, eating and drinking refer to the utilization of the sources of life. Such utilization is not without controls. The component elements of life have to be protected so that their utilization may continue in a sustainable way. Yet even this preservation must be undertaken in an altruistic fashion, and not merely for its benefit to human beings. The Prophet Muhammad said: "Act in your life as though you are living forever and act for the Hereafter as if you are dying tomorrow."

These actions must not be restricted to those which will derive direct benefits. Even if doomsday were expected imminently, humans would be expected to continue their good behaviour, for Muhammad said: "When doomsday comes if someone has a palm shoot in his hand he should plant it." This *hadīth* encapsulates the principles of Islamic environmental ethics. Even when all hope is lost, planting should continue for planting is good in itself. The planting of the palm shoot continues the process of development and will sustain life even if one does not anticipate any benefit from it. In this, the Muslim is like the soldier who fights to the last bullet.

A theory of the sustainable utilization of the ecosystem may be deduced from Islam's assertion that life is maintained with due balance in everything: "Allah knoweth that which every female beareth and that which the wombs absorb and that which they grow. And everything with Him is measured" (Sūrah 13:8). Also: "He unto Whom belongeth the sovereignty of the heavens and the earth, He hath chosen no son nor hath He any partner in the sovereignty. He hath created everything and hath meted out for it a measure" (Sūrah 25:2).

Humans are not the owners, but the maintainers of the due balance and measure which God provided for them and for the animals that live with them.

> And after that He spread the earth,
> And produced therefrom water thereof and the
>   pasture thereof,
> And He made fast the hills,
> A provision for you and for your cattle.
>
> (SŪRAH 79:30–33)

The Qur'ān goes on to say:

> But when the great disaster cometh,
> The day when man will call to mind his [whole]
>   endeavor.
>
> (SŪRAH 79:34–35)

Humans will have a different home (*ma'wā*) or place of abode, different from the Earth and what it contains. The word *ma'wā* is the same word used in modern Arabic for "environment." One cannot help but wonder if these verses are an elaboration on the concept of sustainable development, a task that humans will undertake until their home is changed.

Sayyid Quṭb, commenting on these verses, observes that the Qur'ān, in referring to the origin of ultimate truth, used many correspondences (*muwāfaqāt*)—such as building the heavens, darkening the night, bringing forth human beings, spreading the earth, producing water and plants, and making the mountains fast. All these were provided for human beings and their animals as providence, and are direct signs which constitute proof as to the reality of God's measurement and calculation. Finally, Sayyid Quṭb observes that every part of God's creation was carefully made to fit into the general system, a system that testifies to the Creator's existence and the existence of a day of reward and punishment.

At this point, one must ask whether it is not a person's duty to preserve the proof of the Creator's existence while developing it. Wouldn't the wholesale destruction of the environment be the destruction of much which testifies to the greatness of God?

The concept of the sustained care of all aspects of the environment also fits into Islam's concept of charity, for charity is not only for the present generation but also for those in the future. A story is told of 'Umar ibn al-Khattāb, the famous companion of the Prophet. He once saw that an old man, Khuzaymah ibn Thābit, had neglected his land. 'Umar asked what was preventing him from cultivating it. Khuzaymah explained that he was old and could be expected to die soon. Whereupon, Umar insisted that he should plant it. Khuzaymah's son, who narrated the story, added that his father and 'Umar planted the uncultivated land together.

This incident demonstrates how strongly Islam encourages the sustained cultivation of the land. Land should not be used and then abandoned just because the cultivator expects no personal benefit.

In Islam, law and ethics constitute the two interconnected elements of a unified world view. When considering the environment and its protection, this Islamic attitude may constitute a useful foundation for the formulation of a strategy throughout, at least, the Muslim world. Muslims who inhabit so much of the developing world may vary in local habits and customs but they are remarkably united in faith and in their attitude to life.

Islam is a religion of submission to God, master of all worlds. The Earth and all its inhabitants were created and are dominated by God. All Muslims begin their prayers five times a day with the same words from the Holy Qur'ān: "Praise be to Allah, Lord of the Worlds" (Sūrah 1:1). These opening words of the Qur'ān have become not only the most repeated but also the most loved and respected words for Muslims everywhere. Ibn Kathīr, like many other Qur'ānic commentators, considers that the word "worlds" ('ālamīn) means the different kinds of creatures that inhabit the sky, the land, and the sea. Muslims submit themselves to the Creator who made them and who made all other worlds. The same author mentions that Muslims also submit themselves to the signs of the existence of the Creator and His unity. This secondary meaning exists because "worlds" comes from the same root as signs; thus the worlds are signs of the Creator.

A Muslim, therefore, has a very special relationship with those worlds which in modern times have come to be known as the environment. Indeed, that these worlds exist and that they were made by the same Creator means that they are united and interdependent, each a part of the perfect system of creation. No conflict should exist between them; they should exist in harmony as different parts of the whole. Their coexistence could be likened to an architectural masterpiece in which every detail has been added to complete and complement the structure. Thus the details of creation serve to testify to the wisdom and perfection of the Creator.

THE PRACTICE OF ISLAMIC ENVIRONMENTAL ETHICS

Islam has always had a great influence on the formation of individual Muslim communities and the policy making of Muslim states. Environmental policy has been influenced by Islam and this influence has remained the same throughout the history of the Islamic faith.

The concept of *himā* (protection of certain zones) has existed since the time of the Prophet Muhammad. *Himā* involved the ruler or government's protection of specific unused areas. No one may build on them or develop them in any way. The Mālikī school of Islamic law described the requirements of *himā* to be the following. First, the need of the Muslim public for the maintenance of land in an unused state. Protection is not granted to satisfy an influential individual unless there is a public need. Second, the protected area should be limited in order to avoid inconvenience to the public. Third, the protected

area should not be built on or cultivated. And fourth, the aim of protection (Zuhaylī 5:574) is the welfare of the people, for example, the protected area may be used for some restricted grazing by the animals of the poor.

The concept of *himā* can still be seen in many Muslim countries, such as Saudi Arabia, where it is practised by the government to protect wildlife. In a less formal way it is still practised by some bedouin tribes as a custom or tradition inherited from their ancestors.

The *harīm* is another ancient institution which can be traced back to the time of the Prophet Muhammad. It is an inviolable zone which may not be used or developed, save with the specific permission of the state. The *harīm* is usually found in association with wells, natural springs, underground water channels, rivers and trees planted on barren land or *mawāt*. There is careful administration of the *harīm* zones based on the practice of the Prophet Muhammad and the precedent of his companions as recorded in the sources of Islamic law.

At present the role of Islam in environmental protection can be seen in the formation of different Islamic organizations and the emphasis given to Islam as a motive for the protection of the environment.

Saudi Arabia has keenly sought to implement a number of projects aimed at the protection of various aspects of the environment, for example, the late King Khalid's patronage of efforts to save the Arabian ornyx from extinction.

The Meteorology and Environmental Protection Administration (MEPA) of Saudi Arabia actively promotes the principles of Islamic environmental protection. In 1983 MEPA and the International Union for the Conservation of Nature and Natural Resources commissioned a basic paper on the Islamic principles for the conservation of natural environment.

The Islamic faith has great impact on environmental issues throughout the Arab and Muslim world. The first Arab Ministerial Conference took as its theme "The Environmental Aspects of Development" and one of the topics considered was the Islamic faith and its values. The Amir of Kuwait emphasized the fundamental importance of Islam when he addressed the General Assembly of the United Nations in 1988. He explained that Islam was the basis for justice, mercy, and cooperation between all humankind; and he called for an increase in scientific and technological assistance from the North to help conserve natural and human resources, combat pollution and support sustainable development projects.

Finally, it is imperative to acknowledge that the new morality required to conserve the environment which the World Conservation Strategy emphasizes, needs to be based on a more solid foundation. It is not only necessary to involve the public in conservation policy but also to improve its morals and alter its attitudes. In Muslim countries such changes should be brought about by identifying environmental policies with Islamic teachings. To do this, the public education system will have to supplement the scientific approach to environmental education with serious attention to Islamic belief and environmental awareness.

STUDY QUESTIONS

1. Compare Deen's view of the Islamic environmental ethics with the preceding views on Hinduism and Buddhism. Then compare it with Patrick Dobel's view (Reading 4) of Christian environmental ethics.

2. What insights or practices in Islam have you found that might be helpful in developing a Western environmental ethic? How would Islam contribute toward a global ecumenical environmental ethic?

38   An African Perspective on the Environmental Crisis*

SEGUN OGUNGBEMI

Segun Ogungbemi, a Yoruban from Nigeria, was for some years head and associate professor of philosophy, Moi University, Kenya, and the author of several works in African philosophy, ethics, and philosophy of religion.

Ogungbemi says that three principal factors contribute to the African ecological crisis: (1) ignorance and poverty, (2) misuse of science and technology, and (3) political conflict, including international economic pressures. He illustrates his thesis with regard to land, water, and air and argues that enlightened political leadership is needed in sub-Saharan Africa if environmental issues are to be satisfactorily dealt with.

One of the global problems of our time is the environmental condition of our world. Some of the environmental crises with which human beings have been grappling are of natural causes—earthquakes, volcanic eruptions, storms, droughts, diseases, and the like. Be that as it may, it is evident that man has exacerbated the situation, so that we now talk about an environmental crisis. For instance, there is air and water pollution, depletion of the ozone layers, extinction of fish and animal species, and such like. We are gripped with anxiety because of the danger of global warming. One of the questions which I think agitates our minds is, where are science, technology, and our desire for development leading us? Considering the moral, social and individual value of human existence

This essay was commissioned for the first edition of this volume.
*I am grateful to Professor Louis P. Pojman for sharing some of his books and articles with me. They have inspired me in writing both this article and others.

and the threat which current environmental hazards pose to its sustainability, it seems to me that the need for immediate solutions is one of the most urgent issues which contemporary philosophy ought to address. In this paper, I have examined the nature of the environmental crisis in Africa and provided some moral and practical suggestions.

THE NATURE OF THE ENVIRONMENTAL CRISIS IN AFRICA

Broadly speaking, the nature of the environmental crisis in sub-Saharan Africa can be understood from three perspectives—one that emanates from ignorance and poverty, another from modern science and technology, and the third relative to political conflict and international economics. In other words, if we want to understand the environmental crisis in Africa, we must consider both traditional and modern societies and their contributions to the environmental hazards we now find. The majority of African peoples live in rural areas where traditional modes of living lack some basic amenities, namely, good water supplies, adequate lavatories and the like. Isaac Sindiga explains:

> Clean water supplies are often unavailable and faeces disposal is a problem. Many people do not have pit latrines and help themselves in the bush. Such waste is often collected by rain water and taken to rivers where people take their livestock to water and also fetch water for domestic use.[1]

By polluting the rivers with human waste, our traditional society exposes itself to some . . . "water-borne diseases such as dysentery, typhoid and cholera."[2] This may not necessarily be due to unwillingness to change on the part of our people but it is the case that they are poor. Being poor however, does not necessarily exonerate our people from their contributions to environmental hazards which contribute to the death of many Africans.

The use of fuelwood by our traditional societies as a means of generating heat for cooking and other domestic services also contributes to the exacerbation of our environmental problems. According to Mostafa Kamal Tolba, "Fuelwood accounts for over 80% of Africa's energy use, but most is squandered on open heat fires."[3] Closely related to the issue of fuel-wood as energy for domestic needs is the habit of bush burning (bush burning facilitates hunting). The excessive use of fuelwood and constant bush burning increases air pollution and also depletes forests and other natural habitats.

Having shown some of the contributions made by our traditional society to the general environmental problems of the world today, I need to say that in many ways our rural men and women have lived with nature with respect and awe. Thomas McGinn notes:

> Primitive man is capable of apologizing to mother earth when he digs up to plant crops. Contemporary man has indeed lost a sense of respect through his philosophy of exploitation.[4]

In our traditional relationship with nature, men and women recognize the importance of water, land and air management. To our traditional communities the ethics of not taking more than you need from nature is a moral code. Perhaps this may explain why earth, forests, rivers, and wind and other natural objects are traditionally believed to be both natural and divine. The philosophy behind this belief may not necessarily be religious, but a natural means by which the human environment can be preserved. The ethics of care is essential to traditional understanding of environmental protection and conservation.

One may argue that the ethics of care of traditional Africans is due largely to their inability to exploit nature for their own benefits. For instance, it is evident that Africa is the poorest area in the world. Tolba writes:

> Africa has the world's lowest life expectancy, the highest rural under-development and the severest food shortages. These are the social and economic consequences of Africa's environmental crisis, but they are rarely seen as such.[5]

The lack of development in our traditional communities may also be due to internal strife. Morag Bell explains:

> At the same time lack of progress is partly due to internal politics which have shaken the stability necessary for effective development planning.[6]

It is important to note that whether or not there is development in our traditional communities, the ethics of not taking more than one needs from nature has its own credibility. This will be discussed later. Let us for the moment consider the contributions of modern Africa to the environmental crisis.

Today, modern Africa has benefitted from Western Civilization and industrialization even as the West has in turn benefitted from the exploitation of Africa. In contemporary Africa, however, because of the desire to develop like Europe and the United States of America, African governments and international corporations have engaged in mass destruction of our ecosystems. We all know that three basic natural resources are utilized in any development. These are land, water and air. I shall elaborate on each one of these natural resources as it is used in modern Africa.

I. Land

If one is a physicalist, one will not hesitate to ascribe one's physical substance to the earth. If however, one is a dualist, one will argue that human life is composed fundamentally of corporeal and incorporeal substances—body and mind. This shows our natural or physical affinity to the earth. The earth, which I otherwise will refer to as land, provides most of the necessary ingredients of life for human use, namely, trees, forest, minerals, animals, vegetables, rivers, etc. Our physical developments are primarily based on land use. In modern Africa, the way in which land has been exploited goes contrary to our traditional philosophy. David Okali writes:

> Modern usage of our land by our society does not reflect a similar degree of awareness of the importance of forests and trees for the maintenance of environmental values. The drive to develop has led to wholesale abandonment of traditional practices, and values of forests land management as if development and modernization were incompatible with conservation of forest and protection of trees. The consequence of this has been a break-down in environmental stability we witness in form of severe erosion, increased turbidity and silting-up of steams, flood disasters and degradation of forest land first to grassland and then to desert.[7]

Similarly R. P. Baffour writes:

> The rapid rate of deforestation which is taking place at present in most parts of African forests, where large numbers of valuable trees are being cut down annually and shipped for lumber overseas, should give cause for grave concern to present-day Africa.[8]

There is no doubt about the rapid population growth in Africa, and a need to feed the people requires some improvements in the traditional subsistence farming. In other words, mechanized farming has to compliment subsistence farming. The semi-arid and arid lands have been overutilized to the extent that fertilizers are needed to enrich the soils for maximum yields. Furthermore, modern Africa does not want to eat and drink only what is produced locally; it has been infected with a desire for the Western lifestyle, and to cope with this modern lifestyle it has to import goods from the industrial nations.

This importing requires increased production of export goods, namely, coffee, tea, cocoa, rubber, etc. However, the more agricultural products modern Africa has to produce the more fertilizers and other chemicals are used. The end result is that when it rains these chemicals are washed away into our rivers, lakes and oceans. The health hazards that these chemicals cause affect not only humans but also other species in our waters. With the extensive exportation of agricultural goods to Western Europe and the Americas, modern Africa has boosted the economy of the developed nations at the expense of its own. Apart from boosting the economy of the developed nations at the expense of its own, modern Africa has failed to adequately feed its own peoples. The observation of Paul Ekins is relevant to Africa. He writes:

> Paradoxically, therefore, "development" can end up giving more benefit to the rich countries which provided the initial "aid" than to the poor people in the countries which received it.... It is because of this sort of cycle that increasing numbers of grassroots activists in Southern countries are regarding "development" as dangerous to and exploitative of poor people in poor countries.[9]

In its bid to catch up with developed nations, modern Africa has exploited some of its essential minerals, namely, gold, copper, oil, diamonds, coal, uranium, etc., creating other ecological problems. For instance, where there are oil fields, it is a known fact that the areas are no longer good for agricultural activities. The exploitation of land minerals in modern Africa has provided jobs for many people, but the number is few when compared with the rest of the populace.

II. Water

Africa is blessed with an abundance of water. There are lakes, streams, rivers, and of course the Atlantic and Indian oceans. Water is an essential natural resource. Apart from its aesthetic values, the food values on which Africans depend cannot be overemphasized. Baffour explains:

> The rich shoals of tuna known to exist in the Atlantic lie almost unexploited and it has been known that trawlers as far afield as from Japan have recently been coming all the way from their home waters to fish tuna in the Atlantic and still make enormous profits. It is claimed that schools of tuna in the Atlantic can provide enough proteins for the entire world population for the next 500 years.[10]

Water is also essential to our domestic, agricultural and industrial needs. However, human activities have affected our clean waters. Charles O. Okidi writes:

> One instance was carried in newspapers as "U.S. Firms May Ship Toxic Wastes to Africa." The story was that there were U.S. industries producing wastes so highly toxic and so persistent that the U.S. laws would not permit their disposal in that country. So the companies were negotiating with some countries in Africa to allow the disposal of such wastes in their territories, in exchange for handsome foreign exchange for the national development needs of those African countries. Clearly, it must take a very gruesome sense of humor to accept that as an approach to development. But two African countries were reported to be actually involved in the negotiations.[11]

Similarly, a few years ago some Nigerian students in Italy informed the Nigerian government of a plan to dump toxic wastes on the Nigerian coast. At first the news appeared to be unfounded, but later the Nigerian government was caught up with the reality of the news. Some tons of toxic wastes were dumped at Koko in the then Bendel State of Nigeria. The drums used for transportation of the wastes were later used by local people to store water and other domestic materials. The Italian government was contacted about the incident, and the toxic wastes were cleaned up. However, some Nigerians who used the drums for water storage died. Painful as such human casualty may be, we must not lose sight of members of other species who have perished as a result of the toxic wastes dumped at Koko.

While the industrialized nations have polluted our waters, it must be noted that where African business people have developed industries, similar environmental problems have been created. Okidi writes:

> In the African context, the East African Medical Research Institute warned in 1971 that measures should be taken against pollution of Lake Victoria by industrial and municipal wastes. Up to now no actual remedial programme has been commenced. Yet more industries such as Kenya's molasses factory, breweries and cotton mills have been attracted by the water.[12]

What has happened to Lake Victoria is morally reprehensible, and it is happening to most of Africa's waters, particularly those that are in industrial locations. Water pollution is not limited to industrial areas, but is also found in our rural centres. Okidi observes:

> Africa's central problems are two-fold; preventing water pollution by bacteriological agents and actual delivery of safe drinking water to rural population. It is still possible to pump water from various inland or ground sources, cheaply and with fairly inexpensive treatment to the consumers. However, careless disposal of wastes can still pollute these inland waters as well as ground waters until some unexpected pollution can be found in waters remote from industrial centres.[13]

III. Air

Clean air is another essential resource that human beings and animal species depend on for survival. Without good air even plant life would suffer and our environment would be difficult, if not impossible, to live in. But in Africa, human activities are threatening good air. As already noted, our traditional communities depend on fuelwood for most of their energy needs, and bush burning is common. Both activities affect air quality adversely. Modern lifestyles have encouraged the abuse of good air. Industrial activities have also polluted the air, especially by the burning of industrial wastes.

With the development of modern systems of transportation, there are more cars, commercial vehicles and aeroplanes in African urban and commercial centres than ever before. It is unfortunate though that the cars and commercial vehicles imported into Africa have no emission controls. Driving on our commercial roads during the rush hours, particularly in the cities like Lagos, Ibadan, Kano, Kaduna, Accra, Dakar, Nairobi, Addis-Abbaba, etc., exposes one to a heavily polluted environment.

Further, modern African leaders have engaged themselves in what might be called a national security syndrome. The end result is the constant buildup of modern military equipment. As a matter of fact, as Tolba observes, "Of 37 countries for which data are available, only 10 spend more on agriculture than the military. This does not achieve meaningful security."[14] Since African leaders do not find any external aggressors who could be put in check militarily, they therefore turn against their own people. In other words, African countries are not presently threatened by any foreign aggressors so the leaders who want to consolidate their powers have been using military arms for their own protection. A case in point is Mobutu Seso Seko in Zaire. There are others who have engaged in oppressing their peoples simply because they want to remain in power. What is happening in Sudan, Ethiopia, Somalia, Angola, and Liberia provides other examples. The environmental pollution caused by the air raids and artillery bombardments that have taken place and which continue to take place in the above-named countries is disheartening. Apart from the pollution of the biosphere, the loss of human, animal and fish species are clear indications of leadership-madness of Africa.

POPULATION

On the population growth rate in Africa, Inga Ngel writes:

> At present, Africa's population doubles every twenty years. From 430 million during the mid-eighties, the continent will have to sustain approximately 900 million by the turn of the millennium. The prognosis for 2025 is an unbelievable 1.5 billion people. In order to preserve even the present poor standard of living, the crisis-ridden African States would have to achieve an annual economic growth rate of at least four per cent—an unattainable goal for most of them. Africa's population is growing at an unprecedented rate. Annually, an additional three per cent of people accelerate the destruction of the environment and aggravate social conflicts in the rapid growing cities. The balance between the ecosystem and man, upset for a long time already, is collapsing (Development and Cooperation No. 6/1990).

Bell (1986: 142–143) agrees that there is the problem of population growth in Africa but he is quick to note with caution:

> It has already been suggested that perhaps the most important demographic change in Africa in the recent past has been a marked increase in the population growth rate of the area. While the usual explanation for this trend is a decrease in death rates due to improvements in medical facilities, hygiene and nutrition, such an interpretation must be applied with caution. By international standards, mortality rates in Africa remain high and some investigations suggest that within parts of the continent, they are as high as ever they were....While the average life expectancy at birth is about 72 years in the more developed countries, it is about 57 years in the less developed countries and a mere 47 years in Africa south of the Sahara excluding South Africa....Focusing just on infant and early childhood deaths, which are the leading causes of low life expectancy, a similar pattern arises. Data on the former indicate that while the infant mortality rate is about 20 per 1000 live births in the most developed countries, many African countries have rates of over 150 and in some instances, it exceeds 200 per 1000 live births.

I do not doubt the rapid population growth in contemporary Africa. The more people we have the more effects it has on the environment, for instance, deforestation, decimation of animal species, pollution and the like. There are, however, some issues that have to be taken into consideration when discussing population explosion in Africa, namely, disasters which have taken many lives in Africa.

Generally, reliable data on population in Africa are not available. But, for the moment, let us consider countries in Africa where conflicts and natural disasters have reduced the population in Africa, namely, Somalia, Ethiopia, Nigeria, Kenya, Ghana, Niger, Chad, Togo, Zaire, Cameroun, Liberia, Angola, Sudan, Ruwanda, and South Africa. What we have gained in terms of population growth rate due to improvements in medical facilities and hygiene, among others, has been lost as a result of social conflicts and natural disasters. By the time everything is settled, we may be able to have the true picture of our population. It is no wonder why Bell sounds a note of caution when we talk about population explosion in Africa.

It seems to me that it is not necessarily the case that Africa must reduce its population or watch the pendulum of population indicator. Rather, it is the case that the wealth in the world is not equitably distributed.

> Oxfam, a United Kingdom based humanitarian organisation believes that poverty is the greatest scourge afflicting the human race this decade, with most countries of the South severely affected. "As the 20th Century draws to a close," the organisation says "more than a billion people in the world cannot afford the bare essentials of life." It observes that the rich countries of the North "with only 25 per cent of the world's people consume 80 per cent of the earth's resources... while one in three people in the developing world does not have enough to eat" (*African Concord,* Vol. 6, No. 26, 1991).

The developed countries, particularly the U.S. and the former Soviet Union, invested heavily on the military rather than sharing the wealth of the world more equitably with poor nations. According to Ekins, 1992:5:

> The U.S. in particular still strives to improve the stealth and accuracy of its nuclear weapons, against all deterrence logic. In proceeding with the SDI (the "Star Wars" Strategic Defence Initiative), which by 1989 had cost US$17 billion... the US continues to signal to the USSR and the world in general that it wishes to obtain invulnerability from nuclear attack and so break the balance of deterrence in its favour.

The military aid given to African States has exacerbated the escalation of social and political and religious upheavals in Africa. The effects of wars in African States, particularly in Somalia, Liberia, Sudan, Angola, among others, have had a damaging effect both on humans and the ecosystems. If the wealth in this world had been adequately managed, there would be no need for African nations to reduce their population. One important factor which should be taken very seriously is that if we reduce our population, where are we going to get more geniuses that will contribute to the development of Africa? What Africa needs is good leadership. Many things have gone wrong under the leadership of the military in many parts of Africa, for instance, Nigeria:

> It is not the best season in Nigeria. In fact, this is a season that tries man's souls, a season of vanishing happiness, arrested smiles, gloomy faces, a season when despair is now a compulsory company, a season when men and women tremble with fears about the present and the future (Bayo Onanuga: *African Concord,* Vol. 6, No. 8, 1992).

Writing in the same vein, Adebayo Williams notes:

> From exhaustive research, I have come to the conclusion that if the majority of African leaders were to submit themselves to psychiatric evaluation, there may be no further need to keep innocent people in our various madhouses (*African Concord,* Vol. 6, No. 8, 1992).

One ought not to see Williams as casting aspersions on African leaders but rather, his position ought to be seen as an individual looking at the desperation of his people. For if African leaders had taken proper care of their people, there would be no need for them to go to the developed countries cap in hand begging for food, drugs and other foreign aid.

Generally, nature has a way of reducing population in the world. Recently, there was an earthquake in Egypt and many lives were lost. I believe when our population has reached an alarming situation, nature will invariably apply its brake and have a drastic reduction in our population growth rate. If our population is reduced and there happens to be a major natural disaster (e.g., volcanic eruptions, earthquakes, and others), Africa will be worse off in terms of population. The world ought to learn how to share its natural and human resources.

MILITARY SPENDING

It is observed that several African States have spent more of their income on the military rather than on social and educational development. For instance, Somalia spends about 500% of its income on the military. Ethiopia also spends over 200% of its income on the military. Today, Nigeria has spent well over N2.7 billion ($135,000.00) in Liberia while its people are wallowing in abject poverty. Mobutu Sese Seko of Zaire has plunged his country into a huge debt of about $5 billion. As a matter of fact, Mobutu Sese Seko is one of the richest leaders in Africa and his people are among the poorest.

SOME MORAL AND PRACTICAL SUGGESTIONS

In my discussion of the traditional African attitude to nature, I promised to show its credibility. The moral concept of not taking more than one needs from nature is an effort on the part of our traditional communities to, "keep a reasonable balance among the various resources constituting the ecosystem...."[15] This traditional moral wisdom has been employed for the "proper management" of our natural resources, and is what I have called the *ethics of care*. This ethics of care is not unique to traditional Africa. John Passmore writes:

> The traditional moral teaching of the West, Christian or Utilitarian, has always taught men, however, that they ought not so to act to injure their neighbours. And we have now discovered that the disposal of wastes into sea or air, the destruction of

ecosystems, the procreation of large families and the depletion of resources constitute injury to our fellowmen, present and future. To that extent, conventional morality, without any supplementation whatsoever, suffices to justify our ecological concern, our demand for action against the polluter, the depleter of natural resources, the destroyer of species and wilderness.[16]

But this ethics of care of nature must not be seen as absolute even though it may have a universal appeal and application. Its universalizability can be stretched to a point, I believe, because there are many questions that have to be answered to justify its moral and epistemological warrant. Some of the questions that may be lurking in our minds are: How do we know how much we need, given the nature of human greed? Who judges whether we have been taking more or less than we need from the natural resources? If we have been taking more than we need, what are the penalties and how fair are they?

While I believe we need rapid development in Africa, the question is, can the traditional environmental wisdom be a guiding moral principle? In other words, is the environmental ethic of traditional society applicable to our contemporary situation? I believe its relevance can be seen in a reformulation of it which I term the ethics of nature-relatedness. Let me qualify this. The ethics of nature-relatedness does not imply that natural resources actually have a spiritual nature. Furthermore, it does not attribute the creation of the natural resources to a Supreme Being. That is to say, the ethics of nature-relatedness has no religious affinity. (I am aware that this position is not the traditional view.)

There are three basic elements in the ethics of nature-relatedness, namely, reason, experience and the will. The guiding force among the three elements is reason. The ethics of nature-relatedness must have reason to pilot it because morality is inseparable from reason. The ethics of nature-relatedness asserts that our natural resources do not need man for their existence and functions. As a matter of fact, if these natural resources had any rational capacity they would wonder what kind of beings humans are. The fact of the matter is that human beings cannot do without the natural resources at their disposal. By destroying our natural resources in the name of development we are invariably endangering our own existence. So the ethics of nature-relatedness can be succinctly stated as an ethics that leads human beings to seek to co-exist peacefully with nature and treat it with some reasonable concern for its worth, survival and sustainability. It is an ethics that calls for an alternative approach to our present reckless use of nature.

As we have already noted, the majority of Africans use fuelwood and engage in bush burning. Our industries pollute air and water resources, which in effect endangers our health. Is there anything we can do to reduce the danger of these human activities? Baffour provides a useful suggestion. He writes:

> Talking of sources of power, one should not ignore the possibilities of the use of solar energy which would have enormous advantages to Africa. With large areas of perennially clear and cloudless skies, the possibilities are great indeed. Already in North Africa, and to a limited degree in other parts of Africa, experiments are being conducted in the development of power from solar energy through the use of cells; but not enough work is being done in this field of study and it is commended to scientists and technologists to intensify their study of the possibilities in this field, so that even the remotest parts of Africa may be blessed with power for domestic and cottage industry.[17]

If adequate energy resources are provided for our industrial and domestic consumptions at a reasonable cost, our overdependence on fuelwood, coal, kerosene, gas and petrol would be reduced. I believe solar energy could be our safety valve in this direction.

People in several African countries have been suffering from starvation and famine. One of the causes of these problems is manmade, namely, political conflicts. Furthermore, food production for all Africans south of the Sahara is possible if we turn all the unused land areas from Senegal to Zaire into agricultural centers and use modern techniques of mechanized farming. But this cannot be done without first having all our leaders come to reason together and use their political will for our common good.

In conclusion, the environmental crisis in sub-Saharan Africa has both unique components and some it shares with other areas of the world. Poor health conditions in contemporary Africa can be attributed largely to poverty, ignorance, poor sanitation and rapid population growth. Health education, appropriate economic development, and increased literacy are all needed. There would be natural and monetary resources to address these problems if those which are currently fueling political conflicts were available. Further, plans need to be developed to reduce the amount of industrial and agricultural wastes and properly dispose of them, so that both our industrial and commercial centres and our rural areas are safe from air and water pollution. In addressing these problems, we would not only be saving ourselves from dangerous pollutants, but would be saving our ecosystems for generations to come. Our governments, industrialists, scientists, ethicists and environmentalists have more roles to play in keeping our environment safe.

NOTES

1. Isaac Sindiga, *Ethnomedicine and Health Care in Kenya* (Eldoret: Moi University, Final Technical Report to the International Development Research Center for Project 1992), 6.
2. Ibid., 5.
3. Mostafa Kamal Tolba, *Sustainable Development: Constraints and Opportunities* (London: Butterworths, 1987), 207.
4. Thomas McGinn, "Ecology and Ethics" in *Philosophy for a New Generation* (ed.) A. K. Bierman and James A. Gould (New York: Macmillan, 1977), 159.
5. Tolba, op. cit., 206.
6. Morag Bell, *Contemporary Africa: Development, Culture and the State* (London: Longman, 1986), 19.
7. *Nigerian Tribune* (Ibadan), 3 October 1992.
8. R. P. Baffour, "Science and Technology in Relation to Africa's Development," *The Proceedings of the First International Congress of Africanists* (London: Longmans, 1964), 303.
9. Paul Ekins, *A New World Order* (London: Routledge, 1992), 10.
10. Baffour, op. cit., 307.
11. Charles O. Okidi, "Management of Natural Resources and the Environment for Self-Reliance," *Journal of Eastern African Research and Development*, 14 (1984), 98.
12. Ibid., 98–99.

13. Ibid., 103.
14. Tolba, op. cit., 206.
15. Okidi, op. cit., 97.
16. John Passmore, "Removing the Rubbish: Reflections on the Ecological Craze," *Philosophy for a*

New Generation (ed.) A. K. Bierman and James A. Gould (New York: Macmillan, 1977), 175.
17. Baffour, op. cit., 304–305.

✌ STUDY QUESTIONS

1. What are the greatest environmental problems in Africa, according to Ogungbemi? What causes them?

2. What sorts of things does Ogungbemi recommend as solutions?

3. Evaluate Ogungbemi's discussion on population growth. How does he view this problem? Do you agree with his assessment? Explain.

4. Ogungbemi refers to Africa's desire to emulate materialistic Western lifestyles, claiming that such emulation contributes to Africa's environmental decline. What should Westerners do if this is a fact?

39   Radical Environmentalism and Wilderness Preservation: A Third World Critique

RAMACHANDRA GUHA

Ramachandra Guha is a sociologist and historian at the Centre for Ecological Sciences, Indian Institute for Science, Bangalore, India. He has written extensively on the historical roots of ecological conflict in the East and West. The following is the original abstract he wrote for this article.

I present a Third World critique of the trend in American environmentalism known as deep ecology, analyzing each of deep ecology's central tenets: the distinction between anthropocentrism and biocentrism, the focus on wilderness preservation, the invocation of Eastern traditions, and the belief that it represents the most radical trend within environmentalism. I argue that the anthropocentrism/biocentrism distinction is of little use in understanding the dynamics of environmental degradation, that the implementation of the wilderness agenda is causing serious deprivation in the Third World, that the deep ecologist's interpretation of Eastern tradition is highly selective, and that in other cultural contexts (e.g., West Germany and India) radical environmentalism manifests itself quite differently, with a far greater emphasis on equity and the integration of ecological concerns with livelihood and work. I conclude that despite its claims to universality, deep ecology is firmly rooted in American environmental and cultural history and is inappropriate when applied to the Third World.

Even God dare not appear to the poor man except in the form of bread.

MAHATMA GANDHI

Reprinted from *Environmental Ethics*, Vol. 11 (Spring 1989) by permission. Notes deleted.

I. INTRODUCTION

The respected radical journalist Kirkpatrick Sale recently celebrated "the passion of a new and growing movement that has become disenchanted with the environmental establishment and has in recent years mounted a serious and sweeping attack on it—style, substance, systems, sensibilities and all." The vision of those whom Sale calls the "New Ecologists"—and what I refer to in this article as deep ecology—is a compelling one. Decrying the narrowly economic goals of mainstream environmentalism, this new movement aims at nothing less than a philosophical and cultural revolution in human attitudes toward nature. In contrast to the conventional lobbying efforts of environmental professionals based in Washington, it proposes a militant defence of "Mother Earth," an unflinching opposition to human attacks on undisturbed wilderness. With their goals ranging from the spiritual to the political, the adherents of deep ecology span a wide spectrum of the American environmental movement. As Sale correctly notes, this emerging strand has in a matter of a few years made its presence felt in a number of fields: from an academic philosophy (as in the journal *Environmental Ethics*) to popular environmentalism (for example, the group Earth First!).

In this article I develop a critique of deep ecology from the perspective of a sympathetic outsider. I critique deep ecology not as a general (or even a foot soldier) in the continuing struggle between the ghosts of Gifford Pinchot and John Muir over control of the U.S. environmental movement, but as an outsider to these battles. I speak admittedly as a partisan, but of the environmental movement in India, a country with an ecological diversity comparable to the U.S., but with a radically dissimilar cultural and social history.

My treatment of deep ecology is primarily historical and sociological, rather than philosophical, in nature. Specifically, I examine the cultural rootedness of a philosophy that likes to present itself in universalistic terms. I make two main arguments: first, that deep ecology is uniquely American, and despite superficial similarities in rhetorical style, the social and political goals of radical environmentalism in other cultural contexts (e.g., West Germany and India) are quite different; second, that the social consequences of putting deep ecology into practice on a worldwide basis (what its practitioners are aiming for) are very grave indeed.

II. THE TENETS OF DEEP ECOLOGY

While I am aware that the term *deep ecology* was coined by the Norwegian philosopher Arne Naess, this article refers specifically to the American variant. Adherents of the deep ecological perspective in this country, while arguing intensely among themselves over its political and philosophical implications, share some fundamental premises about human-nature interactions. As I see it, the defining characteristics of deep ecology are fourfold:

First, deep ecology argues that the environmental movement must shift from an "anthropocentric" to a "biocentric" perspective. In many respects, an acceptance of the primacy of this distinction constitutes the litmus test of deep ecology. A considerable effort is expended by deep ecologists in showing that the dominant motif in Western philosophy has been anthropocentric—i.e., the belief that man and his works are the center of the universe—and conversely, in identifying those lonely thinkers (Leopold, Thoreau, Muir, Aldous Huxley, Santayana, etc.) who, in assigning man a more humble place in the natural order, anticipated deep ecological thinking. In the political realm, meanwhile, establishment environmentalism (shallow ecology) is chided for casting its arguments in human-centered terms. Preserving nature, the deep ecologists say, has an intrinsic worth quite apart from any benefits preservation may convey to future human generations. The anthropocentric-biocentric distinction is accepted as axiomatic by deep ecologists, it structures their discourse, and much of the present discussion remains mired within it.

The second characteristic of deep ecology is its focus on the preservation of unspoilt wilderness—and the restoration of degraded areas to a more pristine condition—to the relative (and sometimes absolute) neglect of other issues on the environmental agenda. I later identify the cultural roots and portentous consequences of this obsession with wilderness. For the moment, let me indicate three distinct sources from which it springs. Historically, it represents a playing out of the preservationist (read *radical*) and utilitarian (read *reformist*) dichotomy that has plagued American environmentalism since the turn of the century. Morally, it is an imperative that follows from the biocentric perspective; other species of plants and animals, and nature itself, have an intrinsic right to exist. And finally, the preservation of wilderness also turns on a scientific argument—viz., the value of biological diversity in stabilizing ecological regimes and in retaining a gene pool for future generations. Truly radical policy proposals have been put forward by deep ecologists on the basis of these arguments. The influential poet Gary Snyder, for example, would like to see a 90 percent reduction in human populations to allow a restoration of pristine environments, while others have argued forcefully that a large portion of the globe must be immediately cordoned off from human beings.

Third, there is a widespread invocation of Eastern spiritual traditions as forerunners of deep ecology. Deep ecology, it is suggested, was practiced both by major religious traditions and at a more popular level by "primal" peoples in non-Western settings. This complements the search for an authentic lineage in Western thought. At one level, the task is to recover those dissenting voices within the Judeo-Christian tradition; at another, to suggest that religious traditions in other cultures are, in contrast, dominantly if not exclusively "biocentric" in their orientation. This coupling of (ancient) Eastern and (modern) ecological wisdom seemingly helps consolidate the claim that deep ecology is a philosophy of universal significance.

Fourth, deep ecologists, whatever their internal differences, share the belief that they are the "leading edge" of the environmental movement. As the polarity of the shallow/deep and anthropocentric/biocentric distinctions makes clear, they see themselves as the spiritual, philosophical, and political vanguard of American and world environmentalism.

III. TOWARD A CRITIQUE

Although I analyze each of these tenets independently, it is important to recognize, as deep ecologists are fond of remarking in reference to nature, the interconnectedness and unity of these individual themes.

(1) Insofar as it has begun to act as a check on man's arrogance and ecological hubris, the transition from an anthropocentric (human-centered) to a biocentric (humans as only one element in the ecosystem) view in both religious and scientific traditions is only to be welcomed. What is unacceptable are the radical conclusions drawn by deep ecology, in particular, that intervention in nature should be guided primarily by the need to preserve biotic integrity rather than by the needs of humans. The latter for deep ecologists is anthropocentric, the former biocentric. This dichotomy is, however, of very little use in understanding the dynamics of environmental degradation. The two fundamental ecological problems facing the globe are (i) overconsumption by the industrialized world and by urban elites in the Third World and (ii) growing militarization, both in a short-term sense (i.e., ongoing regional wars) and in a long-term sense (i.e., the arms race and the prospect of nuclear annihilation). Neither of these problems has any tangible connection to the anthropocentric-biocentric distinction. Indeed, the agents of these processes would barely comprehend this philosophical dichotomy. The proximate causes of the ecologically wasteful characteristics of industrial society and of militarization are far more mundane: at an aggregate level, the dialectic of economic and political structures, and at a micro-level, the life style choices of individuals. These causes cannot be reduced, whatever the level of analysis, to a deeper anthropocentric attitude toward nature; on the contrary, by constituting a grave threat to human survival, the ecological degradation they cause does not even serve the best interests of human beings! If my identification of the major dangers to the integrity of the natural world is correct, invoking the bogy of anthropocentrism is at best irrelevant and at worst a dangerous obfuscation.

(2) If the above dichotomy is irrelevant, the emphasis on wilderness is positively harmful when applied to the Third World. If in the U.S. the preservationist/utilitarian division is seen as mirroring the conflict between "people" and "interests," in countries such as India the situation is very nearly the reverse. Because India is a long settled and densely populated country in which agrarian populations have a finely balanced relationship with nature, the setting aside of wilderness areas has resulted in a direct transfer of resources from the poor to the rich. Thus, Project Tiger, a network of parks hailed by the international conservation community as an outstanding success, sharply posits the interests of the tiger against those of poor peasants living in and around the reserve. The designation of tiger reserves was made possible only by the physical displacement of existing villages and their inhabitants; their management requires the continuing exclusion of peasants and livestock. The initial impetus for setting up parks for the tiger and other large mammals such as the rhinoceros and elephant came from two social groups, first, a class of ex-hunters turned conservationists belonging mostly to the declining Indian feudal elite and second, representatives of international agencies, such as the World Wildlife Fund (WWF) and the International Union for the Conservation of Nature and Natural Resources (IUCN), seeking to transplant the American system of national parks onto Indian soil. In no case have the needs of the local population been taken into account, and as in many parts of Africa, the designated wildlands are managed primarily for the benefit of rich tourists. Until very recently, wildlands preservation has been identified with environmentalism by the state and the conservation elite; in consequence, environmental problems that impinge far more directly on the lives of the poor—e.g., fuel, fodder, water shortages, soil erosion, and air and water pollution—have not been adequately addressed.

Deep ecology provides, perhaps unwittingly, a justification for the continuation of such narrow and inequitable conservation practices under a newly acquired radical guise. Increasingly, the international conservation elite is using the philosophical, moral, and scientific arguments used by deep ecologists in advancing their wilderness crusade. A striking but by no means atypical example is the recent plea by a prominent American biologist for the takeover of large portions of the globe by the author and his scientific colleagues. Writing in a prestigious scientific forum, the *Annual Review of Ecology and Systematics,* Daniel Janzen argues that only biologists have the competence to decide how the tropical landscape should be used. As "the representatives of the natural world," biologists are "in charge of the future of tropical ecology," and only they have the expertise and mandate to "determine whether the tropical agroscape is to be populated only by humans, their mutualists, commensals, and parasites, or whether it will also contain some islands of the greater nature—the nature that spawned humans, yet has been vanquished by them." Janzen exhorts his colleagues to advance their territorial claims on the tropical world more forcefully, warning that the very existence of these areas is at stake: "if biologists want a tropics in which to biologize, they are going to have to buy it with care, energy, effort, strategy, tactics, time, and cash."

This frankly imperialist manifesto highlights the multiple dangers of the preoccupation with wilderness preservation that is characteristic of deep ecology. As I have suggested, it seriously compounds the neglect by the American movement of far more pressing environmental problems within the Third World. But perhaps more importantly, and in a more insidious fashion, it also provides an impetus to the imperialist yearning of Western biologists and their financial sponsors, organizations such as the WWF and the IUCN. The wholesale transfer of a movement culturally rooted in American conservation history can only result in the social uprooting of human populations in other parts of the globe.

(3) I come now to the persistent invocation of Eastern philosophies as antecedent in point of time but convergent in their structure with deep ecology. Complex and internally differentiated religious traditions—Hinduism, Buddhism, and Taoism—are lumped together as holding a view of nature believed to be quintessentially biocentric. Individual philosophers such as the Taoist Lao Tzu are identified as being forerunners of deep ecology.

Even an intensely political, pragmatic, and Christian influenced thinker such as Gandhi has been accorded a wholly undeserved place in the deep ecological pantheon. Thus the Zen teacher Robert Aitken Roshi makes the strange claim that Gandhi's thought was not human-centered and that he practiced an embryonic form of deep ecology which is "traditionally Eastern and is found with differing emphasis in Hinduism, Taoism and in Theravada and Mahayana Buddhism." Moving away from the realm of high philosophy and scriptural religion, deep ecologists make the further claim that at the level of material and spiritual practice "primal" peoples subordinated themselves to the integrity of the biotic universe they inhabited.

I have indicated that this appropriation of Eastern traditions is in part dictated by the need to construct an authentic lineage and in part a desire to present deep ecology as a universalistic philosophy. Indeed, in his substantial and quixotic biography of John Muir, Michael Cohen goes so far as to suggest that Muir was the "Taoist of the [American] West." This reading of Eastern traditions is selective and does not bother to differentiate between alternate (and changing) religious and cultural traditions; as it stands, it does considerable violence to the historical record. Throughout most recorded history the characteristic form of human activity in the "East" has been a finely tuned but nonetheless conscious and dynamic manipulation of nature. Although mystics such as Lao Tzu did reflect on the spiritual essence of human relations with nature, it must be recognized that such ascetics and their reflections were supported by a society of cultivators whose relationship with nature was a far more *active* one. Many agricultural communities do have a sophisticated knowledge of the natural environment that may equal (and sometimes surpass) codified "scientific" knowledge; yet, the elaboration of such traditional ecological knowledge (in both material and spiritual contexts) can hardly be said to rest on a mystical affinity with nature of a deep ecological kind. Nor is such knowledge infallible; as the archaeological record powerfully suggests, modern Western man has no monopoly on ecological disasters.

In a brilliant article, the Chicago historian Ronald Inden points out that this romantic and essentially positive view of the East is a mirror image of the scientific and essentially pejorative view normally upheld by Western scholars of the Orient. In either case, the East constitutes the Other, a body wholly separate and alien from the West; it is defined by a uniquely spiritual and nonrational "essence," even if this essence is valorized quite differently by the two schools. Eastern man exhibits a spiritual dependence with respect to nature—on the one hand, this is symptomatic of his prescientific and backward self, on the other, of his ecological wisdom and deep ecological consciousness. Both views are monolithic, simplistic, and have the characteristic effect—intended in one case, perhaps unintended in the other—of denying agency and reason to the East and making it the privileged orbit of Western thinkers.

The two apparently opposed perspectives have then a common underlying structure of discourse in which the East merely serves as a vehicle for Western projections. Varying images of the East are raw material for political and cultural battles being played out in the West; they tell us far more about the Western commentator and his desires than about the "East." Inden's remarks apply not merely to Western scholarship on India, but to Orientalist constructions of China and Japan as well:

> Although these two views appear to be strongly opposed, they often combine together. Both have a similar interest in sustaining the Otherness of India. The holders of the dominant view, best exemplified in the past in imperial administrative discourse (and today probably by that of "development economics"), would place a traditional, superstition-ridden India in a position of perpetual tutelage to a modern, rational West. The adherents of the romantic view, best exemplified academically in the discourses of Christian liberalism and analytic psychology, concede the realm of the public and impersonal to the positivist. Taking their succour not from governments and big business, but from a plethora of religious foundations and self-help institutes, and from allies in the "consciousness industry," not to mention the important industry of tourism, the romantics insist that India embodies a private realm of the imagination and the religious which modern, western man lacks but needs. They, therefore, like the positivists, but for just one

opposite reason, have a vested interest in seeing that the Orien-talist view of India as "spiritual," "mysterious," and "exotic" is perpetuated.

(4) How radical, finally, are the deep ecologists? Notwithstanding their self-image and strident rhetoric (in which the label "shallow ecology" has an opprobrium similar to that reserved for "social democratic" by Marxist-Leninists), even within the American context their radicalism is limited and it manifests itself quite differently elsewhere.

To my mind, deep ecology is best viewed as a radical trend within the wilderness preservation movement. Although advancing philosophical rather than aesthetic arguments and encouraging political militancy rather than negotiation, its practical emphasis—viz., preservation of unspoilt nature—is virtually identical. For the mainstream movement, the function of wilderness is to provide a temporary antidote to modern civilization. As a special institution within an industrialized society, the national park "provides an opportunity for respite, contrast, contemplation, and affirmation of values for those who live most of their lives in the workaday world." Indeed, the rapid increase in visitations to the national parks in postwar America is a direct consequence of economic expansion. The emergence of a popular interest in wilderness sites, the historian Samuel Hays points out, was "not a throwback to the primitive, but an integral part of the modern standard of living as people sought to add new 'amenity' and 'aesthetic' goals and desires to their earlier preoccupation with necessities and conveniences."

Here, the enjoyment of nature is an integral part of the consumer society. The private automobile (and the life style it has spawned) is in many respects the ultimate ecological villain, and an untouched wilderness the prototype of ecological harmony; yet, for most Americans it is perfectly consistent to drive a thousand miles to spend a holiday in a national park. They possess a vast, beautiful, and sparsely populated continent and are also able to draw upon the natural resources of large portions of the globe by virtue of their economic and political dominance. In consequence, America can simultaneously enjoy the material benefits of an expanding economy and the aesthetic benefits of unspoilt nature. The two poles of "wilderness" and "civilization" mutually coexist in an internally coherent whole, and philosophers of both poles are assigned a prominent place in this culture. Paradoxically as it may seem, it is no accident that Star Wars technology and deep ecology both find their fullest expression in that leading sector of Western civilization, California.

Deep ecology runs parallel to the consumer society without seriously questioning its ecological and sociopolitical basis. In its celebration of American wilderness, it also displays an uncomfortable convergence with the prevailing climate of nationalism in the American wilderness movement. For spokesmen such as the historian Roderick Nash, the national park system is America's distinctive cultural contribution to the world, reflective not merely of its economic but of its philosophical and ecological maturity as well. In what Walter Lippman called the American century, the "American invention of national parks" must be exported worldwide. Betraying an economic determinism that would make even a Marxist shudder, Nash believes that environmental preservation is a "full stomach" phenomenon that is confined to the rich, urban, and sophisticated. Nonetheless, he hopes that "the less developed nations may eventually evolve economically and intellectually to the point where nature preservation is more than a business."

The error which Nash makes (and which deep ecology in some respects encourages) is to equate environmental protection with the protection of the wilderness. This is a distinctively American notion, born out of a unique social and environmental history. The archetypal concerns of radical environmentalists in other cultural contexts are in fact quite different. The German Greens, for example, have elaborated a devastating critique of industrial society which turns on the acceptance of environmental limits to growth. Pointing to the intimate links between industrialization, militarization, and conquest, the Greens argue that economic growth in the West has historically rested on the economic and ecological exploitation of the Third World. Rudolf Bahro is characteristically blunt:

> The working class here [in the West] is the richest lower class in the world. And if I look at the problem from the point of view of the whole of

humanity, not just from that of Europe, then I must say that the metropolitan working class is the worst exploiting class in history.... What made poverty bearable in eighteenth or nineteenth-century Europe was the prospect of escaping it through exploitation of the periphery. But this is no longer a possibility, and continued industrialism in the Third World will mean poverty for whole generations and hunger for millions.

Here the roots of global ecological problems lie in the disproportionate share of resources consumed by the industrialized countries as a whole *and* the urban elite within the Third World. Since it is impossible to reproduce an industrial monoculture worldwide, the ecological movement in the West must begin by cleaning up its own act. The Greens advocate the creation of a "no growth" economy, to be achieved by scaling down current (and clearly unsustainable) consumption levels. This radical shift in consumption and production patterns requires the creation of alternate economic and political structures—smaller in scale and more amenable to social participation—but it rests equally on a shift in cultural values. The expansionist character of modern Western man will have to give way to an ethic of renunciation and self-limitation, in which spiritual and communal values play an increasing role in sustaining social life. This revolution in cultural values, however, has as its point of departure an understanding of environmental processes quite different from deep ecology.

Many elements of the Green program find a strong resonance in countries such as India, where a history of Western colonialism and industrial development has benefited only a tiny elite while exacting tremendous social and environmental costs. The ecological battles presently being fought in India have as their epicenter the conflict over nature between the subsistence and largely rural sector and the vastly more powerful commercial-industrial sector. Perhaps the most celebrated of these battles concerns the Chipko (Hug the Tree) movement, a peasant movement against deforestation in the Himalayan foothills. Chipko is only one of several movements that have sharply questioned the nonsustainable demand being placed on the land and vegetative base by urban centers and

industry. These include opposition to large dams by displaced peasants, the conflict between small artisan fishing and large-scale trawler fishing for export, the countrywide movements against commercial forest operations, and opposition to industrial pollution among downstream agricultural and fishing communities.

Two features distinguish these environmental movements from their Western counterparts. First, for the sections of society most critically affected by environmental degradation—poor and landless peasants, women, and tribals—it is a question of sheer survival, not of enhancing the quality of life. Second, and as a consequence, the environmental solutions they articulate deeply involve questions of equity as well as economic and political redistribution. Highlighting these differences, a leading Indian environmentalist stresses that "environmental protection per se is of least concern to most of these groups. Their main concern is about the use of the environment and who should benefit from it." They seek to wrest control of nature away from the state and the industrial sector and place it in the hands of rural communities who live within that environment but are increasingly denied access to it. These communities have far more basic needs, their demands on the environment are far less intense, and they can draw upon a reservoir of cooperative social institutions and local ecological knowledge in managing the "commons"—forest, grasslands, and the waters—on a sustainable basis. If colonial and capitalist expansion has both accentuated social inequalities and signaled a precipitous fall in ecological wisdom, an alternate ecology must rest on an alternate society and polity as well.

This brief overview of German and Indian environmentalism has some major implications for deep ecology. Both German and Indian environmental traditions allow for a greater integration of ecological concerns with livelihood and work. They also place a greater emphasis on equity and social justice (both within individual countries and on a global scale) on the grounds that in the absence of social regeneration environmental regeneration has very little chance of succeeding. Finally, and perhaps most significantly, they have escaped the preoccupation with wilderness preservation so characteristic of American cultural and environmental history.

IV. A HOMILY

In 1958, the economist J. K Galbraith referred to overconsumption as the unasked question of the American conservation movement. There is a marked selectivity, he wrote, "in the conservationist's approach to materials consumption. If we are concerned about our great appetite for materials, it is plausible to seek to increase the supply, to decrease waste, to make better use of the stocks available, and to develop substitutes. But what of the appetite itself? Surely this is the ultimate source of the problem. If it continues its geometric course, will it not one day have to be restrained? Yet in the literature of the resource problem this is the forbidden question. Over it hangs a nearly total silence."

The consumer economy and society have expanded tremendously in the three decades since Galbraith penned these words; yet his criticisms are nearly as valid today. I have said "nearly," for there are some hopeful signs. Within the environmental movement several dispersed groups are working to develop ecologically benign technologies and to encourage less wasteful life styles. Moreover, outside the self-defined boundaries of American environmentalism, opposition to the permanent war economy is being carried on by a peace movement that has a distinguished history and impeccable moral and political credentials.

It is precisely these (to my mind, most hopeful) components of the American social scene that are missing from deep ecology. In their widely noticed book, Bill Devall and George Sessions make no mention of militarization or the movements for peace, while activists whose practical focus is on developing ecologically responsible life styles (e.g., Wendell Berry) are derided as "falling short of deep ecological awareness." A truly radical ecology in the American context ought to work toward a synthesis of the appropriate technology, alternate life style, and peace movements. By making the (largely spurious) anthropocentric-biocentric distinction central to the debate, deep ecologists may have appropriated the moral high ground, but they are at the same time doing a serious disservice to American and global environmentalism.

STUDY QUESTIONS

1. Is Guha's critique of deep ecology sound? How would a full application of deep ecology affect the Third World? Explain.
2. How might deep ecologists like Naess, Devall, or Sessions (Readings 24–26) respond to Guha's criticisms?
3. How might Western environmentalists justify emphasizing quality of life versus sheer survival?
4. Is J. K. Galbraith right that our "appetite for materials" needs to be curbed (or cured)? If so, can you convince your friends?

FOR FURTHER READING

Dwivedi, O. P., and B. N. Tiwari. *Environmental Crisis and Hindu Religion.* New Delhi, India: Gitanjali Publishing House, 1987.

Engel, J. R., and J. G. Engel, eds. *Ethics of Environmental Response.* Tucson: University of Arizona Press, 1990.

Hargrove, Eugene, ed. *Religion and Environmental Crisis.* Athens: University of Georgia Press, 1985.

Johns, David. "Relevance of Deep Ecology to the Third World." *Environmental Ethics* 12 (1990): 233–252.

Noss, John. *Man's Religions,* 7th ed. New York: MacMillan, 1980.

Regan, Tom. *Animal Sacrifices: Religious Perspectives on the Use of Animalism in Science.* Philadelphia: Temple University Press, 1986.

Smart, Ninian. *The Religious Experiences of Mankind.* New York: Scribners, 1969.

Smith, William Cantwell. *Religious Diversity.* New York: Harper and Row, 1976.

Obligations to Future Generations

WHAT ARE OUR MORAL OBLIGATIONS to future generations? Unless a catastrophe occurs, people will be alive on earth 500 or 1000 years from today. What claims do they have on us today, if any? Are they morally considerable? Would it be an evil thing if they never come to exist? Who are the "they" we are talking about? If "they" don't exist, how can we be said to have duties to "them"?

The problem of obligations to future generations is perplexing for a couple of reasons. First, "future people" do not exist, so there are no specific, flesh and blood individuals to whom we have duties. How can we have obligations to nonexistent persons? Second, even if we solve this problem with the notion of hypothetical persons or probable persons, how do we know what they will be like and what their needs and values will be? Third, even if we believe that we have some idea of their needs and values, how can their needs and values compare with those of present living beings, especially our families, friends, and communities? Fourth, there is the question of why we should care about future people any more than we care about people on distant planets. From a self-interested perspective, why should I make sacrifices for people who will live in the distant future. Why should I care about posterity? What has posterity ever done for me?

It is this last question to which Robert Heilbroner takes us in our first reading. Heilbroner, an economist, is perplexed and outraged by the casual way his fellow economists dismiss the question of duties to future generations, as though it's no concern of ours—since the economic model they develop cannot make it rational to save for such a long, distant future. Heilbroner believes we do have such duties, and the strength of his essay is in his insightful analysis of the problem. In our second selection, Garrett Hardin picks up on Heilbroner's theme and develops it, arguing that while both philosophy and economics fail to give us a satisfying answer to the problem of duties to future generations, it is nonetheless one of our highest values, and legitimately so. Through fascinating illustrations of people sacrificing for future generations, he reveals an underlying paradox in our attitudes toward posterity. Hardin then outlines a plan of action, having to do with promoting special interests and education of the young.

In our third reading, Martin Golding sets forth the necessary conditions for having moral duties to others—specifically, they must be recognized as part of our moral community and their good must be recognized as good by our value system so that they can have claims against us. Golding argues that we don't know what kind of people the future will produce, and since we have reason to believe that they will be very different from us, it follows that we probably don't have any obligations to them—except duties of not leaving Earth a cesspool of pollution. Otherwise, the argument from ignorance enjoins us to embrace a hands-off policy.

In our final reading, Derek Parfit rejects Golding's argument from ignorance as well as Heilbroner's and Hardin's claims that reason doesn't guide us with regard to making provisions for posterity. Parfit examines various justifications for intergenerational duties. The traditional view is that one can commit crimes only if one has an identifiable victim. Policy choices regarding energy, however, do not identity specific victims. Parfit argues that these views are wrong. Polices are bad "if those who live are worse off than those who might have lived." We are responsible for environmental policies because we can make a difference in the quality of future lives.

40   What Has Posterity Ever Done for Me?

ROBERT HEILBRONER

Robert Heilbroner was for many years professor of economics at the New School for Social Research in New York. He is the author of several books including *The Worldly Philosophers* and *Marxism: For and Against*.

Heilbroner asks why we should care about future people or whether humanity survives into the distant future. Citing fellow economists who argue that we have no reason to sacrifice for the unknown future, Heilbroner expresses outrage at this callous disregard for future people. Admitting that he cannot give a rational argument for this view, he appeals to Adam Smith's principle of sentiment or inner conscience, which urges us to work for the long range survival of humanity.

Will mankind survive? Who knows? The question I want to put is more searching: Who cares? It is clear that most of us today do not care—or at least do not care enough. How many of us would be willing to give up some minor convenience—say, the use of aerosols—in the hope that this might extend the life of man on earth by a hundred years? Suppose we also knew with a high degree of certainty that humankind could not survive a thousand years unless we gave up our wasteful diet of meat, abandoned all pleasure driving, cut back on every use of energy that was not essential to the maintenance of a bare minimum. Would we care enough for posterity to pay the price of its survival?

I doubt it. A thousand years is unimaginably distant. Even a century far exceeds our powers of empathetic imagination. By the year 2075, I shall probably have been dead for three quarters of a century. My children will also likely be dead, and my grandchildren, if I have any, will be in their dotage. What does it matter to me, then, what life will be like in 2075, much less 3075? Why should I lift a finger to affect events that will have no more meaning for me seventy-five years after my death than those that happened seventy-five years before I was born?

There is no rational answer to that terrible question. No argument based on reason will lead me to care for posterity or to lift a finger in its behalf. Indeed, by every rational consideration, precisely the opposite answer is thrust upon us with irresistible force. As a Distinguished Professor of political economy at the University of London has written in the current winter issue of *Business and Society Review:*

> Suppose that, as a result of using up all the world's resources, human life did come to an end. So what? What is so desirable about an indefinite continuation of the human species, religious convictions apart? It may well be that nearly everybody who is already here on earth would be reluctant to die, and that everybody has an instinctive fear of death. But one must not confuse this with the notion that, in any meaningful sense, generations who are yet unborn can be said to be better off if they are born than if they are not.

Thus speaks the voice of rationality. It is echoed in the book *The Economic Growth Controversy* by a Distinguished Younger Economist from the Massachusetts Institute of Technology:

> ...Geological time [has been] made comprehensible to our finite human minds by the statement that the 4.5 billion years of the earth's history [are] equivalent to once around the world in an SST.... Man got on eight miles before the end, and industrial man got on six feet before the end.... Today we are having a debate about the extent to which man ought to maximize the length of time that he is on the airplane.
>
> According to what the scientists think, the sun is gradually expanding and 12 billion years from now the earth will be swallowed up by the sun. This means that our airplane has time to go round three more times. Do we want man to be on it for all three times around the world? Are we interested in man being on for another eight miles? Are we interested in man being on for another six feet? Or are we only interested in man for a fraction of a millimeter—our lifetimes?
>
> That led me to think: Do I care what happens a thousand years from now?... Do I care when man

gets off the airplane? I think I basically [have come] to the conclusion that I don't care whether man is on the airplane for another eight feet, or if man is on the airplane another three times around the world.

Is it an outrageous position? I must confess it outrages me. But this is not because the economists' arguments are "wrong"—indeed, within their rational framework they are indisputably right. It is because their position reveals the limitations—worse, the suicidal dangers—of what we call "rational argument" when we confront questions that can only be decided by an appeal to an entirely different faculty from that of cool reason. More than that, I suspect that if there is cause to fear for man's survival it is because the calculus of logic and reason will be applied to problems where they have as little validity, even as little bearing, as the calculus of feeling of sentiment applied to the solution of a problem in Euclidean geometry.

If reason cannot give us a compelling argument to care for posterity—and to care desperately and totally—what can? For an answer, I turn to another distinguished economist whose fame originated in his profound examination of moral conduct. In 1759, Adam Smith published "The Theory of Moral Sentiments," in which he posed a question very much like ours, but to which he gave an answer very different from that of his latter-day descendants.

Suppose, asked Smith, that "a man of humanity" in Europe were to learn of a fearful earthquake in China—an earthquake that swallowed up its millions of inhabitants. How would that man react? He would, Smith mused, "make many melancholy reflections upon the precariousness of human life, and the vanity of all the labors of man, which could thus be annihilated in a moment. He would, too perhaps, if he was a man of speculation, enter into many reasonings concerning the effects which this disaster might produce upon the commerce of Europe, and the trade and business of the world in general." Yet, when this fine philosophizing was over, would our "man of humanity" care much about the catastrophe in distant China? He would not. As Smith tells us, he would "pursue his business or his pleasure, take his repose for his diversion, with the same ease and tranquility as if nothing had happened."

But now suppose, Smith says, that our man were told he was to lose his little finger on the morrow. A very different reaction would attend the contemplation of this "frivolous disaster." Our man of humanity would be reduced to a tormented state, tossing all night with fear and dread—whereas "provided he never saw them, he will snore with the most profound security over the ruin of a hundred millions of his brethren."

Next, Smith put the critical question: Since the hurt to his finger bulks so large and the catastrophe in China so small, does this mean that a man of humanity, given the choice, would prefer the extinction of a hundred million Chinese in order to save his little finger? Smith is unequivocal in his answer. "Human nature startles at the thought," he cries, "and the world in its greatest depravity and corruption never produced such a villain as would be capable of entertaining it."

But what stays our hand? Since we are all such creatures of self-interest (and is not Smith the very patron saint of the motive of self-interest?), what moves us to give precedence to the rights of humanity over those of our own immediate well-being? The answer, says Smith, is the presence within us all of a "man within the beast," an inner creature of conscience whose insistent voice brooks no disobedience: "it is the love of what is honorable and noble, of the grandeur and dignity, and superiority of our own characters."

It does not matter whether Smith's eighteenth-century view of human nature in general or morality in particular appeals to the modern temper. What matters is that he has put the question that tests us to the quick. For it is one thing to appraise matters of life and death by the principles of rational self-interest and quite another *to take responsibility for our choice*. I cannot imagine the Distinguished Professor from the University of London personally consigning humanity to oblivion with the same equanimity with which he writes off its demise. I am certain that if the Distinguished Younger Economist from M.I.T. were made responsible for determining the precise length of stay of humanity on the SST, he would agonize

over the problem and end up by exacting every last possible inch for mankind's journey.

Of course, there are moral dilemmas to be faced even if one takes one's stand on the "survivalist" principle. Mankind cannot expect to continue on earth indefinitely if we do not curb population growth, thereby consigning billions or tens of billions to the oblivion of non-birth. Yet, in this case, we sacrifice some portion of life-to-come in order that life itself may be preserved. This essential commitment to life's continuance gives us the moral authority to take measures, perhaps very harsh measures, whose justification cannot be found in the precepts of rationality, but must be sought in the unbearable anguish we feel if we imagine ourselves as the executioners of mankind.

This anguish may well be those "religious convictions," to use the phrase our London economist so casually tosses away. Perhaps to our secular cast of mind, the anguish can be more easily accepted as the furious power of the biogenetic force we see expressed in every living organism. Whatever its source, when we ask if mankind "should" survive, it is only here that we can find a rationale that gives us the affirmation we seek.

This is not to say we will discover a religious affirmation naturally welling up within us as we careen toward Armageddon. We know very little about how to convince men by recourse to reason and nothing about how to convert them to religion. A hundred faiths contend for believers today, a few perhaps capable of generating that sense of caring for human salvation on earth. But, in truth, we do not know if "religion" will win out. An appreciation of the magnitude of the sacrifices required to perpetuate life may well tempt us to opt for "rationality"—to enjoy life while it is still to be enjoyed on relatively easy terms, to write mankind a shorter ticket on the SST so that some of us may enjoy the next millimeter of the trip in first-class seats.

Yet I am hopeful that in the end a survivalist ethic will come to the fore—not from the reading of a few books or the passing twinge of a pious lecture but from an experience that will bring home to us, as Adam Smith brought home to his "man of humanity," the personal responsibility that defies all the homicidal promptings of reasonable calculation. Moreover, I believe that the coming generations, in their encounters with famine, war, and the threatened life-carrying capacity of the globe, may be given just such an experience. It is a glimpse into the void of a universe without man. I must rest my ultimate faith on the discovery by these future generations, as the ax of the executioner passes into their hands, of the transcendent importance of posterity for them.

STUDY QUESTIONS

1. Why should we care about future generations? How would you answer Heilbroner's question, "Why should I lift a finger to affect events that will have no more meaning for me seventy-five years after my death than those that happened seventy-five years before I was born?"
2. Do you agree with Heilbroner that there is "no rational answer to that terrible question"? Defend your answer.
3. Do you think "religious convictions" or simply well-thought-out humanistic concerns (Adam Smith's "man of humanity") should have more weight than logic and rational argument when considering issues such as obligations to posterity? How do you decide?

41   Who Cares for Posterity?

GARRETT HARDIN

Garrett Hardin is emeritus professor of biology at the University of California, Santa Barbara, and the author of several works in biology and ethics, including *The Limits of Altruism* and *Exploring New Ethics for Survival*.

Hardin argues that contemporary philosophy is centered on personal relations, "I-Thou" and "Here-Now" relations, which are not applicable to future generations. He proposes that we incorporate an economic cost–benefit model to overcome the undue self-interest of people so that future generations may have their needs met. One method of ensuring prosperity for posterity is to allow limited special interests or privilege to the guardians of our resources so that future people will have an inheritance. He also advocates the inculcation of an ecological literacy and understanding in the young (sometimes called "ecolacy").

I

Two centuries ago the American poet John Trumbull (1750–1831) posed a question that has ever since disturbed those who want to put a wholly rational foundation under conservation policy. Why, Trumbull asked, should people act

> . . . *as though there were a tie*
> *And obligation to posterity.*
> *We get them, bear them, breed, and nurse:*
> *What has posterity done for us?*

The question is surely an ethical one. One would think that philosophers who have been dealing with ethics for more than two thousand years would by this time have developed a rather impressive intellectual apparatus for dealing with the needs of posterity; but they have not. In a thought-provoking essay on "Technology and Responsibility," Hans Jonas points out that ethical literature is almost wholly individualistic: it is addressed to private conduct rather than to public policy. Martin Buber epitomized this

Reprinted from *The Limits of Altruism* (Indiana University Press, 1977) by permission. Notes deleted.

spirit well when he oriented his ethics around the *I-Thou* dyad. That sounds fine until a close reading reveals that the author means no more than *I-Thou, Here and Now.* The standard ethical dialogue is between people who stand face to face with each other, seeking a reasonable basis for reciprocal altruism. Posterity has no chance to show its face in the here and now.

Except for Jonas's valuable comments, contemporary philosophy still evades the hard problem of caring for posterity's interests. Probably no recent work is well known or spoken of with such awe as John Rawls's *A Theory of Justice,* so we should see what this book has to say about "the problem of justice between generations," as Rawls puts the problem. In §44 the author candidly admits that in his hopefully comprehensive system of analysis the problem "seems to admit of no definite answer." One might suppose that he would then drop the matter but he somehow manages to talk about it for another fourteen pages without adding anything more positive than statements such as "men have a natural duty to uphold and to further just institutions." This pronouncement is less than revolutionary; it is hardly operational. Perhaps we have expected too much from philosophers. Can economists throw any more light on the problem of posterity?

Time is of the essence. In cost–benefit analysis we attempt to list and evaluate all the costs (negative benefits); similarly with all the (positive) benefits; then we strike a balance for the whole, on which action can be based. If the balance is plus, we go ahead; if minus, we stop. The decision is simple if costs and benefits are encountered at practically the same moment. But what if they are separated by a considerable gap in time? What if the benefits come now and the costs do not turn up for a generation? Contrariwise, what if costs have to be paid now for benefits that come later? How do we balance costs against benefits when time is interposed between the two?

To begin with let us take up the benefits-first problem, which throws an interesting light on human nature. When the High Aswan Dam was proposed for the Nile only its expected benefits were publicized: the additional electricity it

would generate and the additional land that could be irrigated with the impounded water. The huge financial cost of the dam was acknowledged, but the world was told that it would be well worth it. It would bring the blessings of "development" to the poor people of Egypt.

People were not told certain other costs that were well known to some agricultural experts. Agriculture in the Nile below Aswan had always depended on a yearly flooding of the flat fields. This flooding accomplished two things: it leached out the salts accumulated from the preceding year's evaporation of irrigation water, and it left behind one millimeter of silt, which served as fertilizer for the next year's crops. This system of agriculture had been successful for six thousand years—a unique record of long-term success. Now technologists proposed to put an end to it.

Had there been any national or international debate on the subject the debaters should have wrestled with this question: Do today's short-term benefits of more electricity and more agricultural land in the upper reaches of the river outweigh tomorrow's losses in the lower valley resulting from salination and loss of fertility? The gains are necessarily short term: all dam-lakes eventually silt up and become useless as generators of electricity and sources of abundant water. The process usually takes only a century or two, and often much less. No economically feasible method has ever been found for reclaiming a silted-up dam-lake. The loss from salination of irrigated land is also virtually permanent; treatment requires periodic flooding, but that is what the High Aswan Dam was designed to prevent. The Tigris-Euphrates valley, in which irrigation was practiced for centuries, was ruined by salination two thousand years ago—and it is still ruined.

How a cost–benefit balance would have been struck had these facts been known to the decision makers we do not know. Probably their reaction would have been that of Mr. Micawber in *David Copperfield:* "Something will turn up." Such is the faith of the technological optimists. "Eat, drink, and be merry—for tomorrow will find a solution to today's problems. We will learn how to dredge out dam-ponds—economically. We will learn how to desalinate farmland—economically. Don't wait until we've solved these problems. Plunge ahead! Science will find an answer in time."

Curiously, economists have more confidence in science and technology than scientists do. Could it be that too much knowledge is a bad thing? Should conservatism in ecological matters be labeled a vice rather than a virtue? So say the technological optimists.

Well, the High Aswan Dam has been built now, and the returns are coming in. They are worse than expected. There has not been time for appreciable salination or significant loss of soil fertility—which no one expected this soon anyway—but other disadvantages we had not foreseen have turned up. Water behind the dam is rising more slowly than had been hoped, because of unexpected leakage into surrounding rock strata and greater than expected evaporation from the surface of the lake. The present steady flow of water in irrigation channels (instead of the former intermittent flow) favors snails that carry parasitic worms. As a result, the painful and debilitating disease of schistosomiasis is more widespread among Egyptians now. There are medical measures that can be taken against the disease and sanitary measures to combat the snails, but both cost money, which is what the Egyptians are short of. In addition, the reduction of the flow of the Nile has opened the delta to erosion by the currents of the Mediterranean; as a result, precious delta farmland is now being swept into the sea. And the stoppage of the annual fertilization of the eastern Mediterranean by flood-borne silt has destroyed 95 percent of the local sardine fisheries. The dam is proving a disaster, and sooner than anyone had thought.

Mr. Micawber, where are you now?

We come now to the opposite problem, that of weighing present costs against future benefits. For this question there is a rational economic theory. Let us see if it is adequate.

Suppose I offer to sell you something that will be worth $100 ten years from now: how much should you be willing to pay for it? If you are the standard "economic man," equipped with a hand calculator, you will say something like this: "Well, let me see: assuming the interest rate of money stays at 6 percent, I cannot afford

to pay you more than $55.84 for this opportunity. So if you want to close the deal you'll have to accept $55.84 or a bit less to get me to opt for $100 ten years from now."

The reasoning is as follows. A person with some money to spare can either put it in the bank at 6 percent interest or invest it in this enterprise. Put in the bank, $55.84 (at compound interest) will amount to $100 ten years later: the proposed investment should be able to do that well. If the investor thinks the proposal is speculative he will make a lower bid (i.e., expect a higher rate of interest). If he is worried about inflation (and thinks he knows another investment that is inflation-proof) he will demand a still lower price.

In economic terms, we "discount" the future value at a discount rate (rate of interest), calling the discounted value the "present value." The present value of $100 ten years from now at a discount rate of 6 percent is $55.84; if the discount rate is 10 percent the present value is only $38.55. The formula for these calculations is:

$$\text{Present value} = \text{Future value} \div e^{bt}$$

where: e = base of natural logarithms (ln)

$$b = \ln(1 + \text{interest rate})$$

and t = time

The economic theory of discounting is a completely rational theory. For short periods of time it gives answers that seem intuitively right. For longer periods, we are not so sure.

A number of years ago I decided to plant a redwood tree in my backyard. As I did so I mused, "What would my economist friends say to this? Would they approve? Or would they say I was an economic fool?"

The seedling cost me $1.00. When mature the tree would (at the then current prices) have $14,000 worth of lumber in it—but it would take two thousand years to reach that value. Calculation showed that the investment of so large a sum of money as $1.00 to secure so distant a gain would be justified only if the going rate of interest was no more than 0.479 percent per year. So low a rate of interest has never been known. Plainly I was being a rather stupid "economic man" in planting that tree. *But I planted it.*

The theory of discounting scratches only the surface of the problem. What about the quid pro quo? The quid ($1.00) is mine to pay; but who gets the quo, two thousand years from now? Not I, certainly. And it is most unlikely that any of my direct descendants will get it either, history being what it is. The most I can hope for is that an anonymous posterity will benefit by my act. Almost the only benefit I get is the thought that posterity will benefit—a curious sort of quo indeed. Why bother?

I am beginning to suspect that rationality— as we now conceive it—may be insufficient to secure the end we desire, namely, taking care of the interests of posterity. (At least, some of us desire that.) I can illustrate my point with a true story, which I shall embellish with a plausible historical explanation.

During the Second World War certain fragments of information, and fragments of wood, coming out of China led the California botanist Ralph Chaney to believe that the dawn redwood, which had been thought to be extinct for hundreds of thousands of years, was still in existence. Fortunately Chaney was a person of initiative and independent means, and he promptly set out for China to look for the tree. Getting to the interior of this war-torn country was no small accomplishment, but he did it. He found the tree. It was in an area that had suffered severe deforestation for several thousand years, and there were fewer than a thousand dawn redwoods left. They were still being cut down for fuel and cabinetmaking. Most of the living specimens were in temple courtyards—and thereby hangs our tale.

What is so special about being in a temple courtyard? Just this: it makes the object sacred. The word *sacred* is not easy to define, but whatever we mean by it we mean something that stands outside the bounds of rationality, as ordinarily understood. Let me illustrate this by a fictional conversation between a priest and a peasant in a Chinese temple a thousand years ago. Knowing almost nothing of Chinese social history I cannot make the conversation idiomatically correct, but I think the sense of it will be right.

A peasant from the deforested countryside, desperate for fuel to cook his rice, has slipped into a temple courtyard and is breaking twigs off the dawn redwood when he is apprehended by the priest.

"Here, here! You can't do that!"

"But, honorable sir, I have to. See, I have a little rice in this bowl, but it is uncooked. I can't eat it that way. I'm starving. If you'll only let me have a few twigs I can cook my rice and live another day."

"I'm sorry," says the priest, "but it is forbidden. This tree is sacred. No one is allowed to harm it."

"But if I don't get this fuel I will die."

"That's too bad: the tree is sacred. If everybody did what you are trying to do there soon wouldn't be any tree left."

The peasant thinks a few moments and then gets very angry: "Do you mean to tell me that the life of a mere tree is more valuable than the life of a human being?"

Now this is a very Westernized, twentieth-century question; I doubt that an ancient Chinese would have asked it. But if he had, how would the priest have replied? He might have repeated his assertion that the tree was sacred; or he might have tried to frighten the peasant by saying that touching it would bring bad luck to him in the future. That which is sacred or taboo is generally protected by legends that tend to make the taboo operational: bad luck, the evil eye, the displeasure of the gods. Are such stories consciously concocted because the idea of posterity is too remote to be effective? Or is it just a coincidence that objects so protected do survive for posterity's enjoyment? Whatever the case, being treated as sacred can protect an object against destruction by impoverished people who might otherwise discount the future in a simplistically rational way.

Once the peasant realized that the tree was sacred (or that its destruction would bring him bad luck) he would probably have slunk out of the courtyard. But suppose we continue to endow him with twentieth-century sentiments and see what happens.

"Sir," says the peasant, "your position is a self-serving one if I ever heard such. It's all well and good for you to be so thoughtful of posterity, for you get your three square meals a day no matter what. But what about me? Why do I have to serve posterity while you stuff your belly? Where's your sense of justice?"

"You're right," admits the priest. "I *am* the beneficiary of special privilege. There's only one thing to do," he says, as he takes off his clothes, "and that is to trade positions. Take your clothes off and trade with me! From now on you are the priest and I am the peasant."

That is a noble gesture—but surely the point is obvious? The gesture solves nothing. The next day, when the priest-turned-peasant comes begging for wood, the peasant-turned-priest must refuse him. If he doesn't the tree will soon be destroyed.

But the dawn redwood did survive. The conversation was fictional but the event—saving the trees by labeling some of them sacred—is true. The ginkgo tree was also saved in this way: it was known only in temple courtyards when Western men first found it in China. Special privilege preserved the trees in the face of vital demands made by an impoverished people.

Are we in the West capable of such severity? I know of only two stories of this sort, both from the USSR. The first dates from 1921, a time of famine there. An American journalist visited a refugee camp on the Volga where almost half the people had already died of starvation. Noticing sacks of grain stacked in great mounds in an adjacent field, he asked the patriarch of the refugee community why the people did not simply overpower the lone soldier guarding the grain and help themselves. The patriarch explained that the sacks contained seed for planting the next season. "We do not steal from the future," he said.

Much the same thing happened again in the Second World War. The siege of Leningrad by the Germans lasted 900 days, killing about a quarter of the population of three million. The cold and starving inhabitants had to eat dogs, cats, rats, and dried glue from furniture joints and wallpaper. All this time truckloads of edible seeds in containers were in storage in the All-Union Institute of Plant Industry. The seeds were a precious repository of genetic variety for Russian agriculture in the future. The seeds were never touched, though hundreds of thousands of people died.

Do these stories show that starving people are just naturally noble and take the long view? No. The behavior of people in prison camps shows that the opposite is the case. Altruism evaporates as egoism takes over. It is egoism of the crudest sort: people will sacrifice every promise of tomorrow for the merest scrap of food today. It is as though the interest rate for discounting the future approached infinity.

Under severe survival conditions morality disappears, as became evident in an experiment carried out by American physiologists during the Second World War. Foreseeing the need to treat starving victims of European concentration camps after the Germans were driven back, and recognizing that there was too little sound physiological knowledge, American scientists called for volunteers to take part in starvation experiments. Some conscientious objectors, members of the Church of the Brethren, volunteered. They were extremely idealistic young men, but as their ribs started to show, their ideals evaporated. They stole food from any place they could get it, including from one another. Many people do not like to face this sort of reality about human nature, but thoughtful religious men have known it for centuries. Thomas Aquinas summarized the situation very well when he said, "Necessity knows no law."

It is futile to ask starving people to act against their own self-interest as they see it, which is an exclusively short-term self-interest. In a desperate community long-term interests can be protected only by institutional means: soldiers and policemen. These agents will be reliable only if they are fed up to some minimum level, higher than the average of the starving population. In discounting the future a man's personal discount rate is directly related to the emptiness of his stomach. Those who are the guardians of the future stores must be put in a favored position to keep their personal discount rates low—that is, to make it possible for them to believe in, and protect, the future.

In a prosperous society the interests of posterity may often be served by the actions of a multitude of people. These actions are (or at least seem to be) altruistic. That cannot happen in a desperately needy society. When necessity is in the saddle we dare not expect altruism from "the people." Only institutions can then take actions that would be called altruistic were individuals to perform them. "An institution," as George Berg has pointed out, "can be considered as an anticipating device designed to pay off its members now for behavior which will benefit and stabilize society later." An army, a police force, and a priesthood are institutions that *can* serve the needs of posterity—which they may or may not do.

Moralists try to achieve desired ends by exhorting people to be moral. They seldom succeed; and the poorer the society (other things being equal) the less their success. Institutionalists try to achieve desired ends by the proper design of institutions, allowing for the inescapable moral imperfection of the people on whose services institutions must depend. The Cardinal Rule is not violated: institution-designers count on people acting egoistically.

If there is complete equality of position and power in a needy society the interests of posterity are unlikely to be taken care of. Seeds for the future will be used for food today by a hungry people acting egoistically. To serve the future a few individuals must be put in the special position of being egoistically rewarded for protecting the seeds against the mass of people not enjoying special privilege. Well-fed soldiers acting egoistically (to preserve their institutional right to be well fed) can protect posterity's interests against the egoistic demands of today's hungry people. It is not superior morality that is most likely to serve posterity but an institutional design that makes wise use of special privilege.

I am not pleading for more special privilege in our own country. So far as posterity's interests are concerned the richer the country the less need it has for special privilege. We are rich. But I do plead for tolerance and understanding of special privilege in other countries, in poor countries. Political arrangements can never be wholly independent of the circumstances of life. We have long given lip service to this principle, recognizing that illiteracy, poverty, and certain traditions make democracy difficult. If we wish to protect posterity's interests in poor countries we must understand that distributional justice is a luxury that cannot be afforded by a country in which population overwhelms the resource base.

In a poor country, if all people are equally poor—if there is no special privilege—the future will be universally discounted at so high a rate that it will practically vanish. Posterity will be cheated; and being cheated it will, in its turn, be still poorer and will discount the future at an even higher rate. Thus a vicious cycle is established. Only special privilege can break this cycle in a poor country. We need not positively approve of special privilege; but we can only do harm if, like the missionaries of old, we seek to prevent it.

Special privilege does not insure that the interests of posterity will be taken care of in a poor country; it merely makes it possible. Those enjoying special privilege may find it in their hearts to safeguard the interests of posterity against the necessarily—and forgivably—short-sighted egoism of the desperately poor who are under the natural necessity of discounting the future at a ruinous rate. We will serve posterity's interests better if we give up the goal of diminishing special privilege in poor countries. We should seek instead to persuade the privileged to create altruistic institutions that can make things better for posterity, thus diminishing the need for special privilege in the future.

Special privilege may be *pro tempore*, as it is for drafted or enlisted soldiers (in the stories told of the USSR); or it may extend over generations by virtue of hereditary privilege. The privileged always seek to make privilege hereditary. There is much to be said against hereditary privilege, from both biological and political points of view; but it has a peculiar psychological merit from the point of view of posterity, a merit pointed out by Edmund Burke (1729–1797) when he said: "People will not look forward to posterity who never look backward to their ancestors." The image evoked by this old-fashioned voice of conservatism is one of landed gentry or nobility, reared in baronial halls lined with the pictures of ancestors, looking out over comfortable estates, which they are determined to keep intact against the demands of the less fortunate, so that their children may enjoy what they enjoy. In some psychological sense posterity and ancestors fuse together in the service of an abstraction called "family."

If Burke's psychology is right (and I think it is), he points to several ways in which posterity may be served despite the strictures of hardheaded economics. A society in which prosperity is less than universal may institutionalize special privilege. (The desired result is not guaranteed: when ill used, special privilege can have the opposite effect, of course.) Where wealth is sufficiently great and more equitably distributed, a society that held Burke's assertion to be true would be expected to modify its institutions in a number of ways. Obviously it would see to it that the teaching of history played a large role in education.

Less obviously, a society interested in posterity might decide that the policy of encouraging a high degree of mobility in the labor force should be reversed. There is considerable anecdotal evidence to show that a person's identification with the past is significantly strengthened by exposure during childhood to the sight of enduring artifacts: family portraits, a stable dwelling place, even unique trees. It is harder for a mobile family to achieve this unconscious identification with the past. It is the conventional wisdom of economics that labor mobility improves the productivity of a nation. In the short run that may be true; but if the Burkean argument presented here is sound it means that short-term economic efficiency is purchased at the expense of long-term failure to conserve resources.

One further and rather curious point needs to be made about this argument. If I believe it to be true that location stability encourages the identification of the past with the future, that belief may have little direct effect on my own actions because my childhood is now beyond reach. Such a "belief" would be a conscious one, and it seems that only unconscious beliefs have much power to cause actions that run contrary to the dictates of simple rationality. I cannot wilfully create within myself the psychological identification whose praises I sing. The most I can do (if I am powerful and clever enough) is modify the environment of other people—of children now growing up—so that they will unconsciously come to give preference to the interests of posterity.

Here is a curious question: if, because of my own childhood I myself lack a strong feeling for place and ancestry (and hence for posterity), what would lead me to try to inculcate it in

others by working to modify their childhood experiences? Isn't this process a sort of lifting one's self by one's bootstraps, a sort of second-order altruism? The problem of posterity is rich in puzzles!

Whatever the answer may be to questions like these, this much should be clear: once a society loses a keen concern for posterity, regaining such a sense will be the work not of a few years but of a generation or more. If civilization should collapse worldwide, the second tragedy would be the loss of the will to rebuild. Under the inescapable condition of dire poverty, augmented no doubt by a rejection of the past that had caused the collapse, effective concern for posterity would virtually disappear—not forever, perhaps, but until historical developments we cannot possibly foresee rekindled a concern for social continuity.

In the light of this conclusion questions of another sort should be raised. Do we yet have the knowledge needed to insure the indefinite survival of any political unit? Do we yet know how to prevent the collapse that overtook all previous civilizations? If we do, then it is safe to create One World (if we can); but if we do not, it is not advisable even to try. If collapse is still an inescapable part of the life cycle of political units then posterity would be poorly served by a fusing of all present states into one. We should instead preserve enough of the economic and social barriers between groupings of humanity so that the cancer of collapse can be localized.

If knowledge of local wretchedness in distant states should lead us altruistically to create a resource commons we would thereby become a party to the ultimate metastasis of collapse. If our understanding of the physiology and pathology of political organizations is less than total, an overriding concern for the needs of the present generation can lead to a total sacrifice of the interests of posterity. I submit that our knowledge of the laws of political behavior is less than total.

✿ STUDY QUESTIONS

1. What is Hardin's critique of rationality, especially economic rationality?
2. What is the significance of Hardin's story about the peasant, desperate for fuel to cook his rice, who

wants to use the dawn redwood branches for firewood?
3. Do you agree with Hardin that we should allow special privileges in some countries to certain

people so long as they preserve our resources for future use? Why doesn't Hardin apply this principle to our country?

4. How does Hardin link a concern for ancestry with concerns for posterity? Is he correct?

5. Consider your situation. Is your family among the prosperous in the United States or Canada? How

about in the world? How much austerity or severity can you imagine experiencing for the sake of future generations?

6. Does Hardin advocate the tearing down of barriers between nations? Why, or why not?

42   Limited Obligations to Future Generations

MARTIN GOLDING

Martin Golding is professor of philosophy at Duke University and the author of several works in philosophy of law, including *Philosophy of Law*.

Golding's essay divides into two parts. In the first part, he seeks to answer three questions: (1) Who are the individuals in whose regard it is maintained that we have such obligations? (2) What do these obligations oblige us to do? and (3) What kind of obligations are they? In answering these questions, Golding argues that we have obligations to those outside our immediate moral community if and only if we can recognize their good as part of our understanding of the good. In the second part of this essay, he asks whether we have reason to believe that future generations will be sufficiently like us (have our values) for us to be able to recognize such a good. Here he is skeptical.

Golding thinks that our only clear obligation to future people is to leave them alone, not to make plans for them. So while he favors pollution control and stewardship of Earth's resources, he is against the population-limiting policies. That is a problem for each generation to deal with, not one for us to impose on other generations.

PRELIMINARY QUESTIONS

Before I turn to the question of the basis of obligations [to future generations]—the necessity of the plural is actually doubtful—there are three general points to be considered: (1) Who are the individuals in whose regard it is maintained that we have such obligations, to whom do we owe such obligations? (2) What, essentially, do obligations to future generations oblige us to do, what are they aimed at? and (3), To what class of obligation do such obligations belong, what kind of obligation are they? Needless to say, in examining a notion of this sort, which is used in everyday discussion and polemic, one

must be mindful of the danger of taking it—or making it out—to be more precise than it is in reality.

1. This cautionary remark seems especially appropriate in connection with the first of the above points. But the determination of the purview of obligations to future generations is both ethically and practically significant. It seems clear, at least, who does not come within their purview. Obligations to future generations are distinct from the obligations we have to our presently living fellows, who are therefore excluded from the purview of the former, although it might well be the case that *what* we owe to future

Reprinted from *The Monist* 56 (January 1972), with permission of the author and publisher. Notes deleted.

generations is identical with (or overlaps) what we owe to the present generation. However, I think we may go further than this and also exclude our most immediate descendants, our children, grandchildren and great-grandchildren, perhaps. What is distinctive about the notion of obligations to future generations is, I think, that it refers to generations with which the possessors of the obligations cannot expect in a literal sense to share a common life. (Of course, if we have obligations to future generations, understood in this way, we *a fortiori* have obligations to immediate posterity.) This, at any rate, is how I shall construe the reference of such obligations; neither our present fellows nor our immediate posterity come within their purview. What can be the basis of our obligations toward individuals with whom we cannot expect to share a common life is a question I shall consider shortly.

But if their inner boundary be drawn in this way, what can we say about their outer limits? Is there a cut-off point for the individuals in whose regard we have such obligations? Here, it seems, there are two alternatives. First, we can flatly say that there are no outer limits to their purview: all future generations come within their province. A second and more modest answer would be that we do not have such obligations towards any assignable future generation. In either case the referent is a broad and unspecified community of the future, and I think it can be shown that we run into difficulties unless certain qualifications are taken into account.

2. Our second point concerns the question of what it is that obligations to future generations oblige us to do. The short answer is that they oblige us to do many things. But an intervening step is required here, for obligations to future generations are distinct from general duties to perform acts which are in themselves intrinsically right, although such obligations give rise to duties to perform specific acts. Obligations to future generations are essentially an obligation to produce—or to attempt to produce—a desirable state of affairs *for* the community of the future, to promote conditions of good living for future generations. The many things that we are obliged to do are founded upon this obligation (which is why I earlier questioned the necessity

of the plural). If we think we have an obligation to transmit our cultural heritage to future generations it is because we think that our cultural heritage promotes, or perhaps even embodies, good living. In so doing we would hardly wish to falsify the records of our civilization, for future generations must also have, as a condition of good living, the opportunity to learn from the mistakes of the past. If, in addition, we believe lying to be intrinsically wrong we would also refrain from falsifying the records; but this would not be because we think we have any special duty to tell the truth to future generations.

To come closer to contemporary discussion, consider, for example, population control, which is often grounded upon an obligation to future generations. It is not maintained that population control is intrinsically right—although the rhetoric frequently seems to approach such a claim—but rather that it will contribute towards a better life for future generations, and perhaps immediate posterity as well. (If population control were intrinsically anything, I would incline to thinking it intrinsically wrong.) On the other hand, consider the elimination of water and air pollution. Here it might be maintained that we have a definite duty to cease polluting the environment on the grounds that such pollution is intrinsically bad or that it violates a Divine command. Given the current mood of neopaganism, even secularists speak of the despoilment of the environment as a sacrilege of sorts. When the building of a new dam upsets the ecological balance and puts the wildlife under a threat, we react negatively and feel that something bad has resulted. And this is not because we necessarily believe that our own interests or those of future generations have been undermined. Both views, but especially the latter (Divine command), represent men as holding sovereignty over nature only as trustees to whom not everything is permitted. Nevertheless, these ways of grounding the duty to care for the environment are distinguishable from a grounding of the duty upon an obligation to future generations, although one who acknowledges such an obligation will also properly regard himself as a trustee to whom not everything is permitted. Caring for the environment is presumably among the many things that the obligation to future generations obliges us to do because we thereby presumably promote conditions of good living for the community of the future.

The obligation—dropping the plural again for a moment—to future generations, then, is not an immediate catalogue of specific duties. It is in this respect rather like the responsibility that a parent has to see to the welfare of his child. Discharging one's parental responsibility requires concern, seeking, and active effort to promote the good *of* the child, which is the central obligation of the parent and out of which grows the specific parental obligations and duties. The use of the term "responsibility" to characterize the parent's obligation connotes, in part, the element of discretion and flexibility which is requisite to the discharging of the obligation in a variety of antecedently unforseeable situations. Determination of the specific duty is often quite problematic even—and sometimes especially—for the conscientious parent who is anxious to do what is good for his child. And, anticipating my later discussion, this also holds for obligations to future generations. There are, of course, differences, too. Parental responsibility is enriched and reinforced by love, which can hardly obtain between us and future generations. (Still, the very fact that the responsibility to promote the child's good is an obligation means that it is expected to operate even in the absence of love.) Secondly, the parental obligation is always towards assignable individuals, which is not the case with obligations to future generations. There is, however, an additional feature of likeness between the two obligations which I shall mention shortly.

3. The third point about obligations to future generations—to what class of obligation do they belong?—is that they are *owed,* albeit owed to an unspecified, and perhaps unspecifiable, community of the future. Obligations to future generations, therefore, are distinct from a general duty, when presented with alternatives for action, to choose the act which produces the greatest good. Such a duty is not owed to anyone, and the beneficiaries of my fulfilling a duty to promote the greatest good are not necessarily individuals to whom I stand in the moral relation

of having an obligation that is owed. But when I owe it to someone to promote his good, he is never, to this extent, merely an incidental beneficiary of my effort to fulfill the obligation. He has a presumptive *right* to it and can assert a claim against me for it. Obligations to future generations are of this kind. There is something which is due to the community of the future from us. The moral relation between us and future generations is one in which they have a claim against us to promote their good. Future generations are, thus, possessors of presumptive rights.

How Can Those Not Yet Born *Now* Have Claims on Us?

This conclusion is surely odd. How can future generations—the not-yet-born—*now* have claims against us? This question serves to turn us finally to consider the basis of our obligations to future generations. I think it useful to begin by discussing and removing one source of the oddity.

It should first be noticed that there is no oddity in investing present effort in order to promote a future state of affairs or in having an owed obligation to do so. The oddity arises only on a theory of obligations and claims (and, hence, of rights) that virtually identifies them with acts of willing, with the exercise of sovereignty of one over another, with the pressing of demands—in a word, with *making* claims. But, clearly, future generations are not now engaged in acts of willing, are not now exercising sovereignty over us, and are not now pressing their demands. Future generations are not now making claims against us, nor will it be *possible* for them to do so. (Our immediate posterity are in this last respect in a different case.) However, the identification of claims with making claims, demanding, is plausible within the field of rights and obligations because the content of a system of rights is historically conditioned by the making of claims. Individuals and groups put forward their claims to the goods of life, demand them as their right; and in this way the content is increasingly expanded towards the inclusion of more of these goods.

Nevertheless, as suggestive a clue as this fact is for the development of a theory of rights, there is a distinction to be drawn between *having* claims and *making* claims. The mere fact that someone claims something from me is not sufficient to establish it as his right, or that he has a claim relative to me. On the other hand, someone may have a claim relative to me whether or not he makes the claim, demands, or is even able to make a claim. (This is not to deny that claiming plays a role in the theory of rights.) Two points require attention here. First, some claims are frivolous. What is demanded cannot really be claimed as a matter of right. The crucial factor in determining this is the *social ideal,* which we may provisionally define as a conception of the good life for man. It serves as the yardstick by which demands, current and potential, are measured. Secondly, whether someone's claim confers an entitlement upon him to receive what is claimed *from me* depends upon my moral relation to him, on whether he is a member of my *moral community.* It is these factors, rather than any actual demanding, which establish whether someone has a claim relative to me.

Who Are the Members of My Moral Community?

Who are the members of my moral community? (Who is my neighbor?) The fact is that I am a member of more than one moral community, for I belong to a variety of groups whose members owe obligations to one another. And many of the particular obligations that are owed vary from group to group. As a result my obligations are often in conflict and I experience a fragmentation of energy and responsibility in attempting to meet my obligations. What I ought to desire for the members of one of these groups is frequently in opposition to what I ought to desire for the members of another of these groups. Moral communities are constituted, or generated, in a number of ways, one of which is especially relevant to our problem. Yet these ways are not mutually exclusive, and they can be mutually reinforcing. This is a large topic and I cannot go into its details here. It is sufficient for our purpose to take brief notice of two possible ways of generating a moral community so as to set in relief the particular kind of moral community that is requisite for obligations to future generations.

A moral community may be constituted by an explicit contract between its members. In this case the particular obligations which the members have towards each other are fixed by the terms of their bargain. Secondly, a moral community may be generated out of a social arrangement in which each member derives benefits from the efforts of other members. As a result a member acquires an obligation to share the burden of sustaining the social arrangement. Both of these are communities in which entrance and participation are fundamentally a matter of self-interest, and only rarely will there be an obligation of the sort that was discussed earlier, that is, a responsibility to secure the good of the members. In general the obligations will be of more specialized kinds. It is also apparent that obligations acquired in these ways can easily come into conflict with other obligations that one may have. Clearly, a moral community comprised of present and future generations cannot arise from either of these sources. We cannot enter into an explicit contract with the community of the future. And although future generations might derive benefits from us, these benefits cannot be reciprocated. Our immediate posterity, who will share a common life with us, are in a better position in this respect; so that obligations towards our children, born and unborn, conceivably *could* be generated from participation in a mutually beneficial social arrangement. This, however, would be misleading.

It seems, then, that communities in which entrance and participation are fundamentally matters of self-interest, do not fit our specifications. As an alternative let us consider communities based upon altruistic impulses and fellow-feeling. This, too, is in itself a large topic, and I refer to it only in order to develop a single point.

The question I began with was: Who are the members of my moral community? Now it is true that there are at least a few people towards whom I have the sentiments that are identified with altruism and sympathetic concern. But are these sentiments enough to establish for me the moral relationship of owing them an obligation? Are these enough to generate a moral community? The answer, I think, must be in the negative so long as these affections towards others remain at the level of animal feeling. The ancient distinction between mere affection, mere liking, and conscious desire is fundamental here. Genuine concern and interest in the well-being of another must be conscious concern. My desire for another's good must in this event be more than impulsive, and presupposes, rather, that I have a *conception* of his good. This conception, which cannot be a bare concept of what is incidentally a good but which is rather a conception of the good *for* him, further involves that he not be a mere blank to me but that he is characterized or described in some way in my consciousness. It is perhaps unnecessary to add that there is never any absolute guarantee that such a conceived good is not, in some sense, false or fragmentary. Nevertheless, an altruism that is literally mindless—if it can be called "altruism" at all—cannot be the basis of moral community.

But even if it be granted that I have a conception of another's good, I have not yet reached the stage of obligation towards him. We are all familiar with the kind of "taking an interest in the welfare of another" that is gracious and gift-like, a matter of *noblesse oblige*. It is not so much that this type of interest-taking tends to be casual, fleeting and fragmentary and stands in contrast to interest-taking that is constant, penetrating and concerned with the other's total good. It is, rather, a form of interest-taking, however "conceptual," that is a manifestation of an unreadiness or even an unwillingness to recognize the other's claim (as distinct, of course, from his claiming), the other's entitlement, to receive his good from me. An additional step is, therefore, required, and I think it consists in this: that I acknowledge this good as a good, that his good is good-to-me. Once I have made this step, I cannot in conscience deny the pertinence of his demand, if he makes one, although whether I should now act so as to promote his good is of course dependent on a host of factors. (Among these factors are moral considerations that determine the permissibility of various courses of action and priorities of duties.) The basis of the obligation is nevertheless secured. . . .

The structure of the situation is highlighted when a stranger puts forward his demand. The question immediately arises, shall his claim be recognized as a matter of right? Initially I have no affection for him. But is this crucial in determining whether he ought to count as a member of my moral community? The determination depends, rather, on what he is like and what are the conditions of his life. One's obligations to a stranger are never immediately clear. If a visitor from Mars or Venus were to appear, I would not know what to desire for him. I would not know whether my conception of the good life is relevant to him and to his conditions of life. The good that I acknowledge might not be good for him. Humans, of course, are in a better case than Martians or Venusians. Still, since the stranger appears as strange, different, what I maintain in my attempt to exclude him is that my conception of the good is not relevant to him, that "his kind" do not count. He, on the other hand, is in effect saying to me: Given your social ideal, you must acknowledge my claim, for it *is* relevant to me given what I am; your good is my good, also. If I should finally come to concede this, the full force of my obligation to him will be manifest to me quite independently of any fellow-feeling that might or might not be aroused. The *involuntary* character of the obligation will be clear to me, as it probably never is in the case of individuals who command one's sympathy. And once I admit him as a member of my moral community, I will also acknowledge my responsibility to secure this good for him even in the absence of any future claiming on his part.

With this we have completed the account of the constitution of the type of moral community that is required for obligations to future generations. I shall not recapitulate its elements. The step that incorporates future generations into our moral community is small and obvious. Future generations are members of our moral community because, and insofar as, our social ideal is relevant to them, given what they are and their conditions of life. I believe that this account applies also to obligations towards our immediate posterity. However, the responsibility that one has to see to the welfare of his children is in addition buttressed and qualified by social understandings concerning the division of moral labor and by natural affection. The basis of the obligations is nevertheless the same in both instances. Underlying this account is the important fact that such obligations fall into the area of the moral life which is independent of considerations of explicit contract and personal advantage. Moral duty and virtue also fall into this area. But I should like to emphasize again that I do not wish to be understood as putting this account forward as an analysis of moral virtue and duty in general.

The Inter-Generational Partnership

As we turn at long last specifically to our obligations to future generations, it is worth noticing that the term "contract" has been used to cover the kind of moral community that I have been discussing. It occurs in a famous passage in Burke's *Reflections on the Revolution in France:*

> Society is indeed a contract. Subordinate contracts for objects of mere occasional interest may be dissolved at pleasure—but the state ought not to be considered as nothing better than a partnership agreement in a trade of pepper and coffee, calico or tobacco, or some other such low concern, to be taken up for a little temporary interest, and to be dissolved by the fancy of the parties. It is to be looked upon with other reverence; because it is not a partnership in things subservient only to the gross animal existence of a temporary and perishable nature.
>
> It is a partnership in all science; a partnership in all art; a partnership in every virtue, and in all perfection. As the ends of such a partnership cannot be obtained in many generations, it becomes a partnership not only between those who are living, but between those who are living, those who are dead and those who are to be born.
>
> Each contract of each particular state is but a clause in the great primaeval contract of eternal society, linking the lower with the higher natures, connecting the visible and invisible world, according to a fixed compact sanctioned by the inviolable oath which holds all physical and all moral natures, each in their appointed place.

The contract Burke has in mind is hardly an explicit contract, for it is "between those who are living, those who are dead and those who are to be born." He implicitly affirms, I think, obligations to future generations. In speaking of the "ends of such a partnership," Burke intends a conception of the good life for man—a social ideal. And, if I do not misinterpret him, I think it also plain that Burke assumes that it is relatively the same conception of the good life whose realization is the object of the efforts of the living, the dead, and the unborn. They all revere the same social ideal. Moreover, he seems to assume that the conditions of life and of the three groups are more or less the same. And, finally, he seems to assume that the same general characterization is true of these groups ("all physical and moral natures, each in their appointed place").

Now I think that Burke is correct in making assumptions of these sorts if we are to have obligations to future generations. However, it is precisely with such assumptions that the notion of obligation to future generations begins to run into difficulties. My discussion, until this point, has proceeded on the view that we *have* obligations to future generations. But do we? I am not sure that the question can be answered in the affirmative with any certainty. I shall conclude this note with a very brief discussion of some of the difficulties. They may be summed up in the question: Is our conception—"conceptions" might be a more accurate word—of the good life for man relevant to future generations?

It will be recalled that I began by stressing the importance of fixing the purview of obligations to future generations. They comprise the community of the future, a community with which we cannot expect to share a common life. It appears to me that the more *remote* the members of this community are, the more problematic our obligations to them become. That they are members of our moral community is highly doubtful, for we probably do not know what to desire for them.

Let us consider a concrete example, namely, that of the maintenance of genetic quality. Sir Julian Huxley has stated:

> [I]f we don't do something about controlling our genetic inheritance, we are going to degenerate. Without selection, bad mutations inevitably tend to accumulate; *in the long run, perhaps 5,000 to 10,000 years from now,* we [*sic*] shall certainly have to do something about it.... Most mutations are deleterious, but we now keep many of them going that would otherwise have died out. If this continues indefinitely... then the whole genetic capacity of man will be much weakened.

This statement, and others like it, raises many issues. As I have elsewhere discussed the problems connected with eugenic programs, positive and negative, I shall not go into details here. The point I would make is this: given that we do not know the conditions of life of the very distant future generations, we do not know what we ought to desire for them even on such matters as genic constitution. The chromosome is "deleterious" or "advantageous" only relative to given circumstances. And the same argument applies against those who would promote certain social traits by means of genetic engineering (assuming that social traits are heritable). Even such a trait as intelligence does not escape immune. (There are also problems in eugenic programs having nothing to do with remoteness.) One might go so far as to say that if we have an obligation to distant future generations it is an obligation not to plan for them. Not only do we not know their conditions of life, we also do not know whether they will maintain the same (or a similar) conception of the good life for man as we do. Can we even be fairly sure that the same general characterization is true both of them and us?

The moral to be drawn from this rather extreme example is that the more distant the generation we focus upon, the less likely it is that we have an obligation to promote its good. We would be both ethically and practically well-advised to set our sights on more immediate generations and, perhaps, solely upon our immediate posterity. After all, even if we do have obligations to future generations, our obligations to immediate posterity are undoubtedly much clearer. The nearer the generations are to us, the more likely it is that our conception of the good life is relevant to them. There is certainly enough work for us to do in discharging our responsibility to promote a good life for them. But it would be unwise, both from an ethical and a practical perspective, to seek to promote the good of the very distant.

And it could also be *wrong*, if it be granted—as I think it must—that our obligations towards (and hence the rights relative to us of) near future generations and especially our immediate posterity are clearer than those of more distant generations. By "more distant" I do not necessarily mean "very distant." We shall have to be highly scrupulous in regard to anything we do for any future generation that also could adversely affect the rights of an intervening generation. Anything else would be "gambling in futures." We should, therefore, be hesitant to act on the dire predictions of certain extreme "crisis ecologists" and on the proposals of those who would have us plan for mere survival. In the main, we would be ethically well-advised to confine ourselves to removing the obstacles that stand in the way of immediate posterity's realizing the social ideal. This involves not only the active task of cleaning up the environment and making our cities more habitable, but also implies restraints upon us. Obviously, the specific obligations that we have cannot be determined in the abstract. This article is not the place for an evaluation of concrete proposals that have been made. I would only add that population limitation schemes seem rather dubious to me. I find it inherently paradoxical that we should have an obligation to future generations (near and distant) to determine in effect the very membership of those generations.

A final point. If certain trends now apparent in our biological technology continue, it is doubtful that we should regard ourselves as being under an obligation to future generations. It seems likely that the man—humanoid(?)—of the future will be Programmed Man, fabricated to order, with his finger constantly on the Delgado button that stimulates the pleasure centers of the brain. I, for one, cannot see myself as regarding the good for Programmed Man as a good-to-me. That we should do so, however, is a necessary condition of his membership in our moral community, as I have argued above. The course of these trends may very well be determined by whether we believe that we are, in the words of Burke, "but a clause in the great primaeval contract of eternal society, linking the lower with the higher natures, connecting the visible and invisible world, according to a fixed compact sanctioned by the inviolable oath which holds all physical and all moral natures, each in their appointed place." We cannot yet pretend to know the outcome of these trends. It appears that whether we have obligations to future generations in part depends on what we do for the present.

STUDY QUESTIONS

1. Carefully analyze Golding's argument. Why must we identify future people's concept of the good with our notion of the good before we have obligations to them? How do you understand this?
2. Look carefully at Golding's use of Burke's idea of an implicit compact (contract or partnership) "between those who are living, those who are dead and those who are to be born." How does Golding interpret this? Is his interpretation too narrow or exactly right? Explain.
3. Golding says, "Population limitation schemes seem rather dubious to me," but he admits that it "will contribute towards a better life for future generations." What are some aims of population limitation besides making life better for future generations?

43 Energy Policy and the Further Future: The Identity Problem

DEREK PARFIT

Derek Parfit is a fellow in philosophy at Oxford University. He has made outstanding contributions to ethical theory and the philosophy of mind. His major work is Reasons and Persons *(1984).*

Here Parfit examines traditional ways of justifying intergenerational rights and duties. On the standard view, we hold that a crime or policy has to have a definite victim before we can call it a crime or a bad *policy. But the policy choices we make regarding energy and resource use will determine who is born so that, as long as future people live worthwhile lives, on the standard view, they cannot blame us for our bad and wasteful policies. Parfit argues (or more accurately, urges us to judge) that the standard view is wrong. The principle he offers (A) is: "It is bad if those who live are worse off than those who might have lived." In this case, it doesn't matter whether different people live. We are responsible for environmental policies since we could have caused human lives to have been better off.*

I have assumed that our acts may have good or bad effects in the further future.[1] Let us now examine this assumption. Consider first

> *The Nuclear Technician:* Some technician lazily chooses not to check some tank in which nuclear wastes are buried. As a result there is a catastrophe two centuries later. Leaked radiation kills and injures thousands of people.

We can plausibly assume that, whether or not this technician checks this tank, the same particular people would be born during the next two centuries. If he had chosen to check the tank, these same people would have later lived, and escaped the catastrophe.

Is it morally relevant that the people whom this technician harms do not yet exist when he makes his choice? I have assumed here that it is not. If we know that some choice either may or will harm future people, this is an objection to this choice even if the people harmed do not yet exist.

Reprinted from *Energy and the Future,* ed. Douglas MacLean and Peter G. Brown (Totowa, NJ: Rowman & Littlefield, 1983). Reprinted by permission of Rowman & Littlefield Publishers, Inc.

(I am to blame if I leave a man-trap on my land, which ten years later maims a five-year-old child.)

Consider next

The Risky Policy: Suppose that, as a community, we have a choice between two energy policies. Both would be completely safe for at least two centuries, but one would have certain risks for the further future. If we choose the Risky Policy, the standard of living would be somewhat higher over the next two centuries. We do choose this policy. As a result there is a similar catastrophe two centuries later, which kills and injures thousands of people.

Unlike the Nuclear Technician's choice, our choice between these policies affects who will be later born. This is not obvious, but is on reflection clear.

Our identity in fact depends partly on when we are conceived. This is so on both the main views about this subject. Consider some particular person, such as yourself. You are the *n*th child of your mother, and you were conceived at time *t*. According to one view, you could not have grown from a different pair of cells. If your mother had conceived her *n*th child some months earlier or later, that child would *in fact* have grown from a different pair of cells, and so would not have been you.

According to the other main view, you could have grown from different cells, or even had different parents. This would have happened if your actual parents had not conceived a child when they in fact conceived you, and some other couple had conceived an extra child who was sufficiently *like* you, or whose life turned out to be sufficiently like yours. On this other view, that child would have been you. (Suppose that Plato's actual parents never had children, and that some other ancient Greek couple had a child who wrote *The Republic, The Last Days of Socrates,* and so on. On this other view, this child would have been Plato.) Those who take this other view, while believing that you could have grown from a different pair of cells, would admit that this would not *in fact* have happened. On both views, it is in fact true that, if your mother had conceived her *n*th child in a different month, that child would not have been you, and *you* would never have existed.

It may help to shift to this example. A fourteen-year-old girl decides to have a child. We try to change her mind. We first try to persuade her that, if she has a child now, that will be worse for her. She says that, even if it will be, that is her affair. We then claim that, if she has a child now, that will be worse for her child. If she waits until she is grown up, she will be a better mother, and will be able to give her child a better start in life.

Suppose that this fourteen-year-old rejects our advice. She has a child now, and gives him a poor start in life. Was our claim correct? Would it have been better for him if she had taken our advice? If she had, *he* would never have been born. So her decision was worse for him only if it is against his interests to have been born. Even if this makes sense, it would be true only if his life was so wretched as to be worse than nothing. Assume that this is not so. We must then admit that our claim was false. We may still believe that this girl should have waited. That would have been better for her, and the different child she would have had later would have received a better start in life. But we cannot claim that, in having *this* child, what she did was worse for *him.*

Return now to the choice between our two energy policies. If we choose the Risky Policy, the standard of living will be slightly higher over the next two centuries. This effect implies another. It is not true that, whichever policy we choose, the same particular people will exist two centuries later. Given the effects of two such policies on the details of our lives, it would increasingly over time be true that people married different people. More simply, even in the same marriages, the children would increasingly be conceived at different times. (Thus the British Miners' Strike of 1974, which caused television to close down an hour early, thereby affected the timing of thousands of conceptions.) As we have seen, children conceived at different times would in fact be different children. So the proportion of those later born who would owe their existence to our choice would, like ripples in a pool, steadily grow. We can plausibly assume that, after two centuries, there would be no one living who would have been born whichever policy we chose. (It may help to think of this example: how many of us could truly claim, "Even if railways had never been invented, I would still have been born"?)

In my imagined case, we choose the Risky Policy. As a result, two centuries later, thousands of people are killed and injured. But if we had chosen the alternative Safe Policy, these particular people would never have existed. Different people would have existed in their place. Is our choice of the Risky Policy worse for anyone?

We can first ask, "Could a life be so bad—so diseased and deprived—that it would not be worth living? Could a life be even worse than this? Could it be worse than nothing, or as we might say 'worth not living'?" We need not answer this question. We can suppose that, whether or not lives could be worth not living, this would not be true of the lives of the people killed in the catastrophe. These people's lives would be well worth living. And we can suppose the same of those who mourn for those killed, and those whom the catastrophe disables. (Perhaps, for some of those who suffer most, the rest of their lives would be worth not living. But this would not be true of their lives as a whole.)

We can next ask: "If we cause someone to exist, who will have a life worth living, do we thereby benefit this person?" This is a difficult question. Call it the question whether *causing to exist can benefit*. Since the question is so difficult, I shall discuss the implications of both answers.

Because we chose the Risky Policy, thousands of people are later killed or injured or bereaved. But if we had chosen the Safe Policy these particular people would never have existed. Suppose we do *not* believe that causing to exist can benefit. We should ask, "If particular people live lives that are on the whole well worth living, even though they are struck by some catastrophe, is this worse for these people than if they had never existed?" Our answer must be "no." If we believe that causing to exist *can* benefit, we can say more. Since the people struck by the catastrophe live lives that are well worth living and would never have existed if we had chosen the Safe Policy, our choice of the Risky Policy is

not only not worse for these people, it *benefits* them.

Let us now compare our two examples. The Nuclear Technician chooses not to check some tank. We choose the Risky Policy. Both these choices predictably cause catastrophes, which harm thousands of people. These predictable effects both seem bad, providing at least some moral objection to these choices. In the case of the technician, the objection is obvious. His choice is worse for the people who are later harmed. But this is not true of our choice of the Risky Policy. Moreover, when we understand this case, we know that this is not true. We know that, even though our choice may cause such a catastrophe, it will not be worse for anyone who ever lives.

Does this make a moral difference? There are three views. It might make all the difference, or some difference, or no difference. There might be no objection to our choice, or some objection, or the objection may be just as strong.

Some claim

Wrongs Require Victims: Our choice cannot be wrong if we know that it will be worse for no one.

This claim implies that there is no objection to our choice. We may find it hard to deny this claim, or to accept this implication.

I deny that wrongs require victims. If we know that we may cause such a catastrophe, I am sure that there is at least some moral objection to our choice. I am inclined to believe that the objection is just as strong as it would have been if, as in the case of the Nuclear Technician, our choice would be worse for future people. If this is so, it is morally irrelevant that our choice will be worse for no one. This may have important theoretical implications.

Before we pursue the question, it will help to introduce two more examples. We must continue to assume that some people can be worse off than others, in morally significant ways, and by more or less. But we need not assume that these comparisons could be even in principle precise. There may be only rough or partial comparability. By "worse off" we need not mean "less happy." We could be thinking, more narrowly, of the standard of living, or, more broadly, of the

FIGURE 1 Effects of Choice on Future Standard of Living

quality of life. Since it is the vaguer, I shall use the phrase "the quality of life." And I shall extend the ordinary use of the phrase "worth living." If one of two groups of people would have a lower quality of life, I shall call their lives to this extent "less worth living."

Here is another example:

> *Depletion:* Suppose that, as a community, we must choose whether to deplete or conserve certain kinds of resources. If we choose Depletion, the quality of life over the next two centuries would be slightly higher than it would have been if we had chosen Conservation, but it may later be much lower. Life at this much lower level would, however, still be well worth living. The effects might be shown as in Figure 1.

This case raises the same problem. If we choose Depletion rather than Conservation, this will lower the quality of life more than two centuries from now. But the particular people who will then be living would never have existed if instead we had chosen Conservation. So our choice of Depletion is not worse for any of these people. But our choice will cause these people to be worse off than the different people who, if we had chosen Conservation, would have later lived. This seems a bad effect, and an objection to our choice, even though it will be worse for no one.

Would the effect be worse, having greater moral weight, if it *was* worse for people? One test of our intuitions may be this. We may remember a time when we were concerned about effects on future generations, but had overlooked my point about personal identity. We may have thought that a policy like Depletion would be against the interests of future people. When we saw that this was false, did we become less concerned about effects on future generations?

I myself did not. But it may help to introduce a different example. Suppose there are two rare conditions X and Y, which cannot be detected without special tests. If a pregnant woman has condition X, this will give to the child she is carrying a certain handicap. A simple treatment would prevent this effect. If a woman has condition Y when she becomes pregnant, this will give to the child she conceives the same particular handicap. Condition Y cannot be treated, but always disappears within two months. Suppose next that we have planned two medical programs, but there are funds for only one; so one must be canceled. In the first program, millions of women would be tested during pregnancy. Those found to have condition X would be treated. In the second program, millions of women would be tested when they intend to try to become pregnant. Those found to have condition Y would be warned to postpone conception for at least two months. We are able to predict that these two programs would achieve results in as many cases. If there is Pregnancy Testing, 1,000 children a year would be born normal rather than handicapped. If there is Pre-Conception Testing, there would each year be born 1,000 normal children, rather than 1,000 different handicapped children. Would these two programs be equally worthwhile?

Let us note carefully what the difference is. As a result of either program, 1,000 couples a year would have a normal rather than a handicapped child. These would be different couples on the two programs. But since the numbers would be the same, the effects on parents and on other people would be morally equivalent. The only difference lies in the effects on the children. Note next that, in judging these effects, we need have no view about the moral status of a fetus. We can suppose that it would take a year before either kind of testing could begin. When we choose between the two programs, none of the children has yet been conceived. And all of the children will become adults. So we are considering effects, not on present fetuses, but on future people. Assume next that the handicap in question, though it is not trivial, is not so severe as to make life doubtfully worth living. Even if it can be against our interests to have been born, this would not be true of those born with this handicap.

Since we cannot afford both programs, which should we cancel? Under one description, both would have the same effects. Suppose that conditions X and Y are the only causes of this handicap. The incidence is now 2,000 a year. Either program would halve the incidence; the rate would drop to 1,000 a year. The difference is this. If we decide to cancel Pregnancy Testing, those who are later born handicapped would be able to claim, "But for your decision, I would have been normal." Our decision will be worse for all these people. If instead we decide to cancel Pre-Conception Testing, there will later be just as many people who are born with this handicap. But none of these could truly claim, "But for your decision, I would have been normal." But for our decision, they would never have existed; their parents would have later had different children. Since their lives, though handicapped, are still worth living, our decision will not be worse for any of these people.

Does this make a moral difference? Or are the two programs equally worthwhile? Is all that matters morally how many future lives will be normal rather than handicapped? Or does it also matter whether these lives would be lived by the very same people?

I am inclined to judge these programs equally worthwhile. If Pre-Conception Testing would achieve results in a few more cases, I would judge it the better program. This matches my reactions to the questions asked above about our choice of the Risky Policy or of Depletion. There too, I think it would be bad if there would later be a catastrophe, killing and injuring thousands of people, and bad if there would later be a lower quality of life. And I think that it would not be *worse* if the people who later live

would themselves have existed if we had chosen the Safe Policy or Conservation. The bad effects would not be worse if they had been, in this way, worse for any particular people.

Let us review the argument so far. If we choose the Risky Policy or Depletion, this may later cause a predictable catastrophe, or a decline in the quality of life. We naturally assume that these would be bad effects, which provide some objection to these two choices. Many think the objection is that our choices will be worse for future people. We have seen that this is false. But does this make a moral difference? There are three possible answers. It might make all the difference, or some difference, or no difference at all. When we see that our choice will be worse for no one, we may decide that there is no objection to this choice, or that there is less objection, or that the objection is just as strong.

I incline to the third answer. And I give this answer in the case of the medical programs. But I know some people who do not share my intuitions. How can we resolve this disagreement? Is there some familiar principle to which we can appeal?

Return to the choice of the Risky Policy, which may cause a catastrophe, harming thousands of people. It may seem irrelevant here that our choice will not be worse for these future people. Can we not deserve blame for causing harm to others, even when our act is not worse for them? Suppose that I choose to drive when drunk, and in the resulting crash cause you to lose a leg. One year later, war breaks out. If you had not lost this leg, you would have been conscripted, and been killed. So my drunken driving saves your life. But I am still morally to blame.

This case reminds us that, in assigning blame, we must consider not actual but predictable effects. I knew that my drunken driving might injure others, but I could not know that it would in fact save your life. This distinction might apply to the choice between our two policies. We know that our choice of the Risky Policy may impose harm on future people. Suppose next that we have overlooked the point about personal identity. We mistakenly believe that, whichever policy we choose, the very same people will later live. We may therefore believe that, if we choose the Risky Policy, this may be worse for future people. If we believe this, our choice can be criticized. We can deserve blame for doing what we *believe* may be worse for others. This criticism stands even if our belief is false—just as I am as much to blame even if my drunken driving will in fact save your life.

Now suppose, however, that we have seen the point about personal identity. We realize that, if we choose the Risky Policy, our choice will not be worse for those people whom it later harms. Note that this is not a lucky guess. It is not like predicting that, if I cause you to lose a leg, that will later save you from death in the trenches. We know that, if we choose the Risky Policy, this may impose harms on several future people. But we also know that, if we had chosen the Safe Policy, those particular people would never have been born. Since their lives will be worth living we *know* that our choice will not be worse for them.

If we know this, we cannot be compared to a drunken driver. So how should we be criticized? Can we deserve blame for causing others to be harmed, even when we know that our act will not be worse for them? Suppose we know that the harm we cause will be fully compensated by some benefit. For us to be sure of this, the benefit must clearly outweigh the harm. Consider a surgeon who saves you from blindness, at the cost of giving you a facial scar. In scarring you, this surgeon does you harm. But he knows that his act is not worse for you. Is this enough to justify his decision? Not quite. He must not be infringing your autonomy. But this does not require that you give consent. Suppose that you are unconscious, so that he is forced to choose without consulting you. If he decides to operate, he would here deserve no blame. Though he scars your face, his act is justified. It is enough for him to know that his act will not be worse for you.

If we choose the Risky Policy, this may cause harm to many people. Since these will be future people, whom we cannot now consult, we are not infringing their autonomy. And we know that our choice will not be worse for them. Have we shown that, in the same way, the objection has been met?

The case of the surgeon shows only that the objection might be met. The choice of the Risky Policy has two special features. Why is the surgeon's act not worse for you? Because it gives you a compensating benefit. Though he scars your face, he saves you from going blind. Why is our choice of the Risky Policy not worse for those future people? Because they will owe their existence to this choice. Is this a compensating benefit? This is a difficult question. But suppose that we answer "no." Suppose we believe that to receive life, even a life worth living, is not to be benefited.[2] There is then a special reason why, if we choose the Risky Policy, this will not be worse for the people who will later live.

Here is the second special feature. If we had chosen the Safe Policy, different people would have later lived. Let us first set aside this feature. Let us consider only the people who, given our actual choice, will in fact later live. These will be the only actual people whom our choice affects. Should the objection to our choice appeal to the effects on these people? Because of our choice, they will later suffer certain harms. This seems to provide an objection. But they owe their existence to this same choice. Does this remove the objection?

Consider a second case involving a fourteen-year-old girl. If this second girl has a child now, she will give him a poor start in life. But suppose she knows that, because she has some illness, she will become sterile within the next year. Unless she has a child now, she can never have a child. Suppose that this girl chooses to have a child. Can she be criticized? She gives her child a poor start in life. But she could not have given *him* a better start in life, and his life will still be worth living. The effects on him do not seem to provide an objection. Suppose that she could also reasonably assume that, if she has this child, this would not be worse for other people. It would then seem that there is no objection to this girl's choice—not even one that is overridden by her right to have a child.

Now return to our earlier case of a fourteen-year-old girl. Like the second girl, the first girl knows that, if she has a child now, she will give him a poor start in life. But she could wait for several years and have another child, who would have a better start in life. She decides not to wait, and has a child now. If we consider the effects only on her actual child, they are just like those of the second girl's choice. But the first girl's choice surely can be criticized. The two choices differ, not in their effects on the actual children, but in the alternatives. How could the second girl avoid having a child to whom she would give a poor start in life? Only by never having a child. That is why her choice seemed not to be open to criticism. She could reasonably assume that her choice would not be worse either for her actual child or for other people. In her case, that seems all we need to know. The first girl's choice has the same effects on her actual child, and on others. But *this* girl could have waited, and given some later child a better start in life. This is the objection to her choice. Her actual child is worse off than some later child would have been.

Return now to the choice between our two social policies. Suppose that we have chosen the Risky Policy. As a result, those who later live suffer certain harms. Is this enough to make our choice open to criticism? I suggest not. Those who later live are like the actual children of the two girls. They owe their existence to our choice, so its effects are not worse for them. The objection must appeal to the alternative.

This restores the second feature that we set aside above. When we chose the Risky Policy, we imposed certain harms on our remote descendants. Were we like the second girl, whose only alternative was to have no descendants? If so, we could not be criticized. But this is not the right comparison. In choosing the Risky Policy, we were like the first girl. If we had chosen the Safe Policy, we would have had different descendants, who would not have suffered such harms.

The objection to our choice cannot appeal only to effects on those people who will later live. It must mention possible effects on the people who, if we had chosen otherwise, would have later lived. The objection must appeal to a claim like this:

> (A) It is bad if those who live are worse off than those who might have lived.

We must claim that this is bad even though it will be worse for no one.

(A) is not a familiar principle. So we have not solved the problem that we reached above. Let us remember what that was. If we choose the Risky Policy, or Depletion, this may later cause a catastrophe or a decline in the quality of life. These seemed bad effects. Many writers claim that, in causing such effects, we would be acting against the interests of future people. Given the point about personal identity, this is not true. But I was inclined to think that this made no moral difference. The objection to these two choices seemed to me just as strong. Several people do not share my intuitions. Some believe that the objections must be weaker. Others believe that they disappear. On their view, our choice cannot be morally criticized if we know that it will be worse for no one. They believe that, as moral agents, we need only be concerned with the effects of our acts on all of the people who are ever actual. We need not consider people who are merely possible—those who never do live but merely might have lived. On this view, the point about identity makes a great moral difference. The effects of our two choices, the predictable catastrophe, and the decline in the quality of life, can be morally totally ignored.

We hoped to resolve this disagreement by appeal to a familiar principle. I suggest now that this cannot be done. To criticize our choice, we must appeal to a claim like (A). And we have yet to explain why (A) should have any weight. To those who reject (A), we do not yet have an adequate reply.

To explain (A), and decide its weight, we would need to go deep into moral theory. And we would need to consider cases where, in the different outcomes of our acts or policies, different numbers of people would exist. This is much too large a task to be attempted here.

I shall therefore end with a practical question. When we are discussing social policies, should we ignore the point about personal identity? Should we allow ourselves to say that a choice like that of the Risky Policy, or of Depletion, might be against the interests of people in the further future? This is not true. Should we pretend that it is? Should we let other people go on thinking that it is?

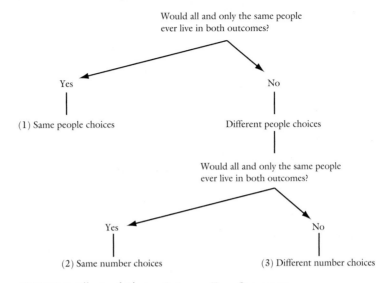

FIGURE 2 Effects of Choice Between Two Outcomes

If you share my intuitions, this seems permissible. We can then use such claims as a convenient form of short-hand. Though the claims are false, we believe that this makes no moral difference. So the claims are not seriously misleading.

Suppose instead that you do not share my intuitions. You believe that, if our choice of Depletion would be worse for no one, this must make a moral difference. It would then be dishonest to conceal the point about identity. But this is what, with your intuitions, I would be tempted to do. I would not *want* people to conclude that we can be less concerned about the more remote effects of our social policies. So I would be tempted to suppress the argument for this conclusion.

Theoretical Footnote: How might the attempt to justify claim (A) take us far into moral theory? Here are some brief remarks. Consider any choice between two outcomes. Figure 2 shows that there are three kinds of choice. These can be distinguished if we ask two questions: "Would all and only the same people ever live in both outcomes?" "Would the same number of people ever live in both outcomes?"

Of these three types of choice, it is the first and third that are important. Most of our moral thinking concerns Same People Choices, where there is a given group of people whom our acts may affect.

We seldom consider Different Number Choices. Those who do have found them puzzling. What this essay has discussed are the second group, Same Number Choices. These are much less puzzling than Different Number Choices. But they are not common. Once we have moved outside Same People Choices—once we are considering acts that would cause different people to exist—it is seldom true that in all of the relevant outcomes the very same numbers would exist.

According to claim (A), it is bad if those who live are worse off than those who might have lived. This claim applies straightforwardly only to Same Number Choices. Can we extend (A) to cover Different Number Choices? One extension would be the so-called "Average View." On this view, it would be worse for there to be more people if the average person would be worse off. The Average View, though popular, can be shown to be implausible.[3] But this does not cast doubt on (A). What it shows is that (A) should not be thought to cover Different Number Choices. We should restate (A) to make this explicit. But (A) *can* be made to cover Same People Choices. Our restatement might be this:

(B) If the same number of lives would be lived either way, it would be bad if people are worse off than people might have been.

The two occurrences of "people" here may refer to *different* people. That is how (B) can cover Same Number Choices. But it can also cover Same People Choices. (B) here implies that it is bad if people are worse off than *they* might have been.

Now consider a more familiar principle. This appeals to the interests of those whom our acts affect. One statement might be this:

> *The Person-Affecting Principle*, or *PAP*: It is bad if people are affected for the worse.

What is the relation between (B) and the PAP?[4] In Same People Choices, these claims coincide. If people are worse off than they might have been, they are affected for the worse. So it will make no difference whether we appeal to (B) or to the PAP.[5]

The two claims diverge only in Same Number Choices. These are what my essay has discussed. Suppose that you share my intuitions, thinking that the point about identity makes no moral difference. You then believe that in Same Number Choices we should appeal to (B) *rather than* the PAP. If we choose Depletion, this will lower the quality of life in the further future. According to (B), this is a bad effect. When we see the point about identity, we see that this effect will be worse for no one. So it is not bad according to the PAP. If we believe that the effect is just as bad, we will here have no use for the PAP. Similar remarks apply to the choice between the two medical programs. If we believe these two programs to be equally worthwhile, we shall again appeal to (B). We shall have no use for the PAP. It draws a moral distinction where, in our view, no distinction should be drawn. It is thus like the claim that it is wrong to enslave whites.

To draw these remarks together: in Same People Choices, (B) and the PAP coincide. In Same Number Choices, we accept (B) rather than the PAP. So, wherever the claims diverge, we prefer (B).

There remain the Different Number Choices. Since we have restricted (B), we shall need some wider claim to cover these. Call this claim (X). I am not sure what (X) should be. But, if you have shared my intuitions, we can expect this. We shall have no further use for (B). It will be implied by (X).[6] So we can expect (X) to inherit (B)'s relations to the PAP. Wherever the claims diverge, we will prefer (X). In Same People Choices, (X) will imply the PAP. It will here make no difference to which we appeal. These are the cases with which most moral thinking is concerned. This explains the reputation of the PAP. This part of morality, the part concerned with human welfare is usually thought of in person-affecting terms. We appeal to the interests of those whom our acts affect. Even after we have found (X), we may continue to use the PAP in most cases. But it will be only a convenient form of short-hand. In some cases, (X) and the PAP will diverge. And we will here appeal to (X) rather than the PAP. We will here believe that, if an effect is bad according to (X), it makes no moral difference whether it is also worse for any particular people. The PAP draws a distinction where, in our view, no distinction should be drawn. We may thus conclude that this part of morality, the part concerned with human welfare, cannot be explained in person-affecting terms. Its fundamental principle will not be concerned with whether acts will be good or bad for those people whom they affect. If this is so, many moral theories need to be revised.

NOTES

1. The first third of this section is adapted from my "Future Generations: Further Problems," Philosophy & Public Affairs 11, no. 2 (Spring 1982).
2. Thus we might say: "We are benefited only if the alternative would not have been worse for us." "If we had never existed, this would not have been worse for us." These and similar arguments I claim not to be decisive in my "Future Generations." Even if it can be in our interests to have been conceived, most of my later claims would still stand.
3. See my "Future Generations," section IX, and Jefferson McMahan's "Problems of Population Theory" in Ethics (October 1981).
4. On the assumption that it cannot be in or against our interests to have been conceived. If we drop this assumption, some of the following claims need to be revised. Again, see my "Future Generations."
5. Does the equivalence go the other way? If people are affected for the worse, does this make them worse off? There is at least one exception: when

they are killed. (B) should be revised to cover such exceptions. Only this ensures that, in Same People Choices, B and the PAP always coincide.

6. Consider the best-known candidates for the role of (X): the Average and Total Views. In their hedonistic forms, the Average View calls for the greatest net sum of happiness per life lived, the Total View simply calls for the greatest total net sum of happiness. When applied to population policy, these two views lie at opposite extremes.

But when applied to Same Number Choices, both imply the hedonistic form of (B). This suggests that, whatever (X) should be, it, too, will imply (B). The difference between the candidates for (X) will be confined to Different Number Choices. This would be like the fact that only in Same Number Choices does (B) diverge from the PAP. I shall discuss these points more fully in my book *Reasons and Persons*, Oxford University Press, 1984.

STUDY QUESTIONS

1. Describe the main thesis of Parfit's essay. How does Parfit set forth the alternatives?
2. Personal identity has to do with being the same person over time. According to traditional ethics, we think that those who are harmed by our actions must be able to say that they would have been better off but for our actions. But in the case of energy or resource depletion, different people will be born than would have been had we had better policies. So, according to this view, these people cannot complain about our bad policies, since but for them, they wouldn't exist. What does Parfit say about the traditional point of view? What do you think?

FOR FURTHER READING

Feinberg, Joel. "The Rights of Animals and Unborn Generations." In his *Rights, Justice and the Bounds of Liberty.* Princeton, NJ: Princeton University Press, 1980.

Partridge, Ernest, ed. *Responsibilities to Future Generations.* Buffalo, NY: Prometheus, 1981.

Reichenbach, Bruce. " On Obligations to Future Generations." *Public Affairs Quarterly* 6.2 (April 1992).

Sikora, R. I., and Brian Barry,eds. *Obligations to Future Generations.* Philadelphia: Temple University Press, 1978.

PART TWO

Practice

Population and Consumption

THE UNIVERSAL DECLARATION ON HUMAN RIGHTS describes the family as the natural and fundamental unit of society. It follows that any choice and decision with regard to the size of the family must irrevocably rest with the family itself and cannot be made by anyone else.[1]

In evaluating population growth one must keep in mind that such growth increases *exponentially* rather than *linearly*. Linear growth increases by adding 1 unit to the sum: 1, 2, 3, 4, 5, and so forth. Exponential growth increases by a fixed percentage of the whole over a given time. It doubles itself: 1, 2, 4, 8, 16, 32, 64, and so forth.

An ancient Chinese story illustrates this. Once a hero defeated the enemies of his country. The emperor had the hero brought before him and promised the hero anything he wanted. The hero produced a chessboard and asked the Emperor for one grain of rice on the first square, two on the second, four on the third, eight on the fourth, and to continue doubling through all 64 squares. The emperor was astonished. "Is that all you request?" he cried. "You could have had half my kingdom, and all you ask for is a little grain?" But the emperor soon discovered that he could not comply with the hero's request. By the time he had gotten to square 32, he found that on that square alone he owed the hero 8.6 billion grains of rice. By the time he got to square 64, he owed over 10,000,000,000,000,000,000 grains of rice, far more than the entire country produced.

We calculate the doubling time of a given amount by using the *rule of 70*. If a sum increases at 1% per annum, it will double in size in 70 years. If it increases at a 2% rate per annum, it will increase fourfold in 70 years.

About 2,000 years ago, 300 million people existed (about the population of the United States in 2006). It reached a billion in the nineteenth century, and by the end of the twentieth century, it reached 6 billion (about 6.3 billion in 2006). A current estimate is that by 2050, the world's population will be 9.3 billion (see Figure 7.1). How serious is this growth? The more people there are, the more food, water, and energy we need and the more pollution we produce. How many people can Earth reasonably sustain?

As more societies industrialize and achieve middle-class lifestyles, they tend to use more resources and produce more pollution, resulting in more environmental degradation. This use is sometimes referred to as *consumption overpopulation* as opposed to

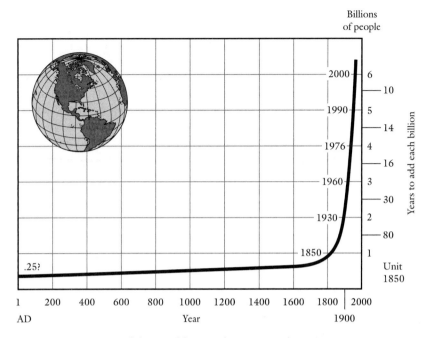

FIGURE 7.1 J Curve of the World's Population Growth

people overpopulation. Many countries are rapidly industrializing, including India and China.

For some environmentalists, the picture is quite gloomy; there are simply not enough land resources. Others argue that our problems are moral and political, not demographic. They say we can solve our urban problems if we have the will to live together in equality and harmony. Technology has radically increased our energy and food resources. Enough food exists for all. The real problem is one of just distribution.

Proponents of this view argue that the wealthy nations should moderate their consumptive passions, pointing out that with only 4.5% of the world's population, the United States uses 33% of its resources, 25% of its nonrenewable energy, and produces 33% of its pollution. The average American's negative impact on the environment is about forty or fifty times that of a person in the Third World. In the affluent West, we must reject consumerism and simplify our lives. Those in the poorer developing nations must be allowed to improve their quality of life through education and appropriate technology.

To provide some data, we begin with a reading by Bill McKibben that succinctly sets forth a case for limiting population growth.

Next we turn to Garrett Hardin's classic article, "The Tragedy of the Commons," in which he argues that unless strong social sanctions are enforced, self-interest will lead people to maximize personal utility, which all too often means violating the carrying capacity of the land. With regard to population, he says that unless we have mutually coercive, mutually agreed-on restrictions on procreation, we will not survive, or survive with enormous misery.

In our third reading, Jacqueline Kasun takes a diametrically opposite point of view from that of McKibben and Hardin. Citing an impressive array of statistics,

Kasun argues that enough food and resources exist to care for a lot more people than presently inhabit Earth and that technology promises to expand our resources efficiently. Population increase, rather than being a liability, is actually a blessing. Such growth stimulates agricultural and economic investment, encourages governments and parents to devote greater resources to education, and inspires both more ideas and the exchange of ideas among people. Contrary to the interests of the ruling elite, we must learn to live creatively with the expanding opportunities that a growing population affords.

Next, "The State of Consumption Today" looks at trends in world consumption, asking especially what will happen as India and China join the ranks of high-consumers.

Finally, Clark Wolf gives a clear overview of the problem of population and possible solutions.

NOTE

1. Secretary General of the United Nations U Thant, *International Planned Parenthood News* 168 (February 1968): 3.

44   A Special Moment in History: The Challenge of Overpopulation and Overconsumption

BILL MCKIBBEN

Bill McKibben is an environmentalist and writer who lives in the Adirondacks in New York State. In this essay he argues that, because of the environmental crisis we face, we are living in a special time, which could determine the near—and long-term—future of the planet. With the world's population heading for another doubling and with more people consuming more resources and creating more pollutants—and with fewer sinks into which to throw them—the decisions we make in the next few decades may well determine the fact of Earth and prospects for future generations. McKibben's article is valuable for the large amount of data on demographics and global warming (see Chapter 11), which it lucidly sets forth and analyzes.

...We may live in a special time. We may live in the strangest, most thoroughly different moment [of history] since human beings took up farming, 10,000 years ago, and time more or less commenced. Since then time has flowed in one direction—toward *more*, which we have taken to be progress. At first the momentum was gradual, almost imperceptible, checked by wars and the Dark Ages and plagues and taboos; but in recent centuries it has accelerated, the curve of every graph steepening like the Himalayas rising from the Asian steppe. We have climbed quite high. Of course, fifty years ago one could have said the same thing, and fifty years before that, and fifty years before *that*. But in each case it would have been premature. We've increased the population fourfold in that 150 years; the amount of food we grow has gone up faster still; the size of our economy has quite simply exploded.

But now—now may be the special time. So special that in the Western world we might each of us consider, among many other things, having only one child—that is, reproducing at a rate as low as that at which human beings have ever voluntarily reproduced. Is this really necessary? Are we finally running up against some limits?

To try to answer this question, we need to ask another: *How many of us will there be in the near future?* Here is a piece of news that may alter the way we see the planet—an indication that we live at a special moment. At least at first blush the news is hopeful. *New demographic evidence shows that it is at least possible that a child born today will live long enough to see the peak of human population.*

Around the world people are choosing to have fewer and fewer children—not just in China, where the government forces it on them, but in almost every nation outside the poorest parts of Africa. Population growth rates are lower than they have been at any time since the Second World War. In the past three decades the average woman in the developing world, excluding China, has gone from bearing six children to bearing four. Even in Bangladesh the average has fallen from six to fewer than four; even in the mullahs' Iran it has dropped by four children. If this keeps up, the population of the world will not quite double again; United Nations analysts offer as their mid-range projection that it will top out at 10 to 11 billion, up from just under six billion at the moment. The world is still growing, at nearly a record pace—we add a New York City every month, almost a Mexico every year, almost an India every decade. But the rate of growth is slowing; it is no longer "exponential," "unstoppable," "inexorable," "unchecked," "cancerous." If current trends hold, the world's population will all but stop growing before the twenty-first century is out.

And that will be none too soon. There is no way we could keep going as we have been. The *increase* in human population in the 1990s has exceeded the *total* population in 1600. The population has grown more since 1950 than it did during the previous four million years. The reasons for our recent rapid growth are pretty clear. Although the Industrial Revolution speeded historical growth rates considerably, it was really the public-health revolution, and its spread to the Third World at the end of the Second World War, that set us galloping. Vaccines and antibiotics came all at once, and right behind came population. In Sri Lanka in the late 1940s life expectancy was rising at least a year every twelve months. How much difference did this make? Consider the United States: if people died throughout this century at the same rate as they did at its beginning, America's population would be 140 million, not 270 million.

If it is relatively easy to explain why populations grew so fast after the Second World War, it is much harder to explain why the growth is now slowing. Experts confidently supply answers, some of them contradictory: "Development is the best contraceptive"—or education, or the empowerment of women, or hard times that force families to postpone having children. For each example there is a counterexample. Ninety-seven percent of women in the Arab sheikhdom of Oman know about contraception, and yet they average more than six children apiece. Turks have used contraception at about the same rate as the Japanese, but their birth rate is twice as high. And so on. It is not AIDS that will slow population growth, except in a few African countries. It is not horrors like the civil war in Rwanda, which claimed half a million lives—a loss the planet can make up for in two days. All that matters is how often individual men and women decide that they want to reproduce.

Will the drop continue? It had better. UN mid-range projections assume that women in the developing world will soon average two children apiece—the rate at which population growth stabilizes. If fertility remained at current levels, the population would reach the absurd figure of 296 billion in just 150 years. Even if it dropped to 2.5 children per woman and then stopped falling, the population would still reach 28 billion.

But let's trust that this time the demographers have got it right. Let's trust that we have rounded the turn and we're in the home stretch. Let's trust that the planet's population really will double only one more time. Even so, this is a case of good news, bad news. The good news is that we won't grow forever. The bad news is that there are six billion of us already, a number the world strains to support. One more near-doubling—four or five billion more people—will nearly double that strain. Will these be the five billion straws that break the camel's back?

BIG QUESTIONS

We've answered the question *How many of us will there be?* But to figure out how near we are to any limits, we need to ask something else: *How big are we?* This is not so simple. Not only do we vary greatly in how much food and energy and water and minerals we consume, but each of us varies over time. William Catton, who was a sociologist at Washington State University before his retirement, once tried to calculate the amount of energy human beings use each day. In hunter-gatherer times it was about 2,500 calories, all of it food. That is the daily energy intake of a common dolphin. A modern human being uses 31,000 calories a day, most of it in the form of fossil fuel. That is the intake of a pilot whale. And the average American uses six times that—as much as a sperm whale. We have become, in other words, different from the people we used to be. Not kinder or unkinder, not deeper or stupider—our natures seem to have changed little since Homer. We've just gotten bigger. We appear to be the same species, with stomachs of the same size, but we aren't. It's as if each of us were trailing a big Macy's-parade balloon around, feeding it constantly.

So it doesn't do much good to stare idly out the window of your 737 as you fly from New York to Los Angeles and see that there's *plenty* of empty space down there. Sure enough, you could crowd lots more people into the nation or onto the planet. The entire world population could fit into Texas, and each person could have an area equal to the floor space of a typical U.S. home. If people were willing to stand, everyone on earth could fit comfortably into half of Rhode Island. Holland is crowded and is doing just fine.

But this ignores the balloons above our heads, our hungry shadow selves, our sperm-whale appetites. As soon as we started farming, we started setting aside extra land to support ourselves. Now each of us needs not only a little plot of cropland and a little pasture for the meat we eat but also a little forest for timber and paper,

a little mine, a little oil well. Giants have big feet. Some scientists in Vancouver tried to calculate one such "footprint" and found that although 1.7 million people lived on a million acres surrounding their city, those people required 21.5 million acres of land to support them—wheat fields in Alberta, oil fields in Saudi Arabia, tomato fields in California. People in Manhattan are as dependent on faraway resources as people on the Mir space station.

Those balloons above our heads can shrink or grow, depending on how we choose to live. All over the earth people who were once tiny are suddenly growing like Alice when she ate the cake. In China per capita income has doubled since the early 1980s. People there, though still Lilliputian in comparison with us, are twice their former size. They eat much higher on the food chain, understandably, than they used to: China slaughters more pigs than any other nation, and it takes four pounds of grain to produce one pound of pork. When, a decade ago, the United Nations examined sustainable development, it issued a report saying that the economies of the developing countries needed to be five to ten times as large to move poor people to an acceptable standard of living—with all that this would mean in terms of demands on oil wells and forests.

That sounds almost impossible. For the moment, though, let's not pass judgment. We're still just doing math. There are going to be lots of us. We're going to be big. But lots of us in relation to what? Big in relation to what? It could be that compared with the world we inhabit, we're still scarce and small. Or not. So now we need to consider a third question.

HOW BIG IS THE EARTH?

Any state wildlife biologist can tell you how many deer a given area can support—how much browse there is for the deer to eat before they begin to suppress the reproduction of trees, before they begin to starve in the winter. He can calculate how many wolves a given area can support too, in part by counting the number of deer. And so on, up and down the food chain. It's not an exact science, but it comes pretty close—at least compared with figuring out the carrying capacity of the earth for human beings, which is an art so dark that anyone with any sense stays away from it.

Consider the difficulties. Human beings, unlike deer, can eat almost anything and live at almost any level they choose. Hunter-gatherers used 2,500 calories of energy a day, whereas modern Americans use seventy-five times that. Human beings, unlike deer, can import what they need from thousands of miles away. And human beings, unlike deer, can figure out new ways to do old things. If, like deer, we needed to browse on conifers to survive, we could crossbreed lush new strains, chop down competing trees, irrigate forests, spray a thousand chemicals, freeze or dry the tender buds at the peak of harvest, genetically engineer new strains—and advertise the merits of maple buds until, everyone was ready to switch. The variables are so great that professional demographers rarely even bother trying to figure out carrying capacity. The demographer Joel Cohen, in his potent book *How Many People Can the Earth Support?* (1995), reports that at two recent meetings of the Population Association of America exactly none of the more than 200 symposia dealt with carrying capacity.

But the difficulty hasn't stopped other thinkers. This is, after all, as big a question as the world offers. Plato, Euripides, and Polybius all worried that we would run out of food if the population kept growing; for centuries a steady stream of economists, environmentalists, and zealots and cranks of all sorts have made it their business to issue estimates either dire or benign. The most famous, of course, came from the Reverend Thomas Malthus. Writing in 1798, he proposed that the growth of population, being "geometric," would soon outstrip the supply of food. Though he changed his mind and rewrote his famous essay, it's the original version that people have remembered—and lambasted—ever since. Few other writers have found critics in as many corners. Not only have conservatives made Malthus's name a byword for ludicrous alarmism, but Karl Marx called his essay "a libel on the human race," Friedrich Engels believed that "we are forever secure from the fear of overpopulation," and even Mao Zedong attacked Malthus by name, adding, "Of all things in the world people are the most precious."

Each new generation of Malthusians has made new predictions that the end was near, and has been proved wrong. The late 1960s saw an upsurge of Malthusian panic. In 1967 William and Paul Paddock published a book called *Famine—1975!*, which contained a triage list: "Egypt: Can't-be-saved.... Tunisia: Should Receive Food.... India: Can't-be-saved." Almost simultaneously Paul Ehrlich wrote, in his best-selling *The Population Bomb* (1968), "The battle to feed all of humanity is over. In the 1970s, the world will undergo famines—hundreds of millions of people will starve to death." It all seemed so certain, so firmly in keeping with a world soon to be darkened by the first oil crisis.

But that's not how it worked out. India fed herself. The United States still ships surplus grain around the world. As the astute Harvard social scientist Amartya Sen points out, "Not only is food generally much cheaper to buy today, in constant dollars, than it was in Malthus's time, but it also has become cheaper during recent decades." So far, in other words, the world has more or less supported us. Too many people starve (60 percent of children in South Asia are stunted by malnutrition), but both the total number and the percentage have dropped in recent decades, thanks mainly to the successes of the Green Revolution. Food production has tripled since the Second World War, outpacing even population growth. We may be giants, but we are clever giants.

So Malthus was wrong. Over and over again he was wrong. No other prophet has ever been proved wrong so many times. At the moment, his stock is especially low. One group of technological optimists now believes that people will continue to improve their standard of living precisely *because* they increase their numbers. This group's intellectual fountainhead is a brilliant Danish economist named Ester Boserup—a sort of anti-Malthus, who in 1965 argued that the gloomy cleric had it backward. The more people, Boserup said, the more progress. Take agriculture as an example: the first farmers, she pointed out, were slash-and-burn cultivators, who might farm a plot for a year or two and then move on, not returning for maybe two decades. As the population grew, however, they had to return more frequently to the same plot. That meant problems:

compacted, depleted, weedy soils. But those new problems meant new solutions: hoes, manure, compost, crop rotation, irrigation. Even in this century, Boserup said, necessity-induced invention has meant that "intensive systems of agriculture replaced extensive systems," accelerating the rate of food production.

Boserup's closely argued examples have inspired a less cautious group of popularizers, who point out that standards of living have risen all over the world even as population has grown. The most important benefit, in fact, that population growth bestows on an economy is to increase the stock of useful knowledge, insisted Julian Simon, the best known of the so-called cornucopians, who died earlier this year. We might run out of copper, but who cares? The mere fact of shortage will lead someone to invent a substitute. "The main fuel to speed our progress is our stock of knowledge, and the brake is our lack of imagination," Simon wrote. "The ultimate resource is people—skilled, spirited, and hopeful people who will exert their wills and imaginations for their own benefit, and so, inevitably, for the benefit of us all."

Simon and his ilk owe their success to this: they have been right so far. The world has behaved as they predicted. India hasn't starved. Food is cheap. But Malthus never goes away. The idea that we might grow too big can be disproved only for the moment—never for good. We might always be on the threshold of a special time, when the mechanisms described by Boserup and Simon stop working. It is true that Malthus was wrong when the population doubled from 750 million to 1.5 billion. It is true that Malthus was wrong when the population doubled from 1.5 billion to three billion. It is true that Malthus was wrong when the population doubled from three billion to six billion. Will Malthus still be wrong fifty years from now?

LOOKING AT LIMITS

The case that the next doubling, the one we're now experiencing, might be the difficult one can begin as readily with the Stanford biologist Peter Vitousek as with anyone else. In 1986 Vitousek decided to calculate how much of the earth's "primary productivity" went to support human beings. He added together the grain we ate, the corn we fed our cows, and the forests we cut for timber and paper; he added the losses in food as we overgrazed grassland and turned it into desert. And when he was finished adding, the number he came up with was 38.8 percent. We use 38.8 percent of everything the world's plants don't need to keep themselves alive; directly or indirectly, we consume 38.8 percent of what it is possible to eat. "That's a relatively large number," Vitousek says. "It should give pause to people who think we are far from any limits." Though he never drops the measured tone of an academic, Vitousek speaks with considerable emphasis: "There's a sense among some economists that we're *so* far from any biophysical limits. I think that's not supported by the evidence."

For another antidote to the good cheer of someone like Julian Simon, sit down with the Cornell biologist David Pimentel. He believes that we're in big trouble. Odd facts stud his conversation—for example, a nice head of iceberg lettuce is 95 percent water and contains just fifty calories of energy, but it takes 400 calories of energy to grow that head of lettuce in California's Central Valley, and another 1,800 to ship it east. ("There's practically no nutrition in the damn stuff anyway," Pimentel says. "Cabbage is a lot better, and we can grow it in upstate New York.") Pimentel has devoted the past three decades to tracking the planet's capacity, and he believes that we're already too crowded—that the earth can support only two billion people over the long run at a middle-class standard of living, and that trying to support more is doing great damage. He has spent considerable time studying soil erosion, for instance. Every raindrop that hits exposed ground is like a small explosion, launching soil particles into the air. On a slope, more than half of the soil contained in those splashes is carried downhill. If crop residue—cornstalks, say—is left in the field after harvest, it helps to shield the soil: the raindrop doesn't hit as hard. But in the developing world, where firewood is scarce, peasants burn those cornstalks for cooking fuel. About 60 percent of crop residues in China and 90 percent in Bangladesh are removed and burned, Pimentel says. When planting season comes, dry soils simply blow away. "Our measuring stations pick up Chinese soil in the Hawaiian air when ploughing time comes," he says. "Every year in Florida we pick up African soils in the wind when they start to plough."

The very things that made the Green Revolution so stunning—that made the last doubling possible—now cause trouble. Irrigation ditches, for instance, water 17 percent of all arable land and help to produce a third of all crops. But when flooded soils are baked by the sun, the water evaporates and the minerals in the irrigation water are deposited on the land. A hectare (2.47 acres) can accumulate two to five tons of salt annually, and eventually plants won't grow there. Maybe 10 percent of all irrigated land is affected.

Or think about fresh water for human use. Plenty of rain falls on the earth's surface, but most of it evaporates or roars down to the ocean in spring floods. According to Sandra Postel, the director of the Global Water Policy Project, we're left with about 12,500 cubic kilometers of accessible runoff, which would be enough for current demand except that it's not very well distributed around the globe. And we're not exactly conservationists—we use nearly seven times as much water as we used in 1900. Already 20 percent of the world's population lacks access to potable water, and fights over water divide many regions. Already the Colorado River usually dries out in the desert before it reaches the Sea of Cortez, making what the mid-century conservationist Aldo Leopold called a "milk and honey wilderness" into some of the nastiest country in North America. Already the Yellow River can run dry for as much as a third of the year. Already only two percent of the Nile's freshwater flow makes it to the ocean. And we need more water all the time. Producing a ton of grain consumes a thousand tons of water—that's how much the wheat plant breathes out as it grows. "We estimated that biotechnology might cut the amount of water a plant uses by ten percent," Pimentel says. "But plant physiologists tell us that's optimistic—they remind us that water's a pretty important part of photosynthesis. Maybe we can get five percent."...

I said earlier that food production grew even faster than population after the Second World War. Year after year the yield of wheat and corn

and rice rocketed up about three percent annually. It's a favorite statistic of the eternal optimists. In Julian Simon's book *The Ultimate Resource* (1981) charts show just how fast the growth was, and how it continually cut the cost of food. Simon wrote, "The obvious implication of this historical trend toward cheaper food—a trend that probably extends back to the beginning of agriculture—is that real prices for food will continue to drop.... It is a fact that portends more drops in price and even less scarcity in the future."

A few years after Simon's book was published, however, the data curve began to change. That rocketing growth in grain production ceased; now the gains were coming in tiny increments, too small to keep pace with population growth. The world reaped its largest harvest of grain per capita in 1984; since then the amount of corn and wheat and rice per person has fallen by six percent. Grain stockpiles have shrunk to less than two months' supply.

No one knows quite why. The collapse of the Soviet Union contributed to the trend—cooperative farms suddenly found the fertilizer supply shut off and spare parts for the tractor hard to come by. But there were other causes, too, all around the world—the salinization of irrigated fields, the erosion of topsoil, the conversion of prime farmland into residential areas, and all the other things that environmentalists had been warning about for years. It's possible that we'll still turn production around and start it rocketing again. Charles C. Mann, writing in *Science,* quotes experts who believe that in the future a "gigantic, multi-year, multi-billion-dollar scientific effort, a kind of agricultural 'person-on-the-moon project,'" might do the trick. The next great hope of the optimists is genetic engineering, and scientists have indeed managed to induce resistance to pests and disease in some plants. To get more yield, though, a cornstalk must be made to put out another ear, and conventional breeding may have exhausted the possibilities. There's a sense that we're running into walls.

We won't start producing *less* food. Wheat is not like oil, whose flow from the spigot will simply slow to a trickle one day. But we may be getting to the point where gains will be small and hard to come by. The spectacular increases may be behind us. One researcher told Mann, "Producing higher yields will no longer be like unveiling a new model of a car. We won't be pulling off the sheet and there it is, a two-fold yield increase." Instead the process will be "incremental, torturous, and slow." And there are five billion more of us to come.

So far we're still fed; gas is cheap at the pump; the supermarket grows ever larger. We've been warned again and again about approaching limits, and we've never quite reached them. So maybe—how tempting to believe it!—they don't really exist. For every Paul Ehrlich there's a man like Lawrence Summers, the former World Bank chief economist and current deputy secretary of the Treasury, who writes, "There are no...limits to carrying capacity of the Earth that are likely to bind at any time in the foreseeable future." And we are talking about the future—nothing can be *proved*.

But we can calculate risks, figure the odds that each side may be right. Joel Cohen made the most thorough attempt to do so in *How Many People Can the Earth Support?* Cohen collected and examined every estimate of carrying capacity made in recent decades, from that of a Harvard oceanographer who thought in 1976 that we might have food enough for 40 billion people to that of a Brown University researcher who calculated in 1991 that we might be able to sustain 5.9 billion (our present population), but only if we were principally vegetarians. One study proposed that if photosynthesis was the limiting factor, the earth might support a trillion people; an Australian economist proved, in calculations a decade apart, that we could manage populations of 28 billion and 157 billion. None of the studies is wise enough to examine every variable, to reach by itself the "right" number. When Cohen compared the dozens of studies, however, he uncovered something pretty interesting: the median low value for the planet's carrying capacity was 7.7 billion people, and the median high value was 12 billion. That, of course, is just the range that the UN predicts we will inhabit by the middle of the next century. Cohen wrote,

> The human population of the Earth now travels in the zone where a substantial fraction of scholars have estimated upper limits on human population size.... The possibility must be considered seriously

that the number of people on the Earth has reached, or will reach within half a century, the maximum number the Earth can support in modes of life that we and our children and their children will choose to want.

EARTH2

Throughout the 10,000 years of recorded human history the planet—the physical planet—has been a stable place. In every single year of those 10,000 there have been earthquakes, volcanoes, hurricanes, cyclones, typhoons, floods, forest fires, sandstorms, hailstorms, plagues, crop failures, heat waves, cold spells, blizzards, and droughts. But these have never shaken the basic predictability of the planet as a whole. Some of the earth's land areas—the Mediterranean rim, for instance—have been deforested beyond recovery, but so far these shifts have always been local.

Among other things, this stability has made possible the insurance industry—has underwritten the underwriters. Insurers can analyze the risk in any venture because they know the ground rules. If you want to build a house on the coast of Florida, they can calculate with reasonable accuracy the chance that it will be hit by a hurricane and the speed of the winds circling that hurricane's eye. If they couldn't, they would have no way to set your premium—they'd just be gambling. They're always gambling a little, of course: they don't know if that hurricane is coming next year or next century. But the earth's physical stability is the house edge in this casino. As Julian Simon pointed out, "A prediction based on past data can be sound if it is sensible to assume that the past and the future belong to the same statistical universe."

So what does it mean that alone among the earth's great pools of money and power, insurance companies are beginning to take the idea of global climate change quite seriously? What does it mean that the payout for weather-related damage climbed from $16 billion during the entire 1980s to $48 billion in the years 1990–1994? What does it mean that top European insurance executives have begun consulting with Greenpeace about global warming? What does it mean that the insurance giant Swiss Re, which paid out $291.5 million in the wake of Hurricane Andrew, ran an ad in the *Financial Times* showing its corporate logo bent sideways by a storm?

These things mean, I think, that the possibility that we live on a new earth cannot be discounted entirely as a fever dream. Above, I showed attempts to calculate carrying capacity for the world as we have always known it, the world we were born into. But what if, all of a sudden, we live on some other planet? On Earth2?

In 1955 Princeton University held an international symposium on "Man's Role in Changing the Face of the Earth." By this time anthropogenic carbon, sulfur, and nitrogen were pouring into the atmosphere, deforestation was already widespread, and the population was nearing three billion. Still, by comparison with the present, we remained a puny race. Cars were as yet novelties in many places. Tropical forests were still intact, as were much of the ancient woods of the West Coast, Canada, and Siberia. The world's economy was a quarter its present size. By most calculations we have used more natural resources since 1955 than in all of human history to that time.

Another symposium was organized in 1987 by Clark University, in Massachusetts. This time even the title made clear what was happening—not "Man and Nature," not "Man's Role in Changing the Face of the Earth," but "The Earth as Transformed by Human Actions." Attendees were no longer talking about local changes or what would take place in the future. "In our judgment," they said, "the biosphere has accumulated, or is on its way to accumulating, such a magnitude and variety of changes that it may be said to have been transformed."

Many of these changes come from a direction that Malthus didn't consider. He and most of his successors were transfixed by *sources*—by figuring out whether and how we could find enough trees or corn or oil. We're good at finding more stuff, as the price rises, we look harder. The lights never did go out, despite many predictions to the contrary on the first Earth Day. We found more oil, and we still have lots and lots of coal. Meanwhile, we're driving big cars again, and why not? As of this writing, the price of gas has dropped below a dollar a gallon across much of the nation. Who can believe in limits while driving

a Suburban? But perhaps, like an audience watching a magician wave his wand, we've been distracted from the real story.

That real story was told in the most recent attempt to calculate our size—a special section in *Science* published last summer. The authors spoke bluntly in the lead article. Forget man "transforming" nature—we live, they concluded, on "a human-dominated planet," where "no ecosystem on Earth's surface is free of pervasive human influence." It's not that we're running out of stuff. What we're running out of is what the scientists call "sinks"—places to put the by-products of our large appetites. Not garbage dumps (we could go on using Pampers till the end of time and still have empty space left to toss them away) but the atmospheric equivalent of garbage dumps.

It wasn't hard to figure out that there were limits on how much coal smoke we could pour into the air of a single city. It took a while longer to figure out that building ever higher smokestacks merely lofted the haze farther afield, raining down acid on whatever mountain range lay to the east. Even that, however, we are slowly fixing, with scrubbers and different mixtures of fuel. We can't so easily repair the new kinds of pollution. These do not come from something going wrong—some engine without a catalytic converter, some waste-water pipe without a filter, some smokestack without a scrubber. New kinds of pollution come instead from things going as they're supposed to go—but at such a high volume that they overwhelm the planet. They come from normal human life—but there are so many of us living those normal lives that something abnormal is happening. And that something is so different from the old forms of pollution that it confuses the issue even to use the word.

Consider nitrogen, for instance. Almost 80 percent of the atmosphere is nitrogen gas. But before plants can absorb it, it must become "fixed"—bonded with carbon, hydrogen, or oxygen. Nature does this trick with certain kinds of algae and soil bacteria, and with lightning. Before human beings began to alter the nitrogen cycle, these mechanisms provided 90–150 million metric tons of nitrogen a year. Now human activity adds 130–150 million more tons. Nitrogen isn't pollution—it's essential. And we are using more of it all the time. Half the industrial nitrogen fertilizer used in human history has been applied since 1984. As a result, coastal waters and estuaries bloom with toxic algae while oxygen concentrations dwindle, killing fish; as a result, nitrous oxide traps solar heat. And once the gas is in the air, it stays there for a century or more.

Or consider methane, which comes out of the back of a cow or the top of a termite mound or the bottom of a rice paddy. As a result of our determination to raise more cattle, cut down more tropical forest (thereby causing termite populations to explode), and grow more rice, methane concentrations in the atmosphere are more than twice as high as they have been for most of the past 160,000 years. And methane traps heat—very efficiently.

Or consider carbon dioxide. In fact, concentrate on carbon dioxide. If we had to pick one problem to obsess about over the next fifty years, we'd do well to make it CO_2—which is not pollution either. Carbon *monoxide* is pollution: it kills you if you breathe enough of it. But carbon *dioxide*, carbon with two oxygen atoms, can't do a blessed thing to you. If you're reading this indoors, you're breathing more CO_2 than you'll ever get outside. For generations, in fact, engineers said that an engine burned clean if it produced only water vapor and carbon dioxide.

Here's the catch: that engine produces a *lot* of CO_2. A gallon of gas weighs about eight pounds. When it's burned in a car, about five and a half pounds of carbon, in the form of carbon dioxide, come spewing out the back. It doesn't matter if the car is a 1958 Chevy or a 1998 Saab. And no filter can reduce that flow—it's an inevitable by-product of fossil-fuel combustion, which is why CO_2 has been piling up in the atmosphere ever since the Industrial Revolution. Before we started burning oil and coal and gas, the atmosphere contained about 280 parts CO_2 per million. Now the figure is about 360. Unless we do everything we can think of to eliminate fossil fuels from our diet, the air will test out at more than 500 parts per million fifty or sixty years from now, whether it's sampled in the South Bronx or at the South Pole.

This matters because, as we all know by now, the molecular structure of this clean, natural, common element that we are adding to every cubic foot of the atmosphere surrounding us traps heat that would otherwise radiate back out to space. Far more than even methane and nitrous oxide, CO_2 causes global warming—the greenhouse effect—and climate change. Far more than any other single factor, it is turning the earth we were born on into a new planet.

Remember, this is not pollution as we have known it. In the spring of last year the Environmental Protection Agency issued its "Ten-Year Air Quality and Emissions Trends" report. Carbon monoxide was down by 37 percent since 1986, lead was down by 78 percent, and particulate matter had dropped by nearly a quarter. If you lived in the San Fernando Valley, you saw the mountains more often than you had a decade before. The air was *cleaner,* but it was also *different*—richer with CO_2. And its new composition may change almost everything.

Ten years ago I wrote a book called *The End of Nature,* which was the first volume for a general audience about carbon dioxide and climate change, an early attempt to show that human beings now dominate the earth. Even then global warming was only a hypothesis—strong and gaining credibility all the time, but a hypothesis nonetheless. By the late 1990s it has become a fact. For ten years, with heavy funding from governments around the world, scientists launched satellites, monitored weather balloons, studied clouds. Their work culminated in a long-awaited report from the UN's Intergovernmental Panel on Climate Change, released in the fall of 1995. The panel's 2,000 scientists, from every corner of the globe, summed up their findings in this dry but historic bit of understatement: "The balance of evidence suggests that there is a discernible human influence on global climate." That is to say, we are heating up the planet—substantially. If we don't reduce emissions of carbon dioxide and other gases, the panel warned, temperatures will probably rise 3.6° Fahrenheit by 2100, and perhaps as much as 6.3°.

You may think you've already heard a lot about global warming. But most of our sense of the problem is behind the curve. Here's the current news: the changes are already well under way. When politicians and businessmen talk about "future risks," their rhetoric is outdated. This is not a problem for the distant future, or even for the near future. The planet has already heated up by a degree or more. We are perhaps a quarter of the way into the greenhouse era, and the effects are already being felt. From a new heaven, filled with nitrogen, methane, and carbon, a new earth is being born. If some alien astronomer is watching us, she's doubtless puzzled. This is the most obvious effect of our numbers and our appetites, and the key to understanding why the size of our population suddenly poses such a risk.

STORMY AND WARM

What does this new world feel like? For one thing, it's stormier than the old one. Data analyzed last year by Thomas Karl, of the National Oceanic and Atmospheric Administration, showed that total winter precipitation in the United States had increased by 10 percent since 1900 and that "extreme precipitation events"—rainstorms that dumped more than two inches of water in twenty-four hours and blizzards—had increased by 20 percent. That's because warmer air holds more water vapor than the colder atmosphere of the old earth; more water evaporates from the ocean, meaning more clouds, more rain, more snow. Engineers designing storm sewers, bridges, and culverts used to plan for what they called the "hundred-year storm." That is, they built to withstand the worst flooding or wind that history led them to expect in the course of a century. Since that history no longer applies, Karl says, "there isn't really a hundred-year event anymore . . . we seem to be getting these storms of the century every couple of years." When Grand Forks, North Dakota, disappeared beneath the Red River in the spring of last year, some meteorologists referred to it as "a 500-year flood"—meaning, essentially, that all bets are off. Meaning that these aren't acts of God. "If you look out your window, part of what you see in terms of the weather is produced by ourselves," Karl says. "If you look out the window fifty years from now, we're going to be responsible for more of it."

Twenty percent more bad storms, 10 percent more winter precipitation—these are enormous numbers. It's like opening the newspaper to read that the average American is smarter by 30 IQ points. And the same data showed increases in drought, too. With more water in the atmosphere, there's less in the soil, according to Kevin Trenberth, of the National Center for Atmospheric Research. Those parts of the continent that are normally dry—the eastern sides of mountains, the plains and deserts—are even drier, as the higher average temperatures evaporate more of what rain does fall. "You get wilting plants and eventually drought faster than you would otherwise," Trenberth says. And when the rain does come, it's often so intense that much of it runs off before it can soak into the soil.

So—wetter and drier. *Different.*

In 1958 Charles Keeling, of the Scripps Institution of Oceanography, set up the world's single most significant scientific instrument in a small hut on the slope of Hawaii's Mauna Loa volcano. Forty years later it continues without fail to track the amount of carbon dioxide in the atmosphere. The graphs that it produces show that this most important greenhouse gas has steadily increased for forty years. That's the main news.

It has also shown something else of interest in recent years—a sign that this new atmosphere is changing the planet. Every year CO_2 levels dip in the spring, when plants across the Northern Hemisphere begin to grow, soaking up carbon dioxide. And every year in the fall decaying plants and soils release CO_2 back into the atmosphere. So along with the steady upward trend, there's an annual seesaw, an oscillation that is suddenly growing more pronounced. The size of that yearly tooth on the graph is 20 percent greater than it was in the early 1960s, as Keeling reported in the journal *Nature,* in July of 1996. Or, in the words of Rhys Roth, writing in a newsletter of the Atmosphere Alliance, the earth is "breathing deeper." More vegetation must be growing, stimulated by higher temperatures. And the earth is breathing earlier, too. Spring is starting about a week earlier in the 1990s than it was in the 1970s, Keeling said. . . .

[It's] not clear that the grain belt will have the water it needs as the climate warms. In

1988, a summer of record heat across the rain belt, harvests plummeted, because the very heat that produces more storms also causes extra evaporation. What *is* clear is that fundamental shifts are under way in the operation of the planet. And we are very early yet in the greenhouse era.

The changes are basic. The freezing level in the atmosphere—the height at which the air temperature reaches 32°F—has been gaining altitude since 1970 at the rate of nearly fifteen feet a year. Not surprisingly, tropical and subtropical glaciers are melting at what a team of Ohio State researchers termed "striking" rates. Speaking at a press conference last spring, Ellen Mosley-Thompson, a member of the Ohio State team, was asked if she was sure of her results. She replied, "I don't know quite what to say. I've presented the evidence. I gave you the example of the Quelccaya ice cap. It just comes back to the compilation of what's happening at high elevations: the Lewis glacier on Mount Kenya has lost forty percent of its mass; in the Ruwenzori range all the glaciers are in massive retreat. Everything, virtually, in Patagonia, except for just a few glaciers, is retreating. . . . We've seen . . . that plants we moving up the mountains. . . . I frankly don't know what additional evidence you need."

As the glaciers retreat, a crucial source of fresh water in many tropical countries disappears. These areas are "already water-stressed," Mosley-Thompson told the Association of American Geographers last year. Now they may be really desperate.

As with the tropics, so with the poles. According to every computer model, in fact, the polar effects are even more pronounced, because the Arctic and the Antarctic will warm much faster than the Equator as carbon dioxide builds up. Scientists manning a research station at Toolik Lake, Alaska, 170 miles north of the Arctic Circle, have watched average summer temperatures rise by about seven degrees in the past two decades. "Those who remember wearing down-lined summer parkas in the 1970s—before the term 'global warming' existed—have peeled down to T-shirts in recent summers," according to the reporter Wendy Hower, writing in the *Fairbanks Daily News-Miner*. It rained briefly at the American base in McMurdo Sound, in Antarctica, during the southern summer of 1997—as strange as if it had snowed in Saudi Arabia. None of this necessarily means that the ice caps will soon slide into the sea, turning Tennessee into beachfront. It simply demonstrates a radical instability in places that have been stable for many thousands of years. One researcher watched as emperor penguins tried to cope with the early breakup of ice: their chicks had to jump into the water two weeks ahead of schedule, probably guaranteeing an early death. They (like us) evolved on the old earth. . . .

The effects of that warming can be found in the largest phenomena. The oceans that cover most of the planet's surface are clearly rising, both because of melting glaciers and because water expands as it warms. As a result, low-lying Pacific islands already report surges of water washing across the atolls. "It's nice weather and all of a sudden water is pouring into your living room," one Marshall Islands resident told a newspaper reporter. "It's very clear that something is happening in the Pacific, and these islands are feeling it." Global warming will be like a much more powerful version of El Niño that covers the entire globe and lasts forever, or at least until the next big asteroid strikes.

If you want to scare yourself with guesses about what might happen in the near future, there's no shortage of possibilities. Scientists have already observed large-scale shifts in the duration of the El Niño ocean warming, for instance. The Arctic tundra has warmed so much that in some places it now gives off more carbon dioxide than it absorbs—a switch that could trigger a potent feedback loop, making warming ever worse. And researchers studying glacial cores from the Greenland Ice Sheet recently concluded that local climate shifts have occurred with incredible rapidity in the past— 18° in one three-year stretch. Other scientists worry that such a shift might be enough to flood the oceans with fresh water and reroute or shut off currents like the Gulf Stream and the North Atlantic, which keep Europe far warmer than it would otherwise be. . . . In the words of Wallace Broecker, of Columbia University, a pioneer in the field, "Climate is an angry beast, and we are poking it with sticks."

But we don't need worst-case scenarios: best-case scenarios make the point. The population of the earth is going to nearly double one more time. That will bring it to a level that even the reliable old earth we were born on would be hard-pressed to support. Just at the moment when we need everything to be working as smoothly as possible, we find ourselves inhabiting a new planet, whose carrying capacity we cannot conceivably estimate. We have no idea how much wheat this planet can grow. We don't know what its politics will be like: not if there are going to be heat waves like the one that killed more than 700 Chicagoans in 1995; not if rising sea levels and other effects of climate change create tens of millions of environmental refugees; not if a 1.5° jump in India's temperature could reduce the country's wheat crop by 10 percent or divert its monsoons....

We have gotten very large and very powerful, and for the foreseeable future we're stuck with the results. The glaciers won't grow back again anytime soon; the oceans won't drop. We've already done deep and systemic damage. To use a human analogy, we've already said the angry and unforgivable words that will haunt our marriage till its end. And yet we can't simply walk out the door. There's no place to go. We have to salvage what we can of our relationship with the earth, to keep things from getting any worse than they have to be.

If we can bring our various emissions quickly and sharply under control, we *can* limit the damage, reduce dramatically the chance of horrible surprises, preserve more of the biology we were born into. But do not underestimate the task. The UN's Intergovernmental Panel on Climate Change projects that an immediate 60 percent reduction in fossil-fuel use is necessary just to stabilize climate at the current level of disruption. Nature may still meet us halfway, but halfway is a long way from where we are now. What's more, we can't delay. If we wait a few decades to get started, we may as well not even begin. It's not like poverty, a concern that's always there for civilizations to address. This is a timed test, like the SAT: two or three decades, and we lay our pencils down. It's *the* test for our generations, and population is a part of the answer....

STUDY QUESTIONS

1. Explain why McKibben thinks we live in a special moment of history. Do you find his arguments cogent and convincing?
2. Doomsdayers have been wrong before in their prediction that the sky is falling. How does McKibben respond to this charge that he and others, like Paul Ehrlich, are unduly pessimistic?
3. What evidence does McKibben bring to bear on the global warming thesis—that humans are responsible for the greenhouse effect, which is having dramatic effects on Earth's climate? How serious is the greenhouse effect?

45   The Tragedy of the Commons

GARRETT HARDIN

Garrett Hardin argues that some social problems have no *technical*—that is, scientific or technological—solution, but must be addressed by moral and political means. Exponential population growth is one such problem. Hardin calls our attention to a study by the British mathematician William Forster Lloyd (1794–1852), which demonstrates that in nonregulated areas (the "commons") individual rationality and self-interest leads to disaster. Hardin applies Lloyd's study to human population growth and argues that voluntary restriction of population by families is not adequate to deal with this problem, since many will not respond to voluntary procreation limitations. We must have "mutual coercion, mutually agreed upon by the majority of the people affected."

A biographical sketch on Garrett Hardin is included within Reading 41.

At the end of a thoughtful article on the future of nuclear war, Wiesner and York[1] concluded that: "Both sides in the arms race are ... confronted by the dilemma of steadily increasing military power and steadily decreasing national security. *It is our considered professional judgment that this dilemma has no technical solution.* If the great powers continue to look for solutions in the area of science and technology only, the result will be to worsen the situation."

I would like to focus your attention not on the subject of the article (national security in a nuclear world) but on the kind of conclusion they reached, namely that there is no technical solution to the problem. An implicit and almost universal assumption of discussions published in professional and semi-popular scientific journals is that the problem under discussion has a technical solution. A technical solution may be defined as one that requires a change only in the techniques of the natural sciences, demanding little or nothing in the way of change in human values or ideas of morality.

In our day (though not in earlier times) technical solutions are always welcome. Because of previous failures in prophecy, it takes courage to assert that a desired technical solution is not possible. Wiesner and York exhibited this courage; publishing in a science journal, they insisted that the solution to the problem was not to be found in the natural sciences. They cautiously qualified their statement with the phrase, "It is our considered professional judgment...." Whether they were right or not is not the concern of the present article. Rather, the concern here is with the important concept of a class of human problems which can be called "no technical solution problems," and, more specifically, with the identification and discussion of one of these.

It is easy to show that the class is not a null class. Recall the game of tick-tack-toe. Consider the problem, "How can I win the game of tick-tack-toe?" It is well known that I cannot, if I assume (in keeping with the conventions of game theory) that my opponent understands the game perfectly. Put another way, there is no "technical solution" to the problem. I can win only by giving a radical meaning to the word "win." I can hit my opponent over the head; or I can drug him; or I can falsify the records. Every way in which I "win" involves, in some sense, an abandonment of the game, as we intuitively understand it. (I can also, of course, openly abandon the game— refuse to play it. This is what most adults do.)

The class of "No technical solution problems" has members. My thesis is that the "population problem," as conventionally conceived, is a member of this class. How it is conventionally conceived needs some comment. It is fair to say that most people who anguish over the population problem are trying to find a way to avoid the evils of overpopulation without relinquishing any of the privileges they now enjoy. They think that farming the seas or developing new strains of wheat will solve the problem—technologically. I try to show here that the solution they seek cannot be found. The population problem cannot be solved in a technical way, any more than can the problem of winning the game of tick-tack-toe.

WHAT SHALL WE MAXIMIZE?

Population, as Malthus said, naturally tends to grow "geometrically," or, as we would now say, exponentially. In a finite world this means that the per capita share of the world's goods must steadily decrease. Is ours a finite world?

A fair defense can be put forward for the view that the world is infinite; or that we do not know that it is not. But, in terms of the practical problems that we must face in the next few generations with the foreseeable technology, it is clear that we will greatly increase human misery if we do not, during the immediate future, assume that the world available to the terrestrial human population is finite. "Space" is no escape.[2]

A finite world can support only a finite population; therefore, population growth must eventually equal zero. (The case of perpetual wide fluctuations above and below zero is a trivial variant that need not be discussed.) When this condition is met, what will be the situation of mankind? Specifically, can Bentham's goal of "the greatest good for the greatest number" be realized?

No—for two reasons, each sufficient by itself. The first is a theoretical one. It is not mathematically possible to maximize for two (or more) variables at the same time. This was clearly stated by von Neumann and Morgenstern,[3] but the principle is implicit in the theory of partial differential equations, dating back at least to D'Alembert (1717–1783).

The second reason springs directly from biological facts. To live, any organism must have a source of energy (for example, food). This energy is utilized for two purposes: mere maintenance and work. For man, maintenance of life requires about 1600 kilocalories a day ("maintenance calories"). Anything that he does over and above merely staying alive will be defined as work, and is supported by "work calories" which he takes in. Work calories are used not only for what we call work in common speech; they are also required for all forms of enjoyment, from swimming and automobile racing to playing music and writing poetry. If our goal is to maximize population it is obvious what we must do: We must make the work calories per person approach as close to zero as possible. No gourmet meals, no vacations, no sports, no music, no literature, no art.... I think that everyone will grant, without argument or proof, that maximizing population does not maximize goods. Bentham's goal is impossible.

In reaching this conclusion I have made the usual assumption that it is the acquisition of energy that is the problem. The appearance of atomic energy has led some to question this assumption. However, given an infinite source of energy, population growth still produces an inescapable problem. The problem of the acquisition of energy is replaced by the problem of its dissipation, as J. H. Fremlin has so wittily shown.[4] The arithmetic signs in the analysis are, as it were, reversed; but Bentham's goal is still unobtainable.

The optimum population is, then, less than the maximum. The difficulty of defining the optimum is enormous; so far as I know, no one has seriously tackled this problem. Reaching an acceptable and stable solution will surely require more than one generation of hard analytical work—and much persuasion.

We want the maximum good per person; but what is good? To one person it is wilderness, to another it is ski lodges for thousands. To one it is estuaries to nourish ducks for hunters to shoot; to another it is factory land. Comparing one good with another is, we usually say, impossible because goods are incommensurable. Incommensurables cannot be compared.

Theoretically this may be true; but in real life incommensurables *are* commensurable. Only a criterion of judgment and a system of weighting are needed. In nature the criterion is survival. Is it better for a species to be small and hideable, or large and powerful? Natural selection commensurates the incommensurables. The compromise achieved depends on a natural weighting of the values of the variables.

Man must imitate this process. There is no doubt that in fact he already does, but unconsciously. It is when the hidden decisions are made explicit that the arguments begin. The problem for the years ahead is to work out an acceptable theory of weighting. Synergistic effects, non-linear variation, and difficulties in discounting the future make the intellectual problem difficult, but not (in principle) insoluble.

Has any cultural group solved this practical problem at the present time, even on an intuitive level? One simple fact proves that none has: there is no prosperous population in the world today that has, and has had for some time, a growth rate of zero. Any people that has intuitively identified its optimum point will soon reach it, after which its growth rate becomes and remains zero.

Of course, a positive growth rate might be taken as evidence that a population is below its optimum. However, by any reasonable standards, the most rapidly growing populations on earth today are (in general) the most miserable. This association (which need not be invariable) casts doubt on the optimistic assumption that the positive growth rate of a population is evidence that it has yet to reach its optimum.

We can make little progress in working toward optimum population size until we explicitly exorcize the spirit of Adam Smith in the field of practical demography. In economic affairs, *The Wealth of Nations* (1776) popularized the "invisible hand," the idea that an individual who "intends only his own gain," is, as it were, "led by an invisible hand to promote...the public interest."[5] Adam Smith did not assert that this was invariably true, and perhaps neither did any of his followers. But he contributed to a dominant tendency of thought that has ever since interfered with positive action based on rational analysis, namely, the tendency to assume that decisions reached individually will, in fact, be the best decisions for an entire society. If this assumption is correct it justifies the continuance of our present policy of laissez-faire in reproduction. If it is correct we can assume that men will control their individual fecundity so as to produce the optimum population. If the assumption is not correct, we need to reexamine our individual freedoms to see which ones are defensible.

TRAGEDY OF FREEDOM IN A COMMONS

The rebuttal to the invisible hand in population control is to be found in a scenario first sketched in a little-known pamphlet[6] in 1833 by a mathematical amateur named William Forster Lloyd (1794–1852). We may well call it "the tragedy of the commons," using the word "tragedy" as the philosopher Whitehead used it:[7] "The essence of dramatic tragedy is not unhappiness. It resides in the solemnity of the remorseless working of things." He then goes on to say, "This inevitableness of destiny can only be illustrated in terms of human life by incidents which in fact involve unhappiness. For it is only by them that the futility of escape can be made evident in the drama."

The tragedy of the commons develops in this way. Picture a pasture open to all. It is to be expected that each herdsman will try to keep as many cattle as possible on the commons. Such an arrangement may work reasonably satisfactorily for centuries because tribal wars, poaching, and disease keep the numbers of both man and beast well below the carrying capacity of the land. Finally, however, comes the day of reckoning, that is, the day when the long-desired goal of social stability becomes a reality. At this point, the inherent logic of the commons remorselessly generates tragedy.

As a rational being, each herdsman seeks to maximize his gain. Explicitly or implicitly, more or less consciously, he asks, "What is the utility *to me* of adding one more animal to my herd?" This utility has one negative and one positive component.

1. The positive component is a function of the increment of one animal. Since the herdsman receives all the proceeds from the sale of the additional animal, the positive utility is nearly +1.
2. The negative component is a function of the additional overgrazing created by one or more animal. Since, however, the effects of overgrazing are shared by all the herdsmen, the negative utility for any particular decision-making herdsman is only a fraction of −1.

Adding together the component partial utilities, the rational herdsman concludes that the only sensible course for him to pursue is to add another animal to his herd. And another; and another....But this is the conclusion reached by each and every rational herdsman sharing a commons. Therein is the tragedy. Each man is locked into a system that compels him to increase his herd without limit—in a world that is limited. Ruin is the destination toward which all men rush, each pursuing his own best interest in a society that believes in the freedom of the commons. Freedom in a commons brings ruin to all.

Some would say that this is a platitude. Would that it were! In a sense, it was learned thousands of years ago, but natural selection favors the forces of psychological denial.[8] The individual benefits as an individual from his ability to deny the truth even though society as a whole, of which he is a part, suffers. Education can counteract the natural tendency to do the wrong thing, but the inexorable success of generations requires that the basis for this knowledge be constantly refreshed.

A simple incident that occurred a few years ago in Leominster, Massachusetts, shows how perishable the knowledge is. During the Christmas shopping season the parking meters downtown were covered with plastic bags that bore tags reading: "Do not open until after Christmas. Free parking courtesy of the mayor and city council." In other words, facing the prospect of an increased demand for already scarce space, the city fathers reinstituted the system of the commons. (Cynically, we suspect that they gained more votes than they lost by this retrogressive act.)

In an approximate way, the logic of the commons has been understood for a long time, perhaps since the discovery of agriculture or the invention of private property in real estate. But it is understood mostly only in special cases which are not sufficiently generalized. Even at this late date, cattlemen leasing national land on the western ranges demonstrate no more than an ambivalent understanding, in constantly pressuring federal authorities to increase the head count to the point where overgrazing produces erosion and weed-dominance. Likewise, the oceans of the world continue to suffer from the survival of the philosophy of the commons. Maritime nations still respond automatically to the shibboleth of the "freedom of the seas." Professing to believe in the "inexhaustible resources of the oceans," they bring species after species of fish and whales closer to extinction.[9]

The National Parks present another instance of the working out of the tragedy of the commons. At present they are open to all, without limit. The parks themselves are limited in extent—there is only one Yosemite Valley—whereas population seems to grow without limit. The values that visitors seek in the parks are steadily eroded. Plainly, we must soon cease to treat the parks as commons or they will be of no value to anyone.

What shall we do? We have several options. We might sell them off as private property. We might keep them as public property, but allocate the right to enter them. The allocation might be on the basis of wealth, by the use of an auction system. It might be on the basis of merit, as defined by some agreed-upon standards. It might be by lottery. Or it might be on a first-come, first-served basis, administered to long queues. These, I think, are all the reasonable possibilities. They are all objectionable. But we must choose—or acquiesce in the destruction of the commons that we call our National Parks.

POLLUTION

In a reverse way, the tragedy of the commons reappears in problems of pollution. Here it is not a question of taking something out of the commons, but of putting something in—sewage, or chemical, radioactive, and heat wastes into water; noxious and dangerous fumes into the air, and distracting and unpleasant advertising signs into the line of sight. The calculations of utility are much the same as before. The rational man finds that his share of the cost of the wastes he discharges into the commons is less than the cost of purifying his wastes before releasing them. Since this is true for everyone, we are locked into a system of "fouling our own nest," so long as we behave only as independent, rational, free-enterprisers.

The tragedy of the commons as a food basket is averted by private property, or something formally like it. But the air and waters surrounding us cannot readily be fenced, and so the tragedy of the commons as a cesspool must be prevented by different means, by coercive laws or taxing devices that make it cheaper for the polluter to treat his pollutants than to discharge them untreated. We have not progressed as far with the solution of this problem as we have with the first. Indeed, our particular concept of private property, which deters us from exhausting the positive resources of the earth, favors pollution. The owner of a factory on the bank of a stream—whose property extends to the middle of the stream—often has difficulty seeing why it is not his natural right to muddy the waters flowing past his door. The law, always behind the times, requires elaborate stitching and fitting to adapt it to this newly perceived aspect of the commons.

The pollution problem is a consequence of population. It did not much matter how a lonely

American frontiersman disposed of his waste. "Flowing water purifies itself every 10 miles," my grandfather used to say, and the myth was near enough to the truth when he was a boy, for there were not too many people. But as population became denser, the natural chemical and biological recycling processes became overloaded, calling for a redefinition of property rights.

HOW TO LEGISLATE TEMPERANCE?

Analysis of the pollution problem as a function of population density uncovers a not generally recognized principle of morality, namely: *the morality of an act is a function of the state of the system at the time it is performed.*[10] Using the commons as a cesspool does not harm the general public under frontier conditions, because there is no public; the same behavior in a metropolis is unbearable. A hundred and fifty years ago a plainsman could kill an American bison, cut out only the tongue for his dinner, and discard the rest of the animal. He was not in any important sense being wasteful. Today, with only a few thousand bison left, we would be appalled at such behavior.

In passing, it is worth noting that the morality of an act cannot be determined from a photograph. One does not know whether a man killing an elephant or setting fire to the grassland is harming others until one knows the total system in which his act appears. "One picture is worth a thousand words" said an ancient Chinese; but it may take 10,000 words to validate it. It is as tempting to ecologists as it is to reformers in general to try to persuade others by way of the photographic shortcut. But the essence of an argument cannot be photographed: it must be presented rationally—in words.

That morality is system-sensitive escaped the attention of most codifiers of ethics in the past. "Thou shalt not . . ." is the form of traditional ethical directives which make no allowance for particular circumstances. The laws of our society follow the pattern of ancient ethics, and therefore are poorly suited to governing a complex, crowded, changeable world. Our epicyclic solution is to augment statutory law with administrative law. Since it is practically impossible to spell out all the conditions under which it is safe to burn trash in the backyard or to run an automobile without smog-control, by law we delegate the details to bureaus. The result is administrative law, which is rightly feared for an ancient reason—*Quis custodiet ipsos custodes?*—"Who shall watch the watchers themselves?" John Adams said that we must have "a government of laws and not men." Bureau administrators, trying to evaluate the morality of acts in the total system, are singularly liable to corruption, producing a government by men, not laws.

Prohibition is easy to legislate (though not necessarily to enforce); but how do we legislate temperance? Experience indicates that it can be accomplished best through the mediation of administrative law. We limit possibilities unnecessarily if we suppose that the sentiment of *Quis custodiet* denies us the use of administrative law. We should rather retain the phrase as a perpetual reminder of fearful dangers we cannot avoid. The great challenge facing us now is to invent the corrective feedbacks that are needed to keep custodians honest. We must find ways to legitimate the needed authority of both the custodians and the corrective feedbacks.

FREEDOM TO BREED IS INTOLERABLE

The tragedy of the commons is involved in population problems in another way. In a world governed solely by the principle of "dog eat dog"—if indeed there ever was such a world—how many children a family had would not be a matter of public concern. Parents who bred too exuberantly would leave fewer descendants, not more, because they would be unable to care adequately for their children. David Lack and others have found that such a negative feedback demonstrably controls the fecundity of birds.[11] But men are not birds, and have not acted like them for millenniums, at least.

If each human family were dependent only on its own resources; *if* the children of improvident parents starved to death; *if,* thus, overbreeding brought its own "punishment" to the germ line—*then* there would be no public interest in controlling the breeding of families. But our society is deeply committed to the welfare state,[12] and hence is confronted with another aspect of the tragedy of the commons.

In a welfare state, how shall we deal with the family, the religion, the race, or the class (or indeed any distinguishable and cohesive group) that adopts overbreeding as a policy to secure its own aggrandizement?[13] To couple the concept of freedom to breed with the belief that everyone born has an equal right to the commons is to lock the world into a tragic course of action.

Unfortunately this is just the course of action that is being pursued by the United Nations. In late 1967, some 30 nations agreed to the following:[14]

> The Universal Declaration of Human Rights describes the family as the natural and fundamental unit of society. It follows that any choice and decision with regard to the size of the family must irrevocably rest with the family itself, and cannot be made by anyone else.

It is painful to have to deny categorically the validity of this right; denying it, one feels as uncomfortable as a resident of Salem, Massachusetts, who denied the reality of witches in the 17th century. At the present time, in liberal quarters, something like a taboo acts to inhibit criticism of the United Nations. There is a feeling that the United Nations is "our last and best hope," that we shouldn't find fault with it; we shouldn't play into the hands of the archconservatives. However, let us not forget what Robert Louis Stevenson said: "The truth that is suppressed by friends is the readiest weapon of the enemy." If we love the truth we must openly deny the validity of the Universal Declaration of Human Rights, even though it is promoted by the United Nations. We should also join with Kingsley Davis[15] in attempting to get Planned Parenthood–World Population to see the error of its ways in embracing the same tragic ideal.

CONSCIENCE IS SELF-ELIMINATING

It is a mistake to think that we can control the breeding of mankind in the long run by an appeal to conscience. Charles Galton Darwin made this point when he spoke on the centennial of the publication of his grandfather's great book. The argument is straightforward and Darwinian.

People vary. Confronted with appeals to limit breeding, some people will undoubtedly respond to the plea more than others. Those who have more children will produce a larger fraction of the next generation than those with more susceptible consciences. The difference will be accentuated, generation by generation.

In C. G. Darwin's words: "It may well be that it would take hundreds of generations for the progenitive instinct to develop in this way, but if it should do so, nature would have taken her revenge, and the variety *Homo contracipiens* would become extinct and would be replaced by the variety *Homo progenitivus*."[16]

The argument assumes that conscience or the desire for children (no matter which) is hereditary—but hereditary only in the most general formal sense. The result will be the same whether the attitude is transmitted through germ cells, or exosomatically, to use A. J. Lotka's term. (If one denies the latter possibility as well as the former, then what's the point of education?) The argument has here been stated in the context of the population problem, but it applies equally well to any instance in which society appeals to an individual exploiting a commons to restrain himself for the general good—by means of his conscience. To make such an appeal is to set up a selective system that works toward the elimination of conscience from the race.

PATHOGENIC EFFECTS OF CONSCIENCE

The long-term disadvantage of an appeal to conscience should be enough to condemn it; it has serious short-term disadvantages as well. If we ask a man who is exploiting a commons to desist "in the name of conscience," what are we saying to him? What does he hear?—not only at the moment but also in the wee small hours of the night when, half asleep, he remembers not merely the words we used but also the nonverbal communication cues we gave him unawares? Sooner or later, consciously or subconsciously, he senses that he has received two communications, and that they are contradictory: (i) (intended communication) "If you don't do as we ask, we will openly condemn you for not acting like a responsible citizen"; (ii) (the unintended communication) "If you *do* behave as we ask, we will secretly condemn you for a simpleton who can be shamed into standing aside while the rest of us exploit the commons."

Everyman then is caught in what Bateson has called a "double bind." Bateson and his co-workers have made a plausible case for viewing the double bind as an important causative factor in the genesis of schizophrenia.[17] The double bind may not always be so damaging, but it always endangers the mental health of anyone to whom it is applied. "A bad conscience," said Nietzsche, "is a kind of illness."

To conjure up a conscience in others is tempting to anyone who wishes to extend his control beyond the legal limits. Leaders at the highest level succumb to this temptation. Has any President during the past generation failed to call on labor unions to moderate voluntarily their demands for higher wages, or to steel companies to honor voluntary guidelines on prices? I can recall none. The rhetoric used on such occasions is designed to produce feelings of guilt in noncooperators.

For centuries it was assumed without proof that guilt was a valuable, perhaps even indispensable, ingredient of the civilized life. Now, in this post-Freudian world, we doubt it.

Paul Goodman speaks from the modern point of view when he says: "No good has ever come from feeling guilty, neither intelligence, policy, nor compassion. The guilty do not pay attention to the object but only to themselves, and not even to their own interests, which might make sense, but to their anxieties."[18]

One does not have to be a professional psychiatrist to see the consequences of anxiety. We in the Western world are just emerging from a dreadful two-centuries-long Dark Ages of Eros that was sustained partly by prohibition laws, but perhaps more effectively by the anxiety-generating mechanisms of education. Alex Comfort has told the story well in *The Anxiety Makers;*[19] it is not a pretty one.

Since proof is difficult, we may even concede that the results of anxiety may sometimes, from certain points of view, be desirable. The larger question we should ask is whether, as a matter of policy, we should ever encourage the use of a technique the tendency (if not the intention) of which is psychologically pathogenic. We hear much talk these days of responsible parenthood; the coupled words are incorporated into the titles of some organizations devoted to birth control. Some people have proposed massive propaganda campaigns to instill responsibility into the nation's (or the world's) breeders. But what is the meaning of the word responsibility in this context? Is it not merely a synonym for the word conscience? When we use the word responsibility in the absence of substantial sanctions are we not trying to browbeat a free man in a commons into acting against his own interest? Responsibility is a verbal counterfeit for a substantial *quid pro quo*. It is an attempt to get something for nothing.

If the word responsibility is to be used at all, I suggest that it be in the sense Charles Frankel uses it.[20] "Responsibility," says this philosopher, "is the product of definite social arrangements." Notice that Frankel calls for social arrangements—not propaganda.

MUTUAL COERCION MUTUALLY AGREED UPON

The social arrangements that produce responsibility are arrangements that create coercion, of some sort. Consider bank-robbing. The man who takes money from a bank acts as if the bank were a commons. How do we prevent such action? Certainly not by trying to control his behavior solely by a verbal appeal to his sense of responsibility. Rather than rely on propaganda we follow Frankel's lead and insist that a bank is not a commons; we seek the definite social arrangements that will keep it from becoming a commons. That we thereby infringe on the freedom of would-be robbers we neither deny nor regret.

The morality of bank-robbing is particularly easy to understand because we accept complete prohibition of this activity. We are willing to say "Thou shalt not rob banks," without providing for exceptions. But temperance also can be created by coercion. Taxing is a good coercive device. To keep downtown shoppers temperate in their use of parking space we introduce parking meters for short periods, and traffic fines for longer ones. We need not actually forbid a citizen to park as long as he wants to; we need merely make it increasingly expensive for him to do so. Not prohibition, but carefully biased options are what we offer him. A Madison Avenue man might call this persuasion; I prefer the greater candor of the word coercion.

Coercion is a dirty word to most liberals now, but it need not forever be so. As with the four-letter words, its dirtiness can be cleansed away by exposure to light, by saying it over and over without apology or embarrassment. To many, the word coercion implies arbitrary decisions of distant and irresponsible bureaucrats; but this is not a necessary part of its meaning. The only kind of coercion I recommend is mutual coercion, mutually agreed upon by the majority of the people affected.

To say that we mutually agree to coercion is not to say that we are required to enjoy it, or even to pretend we enjoy it. Who enjoys taxes? We all grumble about them. But we accept compulsory taxes because we recognize that voluntary taxes would favor the conscienceless. We institute and (grumblingly) support taxes and other coercive devices to escape the horror of the commons.

An alternative to the commons need not be perfectly just to be preferable. With real estate and other material goods, the alternative we have chosen is the institution of private property coupled with legal inheritance. Is this system perfectly just? As a genetically trained biologist I deny that it is. It seems to me that, if there are to be differences in individual inheritance, legal possession should be perfectly correlated with biological inheritance—that those who are biologically more fit to be the custodians of property and power should legally inherit more. But genetic recombination continually makes a mockery of the doctrine of "like father, like son" implicit in our laws of legal inheritance. An idiot can inherit millions, and a trust fund can keep his estate intact. We must admit that our legal system of private property plus inheritance is unjust—but we put up with it because we are not convinced, at the moment, that anyone has

invented a better system. The alternative of the commons is too horrifying to contemplate. Injustice is preferable to total ruin.

It is one of the peculiarities of the warfare between reform and the status quo that it is thoughtlessly governed by a double standard. Whenever a reform measure is proposed it is often defeated when its opponents triumphantly discover a flaw in it. As Kingsley Davis has pointed out,[21] worshippers of the status quo sometimes imply that no reform is possible without unanimous agreement, an implication contrary to historical fact. As nearly as I can make out, automatic rejection of proposed reforms is based on one of two unconscious assumptions: (i) that the status quo is perfect; or (ii) that the choice we face is between reform and no action; if the proposed reform is imperfect, we presumably should take no action at all, while we wait for a perfect proposal.

But we can never do nothing. That which we have done for thousands of years is also action. It also produces evils. Once we are aware that the status quo is action, we can then compare its discoverable advantages and disadvantages with the predicted advantages and disadvantages of the proposed reform, discounting as best we can for our lack of experience. On the basis of such a comparison, we can make a rational decision which will not involve the unworkable assumption that only perfect systems are tolerable.

RECOGNITION OF NECESSITY

Perhaps the simplest summary of this analysis of man's population problems is this: the commons, if justifiable at all, is justifiable only under conditions of low-population density. As the human population has increased, the commons has had to be abandoned in one aspect after another.

First we abandoned the commons in food gathering, enclosing farm land and restricting pastures and hunting and fishing areas. These restrictions are still not complete throughout the world.

Somewhat later we saw that the commons as a place for water disposal would also have to be abandoned. Restrictions on the disposal of domestic sewage are widely accepted in the Western world; we are still struggling to close the commons to pollution by automobiles, factories, insecticide sprayers, fertilizing operations, and atomic energy installations.

In a still more embryonic state is our recognition of the evils of the commons in matters of pleasure. There is almost no restriction on the propagation of sound waves in the public medium. The shopping public is assaulted with mindless music, without its consent. Our government is paying out billions of dollars to create supersonic transport which will disturb 50,000 people for every one person who is whisked from coast to coast 3 hours faster. Advertisers muddy the airwaves of radio and television and pollute the view of travelers. We are a long way from outlawing the commons in matters of pleasure. Is this because our Puritan inheritance makes us view pleasure as something of a sin, and pain (that is, the pollution of advertising) as the sign of virtue?

Every new enclosure of the commons involves the infringement of somebody's personal liberty. Infringements made in the distant past are accepted because no contemporary complains of a loss. It is the newly proposed infringements that we vigorously oppose; cries of "rights" and "freedom" fill the air. But what does "freedom" mean? When men mutually agreed to pass laws against robbing, mankind became more free, not less so. Individuals locked into the logic of the commons are free only to bring on universal ruin; once they see the necessity of mutual coercion, they become free to pursue other goals. I believe it was Hegel who said, "Freedom is the recognition of necessity."

The most important aspect of necessity that we must now recognize, is the necessity of abandoning the commons in breeding. No technical solution can rescue us from the misery of overpopulation. Freedom to breed will bring ruin to all. At the moment, to avoid hard decisions many of us are tempted to propagandize for conscience and responsible parenthood. The temptation must be resisted, because an appeal to independently acting consciences selects for the disappearance of all conscience in the long run, and an increase in anxiety in the short.

The only way we can preserve and nurture other and more precious freedoms is by relinquishing the freedom to breed, and that very soon. "Freedom is the recognition of necessity"—and it is the role of education to reveal to all the necessity of abandoning the freedom to breed. Only so, can we put an end to this aspect of the tragedy of the commons.

NOTES

1. J. B. Wiesner and H. F. York, *Sci. Amer.* 211 (No. 44), 27 (1964).
2. G. Hardin, *J. Hered.* 50, 68 (1959); S. von Hoernor, *Science* 137, 18 (1962).
3. J. von Neumann and O. Morgenstern, *Theory of Games and Economic Behavior* (Princeton Univ. Press, Princeton, NJ: 1947), p. 11.
4. J. H. Fremlin, *New Sci.*, No. 415 (1964), p. 285.
5. A. Smith, *The Wealth of Nations* (Modern Library, New York, 1937), p. 423.
6. W. F. Lloyd, *Two Lectures on the Checks to Population* (Oxford Univ. Press, Oxford, England, 1833), reprinted (in part) in *Population, Evolution, and Birth Control,* G. Hardin, Ed. (Freeman, San Francisco, 1964), p. 37.
7. A. N. Whitehead, *Science and the Modern World* (Mentor, New York, 1948), p. 17.
8. G. Hardin, Ed., *Population, Evolution and Birth Control* (Freeman, San Francisco, 1964), p. 56.
9. S. McVay, *Sci. Amer.* 216 (No. 8), 13 (1966).
10. J. Fletcher, *Situation Ethics* (Westminster, Philadelphia, 1966).
11. D. Lack, *The Natural Regulation of Animal Numbers* (Clarendon Press, Oxford, 1954).
12. H. Girvetz, *From Wealth to Welfare* (Stanford Univ. Press, Stanford, Calif., 1950).
13. G. Hardin, *Perspec. Biol. Med.* 6, 366 (1963).
14. U Thant, *Int. Planned Parenthood News,* No. 168 (February 1968), p. 3.
15. K. Davis, *Science,* 158, 730 (1967).
16. S. Tax, Ed., *Evolution After Darwin* (Univ. of Chicago Press, Chicago, 1960), vol. 2, p. 469.
17. G. Bateson, D. D. Jackson, J. Haley, and J. Weakland, *Behav. Sci.* 1, 251 (1956).
18. P. Goodman, *New York Rev. Books* 1968, 10 (8), 22 (23 May 1968).
19. A. Comfort, *The Anxiety Makers* (Nelson, London, 1967).
20. C. Frankel, *The Case for Modern Man* (Harper New York, 1955), p. 203.
21. J. D. Roslansky, *Genetics and the Future of Man* (Appleton-Century-Crofts New York, 1966), p. 177.

📚 STUDY QUESTIONS

1. What does Hardin mean when he says that the problem of population growth has no technical solution?
2. Explain the idea of the "tragedy of the commons" as first set forth by William Forster Lloyd. How does it work?
3. What does Hardin mean when he says, "Freedom in a commons brings ruin to all"? How does he define true "freedom" at the end of his essay?
4. How does Hardin apply the tragedy of the commons to human population growth? Do you agree with his analysis? Explain.
5. What does Hardin mean by "conscience is self-eliminating"? What is wrong with appealing to conscience to solve environmental problems?
6. How serious is the current population growth? What do you think should be done about it?

46   The Unjust War against Population

JACQUELINE KASUN

Jacqueline Kasun is professor of economics at Humboldt State University in Arcata, California. Her writings have appeared in *The Wall Street Journal, The American Spectator*, and *The Christian Science Monitor*. She is the author of *The War Against Population* (1988) from which this selection is taken.

    Kasun argues that Doomsdayers like the Smithsonian Institution and Garrett Hardin are carrying out an irrational campaign against our freedom to propagate. The idea that humanity is multiplying at a horrendous rate is one of the unexamined dogmas of our time. Kasun offers evidence to the contrary and charges the Doomsdayers with bad faith and with attempting to take control of our families, churches, and other voluntary institutions around the globe.

It was a traveling exhibit for schoolchildren. Titled "Population: The Problem Is Us," it toured the country at government expense in the mid-1970s. It consisted of a set of illustrated panels with an accompanying script that stated:

> . . . there are too many people in the world. We are running out of space. We are running out of energy. We are running out of food. And, although too few people seem to realize it, we are running out of time.[1]

It told the children that "the birth rate must decrease and/or the death rate must increase" since resources were all but exhausted and mass starvation loomed. It warned that, "driven by starvation, people have been known to eat dogs, cats, bird droppings, and even their own children," and it featured a picture of a dead rat on a dinner plate as an example of future "food sources." Overpopulation, it threatened, would lead not only to starvation and cannibalism but to civil violence and nuclear war.

The exhibit was created at the Smithsonian Institution, the national museum of the U.S. government, using federal funds provided by the National Science Foundation, an agency of the U.S. government.

Concurrently, other American schoolchildren were also being treated to federally funded "population education," instructing them on "the growing pressures on global resources, food, jobs, and political stability." They read Paul Ehrlich's book, *The Population Bomb*. They were taught, falsely, that "world population is increasing at a

Reprinted from *The War against Population* (San Francisco: Ignatius, 1988) by permission. Notes edited.

rate of 2 percent per year whereas the food supply is increasing at a rate of 1 percent per year," and equally falsely, that "population growth and rising affluence have reduced reserves of the world's minerals." They viewed slides of the "biological catastrophes" that would result from overpopulation and held class discussions on "what responsible individuals in a 'crowded world' should or can do about population growth." They learned that the world is like a spaceship or a crowded lifeboat, to deduce the fate of mankind, which faces a "population crisis." And then, closer to home, they learned that families who have children are adding to the problems of overpopulation, and besides, children are a costly burden who "need attention... 24 hours a day" and spoil marriages by making their fathers "jealous" and rendering their mothers "depleted." They were told to "say good-bye" to numerous wildlife species doomed to extinction as a result of the human population explosion.

This propaganda campaign in the public schools, which indoctrinated a generation of children, was federally funded, despite the fact that no law had committed the United States to this policy. Nor, indeed, had agreement been reached among informed groups that the problem of "overpopulation" even existed. To the contrary, during the same period the government drive against population was gaining momentum, contrary evidence was proliferating. One of the world's most prominent economic demographers, Colin Clark of Oxford University, published a book titled *Population Growth: The Advantages;* and economists Peter Bauer and Basil Yamey of the London School of Economics discovered that the population scare "relies on misleading statistics... misunderstands the determinants of economic progress... misinterprets the causalities in changes in fertility and changes in income" and "envisages children exclusively as burdens." Moreover, in his major study of The *Economics of Population Growth,* Julian Simon found that population growth was economically beneficial. Other economists joined in differing from the official antinatalist position.

Commenting on this body of economic findings, Paul Ehrlich, the biologist-author of

The Population Bomb, charged that economists "continue to whisper in the ears of politicians all kinds of nonsense." If not on the side of the angels, Ehrlich certainly found himself on the side of the U.S. government, which since the mid-1960s has become increasingly committed to a worldwide drive to reduce the growth of population. It has absorbed rapidly increasing amounts of public money, as well as the energies of a growing number of public agencies and publicly subsidized private organizations.

The spirit of the propaganda has permeated American life at all levels, from the highest reaches of the federal bureaucracy to the chronic reporting of overpopulation problems by the media and the population education being pushed in public schools. It has become so much a part of daily American life that its presuppositions and implications are scarcely examined; though volumes are regularly published on the subject, they rarely do more than restate the assumptions as a prelude to proposing even "better" methods of population planning.

But even more alarming are some neglected features inherent in the proposed needs and the probable results of population planning. The factual errors are egregious, true, and the alarmists err when they claim that world food output per person and world mineral reserves are decreasing—that, indeed, the human economic prospect has been growing worse rather than more secure and prosperous by all available objective standards. But these are not the most significant claims made by the advocates of government population planning. The most fundamental, which is often tacit rather than explicit, is that the world faces an unprecedented problem of "crisis" proportions that defies all familiar methods of solution.

Specifically, it is implied that the familiar human response to scarcity—that of economizing—is inadequate under the "new" conditions. Thus the economist's traditional reliance on the individual's ability to choose in impersonal markets is disqualified. Occasionally it is posited that the market mechanism will fail due to "externalities," but it is more often said that mankind is entering by a quantum leap into a new age in which all traditional methods and values are inapplicable. Sometimes it is implied that the uniqueness of this new age inheres in its new technology, and at other times that human nature itself is changing in fundamental respects.

Whatever the cause of this leap into an unmapped future, the widely held conclusion is that since all familiar human institutions are failing and will continue to fail in the "new" circumstances, they must be abandoned and replaced. First among these supposedly failing institutions is the market mechanism, that congeries of institutions and activities by which individuals and groups carry out production and make decisions about the allocation of resources and the distribution of income. Not only the market, but democratic political institutions as well are held to be manifestly unsuitable for the "new" circumstances. Even the traditional family is labeled for extinction because of its inability to adapt to the evolving situation. The new school family life and sex education programs, for example, stress the supposed decline of the traditional family—heterosexual marriage, blood or adoptive relationships—and its replacement by new, "optional" forms, such as communes and homosexual partnerships. Unsurprisingly, traditional moral and ethical teachings must be abandoned.

The decision to repudiate the market is of interest not only to economists but to both those capitalists and market socialists who have seen how impersonal markets can mediate the innate conflict between consumer desires and resource scarcity. The most elegant models of socialism have incorporated the market mechanism into their fundamental design. Adam Smith's "invisible hand," which leads men to serve one another and to economize in their use of resources as they pursue their own self-interest, is relied upon to a considerable extent in a number of socialist countries. John Maurice Clark called it "our main safeguard against exploitation" because it performs "the simple miracle whereby each one increases his gains by increasing his services rather than by reducing them," and Walter Eucken said it protects individuals by breaking up the great concentrations of economic power. The common element here

is, of course, the realization that individual decision-making leads not to chaos but to social harmony.

This view is denied by the population planners and it is here that the debate is, or should be, joined. Why are the advocates of government population planning so sure that the market mechanism cannot handle population growth? Why are they so sure that the market will not respond as it has in the past to resource scarcities—by raising prices so as to induce consumers to economize and producers to provide substitutes? Why can individual families not be trusted to adjust the number of their children to their incomes and thus to the given availability of resources? Why do the advocates of government population control assume that human beings must "overbreed," both to their own detriment and to that of society?

It is occasionally averred that the reason for this hypothetical failure is that individuals do not bear the full costs of their childbearing decisions but transfer a large part to society and therefore tend to have "too many" children. This is a dubious claim, for it overlooks the fact that individual families do not receive all the benefits generated by their childbearing. The lifetime productivity and social contribution of children flows largely to persons other than their parents, which, it might be argued, leads families to have fewer children than would be in the best interests of society. Which of these "externalities" is the more important, or whether they balance one another, is a question that waits not merely for an answer but for a reasoned study.

Another reason commonly given for the alleged failure of personal decisions is that individuals do not know how to control the size of their families. But a deeper look makes it abundantly clear that the underlying reason is that the population planners do not believe that individuals, even if fully informed, can be relied upon to make the proper choice. The emphasis on "outreach" and the incentives that pervade the United States' domestic and foreign population efforts testify to this, as will be shown in more depth shortly.

More important than these arguments, however, is the claim that new advances in technology are not amenable to control by market forces—a traditional argument in favor of socialism. From the time of Saint Simon to that of Veblen and on to our own age, the argument has been advanced that the market forces of supply-and-demand are incapable of controlling the vast powers of modern technology. At the dawn of the nineteenth century Saint Simon called for the redesigning of human society to cope with the new forces being unleashed by science. Only planned organization and control would suffice, he claimed. "Men of business" and the market forces which they represented would have to be replaced by planning "experts." In the middle of the nineteenth century Marx created a theoretic model of the capitalist market that purported to prove that the new technological developments would burst asunder the forms of private property and capitalist markets. Three-quarters of a century later Veblen spoke for the planning mentality when he wrote in 1921:

> The material welfare of the community is unreservedly bound up with the due working of this industrial system, and therefore with its unreserved control by the engineers, who alone are competent to manage it. To do their work as it should be done these men of the industrial general staff must have a free hand, unhampered by commercial considerations. . . .

In our own time, Heilbroner expresses a similar but even more profound distrust of market forces:

> . . . the external challenge of the human prospect, with its threats of runaway populations, obliterative war, and potential environmental collapse, can be seen as an extended and growing crisis induced by the advent of a command over natural processes and forces that far exceeds the reach of our present mechanisms of social control.

Heilbroner's position is uniquely modern in its pessimism. Unlike Marx and Veblen, who believed that the profit-seeking aspects of supply-and-demand unduly restricted the new technology from fulfilling its *beneficent* potential, Heilbroner sees the market as incapable of controlling an essentially *destructive* technology. Technology, in Heilbroner's view, brings nuclear arms, industrial pollution, and the reduction in death rates that is responsible for the population "explosion"; all of these stubbornly resist control by the market or by benign technological advance. Heilbroner has little hope that pollution-control technology, for example, will be able to offset the bad effects of industrial pollution.

An additional argument is that mankind is rapidly approaching, or has reached, the "limits to growth" or the "carrying capacity" of an earth with "finite" resources. Far from being a new position, it dates back to Thomas Malthus' *Essay on the Principle of Population* (1798), which held that the growth of population must inevitably outrun the growth of food supply. It must be one of the curiosities of our age that though Malthus' forecast has proved mistaken— that, in fact, the living standards of the average person have reached a level probably unsurpassed in history—doom is still pervasively forecast. The modern literature of "limits" is voluminous, including such works as the much-criticized *Limits to Growth* published by the Club of Rome, and the Carter administration's *Global 2000*. In common, these works predict an impending exhaustion of various world economic resources which are assumed to be absolutely fixed in quantity and for which no substitutes can be found. The world is likened to a "spaceship," as in Boulding's and Asimov's writings; or, even more pessimistically, an overloaded "lifeboat," as in Garrett Hardin's articles.

Now, in the first place, as for the common assumption in this literature that the limits are fixed and known (or, as Garrett Hardin puts it, each country's "lifeboat" carries a sign that indicates its "capacity"), no such knowledge does in fact exist—for the earth, or for any individual country, or with regard to any resource. No one knows how much petroleum exists on earth or how many people can earn their living in Illinois. What is known is that the types and quantities of economic resources are continually changing, as is the ability of given areas to support life. In the same territories in which earlier men struggled and starved, much larger populations today support themselves in comfort. The difference, of course, lies in the *knowledge* that human beings bring to the task of discovering and managing resources.

But then, secondly, the literature of limits rules out all such increasing knowledge. Indeed, in adopting the lifeboat or spaceship metaphor, the apostles of limits not only rule out all new knowledge, but the discovery of new resources, and in fact, virtually all production. Clearly, if the world is really a spaceship or a lifeboat, then both technology and resources are absolutely fixed, and beyond a low limit, population growth would be disastrous. Adherents of the view insist that that limit is either being rapidly approached or has been passed, about which more later. Important here is that even this extreme view of the human situation does not rule out the potential of market forces. Most of mankind throughout history has lived under conditions that would be regarded today as extreme, even desperate, deprivation. And over the millennia private decisions and private transactions have played an important, often a dominant, role in economic life. The historical record clearly shows that human beings can act and cooperate on their own in the best interests of survival, even under very difficult conditions. But history notwithstanding, the claims that emergencies of one kind or another require the centralized direction of economic life have been recurrent, especially during this century, which, ironically, has been the most economically prosperous. Today's advocates of coercion—the proponents of population control—posit the imminent approach of resource exhaustion, a condition wherein human beings will abandon all semblance of rational and civilized behavior.

To ward off their "emergency," the proponents of population control call for the adoption of measures that they admit would not be normally admissible. This is surely ample reason for a thoughtful and thorough examination of measures already being propagated.

Social and economic planning require an administrative bureaucracy with powers of enforcement. Modern economic analysis clearly shows that there are no impersonal, automatic mechanisms in the public sector that can simply and perfectly compensate for private market "failure." The public alternative is fraught with inequity and inefficiency, which can be substantial and exceedingly important. Although the theory of bureaucratic behavior has received less attention than that of private consumer choice, public administrators have also proved subject to greed, which hardly leads to social harmony. Government employees and contractors have the same incentives to avoid competition and form monopolies as private firms. They can increase their incomes by padding their costs and bloating their projects, and excuse it by exaggerating the need for their services and discrediting alternative solutions.

Managers of government projects have no market test to meet since they give away their products, even force them on an unwilling public, while collecting the necessary funds by force through the tax system. They can use their government grants to lobby for still more grants and to finance legal action to increase their power. They can bribe other bureaucrats and grants recipients to back their projects with the promise of reciprocal services. Through intergovernmental grants and "subventions" they can arrange their financial affairs so that apparently no one is accountable for any given decision or program. In short, the record of bureaucratic behavior confirms the statement of the great socialist scholar Oskar Lange, that "the real danger of socialism is that of a bureaucratization of economic life." The danger may well be more serious than we realize—it could be nothing less than totalitarianism.

Finally, proponents of the "population crisis" believe that not only must the *agencies* and *methods* of control be changed under the "new" circumstances but also the *criteria for choice*. Since, they argue, the technological and demographic developments of the modern age render all traditional standards of value and goodness either obsolete or questionable, these must be revised—under the leadership, of course, of those who understand the implications of the new developments.

Above all, they hold that the traditional concept of the value and dignity of the individual human being must be overhauled. The good of the *species,* as understood fully only by the advocates of the new views, must in all cases supersede the good as perceived and sought after by individuals.

Clearly, in the late twentieth century a worldview has emerged that calls into question not only the presuppositions of much of economics, but some basic political and philosophical thought as well. The history of our age may be determined by the outcome of the confrontation between these views.

It must be emphasized that the essential issue is not birth control or family planning. People have throughout history used various means to determine the size of their families, generating a great deal of discussion and debate. But the critical issue raised by recent history, especially in the United States, is whether government has the right or duty to preside over the reproductive process...for what reasons, to what extent?

Recent official action in the United States has proceeded as if the question had already been answered. The fact is, however, that it has been neither explicitly asked nor discussed, even as we rush toward a future shaped by its affirmative answer. It is this question that must be examined.

SCARCITY OR LIFEBOAT ECONOMICS: WHICH IS RIGHT?

The fact of scarcity is the fundamental concern of economics. As one leading textbook puts it in its opening pages, "wants exceed what is available."[2] It pertains to the rich as well as to the poor, since scarcity is not the same thing as poverty. As another text tells students, "higher production levels seem to bring in their train ever-higher consumption standards. Scarcity remains."[3]

Yet another explains,

> we are not able to produce all of everything that everyone wants free; thus we must "economize" our resources, or use them as efficiently as possible...human wants, if not infinite, go...far beyond the ability of our productive resources to satisfy them....[4]

That scarcity is no less real in affluent societies than in poor ones is explained in more general terms by other economists who stress the need to make *choices* whenever alternatives exist. In the words of McKenzie and Tullock,

> the individual makes *choices* from among an array of alternative options...in each choice situation, a person must always forgo doing one or more

things when doing something else. Since *cost* is the most highly valued alternative forgone, all rational behavior involves a cost.[5]

Clearly, the affluent person or society faces a large list of highly valued alternatives, and is likely to have a difficult choice to make—to be more acutely aware of the scarcity and the need to give up one thing in order to have another. It follows that scarcity does not lessen with affluence but is more likely to increase.

Simply put, economists understand scarcity as the inescapable fact that candy bars and ice cream cannot be made out of the same milk and chocolate. A choice must be made, regardless of how much milk and chocolate there is. And the decision to produce milk and chocolate rather than cheese and coffee is another inescapable choice. And so the list continues, endlessly, constituting the core of economics. How to choose what to produce, for whom, and how, is the very stuff of economics.

It is important to notice how different these traditional economic concepts of scarcity and choice are from the notions of "lifeboat economics." In Garrett Hardin's metaphor, the lifeboat's capacity is written on its side. The doomsday literature of limits is shot through with the conceit of absolute capacity, which is alien to economics. Not the least of the differences is that in economics humanity is viewed not only as the *raison d'être* of other forms of wealth but as one of the sources of wealth; human labor and ingenuity are resources, means for creating wealth. In the lifeboat, human beings are pure burdens, straining the capacity of the boat. Which of these views is closer to reality?

Is the earth rapidly approaching or has it surpassed its capacity to support human life? But before delving into the existence and nature of limits, keep in mind that the notion of a limited carrying capacity is not the only argument for population control. The view of people, or at least of more people, as simply a curse or affliction has its adherents. Thus Kingsley Davis writes of the plague," and Paul Ehrlich speaks with obvious repugnance of "people, people, people, people." Other writers, both old and new, attribute, if not a negative, at least a zero value to people. Thus John D. Rockefeller III, submitting the final report of the Commission on Population Growth and the American Future, wrote:

> in the long run, no substantial benefits will result from further growth of the Nation's population, rather…the gradual stabilization of our population would contribute significantly to the Nation's ability to solve its problems. We have looked for, and have not found, any convincing economic argument for continued population growth. The health of our country does not depend on it, nor does the vitality of business nor the welfare of the average person.[6]

The notion embodied in this statement—that, to validate its claim to existence, a human life should justify itself by contributing to such things as the "vitality of business"—is a perfect example of the utilitarian ethic. Though economics has skirted utilitarianism at times, it was never in this sense, but rather in its belief that human beings could be rational in making choices. Economics has been content to value all things in terms of what they mean to individual human beings; it has never valued human beings in terms of supposedly higher values.

The idea that the earth is incapable of continuing to support human life suffuses United States governmental publications. The House Select Committee on Population reported in 1978 that

> the four major biological systems that humanity depends upon for food and raw materials—ocean fisheries, grasslands, forests, and croplands—are being strained by rapid population growth to the point where, in some cases, they are actually losing productive capacity.[7]

The Carter administration's *Global 2000* report, which was much criticized by research experts, predicted:

> With the persistence of human poverty and misery, the staggering growth of human population, and ever increasing human demands, the possibilities of further stress and permanent damage to the planet's resource base are very real.

Such statements have been duly broadcast by the media despite the facts, which tell a quite different story.

In the first place, world food production has increased considerably faster than population in recent decades. The increase in per capita food output between 1950 and 1977 amounted to either 28 percent or 37 percent, depending on whether United Nations or United States Department of Agriculture figures are used, as Julian Simon has shown. Clearly, this is a very substantial increase. More recent United Nations and U.S. Department of Agriculture data show that world food output has continued to match or outstrip population growth in the years since 1977. Some of the most dramatic increases have occurred in the poorest countries, those designated for "triage" by the apostles of doom. For example, rice and wheat production in India in 1983 was almost three-and-a-half times as great as in 1950. This was considerably more than twice the percentage increase in the population of India in the same period.[8]

In a recent article written at the Harvard Center for Population Studies, Nick Eberstadt calls attention to the great increases in the world food supply in recent decades. He points out that only about 2 percent of the world's population suffers from serious hunger, in contrast to the much larger estimates publicized by the Food and Agricultural Organization of the United Nations in its applications for grants to continue its attempts to "solve" the world hunger problem. Eberstadt notes that the improving world food situation is probably reflected by the fact that "in the past thirty years, life expectancy in the less developed countries, excluding China, has risen by more than a third," and that "in the past twenty years in these same nations, death rates for one-to-four-year-olds, the age group most vulnerable to nutritional setback, have dropped by nearly half."

He points out that the much-decried increase in food imports by some less-developed countries is not a cause for alarm, but actually requires a smaller proportion of their export earnings to finance than in 1960.

In 1980, according to Eberstadt, even the poorest of the less-developed countries had to use less than 10 percent of their export earnings to pay for their food imports. The good news is underscored by the fact that these countries have been able to export their manufactured and other nonfood items so much in recent years that it is profitable—it is the efficient choice—for them to export these products in exchange for food, just as developed countries do.

The recent famine in Africa may seem to belie these optimistic findings. Africa, however, is a continent torn by war; farmers cannot cultivate and reap in battle zones, and enemy troops often seize or burn crops. Collectivist governments, also endemic in Africa, often seize crops and farm animals without regard for farmers' needs. War and socialism are two great destroyers of the food supply in Africa, as they have been in other continents.

The impressive increases in food production that have occurred in recent decades have barely scratched the surface of the available food-raising resources, according to the best authorities. Farmers use less than half of the earth's arable land and only a minute part of the water available for irrigation. Indeed, three-fourths of the world's available crop-land requires no irrigation.

How large a population could the world's agricultural resources support using presently known methods of farming? Colin Clark, former director of the Agricultural Economic Institute at Oxford University, classified world land-types by their food-raising capabilities and found that if all farmers were to use the best methods, enough food could be raised to provide an American-type diet for 35.1 billion people, more than seven times the present population. Since the American diet is a very rich one, Clark found that it would be possible to feed three times as many again, or more than twenty-two times as many as now exist, at a Japanese standard of food intake. Clark's estimate assumed that nearly half of the earth's land area would remain in conservation areas, for recreation and the preservation of wildlife.

Roger Revelle, former director of the Harvard Center for Population Studies, estimated that world agricultural resources are capable of providing an adequate diet (2,500 kilocalories per day), as well as fiber, rubber, tobacco, and beverages, for 40 billion people, or eight times the present number. This, he thought, would require the use of less than one-fourth—compared with one-ninth today—of the earth's ice-free land area. He presumed that average yields would be about one-half those presently produced in the United States Midwest. Clearly, better yields and/or the use of a larger share of the land area would support over 40 billion persons.

Revelle has estimated that the less-developed continents, those whose present food supplies are most precarious, are capable of feeding 18 billion people, or six times their present population. He has estimated that the continent of Africa alone is capable of feeding 10 billion people, which is twice the amount of the present world population and more than twenty times the 1980 population of Africa. He sees "no known physical or biological reason" why agricultural yields in Asia should not be greatly increased. In a similar vein, the Indian economist Raj Krishna has written that

> ...the amount of land in India that can be brought under irrigation can still be doubled ... Even in Punjab, the Indian state where agriculture is most advanced, the yield of wheat can be doubled. In other states it can be raised three to seven times. Rice yields in the monsoon season can be raised three to 13 times, rice yields in the dry season two to three-and-a-half times, jowar (Indian millet) yields two to 11 times, maize yields two to 10 times, groundnut yields three-and-a-half to five-and-a-half times and potato yields one-and-a-half to five-and-a-half times.[9]

What Mr. Krishna is, in fact, saying is that Indian agriculture is potentially capable of feeding not only the people of India but the entire population of the world!

Revelle sums up his conclusions and those of other experts by quoting Dr. David Hopper, another well-known authority on agriculture:

> The world's food problem does not arise from any physical limitation on potential output or any danger of unduly stressing the environment. The limitations on abundance are to be found in the social and political structures of nations and in the economic relations among them. The unexploited global food resource is there, between Cancer and Capricorn. The successful husbandry of that resource depends on the will and actions of men.[10]

Obviously, such great expansions of output would require large inputs of fertilizer, energy, and human labor, as Revelle puts it:

Most of the required capital facilities can be constructed in densely populated poor countries by human labor, with little modern machinery: in the process much rural unemployment and under-employment can be alleviated.

In other words, as Clark has noted, future generations can and will build their own farms and houses, just as in the past.

With regard to fertilizer, Clark has pointed out that the world supply of the basic ingredients, potash and sulphates, is adequate for several centuries, while the third major ingredient, nitrogen, is freely available in the atmosphere, though requiring energy for extraction. Since the world's coal supply is adequate for some 2,000 years, this should pose no great problem. Revelle states that

> in principle ... most—perhaps all—of the energy needed in modern high-yielding agriculture could be provided by the farmers themselves. For every ton of cereal grain there are one to two tons of humanly inedible crop residues with an energy content considerably greater than the food energy in the grain.

Surprisingly, in view of the recurrent alarms about desertification, urban encroachment, and other forces supposedly reducing the amount of world agricultural land, it is actually increasing. Julian Simon has drawn attention to the data indicating this trend:

> A demographer, Joginder Kumar, found in a study at the University of California at Berkeley that there was 9 percent more total arable land in 1960 than in 1950 in 87 countries for which data were available and which constituted 73 percent of the world's total land area. And United Nations data show a 6 percent rise in the world's arable, permanent cropland from around 1963 to 1977 (the last date for which data are available).[11]

And UN data show a further increase of almost 1 percent between 1977 and 1980. Simon also notes that

> there are a total of 2.3 billion acres in the United States. Urban areas plus highways, nonagricultural roads, railroads, and airports total 61 million acres—just 2.7 percent of the total. Clearly,

there is little competition between agriculture and cities and roads.

And that,

> furthermore, between 1.25 million and 1.7 million acres of cropland are being created yearly with irrigation, swamp drainage, and other reclamation techniques. This is a much larger quantity of new farmland than the amount that is converted to cities and highways each year.

Simon's point is significant: a very small share of the total land area is used for urban purposes— less than 3 percent in the United States. This is probably a high percentage by world standards since the United States has a peculiarly sprawling type of development. Doxiadis and Papaioannou have estimated that only three-tenths of 1 percent of the land surface of the earth is used for "human settlements."

Similarly, the biologist Francis P. Felice has shown that all the people in the world could be put into the state of Texas, forming one giant city with a population density less than that of many existing cities, and leaving the rest of the world empty. Each man, woman, and child in the 1984 world population could be given more than 1,500 square feet of land space in such a city (the average home in the United States ranges between 1,400 and 1,800 square feet). If one-third of the space of this city were devoted to parks and one-third to industry, each family could still occupy a single-story dwelling of average U.S. size.

In like vein, R. L. Sassone has calculated that there would be standing room for the entire population of the world within one-quarter of the area of Jacksonville, Florida.

Evidently, if the people of the world are floating in a lifeboat, it is a mammoth one quite capable of carrying many times its present passengers. An observer, in fact, would get the impression that he was looking at an empty boat, since the present occupants take up only a fraction of 1 percent of the boat's space and use less than one-ninth of its ice-free land area to raise their food and other agricultural products. The feeling of the typical air passenger that he is looking down on a mostly empty earth is correct.

On the extremely unlikely assumption that no improvements take place in technology and that population growth continues at its present rate, it will be more than a century and a quarter before world population will approach the limit of the support capacity estimated by Revelle, and almost two centuries before the limit estimated by Clark is reached. And, again on these wild surmises, what will the world be like then? At least one-half of the world's land area will still be in conservation and wildlife areas; and human settlements will occupy no more than 8 percent of the land. In a word, although by our assumptions, average living standards will no longer be able to rise, the boat will still be mostly empty.

Yet despite the optimism for human life in agriculture, and although most of the people in the less-developed world are still engaged in such work, we do live in the industrial age. Among the roughly one-third of the people who live in industrial countries, only a small proportion are farmers. In the United States, for example, one out of thirty people in the labor force is a farmer.

Even the most superficial view of the industrial economy shows how vastly it differs from the economy of agriculture. It uses a high proportion of fossil fuels and metal inputs; it is relatively independent of climate and seasons; a high proportion of its waste products are "nonbiodegradable"; and it requires clustering rather than dispersal of its productive units, which encourages urbanization. While depending on agriculture for much of its resources, including its initial stock of capital, it has contributed greatly to the productivity and security of agriculture by providing energy, labor-saving machinery, and chemical fertilizers. Above all, perhaps, it has provided agriculture with cheap, fast transportation, so that local crop failures no longer mean famine.

It is generally agreed that industrialization has been important in reducing mortality and hence increasing population. And concerns regarding the limits of industry match those over the capacity of agriculture. How far can we go with the industrial process before we run out of the minerals and energy that are essential to it? How much "disruption" of nature does the industrial system create and how much can the earth and its inhabitants endure?

It is quite evident that, with few exceptions, intellectuals have never much liked the industrial process. Its noise, smoke—its obliteration of natural beauty—have never endeared it to the more genteel classes, or perhaps to anybody. But where its unattractive characteristics were once regarded as an unavoidable cost, given the benefits for human beings, now there is a growing conviction—especially among environmentalists—that these costs are unendurable and could be avoided by simply dispensing with part of the population. This is a simple choice from a set of complex alternatives, which raises much more far-reaching questions than whether we are simply "running out of everything."

First, though, the question: Are we running out of everything? If we are, the industrialization process, as well as all the benefits and problems it creates, will soon be at an end. (For those who dislike industry this should be good news indeed, though they shy away from the argument.)

On this score, the signs are clear. There is very little probability of running out of anything essential to the industrial process at any time in the foreseeable future. Over the past decades there have been recurrent predictions of the imminent exhaustion of all energy and basic metals, none of which has come about. And properly so, because it is a familiar chemical principle that nothing is ever "used up." Materials are merely changed into other forms. Some of these forms make subsequent recycling easier, others less so. It is cheaper to retrieve usable metals from the city dump than from their original ore, but once gasoline has been burned it cannot be reused as gasoline. Economists gauge the availability of basic materials by measuring their price changes over time. A material whose price has risen over time (allowing for changes in the average value of money) is becoming more scarce, while one whose price has fallen is becoming more abundant, relative to the demand for it. Two major economic studies of the availability of basic metals and fuels found no evidence of increasing scarcity over the period 1870–1972. And in 1984 a group of distinguished resource experts reported that the cost trends of non-fuel minerals for the period 1950–1980 "fail to support the increasing scarcity hypothesis."

Julian Simon has recently noted the trend of decreasing scarcity for all raw materials:

> An hour's work in the United States has bought increasingly more of copper, wheat, and oil (representative and important raw materials) from 1800 to the present. And the same trend has almost surely held throughout human history. Calculations of expenditures for raw materials as a proportion of total family budgets make the same point even more strongly. These trends imply that the raw materials have been getting increasingly available and less scarce relative to the most important and most fundamental element of life, human work-time. The prices of raw materials have even been falling relative to consumer goods and the Consumer Price Index. All the items in the Consumer Price Index have been produced with increasing efficiency in terms of labor and capital over the years, but the decrease in cost of raw materials has been even greater than that of other goods, a very strong demonstration of progressively decreasing scarcity and increasing availability of raw materials.[12]

Simon also noted that the real price of electricity had fallen at the end of the 1970s to about one-third its level in the 1920s.

Even the Carter administration's gloomy *Global 2000* report admitted that "the real price of most mineral commodities has been constant or declining for many years," indicating less scarcity. Yet the report, in the face of all the evidence of a historical decline in industrial resource scarcity, trumpets an imminent reversal of the trend and an abrupt increase in the prices and scarcity of raw materials.

Other analysts disagree. As Ansley Coale points out, metals exist in tremendous quantities at lower concentrations. Geologists know that going from a concentration of 6 percent to 5 percent multiplies the available quantities by factors of ten to a thousand, depending on the metal.

Ridker and Cecelski of Resources for the Future are equally reassuring, concluding, "in the long run, most of our metal needs can be supplied by iron, aluminum, and magnesium, all of which are extractable from essentially inexhaustible sources."[13]

Even should scarcities of such materials develop, the economic impact would be small:

> metals...are only a small fraction of the cost of finished goods. The same is true with energy.... In the United States, for example, non-fuel minerals account for less than one-half of one percent of the total output of goods and services, and energy costs comprise less than one percent.

In the case of fuels, the United States has currently reduced its own sources of low-cost petroleum. This can hardly be described as a "crisis," since higher-cost petroleum supplies are still available here while large reserves of low-cost petroleum remain and are being discovered in other parts of the world, though cartel influences are presently affecting prices. Extremely large deposits of coal remain in the United States and throughout the world, enough for a thousand years, possibly more than twice that, at foreseeable rates of increase in demand.

Summarizing the conclusions of a group of energy experts in 1984, Simon and Kahn wrote:

> Barring extraordinary political problems, we expect the price of oil to go down...there is no basis to conclude...that humankind will ever face a greater shortage of oil in economic terms than it does now; rather, decreasing shortage is the more likely...

Speaking of all kinds of energy, they concluded:

> The prospect of running out of energy is purely a bogeyman. The availability of energy has been increasing, and the meaningful cost has been decreasing, over the entire span of humankind's history. We expect this benign trend to continue at least until our sun ceases to shine in perhaps 7 billion years....

Furthermore, the United States has tremendous, unexploited opportunities to economize on energy. Because energy has been so cheap, Americans drive their cars more than any other people and, in some parts of the United States, heat their houses without insulation and even with open windows. A reduction in U.S. energy consumption by one-half would put us on a par with the people of western Europe, whose living standards are as high as ours.

Although history teaches that we can expect great technological changes in the future, the nature of these changes is unknown. To attempt, then, to determine the safe capacity of our lifeboat, it seems the better part of wisdom not to anticipate any miraculous rescues, such as breakthroughs in the use of solar or nuclear power. Old-fashioned as it may seem, the coal on board alone will provide us with energy for at least a millennium, to say nothing of the petroleum and natural gas—and solar and nuclear possibilities—all of which remain substantial.

The message is clear. The boat is extremely well stocked. The industrial system will not grind to a halt for lack of supplies.

But what about the disruption (an obscure term, and so all the more dreaded) supposedly created by population growth and/or industrialization? As Heilbroner puts it: "The sheer scale of our intervention into the fragile biosphere is now so great that we are forced to proceed with great caution lest we inadvertently bring about environmental damage of an intolerable sort."

Man has, of course, been intervening in the biosphere for thousands of years. Perhaps the most massive human intervention was the invention of agriculture. It is not certain that modern industry, which is confined to much smaller areas, is having even an equal effect. Both humanity and the rest of the biosphere have apparently survived the agricultural intervention rather well; in fact, well enough so that our present anxiety is whether too many of us have survived.

"Too many for what?" springs to mind. The fact that more people are now living longer, healthier, better-fed, and more comfortable lives, and have been for many decades, rather suggests that the interventions have been the very opposite of intolerable. According to a number of authorities, the best overall index of environmental quality is life expectancy, which has been increasing throughout the world during this century. It is precisely because of this increase that population has grown even though birth rates have fallen. It is possible, of course, that what the population alarmists really mean is that there are too many *other* people for their taste,

or for those who prefer solitude, which is quite another thing....

These and other economists have spelled out the case against the assumptions and teachings of the population-bombers: population growth permits the easier acquisition as well as the more efficient use of the economic infrastructure—the modern transportation and communications systems, and the education, electrification, irrigation, and waste disposal systems. Population growth encourages agricultural investment—clearing and draining land, building barns and fences, improving the water supply. Population growth increases the size of the market, encouraging producers to specialize and use cost-saving methods of large-scale production. Population growth encourages governments, as well as parents, philanthropists, and taxpayers, to devote more resources to education. If wisely directed, these efforts can result in higher levels of competence in the labor force. Larger populations not only inspire more ideas but more *exchanges,* or improvements, of ideas among people, in a ratio that is necessarily more than proportional to the number of additional people. (For example, if one person joins an existing couple, the possible number of exchanges does not increase by one-third but triples.) One of the advantages of cities, as well as of large universities, is that they are mentally stimulating, that they foster creativity.

The arguments and evidence that population growth does not lead to resource exhaustion, starvation, and environmental catastrophe, fail to persuade the true believers in the population bomb. They have, after all, other rationalizations for their fears of doom. Another recurring theme of the doomsdayers is, in the words of a public affairs statement by the U.S. Department of State, that population growth increases the size of the "politically volatile age group—those 15–24 years," which contributes to political unrest. Ambassador Richard Elliot Benedick, coordinator of population affairs in the U.S. State Department, spelled out the concern for the Senate Foreign Relations Committee in 1980:

> Rapid population growth...creates a large proportion of youth in the population. Recent experience, in Iran and other countries, shows that this

younger age group—frequently unemployed and crowded into urban slums—is particularly susceptible to extremism, terrorism, and violence as outlets for frustration.[14]

The ambassador went on to enumerate a long list of countries of economic and strategic importance to the United States where, he claimed, population growth was encouraging "political instability." The list included Turkey, Egypt, Iran, Pakistan, Indonesia, Mexico, Venezuela, Nigeria, Bolivia, Brazil, Morocco, the Philippines, Zimbabwe, and Thailand—countries of special importance to the United States because of their "strategic location, provision of military bases or support, and supply of oil or other critical raw materials." While he admitted that it is "difficult to be analytically precise in pinpointing exact causes of a given historical breakdown in domestic or international order," he nevertheless insisted that "unprecedented demographic pressures" were of great significance.

No results of scientific research support Benedick's belief; it is simply another one of those unverified *assumptions* that advocates of population control rely upon to make their case. It may be, of course, that Ambassador Benedick is right: that the young tend to be more revolutionary and that public bureaucracies who want to stay in power would be wise to encourage the aging of the population through lower birth rates. As public bureaucracies increase their power in this age of growth of government, we may see an increasing manipulation of the population so as to ensure an older and more docile citizenry. However, putting aside the ethical implications and the welfare of society, and speaking only of the self-interest of the ruling bureaucracy, the risks are obvious. Such policy could arouse a deep antagonism among those on the check list, especially if they are citizens of countries who perceive the policy as a tool of outside interference in their most intimate national affairs.

The question, then, is resolved in favor of the economic notion of scarcity rather than the lifeboat model of absolute limits being the more nearly correct. While resources are always scarce relative to the demands that human beings place upon them, there is no indication of imminent, absolute limits. The limits are so far beyond the levels of our present use of resources as to be nearly invisible, and are actually receding as new knowledge develops. Ironically, though, the perception of economic scarcity may increase along with increasing wealth and income. There is no evidence whatsoever that slower rates of population growth encourage economic growth or economic welfare; on the contrary, the developing countries with *higher* rates of population growth have had higher average rates of per-capita-output growth in the period since 1950. It may, of course, be in the interests of a ruling bureaucracy to rid itself of those people it finds troublesome, but the policy can hardly promote the general welfare, and it would prove very costly, even to the ruling elites.

NOTES

1. *Projectbook for the Exhibition "Population: The Problem Is Us": A Book of Suggestions or Implementing the Exhibition in Your Own Institution* (Washington: The Smithsonian Institution, undated, circulated in late 1970s), p. 9.

2. Armen A. Alchian and William R Allen, *University Economics,* 3rd ed. (Belmont: Wadsworth Publishing Co., 1972), p. 7.

3. Paul A. Samuelson, *Economics,* 11th ed. (New York: McGraw Hill, 1980), p. 17.

4. George Leland Bach, *Economics: An Introduction to Analysis and Policy,* 10th ed. (Englewood Cliffs: Prentice-Hall, Inc., 1980), p. 3.

5. Richard B. McKenzie and Gordon Tullock, *Modern Political Economy* (New York: McGraw-Hill 1978), p. 18.

6. John D. Rockefeller III, Letter to the President and Congress, transmitting the Final Report on the Commission on Population Growth and the American Future, dated March 27, 1972.

7. Select Committee on Population, Report, "World Population: Myths and Realities," U.S. House of Representatives, 95th Congress, 2nd Session (Washington: U.S. Government Printing Office, 1978), p. 5.

8. *The Global 2000 Report to the President: Global Future: Time to Act,* prepared by the Council on Environmental Quality and the U.S. Department of State (Washington: U.S. Government Printing Office, January 1981), p. ix.

9. Raj Krishna, "The Economic Development of India," *Scientific American,* vol. 243, no. 3. September 1980, pp. 173–174.

10. Revelle, "The World Supply of Agricultural Land," op. cit., p. 184, quoting W. David Hopper, "The Development of Agriculture in Developing Countries," *Scientific American*, September 1976, pp. 197–205.

11. Julian L. Simon, "Worldwide, Land for Agriculture Is Increasing, Actually," *New York Times*, October 7, 1980, p. 23.

12. Simon, "Global Confusion," op. cit., p. 11.

13. Ronald G. Ridker and Elizabeth W. Cecelski, "Resources, Environment, and Population: The Nature of Future Limits," *Population Bulletin*, vol. 34, no. 3, August 1979, p. 29.

14. Richard Elliot Benedick, Statement before the Senate Foreign Relations Committee, April 29, 1980, reprinted in *Department of State Bulletin*, vol. 80, no. 2042, September 1980, p. 58.

STUDY QUESTIONS

1. How strong is Kasun's case that the "Population Control Industry" is misleading us about the dangers of our present population growth?

2. According to Kasun, what is the truth about population growth in relation to scarcity of resources?

3. Compare Kasun's arguments with Hardin's. Which one has the stronger case, and why?

4. Evaluate the anthropocentric viewpoint in Kasun's essay.

5. Do you think Kasun ignores quality-of-life issues?

47   The State of Consumption Today

GARY GARDNER, ERIK ASSADOURIAN, AND RADHIKA SARIN

The authors are researchers for the Worldwatch Institute. This article, from State of the World 2004, examines the relation between population, consumption, and quality of life trends in the world. Moral questions arise both from the current disparities (for instance "the 12% of the world living in North America and Western Europe account for 60% of global private consumer spending, whereas the one-third living in South Asia and sub-Sahara Africa account for only 3.2%"), as well as our future commitment to a way of life that is at best questionable.

China has a well-deserved reputation as the land of the bicycle. Throughout the twentieth century, the streets of her cities were filled with literally millions of bikes, not only providing personal transportation but also serving as delivery vehicles—carrying everything from construction materials to chickens on their way to market. As recently as the early 1980s, few private cars were found on China's streets.[1]

A visitor from the 1980s who returns to Beijing, Shanghai, or other Chinese cities today will hardly recognize them. By 2002 there were 10 million private cars, and growth in ownership was accelerating: every day in 2003 some 11,000 more cars merged into the traffic on Chinese roads—4 million new private cars during the year. Auto sales increased by 60 percent in 2002 and by more than 80 percent in the first half of 2003. By 2015, if growth continues apace, industry analysts expect 150 million cars to be jamming China's streets—18 million more than were

---

Units of measure throughout this book are metric unless common usage dictates otherwise.

Reprinted from *State of the World 2004* by permission.

driven on U.S. streets and highways in 1999. The emerging class of Chinese consumers is enthusiastically embracing the increased mobility and higher social status that the automobile now represents—millions wait months and take on significant debt in order to become pioneer members of China's new automobile culture.[2]

The advantages of this development path are clear to the government officials who are encouraging it. Each new Chinese-made car provides two new jobs to Chinese workers, and the income they receive then stimulates other sectors of the Chinese economy. Moreover, the rush to meet demand is attracting massive investments by foreign companies—General Motors has spent $1.5 billion on a new factory in Shanghai, while Volkswagen has committed $7 billion over the next five years to increase its production capacity.[3]

China is of course following a well-blazed trail, albeit roughly eight decades after widespread use of the automobile first caught on in the United States. Yet China's automobile story is tied to neither the Chinese nor the automobile. From fast food to disposable cameras and from Mexico to South Africa, a good deal of the world is now entering the consumer society at a mind-numbing pace. By one calculation, there are now more than 1.7 billion members of "the consumer class" today—nearly half of them in the "developing" world. A lifestyle and culture that became common in Europe, North America, Japan, and a few other pockets of the world in the twentieth century is going global in the twenty-first.[4]

The consumer society clearly has a strong allure, and carries with it many economic benefits. And it would certainly be unfair to argue that advantages gained by an earlier generation of consumers should not be shared by those who come later. Yet the headlong growth of consumption in the last decade—and the staggering projections that flow logically from that growth—suggest that the world as a whole will soon run smack into a stark dilemma. If the levels of consumption that several hundred million of the most affluent people enjoy today were replicated across even half of the roughly 9 billion people projected to be on the planet in 2050, the impact on our water supply, air quality, forests, climate, biological diversity, and human health would be severe.[5]

Despite the dangers ahead, there is little evidence that the consumption locomotive is braking—not even in countries like the United States, where most people are amply supplied with the goods and services needed to lead a dignified life. As of 2003 the United States had more private cars than licensed drivers, and gas-guzzling sport-utility vehicles were one of the best-selling vehicles. New houses were 38 percent bigger in 2002 than in 1975, despite having fewer people in each household on average. Americans themselves are larger as well—so much bigger, in fact, that a multi-billion-dollar industry has emerged to cater to the needs of large Americans, supplying them with oversized clothing, sturdier furniture, even supersized caskets. If the consumption aspirations of the wealthiest of nations cannot be satiated, the prospects for corralling consumption everywhere before it strips and degrades our planet beyond recognition would appear to be bleak.[6]

Yet there are many reasons to be hopeful. Consumer advocates, economists, policy-makers, and environmentalists have developed creative options for meeting people's needs while dampening the environmental and social costs associated with mass consumption. In addition to helping individuals find the balance between too much and too little consumption, they stress placing more emphasis on publicly provided goods and services, on services in place of goods, on goods with high levels of recycled content, and on genuine choice for consumers. Together, these measures can help deliver a high quality of life with a minimum of environmental abuse and social inequity. The key is to look critically not only at the "how much" of consumption, but also the "how."...

Consumption is not a bad thing. People must consume to survive, and the world's poorest will need to consume more if they are to lead lives of dignity and opportunity. But consumption threatens the well-being of people and the environment when it becomes an end in itself—when it is an individual's primary goal in life, for example, or the ultimate measure of the success of a government's economic policies. The economies of mass consumption that produced a world of abundance for many in the twentieth century face a different challenge in the twenty-first: to focus not on the indefinite accumulation of goods but

---

BOX 7.1 What About Population?

The United Nations Population Division projects that world population will increase 41 percent by 2050, to 8.9 billion people. Just as growing acquisition of appliances and cars can eliminate energy savings achieved by efficiency improvements, this increase in human numbers threatens to offset any progress in reducing the amount of goods that each person consumes. For example, even if the average American eats 20 percent less meat in 2050 than in 2000, total meat consumption in the United States will be roughly 5 million tons greater in 2050 due to population growth alone.

With 99 percent of global population growth projected to occur in developing nations, these countries need to consider carefully the twin goals of population stabilization and increased consumption for human development. The industrial world can help developing countries stabilize their populations by supporting family planning, education, and the improvement of women's status. And it can lower the impact of increased consumption by assisting with the adoption of cleaner, more efficient technologies.

But it would be a mistake to think of population growth as a challenge facing only poor nations. When population growth and high levels of consumption mix, as they do in the United States, the significance of the former balloons. For example, although the U.S. population increases by roughly

3 million a year, whereas India's increases by nearly 16 million, the additional Americans have greater environmental impact. They are responsible for 15.7 million tons of additional carbon to the atmosphere, compared with only 4.9 million tons in India. Wealthy countries with expanding populations need to look at the impact of both their consumption and their population policies.

Other less discussed demographic trends mix with consumption in surprising ways as well. For instance, as a result of rising incomes, urbanization, and smaller families, the number of people living under one roof fell between 1970 and 2000 from 5.1 to 4.4 in developing countries and from 3.2 to 2.5 in industrial countries, while the total number of households increased. Each new house requires space and materials, of course. In addition, savings gained from having more people share energy, appliances, and home furnishings are lost when fewer people live in the same house. Thus a one-person household in the United States uses 17 percent more energy per person than a two-person household does. So even in some European nations and Japan, where total population is not growing much if at all, changing household dynamics should be examined as drivers of increased consumption.

Source: See endnote 7.

---

instead on a better quality of life for all, with minimal environmental harm.

CONSUMPTION BY THE NUMBERS

By virtually any measure—household expenditures, number of consumers, extraction of raw materials—consumption of goods and services has risen steadily in industrial nations for decades, and it is growing rapidly in many developing countries. The numbers tell the story of a world being transformed by a consumption revolution.

Private consumption expenditures—the amount spent on goods and services at the household level—topped $20 trillion in 2000, up from

$4.8 trillion in 1960 (in 1995 dollars). Some of this fourfold increase occurred because of population growth (see Box 7.1), but much of it was due to advancing prosperity in many parts of the globe. These overall numbers mask enormous disparities in spending. The 12 percent of the world living in North America and Western Europe account for 60 percent of global private consumer spending, while the one third living in South Asia and sub-Saharan Africa account for only 3.2 percent. (See Table 7.1.)[7]

In 1999, some 2.8 billion people—two of every five humans on the planet—were living on less than $2 a day, which the United Nations and the World Bank say is the minimum for meeting basic needs. Roughly 1.2 billion people were

TABLE 7.1 Consumer Spending and Population, by Region, 2000

Region	Share of World Private Consumption Expenditures	Share of World Population
	(percent)	(percent)
United States and Canada	31.5	5.2
Western Europe	28.7	6.4
East Asia and Pacific	21.4	32.9
Latin America and the Caribbean	6.7	8.5
Eastern Europe and Central Asia	3.3	7.9
South Asia	2.0	22.4
Australia and New Zealand	1.5	0.4
Middle East and North Africa	1.4	4.1
Sub-Saharan Africa	1.2	10.9

Source: See endnote 7.

living in "extreme poverty," measured by an average daily income of less than $1. Among the poorest are hundreds of millions of subsistence farmers, who by definition do not earn wages and who seldom engage in money-based market transactions. For them, and for all of the world's poor, consumption expenditures are focused almost entirely on meeting basic needs.[8]

Although most consumer spending occurs in the wealthier regions of the world, the number of consumers is spread a bit more evenly between industrial and developing regions. This is clear from research done by former U.N. Environment Programme (UNEP) consultant Matthew Bentley, who describes the existence of a global "consumer class." These people have incomes over $7,000 of purchasing power parity (an income measure adjusted for the buying power in local currency), which is roughly the level of the official poverty line in Western Europe. The global consumer class itself ranges widely in levels of wealth, but

members are typically users of televisions, telephones, and the Internet, along with the culture and ideas that these products transmit. This global consumer class totals some 1.7 billion people—more than a quarter of the world. (See Table 7.2.)[9]

Almost half of this global consumer class lives in developing nations, with China and India alone claiming more than 20 percent of the global total. (See Table 7.3.) In fact, these two countries' combined consumer class of 362 million people is larger than this class in all of Western Europe (although the average Chinese or Indian member of course consumes substantially less than the average European). Much of the rest of the developing world is not represented in this surge of new consumption, however: sub-Saharan Africa's consumer class, the smallest, has just 34 million people. Indeed, the region has essentially been a bystander to the prosperity experienced in most of the world in recent decades. Measured in terms of private consumption expenditures per person, sub-Saharan Africa in 2001 was 20 percent worse off than two decades earlier, creating a yawning gap between that region and the industrial world.[10]

In addition to having large consumer blocs, developing countries tend to have the greatest potential to expand the ranks of consumers. For example, China and India's large consumer set constitutes only 16 percent of the region's population, whereas in Europe the figure is 89 percent. Indeed, in most developing countries the consumer class accounts for less than half of the population—often much less—suggesting considerable room to grow. Based on population projections alone, the global consumer class is conservatively projected to hold at least 2 billion people by 2015.[11]

These numbers suggest that the story of consumption in the twenty-first century could be as much about emerging consumer nations as about traditional ones. In a 2003 Background Paper, the U.N. Environment Programme noted that boosting Asian car ownership rates to the world average would add 200 million cars to the global fleet—one and a half times the number of cars currently found in the United States. Concerns about the impact of developments like these suggest the urgency of pursuing alternative, sustainable paths to prosperity in the region. At the same time, worries about potential increases in Asian consumption

TABLE 7.2 Consumer Class, by Region, 2002

Region	Number of People Belonging to the Consumer Class	Consumer Class as Share of Regional Population	Consumer Class as Share of Global Consumer Class[1]
	(million)	(percent)	(percent)
United States and Canada	271.4	85	16
Western Europe	348.9	89	20
East Asia and Pacific	494.0	27	29
Latin America and the Caribbean	167.8	32	10
Eastern Europe and Central Asia	173.2	36	10
South Asia	140.7	10	8
Australia and New Zealand	19.8	84	1
Middle East and North Africa	78.0	25	4
Sub-Saharan Africa	34.2	5	2
Industrial Countries	912	80	53
Developing Countries	816	17	47
World	1,728	28	100

[1]Total does not add 100 due to rounding.
Source: See endnote 9.

are misplaced if they obscure the need for reform in wealthy countries, where high levels of consumption have been the norm for decades. The early industrializing countries in Europe and North America, along with Japan and Australia, are responsible for the bulk of global environmental degradation associated with consumption.[12]

Consumption trends cover virtually every conceivable good and service, and these can be categorized in many ways. Of particular interest are fundamentals such as food and water; trends for these give a sense of whether basic needs are being met. Other consumer items indicate the degree to which life options are expanding for people, and how much more comfortable life is becoming.

In terms of basic needs, trends are mixed. Daily intake of calories has increased in both the industrial and the developing worlds since 1961 as food supplies have become bountiful, at least at the global level. Yet the U.N. Food and Agriculture Organization (FAO) reports that 825 million people are still undernourished and that the average person in the industrial world took in 10 percent more calories daily in 1961 (2,947 calories) than the average person in the developing world consumes today (2,675 calories). The existence of hunger in the face of record food supplies reflects the fact that food remains expensive for

TABLE 7.3 Top 10 National Consumer Class Populations, 2002

Country	Number of People In Consumer Class, 2002	Share of National Population
	(million)	(percent)
United States	242.5	84
China	239.8	19
India	121.9	12
Japan	120.7	95
Germany	76.3	92
Russian Federation	61.3	43
Brazil	57.8	33
France	53.1	89
Italy	52.8	91
United Kingdom	50.4	86

Source: See endnote 10.

TABLE 7.4 Share of Household Expenditures Spent on Food

Country	Per Capita Household Expenditures, 1998	Share Spent on Food
	(dollars)[1]	(percent)
Tanzania	375	67
Madagascar	608	61
Tajikistan	660	48
Lebanon	6,135	31
Hong Kong	12,468	10
Japan	13,568	12
Denmark	16,385	16
United States	21,515	13

[1]Purchasing power parity.
Source: See endnote 13.

much of the world's poor relative to their meager incomes. In Tanzania, for instance, where per capita household expenditures were $375 in 1998, 67 percent of household spending went to food. In Japan, per capita household expenditures stood at $13,568 that year, but only 12 percent of that was spent on food. (See Table 7.4.)[13]

Not only do the world's wealthy take in more calories than the poor, but those calories are likelier to come from more resource-intensive foods, such as meat and dairy products, which are produced using large quantities of grain, water, and energy. People in industrial countries get 856 of their daily calories from animal products, while in developing countries the figure is 350. Still, meat consumption is rising in the more prosperous regions of the developing world as incomes and urbanization rates increase. Half of the world's pork is eaten in China, for example, while Brazil is the second largest consumer of beef, after the United States. And meat is increasingly consumed as fast food, which is often more energy-intensive to produce. According to a recent marketing research study, the fast-food industry in India is growing by 40 percent a year and is expected to generate over a billion dollars in sales by 2005. Meanwhile, a quarter of India's population remains undernourished—a number virtually unchanged over the past decade.[14]

Clean water and adequate sanitation, which are instrumental in preventing the spread of infectious disease, are also basic consumption needs. As with most goods, access to water and sanitation is skewed in favor of wealthier populations, although this situation has improved for poorer people somewhat in the past decade. In 2000, 1.1 billion people did not have access to safe drinking water, defined as the availability of at least 20 liters per person per day from a source within one kilometer of the user's dwelling. And two out of every five people did not have adequate sanitation facilities, such as a connection to a sewer or septic tank, or even a simple pit latrine. People in rural areas suffer the most. In 2000, only 40 percent of people living in rural areas were using adequate sanitation facilities, compared with 85 percent of urban inhabitants.[15]

As incomes rise, people gain access to nonfood consumer items that indicate greater prosperity. Paper use, for example, tends to increase as people become more literate and as communications links increase. Globally, paper use increased more than sixfold between 1950 and 1997 and has doubled since the mid-1970s; the average Briton used 16 times more paper at the end of the twentieth century than at its start. Indeed, most of the world's paper is produced and consumed in industrial countries: the United States alone produces and uses a third of the world's paper, and Americans use more than 300 kilograms each annually. In developing nations as a whole, in contrast, people use 18 kilograms of paper each year. In India, the annual figure is 4 kilos, and in 20 nations in Africa, it is less than 1 kilo. UNEP estimates that 30–40 kilos of paper are the minimum needed to meet basic literacy and communication needs.[16]

Rising prosperity also opens access to goods that promise new levels of comfort, convenience, and entertainment to millions. (See Table 7.5.) In 2002, 1.12 billion households, about three quarters of the world's people, owned at least one television set. Watching TV has become a leading form of leisure, with the average person in the industrial world spending three hours—half of their daily leisure time—in front of a television each day. The TV offers viewers access to local news and entertainment, but also exposure

TABLE 7.5 Household Consumption, Selected Countries, Circa 2000

Country	Household Consumption Expenditure	Electric Power	Television Sets	Telephone Mainlines	Mobile Phones	Personal Computers
	(1995 dollars per person)	(kilowatt-hours per person)	(per thousand population)			
Nigeria	194	81	68	6	4	7
India	294	355	83	40	6	6
Ukraine	558	2,293	456	212	44	18
Egypt	1,013	976	217	104	43	16
Brazil	2,779	1,878	349	223	167	75
South Korea	6,907	5,607	363	489	621	556
Germany	18,580	5,963	586	650	682	435
United States	21,707	12,331	835	659	451	625

Source: See endnote 17.

to countless consumer products that are shown in advertisements and during programs. And the view emerging from the screen is increasingly global in scope. Of the 1.12 billion households with TVs, 31 percent subscribed to a cable television service, often exposing them to a global entertainment culture.[17]

Many of these conveniences were considered luxuries when first introduced but are now perceived to be necessities. Indeed, where societal infrastructures have developed around them, some of these consumer goods have become integral to day-to-day life. Telephones, for example, have become an essential tool of communication—in 2002, there were 1.1 billion fixed-lines and another 1.1 billion mobile lines. A significant percentage of the world's people, including the vast majority of the world's global consumers, now has at least basic access to telephones. Communications have also advanced with the introduction of the Internet. This most recent addition to modern communications now connects about 600 million users.[18]

A large share of consumer spending focuses on goods that are arguably unnecessary for comfort or survival but that make life more enjoyable. These purchases include everything from seemingly minor daily indulgences, such as sweets and soda,

to major purchases, such as ocean cruises, jewelry, and sports cars. Expenditures on these products are not necessarily an indictment of the global consumer class, since reasonable people can disagree on what constitutes excessive consumption. But the sums spent on them are an indication of the surplus wealth that exists in many countries. Indeed, figures on consumer spending at the extreme undercut the perception that many of the unmet basic needs of the world's poor are too costly to address. Providing adequate food, clean water, and basic education for the world's poorest could all be achieved for less than people spend annually on makeup, ice cream, and pet food. (See Table 7.6.)[19]

The growing frenzy of consumption during the twentieth century led to greater use of raw materials, which complements household expenditures and numbers of consumers as a measure of consumption. Between 1960 and 1995, world use of minerals rose 2.5-fold, metals use increased 2.1-fold, wood products 2.3-fold, and synthetics, such as plastics, 5.6-fold. This growth outpaced the increase in global population and occurred even as the global economy shifted to include more service industries such as telecommunications and finance, which are not as materials-intensive as manufacturing, transportation, and

TABLE 7.6 Annual Expenditure on Luxury Items Compared with Funding Needed to Meet Selected Basic Needs

Product	Annual Expenditure	Social or Economic Goal	Additional Annual Investment Needed to Achieve Goal
Makeup	$18 billion	Reproductive health care for all women	$12 billon
Pet food in Europe and United States	$17 billion	Elimination of hunger and malnutrition	$19 billion
Perfumes	$15 billion	Universal literacy	$5 billion
Ocean cruises	$14 billion	Clean drinking water for all	$10 billion
Ice cream in Europe	$11 billion	Immunizing every child	$1.3 billion

Source: See endnote 19.

other once-dominant industries. The doubling of metals use, for example, happened even as metals became less critical to generating wealth: in 2000, the global economy used 45 percent fewer metals than three decades earlier to generate a dollar's worth of economic output.[20]

Fuel and materials consumption reflects the same pattern of global inequity found in final goods consumption. The United States alone, with less than 5 percent of the global population, uses about a quarter of the world's fossil fuel resources—burning up nearly 25 percent of the coal, 26 percent of the oil, and 27 percent of the world's natural gas. Add consumption by other wealthy nations, and the dominance of just a few countries in global materials use is clear. In terms of metals use, the United States, Canada, Australia, Japan, and Western Europe—with among them 15 percent of the world's population—use 61 percent of the aluminum produced each year, 60 percent of lead, 59 percent of copper, and 49 percent of steel. Use is high on a per person basis as well, especially relative to use in poorer nations. The average American uses 22 kilograms of aluminum a year, while the average Indian uses 2 kilos and the average African, less than 1 kilo.[21]

Meanwhile, the world's growing appetite for paper makes increasing demands on the world's forests. Virgin wood stocks destined for paper production, for instance, account for approximately 19 percent of the world's total wood harvest and 42 percent of wood harvested for "industrial" uses (everything but fuelwood). By 2050, pulp and paper manufacture could account for over half of the world's industrial wood demand.[22]

Consumption of raw materials such as metals and wood could, in principle, be largely independent of the consumption of goods and services, since many products could be remanufactured or made from recycled materials. But materials in most economies in the twentieth century did not circulate for even a second or third use. Even today, recycling provides only a small share of the materials used in economies worldwide. About half of the lead used today comes from recycled sources, as does a third of the aluminum, steel, and gold. Only 13 percent of copper is from recycled sources, down from 20 percent in 1980. Meanwhile, recycling of municipal waste generally remains low, even in nations that can afford recycling infrastructure. The 24 nations in the Organisation for Economic Co-operation and Development (OECD) that provide data on this, for example, have an average recycling rate of only 16 percent for municipal waste; half of them recycle less than 10 percent of their waste.[23]

Meanwhile, the share of total paper fiber supply coming from recycled fiber has grown only modestly, from 20 percent in 1921 to 38 percent today. This small increase, in the face of far greater increases in paper consumption, means that the amount of paper not recycled is higher than ever. In light of FAO projections that global paper consumption will increase by nearly 30 percent between 2000 and 2010, the share of paper that is recycled is especially critical, and it will have a large impact on the health of the world's forests in coming years.[24]

DISPARATE DRIVERS, COMMON RESULT

The global appetite for goods and services is driven by a set of largely independent influences, from technological advances and cheap energy to new business structures, powerful communications media, population growth, and even the social needs of human beings. These disparate drivers—some are natural endowments, others accidents of history, still others human innovations—have interacted to send production and demand to record levels. In the process, they have created an economic system of unprecedented bounty and unparalleled environmental and social impact.

The story starts with the consumer. Mainstream economists since Adam Smith have claimed that consumers are "sovereign" actors who make rational choices in order to maximize their gratification. Instead, consumers make imperfect decisions using a set of judgments that are shaped by incomplete and biased information. Their decisions are primarily driven by advertising, cultural norms, social influences, physiological impulses, and psychological associations, each of which can boost consumption.[25]

Physiological drives play a central role in stimulating consumption. The innate desire for pleasurable stimulation and the alleviation of discomfort are powerful motivators that have evolved over millennia to facilitate survival, as when hunger leads a person to search for food. These impulses are reinforced by consumers' experiences. Products that have satisfied us in the past are remembered as pleasurable, bolstering the desire to consume them again. In consumer societies where food and other goods are abundant, these impulses are leading to unhealthful levels of consumption, in part because they are further stimulated by advertising. Indeed, recent psychological studies have revealed that these impulses can even be primed subconsciously, arousing a desire for increased consumption, as for a thirst-quenching beverage after a feeling of thirst is aroused.[26]

Consumption habits also have social roots. Consumption is in part a social act through which people express their personal and group identity—choosing the newspaper of a particular political party, for instance, or the fashions favored by a peer group. Social motivators can be insatiable drivers of consumption, in contrast to the desire for food, water, or other goods, which is circumscribed by capacity limits. In 1954, the average Briton, for example, could count on an ample material base—enough food, clothing, shelter, and access to transportation to live a dignified life. So the increased spending that accompanied a doubling of wealth by 1994 was likely an attempt to satisfy social and psychological needs. Beyond the first pair of shoes, for instance, shoe ownership may not be about protecting a person's feet but about comfort, style, or status. Such desires can be boundless and therefore have the potential of driving consumption ever upward.[27]

Cornucopian stocks of goods, the product of huge increases in production efficiency since the Industrial Revolution, further stimulate humans' social and psychological proclivity to consume. Modern industrial workers now produce in a week what took their eighteenth-century counterparts four years. Innovations such as Henry Ford's assembly line slashed production time per automobile chassis from 12.5 hours in 1913 to 1.5 hours in 1914—and have been greatly improved since then. Today, a Toyota plant in Japan rolls out 300 completed Lexuses per day, using only 66 workers and 310 robots. Efficiency increases like these have reduced costs dramatically and fueled sales. This is perhaps most evident in the semiconductor industry, where production efficiencies helped to drive the cost per megabit of computing power from roughly $20,000 in 1970 to about 2¢ in 2001. Such order-of-magnitude increases in computing power at greatly reduced prices have spurred the modern computer revolution.[28]

Globalization has also lowered prices and stimulated consumption. Since 1950, successive rounds of trade negotiations have driven tariffs on many products steadily lower, with real consequences for individual consumers: Australians, for example, pay on average A$2,900 less for a car today because of tariff reductions that took effect after 1998. And the World Trade Organization's 1996 Information Technology Agreement has eliminated tariffs entirely for most computers and other information technologies, often reducing a product's cost by 20–30 percent. The eight rounds of global trade negotiations since 1950 are credited as a major spur to economic expansion worldwide.[29]

A globalizing world has also allowed large corporations to look across national borders for cheaper labor—and to pay workers as little as pennies per hour....Export processing zones (EPZs), minimally regulated manufacturing areas that produce goods for global commerce, have multiplied in the past three decades in response to the demand for inexpensive labor and a desire to boost exports. From 79 EPZs in 25 countries in 1975, the number expanded to some 3,000 in 116 nations by 2002, with the zones employing some 43 million workers who assemble clothing, sneakers, toys, and other goods for far less than it would cost in industrial nations. The zones boost the availability of inexpensive goods for global consumers, but are often criticized for fostering abuses of labor and human rights.[30]

Meanwhile, technological innovations of all kinds have increased production efficiency, often by raising the capacity of people and machinery to extract resources. Today's "supertrawler" fishing vessels, for example, can process hundreds of tons of fish per day. They are part of the reason that communities of many oceanic fish have suffered declines on the order of 80 percent within 15 years of the start of commercial exploitation. Mining equipment is also more muscular: in the United States, mining companies now engage in "mountaintop removal," which can leave a mountain dozens of meters shorter than its original height. In addition, the capacity of hauling trucks increased some eightfold, from 32 tons to 240 tons, between 1960 and the early 1990s. And output per U.S. miner more than tripled in the same period. Finally, chip mills—facilities that grind whole trees into wood chips for paper and pressed lumber products—can convert more than 100 truckloads of trees into chips every day. These

advances in humanity's ability to exploit vast swaths of resources, and at lower cost, help supply markets with inexpensive goods—a prod to greater consumption.[31]

In consumer societies where food and other goods are abundant, impulses are leading to unhealthful levels of consumption.

Cheap energy and improved transportation have also fueled production, lowering costs and facilitating increased distribution. Despite a spike in oil prices in the 1970s, the inflation-adjusted price of oil was only 7 percent higher in the 1997–2001 period than in 1970–74, for example. And reductions in transportation costs have helped make goods affordable to more people. Air freight rates dropped by nearly 3 percent annually for most international routes between 1980 and 1993, which helps to explain why perishables such as apples from New Zealand or grapes from Chile are now commonly found in European and North American supermarkets. Expanded markets also allow companies to increase the division of labor used in producing and delivering goods and services and to achieve greater economies of scale, each of which further lowers the costs of production.[32]

The unparalleled pace of these technological and transportation developments in the twentieth century led to increasingly rapid adoption of new products. In the United States, it took 38 years for the radio to reach an audience of 50 million people, 13 years for television to reach the same number, and only 4 years for the Internet to do the same. This has kept production lines humming in the information technologies industries, where Moore's Law—the rule of thumb that microprocessor capacity will double every 18 months—has prompted regular introductions of ever-more powerful computers and other digital products. The regular supply of new products, in turn, has prompted rapid turnover of these products in the last two decades—increasing consumption even further.[33]

Forces driving consumption are even found in the economic realities facing modern corporations. Most companies have substantial fixed costs—for heavy machinery, factory buildings, and delivery vehicles needed to produce and sell their products. Today's state-of-the-art semiconductor manufacturing plant, for instance, now costs around $3 billion, a huge investment that must be paid for even when sales are poor. Fixed costs therefore represent financial risk. This danger can be reduced by increasing output and sales so that fixed costs are spread over a greater volume of products and a greater diversity of markets. Thus the ongoing pressure to cover fixed costs creates an urgency to expand production—and to find new customers to buy the steady output of goods.[34]

The need for new customers gives business a strong incentive to develop a host of new tools designed to stimulate consumer demand, many of which play on the physiological, psychological, and social needs of human beings. Advertising has perhaps been the most powerful of these tools. Today advertising pervades nearly all aspects of the media, including commercial broadcasting, print media, and the Internet. Global spending on advertising reached $446 billion in 2002 (in 2001 dollars), an almost ninefold increase over 1950. (See Figure 7.2.) More than half of this is spent in the United States, where ads account for about two thirds of the space in the average newspaper, almost half of the mail that Americans receive, and about a quarter of network television programming. But advertising is surging in the rest of the world as well. Non-U.S. advertising expenditures have risen three and a half times over 20 years, with emerging markets showing particularly rapid growth. In China, ad spending increased by 22 percent in 2002 alone.[35]

Advertising is increasingly targeted and sophisticated, as seen in efforts to place products in movies and television programs. In recent studies, more than half of the cases of new smoking among teenagers could be traced to their exposure to smoking in movies, for example. And despite a 1990 voluntary "ban" on product placements by the tobacco industry, in the United States actual placements have almost doubled, with 85 percent of the top 250 movies between 1988 and 1997 containing smoking. Indeed, smoking is three times more prevalent in the movies than in the actual U.S. population. With Hollywood earning perhaps half of its revenues from movie sales outside the United States, smoking in movies continues to shape global smoking patterns as well. And non-American studios increasingly serve as vehicles for tobacco advertising. Some three fourths of the films produced between 1991 and 2002 by Bollywood (India's equivalent of Hollywood) included scenes with smoking.[36]

Innovative business practices have also helped boost consumer demand. The introduction of the credit card in the United States in the 1940s helped to increase total consumer credit almost elevenfold between 1945 and 1960. Today, heavy use of credit cards is promoted vigorously, since the profits of companies issuing the cards depend on having consumers maintain large monthly balances. In 2002, 61 percent of American credit card users carried an outstanding monthly balance, which on average was $12,000 at an interest rate of 16 percent....At this rate, a cardholder would pay about $1,900 a year in finance charges—more than the average per capita income (in purchasing power parity) in at least 35 countries.[37]

Credit is also spurring spending in Asia, Latin America, and Eastern Europe. In East Asia, the household share of total bank lending increased from 27 percent in 1997 to 40 percent in 2000. In several countries, major automobile

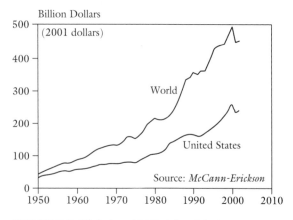

FIGURE 7.2 Global and U.S. Advertising Expenditures, 1950–2002

manufacturers are expanding their product lines because of this explosion in credit lending. General Motors official Philip Murtaugh underlines the importance of credit in China: "Once we establish the type of comprehensive GM financing systems we have in the U.S., we expect to see a huge jump in purchases."[38]

Finally, government policies are sometimes responsible for priming the consumption pump. Economic subsidies, now totaling around $1 trillion globally each year, can ripple throughout an economy, stimulating consumption along the way. The U.S. government, for instance, has subsidized suburban homebuilding since World War II with tax benefits and other enticements. Roomy suburban homes helped spur the consumption of a wide array of consumer durables, including refrigerators, televisions, furniture, washing machines, and automobiles. Cars, in turn, require vast quantites of raw materials: a third of U.S. iron and steel, a fifth of the aluminum, and two thirds of the lead and rubber. And the spread of suburbs led to greater public spending for new roads, firehouses, police stations, and schools. The Center for Neighborhood Technology in Chicago found in the late 1990s that low-intensity development is about 2.5 times more materials-intensive than high-intensity development. Thus the decision to subsidize suburban homebuilding had a profound effect on U.S. consumption patterns in the last half of the twentieth century.[39]

PROBLEMS IN PARADISE

In *Natural Capitalism,* their 1999 analysis of industrial economies, Paul Hawkins, Amory Lovins, and Hunter Lovins suggested that the United States generates a gargantuan amount of what the authors called "waste"—any expenditure for which no value is received. These outlays pay for a host of unintended byproducts of the American economic system, including air and water pollution, time spent idle in traffic, obesity, and crime, among many others. By the authors' calculations, this waste cost the United States at least $2 trillion in the mid-1990s—some 22 percent of the value of the economy. The estimate can only be a rough one, but the analysis is useful in calling attention in a comprehensive way to the little-noticed underbelly of modern industrial economies. The environmental and social toll of industrial economies is becoming difficult to ignore.[40]

Indeed, the very existence of waste in the more traditional sense—from households, mines, construction sites, and factories—shows that industrial economies are defective in their design. In contrast to the goods and services produced by the millions of other species on our planet, which generate useful byproducts but not worthless waste, human economies are designed with little attention to the residuals of production and consumption. The impact of this design flaw is enormous, starting with the extraction process. For every usable ton of copper, for example, 110 tons of waste rock and ore are discarded. As metals become rarer, the wastes tend to increase: roughly 3 tons of toxic mining waste are produced in mining the amount of gold needed in a single wedding ring.[41]

Nearly all the world's ecosystems are shrinking to make way for humans and their homes, farms, malls, and factories.

Consumer waste is equally sobering, especially in wealthy countries. The average resident of an OECD country generates 560 kilos of municipal waste per year, and all but three of the 27 reporting countries generated more per person in 2000 than in 1995. Even in nations considered leaders in environmental policy, such as Norway, reducing waste flows is a continuing challenge. In 2002, the average Norwegian generated 354 kilograms of waste, 7 percent more than the previous year. The share of waste recycled also grew, but it has stalled at less than half of total waste generated. Meanwhile, Americans remain the world's waste champions, producing 51 percent more municipal waste per person than the average resident of any other OECD country. The glimmer of good news from the United States is that per person rates appear to have plateaued in the 1990s. Still, the high waste levels per American, coupled with continuing growth of the U.S. population, adds up to a lot of trash.[42]

TABLE 7.7 Global Natural Resource and Environmental Trends

Environmental Indicator	Trend
Fossil fuels and atmosphere	Global use of coal, oil, and natural gas was 4.7 times higher in 2002 than in 1950. Carbon dioxide levels in 2002 were 18 percent higher than in 1960, and estimated to be 31 percent higher since the onset of the Industrial Revolution in 1750. Scientists have linked the warming trend during the twentieth century to the buildup of carbon dioxide and other heat-trapping gases.
Ecosystem degradation	More than half of Earth's wetlands, from coastal swamps to inland floodplains, have been lost, largely due to draining or filling for human settlements or agriculture. About half of the world's original forest cover is also gone, while another 30 percent of it is degraded or fragmented. In 1999, global use of wood for fuel, lumber, paper, and other wood products was more than double that in 1950.
Sea level	Sea level rose 10–20 centimeters in the twentieth century, an average of 1–2 millimeters per year, as a result of melting continental ice masses and the expansion of oceans due to climate change. Small island nations, though accounting for less than 1 percent of global greenhouse emissions, are at risk of being inundated by rising sea levels.
Soil/land	Some 10–20 percent of the world's cropland suffers from some form of degradation, while over 70 percent of the world's rangelands are degraded. Over the past half-century, land degradation has reduced food production by an estimated 13 percent on cropland and 4 percent from pasture.
Fisheries	In 1999, total fish catch was 4.8 times the amount in 1950. In just the past 50 years, industrial fleets have fished out at least 90 percent of all large ocean predators—tuna, marlin, swordfish, sharks, cod, halibut, skate, and flounder.
Water	Overpumping of groundwater is causing water tables to decline in key agricultural regions in Asia, North Africa, the Middle East, and the United States. The quality of groundwater is also deteriorating as a result of runoff of fertilizers and pesticides, petrochemicals that leak out of storage tanks, chlorinated solvents and heavy metals discarded by industries, and radioactive wastes from nuclear facilities.

Source: See endnote 43.

Trends in resource use and ecosystem health indicate that natural areas are also under stress from growing consumption pressures. (See Table 7.7.) An international team of ecologists, economists, and conservation biologists published a study in *Science* in 2002 indicating that nearly all the world's ecosystems are shrinking to make way for humans and their homes, farms, malls, and factories. Seagrass and algae beds, the study says, are declining by 0.01–0.02 percent each year, tropical forests by 0.8 percent, marine fisheries by 1.5 percent, freshwater ecosystems (swamps, floodplains, lakes, and rivers) by 2.4 percent, and mangroves by a staggering 2.5 percent. It also cited large but harder to quantify annual losses of coral reefs, rangeland, and cropland. Only temperate and boreal forests showed a resurgence, increasing by 0.1 percent annually after decades of decline. Consistent findings of global environmental decline are found in the Living Planet Index, a tool developed by WWF International to measure the health of forests, oceans, freshwater systems, and other natural systems. The Index shows a 35-percent decline in the planet's ecological health since 1970. (See Figure 7.3.)[43]

One measure of the impact of human consumption on global ecosystems is provided by the "ecological footprint" accounting system, which measures the amount of productive land an economy requires to produce the resources it needs and to assimilate its wastes. Calculations done by the California-based group Redefining Progress show that Earth has 1.9 hectares of

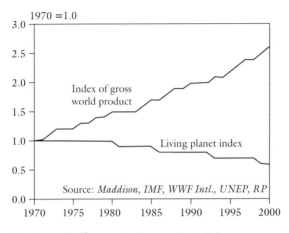

1970 = 1.0

Index of gross world product

Living planet index

Source: *Maddison, IMF, WWF Intl., UNEP, RP*

FIGURE 7.3 Changes in Economic Activity and Ecosystem Health, 1970–2000

biologically productive land per person to supply resources and absorb wastes. Yet the environmental demands of the world's economies are so large that the average person today uses 2.3 hectares worth of productive land. This overall number masks, of course, a tremendous range of ecological footprints—from the 9.7 hectares claimed by the average American to the 0.47 hectares used by the average Mozambican. Footprint analysis shows that total consumption levels had already exceeded the planet's ecological capacity by the late 1970s or early 1980s. Such overconsumption is possible only by drawing down stocks of resource reserves, as when wellwater is pumped to the point that groundwater levels decrease.[44]

Aggressive pursuit of a mass consumption society also correlates with a decline in health indicators in many countries. "Diseases of consumption" continue to surge. Smoking, for example, a consumer habit fueled by tens of billions of dollars in advertising, contributes to around 5 million deaths worldwide each year. In 1999, tobacco-related medical expenditures and productivity losses cost the United States more than $150 billion—almost 1.5 times the revenue of the five largest multinational tobacco companies that year. Similarly, overweight and obesity, generally the result of poor diet and an increasingly sedentary lifestyle, affect more than a billion people, lowering day-to-day life quality, costing societies billions in health care, and contributing to rapid increases in diabetes. In the

United States, an estimated 65 percent of adults are overweight or obese, leading to an annual loss of 300,000 lives and to at least, $117 billion in health care costs in 1999.[45]

The failure of additional wealth and consumption to help people have satisfying lives may be the most eloquent argument for reevaluating our approach to consumption.

Overall "social health" has declined in the United States in the past 30 years as well, according to Fordham University's Index of Social Health. This documents increases in poverty, teenage suicide, lack of health insurance coverage, and income inequity since 1970. And despite higher levels of consumption than in most other industrial nations, the United States scores worse on numerous indices of development: it ranks last among 17 OECD countries measured in the U.N. Development Programme's Human Poverty Index for industrial countries, for instance, which compiles indicators of poverty, functional illiteracy, longevity, and social inclusion.[46]

An OECD study has also documented disengagement from civic involvement in some industrial nations, especially the United States and Australia. In both countries, rates of membership in formal organizations have fallen, as has the intensity of participation in terms of meeting attendance and willingness to take on leadership roles. Meanwhile, informal social interactions—playing cards with neighbors, going on picnics, and the like—have also declined markedly in both countries, as have levels of trust among people and in institutions. The data on other prosperous countries are more encouraging, although early signs of social disengagement are evident. Organizational membership remains high in many European nations, but the level of involvement and of personal interaction has shown declines in some, and membership is often more transient than in the past. Even in Sweden, which appears to have strong social and community networks, signs of concern are appearing: political engagement is increasingly passive, and levels of trust in institutions are declining.[47]

Harvard Professor of Public Policy Robert Putnam has identified time limitations, residential sprawl, and high rates of television viewing as three features of American society that may explain a decline in civic engagement, together accounting for about half of the situation. All three are linked to high consumption: time pressures are often linked to the need to work long hours to support consumption habits, sprawl is a function of car dependence and the desire for larger homes and properties, and heavy television viewing helps promote consumption through exposure to advertising and programming that often romanticizes the consumer lifestyle.[48]

Perhaps the most damning evidence that continued consumption is generating diminishing benefits is found in studies that compare the ever-rising level of personal wealth in rich countries with the stagnant share of people in these nations who claim to be "very happy." Although self-reported happiness among the poor tends to rise with increased income, studies show that the linkage between happiness and rising income is broken once modest levels of income are reached. The failure of additional wealth and consumption to help people have satisfying lives may be the most eloquent argument for reevaluating our current approach to consumption.[49]

Disappointment in the ability of consumption to deliver lives of fulfillment is producing discontent among scholars, policymakers, and the public. A slew of books published in the 1990s documented dissatisfaction with societies organized around consumption. The titles tell the story: *The Overspent American, The Overworked American, An All-Consuming Century, Confronting Consumption,* and *The High Price of Materialism,* among others. Although the analyses differ, all these authors express the view that consumption-oriented societies are not sustainable, for environmental or social reasons.

Discontent with a commitment to high consumption was evident at the policy and grassroots levels as well. Several European governments are implementing or considering reforms to working hours and family leave benefits, for example. And some people in Europe and the United States are starting to adopt simpler lifestyles. Slowly but steadily, people's interest in recasting consumption in a supporting rather than the leading role is now evident.[50]

A NEW ROLE FOR CONSUMPTION?

Despite the problems associated with a consumer society, and notwithstanding the tentative steps taken to shift societies to a less damaging path, most people in industrial countries are still on an upward consumption track, and many in developing countries remain mired in poverty. In order to advance the tentative interest in a new role for consumption, any vision will need to include responses to four key questions:

- Is the global consumer class experiencing a higher quality of life from its growing levels of consumption?
- Can societies pursue consumption in a balanced way, especially in putting consumption in harmony with the natural environment?
- Can societies reshape consumer options to offer genuine choice?
- Can societies make a priority of meeting the basic needs of all?

All things considered, are consumers benefiting from the global consumer culture? Individuals, the important arbiters of this question, might consider the personal costs associated with heavy levels of consumption: the financial debt; the time and stress associated with working to support high consumption; the time required to clean, upgrade, store, or otherwise maintain possessions; and the ways in which consumption replaces time with family and friends.

Individuals as well as policymakers might consider the seeming paradox that quality of life is often improved by operating within clear limits on consumption. Forests, for example, can be available to all indefinitely if they are harvested no faster than the rate of regrowth. Similarly, someone who adopts clear parameters of personal well-being—exercising daily and eating well, for example—is likely to have a higher quality of life than a person who consumes in an open-ended and unrestrained way. Indeed, the underlying premise of mass consumption economics—that unlimited consumption is acceptable, even desirable—is fundamentally at odds with life patterns of the natural world and with the teaching on moderation that is common to philosophers and religious leaders across many cultures and throughout much of human history.

The underlying premise of mass consumption economics—that unlimited consumption is acceptable, even desirable—is fundamentally at odds with life patterns of the natural world.

Second, is our consumption in balance economically, socially, and environmentally? In societies of mass consumption, laws and economic incentives often encourage people to cross key economic, environmental, and social thresholds. Banks and credit agencies urge consumers to take on heavy burdens of debt; businesses and individuals use forests, groundwater, and other renewable resources beyond their rates of renewal; and employers often reward workers for spending long hours on the job. Each of these excesses exacts a price in personal or societal well-being. Numerous imaginative ways for bringing consumption choices in better harmony with social and environmental needs—from legislation mandating levels of recycled content to product "take back" laws that make producers responsible for the products and waste they create—are available.

Third, are consumers given genuine choices that help them to meet their needs? Clearly, mass consumption societies offer more products and services than any other economic system in human history. Yet consumers do not always find what they need. Consider transportation: safe and convenient access to just five transportation alternatives—walking, cycling, mass transit, car-sharing, or private cars—may offer more real options for getting people where they want to go than a choice of 100 models at a car dealership

would. And where genuine choice is present, the most desirable choice may not be affordable, as happens with organic food in some countries. Governments need to reshape economic incentives and regulations to ensure that businesses offer affordable options that meet consumers' needs. They also have a role in curbing consumption excess, primarily by removing incentives to consume—from subsidized energy to promotion of low-density development.

Last, can societies create a consumption ethic that gives priority to meeting the basic needs of all? Physical well-being—including sufficient access to healthy food, clean water and sanitation, education, health care, and physical security—is the foundation of all individual and societal achievement. Neglecting these basics will inevitably limit the capacity of many to realize their personal potential—and their ability to make meaningful contributions to society. In a world in which there are more people living on less than $2 per day than there are in the global consumer class, the continued pursuit of greater wealth by the rich when there is little evidence that it increases happiness raises serious ethical questions.

Beyond the ethical imperative to care for all is a self-serving motive. Lack of attention to the needs of the poorest can result in greater insecurity for the prosperous and in increased spending on defensive measures. The need to spend billions of dollars on wars, border security, and peacekeeping arguably is linked to a disregard for the world's pressing social and environmental problems. The same is true at the community level. Expenditures for private education, gated communities, and home alarm systems are just a few of the ways that failing to invest in the poorest comes back to haunt the wealthy. Meeting the basic needs of all, it seems, is both right and smart.

Addressing these four questions would give consumption a less central place in our lives and would free up time for community building and strengthening interpersonal relationships—factors that psychologists tell us are essential for a satisfying life. By reorienting societal priorities toward improving people's well-being rather than merely accumulating goods, consumption can act not as the engine that drives the economy but as a tool that delivers an improved quality of life.

NOTES

1. Wayne W. J. Xing, "Shifting Gears," *The China Business Review,* November-December 1997.

2. "China's Private Car Ownership Tops 10 Million," *People's Daily,* 14 June 2003; 11,000 a day is a Worldwatch calculation based on the data in Liu Wei, "China's Demand of Cars to Exceed 4.2 Million in 2003," *People's Daily,* 30 July 2003; auto sales from "Car Sales Booming in China," *All Things Considered,* National Public Radio, 17 September 2003; "150 mn Chinese Families to Buy Cars in Next 15 Years," *People's Daily,* 12 March 2003; U.S. auto fleet from Ward's Communications, *Ward's Motor Vehicle Facts & Figures 2001* (Southfield, MI: 2001), p. 38; attitudes of Chinese from "Car Sales Booming," op. cit. this note.

3. Julie Chao, "Pacific Currents: China Trying to Cope With Burgeoning Car Culture," *Seattle Post-Intelligencer,* 8 September 2003; foreign investments from Clay Chandler, "China Goes Car Crazy: Suburbs, Drive-ins, Car Washes—This Revolution Has Wheels," *Fortune,* 11 August 2003.

4. Matthew Bentley, *Sustainable Consumption: Ethics, National Indices and International Relations* (PhD dissertation, American Graduate School of International Relations and Diplomacy, Paris, 2003).

5. Population projection from United Nations, *World Population Prospects, The 2002 Revision* (New York: 2003).

6. U.S. Department of Transportation, Bureau of Transportation Statistics, *National Household Travel Survey 2001 Highlights Report* (Washington, DC: 2003); SUVs from Oak Ridge National Laboratory, *Transportation Energy Data Book,* Edition 22 (Oak Ridge, TN: September 2002), p. 7–1; house size from Joint Center for Housing Studies, *State of the Nation's Housing 2003* (Cambridge, MA: Harvard University, 2003), p. 32; household size from U.S. Department of Agriculture, Economic Research Service, *Race and Ethnicity in Rural America: Marital Status and Household Structure,* at www.ers.usda.gov/Briefing/RaceAndEthnic/familystructure.htm, updated 24 December 2002; obesity industry from Jui Chakravorty, "Catering to Obese Becoming Big Business," *Reuters,* 4 October 2003.

7. Private consumption expenditures (in 1995 dollars) are Worldwatch calculations based on World Bank, *World Development Indicators Database,* at media.worldbank.org/secure/data/qquery.php, viewed 2 June 2003. Box 7.1 from the following: United Nations, op. cit. note 5, p. 1; Americans' projected meat consumption and all population data from United Nations Population Division, online database, at esa.un.org/unpp, viewed 20 September 2003, and from U.N. Food and Agriculture Organization (FAO), *FAOSTAT Statistical Database,* at apps.fao.org, updated 30 June 2003; carbon emissions are Worldwatch calculations based on data in Molly O. Sheehan, "Carbon Emissions and Temperature Climb," in Worldwatch Institute, *Vital Signs 2003* (New York: W.W. Norton & Company, 2003), pp. 40–41; household size and energy use from Nico Keilman, "The Threat of Small Households," *Nature,* 30 January 2003, p. 489. Table 7.1 contains Worldwatch calculations based on population and private consumption expenditures data from World Bank, op. cit. this note; totals add up to 98 and 99 percent because data are unavailable for a few small countries.

8. Poverty numbers are World Bank estimates cited on Millennium Development Goals Web site, at www.developmentgoals.com/Poverty.htm.

9. Table 7.2 from Bentley, op. cit. note 4. Share of global consumer class is a Worldwatch calculation.

10. Table 7.3 from Bentley, op. cit. note 4; expenditures in sub-Saharan Africa (in 1995 dollars) from World Bank, op. cit. note 7.

11. Bentley, op. cit. note 4.

12. U.N. Environment Programme (UNEP), "UNEP Urges Asia-Pacific Towards a Cleaner, Greener Development Path," press release (Nairobi: 19 May 2003); U.S. auto fleet from Ward's Communications, op. cit. note 2, p. 38; Matthew Bentley, "Forging New Paths to Sustainable Development," UNEP Background Paper, Asia Pacific Expert Meeting on Promoting Sustainable Consumption and Production Patterns, Yogyakarta, Indonesia, 21–23 May 2003.

13. Daily calories from FAO, op. cit. note 7; number of undernourished from idem, *The State of Food Insecurity in the World,* as cited in United Nations Statistical Division, *Millennium Indicators Database,* at unstats.un.org/unsd/mi/mi_series_xrxx.asp?row_id=640, viewed 23 October 2003; Table 7.4 from World Bank, *World Development Indicators 2000* (Washington, DC: 2000), pp. 222–24.

14. Calories from animal products from FAO, op. cit. note 7; meat consumption from Danielle Nierenberg, "Meat Production and Consumption Grow," in Worldwatch Institute, op. cit. note 7, p. 30; fast food in India from Saritha Rai, "Taste of India in U.S. Wrappers," *New York Times,* 29 April 2003, and from Seth Mydans, "Clustering

in Cities, Asians Are Becoming Obese," *New York Times,* 13 March 2003; undernourished in India from U.N. Development Programme (UNDP), *Human Development Report 2003* (New York: Oxford University Press, 2003), p. 199.

15. Data on clean water and sanitation from UNICEF, *The State of the World's Children 2003* (New York: 2003), p. 95; definitions of "safe drinking water" and "adequate sanitation" from UNDP, op. cit. note 14, pp. 357–58.

16. Janet Abramovitz and Ashley Matoon, Paper Cuts: Recovering the Paper Landscape, Worldwatch Paper 149 (Washington, DC: Worldwatch Institute, December 1999), pp. 6, 11–12.

17. Table 7.5 from World Bank, op. cit. note 7; households with televisions and number with cable service from International Telecommunication Union (ITU), *World Telecommunication Development Report 2002* (Geneva: 2002); average television habits from Robert Kubey and Mihaly Csikszentmihalyi, "Television Addiction Is No Mere Metaphor," *Scientific American,* February 2002, pp. 74–80.

18. Phones from ITU, op. cit. note 17; Internet users from idem, "Internet Indicators: Hosts, Users and Number of PCs," at www.itu.int/ITU-D/ict/statistics/at_glance/Internet02.pdf, viewed 9 October 2003.

19. Table 7.6 from the following: makeup and perfumes from "Posts of Promise," *The Economist,* 24 May 2003, pp. 69–71; pet food and ice cream from UNDP, *Human Development Report 1998* (New York: Oxford University Press, 1998), p. 37; ocean cruises from Lisa Mastny, "Cruise Industry Buoyant," in Worldwatch Institute, *Vital Signs 2002* (New York: W.W. Norton & Company, 2002), p. 122; additional annual investments needed from Michael Renner, "Military Expenditures on the Rise," in Worldwatch Institute, op. cit. note 7, p. 119, except for immunizing estimate from Erik Assadourian, "Consumption Patterns Contribute to Mortality," in Worldwatch Institute, op. cit. note 7, p. 108.

20. Materials increases from Gary Gardner and Payal Sampat, *Mind Over Matter: Recasting the Role of Materials in Our Lives,* Worldwatch Paper 144 (Washington, DC: Worldwatch Institute, December 1998), p. 16; metals intensity from Payal Sampat, "Metals Production Climbs," in Worldwatch Institute, op. cit. note 19, pp. 66–67.

21. Fossil fuel use from Janet L. Sawin, "Fossil Fuel Use Up," in Worldwatch Institute, op. cit. note 7, pp. 34–35; metals from Payal Sampat,

"Scrapping Mining Dependence," in Worldwatch Institute, *State of the World 2003* (New York: W.W. Norton & Company, 2003), p. 113.

22. Abramovitz and Mattoon, op. cit. note 16, p. 20.

23. Sampat, op. cit. note 21, p. 114; Organisation for Economic Co-operation and Development (OECD), OECD *Environmental Data Compendium 2002* (Paris: 2003), p. 14.

24. Data and FAO projections from Abramovitz and Mattoon, op. cit. note 16, pp. 20–21, 40, 52.

25. Peter Lunt, "Psychological Approaches to Consumption: Varieties of Research—Past, Present and Future," in Daniel Miller, ed., *Acknowledging Consumption* (London: Routledge, 1995), pp. 238–63.

26. Ibid.; John A. Bargh, "Losing Consciousness: Automatic Influences on Consumer Judgment, Behavior, and Motivation," *Journal of Consumer Research,* September 2002, pp. 280–85.

27. Tim Jackson and Nic Marks, "Consumption, Sustainable Welfare and Human Needs," *Ecological Economics,* vol. 28, no. 3 (1999), pp. 421–42.

28. J. R. McNeill, *Something New Under the Sun: An Environmental History of the 20th Century World* (New York: W.W. Norton & Company, 2001), p. 315; Toyota plant from Thomas L. Friedman, *The Lexus and the Olive Tree* (New York: Farrar, Strauss, Giroux, 1999), p. 26; semiconductor costs from "Cost per Megabit Trends," IC Knowledge Web site, at www.icknowledge.com/economic/productcosts2.html, viewed 2 September 2003.

29. Australians from "Freer Trade Cuts the Cost of Living," at WTO website at www.wto.org/english/thewto_e/whatis_e/10ben_e/10b04_e.htm, viewed 17 October 2003; "Kingdom of Bahrain Joins WTO's Information Technology Agreement," 18 July 2003, at www.wto. org/english/news_e/news03_e/news_bahrain_ita_18jul03_e.htm, viewed 17 October 2003; cost reductions from Telecommunications Industry Association, "Information Technology Agreement Promises to Eliminate Tariffs on Most IT Products by the Year 200," *PulseOnline Newsletter Archive,* October 1997, at www.tiaonline.org/media/pulse/1997/pulse1097-3.cfm, viewed 17 October 2003.

30. International Labour Organization, Committee on Employment and Social Policy, *Employment and Social Policy in Respect of Export Processing Zones* (Geneva: November 2002); Jim Lobe, "Unions Assail WTO for Ignoring Worker Rights," *One World US,* 8 September 2003; International Confederation of Free Trade Unions, *Export Processing*

Zones—Symbols of Exploitation and a Development Dead-End (Brussels: September 2003).

31. Ransom A. Myers and Boris Worm, "Rapid Worldwide Depletion of Predatory Fish Communities," *Nature,* 15 May 2003, pp. 280–83; mining from Craig B. Andrews, *Mineral Sector Technologies: Policy Implications for Developing Countries,* Industry and Energy Division Note No. 19 (Washington, DC: World Bank, 1992), and from Craig Andrews, discussion with Claudia Meulenberg, Worldwatch Institute, 22 September 2003; Dogwood Alliance, "Paper and Chipboard Production," at www.dogwoodalliance .org/chipmill.asp#chipboard, viewed 22 October 2003.

32. Oil prices from Organization of the Petroleum Exporting Countries, *OPEC Annual Statistics Bulletin 2001* (Vienna: 2001), p. 119; air freight rates from David Hummels, "Have International Transportation Costs Declined?" draft (Chicago: University of Chicago, November 1999), pp. 4–5; division of labor from Nathan Rosenberg, "Technology," in Glenn Porter, ed., *Encyclopedia of American Economic History,* vol. 1 (New York: Charles Scribner's Sons, 1980), pp. 294–308.

33. ITU, *Telecommunications Indicators in the World, 2000,* at www.rtnda.org/resources/wiredweb/ text.html; Moore's Law from Webopedia, at www.webopedia.com/TERM/M/Moores_Law .html, viewed 9 October 2003.

34. Semiconductor costs from Joseph I. Lieberman, *White Paper: National Security Aspects of the Global Migration of the U.S. Semiconductor Industry* (Washington, DC: Office of Senator Lieberman, June 2003); fixed costs from Rosenberg, op. cit. note 32.

35. Global, U.S., and Chinese advertising spending from Bob Coen, *Universal McCann's Insider's Report on Advertising Expenditures,* June 2003, at www.mccann.com/insight/bobcoen.html, viewed 9 October 2003; Figure 7.2 from ibid. and from Bob Coen, *Estimated World Advertising Expenditures,* at www.mccann.com/insight/bobcoen. html, viewed 9 October 2003; newspapers and mail from John de Graff, David Wann, and Thomas Naylor, *Affluenza: The All-Consuming Epidemic* (San Francisco, CA: Berrett-Koehler Publishers, Inc., 2001), p. 149; "Television Clutter in Prime Time and Early Morning Reach All Time Highs," press release (New York: American Association of Advertising Agencies and Association of National Advertisers, Inc., 12 April 1999).

36. Teen smoking from Madeline A. Dalton et al., "Effect of Viewing Smoking in Movies on Adolescent Smoking Initiation: A Cohort Study," *The Lancet,* 10 June 2003, pp. 281–85; ban and increase from Stanton A. Glantz, "Smoking in Movies: A Major Problem and a Real Solution," *The Lancet,* 10 June 2003, p. 258; 85 percent and revenue from foreign sales from James D. Sargeant et al., "Brand Appearances in Contemporary Cinema Films and Contribution to Global Marketing of Cigarettes," *The Lancet,* 6 January 2001, pp. 29–32; three times more prevalent from A. R. Hazan, H. L. Lipton, and S. A. Glantz, "Popular Films Do Not Reflect Current Tobacco Use," *American Journal of Public Health,* vol. 84, no. 6 (1994), pp. 998–1000; World Health Organization (WHO), *'Bollywood': Victim or Ally? A WHO Study on the Portrayal of Tobacco in Indian Cinema* (Geneva: February 2003).

37. Consumer credit growth from Lizabeth Cohen, *A Consumer's Republic: The Politics of Mass Consumption in Postwar America* (New York: Alfred A. Knopf, 2003), pp. 123–24; 61 percent from Robert D. Manning, "Perpetual Debt, Predatory Plastic: From the Company Store to the World of Late Fees and Overlimit Penalties," *Southern Exposure,* summer 2003, p. 51; per capita income from World Bank, *World Development Indicators 2003* (Washington, DC: 2003), pp. 14–16.

38. Credit growth and quote from Joshua Kurlantzick, "Charging Ahead: America's Biggest New Export— Credit Cards—Could Bring Down the World Economy," *Washington Monthly,* May 2003, pp. 28–29.

39. Economic subsidies from OECD, *Towards Sustainable Consumption: An Economic Conceptual Framework* (Paris: Environment Directorate, June 2002), p. 41; suburban home subsidies from Cohen, op. cit. note 37; Scott Bernstein, Center for Neighborhood Technology, Chicago, discussion with Gary Gardner, 20 August 1998.

40. Paul Hawken, Amory Lovins, and L. Hunter Lovins, *Natural Capitalism: Creating the Next Industrial Revolution* (Boston: Little, Brown, and Company, 1999), pp. 57–60.

41. Sampat, op. cit. note 21, p. 117.

42. OECD, *OECD Environmental Data 2002* (Paris: 2002), p. 11; "Norway—Household Waste Increases More Than Ever," *Warmer Bulletin,* 28 June 2003.

43. Andrew Balmford et al., "Economic Reasons for Conserving Wild Nature," *Science,* 9 August 2002; Living Planet Index from WWF International, UNEP, and Redefining Progress *Living Planet Report 2002,* at www.panda.org/news _facts/publications/general/livingplanet/index

.cfm, p. 21. Table 7.7 from various editions of Worldwatch Institute's *Vital Signs* as follows: fossil fuel use, carbon emissions, and sea level rise from *Vital Signs 2003;* forests, wood use, cropland, rangelands, food production, and water deficit from *Vital Signs 2002;* wetlands from *Vital Signs 2001;* groundwater from *Vital Signs 2000;* in addition, large predator fish depletion from Myers and Worm, op. cit. note 31. Figure 7.3 from WWF International, UNEP, and Redefining Progress, op. cit. this note, and from Angus Maddison, *The World Economy: A Millennial Perspective* (OECD, Paris: 2001), pp. 272–321, with updates from International Monetary Fund, *World Economic Outlook Database* (Washington, DC: December 2002).

44. WWF International, UNEP, and Redefining Progress, op. cit. note 43; Mathis Wackernagel et al., "Tracking the Ecological Overshoot of the Human Economy," *Proceedings of the National Academy of Sciences,* 9 July 2002, p. 9268.

45. Deaths from Majid Ezzati and Alan D. Lopez, "Estimates of Global Mortality Attributable to Smoking in 2000," *The Lancet,* 13 September 2003, pp. 847–52; $150 billion from "Annual Smoking-Attributable Mortality, Years of Potential Life Lost, and Economic Costs—United States, 1995–1999," *Morbidity and Mortality Weekly Report,* 12 April 2002, p. 303; revenue from Judith Mackay and Michael Eriksen, *The Tobacco Atlas* (Geneva: WHO, 2002), p. 50; overweight and obesity from WHO and FAO, *Joint WHO/FAO Expert Consultation on Diet, Nutrition and the Prevention of Chronic Diseases* (Geneva: 2002); National Center for Health Statistics, *Health, United States, 2003* (Hyattsville, MD: 2003); U.S. Department of Health and Human Services, *The Surgeon General's Call to Action to Prevent and Decrease Overweight and Obesity, 2001* (Washington, DC: 2001).

46. The Fordham Institute for Innovation in Social Policy, *The Social Report 2003* (New York: 2003); UNDP, op. cit. note 14, pp. 248–49.

47. OECD, *The Well Being of Nations: The Role of Human and Social Capital* (Paris: 2001), pp. 99–103.

48. Robert Putnam, *Bowling Alone: The Collapse and Revival of American Community* (New York: Simon & Schuster, 2000), pp. 189–246.

49. Michael Bond, "The Pursuit of Happiness," *New Scientist,* 4 October 2003, pp. 40–47.

50. Anders Hayden, "Europe's Work-Time Alternatives," in John de Graaf, ed., *Take Back Your Time* (San Francisco: Berrett Koehler, 2003), p. 204.

✿ STUDY QUESTIONS

1. What is meant by the 'consumer class' or 'consumer society'? How does it differ from other classes and societies?

2. Examine and comment on Table 7.1 and the associated text.

3. Using the data in text and tables, summarize the current global distribution of population and consumption.

4. Is consumption a moral issue? That is, is it wrong to overconsume? Summarize the author's views on this and respond with your own.

---

48 Population and the Environment

CLARK WOLF

Clark Wolf is a professor of philosophy at Iowa State University. In this essay he provides a balanced overview of issues relating population dynamics to the environment. He discusses the original debate on population between Thomas Malthus and the Marquis Condorcet and shows how this debate continues today between the Doomsdayers and Cornucopians, those who hold the Notestein Demographic Transition Hypothesis. Clark shows the problems with this theory, but in the end he judges that something like it is our most promising policy.

He argues that by empowering via educational and economic opportunities, we will enable people to prosper with fewer children. We will also have to institute social security systems so that people do not overly rely on children for their security in old age.

HOW MANY PEOPLE ARE THERE?

While people have been concerned about human population growth for thousands of years, the existence of what we would now consider large human populations is a relatively recent phenomenon: the human population of the earth did not reach the first billion until the early nineteenth century—long after the publication of Thomas Malthus's famous *Essay on the Principles of Population* in 1798. Population did not reach two billion until the early twentieth century (between 1925 and 1935). The third, fourth, and fifth billions arrived around 1960, 1975, and 1990, respectively, the sixth arriving with the new millennium.

Most estimates put the current (turn of the century) human population of the earth quite near 6 billion. The present rate of population growth, however, is between 1.6 and 1.7 percent per year. If that rate of growth were to remain stable, we would expect an additional billion people in about ten years, and would expect the current population to double in size in less than fifty years. However, while most demographers expect population size to continue to grow well into the twenty-first century, many also predict that the *rate* of growth will decline during the next twenty years, and that world population may even stabilize at some time during the mid-twenty-first century. There is little agreement, however, about what mechanism is likely to cause the rate of growth to diminish, or about the population levels that may be achieved before we reach stability or decline in total population size. Some argue that human population is likely to keep growing until environmental destruction and consequent resource scarcity causes widespread famine, bringing the death rate high enough to compensate for the birth rate. Others more hopefully propose

that fertility rates may fall as economic and human development give people (and especially women) more control over their reproductive lives.

Is the increase in human population a problem, and if so, what kind of problem is it? Concerns about population growth usually identify the problem in one of two ways: first, human population growth may imply proliferation of destitution and misery for present and future generations of human beings. Some theorists have argued that population increase will go hand in hand with increasing poverty, since there will be less of everything to go around. But those who find this view untenable may still have a (second) good reason to be concerned, since the growing human population may unsustainably exploit resources and destroy the earth's great ecosystems. There is a third important reason why population growth and high human fertility should be regarded as a serious problem: the high fertility rates that lead to rapid population growth impose inordinate personal costs and an unacceptably high risk of death on women in their reproductive years.

Important elements of the current population debate were first articulated in an exchange between the Marquis de Condorcet and Thomas Malthus at the end of the eighteenth century. I begin by exploring the main themes in this exchange, tracing the influence of this classical debate in contemporary theories of population, and examining the role these theories play in development economics, including consideration of the policy implications of contemporary theories. Next I discuss paradoxes that arise when we try to use common normative criteria to evaluate potential changes in population. Finally, I consider the significance of population growth for environmental philosophy and policy.

Reprinted from *A Companion to Environmental Philosophy*, ed. Dale Jamieson (Blackwell Publishing, 2001).

CLASSIC DISCUSSIONS OF POPULATION: CONDORCET AND MALTHUS

In 1793, Antoine-Nicolas, Marquis de Condorcet argued that the advancement of science and knowledge will lead to the continued improvement of human institutions, and that the human condition will approach perfection as our knowledge increases. Even the length of human life, claimed Condorcet, may be expected to approach infinity as knowledge of medical science becomes more perfect. Since increasing population size poses a potential threat to improvement, he considered the likelihood that the number of people in the world might eventually exceed the means of subsistence, and that this might lead either to "a continual diminution of happiness and population," or alternately to "an oscillation between good and bad" which would be "a perennial source of more or less periodic disaster." This problem, argued Condorcet, will be solved once.

> the absurd prejudices of superstition will have ceased to corrupt and degrade the moral code by its harsh doctrines instead of purifying and elevating it. We can assume that by then men will know that if they have a duty towards those who are not yet born, it is not to give them existence but to give them happiness; their aim should be to promote the general welfare of the human race or of the society in which they live or of the family to which they belong, rather than foolishly to encumber the earth with useless and wretched beings. (Condorcet 1955 [1793], p. 189)

It is usually assumed (for example by Malthus) that by "the absurd prejudices of superstition," Condorcet meant to refer to puritanical attitudes toward the use of birth control. It is clear enough that this was at least part of his intent. But in the context of the *Sketch,* it is plausible to read him as meaning more than this: Condorcet believed that the progressive improvement of knowledge and human institutions, including especially the recognition of fully equal rights for women, would lead people to have greater control over their lives generally. Voluntary fertility reduction would, he believed, be a natural consequence of these improvements. It is because of this broader project that Condorcet is usually associated with the view that fertility reduction will naturally follow from human development and improvement in the conditions of life.

It was largely in response to Condorcet's *Sketch* that Thomas Malthus wrote the first edition of his *Essay on the Principles of Population* (1798). In this work (usually called the *First Essay*) Malthus argues that human population will increase geometrically until checked by some countervailing force, while the "means for subsistence" can be expected to increase only arithmetically. Because of this, the size of the human population will grow until it eventually reaches a plateau when the earth's capacity to meet needs has been stretched to its extreme limit. At this point, it will stabilize as starvation causes the death rate to rise to the level of the fertility rate. If the means of subsistence increase (due, perhaps, to colonization of new territories or increase in productive efficiency) population will again rise to a new famine equilibrium. Malthus recognized two categories of check on population growth: "positive checks" are causes of increased mortality, while "preventive checks" are the causes of decreased fertility. Elsewhere in the *First Essay,* he argues that these checks, both positive and preventive, "may be fairly resolved into misery and vice." When starvation, disease, or war increase the death rate, population is checked by misery. Of the other category, he remarks that "Promiscuous intercourse, unnatural passions, violations of the marriage bed, and improper arts to conceal the consequences of irregular connections are preventive checks that clearly come under the head of vice" (Malthus, 1989 [1803], p. 18).

Puritanical Malthus was shocked by Condorcet's suggestion that birth control would allow people to gain more rational control over their reproductive lives. But in later editions of the *Essay* he added "moral restraint" as a third category of preventive check, if people can acquire the moral fortitude to abstain from marriage and from "irregular gratifications." Still, Malthus seems to have regarded this last check as much too weak to counteract the forces leading to rapid population growth. So population should be expected to rise to the level permitted by the availability of "means of subsistence," at which point "misery and vice" will bring this growth to a stop. Even then, "misery" will be the most prevalent check on population growth, since "vice" is not very effective as a means of fertility reduction while starvation and deprivation can be cruelly efficient causes of increased mortality.

While his analysis was already quite bleak enough, it was his prescriptions for policy that brought Malthus undeserved notoriety as a gloomy misanthrope. He saw efforts to ameliorate poverty as doomed to ultimate failure since they must ultimately cause an increase in population and a consequent increase in misery and suffering. Improving the conditions of life for the poor, he argued in the *First Essay,* simply facilitates faster rates of reproduction, leading to a new and more populous famine equilibrium at a later date. Malthus's views have often been dismissed as "cruel," but his express aim was to describe policies that would minimize human misery. It can hardly be acceptable simply to argue that such a view is cruel: it must be shown that there are alternative policies that are likely to do better. While contemporary theorists have improved upon Malthus's analysis, key elements of his theory have yet to be disconfirmed.

THE CONTEMPORARY DEBATE: POPULATION, DEVELOPMENT, AND THE ENVIRONMENT

The Malthusian view of the population problem is still prevalent in popular discussions of population, and many still see the Condorcet–Malthus exchange as having set out the essential elements of the current debate. Two fundamental features of Malthus's analysis are carried on in contemporary discussion: the Malthusian view that resource availability sets limits to growth is carried on in the contemporary notion of a "carrying capacity" for the earth. And Malthus's insight that fertility should be analyzed in terms of the factors that influence individual decision-making is carried on in economic models of fertility. While Condorcet's enlightenment optimism has few contemporary adherents, an important insight of his analysis has been resurrected in recent work on population and development: as Condorcet implies, the best way to reduce fertility may well

be to improve the circumstances of life for the poor and to work to guarantee equal opportunities for women. Environmental philosophers should pay particular attention to this insight, since it implies that human development must be a centerpiece of any effective plan for global environmental protection.

Carrying Capacity

The concept of "carrying capacity" was developed by ecologists, who have used it to refer to the Malthusian notion of an upper limit on population size set by the availability of resources. One way to estimate the carrying capacity of an environment is as follows: first estimate the quantity of renewable resource necessary to support an individual organism (whether human or non-human). Then estimate the total quantity of renewable resources available. The carrying capacity of this environment is determined by dividing the total quantity of renewable resources by the quantity needed to support an individual organism.

So understood, the carrying capacity of an environment represents the maximum population level that can possibly be held stable over time. However, this possibility is only theoretical, not practical: once carrying capacity is reached, it can be held stable only if each organism consumes just barely enough to stay alive. Since such perfectly egalitarian distribution is as unlikely in non-human populations as it is in human populations, it is not practically possible to hold the carrying capacity maximum as a stable equilibrium. It would be far better for each organism if population could stabilize far below the carrying capacity limit. However, on this conception, environmental carrying capacity can even be *exceeded* for limited periods of time, while non-renewable resources are used up, or when renewable resources are consumed faster than they can be renewed. Such over-exploitation is bound to be followed by a "crash," during which resource scarcity and consequent increased mortality (Malthus's "misery") will reduce population to a level that can be supported. The dynamics of population growth and decline can be represented by a "flow chart" such as that given in Figure 7.4. Some, like the biologist Garrett Hardin (1993), continue to make the case for the Malthusian

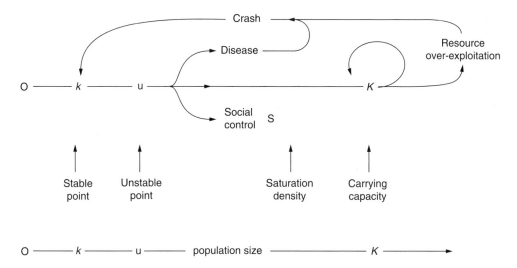

FIGURE 7.4 Carrying capacity understood in the context of population dynamics. "As population size increases form left to right, the population may reach one of two equilibria: k is the population size set by predation, while K is set by resources. Social control might cause a stable population to be maintained below K. Resource over-exploitation or disease might cause a population crash." Source: Ron Pulliam and Nick Haddad, 1994, "Human Population Growth an the Carrying Capacity Concept." *Bulletin of the Ecological Society of America* 75 (1994)

view by applying the notion of a carrying capacity to the human population of the earth.

But this conception of environmental carrying capacity was originally developed for demographic analysis of *animal* populations, and may not be easily applied to human populations. One reason for this is the ambiguity of the term "resource." Resources are not homogeneous, as the account above suggests, and in important respects resource availability is a function of technology. In particular, resource availability can vary when new technologies increase or decrease productive efficiency. Fertilizers can increase crop yields, shifts to reliance on new sources of energy may change energy needs, and improved communications systems may reduce travel needs. With technological change, we may be able to find substitutes for resources on which we now rely. For these reasons, the "human carrying capacity of the earth" is not a fixed quantity as the model above implies: carrying capacity varies with technology and with changes in productive efficiency.

Contemporary technological optimists rival Condorcet in their confidence that reason and human creativity will enable us to increase the carrying capacity of the earth so that shortages will not be a significant problem for the much larger human populations to come. Such considerations have led some to reject the notion of a "carrying capacity" altogether, since people themselves may be considered a resource for others. On this view, resources necessarily increase as populations grow, and the notion that resource scarcity could result from population growth becomes unthinkable. A moderate version of this view is reflected in ex-US President George Bush's observation that "Population growth itself is a neutral phenomenon...every human being represents hands to work, and not just another mouth to feed" (quoted in Cohen 1995, p. 38). A more extreme version is found in the work of the economist Julian Simon, who, like Condorcet before him, follows this technological optimism to its logical extreme: since human creativity is an "infinite" capacity, the set of resources available to human beings must itself be infinite. Applied to an infinite resource base, the account of "carrying capacity" given above implies that population may also grow infinitely. Population growth, urges Simon (1996), should not be inhibited. It should be encouraged.

While this optimistic view is often dismissed out of hand by economists and environmentalists, it is not all wrong, and it continues to have great influence in discussions of population. Simon is right to point out that the term "resource" is ambiguous, and that the earth's "carrying capacity" may increase (or decrease) with technological change. The ecological conception of carrying capacity, so useful in its application to animal species, may not neatly describe the demographic behavior of our own species. But neither creativity nor resources are "infinite" in the sense implied by Simon, and it would be premature to conclude that the carrying capacity concept is irrelevant for the analysis of human populations. For example, there is evidence that when fertility is higher, fewer resources are spent on education and nutrition for each child (Nancy Birdsall, in Lindahl-Kiessling and Landberg 1994, p. 178). If creative innovation requires education and resources, then there is reason to believe that per capita productivity may decrease as fertility and population size increase, as J. S. Mill (1806–73) predicted long ago: "It is vain to say that all mouths which the increase of mankind brings into existence bring with them hands. The new mouths require as much food as the old ones, and the hands do not produce as much" (J. S. Mill, *Principles of Political Economy*, Book 1, ch. XIII).

Beyond these internal problems with the optimistic view, there are external problems as well. Some "resources" are indispensable, and it is unlikely that technology will provide adequate substitutes (breathable air, for example). Others are valued in themselves, independently of their contribution to human well-being (ecosystems and wildlands). Their loss could not be compensated by replacement technologies, and we may have good reason to preserve and protect them independently of their contribution to human well-being. Even if the needs of an enormous human population could somehow be met without the earth's great natural systems, we would still have good reason to prevent environmental destruction.

The concept of carrying capacity will require revisions before it can be neatly applied to human populations. Still, those who are unconvinced by Condorcet's case for the infinite prospects for human reason and the perfectibility of the human condition will recognize that human and environmental limitations do ultimately impose upper limits on human population size, as Malthus recognized. For these reasons, it is quite clear that the concept of carrying capacity has continued relevance to issues concerning human population growth, and that it will be valuable to develop a conception of "carrying capacity" that is more readily applicable to human populations (Cohen 1995).

Focus on Individual Fertility Decisions

A second Malthusian insight that retains considerable influence in contemporary discussions of population is that demographic change should be studied with an eye to the determinants of individual fertility decisions. While Malthus himself spent large portions of his later work investigating the factors that influence people's individual reproductive choices, Gary Becker and H. G. Lewis (1976) may be credited as the first to develop this Malthusian insight into a full theory by representing reproductive choice using the tools of microeconomic analysis. Becker and Lewis represent children as "consumer goods," and hypothesize that parents will "consume children" at efficient rates (that is, they will have an "efficient" number of them) balancing "quantity," the number of children they will have, against "quality," reflected in the resources they will be able to provide for their children. They assume that children who are provided with more resources will be "better children," and more satisfying to their parents. On these assumptions, it is possible to show that rational parents will make "optimal" choices, likely to benefit children and parents alike.

In spite of its virtues, the Becker–Lewis model does not provide any analysis of the criteria parents use in evaluating the "quality" of their children. They assume that the benefits children provide for their parents are primarily the "psychic benefits"of seeing their children prosper. This may reflect fertility choices in developed countries like the United States, but it leaves out a crucial fertility motive operant in developing countries, where children provide the primary means for old-age security. The difference matters a great deal, for if parents' concerns are primarily self-regarding (desire to have children who can and will support parents in old age), they will make quite different decisions from what they would if their concerns were altruistic (desire to see children prosper). The extent to which parents' rational decisions will reflect the interests of their children may thus be contingent on childhood mortality rates, on the likelihood that children will support their elderly parents, and on the existence of alternate means of economic security for the elderly. In less developed countries, where childhood mortality is high, where cultural norms assign children weighty obligations to care for their parents, and where there are no effective institutions providing support for older people, it may be rational for parents to have as many children as possible in order to maximize the likelihood that they will have children to care for them in old age. On the other hand, in developed countries where childhood mortality is low, where children do not generally bear financial responsibility for their parent's well-being, and where many people prepare financially for their retirement, parental choices may reflect the interests of children as suggested by Becker and Lewis.

The most helpful insight to come from this model of reproductive choice is that parents' reproductive decisions may be influenced by increasing the opportunity cost of fertility. The opportunity costs of a choice are measured by the value of the options one sets aside in making it. So the opportunity costs of fertility are measured by the value of the opportunities parents will be unable to use if they have additional children. The income that might have been gained if parents were wage-earners rather than child-caretakers is only one kind of opportunity cost of fertility. While programs such as China's one-child policy raise the direct costs of fertility by punishing parents and children alike, alternatives that provide parents with employment and social security improve their welfare, thus increasing the opportunity cost of fertility. When these opportunity costs are high, it is far more likely that parents will make reproductive choices with the welfare of their prospective children in mind. In such circumstances, it is far more likely that parents will choose to have fewer children and to provide each with a better start in life.

Among the most effective means for increasing the opportunity cost of fertility are the improvement of educational and employment opportunities for women, promotion of women's autonomy, and elimination of sexist barriers to equal opportunity. These means are desirable for their own sakes as well as for their implications for population. High fertility rates impose excessive burdens on women, including high mortality rates due to the stresses of pregnancy and childbirth as well as the labor involved in childcare. In most developing countries, maternal mortality is the largest single cause of death for women in their reproductive years: the maternal mortality rate in some areas in sub-Saharan Africa is as high as one in fifty. Since women in these areas typically have seven or more children during their reproductive years, the chance for each woman that she will not survive those years is about one in six. Partha Dasgupta grimly remarks that the reproductive cycle in this woman's life involves her "playing Russian roulette" (Partha Dasgupta, in Graham-Smith 1994, p. 157). This tragic state of affairs has hopeful implications for fertility policy, since fertility rates tend to fall toward stable levels when women have better opportunities for education and employment, access to effective birth control, and more autonomous control over their reproductive lives.

Here, Condorcet's hopeful analysis seems to have been correct: as he suggested, the best way to implement policies for fertility reduction may be to improve the conditions of life for the worst off members of society, and to work toward social and economic equality for women. Malthus was wrong to think that fertility will always increase when people are better off. Development theorists have taken Condorcet's hypothesis seriously, and have confirmed the causal connections among the problems of social inequality, poverty, women's rights, fertility, and environmental degradation. High fertility rates typically exacerbate poverty and social inequalities since fertility is strongly linked to affluence and class differences. In some developing countries, the fertility rate of the poor is twice that of the wealthy. Combined with data showing that fewer resources are used to provide for children in large families, this statistic reflects exacerbation of both poverty and social inequality, which in turn contribute to increased rates of environmental destruction.

The popular slogan "Development is the best contraceptive" expresses Condorcet's optimism that this cycle may be broken by policies that improve the conditions of life for women and for the poor. Since we have good independent reasons for pursuing development efforts for this kind, this is a hopeful conclusion.

FERTILITY AND DEVELOPMENT

The success or failure of this conclusion depends, however, on the nature of the development process. Economist Simon Kuznets famously hypothesized that initial income inequalities resulting from early stages of economic development should gradually level out as the benefits of economic prosperity are more broadly distributed. Frank Notestein proposed a corresponding hypothesis that fertility rates in developing countries will initially spike upwards, but that they too should level off or even decline as the changes due to economic development lead couples to choose smaller families. This second hypothesis (the "Notestein Demographic Transition Hypothesis") is based on the assumption that effective economic development will raise the opportunity costs of having children, since children will be selected among a broader range of desirable alternatives. Economic development is also supposed to diminish the motive to have children as protection for old-age security, as social institutions provide alternate means for protection of well-being in old age.

But like many efforts in "ideal theory," these optimistic economic hypotheses seem to apply poorly to the real world. As Lester Brown notes, many developing countries seem trapped in the second stage where fertility spikes upward, but are "unable to achieve the economic and social gains that are counted upon to reduce births" (Brown et al. 1987, p. 20). Perhaps it is the failure of Kuznets's hypothesis that explains the failure of Notestein's Demographic Transition Hypothesis: fertility rates do not fall in the poor sectors of the population, because the purported benefits of economic development are often not distributed widely within the population, and because economic development often increases social inequalities instead of alleviating

them, when a powerful minority manages to reap the economic benefits.

What explains the frequent failure of Kuznets's hypothesis? No single explanation may apply in all cases where development has failed to improve the welfare of the poor. But there may be institutional barriers that were not adequately taken into account by optimistic development theorists: it is often in the interest of those who become wealthy in the early stages of the development process to do what they can to prevent the benefits of economic prosperity from being more widely distributed. In many cases, high profit margins and low production costs depend on the existence of a large and impoverished labor force. Furthermore, those who have an economic interest in perpetuating social and economic inequalities are often the same people who have power over social institutions, and can effectively put in place barriers that retard or prevent a broader distribution of development benefits. Thus we might expect to see the prosperous and the powerful working to thwart efforts to improve general welfare, and resisting efforts to more widely distribute democratic control of political institutions. When economic development does not bring the expected benefits for an impoverished majority, fertility and maternal mortality rates should not be expected to fall. Increasingly large and densely packed human populations in turn lead to increasing rates of environmental exploitation and destruction. This may explain much of what we see when we look at the developing world.

Unless development improves the lives of the poor, it is unlikely to have desirable effects on human fertility or population growth, nor is it likely to decrease the rate of environmental destruction. These considerations suggest an alternative model for development, quite different from the "top-down," large-scale industrial strategy that has traditionally been favored by organizations like the World Bank and the International Monetary Fund. Development projects that import large industries into developing regions rarely reduce social inequality, since the benefits may not "trickle down" to those who need them most. Such "development" sometimes makes the poor even worse off, since it can be highly destructive to traditional small-scale economies and ways of life. An alternative "bottom-up" approach would focus on improving the opportunities of the poor instead of focusing on industrial growth or increasing GNP. If human development is sacrificed to economic development, fertility levels are unlikely to decrease.

Policies aimed specifically at population control have often been repressive, and have had high social costs. Amartya Sen (1994) distinguishes between "Collaboration" and "Override" as alternative strategies for addressing the population problem: the former changes fertility incentives by increasing opportunities, while the latter operates by limiting people's ability to make their own choices or by punishing those who have more children than policies permit. China's aggressive efforts to control population by imposing punitive sanctions on couples who exceed their quota of children is a prime example of a coercive strategy. Not only do such strategies penalize parents and their children, they are also likely to be less effective in the long run: when population policies are repressive, it is in each person's interest to attempt to skirt them and to avoid their effects and costs. In societies marked by traditional sexism, the costs of coercive policies are likely to fall most heavily on women. In China, this is reflected in the marked rise in female mortality rates following the imposition of family quotas. But when population policies endeavor to provide people with incentives and opportunities, to raise the opportunity cost of fertility, then lower fertility becomes individually rational. Three kinds of collaborative measure for fertility reduction are most clearly implied by this strategy of increasing the opportunity costs of fertility:

1. Efforts to expand women's educational opportunities are likely to have the effect of lowering fertility. Such access will not only improve women's employment prospects, but will also result in later marriage and reproduction so that each is likely to have fewer children overall.
2. Efforts to provide women with employment opportunities can have a similar effect: when women are prohibited from work, as they have traditionally been in much of the world, the opportunity costs of fertility are extremely low. Generally increased economic opportunity for both women and men will increase the opportunity cost of children, but since women have suffered radically diminished opportunities in every culture and every country in the world, and since women are still the primary caretakers for children worldwide, it is especially important to expand opportunities for women....
3. Since the need for old-age security is a prime incentive to have children in most developing countries, institutions that increase the economic security of the elderly remove an important destructive incentive to have children. The motive to have children to provide for one's old age is destructive in the sense that it passes costs on to the succeeding generation, whose interests are not adequately represented in the decisions of their parents. There is empirical evidence that old-age pension and effective social security systems do indeed reduce fertility.

The account of the population problem given here has not emphasized the distribution of contraceptives as a means for population control, but of course the availability of contraceptives can be crucial for people's autonomous control over their reproductive lives. Where policies aimed at human development are accompanied by increased access to contraceptives, they will be more effective. But when efforts to control population growth focus on the distribution of contraceptives at the expense of attention to human development, they are unlikely to be effective, and are likely to be viewed with skepticism by those they are intended to help....

POPULATION ETHICS AND ENVIRONMENTAL PHILOSOPHY

Environmental philosophers have not generally devoted great attention to the growth of human population, but it is clear that population growth is one of the most important environmental problems of our time. Unless human population growth can be slowed and stabilized, it is unlikely that efforts to reduce the rate of environmental destruction can be successful. Many environmentalists naively accept the Malthusian argument that human development will simply provide grist for human population explosions in poor, environmentally stressed parts of the world. Some feed the misanthropic image of environmentalists by proposing that we should control the population problem by letting people starve. But if the best way to reduce fertility is to encourage human development in poor countries, then this Malthusian strategy is unlikely to achieve the desired aims. This is an important and hopeful implication for several reasons: first, it implies that the best way to address the population problem is to pursue social goals such as human development and women's equality. These are goals that we already have sufficient independent reason to support. Second, it implies that environmentalists must also be concerned with issues of social justice and human development. If it is true that the growth of human population is among the greatest of all threats to the world's ecosystems, and that this problem can most effectively be addressed by policies that work toward human development and social justice, then environmentalists must focus on social justice if we hope to preserve the fragile natural systems of the earth. . . .

REFERENCES

Becker, Gary and Lewis, H. G. (1976) "Interaction between the quantity and quality of children," in *The Economic Approach to Human Behavior,* Gary Becker (Chicago: University of Chicago Press). [This groundbreaking paper argues that fertility control will arise naturally as parents make rational trade-offs between the number of children they will have, and the benefits they will be able to provide for each child.]

Broome, John (1992) *Counting the Cost of Global Warming* (Cambridge: White Horse Press). [This book presents a clear account of the economic problems of population choice.]

Brown, Lester R., Chandler, William, Flavin, Christopher, Postel, Sandra, Starke, Linda, and Wolf, Edward (1984) *State of the World: 1984* (New York: Norton). [Part of the 1984 edition of this annual report focuses on population growth and economic development.]

Cohen, Joel (1995) *How Many People Can the Earth Support?* (New York: W. W. Norton Company). [This is currently the most accessible and clear account of the "carrying capacity" concept applied to the earth's human population.]

Condorcet, Antoine-Nicolas (1955[1793]) *Sketch for a Historical Picture of The Progress of The Human Mind,* trans. June Barraclough (Westport Ct: Hyperion Press). [Condorcet's *Sketch* was the goad that prompted Malthus to write his *Essay on the Principles of Population,* and is one of the classic sources on population theory.]

Graham-Smith, Sir Francis, ed. (1994) *Population: The Complex Reality* (London: The Royal Society). [This excellent collection contains a wide variety of papers on the causes and implications of human population growth.]

Hardin, Garret (1993) *Living Within Limits* (New York: Oxford). [One of the clearest contemporary "Malthusian" accounts of human population growth.]

Lindahl-Kiessling, Kerstin and Landberg, Hans, eds. (1994) *Population, Economic Development, and the Environment* (Oxford: Oxford University Press). [This collection contains many seminal papers on population growth and economic development.]

Malthus, Thomas (1989 [1803]) *An Essay on the Principle of Population,* ed. Patricia James (Cambridge: Cambridge University Press). [Malthus's work is the most famous source on population theory.]

Ng, Yew-Kwang (1989) "What should we do about future generations? The impossibility of Parfit's theory X," *Economics and Philosophy* 5, pp. 235–53. [Ng defends a total utilitarian theory of population.]

Parfit, Darek (1984) *Reasons and Persons* (Oxford: Oxford University Press). [Parfit's book brilliantly articulates the paradoxes of population theory, and is the source of most of the philosophical discussions of population.]

Sen, Amartya (1994) "Population: delusion and reality," *New York Review of Books* 41, no. 15 (September 22), pp. 62–71. [In this paper Sen explains the relationship between population growth and human development.]

Simon, Julian L. (1996) *The Ultimate Resource II* (Princeton: Princeton University Press). [Simon argues that population is not a problem, and that free markets will adequately meet human needs no matter how large the human population of the earth grows.]

Temkin, Larry S. (1987) "Intransitivity and the mere addition paradox," *Philosophy and Public Affairs,* 16, pp. 138–87. [This paper offers a tentative solution to one of the paradoxes of population theory identified by Parfit 1984.]

✎ FOR FURTHER READING

Bouvier, Leon and Lindsey Grant, *How Many Americans?* (San Francisco: Sierra Club Books, 1994).

Cohen, Joel E., *How Many People Can the Earth Support?* (New York: Norton, 1995).

Ehrlich, Paul, *The Population Bomb* (New York: Ballantine, 1968).

Ehrlich, Paul and Anne Ehrlich, *Betrayal of Science and Reason* (Washington, DC: Island Press, 1996).

Kasun, Jacqueline, *The War against Population* (San Francisco: Ignatius, 1988).

Grant, Lindsey, *Juggernaut: Growth on a Finite Planet* (Santa Ana, CA: Seven Locks Press, 1996).

Hardin, Garrett, *Living within Limits: Ecology, Economics and Population Taboos* (Oxford University Press, 1992).

Malthus, Thomas, "On Population" (1830) in *Three Essays on Population: Thomas Malthus, Julian Huxley and Frederick Osborn* (New York: Mentor, 1956).

Myers, Norman and Julian Simon, *Scarcity or Abundance? A Debate on the Environment* (New York: Norton, 1994). A debate between Norman Myers and Julian Simon.

Simon, Julian, *The Ultimate Resource 2* (Princeton: Princeton University Press, 1996) (revised edition).

Food Ethics

Hunger is a child with shriveled limbs and a swollen belly. It is the grief of parents, or a person gone blind for lack of vitamin A.[1]

The victim of starvation burns up his own body fats, muscles and tissues for fuel. His body quite literally consumes itself and deteriorates rapidly. The kidneys, liver and endocrine system often cease to function properly. A shortage of carbohydrates, which play a vital role in brain chemistry, affects the mind. Lassitude and confusion set in, so that starvation victims often seem unaware of their plight. The body's defenses drop; disease kills most famine victims before they have time to starve to death. An individual begins to starve when he has lost about a third of his normal body weight. Once this loss exceeds 40%, death is almost inevitable.[2]

TEN THOUSAND PEOPLE starve to death every day, another 2 billion (out of a global population of over 6 billion) are malnourished, and 460 million are permanently hungry. Almost half of these are children. More than one-third of the world goes to bed hungry each night. In recent years, devastating famines have occurred in Bangladesh (1974), Ethiopia (1972–74, 1984), Cambodia (1978), Chad and Sudan (1985), and in many of the other 43 countries making up the sub-Saharan region of Africa throughout the 1970s and 1980s, including the recent famine in Somalia. Since the 1960s conditions have deteriorated in many parts of the world.[3]

On the other hand, another third of the world lives in affluence. Imagine ten children eating at a table. The three healthiest eat the best food and throw much of it away or give it to their pets. Two other children get just enough to get by on. The other five do not get enough food. Three of them who are weak manage to stave off hunger pangs by eating bread and rice, but the other two are unable to do even that and die of hunger-related diseases, such as pneumonia and dysentery. Such is the plight of children in the world.

In the United States, enough food is thrown into the garbage each day to feed an entire nation, more money is spent on pet food than on aid to the world's starving, and many people are grossly overweight.

Problems of global scarcity, poverty, hunger, and famine are among the most urgent facing us. What is our duty to the hungry in our country and in other lands? What obligations do we have toward the poor abroad? What rights do the starving have against us? To what extent, if any, should hunger relief be tied to population control?

We begin with Garrett Hardin's famous article, "Lifeboat Ethics," in which Hardin argues that affluent societies, like lifeboats, ought to ensure their survival by preserving a safety factor of resources. Giving away its resources to needy nations or admitting needy immigrants is like taking on additional passengers who threaten to capsize the lifeboat. We help neither them nor ourselves. Aiming at perfect distributive justice ends up a perfect catastrophe. Furthermore, we have a duty to our children and grandchildren, which will be compromised if we endeavor to help the poor.

In our second reading, William Murdoch and Allan Oaten take strong issue with Hardin's assessment. They argue that Hardin's arguments rest on misleading metaphors, *lifeboat, commons,* and *ratchet,* and a fuller analysis will reveal that the situation is far more hopeful than Hardin claims. We are responsible for the plight of the poor and must take steps to alleviate their suffering.

In our third reading, Mylan Engel, Jr. links world hunger with environmental integrity and animal rights and argues that by changing the way we eat, we could save millions of lives and feed the whole world. He argues that even by our present moral values we have a moral duty to become vegetarians. We then examine genetically modified foods, with Jonathon Rauch arguing that they are potentially the solution to world hunger and Mae-Wan Ho presenting evidence that they are not only dangerous for the environment but are also taking autonomy away from individual farmers. Finally, Tristam Coffin and Michael Allen Fox examine the impact of the meat industry upon the world's food supply and the environment.

NOTES

1. Arthur Simon, *Bread for the World* (New York: Paulist Press, 1975).
2. *Time Magazine,* November 11, 1974.
3. Statistics in this introduction come from the U.N. Food and Agriculture Organization. Some of the discussion is based on Arthur Simon, op. cit.

49   Lifeboat Ethics

GARRETT HARDIN

A biographical sketch of Garrett Hardin is found at the beginning of Reading 41.

He argues that the proper metaphor that characterizes our global ecological situation is not "spaceship" but "lifeboat." The spaceship metaphor is misleading since Earth has no captain to steer it through its present and future problems. Rather, each rich nation is like a lifeboat in an ocean in which the poor of the world are swimming and in danger of drowning. Hardin argues that affluent societies, like lifeboats, ought to ensure their own survival by preserving a safety factor of resources. For a society to give away its resources to needy nations or to admit needy immigrants is like taking on additional passengers who would threaten to cause the lifeboat to capsize. Under these conditions, it is our moral duty to refrain from aiding the poor.

Reprinted from "Living on a Lifeboat," *Bioscience* 24 (1974) by permission.

No generation has viewed the problem of the survival of the human species as seriously as we have. Inevitably, we have entered this world of concern through the door of metaphor. Environmentalists have emphasized the image of the earth as a spaceship—Spaceship Earth. Kenneth Boulding . . . is the principal architect of this metaphor. It is time, he says, that we replace the wasteful "cowboy economy" of the past with the frugal "spaceship economy" required for continued survival in the limited world we now see ours to be. The metaphor is notably useful in justifying pollution control measures.

Unfortunately, the image of a spaceship is also used to promote measures that are suicidal. One of these is a generous immigration policy, which is only a particular instance of a class of policies that are in error because they lead to the tragedy of the commons. . . . These suicidal policies are attractive because they mesh with what we unthinkably take to be the ideals of "the best people." What is missing in the idealistic view is an insistence that rights and responsibilities must go together. The "generous" attitude of all too many people results in asserting inalienable rights while ignoring or denying matching responsibilities.

For the metaphor of a spaceship to be correct the aggregate of people on board would have to be under unitary sovereign control. . . . A true ship always has a captain. It is conceivable that a ship could be run by a committee. But it could not possibly survive if its course were determined by bickering tribes that claimed rights without responsibilities.

What about Spaceship Earth? It certainly has no captain, and no executive committee. The United Nations is a toothless tiger, because the signatories of its charter wanted it that way. The spaceship metaphor is used only to justify spaceship demands on common resources without acknowledging corresponding spaceship responsibilities.

An understandable fear of decisive action leads people to embrace "incrementalism"— moving toward reform by tiny stages. As we shall see, this strategy is counterproductive in the area discussed here if it means accepting rights before responsibilities. Where human survival is at stake, the acceptance of responsibilities is a precondition to the acceptance of rights, if the two cannot be introduced simultaneously.

LIFEBOAT ETHICS

Before taking up certain substantive issues let us look at an alternative metaphor, that of a lifeboat. In developing some relevant examples the following numerical values are assumed. Approximately two-thirds of the world is desperately poor, and only one-third is comparatively rich. The people in poor countries have an average per capita GNP (Gross National Product) of about $200 per year; the rich, of about $3,000. (For the United States it is nearly $5,000 per year.) Metaphorically, each rich nation amounts to a lifeboat full of comparatively rich people. The poor of the world are in other, much more crowded lifeboats. Continuously, so to speak, the poor fall out of their lifeboats and swim for a while in the water outside, hoping to be admitted to a rich lifeboat, or in some other way to benefit from the "goodies" on board. What should the passengers on a rich lifeboat do? This is the central problem of "the ethics of a lifeboat."

First we must acknowledge that each lifeboat is effectively limited in capacity. The land of every nation has a limited carrying capacity. The exact limit is a matter for argument, but the energy crunch is convincing more people every day that we have already exceeded the carrying capacity of the land. We have been living on "capital"— stored petroleum and coal—and soon we must live on income alone.

Let us look at only one lifeboat—ours. The ethical problem is the same for all, and is as follows. Here we sit, say 50 people in a lifeboat. To be generous, let us assume our boat has a capacity of 10 more, making 60. (This, however, is to violate the engineering principle of the "safety factor." A new plant disease or a bad change in the weather may decimate our population if we don't preserve some excess capacity as a safety factor.)

The 50 of us in the lifeboat see 100 others swimming in the water outside, asking for admission to the boat, or for handouts. How shall we respond to their calls? There are several possibilities.

One. We may be tempted to try to live by the Christian ideal of being "our brother's keeper," or by the Marxian ideal . . . of "from each according to his abilities, to each according to his needs." Since the needs of all are the same, we take all the needy into our boat, making a total of 150 in a boat with a capacity of 60. The boat is swamped, and everyone drowns. Complete justice, complete catastrophe.

Two. Since the boat has an unused excess capacity of 10, we admit just 10 more to it. This has the disadvantage of getting rid of the safety factor, for which action we will sooner or later pay dearly. Moreover, *which* 10 do we let in? "First come, first served?" The best 10? The neediest 10? How do we *discriminate*? And what do we say to the 90 who are excluded?

Three. Admit no more to the boat and preserve the small safety factor. Survival of the people in the lifeboat is then possible (though we shall have to be on our guard against boarding parties).

The last solution is abhorrent to many people. It is unjust, they say. Let us grant that it is.

"I feel guilty about my good luck," say some. The reply to this is simple: *Get out and yield your place to others.* Such a selfless action might satisfy the conscience of those who are addicted to guilt but it would not change the ethics of the lifeboat. The needy person to whom a guilt-addict yields his place will not himself feel guilty about his sudden good luck. (If he did he would not climb aboard.) The net result of conscience-stricken people relinquishing their unjustly held positions is the elimination of their kind of conscience from the lifeboat. The lifeboat, as it were, purifies itself of guilt. The ethics of the lifeboat persist, unchanged by such momentary aberrations.

This then is the basic metaphor within which we must work out our solutions. Let us enrich the image step by step with substantive additions from the real world.

REPRODUCTION

The harsh characteristics of lifeboat ethics are heightened by reproduction, particularly by reproductive differences. The people inside the lifeboats of the wealthy nations are doubling in numbers every 87 years; those outside are doubling every 35 years, on the average. And the relative difference in prosperity is becoming greater.

Let us, for a while, think primarily of the U.S. lifeboat. As of 1973 the United States had a population of 210 million people, who were increasing by 0.8% per year, that is, doubling in number every 87 years.

Although the citizens of rich nations are outnumbered two to one by the poor, let us imagine an equal number of poor people outside our lifeboat—a mere 210 million poor people reproducing at a quite different rate. If we imagine these to be the combined populations of Colombia, Venezuela, Ecuador, Morocco, Thailand, Pakistan, and the Philippines, the average rate of increase of the people "outside" is 3.3% per year. The doubling time of this population is 21 years.

Suppose that all these countries, and the United States, agreed to live by the Marxian ideal, "to each according to his needs," the ideal of most Christians as well. Needs, of course, are determined by population size, which is affected by reproduction. Every nation regards its rate of reproduction as a sovereign right. If our lifeboat were big enough in the beginning it might be possible to live *for a while* by Christian-Marxian ideals. *Might.*

Initially, in the model given, the ratio of non-Americans to Americans would be one to one. But consider what the ratio would be 87 years later. By this time Americans would have doubled to a population of 420 million. The other group (doubling every 21 years) would now have swollen to 3,540 million. Each American would have more than eight people to share with. How could the lifeboat possibly keep afloat?

All this involves extrapolation of current trends into the future, and is consequently suspect. Trends may change. Granted: but the change will not necessarily be favorable. If—as seems likely—the rate of population increase falls faster in the ethnic group presently inside the lifeboat than it does among those now outside, the future will turn out to be even worse than mathematics predicts, and sharing will be even more suicidal.

RUIN IN THE COMMONS

The fundamental error of the sharing ethic is that it leads to the tragedy of the commons. Under a system of private property the man (or group of men) who own property recognize their responsibility to care for it, for if they don't they will eventually suffer. A farmer, for instance, if he is intelligent, will allow no more cattle in a pasture than its carrying capacity justifies. If he overloads the pasture, weeds take over, erosion sets in, and the owner loses in the long run.

But if a pasture is run as a commons open to all, the right of each to use it is not matched by an operational responsibility to take care of it. It is no use asking independent herdsmen in a commons to act responsibly, for they dare not. The considerate herdsman who refrains from overloading the commons suffers more than a selfish one who says his needs are greater. (As Leo Durocher says, "Nice guys finish last.") Christian-Marxian idealism is counterproductive. That it *sounds* nice is no excuse. With distribution systems, as with individual morality, good intentions are no substitute for good performance.

A social system is stable only if it is insensitive to errors. To the Christian-Marxian idealist a selfish person is a sort of "error." Prosperity in the system of the commons cannot survive errors. If *everyone* would only restrain himself, all would be well; but it takes *only one less than everyone* to ruin a system of voluntary restraint. In a crowded world of less than perfect human beings—and we will never know any other—mutual ruin is inevitable in the commons. This is the core of the tragedy of the commons.

WORLD FOOD BANKS

In the international arena we have recently heard a proposal to create a new commons, namely an international depository of food reserves to which nations will contribute according to their abilities, and from which nations may draw according to their needs. Nobel laureate Norman Borlaug has lent the prestige of his name to this proposal.

A world food bank appeals powerfully to our humanitarian impulses. We remember John Donne's celebrated line, "Any man's death diminishes me." But before we rush out to see for whom the bell tolls let us recognize where the greatest political push for international granaries comes from, lest we be disillusioned later. Our experience with Public Law 480 clearly reveals the answer. This was the law that moved billions of dollars worth of U.S. grain to food-short, population-long countries during the past two decades. When P.L. 480 first came into being, a headline in the business magazine *Forbes*...revealed the power behind it: "Feeding the World's Hungry Millions: How It Will Mean Billions for U.S. Business."

And indeed it did. In the years 1960 and to 1970 a total of $7.9 billion was spent on the "Food for Peace" program as P.L. 480 was called. During the years 1948 to 1970 an additional $49.9 billion were extracted from American taxpayers to pay for other economic aid programs, some of which went for food and food-producing machinery. (This figure does *not* include military aid.) That P.L. 480 was a give-away program was concealed. Recipient countries went through the motions of paying for P.L. 480 food—with IOU's. In December 1973 the charade was brought to an end as far as India was concerned when the United States "forgave" India's $3.2 billion debt....Public announcement of the cancellation of the debt was delayed for two months: one wonders why.

The search for a rational justification can be short-circuited by interjecting the word "emergency." Borlaug uses this word. We need to look sharply at it. What is an "emergency"? It is surely something like an accident, which is correctly defined as *an event that is certain to happen, though with a low frequency*....A well-run organization prepares for everything that is certain, including accidents and emergencies. It budgets for them. It saves for them. It expects them—and mature decision-makers do not waste time complaining about accidents when they occur.

What happens if some organizations budget for emergencies and others do not? If each organization is solely responsible for its own well-being, poorly managed ones will suffer. But they should be able to learn from experience. They have a chance to mend their ways and learn to budget for infrequent but certain emergencies. The weather, for instance, always varies and periodic crop failures are certain. A wise and competent government saves out of the production of the good years in anticipation of bad years that are sure to come. This is not a new idea. The Bible tells us that Joseph taught this policy to Pharaoh in Egypt more than 2,000 years ago. Yet it is literally true that the vast majority of the governments of the world today have no such policy. They lack either the wisdom or the competence, or both. Far more difficult than the transfer of wealth from one country to another is the transfer of wisdom between sovereign powers or between generations.

"But it isn't their fault! How can we blame the poor people who are caught in an emergency? Why must we punish them?" The concepts of blame and punishment are irrelevant. The question is, what are the operational consequences of establishing a world food bank? If it is open to every country every time a need develops, slovenly rulers will not be motivated to take Joseph's advice. Why should they? Others will bail them out whenever they are in trouble.

Some countries will make deposits in the world food bank and others will withdraw from it: there will be almost no overlap. Calling such a depository-transfer unit a "bank" is stretching the metaphor of *bank* beyond its elastic limits. The proposers, of course, never call attention to the metaphorical nature of the word they use.

THE RATCHET EFFECT

An "international food bank" is really, then, not a true bank but a disguised one-way transfer device for moving wealth from rich countries to poor. In the absence of such a bank, in a world inhabited by individually responsible sovereign nations, the population of each nation would repeatedly go through a cycle of the sort shown in Figure 1. P_2 is greater than P_1, either in absolute numbers or because a deterioration of the food supply has removed the safety factor and produced a dangerously low ratio of resources to population. P_2 may be said to represent a state of overpopulation, which becomes obvious upon the appearance of an "accident," e.g., a crop failure. If the "emergency" is not met by outside help, the population drops back to the "normal" level—the "carrying capacity" of the environment—or even below. In the absence of population control by a sovereign, sooner or later the population grows to P_2 again and the cycle repeats. The long-term population curve . . . is an irregularly fluctuating one, equilibrating more or less about the carrying capacity.

A demographic cycle of this sort obviously involves great suffering in the restrictive phase, but such a cycle is normal to any independent country with inadequate population control. The third-century theologian Tertullian . . . expressed what must have been the recognition of many wise men when he wrote: "The scourges of pestilence, famine, wars, and earthquakes have come to be regarded as a blessing to overcrowded nations, since they serve to prune away the luxuriant growth of the human race."

Only under a strong and farsighted sovereign—which theoretically could be the people themselves, democratically organized—can a population equilibrate at some set point below the carrying capacity, thus avoiding the pains

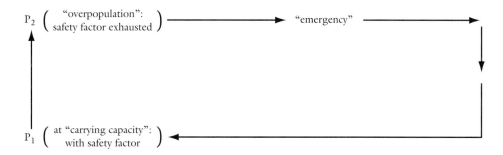

FIGURE 1 The population cycle of a nation that has no effective, conscious population control, and which receives no aid from the outside. P_2 is greater than P_1.

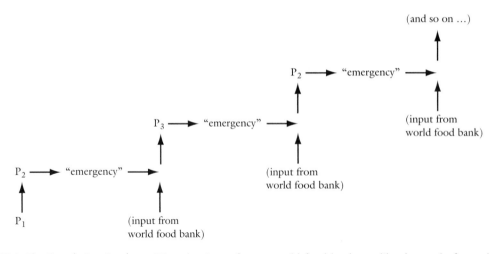

FIGURE 2 The Population Escalator. Note that input from a world food bank acts like the pawl of a ratchet, preventing the normal population cycle shown in Figure 1 from being completed. P_{n+1} is greater than P_n and the absolute magnitude of the "emergencies" escalates. Ultimately the entire system crashes. The crash is not shown, and few can imagine it.

normally caused by periodic and unavoidable disasters. For this happy state to be achieved it is necessary that those in power be able to contemplate with equanimity the "waste" of surplus food in times of bountiful harvests. It is essential that those in power resist the temptation to convert extra food into extra babies. On the public relations level it is necessary that the phrase "surplus food" be replaced by "safety factor."

But wise sovereigns seem not to exist in the poor world today. The most anguishing problems are created by poor countries that are governed by rulers insufficiently wise and powerful. If such countries can draw on a world food bank in times of "emergency," the population *cycle* of Figure 1 will be replaced by the population *escalator* of Figure 2. The input of food from a food bank acts as the pawl of a ratchet, preventing the population from retracing its steps to a lower level. Reproduction pushes the population upward, inputs from the world bank prevent its moving downward. Population size escalates, as does the absolute magnitude of "accidents" and "emergencies." The process is brought to an end only by the total collapse of the whole system, producing a catastrophe of scarcely imaginable proportions.

Such are the implications of the well-meant sharing of food in a world of irresponsible reproduction.

All this is terribly obvious once we are acutely aware of the pervasiveness and danger of the commons. But many people still lack this awareness and the euphoria of the "benign demographic transition" . . . interferes with the realistic appraisal of pejoristic mechanisms. As concerns public policy, the deductions drawn from the benign demographic transition are these:

1. If the per capita GNP rises the birth rate will fall; hence, the rate of population increase will fall, ultimately producing ZPG (Zero Population Growth).
2. The long-term trend all over the world (including the poor countries) is of a rising per capita GNP (for which no limit is seen).
3. Therefore, all political interference in population matters is unnecessary; all we need to do is foster economic "development"—*note the metaphor*—and population problems will solve themselves.

Those who believe in the benign demographic transition dismiss the pejoristic mechanism of Figure 2 in the belief that each input of food from the world fosters development within a poor country thus resulting in a drop in the rate of population increase. Foreign aid has proceeded on this assumption for more than two decades. Unfortunately it has produced no indubitable instance of the asserted effect. It has, however, produced a library of excuses. The air is filled with plaintive calls for more massive foreign aid appropriations so that the hypothetical melioristic process can get started.

The doctrine of demographic laissez-faire implicit in the hypothesis of the benign demographic transition is immensely attractive. Unfortunately there is more evidence against the melioristic system than there is for it. . . . On the historical side there are many counterexamples. The rise in per capita GNP in France and Ireland during the past century has been accompanied by a rise in population growth. In the 20 years following the Second World War the same positive correlation was noted almost everywhere in the world. Never in world history before 1950 did the worldwide population growth reach 1% per annum. Now the average population growth is over 2% and shows no signs of slackening.

On the theoretical side, the denial of the pejoristic scheme of Figure 2 probably springs from the hidden acceptance of the "cowboy economy" that Boulding castigated. Those who recognize the limitations of a spaceship, if they are unable to achieve population control at a safe and comfortable level, accept the necessity of the corrective feedback of the population cycle shown in Figure 1. No one who knew in his bones that he was living on a true spaceship would countenance political support of the population escalator shown in Figure 2.

ECO-DESTRUCTION VIA THE GREEN REVOLUTION

The demoralizing effect of charity on the recipient has long been known. "Give a man a fish and he will eat for a day: teach him how to fish and he will eat for the rest of his days." So runs an ancient Chinese proverb. Acting on this advice the Rockefeller and Ford Foundations have financed a multipronged program for improving agriculture in the hungry nations. The result, known as the "Green Revolution," has been quite remarkable. "Miracle wheat" and "miracle rice" are splendid technological achievements in the realm of plant genetics.

Whether or not the Green Revolution can increase food production is doubtful . . . , but in any event not particularly important. What is missing in this great and well-meaning humanitarian effort is a firm grasp of fundamentals. Considering the importance of the Rockefeller Foundation in this effort it is ironic that the late Alan Gregg, a much-respected vice president of the Foundation, strongly expressed his doubts of the wisdom of all attempts to increase food production some two decades ago. (This was before Borlaug's work—supported by Rockefeller—had resulted in the development of "miracle wheat.") Gregg . . . likened the growth and spreading of humanity over the surface of the earth to the metastasis of cancer in the human body, wryly remarking that "Cancerous growths demand food; but, as far as I know, they have never been cured by getting it."

"Man does not live by bread alone"—the scriptural statement has a rich meaning even in the material realm. Every human being born constitutes a draft on all aspects of the environment—food, air, water, unspoiled scenery, occasional and optional solitude, beaches, contact with wild animals, fishing, hunting—the list is long and incompletely known. Food can, perhaps, be significantly increased: but what about clean beaches, unspoiled forests, and solitude? If we satisfy the need for food in a growing population we necessarily decrease the supply of other goods, and thereby increase the difficulty of equitably allocating scarce goods. . . .

The present population of India is 600 million, and it is increasing by 15 million per year. The environmental load of this population is already great. The forests of India are only a small fraction of what they were three centuries ago. Soil erosion, floods, and the psychological costs of crowding are serious. Every one of the net 15 million lives added each year stresses the Indian environment more severely. *Every life saved this year in a poor country diminishes the quality of life for subsequent generations.*

Observant critics have shown how much harm we wealthy nations have already done to poor nations through our well-intentioned but misguided attempts to help them.... Particularly reprehensible is our failure to carry out postaudits of these attempts.... Thus we have shielded our tender consciences from knowledge of the harm we have done. Must we Americans continue to fail to monitor the consequences of our external "do-gooding"? If, for instance, we thoughtlessly make it possible for the present 600 million Indians to swell to 1,200 millions by the year 2001—as their present growth rate promises—will posterity in India thank us for facilitating an even greater destruction of *their* environment? Are good intentions ever a sufficient excuse for bad consequences?

IMMIGRATION CREATES A COMMONS

I come now to the final example of a commons in action, one for which the public is least prepared for rational discussion. The topic is at present enveloped by a great silence which reminds me of a comment made by Sherlock Holmes in A. Conan Doyle's story, "Silver Blaze." Inspector Gregory had asked, "Is there any point to which you would wish to draw my attention?" To this Holmes responded:

> "To the curious incident of the dog in the night-time."
>
> "The dog did nothing in the night-time," said the Inspector.
>
> "That was the curious incident," remarked Sherlock Holmes.

By asking himself what would repress the normal barking instinct of a watchdog Holmes realized that it must be the dog's recognition of his master as the criminal trespasser. In a similar way we should ask ourselves, what repression keeps us from discussing something as important as immigration?

It cannot be that immigration is numerically of no consequence. Our government acknowledges a *net* flow of 400,000 a year. Hard data are understandably lacking on the extent of illegal entries, but a not implausible figure is 600,000 per year.... The natural increase of the resident population is now about 1.7 million per year. This means that the yearly gain from immigration is at least 19%, and may be 37%, of the total increase. It is quite conceivable that educational campaigns like that of Zero Population Growth, Inc., coupled with adverse social and economic factors—inflation, housing shortage, depression, and loss of confidence in national leaders—may lower the fertility of American women to a point at which all of the yearly increase in population would be accounted for by immigration. Should we not at least ask if that is what we want? How curious it is that we so seldom discuss immigration these days!

Curious, but understandable—as one finds out the moment he publicly questions the wisdom of the status quo in immigration. He who does so is promptly charged with *isolationism, bigotry, prejudice, ethnocentrism, chauvinism,* and *selfishness.* These are hard accusations to bear. It is pleasanter to talk about other matters, leaving immigration policy to wallow in the cross-currents of special interests that take no account of the good of the whole—*or of the interests of posterity.*

We Americans have a bad conscience because of things we said in the past about immigrants. Two generations ago the popular press was rife with references to *Dagos, Wops, Pollacks, Japs, Chinks,* and *Krauts*—all pejorative terms which failed to acknowledge our indebtedness to Goya, Leonardo, Copernicus, Hiroshige, Confucius, and Bach. Because the implied inferiority of foreigners was *then* the justification for keeping them out, it is *now* thoughtlessly assumed that restrictive policies can only be based on the assumption of immigrant inferiority. *This is not so.*

Existing immigration laws exclude idiots and known criminals; future laws will almost certainly continue this policy. But should we also consider the quality of the average immigrant, as compared with the quality of the average resident? Perhaps we should, perhaps we shouldn't. (What is "quality" anyway?) But the quality issue is not our concern here.

From this point on, *it will be assumed that immigrants and native-born citizens are of exactly equal quality,* however quality may be defined. The focus is only on quantity. The conclusions reached depend on nothing else, so all charges of ethnocentrism are irrelevant.

World food banks move food to the people, thus facilitating the exhaustion of the environment of the poor. By contrast, unrestricted immigration moves people to the food, thus speeding up the destruction of the environment in rich countries. Why poor people should want to make this transfer is no mystery: but why should rich hosts encourage it? This transfer, like the reverse one, is supported by both selfish interests and humanitarian impulses.

The principal selfish interest in unimpeded immigration is easy to identify; it is the interest of the employers of cheap labor, particularly that needed for degrading jobs. We have been deceived about the forces of history by the lines of Emma Lazarus inscribed on the Statue of Liberty:

> *Give me your tired, your poor*
> *Your huddled masses yearning to breathe free,*
> *The wretched refuse of your teeming shore,*
> *Send these, the homeless, tempest-tossed, to me:*
> *I lift my lamp beside the golden door.*

The image is one of an infinitely generous earth-mother, passively opening her arms to hordes of immigrants who come here on their own initiative. Such an image may have been adequate for the early days of colonization, but by the time these lines were written (1886) the force for immigration was largely manufactured inside our own borders by factory and mine owners who sought cheap labor not to be found among laborers already here. One group of foreigners after another was thus enticed into the United States to work at wretched jobs for wretched wages.

At present, it is largely the Mexicans who are being so exploited. It is particularly to the advantage of certain employers that there be many illegal immigrants. Illegal immigrant workers dare not complain about their working conditions for fear of being repatriated. Their presence reduces the bargaining power of all Mexican-American laborers. Cesar Chavez has repeatedly pleaded with congressional committees to close the doors to more Mexicans so that those here can negotiate effectively for higher wages and decent working conditions. Chavez understands the ethics of a lifeboat.

The interests of the employers of cheap labor are well served by the silence of the intelligentsia of the country. WASPs—White Anglo-Saxon Protestants—are particularly reluctant to call for a closing of the doors to immigration for fear of being called ethnocentric bigots. It was, therefore, an occasion of pure delight for this particular WASP to be present at a meeting when the points he would like to have made were made better by a non-WASP speaking to other non-WASPS. It was in Hawaii, and most of the people in the room were second-level Hawaiian officials of Japanese ancestry. All Hawaiians are keenly aware of the limits of their environment, and the speaker had asked how it might be practically and constitutionally possible to close the doors to more immigrants to the islands. (To Hawaiians, immigrants from the other 49 states are as much of a threat as those from other nations. There is only so much room in the islands, and the islanders know it. Sophistical arguments that imply otherwise do not impress them.)

Yet the Japanese-Americans of Hawaii have active ties with the land of their origin. This point was raised by a Japanese-American member of the audience who asked the Japanese-American speaker: "But how can we shut the doors now? We have many friends and relations in Japan that we'd like to bring to Hawaii some day so that they can enjoy this beautiful land."

The speaker smiled sympathetically and responded slowly: "Yes, but we have children now and someday we'll have grandchildren. We can bring more people here from Japan only by giving away some of the land that we hope to pass on to our grandchildren some day. What right do we have to do that?"

To be generous with one's own possessions is one thing; to be generous with posterity's is quite another. This, I think, is the point that must be gotten across to those who would, from a commendable love of distributive justice, institute a ruinous system of the commons, either in the form of a world food bank or that of unrestricted immigration. Since every speaker is a member of some ethnic group it is always possible to charge him with ethnocentrism. But even after purging an argument of ethnocentrism the rejection of the commons is still valid and necessary if we are to save at least some parts of the world from environmental ruin. Is it not desirable that at least some of the grandchildren of people now living should have a decent place in which to live?

Plainly many new problems will arise when we consciously face the immigration question and seek rational answers. No workable answers can be found if we ignore population problems. And—if the argument of this essay is correct—so long as there is no true world government to control reproduction everywhere it is impossible to survive in dignity if we are to be guided by Spaceship ethics. Without a world government that is sovereign in reproductive matters mankind lives, in fact, on a number of sovereign lifeboats. For the foreseeable future survival demands that we govern our actions by the ethics of a lifeboat. Posterity will be ill served if we do not.

✦ STUDY QUESTIONS

1. What is Hardin's case against helping poor, needy countries? What is the significance of the lifeboat metaphor?
2. What is the relationship of population policies to world hunger?
3. Explain the "ratchet effect." Is Hardin right that in bringing aid to countries who do not control their population we act immorally?

---

50   Population and Food: A Critique of Lifeboat Ethics

WILLIAM W. MURDOCH
AND ALLAN OATEN

William Murdoch is professor of biological science at the University of California at Santa Barbara and is the author of *Environment: Resources, Pollution and Society* (2nd ed., 1975). Allan Oaten is also a biologist who has taught at the University of California at Santa Barbara and specializes in mathematical biology and statistics.

Murdoch and Oaten begin by attacking Hardin's metaphors of "lifeboat," "commons," and "ratchet" as misleading. They then argue that other factors are needed to understand the population and hunger problem, including parental confidence in the future, low infant mortality rates, literacy, health care, income and employment, and an adequate diet. They claim that once the socioeconomic conditions are attended to, population size will take care of itself. Nonmilitary foreign aid to Third World countries is both just and necessary if we are to prevent global disaster.

Reprinted from "Population and Food: Metaphors and the Reality," *Bioscience* 25 (1975) by permission. Notes deleted.

MISLEADING METAPHORS

[Hardin's] "Lifeboat" Article actually has two messages. The first is that our immigration policy is too generous. This will not concern us here. The second, and more important, is that by helping poor nations we will bring disaster to rich and poor alike:

> Metaphorically, each rich nation amounts to a lifeboat full of comparatively rich people. The poor of the world are in other, much more crowded lifeboats. Continuously, so to speak, the poor fall out of their lifeboats and swim for a while in the water outside, hoping to be admitted to a rich lifeboat, or in some other way to benefit from the "goodies" on board. What should the passengers on a rich lifeboat do? This is the central problem of "the ethics of a lifeboat." (Hardin)

Among these so called "goodies" are food supplies and technical aid such as that which led to the Green Revolution. Hardin argues that we should withhold such resources from poor nations on the grounds that they help to maintain high rates of population increase, thereby making the problem worse. He foresees the continued supplying and increasing production of food as a process that will be "brought to an end only by the total collapse of the whole system, producing a catastrophe of scarcely imaginable proportions."

Turning to one particular mechanism for distributing these resources, Hardin claims that a world food bank is a commons—people have more motivation to draw from it than to add to it; it will have a ratchet or escalator effect on population because inputs from it will prevent population declines in over-populated countries. Thus "wealth can be steadily moved in one direction only, from the slowly-breeding rich to the rapidly-breeding poor, the process finally coming to a halt only when all countries are equally and miserably poor." Thus our help will not only bring ultimate disaster to poor countries, but it will also be suicidal for us.

As for the "benign demographic transition" to low birth rates, which some aid supporters have predicted, Hardin states flatly that the weight of evidence is against this possibility.

Finally, Hardin claims that the plight of poor nations is partly their own fault: "wise sovereigns seem not to exist in the poor world today. The most anguishing problems are created by poor countries that are governed by rulers insufficiently wise and powerful." Establishing a world food bank will exacerbate this problem: "slovenly rulers" will escape the consequences of their incompetence—"Others will bail them out whenever they are in trouble"; "Far more difficult than the transfer of wealth from one country to another is the transfer of wisdom between sovereign powers or between generations."

What arguments does Hardin present in support of these opinions? Many involve metaphors: lifeboat, commons, and ratchet or escalator. These metaphors are crucial to his thesis, and it is, therefore, important for us to examine them critically.

The lifeboat is the major metaphor. It seems attractively simple, but it is in fact simplistic and obscures important issues. As soon as we try to use it to compare various policies, we find that most relevant details of the actual situation are either missing or distorted in the lifeboat metaphor. Let us list some of these details.

Most important, perhaps, Hardin's lifeboats barely interact. The rich lifeboats may drop some handouts over the side and perhaps repel a boarding party now and then, but generally they live their own lives. In the real world, nations interact a great deal, in ways that affect food supply and population size and growth, and the effect of rich nations on poor nations has been strong and not always benevolent.

First, by colonization and actual wars of commerce, and through the international marketplace, rich nations have arranged an exchange of goods that has maintained and even increased the economic imbalance between rich and poor nations. Until recently we have taken or otherwise obtained cheap raw material from poor nations and sold them expensive manufactured goods that they cannot make themselves. In the United States, the structure of tariffs and internal subsidies discriminates selectively against poor nations. In poor countries, the concentration on cash crops rather than on food crops, a legacy of colonial times, is now actively encouraged by western multinational corporations. . . . Indeed, it is claimed that in famine-stricken Sahelian Africa, multinational agribusiness has recently taken land out of food production for cash crops.... Although we often self-righteously take the "blame" for lowering the death rates of poor nations during the 1940s and 1950s, we are less inclined to accept responsibility for the effects of actions that help maintain poverty and hunger. Yet poverty directly contributes to the high birth rates that Hardin views with such alarm.

Second, U.S. foreign policy, including foreign aid programs, has favored "pro-Western" regimes, many of which govern in the interests of a wealthy elite and some of which are savagely repressive. Thus, it has often subsidized a gross maldistribution of income and has supported political leaders who have opposed most of the social changes that can lead to reduced birth rates. In this light, Hardin's pronouncements on the alleged wisdom gap between poor leaders and our own, and the difficulty of filling it, appear as a grim joke: our response to leaders with the power and wisdom Hardin yearns for has often been to try to replace them or their policies as soon as possible. Selective giving and withholding of both military and non-military aid has been an important ingredient of our efforts to maintain political leaders we like and to remove those we do not. Brown..., after noting that the withholding of U.S. food aid in 1973 contributed to the downfall of the Allende government in Chile, comments that "although Americans decry the use of petroleum as a political weapon, calling it 'political blackmail,' the United States has been using food aid for political purposes for twenty years—and describing this as 'enlightened diplomacy.'"

Both the quantity and the nature of the supplies on a lifeboat are fixed. In the real world, the quantity has strict limits, but these are far from having been reached (University of California Food Task Force 1974). Nor are we forced to devote fixed proportions of our efforts and energy to automobile travel, pet food, packaging, advertising, corn-fed beef, "defense" and other diversions, many of which cost far more than foreign aid does. The fact is that enough food is now produced to feed the world's population adequately. That people are malnourished is due to distribution and to economics, not to agricultural limits (United Nations Economic and Social Council 1974).

Hardin's lifeboats are divided merely into rich and poor, and it is difficult to talk about birth rates on either. In the real world, however, there are striking differences among the birth rates of the poor countries and even among the birth rates of different parts of single countries. These differences appear to be related to social conditions (also absent from lifeboats) and may guide us to effective aid policies.

Hardin's lifeboat metaphor not only conceals facts, but misleads about the effects of his proposals. The rich lifeboat can raise the ladder and sail away. But in real life, the problem will not necessarily go away just because it is ignored. In the real world, there are armies, raw materials in poor nations, and even outraged domestic dissidents prepared to sacrifice their own and others' lives to oppose policies they regard as immoral.

No doubt there are other objections. But even this list shows the lifeboat metaphor to be dangerously inappropriate for serious policy making because it obscures far more than it reveals. Lifeboats and "lifeboat ethics" may be useful topics for those who are shipwrecked; we believe they are worthless—indeed detrimental—in discussions of food-population questions.

The ratchet metaphor is equally flawed. It, too, ignores complex interactions between birth rates and social conditions (including diets), implying as it does that more food will simply mean more babies. Also, it obscures the fact that the decrease in death rates has been caused at least as much by developments such as DDT, improved sanitation, and medical advances, as by increased food supplies, so that cutting out food aid will not necessarily lead to population declines.

The lifeboat article is strangely inadequate in other ways. For example, it shows an astonishing disregard for recent literature. The claim that we can expect no "benign demographic transition" is based on a review written more than a decade ago.... Yet, events and attitudes are changing rapidly in poor countries: for the first time in history, most poor people live in countries with birth control programs; with few exceptions, poor nations are somewhere on the demographic transition to lower birth rates...; the population-food squeeze is now widely recognized, and governments of poor nations are aware of the relationship. Again, there is a considerable amount of evidence that birth rates can fall rapidly in poor countries given the proper social conditions (as we will discuss later); consequently, crude projections of current populations growth rates are quite inadequate for policy making.

THE TRAGEDY OF THE COMMONS

Throughout the lifeboat article, Hardin bolsters his assertions by reference to the "commons."...The thesis of the commons, therefore, needs critical evaluation.

Suppose several privately owned flocks, comprising 100 sheep altogether, are grazing on a public commons. They bring in an annual income of $1.00 per sheep. Fred, a herdsman, owns only one sheep. He decides to add another. But 101 is too many: the commons is overgrazed and produces less food. The sheep lose quality and income drops to 90¢ per sheep. Total income is now $90.90 instead of $100.00. Adding the sheep has brought an overall loss. But Fred has gained: *his* income is $1.80 instead of $1.00. The gain from the additional sheep, which is his alone, outweighs the loss from overgrazing, which he shares. Thus he promotes his interest at the expense of the community.

This is the problem of the commons, which seems on the way to becoming an archetype. Hardin, in particular, is not inclined to underrate its importance: "One of the major tasks of education today is to create such an awareness of the dangers of the commons that people will be able to recognize its many varieties, however disguised"...and "All this is terribly obvious once we are acutely aware of the pervasiveness and danger of the commons. But many people still lack this awareness...."

The "commons" affords a handy way of classifying problems: the lifeboat article reveals that sharing, a generous immigration policy, world food banks, air, water, the fish populations of the ocean, and the western range lands are, or produce, a commons. It is also handy to be able to dispose of policies one does not like and "only a particular instance of a class of policies that are in error because they lead to the tragedy of the commons."

But no metaphor, even one as useful as this, should be treated with such awe. Such shorthand can be useful, but it can also mislead by discouraging and obscuring important detail. To dismiss a proposal by suggesting that "all you need to know about this proposal is that it institutes a commons and is, therefore, bad" is to assert that the proposed commons is worse than the original problem. This might be so if the problem of the commons were, indeed, a tragedy—that is, if it were insoluble. But it is not.

Hardin favors private ownership as the solution (either through private property or the selling of pollution rights). But, of course, there are solutions other than private ownership; and private ownership itself is no guarantee of carefully husbanded resources.

One alternative to private ownership of the commons is communal ownership of the sheep—or, in general, of the mechanisms and industries that exploit the resource—combined with communal planning for management. (Note, again, how the metaphor favors one solution: perhaps the "tragedy" lay not in the commons but in the sheep. "The Tragedy of the Privately Owned Sheep" lacks zing, unfortunately.) Public ownership of a commons has been tried in Peru to the benefit of the previously privately owned anchovy fishery.... The communally owned agriculture of China does not seem to have suffered any greater over-exploitation than that of other Asian nations.

Another alternative is cooperation combined with regulation. For example, Gulland...has shown that Antarctic whale stocks (perhaps the epitome of a commons since they are internationally exploited and no one owns them) are now being properly managed, and stocks are increasing. This has been achieved through cooperation in the International Whaling Commission, which has by agreement set limits to the catch of each nation.

In passing, Hardin's private ownership argument is not generally applicable to nonrenewable resources. Given discount rates, technology substitutes, and no more than an average regard for posterity, privately owned nonrenewable resources, like oil, coal and minerals, are mined at rates that produce maximum profits, rather than at those rates that preserve them for future generations. . . .

BIRTH RATES: AN ALTERNATIVE VIEW

Is the food-population spiral inevitable? A more optimistic, if less comfortable, hypothesis, presented by Rich and Brown, is increasingly tenable: contrary to the "ratchet" projection, population growth rates are affected by many complex conditions beside food supply. In particular, a set of socioeconomic conditions can be identified that motivate parents to have fewer children; under these conditions, birth rates can fall quite rapidly, sometimes even before birth control technology is available. Thus, population growth can be controlled more effectively by intelligent human intervention that sets up the appropriate conditions than by doing nothing and trusting to "natural population cycles."

These conditions are: parental confidence about the future, an improved status of women, and literacy. They require low infant mortality rates, widely available rudimentary health care, increased income and employment, and an adequate diet above subsistence levels. Expenditure on schools (especially elementary schools), appropriate health services (especially rural para-medical services), and agriculture reform (especially aid to small farmers) will be needed, and foreign aid can help here. It is essential that these improvements be spread across the population; aid can help here, too, by concentrating on the poor nations' poorest people, encouraging necessary institutional and social reforms, and making it easier for poor nations to use their own resources and initiative to help themselves. It is *not* necessary that per capita GNP be very high, certainly not as high as that of the rich countries during their gradual demographic transition. In other words, low birth rates in poor countries are achievable long before the conditions exist that were present in the rich countries in the late 19th and early 20th centuries.

Twenty or thirty years is not long to discover and assess the factors affecting birth rates, but a body of evidence is now accumulating in favor of this hypothesis. Rich and Brown show that at least 10 developing countries have managed to reduce their birth rates by an average of more than one birth per 1,000 population per year for periods of 5 to 16 years. A reduction of one birth per 1,000 per year would bring birth rates in poor countries to a rough replacement level of about 16/1,000 by the turn of the century, though age distribution effects would prevent a smooth population decline. We have listed these countries in Table 1, together with three other nations, including China, that are poor and yet have brought their birth rates down to 30 or less, presumably from rates of over 40 a decade or so ago.

These data show that rapid reduction in birth rates is possible in the developing world. No doubt it can be argued that each of these cases is in some way special. Hong Kong and Singapore are relatively rich; they, Barbados, and Mauritius are also tiny. China is able to exert great social pressure on its citizens; but China is particularly significant. It is enormous; its per capita GNP is almost as low as India's; and it started out in 1949 with a terrible health system. Also, Egypt, Chile, Taiwan, Cuba, South Korea, and Sri Lanka are quite large, and they are poor or very poor (Table 1). In fact, these examples represent an enormous range of religion, political systems, and geography and suggest that such rates of decline in the birth rate can be achieved whenever the appropriate conditions are met. "The common factor in these countries is that the *majority* of the population has shared in the economic and social benefits of significant national progress. . . . [M]aking health, education and jobs more broadly available to lower income groups in poor countries contribute[s] significantly toward the motivation for smaller families that is the prerequisite of major reduction in birth rates." . . .

The converse is also true. In Latin America, Cuba (annual per capita income $530), Chile ($720), Uruguay ($820), and Argentina ($1,160) have moderate to truly equitable distribution of goods and services and relatively low birth rates (27, 25, 23, and 22, respectively). In

TABLE 1 Declining Birth Rates and Per Capita Income in Selected Developing Countries (These Are Crude Birth Rates, Uncorrected for Age Distribution.)

Country	Time Span	Births/1,000/year		
		Avg. Annual Decline in Crude Birth Rate	Crude Birth Rate 1972	$ per Capita Per Year 1973
Barbados	1960–69	1.5	22	570
Taiwan	1955–71	1.2	24	390
Tunisia	1966–71	1.8	35	250
Mauritius	1961–71	1.5	25	240
Hong Kong	1960–72	1.4	19	970
Singapore	1955–72	1.2	23	920
Costa Rica	1963–72	1.5	32	560
South Korea	1960–70	1.2	29	250
Egypt	1966–70	1.7	37	210
Chile	1963–70	1.2	25	720
China			30	160
Cuba			27	530
Sri Lanka			30	110

contrast, Brazil ($420), Mexico ($670), and Venezuela ($980) have very unequal distribution of goods and services and high birth rates (38, 42, and 41, respectively). Fertility rates in poor and relatively poor nations seem unlikely to fall as long as the bulk of the population does not share in increased benefits....

...As a disillusioning quarter-century of aid giving has shown, the obstacles of getting aid to those segments of the population most in need of it are enormous. Aid has typically benefited a small rich segment of society, partly because of the way aid programs have been designed but also because of human and institutional factors in the poor nations themselves.... With some notable exceptions, the distribution of income and services in poor nations is extremely skewed—much more uneven than in rich countries. Indeed, much of the population is essentially outside the economic system. Breaking this pattern will be extremely difficult. It will require not only aid that is designed specifically to benefit the rural poor, but also important institutional changes such as decentralization of decision making and the development of greater autonomy and stronger links to regional and national market for local groups and industries such as cooperative farms.

Thus, two things are being asked of rich nations and of the United States in particular: to increase nonmilitary foreign aid, including food aid, and to give it in ways, and to governments, that will deliver it to the poorest people and will improve their access to national economic institutions. These are not easy tasks, particularly the second, and there is no guarantee that birth rates will come down quickly in all countries. Still, many poor countries have, in varying degrees, begun the process of reform, and recent evidence suggests that aid and reform together can do much to solve the twin problems of high birth rates and economic underdevelopment. The tasks are far from impossible. Based on the evidence, the policies dictated by a sense of decency are also the most realistic and rational.

✎ STUDY QUESTIONS

1. What are the criticisms leveled against Hardin's arguments?
2. What is Murdoch and Oaten's view on the question of population growth? What is the gradual demographic transition theory? Is their view plausible?

3. Compare Hardin's arguments with Murdoch and Oaten's response. Where does the evidence lie?
4. What are the disanalogies between a lifeboat and the United States?

51 Hunger, Duty, and Ecology: On What We Owe Starving Humans

MYLAN ENGEL, JR.

Mylan Engel, Jr. is associate professor of philosophy at Northern Illinois University. His primary areas of interest include epistemology, philosophy of religion, and practical ethics. His current research centers on the following issues: personal and doxastic justification in epistemology; epistemic contextualism, skepticism, and closure; rational belief in the absence of reasons; human obligations toward nonhuman animals; and our duties to those living in absolute poverty. Engel has provided the following abstract of his article.

An argument is advanced for the moral obligatoriness of (O_1) supporting famine relief organizations through financial contributions and (O_2) refraining from squandering food in situations of food scarcity. Unlike other ethical arguments for the obligation to assist the world's absolutely poor, my argument is not predicated on any highly contentious ethical theory which can you reject. Rather, it is predicated on *your* own beliefs. The argument shows that the things you currently believe already commit you to the obligatoriness of helping to reduce malnutrition and famine-related diseases by sending a nominal percentage of your income to famine-relief organizations and by not squandering food that could be fed to them. Being consistent with your own beliefs implies that to do any less is to be profoundly immoral.

HUNGER, DUTY, AND ECOLOGY: ON WHAT WE OWE STARVING HUMANS

You probably remember many of the tragic events of September 11, 2001. Nineteen terrorists hijacked four commercial airliners, crashing two of them into the World Trade Center towers, one into the Pentagon, and one in a field in Pennsylvania. Approximately 3,200 innocent individuals died needlessly. People around the world stared at their television sets in horror and disbelief as the news media aired clips of the attack 'round the clock. The tragedy immediately roused President Bush to declare "war on terrorism." Volunteers from all across America traveled to New York at their own expense to aid in the rescue and clean-up efforts. Charitable contributions poured into the American Red Cross, which in turn wrote checks totaling $143.4 million in emergency aid (averaging $45,837 per family). The U.S. government put together a $5 billion relief package that will provide $1.6 million to each of the victim's families. The United States has spent billions more on its military efforts to root out Osama bin Laden and his al-Qaeda terrorist network. As the dust from the 9/11 attacks has finally settled, it is safe to say that Americans are now taking terrorism seriously.

Here are some of the tragic events that took place on 9/11 that you probably don't recall. On that infamous day, more then 33,000 innocent children under the age of five died *senseless, needless* deaths—18,000 died from malnutrition and another 15,300 died of untreated poverty-related diseases. It must be stressed that almost all of these deaths were *unnecessary*. They could have *easily been prevented*. The United States alone grows enough grain and soybeans to feed the world's human population several times over. Given this overabundance of food, the lives of those children who starved to death on 9/11 could have easily been saved, had we only diverted a relatively modest portion of this food to them. As for the disease-related deaths, 19% of the 33,000 children who lost their lives on 9/11 died from the dehydrating effects of chronic diarrhea. Almost all of these 6,350 diarrheal dehydration deaths could have been prevented by administering each child a single packet of oral rehydration salts (cost per packet: 15 cents). Another 19% of these children died from acute respiratory infections. Most of them could have been saved with a course of antibiotics (cost: 25 cents). Most of the 2,300 children who died from measles could have been saved with vitamin A therapy (cost per capsule: less than 10 cents). What makes the deaths of these children particularly tragic is that virtually all of them were readily preventable. They occurred only because otherwise good people did nothing to prevent them.

Despite the fact that the number of innocent children who died needlessly on 9/11 was ten times greater than the number of innocent people who lost their lives in the 9/11 terrorist attack, compassionate conservative President Bush did not declare war on hunger or on poverty. The U.S. Government did not immediately institute a multibillion dollar relief package for the world's absolutely poor. People did not make out generous checks to famine-relief organizations. The media did not so much as mention the tragedy of so many innocent young lives lost. And, as if 9/11 wasn't enough for us to deal with, on 9/12 another 33,000 innocent children under the age of five died unnecessarily, and another 33,000 on 9/13. In the 22 months that have transpired since the 9/11 tragedy, more than 22 million innocent children under the age of five have died needlessly. By any objective measure, the tragedy of the 9/11 attack pales in comparison with the tragedy of world hunger and famine-related disease. Each year the latter claims 3,800 times more innocent lives than the 9/11 attack. Despite the magnitude of the tragedy of global hunger and childhood malnutrition, the overwhelming majority of affluent and moderately affluent people, including most philosophers, send no money to famine-relief organizations. Of the 4 million people who receive solicitations from UNICEF each year, less than 1% donate anything at all. For most of us, world hunger doesn't even register a blip on our moral radar screens, much less present itself as a serious moral problem requiring action on our part.

My aim in the present paper is an ambitious one. I hope to convince you (and others) to *take hunger seriously*. How? By showing you that your beliefs already commit you to the view that global hunger and *absolute poverty*[1] impose serious moral obligations on moderately affluent people. Starting with your beliefs as premises, I shall argue that affluent and moderately affluent people, like you and me, are morally obligated:

(O₁) to provide modest financial support for famine-relief organizations and/or other humanitarian organizations working to reduce the amount of unnecessary pain, suffering, and death in the world, and

(O₂) to refrain from squandering food that could be fed to the world's absolutely poor.

1. PRELIMINARIES

The central questions this essay addresses are not new: Is it morally permissible for moderately affluent people who have the financial means to prevent some innocent children from starving to death to do nothing to reduce the number of children suffering from starvation? Are moderately affluent people morally obligated to send money to famine-relief organizations to help reduce world hunger and absolute poverty? If so, what is the extent of their obligation—i.e., just how much money must they send to these humanitarian organizations if they are to avoid being immoral?

These questions took center stage in the 1970s when a spate of philosophers offered arguments defending the view that affluent and moderately affluent people are morally required to provide financial support to organizations working to alleviate hunger, malnutrition, and absolute poverty around the world. Arguments from practically every theoretical perspective in normative ethics (except for libertarianism, which will be discussed later) were advanced: utilitarian arguments, Kantian arguments, human rights-based arguments, and ideal contractarian arguments. Working backwards, Jan Narveson (1977) rejects the libertarian "Nobody needs to help anybody" stance as unreasonable and, using a Rawlsean approach, he tentatively defends the view that one is free to acquire more property than one's neighbor, but only if one is "willing to contribute a certain amount of one's wealth to those in undeserved misfortune, once one gets beyond a certain minimal amount—a fraction which perhaps increases as one gets more and more." William Aiken (1977) argues that the moral right to be saved from starvation derives from the more general moral right to be saved from preventable death due to deprivation and that this latter right generates a stringent corresponding moral obligation on the part of those in a position to prevent such deaths. As Aiken puts it:

> Until it is true that I cannot help another without putting myself in an equivalent position of need (that is, dying of deprivation), I have a *prima facie* obligation to honor others' right to be saved from preventable death due to deprivation.[2]

The Kantian argument is predicated on Kant's claim that we have an imperfect duty to help those in dire need. As I interpret Kant, the duty is imperfect, since (i) there is no specific person to whom we owe it; (ii) since we owe it to persons generally and because we cannot possibly help *every* person in dire need, we are free to fulfill the duty in various ways as various opportunities to help present themselves; and (iii) the duty is a general duty that is never completely satisfied—i.e., no matter how many people in dire need we help, we are still obligated to help other people in dire need when we can do so. It is not a duty that we should fulfill *only* when some especially salient case presents itself. It is a duty that we should fulfill *whenever* we can, provided that doing so won't prevent us from our doing any of our other overriding duties. Most of us living in affluent nations have relatively few nearby opportunities to help people in dire need (because most of the people we regularly encounter are not in dire need). But there are millions of people elsewhere who are in dire need (of food, medicine, etc.), some of whom we can help by sending money to organizations like OXFAM, and so, on Kantian grounds, we ought to send money to these organizations whenever doing so will not prevent us from carrying out any of our other duties. Emphasizing consequentialist reasoning, Peter Unger (1996) argues that our *primary basic moral values* entail the following Pretty Demanding Dictate:

(P₁) On pain of living a life that's seriously immoral, a typical well-off person, like you and me, must give away most of her financially valuable assets, and much of her income, directing the funds to lessen efficiently the serious suffering of others.

In his seminal article "Famine, Affluence, and Morality," Peter Singer (1972) offers a utilitarian argument to the effect that we ought to send famine-relief organizations "as much money as possible, that is, at least up to the point at which by giving more one would begin to cause serious suffering for oneself and one's dependents—perhaps even beyond this point to the point of marginal utility." Singer begins his argument with the following much-discussed example:

> *The Pond*: Suppose that on my way to give a lecture I notice that a small child has fallen

in [a pond] and is in danger of drowning. Would anyone deny that I ought to wade in and pull the child out? This will mean getting my clothes muddy and either canceling my lecture or delaying it until I can find something dry to change into, but compared with the avoidable death of the child this is insignificant.

The Pond example is supposed to motivate the following principle:

(P_1) If it is in our power to prevent something very bad from happening, without thereby sacrificing anything of comparable moral significance, we ought to do it.[3]

Singer takes (P_2) to be uncontroversial and thinks it explains why we ought to pull the child from the pond. Given (P_2), Singer reasons as follows: Since absolute poverty is very bad, we ought to prevent as much absolute poverty as we can, without thereby sacrificing anything of comparable moral significance. Since most of the material possessions with which we surround ourselves pale in significance compared to an innocent child's life, we ought to forego such luxuries and save children instead.

These arguments taken together present us with a certain sort of puzzle. First, each of these arguments is initially quite compelling, at least if one accepts the normative framework within which the argument is couched. For example, it seems that any hedonistic or preference act-utilitarian is committed to Singer's principle (P_2), regardless whether The Pond justifies (P_2). Because the other premises in Singer's argument are uncontroversial, it looks as if any hedonistic or preference act-utilitarian must accept Singer's robust conclusion. In short, these arguments provide strong utilitarian, Kantian, rights-based, and contractrian reasons for thinking that we have a moral duty to assist those in absolute poverty. Second, utilitarianism, Kantian ethics, human rights-based ethics, and contractarianism are among the most widely accepted theories in normative ethics. Most philosophers working in ethics today claim to accept some version of one of these theories. Third,

with the possible exception of Narveson's view, all of the arguments just considered draw highly demanding conclusions. These arguments (especially Singer's, Unger's, and Aiken's) conclude that we are morally obligated to send sizeable portions of our wealth and income to famine-relief organizations like CARE and that we should continue doing so up to the point where further contributions would reduce us to the same level of need as those we are trying to help. Fourth, few people, philosophers included, contribute anything to CARE, OXFAM, or UNICEF, and almost no people contribute sizeable portions of their income to these organizations, even after they have heard the arguments. What has gone wrong?

Perhaps such highly demanding views are psychologically overwhelming and hence counterproductive. Shelly Kagan considers such an objection. As he puts it:

> [I]f morality demands too much...then when people fall short of its requirements (as doubtless they will do) they will say to themselves that they might as well obey none of morality's requirements at all. Given this all-or-nothing attitude, it is important that morality's requirements not be too severe—for were they severe morality would fall into wide neglect.

Call this objection *Too Much*. According to Too Much, what has gone wrong is that the overly demanding moral principles advocated by Singer, Unger, and Aiken have generated a counterproductive kind of futility thinking: "If I can't live up to the ideal, I shouldn't even try to approximate it." But Too Much is a psychological thesis. Even if true, it has no bearing on what our *actual* moral duties are. It is only concerned with what moral duties and principles we should publicly espouse. In short, Too Much can be restated as follows: "There may be good consequentialist reasons for *understating* the extent of people's *actual* moral obligations, namely, that by doing so people will fulfill more of their *actual* obligations than they otherwise would have." Such an observation tells us nothing about what our *actual* duties are nor does it do anything to *reduce* or *minimize* those actual duties. Plus,

Too Much is probably false. It is highly doubtful that people engage in the sort of all-or-nothing thinking that Too Much predicts, for as Kagan observes:

> Many people disobey the speed limit; few consequently feel free to run down pedestrians. I see no reason why we couldn't teach people to think, "Well, I'm not doing all I should—but only a *monster* would fail to do at least..."

If all-or-nothing futility thinking isn't to blame, then our puzzle remains. Why have such seemingly compelling arguments been so ineffective in evoking behavioral change? I think the answer is more straightforward than Too Much. Moral arguments often tell people that they ought to do things they don't want to do. Typically, when people are presented with an argument telling them that they ought to do *X*—where *X* is something they would rather not do—they look for reasons to reject that argument. One of the most common reasons that I have heard philosophers give for rejecting the arguments of Singer and company runs roughly as follows:

> Singer's preference utilitarianism is irremediably flawed, as are Kant's ethics, Aiken's theory of human rights, and Rawlsean contractarianism. The literature is peppered with devastating objections to these views. Because all of the aforementioned arguments are predicated on flawed ethical theories, all these arguments are also flawed. Until someone can provide me with clear moral reasons grounded in a true moral theory for sending large portions of my income to famine-relief organizations, I will continue to spend my money on what I please.

Such a self-serving reply is both disingenuous and sophistical. It is disingenuous because, as noted earlier, utilitarianism, Kantian ethics, human rights-based ethics, and contractarianism are among the most widely accepted theories in normative ethics. In other contexts, philosophers typically embrace one of these four theoretical approaches to ethics. It is sophistical because a similar reply can be used to "justify" or rationalize virtually any behavior. Because no moral theory to date is immune to objection, one

could, for example, "justify" rape on the grounds that all of the arguments against rape are predicated on flawed ethical theories.

The speciousness of such a "justification" of rape is obvious. No one who seriously considers the brutality of rape can think that it is somehow justified/permissible *simply because* all current ethical theories are flawed. But such specious reasoning is often used to "justify" allowing millions of innocent children to starve to death each year. I aim to block this spurious reply by providing an argument for the moral obligatoriness of (O_1) and (O_2), which does not rest on any particular, highly contentious ethical theory. Rather, it rests on beliefs you already hold.[4]

One caveat before we begin. Ethical arguments are often context-dependent in that they presuppose a specific audience in a certain set of circumstances. Recognizing what that intended audience and context are can prevent confusions about the scope of the ethical claim being made. My argument is context-dependent in precisely this way. It is not aimed at those relatively few people in developed nations who are so impoverished that they couldn't contribute to famine relief without extreme sacrifice. Rather, it is directed at people like you who are relatively well-off and who could easily contribute to famine relief with minimal sacrifice. I intend to show that your beliefs commit you to the view that it is morally wrong not to support famine-relief organizations (or other organizations working to reduce unnecessary suffering) for anyone who is in the circumstances in which you typically find yourself and *a fortiori* that it is morally wrong for you not to support such organizations. Enough by way of preamble, on to your beliefs.

2. THE THINGS YOU BELIEVE

The beliefs attributed to you herein would normally be considered noncontentious. In most contexts, we would take someone who didn't hold these beliefs to be either morally defective or irrational. Of course, in most contexts, people aren't being asked to part with their hard-earned cash. Still, even with that two-week luxury cruise in the Bahamas on the line, you will, I think, readily admit to believing the following propositions:

(B_1) Other things being equal, a world with less (more) pain and suffering is better (worse) than a world with more (less) pain and suffering.

(B_2) A world with less (more) *unnecessary* suffering is better (worse) than a world with more (less) *unnecessary* suffering.[5]

For those who have doubts as to whether or not they really do believe these two propositions, compare our world α as it actually is—where millions of innocent children suffer slow painful deaths from starvation each year—with possible world W_1, where W_1 is like our world in all respects except for two, namely, in W_1 every child has sufficient food to eat and every country has instituted effective population measures that have reduced human population to sustainable levels. W_1 is clearly a better world than α, and you know that it is. After all, unnecessary suffering is intrinsically bad and α contains vastly more unnecessary suffering than W_1.

Unnecessary suffering isn't the only thing you disvalue, as is evidenced by your belief:

(B_3) A world with fewer (more) *unnecessary* childhood deaths is better (worse) than a world with more (fewer) *unnecessary* childhood deaths.

Because you believe (B_3) and also believe that *unnecessary* suffering is intrinsically bad, you no doubt believe both:

(B_4) It is bad when an innocent child under the age of 5 dies instantly in an automobile accident, and

(B_5) It is even worse when an innocent child under the age of 5 suffers a slow painful death from starvation.

These beliefs together commit you to the belief:

(B_6) Other things being equal, the world would be: (i) better if there were fewer children starving to death, (ii) much better if there were no children starving to death, and

(iii) worse if there were more children starving to death.

Having reflected upon Singer's Pond, you surely believe:

(B_7) It is wrong to let an innocent child under age 5 drown *when one can easily save that child with no risk and with minimal cost to oneself.*

The fact that you accept (B_7) demonstrates that you believe that there are at least some positive duties—i.e., duties to benefit others. So, you probably believe:

(B_8) We ought to take steps to make the world a better place, *especially those steps that require little effort and minimal sacrifice on our part.*

But even if you reject (B_8) on the grounds that we have no positive duties (or very limited positive duties), you still think there are negative duties to do no harm, and so you believe:

($B_{8'}$) One ought to avoid making the world a worse place, *at least whenever one can do so with minimal effort and negligible sacrifice.*

You also believe:

(B_9) A morally good person will take steps to make the world a better place and even stronger steps to avoid making the world a worse place, and

(B_{10}) Even a "minimally decent person"[6] would take steps to help reduce the amount of unnecessary pain, suffering, and death in the world *if s/he could do so with little effort on her/his part.*

You also have beliefs about the sort of person you are. You believe one of the following propositions when the reflexive pronoun is indexed to yourself:

(B_{11}) I am a morally good person; or

(B_{12}) I am at least a minimally decent person.

You also believe of yourself:

(B_{13}) I am the sort of person who certainly would take steps to help reduce the amount of unnecessary pain, suffering, and death in the world *if I could do so with little effort on my part,* and

(B_{14}) I am an intellectually honest individual.

Finally, like most people, you believe:

(B_{15}) It is wrong to kill an innocence person unjustly.

And so you believe:

(B_{16}) It is wrong to kill innocent children between the ages of 2 and 5 as a means of population control, when equally effective nonlethal means of population control are readily available.

Even where *unjust killing* is not involved, you believe:

(B_{17}) Other things being equal, it is better when a person lives out her natural lifespan than when she dies prematurely.

Because you believe (B_7), (B_8), (B_{10}), and (B_{17}), presumably you also believe:

(B_{18}) Other things being equal, it is wrong to let an innocent person die *when one can prevent that death with minimal effort and negligible sacrifice.*

Because (B_{18}) is completely general in its application, it commits you to the following belief as well:

(B_{19}) Other things being equal, it is wrong to let an innocent person die as a means of population control *when one can prevent that death with minimal effort and negligible sacrifice* and when equally effective nonlethal means of population control are readily available.

3. WHY YOU ARE COMMITTED TO THE MORAL OBLIGATORINESS OF (O_1)

The burden of the present section is to show that your beliefs (B_1)–(B_{19}) already commit you to obligation (O_1). Using different subsets of [(B_1), (B_2), ..., (B_{19})], I will argue that anyone who believes (B_1)–(B_{19}) is committed to accepting two commonsensical, minimally demanding,

normative principles and that these two principles entail that we are morally obligated (O_1) to send a modest portion of our income to famine-relief organizations and/or other organizations working to reduce unnecessary suffering. Because each of these normative principles independently entails obligation (O_1), you don't have to believe all of (B_1)–(B_{19}) for my argument to succeed. However, the more of these propositions you believe, the greater *your* commitment to the obligatoriness of (O_1).

Upon closer inspection, the arguments for demanding dictates like those advocated by Unger and Singer break down. For example, Unger's argument for his Pretty Demanding Dictate is predicated on *The Weak Principle of Ethical Integrity:*

> Other things being even nearly equal, if it's **all right** for you to impose losses on others with the result that there's a significant lessening in the serious losses suffered by others overall, then, if you're to avoid doing what's seriously wrong, *you **can't fail to impose** much lesser losses on yourself,* nor can you fail to accept such lesser losses, when the result's a *much more* significant lessening of such serious losses overall. (Unger's italics; bold emphasis mine)

But this principle is false. The fact that it would be *permissible* for you to impose certain losses on others does not entail that it is *obligatory* for you to impose lesser losses on yourself. It only entails that it would be *permissible* for you to impose such losses on yourself, and that has never been in doubt. What is at issue is whether or not we are *obligated* to impose such losses on ourselves. Because Unger's argument is predicated on a false normative principle, his argument for Pretty Demanding Dictate is unsound.

In order for Singer's argument for the obligation to assist to be sound, his principle (P_2) must be true, but is (P_2) true? Singer suggests that it is the truth of (P_2) that accounts for the wrongness of letting the child drown. To be sure, (P_2) entails that it is wrong to let the child drown, but so do many other weaker principles. Consider the following highly specific principle:

(P_3) If one encounters a young child drowning in a shallow pond and one can save the child without personal risk and without ruining more than $400 worth of clothes, then one ought to save the child.

Like (P_2), (P_3) also entails that it is wrong to let the child drown. So, it is not clear that it is (P_2)'s truth that accounts for the wrongfulness of letting the child drown. Perhaps, it is the truth of (P_3) instead. To be sure, one can rightfully object that (P_3) is not couched at the appropriate level of generality for a normative principle. The point of mentioning (P_3) is just to show that there are considerably weaker principles than (P_2) that can account for the wrongness of letting the child drown. Because other weaker principles can account for the wrongfulness of letting the child drown, Singer's example does not show that (P_2) is true. Here is a more plausible principle:

(P_4) Other things being equal, if you can prevent an innocent person from dying with minimal effort, with no noticeable reduction in your standard of living or the standard of living of your dependents, with no risk to yourself or others, and without thereby failing to fulfill any other more pressing obligation, then you ought to do so.

Unlike (P_3), (P_4) is sufficiently general to provide normative guidance in a wide variety of circumstances. Moreover, (P_4) also entails that it would be wrong of you to let the child drown. Granted, if you wade into the pond, you will ruin your cotton twill pants, your oxford cloth shirt, and your tweed jacket, but being a professor you have several tweed jackets, several pairs of Dockers, and numerous oxford cloth shirts. Even if the clothes you are wearing are completely ruined, there will be no noticeable difference in your standard of living. You will simply wear different clothes that are already hanging in your closet. My modest principle (P_4) has another thing going for it, as well. Anyone, like you, who believes (B_3), $(B_{8'})$, (B_{10}), (B_{12}), (B_{17}), and (B_{18}) is already committed to (P_4), on pain of inconsistency.

Your beliefs [(B_1), (B_2), (B_8), and (B_{10})] also commit you to another minimalistic principle:

(P_5) If you can help to reduce the amount of unnecessary suffering in the world with minimal effort on your part, with no risk to yourself or others, with no noticeable reduction in your standard of living or the standard of living of your dependents, and without thereby failing to fulfill any other more pressing obligation, then you ought to do so.

Now here's the rub. Any affluent or moderately affluent person who is committed to (P_4) and (P_5) is already committed to the obligatoriness of sending a portion of her income to famine relief organizations and/or other organizations working to reduce unnecessary suffering. Consider the implications of your commitment to (P_4). According to (P_4), you ought to prevent a person from dying if you can do so with minimal effort and no noticeable reduction in your standard of living or that of your dependents, all else being equal. By sending a modest portion of your income to OXFAM, CARE, or UNICEF, you can prevent many innocent children from dying unnecessarily. Plus, you can do so with no noticeable reduction in your or your dependents' standards of living, and your doing so will not prevent you from fulfilling any more pressing obligation. So, according to (P_4), you ought to do so. It is worth noting that your belief (B_{18})—it is wrong to let an innocent person die *when one can prevent that death with minimal effort and minimal sacrifice on one's part*—entails the same result. By not sending money to famine-relief organizations like those listed above, you are letting numerous innocent children under the age of 5 die when you could have easily prevented their deaths with *little effort* (writing out a check) and *minimal sacrifice* on your part (no noticeable reduction in your standard of living). (B_{18}) entails that it is wrong of you to let these children die. Thus, your beliefs about the intrinsic badness of unnecessary childhood deaths and our duties to help prevent such deaths commit you to the obligatoriness of sending a portion of your income to organizations like OXFAM, CARE, and UNICEF to prevent some of those innocent children from dying.

Your beliefs about the intrinsic badness of unnecessary suffering [(B_1) and (B_2)] and your beliefs about our duties to minimize such suffering [(B_8), (B_{10}), (B_{12}), and (B_{13})] together commit you to the view that you ought to help reduce the amount of unnecessary suffering in the world when you can do so with minimal effort, with no risk to yourself or others, and with no noticeable reduction in your standard of living [i.e., they commit you to (P_5)]. Children living in absolute poverty don't only *die* from starvation. They *suffer* terribly from unrelenting hunger and its attendant diseases, including impaired brain development, measles, chronic diarrhea, chronic fatigue, and wasting. Sending a modest portion of your income to OXFAM, CARE, or UNICEF will enable these organizations to provide food, clean water, and needed medications to numerous malnourished children, thereby alleviating their suffering and greatly reducing their risk of disease. Because you can easily do so (by making out a check) with no risk to yourself or to others, with no noticeable reduction in your standard of living, and without failing to perform any other more serious obligation, your beliefs, together with their concomitant, (P_5), entail that you ought to do so.

Your other beliefs support the same conclusion. You believe (B_9)—a morally good person will take steps to make the world a better place and even stronger steps to avoid making the world a worse place—and (B_{10})—even a "minimally decent person" would take steps to help reduce the amount of unnecessary pain, suffering, and death in the world *if s/he could do so with little effort on her/his part*. You also believe that you are a morally good person [(B_{11})], or at least a minimally decent one [(B_{12})], and that you are the kind of person who would take steps to help reduce the amount of pain, suffering, and death in the world *if you could do so with little effort on your part* [(B_{13})]. As we have already seen, *with minimal effort and negligible sacrifice*, you could take steps to help reduce both the number of unnecessary childhood deaths and the amount of unnecessary suffering experienced by these impoverished children just by writing out a modest check to OXFAM, CARE, UNICEF, or some other humanitarian organization working effectively to reduce the amount of unnecessary suffering in the world. Given (B_{10}), you ought to provide modest support to one (or more) of these organizations. Given (B_{12}) and (B_{13}), if you really are the kind of person

you think you are, you will provide such support to one (or more) of these organizations.

We have just seen that consistency with your other beliefs requires that you send a portion of your income to famine-relief organizations and/or other organizations working to reduce unnecessary suffering and prevent unnecessary death. But how much of your money are you obligated to send to such worthy organizations? Here I must appeal to your belief (B_{14}). Because you take yourself to be an intellectually honest individual, you must honestly ask yourself how much can you afford to send to famine relief organizations with no noticeable reduction in your standard of living (or in the standard of living of your dependents). Granted, just how much money you can send without noticeably reducing your standard of living will depend on what stage of life you are in and on the extent of your financial resources. Even so, I submit that, like most moderately affluent people, you could easily divert 2% of your income to such worthy causes as famine relief and global population control without the slightest noticeable change in your current standard of living. I arrived at this number in the following highly scientific manner. I asked my teaching assistant who makes $9,000 per year if he could send 1% of his income ($90 per year, $7.50 per month) to famine-relief organizations with no noticeable difference in his current standard of living, and he said, "Yes." Almost everyone reading this article, except for students who are being forced to read it for a class, makes considerably more money than my teaching assistant; and although it may be true that you have more financial obligations than my T.A. (your house payment, insurance, college tuition for your children, etc. versus his rent, insurance, student fees, etc.), still, given the law of marginal utility, if he can afford to send 1% of his income with no noticeable reduction in his standard of living, you can almost certainly afford to send 2% of your income without noticeably reducing your standard of living. As overpaid philosophy professors, many of you make $40,000 a year. Two percent of $40,000 is $800/year or $15/week. Sending $15/week to famine-relief organizations would prevent more than 250 innocent children under age 5 from dying annually, and your life wouldn't be worse off in any noticeable way. Did your standard of living change *in any noticeable way* when George "Read My Lips" Bush increased your taxes by 2% (while promising to cut them)? No. So, it is extremely doubtful that you would be able to notice a 2% reduction in your current income level, especially if you have your credit card billed automatically for $60 each month. It would be just another monthly payment that you wouldn't even notice.

Many of you could send an even greater percentage of your income (perhaps as much as 5% of your income) with no noticeable reduction in your standard of living. As I said earlier, this is where intellectual honesty comes in. You must honestly determine what percentage of your income you could send to famine-relief organizations without noticeably reducing your standard of living and without thereby failing to fulfill any other overriding obligations, for, according to your own beliefs, that percentage is the *minimum* amount that you are morally required to send to famine-relief organizations and/or other organizations working to reduce unnecessary suffering. One thing seems reasonably clear: You could easily send 1% of your income to such worthy organizations as OXFAM, CARE, UNICEF, and IPPF with no noticeable difference in your standard of living or the standard of living of any of your dependents. Because your beliefs commit you to (P4) and (P5), your beliefs commit you to contributing at the very least 1% of your income, and probably 2% or more, to such important organizations. To do any less is seriously immoral, *by your own standards.*

What about students? Because students also accept (B₁)–(B₁₉), their beliefs likewise entail that if they can reduce the number of innocent children starving to death *with minimal effort and negligible sacrifice on their part,* then they ought to do so. The question is whether they can do so with minimal effort and sacrifice. If you're a student, money's tight, right? As a student struggling to pay your own bills, can you really be morally obligated to support organizations working to save the lives of innocent impoverished children? The answer will no doubt vary from student to student, but here again, intellectual honesty must play a role. Would your life really be any worse off, say, if you had one less beer ($2.00) or café latté ($2.50) per week, or one less pack of cigarettes ($4.00) per month? Or suppose you bought one less CD ($15.00) every two months. Would that really make your life noticeably worse off? (How many CDs sit unused on your shelf anyway?) If we are honest with ourselves, most of us, *including most students,* have to admit that we make lots of frivolous purchases. Reducing the number of these frivolous purchases ever so slightly won't make any noticeable difference in our quality of life, and, in some cases, reducing the number of these purchases would actually improve both our health and the quality of our lives—e.g., reducing the number of cigarettes one smokes or the number of high-fat café lattés one drinks. By way of illustration, suppose you drank one fewer café lattés per week. As a result, you would save $10 per month. By simply sending the $10 saved each month to OXFAM, you would, over the course of a year, prevent 40 children from dying soon, and your standard of living would remain essentially the same. If you are absolutely crazy about café lattés and feel your life wouldn't be complete without a latté a day, then you must honestly ask yourself whether you could cut back on some other frivolous purchases without noticeably reducing the quality of your life. Even buying just one fewer CD *per year* and sending that $15.00 to UNICEF would prevent 5 children from dying soon. The point is simply this: By cutting out a frivolous purchase here or there, even students could help to reduce the number of innocent children suffering and dying from absolute poverty and malnutrition *with minimal effort and no noticeable reduction in their standards of living.*

The moral of the present section is clear: Consistency with your own beliefs forces you to admit: (i) that you are morally obligated to send a portion of your income to famine-relief organizations and/or other organizations working to reduce the amount of unnecessary pain, suffering, and death in the world and (ii) that the minimum you are obligated to send is whatever amount you could send with no noticeable reduction in your or your dependents' standards of living and without thereby failing to meet any of your other more stringent obligations. For most of us, that means sending 2% of our income to such organizations (which amounts to around 1.5% of your income after taxes). For most students, it means cutting back on a few frivolous purchases and sending the money saved to one of these organizations. To make fulfilling this obligation as easy and effortless as possible, I have provided the addresses and phone numbers for OXFAM, CARE, UNICEF, and IPPF at the end of this article.

4. WHY YOU ARE COMMITTED TO THE MORAL OBLIGATORINESS OF (O_2)

You have just seen that your beliefs entail that you are obligated:

(O_1) To send a modest portion of our income to humanitarian organizations working to reduce the amount of unnecessary suffering in the world.

But our duties to the world's absolutely poor don't stop with (O_1). As we shall presently see, your beliefs also entail that we are obligated:

(O_2) To refrain from squandering food that could be fed to the world's absolutely poor, especially when doing so involves no risk to ourselves or others.

A. Malnutrition

When we think of malnutrition, images of poor starving children wasting away in undeveloped nations quickly come to mind. We don't think of the obese people suffering from diabetes, hypertension, and heart disease that are all too common in developed countries. But these latter people are clearly malnourished, as well. The fact is that there are two kinds of malnutrition—undernutrition and overnutrition—and both of them result in preventable disease, unnecessary suffering, and premature death. *Undernutrition* arises when a person consumes insufficient calories and/or insufficient macro-and micro-nutrients to meet the basic energy and nutrient requirements for normal biological and metabolic function. Undernutrition causes a wide variety of deficiency diseases including: tissue wasting (due to protein deficiency); brain underdevelopment (due to inadequate fat consumption prior to age 2); blindness (vitamin A deficiency); scurvy (vitamin C deficiency), beriberi (thiamin deficiency), and pellagra (niacin and protein deficiency); and death from starvation (insufficient calories). These diseases, so common in undeveloped countries, are virtually nonexistent in developed nations. *Overnutrition* arises when one consumes too many calories, excess fat, excess saturated fat, excess protein, excess cholesterol, excess refined sugar, and excess sodium. Overnutrition gives rise to a wide variety of diseases of excess: coronary artery disease, stroke and other arteriosclerotic diseases (excess cholesterol, saturated fat, transfatty acids, and iron); obesity (excess fat and calories); hypertension (excess fat, calories, and sodium), diabetes mellitus (excess fat, calories, and refined sugar), some forms of cancer (excess fat), and osteoporosis (excess protein consumption, coupled with inactivity). These diseases, rampant in developed countries, are practically unheard of in underdeveloped countries. As we shall see, both forms of malnutrition have the same root cause, a form of agriculture that (i) fosters overnutrition and (ii) systematically requires the overnourished to squander food that could have been made available to the undernourished.

B. Day-Old Bread: Why Squandering Food in a World of Scarcity Is Morally Wrong

Day-Old Bread: Suppose there is a small bakery in my neighborhood that sells its day-old bread at one-third of the regular price. The bakery doesn't want to run out of bread for its full-paying customers, so it typically bakes twelve more loaves of bread than it anticipates needing. Also suppose there is a small homeless shelter for battered women and children in the neighborhood. It can afford to buy only the discounted day-old bread. When there is no day-old bread available, these people go without bread for the day. Suppose I know all these facts, but I, nevertheless, start buying the remaining twelve loaves of bread (in addition to the loaf I regularly buy) right before the bakery closes each day just because I like the way it makes my kitchen smell. As a result, there is no longer any day-old bread available. Of course, I can't eat that much bread. So, the next day, when that fresh-baked smell is gone, I simply throw all twelve loaves of bread in the garbage. By squandering food in this way, I have knowingly caused the women and children in the shelter to go hungry, and I have done so just to satisfy my trivial desire to have my kitchen smell a certain way. Finally, suppose I keep up my bread-purchasing habit for so long that some of these women and children end up dying from hunger-related diseases.

Have I done anything wrong? Your beliefs entail that I have. You believe that a world with more *unnecessary* suffering is worse than a world with less *unnecessary* suffering [(B_2)], and you also believe that we ought to avoid making the world a worse place when we can do so with minimal effort and negligible sacrifice [$(B_{8'})$]. In Day-Old Bread, I have knowingly squandered food that these women and children would have been able to eat and have, thus, knowingly caused them to suffer unnecessarily just so that I could experience a certain olfactory sensation. I have knowingly made the world a worse place by increasing the amount of unnecessary suffering it contains for an entirely trivial reason. Here, I have actively and knowingly made others worse off. One thing I could have easily done to avoid making the world a worse place would have been to purchase only the bread I need, leaving the rest for others to consume. Perhaps, it would not be wrong of me to purchase vastly more bread than I need in a world where everyone's food needs were adequately met, but as your beliefs rightly reveal, it is wrong of me to waste food that could be fed to severely undernourished humans who desperately need that food. Simply put, your beliefs entail that we are obligated to (O_2)—to refrain from squandering food that could be fed to others who desperately need it.

Multi-Squanderer Scenario: Suppose I am not unique in my desire to smell fresh-baked bread. Suppose that there are people in every

community in America who enjoy the smell of fresh-baked bread as much as I do and who, like me, buy up all the available bread at their local bakeries just before closing time so that there is no day-old bread available anywhere in the country. And suppose that, as a result, women and children in shelters all across North America are starving to death, just so lots of other North Americans can enjoy the smell of fresh-baked bread. Does the fact that lots of other people are squandering bread in this way make it any less wrong of me to squander the bread from my local bakery? Not one bit. The fact that other people are behaving immorally does not justify my doing so. Given your beliefs, the only difference between Day-Old Bread and Multi-Squanderer Scenario is that in the latter case lots of other people are just as morally culpable as I am.

C. Eating in a World of Scarcity: (O_2)'s Implications

Day-Old Bread illustrates that your beliefs commit you to the moral obligatoriness of not squandering food that could be fed to the world's absolutely poor. You are not alone in this commitment. Anyone who believes (B_1)–(B_{19}), and that includes almost everyone, is committed to the obligatoriness of (O_2). Even without appealing to (B_1)–(B_{19}), almost everyone would agree that it is wrong to knowingly throw away bread that could save other people's lives and that, therefore, we are obligated not to squander food in this way. What most people don't realize is that in order to fulfill obligation (O_2), they must radically change the way they eat.

If you are like most moderately affluent people, you eat meat and lots of it: Bacon or sausage for breakfast, one or two quarter-pound hamburgers for lunch, and steak, pork chops, or chicken for dinner. For most people in affluent nations, eating this way is normal—it's how they were raised to eat—and it seems not only permissible, but downright wholesome. But things are not always as they seem. The burden of the present section is to show that anyone who believes (B_1)–(B_{19}) is already committed, on pain of inconsistency, to the immorality of eating most meat. Elsewhere, I have argued that beliefs like (B_1), (B_2), (B_8), $(B_{8'})$, and (B_{10}) commit us to the immorality of eating meat and other animal products because of the enormous amount of unnecessary *animal* suffering modern animal factories generate.[7] Here, I am interested in the untold *human* suffering that such a system of agriculture produces.

The numbers used in Day-Old Bread were not chosen at random. They were chosen because it takes 12.9 pounds of grain to produce one pound of beef. This grain could be fed directly to the world's starving poor, but instead it is fed to intentionally bred cows—cows that would not have existed and, hence, would not have needed to be fed, had we not artificially inseminated their mothers. These cows, in turn, convert that grain to manure. By cycling grain through cattle to produce animal protein, we lose 90% of that grain's protein, 96% of its calories, 100% of its carbohydrates, and 100% of its fiber. By cycling grain through cattle so that affluent people can eat meat, starving *humans* are being deprived of that grain so that *cows* can be fed. As a result, while more than 1 billion humans experience chronic hunger, cows in feedlots never go hungry. Playing off our Day-Old Bread analogy, those 12.9 pounds of grain could have been converted to 12.9 loaves of bread that could have, in turn, been fed to the world's starving poor. Instead, that grain/bread is wasted, just so people in affluent nations can eat meat and other animal products. There is no way around it: Whenever one purchases a pound of beef, one is supporting a system of agriculture that effectively squanders 12.9 pounds of grain for every pound of beef produced.

Although beef production is one of the most inefficient means of food production, all forms of animal agriculture are highly inefficient. Of the 12 million tons of grain protein produced in the United States in 1991, 10 millions tons were fed to livestock, leaving only 2 million tons for human consumption. Of the 9.2 million tons of legume protein produced in the United States that year, 9 million tons were fed to livestock, leaving only 0.2 million ton for human consumption. For the 21 million tons of plant protein fed to livestock, we received only 7 million tons of livestock protein in return (a 33% protein-conversion efficiency rate). The end result is a net loss of 14 million tons of protein, protein that could have saved the lives of starving children had it not been squandered on livestock production. And protein isn't the only macronutrient we lose by feeding grain to livestock. We also lose all of that grain's carbohydrates and fiber (meat contains no carbohydrates or fiber) and approximately 90% of its caloric energy. I noted at the outset that the United States grows more than enough grain and soybeans to feed the world's entire human population. Unfortunately, most of that grain is squandered on livestock production. Of the estimated 740 kg of grain grown in the United States per person per year, 663 kg are fed to livestock, leaving only 77 kg for human consumption.[8] Were we to forego foods of animal origin and eat that grain directly, there would be more than enough grain left over to feed the world's starving human population.

The irony is that the same system of agriculture that deprives starving humans of grain, thereby contributing to undernutrition in poor nations, is also one of the primary causes of overnutrition in affluent nations. It is now an established fact that diets high in saturated fat and cholesterol greatly increase the risk of several chronic degenerative diseases, including heart disease, hypertension, obesity, diabetes, and some forms of cancer. We also know that meat and animal products are the principal sources of saturated fat and cholesterol in standard Western diets. The evidence is so compelling that the American Dietetic Association, the leading nutritional organization in the United States, now maintains:

> Scientific data suggest positive relationships between a vegetarian diet and reduced risk for several chronic degenerative diseases and conditions, including obesity, coronary artery disease, hypertension, diabetes mellitus, and some types of cancer.- *It is the position of The American Dietetic Association (ADA) that appropriately planned vegetarian diets are healthful, are nutritionally adequate, and provide health benefits in the prevention and treatment of certain diseases.*[9]

The ADA also holds:

> Well-planned vegan and lacto-ovo vegetarian diets are appropriate for all stages of the life cycle, including during pregnancy and lactation. Appropriately planned vegan and lacto-ovo vegetarian diets satisfy nutrient needs of infants, children, and adolescents and promote normal growth.

One result of feeding our children a meat-based diet—childhood obesity—is both ironic and sad. While children in underdeveloped countries are starving to death, more than one-fifth of U.S. children are obese. In addition, the damage to coronary arteries arising from a meat-based diet begins remarkably early. Dr. Spock points out: "Fatty deposits are now typically found in the coronary arteries of children on a typical American diet by the age of three. And by the age of twelve, they are found in 70% of children." As a result, Dr. Spock recommends vegan diets for all children over the age of 2. These last observations demonstrate that our duty not to squander food is not overridden by a biological need to consume meat and animal products. There is no such need. Neither adults nor children need to consume any animal products at all. As the ADA has averred, appropriately planned vegan diets—diets devoid of meat and animal products—are *nutritionally adequate* for all stages of the life cycle. If Dr. Spock is right, appropriately planned vegan diets are *nutritionally superior* to meat-based diets. Either way, we have no need for meat and animal products. We eat them only because we like the way they taste.

Does the desire for a particular taste sensation justify us in squandering food that could be fed to starving children? No. In Day-Old Bread, we saw that your beliefs entail the wrongness of squandering 12 loaves of bread just so one can experience a particular olfactory sensation. By doing so, one not only fails to benefit others, one actively makes others worse off. Of course, by purchasing meat because one likes its taste, one is squandering 12 pounds of grain, just to experience a particular gustatory sensation, and in so doing, one is actively making others—those in desperate need of that grain—worse off. Surely, the fact that it is a *gustatory* sensation, rather than an *olfactory* sensation, is not morally relevant. Because your beliefs entail that it is wrong to squander bread in Day-Old Bread, your beliefs also entail that it is wrong to squander grain by purchasing meat. Hence, your commitment to the obligatoriness of not squandering grain commits you to the obligatoriness of adopting a predominantly plant-based diet devoid of meat and animal products obtained from grain-fed animals. Because virtually all commercially produced meat (including beef, pork, chicken, turkey, and farm-raised fish), dairy products, and eggs come from grain-fed animals, consistency with your own beliefs requires that you adopt a quasi-vegan diet devoid of beef, pork, chicken, turkey, farm-raised fish, dairy products, and eggs.[10]

One might object that (O_2) does not entail that the obligatoriness of adopting such a diet on the grounds that the difficulty of planning a nutritionally balanced quasi-vegan diet for oneself and one's family simply makes such a diet too risky. Such an objection is entirely unfounded. It is extremely easy to eat a nutritionally balanced vegan diet. No special food combining is necessary. All one need do is eat sufficient calories centered around the Physicians Committee for Responsible Medicine's *new* four food groups: I. Whole Grains (5+ servings/day), II. Vegetables (3+ servings/day), III. Fruits (3+ servings/day), and IV. Legumes (2+ servings/day). Anyone who eats the recommended daily servings from these new four groups will be eating a nutritionally sound plant-based diet. And far from being risky, such a diet will reduce one's risk of heart disease, cancer, stroke, hypertension, obesity, and diabetes.

There is no justification for squandering precious grain reserves in a world of food scarcity. This conclusion is not derived from some highly contentious ethical theory you likely reject, but from beliefs you already hold. Consistency with your own beliefs entails that it's wrong to squander food that could be fed to the world's starving poor for trivial reasons like taste or smell. Because modern meat, dairy, and egg production necessarily squanders grain that could be fed directly to humans, *your own beliefs* entail that it is wrong to consume these products, which, in turn, entails that quasi-vegan diets are obligatory.

5. OBJECTIONS AND REPLIES

A. The Iteration Objection

In Section 3, after showing that Singer's and Unger's attempts to defend highly demanding dictates fail, I argued that your beliefs commit you to two *much less demanding* normative principles (P_4) and (P_5), which, in turn, entail that you are obligated to (O_1)—to send a modest portion of your income to famine-relief organizations and/or other organizations working to reduce unnecessary suffering. The present worry is that these two principles will ultimately reduce to the very same highly demanding dictate from which I was aiming to distance myself. Because *standards of living* are vague and lack precise boundaries, there can be a repeated series of non-noticeable reductions in one's standard of living, such that, before long, one is radically worse off than one's original starting position, and noticeably so.

My response is quite simple. Neither (P_4) nor (P_5) is intended to be iterated in this way. In fact, (P_4) and (P_5) are intended to be compatible with gradual increases in one's standard of living so as to enable one to do even more to help reduce the amount of unnecessary suffering down the road. To block the iteration objection and to make explicit the kinds of principles your beliefs clearly commit you to, (P_4) and (P_5)—as they apply to *moderately affluent* people—should be restricted as follows: The principles never require a moderately affluent person to have a standard of living *noticeably* lower than the highest standard of living she has ever enjoyed. Even with this restriction in place, (P_4) and (P_5) still entail that most of us are morally required to send at least 2% of our income to famine-relief organizations and/or other organizations working to reduce unnecessary suffering. The reason is this: Because standards of living typically continue to improve the longer people are in the workforce, most people are currently enjoying their highest standards of living. (P_4) and (P_5) require these people to provide whatever amount of financial assistance they can provide without noticeably lowering their standard of living from its current optimal level.

B. The Libertarian Objection: There Are No Positive Duties

Strict libertarians insist that although we have negative duties to do no harm, we have *no* positive duties to assist others. Thus, on the libertarian view, it would not be wrong of you to let the child drown in Singer's Pond. Libertarians maintain that even though you could save the child with minimal sacrifice and no risk to yourself, you have absolutely no positive obligation to assist the child in any way. Because they deny the existence of positive duties, libertarians contend that it also would *not* be wrong of you *not* to save the lives of numerous starving children by sending a modest portion of your income to famine-relief organizations. Granted, libertarians do think that it would be *good* of you to wade in and save the child. They also think it would be *good* of you to send money to such worthy causes as famine relief, but these actions would be entirely supererogatory on your part. Thus, the libertarian objection runs as follows: Because there are *no* positive duties, we have *no* obligation to send money to famine-relief organizations, even though that money would save the lives of numerous innocent children.

As noted earlier, Narveson claims that such a libertarian "nobody-needs-to-help-anybody" stance is unreasonable. A variation on the trolley problem suggests that he is right. Suppose that six innocent people are trapped on the tracks and a runaway trolley is barreling down on them. Fortunately, you just happen to be standing right next to a switch which, if flipped, will divert the trolley onto a second track. Even more fortunately, unlike typical trolley problems where three people are trapped on the second track and you have to decide between killing three and letting six die, in the present trolley case, no one is on the other track and so, if the switch is flipped, the train will be diverted to the second track where it will roll safely to a stop with no one being injured. The question is this: Are you morally required to flip the switch and save the six people? Not according to the libertarian. Even though you are standing right next to the switch and can flip the switch with little effort and no sacrifice on your part, with no risk to yourself or others, and without thereby violating any other obligations, the libertarian maintains that it would *not* be wrong of you to let the six die by not flipping the switch.

Such a position strikes most of us as morally outrageous. You *should* flip the switch, and it would be *clearly wrong* of you not to do so. And you, no doubt, agree. Because you believe that one should wade into the pond to save the child [(B_7)], you surely think it would be wrong not to flip the switch. I realize that a die-hard libertarian might remain unconvinced, but you are not a die-hard libertarian. You believe that there are both positive and negative duties. Thus, the libertarian objection under consideration gives *you* absolutely no reason to think that (O_1) is not obligatory.

C. Malthusian Musings

A common reason offered for not sending money to famine-relief organizations is that doing so will just exacerbate the problem. If lots more children under age 5 survive, then when they reach puberty and start having their own children, there will be even more mouths to feed, and as a result, there will be even more human suffering due to starvation. In short, it is better to let 12 million children starve to death each year than to save them and have two or three times that many children starving 15 years from now.

Couched in the more scientific language of ecology, the Malthusian objection runs as follows: Left unchecked, organisms will reproduce until they reach the carrying capacity K of their respective ecosystems. Once they exceed K, there will be a major crash in the population size of that organism. By feeding starving humans, the anti-assistance argument goes, we are simply speeding up the time at which we exceed the Earth's K for humans (hereafter K_h). Better to let 12 million children starve to death each year than to exceed K_h and have an even more devastating population crash.

The first thing to note is that we don't think Malthusian worries about exceeding K_h give us a good reason to let our own children starve. But if

we don't let our children starve, then, as adults, they will probably procreate, thereby hastening the time when K_h is exceeded. If ecologically based, global human population concerns give us a reason to let distant children die, they give us an equally good reason to let our own children die. You wouldn't think of letting your own children die to help reduce human population. Thus you must not find letting children starve to death to be a legitimate way to curb human population growth.

Second, there are other more effective ways of reducing human population growth: improving educational opportunities and employment opportunities *for women* (which drives up the opportunity cost of procreation), improving the economic security of the elderly, providing ready access to birth control, and providing abortion services.[11] Even more draconian policies, like mandatory sterilization after having one child, are preferable to letting children starve to death. Because there are numerous more effective means of curbing population growth than letting innocent children starve, anyone who accepts (B_{19}) must think it wrong to let innocent children starve as a means of population control.

Third, demographic studies repeatedly show that childhood morality rates and birthrates are positively correlated—as childhood mortality rates decline, so do birthrates—and so, supporting famine-relief organizations working to reduce the number of unnecessary childhood deaths is, paradoxically, a way of slowing population growth. But suppose you question the validity of these studies. Suppose you dig in your Malthusian heels and insist that feeding the world's starving children will increase the number of humans suffering from starvation down the road. Such insistence does not absolve you from obligation (O_1); it just means that you are obligated to fulfill it in a different way. Instead of being required to send money to a famine-relief organization, you will be obligated to send money to humanitarian organizations, like the IPPF, that are working to reduce the rate of population growth in underdeveloped countries through effective birth control measures.

Fourth, those who take Malthusian concerns seriously are even more obligated to refrain from

THE FAR SIDE® BY GARY LARSON

"Lord, we thank thee."

consuming meat and other animal products, because intentionally breeding millions of cows and pigs and billions of chickens greatly reduces the world's K_h. Intentionally adding billions of farm animals to the world greatly increases the number of animal mouths that must be fed and, thus, greatly reduces the amount of food available for human consumption.

6. CONCLUSION

The implications of your beliefs are clear. Given your beliefs, it follows that we are morally obligated to (O_1)—to send a modest portion of our income to famine-relief organizations and/or other organizations working to reduce the amount of unnecessary pain, suffering, and death in the world—and to (O_2)—to refrain from squandering food that could be fed to the world's absolutely poor. (O_2), in turn, entails that we are obligated to adopt a quasi-vegan diet, rather than squander grain on a meat-based diet. These conclusions were not derived from some highly contentious ethical theory that you can easily reject, but from your own firmly held beliefs. Consequently, consistency

Appendix

Oxfam America
26 West St.
Boston, MA 02111
1-800-OXFAM US
 [1-800-693-2687].

International Planned Parenthood Federation (IPPF)
902 Broadway, 10th Floor
New York, NY 10010

United Nations Children's Fund
333 East 38th St.
New York, NY 10016
UNICEF: 1-800-FOR KIDS [1-800-367-5437]

CARE
151 Ellis St.
Atlanta, GA 30303
1-800-521-CARE
 [1-800-521-2273]

demands that you embrace these obligations and modify your behavior accordingly.

NOTES

1. Following Peter Singer (who borrows the term from Robert McNamara), I use 'absolute poverty' to refer to "a condition of life so characterised by malnutrition, illiteracy, disease, squalid surroundings, high infant mortality and low life expectancy as to be beneath any reasonable definition of human decency" [Singer, *Practical Ethics,* Second Edition (Cambridge: Cambridge University Press, 1993), p. 219.]. Singer reports that, according to the Worldwatch Institute, as many as 1.2 billion people live in absolute poverty (pp. 219–20).

2. William Aiken, "The Right to Be Saved from Starvation" in *World Hunger and Moral Obligation,* eds. W. Aiken and H. LaFollette (Englewood Cliffs, NJ: Prentice-Hall, 1977), pp. 86 and 93. Aiken argues that one's right to be saved from starvation is claimable against all persons who satisfy three minimal conditions: (i) they must know that the person is starving, (ii) they must have the means necessary to save the person, and (iii) they must be able to save the person without placing themselves in an equally bad or worse situation than the person they are saving (pp. 91–93).

3. By "without sacrificing anything of comparable moral significance" Singer means "without causing anything else comparably bad to happen, or doing something that is wrong in itself, or failing to promote some moral good, comparable in significance to the bad thing that we prevent." ("Famine, Affluence, and Morality," *Philosophy and Public Affairs,* vol. 1, no. 3 (Spring 1972), p. 234).

4. Obviously, if you do not hold these beliefs (or enough of them), my argument will have no force for you, nor is it intended to. It is only aimed at those of you who do hold these widespread commonsense beliefs.

5. By "*unnecessary* suffering" I mean suffering which serves no greater, outweighing justifying good. If some instance of suffering is required to bring about a greater good (e.g., a painful root canal may be the only way to save a person's tooth), then that suffering is *not* unnecessary. Thus, in the case of (B_2), no *ceteris paribus* clause is needed, because if other things are *not* equal such that the suffering in question is justified by an overriding justifying good that can only be achieved by allowing that suffering, then that suffering is *not* unnecessary.

6. By a "minimally decent person" I mean a person who does the very minimum required by morality and no more. I borrow this terminology from Judith Jarvis Thomson who distinguishes a *good* Samaritan from a *minimally decent* Samaritan. See her "A Defense of Abortion," *Philosophy and Public Affairs* 1 (1971): 62–65.

7. See my "The Immorality of Eating Meat" in *The Moral Life,* ed. Louis Pojman (New York and Oxford: Oxford University Press, 2000), pp. 856–889. There I documented that the routine unanaesthetized mutilations (castration, branding, dehorning, debeaking, dubbing, tail docking, and tooth pulling) and abysmal living conditions which farm animals are forced to endure in factory farms, along with inhumane transportation and slaughter processes, greatly increase the amount of unnecessary suffering in the world; and I argued that because you could easily take steps to help reduce such unnecessary suffering by eating something other than meat, consistency with your beliefs forces you to admit that eating meat is morally wrong.

8. Data on protein production and consumption and grain production and consumption taken from *Food, Energy, and Society,* Revised Edition, eds. David Pimentel and Marcia Pimentel (Niwot, CO: University of Colorado Press, 1996), pp. 77–78.

9. "Position of the American Dietetic Association: Vegetarian Diets," *Journal of the American Dietitic Association* 97 (November 1997): 1317. For those wishing to learn more about sound vegetarian nutrition, the ADA has published this article in its entirety at: www.eatright.org/adap1197.html.

10. (O_2) does not entail that it is wrong to eat meat *per se*, e.g. it does *not* entail that eating the flesh of wild animals is wrong. Hence, the use of 'quasi-vegan' in the text. However, (O_2) does entail that it is wrong to eat virtually all commercially produced meat and animal products because these products are obtained from grain-fed animals and their production necessarily squanders grain which could have been fed to starving humans.

11. Regardless of one's views on abortion, presumably it would be better to abort a fetus quickly and relatively painlessly than to let that fetus be born only to starve to death slowly and painfully.

STUDY QUESTIONS

1. Examine Engel's arguments for his two main principles. Discuss their premises. Do you see any problems with them?
2. Is Engel correct that virtually all major moral theories contain principles that require us to make some modest sacrifices for the welfare of the absolutely poor?
3. Examine the objections that Engel discusses against his position. Does he defeat them? Are there other objections you can think of?
4. How much should we give to the absolutely poor? Is Engel too lenient, too stringent, or about right?
5. Examine Engel's Day-Old Bread example and discuss its implications.

52   Can Frankenfood Save the Planet?

JONATHAN RAUCH

Jonathan Rauch is a writer for the *Atlantic Monthly*. In this essay he presents evidence to the effect that genetically engineered food could provide enough nutrition to save future generations from starvation. He argues that environmentalists who oppose genetically modified food are actually working against the best interests of humankind and their pets.

That genetic engineering may be the most environmentally beneficial technology to have emerged in decades, or possibly centuries, is not immediately obvious. Certainly, at least, it is not obvious to the many U.S. and foreign environmental groups that regard biotechnology as a bête noire. Nor is it necessarily obvious to people who grew up in cities, and who have only an inkling of what happens on a modern farm. Being agriculturally illiterate myself, I set out to look at what may be, if the planet is fortunate, the farming of the future.

It was baking hot that April day. I traveled with two Virginia state soil-and-water-conservation officers and an agricultural-extension agent to an area not far from Richmond. The farmers there are national (and therefore world) leaders in the application of what is known as continuous no-till farming. In plain English, they don't plough. For thousands of years, since the dawn of the agricultural revolution, farmers have ploughed, often several times a year; and with ploughing has come runoff that pollutes rivers and blights aquatic habitat, erosion that wears away the land, and the release into the atmosphere

of greenhouse gases stored in the soil. Today, at last, farmers are working out methods that have begun to make ploughing obsolete.

At about one-thirty we arrived at a 200-acre patch of farmland known as the Good Luck Tract. No one seemed to know the provenance of the name, but the best guess was that somebody had said something like "You intend to farm this? Good luck!" The land was rolling, rather than flat, and its slopes came together to form natural troughs for rainwater. Ordinarily this highly erodible land would be suitable for cows, not crops. Yet it was dense with wheat— wheat yielding almost twice what could normally be expected, and in soil that had grown richer in organic matter, and thus more nourishing to crops, even as the land was farmed. Perhaps most striking was the almost complete absence of any chemical or soil runoff. Even the beating administered in 1999 by Hurricane Floyd, which lashed the ground with nineteen inches of rain in less than twenty-four hours, produced no significant runoff or erosion. The land simply absorbed the sheets of water before they could course downhill.

Reprinted from the *Atlantic Monthly* (October 2003) by permission of the author.

At another site, a few miles away, I saw why. On land planted in corn whose shoots had only just broken the surface, Paul Davis, the extension agent, wedged a shovel into the ground and dislodged about eight inches of topsoil. Then he reached down and picked up a clump. Ploughed soil, having been stirred up and turned over again and again, becomes lifeless and homogeneous, but the clump that Davis held out was alive. I immediately noticed three squirming earthworms, one grub, and quantities of tiny white insects that looked very busy. As if in greeting, a worm defecated. "Plant-available food!" a delighted Davis exclaimed.

This soil, like that of the Good Luck Tract, had not been ploughed for years, allowing the underground ecosystem to return. Insects and roots and microorganisms had given the soil an elaborate architecture, which held the earth in place and made it a sponge for water. That was why erosion and runoff had been reduced to practically nil. Crops thrived because worms were doing the ploughing. Crop residue that was left on the ground, rather than ploughed under as usual, provided nourishment for the soil's biota and, as it decayed, enriched the soil. The farmer saved the fuel he would have used driving back and forth with a heavy plough. That saved money, and of course it also saved energy and reduced pollution. On top of all that, crop yields were better than with conventional methods.

The conservation people in Virginia were full of excitement over no-till farming. Their job was to clean up the James and York Rivers and the rest of the Chesapeake Bay watershed. Most of the sediment that clogs and clouds the rivers, and most of the fertilizer runoff that causes the algae blooms that kill fish, comes from farmland. By all but eliminating agricultural erosion and runoff—so Brian Noyes, the local conservation-district manager, told me—continuous no-till could "revolutionize" the area's water quality.

Even granting that Noyes is an enthusiast, from an environmental point of view no-till farming looks like a dramatic advance. The rub—if it is a rub—is that the widespread elimination of the plough depends on genetically modified crops.

It is only a modest exaggeration to say that as goes agriculture, so goes the planet. Of all the human activities that shape the environment, agriculture is the single most important, and it is well ahead of whatever comes second. Today about 38 percent of the earth's land area is cropland or pasture—a total that has crept upward over the past few decades as global population has grown. The increase has been gradual, only about 0.3 percent a year; but that still translates into an additional Greece or Nicaragua cultivated or grazed every year.

Farming does not go easy on the earth, and never has. To farm is to make war upon millions of plants (weeds, so-called) and animals (pests, so-called) that in the ordinary course of things would crowd out or eat or infest whatever it is a farmer is growing. Crop monocultures, as whole fields of only wheat or corn or any other single plant are called, make poor habitat and are vulnerable to disease and disaster. Although fertilizer runs off and pollutes water, farming without fertilizer will deplete and eventually exhaust the soil. Pesticides can harm the health of human beings and kill desirable or harmless bugs along with pests. Irrigation leaves behind trace elements that can accumulate and poison the soil. And on and on.

The trade-offs are fundamental. Organic farming, for example, uses no artificial fertilizer, but it does use a lot of manure, which can pollute water and contaminate food. Traditional farmers may use less herbicide, but they also do more ploughing, with all the ensuing environmental complications. Low-input agriculture uses fewer chemicals but more land. The point is not that farming is an environmental crime—it is not—but that there is no escaping the pressure it puts on the planet.

In the next half century the pressure will intensify. The United Nations, in its midrange projections, estimates that the earth's human population will grow by more than 40 percent, from 6.3 billion people today to 8.9 billion in 2050. Feeding all those people, and feeding their billion or so hungry pets (a dog or a cat is one of the first things people want once they move beyond a subsistence lifestyle), and providing the increasingly protein-rich diets that an increasingly wealthy world will expect—doing all of that will require food output to at least double, and possibly triple.

But then the story will change. According to the UN's midrange projections (which may, if anything, err somewhat on the high side), around 2050 the world's population will more or less level off. Even if the growth does not stop, it will slow. The crunch will be over. In fact, if in 2050 crop yields are still increasing, if most of the world is economically developed, and if population pressures are declining or even reversing—all of which seems reasonably likely—then the human species may at long last be able to feed itself, year in and year out, without putting any additional net stress on the environment. We might even be able to grow everything we need while *reducing* our agricultural footprint: returning cropland to wilderness, repairing damaged soils, restoring ecosystems, and so on. In other words, human agriculture might be placed on a sustainable footing forever: a breathtaking prospect.

The great problem, then, is to get through the next four or five decades with as little environmental damage as possible. That is where biotechnology comes in.

One day recently I drove down to southern Virginia to visit Dennis Avery and his son, Alex. The older Avery, a man in late middle age with a chinstrap beard, droopy eyes, and an intent, scholarly manner, lives on ninety-seven acres that he shares with horses, chickens, fish, cats, dogs, bluebirds, ducks, transient geese, and assorted other creatures. He is the director of global food issues at the Hudson Institute, a conservative think tank; Alex works with him, and is trained as a plant physiologist. We sat in a sunroom at the back of the house, our afternoon conversation punctuated every so often by dog snores and rooster crows. We talked for a little while about the Green Revolution, a dramatic advance in farm productivity that fed the world's burgeoning population over the past four decades, and then I asked if the challenge of the next four decades could be met.

"Well," Dennis replied, "we have tripled the world's farm output since 1960. And we're feeding twice as many people from the same land. That was a heroic achievement. But we have to do what some think is an even more difficult thing in this next forty years, because the Green Revolution had more land per person and more water per person—"

"—and more potential for increases," Alex added, "because the base that we were starting from was so much lower."

"By and large," Dennis went on, "the world's civilizations have been built around its best farmland. And we have used most of the world's good farmland. Most of the good land is already heavily fertilized. Most of the good land is already being planted with high-yield seeds. [Africa is the important exception.] Most of the good irrigation sites are used. We can't triple yields again with the technologies we're already using. And we might be lucky to get a fifty percent yield increase if we froze our technology short of biotech."

"Biotech" can refer to a number of things, but the relevant application here is genetic modification: the selective transfer of genes from one organism to another. Ordinary breeding can cross related varieties, but it cannot take a gene from a bacterium, for instance, and transfer it to a wheat plant. The organisms resulting from gene transfers are called "transgenic" by scientists—and "Frankenfood" by many greens.

Gene transfer poses risks, unquestionably. So, for that matter, does traditional crossbreeding. But many people worry that transgenic organisms might prove more unpredictable. One possibility is that transgenic crops would spread from fields into forests or other wild lands and there become environmental nuisances, or worse. A further risk is that transgenic plants might cross-pollinate with neighboring wild plants, producing "superweeds" or other invasive or destructive varieties in the wild. Those risks are real enough that even most biotech enthusiasts—including Dennis Avery, for example—favor some government regulation of transgenic crops.

What is much less widely appreciated is biotech's potential to do the environment good. Take as an example continuous no-till farming, which really works best with the help of transgenic crops. Human beings have been ploughing for so long that we tend to forget why we started doing it in the first place. The short answer: weed control. Turning over the soil between plantings smothers weeds and their seeds. If you don't plough, your land becomes a weed garden—unless you use herbicides to kill the weeds. Herbicides, however, are expensive, and can be complicated to apply. And they tend to kill the good with the bad.

In the mid-1990s the agricultural-products company Monsanto introduced a transgenic soybean variety called Roundup Ready. As the name implies, these soybeans tolerate Roundup, an herbicide (also made by Monsanto) that kills many kinds of weeds and then quickly breaks down into harmless ingredients. Equipped with Roundup Ready crops, farmers found that they could retire their ploughs and control weeds with just a few applications of a single, relatively benign herbicide—instead of many applications of a complex and expensive menu of chemicals. More than a third of all U.S. soybeans are now grown without ploughing, mostly owing to the introduction of Roundup Ready varieties. Ploughless cotton farming has likewise received a big boost from the advent of bioengineered varieties. No-till farming without biotech is possible, but it's more difficult and expensive, which is why no-till and biotech are advancing in tandem.

In 2001 a group of scientists announced that they had engineered a transgenic tomato plant able to thrive on salty water—water, in fact, almost half as salty as seawater, and fifty times as salty as tomatoes can ordinary abide. One of the researchers was quoted as saying, "I've already transformed tomato, tobacco, and canola. I believe I can transform any crop with this gene"—just the sort of Frankenstein hubris that makes environmentalists shudder. But consider the environmental implications. Irrigation has for millennia been a cornerstone of agriculture, but it comes at a price. As irrigation water evaporates, it leaves behind traces of salt, which accumulate in the soil and gradually render it infertile. (As any Roman legion knows, to destroy a nation's agricultural base you salt the soil.) Every year the world loses about 25 million acres—an area equivalent to a fifth of California—to salinity; 40 percent of the world's irrigated land, and 25 percent of America's, has been hurt to some degree. For decades traditional plant breeders tried to create salt-tolerant crop plants, and for decades they failed.

Salt-tolerant crops might bring millions of acres of wounded or crippled land back into production. "And it gets better," Alex Avery told me. The transgenic tomato plants take up and sequester in their leaves as much as six or seven percent of their weight in sodium. "Theoretically," Alex said, "you could reclaim a salt-contaminated field by growing enough of these crops to remove the salts from the soil."

His father chimed in: "We've worried about being able to keep these salt-contaminated fields going even for decades. We can now think about *centuries*."

One of the first biotech crops to reach the market, in the mid-1990s, was a cotton plant that makes its own pesticide. Scientists incorporated into the plant a toxin-producing gene from a soil bacterium known as *Bacillus thuringiensis*. With Bt cotton, as it is called, farmers can spray much less, and the poison contained in the plant is delivered only to bugs that actually eat the crop. As any environmentalist can tell you, insecticide is not very nice stuff—especially if you breathe it, which many Third World farmers do as they walk through their fields with backpack sprayers.

Transgenic cotton reduced pesticide use by more than two million pounds in the United States from 1996 to 2000, and it has reduced pesticide sprayings in parts of China by more than half. Earlier this year the Environmental Protection Agency approved a genetically modified corn that resists a beetle larva known as rootworm. Because rootworm is American corn's most voracious enemy, this new variety has the potential to reduce annual pesticide use in America by more than 14 million pounds. It could reduce or eliminate the spraying of pesticide on 23 million acres of U.S. land.

All of that is the beginning, not the end. Bioengineers are also working, for instance, on crops that tolerate aluminum, another major contaminant of soil, especially in the tropics. Return an acre of farmland to productivity, or double yields on an already productive acre, and, other things being equal, you reduce by an acre the amount of virgin forest or savanna that will be stripped and cultivated. That may be the most important benefit of all.

Of the many people I have interviewed in my twenty years as a journalist, Norman Borlaug must be the one who has saved the most lives. Today he is an unprepossessing eighty-nine-year-old man of middling height, with crystal-bright blue eyes and thinning white hair. He still loves to talk about plant breeding, the discipline that won him the 1970 Nobel Peace Prize: Borlaug led efforts to breed the staples of the Green Revolution. (See "Forgotten Benefactor of Humanity," by Gregg Easterbrook, an article on Borlaug in the January 1997 *Atlantic*.) Yet the renowned plant breeder is quick to mention that he began his career, in the 1930s, in forestry, and that forest conservation has never been far from his thoughts. In the 1960s, while he was working to improve crop yields in India and Pakistan, he made a mental connection. He would create tables detailing acres under cultivation and average yields—and then, in another column, he would estimate how much land had been saved by higher farm productivity. Later, in the 1980s and 1990s, he and others began paying increased attention to what some agricultural economists now call the Borlaug hypothesis: that the Green Revolution has saved not only many human lives but, by improving the productivity of existing farmland, also millions of acres of tropical forest and other habitat—and so has saved countless animal lives.

From the 1960s through the 1980s, for example, Green Revolution advances saved more than 100 million acres of wild lands in India. More recently, higher yields in rice, coffee, vegetables, and other crops have reduced or in some cases stopped forest-clearing in Honduras, the Philippines, and elsewhere. Dennis Avery estimates that if farming techniques and yields had not improved since 1950, the world would have lost an additional 20 million or so square miles of wildlife habitat, most of it forest. About 16 million square miles of forest exists today. "What I'm saying," Avery said, in response to my puzzled expression, "is that we have saved every square mile of forest on the planet."

Habitat destruction remains a serious environmental problem; in some respects it is the most serious. The savannahs and tropical forests of Central and South America, Asia, and Africa by and large make poor farmland, but they are the earth's storehouses of biodiversity, and the forests are the earth's lungs. Since 1972 about 200,000 square miles of Amazon rain forest have been cleared for crops and pasture; from 1966 to 1994 all but three of the Central American countries cleared more forest than they left standing. Mexico is losing more than 4,000 square miles of forest a year to peasant farms; sub-Saharan Africa is losing more than 19,000.

That is why the great challenge of the next four or five decades is not to feed an additional three billion people (and their pets) but to do so without converting much of the world's prime habitat into second or third-rate farmland. Now, most agronomists agree that some substantial yield improvements are still to be had from advances in conventional breeding, fertilizers, herbicides, and other Green Revolution standbys. But it seems pretty clear that biotechnology holds more promise—probably much more. Recall that world food output will need to at least double and possibly triple over the next several decades. Even if production could be increased that much using conventional technology, which is doubtful, the required amounts of pesticide and fertilizer and other polluting chemicals would be immense. If properly developed, disseminated, and used, genetically modified crops might well be the best hope the planet has got.

If properly developed, disseminated, and used. That tripartite qualification turns out to be important, and it brings the environmental community squarely, and at the moment rather jarringly, into the picture.

Not long ago I went to see David Sandalow in his office at the World Wildlife Fund, in Washington, D.C. Sandalow, the organization's executive vice-president in charge of conservation programs, is a tall, affable, polished, and slightly reticent man in his forties who holds degrees from Yale and the University of Michigan Law School.

Some weeks earlier, over lunch, I had mentioned Dennis Avery's claim that genetic modification had great environmental potential. I was surprised when Sandalow told me he agreed. Later, in our interview in his office, I asked him to elaborate. "With biotechnology," he said, "there are no simple answers. Biotechnology has huge potential benefits and huge risks, and we need to address both as we move forward. The huge potential benefits include increased productivity of arable land, which could relieve pressure on forests. They include decreased pesticide usage. But the huge risks include severe ecological disruptions—from gene flow and from enhanced invasiveness, which is a very antiseptic word for some very scary stuff."

I asked if he thought that, absent biotechnology, the world could feed everybody over the next forty or fifty years without ploughing down the rain forests. Instead of answering directly he said, "Biotechnology could be part of our arsenal if we can overcome some of the barriers. It will never be a panacea or a magic bullet. But nor should we remove it from our tool kit."

Sandalow is unusual. Very few credentialed greens talk the way he does about biotechnology, at least publicly. They would readily agree with him about the huge risks, but they wouldn't be caught dead speaking of huge potential benefits—a point I will come back to. From an ecological point of view, a very great deal depends on other environmentalists' coming to think more the way Sandalow does.

Biotech companies are in business to make money. That is fitting and proper. But developing and testing new transgenic crops is expensive and commercially risky, to say nothing of politically controversial. When they decide how to invest their research-and-development money, biotech companies will naturally seek products for which farmers and consumers will pay top dollar. Roundup Ready products, for instance, are well suited to U.S. farming, with its high levels of capital spending on such things as herbicides and automated sprayers. Poor farmers in the developing world, or course, have much less buying power. Creating, say, salt-tolerant cassava suitable for growing on hardscrabble African farms might save habitat

as well as lives—but commercial enterprises are not likely to fall over one another in a rush to do it.

If earth-friendly transgenics are developed, the next problem is disseminating them. As a number of the farmers and experts I talked to were quick to mention, switching to an unfamiliar new technology—something like no-till—is not easy. It requires capital investment in new seed and equipment, mastery of new skills and methods, a fragile transition period as farmer and ecology readjust, and an often considerable amount of trial and error to find out what works best on any given field. Such problems are only magnified in the Third World, where the learning curve is steeper and capital cushions are thin to nonexistent. Just handing a peasant farmer a bag of newfangled seed is not enough. In many cases peasant farmers will need one-on-one attention. Many will need help to pay for the seed, too.

Finally there is the matter of using biotech in a way that actually benefits the environment. Often the technological blade can cut either way, especially in the short run. A salt-tolerant or drought-resistant rice that allowed farmers to keep land in production might also induce them to plough up virgin land that previously was too salty or too dry to farm. If the effect of improved seed is to make farming more profitable, farmers may respond, at least temporarily, by bringing more land into production. If a farm becomes more productive, it may require fewer workers; and if local labor markets cannot provide jobs for them, displaced workers may move to a nearby patch of rain forest and burn it down to make way for subsistence farming. Such transition problems are solvable, but they need money and attention.

In short, realizing the great—probably unique—environmental potential of biotech will require stewardship. "It's a tool," Sara Scherr, an agricultural economist with the conservation group Forest Trends, told me, "but it's absolutely not going to happen automatically."

So now ask a question: Who is the natural constituency for earth-friendly biotechnology?

Who cares enough to lobby governments to underwrite research—frequently unprofitable research—on transgenic crops that might restore soils or cut down on pesticides in poor countries? Who cares enough to teach Asian or African farmers, one by one, how to farm without ploughing? Who cares enough to help poor farmers afford high-tech, earth-friendly seed? Who cares enough to agitate for programs and reforms that might steer displaced peasants and profit-seeking farmers away from sensitive lands? Not politicians, for the most part. Not farmers. Not corporations. Not consumers.

At the World Resources Institute, an environmental think tank in Washington, the molecular biologist Don Doering envisions transgenic crops designed specifically to solve environmental problems: crops that might fertilize the soil, crops that could clean water, crops tailored to remedy the ecological problems of specific places. "Suddenly you might find yourself with a virtually chemical-free agriculture, where your cropland itself is filtering the water, it's protecting the watershed, it's providing habitat," Doering told me. "There is still so little investment in what I call design-for-environment." The natural constituency for such investment is, of course, environmentalists.

But environmentalists are not acting such a constituency today. They are doing the apposite. For example, Greenpeace declares on its Web site: "The introduction of genetically engineered (GE) organisms into the complex ecosystems of our environment is a dangerous global experiment with nature and evolution . . . GE organisms must not be released into the environment. They pose unacceptable risks to ecosystems, and have the potential to threaten biodiversity, wildlife and sustainable forms of agriculture."

Other groups argue for what they call the Precautionary Principle, under which no transgenic crop could be used until proven benign in virtually all respects. The Sierra Club says on its Web site,

> In accordance with this Precautionary Principle, we call for a moratorium on the planting of all genetically engineered crops and the release of all GEOs [genetically engineered organisms] into the environment, *including those now approved*. Releases should be delayed until extensive, rigorous research is done which determines the long-term environmental and health impacts of each GEO and there is public debate to ascertain the need for the use of each GEO intended for release into the environment. [italics added]

Under this policy the cleaner water and healthier soil that continuous no-till farming has already brought to the Chesapeake Bay watershed would be undone, and countless tons of polluted runoff and eroded topsoil would accumulate in Virginia rivers and streams while debaters debated and researchers researched. Recall David Sandalow: "Biotechnology has huge potential benefits and huge risks, and we need to address both as we move forward." A lot of environmentalists would say instead, "*before* we move forward." That is an important difference, particularly because the big population squeeze will happen not in the distant future but over the next several decades.

For reasons having more to do with policies than with logic, the modern environmental movement was to a large extent founded on suspicion of markets and artificial substances. Markets exploit the earth; chemicals poison it. Biotech touches both hot buttons. It is being pushed forward by greedy corporations, and it seems to be the very epitome of the unnatural.

Still, I hereby hazard a prediction. In ten years or less, most American environmentalists (European ones are more dogmatic) will regard genetic modification as one of their most powerful tools. In only the past ten years or so, after all, environmentalists have reversed field and embraced market mechanisms—tradable emissions permits and the like—as useful in the fight against pollution. The environmental logic of biotechnology is, if anything, even more compelling. The potential upside of genetic modification is simply too large to ignore—and therefore environmentalists will not ignore it. Biotechnology will transform agriculture, and in doing so will transform American environmentalism.

📖 STUDY QUESTIONS

1. Discuss the promise of genetically modified food. What environmental problems can it solve? How can it help alleviate world hunger?
2. Discuss the risks involved in producing genetically modified food. Why are so many environmentalists against it?
3. How do you think we should proceed with regard to genetically modified food?

53   The Unholy Alliance

MAE-WAN HO

Mae-Wan Ho, trained as a geneticist, is a leading social and environmental activist. She is the author of numerous books and articles, including most recently *Genetic Engineering, Dream or Nightmare?* She proposes an immediate moratorium on genetically modified foods until their safety, in all phases, can be properly tested.

> Genetic engineering biotechnology is inherently hazardous. It could lead to disasters far worse than those caused by accidents to nuclear installations. In the words of the author, "genes can replicate indefinitely, spread and recombine." For this reason the release of a genetically engineered micro-organism that is lethal to humans could well spell the end of humanity. Unfortunately the proponents of this terrifying technology share a genetic determinist mindset that leads them to reject the inherently dangerous nature of their work. What is particularly worrying at first sight is the irresistible power of the large corporations which are pushing this technology.

Suddenly, the brave new world dawns.

Suddenly, as 1997 begins and the millennium is drawing to a close, men and women in the street are waking up to the realization that genetic engineering biotechnology is taking over every aspect of their daily lives. They are caught unprepared for the avalanche of products arriving, or soon to arrive, in their supermarkets: rapeseed oil, soybean, maize, sugar beet, squash, cucumber.... It started as a mere trickle less than three years ago—the BST-milk from cows fed genetically engineered bovine growth hormone to boost milk yield, and the tomato genetically engineered to prolong shelf-life. They had provoked so much debate and opposition, as did indeed, the genetic screening tests for an increasing number of diseases. Surely, we wouldn't, and shouldn't, be rushed headlong into the brave new world.

Back then, in order to quell our anxiety, a series of highly publicized "consensus conferences" and "public consultations" were carried out. Committees were set up by many European governments to consider the risks and the ethics, and the debates continued. The public were, however, only dimly aware of critics who deplored "tampering with nature" and "scrambling the genetic code of species" by introducing human genes into animals, and animal genes into vegetables. Warnings of unexpected effects on agriculture and biodiversity, of the dangers of irreversible "genetic pollution," warnings of genetic discrimination and the return of eugenics, as genetic screening and prenatal diagnosis became widely available, were marginalized. So

From *The Ecologist,* Vol. 27, No. 4, July/August 1997. Used by permission.

too were condemnations of the immorality of the "patents on life"—transgenic animals, plants and seeds, taken freely by geneticists of developed countries from the Third World, as well as human genes and human cell lines from indigenous peoples.

By and large, the public were lulled into a false sense of security, in the belief that the best scientists and the new breed of "bioethicists" in the country were busy considering the risks associated with the new biotechnology and the ethical issues raised. Simultaneously, glossy information pamphlets and reports, which aimed at promoting "public understanding" of genetic "modification" were widely distributed by the biotech industries and their friends, and endorsed by government scientists. "Genetic modification," we are told, is simply the latest in a "seamless" continuum of biotechnologies practised by human beings since the dawn of civilization, from bread and wine-making, to selective breeding. The significant advantage of genetic modification is that it is much more "precise," as genes can be individually isolated and transferred as desired.

Thus, the possible benefits promised to humankind are limitless. There is something to satisfy everyone. For those morally concerned about inequality and human suffering, it promises to feed the hungry with genetically modified crops able to resist pests and diseases and to increase yields. For those who despair of the present global environmental deterioration, it promises to modify strains of bacteria and higher plants that can degrade toxic wastes or mop up heavy metals (contaminants). For those hankering after sustainable agriculture, it promises to develop Greener, more environmentally friendly transgenic crops that will reduce the use of pesticides, herbicides and fertilizers.

That is not all. It is in the realm of human genetics that the real revolution will be wrought. Plans to uncover the entire genetic blueprint of the human being would, we are told, eventually enable geneticists to diagnose, in advance, all the diseases that an individual will suffer in his or her lifetime, even before the individual is born, or even as the egg is fertilized *in vitro*. A whole gamut of specific drugs tailored to individual genetic needs can be designed to cure all

diseases. The possibility of immortality is dangling from the horizons as the "longevity gene" is isolated.

There are problems, of course, as there would be in any technology. The ethical issues have to be decided by the public. (By implication, the science is separate and not open to question.) The risks will be minimized. (Again, by implication, the risks have nothing to do with the science.) After all, nothing in life is without risk. Crossing roads is a risk. The new biotechnology (i.e. genetic engineering biotechnology) is under very strict government regulation, and the government's scientists and other experts will see to it that neither the consumer nor the environment will be unduly harmed.

Then came the relaxation of regulation on genetically modified products, on grounds that over-regulation is compromising the "competitiveness" of the industry, and that hundreds of field trials have demonstrated the new biotechnology to be safe. And, in any case, there is no essential difference between transgenic plants produced by the new biotechnology and those produced by conventional breeding methods. (One prominent spokesperson for the industry even went as far as to refer to the varieties produced by conventional breeding methods, *retrospectively,* as "transgenics."[1] This was followed, a year later, by the avalanche of products approved, or seeking, approval marketing, for which neither segregation from non-genetically engineered produce nor labelling is required. One is left to wonder why, if the products are as safe and wonderful as claimed, they could not be segregated, as organic produce has been for years, so that consumers are given the choice of buying what they want.

A few days later, as though acting on cue, the Association of British Insurers announced that, in future, people applying for life policies will have to divulge the results of any genetic tests they have taken. This is seen, by many, as a definite move towards open genetic discrimination. A few days later, a scientist of the Roslin Institute near Edinburgh announced that they had successfully "cloned" a sheep from a cell taken from the mammary gland of an adult animal. "Dolly," the cloned lamb, is now seven months

I should, right away, dispel the myth that genetic engineering is just like conventional breeding techniques. It is not. Genetic engineering bypasses conventional breeding by using the artificially constructed vectors to multiply copies of genes, and in many cases, to carry and smuggle genes into cells. Once inside cells, these vectors slot themselves into the host genome. In this way, *transgenic* organisms are made carrying the desired *transgenes*. The insertion of foreign genes into the host genome has long been known to have many harmful and fatal effects including cancer; and this is born out by the low success rate of creating desired transgenic organisms. Typically, a large number of eggs or embryos have to be injected or infected with the vector to obtain a few organisms that successfully express the transgene.

The most common vectors used in genetic engineering biotechnology are a chimaeric recombination of natural genetic parasites from different sources, including viruses causing cancers and other diseases in animals and plants, with their pathogenic functions 'crippled,' and tagged with one or more antibiotic resistance 'marker' genes, so that cells transformed with the vector can be selected. For example, the vector most widely used in plant genetic engineering is derived from a tumour-inducing plasmid carried by the soil bacterium *Agrobacterium tumefaciens*. In animals, vectors are constructed from *retroviruses* causing cancers and other diseases. A vector currently used in fish has a framework from the Moloney marine leukaemic virus, which causes leukaemia in mice, but can infect all mammalian cells. It has bits from the Rous Sarcoma virus, causing sarcomas in chickens, and from the vesicular stomatitis virus, causing oral lesions in cattle, horses, pigs and humans. Such mosaic vectors are particularly hazardous. Unlike natural parasitic genetic elements which have various degrees of host specificity, vectors used in genetic engineering, partly by design, and partly on account of their mosaic character, have the ability to overcome species barriers, and to infect a wide range of species. Another obstacle to genetic engineering is that all organisms and cells have natural defence mechanisms that enable them to destroy or inactivate foreign genes, and transgene instability is a big problem for the industry. Vectors are now increasingly constructed to overcome those mechanisms that maintain the integrity of species. The result is that the artificially constructed vectors are especially good at carrying out horizontal gene transfer.

Let me summarize why rDNA technology differs radically from conventional breeding techniques.

1. Genetic engineering recombines genetic material in the laboratory between species that do not interbreed in nature.
2. While conventional breeding methods shuffle different forms (alletes) of the same genes, genetic engineering enables completely new (exotic) genes to be introduced with unpredictable effects on the physiology and biochemistry of the resultant transgenic organism.
3. Gene multiplications and a high proportion of gene transfers are mediated by vectors which have the following undesirable characteristics:
   a. many are derived from disease-causing viruses, plasmids and mobile genetic elements—parasitic DNA that have the ability to invade cells and insert themselves into the cell's genome causing genetic damages.
   b. they are designed to break down species barriers so that they can shuttle genes between a wide range of species. Their wide host range means that they can infect many animals and plants, and in the process pick up genes from viruses of all these species to create new pathogens.
   c. they routinely carry genes for antibiotic resistance, which is already a big health problem.
   d. they are increasingly constructed to overcome the recipient species' defence mechanisms that break down or inactivate foreign DNA.

old. Of course it took nearly 300 trials to get one success, but no mention is made of the vast majority of the embryos that failed. Is that ethical? If it can be done on sheep, does it mean it can be done for human beings? Are we nearer to cloning human beings? The popular media went wild with heroic enthusiasm at one extreme to the horror of Frankenstein at the other. Why is this work only coming to public attention now, when the research has actually been going on for at least 10 years?[2]

The public are totally unprepared. They are being plunged headlong, against their will, into the brave new genetically engineered world, in which giant, faceless multinational corporations will control every aspect of their lives, from the food they can eat, to the baby they can conceive and give birth to.

Isn't it a bit late in the day to tell us that?, you ask. Yes and no. Yes, because I, who should, perhaps, have known better, was caught unprepared like the rest. And no, because there have been so many people warning us of that eventuality, who have campaigned tirelessly on our behalf, some of them going back to the earliest days of genetic engineering in the 1970s—although we have paid them little heed. No, it is not too late, if only because that is precisely what we tend to believe, and are encouraged to believe. A certain climate is created—that of being rapidly overtaken by events—reinforcing the feeling that the tidal wave of progress brought on by the new biotechnology is impossible to stem, so that we may be paralysed into accepting the inevitable. No, because we shall not give up, for the consequence of giving up is the brave new world, and soon after that, there may be no world at all. The gene genie is fast getting out of control. The practitioners of genetic engineering biotechnology, the regulators and the critics alike, have *all* underestimated the risks involved, which are *inherent* to genetic engineering biotechnology, particularly as misguided by an outmoded and erroneous world-view that comes from bad science. The dreams may already be turning into nightmares.

That is why people like myself are calling for an immediate moratorium on further releases and marketing of genetically engineered products, and for an independent public enquiry to be set up to look into the risks and hazards involved, taking into account the most comprehensive, scientific knowledge in addition to the social, moral implications. This would be most timely, as public opposition to genetic engineering biotechnology has been gaining momentum throughout Europe and the USA.

In Austria, a record 1.2 million citizens, representing 20 per cent of the electorate, have signed a people's petition to ban genetically engineered foods, as well as deliberate releases of genetically modified organisms and patenting of life. Genetically modified foods were also rejected earlier by a lay people consultation in Norway, and by 95 percent of consumers in Germany, as revealed by a recent survey. The European Parliament has voted by an overwhelming 407 to 2 majority to censure the Commission's authorization, in December 1996, for imports of Ciba-Geigy's transgenic maize into Europe, and is calling for imports to be suspended while the authorization is re-examined. The European Commission has decided that in the future genetically engineered seeds will be labelled, and is also considering proposals for retroactive labelling. Commissioner Emma Bonino is to set up a new scientific committee to deal with genetically engineered foods, members of which are to be completely independent of the food industry. Meanwhile, Franz Fischler, the European Commissioner on Agriculture, supports a complete segregation and labelling of production lines of genetically modified and non-genetically modified foods.

In June this year, President Clinton imposed a five-year ban on human cloning in the USA, while the UK House of Commons Science and Technology Committee (STC) wants British law to be amended to ensure that human cloning is illegal. The STC, President Chirac of France and German Research Minister Juergen Ruettgers are also calling for an international ban on human cloning.

Like other excellent critics before me,[3] I do not think there is a grand conspiracy afoot, though there are many forces converging to a single terrible end. Susan George comments, "They don't have to conspire if they have the same world-view, aspire to similar goals and take concerted steps to attain them."[4]

I am one of those scientists who have long been highly critical of the reductionist mainstream scientific world-view, and have begun to work towards a radically different approach for understanding nature.[5] But I was unable, for a long time, to see how much science really matters in the affairs of the real world, not just in terms of practical inventions like genetic engineering, but in how that scientific world-view takes hold of people's unconscious, so that they take action, involuntarily, unquestioningly, to shape the world to the detriment of human beings. I was so little aware of how that science is used, without conscious intent, to intimidate and control, to obfuscate, to exploit and oppress; how that dominant world-view generates a selective blindness to make scientists themselves ignore or misread scientific evidence.

The point, however, is not that *science* is bad—but that there can be *bad science* that ill-serves humanity. Science can often be wrong. The history of science can just as well be written in terms of the mistakes made than as the series of triumphs it is usually made out to be. Science is nothing more, and nothing less, than a system of concepts for understanding nature and for obtaining reliable knowledge that enables us to live sustainably with nature. In that sense, one can ill-afford to give up science, for it is through our proper understanding and knowledge of nature that we can live a satisfying life, that we can ultimately distinguish the good science, which serves humanity, from the bad science that does not. In this view, science is imbued with moral values from the start, and cannot be disentangled from them. Therefore it is bad science that purports to be "neutral" and divorced from moral values, as much as it is bad science that ignores scientific evidence.

It is clear that I part company with perhaps a majority of my scientist colleagues in the mainstream, who believe that science can never be wrong, although it can be misused. Or else they carefully distinguish science, as neutral and value-free, from its application, technology, which can do harm or good.[6] This distinction between science and technology is spurious, especially in the case of an experimental science like genetics, and almost all of biology, where the techniques determine what sorts of question are asked and hence the range of answers that are important, significant and relevant to the science. Where would molecular genetics be without the tools that enable practitioners to recombine and manipulate our destiny? It is an irresistibly

heroic view, except that it is totally wrong and misguided.

It is also meaningless, therefore, to set up Ethical Committees which do not question the basic scientific assumptions behind the practice of genetic engineering biotechnology. Their brief is severely limited, often verging on the trivial and banal—such as whether a pork gene transferred to food plants might be counter to certain religious beliefs—in comparison with the much more fundamental questions of eugenics, genetic discrimination and, indeed, whether gene transfers should be carried out at all. They can do nothing more than make the unacceptable acceptable to the public.

The debate on genetic engineering biotechnology is dogged by the artificial separation imposed between "pure" science and the issues it gives rise to. "Ethics" is deemed to be socially determined, and therefore negotiable, while the science is seen to be beyond reproach, as it is the "laws" of nature. The same goes for the distinction between "technology"—the application of science—from the science. Risk assessments are to do with the technology, leaving the science equally untouched. The technology can be bad for your health, but not the science. In this article, I shall show why science cannot be separated from moral values nor from the technology that shapes our society. In other words, bad science is unquestionably bad for one's health and well-being, and should be avoided at all costs. Science is, above all, fallible and negotiable, because we have the choice, to do or not to do. It should be negotiated for the public good. That is the only ethical position one can take with regard to science. Otherwise, we are in danger of turning science into the most fundamentalist of religions, that, working hand in hand with corporate interests, will surely usher in the brave new world.

BAD SCIENCE AND BIG BUSINESS

What makes genetic engineering biotechnology dangerous, in the first instance, is that it is an unprecedented, close alliance between two great powers that can make or break the world: science and commerce. Practically all established molecular geneticists have some direct or indirect connection with industry, which will set limits on what the scientists can and will do research on, not to mention the possibility of compromising their integrity as independent scientists.[7]

The worst aspect of the alliance is that it is between the most reductionist science and multinational monopolistic industry at its most aggressive and exploitative. If the truth be told, it is bad science working together with big business for quick profit, aided and abetted by our governments for the banal reason that governments wish to be re-elected to remain in 'power.'[8]

Speaking as a scientist who loves and believes in science, I have to say it is bad science that has let the world down and caused the major problems we now face, not the least among which is by promoting and legitimizing a particular world-view. It is a reductionist, manipulative and exploitative world-view. Reductionist because it sees the world as bits and pieces, and denies there are organic wholes such as organisms, ecosystems, societies and community of nations. Manipulative and exploitative because it regards nature and fellow human beings as objects to be manipulated and exploited for gain; life being a Darwinian struggle for survival of the fittest.

It is by no means coincidental that the economic theory currently dominating the world is rooted in the same *laissez-faire* capitalist ideology that gave rise to Darwinism. It acknowledges no values other than self-interest, competitiveness and the accumulation of wealth, at which the developed nations have been very successful. Already, according to the 1992 United Nations Development Programme Report, the richest fifth of the world's population has amassed 82.7 per cent of the wealth, while the poorest fifth gets a piddling 1.4 per cent. Or, put in another way, there are now 477 billionaires in the world whose combined assets are roughly equal to the combined annual incomes of the poorer half of humanity—2.8 billion people.[9] Do we need to be more "competitive" still to take from the poorest their remaining pittance? That is, in fact, what we are doing.

The governmental representatives of the superpowers are pushing for a "globalized economy" under trade agreements which erase all economic borders. "Together, the processes of deregulation and globalization are undermining the power of both unions and governments and placing the power of global corporations and finance beyond the reach of public accountability."[10] The largest corporations continue to consolidate that power through mergers, acquisitions and strategic alliances. Multinational corporations now comprise 51 of the world's 100 largest economies: only 49 of the latter are nations. By 1993, agricultural biotechnology was being controlled by just 11 giant corporations, and these are now undergoing further mergers. The OECD (Organization for Economic Co-operation and Development) member countries are at this moment working in secret in Paris on the Multilateral Agreements on Investment (MAI), which is written by and for corporations to prohibit any government from establishing performance or accountability standards for foreign investors. European Commissioner, Sir Leon Brittan, is negotiating in the World Trade Organization, on behalf of the European Community, to ensure that no barriers of any kind should remain in the South to dampen exploitation bythe North, and at the same time, to protect the deeply unethical "patents of life" through Trade Related Intellectual Property Rights (TRIPS) agreements.[11] So, in addition to gaining complete control of the food supply of the South through exclusive rights to genetically engineered seeds, the big food giants of the North can asset-strip the South's genetic and intellectual resources with impunity, up to and including genes and cell lines of indigenous peoples.

There is no question that the mindset that leads to and validates genetic engineering is *genetic determinism*—the idea that organisms are determined by their genetic makeup, or the totality of their genes. Genetic determinism derives from the marriage of Darwinism and Mendelian genetics. For those imbued with the mindset of genetic determinism, the major problems of the world can be solved simply by identifying and manipulating genes, for genes determine the characters of organisms; so by identifying a gene we can predict a desirable or undesirable trait, by changing a gene we change the trait, by transferring a gene we transfer the corresponding trait.

The Human Genome Project was inspired by the same genetic determinism that locates the "blueprint" for constructing the human being in the human genome. It may have been a brilliant political move to capture research funds and, at the same time, to revive a flagging pharmaceutical industry, but its scientific content was suspect from the first.

Genetic engineering technology promises to work for the benefit of mankind; the reality is something else.

- It displaces and marginalizes all alternative approaches that address the social and environmental causes of malnutrition and ill-health, such as poverty and unemployment, and the need for a sustainable agriculture that could regenerate the environment, guarantee long-term food security and, at the same time, conserve indigenous biodiversity.
- Its purpose is to accommodate problems that reductionist science and industry have created in the first place—widespread environmental deterioration from the intensive, high-input agriculture of the Green Revolution, and accumulation of toxic wastes from chemical industries. What's on offer now is more of the same, except with new problems attached.
- It leads to discriminatory and other unethical practices that are against the moral values of societies and community of nations.
- Worst of all, it is pushing a technology that is untried, and, according to existing knowledge, is inherently hazardous to health and biodiversity.

Let me enlarge on that last point here, as I believe it has been underestimated, if not entirely overlooked by the practitioners, regulators and many critics of genetic engineering biotechnology alike, on account of a certain blindness to concrete scientific evidence, largely as a result of their conscious or unconscious commitment to an old, discredited paradigm. The most immediate hazards are likely to be in public health—which has already reached a global crisis, attesting to the failure of decades of reductionist medical practices—although the hazards to biodiversity will not be far behind.

GENETIC ENGINEERING BIOTECHNOLOGY IS INHERENTLY HAZARDOUS

According to the 1996 World Health Organization Report, at least 30 new diseases, including AIDS, Ebola and Hepatitis C, have emerged over the past 20 years, while old infectious diseases such as tuberculosis, cholera, malaria and diphtheria are coming back worldwide. Almost every month now in the UK we hear reports on fresh outbreaks: *Streptococcus,* meningitis, *E. coli.* Practically all the pathogens are resistant to antibiotics, many to multiple antibiotics. Two strains of *E. coli* isolated in a transplant ward outside Cambridge in 1993 were found to be resistant to 21 out of 22 common antibiotics.[12] A strain of *Staphylococcus* isolated in Australia in 1990 was found to be resistant to 31 different drugs.[13] Infections with these and other strains will very soon become totally invulnerable to treatment. In fact, scientists in Japan have already isolated a strain of *Staphylococcus aureus* that is resistant even to the last resort antibiotic, vancomycin.[14]

Geneticists have now linked the emergence of pathogenic bacteria and of antibiotic resistance to *horizontal gene transfer*—the transfer of genes to unrelated species, by infection through viruses, though pieces of genetic material, DNA, taken up into cells from the environment, or by unusual mating taking place between unrelated species. For example, horizontal gene transfer and subsequent genetic recombination have generated the bacterial strains responsible for the cholera outbreak in India in 1992,[15] and the Streptococcus epidemic in Tayside in 1993.[16] The *E. coli* 157 strain involved in the recent outbreaks in Scotland is believed to have originated from horizontal gene transfer from the pathogen, *Shigella.*[17] Many unrelated bacterial pathogens, causing diseases from bubonic plague to tree blight, are found to share an entire set of genes for invading cells, which have almost certainly spread by horizontal gene transfer.[18] Similarly, genes for antibiotic resistance have spread horizontally and recombined with one another to generate multiple antibiotic resistance throughout the bacterial populations.[19] Antibiotic resistance genes spread readily by contact between human beings, and from bacteria inhabiting the gut of farm animals to those in human beings.[20] Multiple antibiotic resistant strains of pathogens have been endemic in many hospitals for years.[21]

What is the connection between horizontal gene transfer and genetic engineering? Genetic engineering is a technology designed specifically to transfer genes horizontally between species that do not interbreed. It is designed to break down species barriers and, increasingly, to overcome the species' defence mechanisms which normally degrade or inactivate foreign genes.[22] For the purpose of manipulating, replicating and transferring genes, genetic engineers make use of recombined versions of precisely those genetic parasites causing diseases including cancers, and others that carry and spread virulence genes and antibiotic resistance genes. Thus the technology will contribute to an increase in the frequency of horizontal gene transfer of those genes that are responsible for virulence and antibiotic resistance, and allow them to recombine to generate new pathogens.

What is even more disturbing is that geneticists have now found evidence that the presence of antibiotics typically increases the frequency of horizontal gene transfer 100-fold or more, possibly because the antibiotic acts like a sex hormone for the bacteria, enhancing mating and exchange of genes between unrelated species.[23] Thus, antibiotic resistance and multiple antibiotic resistance cannot be overcome simply by making new antibiotics, *for antibiotics create the very conditions to facilitate the spread of resistance*. The continuing profligate use of antibiotics in intensive farming and in medicine, in combination with the commercial-scale practice of genetic engineering, may already be major contributing factors for the accelerated spread of multiple antibiotic resistance among new and old pathogens that the WHO 1996 Report has identified within the past 10 years. For example, there has been a dramatic rise both in terms of incidence and severity of cases of infections by *Salmo-nella*,[24] with some countries in Europe witnessing a staggering 20-fold increase in incidence since 1980.

That is not all. One by one, those assumptions on which geneticists and regulatory committees have based their assessment of genetically engineered products to be "safe" have fallen by the wayside, especially in the light of evidence emerging within the past three to four years. However, there is still little indication that the new findings are being taken on board. On the contrary, regulatory bodies have succumbed to pressure from the industry to relax already inadequate regulations. Let me list a few more of the relevant findings in genetics.

We have been told that horizontal gene transfer is confined to bacteria. That is not so. It is now known to involve practically all species of animal, plant and fungus. It is possible for any gene in any species to spread to any other species, especially if the gene is carried on genetically engineered gene-transfer vectors. Transgenes and antibiotic resistance marker genes from transgenic plants have been shown to end up in soil fungi and bacteria.[25] The microbial populations in the environment serve as the gene-transfer highway and reservoir, supporting the replication of the genes and allowing them to spread and recombine with other genes to generate new pathogens.[26]

We have been assured that "crippled" laboratory strains of bacteria and viruses do not survive when released into the environment. That is not true. There is now abundant evidence that they can either survive quite well and multiply, or they can go dormant and reappear after having acquired genes from other bacteria to enable them to multiply.[27] Bacteria co-operate much more than they compete. They share their most valuable assets for survival.

We have been told that DNA is easily broken down in the environment. Not so. DNA can remain in the environment where they can be picked up by bacteria and incorporated into their genome.[28] DNA is, in fact, one of the toughest molecules. Biochemists jumped with joy when they didn't have to work with proteins anymore, which lose their activity very readily. By contrast, DNA survives rigorous boiling, so when they approve processed food on grounds that there can be no DNA left, ask exactly how the processing is done, and whether the appropriate tests for the presence of DNA have been carried out.

The survival of "crippled" laboratory strains of bacteria and viruses and the persistence of DNA in the environment are of particular relevance to the so-called "contained" users producing transgenic pharmaceuticals, enzymes and food additives. "Tolerated" releases and transgenic wastes from such users may already have released large amounts of transgenic bacteria and viruses as well as DNA into the environment since the early 1980s when commercial genetic engineering biotechnology began.

We are told that DNA is easily digested by enzymes in our gut. Not true. The DNA of a virus has been found to survive passage through the gut of mice. Furthermore, the DNA readily finds its way into the bloodstream, and into all kinds of cell[s] in the body.[29] Once inside the cell, the DNA can insert itself into the cell's genome, and create all manner of genetic disturbances, including cancer.[30]

There are yet further findings pointing to the potential hazards of generating new disease-causing viruses by recombination between artificial viral vectors and vaccines and other viruses in the environment. The viruses generated in this way will have increased host ranges, infecting and causing diseases in more than one species, and hence very difficult to eradicate. *We are already seeing such viruses emerging.*

- Monkeypox, a previously rare and potentially fatal virus caught from rodents, is spreading through central Zaire.[31] Between 1981–1986 only 37 cases were known, but there have been at least 163 cases in one eastern province of Zaire alone since July 1995. For the first time, humans are transmitting the disease directly from one to the other.
- An outbreak of hantavirus infection hit southern Argentina in December 1996, the first time the virus was transmitted from person to person.[32] Previously, the virus was spread by breathing in the aerosols from rodent excrement or urine.
- New highly virulent strains of infectious bursal disease virus (IBDV) spread rapidly throughout most of the poultry industry in the Northern Hemisphere, and are now infecting Antarctic penguins, and are suspected of causing mass mortality.[33]
- New strains of distemper and rabies viruses are spilling out from towns and villages to plague some of the world's rarest wild animals in Africa:[34] lions, panthers, wild dogs, giant otter.

None of the plethora of new findings has been taken on board by the regulatory bodies. On the contrary, safety regulations have been relaxed. The public is being used, against its will, as guinea pigs for genetically engineered products, while new viruses and bacterial pathogens may be created by the technology every passing day.

The present situation is reminiscent of the development of nuclear energy which gave us the atom bomb, and the nuclear power stations that we now know to be hazardous to health and also to be environmentally unsustainable on account of the long-lasting radioactive wastes they produce. Joseph Rotblat, the British physicist who won the 1995 Nobel Prize after years of battling against nuclear weapons, has this to say. "My worry is that other advances in science may result in other means of mass destruction, maybe more readily available even than nuclear weapons. Genetic engineering is quite a possible area, because of these dreadful developments that are taking place there."[35]

The large-scale release of transgenic organisms is much worse than nuclear weapons or radioactive nuclear wastes, as genes can replicate indefinitely, spread and recombine. There may yet be time enough to stop the industry's dreams turning into nightmares if we act now, before the critical genetic "melt-down" is reached.

NOTES

1. The first time I heard the word "transgenic" being used on cultivars resulting from conventional breeding methods was from Henry Miller, a

prominent advocate for genetic engineering bio-technology, in a public debate with myself, organized by the Oxford Centre for Environment, Ethics and Society, in Oxford University on February 20, 1997.

2. "Scientists scorn sci-fi fears over sheep clone," *The Guardian,* February 24, 1997, p.7. Lewis Wolpert, development biologist at University College London was reported as saying, "It's a pretty risky technique with lots of abnormalities." Also report and interview in the Eight O'Clock News, BBC Radio 4, February 24, 1997.

3. As for instance, Spallone, 1992.

4. George, 1988, p.5.

5. My colleague Peter Saunders and I began working on an alternative approach to neo-Darwinian evolutionary theory in the 1970s. Major collections of multi-author essays appeared in Ho and Saunders, 1984: Pollard , 1981: Ho and Fox, 1988.

6. Lewis Wolpert, who currently heads the Committee for the Public Understanding of Science, argues strenuously for this 'fundamentalist' view of science. See Wolpert, 1996.

7. See Hubbard and Wald, 1993.

8. This was pointed out to me by Martin Khor, during a Course on Globalization and Economics that he gave at Schumacher College, February 3–10, 1997.

9. See Korten, 1997.

10. Korten, 1997, p.2.

11. See Perlas, 1994; also WTO: New setback for the South, *Third World Resurgence* issue 77/78, 1997, which contains many articles reporting on the WTO meeting held in December 1996 in Singapore.

12. Brown *et al.,*1993.

13. Udo and Grubb, 1990.

14. "Superbug spectre haunts Japan," Michael Day, *New Scientist* 3 May, 1997, p.5.

15. See Bik *et al,* 1995; Prager *et al.,* 1995; Reidl and Makalanos, 1995.

16. Whatmore *et al.,* 1994; Kapur*et al.,* 1995; Schnitzler *et al.,* 1995; Upton *et al.,* 1996.

17. Professor Hugh Pennington, on BBC Radio 4 News, February 1997.

18. Barinaga, 1996.

19. Reviewed by Davies, 1994.

20. Tschape, 1994.

21. See World Health Report, 1996; also Garret, 1995, chapter 13, for an excellent account of the history of antibiotic resistance in pathogens.

22. See Ho and Tappeser, 1997.

23. See Davies, 1994.

24. WHO Fact Sheet No. 139, January 1997.

25. Hoffman *et al.,* 1994; Schluter *et al.,* 1995.

26. See Ho, 1996a.

27. Jager and Tappeser, 1996, have extensively reviewed the literature on the survival of bacteria and DNA released into different environments.

28. See Lorenz and Wackernagel, 1994.

29. See Schubert *et al.,* 1994; also *New Scientist* January 24, p.24, featured a short report on recent findings of the group that were presented at the International Congress on Cell Biology in San Francisco, December 1996.

30. Wahl *et al.,* 1984; see also relevant entries in Kendrew, 1995, especially "slow transforming retroviruses" and "Transgenic technologies."

31. "Killer virus piles on the misery in Zaire" Debora MacKenzie, *New Scientist* April 19, 1997, p.12.

32. "Virus gets personal," *New Scientist* April 26, 1997, p.13.

33. "Poultry virus infection in Antarctic penguins," Heather Gardner, Knowles Kerry and Martin Riddle, *Nature* 387, May 15, 1997, p.245.

34. See Pain, 1997.

35. Quoted in "The spectre of a human clone" *The Independent,* February 26, 1997, p.1.

✍ STUDY QUESTIONS

1. What is a 'vector,' and how are vectors used in modifying organisms?

2. What is horizontal gene transfer, and what are the concerns about it?

3. It is often claimed that genetic modification of food is not substantively different from conventional food breeding. Discuss three of Ho's reasons for disputing this claim.

4. We are typically taught that the aim of science is 'knowledge.' Although Ho does not disagree that this is *an* aim of science, she believes that science now more often aims to serve the ends of business. Discuss some of her examples.

54   The World Food Supply: The Damage Done by Cattle-Raising

TRISTRAM COFFIN

Tristram Coffin was the editor of *The Washington Spectator*, a public concerns newsletter.

This article from *The Washington Spectator* reports on the ecological costs of cattle-raising. For example, in California it takes 5214 gallons of water to produce one edible pound of beef, as compared to 23 gallons for the same amount of tomatoes. In addition, lowering one's meat diet is likely to result in greater health. Coffin calls on us to change our diet, for our own good and the good of humankind, from one heavy in meat to more grains, vegetables, and fruits.

In this century, the number and impacts of livestock have swelled apace with human population and affluence. Since mid-century human numbers have doubled to [5.8] billion, while the number of four-legged livestock—cattle, pigs, sheep, goats, horses, buffalo and camels—has grown from 2.3 billion to 4 billion. At the same time, the fowl population multiplied from about 3 billion to nearly 11 billion. There are now three times as many domestic animals as people.[1]

"Currently, sufficient land, energy and water exist to feed well over twice the world's population" (*Earth Save Foundation*). But this is not the whole story. The Foundation adds, "Yet half of the world's grain harvest is fed to livestock, while millions of humans go hungry. In 1984 when thousands of Ethiopians were dying from famine, Ethiopia continued growing and shipping millions of dollars worth of livestock to the United States and other European countries."

Worldwatch Institute reports: "Rings of barren earth spread out from wells on the grasslands of Soviet Turkmenia. Heather and lilies wilt in the nature preserves of the southern Netherlands.

"Forests teeming with rare forms of plant and animal life explode in flame in Costa Rica. Water tables fall and fossil fuels are wasted in the U.S. Each of these cases of environmental decline issues from a single source: the global livestock industry."

The simple fact is that the livestock industry is a better paying customer than are hungry human beings. In turn, the industry is supported by the lusty appetite for meat of well-to-do individuals. Since 1985, North Americans have been eating 50% more beef, 280% more poultry and 33% more dairy products. In its tract "Our Food, Our World," the Foundation points out that this is a diet with one-third more fat, one-fifth less carbohydrate, and levels of protein consumption "far exceeding official recommendation."

"This increased demand for animal products has resulted in a vast reallocation of resources, has promoted the degradation of global systems, and has disrupted indigenous cultures. The impact on human health has been equally devastating."

Worldwatch advises: "Feeding the world's current population on an American style diet would require two and a half times as much grain as the world's farmers produce for all purposes. A future world of 8 to 14 billion people eating the American ration of 220 grams a day can be nothing but a flight of fancy." Why? "In the U.S., over one-third of all raw materials—including fossil fuels—consumed for all purposes are devoted to the production of livestock" [*Earth Save*].

Example: it takes 16 pounds of grain and soy to produce one pound of beef. One half the Earth's land mass is grazed for livestock, as compared to the 2% used for fruits and vegetables.

Growing cattle crops is an "extremely energy-intensive process. Farmers must pump water, plow, cultivate and fertilize the fields, then harvest and transport the crops. The

Reprinted from *The Washington Spectator*, ed. Tristram Coffin, Vol. 19.2 (January 15, 1993).

number of calories of fossil fuel expended to produce one calorie of protein from beef is 78, as compared to 2 calories to produce the same one calorie of soybeans." The energy used to produce one pound of grain-fed beef is equal to one gallon of gasoline, according to *Earth Save*.

What about water? "Our Food, Our World" estimates that livestock production accounts for more than half of all water consumed. In California it takes 5214 gallons of water to produce one edible pound of beef, as compared to 23 gallons for the same amount of tomatoes...Water tables, like the Ogallala aquifer under the Great Plains states, are fast being depleted."

Marc Reisner writes in his book *California Desert*, "It offends me that we give three times more water to grow cows than we give to people in California."

The Growth of Deserts—"Our Food, Our World" contends that livestock grazing and overuse of land to grow food crops for cattle have played a major role in the growth of deserts. "Regions most affected by desertification are all cattle-producing areas, including the western half of the U.S., Central and South America, Australia and sub-Saharan Africa. The main causes of desertification are overgrazing of livestock, overcultivation of land, improper irrigation techniques, deforestation [to clear land for cattle raising as is now occurring in the Brazilian Rain Forest].

Why? "Under persistent grazing, the bare ground becomes impermeable to rainwater, which then courses off the surface, carrying away topsoil and scouring stream beds into deep gullies. Upstream, water tables fall for lack of replenishment; downstream, flooding occurs more frequently and sediment clogs waterways, dams and estuaries. In drier climates wind sweeps away the destabilized soil."

The U.N. Environment Program estimates that 73% of the world's 3.3 billion hectares of dry rangeland is at least moderately desertified, having lost more than 25% of its carrying capacity. "There is little debate that degradation is occurring in environments where rainfall is more plentiful and regular. The perennial plants that flourish in these zones are easily disrupted by cattle; clay soils are easily compacted and rendered impervious to water; and rains often arrive

in strong, sudden downpours, sluicing away soils destabilized by cattle" (Worldwatch Institute).

Philip Fradkin, writing in *Audubon* magazine, says: "The impact of countless hooves and mouths over the years has done more to alter the type of vegetarian and land forms of the West than all the water projects, strip mines, power plants, freeways, and subdivision developments combined."

A few pertinent facts: Each year, an estimated 125,000 square miles of rainforest are destroyed, together with the loss of 1,000 plant and animal species. In Central America cattle ranching has destroyed more rainforests than has any other activity. A quarter of Central American rainforests have been cleared for pasture. This creates a profitable market for cattle sold to the U.S. market.

Livestock production creates other environmental problems—the pollution of the atmosphere by carbon dioxide and methane, of water by animal wastes and pesticides. Worldwatch Institute states: "The millions of tons of animal waste that accumulate at modern production facilities can pollute rivers and groundwater if precautions are not taken. If they get into rivers or open bodies of water, nitrogen and phosphorus in manure overfertilize algae, which grow rapidly, deplete oxygen supplies, and suffocate aquatic ecosystems. From the hundreds of algae-choked Italian lakes to the murky Chesapeake Bay, and from the oxygen-starved Baltic Sea to the polluted Adriatic, animal wastes add to the nutrient loads from fertilizer runoff, human sewage and urban and industrial pollution."

In the Netherlands, the 14 million animals in feeding houses in the southern part of the nation "excrete more nitrogen- and phosphorus-rich manure than the soil can absorb...pushing freshwater ecosystems into decline."

And, "manure nitrogen, mixed with nitrogen from artificial fertilizers, percolates through the soil into the underground water tables as nitrates....In the U.S., roughly one-fifth of the wells in livestock states, such as Iowa, Kansas and Nebraska, have nitrate levels that exceed health standards. Manure nitrogen also escapes into the air as gaseous ammonia, a pollutant that causes acid rain."

The *Earth Save* study looks at three problems:

- "The metabolic processes of cattle result in the emission of large quantities of methane.

Each cow produces 1 pound of methane for every 2 pounds of meat it yields. The amount of methane emitted by the world's cattle annually: 100 million tons." 20% of total world methane emissions comes from cattle.

- Wastes from factory farmers, feedlots and dairies create a buildup of toxins in the land and water. The E.P.A. estimates that almost half the wells and surface streams in the U.S. are "contaminated by agricultural pollutants."

- Chemical pesticides are used so widely and in such large quantities that they "poison the environment and the human food chain. The increase in overall pesticide use since 1945, when petro-chemical based agriculture became popular, is 3,300%."

Loss of Forests—Not only rangeland, but forests, too, suffer from heavy livestock production. The Worldwatch study reports, "Forests suffer, as branches are cut for fodder or entire stands are leveled to make way for pastures. The roster of impacts from forest clearing includes the loss of watershed protection, loss of plant and animal species, and on a larger scale, substantial contributions of the greenhouse gas carbon dioxide to the atmosphere."

Examples: in Latin America, more than 20 million hectares of moist tropical forests have been cleared for cattle pasture. The U.N. Food and Agricultural Organization says that Central America has lost more than a third of its forest since the early 1960s. Nearly 70% of the deforested land in Panama and Costa Rica is now pasture.

"Eradicating tree cover sets the wheels of land degradation in motion. Shallow, acidic, and nutrient-poor, tropical soils lose critical phosphorus and other nutrients when the forest is converted to pasture. . . . Most pasture is abandoned within a decade for land newly carved from the forest . . . Forest destruction for ranching also contributes to climate change. When living plants are cut down and burned, or when they decompose, they release carbon into the atmosphere as the greenhouse gas carbon dioxide. In the atmosphere, carbon dioxide traps the heat of the sun, warming the earth.- The expansion of pastures into Latin American forests has released an estimated 1.4 billion tons of carbon into the atmosphere."

Worldwatch points out that methane, a by-product of cattle-raising, is the second most important greenhouse gas.

Effect on Health—Earth Save warns, "Animal products contain large quantities of saturated fat, cholesterol and protein and no dietary fiber. The impact of this diet on human health has been devastating. . . . Fortunately, by observing a low-fat diet free of animal products, some diseases can be commonly prevented, consistently improved and sometimes cured." Some fats are associated with most of the diseases of affluence that are among the leading causes of death in industrialized countries: heart disease, stroke, breast and colon cancer. The study laments that physicians generally are taught to cure disease, but not how to prevent it. The majority "are taught little about nutrition as a preventative measure," but many are inquiring into this possibility.

"*Great Protein Fiasco*"—The Worldwatch study comments: "The adverse health impacts of excessive meat-eating stem in large part from what nutritionists call the *great protein fiasco*—a mistaken belief by many Westerners that they need to consume large quantities of protein. This myth, propagated as much as a century ago by health officials and governmental dietary guidelines, has resulted in Americans and other members of industrial societies ingesting twice as much protein as they need. Among the affluent, the protein myth is dangerous because of the saturated fats that accompany concentrated protein in meat and dairy products."

Low-fat diets are now recommended by the U.S. Surgeon General, the U.S. National Research Council, the American Heart Association, and the World Health Organization. They recommend lowering fat consumption to no more than 30% of calories, as compared to the U.S. norm of 37%. [Many health specialists recommend lowering the fat consumption to 10 to 15%—ed. note.]

Higher meat consumption among the well-to-do may also create a problem for the poor, "as the share of farmland devoted to feed cultivation expands, reducing production of food staples," says the Worldwatch study. It points out that in Egypt, for example, "over the past quarter-century, corn grown for animal feed has taken over cropland from wheat, rice, sorghum and millet—all staple grains fed to livestock rose from 10 to 36%."

Much the same is true in Mexico, where 30% of the grain is fed to livestock, "although 22% of the country's people suffer from malnutrition." The share of cropland growing animal food and fodder went up from 5% in 1960 to 23% in 1980. A study of agriculture in 23 third world countries showed that in 13 countries, farmers had shifted more than 10% of grain land from food crops to feed crops in the last 25 years. In nine countries, "the demand for meat among the rich was squeezing out staple production for the poor."

The picture in the U.S.: more than a million farms and ranches raise young beef, while four big companies slaughter nearly 60% of them. Since 1962, the number of huge American beef feedlots, capable of holding 16,000 head of cattle, has risen from 23 to 189. At the same time, small feedlots, holding no more than 1,000 have dropped by 117,000.

The big operations have no trouble getting government support, such as guaranteed minimum prices, government storage of surpluses, feed subsidies, import levies and product insurance. The Organization for Economic Cooperation and Development reports that in 1990 government programs in the industrial democracies gave subsidies to animal farmers and feed growers worth $120 billion.

What is the answer? The *Los Angeles Times* states: "The Seeds of Change [a group based in Santa Fe, NM] philosophy holds that adopting a plant-based diet is the best solution for improving individual health and lessening the toll of the human race on our Earth's limited resources." Seeds of Change founder Gabriel Howearth recommends:

> Bush acorn squash and bush buttercup squash, both high in vitamin A and free amino acids. Jerusalem artichokes, a native North American food plant with a varied vitamin balance and useful digestive enzymes. Hopi blue starch corn grown without irrigation in the Southwest and a traditional staple of the Hopi Indians... Okra, containing high amounts of vitamin C and amino acids, good in vegetable soup, stew and gumbo. Amaranth, a high-protein garden grain.

Howearth's goal "is to get all kinds of people, even those who work and have limited leisure time, to grow their own food—in their backyards, on their balconies, or on their rooftops."

This is not a goal everyone can follow. What many can do is change their diet from heavy meats to more vegetables and fruits. They will be less likely to become ill, and they will help save the planet Earth.

NOTE

1. From *The Worldwatch Institute,* quoted in "World Food Supply: The Damage Done by Cattle-Raising." *The Washington Spectator* (Jan. 15, 1993).

🐝 **STUDY QUESTIONS**

1. Go over the figures and damage caused by cattle-raising, mentioned in this essay. Are you convinced by the article that the situation is as bad as it is made out to be? Explain your answer.

2. If the raising of cattle and other livestock is so damaging to the environment and our health, what should we be doing about it?

55   Vegetarianism and Treading Lightly on the Earth

MICHAEL ALLEN FOX

Michael Allen Fox was educated at Cornell University and the University of Toronto, taught philosophy for thirty-nine years at Queen's University in Canada, and is now retired and living in Australia, where he is Adjunct Professor of Social Science at the University of New England.

He has published work in such journals as *Ethics, Environmental Ethics, Environmental Values, Ethics and the Environment,* and *International Journal of Applied Ethics,* and his most recent books are *Deep Vegetarianism* (also translated into Chinese) and *The Accessible Hegel.*

The meat-based diet that is the prevailing choice in affluent, industrialized parts of the world is unhealthy and environmentally unsustainable in a number of ways. These claims are explained and documented in some detail in this essay. The negative effects of meat production on species diversity in particular are illustrated with special reference to rain forest destruction for cattle grazing. Also investigated here is the link between animal agriculture and the manipulative or dominating mindset that encourages viewing animals and ecosystems generally just as resources to be exploited at will. In contrast, it is argued, a vegetarian food system would enable us to take greater responsibility for our actions by minimizing our impact on the planet and help us regain a sense of being part of nature rather than existing apart from it.

MOVING AWAY FROM MEAT

I begin with a basic assumption: Scientific evidence increasingly reveals that a vegetarian— even a vegan—diet is from a nutritional standpoint, at least as healthy as, and in all probability healthier than, one that features meat (Anonymous 1988a; Anonymous 1988b; US National Research Council 1989; Barnard 1990; Chen 1990; Lappé 1992; White and Frank 1994; Melina & Davis 2003; Rice 2003; Saunders 2003). But beyond this important finding, many people are coming to understand that the amount of meat they consume individually and collectively has a profound effect on the way we use and manage natural resources—forests, land, water, and nonrenewable energy. To put it simply, the greater our dependence on meat and other animal products, the more we overexploit these resources to satisfy our food preferences. And if (as I argue here) the prevailing form of agroindustry significantly abuses and damages the environment, then it follows that the more meat we consume, the more the well-being of the planet, and consequently our own well-being, will suffer. This insight leads to an awareness that the dietary orientation of unhealthy, meat-dependent societies needs to change, not only for the good of each of their members, but also for the benefit of nature as a whole.

Many of us live in societies that encourage individuality, self-reliance, self-development, and the cultivation of personal taste. These are good things, to be sure. However, we are bombarded all the time by messages that encourage us to pursue the construction of selfhood by means of consumer choices—that is, by acting out self-centered desires and fantasies in our role as powerful purchasers within the global market system. We are all conditioned to view what we purchase as consumers simply as an expression of personal freedom, of consequence to ourselves alone. Numerous vested interests energetically promote this outlook: business leaders, industry spokespersons, the media, politicians, advertisers, and image-makers, to name a few. It therefore takes major effort to develop a contrasting form of awareness, namely, one that acknowledges that what we decide to buy has wider consequences. Many of these consequences have an impact on the environment. When we begin to appreciate the connections between our purchases and the environment, we start to question our choices and the influences that helped bring them about. Being sensitized by ecological issues, as a growing number of citizens are today, opens our minds to the possibility of change through the formation of new values. The process of becoming a vegetarian is often part of this creative ferment.

THE ENVIRONMENTAL IMPACT OF DIETARY CHOICE

The eco-destructive side of the meat industry's operations has been demonstrated with ample documentation from both government and non-government sources (Robbins 1987; Fiddes 1991; Durning & Brough 1995; Hill 1996; Fox 1999; Rice 2003; Gold 2004; Tudge 2004a, 2004b). These effects include:

- toxic chemical residues in the food chain
- pharmaceutical additives in animal feeds
- polluting chemicals and animal wastes from feedlot runoff in waterways and underground aquifers
- loss of topsoil caused by patterns of relentless grazing
- domestic and foreign deforestation and desertification resulting from the clearing of land for grazing and cultivating animal feed
- threatened habitats of wild species of plants and animals
- intensive exploitation of water and energy supplies
- ozone depletion caused by extensive use of fossil fuels and significant production of methane gas by cattle

A brief case study will help place these complex problems in context and help us comprehend their interconnections.

Canada is a typical Western industrialized country with a population only one-tenth that of the United States. Since the time of white settlement, expanding agriculture has been the major factor in an 85% reduction of wetlands (Government of Canada 1991: 9–9, 9–15). Agricultural acreage has increased fourfold since 1900, and the total area under irrigation more than doubled between 1970 and 1988 (Government of Canada 1991: 26–6, 9–14). We infer that the consumption of meat is a powerful force here, given that in North America some 95% of oats and 80% of corn crops end up as livestock feed (Animal Alliance of Canada 1991; Government of Canada 1991; Agriculture Canada 1994).

Farm animals in Canada produce 322 million liters (85 million U.S. gal) of manure *daily*, an overwhelming proportion of which comes from cattle. Each marketed kilogram (2.2 lb) of edible beef generates at least 40 kg (88 lb) of manure, and each marketed kilogram of pork 15 kg (33 lb). These wastes, plus the runoff of water used to clean farm buildings and equipment and pesticide residues and other agricultural chemicals, are often poorly handled, causing the contamination of waterways and soil, as well as air pollution (Government of Canada 1991: 9–26).

Now consider that to produce each quarter-pound hamburger costs the environment 11,000 L (2,904 gal) of water. This amounts to 96,800 L (25,555 gal) per kilogram. Meanwhile, a kilo of rice or cheese requires 5,000 L (1,320 gal) of water to produce, and a kilo of wheat only 1,000 L (264 gal) (Pearce 2006). Which is a better investment in the earth's future?

Finally, reflect on the accelerating demand for meat worldwide. As an example, whereas annual meat consumption in China averaged 4 kg (8.8 lb) in the 1960s, it is about 60 kg (132 lb) today (Porritt 2006).[1] This trend has prompted the prestigious World Watch Institute to focus attention on global problems of meat production in the latest edition of its *State of the World* report (Starke 2006).

Obviously not all of the environmentally negative effects of today's unsound agricultural practices can be blamed on livestock management. And clearly some of the abuses already listed can be reduced or eliminated by a dedicated approach to recycling animal manure (and even human waste) into fertilizer, the use of natural means of pest control instead of harmful chemicals, and like measures. So it has been argued that the proper target of criticism is not meat production per se, but rather the intensive rearing methods used by contemporary agribusiness. There is some point to this rejoinder, and those who obtain meat from their own or others' free-range, organic, or biodynamic operations surely contribute less to the environmental toll on the planet. But, given the rate at which smaller-scale family farms are being forced out of competition (and out of existence) by larger and larger corporate conglomerates (Berry 1996), the opportunities for obtaining "environmentally friendly" meat are extremely rare. Taking current agricultural trends into account, then, only a tiny fraction of the population can conceivably exercise this option, and an even tinier group desires to do so in the first place. But the bottom line is that vegetarians are able to live more lightly on the land than do meat eaters of any description.

Is there evidence to back up this assertion? The short answer is yes. Consider the following observations.

> Substituting a grass-feeding livestock system (using only ruminant animals) for the current grain and grass system was found to reduce the energy inputs about 60% and land resources about 8%....[In addition, it] would free up about 300 million tons of grain for export each year. This amount of grain is sufficient to feed a human population of 400 million a vegetarian-type diet for an entire year (Pimentel 1990: 12).
>
> All the grain fed to livestock could feed five times as many people. *(Proponents of intensive animal agriculture claim that we only put animals on land that could not support plant production. But we could grow more than enough plant food for human consumption if we used even a fraction of the land that is now used to grow plant food for livestock consumption.)* (Animal Alliance of Canada 1991)

Merely making animal agriculture more ecologically efficient would greatly reduce resource depletion and increase global food supplies. Imagine what a gradual and complete conversion of the meat economy to a vegetarian economy worldwide could achieve.

One of the accomplishments of environmental philosophy in its relatively short history is the establishment of ecologically informed ethical thinking. If this phrase stands for anything, it certainly must entail that an overarching goal of human life ought to minimize the harmful impact our existence—as individuals and as collectivities—has upon the biosphere. It follows that we also ought to make lifestyle choices that help secure this objective. Now a diet that relies heavily on meat appears affordable and environmentally sustainable only to those who (a) are unaware of the larger ecological costs of meat production; (b) assume that these costs do not have to be factored into our choices and a calculation of their consequences; or (c) believe that the costs can be passed on to others—people in developing nations, our children, and other future persons. We all have to eat and the

earth inevitably has to absorb the impact of our pursuing this natural end, but we should aim to reduce and confine the ecological stresses that are under our species' control. Vegetarianism seems plainly to be the best way to manage the environmental harm and degradation caused by humans' quest for nourishment. Some of the eco-destructive effects of the meat industry listed earlier are not caused by plant-based agriculture, and with respect to other results, the effects are less severe. By enabling us to eat lower down on the food chain, a vegetarian regime makes more efficient use of solar and caloric energy inputs. (For example, by concentrating on plant sources of protein—such as soya, beans, and nuts—we get at it more directly than we do by eating animals who have processed cellulose into protein for us.) As an energy-saving diet, vegetarianism lightens the exploitative load we place upon the earth's ecosystems.

MEAT PRODUCTION AS A THREAT TO BIODIVERSITY

We have seen that the global environmental consequences of the meat production system are serious. They are also pervasive. To show this, I want to shift attention now to the effects of animal agriculture on planetary biodiversity and on our attitudes toward nature as a whole.

There are many causes of species extinction, both natural and human. In relation to human factors, no single activity accounts totally for the sort of ecocide that undermines species viability. We should not expect, therefore, that the process whereby the flesh of animals appears on our tables explains by itself why certain ecosystems and the life-forms they support are either under threat or beyond recovery.

Let us begin by getting some idea of the scope of species eradication by humans. According to E. O. Wilson, who has conducted one of the most detailed studies of the problem, rain forest extinctions for which our species are responsible occur at between 1,000 and 10,000 times the natural rate (Wilson 1993). Wilson approximates that 27,000 species per year (74 per day, 3 per hour) are perishing at our hands. A more recently completed twenty-year study by the World Conservation Union shows that "at least one in eight plant species in the world—and nearly one in three in the United States—are under threat of extinction" (Stevens 1998). This appalling pace of destruction stems from several major dynamics, including the clearing of foreign and domestic forests for agricultural purposes and development, drainage and filling of wetlands, damming of rivers, use and abuse of coral reefs, and relentless high-tech ocean fishing. Among these, deforestation and overfishing are the most evident areas in which a relationship between human diet and species extinction is to be discovered. I shall focus here on the devastation of the irreplaceable rain forests of Latin America.

Most people who follow the news are conscious that global rain forests perform unique functions within the regulative cycles of the biosphere, helping to maintain global temperature, providing fresh supplies of oxygen and water to the atmosphere, and sheltering the most complex web of life imaginable. It is reported that 40% to 50% of the world's plant and animal species dwell in rain forests (McKisson & MacRae-Campbell 1990). This superabundance of life-forms yields a wide range of raw materials used in the manufacture of all manner of consumer goods and pharmaceuticals, upon which the quality of human life crucially depends. Products of great value include hardwoods, rattan, natural rubber, waxes, essential oils, fruits, and nuts. One-quarter of all drug compounds obtained from pharmacies contain rain forest ingredients, whereas for most of the world's people, traditional medicines extracted from plants are used exclusively to treat ailments (Collins 1990; UN Food and Agricultural Organization 1995). Notwithstanding all this, a Smithsonian-sponsored research team found that an area of Amazon-basin rain forest equivalent to seven football fields is being cleared *per minute* for grazing land (Smithsonian Institution 2002). Sadly, "fewer than one percent of tropical rain forest plants have been chemically screened for useful medicinal properties" (Collins 1990: 32). Meanwhile, "studies in Peru, the Brazilian Amazon, the Philippines and Indonesia suggest that harvesting forest products sustainably is at least twice as profitable as clearing [the forests] for timber or to provide land for agriculture" (UN Food and Agricultural Organization 1995: 62).

That the rain forests are the earth's principal networks of species diversity seems unarguable.

But why does this diversity matter so much? Thomas E. Lovejoy, a conservation biologist, places the matter in perspective:

> Assuming that the [earth's] biota contains ten million species, they then represent ten million successful sets of solutions to a series of biological problems, any one of which could be immensely valuable to us in a number of ways.... The point ... is not that the "worth" of an obscure species is that it may someday produce a cure for cancer. The point is that the biota as a whole is continually providing us with new ways to improve our biological lot, and that species that may be unimportant on our current assessment of what may be directly useful may be important tomorrow (Lovejoy 1986:16–17).

Wilson has commented that "biodiversity is our most valuable but least appreciated resource" (Wilson 1993: 281), and Collins remarks that the rain forests comprise a unique "genetic library" of virtually untapped information (Collins 1990: 32).

Solid, human-centered reasons for preserving biological diversity are to be found in these reflections. But might there not be additional good grounds for promoting species diversity? We have no difficulty in valuing other species instrumentally—in terms of what they can do for us. Perhaps we can also value them for their own sake—that is, for having a marvellous way of being that is worthy of celebrating quite independently of any actual or potential use we might make of them, and no matter how remotely related to ourselves they may be.

We are now in a position to consider the role that animal agriculture plays in undermining species diversity on the planet. Former U.S. Vice President Al Gore has written that "at the current rate of deforestation, virtually all of the tropical rain forests will be gone partway through the next century" (Gore 1993: 119)—that is, the century we live in now.[2] It is difficult to establish a precise correlation between animal agriculture and rain forest decimation, but it should be noted that the World Watch Institute has observed that "the human appetite for animal flesh is a driving force behind virtually every major category of environmental damage now threatening the human future" (World Watch Institute 2004). Rain forests are cleared by humans seeking firewood, settlement space, farm plots, monocultural plantations, expanded land holdings, oil, minerals, pastureland for cattle, and more recently, soybean cultivation.[3] Hydroelectric projects, roads, and other development schemes also take their toll. Even though these pressures are numerous and diverse, grazing may be identified as a major threat (Greenpeace International 2006a).[4]

Conversion of tropical rain forests to pasture-land for cattle has proceeded at a remarkable pace in Central America since the middle of the twentieth century. The inherent nature of rain forests is such that when they are cleared, only poor quality, unsustainable pastureland remains, and this contributes to the dynamics of expanding destruction as new grazing areas are sought to replace older, exhausted ones. Norman Myers contends that from Mexico to Brazil "the number one factor in elimination of Latin America's tropical forests is cattlegrazing" (Myers 1984: 127). Most of the beef produced in this region is exported to the American market, although an increasing portion goes to Western Europe and Japan (Myers 1984; Rifkin 1992). The United States contains only 5% of the world's population, yet it produces, imports, and consumes more beef than any other country (Myers 1984). The beef imported from Latin America ends up as fast food burgers, processed meats, and pet foods.[5] Myers notes that "convenience foods . . . constitute the fastest-growing part of the entire food industry in the United States"; 50% of all meals are now consumed in either fast food or institutional settings (Myers 1984: 130). These patterns demonstrate forcefully the connection between meat eating and rain forest destruction. We cannot save the forests just by saying no to fast-food hamburgers, but we can help turn things around if enough of us set an example by reducing the meat in our diets and if, in this way, we set an example for others.

MEAT PRODUCTION AND THE DOMINATION OF NATURE

The case of rain forest decimation for cattle grazing is a typical ecological horror story. But viewed through a slightly different prism, what we encounter here is one of the many forms of the human domination and manipulation of nature. I mean to point out here by that the range of our activities starkly display our species' tendency to treat nature and natural biological systems purely as instruments for achieving human and often very narrow, shortsighted objectives.

According to the manipulative mindset, nature or parts of nature (such as members of nonhuman species) merely constitute resources or materials for our use and disposal as we see fit. The slash-and-burn practice that seals the fate of rain forests as obstacles that are "in the way" of profit to be extracted from low-cost meat provides but one example of this mentality at work in the world. Whereas the rain forests are treated as dispensable, the animals subsequently bred on this land are themselves no more than commodities destined for some distant stockyard—just further contents of the organic cash till that is nature.

But the attitude evident here, which permits the ruthless exploitation of cattle from rain forest regions, is in reality no different from that which endorses the widespread practice of animal confinement on factory farms. Animals there have manifestly become machines or artefacts of production and reproduction (Mason & Singer 1990; Rice 2003; Gold 2004). New developments may yield even more ominous scenarios. Researchers have considered or are actively considering the application of genetic techniques to create freakish monster animals and to clone superproductive animals (U.S. Congress, Office of Technology Assessment 1985; British Medical Association 1992; Fox 1992; Spallone 1992). Other scientific fantasies include: animals with modified physiologies that experience little or no stress (Mason & Singer 1990), animals with no pain receptors (Rollin 1995), and the manufacture of synthetic meat (Edelman et al. 2005; Reuters 2005). Greed is driving some of these developments; the thinking behind others must be that if the experiments are successful and lead to economical avenues of meat production, then it will be all right to treat the animal-artifacts that result as mere things, and hence the major ethical objections to factory farming will simply melt away.[6]

What does all this add up to? The meat industry, itself feeding off human demand for certain types of food, is ushering in an era of activities that are totally lacking in compassion or a sense of connection with nature. Although we seem to be learning to connect to nature on one level—concern over ecological issues—on another level we have become out of touch with what matters most. The vast majority would not wish to visit a slaughterhouse for any reason,[7] and from what people know of modern livestock production processes, they would never want their pet or any animal they cared about to be treated the way food animals routinely are, let alone how they may be treated in the future. But at the same time, the consumers' selection of meat and meat products as foods of choice goes on with apparently little thought. In this manner, we accustom ourselves to accept the domination and manipulation of nature that as sensitive, caring people we ought to be aware of and reject. We thus find ourselves caught in a trap of our own making. We can, however, seek a way out by being reflective and deciding in favor of a lifestyle that does not rest upon the subjugation of the earth and the suffering of nonhuman forms of life. This is the vegetarian option, which is where I started.

CONCLUSION: A VEGETARIAN ETHIC

Vegetarianism encourages us to think of ourselves as *part of* nature rather than *apart from* nature. The vegetarian outlook recognizes the importance of ecologically sustainable human activity and affirms the requirement that we seek to minimize our impact on the planet, and this recognition includes the amount of harm we do in the course of looking after our essential needs. Mindfulness of both short- and long-term consequences of individual choice and collective behavior are hallmarks of a commitment to vegetarianism as a way of life. This choice also entails compassionate cohabitation with other species and respect for the earth to the greatest extent that these precepts can be followed, both in one's personal activities and in social policy and planning. The vegetarian way of life offers us a chance to re-establish contact with the land, eat locally grown foods, and recover connections with nature. Finally, vegetarianism is liberating in the sense that it frees us *from* the exploitation of animals and nature, while it frees us *to* discover who we are in more positive, life-affirming ways that are healthy for both humans and the planet that is our home.

NOTES

1. Also of interest here, it has been reported that nearly 15% of the Chinese population is now overweight, and childhood obesity in China has increased by 28 times over the past decade and a half, the causes of this being cited as greater meat consumption and lack of exercise (Guardian Weekly 2006).

2. See also his acclaimed environmental documentary film *An Inconvenient Truth* (2006).

3. Rain forest destruction for the purpose of creating soya plantations will cause concern among vegetarians, but this process is in fact geared toward supplying feed for livestock animals, not food for humans (Greenpeace International 2006b).

4. The radical transformation and degradation of *American* land by animal agriculture should not be underestimated and likewise presents a tragic story (Berry 1996; University of Washington Students n.d.).

5. Fast-food giants Burger King and McDonald's have pledged to stop using rain-forest-grown beef; others have made no such commitment. Greenpeace has recently charged that McDonald's beef and Kentucky Fried Chicken's chicken are fed on soya grown in cleared Amazon rain forests (Greenpeace International 2006c).

6. The case of synthetic or laboratory-grown meat is represented by smug journalists as a big "problem" for vegetarianism because its ethical position in regard to meat eating would supposedly be undermined by the prospect of animal flesh being produced without pain, suffering, and killing. But first, this view shows little understanding of what vegetarianism is all about (see the final section of this article and Fox 1999). Second, synthetic meat is merely a possibility today; we are very far from seeing it drive conventional factory farms out of business. And if it did, this would cause as big an economic upheaval as a large-scale transition to vegetarianism. Third, if meat eaters so desperately want meat that they will queue up for fake, laboratory-cultured versions, let them do so and leave the fresh, healthy, naturally grown plants to the rest of us.

7. I have, and it is a profoundly disturbing experience. For readers with strong stomachs who might be willing to "visit" an abattoir through the pages of a book, I recommend Coe (1995) and Eisnetz (1997).

REFERENCES

Agriculture Canada, Market Information Service. 1994. *Livestock Market Report, 1993.* Ottawa: Agriculture Canada.

Animal Alliance of Canada. 1991. "Enviro Facts about Livestock Production (compiled from World Watch Paper No. 103). Toronto: Animal Alliance of Canada.

Anonymous. 1988a. "Position of the American Dietetic Association: Vegetarian Diets." *Journal of the American Dietetic Association* 3: 351–355.

Anonymous. 1988b. "The Vegetarian Advantage." *Health* 20 (October): 18.

Barnard, Neal D. 1990. *The Power of Your Plate.* Summertown, TN: Book Publishing.

Berry, Wendell. 1996. *The Unsettling of American Culture and Agriculture.* Berkeley: University of California Press.

British Medical Association. 1992. *Our Genetic Future: The Science and Ethics of Genetic Technology.* Oxford: Oxford University Press.

Chen, Junshi. 1990. *Diet, Lifestyle and Mortality in China: A Study of 65 Chinese Counties.* Ithaca, NY: Cornell University Press.

Coe, Sue. 1995. *Dead Meat.* New York: Four Walls Eight Windows.

Collins, Mark, ed. 1990. *The Last Rain Forests: A World Conservation Atlas.* New York: Oxford University Press.

Durning, Alan T. and Brough, Holly B. 1995. "Animal Farming and the Environment." In *Just Environments: Intergenerational, International and Interspecies Issues.* Ed. David E. Cooper and Joy A. Palmer. London: Routledge.

Edelman, P. D. et al. 2005. "*In Vitro*-Cultured Meat Production." *Tissue Engineering* 11, No. 5/6: 659–662.

Eisnetz, Gail. 1997. *Slaughterhouse.* Buffalo: Prometheus Books.

Fiddes, Nick. 1991. *Meat: A Natural Symbol.* London: Routledge.

Fox, Michael Allen. 1999. *Deep Vegetarianism.* Philadelphia: Temple University Press.

Fox, Michael W. 1992. *Superpigs and Wondercorn: The Brave New World of Biotechnology and Where It All May Lead.* New York: Lyons & Burford.

Gold, Mark. 2004. "The Global Benefits of Eating Less Meat" (a 76-page report). Compassion in World Farming Trust. www.cifw.org.uk/education/eat.html

Gore, Albert. 1993. *Earth in the Balance: Ecology and the Human Spirit.* New York: Plume.

Government of Canada. 1991. *The State of Canada's Environment.* Ottawa: Supply and Services Canada.

Greenpeace International. 2006a. *Eating Up the Amazon* (a 64-page report). 6 April.

Greenpeace International. 2006b. "Greenpeace closes Amazon soya facilities in Brazil and Europe." 22 May press release. www.greenpeace.org.uk/forests

Greenpeace International. 2006c. "Greenpeace prevents soya from Amazon rain forest destruction Entering Europe." 7 April press release. www.greenpeace.org/international/press/releases/greenpeace-prevents-soya-from-2

Guardian Weekly. 2006. "China's Expanding Girth." 25–31 August: 2.

Hill, John Lawrence. 1996. *The Case for Vegetarianism: Philosophy for a Small Planet.* Lanham, MD: Rowman & Littlefield.

Lappé, Frances Moore. 1992. *Diet for a Small Planet* (20th ed.). New York: Ballantine.

Lovejoy, Thomas E. 1986. "Species Leave the Ark One by One." In *The Preservation of Species: The Value of Biological Diversity.* Ed. Brian G. Norton. Princeton: Princeton University Press.

Mason, Jim and Singer, Peter. 1990. *Animal Factories* (rev. ed.). New York: Harmony Books.

McKisson, Nicki and MacRae-Campbell, Linda. 1990. *The Future of Our Tropical Rainforests.* Tucson: Zephyr Press.

Melina, Vesanto and Davis, Brenda. 2003. *The New Becoming Vegetarian: The Essential Guide to a Healthy Vegetarian Diet* (2nd rev. ed.). Summertown, TN: Healthy Living Publications.

Myers, Norman. 1984. *The Primary Source: Tropical Forests and Our Future.* New York: Norton.

Pearce, Fred. 2006. "The Parched Planet." *New Scientist,* 26 February: 32–36.

Pimentel, David. 1990. "Environmental and Social Implications of Waste in U.S. Agriculture and Food Sectors." *Journal of Agricultural Ethics* 3: 5–20.

Porritt, Jonathon. 2006. "Hard facts to swallow." *Guardian Weekly,* 13–19 January: 18.

Rice, Pamela. 2004. *101 Reasons Why I'm a Vegetarian.* New York: Lantern Books.

Reuters. 2005. "Scientists propose growing artificial meat." 7 July dispatch. www.msnbc.msn.com/id/8498629/

Rifkin, Jeremy. 1992. *Beyond Beef: The Rise and Fall of the Cattle Culture.* New York: Dutton.

Robbins, John. 1987. *Diet for a New America*. Walpole, NH: Stillpoint.

Rollin, Bernard E. 1995. *The Frankenstein Syndrome: Ethical and Social Issues in The Genetic Engineering of Animals*. New York: Cambridge University Press.

Saunders, Kerrie K. 2003. *The Vegan Diet as Chronic Disease Prevention: Evidence Supporting the New Four Food Groups*. New York: Lantern Books.

Smithsonian Institution. 2002. "Smithsonian researchers show Amazonian deforestation accelerating." *Science Daily Online*, 15 January. www.sciencedaily.com/releases/2002/01/020115075118.htm

Spallone, Pat. 1992. *Generation Games: Genetic Engineering and the Future for Our Lives*. Philadelphia: Temple University Press.

Starke, Linda, ed. 2006. *State of the World 2006*. Washington, DC: World Watch Institute.

Stevens, William K. 1998. "Plant Species Threats Cited." *The Globe and Mail* (Toronto), 9 April: A15.

Tudge, Colin. 2004a. "It's a Meat Market." *New Scientist*, 13 March: 19.

———, 2004b. *So Shall We Reap: What's Gone Wrong with the World's Food—and How to Fix It*. Harmondsworth, Middlesex: Penguin.

U.N. Food and Agricultural Organization. 1995. *Dimensions of Need: An Atlas of Food and Agriculture*. Santa Barbara: ABC-CLIO.

University of Washington Students n.d. "Rape of Mother Earth." www.students.washington.edu/careuw/rapeofmotherearth.pdf

U.S. Congress, Office of Technology Assessment. 1985. *Technology, Public Policy, and the Changing Structure of American Agriculture: A Special Report for the 1985 Farm Bill*. Washington, DC: US Government Printing Office.

U.S. National Research Council. 1989. *Diet and Health: Implications for Reducing Chronic Disease Risk*. Washington, DC: National Academy Press.

White, Randall and Frank, Erica. 1994. "Health Effects and Prevalence of Vegetarianism." *Western Journal of Medicine* 160: 465–471.

Wilson, Edward O. 1993. *The Diversity of Life*. New York: Norton.

World Watch. 2004. "Is Meat Sustainable?" (editorial). *World Watch Magazine* 17(4), July/August.

STUDY QUESTIONS

1. Fox argues that our food choices have consequences that extend beyond our personal lives and that we should take responsibility for them. What do you think of his argument?

2. If you were convinced that eating meat is morally wrong, would you give it up? Why, or why not?

3. Toward the end of this reading, Fox alleges that humans have a "manipulative mindset" in relation to the natural world. Is animal agriculture part of this mindset? Discuss.

4. What sort of diet, in your opinion, would be consistent with the principle that humans ought to minimize their impact on the biosphere? Explain your answer.

5. If synthetic meat (meat made in laboratories) were widely available, would there remain any moral objection to eating meat? Defend your answer.

FOR FURTHER READING

Aiken, William, and Hugh LaFollette, eds., *World Hunger and Moral Obligation*, 2nd ed., Englewood Cliffs, N.J.: Prentice Hall, 1996. The best collection of readings available, containing four of the readings in this chapter, plus others of great importance.

Ehrlich, Paul. *The Population Bomb*. New York: Ballantine Books, 1971. An important work, warning of the dangers of the population explosion.

Lappé, Francis, and Joseph Collins. *Food First: Beyond the Myth of Scarcity*. New York: Ballantine Books, 1978). An attack on Neo-Malthusians like Hardin in which the authors argue that we have abundant resources to solve the world's hunger problems.

O'Neill, Onora. *Faces of Hunger*. London: Allen & Unwin, 1986. A penetrating Kantian discussion of the principles and problems surrounding world hunger.

Rifkin, Jeremy. *Beyond Beef*. New York: Plume, 1993.

Simon, Arthur. *Bread for the World*. New York: Paulist Press, 1975. A poignant discussion of the problem of world hunger from a Christian perspective with some thoughtful solutions.

Pollution: General Considerations

ON MARCH 24, 1989, the oil tanker *Exxon Valdez* ran aground off the Alaskan coast, spilling 1.26 million barrels of oil into Prince William Sound. It was the worst oil spill in history. The pristine beauty of the Alaskan Coast with its wealth of birds, fish, and wildlife was degraded. Five hundred square miles of the Sound were polluted. Millions of fish, birds, and wildlife were killed, and fishermen lost their means of livelihood. The fishing industry, which earns $100 million annually in Prince William Sound, ground to an abrupt halt. The Exxon Corporation was unprepared for an accident of this magnitude. It had only 69 barrels of oil dispersant on hand in Alaska, when something like 10,000 barrels were needed to clean up the spill. The ship's captain, Joseph Hazelwood, was found guilty of negligence and operating the tanker under the influence of alcohol, and Exxon was fined $100 million. Greenpeace put an ad in newspapers, showing Joseph Hazelwood's face, with the caption: "It wasn't his driving that caused the Alaskan oil spill. It was yours. The spill was caused by a nation drunk on oil. And a government asleep at the wheel."

Modern industrial society has provided enormous benefits, making our lives far more comfortable and freeing us from backbreaking drudgery. From electric lighting, washing machines, air conditioners, and gas-driven automobiles to medical miracles, supersonic airplanes, and microchip computers, our lives have been enriched with possibilities that existed only in dreams or in science fiction a little more than a century ago. Yet with these life-enhancing, technological wonders have come waste and pollution. This pollution in turn threatens to undo the benefits technology has brought us. How great is that threat?

Pollution may be broadly defined as any unwanted state or change in the properties of air, water, soil, liquid, or food that can have a negative impact on the health, well-being, or survival of human beings or other living organisms. Most pollutants are undesirable chemicals that are produced as by-products when a resource is converted into energy or a commodity. Types of pollution include contaminated water, chemically polluted air (such as smog), toxic waste in the soil, poisoned food, high levels of radiation, and noise. They also include acid rain and second-hand cigarette smoke because these can have a deleterious effect on our health.

ATLANTA—Most Americans will never encounter the parasite that contaminated Milwaukee's water. But 21 million people use water systems that aren't protected from the bug, and others swallow it when water plants improperly clean their filters, experts said Friday.

"Just a little lack of rigor can result in one of these outbreaks," said Jack Hoffbuhr of the American Water Works Association, a nonprofit foundation that tracks drinking water. "But I think most people can rest assured this is not common."

Thousands of Milwaukee residents were stricken by cryptosporidium, a protozoan about one-hundredth the size of a speck of dust. It causes severe diarrhea.

Mostly found in developing countries, it's the major cause of travelers' diarrhea. But 2 percent of the diarrhea cases in U.S. hospitals are caused by the bug, which can kill people who have weak immune systems.

"The bad news is there's no treatment for it, but the good news is it runs its course in about 14 days in healthy people," said Dr. Dennis Juranek of the U.S. Centers for Disease Control and Prevention.

Cryptosporidia lives in the intestines of animals and humans and is spread by contact with anything from diapers to water tainted by farm runoff.

Filters are the only protection from the parasite, which cannot be killed by chlorine or other chemicals, Juranek said.

Don't Drink The Water

About 21 million Americans drink unfiltered surface water. Most live in mountainous areas where people think the water's safe because it appears do clear, the Centers for Disease Control and Prevention said. A 1992 Oregon bacteria outbreak was caused by an unfiltered spring.

The earth naturally filters crypotosporidia in ground water, which is the primary source for 92 percent of the nation's water systems. But cities that draw water from rivers or lakes—such as Milwaukee—are required to chemically treat their water but not to filter it, Juranek said.

The U.S. Environmental Protection Agency is studying whether to require filtering for all water systems because of cryptosporidia, Juranek said.

People worried about the parasite shouldn't rely on home filters, Juranek and Hoffbuhr said. Most on the market won't screen out crypotosporidia, and the few that will are expensive and only produce about five gallons of water a day.

"My recommendation is boiling the water," Hoffbuhr said. "That's a fairly easy process to do and you don't have to buy those gizmos."

Source: CDC Report to wire service, 4–10–93.

Three factors determine the severity of a pollutant: its chemical nature (how harmful it is to various types of living organisms), its concentration (the amount per volume of air, water, soil, or body weight), and its persistence (how long it remains in the air, water, soil, or body).

We divide a pollutant's persistence into three types: degradable, slowly degradable, and nondegradable. Degradable pollutants, such as human sewage and contaminated soil, are usually broken down completely or reduced to acceptable levels by natural chemical processes. Slowly degradable pollutants, such as DDT, plastics, aluminum cans, and chlorofluorocarbons (CFCs) often take decades to degrade to acceptable levels. Nondegradable pollutants, such as lead and mercury, are not broken down by natural processes.

We know little about the short- and long-range harmful potential of most of the more than 70,000 synthetic chemicals in commercial use on people and the environment. The Environmental Protection Agency (EPA) estimates that 80% of cancers are caused by pollution. We know that half of our air pollution is caused by the internal combustion engines of motor vehicles and that coal-burning stationary power plants produce unacceptable amounts of sulfur dioxide (SO_2). The World Health Organization (WHO) estimates that about 1 billion urban people (about one-fifth of humanity) are being exposed to health hazards from air pollution and that emphysema, an incurable lung disease, is rampant in our cities. Studies tell us that smog is hazardous to our health and that it has caused thousands of deaths in such cities as London, New York, and Los Angeles.

In the United States, 80% of our freshwater aquifers are in danger, so a large percentage (estimates are more than 30%) of our population is drinking contaminated water (see the box on p. 506). By 1991 the EPA had listed 1211 hazardous waste sites for cleanup, with an estimated cost of cleanup per site of $26 million. Acid rain is killing our forests and lakes.

In our first reading, Hilary French documents the dire consequences of air pollution. Her essay provides hard data around which rational discussion can take place.

Our second reading contains a sharp indictment of corporate capitalism by George Bradford. Reacting to what he perceived to be a condoning of the tragedy of Bhopal, India (where a Union Carbide factory exploded, killing 3000 people in 1984), by the *Wall Street Journal,* Bradford lashes out at the whole economic and social philosophy that permitted and is responsible for this and many other threats to humanity. In the Third World, businesses cut costs by having lax safety standards. Chemicals that are banned in the United States and Europe are produced overseas. Even in the United States and Europe, our industrial culture continues to endanger our lives. We must throw "off this Modern Way of Life," argues Bradford, for it only constitutes a "terrible burden" that threatens to crush us all.

Our third reading, "People or Penguins: The Case for Optimal Pollution" by William Baxter, is essentially clarificatory in that it sets forth the relationship between resources and pollution, showing that we cannot have the good of resource use without the bad of pollution. The point is to decide on the proper balance. Those like Baxter, who take a decidedly anthropocentric point of view, argue that we ought to risk pollution that might endanger other species (as DDT does) if it promotes human advantage.

56   You Are What You Breathe

HILARY FRENCH

Hilary French is a staff researcher for the Worldwatch Institute.

In this essay, French provides a detailed, documented account of the devastating global effects of air pollution. Because the wind carries the polluted air from one nation to another, this problem requires international as well as national action and cooperation. If we are to solve the problem, our lifestyles will have to change.

Asked to name the world's top killers, most people wouldn't put air pollution high on their lists. A nuisance, at best, but not a terribly serious threat to health.

The facts say otherwise. In greater Athens, for example, the number of deaths rises sixfold on heavily polluted days. In Hungary, the government attributes 1 in 17 deaths to air pollution. In Bombay, breathing the air is equivalent to smoking 10 cigarettes a day. And in Beijing, air-pollution-related respiratory distress is so common that it has been dubbed the "Beijing Cough."

Air pollution is truly a global public health emergency. United Nations statistics show that more than one billion people—a fifth of humanity—live in areas where the air is not fit to breathe. Once a local phenomenon primarily affecting city dwellers and people living near factories, air pollution now reaches rural as well as urban dwellers. It's also crossing international borders.

In the United States alone, roughly 150 million people live in areas whose air is considered unhealthy by the Environmental Protection Agency (EPA). According to the American Lung Association, this leads to as many as 120,000 deaths each year.

A century ago, air pollution was caused primarily by the coal burned to fuel the industrial revolution. Since then, the problem and its causes have become more complex and widespread. In some parts of the world, including much of Eastern Europe and China, coal continues to be the main source of pollution. Elsewhere, automobiles and industries are now the primary cause.

Adding to the miasma, industries are emitting pollutants of frightening toxicity. Millions of tons of carcinogens, mutagens, and poisons pour into the air each year and damage health and habitat near their sources and, via the winds, sometimes thousands of miles away. Many regions that have enjoyed partial success combating pollution are finding their efforts overwhelmed as populations and economies grow and bring in more power plants, home furnaces, factories, and motor vehicles.

Meanwhile, global warming has arisen as the preeminent environmental concern; this sometimes conveys the misleading impression that conventional air pollution is yesterday's problem. But air pollutants and greenhouse gases stem largely from fossil fuels burned in energy, transportation, and industrial systems. Having common roots, the two problems can also have common solutions. Unfortunately, policymakers persist in tackling them separately, which runs the risk of lessening one while exacerbating the other.

Air pollution has proven so intractable a phenomenon that a book could be written about the history of efforts to combat it. Law has followed law. As one problem has largely been solved, a new one has frequently emerged to take its place. Even some of the solutions have become part of the problem: The tall smokestacks built in the 1960s and 1970s to disperse emissions from huge coal-burning power plants became conduits to the upper atmosphere for the pollutants that form acid rain.

Turning the corner on air pollution requires moving beyond patchwork, end-of-the-pipe approaches to confront pollution at its sources. This will mean reorienting energy, transportation, and industrial structures toward prevention.

CHEMICAL SOUP

Although air pollution plagues countries on all continents and at all levels of development, it comes in many different varieties. The burning of fossil fuels—predominantly coal—by power plants, industries, and home furnaces was the first pollution problem recognized as a threat to human health. The sulfur dioxide and particulate emissions associated with coal burning—either alone or in combination—can raise the incidence of respiratory diseases such as coughs and colds, asthma, bronchitis, and emphysema. Particulate matter (a general term for a complex and varying mixture of pollutants in minute solid form) can carry toxic metals deep into the lungs.

Pollution from automobiles forms a second front in the battle for clean air. One of the worst auto-related pollutants is ozone, the principal ingredient in urban smog. Formed when sunlight causes hydrocarbons (a by-product of many

TABLE 1 Health Effects of Pollutants from Automobiles[1]

Pollutant	Health Effect
Carbon monoxide	Interferes with blood's ability to absorb oxygen; impairs perception and thinking; slows reflexes; causes drowsiness; and so can cause unconsciousness and death; if inhaled by pregnant women, may threaten growth and mental development of fetus.
Lead	Affects circulatory, reproductive, nervous, and kidney systems; suspected of causing hyperactivity and lowered learning ability in children; hazardous even after exposure ends.
Nitrogen oxides	Can increase susceptibility to viral infections such as influenza. Can also irritate the lungs and cause bronchitis and pneumonia.
Ozone	Irritates mucous membranes of respiratory system; causes coughing, choking, and impaired lung function; reduces resistance to colds and pneumonia; can aggravate chronic heart disease, asthma, bronchitis, and emphysema.
Toxic emissions	Suspected of causing cancer, reproductive problems, and birth defects. Benzene is a known carcinogen.

[1]Automobiles are a primary source, but not the only source, of these pollutants.

Sources: National Clean Air Coalition and the U.S. Environmental Protection Agency.

industrial processes and engines) to react with nitrogen oxides (produced by cars and power plants), ozone can cause serious respiratory distress. Recent U.S. research suggests that ground-level ozone causes temporary breathing difficulty and long-term lung damage at lower concentrations than previously believed.

Other dangerous pollutants spewed by automobiles include nitrogen dioxide, carbon monoxide, lead, and such toxic hydrocarbons as benzene, toluene, xylene, and ethylene dibromide (see Table 1).

At elevated levels, nitrogen dioxide can cause lung irritation, bronchitis, pneumonia, and increased susceptibility to viral infections such as influenza. Carbon monoxide can interfere with the blood's ability to absorb oxygen; this impairs perception and thinking, slow reflexes, and causes drowsiness and—in extreme cases—unconsciousness and death. If inhaled by a pregnant woman, carbon monoxide can threaten the fetus's physical and mental development.

Lead affects the circulatory, reproductive, nervous, and kidney systems. It is suspected of causing hyperactivity and lowered learning ability in children. Because it accumulates in bone and tissue, it is hazardous long after exposure ends.

Concern is growing around the world about the health threat posed by less common but extremely harmful airborne toxic chemicals such as benzene, vinyl chloride, and other volatile organic chemicals produced by automobiles and industries. These chemicals can cause a variety of illnesses, such as cancer and genetic and birth defects, yet they have received far less regulatory attention around the world than have "conventional" pollutants.

WHERE THE BREATHING ISN'T EASY

With the aid of pollution control equipment and improvements in energy efficiency, many Western industrialized countries have made significant strides in reducing emissions of sulfur dioxide and particulates. The United States, for example cut sulfur oxide emissions by 28 percent between 1970 and 1987 and particulates by 62 percent (see Figure 1). In Japan, sulfur dioxide emissions fell by 39 percent from 1973 to 1984.

The same cannot be said for Eastern Europe and the Soviet Union, where hasty industrialization after World War II, powered by abundant high-sulfur brown coal, has led to some of the worst air pollution ever experienced. Pollution control technologies have been virtually nonexistent. And, because of heavily subsidized fuel prices and the absence

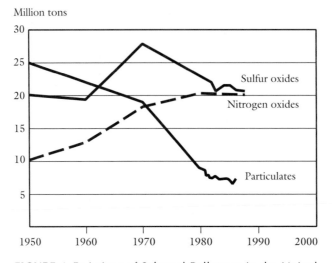

Million tons

FIGURE 1 Emissions of Selected Pollutants in the United States, 1950–1987. Source: Worldwatch Institute, based on Summers and Heston.

of market forces governing production, these countries never made the impressive gains in energy efficiency registered in the West after the oil shocks of the 1970s.

Many developing countries also confront appalling air pollution problems. The lack of adequate pollution control technologies and regulations, plus plans to expand energy and industrial production, translates into worsening air quality in many cities. Urbanization in much of the Third World means that increasing numbers of people are exposed to polluted city air.

A 1988 report by the United Nations' Environment Program (UNEP) and the World Health Organization (WHO) gives the best picture to date of the global spread of sulfur dioxide and particulate pollution (see Table 2). Of the 54 cities with data available on sulfur dioxide pollution for 1980 to 1984, 27 were on the borderline or in violation of the WHO health standard.

High on the list were Shenyang, Tehran, and Seoul, as well as Milan, Paris, and Madrid; this indicates that sulfur dioxide problems have by no means been cured in industrial countries. Though conditions are gradually improving in most of the cities surveyed, several in the Third World reported a worsening trend.

TABLE 2 Violations of Sulfur Dioxide and Suspended Particulate Matter Standards, Selected Cities[1]

City	Sulfur Dioxide	Particulates[2]
	(number of days above WHO standard)	
New Delhi	6	294
Xian	71	273
Beijing	68	272
Shenyang	146	219
Tehran	104	174
Bangkok	0	97
Madrid	35	60
Kuala Lampur	0	37
Zagreb	30	34
Sao Paulo	12	31
Paris	46	3
New York	8	0
Milan	66	n.a.
Seoul	87	n.a.

[1]Averages of readings at a variety of monitoring sites from 1980 to 1984.

[2]For Madrid, Sao Paulo, and Paris, the reading is of smoke rather than particulates.

Sources: United Nations' Environment Program and World Health Organization, Assessment of Urban Air Quality (Nairobi: Global Environment Monitoring System, 1988).

Suspended particulate matter poses an even more pervasive threat, especially in the developing world, where the appropriate control technologies have not been installed and conditions are frequently dusty. Fully 37 of the 41 cities monitored for particulates averaged either borderline or excessive levels. Annual average concentrations were as much as five times the WHO standard in both New Delhi and Beijing.

Ozone pollution, too, has become a seemingly intractable health problem in many parts of the world. In the United States, 1988 ushered in one of the hottest and sunniest years on record, and also one of the worst for ground-level ozone in more than a decade. According to the Natural Resources Defense Council, the air in New York City violated the federal health standard on 34 days—two to three times a week, all summer long. In Los Angeles, ozone levels surged above the federal standard on 172 days. At last count 382 counties, home to more than half of all Americans, were out of compliance with the EPA ozone standard.

Ozone is becoming a problem elsewhere, too. In Mexico City, the relatively lenient government standard of a one-hour ozone peak of 0.11 parts per million not to be exceeded more than once daily is topped more than 300 days a year—nearly twice as often as Los Angeles violates its much stricter standard.

The other automobile-related pollutants also constitute a far-flung health threat. The WHO/ UNEP report estimates that 15 to 20 percent of urban residents in North America and Europe are exposed to unacceptably high levels of nitrogen dioxide, 50 percent to unhealthy carbon monoxide concentrations, and a third to excessive lead levels. In a study in Mexico City, lead levels in the blood of 7 out of 10 newborns were found to exceed WHO standards. "The implication for Mexican society, that an entire generation of children will be intellectually stunted, is truly staggering," says Mexican chemist and environmental activist Manuel Guerra.

Airborne toxic chemical emissions present no less of a danger. In the United States, the one country that has begun to tally total emissions, factories reported 1.3 million tons of hazardous emissions in 1987, including 118,000 tons of carcinogens. According to the EPA, these emissions cause about 2,000 cancer deaths a year.

These deaths fall disproportionately on certain communities. For example, in West Virginia's Kanawha Valley—home to a quarter of a million people and 13 major chemical plants—state health department records show that, between 1968 and 1977, the incidence of respiratory cancer was more than 21 percent above the national average. According to EPA statistics, a lifetime of exposure to the airborne concentrations of butadiene, chloroform, and ethylene oxide in this valley could cause cancer in 1 resident in 1,000.

Unfortunately, data are not so extensive for other countries. Wherever uncontrolled polluting industries such as chemical plants, smelters, and paper mills exist, however, emission levels are undoubtedly high. Measurements of lead and cadmium in the soil of the upper Silesian towns of Olkosz and Slawkow in Poland, for instance, are among the highest recorded anywhere in the world.

The health damage inflicted by air pollution comes at great human cost; it also carries an economic price tag. The American Lung Association estimates that air pollution costs the United States $40 billion annually in health care and lost productivity.

CLEARING THE AIR

In the Western industrial world, the last 20 years has been a period of intense political and scientific activity aimed at restoring clean air. The approaches to date, however, have tended to be technological Band-Aids rather than efforts to address the roots of the problem.

Scrubbers, nitrogen-oxides control technologies, and new cleaner-burning coal technologies can all reduce emissions dramatically, but they are not the ultimate solutions. For one, they can create environmental problems of their own, such as the need to dispose of scrubber ash, a hazardous waste. Second, they do little if anything to reduce carbon dioxide emissions, so make no significant contribution to slowing global warming.

For these reasons, technologies of this kind are best viewed as a bridge to the day when energy-efficient societies are the norm and pollution-free sources such as solar, wind, and water power provide the bulk of the world's electricity.

Improving energy efficiency is a clean air priority. Such measures as more-efficient refrigerators and lighting can markedly and cost-effectively reduce electricity consumption; this will in turn reduce emissions. Equally important, the savings that results from not building power plants because demand has been cut by efficiency can more than offset the additional cost of installing scrubbers at existing plants.

Using conservative assumptions, the Washington, D.C.–based American Council for an Energy Efficient Economy concluded that cutting sulfur dioxide emissions steeply with a scrubbers/conservation combination could actually save consumers in the Midwest up to $8 billion.

Similar rethinking can help reduce auto emissions. To date, modifying car engines and installing catalytic converters have been the primary strategies employed to lower harmful emissions. These devices reduce hydrocarbon emissions by an average of 87 percent, carbon monoxide by an average of 85 percent, and nitrogen oxides by 62 percent over the life of a vehicle. Although catalytic converters are sorely needed in countries that don't require them, they alone are not sufficient. Expanding auto fleets are overwhelming the good they do, even in countries that have mandated their use.

Alternative fuels, such as methanol, ethanol, natural gas, hydrogen, and electricity, are being pushed by many governments as the remedy for the air pollution quagmire. Although these fuels may have some role to play eventually, they can by no means be viewed as a panacea.

Reducing air pollution in cities is likely to require a major shift away from automobiles as the cornerstone of urban transportation systems. As congestion slows traffic to a crawl in many cities, driving to work is becoming unattractive anyway. Convenient public transportation, car pooling, and measures that facilitate bicycle commuting are the cheapest, most effective ways for metropolitan areas to proceed.

Driving restrictions already exist in many of the world's cities. For example, Florence has turned its downtown into a pedestrian mall during daylight hours. Budapest bans motor traffic from all but two streets in the downtown area during particularly polluted spells. In Mexico City and Santiago, one-fifth of all vehicles are kept off the streets each weekday based on their license-plate numbers.

As with power plant and auto emissions, efforts to control airborne toxic chemicals will be most successful if they focus on minimizing waste rather than simply on controlling emissions. Such a strategy also prevents waste from being shifted from one form to another. For instance, control technologies such as scrubbers and filters produce hazardous solid wastes that must be disposed on land.

The Congressional Office of Technology Assessment has concluded it is technically and economically feasible for U.S. industries to lower production of toxic wastes and pollutants by up to 50 percent within the next few years. Similar possibilities exist in other countries.

Freedom of environmental information can also be a powerful regulatory tool. In the United States, "right-to-know" legislation requiring industries to release data on their toxic emissions has been instrumental in raising public awareness of the threat and spurring more responsible industrial behavior. The Monsanto Company, a major chemical producer, was so embarrassed by the enormous pollution figures it was required to release in 1989 that it simultaneously announced its intention to cut back emissions 90 percent by 1992.

Few European countries have released information about emissions from industrial plants, although that may change if the European Economic Community (EEC) issues a directive now in draft form on freedom of information regarding environmental matters. The recent political transformation in Eastern Europe and the Soviet Union are gradually improving the environmental data flow, although much progress in this area remains to be made.

SOLUTION FROM SMOG CITY

In most parts of the world, air pollution is now squarely on the public policy agenda. This is a promising sign. Unfortunately, the public's desire for clean air has not yet been matched with the political leadership needed to provide it. Recent developments at the national and international levels, though constituting steps forward, remain inadequate to the task.

In the United States, for example, recent major amendments to the Clean Air Act of 1970 will cut acid rain emissions in half, tighten emissions standards for automobiles significantly, and require much stricter control of toxic air pollutants.

Almost any legislation would be an improvement. Twenty years after the act became law, 487 counties still are not in compliance. But the legislation fails to address the problem at a fundamental level by not encouraging energy efficiency, waste reduction, and a revamping of transportation systems and urban designs.

Los Angeles—with the worst air quality in the United States—is one of the first regions in the world to really understand that lasting change will not come through mere tinkering. Under a bold new air-quality plan embracing the entire region, the city government will discourage automobile use, boost public transportation, and control household and industrial activities that contribute to smog.

For example, paints and solvents will have to be reformulated to produce fewer ozone-forming fumes; gasoline-powered lawn mowers and lighter fluid will be banned; carpooling will be mandated; and the number of cars per family limited. Even though the plan has been approved by all of the relevant state and federal agencies, implementing it at the local level will be a challenge.

Most of Europe, though quicker than the United States to cut back sharply on the emissions that cause acid rain, has been slower to tackle urban air quality. Non-EEC countries such as Austria, Norway, Sweden, and Switzerland have had strong auto emissions control legislation in place for several years, but until recently the EEC had been unable to agree on its own stringent standards.

This finally changed in June 1989, when the EEC Council of Environmental Ministers ended a nearly four-year debate and approved new standards for small cars. These will be as tough as those now in effect in the United States. To meet them, small cars will have to be equipped with catalytic converters. Although an important step forward, it's somewhat ironic that Europe sees its adoption of U.S. standards as a major victory at the same time the United States realizes these regulations don't go far enough.

In Eastern Europe and the Soviet Union, air pollution emerged as a pressing political issue as *glasnost* and the revolutions of 1989 opened up public debate. Air pollution in much of the region is taking a devastating toll on human health. Fledgling governments in Eastern Europe are under pressure to show some improvements.

A HELPFUL HAND

To make a dent in their pollution, Eastern Europe and the Soviet Union will need Western technologies and a dose of domestic economic and environmental reform. Given current economic conditions in these countries, money for purchasing pollution control, energy efficiency, renewable energy, and waste reduction technologies will have to come in part in the form of environmental aid from the West.

Aid of this kind can be classified as enlightened philanthropy, since stemming pollution in Eastern Europe, where even rudimentary controls are still lacking, can yield a far greater return on the investment than taking further incremental steps at home. To illustrate this point, Sweden receives 89 percent of the sulfur that contributes to the acid rain poisoning its lakes and forests from other countries. Because much of this is of Eastern European origin, anything Sweden does to combat emissions there helps at home.

Air pollution is beginning to emerge on the political agenda in the Third World as well. In Cubatão, Brazil, a notoriously polluted industrial city known as "the Valley of Death," a five-year-old government cleanup campaign is starting to make a dent in the problem. Total emissions of particulates, for instance, were cut from 521,600 pounds a day in 1984 to 156,000 in 1989.

Mexico City, too, is embarking on an ambitious cleanup. With the support of the World Bank, Japan, the United States, and West Germany, the municipal government is introducing a package of measures aimed at cutting automotive pollution dramatically over the next two to three years. As part of the plan, driving will be restricted on certain days. In March 1991, Mexican President Carlos Salinas de Gortari ordered the shutdown of a large oil refinery on the outskirts of Mexico City that has long been a major contributor to the city's pollution problem.

Industrial countries are involved in a variety of efforts to assist developing countries with air pollution problems. The International Environmental Bureau in Switzerland and the World Environment Center in New York City help facilitate transfer of pollution control information and technology to the Third World. The World Bank is exploring ways to step up its air pollution control activities. One proposed project involving the World Bank and the UN Development Program would help Asian governments confront urban air pollution, among other environmental problems.

Legislation passed by the U.S. Congress requires the Agency for International Development to encourage energy efficiency and renewable energy through its programs in the interests of slowing global warming. This step will reduce air pollution at the same time.

While the means are available to clear the air, it will be a difficult task. In the West, powerful businesses such as auto manufacturers and electric utilities will strongly resist measures that appear costly. In Eastern Europe, the Soviet Union, and the developing world, extreme economic problems coupled with shortages of hard currency mean that money for pollution prevention and control is scarce.

Overcoming these barriers will require fundamental modifications of economic systems. As long as air pollution's costs remain external to economic accounting systems, utilities, industries, and individuals will have little incentive to reduce the amount of pollution they generate. Taxes, regulations, and public awareness can all be harnessed to bring the hidden costs of air pollution out into the open.

On the promising side, faced with mounting costs to human health and the environment, people on every continent are beginning to look at pollution prevention through a different economic lens. Rather than a financial burden, they're seeing that it is a sound investment. The old notion that pollution is the price of progress seems finally to be becoming a relic of the past.

✺ STUDY QUESTIONS

1. What conclusions should we come to after reading French's assessment of the hazards of air pollution? What does the data signify for the future?
2. If you were to propose a plan to solve the problem of air pollution, how would you begin? What sort of measures would you take both locally and nationally? How would you deal with other nations who are polluting the atmosphere?
3. Is air pollution an area that the United Nations should be involved in? Explain your reasoning.

57   We All Live in Bhopal

GEORGE BRADFORD

George Bradford is an editor of *The Fifth Estate*.

In this essay, Bradford argues that in the Third World, as well as in Europe and the United States, industrial capitalism is harming hundreds of thousands of people and imposing a

George Bradford, "We All Live in Bhopal," in *Fifth Estate* (4632 Second, Detroit, MI 48201), Winter 1985: Vol. 19 No. 4 (319). Reprinted in J. Zerzan and Alice Carnes, *Questioning Technology* (Santa Cruz, CA: Freedom Press, 1988). Reprinted by permission frightful risk on millions more by unsafe practices that pollute our air, water, soil, and food. Taking the tragic explosion of the Union Carbide insecticide plant in Bhopal, India, as his point of departure, he recounts a tale of corporate negligence and moral culpability. Calling these large corporations "corporate vampires," Bradford accuses them of turning industrial civilization into "one vast, stinking extermination camp."

Our modern way of life, dependent on dangerous industrial institutions, reeks with harmful pollution. We must rid ourselves of it before we are crushed by it.

The cinders of the funeral pyres at Bhopal are still warm, and the mass graves still fresh, but the media prostitutes of the corporations have already begun their homilies in defense of industrialism and its uncounted horrors. Some 3,000 people were slaughtered in the wake of the deadly gas cloud, and 20,000 will remain permanently disabled. The poison gas left a 25 square mile swath of dead and dying, people and animals, as it drifted southeast away from the Union Carbide factory. "We thought it was a plague," said one victim. Indeed it was: a chemical plague, an *industrial plague.*

Ashes, ashes, all fall down!

A terrible, unfortunate, "accident," we are reassured by the propaganda apparatus for Progress, for History, for "Our Modern Way of Life." A price, of course, has to be paid—since the risks are necessary to ensure a higher Standard of Living, a Better Way of Life.

The *Wall Street Journal,* tribune of the bourgeoisie, editorialized, "It is worthwhile to remember that the Union Carbide insecticide plant and the people surrounding it were where they were for compelling reasons. India's agriculture has been thriving, bringing a better life to millions of rural people, and partly because of the use of modern agricultural technology that includes applications of insect killers." The indisputable fact of life, according to this sermon, is that universal recognition that India, like everyone else, "needs technology. Calcutta-style scenes of human deprivation can be replaced as fast as the country imports the benefits of the West's industrial revolution and market economics." So, despite whatever dangers are involved, "the benefits outweigh the costs" (Dec. 13, 1984).

The *Journal* was certainly right in one regard—the reasons for the plant and the people's presence there are certainly compelling: capitalist market relations and technological invasion are as compelling as a hurricane to the small communities from which those people were uprooted. It conveniently failed to note, however, that countries like India do not import the *benefits* of industrial capitalism; those benefits are *exported* in the form of loan repayments to fill the coffers of the bankers and corporate vampires who read the *Wall Street Journal* for the latest news of their investments. The Indians only take the risks and pay the costs; in fact, for them, as for the immiserated masses of people living in the shantytowns of the Third World, there are no risks, only certain hunger and disease, only the certainty of death squad revenge for criticizing the state of things as they are.

GREEN REVOLUTION A NIGHTMARE

In fact, the Calcutta-style misery is the result of Third World industrialization and the so called industrial "Green Revolution" in agriculture. The Green Revolution, which was to revolutionize agriculture in the "backward" countries and produce greater crop yields, has only been a miracle for the banks, corporations and military dictatorships who defend them. The influx of fertilizers, technology, insecticides and bureaucratic administration exploded millennia-old rural economies based on subsistence farming, creating a class of wealthier farmers dependent upon western technologies to produce cash crops such as coffee, cotton and wheat for export, while the vast majority of farming communities were destroyed by capitalist market competition and sent like refugees into the growing cities. These victims, paralleling the destroyed peasantry of Europe's Industrial Revolution several hundred years before, joined either the permanent underclass of unemployed and underemployed slumdwellers eking out a survival on the tenuous margins of civilization, or became proletarian fodder in the Bhopals, Sao Paulos and Djakartas of an industrializing world—an industrialization process, like all industrialization in history, paid for by the pillage of nature and human beings in the countryside.

Food production goes up in some cases, of course, because the measure is only quantitative—some foods disappear while others are produced year round, even for export. *But subsistence is destroyed*. Not only does the rural landscape begin to suffer the consequences of constant crop production and use of chemicals, but the masses of people—laborers on the land and in the teeming hovels growing around the industrial plants—go hungrier in a vicious cycle of exploitation, while the wheat goes abroad to buy absurd commodities and weapons.

But subsistence is culture as well: culture is destroyed with subsistence, and people are further trapped in the technological labyrinth. The ideology of progress is there, blared louder than ever by those with something to hide, a cover-up for plunder and murder on levels never before witnessed.

INDUSTRIALIZATION OF THE THIRD WORLD

The industrialization of the Third World is a story familiar to anyone who takes even a glance at what is occurring. The colonial countries are nothing but a dumping ground and pool of cheap labor for capitalist corporations. Obsolete technology is shipped there along with the production of chemicals, medicines and other products banned in the developed world. Labor is cheap, there are few if any safety standards, and *costs are cut*. But the formula of cost-benefit still stands: the costs are simply borne by others, by the victims of Union Carbide, Dow, and Standard Oil.

Chemicals found to be dangerous and banned in the US and Europe are produced instead overseas—DDT is a well-known example

of an enormous number of such products, such as the unregistered pesticide Leptophos exported by the Velsicol Corporation to Egypt which killed and injured many Egyptian farmers in the mid-1970's. Other products are simply dumped on Third World markets, like the mercury-tainted wheat which led to the deaths of as many as 5,000 Iraqis in 1972, wheat which had been imported from the US. Another example was the wanton contamination of Nicaragua's Lake Managua by a chlorine and caustic soda factory owned by Pennwalt Corporation and other investors, which caused a major outbreak of mercury poisoning in a primary source of fish for the people living in Managua.

Union Carbide's plant at Bhopal did not even meet US safety standards according to its own safety inspector, but a UN expert on international corporate behavior told the *New York Times*, "A whole list of factors is not in place to insure adequate industrial safety" throughout the Third World. "Carbide is not very different from any other chemical company in this regard." According to the *Times*, "In a Union Carbide battery plant in Jakarta, Indonesia, more than half the workers had kidney damage from mercury exposure. In an asbestos cement factory owned by the Manville Corporation 200 miles west of Bhopal, workers in 1981 were routinely covered with asbestos dust, a practice that would never be tolerated here." (12/9/84)

Some 22,500 people are killed every year by exposure to insecticides—a much higher percentage of them in the Third World than use of such chemicals would suggest. Many experts decried the lack of an "industrial culture" in the "underdeveloped" countries as a major cause of accidents and contamination. But where an "industrial culture" thrives, is the situation really much better?

INDUSTRIAL CULTURE AND INDUSTRIAL PLAGUE

In the advanced industrial nations an "industrial culture" (and little other) exists. Have such disasters been avoided as the claims of these experts would lead us to believe?

Another event of such mammoth proportions as those of Bhopal would suggest otherwise—in that case, industrial pollution killed some 4,000 people in a large population center. That was London, in 1952, when several days of "normal" pollution accumulated in stagnant air to kill and permanently injure thousands of Britons.

Then there are the disasters closer to home or to memory, for example, the Love Canal (still leaking into the Great Lakes water system), or the massive dioxin contaminations at Seveso, Italy and Times Creek, Missouri, where thousands of residents had to be permanently evacuated. And there is the Berlin and Farro dump at Swartz Creek, Michigan, where C-56 (a pesticide by-product of Love Canal fame), hydrochloric acid and cyanide from Flint auto plants had accumulated. "They think we're not scientists and not even educated," said one enraged resident, "but anyone who's been in high school knows that cyanide and hydrochloric acid is what they mixed to kill the people in the concentration camps."

A powerful image: industrial civilization as one vast, stinking extermination camp. We all live in Bhopal, some closer to the gas chambers and to the mass graves, but all of us close enough to be victims. And Union Carbide is obviously not a fluke—the poisons are vented in the air and water, dumped in rivers, ponds and streams, fed to animals going to market, sprayed on lawns and roadways, sprayed on food crops, every day, everywhere. The result may not be as dramatic as Bhopal (which then almost comes to serve as a *diversion,* a deterrence machine to take our minds off the pervasive reality which Bhopal truly represents), but it is as deadly. When ABC News asked University of Chicago professor of public health and author of *The Politics of Cancer,* Jason Epstein, if he thought a Bhopal-style disaster could occur in the US, he replied: "I think what we're seeing in America is far more slow—not such large accidental occurrences, but a slow, gradual leakage with the result that you have excess cancers or reproductive abnormalities."

In fact, birth defects have doubled in the last 25 years. And cancer is on the rise. In an interview with the *Guardian,* Hunter College professor David Kotelchuck described the "Cancer Atlas"

maps published in 1975 by the Department of Health, Education and Welfare. "Show me a red spot on these maps and I'll show you an industrial center of the US," he said. "There aren't any place names on the maps but you can easily pick out concentrations of industry. See, it's not Pennsylvania that's red it's just Philadelphia, Erie and Pittsburgh. Look at West Virginia here, there's only two red spots, the Kanawha Valley, where there are nine chemical plants including Union Carbide's, and this industrialized stretch of the Ohio River. It's the same story wherever you look."

There are 50,000 toxic waste dumps in the United States. The EPA admits that *ninety per cent* of the 90 billion pounds of toxic waste produced annually by US industry (70 per cent of it by chemical companies) is disposed of "improperly" (although we wonder what they would consider "proper" disposal). These deadly products of industrial civilization—arsenic, mercury, dioxin, cyanide, and many others—are simply dumped, "legally" and "illegally," wherever convenient to industry. Some 66,000 different compounds are used in industry. Nearly a billion tons of pesticides and herbicides comprising 225 different chemicals were produced in the US last year, and an additional 79 million pounds were imported. Some two per cent of chemical compounds have been tested for side effects. There are 15,000 chemical plants in the United States, daily manufacturing mass death.

All of the dumped chemicals are leaching into our water. Some three to four thousand wells, depending on which government agency you ask, are contaminated or closed in the US. In Michigan alone, 24 municipal water systems have been contaminated, and a thousand sites have suffered major contamination. According to the Detroit *Free Press,* "The final toll could be as many as 10,000 sites" in Michigan's "water wonderland" alone (April 15, 1984).

And the coverups go unabated here as in the Third World. One example is that of dioxin; during the proceedings around the Agent Orange investigations, it came out that Dow Chemical had lied all along about the effects of dioxin. Despite research findings that dioxin is "exceptionally toxic" with "a tremendous potential for producing chlor-acne and systemic injury," Dow's top toxicologist, V. K Rowe, wrote in 1965, "We are not in any way attempting to hide our problems under a heap of sand. But we certainly do not want to have any situations arise which will cause the regulatory agencies to become restrictive."

Now Vietnam suffers a liver cancer epidemic and a host of cancers and health problems caused by the massive use of Agent Orange there during the genocidal war waged by the US. The sufferings of the US veterans are only a drop in the bucket. And dioxin is appearing everywhere in our environment as well, in the form of recently discovered "dioxin rain."

GOING TO THE VILLAGE

When the Indian authorities and Union Carbide began to process the remaining gases in the Bhopal plant, thousands of residents fled, despite the reassurances of the authorities. The *New York Times* quoted one old man who said, "They are not believing the scientists or the state government or anybody. They only want to save their lives."

The same reporter wrote that one man had gone to the train station with his goats, "hoping that he could take them with him—anywhere, as long as it was away from Bhopal" (Dec. 14, 1984). The same old man quoted above told the reporter, "All the public has gone to the village." The reporter explained that "going to the village" is what Indians do when trouble comes.

A wise and age-old strategy for survival by which little communities always renewed themselves when bronze, iron and golden empires with clay feet fell to their ruin. But subsistence has been and is everywhere being destroyed, and with it, culture. What are we to do when there is no village to go to? When we all live in Bhopal, and Bhopal is everywhere? The comments of two women, one a refugee from Times Creek, Missouri, and another from Bhopal, come to mind. The first woman said of her former home, "This was a nice place once. Now we have to bury it." The other woman said, "Life cannot come back. Can the government pay for the lives? Can you bring those people back?"

The corporate vampires are guilty of greed, plunder, murder, slavery, extermination and devastation. And we should avoid any pang of sentimentalism when the time comes for them to pay for their crimes against humanity and the natural world. But we will have to go beyond them, to ourselves: subsistence, and with it culture, has been destroyed. We have to find our way back to the village, out of industrial civilization, out of this exterminist system.

The Union Carbides, the Warren Andersons, the "optimistic experts" and the lying propagandists all must go, but with them must go the pesticides, the herbicides, the chemical factories and the chemical way of life which is nothing but death.

Because this is Bhopal, and it is all we've got. This "once nice place" can't be simply buried for us to move on to another pristine beginning. The empire is collapsing. We must find our way back to the village, or as the North American natives said, "back to the blanket," and we must do this not by trying to save an industrial civilization which is doomed, but in that renewal of life which must take place in its ruin. By throwing off this Modern Way of Life, we won't be "giving things up" or sacrificing, but throwing off a terrible burden. Let us do so soon before we are crushed by it.

STUDY QUESTIONS

1. Does Bradford make his case that Western industrial society is dangerous to humanity and nature and needs to be rejected? What are the implications of Bradford's indictment? What sort of world do you think that he would want us to live in? Is Bradford a "Luddite"? (Luddites were people in England in the early nineteenth century who went around destroying machines because they believed that the Industrial Revolution was evil.)

2. Is the anger that comes through in this article justified? Is modern industrial practice really morally irresponsible? Explain your answer.

3. How might someone in the business community respond to Bradford's essay? Can our industrial practices be defended?

58   People or Penguins: The Case for Optimal Pollution

WILLIAM F. BAXTER

William Baxter is professor of law at Stanford University and the author of *People or Penguins: The Case for Optimal Pollution* (1974) from which this selection is taken.

In this essay, Baxter aims at clarifying the relationship between resource use and pollution. They are the opposite sides of the same coin, the privilege and its price, the good and the bad. Baxter argues that we cannot have a pollution-free society without harming humans. If we are humanists, committed to promoting the human good above all else, as he is, we should be willing to allow pollution where it harms animals and trees if overall benefits accrue to human beings.

I start with the modest proposition that, in dealing with pollution, or indeed with any problem, it is helpful to know what one is attempting to accomplish. Agreement on how and whether to pursue a particular objective, such as pollution control, is not possible unless some more general objective has been identified and stated with reasonable precision. We talk loosely of having clean air and clean water, of preserving our wilderness areas, and so forth. But none of these is a sufficiently general objective: each is more accurately viewed as a means rather than as an end.

With regard to clean air, for example, one may ask, "how clean?" and "what does clean mean?" It is even reasonable to ask, "why have clean air?" Each of these questions is an implicit demand that a more general community goal be stated—a goal sufficiently general in its scope and enjoying sufficiently general assent among the community of actors that such "why" questions no longer seem admissible with respect to that goal.

If, for example, one states as a goal the proposition that "every person should be free to do whatever he wishes in contexts where his actions do not interfere with the interests of other human beings," the speaker is unlikely to be met with a response of "why." The goal may be criticized as uncertain in its implications or difficult to implement, but it is

so basic a tenet of our civilization—it reflects a cultural value so broadly shared, at least in the abstract—that the question "why" is seen as impertinent or imponderable or both.

I do not mean to suggest that everyone would agree with the "spheres of freedom" objective just stated. Still less do I mean to suggest that a society could subscribe to four or five such general objectives that would be adequate in their coverage to serve as testing criteria by which all other disagreements might be measured. One difficulty in the attempt to construct such a list is that each new goal added will conflict, in certain applications, with each prior goal listed; and thus each goal serves as a limited qualification on prior goals.

Without any expectation of obtaining unanimous consent to them, let me set forth four goals that I generally use as ultimate testing criteria in attempting to frame solutions to problems of human organization. My position regarding pollution stems from these four criteria. If the criteria appeal to you and any part of what appears hereafter does not, our disagreement will have a helpful focus: which of us is correct, analytically, in supposing that his position on pollution would better serve these general goals. If the criteria do not seem acceptable to you, then it is to be expected that

Reprinted with permission of Columbia University Press from William F. Baxter, *People or Penguins: The Case for Optimal Pollution* (1974).

our more particular judgments will differ, and the task will then be yours to identify the basic set of criteria upon which your particular judgments rest.

My criteria are as follows:

1. The spheres of freedom criterion stated above.
2. Waste is a bad thing. The dominant feature of human existence is scarcity—our available resources, our aggregate labors, and our skill in employing both have always been, and will continue for some time to be, inadequate to yield to every man all the tangible and intangible satisfactions he would like to have. Hence, none of those resources, or labors, or skills, should be wasted—that is, employed so as to yield less than they might yield in human satisfactions.
3. Every human being should be regarded as an end rather than as a means to be used for the betterment of another. Each should be afforded dignity and regarded as having an absolute claim to an evenhanded application of such rules as the community may adopt for its governance.
4. Both the incentive and the opportunity to improve his share of satisfactions should be preserved to every individual. Preservation of incentive is dictated by the "no-waste" criterion and enjoins against the continuous, totally egalitarian redistribution of satisfactions, or wealth; but subject to that constraint, everyone should receive, by continuous redistribution if necessary, some minimal share of aggregate wealth so as to avoid a level of privation from which the opportunity to improve his situation becomes illusory.

The relationship of these highly general goals to the more specific environmental issues at hand may not be readily apparent, and I am not yet ready to demonstrate their pervasive implications. But let me give one indication of their implications. Recently scientists have informed us that use of DDT in food production is causing damage to the penguin population. For the present purposes let us accept that assertion as an indisputable scientific fact. The scientific fact is often asserted as if the correct implication—that we must stop agricultural use of DDT—followed from the mere statement of the fact of penguin damage. But plainly it does not follow if my criteria are employed.

My criteria are oriented to people, not penguins. Damage to penguins, or sugar pines, or geological marvels is, without more, simply irrelevant. One must go further, by my criteria, and say: Penguins are important because people enjoy seeing them walk about rocks; and furthermore, the well-being of people would be less impaired by halting use of DDT than by giving up penguins. In short, my observations about environmental problems will be people-oriented, as are my criteria. I have no interest in preserving penguins for their own sake.

It may be said by way of objection to this position, that it is very selfish of people to act as if each person represented one unit of importance and nothing else was of any importance. It is undeniably selfish. Nevertheless I think it is the only tenable starting place for analysis for several reasons. First, no other position corresponds to the way most people really think and act—i.e., corresponds to reality.

Second, this attitude does not portend any massive destruction of nonhuman flora and fauna, for people depend on them in many obvious ways, and they will be preserved because and to the degree that humans do depend on them.

Third, what is good for humans is, in many respects, good for penguins and pine trees—clean air for example. So that humans are, in these respects, surrogates for plant and animal life.

Fourth, I do not know how we could administer any other system. Our decisions are either private or collective. Insofar as Mr. Jones is free to act privately, he may give such preferences as he wishes to other forms of life: he may feed birds in winter and do less with himself, and he may even decline to resist an advancing polar bear on the ground that the bear's appetite is more important than those portions of himself that the bear may choose to eat. In short my basic premise does not rule out private altruism to competing life-forms. It does rule out, however, Mr. Jones' inclination to feed Mr. Smith to the bear, however hungry the bear, however despicable Mr. Smith.

Insofar as we act collectively on the other hand, only humans can be afforded an opportunity to participate in the collective decisions. Penguins cannot vote now and are unlikely subjects for the franchise—pine trees more unlikely still. Again each individual is free to cast his vote so as to benefit sugar pines if that is his inclination. But many of the more extreme assertions that one hears from some conservationists amount to tacit assertions that they are specially appointed representatives of sugar pines, and hence that their preferences should be weighted more heavily than the preferences of other humans who do not enjoy equal rapport with "nature." The simplistic assertion that agricultural use of DDT must stop at once because it is harmful to penguins is of that type.

Fifth, if polar bears or pine trees or penguins, like men, are to be regarded as ends rather than means, if they are to count in our calculus of social organization, someone must tell me how much each one counts, and someone must tell me how these life-forms are to be permitted to express their preferences, for I do not know either answer. If the answer is that certain people are to hold their proxies, then I want to know how those proxy-holders are to be selected: self-appointment does not seem workable to me.

Sixth, and by way of summary of all the foregoing, let me point out that the set of environmental issues under discussion—although they raise very complex technical questions of how to achieve any objective—ultimately raise a normative question: what ought we to do. Questions of ought are unique to the human mind and world—they are meaningless as applied to a nonhuman situation.

I reject the proposition that we ought to respect the "balance of nature" or to "preserve the environment" unless the reason for doing so, express or implied, is the benefit of man.

I reject the idea that there is a "right" or "morally correct" state of nature to which we should return. The word "nature" has no normative connotation. Was it "right" or "wrong" for the earth's crust to heave in contortion and create mountains and seas? Was it "right" for the first amphibian to crawl up out of the primordial ooze? Was it "wrong" for plants to reproduce themselves and alter the atmospheric composition in favor of oxygen? For animals to alter the atmosphere in favor of carbon dioxide both by breathing oxygen and eating plants? No answers can be given to these questions because they are meaningless questions.

All this may seem obvious to the point of being tedious, but much of the present controversy over environment and pollution rests on tacit normative assumptions about just such nonnormative phenomena: that it is "wrong" to impair penguins with DDT, but not to slaughter cattle for prime rib roasts. That it is wrong to kill stands of sugar pines with industrial fumes, but not to cut sugar pines and build housing for the poor. Every man is entitled to his own preferred definition of Walden Pond, but there is no definition that has any moral superiority over another, except by reference to the selfish needs of the human race.

From the fact that there is no normative definition of the natural state, it follows that there is no normative definition of clean air or pure water—hence no definition of polluted air—or of pollution—except by reference to the needs of man. The "right" composition of the atmosphere is one which has some dust in it and some lead in it and some hydrogen sulfide in it—just those amounts that attend a sensibly organized society thoughtfully and knowledgeably pursuing the greatest possible satisfaction for its human members.

The first and most fundamental step toward solution of our environmental problems is a clear recognition that our objective is not pure air or water but rather some optimal state of pollution. That step immediately suggests the question: How do we define and attain the level of pollution that will yield the maximum possible amount of human satisfaction?

Low levels of pollution contribute to human satisfaction but so do food and shelter and education and music. To attain ever lower levels of pollution, we must pay the cost of having less of these other things. I contrast that view of the cost of pollution control with the more popular statement that pollution control will "cost" very large numbers of dollars. The popular statement is true in some senses, false in others; sorting out the true and false senses is of some importance. The first step in that sorting process is to achieve a clear understanding of the difference between dollars and resources. Resources are the wealth of our nation; dollars are merely claim checks upon those resources. Resources are of vital importance; dollars are comparatively trivial.

Four categories of resources are sufficient for our purposes: At any given time a nation, or a planet if you prefer, has a stock of labor, of technological skill, of capital goods, and of natural resources (such as mineral deposits, timber, water, land, etc.). These resources can be used in various combinations to yield goods and services of all kinds—in some limited quantity. The quantity will be larger if they are combined efficiently, smaller if combined inefficiently. But in either event the resource stock is limited, the goods and services that they can be made to yield are limited; even the most efficient use of them will yield less than our population, in the aggregate, would like to have.

If one considers building a new dam, it is appropriate to say that it will be costly in the sense that it will require x hours of labor, y tons of steel and concrete, and z amount of capital goods. If these resources are devoted to the dam, then they cannot be used to build hospitals, fishing rods, schools, or electric can openers. That is the meaningful sense in which the dam is costly.

Quite apart from the very important question of how wisely we can combine our resources to produce goods and services, is the very different question of how they get distributed—who gets how many goods? Dollars constitute the claim checks which are distributed among people and which control their share of national output. Dollars are nearly valueless pieces of paper except to the extent that they do represent claim checks to some fraction of the output of goods and services. Viewed as claim checks, all the dollars outstanding during any period of time are worth, in the aggregate, the goods and services that are available to be claimed with them during that period—neither more nor less.

It is far easier to increase the supply of dollars than to increase the production of goods and services—printing dollars is easy. But printing more dollars doesn't help because each dollar

then simply becomes a claim to fewer goods, i.e., becomes worth less.

The point is this: many people fall into error upon hearing the statement that the decision to build a dam, or to clean up a river, will cost $X million. It is regrettably easy to say: "It's only money. This is a wealthy country, and we have lots of money." But you cannot build a dam or clean a river with $X million—unless you also have a match, you can't even make a fire. One builds a dam or cleans a river by diverting labor and steel and trucks and factories from making one kind of goods to making another. The cost in dollars is merely a shorthand way of describing the extent of the diversion necessary. If we build a dam for $X million, then we must recognize that we will have $X million less housing and food and medical care and electric can openers as a result.

Similarly, the costs of controlling pollution are best expressed in terms of the other goods we will have to give up to do the job. This is not to say the job should not be done. Badly as we need more housing, more medical care, and more can openers, and more symphony orchestras, we could do with somewhat less of them, in my judgment at least, in exchange for somewhat cleaner air and rivers. But that is the nature of the trade-off, and analysis of the problem is advanced if that unpleasant reality is kept in mind. Once the trade-off relationship is clearly perceived, it is possible to state in a very general way what the optimal level of pollution is. I would state it as follows:

People enjoy watching penguins. They enjoy relatively clean air and smog-free vistas. Their health is improved by relatively clean water and air. Each of these benefits is a type of good or service. As a society we would be well advised to give up one washing machine if the resources that would have gone into that washing machine can yield greater human satisfaction when diverted into pollution control. We should give up one hospital if the resources thereby freed would yield more human satisfaction when devoted to elimination of noise in our cities. And so on, trade-off by trade-off, we should divert our productive capacities from the production of existing goods and services to the production of a cleaner, quieter, more pastoral nation up to—and no further than—the point at which we value more highly the next washing machine or hospital that we would have to do without than we value the next unit of environmental improvement that the diverted resources would create.

Now this proposition seems to me unassailable but so general and abstract as to be unhelpful— at least unadministerable in the form stated.

It assumes we can measure in some way the incremental units of human satisfaction yielded by very different types of goods... But I insist that the proposition stated describes the result for which we should be striving—and again, that it is always useful to know what your target is even if your weapons are too crude to score a bull's eye.

🐛 STUDY QUESTIONS

1. Evaluate the four tenets of Baxter's environmental philosophy.

   a. Which do you agree with, and which do you disagree with? Explain why.

   b. Is human benefit the only morally relevant criterion with regard to our behavior to animals and the environment?

   c. Do penguins and sugar pine trees have intrinsic value? Or is their value entirely instrumental, derived from benefits to humans?

2. Do you agree with Baxter that pollution is just the opposite side of the coin of resource use? Do you also agree that on the principle that "waste is a bad thing" we are led to use resources for human good and thus bring about some level of pollution?

3. Compare Baxter's analysis with those of Bradford and French. What are their similarities and differences? Does Baxter shed any light on the matter?

🐛 FOR FURTHER READING

Bernards, Neal, ed. *The Environmental Crisis.* San Diego, CA: Greenhaven Press, 1991.

Bogard, William. *The Bhopal Tragedy: Language, Logic and Politics in the Production of a Hazard.* Boulder, CO: Westview, 1989.

Brown, Lester. *The Twenty Ninth Day.* New York: Norton, 1978.

———, ed. *The Worldwatch Reader.* Washington, DC: Worldwatch Institute, 1991.

Brown, Michael. *The Toxic Cloud.* New York: Harper & Row, 1987.

Gore, Albert. *Earth in the Balance.* Boston: Houghton Mifflin, 1992.

Keeble, John. *Out of the Channel: The Exxon Valdez Spill.* New York: HarperCollins, 1991.

Lomborg, Bjorn. *The Skeptical Environmentalist.* New York: Routledge, 2001.

McKibbern, Bill. *The End of Nature.* New York: Random House, 1989.

Postel, Sandra. *Defusing the Toxic Threat: Controlling Pesticides and Industrial Waste.* Washington, DC: Worldwatch Institute, 1987.

Ray, Dixy Lee, and Lou Guzzo. *Trashing the Planet.* Washington, DC: Regnery Gateway, 1990.

Silver, Cheryl Pollack. *Protecting Life on Earth: Steps to Save the Ozone Layer.* Washington, DC: Worldwatch Institute, 1988.

Simon, Julian. *The Ultimate Resource.* Princeton, NJ: Princeton University Press, 1981.

Wellburn, Alan. *Air Pollution and Acid Rain.* New York: Wiley, 1988.

Pesticides

IN 1962 RACHEL CARSON published Silent Spring in which she documented the effects of DDT and other pesticides on human health. She charged that these "elixers of death" were causing widespread cancer and genetic mutations, as well as wreaking havoc on birds, fish, and wildlife. Pesticides have the paradoxical consequence of producing a greater insect problem than the one they are combating because evolution selects for pesticide-resistant insects. The new "improved" insects are more lethal and in turn require more potent pesticides, which in turn lead to even more potent insects, which in turn require a still more potent pesticide....

A further danger of pesticides is biological magnification, the increased concentration of pollutants in living organisms. Many synthetic chemicals, such as DDT and PCB, are soluble in fat but insoluble in water and are slowly degradable by natural processes. That is, when the organism takes in DDT or PCB, the chemical becomes concentrated in the fatty tissue of the animal and is degraded very slowly. When a large fish consumes plankton or small fish with these pesticides, the chemicals become more concentrated still (Figure 1). Sufficient levels of these chemicals in an organism can harm the organism. High DDT levels in birds cause a calcium deficiency in their egg shells, so the shells are much thinner than normal. These shells break easily and so fail to protect the chicks inside the egg. Such pollution was responsible for the extinction or drastic decline of the peregrine falcon, California brown pelican, osprey, and bald eagles in the 1960s.

Carson argued that because of this inappropriate use of poisons ("biocides"), we were heading toward a time when our nation's springs would be silent with death. The book startled the nation and in 1972 led to a government ban on the use of DDT. But other pesticides, it is claimed, are still being used that are harming human beings and other species. So the message of *Silent Spring* remains relevant to our world today.

In our second reading, entomologist David Pimentel assesses the progress and problems of pesticide use since *Silent Spring* was written. On the one hand, much progress has been made so that the poisons in pesticides affect humans and wildlife less directly. But unfortunately, pesticide-resistant insects have replaced their less damaging ancestors. Furthermore, pesticides have destroyed some of the natural

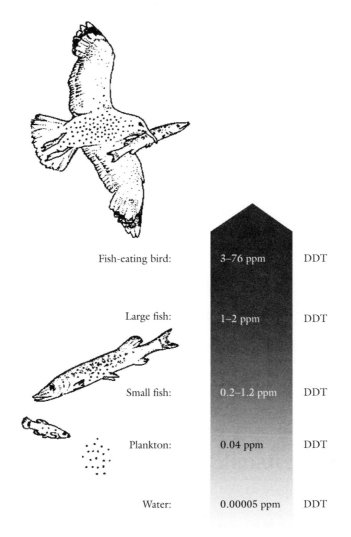

Fish-eating bird: 3–76 ppm DDT

Large fish: 1–2 ppm DDT

Small fish: 0.2–1.2 ppm DDT

Plankton: 0.04 ppm DDT

Water: 0.00005 ppm DDT

FIGURE 1 Biological Magnification. In 1967 fish-eating birds from a Long Island salt marsh estuary contained almost a million times more DDT than could be found in the water. At each step of the food chain, DDT was concentrated, as organisms consumed and absorbed more DDT than they were able to excrete. "PPM" stands for parts per million. (Adapted from W. Keeton, *Biological Science,* 3rd ed. [New York: Norton, 1980].)

enemies of certain pests, so more crops are now lost to insects than they were when *Silent Spring* was written. However, because of better overall agricultural techniques and fertilizers, the total picture is positive.

Our third reading looks at the attempts to combat malaria around the world. DDT remains the most effective method of killing mosquitoes, and in fact for many years there was hope that this miracle chemical would wipe out malaria.

Our fourth reading, "The Blessings of Pesticides" by Dixy Lee Ray and Louis Guzzo, accuses Carson of "lyrical hysteria." They seek to show that the overall effects of pesticides like DDT have been beneficial. They defend the use of PCBs, dioxin, Alar, and DDT, arguing that the benefits far outweigh the problems. Without these insecticides and herbicides, we would not have our present abundance of fresh fruits and vegetables.

59   Silent Spring

RACHEL CARSON

Rachel Carson (1907–1964) was for many years a marine biologist with the U.S. Fish and Wildlife Service. She is the author of *The Sea Around Us, The Edge of the Sea,* and *Silent Spring* (1962) from which the present selection is excerpted: *Silent Spring* is viewed by many as the book that launched the modern environmental movement. Her biographer, Paul Brooks, relates that Carson had noticed that pesticide and herbicide spraying had been followed by "wholesale destruction of wildlife and its habitat, and clearly endangering human life." Unable to interest others in the problem, she began to publish her findings. After several rejections, *The New Yorker* serialized parts of *Silent Spring*. The public suddenly took notice of the message that pesticides were endangering the environment as well as human beings. Her work led to the eventual government banning of DDT in 1972.

In this excerpt from *Silent Spring*, Carson describes a world ruined by chemical pollutants and argues that this is the kind of world we are heading toward with our indiscriminate use of harmful chemicals like DDT.

1. A FABLE FOR TOMORROW

There was once a town in the heart of America where all life seemed to live in harmony with its surroundings. The town lay in the midst of a checkerboard of prosperous farms, with fields of grain and hillsides of orchards where, in spring, white clouds of bloom drifted above the green fields. In autumn, oak and maple and birch set up a blaze of color that flamed and flickered across a backdrop of pines. Then foxes barked in the hills and deer silently crossed the fields, half hidden in the mists of the fall mornings.

Along the roads, laurel, viburnum and alder, great ferns and wildflowers delighted the traveler's eye through much of the year. Even in winter the roadsides were places of beauty, where countless birds came to feed on the berries and on the seed heads of the dried weeds rising above the snow. The countryside was, in fact, famous for the abundance and variety of its bird life, and when the flood of migrants was pouring through in spring and fall people traveled from great distances to observe them. Others came to fish the streams, which flowed clear and cold out of the hills and contained shady pools where trout lay. So it had been from the days many years ago when the first settlers raised their houses, sank their wells, and built their barns.

Then a strange blight crept over the area and everything began to change. Some evil spell had settled on the community: mysterious maladies swept the flocks of chickens; the cattle and sheep sickened and died. Everywhere was a shadow of death. The farmers spoke of much illness among their families. In the town the doctors had become more and more puzzled by new kinds of sickness appearing among their patients. There had been several sudden and unexplained deaths, not only among adults but even among children, who would be stricken suddenly while at play and die within a few hours.

There was a strange stillness. The birds, for example—where had they gone? Many people spoke of them, puzzled and disturbed. The feeding stations in the backyards were deserted. The few birds seen anywhere were moribund; they trembled violently and could not fly. It was a spring without voices. On the mornings that had once throbbed with the dawn chorus of robins, catbirds, doves, jays, wrens, and scores of other bird voices there was now no sound; only silence lay over the fields and woods and marsh.

On the farms the hens brooded, but no chicks hatched. The farmers complained that they were unable to raise any pigs—the litters were small and the young survived only a few days. The apple trees were coming into bloom but no bees droned among the blossoms, so there was no pollination and there would be no fruit.

The roadsides, once so attractive, were now lined with browned and withered vegetation as though swept by fire. These, too, were silent, deserted by all living things. Even the streams were now lifeless. Anglers no longer visited them, for all the fish had died.

In the gutters under the eaves and between the shingles of the roofs, a white granular powder still showed a few patches; some weeks before it had fallen like snow upon the roofs and the lawns, the fields and streams.

No witchcraft, no enemy action had silenced the rebirth of new life in this stricken world. The people had done it themselves.

This town does not actually exist, but it might easily have a thousand counterparts in America or elsewhere in the world. I know of no community that has experienced all the misfortunes I describe. Yet every one of these disasters has actually happened somewhere, and many real communities

have already suffered a substantial number of them. A grim specter has crept upon us almost unnoticed, and this imagined tragedy may easily become a stark reality we all shall know.

What has already silenced the voices of spring in countless towns in America? This book is an attempt to explain.

2. THE OBLIGATION TO ENDURE

The history of life on earth has been a history of interaction between living things and their surroundings. To a large extent, the physical form and the habits of the earth's vegetation and its animal life have been molded by the environment. Considering the whole span of earthly time, the opposite effect, in which life actually modifies its surroundings, has been relatively slight. Only within the moment of time represented by the present century has one species—man—acquired significant power to alter the nature of his world.

During the past quarter century this power has not only increased to one of disturbing magnitude but it has changed in character. The most alarming of all man's assaults upon the environment is the contamination of air, earth, rivers, and sea with dangerous and even lethal materials. This pollution is for the most part irrecoverable, the chain of evil it initiates not only in the world that must support life but in living tissues is for the most part irreversible. In this now universal contamination of the environment, chemicals are the sinister and little-recognized partners of radiation in changing the very nature of the world—the very nature of its life. Strontium 90, released through nuclear explosions into the air, comes to earth in rain or drifts down as fallout, lodges in soil, enters into the grass or corn or wheat grown there, and in time takes up its abode in the bones of a human being, there to remain until his death. Similarly, chemicals sprayed on croplands or forests or gardens lie long in soil, entering into living organisms, passing from one to another in a chain of poisoning and death. Or they pass mysteriously by underground streams until they emerge and, through the alchemy of air and sunlight, combine into new forms that kill vegetation, sicken cattle, and work unknown harm on those who drink from once pure wells. As Albert Schweitzer has said, "Man can hardly even recognize the devils of his own creation."

It took hundreds of millions of years to produce the life that now inhabits the earth—eons of time in which that developing and evolving and diversifying life reached a state of adjustment and balance with its surroundings. The environment, rigorously shaping and directing the life it supported, contained elements that were hostile as well as supporting. Certain rocks gave out dangerous radiation; even within the light of the sun, from which all life draws its energy, there were short-wave radiations with power to injure. Given time—time not in years but in millennia—life adjusts, and a balance has been reached. For time is the essential ingredient; but in the modern world there is no time.

The rapidity of change and the speed with which new situations are created follow the impetuous and heedless pace of man rather than the deliberate pace of nature. Radiation is no longer merely the background radiation of rocks, the bombardment of cosmic rays, the ultraviolet of the sun that have existed before there was any life on earth; radiation is now the unnatural creation of man's tampering with the atom. The chemicals to which life is asked to make its adjustment are no longer merely the calcium and silica and copper and all the rest of the minerals washed out of the rocks and carried in rivers to the sea; they are the synthetic creations of man's inventive mind, brewed in his laboratories, and having no counterparts in nature.

To adjust to these chemicals would require time on the scale that is nature's; it would require not merely the years of a man's life but the life of generations. And even this, were it by some miracle possible, would be futile, for the new chemicals come from our laboratories in an endless stream; almost five hundred annually find their way into actual use in the United States alone. The figure is staggering and its implications are not easily grasped—500 new chemicals to which the bodies of men and animals are required somehow to adapt each year, chemicals totally outside the limits of biologic experience.

Among them are many that are used in man's war against nature. Since the mid-1940's over 200 basic chemicals have been created for use in killing insects, weeds, rodents, and other organisms described in the modern vernacular as "pests"; and they are sold under several thousand different brand names.

These sprays, dusts, and aerosols are now applied almost universally to farms, gardens, forests, and homes—nonselective chemicals that have the power to kill every insect, the "good" and the "bad," to still the song of birds and the leaping of fish in the streams, to coat the leaves with a deadly film, and to linger on in soil—all this though the intended target may be only a few weeds or insects. Can anyone believe it is possible to lay down such a barrage of poisons on the surface of the earth without making it unfit for all life? They should not be called "insecticides," but "biocides."

The whole process of spraying seems caught up in an endless spiral. Since DDT was released for civilian use, a process of escalation has been going on in which ever more toxic materials must be found. This has happened because insects, in a triumphant vindication of Darwin's principle of the survival of the fittest, have evolved super races immune to the particular insecticide used, hence a deadlier one has always to be developed—and then a deadlier one than that. It has happened also because, for reasons to be described later, destructive insects often undergo a "flareback," or resurgence, after spraying, in numbers greater than before. Thus the chemical war is never won, and all life is caught in its violent crossfire.

Along with the possibility of the extinction of mankind by nuclear war, the central problem of our age has therefore become the contamination of man's total environment with such substances of incredible potential for harm—substances that accumulate in the tissues of plants and animals and even penetrate the germ cells to shatter or alter the very material of heredity upon which the shape of the future depends.

Some would-be architects of our future look toward a time when it will be possible to alter the human germ plasm by design. But we may easily be doing so now by inadvertence, for many chemicals, like radiation, bring about gene mutations. It is ironic to think that man might determine his own future by something so seemingly trivial as the choice of an insect spray.

All this has been risked—for what? Future historians may well be amazed by our distorted sense of proportion. How could intelligent beings seek to control a few unwanted species by a method that contaminated the entire environment and brought the threat of disease and death even to their own kind? Yet this is precisely what we have done. We have done it, moreover, for reasons that collapse the moment we examine them. We are told that the enormous and expanding use of pesticides is necessary to maintain farm production. Yet is our real problem not one of *overproduction?* Our farms, despite measures to remove acreages from production and to pay farmers *not* to produce, have yielded such a staggering excess of crops that the American taxpayer in 1962 is paying out more than one billion dollars a year as the total carrying cost of the surplus-food storage program. And is the situation helped when one branch of the Agriculture Department tries to reduce production while another states, as it did in 1958, "It is believed generally that reduction of crop acreages under provisions of the Soil Bank will stimulate interest in use of chemicals to obtain maximum production on the land retained in crops."

All this is not to say there is no insect problem and no need of control. I am saying, rather, that control must be geared to realities, not to mythical situations, and that the methods employed must be such that they do not destroy us along with the insects.

The problem whose attempted solution has brought such a train of disaster in its wake is an accompaniment of our modern way of life. Long before the age of man, insects inhabited the earth—a group of extraordinarily varied and adaptable beings. Over the course of time since man's advent, a small percentage of the more than half a million species of insects have come into conflict with human welfare in two principal ways: as competitors for the food supply and as carriers of human disease.

Disease-carrying insects become important where human beings are crowded together, especially under conditions where sanitation is poor, as in time of natural disaster or war or in situations of extreme poverty and deprivation. Then control of some sort becomes necessary. It is a sobering fact, however, as we shall presently see, that the method of massive chemical control has had only limited success, and also threatens to worsen the very conditions it is intended to curb.

Under primitive agricultural conditions the farmer had few insect problems. These arose with the intensification of agriculture—the devotion of immense acreages to a single crop. Such a system set the stage for explosive increases in specific insect populations. Single-crop farming does not take advantage of the principles by which nature works; it is agriculture as an engineer might conceive it to be. Nature has introduced great variety into the landscape, but man has displayed a passion for simplifying it. Thus he undoes the built-in checks and balances by which nature holds the species within bounds. One important natural check is a limit on the amount of suitable habitat for each species. Obviously then, an insect that lives on wheat can build up its population to much higher levels on a farm devoted to wheat than on one in which wheat is intermingled with other crops to which the insect is not adapted.

The same thing happens in other situations. A generation or more ago, the towns of large areas of the United States lined their streets with the noble elm tree. Now the beauty they hopefully created is threatened with complete destruction as disease sweeps through the elms, carried by a beetle that would have only limited chance to build up large populations and to spread from tree to tree if the elms were only occasional trees in a richly diversified planting.

Another factor in the modern insect problem is one that must be viewed against a background of geologic and human history: the spreading of thousands of different kinds of organisms from their native homes to invade new territories. This worldwide migration has been studied and graphically described by the British ecologist Charles Elton in his recent book *The Ecology of Invasions.* During the Cretaceous Period, some hundred million years ago, flooding seas cut many land bridges between continents and living things found themselves confined in what Elton calls "colossal separate nature reserves." There, isolated from others of their kind, they developed many new species. When some of the land masses were joined again, about 15 million years ago, these species began to move out into new territories—a movement that is not only still in progress but is now receiving considerable assistance from man.

The importation of plants is the primary agent in the modern spread of species, for animals have almost invariably gone along with the plants, quarantine being a comparatively recent and not completely effective innovation. The United States Office of Plant Introduction alone has introduced almost 200,000 species and varieties of plants from all over the world. Nearly half of the 180 or so major insect enemies of plants in the United States are accidental imports from abroad, and most of them have come as hitchhikers on plants.

In new territory, out of reach of the restraining hand of the natural enemies that kept down its numbers in its native land, an invading plant or animal is able to become enormously abundant. Thus it is no accident that our most troublesome insects are introduced species.

These invasions, both the naturally occurring and those dependent on human assistance, are likely to continue indefinitely. Quarantine and massive chemical campaigns are only extremely expensive ways of buying time. We are faced, according to Dr. Elton, "with a life-and-death need not just to find new technological means of suppressing this plant or that animal"; instead we need the basic knowledge of animal populations and their relations to their surroundings that will "promote an even balance and damp down the explosive power of outbreaks and new invasions."

Much of the necessary knowledge is now available but we do not use it. We train ecologists in our universities and even employ them in our government agencies but we seldom take their advice. We allow the chemical death rain to fall as though there were no alternative, whereas in fact there are many, and our ingenuity could soon discover many more if given opportunity.

Have we fallen into a mesmerized state that makes us accept as inevitable that which is inferior or detrimental, as though having lost the will or the vision to demand that which is good? Such thinking, in the words of the ecologist Paul Shepard, "idealizes life with only its head out of

water, inches above the limits of toleration of the corruption of its own environment....Why should we tolerate a diet of weak poisons, a home in insipid surroundings, a circle of acquaintances who are not quite our enemies, the noise of motors with just enough relief to prevent insanity? Who would want to live in a world which is just not quite fatal?"

Yet such a world is pressed upon us. The crusade to create a chemically sterile, insect-free world seems to have engendered a fanatic zeal on the part of many specialists and most of the so-called control agencies. On every hand there is evidence that those engaged in spraying operations exercise a ruthless power. "The regulatory entomologists...function as prosecutor, judge and jury, tax assessor and collector and sheriff to enforce their own orders," said Connecticut entomologist Neely Turner. The most flagrant abuses go unchecked in both state and federal agencies.

It is not my contention that chemical insecticides must never be used. I do contend that we have put poisonous and biologically potent chemicals indiscriminately into the hands of persons largely or wholly ignorant of their potentials for harm. We have subjected enormous numbers of people to contact with these poisons, without their consent and often without their knowledge. If the Bill of Rights contains no guarantee that a citizen shall be secure against lethal poisons distributed either by private individuals or by public officials, it is surely only because our forefathers, despite their considerable wisdom and foresight, could conceive of no such problem.

I contend, furthermore, that we have allowed these chemicals to be used with little or no advance investigation of their effect on soil, water, wildlife, and man himself. Future generations are unlikely to condone our lack of prudent concern for the integrity of the natural world that supports all life.

There is still very limited awareness of the nature of the threat. This is an era of specialists, each of whom sees his own problem and is unaware of or intolerant of the larger frame into which it fits. It is also an era dominated by industry, in which the right to make a dollar at whatever cost is seldom challenged. When the public protests, confronted with some obvious evidence of damaging results of pesticide applications, it is fed little tranquilizing pills of half truth. We urgently need an end to these false assurances, to the sugar coating of unpalatable facts. It is the public that is being asked to assume the risks that the insect controllers calculate. The public must decide whether it wishes to continue on the present road, and it can do so only when in full possession of the facts. In the words of Jean Rostand, "The obligation to endure gives us the right to know."

✿ STUDY QUESTIONS

1. What is the message of *Silent Spring*? How does Carson communicate her message?
2. Why should "insecticides" be called "biocides"? Is Carson persuasive? Has she made her case, or is she engaging in rhetoric?
3. Does Carson believe that we should ban all chemical pesticides?

60   Is Silent Spring Behind Us?

DAVID PIMENTEL

David Pimentel is professor of entomology at Cornell University and the author of *Ecological Effects of Pesticides on Nontarget Species* (1971).

In this selection, Pimentel assesses the progress of the pesticide problem since Rachel Carson's *Silent Spring*. Assembling an array of information, he details the ways in which the situation has improved and in which it has deteriorated.

Is *silent spring* behind us? Have environmental problems associated with pesticide use improved? The answer is a qualified "yes."

Rachel Carson's warning in 1962 generated widespread concern, but many years elapsed before action was taken to halt some of the environmental damage being inflicted by pesticides on our sensitive natural biota. More than 20 years later we still have not solved all the pesticide environmental problems, although some real progress has been made.

FEWER PESTICIDE PROBLEMS DURING THE PAST TWO DECADES

Chlorinated insecticides, such as DDT, dieldrin, and toxaphene, are characterized by their spread and persistence in the environment. The widespread use of chlorinated insecticides from 1945 to 1972 significantly reduced the populations of predatory birds such as eagles, peregrine falcons, and ospreys. Trout, salmon, and other fish populations were seriously reduced, and their flesh was contaminated with pesticide residues. Snakes and other reptile populations, as well as certain insect and other invertebrate populations that were highly sensitive to the chlorinated insecticides were reduced.

Since the restriction on the use of chlorinated insecticides went into effect in 1972, the quantities of these residues in humans and in terrestrial and aquatic ecosystems have slowly declined. From 1970 to 1974, for example, DDT residues in human adipose tissue declined by about one-half in Caucasians who were 0–14 years of age (see Table 1). The declines in other Caucasian age groups and in blacks have not been as great. In agricultural soils, DDT residues have declined by

Reprinted from *Silent Spring Revisited*, ed. G. J. Marco, R. M. Hollingworth, W. Durham (Washington, D.C.: American Chemical Society, 1987) by permission. Notes deleted.

TABLE 1 Total DDT Equivalent Residues in Human Adipose Tissue from General U.S. Population by Race

Age (years)	1970	1971	1972	1973	1974
Caucasians					
0–14	4.16	3.32	2.79	2.59	2.15
15–44	6.89	6.56	6.01	5.71	4.91
45 and above	8.01	7.50	7.00	6.63	6.55
Negroes					
0–14	5.54	7.30		4.68	3.16
15–44	10.88	13.92	11.32	9.97	9.18
45 and above	16.56	19.57	15.91	14.11	11.91

Note: All residues are measured in parts per million lipid weight.

about one-half or from 0.015 parts per million (ppm) in 1968 to 0.007 ppm in 1973. The decline of DDT in soil led to a decline in the amount of DDT running into aquatic ecosystems and resulted in a significant decline in DDT residues found in various fish. For example, in lake trout caught in the Canadian waters of eastern Lake Superior, DDT residues declined from 1.04 ppm in 1971 to only 0.05 ppm in 1975. In aquatic birds that feed on fish, DDT residues also declined. For example, DDT residues in brown pelican eggs collected in South Carolina declined from 0.45 ppm in 1968 to only 0.004 ppm in 1975.

Because DDT and other organochlorine residues in terrestrial ecosystems have declined, various populations of birds, mammals, fishes, and reptiles have started to recover and increase in number. For example, peregrine falcons have been bred in the laboratory and then successfully released in the environment. Limited data do exist on the recoveries of a few animal species, but we do not know the recovery rates for those animal populations that were seriously affected by chlorinated insecticides. Those species with short generation times and high reproductive rates, like insects, have probably recovered best.

New pesticide regulations established in the early 1970s restricted the use of highly persistent pesticides, which include chlorinated insecticides. DDT, toxaphene, and dieldrin, for example, persist in the environment for 10 to 30 years. Two major problems are associated with the use of highly persistent pesticides. Annual applications of chlorinated insecticides add to the total quantity of insecticides in the environment because they degrade slowly. This persistence in the environment increases the chances for the chemicals to move out of the target area into the surrounding environment.

The amount of chlorinated insecticide residues in the environment since most of the chlorinated insecticides were banned has been declining. But because these insecticides are relatively stable, some will persist 30 years or more, and some will be present in the U.S. environment until the end of this century. Fortunately these residues are relatively low, so their effect on most organisms should be minimal.

Persistence of chlorinated insecticides in the environment is only one of the problems created by these chemicals. Their solubility in fats and oils resulted in their accumulation in the fatty tissues of animals, including humans. Thus, bioaccumulation of chlorinated insecticides is a serious environmental problem. Organisms like water fleas and fish, for example, concentrated DDT and other chlorinated insecticides from a dosage of 1 part per billion (ppb) in the environment to levels in their tissues of 100,000 times that. Bioaccumulation continues in the environment with several pesticides (e.g., parathion and 2,4–D), but restricting the use of chlorinated insecticides has reduced this environmental problem.

Movement and magnification of pesticides in the food chain also occurs, but must be carefully documented. Some organisms concentrate pesticides in their bodies 100,000-fold over levels in the ambient environment, and this condition might mistakenly be interpreted as a case of biomagnification in the food chain. Biomagnification in the food chain has been documented with birds like osprey and gulls that feed on fish and has proven to be a serious problem to these predaceous birds.

INCREASED PESTICIDE PROBLEMS DURING THE PAST TWO DECADES

Although restricted use of chlorinated insecticides has relieved some environmental problems, the escalation of pesticide use since 1970 has intensified several other environmental and social problems. Pesticide production and use has increased 2.3-fold since 1970, from around 1.0 to nearly 1.5 billion pounds annually.

Recent research has documented the fact that certain pesticide use may actually increase pest problems. For example, herbicides like 2,4-D used at recommended dosages on corn increased the susceptibility of corn to both insects and plant pathogens. Also the reproduction of certain insects can be stimulated by low dosages of certain insecticides, as occurred in the Colorado potato beetle. For example, sublethal doses of parathion increase egg production by 65%. In addition, most of the insecticides that replaced the chlorinated insecticides are more toxic per unit weight than the chlorinated insecticides.

If one pesticide is more toxic and more biologically active than another, it is not necessarily hazardous to the environment. Risk depends on the dosage and method of application of the specific pesticide. If one pesticide's per-unit weight is more toxic than another, the more toxic chemical is usually applied at a lower dosage that will cause about a 90% kill in the pest population. Thus, a highly toxic material used at a low dosage can achieve about the same mortality as a low-toxicity material. Both high- and low-toxicity pesticides affect pests and nontarget organisms in a similar manner, but the risks to humans handling highly toxic pesticides are far greater than when handling pesticides with a low toxicity. Humans handling highly toxic pesticides like parathion are more likely to be poisoned than those handling pesticides of low toxicity like DDT. If one spills DDT and wipes the pesticide off the skin, no harm is done. However, a similar accident with parathion often leads to poisoning severe enough to require hospitalization.

Human Poisonings

Humans are exposed to pesticides by handling and applying them, by contacting them on treated vegetation, and, to a lesser extent, from their presence in food and water supplies. The number of annual human pesticide poisonings has been estimated at about 45,000; about 3000 of these are sufficiently severe to require hospitalization. The number of annual accidental deaths caused by pesticides is about 50. Accurate data on human pesticide poisonings still are not available 20 years after *Silent Spring*.

Furthermore, detecting the causes of cancer from pesticides is exceedingly difficult because of the long lag time prior to illness and the wide variety of cancer-producing factors that humans are exposed to in their daily activities. No one knows if less human cancer is caused by pesticides now than 20 years ago. Probably less than 1% of human cancers today are caused by pesticides.

We are constantly exposed to pesticides. Despite efforts to keep pesticides out of our food and water, about 50% of U.S. foods sampled by the Food and Drug Administration (FDA) contain detectable levels of pesticides. Improvements in analytical chemical procedures are helping us detect smaller and smaller quantities of pesticides in food and water. These extremely low dosages should have little or no public health effect.

Domestic Animal Poisonings

Because domestic animals are present on farms and near homes where pesticides are used, many of these animals are poisoned. Dogs and cats are most frequently affected because they often wander freely about the home and farm and have ample opportunity to come in contact with pesticides.

A major loss of livestock products (about $3 million annually) occurs when pesticide residues are found in these products. This problem will probably continue as the quantity of pesticides used continues to rise.

Bee Poisonings

Honeybees and wild bees are essential to the pollination of fruits, vegetables, forage crops, and natural plants. Pesticides kill bees, and the losses to agriculture from bee kills and the related reduction of pollination are estimated to be $135 million each year. Evidence suggests that bee poisonings are probably greater now than in 1962 for several reasons. More highly toxic insecticides are being used, and greater quantities of insecticides are being dispensed. In addition, more pesticide is being applied by aircraft, and aircraft applications are employing ultra low volume (ULV) application equipment. ULV applications require smaller droplets for coverage, and this practice tends to increase pesticide drift problems.

Crop Losses

Although pesticides are employed to protect crops from pests, some crops are damaged as a result of pesticidal treatments. Heavy pesticide use damages crops and causes declines in yields because: (1) herbicide residues that remain in the soil after use on one crop injure chemically sensitive crops planted in rotation, (2) certain desired crops cannot be planted in rotation because of knowledge of potential hazard injury, (3) excessive residues of pesticides remain on the harvested crop and result in its destruction or devaluation, (4) pesticides that are applied improperly or under unfavorable environmental conditions result in drift and other problems, and (5) pesticides drift from a treated crop to nearby crops and destroy natural enemies or the crop itself.

Although an accurate estimate of the negative impact of pesticides on crops in agriculture is extremely difficult to obtain, a conservative estimate is about $70 million annually. The problem is probably worse today than in Carson's time because 7 times more pesticide is being applied today than 20 years ago, and its use is more widespread. This statement is especially true of herbicides.

Reduced Populations of Natural Enemies

In undisturbed environments, most insect and mite populations remain at low densities because a wide array of factors, including natural enemies, control them. When insecticides or other pesticides are applied to crops to control one or more pest species, natural enemy populations are sometimes destroyed, and subsequently pest outbreaks occur.

For example, before the synthetic pesticide era (1945) the major pests of cotton in the United States were the boll weevil and cotton leafworm. When extensive insecticide use began in 1945, several other insect and mite species became serious pests. These include the cotton bollworm, tobacco budworm, looper, cotton aphid, and spider mites. In some regions where pesticides are used to control the boll weevil, as many as five additional treatments have to be made to control bollworms and budworms because their natural enemies have been destroyed. This cycle has meant more pesticide use, more natural enemies destroyed, greater pest populations, and more pesticides used.

Pesticide Resistance

In addition to destroying natural enemies, the widespread use of pesticides often causes pest populations to develop resistance and pass it on to their progeny. More than 420 species of insects and mites and several weed species have developed resistance to pesticides. Pesticide resistance in pests results in additional sprays of some pesticides or the use of alternative and often more expensive pesticides. Again the process of pest control escalates the cycle of pesticide use and the development of resistance.

An estimated $133 million worth of added sprays or more expensive pesticides has been employed to deal with the resistance problem annually. This dollar cost, of course, does not include the side effects apparent in the environment and in public health from using more pesticides and more toxic pesticides.

Fishery Losses

Pesticides in treated cropland often run off and move into aquatic ecosystems. Water-soluble pesticides are easily washed into streams and lakes, whereas other pesticides are carried with soil sediments into aquatic ecosystems. Each year several million tons of soil, and with it, pesticides, are washed into streams and lakes.

At present only a small percentage of fish kills are reported because of the procedures used in reporting fish losses. For example, 20% of the reported fish kills give no estimate of the number of dead fish because fish kills often cannot be investigated quickly enough to determine the primary cause. Also, fast-moving waters rapidly dilute all pollutants, including pesticides, and thus make the cause of the kill difficult to determine. Dead fish are washed away or sink to the bottom, so accurate counts are not possible.

Samples of water recently confirmed a steadily decreasing concentration of pesticides found in surface waters and streams from 1964 to 1978. This reduction is apparently related to the replacement of persistent pesticides with less persistent materials. Despite the reduced pesticide residues in streams, an estimated $800,000 or more in fish is lost annually (each fish was calculated to have a value of 40 cents). This estimate of nearly $1 million probably is several times too low and does not confirm that *Silent Spring* is behind us.

Impacts on Wildlife and Microorganisms

Too little information exists to make even a conservative estimate of the populations of vertebrates, invertebrates, and microorganisms that are adversely affected by pesticides. Most invertebrates and microorganisms perform many essential functions to agriculture, forestry, and other segments of human society; such as preventing the accumulation of water, cleaning water or soil of pollutants, recycling vital chemical elements within the ecosystem, and conserving soil and water. An estimated 200,000 species of plants and animals exist in the United States and, at best, we have information on the effects of pesticides on less than 1000 species. Most of these data are based on "safe concentration" tests conducted in the laboratory. This situation confirms that little is known about pesticide effects on the natural environment. At present evaluation must be based on indicator species.

STATUS OF INTEGRATED PEST MANAGEMENT

Integrated pest management (IPM), introduced more than a decade ago, aimed to reduce pesticide use by monitoring pest populations and using pesticides only when necessary as well as augmenting pest control with alternative nonchemical strategies. What happened? IPM has not been successful, and in fact, more of all kinds of pesticides are being used in the United States and throughout the world than ever before.

The reasons for the poor performance of IPM are complex. First, IPM technology, even if it is simply monitoring pest and natural enemy populations, requires a great deal more basic information than scientists now have. This fact signals the pressing need for basic research on the ecology of pests, their natural enemies, and their environment. Also, the use of this basic information to develop control programs is much more sophisticated than routine application of pesticides. Because this technology is more sophisticated, trained manpower is needed, and often the farmer is not trained and cannot be expected to carry out effective IPM programs.

Pesticides are unquestionably simple and quick to use. They have a significant psychological advantage over IPM and especially over nonchemical controls like biological control. Biological controls gradually bring pest populations under control, but do not give the immediate satisfaction of direct kill like pesticides do. However, as research continues and greater ecological knowledge of pests and agroecosystems increases, IPM has the potential to improve pest control.

WHY ARE LOSSES DUE TO PESTS GREATER TODAY THAN 40 YEARS AGO?

Currently, an estimated 37% of all crops is lost annually to pests (13% to insects, 12% to plant pathogens, and 12% to weeds) in spite of the combined use of pesticidal and nonchemical controls. According to a survey of data collected from 1942 to the present, crop losses from weeds declined slightly from 13.8% to 12% because of a combination of improved herbicidal, mechanical, and cultural weed control practices. During the same period, losses from plant pathogens increased slightly from 10.5% to 12%.

On average, however, crop losses due to insects have increased nearly twofold (from 7% to about 13%) from the 1940s to the present in spite of a 10-fold increase in insecticide use. Thus far the impact of this loss in terms of production has been effectively offset through the use of higher yielding varieties and increased use of fertilizers.

The substantial increase in crop losses caused by insects can be accounted for by some of the major changes that have taken place in U.S. agriculture since the 1940s. These changes include

- planting of crop varieties that are increasingly susceptible to insect pests;
- destruction of natural enemies of certain pests, which in turn creates the need for additional pesticide treatments;
- increase in the development of pesticide resistance in insects;
- reduced crop rotations and crop diversity and an increase in the continuous culture of a single crop;
- reduced FDA tolerance and increased cosmetic standards of processors and retailers for fruits and vegetables;
- reduced field sanitation including less destruction of infected fruit and crop residues;
- reduced tillage, leaving more crop remains on the land surface to harbor pests for subsequent crops;

- culturing crops in climatic regions where they are more susceptible to insect attack;
- use of pesticides that alter the physiology of crop plants and make them more susceptible to insect attack.

CONCLUSION

Progress has been made on pesticide problems, but *Silent Spring* is not entirely behind us. Pesticide use continues, and the quantities of pesticides applied grow annually despite support for IPM control. In future decades, as the world population grows rapidly and agricultural production is stretched to meet food needs, we should not forget Carson's warnings.

Pesticides will continue to be effective pest controls, but the challenge now is to find ways to use them judiciously to avoid many of the environmental hazards and human poisonings that exist today. With this goal for research and development we can achieve effective, relatively safe pest control programs.

✎ STUDY QUESTIONS

1. Go over Pimentel's discussion and describe the ways the pesticide problem has improved and how it has deteriorated.

2. Can you suggest ways to improve our situation still further?

61   Combating Malaria

ANNE PLATT MCGINN

Ann McGinn is a senior researcher for the Worldwatch Institute. Malaria kills more people than AIDS each year, yet it has a relatively low profile. A worldwide program to eradicate malaria started in the 1950s, but it was gradually phased out as the deleterious health effects of DDT became known. As the use of DDT went down, malaria started to increase. This article, however, argues against promoting the use of DDT although it would save lives in the short run, suggesting that other public health methods are available.

No other disease in the course of human history has had as profound an effect on human development and well-being as malaria. Africans in

Neolithic times, ancient Chinese and Greeks, Roman emperors, and hundreds of millions of other people—rich and poor—have died from

Reprinted from *State of the World 2003* (W. W. Norton 2003) by permission.

this disease. For centuries, Africa was known as the White Man's Grave because so many Europeans who went there lost their lives to malaria. During the early stages of World War II, General Douglas MacArthur lost more soldiers in the Pacific arena to malaria-carrying mosquitoes than to the Japanese. Today, up to 7,000 people, primarily children in sub-Saharan Africa, die from this disease every day. "There is no doubt that malaria has caused the greatest harm to the greatest number," notes Sir Frank Macfarlane Burnet, a Nobel Prize-winning immunologist.[1]

Malaria is still known as the King of Diseases in Hindi, and with good reason: for each person who dies from malaria itself, another three who have it succumb to more mundane problems such as malnutrition, anemia, or diarrhea. The death toll from malaria and malaria-related illnesses exceeds that of AIDS, which now kills about 3 million people annually.[2]

Despite its unrelenting grip on humanity and the fact that about 2.5 billion people are at risk of contracting the disease, malaria is a relatively low public health priority on the international scene. It rarely makes the news. Between 1975 and 1999, only 4 of the 1,393 new drugs developed worldwide were antimalarials.[3]

The low priority assigned to malaria would be easier to understand if the threat were static. Unfortunately, it is not. Although the geographic range of the disease has contracted substantially since the mid-twentieth century, over a few decades malaria has been gathering strength in several different dimensions. The parasites now resist most anti-malarial drugs, making treatment vastly more complicated and expensive. Poverty, war, and civil strife make it hard for governments to implement preventive and curative measures. Environmental change and human migrations have always exacerbated the potential for this disease to spread, but the global scale of these factors today makes malaria even more difficult to contain.[4]

Like so many problems that are especially acute in developing countries, malaria costs more to ignore than to treat. Malaria costs Africa some $3–12 billion a year, but it could be controlled with available prevention and treatment measures for much less. By 2007, about $2.5 billion a year will be needed to control malaria globally, according to recent estimates. Although such an investment would pay off in human and economic terms, it is not being made. International funding for malaria research currently comes to about $150 million annually, only about 5 percent as much as proposed U.S. government funding for AIDS research in 2003.[5]

The reality is that malaria is a disease of poor countries. If it were a constant threat in industrial countries, the story would be completely different. Although the funding situation looks much better today than it has in years, the newly created Global Fund to Fight AIDS, Tuberculosis & Malaria and the Medicines for Malaria Venture are still vastly underfinanced compared with the scale of the problem. Moreover, money alone is not enough to fight malaria. It will take political will and concerted international cooperation to confront this global threat. And it will take a change in mindset: people must appreciate that human and environmental health are intimately linked on a local and global scale. Adopting this thinking is perhaps the greatest challenge—and the greatest opportunity—for curbing malaria.

A MODERN AND GROWING THREAT

Malaria is predominantly a disease of the tropics (see Figure 2), but as recently as 60 years ago it was found throughout the more temperate regions of southern Europe, North Africa, East Asia, and the southeastern United States. Although the disease's geographic reach has shrunk, more than 40 percent of the world's population now lives in areas where malaria transmission occurs regularly. Elsewhere, people are at risk from the occasional outbreak of "airport malaria," when infected mosquitoes hitchhike on international aircraft and bite people living near airports.[6]

By virtue of ecology, demographics, and climate, sub-Saharan Africa is home to some 90 percent of the world's malaria cases and deaths. In the early 1990s, outpatient clinics throughout the region routinely treated more people for malaria than for any other disease. (The rapid spread of HIV/AIDS has undoubtedly altered

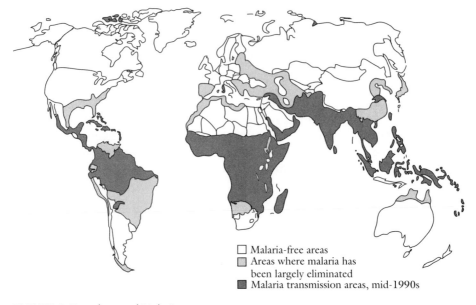

☐ Malaria-free areas
▨ Areas where malaria has
   been largely eliminated
■ Malaria transmission areas, mid-1990s

FIGURE 2 Prevalence of Malaria
Source: Gallup and Sachs

the resources dedicated to malaria, but not the absolute burden from the disease.) The mosquito species most closely adapted to human blood and the most debilitating malaria parasites are common in these areas, taking an especially high toll on pregnant women and the very young. Children may have as many as five different strains of malaria in their bodies at once. In many areas of Africa, the parasite is almost always circulating in people's blood, though not always at levels high enough to be detected by a microscope. Whether or not these parasites cause severe, debilitating disease depends on the person's immunity and genetic susceptibility, among other factors.[7]

In Africa, the typical person infected with malaria lives where a large share of the population gets the disease each year, where infected people are disabled, weakened, or occasionally killed by it, and where people suffer from many bouts of the illness during their lifetimes. In contrast, environmental and human factors and the mosquito species that carry malaria are all quite different in much of Asia and the Americas, manifesting a different disease. (See Table 2). In these areas, people of all ages are affected by malaria, but they rarely die from it.[8]

A severe bout of malaria can trigger prolonged, repeated illness and chronic anemia and can have life-long effects on cognitive development, behavior, and educational achievement. In Kenya, one in 20 children is so anemic from repeated bouts with malaria that in the United States the child would be rushed to a hospital for an emergency blood transfusion. In sub-Saharan Africa, children suffer about 600,000 attacks of cerebral malaria—a severe infection in the brain—each year, with one in five patients dying. Those fortunate enough to survive suffer from a range of neurological difficulties, including learning disorders, behavioral problems, speech disorders, hearing impairment, paralysis, epilepsy, and cerebral palsy.[9]

Pregnant women are especially vulnerable to malaria. In sub-Saharan Africa, as many as 400,000 pregnant women contracted severe anemia induced by malaria in 1995. Up to 10,000 of them died. Pregnant women with malaria are at higher risk of miscarriages, stillbirths, and having babies with low birth weight. In sub-Saharan Africa, malaria is directly responsible for about 30 percent of childhood deaths and is a contributing factor in up to 60 percent of infant and child deaths.[10]

TABLE 2 Malaria in Asia and the Americas Versus Africa

Characteristic	Asia and Americas	Africa
Risk of infection	Very low	Very high
Acquired immunity	No	Yes
Case fatality following infection	High	Low due to immunity
Population at risk of death	All ages	Infants, young children, and women pregnant for first time
History of vector control	Effective	Not widely applied

Source: J.Kevin Baird, "Resurgent Malaria at the Millennium," *Drugs,* April 2000, p. 734.

Where infant and child mortality rates are high, parents often react by having more children. Higher fertility rates, in turn, prompt lower investments in education per child. Moreover, children who are sick with malaria have higher rates of school absenteeism, which increases the chances they will fail classes, possibly repeat a school year, or drop out entirely. In Kenya, primary school students miss up to 11 percent of school days per year because of malaria.[11]

The problem with malaria is not just medical, but also the way it deepens the poverty of people who are just barely scraping along. Many of the 1.2 billion people who live on $1 a day in developing countries are at risk for malaria. In some areas, malaria-stricken households spend up to $40 a month on malaria prevention and treatment. Devoting as much as one third of their total income to fighting this plague, families also suffer a loss of income when a wage-earning member is home sick.[12]

A country that is branded high-risk for malaria is essentially isolated from the global economy. It typically loses potential foreign investment, tourism revenue, and trade because companies, governments, and travelers are reluctant to be in areas where people could contract malaria. This isolation strengthens the cycle of disease and poverty. As noted earlier, malaria costs Africa some $3–12 billion each year, an estimated 1–4 percent of the continent's collective gross domestic products. Over the past 35 years, this one disease has led to nearly $100 billion in losses from Africa's economy, roughly five times as much as the continent received in international development aid in 1999.[13]

After progress against the disease in the 1960s, malaria is now staging a strong global comeback. (See Figure 3). From 1970 to 1997, global mortality rates from malaria (the number of deaths per 100,000 population) increased by 13 percent. Death rates in sub-Saharan Africa jumped by 54 percent during this time. By 1997, Africa's death rate from malaria stood at 165 per 100,000 people, nine times the global average that year. Children are now suffering even more from malaria. From mid-century to the 1990s, mortality rates from all diseases among African children under the age of five declined by 34 percent. But malaria-specific death rates among children have increased 30 percent since the 1960s, offsetting nearly all the gains made in other childhood illnesses.[14]

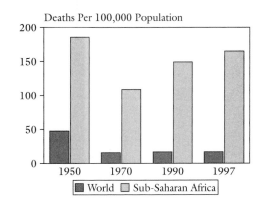

FIGURE 3 Malaria Mortality Rate, 1950, 1970, 1990, and 1997
Source: WHO

Despite our long history with this disease, malaria remains one of the world's leading health threats. Officially, some 300–500 million cases of clinical malaria occur each year, and at least 1 million people die from malaria, but these data are vast underestimates. Because many illnesses and deaths occur at home and are never formally registered, the actual number could be as much as three times as high. Recent studies show, for example, that people in malarious areas suffer at least 1 billion high-fever episodes each year that resemble malaria and should be considered for malaria treatment. If effective control strategies are not introduced, the number of malaria cases could double in the next 20 years, simply due to population growth in areas with high rates of this disease.[15]

Three key factors explain why malaria is getting worse. First, virtually all areas where the disease is endemic (native) have seen drug-resistant strains of the parasite emerge. Chloroquine was the drug of choice for fighting malaria for generations. It was long added to table salt to dose entire populations and prevent malaria. But overuse and misuse have promoted the survival of drug-resistant strains. Now chloroquine is useless in virtually all malaria-ridden areas of the world—more than 100 countries.[16]

The loss of chloroquine is especially great because it is cheaper and easier to administer than other anti-malarial drugs. It is also fast-acting: patients normally feel better within 24 hours. These characteristics contributed to both its usefulness and, more recently, its downfall. *Plasmodium falciparum,* the deadliest of the four malaria parasites, has become even tougher and more expensive to treat after decades of exposure to chloroquine and other anti-malarial drugs. Consequently, death rates are rising.[17]

Replacement drugs are suffering a similar fate. In parts of Southeast Asia and East Africa, for example, multi-drug-resistant parasites have already developed from the heavy use of the second-line anti-malarial drug, sulfadoxine/pyrimethamine. And in northwestern Thailand, local parasites are becoming resistant to every known anti-malarial drug.[18]

While the available medical arsenal shrinks, some scientists have concentrated on genetic blueprints to find clues for new therapeutic agents. In 2002, a group of international scientists decoded the genome sequences for the most dangerous malaria parasite and mosquito. Although such information will be useful for developing new anti-malarial medicines and narrowing the search for a reliable vaccine, widespread application of such tools is still years away.[19]

Second, malaria is gaining ground because of environmental and social changes. The disease occurs where people are poor and the environmental conditions are right. Irrigation, dam building, deforestation, and other activities can boost the chances that malaria will spread, particularly in the world's "malaria belt." In countries as varied as Afghanistan and Sierra Leone, the lack of basic sanitation and medicines in areas disrupted by war has helped spread the disease, as has the interruption of health coverage in places like North and South Korea and Tajikistan. Even though malaria is regarded as predominantly a rural disease, people living in rapidly expanding tropical cities are not immune to its spread, especially as some mosquitoes now show signs of adapting to the urban landscape.[20]

To make matters worse, climatic instability may allow malaria parasites and mosquitoes to survive in places that have been free of them for years. By 2050, for example, some experts predict a return of malaria to the southern United States, southern Brazil, western China, and regions across Central Asia due to climate change.[21]

The third reason for the global resurgence of malaria is the scant use of safe, effective, and affordable means to control the mosquito that carries the disease. Given the absence of a reliable way to kill the parasite, controlling, repelling, or simply killing mosquitoes that bear it—a practice known as vector control—remains fundamental to controlling malaria today. This has led to the use of toxic insecticides, including one of the most notorious—DDT. (See Box 1.)[22]

While the use of DDT may seem necessary, especially in light of the global resurgence of malaria, there are good reasons for thinking that progress against the disease may allow us to minimize this approach. Insecticide-treated bednets, indoor spraying of less persistent insecticides,

BOX 1 The Environmental and Health Impacts of DDT

DDT (dichlorodiphenyl trichloroethane) is a persistent organic pollutant—one of a group of synthetic compounds that share four common properties: they are toxic, they bioaccumulate in the food chain, they persist in the environment, and they have a high potential to travel long distances from their source. Animals and people bioaccumulate DDT in their bodies, primarily from the food they eat. As the chemicals move up the food chain, each link or species takes up the previous link's exposure, adding it to their own and magnifying the effects. Arctic cod and turbot, for example, have up to 1,000 times higher concentrations of DDT per gram of fat than the zooplankton they consume. One of the most commonly detected synthetic chemicals in humans is DDE—a highly persistent breakdown product of DDT.

Most of the problems with DDT relate to environmental contamination and its effects on animals. In 1999, the U.S. National Academy of Sciences stated that "it is now well-established that the DDT metabolite, DDE...causes eggshell thinning" and that the bald eagle population in the United States declined "primarily because of exposure to DDT and its metabolites."

In its 2000 toxicological profile of DDT and DDE, the U.S. Agency for Toxic Substances and Disease Registry (ATSDR) cited studies of the hormone-disrupting impacts of DDT and DDE in wildlife and laboratory animals. It noted that "key endocrine processes can be profoundly affected by exposure to extremely small amounts of active chemicals during critical windows of embryonic, fetal, and neonatal development" ATSDR also noted that these studies raise concerns about human health effects.

DDT has already been linked to human disorders. In a 2001 study, researchers focused on samples of mothers' blood that had been stored when babies were born during the 1950s and 1960s. They used new chemical techniques to measure DDE levels, and then looked at the relationship between these and the likelihood of premature birth. They found a strong association. The higher the contamination level, the more likely a preterm birth was. They also showed that contamination was linked to the baby's size, with babies more likely to be small for their gestational age if their mothers had higher DDE levels. Premature babies not only have a higher death rate, they are also more likely to suffer from neurodevelopmental handicaps, chronic respiratory problems, and infections. The authors warn that "in tropical countries, where DDT is used for malaria control, blood concentrations of DDE can greatly exceed the range observed" in the sample they studied.

Workers in DDT production facilities and malaria control programs have also developed chronic health effects. For example, retired DDT-exposed malaria control workers in Costa Rica performed, on average, up to 20 percent worse on a series of tests than a control group of retired drivers and guards. The longer the malaria control worker had been on the job, the greater the decline in their performance. Their reaction times were slower, they had lower verbal attention and visual motor skills, and they showed more problems with dexterity and sequencing. They also experienced more psychiatric and neuropsychological symptoms than the control group.

Source: See endnote 22.

and carefully designed environmental measures to control larval breeding, for example, all help reduce the burden of malaria. Despite their proven benefits, these measures are not widely applied in regions that desperately need protection. Ensuring that these and other tested tools are available and adopted and that outside funding is secured to purchase and distribute them is a central challenge to combating malaria in the world's poorest regions.

THE BIOLOGY AND EVOLUTION OF THE DISEASE

Malaria is principally a vector-borne disease (one carried by an intermediary, in this case a mosquito) that is caused by four protozoan parasites in the genus *Plasmodium*. The malaria parasite is a highly complex organism that goes through four distinct stages in its lifecycle that cannot be completed without access to both a mosquito

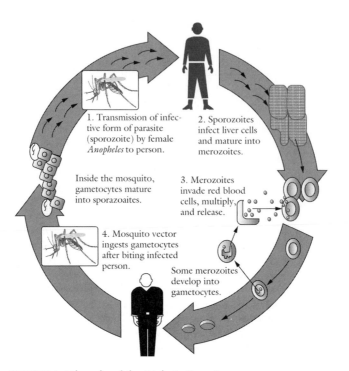

1. Transmission of infective form of parasite (sporozoite) by female *Anopheles* to person.

2. Sporozoites infect liver cells and mature into merozoites.

Inside the mosquito, gametocytes mature into sporazoaites.

3. Merozoites invade red blood cells, multiply, and release.

4. Mosquito vector ingests gametocytes after biting infected person.

Some merozoites develop into gametocytes.

FIGURE 4 Lifecycle of the Malaria Parasite

and a mammal. These parasites are spread exclusively by certain mosquitoes belonging to the genus *Anopheles*. Understanding the interplay between parasite, vector, human host, and environment is important to appreciating why it is so difficult to control the various forms of malaria. Indeed, malaria is not a single disease, but a disease complex, a host of illnesses that are related by ecology.[23]

A malaria infection begins with a single mosquito bite. (See Figure 4). A female *Anopheles* mosquito needs blood from a human (or other mammal) to make eggs. She repeatedly probes the skin with her mouthpiece, basically a pair of sharp, needle-like tubes. With each exploratory prick, one tube sends a mix of anti-coagulation compounds and other chemicals into the bloodstream, ensuring a steady supply of human blood up into her body. When she hits a capillary, the other tube sucks up a micro-liter or two of blood, which triples the mosquito's body weight. Sometimes her saliva contains thousands of thread-like sporozoites, the infective form of malaria parasite. Only about 1 percent of a

mosquito's sporozoites are deposited with each meal. Within minutes of being transferred from mosquito to person, the sporozoites move from the bloodstream to the liver, well before the body can muster an effective defense.[24]

In the second stage of the parasite's life, sporozoites multiply asexually in the liver. Each one matures into tens of thousands of merozoites, a round form of the parasite, that are contained in a schizont, which is like a hard capsule. In about a week's time, the schizonts rupture, spewing forth millions of merozoites that invade the body's red blood cells, where they feed on the oxygen-carrying hemoglobin.[25]

At this stage, some 7–20 days after the initial mosquito bite, a person will feel the first signs of infection: high fever, chills, and profuse sweating. These symptoms come in waves as the merozoites continue to reproduce in cycles. By the time the body's immune system responds to these symptoms, the process of amplification is well under way. The parasite load increases 20-fold every 48 hours. As the parasite infects red blood cells, it starves the brain and other tissues of oxygen and blood, triggering severe anemia, coma, and sometimes death.[26]

Some of the parasites in red blood cells do not stay in the body, however. Instead, they develop into a sexual, egg-like form known as a gametocyte. Gametocytes are taken up by other mosquitoes when they bite an infected person, prompting the fourth and final stage in the life of the malaria parasite. Once inside *Anopheles*, gametocytes spend about 9–12 days maturing into another crop of infective sporozoites. These are then transmitted to other victims via a mosquito bite, continuing the cycle of disease.[27]

Of the roughly 380 mosquito species in the genus *Anopheles*, about 60 are able to transmit malaria in people. Many of these same species are widespread throughout the tropics and warm temperate zones and are very efficient at spreading the disease. Species in the *An. gamebiae* complex are the most important vectors in Africa.[28]

Malaria has an extremely high potential for transmission, as is apparent from a measurement that epidemiologists call the basic reproduction number (BRN). The BRN indicates, on average, how many new cases a single infected person is likely to cause. For example, among the diseases caused by pathogens that travel directly from person to person without an intermediary like a mosquito, measles is one of the most contagious. The BRN for measles is 12–14, meaning that someone with measles is likely to infect about a dozen other people. (There is an inherent limit in this process: as a pathogen spreads through any particular area, it will encounter fewer and fewer susceptible people who are not already sick, and the outbreak will eventually subside.) HIV/AIDS is on the other end of the scale: it is deadly, but it moves through a population slowly. On average, each AIDS patient infects one other person. Its BRN is just above one, the minimum necessary for the pathogen's survival.[29]

With malaria, the BRN varies considerably but is generally higher in sub-Saharan Africa than elsewhere. Malaria can have a BRN as high as 100: conceivably, an infected person can be bitten by more than 100 mosquitoes in one night, each of which can become infected and able to transmit the infection.[30]

To comprehend why malaria has such a strong hold on sub-Saharan Africa, it helps to understand the evolution of the disease. Before the introduction of agriculture, people contracted malaria on the continent but never in large numbers. Movement to and from areas with mosquitoes offered some relief for victims. Then people began to settle down and clear areas of the rainforest to grow yams and other root crops. These islands of cultivation within forests became ideal breeding grounds for mosquitoes. They were sunlit and had clean water. With a semi-permanent population of people to feed on, the mosquito vectors developed a strong preference for human blood. As the landscape changed and human population increased, malaria became more entrenched. Mosquitoes that fed almost exclusively on people rather than cattle, birds or primates emerged as the primary vectors.[31]

Africa is home to the mosquito that is best suited to spreading malaria, one of the most deadly and efficient malaria vectors, *An. gambiae*. Unlike other mosquitoes, *An. gambiae* have a high affinity for human blood and bite people rather than animals 95 percent of the time. Thus, they can maintain disease transmission at extremely low mosquito population densities. These efficient vectors encouraged the emergence of a more virulent species of the malaria parasite, *P. falciparum*. During epidemic bursts of disease, a fast-growing, more aggressive parasite had an advantage over slower-growing ones. It could complete development to disease faster and take advantage of frequent transmission.[32]

Additional evidence of malaria's long and deadly history in Africa comes from the persistence of the sickle-cell trait, a defective form of hemoglobin in the blood. People living throughout the tropics may have this genetic mutation because it confers partial immunity to the most lethal forms of malaria. But people who live in areas of highly endemic malaria, such as tropical sub-Saharan Africa, India, and the Middle East, are most likely to have it. Experts believe that sickle-cell hemoglobin causes red blood cells to "sickle" (collapse) when oxygen in the blood-stream is low.[33]

In the absence of sickle-cell hemoglobin, a person experiences the worst effects of malaria.

If a child inherits the sickle-cell hemoglobin gene from one parent and a normal hemoglobin gene from the other, the child gains the advantage of a partial genetic defense: a single dose of the gene does not prevent the child from acquiring malaria infections, but it fends off the worst effects and virtually guarantees the survival of the child, despite numerous bouts with the disease. If a child inherits the gene from both parents, however, he or she will die from sickle-cell anemia before reaching reproductive age. The evolution of this trait underscores the fact that malaria was an ancient killer of immense proportions. (Other, milder forms of blood diseases, such as thalassemia, persist in populations of southern Europe and Asia, conferring some protection against the less virulent forms of malaria found in those areas.)[34]

Malaria transmission in Africa is highly variable. Depending on where people live in endemic areas of Africa, they receive anywhere from 1 to 1,000 infective bites per person a year. In contrast, people in Southeast Asia and South America generally suffer 1 infective mosquito bite at most each year. The average Tanzanian gets bitten more each night than the average Thai or Vietnamese does in a year because the vector and humans are so closely associated. (Not every bite by an infected mosquito results in malaria; the process has about a 10 percent success rate.) The less efficient vectors that are common in Asia and the Americas mean that the risk of infection is low and infrequent for people. But the infections that do happen can take a stiff toll, quickly progressing to severe forms of disease that are sometimes life-threatening.[35]

In Africa, frequent infectious mosquito bites manifest a very different picture of disease and health. In much of sub-Saharan Africa, malaria is a chronic infection that causes recurring bouts of devastating fever, life-draining anemia, and general weakening of the body. But older children who manage to survive repeated cases of malaria early in life acquire partial immunity. Unlike immunity to other diseases, which confers total protection from illness, people who are immune to malaria are protected only from the worst effects of the disease; they remain susceptible to the illness throughout life and will lose this

protection if infections stop recurring. Children are especially vulnerable, as their bodies have not had time to develop even this partial immunity. Most children in this area battle several bouts of the illness each year and become weaker, until they finally succumb to it.[36]

The course of infection has a direct bearing on control measures. For example, children who are exposed to fewer infective bites experience a lower level of parasites in their blood. Even in the absence of complete elimination, effective, locally tailored control efforts can save many lives and reduce the burden of disease. The critical point is that in highly endemic areas such efforts need to be maintained over the long term to have any hope of keeping the ever-evolving *Anopheles* and malaria parasite in check.[37]

THE FALSE PROMISE OF ERADICATION

"Malaria" comes from the Italian term "malaria." For centuries, European physicians had attributed the disease to "bad air." Apart from a tradition of associating bad air with swamps—a useful prejudice, given the amount of mosquito habitat there—early medicine was largely ineffective against the disease. It wasn't until the mid-1890s that scientists identified the parasites and mosquitoes that transmit malaria and began to understand how the disease works.[38]

These discoveries had an immediate impact. The U.S. administration of Theodore Roosevelt recognized malaria and yellow fever (another mosquito-borne disease) as perhaps the most serious obstacles to the construction of the Panama Canal. (An earlier and unsuccessful French attempt to build the canal is estimated to have lost between 10,000 and 20,000 workers to disease.) So American workers put up screens, filled in swamps, dug ditches, poured oil into standing water to suffocate air-breathing larvae, and swatted adult mosquitoes. This intensive effort worked: the incidence of malaria declined. On average, just 2 percent of Americans were hospitalized with malaria, compared with 30 percent of workers during the French project. Malaria could be suppressed, it turned out, with a great deal of mosquito netting and by eliminating as much mosquito habitat as possible. But such elaborate and labor-intensive campaigns were difficult and costly to sustain, especially in poor and often remote areas of the tropics.[39]

That is why DDT proved so appealing. In 1939, Swiss chemist Paul Müller discovered that dichlorodiphenyl trichloroethane was an extremely potent pesticide. First used in World War II as a delousing agent, DDT was later used to kill malaria-carrying mosquitoes before Allied soldiers moved through southern Europe, North Africa, and Asia. In 1948, Müller won a Nobel Prize for his work, and DDT was hailed as a miracle chemical. For the control of mosquito-borne diseases, it was seen as a panacea.[40]

A decade later, DDT had inspired another kind of war—a global assault on malaria. For the first time, malaria eradication seemed not only feasible but imminent. With DDT in hand, the recently formed World Health Organization (WHO) launched a global program to eliminate malaria. In 1957, more than 66 nations enlisted in the cause. Funding for DDT factories was donated to poor countries, and production of the insecticide climbed, as did distribution of anti-malarial medicine, chloroquine.[41]

The goal of the global program was not to kill every single mosquito but to reduce the daily rate of survival for mosquitoes and thereby reduce the frequency of bites and transmission. By suppressing the mosquitoes, human populations were relieved of new infections and had an opportunity to cleanse their bodies of the parasite in circulation. Once a local human population was cleared of infection, mosquitoes could go about biting people without picking up the parasite—at least, that was the theory.[42]

Rather than spraying DDT outdoors, as in the 1940s, mosquito control experts fine-tuned their approach. They used DDT selectively indoors. After mosquitoes take their blood meal, they usually rest in the vicinity, on a wall inside a house. If those walls were coated with a thin film of insecticide, the mosquitoes would absorb a lethal dose. (DDT is also known to have a repellent effect, prompting mosquitoes to quickly flee outdoors or avoid biting people indoors at all.) Unlike other insecticides that can lose their

potency in a matter of days, DDT is long-lasting: one dousing could protect a family for six months. In the early euphoria, DDT did not seem to cause any harm to other species. And it was cheap.[43]

Relying heavily on DDT, the global program saved millions of lives. The islands of Taiwan, Jamaica, and Sardinia were soon declared malaria-free. Tropical countries such as Sri Lanka and India witnessed stunning declines in the incidence of malaria. Temperate countries rooted it out entirely. By 1961, malaria had been eliminated or dramatically reduced in 37 countries.[44]

But the strategy relied on a centralized approach that proved difficult to maintain over time. Logistical problems were hard to overcome, and local variations in mosquito behavior and patterns of disease transmission were often ignored. At the same time, mosquitoes evolved resistance to the pesticide. This was reported as early as 1948, only one year into a major public health campaign to use DDT (an effort to suppress mosquitoes and flies in Greece). This knowledge was, in large part, why the global campaign became so urgent. Time was of the essence, given the estimated three years that was needed to clear the protozoan from human circulation and the four to seven years it seemed to take mosquitoes to become resistant to DDT.[45]

By the late 1960s, the urgent campaign ground to a halt. The political landscape had shifted considerably with respect to DDT, thanks in large part to Rachel Carson's influential book, *Silent Spring,* which was published in 1962. No longer were people willing to accept protection for human health at such a high ecological cost. Thus in spite of initial successes, the global program was abandoned in 1969. That year, WHO significantly revised its strategy from malaria eradication to control. While control was a far more realistic and achievable goal, it had far less appeal to countries and health agencies with limited financial resources and many other pressing health concerns. Eradication had been sold as a time-limited opportunity; controlling malaria required maintaining a solid effort almost indefinitely.[46]

In many ways, the global program of the 1960s has made the modern malaria problem far worse. It introduced the dynamics of insecticide and drug resistance, it encouraged some

TABLE 3 Level and Changes in Malaria Prevalence Between 1965 and 1994, by Climate Zone

Predominant Climate	Malaria Index 1965[1]	Average Change, 1965–94
Temperate	0.2	−0.2
Desert	27.8	−8.8
Subtropical	61.7	−5.0
Tropical	64.9	+0.5

[1]Index ranges from 0 to 100.

Source: John Luke Gallup and Jeffrey D. Sachs, "The Economic Burden of Malaria," *American Journal of Tropical Medicine & Hygiene*, January/February 2001 (supp.). p. 88.

vectors to change their behavior, it virtually eliminated malariology as a specialty, it created a void in interest and funding for malaria control that is only now turning around, and it engendered the idea of DDT as a first resort against mosquitoes. While most countries experienced a decline in the prevalence of malaria between 1965 and 1994, tropical countries actually registered an increase. (See Table 3.)[47]

ENVIRONMENTAL AND SOCIAL CHANGES ALTER THE BALANCE

During the mid-twentieth century, indoor spraying with DDT helped eradicate *An. darlingi* in Guyana and, along with it, the fear of malaria. Aided by disease control measures, Guyanese society slowly developed. Trade improved and the economy began to grow. Horses, donkeys, oxen, and other work animals were replaced by motorized vehicles. But as the society gradually modernized, malaria came back.[48]

Officials responded by spraying DDT, as it had worked in earlier campaigns. It did not work this time, however, because the primary vector was a different species—one that bit people outdoors. *An aquasalis* had always been present in Guyana, but it had never been a serious problem because it fed on animals. Once the vectors lost their primary source of food, the mosquitoes adapted to human blood and started spreading the infection to city-dwellers. By this time people had lost their previous immunity, so the health risks were much greater.[49]

Thus some of the projects and trends that have been central to rural economic development ironically can make malaria a more formidable foe. Human-induced environmental changes create new habitat areas for mosquitoes to breed in and expand their range, and the overuse of antimalarial drugs can affect the severity of the disease. When irrigation is introduced, when dams or roads are built, or when certain crops are cultivated, mosquitoes are often not far behind.[50]

There is also a direct human element: such changes attract people looking for work. Often these workers and their families have little or no previous exposure to malaria and are susceptible to the full-blown disease. Migrating human populations carry the malaria parasite with them to new areas and inadvertently infect others. Interactions between mosquitoes, people, and the environment determine the opportunities for *Anopheles* to develop more lethal fangs, so to speak, because more infective mosquito bites translate into more new cases of human disease. But as Guyana's experience demonstrates, the consequences of a changing environment are often difficult to predict.[51]

In Sri Lanka, for example, the Mahawehli River project of the late 1970s brought water to seasonally dry areas, increasing the amount of land under cultivation. But malaria became prevalent again in areas where it had been nearly eradicated. In Ethiopia's northern province of Tigray, children living near recently constructed small dams showed a sevenfold increase in malaria incidence compared with children living in villages far from the dams. Moreover, Ethiopian researchers found that the dams strengthened malaria's grip, extending its season from a brief period just after the rains to a nearly year-round occurrence.[52]

Between 1974 and 1991, Brazil witnessed a 10-fold increase in malaria cases, largely due to logging in the Amazon. Expansion into frontier areas brought non-immune, susceptible people into newly disrupted forest areas. Health services were largely nonexistent. The people were poor and often had little education or access to political power. Housing consisted of temporary shelters made from palm fronds, so indoor spraying was out of the question. The vector, *An. darlingi*, thrived in the newly exposed forest fringe areas because it prefers partial shade and deep, sunlit water to the rainforest, where there is too little sunlight and the water is too acidic for its tastes. Breeding on the forest edge also gave this mosquito easy access to human blood.[53]

Gold mining in the Amazon also contributed to the spread of malaria. Miners use mercury to extract the gold from ore, washing the mix in pits filled with water. Once the pits are abandoned, they collect rainwater that is less acidic than streams in the region and therefore attractive to *An. darlingi*.[54]

In addition to changes in the landscape, mosquitoes are also sensitive to their microenvironment. Malaria patterns often vary from one part of a village to another, depending on the mosquito species, sources of standing water, and characteristics of the built environment, for example. Throughout rural Africa, mud bricks are the most common choice of housing materials. A mixture of water and easily crumbled soil provides an almost endless source of construction material and malaria-bearing mosquitoes. The problem is that mud brick houses require frequent replastering and repair, so people create pits adjacent to or very close to their home for when they need more construction materials. Because the pits are so close to people, the source of *Anopheles'* fuel for reproduction, they are quickly inhabited by mosquito larvae. Based on field research in Ethiopia and Namibia, scientists have recently shown that windblown pollen from nearby corn fields settles in these pits and serves as a ready source of food for mosquito larvae.[55]

Changes in water flow can limit the spread of malaria by altering or removing larval habitats. In Karnataka, India, for example, *An. fluviatilis* (one of six epidemiologically important vectors in India) disappeared as coffee plantations, deforestation, and dams virtually eliminated the streams where this species bred. During the 1950s in the southeastern United States, the Tennessee Valley Authority (TVA) built a series of dams and flood control projects. Conscious of the need to control *Anopheles* larvae, engineers constructed the sides of the artificial canals with carefully angled slopes, so periodic changes in water levels would leave the mosquitoes high and dry.[56]

Urban areas have long been free from endemic malaria because of better housing, access to medical treatment, and water pollution. *Anopheles* typically do not lay their eggs in water bodies that are contaminated with high organic content or chemical pollution. They usually prefer clean, still or slowly moving fresh water, not the polluted water found in crowded urban areas. A notable exception is *An. stephensi,* which is endemic in some cities in South Asia, where it lays its eggs in household water storage tanks and cement rooftop cisterns. However, the urban landscape is changing in favor of other mosquitoes. In Accra, Ghana, for instance, researchers have found *An. gambiae* breeding in household water containers, a sign that these species can adapt to the urban environment.[57]

Recent evidence also shows that malaria is gaining ground in densely populated settlements surrounding urban areas in Africa. People migrating from rural areas to the edges of cities typically retain rural activities and habits for a time, such as household gardens, irrigation, and informal housing materials. These bring with them the pattern of rural transmission, and disease consequently spreads. Over time, as these areas become more settled, they become less susceptible to local malaria transmission because the water is usually too polluted to support *Anopheles*.[58]

As in Guyana, environmental factors also interact with economic circumstances in unpredictable ways. This was the case in several farming communities in Tanzania. Scientists who analyzed entomological data predicted that the incidence of malaria would be higher in villages where people grew rice and where paddies provided breeding grounds with higher rates of vector survival and density than where farmers grew sugarcane or savannah crops. What these researchers initially failed to appreciate, however, is that the villagers growing rice had more income and were able to buy bednets and arm themselves with anti-malarial drugs, so they had less exposure to malaria.[59]

The growing problem of drug resistance is complicating the malaria picture worldwide even further. This is especially true in Africa. Chloroquine-resistant strains of *P. falciparum* first appeared in East Africa in 1978. Within 10 years, authorities reported chloroquine resistance in virtually every country in sub-Saharan Africa. The effects of this development were immediate. In the 1980s, several African countries showed a two- to three-fold increase in deaths and hospital admissions for severe malaria, a trend that coincided with the spread of chloroquine resistance. Health officials in Kinshasa reported that not only were children getting more severe forms of the disease and dying more frequently, but the incidence of related health problems, especially anemia and HIV/AIDS, was higher too. (Children who have severe anemia require frequent blood transfusions, which raises the risks of HIV transmission.) Today, hundreds of thousands of African children succumb to malaria each year because *P. falciparum* is no longer susceptible to chloroquine.[60]

Despite these failures, most African countries have yet to change their drug policies. Chloroquine is still widely used as a first step in treating malaria because most people cannot afford other drugs, which can cost 5–10 times more per dose, because it is widely available without a prescription, and because decades of chloroquine use have made it difficult to phase in alternatives. Even if such drugs were readily available, parasites in some areas already resist them. Complicating the situation is the fact that many patients who receive chloroquine become asymptomatic: they show no outward signs of illness, but they still have drug-resistant strains of the parasite circulating in their blood. These people become a reservoir of the more complicated form of the disease.[61]

MEXICO'S APPROACH

Communities struggling to counteract the effects of malaria, whether from environmental, economic, or social changes, may benefit from an approach to disease control that Mexico has successfully developed. It is based on community involvement, widespread prevention, locally tailored treatments, and use of the least toxic option first.

As recently as the mid-twentieth century, malaria was one of the top 10 causes of death in Mexico; roughly 2.4 million people were infected annually. The country began an indoor spraying program with DDT in the late 1940s, well before

the WHO effort was launched. In 1955, Mexico expanded the program into a National Eradication Campaign, which continued through the early 1960s. The campaign did not achieve its ostensible goal, but it did push the number of cases down to about 20,000 annually, a level that remained relatively constant throughout the 1970s. The campaign also largely eliminated the most dangerous species of the parasite, *P. falciparum.*[62]

By 2000, Mexico had achieved its goal of phasing out DDT seven years ahead of schedule.

Mexico could well have continued using DDT had the chemical not become a major trade liability. In 1972, the United States banned DDT and began to reject shipments of imported Mexican produce that were contaminated with the chemical. At first, the Mexican response was confined largely to farmers in the northern part of the country. They were heavily dependent on exports, so they switched to other pesticides to get their crops into the United States. Farther south, farmers relied on crops for local consumption rather than for export income, so DDT remained in use as an agricultural pesticide through the mid-1980s.[63]

But by the early 1990s, DDT had become a domestic issue as well. The Mexican public was growing increasingly uneasy about the high levels of DDE (a breakdown product of DDT) in the milk of nursing mothers. These domestic concerns reinforced the trade issue: in the 1994 North American Free Trade Agreement, Mexico, the United States, and Canada agreed to develop a regional approach to persistent pollutants. DDT became the first order of business; in 1997, Mexico agreed to a 10-year plan to phase out the pesticide entirely.[64]

In the meantime, however, malaria was re-emerging. In the early 1980s, annual infections rose to 133,000. The timing was unfortunate: a severe economic recession cut into production and supplies of DDT; financial resources for malaria control evaporated. Another outbreak occurred in 1988. The following year the federal government delegated malaria control to the states, which revived the rural networks set up decades ago under the eradication program. Over the next eight years, certified community volunteers collected blood samples, which were sent to regional laboratories for testing. The presence of parasites triggered visits from medical teams and from mosquito control personnel. DDT was sprayed on the inside walls of houses to kill adult mosquitoes; outside, less persistent insecticides were sprayed on standing water to kill larvae.[65]

Because it was highly targeted and sensitive to environmental conditions, this new mosquito control strategy was a vast improvement over the old, broadcast spraying techniques. But as concerns about pesticides spread, mosquito control came under greater scrutiny. The pesticide teams were called "cat killers" because so many neighborhood cats died after their visits. In some areas, poor people complained that the teams washed their equipment in streams, killing the fish they depended on for food. And in the state of Oaxaca, organic farmers and environmentalists categorically opposed the use of DDT.[66]

As a result of this public pressure, reliance on DDT diminished greatly by the mid-1990s, replaced by less persistent pyrethroid pesticides. (Indoors, deltamethrin was used instead of DDT; outdoors, permethrin replaced malathion.) These were incorporated into an "integrated vector management" approach that includes the occasional application of pyrethroids but no DDT. Local officials now reserve indoor repellant spraying for areas where the need has been carefully determined. They use a combination of remote sensing maps, geographic information systems, and on-the-ground sampling to pinpoint areas to target spraying and larvicides. Other environmental management techniques, such as water removal and personal protection measures, are also used. Mosquito habitat is reduced without using pesticides at all, by removing algae that serves as a breeding site and source of food for some mosquitoes, for instance.[67]

Since the 1988 outbreak, malaria has been largely confined to several "hotspots" on the Pacific coast of Mexico—poor parts of the states

of Oaxaca and Chiapas. These areas are common destinations for immigrants from Central America. Blood screening and mosquito control programs are now largely limited to these areas.[68]

Mexico's approach has worked. In 2000, the only Mexican manufacturer of DDT, Tekchem, halted all production. Mexico had achieved its goal of phasing out DDT seven years ahead of schedule. And despite the 1988 outbreak, no one is known to have died from locally acquired malaria in Mexico since 1982.[69]

Mexico's experience offers several lessons for malaria control efforts in other parts of the world. Environmental management is a central focus of the program, with several interventions acting at once (such as different combinations of larvicides, vegetation clearance, drainage of standing water, house screening, and surveillance of mosquito larvae). The malaria control strategies rely on a wide range of expertise, including people knowledgeable about entomology, hydrology, epidemiology, ecology, and clinical aspects of malaria. Community participation and local knowledge about malaria and the environmental impacts of control measures are highly valued and help tailor solutions. Last, the program has been fine-tuned over a number of years, adjusting to changing demographics, public perceptions, and scientific knowledge.[70]

THE CHALLENGE IN AFRICA

In December 2000, representatives of governments, environmental groups, and industry associations from more than 100 countries met in Johannesburg, South Africa, for the final round of negotiations on the Stockholm Convention on Persistent Organic Pollutants (POPs). One of the remaining sticking points in the treaty talks was DDT, which had been banned from agricultural use in nearly 90 countries. Its role in disease control was highly controversial, especially in light of South Africa's recent experience with malaria.[71]

South Africa had stopped using DDT to fight malaria in 1996—a move that was not questioned at the time, since decades of DDT use had greatly reduced *Anopheles* populations and largely eliminated one of the most troublesome vectors, the appropriately named *An. funestus* ("funestis" means death-bearing or funereal). Like Mexico, South Africa seemed to have beaten the DDT habit the chemical had been used to achieve a worthwhile objective; it had then been set aside. Mosquito control could henceforth be accomplished with pyrethroids. And the plan worked—until a year before the POPs summit.[72]

In 1999, malaria infections in South Africa rose to 61,000 cases, a level not seen in decades. *An funestus* reappeared as well, in KwaZulu-Natal, in a form resistant to pyrethroids. In early 2000, the authorities reintroduced DDT in an indoor spraying program. By the middle of the year, the number of infections had dropped by half. Initially, the spraying program was criticized. But what reasonable alternative was there? This is said to be the African predicament, although the South African situation is hardly representative of sub-Saharan Africa as a whole. What happened in South Africa suggests that DDT will remain an important tool for malaria control in epidemic situations in parts of Africa where the mode of transmission is susceptible, such as an outbreak that occurred in Madagascar in the late 1980s.[73]

Since its first use in the 1940s, DDT has saved countless millions of lives, and under specific conditions it still helps to reduce the transmission of malaria. But to imply that routine—let alone increased—use of DDT is key to controlling malaria today, especially in Africa, where human suffering and the need for treatment and control are greatest, is misleading. As the Pan-American Health Organization recently concluded, indoor insecticide spraying is inadequate in much of the developing world because of changing environmental conditions, migrating human populations, and informal housing and shelters. Even at the height of the global program in the 1960s, WHO planners limited efforts to Ethiopia, South Africa, and southern Rhodesia (now Zimbabwe), where eradication was thought to be feasible.[74]

Although the global campaign largely passed Africa by, DDT has not. Many African countries have attempted mosquito control during particularly severe outbreaks, but the primary use of DDT on the continent has been as an agricultural

insecticide. Consequently, in parts of West Africa especially, DDT resistance is now widespread in *An. gambiae*. But even if it were possible to reduce *An. gambiae* populations substantially, that alone would not effectively control malaria because *An. gambiae* is such a highly efficient vector that it challenges the theoretical underpinnings of house spraying and vector control. This mosquito can bite people up to 2,000 times more frequently than is needed to maintain endemic malaria.[75]

In Africa, the key to progress includes the general suppression of mosquito populations in their larval and adult stages, a shortening of mosquito longevity, and the reduction of human-vector contact. To this end, a very promising option is bednets—mosquito netting or other material that is treated with a pyrethroid insecticide, such as deltamethrin or permethrin, and that is suspended over a person's bed or hammock.[76]

Bednets alone cannot eliminate malaria, but they can deflect some of the burden. Because *Anopheles* generally feed in the evening and at night, a bednet can radically reduce the number of infective bites that a person is subjected to. The individual would probably still have the parasite in his or her blood, but most of the time it would be at a level low enough for normal functioning.[77]

Even though bednets do not prevent infection, they can in a sense prevent a good deal of disease. Children who sleep under bednets have shown declines in malaria incidence of 14–63 percent and in overall mortality of up to 25 percent. Pregnant women who use bednets tend to give birth to healthier babies. Treated bednets also have a significant communal benefit. People sleeping near a treated bednet in the same bedroom, house, or even neighborhood benefit from a "herd effect" as the nets reduce the number of mosquitoes, the number of infections, and the number of severe cases.[78]

In parts of Burkina Faso, Chad, Mali, and Senegal, bednets are becoming standard household items. In the tiny West African nation of The Gambia, somewhere between 50 and 80 percent of people have bednets. Sadly, these places are notable exceptions. In much of Africa, where transmission rates are high, people have only begun to learn or hear about bednets, let alone use them regularly.[79]

And bednets are hardly a panacea. They have to be used properly and re-treated with insecticide occasionally. Many people cannot afford to buy the net or insecticide. And the insecticides themselves pose a risk to human and environmental health. Plus, there is still the problem of insecticide resistance, although the nets themselves are hardly likely to be the main cause of it. (Pyrethroids are used extensively in agriculture as well.) Nevertheless, a recent U.S. Agency for International Development study concluded that the public health benefits from these materials justify their "apparently modest risks." Quite simply, bednets can help transform malaria from chronic disaster to manageable disease.[80]

So it is unfortunate that in much of central and southern Africa, the nets are a rarity. It is even more unfortunate that as recently as 1998, 28 African countries levied import tariffs on bednets; most people in these countries would have trouble paying for a net even without the tax. This problem was addressed in the Abuja Declaration, a plan of action to control malaria signed by the Heads of State from 44 African countries in April 2000. The Declaration included a pledge to remove "malaria taxes." Since then, 15 countries have acted on the pledge, although in some cases only by reducing rather than eliminating the taxes. In the meantime, several million Africans have died from malaria.[81]

This failure to follow through with the Abuja Declaration casts the concern about DDT in a rather poor light. To date, 28 of the countries that have signed the POPs treaty have indicated that they are reserving the right to use DDT as a public health measure; 18 of these countries are in Africa. And of those, 10 are apparently still taxing or imposing tariffs on bednets. (Among the African countries that have not signed the POPs treaty, some are almost certainly both using DDT and taxing bednets, but the exact number is difficult to ascertain because the status of DDT is not always clear.) A strong case can be made for the use of DDT in situations like the one South Africa encountered in 1999— an infrequent flare-up of the disease in a context that lends itself to control. Throughout most of

sub-Saharan Africa, however, routine spraying of DDT for malaria control is difficult to imagine given the vertical, top-down structure needed to implement it.[82]

Bednets alone cannot eliminate malaria, but they can deflect some of the burden.

In recent years, some scientists have presented the use of DDT as an all-or-nothing situation for malaria control. They argue that rich, northern countries successfully abolished endemic malaria 40 years ago by using DDT, and are now trying to convince other countries not to use it. Without DDT, proponents argue, millions of people in poor countries will die.[83]

The justification for such use sets up a false dichotomy—DDT or disease—thereby perpetuating both. This line of argument also oversimplifies the complexities of malaria control and trivializes the efforts of malariologists, public health officials, and vector control experts who carefully adjust solutions to local conditions. Moreover, it fails to acknowledge that in northern, temperate countries, public health applications of DDT coincided with overall improvements in housing, water drainage, and economic development—conditions that have yet to be met in much of the tropical South.[84]

The most effective programs today rely on a range of tools, including drug policies, environmental management, strengthened health systems, community involvement, and the selective and appropriate use of methods for vector control and personal protection, such as bednets. In some areas, controlling the larvae and vector will require a change in housing materials. This, in turn, requires investment in other materials that are sometimes less convenient and costlier. Real prevention in Africa requires combining anti-malaria measures with anti-poverty programs that can reinforce economic development so that people and governments can afford adequate health care, education, and social services that help interrupt the cycle of poverty and disease.[85]

IMPROVING PUBLIC HEALTH, ENGAGING PEOPLE

Malaria is complex, but combating it does not have to be complicated. (See Box 2.) When simple, easy-to-use, low-tech preventive tools are made available, their benefits are undeniable. Just as condoms have proved effective in preventing HIV/AIDS and oral rehydration salts have helped ameliorate diarrheal diseases, malaria control through a combination of insecticide-treated bednets, better case detection and treatment, elimination of mosquito habitat, and insecticide spraying as a last resort will reduce malaria's human toll.

Not only does a multifaceted approach make sense from a public health perspective, it is a wise economic course as well. "One healthy year of life is gained for every $1 to $8 spent on effectively treating malaria cases, which makes malaria treatment as cost-effective a public health investment as measles vaccinations," according to Dr. Ann Mills of the London School of Hygiene and Tropical Medicine. An annual investment of $2.5 billion—just 1¢ for every $100 of the gross domestic product in industrial countries—would

go a long way toward combating malaria in Africa. And its rewards would be reaped many times over in human, social, and economic benefits.[86]

One of the first steps is to make the most of simple solutions and technologies and adjust them to local conditions. In Namibia, for example, irrigation water is a necessity for agriculture and nourishment, but it also serves as a catalyst for malaria. Farmers in this semiarid nation have found that fixing leaky pipes is sometimes all that is needed to keep malaria in check. In Chennai, India, public health specialists have worked with community representatives to design better lids on water tanks to stop *Anopheles* from breeding.[87]

A second area for action is for policymakers to abolish malaria taxes. As noted earlier, many African countries still have taxes or tariffs on imported nets and insecticides, which is undercutting disease control efforts. In Senegal, for example, foreign net manufacturers have refused to enter the market until the government eliminates taxes and tariffs on bednets, despite a proven need and demand for such products.[88]

Health economists have shown that insecticide-treated nets are as cost-effective as childhood vaccinations, arguing that nets should be provided for free or at least at a subsidized price. China has the largest insecticide-treated net program in the world. In Viet Nam, users buy their own nets and the government provides insecticide for free in regular net treatment services. In Zambia, the government is creating a voucher system to help the poor buy into the system. People who qualify would pick up vouchers in health clinics to be redeemed at a local store for nets.[89]

Many tropical disease experts argue that malaria eradication eradicated the malariologists. Research since the 1960s has focused heavily on vaccines, genetically modified mosquitoes, and genome sequencing, sometimes at the expense of research on the environmental aspects of malaria transmission. Given the scale of tropical ecosystem degradation today, it is imperative that funding for such research is increased. Monitoring the mosquitoes and characteristics of malaria transmission before projects are approved and during the implementation phase can sensitize agricultural officials, urban planners, economists, and health officials to

---

BOX 2 Essential Strategies for Dealing with Malaria

- Make the most of simple, cost-effective tools.
- Abolish so-called malaria taxes and distribute insecticide-treated bednets.
- Fund research on the environmental dimensions of malaria.
- Fund demonstration projects on and further the use of integrated vector management strategies.
- Provide financial assistance to poorer countries.
- Engage public-private partnerships to reach people.
- Use more targeted diagnosis and treatment.
- Slow drug resistance.
- Incorporate malaria treatment into existing programs.
- Invest in malaria drug and combination therapy development and distribution.

the nature of malaria and offer an early warning system for outbreaks of disease. Increased awareness, in turn, sparks greater responsiveness to its control and better preparedness.[90]

Although it is difficult to predict the effect of environmental changes on the spread of malaria, officials can better anticipate the spread of disease and adopt some basic safeguards in their work. To offset the negative effects of dams, for example, authorities and engineers can site them at higher altitudes or away from communities and can manage water levels carefully, much as U.S. authorities did with TVA dams. Irrigated rice paddies have long been associated with malaria, but draining paddies intermittently will kill mosquito larvae that hatch there. As shown in many Asian countries, this practice has the additional benefit of raising rice yields by bringing more oxygen to the plants' roots.[91]

Researchers with the Kenya-based International Centre for Insect Physiology and Ecology are forging new ground in the search for natural insect repellants. They have studied the chemical defense tactics that plants use to repel insects and to deter feeding and reproduction. Researchers have now identified at least a dozen plants native to East Africa that proved successful in lab tests at fending off *An. gambiae,* the primary vector in Africa. Biologists and ethnobotanists are also testing native plants in South Asia and the Amazon basin.[92]

Paying for research and the implementation of costly alternatives is an enormous challenge. The United States and other well-off nations need to invest in the research and assistance programs critical to helping poorer nations combat malaria in a healthier way. The highest priority for existing funding mechanisms is to build stronger capacity in developing nations for delivering malaria control services, including case detection and management and focused vector control.

Public-private partnerships also have an important role to play. In the mid-1990s, for example, public authorities teamed up with the private sector in the Ifakara district of rural Tanzania to promote insecticide-treated bednets. Health officials educated people about their use and maintenance, and the local government subsidized their purchase. The private sector focused on publicizing the benefits of using nets, marketing them, and distributing them widely. By encouraging market competition and footing part of the bill for the cost of nets, the government was able to leverage its resources to bring prices down. Between 1997 and 1999, there was a sixfold increase in net ownership, a 60-percent drop in severe anemia, and a 27-percent increase in survival rates among children who slept under a net.[93]

Even with new programs in place, malaria has continued to kill one child every 30 seconds in sub-Saharan Africa.

Greater public education is vital in order to target malaria diagnosis and treatment more effectively. In the Tigray region of northern Ethiopia, for instance, nearly half of the population is at risk of malaria, yet most people have no access to formal health services. Mothers in the local community started a network in 1992 to teach each other how to diagnose and treat malaria at home. Today, more than 700 volunteers work to use proper drugs to treat malaria early on, before it becomes life-threatening. Nearly a half-million people are protected by this network of mothers each year in Ethiopia.[94]

People on the frontlines who dispense drugs and determine treatment protocols also need education and better information on drug efficacies and the spread of drug-resistant parasites. In 1998, health officials and researchers from Kenya, Rwanda, Tanzania, and Uganda teamed up to create the East African Network for Monitoring Antimalarial Treatment to share data, monitor drug resistance, develop more effective treatment policies, and reduce malaria. Based on improved communication, this new approach has been vital to detecting the presence of drug-resistant cases and selecting the appropriate treatment. Other countries could develop similar online, publicly available data bases to monitor drug resistance.[95]

To reach the youngest victims of disease, the Integrated Management of Childhood Illness program now includes malaria as one of its five key health conditions. Health care providers and staff learn to diagnose and treat malaria as part of their basic training. A new important tool to protect children is artemisinin suppositories. (Artemisinin and related compounds come from an ancient Chinese herb known as qinghaosu. Artesunates have proved to be among the safest, most effective, fastest-acting of all anti-malarials.) The suppositories could significantly reduce deaths in children, who often develop severe malaria quickly and commonly are unable to get the necessary hospital-based care in time.[96]

In Tanzania, health researchers recently established a program to dispense anti-malarials with routine vaccinations. Combining intermittent, preventive malaria treatment with vaccines reduces the number of clinical cases of malaria and the rate of severe anemia and is a good way to reach children who would otherwise receive no treatment. The vaccine programs are already in place and the malaria component can be added on easily. Similarly, intermittent drug treatment and the provision of free bednets for pregnant women are important low-cost ways to prevent the effects of malaria in pregnancy, and they can be readily added to existing prenatal care programs.[97]

In Southeast Asia, it makes sense to invest in better diagnosis methods because the drugs for drug-resistant malaria are expensive and few fevers are actually malaria. One of the latest tools in Cambodia's fight against malaria is a rapid diagnostic kit that is similar to a home-based pregnancy test. The person using the rapid diagnostic test (known as a dipstick) pricks the patient's finger, swipes the blood on a reactive strip, and in a matter of minutes has results that are easy to interpret. Because there is no need for costly equipment, dipsticks are especially useful in areas far from clinical settings or where power supplies are unreliable, and they can reduce the reliance on presumptive treatment, with its unintended results.[98]

Recently, Cambodian authorities joined with private marketers to supply dipstick tests and the latest anti-malarial combination therapy (mefloquine and artesunate) to treat multi-drug-resistant strains. This combination therapy is effective even when the malaria parasite has developed high levels of resistance to mefloquine because it takes longer for genes to resist two different drug compounds at the same time. These efforts have reduced significantly the number of severe cases of malaria, as people are diagnosed earlier and have effective treatments readily available. In frontier areas with seasonal outbreaks and low transmission rates, such as the Brazilian Amazon, or in emergency situations, packets of dipsticks and prepackaged anti-malarial drugs are now proving extremely useful.[99]

Minimal investment in malaria drug development is still a major roadblock. The malaria parasite is about 100 times more complex than the virus that causes AIDS, but it receives only about one tenth as much funding for research. While most pharmaceutical companies have turned a blind eye on malaria because it is seen as a money-losing venture, there are a few notable exceptions. In May 2001, for example, WHO announced a partnership with Swiss-based Novartis AG to distribute the company's new combination therapy anti-malarial drug, Coartem, at greatly reduced cost to poor countries.[100]

In May 1998, Gro Harlem Brundtland became Director-General of WHO. One of her first priorities was to address malaria and other diseases of poverty. Under her leadership, WHO has taken a more active role in advocating for renewed attention and funding for malaria. In the past five years, four major international initiatives were launched to raise the profile of malaria control and to tackle issues of funding, research coordination, and public and private cooperation. All represent a new infusion of political interest and financial commitments.[101]

Even with these new programs in place, malaria has continued to kill one child every 30 seconds in sub-Saharan Africa. The new visibility that this disease has achieved is just a first step in dedicating resources and taking action to stop malaria. But these programs signal a much needed move away from the view of malaria as strictly a health issue, and as a poor person's disease at that, and towards an understanding that malaria is a truly global challenge of improving public health, securing economic and social well-being, and advancing sustainable development.[102]

NOTES

1. Figure of 7,000 based on range of annual deaths from Joel G. Breman, "The Ears of the Hippopotamus: Manifestations, Determinants, and Estimates of the Malaria Burden," *American Journal of Tropical Medicine & Hygiene*, January/February 2001 (supp.), p. 1; history and Burnet quote from Andrew Nikiforuk, *The Fourth Horseman: A Short History of Epidemics, Plagues, Famine and Other Scourges* (New York: M. Evans & Company, Inc., 1991), p. 14, 17–18.

2. Hindi from Nikiforuk, op. sit. note 1, p. 17; Ann Hwang, "AIDS Passes 20-Year Mark," in Worldwatch Institute, *Vital Signs 2002* (New York: W.W. Norton & Company, 2002), pp. 90–91.

3. Population at risk from World Health Organization (WHO), *The World Health Report 1999* (Geneva: 1999), p. 49; Patrice Trouiller et al., "Drug Development for Neglected Diseases: A Deficient Market and a Public-Health Policy Failure," *The Lancet*, 22 June 2002, pp. 2188–94.

4. WHO, *WHO Expert Committee on Malaria: Twentieth Report*, WHO Technical Report Series No. 892 (Geneva: 2000).

5. Figure of $3–12 billion from WHO, "Economic Costs of Malaria Are Many Times Higher than Previously Estimated," press release (Geneva: 25 April 2000); $2.5 billion from Report of the Commission on Macroeconomics and Health, *Macroeconomics and Health: Investing in Health for Economic Development* (Geneva: WHO, 20 December 2001), p. 161; $150 million estimate from Jeffrey D. Sachs, Center for International Development, Harvard University, Cambridge, MA, e-mail to author, 5 March 2002; U.S. Department of Health and Human Services, "HHS Budget for HIV/AIDS Increase 8 Percent," press release (Washington, DC: 4 February 2002).

6. Figure 2 adapted from John Luke Gallup and Jeffrey D. Sachs, "The Economic Burden of Malaria," *American Journal of Tropical Medicine & Hygiene*, January/February 2001 (supp.), p. 86; geography from ibid.; percent from WHO, op. cit. note 3; Norman G. Gratz, Robert Steffen, and William Cocksedge, "Why Aircraft Disinsection?" *Bulletin of the World Health Organization*, August 2000, pp. 995–1004.

7. Figure of 90 percent from WHO, op. cit. note 4, p. 3, and from Joel G. Breman, Andréa Egan, and Gerald T. Keusch, "The Intolerable Burden of Malaria: A New Look at the Numbers," *American Journal of Tropical Medicine & Hygiene*, January/February 2001 (supp.), p. iv; outpatient clinics from UNICEF Programme Division and WHO, "The Global Malaria Burden," *The Prescriber*, January 2000; five strains from Donovan Webster, "Malaria Kills One Child Every 30 Second," *Smithsonian*, September 2000, p. 40; B. Greenwood, "Malaria Mortality and Morbidity in Africa," *Bulletin of the World Health Organization*, August 1999, p. 617.

8. J. Kevin Baird, "Resurgent Malaria at the Millennium," *Drugs*, April 2000, pp. 721, 733–36.

9. Sean C. Murphy and Joel G. Breman, "Gaps in the Childhood Malaria Burden in Africa: Cerebral Malaria, Neurological Sequelae, Anemia, Respiratory Distress, Hypoglycemia, and Complications of Pregnancy," *American Journal of Tropical Medicine & Hygiene*, January/February 2001 (supp.), pp. 57–67; Kenya from Ellen Ruppel Shell, "Resurgence of a Deadly Disease," *Atlantic Monthly*, August 1997, p. 49; cerebral malaria from P. A. Holding and R. W. Snow, "Impact of *Plasmodium falciparum* Malaria on Performance and Learning: Review of the Evidence," *American Journal of Tropical Medicine & Hygiene*, January/February 2001 (supp.), pp. 68–75.

10. Helen L. Guyatt and Robert W. Snow, "The Epidemiology and Burden of *Plasmodium falciparum-related* Anemia among Pregnant Women in Sub-Saharan Africa," *American Journal of Tropical Medicine & Hygiene*, January/February 2001 (supp.), pp. 36–44; miscarriages, stillbirths, and low birth weight from Murphy and Breman, op. cit. note 9, p. 57; 30 percent and 60 percent from Jeffrey Sachs and Pia Malaney, "The Economic and Social Burden of Malaria," *Nature*, 7 February 2002, p. 682.

11. Sachs and Malaney, op. cit. note 10, pp. 682–83; Catherine Goodman, Paul Coleman, and Anne Mills, *Economic Analysis of Malaria Control in Sub-Saharan Africa* (Geneva: Global Forum for Health Research, May 2000), pp. 162–63.

12. Number living in poverty from Molly O. Sheehan, "Poverty Persists," in Worldwatch Institute, op. cit. note 2, pp. 148–49; Goodman, Coleman, and Mills, op. cit. note 11, pp. 159–73.

13. Isolating cycle from Sachs and Malaney, op. cit. note 10, p. 684; costs and development aid from WHO, op. cit. note 5.

14. Figure 3 from WHO, op. cit. note 3, p. 50; Thomas C. Nchinda, "Malaria: A Reemerging

Disease in Africa," *Emerging Infectious Diseases,* July-September 1998, pp. 398–403; Robert W. Snow, Jean-François Trape, and Kevin Marsh, "The Past, Present and Future of Childhood Malaria Mortality in Africa," *Trends in Parasitology,* December 2001, pp. 593–97.

15. Official estimates from WHO, op. cit. note 3, p. 49; three times higher from Ebrahim Samba, "The Malaria Burden and Africa," *American Journal of Tropical Medicine & Hygiene,* January/February 2001 (supp.), p. ii; high-fever episodes and potential doubling from Breman, op. cit. note 1, pp. 1, 7.

16. Andrew Spielman and Michael D'Antonio, *Mosquito: A Natural History of Our Most Persistent and Deadly Foe* (New York: Hyperion, 2001), p. 95; Jean-François Trape, "The Public Health Impact of Chloroquine Resistance in Africa," *American Journal of Tropical Medicine & Hygiene,* January/February 2001 (supp.), p. 15.

17. Baird, op. cit. note 8, pp. 719, 728–30; WHO, op. cit. note 3, p. 52.

18. Replacement drugs from Nchinda, op. cit. note 14, and from WHO, op. cit. note 4, pp. 5, 31; Thailand from Eliot Marshall, "Reinventing an Ancient Cure for Malaria," *Science,* 20 October 2000, p. 437.

19. Martin Enserink and Elizabeth Pennisi, "Researchers Crack Malaria Genome," *Science,* 15 February 2002, p. 1207; Malcolm J. Gardner et al., "Genome Sequence of the Human Malaria Parasite *Plasmodium falciparum,*" *Nature,* 3 October 2002, pp. 498–511; Robert A. Holt et al., "The Genome Sequence of the Malaria Mosquito *Anopheles gambiae,*" *Science,* 4 October 2002, pp. 129–49.

20. Malaria belt from Webster, op. cit. note 7, p. 36; Afghanistan and Sierra Leone from UNICEF Programme Division and WHO, op. cit. note 7; North and South Korea, Tajikistan, and Urban areas from WHO, op. cit. note 4, p. 6; urban malaria also from Vincent Robert et al., "Malaria Transmission in Urban Africa," *American Journal of Tropical Medicine & Hygiene* (in press).

21. David J. Rogers and Sarah E. Randolph, "The Global Spread of Malaria in a Future, Warmer World," *Science,* 8 September 2000, pp. 1763–66.

22. Box 1 from the following: J. B. Opschoor and D. W. Pearce, "Persistent Pollutants: A Challenge for the Nineties," in J. B. Opschoor and David Pearce, eds., *Persistent Pollutants: Economics and Policy* (Boston, MA: Kluwer Academic Publishers,

1991); cod and turbot from World Wildlife Fund (WWF), *Resolving the DDT Dilemma: Protecting Human Health and Biodiversity* (Washington, DC: June 1998), p. 11; DDE from Matthew P. Longnecker, Walter J. Rogan, and George Lucier, "The Human Health Effects of DDT (Dichlorodiphenyltrichloroethane) and PCBs (Polychlorinated Biphenyls) and an Overview of Organochlorines in Public Health," *Annual Review of Public Health,* vol. 18 (1997), pp. 211–44; animal effects from H. Burlington and V.F. Lindeman, "Effect of DDT on Testes and Secondary Sex Characteristics of White Leghorn Cockerels," *Proceedings of the Society for Experimental Biology and Medicine,* vol. 74 (1950), pp. 48–51, and from V. Turusov, V. Rakitsky, and L. Tomatis, "Dichlorodiphenyltrichloroethane (DDT): Ubiquity, Persistence, and Risks," *Environmental Health Perspectives,* February 2002, pp. 125–28; Committee on Hormonally Active Agents in the Environment, Board on Environmental Studies and Toxicology, National Research Council, *Hormonally Active Agents in the Environment* (Washington, DC: National Academy Press, 2000), pp. 165, 289; Agency for Toxic Substances and Disease Registry, "Toxicological Profile for DDT, DDE, DDD: Draft for Public Comment" (Atlanta, GA: September 2000); W. R. Kelce et al., "Persistent DDT Metabolite p,p'-DDE Is a Potent Androgen Receptor Antagonist," *Nature,* 15 June 1995, pp. 581–85; Matthew P. Longnecker et al., "Association Between Maternal Serum Concentration of the DDT Metabolite DDE and Preterm and Small-for-Gestational-Age Babies at Birth," *The Lancet,* 14 July 2001, pp. 110–14; Greenpeace International, *Unseen Poisons: Levels of Organochlorine Chemicals in Human Tissues* (Amsterdam: June 1998); Costa Rica from Berna van Wendel de Joode et al., "Chronic Nervous-System Effects of Long-Term Occupational Exposure to DDT," *The Lancet,* 31 March 2001, pp. 1014–16.

23. Institute of Medicine (IOM), *Malaria: Obstacles and Opportunities* (Washington, DC: National Academy Press, 1991), pp. 90–129; Leonard Jan Bruce-Chwatt, *Essential Malariology* (London: William Heinemann Medical Books, Ltd., 1980), pp. 10–30, 97–124; Andy Coghlan, "Four-Pronged Attack," *New Scientist,* 20 February 1999, p. 11.

24. Figure 4 from U.S. Navy Bureau of Medicine and Surgery, Navy Environmental Health Center, *Navy Medical Department Pocket Guide to Malaria Prevention and Control,* Technical

Manual (Iowa City: University of Iowa, Virtual Naval Hospital, 2000); IOM, op. cit. note 23; microliters from Martin Enserink, "Building a Disease-Fighting Mosquito," *Science*, 20 October 2000, p. 440; share deposited from J. C. Beier et al., "Quantitation of Malaria Sporozoites Transmitted *in vitro* During Salivation by Wild Afrotropical *Anopheles*," *Medical and Veterinary Entomology*, vol. 5 (1991), pp. 71–79; rapid dispersal period from Gary Taubes, "Malaria Parasite Outwits the Immune System," *Science*, 20 October 2000, p. 435.

25. Taubes, op. cit. note 24.

26. Bruce-Chwatt, op. cit. note 23, pp. 13–29, 35–41; 20-fold from Taubes, op. cit. note 24.

27. J. C. Beier, "Malaria Parasite Development in Mosquitoes," *Annual Review of Entomology*, vol. 43 (1998), pp. 519–43.

28. IOM, op. cit. note 23, p. 27; Bruce-Chwatt, op. cit. note 23, pp. 97–114.

29. Bruce-Chwatt, op. cit. note 23, pp. 158–59; explanation and examples from Spielman and D'Antonio, op. cit. note 16, pp. 96–97.

30. Spielman and D'Antonio, op. cit. note 16, p. 97.

31. Mario Coluzzi, "The Clay Feet of the Malaria Giant and Its African Roots: Hypotheses and Inferences About Origin, Spread and Control of *Plasmodium falciparum*," *Parassitologia*, September 1999, pp. 277–83; Robert S. Desowitz, *The Malaria Capers: More Tales of Parasites and People, Research and Reality* (New York: W.W. Norton & Company, 1991), pp. 146–47.

32. Figure of 95 percent from Malcolm Gladwell, "The Mosquito Killer," *New Yorker*, 2 July 2001, p. 45; emergence of parasite from Coluzzi, op. cit. note 31.

33. Bruce-Chwatt, op. cit. note 23, pp. 58–59; Desowitz, op. cit. note 31, p. 148; Gallup and Sachs, op. cit. note 6, p. 89.

34. Bruce-Chwatt, op. cit. note 23, pp. 58–59; Desowitz, op. cit. note 31, p. 148; Gallup and Sachs, op. cit. note 6, p. 89; A. Ashley-Koch, Q. Yang, and R.S. Olney, "Sickle Hemoglobin (HbS) Allele and Sickle Cell Disease: A HuGE Review," *American Journal of Epidemiology*, May 2000, pp. 839–45; K. Pattanapanyasat et al., "Impairment of *Plasmodium falciparum* Growth in Thalassemic Red Blood Cells: Further Evidence by Using Biotin Labeling and Flow Cytometry," *Blood*, 1 May 1999, pp. 3116–19.

35. Range of bites in Africa from J. C. Beier, G. F. Killeen, and J. I. Githure, "Short Report: Entomologic Inoculation Rates and *Plasmodium falciparum* Malaria Prevalence in Africa," *American Journal of Tropical Medicine & Hygiene*, July 1999, pp. 109–13, and from Yeya Tiémoko Touré and Mario Coluzzi, "The Challenges of Doing More Against Malaria, Particularly in Africa," *Bulletin of the World Health Organization*, December 2000, p. 1376; success rate from J. Kevin Baird, Parasitic Diseases Program, U.S. Naval Medical Research Unit, Jakarta, Indonesia, e-mail to author, 18 August 2002; risk and toll from Baird, op. cit. note 8, pp. 719–43.

36. Baird, op. cit. note 8, pp. 734–37; partial immunity and course of infection from Shell, op. cit. note 9, pp. 47–49.

37. Baird, op. cit. note 8, pp. 734–37; P. D. McElroy et al., "Dose- and Time-Dependent Relations between Infective *Anopheles* Inoculation and Outcomes of *Plasmodium falciparum* Parasitemia among Children in Western Kenya," *American Journal of Epidemiology*, May 1997, pp. 945–56.

38. W. F. Bynum, "Mosquitoes Bite More Than Once," *Science*, 4 January 2002, pp. 47–48; Desowitz, op. cit. note 31, pp. 143–52.

39. David McCullough, *The Path Between the Seas: The Creation of the Panama Canal, 1870–1914* (New York: Simon and Schuster, 1977); percentages from Spielman and D'Antonio, op. cit. note 16, p. 125.

40. Bruce-Chwatt, op. cit. note 23, p. 4; Gladwell, op. cit. note 32, pp. 42–44.

41. IOM, op. cit. note 23, pp. 41–43; Spielman and D'Antonio, op. cit. note 16, pp. 157–59.

42. IOM, op. cit. note 23, pp. 41–42; Gladwell, op. cit. note 32, pp. 47–48.

43. WWF, op. cit. note 22, p. 3; Spielman and D'Antonio, op. cit. note 16, p. 165; Bruce-Chwatt, op. cit. note 23, p. 4.

44. Gladwell, op. cit. note 32, p. 50; Spielman and D'Antonio, op. cit. note 16, pp. 157–59; Bruce-Chwatt, op. cit. note 23, pp. 280–85.

45. Spielman and D'Antonio, op. cit. note 16, pp. 148–50; IOM, op. cit. note 23, p. 42.

46. IOM, op. cit. note 23, p. 44; Desowitz, op. cit. note 31, p. 213–16.

47. Desowitz, op. cit. note 31, pp. 217–18; M.A. Farid, "The Malaria Campaign—Why Not Eradication?" *World Health Forum*, vol. 19 (1998), pp. 417–27.

48. Spielman and D'Antonio, op. cit. note 16, pp. 179–83.

49. Ibid.

50. David Brewster, "Is It Worth a Dam If It Worsens Malaria?" *British Medical Journal,* 11 September 1999, pp. 651–52.

51. J. F. Walsh, D. H. Molyneux, and M. H. Birley, "Deforestation: Effects on Vector-borne Disease," *Parasitology,* vol. 106 (1993) (supp.), pp. S55–75; migrations from R. Danis-Lozano et al., "Risk Factors for *Plasmodium vivax* Infection in the Lacandon Forest, Southern Mexico," *Epidemiology and Infection,* June 1999, pp. 461–69; Beier, Killeen, and Githure, op. cit. note 35.

52. Sri Lanka from R. Ramasamy et al., "Malaria Transmission at a New Irrigation Project in Sri Lanka: The Emergence of *Anopheles annularis* as a Major Vector," *American Journal of Tropical Medicine & Hygiene,* November 1992, pp. 547–53, and from Spielman and D'Antonio, op. cit. note 16, p. 176; Tigray from Brewster, op. cit. note 50, pp. 651–52, and from Tedros A. Ghebreyesus et al., "Incidence of Malaria among Children Living Near Dams in Northern Ethiopia: Community Based Incidence Survey," *British Medical Journal,* 11 September 1999, pp. 663–66.

53. Burton H. Singer and Marcia Caldas de Castro, "Agricultural Colonization and Malaria on the Amazon Frontier," *Annals of the New York Academy of Sciences,* December 2001, pp. 187, 191.

54. Ibid., p. 189.

55. Y. Ye-Ebiyo, R. J. Pollack, and A. Spielman, "Enhanced Development in Nature of Larval *Anopheles arabiensis* Mosquitoes Feeding on Maize Pollen," *American Journal of Tropical Medicine & Hygiene,* July/August 2000, pp. 90–93; Spielman and D'Antonio, op. cit. note 16, pp. 220–21.

56. V. P. Sharma, "Re-emergence of Malaria in India," *Indian Journal of Medical Research,* January 1996, p. 32; Tennessee Valley Authority from Spielman and D'Antonio, op. cit. note 16, pp. 152–53.

57. Preferences from Walsh, Molyneux, and Birley, op. cit. note 51, from Spielman and D'Antonio, op. cit. note 16, p. 211, and from Donald R. Roberts and Kevin Baird, "DDT Is Still Needed for Disease Control," *Pesticide Safety News,* first trimester 2002, p. 2; McWilson Warren et al., "Malaria in Urban and Peri-Urban Areas in Sub-Saharan Africa," Environmental Health Project, Activity Report No. 71 (Washington, DC: U.S. Agency for International Development (USAID), August 1999), and from Robert et. al., op. cit. note 20.

58. Warren et al., op. cit. note 57.

59. J. N. Ijumba, F. W. Mosha, and S. W. Lindsay, "Malaria Transmission Risk Variations Derived from Different Agricultural Practices in an Irrigated Area of Northern Tanzania," *Medical and Veterinary Entomology,* March 2002, pp. 28–38.

60. U. D'Alessandro and H. Buttiens, "History and Importance of Antimalarial Drug Resistance," *Tropical Medicine & International Health,* November 2001, pp. 845–48; deaths, hospital admissions, and today from Trape, op. cit. note 16, pp. 12–17.

61. Cost from WHO, op. cit. note 3, p. 59; without prescription from Donald G. McNeil Jr., "New Drug for Malaria Pits U.S. Against Africa," *New York Times,* 28 May 2002; complicated nature from Trape, op. cit. note 16, p. 15.

62. Ministry of Health, Mexico, "Experience in Reducing Use of DDT in Mexico," prepared for the Intergovernmental Forum on Chemical Safety Experts Meeting on POPs, Manila, Philippines, 17–19 June 1996; 20,000 average annual cases between 1959 and 1975 (except for peak in 1968–71 of 60,000) from Lizbeth López-Carrillo et al., "Is DDT Use a Public Health Problem in Mexico?" *Environmental Health Perspectives,* June 1996, p. 585.

63. Ministry of Health, op. cit. note 62.

64. López-Carrillo et al., op. cit. note 62, pp. 584–88; Ministry of Health, op. cit. note 62; Keith E. Chanon et al., "Cooperative Actions to Achieve Malaria Control Without the Use of DDT," *International Journal of Hygiene and Environmental Health* (in press).

65. Rise in annual infections from Roberts and Baird, op. cit. note 57; Fernando Bejarano González, "The Phasing Out of DDT in Mexico," *Pesticide Safety News,* fourth trimester 2001; H. Gómez Dantés and A. E. Birn, "Malaria and Social Movements in Mexico: The Last 60 Years," *Parasitologia,* June 2000, pp. 69–85.

66. González, op. cit. note 65.

67. Pan American Health Organization (PAHO), *Report on the Status of Malaria Programs in the Americas (Based on 2000 Data),* Forty-third Directing Council, Fifty-third Session of the Regional Committee, Washington, DC, 24–28 September 2001 (Washington, DC: 19 September 2001), p. 8; Gómez-Dantés and Birn, op. cit. note 65, p. 80.

68. José Manuel Galindo Jaramillo, "Promoting Health Through Sustainable Development,"

presentation at World Summit on Sustainable Development, Preparatory Commission 3, United Nations, New York, 1 April 2002; José Manuel Galindo Jaramillo, North American Commission for Environmental Cooperation, Mexico City, e-mail to author, 31 July 2002.

69. Rich Liroff, "DDT's Future Under the Stockholm Convention," *Pesticide Safety News,* first trimester 2002, p. 3; Jaramillo, e-mail to author, op. cit. note 68.

70. Burton Singer, "We Can Do Something About Malaria Today," *HMS Beagle* (BioMedNet magazine, at <bmn.com>, Elsevier Science Limited), 13 October 2000.

71. U.N. Environment Programme (UNEP), "Governments Finalize Persistent Organic Pollutants Treaty," press release (Johannesburg: 10 December 2000).

72. Henk Bouwman, "Malaria Control and the Paradox of DDT," *Africa: Environment and Wildlife,* May 2000, p. 56.

73. Ibid.; South African Broadcasting Corporation, "Malaria Below Acceptable Levels," at <www.sabcnews.com/south_africa/health>, viewed 17 August 2002; Roger Thurow, "Choice of Evils: As a Tropical Scourge Makes a Comeback, So, Too, Does DDT," *Wall Street Journal,* 26 July 2001.

74. PAHO, "Situation of Malaria Programs in the Americas," *Epidemiological Bulletin,* March 2001; Peter Trigg and Anatoli Kondrachine, "The Global Malaria Control Strategy," *World Health,* May/June 1998, p. 4.

75. Resistance from B. Sina and K. Aultman, "Resisting Resistance," *Trends in Parasitology,* July 2001, pp. 305–06, and from M. Akogbeto, H. Noukpo, and G. Ahoueya, "Overview of Factors Influencing the Emergence of Insecticide Resistance," presentation at Multilateral Initiative on Malaria Conference, Insecticide Resistance in Malaria Vectors, Harare, Zimbabwe, 5–9 March 2001; frequency of bites from Gallup and Sachs, op. cit. note 6, p. 89.

76. WHO, op. cit. note 4, pp. 57–64; Gerry F. Killeen, Ulrike Fillinger, and Bart G. J. Knols, "Advantages of Larval Control for African Malaria Vectors: Low Mobility and Behavioural Responsiveness of Immature Mosquito Stages Allow High Effective Coverage," *Malaria Journal,* 21 June 2002, pp. 1–7; Michael Macdonald, USAID Environmental Health Project, Arlington, VA, e-mail to author, 19 March 2002.

77. Geoffrey A. T. Targett and Brain M. Greenwood, "Impregnated Bednets," *World Health,* May/June 1998, pp. 10–11; Martin Enserink, "Bed Nets Prove Their Mettle Against Malaria," *Science,* 14 December 2001, p. 2271; Macdonald, op. cit. note 76.

78. Incidence from WHO, "Malaria Major Killer in Africa—But Bednets Can Save Lives," press release (Geneva: 25 April 2001), and from C. Lengeler, "Insecticide-treated Bednets and Curtains for Preventing Malaria," *Cochrane Database of Systematic Reviews,* 2000 (2): CD000363 (software update); 25 percent from U. D'Alessandro et al., "Mortality and Morbidity from Malaria in Gambian Children after Introduction of an Impregnated Bednet Programme," *The Lancet,* 25 February 1995, pp. 479–83, and from Joanna R. M. Armstrong Schellenberg et al., "Effect of Large-scale Social Marketing of Insecticide-treated Nets on Child Survival in Rural Tanzania," *The Lancet,* 21 April 2001, pp. 1241–47; herd effect from Enserink, op. cit. note 77.

79. Malaria Consortium et al., "Chapter 4: Challenges to Expanding Coverage and Use," in *Insecticide Treated Nets in the 21st Century: Report of the Second International Conference on Insecticide Treated Nets, held in Dar es Salaam, Tanzania, 11–14 October 1999* (London: Malaria Consortium of the London School of Hygiene & Tropical Medicine, 1999), p. 4–3.

80. USAID, Bureau for Africa, Office of Sustainable Development, Division of Agriculture, Natural Resources and Rural Enterprise, *Programmatic Environmental Assessment for Insecticide-Treated Materials in USAID Activities in Sub-Saharan Africa* (Washington, DC: January 2002).

81. Program for Appropriate Technology in Health Canada, *Barriers to Trade in Mosquito Nets and Insecticides in Sub-Saharan Africa* (Ottawa, ON, Canada: April 1998); Kabir Cham, *List of African Countries Which Have Reduced and/or Waived Taxes and Tariffs on Nets, Netting Materials and Insecticides* (Geneva: WHO, Roll Back Malaria, March 2002).

82. DDT user status from WHO, "Final DDT Agreement Endorses RBM Objectives," *RBM News,* February 2001, p. 6; United Nations Treaty Collection, "List of Signatories and Parties to the Stockholm Convention (as of 4 October 2002)" at <www.pops.int/documents/signature/sign

status.htm>, viewed 16 October 2002; UNEP, "Revised List of Requests for Specific Exemptions in Annex A and Annex B and Acceptable Purposes in Annex B Received by the Secretariat Prior to the Commencement of the Conference of Plenipotentiaries on 22 May 2001" (Geneva: 14 June 2001); possible existing taxes based on Cham, op. cit. note 81.

83. Amir Attaran et al., "Balancing Risks on the Backs of the Poor," *Nature Medicine,* July 2000, pp. 729–31; Todd Seavey, *The DDT Ban Turns 30—Millions Dead of Malaria Because of Ban, More Deaths Likely* (Washington, DC: American Council on Science and Health, June 2002).

84. Spielman and D'Antonio, op. cit. note 16, pp. 219–20.

85. J. F. Trape et al., "Combating Malaria in Africa," *Trends in Parasitology,* May 2002, pp. 224–30; housing from Spielman and D'Antonio, op. cit. note 16, pp. 220–21; Malaria Consortium, *Malaria and Poverty: Opportunities to Address Malaria through Debt Relief and Poverty Reduction Strategies,* background paper for the Fourth RBM Global Partners Meeting, Washington, DC, 18–19 April 2001 (London: Malaria Consortium of the London School of Hygiene & Tropical Medicine, April 2001).

86. Mills quoted in WHO, op. cit. note 5; $2.5 billion from Commission on Macroeconomics and Health, op. cit. note 5; 1¢ for every $100 is a Worldwatch estimate based on industrial-country gross domestic product in David Malin Roodman, "Economic Growth Falters," in Worldwatch Institute, op. cit. note 2, p. 58.

87. S. Meek, J. Hill, and J. Webster, *The Evidence Base for Interventions to Reduce Malaria Mortality in Low and Middle-Income Countries,* Commission on Macroeconomics and Health, Working Paper Series No. WG5:6 (London: Malaria Consortium of the London School of Hygiene & Tropical Medicine, September 2001), p. 26.

88. David McGuire, NetMark Africa (USAID and the Academy for Educational Development), Washington, DC, discussion with author, 12 December 2001.

89. Cost-effectiveness from D. B. Evans, G. Azene, and J. Kirigia, "Should Governments Subsidize the Use of Insecticide-impregnated Mosquito Nets in Africa? Implications of a Cost-effectiveness Analysis," *Health Policy and Planning,*

June 1997, pp. 107–14; China and Viet Nam from WHO, op. cit. note 3, p. 55, and from Tran Duc Hinh, "Use of Insecticide-Impregnated Bed Nets for Malaria Control in Vietnam," *Mekong Malaria Forum* (Regional Malaria Control Programme in Cambodia, Laos, and Vietnam), April 2000; Zambia from McGuire, op. cit. note 88, and from Michael Macdonald, USAID Environmental Health Project, Arlington, VA, e-mail to author, 14 February 2002.

90. Malariologists eradicated from Farid, op. cit. note 47, p. 426; A. J. McMichael and R. Beaglehole, "The Changing Global Context of Public Health," *The Lancet,* 5 August 2000, pp. 495–99; M. F. Myers et al., "Forecasting Disease Risk for Increased Epidemic Preparedness in Public Health," *Advances in Parasitology,* vol. 47 (2000), pp. 309–30.

91. Difficulties of predictions from P. Carnevale et al., "Diversity of Malaria in Rice Growing Areas of the Afrotropical Region," *Parassitologia,* September 1999, pp. 273–76; high altitudes from Brewster, op. cit. note 50; benefits of draining rice paddies from Gladwell, op. cit. note 32, p. 51.

92. A. Seyoum et al., "Traditional Use of Mosquito-Repellent Plants in Western Kenya and Their Evaluation in Semi-field Experimental Huts Against *Anopheles gambiae:* Ethnobotanical Studies and Application by Thermal Expulsion and Direct Burning," *Transactions of the Royal Society of Tropical Medicine & Hygiene,* May/June 2002, pp. 225–31; G. P. Bhat and N. Surolia, "In vitro Antimalarial Activity of Extracts of Three Plants Used in the Traditional Medicine of India," *American Journal of Tropical Medicine & Hygiene,* October 2001, pp. 304–08; S. J. Moore, A. Lenglet, and N. Hill, "Field Evaluation of Three Plant-Based Insect Repellents Against Malaria Vectors in Vaca Diez Province, the Bolivian Amazon," *Journal of the American Mosquito Control Association,* June 2002, pp. 107–10.

93. S. Abdulla et al., "Impact on Malaria Morbidity of a Programme Supplying Insecticide Treated Nets in Children Aged Under 2 Years in Tanzania: Community Cross Sectional Study," *British Medical Journal,* 3 February 2001, pp. 270–73; child survival from Schellenberg et al., op. cit. note 78.

94. G. Kidane and R. H. Morrow, "Teaching Mothers to Provide Home Treatment of Malaria in

Tigray, Ethiopia: A Randomised Trial," *The Lancet,* 12 August 2000, pp. 550–55; "Ethiopia Mothers Spread Home Treatment Message," *RBM News,* December 2000, p. 3.

95. East African Network for Monitoring Antimalarial Treatment, "Monitoring Antimalarial Drug Resistance within National Malaria Control Programmes: The EANMAT Experience," *Tropical Medicine & International Health,* November 2001, pp. 891–98.

96. Integrated Management of Childhood Illness from WHO, op. cit. note 3, pp. 57–58; artemisinins from Robert G. Ridley, "Medical Need, Scientific Opportunity and the Drive for Antimalarial Drugs," *Nature,* 7 February 2002, pp. 686–93; suppositories from WHO, *Communicable Diseases 2000: Highlights of Activities in 1999 and Major Challenges for the Future* (Geneva: January 2000), p. 82, and from Julie McLaughlin, Africa Region, World Bank, Washington, DC, e-mail to author, 25 September 2002.

97. David Schellenberg et al., "Intermittent Treatment for Malaria and Anaemia Control at Time of Routine Vaccinations in Tanzanian Infants: A Randomized, Placebo-Controlled Trial," *The Lancet,* 12 May 2001, pp. 1471–77; Catherine A. Goodman, Paul C. Coleman, and Anne J. Mills, "The Cost-Effectiveness of Antenatal Malaria Prevention in Sub-Saharan Africa," *American Journal of Tropical Medicine & Hygiene,* January/February 2001 (supp.), pp. 45–56; Helen L. Guyatt et al., "Free Bednets to Pregnant Women through Antenatal Clinics in Kenya: A Cheap, Simple and Equitable Approach to Delivery," *Tropical Medicine & International Health,* May 2002, pp. 409–20.

98. Joanne McManus, "Finding a Cure," *Far Eastern Economic Review,* 23 November 2000, p. 43.

99. Ibid.; frontier areas and emergencies from WHO, op. cit. note 4, pp. 18–26, 60; E. K. Ansah et al., "Improving Adherence to Malaria Treatment for Children: The Use of Pre-Packed Chloroquine Tablets vs. Chloroquine Syrup," *Tropical Medicine & International Health,* vol. 6, no. 7 (2001), pp. 496–504.

100. Comparison of malaria and AIDS from Dr. Stephen Hoffman, Celera Genomics, Rockville, MD, discussion with author, 19 July 2002; Novartis from Novartis International AG, *Novartis Annual Report 2001* (Basel: 2002), from "Poor Countries Get Deal on Malaria Drug,"

USA Today, 24 May 2001, and from Gautam Naik, "New Malaria Strain Hits Africa," *Asian Wall Street Journal,* 30 July 2001.

101. Gro Harlem Brundtland from Moisés Naím, "The Global War for Public Health," *Foreign Policy,* January/February 2002, pp. 24–36; Eliot Marshall, "A Renewed Assault on an Old and Deadly Foe," *Science,* 20 October 2000, pp. 428–30; Global Fund from "Global Fund to Fight AIDS, Tuberculosis, and Malaria: Overview," at <www.globalfundatm.org/overview.html>, viewed 27 September 2002, with confirmed funds from "Q&A on the Progress of the Global Fund, July 2002," at <www.globalfundatm.org/faq_finaltopublic.html#3>, viewed 4 October 2002, and approved projects from "Proposals/Components Approved for Funding with No or Minor Adjustments," at <www.globalfundatm.org/files/Proposalslist_40.doc> viewed 4 October 2002; Roll Back Malaria (RBM) from Barbara Crossette, "U.N. and World Bank Unite To Wage War on Malaria," *New York Times,* 31 October 1998, with $24 million from Gunther Baugh, Resource Mobilization and Administration, RBM Secretariat, e-mail to Suprotik Basu, Malaria Team, World Bank, 11 October 2002; Medicines for Malaria Venture (MMV) from Jocelyn Kaiser, "Raising the Stakes in the Race for New Malaria Drugs," *Science,* 25 September 1998, p. 1930, with current MMV budget, quote, and projects from Declan Butler, "What Difference Does a Genome Make?" *Nature,* 3 October 2002, pp. 426–28, and from Geoffrey Cowley, "Bill's Biggest Bet Yet," *Newsweek,* 4 February 2002, pp. 44–52; Multilateral Initiative on Malaria in Africa funding from "Anteing Up for a World War on Malaria," *Science,* 29 August 1997, p. 1207, from Médicins Sans Frontiéres, Access to Essential Medicines Campaign and the Drugs for Neglected Diseases Working Group, *Fatal Imbalance: The Crisis in Research and Development for Drugs for Neglected Diseases* (Geneva: September 2001), and current budget from Andréa Egan, Multilateral Initiative on Malaria, National Institutes of Health, Bethesda, MD, e-mail to author, 1 October 2002.

102. Webster, op. cit. note 7; Gro Harlem Brundtland, "Health: A Pathway to Sustainable Development," *Journal of the American Medical Association,* 10 July 2002, p. 156.

1. Briefly outline the stages of malaria and how DDT works to kill it.

2. Summarize the history of the use of DDT in malaria eradication.

3. Write a one-page policy statement for the United Nations on whether or not the U.N. should promote the use of DDT in malaria-ridden areas.

62   The Blessings of Pesticides

DIXY LEE RAY AND LOUIS GUZZO

Dixy Lee Ray is a chemical biologist, and Louis Guzzo is a freelance writer.

In this article, Ray and Guzzo defend the use of chemical pesticides like DDT, Alar, PCBs, dioxins, and even asbestos. They argue that environmentalists like Rachel Carson and Paul Ehrlich are scaremongers, promoting lyrical hysteria in their ill-conceived battle against pesticides. On the whole, these pesticides are beneficial to humans and should be used discreetly—regulated, and controlled, but not banned.

No consideration of pesticides and their role in public health and agriculture would be complete without recounting the story of DDT. The events surrounding its use, overuse, and its being banned in the U.S. are dramatic. DDT was the first, best, and most remarkable of modern pesticides. Its history is a tale of triumph that ended in tragedy.

DDT, the convenient name for 1,1,1-tri-chloro-2,2-bis (p-chloro-phenyl) ethane, was first synthesized in 1877 and patented as an insecticide in 1939 by a Swiss chemist, Dr. Paul Muller. Its remarkable effectiveness against insects, specifically clothes moths and ectoparasites of both animals and plants, made it a welcome substitute for the toxic insecticides then in common use—arsenic, mercury, fluorine, and lead. In 1942, it was shown to kill body lice without adverse effect on humans, and it was used by all Allied troops during World War II. The result was that no Allied soldier was stricken with typhus fever (carried by lice) for the first time in the history of warfare. In World War I, by contrast, more soldiers died from typhus than from bullets.

Mosquito-borne malaria has always been man's worst disease, judged by the number of its victims. Until DDT came along, about 200 million people were stricken annually with malaria, and about two million of them died each year. Beginning in 1946, a large-scale spraying program directed against the malaria-carrying mosquito brought an immediate and dramatic decrease in these numbers. It is important to emphasize that this spraying was not indiscriminate, nor was it conducted in the natural environment. It was performed inside homes, on the interior walls. The unique behavior of the malarial mosquito—feeding at night on sleeping victims and then flying to the nearest vertical structure to rest and digest its meal—made this the ideal way to catch the largest number of adult insects.

Public health statistics from Sri Lanka testify to the effectiveness of the spraying program. In 1948, before use of DDT, there were 2.8 million cases of malaria. By 1963, there were only 17. Low levels of infection continued until the late 1960s, when the attacks on DDT in the U.S.

Reprinted from *Trashing the Planet* (Washington, D.C.: Regnery Gateway, 1990), by permission. Notes deleted.

convinced officials to suspend spraying. In 1968, there were one million cases of malaria. In 1969, the number reached 2.5 million, back to the pre-DDT levels. Moreover, by 1972, the largely unsubstantiated charges against DDT in the United States had a worldwide effect. In 1970, of two billion people living in malarial regions, 79 percent were protected and the expectation was that malaria would be eradicated. Six years after the United States banned DDT, there were 800 million cases of malaria and 8.2 million deaths per year. Even worse, because eradication programs were halted at a critical time, resistant malaria is now widespread and travelers could take it home. Much of the southern United States is favorable to the malarial mosquito. Malaria, yellow fever, and other diseases for which mosquitoes are the vector, used to be endemic in the South; mosquitoes have recently undergone an explosive population growth since their breeding grounds are now "protected" under federal law.

In 1948, Dr. Muller was awarded the Nobel Prize in medicine because of the medical importance of DDT. Dr. Samuel Simmons, chief of the technology branch of the Communicable Disease Center of the U.S. Public Health Service, said in 1959:

> The total value of DDT to mankind is inestimable. Most of the peoples of the globe have received benefit from it either directly by protection from infectious diseases and pestiferous insects or indirectly by better nutrition, cleaner food, and increased disease resistance. The discovery of DDT will always remain an historic event in the fields of public health and agriculture.

After initial success in controlling typhus and malaria, DDT was also used against yellow fever, sleeping sickness, plague, and encephalitis, all transmitted by insects and all epidemic at various times in the past in the United States.

"With the introduction of DDT to control the vectors of disease," wrote Claus and Bolander in 1977, "it seemed, for the first time in history, that man could look forward to a life of dignity, freed from the scourges of maiming disease and famine. It is no wonder, then, that its applications were greeted with general high enthusiasm."

Was the prospect of more people living better also anathema to the population-control and zero-growth organizations? There is some reason to believe so.

Plant pests also succumbed to DDT. It proved effective against spruce budworm, gypsy moth, tussock moth, pine weevil, and cotton boll weevil. So effective was DDT against such a variety of insects that it was inevitably overused. The attitude, "if a little bit is good, then more must be better," is a common human failing. Before any steps were taken to curtail and control DDT, it became ubiquitous in soil, water, and in the bodies of many living organisms. Even though no harm has ever been demonstrated to have been caused by DDT, its widespread presence in the environment was enough to give rise to alarm.

Contrary to common belief, DDT is not a persistent pesticide in the natural environment. Only in the unusual circumstances where soil is dark, dry, and devoid of microorganisms will DDT persist. Under normal environmental conditions, DDT loses its toxicity to insects in a few days, usually no more than two weeks. But its overuse did result in DDT being detected, albeit in small amounts, in soil, in water both salt and fresh, in the bodies of fish, birds, and domestic animals, and in man. This energized the opposition to its use that had first been sparked by the lyrical hysteria of Rachel Carson's book, *Silent Spring*.

The growing chorus from self-proclaimed environmentalists demanding that DDT be totally banned led to a public hearing in 1971. It should be noted that the Environmental Protection Agency, the agency responsible for regulating pesticides and for making the final decision about their use, actually took part in the hearing, testifying against DDT, along with the Environmental Defense Fund and other activist groups. The attack on DDT rested on three main allegations: that DDT caused the death of many birds and could lead to the extinction of some bird populations; that DDT was so stable that it could never be eliminated from the environment, and that DDT might cause cancer in humans. None of these charges has ever been substantiated.

It was alleged that DDT was toxic to birds that might ingest it from eating insects, earthworms, or seeds in sprayed areas. It was also charged that sublethal amounts of DDT in the bodies of birds caused them to lay eggs with thin shells that provided insufficient protection, resulting in the death of many chicks. These charges have been repeated so often that they are widely believed, even though they are, at best, "factoids," untrue in most instances.

Actual counts of bird populations, conducted annually by the Audubon Society at Christmastime, have shown that many bird populations were in fact increasing throughout the years of heaviest DDT spraying. For example, between 1941 and 1971, there was a 12 percent increase in robins, 21 times more cowbirds, 8 times more blackbirds, and 131 times more grackles. Gulls also increased, especially along the East Coast. Aside from robins—possibly America's most abundant bird, which some hysterical environmentalists said was "doomed" by DDT—it is the birds of prey that caught most of the anti-DDT attention, especially the osprey and the peregrine falcon. At the Hawk Mountain Sanctuary in Pennsylvania, annual surveys show 191 ospreys in 1946, compared to 600 in 1970. Each year showed some population increase. For the peregrine falcon, the numbers fluctuated from a low of 14 in 1965 to a high of 32 in 1969. Dr. Joseph Hickey, an authority on peregrines, testified at the DDT hearings that the falcon population had been declining since 1890. Its fate is more closely related to the availability of prey and nesting sites than to pesticides. For all hawks, the annual counts showed an increase from 9,291 in 1957 to 20,196 in 1967. Since it was protected by the endangered species designation, populations of the American Bald Eagle have increased significantly. Although environmentalists claim that this resurgence is due to banning DDT, there is no supportive evidence.

In the case of thin egg shells, it is a phenomenon that predates use of DDT. It has been known for decades. There are many causes: diets low in calcium or Vitamin D, fright, high nocturnal temperatures, various toxic substances, and diseases such as Newcastle's disease. Experiments designed to show a toxic effect from eating DDT failed, even though the experimenters fed their birds (pheasant and quail) from 6,000 to 20,000 times more DDT than the 0.3 parts per million residue of DDT found in food. Quail fed 200 parts per million in all their food throughout the reproductive period nevertheless hatched 80 percent of their chicks, compared with an 84 percent hatch in the control groups. No shell-thinning was reported. With pheasants handled in the same way, the DDT-treated birds hatched 80.6 percent of their eggs, compared with only 57.4 percent in the control groups.

DDT rapidly breaks down harmlessly in the natural environment. But in 1968, when DDT was still in wide use, a residue detected in food was measurable. An average daily human intake could reach 0.065 milligrams. To study the effect on humans, volunteer groups were fed up to 35 milligrams of DDT per day for periods of 21 and 27 months, with no ill effects then or in the nearly 30 years since. Most of the DDT is excreted, with some small residue, up to 12 parts per million, stored in human fat. No harm whatsoever has been detected from these trivial amounts. In sea water, which ultimately receives all the runoff from the land, more than 93 percent of all DDT is broken down in 38 days, but one part per *trillion* can be detected in inshore waters. Compare this to the irresponsible and unscientific claim by butterfly specialist and environmental guru Paul Ehrlich who charged that DDT in sea water would kill all algae (phytoplankton) and thus deprive the earth of 40 percent of its oxygen.

Finally, as for DDT being a cancer-causing agent, if one concludes that all growths, even benign tumors and lumps, are cancer, then the answer must be yes, but.... The "but" is important. If one accepts as "cancer" only malignant growths that can metastisize, then the answer is an unequivocal no. DDT is not a carcinogen. Laboratory studies have reported liver deformations in mice, but not in any other experimental animal (including rats). This is the basis for the charge that DDT is "cancer-causing." The doses, given by injection, required to cause the deformation of a mouse's liver were about 100,000 times higher than any possible ingestion from DDT residues in food.

The National Cancer Institute reviewed the mouse experiment results and, in 1978, declared DDT was not a carcinogen. It is also interesting to note that deaths from liver cancer in the United States actually *decreased* by 30 percent during the years of heaviest DDT use (1944 to 1972). Moreover, millions of people were exposed to DDT during the malarial spraying programs, and those who did the spraying, 130,000 men, were exposed to high concentrations with no ill effects.

These data and much more were presented at the 1971 hearing and the recommendation, after considering 300 technical documents and the testimony of 150 scientists, was that a total ban on DDT was not desirable, based on the scientific evidence. The hearing examiner declared in his final decision: "There is a present need for the continued use of DDT for the essential uses defined in this case."

That was in April 1972. Nevertheless, two months later, on June 14, 1972, William Ruckelshaus, EPA administrator, banned all uses of DDT unless an essential public purpose could be proved. Why did he do it? Two years earlier, Ruckelshaus had stated his support of DDT, citing its "amazing and exemplary record of safe use." Was he trying to curry favor with the environmental activist organizations? (When he left the EPA, he signed membership solicitation letters for the Environmental Defense Fund, the organization that led the fight against DDT.) Or was he trying to demonstrate muscle and establish the power of the EPA?

Years later, Ruckelshaus admitted that "decisions by the government involving the use of toxic substances are political...[and] the ultimate judgment remains political....[In] the case of pesticides, the power to make this judgment has been delegated to the Administrator of EPA."

The banning of DDT could not be justified on scientific grounds—regulation yes, control yes, but a total ban no. Had Ruckelshaus taken that position, instead of prohibition, back in 1972, we would still have the benefits of this important chemical today. The most important fallout from the Ruckelshaus decision on DDT was that it gave credibility to *pseudoscience,* it created an atmosphere in which scientific evidence can be pushed aside by emotion, hysteria, and political pressure. It has done inestimable damage. The technique of making unsubstantiated

charges, endlessly repeated, has since been used successfully against asbestos, PCBs, dioxin, and, of course, Alar.

DDT and other insecticides, herbicides, fungicides, and rodenticides have had a tremendous effect on agriculture. So, indeed, have other chemicals, fertilizers, improved varieties of crops, and better understanding of soil treatment and crop management. All of these, in an informed, integrated program of pest management, have led to an abundance in food production undreamed of a few decades ago. Never again need there be a disaster like the famine in the 1840s in Ireland that was caused by a fungus, Fusarium, the late potato blight. That catastrophe led to the death of one third of Ireland's population from starvation, another third emigrated, and the bitterness that exists between the Irish and the English was intensified yet further. How much of the tragedy of the Emerald Isle might have been averted if a good fungicide like captan had been available?

The potato makes a good object lesson for those who think "nature knows best" and who believe manure and crop rotation are all that's needed. In the 1920s, given good soil and animal fertilizer, an exceptional yield was 75 100-pound sacks of potatoes per acre. By 1940, the best methods were producing 82 sacks per acre. Then came the introduction of modern agriculture, with its chemicals and pesticides. The results look this:

Year	100-Pound Sacks Per Acre
1950	165
1960	208
1970	247
1980s	275

The dramatic increase didn't happen without help—from technology. With the very modern problem of agricultural surpluses in this country, we forget that in the 6,000 years of known human history, such food surpluses are new and unique.

In the 1930s, soil erosion became a serious problem in the United States, dramatized by the "dust bowl" experience in the farm areas of the Midwest. Contour plowing, windbreaks, and better soil management helped, but the most important innovation involved the introduction of herbicides for weed control, thereby making extensive tillage and disturbance of the soil unnecessary.

Pesticides have reduced America's food costs 33 percent by controlling weeds, insects, mold, and rot in vegetables and fruits. They have helped to keep our food and our homes clean by controlling rats, mice, and cockroaches. Through the use of wood preservatives in pressure-treated lumber for fences, porches, decks, and homes, we have saved a forest of trees two times the size of New England.

Modern agriculture has made it possible to grow more food, poultry, dairy products, and fiber on less land. This means that more land can be returned to woodlot, forest, and recreational uses. Of the 3.6 million square miles that constitute the United States, 32 percent—or 1.13 million square miles—are forests or woodlots. Because of this, the average annual wood growth is now three and a half times more than it was in 1920. Tree-growing areas increased 18 percent from 1952 to 1977. Forests in America continue to increase in size, even while supplying a substantial portion of the world's timber needs. Better forest management, improved seedlings, and informed use of fertilizers and pesticides have made this possible. The main danger to our forests today comes from federal lands (national parks, national forests, and wilderness areas), where no management is allowed, because "nature knows best." They now serve as foci for the production and dissemination of forest pests.

The fact is, we are about 10,000 years past the point where we can consider any part of nature untouched by humans or their activities. We cannot return to that faraway time. Besides, most farms maintain uncropped areas that are important to perpetuate wildlife, and there are more than two million farm ponds in the United States where wild species thrive.

By nature, plants require many different elements to survive and grow. But nature did not distribute these elements evenly. It is up to man to supply them. For *good* plant growth, calcium, phosphorus, potassium, magnesium, and nitrogen all must be supplied. This is the function of fertilizer. The ammonia arising from cattle urine is the same as that supplied from a chemical solution. It is a myth that "man-made" or synthetic compounds are dangerous and toxic, whereas the same compounds found in nature— for example, "natural chemicals"—are safe. There is no chemical difference between them.

But ignorant opponents of all man's efforts to improve human life on this earth have continued to insist that extremely low levels of industrial chemicals can be toxic or carcinogenic and that everything "synthetic" is somehow uniquely dangerous and will cause cancer. This is not true. It is the *dose*—the size or amount of exposure— that is important. The amount of natural pesticides we eat every day is at least 10,000 times the level of pesticide residue from agricultural use of synthetics.

Arsenic, cadmium, and chromium are all officially identified as carcinogens, yet they are all naturally present in every cell in our bodies. How much arsenic do we normally have? One hundred thousand molecules per cell. How much cadmium? Two million molecules per cell. How much chromium? Seven hundred thousand per cell. To believe, as the "one molecule can cause cancer" adherents do, that one extra molecule out of several hundred thousand will disrupt the DNA molecule and cause cancer stretches credulity beyond imagination. The theory, to put it bluntly, is nonsensical scare-mongering.

People, however, are attracted to horror stories, and since the news media are primarily in the entertainment business, scientific accuracy has a very low priority. At a recent symposium sponsored by the Smithsonian Institution, Ben Bradlee, editor of *The Washington Post*, said: "To hell with the news! I'm no longer interested in news. I'm interested in causes. We don't print the truth. We don't pretend to print the truth. We print what people tell us. It's up to the public to decide what's true."

Careful studies have established that 99.99 percent of the carcinogenic materials ingested daily are either natural or produced by drinking alcohol, cooking, or smoking. The simple way to avoid any problem is to eat a balanced diet with a reasonable variety of different foods. To avoid consuming carcinogens or other toxic substances, one would have to refrain from eating carrots, radishes, onions, olives, melons, ham, shrimp, potatoes, parsley, butter rolls, broccoli, watercress, avocado, lemons, cheese, bananas, apples, oranges, tea, milk, wine, water, and much else besides.

Nitrite, nitrate, and nitrosamines can be avoided only by eliminating most vegetables, especially beets, celery, lettuce, radishes, rhubarb, mustard kale, turnips, cabbage, and . . .

Well, it gets silly. Yet, if any of these foods were subject to tests similar to those used to screen synthetic chemicals, they would all be banned.

⚘ STUDY QUESTIONS

1. How strong are Ray and Guzzo's arguments? How can intelligent people and scientists so strongly disagree, as they do, over the effects of pesticides and herbicides such as DDT, Alar, PCBs, and even asbestos?

2. Do Ray and Guzzo make a convincing case that media hype and lyrical environmental hysteria have led a panic-stricken propaganda campaign against the reasonable use of pesticides?

⚘ FOR FURTHER READING

Bernards, Neal, ed. *The Environmental Crisis.* San Diego, CA: Greenhaven Press, 1991.

Carson, Rachel. *Silent Spring.* Boston: Houghton Mifflin, 1962.

Fumento, Michael. *Science Under Siege: Balancing Technology and the Environment.* New York: Morrow, 1993.

Gilbert, Susan. "America Tackles the Pesticide Crisis." *The New York Times Magazine* (Oct. 8, 1989).

Graham, Frank. *Since Silent Spring.* Boston: Houghton Mifflin, 1962.

Marco, Gino, Robert Hollingworth, and William Durham, eds. *Silent Spring Revisited.* Washington, D.C.: American Chemical Society, 1987.

Climate Change

ON JULY 23, 1988, DR. JAMES HANSEN, Director of the National Aeronautics and Space Administration (NASA) Goddard Institute for Space Studies, told the U.S. Senate Committee on Energy and Natural Resources, "It's time to stop waffling so much and say that this evidence is pretty strong that the greenhouse effect is here." Occurring in Washington, D.C., during the hottest summer on record, Hansen's testimony found a receptive audience. Newspapers issued headlines announcing the greenhouse effect and gave Hansen's testimony pride of place. Many scientists agreed with Hansen's assessment, although they were generally reluctant to give it the depth of conviction that Hansen expressed. Other scientists demurred, arguing that the evidence for global warming was ambiguous.

What is the greenhouse effect? Atmospheric gases keep our planet warm in a manner analogous to the glass panes of a greenhouse. The Sun's rays (energy in the form of light) are allowed in through the glass, but the heat that is then generated is trapped by the glass. The same phenomenon occurs when you keep your car windows closed on a sunny day. The heat is trapped inside, so it is warmer in the car than it is outside.

Likewise, the Sun's energy reaches Earth in the form of light, infrared radiation, and small amounts of ultraviolet radiation. Earth's surface absorbs much of this solar energy, some of which is used for photosynthesis, and transforms it to heat energy, which rises back into the troposphere (the innermost layer of the atmosphere, occupying the area about 11 miles above sea level). But water vapor (mostly in the form of clouds), carbon dioxide (CO_2), methane, and other gases block some of the heat energy from escaping, like the panes of the greenhouse. They absorb the heat and warm Earth. Without this heat-trapping blanket, Earth's surface would cool to about 0°F (−18°C) instead of maintaining an average temperature of 57°F (14°C). Most of our planet would be frozen like Mars.

The problem, then, is not the greenhouse process but its *increased* activity. It's too much of a good thing. For the past 8000 years, Earth's average temperature has never been warmer than 1°C, and the last time it was 2°C warmer was 125,000 years ago. Hansen and others have presented evidence that Earth has begun to get warmer and by current trends the polar ice caps will gradually melt, causing a rise in the ocean's level of anywhere from 6 to 9 feet. Millions of people living on islands and along coastlines would be displaced as their land was flooded by the oceans. While people in northern Canada, northern Russia, and Greenland might rejoice over warmer weather, most of the temperate zones would become much warmer. Air conditioner use would increase, demanding more energy and creating more pollution, which in turn would create a greater greenhouse effect. Weather patterns would change, negatively affecting agriculture and causing global starvation.

While scientists debate whether the evidence points to a significant trend in global warming, a consensus exists that prudence requires us to lower greenhouse gases (CO_2, methane, ozone, and others) wherever possible. The debate is over the seriousness of the threat.

In the last couple of years the issue of climate change has finally gotten the public's attention. There is little doubt that global warming is taking place, and there is little doubt that humans may be contributing to it. Indeed, almost all scientists believe we are the cause of this warming, but there is still dissent on how much of it we are causing and whether or not we should slow down our fossil fuel burning (and thus supposedly slow down our economies). By now many readers will have seen Al Gore's movie *An Inconvenient Truth*. If Gore and the majority of climate scientists are correct, then of course it makes economic sense to do whatever we can to reduce emissions.

The first reading includes a section on global warming from the Pew Center on Global Climate Change, including a discussion of whether global warming caused Hurricane Katrina. Polar ice sheets are melting, hurricanes are becoming stronger and more common, ecologies are changing, and numerous other effects are occurring. If the trend continues, substantial coastal areas around the world may be flooded and the climate of the planet completely changed. The second reading, "Ethics and Global Climate Change," focuses less on the science, instead surveying the numerous ethical questions that arise from the science and its uncertainties. The changing climate is one of the fastest moving fields of environmental ethics; as of August 2006, the readings are as up to date as possible, but readers are advised to seek further information. The Pew Center on Global Climate Change is an excellent place to start.

63   Understanding the Causes of Global Climate Change

PEW CENTER ON GLOBAL CLIMATE CHANGE

The Pew Center on Global Climate Change is a nonprofit organization dedicated to bringing "together business leaders, policy makers, scientists, and other experts to bring a new approach to a complex and often controversial issue. Our approach is based on sound science, straight talk, and a belief that we can work together to protect the climate while sustaining economic growth." For further up-to-date information, visit their web site (from which this section was taken) at http://www.pewclimate.org.

Reprinted by permission of the Pew Center on Global Climate Change (http://www.pewclimate.org/).
Notes deleted.

Average air temperatures at the Earth's surface have increased by approximately 0.6°C (1°F) over the 20th century. Analysis of the various human and natural influences on the global climate indicates that this warming cannot be explained without taking into account human emissions of greenhouse gases (GHGs). Furthermore, current analyses indicate that GHGs have been the dominant force driving temperature increases over the past 50 years.

INTRODUCTION

Recent decades have seen record-high average global surface air temperatures. The years 1998, 2002, and 2003 were the three warmest years recorded in the instrumental record (which dates back to the mid-1800s). In fact, all of the top 10 warmest years on record have occurred since 1990. These record warm years are the result of a century of global warming. Between 1900 and 2000, global surface air temperatures increased by 0.4–0.8°C (0.7–1.4°F). Over the past 30 years, temperatures in the lower atmosphere, or troposphere, have warmed by 0.07–0.1°C (0.1–0.2°F) per decade.

This warming has resulted from numerous factors that influence climate. Some of these factors are natural, such as changes in solar radiation and volcanic activity. Others, particularly emissions of greenhouse gases (GHGs) and land-use changes, are human in origin. Determining their relative contributions to observed climate change is a difficult task. Nevertheless, the current scientific consensus is that, at least over the past 50 years, the major factor driving observed temperature increases has been human emissions of GHGs.

How have scientists arrived at this conclusion? Climate varies considerably over annual to millennial time-scales, and a change in global temperatures alone does not indicate human influence. The attribution of climate change to specific factors requires an analysis of the long-term temperature increases and the factors that could be responsible for those increases.

CLIMATE OVER THE PAST MILLENNIUM

Determining climate patterns over many centuries is difficult because of the absence of instrumental temperature records before the mid-1800s. A number of attempts at reconstructing a temperature record of the northern hemisphere over the past 1000 years have used "proxy" indicators of temperature, such as tree rings, coral reefs, and ice cores.

Despite significant uncertainties, the studies yield consistent results, indicating that the Northern Hemisphere was in a relative warm phase between 1000 and 1400 AD; followed by a prolonged cool phase until the 1800s. These studies also indicate that the last 50 years were probably warmer than any time period during the previous 1000 years ... and recent data suggest that recent temperatures may be unprecedented over the past 2000 years.

THE FACTORS INFLUENCING CLIMATE

Climate varies considerably over time. This variability is a response to climate "forcings"—factors that cause warming or cooling of the atmosphere. Over most of the Earth's history, such forcings have been exclusively natural, and include variability in solar radiation, the Earth's orbit, and the frequency or intensity of volcanic activity. However, since the industrial revolution, human activities have had an increasing influence on the global climate system.

Greenhouse gases. Collectively, GHGs have enhanced the greenhouse effect, contributing to global warming over the past century. Carbon dioxide (CO_2), methane (CH_4), nitrous oxide (N_2O), and tropospheric ozone have all increased well above their pre-industrial concentrations. Various industrial GHGs that were previously absent from the atmosphere have also accumulated.

Land use changes. Land-use changes have influenced the reflectivity of the Earth's surface, resulting in either a warming or a cooling depending on the change. Deforestation and agricultural activities have a net cooling effect because cleared land surfaces reflect more solar radiation than rough or forested lands. Increased urbanization causes localized warming at the Earth's surface, known as the "Urban Heat Island" (UHI) effect. Despite suggestions that UHIs have contributed significantly to recent warming, analysis of 20th century temperature observations indicates that they have had a relatively small effect on global warming trends. On a global scale, the net effects of land-use change are believed to have caused a net cooling of global temperatures since the industrial revolution.

Aerosols. Atmospheric particles, or aerosols, from industry and fossil fuel combustion also can cool or heat the Earth's surface and atmosphere. Sulfate aerosols reflect sunlight and contribute to cloud formation, both of which have a cooling effect. Black carbon aerosols (soot) warm the atmosphere by absorbing solar radiation, and have probably contributed significantly to observed global warming. They also shade the Earth's surface, which has a minor cooling effect. Although the exact magnitude of warming caused by black carbon aerosols is uncertain, some scientists have suggested that reductions in black carbon emissions as well as CO_2 may help slow the rate of global warming over the near-term.

Cosmic rays. In recent years, the influence of cosmic rays on the formation of clouds has been considered as a potential factor in long-term climate change. However, trends in cosmic rays and clouds over the 20th century suggest that cosmic rays are not a major factor influencing the climate change that is currently being observed.

Collectively, some of these factors have had an important influence on the global climate over the past 50 years.... [T]he dominant force has been GHGs, which have had a net warming effect. Natural changes in solar radiation have contributed to warming as well, but these are minor relative to the effects of GHGs. Other factors appear to have had a cooling effect, but not large enough to offset warming caused by GHGs.

CLIMATE CHANGE OVER THE 20TH CENTURY

There is uniform consensus that average surface air temperatures over the 20th century increased between 1900–1940, decreased slightly between 1940–1970, and increased again from 1970 to the present, based on the instrumental temperature record. The first step in determining the causes of climate change is to compare this pattern of warming with what is known about the various factors that have influenced climate over the 20th century.

1900–1940. Although the burning of fossil fuels was commonplace as early as the 1700s, CO_2 concentrations were only about 295 parts per million (ppm) by 1900, just 7% higher than pre-industrial levels of 270 ppm. The warming associated with this CO_2 increase is considered to be too small to account for the observed warming. However, natural factors, particularly increases in solar radiation and a decline in volcanic activity, are well correlated with temperature over this time period, indicating that the warming was predominantly due to these two factors.

1940–1970. The cooling observed between 1940–1970 has been the cause of much speculation, because it is inconsistent with the larger picture of global warming over the 20th century. By 1970, concentrations of CO_2 were approximately 330 ppm, 20% above pre-industrial levels, yet cooling occurred. Again, natural factors appear to have played an important role. Solar radiation decreased between 1940–70, partly explaining the observed cooling. In addition, rapid increases in human emissions of sulfate aerosols probably played a significant role by shading the Earth's surface from solar radiation.

1970-present. Since 1970, atmospheric CO_2 has increased further to ~370 ppm, 30% above pre-industrial levels. By 2000, other GHGs, such as methane and nitrous oxide, were 100% and 15%, respectively, above their pre-industrial levels. The warming caused by this substantial increase in GHGs has exceeded the cooling associated with sulfate aerosols. Sulfur emissions were declining in the United States and Europe by the late 20th century due to air pollution regulations, although global emissions continue to increase. Solar radiation has been relatively stable over the late 20th century, except for the 11-year cycle of sunspot activity, which is not sufficient to account for the observed warming.

Katrina and Global Warming

Was Katrina's Power a Product of Global Warming?

With a unique confluence of geography, expansive lowlands (particularly in the New Orleans area), wetland loss, deforestation, rapid development, large populations of the poor, and a heavy concentration of industry, the Gulf Coast is extremely vulnerable to hurricanes, with or without global warming. Katrina is not the first category 5 hurricane to hit the Gulf Coast (it actually weakened slightly to category 4 shortly before landfall in Louisiana and Mississippi); in fact, of the three previous similar events, two of them occurred in 1935 and 1969, prior to the period of most of the human-induced global warming that has occurred so far. Clearly, then, global warming is not required for an extremely intense hurricane to strike.

But can science tell us whether Katrina's destructiveness was related to global warming? Not directly: science, as a method, is not good at assigning causation for uncontrolled events, and no single weather event can be linked directly to a long-term driver, such as global warming. This inability to draw a definite conclusion, however, in no sense justifies the conclusion that global warming did not influence Katrina.

What science does offer on this question is a general understanding of the physics of tropical storms that can inform reasonable assessment. Because hurricanes draw strength from heat in ocean surface waters, warming the water should generate more powerful hurricanes, on average. Indeed, sea surface temperature records show that the oceans are more than 1 degree F warmer on average today compared to a century ago. On short time scales (days to months), temperatures fluctuate above and below the long-term average, and the water can be warmer or cooler than the average on any given day. But the higher the average, the more likely the water will be warm enough to produce a strong storm on any given day during the hurricane season. Case in point: while Katrina was strengthening from a tropical storm to a category 5 hurricane, as it passed between the Florida Keys and the Gulf Coast, the surface waters in the Gulf of Mexico were unusually warm—about 2 degrees F warmer than normal for this time of year. Form this "first-principles" perspective, then, it is no surprise that Katrina became a very powerful storm. While there is no method to determine whether global warming played a role, it is reasonable to say it increased the probability that the Gulf surface water would be unusually warm on any given day, as it was on August 29 when Katrina's intensity peaked.

Beyond inferences from our understanding of storm physics, is there evidence that storms are actually becoming more intense, as we would expect? A study published recently in Nature found that since the early 1950s, the average intensity of tropical storms has increased globally, and this trend correlates very well through time with the increase in average sea surface temperatures in the tropics. These data show a real trend that fits expectations from our basic understanding of climate, and a powerful storm like Katrina makes sense in this context.

So, although we cannot be certain global warming intensified Katrina per se, it clearly has created circumstances under which powerful storms are more likely to occur at this point in history (and in the future) than they were in the past. Moreover, it would be scientifically unsound to conclude that Katrina was not intensified by global warming. A reasonable assessment of the science suggests that we will face similar events again and that powerful storms are likely to happen more often than we have been accustomed to in the past.

Source: The Pew Center on Global Climate Change. Used with permission.

SUPPORTING EVIDENCE FROM CLIMATE MODELS

Analysis of the factors that can force climate changes and corresponding temperature changes over the 20th century provide strong evidence of a human influence on climate. Furthermore, statistical analyses detect human influences on climate that are distinct from natural variability. When only natural factors or human factors are included in climate models, results differ significantly from observations during certain time periods. Thus, climate models perform best at reproducing 20th century climate observations when they include both human and natural factors. Furthermore, despite the importance of both natural and human factors in driving climate, human factors account for the majority of the observed increase in globally averaged surface air temperatures over the past 50 years. Thus, recent trends in surface air temperatures and atmospheric temperatures are the result of a significant human influence, specifically increases in atmospheric GHG concentrations.

CONCLUSIONS

The current state of knowledge regarding 20th century temperature changes is clear. Temperatures of recent decades, at least in the northern hemisphere, are likely warmer than at any point during at least the previous millennium, and the probability that an unknown factor other than GHGs can account for this warming is low. Thus, despite the long-term natural variability of the climate system, current scientific evidence indicates there is a significant human influence on current climate trends. This human contribution to global warming is projected to grow increasingly strong in future decades as human emissions of long-lived GHGs continue to alter the composition of the atmosphere.

❧ STUDY QUESTIONS

1. In a paragraph, summarize the evidence that shows the observed changes in world climate are due to human activity.
2. Browse The Pew Center on Global Climate Change's website: http://www.pewclimate.org/. What are the dangers of global warming?
3. Go to the above website, and also to http://www.ipcc.ch/, the website of the Intergovernmental Panel on Climate Change (IPCC). What new developments have occurred since the publication of this book?

64   Ethics and Global Climate Change

STEPHEN M. GARDINER

Stephen Gardiner is professor of philosophy at the University of Washington. This article is perhaps the most comprehensive examination of the ethical issues surrounding the complexities of climate change. Gardiner attempts to make climate change more accessible to philosophers and nonexperts and then challenges us to see it as a moral issue.

Very few moral philosophers have written on climate change. This is puzzling, for several reasons. First, many politicians and policy makers claim that climate change is not only the most serious environmental problem currently facing the world, but also one of the most important international problems per se. Second, many of those working in other disciplines describe climate change as fundamentally an ethical issue.

Third, the problem is theoretically challenging, both in itself and in virtue of the wider issues it raises. Indeed, some have even gone so far as to

Reprinted from *Ethics* 114 (April 2004): 555–600. © 2004 by The University of Chicago. All rights reserved. Notes deleted.

suggest that successfully addressing climate change will require a fundamental paradigm shift in ethics (Jamieson 1992, p. 292.)

Arguably, then, there is a strong presumption that moral philosophers should be taking climate change seriously. So, why the neglect? In my view, the most plausible explanation is that study of climate change is necessarily interdisciplinary, crossing boundaries between (at least) science, economics, law, and international relations.

This fact not only creates an obstacle to philosophical work (since amassing the relevant information is both time-consuming and intellectually demanding) but also makes it tempting to assume that climate change is essentially an issue for others to resolve. Both factors contribute to the current malaise—and not just within philosophy, but in the wider community too.

My aims in this survey, then, will be twofold. First, I will try to overcome the interdisciplinary obstacle to some extent, by making the climate change issue more accessible to both philosophers and non-philosophers alike. Second, by drawing attention to the ethical dimensions of the climate change problem, I will make the case that the temptation to defer to experts in other disciplines should be resisted. Climate change is fundamentally an ethical issue. As such, it should be of serious concern to both moral philosophers and humanity at large.

The interdisciplinary nature of the climate change problem once prompted John Broome to imply that a truly comprehensive survey of the relevant literature would be impossible (Broome 1992, p. viii). I shall not attempt the impossible. Instead, I shall present an overview of the most major and recent work relevant to philosophical discussion. Inevitably, this overview will be to some extent selective and opinionated. Still, I hope that it will help to reduce the interdisciplinary obstacles to philosophical work on climate change, by giving both philosophers and the public more generally some sense of what has been said so far and what might be at stake. In my view, the ethics of global climate change is still very much in its infancy. Hopefully, this small contribution will encourage its development.

I. TERMINOLOGY

While global warming has catastrophic communications attached to it, climate change sounds a more controllable and less emotional challenge.

FRANK LUNTZ

Potential confusion about the climate change problem begins even with the terms used to describe it: from 'greenhouse effect' to 'global warming' to the more recently favored 'climate change.' To begin with, many people spoke of 'the greenhouse effect.' This refers to the basic physical mechanism behind projected changes in the climate system. Some atmospheric gases (called 'greenhouse gases' [GHG]) have asymmetric interactions with radiation of different frequencies: just like glass in a conventional greenhouse, they allow shortwave incoming solar radiation through but reflect some of the Earth's outgoing long-wave radiation back to the surface. This creates "a partial blanketing effect," which causes the temperature at the surface to be higher than would otherwise be the case (Houghton 1997, pp. 11–12). Humans are increasing the atmospheric concentrations of these gases through industrialization. This would, other things being equal, be expected to result in an overall warming effect.

The basic greenhouse mechanism is both well understood and uncontroversial. Still, the term 'greenhouse effect' remains unsatisfactory to describe the problem at hand. There are two reasons. First, there is a purely natural greenhouse effect, without which the earth would be much colder than it is now. Hence, it is not accurate to say that "the greenhouse effect" as such is a problem; in fact, the reverse is true: without some greenhouse effect, the Earth would be much less hospitable for life as we know it. The real problem is the enhanced, human-induced, greenhouse effect. Second, it is not the greenhouse effect in isolation which causes the climate problem. Whether an increase in the concentration of greenhouse gases does in fact cause the warming we would otherwise expect depends on how the immediate effects of an increase in low frequency radiation play out in the overall climate system. But that system is complex, and its details are not very well understood.

For a while, then, the term 'global warming' was favored. This term captures the point that it is the effects of increased levels of greenhouse gases which are of concern. However, it also has its limitations. In particular, it highlights a specific effect, higher temperatures, and thus suggests a one-dimensional problem. But while it is true that rising temperature has been a locus for concern about increasing human emissions of greenhouse gases, it is not true that temperature as such defines either the core problem or even (arguably) its most important aspects. Consider, for example, the following. First, a higher global temperature does not in itself constitute the most important impact of climate change. Indeed, considered in isolation, there might be no particular reason to prefer the world as it is now to one several degrees warmer. However, second, this thought is liable to be misleading. For presumably if one is imagining a warmer world and thinking that it may be appealing, one is envisioning the planet as it might be in a stable, equilibrium state at the higher level, where humans, animals, and plants have harmoniously adapted to higher temperatures. But the problem posed by current human behavior is not of this kind. The primary concern of many scientists is that an enhanced greenhouse effect puts extra energy into the earth's climate system and so creates an imbalance. Hence, most of the concern about present climate change has been brought about because it seems that change is occurring at an unprecedented rate, that any equilibrium position is likely to be thousands, perhaps tens or hundreds of thousands, of years off, and that existing species are unlikely to be able to adapt quickly and easily under such conditions. Third, though it is at present unlikely, it is still possible that temperature might go down as a result of the increase in atmospheric greenhouse gas concentrations. But this does not cast any doubt on the serious nature of the problem. This is partly because a rapid and unprecedented lowering of temperature would have similar kinds of adverse effects on human and nonhuman life and health as a rapid warming, and partly because the effects most likely to cause cooling (such as a shutdown of the thermohaline circulation [THC] which supports the Gulf Stream current to Northern Europe [discussed in the next section]) may well be catastrophic even in relation to the other projected effects of global warming.

For all these reasons, current discussion tends to be carried out under the heading 'climate change.' This term captures the fact that it is interference in the climate system itself which is the crucial issue, not what the particular effects of that interference turn out to be. The fundamental problem is that it is now possible for humans to alter the underlying dynamics of the planet's climate and so the basic life-support system both for themselves and all other forms of life on Earth. Whether the alteration of these dynamics is most conveniently tracked in terms of increasing, declining, or even stable temperatures is of subsidiary interest in comparison to the actual changes in the climate itself and their consequences for human, and nonhuman, life.

II. CLIMATE SCIENCE

Almost no one would deny that in principle our actions and policies should be informed by our best scientific judgments, and it is hard to deny that our best scientific judgments about climate change are expressed in the IPCC reports.

JAMIESON, 1998, P. 116

Recent scientific evidence shows that major and widespread climate changes have occurred with startling speed.... Climate models typically underestimate the size, speed, and extent of those changes.... Climate surprise to be expected.

U.S. NATIONAL RESEARCH COUNCIL, 2002, P. 1

What do we know about climate change? In 1988, the Intergovernmental Panel on Climate Change (IPCC) was jointly established by the World Meteorological Association and the United Nations Environment Program to provide member governments with state of the art assessments of "the science, the impacts, and the economics of—and the options for mitigating and/or adapting to—climate change" (IPCC 2001*c*, p. vii). The IPCC has, accordingly, submitted three comprehensive reports, in 1990, 1995, and 2001. The results have remained fairly consistent across all three reports, though the level of confidence in those results has increased. The main findings of the most recent are as follows.

The IPCC begins with an account of patterns of climate change observed so far. On temperature, they report: "The global average surface temperature has increased over the 20th century by about 0.6°C"; "Globally, it is very likely that the 1990s was the warmest decade and 1998 the warmest year in the instrumental record, since 1861"; and "The increase in temperature in the 20th century is likely to have been the largest of any century during the past 1,000 years" (IPCC 2001c, p. 152). For other phenomena, they say that snow cover and ice extent have decreased, global average sea level has risen, and ocean heat content has increased. They also cite evidence for increases in the amount of precipitation in some regions; the frequency of heavy precipitation events; cloud cover in some latitudes; and the frequency, persistence, and intensity of El Nino phenomenon.

The IPCC also surveys the literature on relevant human activities. They conclude that since preindustrial times (1750 is the usual benchmark), humans have altered "the atmosphere in ways that are expected to affect the climate" by markedly increasing the concentrations of greenhouse gases (IPCC 2001c, p. 154). The main culprit is carbon dioxide, for which "the concentration has increased by 31% since 1750"; "the present CO_2 concentration has not been exceeded during the past 420,000 years and likely not during the past 20 million years"; and "the current rate of increase is unprecedented during at least the past 20,000 years...at about 1.5 ppm [parts per million] (0.4%) per year" (IPCC 2001c, p. 155). The main anthropogenic sources of CO_2 are the burning of fossil fuels (about 75 percent) and changes in land-use patterns (principally, deforestation). Of secondary importance is methane, where the present atmospheric concentration "has increased by...151% since 1750; and has not been exceeded during the past 420,000 years," and "slightly more than half of current...emissions are anthropogenic (e.g., use of fossil fuels, cattle, rice agriculture and landfills)" (IPCC 2001c, pp. 156–57). Molecule for molecule, methane is a more potent greenhouse gas than carbon dioxide.

Still, because CO_2 lasts much longer in the atmosphere (about 5–200 years, as opposed to methane's 12 years), it is the more important anthropogenic greenhouse gas.

The IPCC also tries to predict future climate. To do so, it uses computer models to simulate a variety of different possible future scenarios, incorporating different assumptions about economic growth, world population, and technological change. The basic results are as follows. First, carbon dioxide emissions due to the burning of fossil fuels are "virtually certain to be the dominant influence on the trends in atmospheric CO_2 concentration during the 21st century," and by 2100, that concentration should be 90–250 percent above preindustrial levels (of 280 parts per million), at 540–970 parts per million (IPCC 2001c, pp. 158–59). Second, if this occurs, the full range of model scenarios predict that surface temperature will increase by 1.4–5.8°C over the century. The IPCC states that this is not only a much larger projected rate of warming than that observed during the twentieth century but one "very likely...without precedent during at least the last 10,000 years." Third, models indicate that "stabilisation of atmospheric CO_2 concentrations at 450, 650 or 1,000 ppm would require global anthropogenic CO_2 emissions to drop below 1990 levels, within a few decades, about a century, or about two centuries, respectively, and continue to decrease steadily thereafter. Eventually CO_2 emissions would need to decline to *a very small fraction* of current emissions" (IPCC 2001c, p. 160; emphasis added).

Alarming as the IPCC predictions are, we should also pay attention to the fact that they might be overly optimistic. For some authors argue that the current climate models typically underestimate the potential for nonlinear threshold effects (U.S. National Research Council 2002; Gagosian 2003). One well-known threat of this sort is the potential collapse of the West Antarctic Ice Sheet (WAIS), which would eventually raise global sea levels by 4–6 meters. But the recent literature registers even greater concern about a lesser-known issue: the possibility of a weakening or shutdown of the deep circulation system which drives the world's ocean currents.

This system, known as "the Ocean Conveyor," distributes "vast quantities of heat around our planet, and thus plays a fundamental role in governing Earth's climate . . . [and] in the distribution of life-sustaining water" (Gagosian 2003, p. 4).

The Ocean Conveyor has been called the climate's "Achilles Heel" (Broecker 1997), because it appears to be a major threshold phenomenon. There are two grounds for concern. First, there is strong evidence that in the past the conveyor has slowed, and slowed very quickly, with significant climatic consequences. One such event, 12,700 years ago, saw a drop in temperatures in the North Atlantic region of around 5 degrees Celsius in a single decade. This apparently caused icebergs to spread as far south as the coast of Portugal and has been linked to widespread global drought. Second, the operation of the conveyor is governed by factors that can be affected by climate change. In particular, the world's currents are driven by the sinking of a large volume of salty water in the North Atlantic region. But this process can be disrupted by an influx of fresh water, which both dilutes the salty water and can also create a lid over it, restricting heat flow to the atmosphere.

The possibility of dramatic climate shifts of this sort complicates the picture of a global warming world in several ways. First, it suggests that gradual warming at the global level could cause, and coexist with, dramatic cooling in some regions. (Among other things, this has serious ramifications for our ability to plan for future changes.) Second, it envisages that the major losers from climate change may not be the usual suspects, the less developed countries (LDCs). For it is the rich countries bordering the North Atlantic that are particularly vulnerable to Conveyor shifts. Climate models predict that "the North Atlantic region would cool 3 to 5 degrees Celsius if conveyor circulation were totally disrupted," producing winters "twice as cold as the worst winters on record in the eastern United States in the past century" for a period of up to a century (Gagosian 2003, p. 7).

The IPCC does not emphasize the problem of the Ocean Conveyor. For one thing, though it acknowledges that most models predict a weakening of the conveyor during the twenty-first century, it emphasizes that such changes are projected to be offset by the more general warming; for another, it suggests that a complete shutdown is unlikely during the twenty-first century (though increasingly likely thereafter) (IPCC 2001c, p. 16). Hence, the IPCC's attitude is relatively complacent. Still, it is not clear what justifies such complacency. On the one hand, even if the threshold will not be reached for 100 years, this is still a matter of serious concern for future generations, since once the underlying processes which will breach it are in motion, it will be difficult, if not impossible, to reverse them. On the other hand, the current models of thermohaline circulation are not very robust, primarily because scientists simply do not know where the threshold is. And some models do predict complete shutdown within a range which overlaps with IPCC projections for the twenty-first century (IPCC 2001c, p. 440).

III. SCIENTIFIC UNCERTAINTY

Scientists aren't any time soon going to give politicians some magic answer. Policy makers for a long, long time are going to have to deal with a situation where it's not clear what the costs and benefits are, where lots of people disagree about them, and they can't wait until everything is resolved.

ROBERT J. LAMPERT

Should the public come to believe that the scientific issues are settled, their views about global warming will change accordingly. Therefore, you need to continue to make the lack of scientific certainty a primary issue.

FRANK LUNTZ, IN LEE 2003

It is sometimes argued that the uncertainty of the scientist's predictions is a reason for not acting at present, and that we should wait until some further research has been concluded. This argument is poor economics.

BROOME, 1992, P. 17

Politically, the most common objection raised to action on climate change is that of scientific uncertainty. In this section, I will explain why most writers on the subject believe this objection to be a red herring.

The first thing to note is that, at least in economics, uncertainty is a technical term, to be distinguished from risk. In the technical sense, a risk involves a known, or reliably estimable, probability, whereas an uncertainty arises when such probabilities are not available. So to say that there is scientific uncertainty surrounding global warming is to claim that we do not know, and cannot reliably estimate, the probability that climate change will occur, nor its extent if it does occur.

This distinction is useful, because the first problem with the objection from scientific uncertainty is that the IPCC does not seem to view global warming as uncertain in the technical sense. As we have seen, the 2001 Scientific Assessment explicitly assigns probabilities to its main climate predictions, making the situation one of risk, rather than uncertainty. Furthermore, these probabilities are of considerable magnitude. (For example, the IPCC says that it is "very likely" that in the twenty-first century there will be "higher maximum temperatures and more hot days over nearly all land areas" [IPCC 2001c, p. 162], by which they mean a probability of 90–99 percent [IPCC 2001c, p. 152, n. 7].) Given that many of the effects assigned high probabilities are associated with significant costs, they would seem to justify some kinds of action.

But perhaps the idea is that the IPCC's probability statements are not reliable, so that we should ignore them, treat the situation as genuinely uncertain, and hence refuse to act. Still, there is a difficulty. For, to an important extent, some kind of uncertainty "is an inherent part of the problem" (Broome 1992, p. 18). Arguably, if we knew exactly what was going to happen, to whom, and whose emissions would cause it, the problem might be more easily addressed; at the very least, it would have a very different shape. Hence, to refuse to act because of uncertainty is either to refuse to accept the global warming problem as it is (insisting that it be turned into a more respectable form of problem before one will address it) or else to endorse the principle that to "do nothing" is the appropriate response to uncertainty. The former is a head-in-the-sand approach and clearly unacceptable, but

the latter is also dubious and does not fit our usual practice.

The third, and perhaps most crucial, point to make about the problem of uncertainty is that it is important not to overplay it. For one thing, many decisions we have to make in life, including many important decisions, are also subject to considerable uncertainties. For another, all uncertainties are not created equal. On the one hand, the reason I am unable to assign probabilities may be that I know absolutely nothing about the situation, or else that I have only one past instance to go on. But I may also be uncertain in circumstances where I have considerable information.

Now it seems clear that uncertainty in the first kind of case is worse than uncertainty in the second, and potentially more paralyzing. Furthermore, and this is the crucial point, it seems reasonably clear that scientific uncertainty about global warming is of the second kind. As Donald Brown argues: "A lot of climate change science has never been in question, . . . many of the elements of global warming are not seriously challenged even by the scientific skeptics, and . . . the issues of scientific certainty most discussed by climate skeptics usually deal with the magnitude and timing of climate change, not with whether global warming is a real threat" (Brown 2002, p. 102). To see this, let us briefly examine a number of sources of uncertainty about global warming.

The first concerns the direct empirical evidence for anthropogenic warming itself. This has two main aspects. First, systematic global temperature records, based on measurements of air temperature on land and surface-water temperature measurements at sea, exist only from 1860, and satellite-based measurements are available only from 1979. The direct evidence for recent warming comes from the former. But skeptics suggest that the satellite measurements do not match the surface readings and do not provide evidence for warming. Second, there is no well-defined baseline from which to measure change. While it is true that the last couple of decades have been the warmest in human history, it is also true that the long-term climate record displays significant short-term variability and that, even accounting for this, climate seems to have been remarkably stable since the end of the last Ice Age 10,000 years ago, as compared with the preceding 100,000 years. Hence, global temperatures have fluctuated considerably over the long-term record, and it is clear that these fluctuations have been naturally caused.

The skeptics are right, then, when they assert that the observational temperature record is a weak data set and that the long-term history of the climate is such that even if the data were more robust, we would be rash to conclude that humans are causing it solely on this basis. Still, it would be a mistake to infer too much from the truth of these claims. For it would be equally rash to dismiss the possibility of warming on these grounds. For, even though it might be true that the empirical evidence is consistent with there being no anthropogenic warming, it is also true that it provides just the kind of record we would expect if there were a real global warming problem.

This paradox is caused by the fact that our epistemological position with respect to climate change is intrinsically very difficult: it may simply be impossible to confirm climate change empirically from this position. This is because our basic situation may be a bit like that of a coach who is asked whether the current performance of a fifteen-year-old athlete shows that she will reach the highest level of her sport. Suppose the coach has the best evidence that she can have. It will still only be evidence for a fifteen-year-old. It will be at most consistent with reaching the highest level. It cannot be taken as a certain prediction. But that does not mean it is no prediction at all, or worthless. It is simply the best prediction she is currently in a position to make.

Fortunately, for the climate change problem, the concern with the empirical record is not the end of the matter. For the temperature record is far from our only evidence for warming. Instead, we also have strong theoretical grounds for concern. First, the basic physical and chemical mechanisms which give rise to a potential global warming effect are well understood. In particular, there is no scientific controversy over the claims (*a*) that in itself a higher concentration of greenhouse gas molecules in the upper atmosphere would cause more heat to be retained by the earth and less radiated out into the solar system, so that other things being equal, such an increase would cause global temperatures to rise; and (*b*) that human activities since the industrial revolution have significantly increased the atmospheric concentration of greenhouse gases. Hence, everyone agrees that the basic circumstances are such that a greenhouse effect is to be expected.

Second, the scientific dispute, insofar as there is one, concerns the high level of complexity of the global climate system, given which there are the other mechanisms that might be in play to moderate such an effect. The contentious issue here is whether there might be negative feedbacks that either sharply reduce or negate the effects of higher levels of greenhouse gases, or even reduce the amount of them present in the atmosphere. However, current climate models suggest that most related factors will likely exhibit positive feedbacks (water vapor, snow, and ice), while others have both positive and negative feedbacks whose net effect is unclear (e.g., clouds, ocean currents). Hence, there is genuine scientific uncertainty. But this does not by itself justify a skeptical position about action on climate change. For there may be no more reason to assume that we will be saved by unexpectedly large negative feedbacks than that the warming effect will be much worse than we would otherwise anticipate, due to unexpectedly large positive feedbacks.

This is the basic scientific situation. However, there further aspects of uncertainty are worth mentioning. First, the conclusions about feedback are also open to doubt because considerable uncertainties remain about the performance of the models. In particular, they are not completely reliable against past data. This is to be expected because the climate is a highly complex system which is not very well understood. Still, it clouds the overall picture. Second, as mentioned earlier, the current models tend to assume that atmospheric feedbacks scale linearly with surface warming, and they do not adequately account for possible threshold effects, such as the possible collapse of the West Antarctic Ice Sheet. Hence, they may underestimate the potential risks from global warming. Finally, there is a great deal of uncertainty about the distribution of climate change. Though global rises may seem small, they disguise considerable variation within years and across regions. Furthermore, though it is very difficult to predict which regions will suffer most, and in what ways, such evidence as there is suggests that, at least in the medium term, the impact will be heaviest in the tropical and subtropical regions (where most of the LDCs are), and lighter in the temperate regions (where most of the richer countries are).

In conclusion, there are substantial uncertainties surrounding both the direct empirical evidence for warming and our theoretical understanding of the overall climate system. But these uncertainties cut both ways. In particular, while it is certainly conceivable (though, at present, unlikely) that the climate change problem will turn out to be chimerical, it is also possible that global warming will turn out to be much worse than anyone has yet anticipated. More importantly, the really vital issue does not concern the presence of scientific uncertainty, but rather how we decide what to do under such circumstances. To this issue we now turn.

IV. ECONOMICS

Economic analyses clearly show that it will be far more expensive to cut CO_2 emissions radically than to pay the costs of adaptation to the increased temperatures.

LOMBORG, 2001, P. 318

Cost-benefit analysis, when faced with uncertainties as big as these, would simply be self-deception. And in any case, it could not be a successful exercise, because the issue is too poorly understood, and too little accommodated in the current economic theory.

BROOME, 1992, P. 19

As it turns out, many recent skeptics no longer cite scientific uncertainty as their reason for resisting action on climate change. Instead, they claim to accept the reality of human-induced climate change but argue that there is a strong economic rationale for refusing to act. Prevention, they insist, is more expensive than adaptation; hence, both present and future generations would be better

off if we simply accepted that there will be climate change and tried to live with it. Furthermore, they assert, money that might be spent on prevention would be better spent helping the world's poor. I will consider the first of these arguments in this section and the second later on.

Several attempts have been made to model the economic implications of climate change. Politically prominent among these is the DICE model proposed by the Yale economist William Nordhaus. The DICE model is an integrated assessment model. Integrated assessment (IA) models combine the essential elements of biophysical and economic systems in an attempt to understand the impact of climate and economic policies on one another. Typically, such models aim to find a climate policy which will maximize the social welfare function. And many give the surprising result that only limited abatement should occur in the next twenty to thirty years, since the costs of current reductions are too high in comparison to the benefits. Hence, proponents of these models argue that, based on economic costs, the developed world (and the United States in particular) should pursue adaptation rather than abatement. This is the argument embraced by Lomborg, who cites Nordhaus's work as his inspiration.

1. The Cost Argument

A full response to Lomborg's proposal requires addressing both the argument about costs and the more general argument for an adaptation, rather than mitigation, strategy. Let us begin with the cost argument.

The first point to make is that, even if Nordhaus's calculations were reliable, the costs of climate change mitigation do not seem unmanageable. As Thomas Schelling puts it:

> The costs in reduced productivity are estimated at two percent of GNP forever. Two percent of GNP seems politically unmanageable in many countries. Still, if one plots the curve of US per capita GNP over the coming century with and without the two percent permanent loss, the difference is about the thickness of a line drawn with a number two pencil, and the doubled per capita income that would have been achieved by 2060 is reached in 2062. If someone could wave a wand and phase

in, over a few years, a climate-mitigation program that depressed our GNP by two percent in perpetuity, no one would notice the difference. (Schelling 1997)

Even Lomborg agrees with this. For he not only cites the 2 percent figure with approval but adds, "there is no way that the cost [of stabilizing abatement measures] will send us to the poorhouse" (Lomborg 2001, p. 323).

The second point is that Nordhaus's work is extremely controversial. For one thing, some claim that his model is simplistic, both in itself and, especially, relative to the climate models. Indeed, one commentator goes so far as to say that "the model is extremely simple—so simple that I once, during a debate, dubbed it a toy model" (Gundermann 2002, p. 150). For another others offer rival models which endorse the exact opposite to Nodhaus's conclusion: that action now (in the form of carbon taxes, etc.) would be more beneficial in the long term than waiting, even perhaps if global warming does not actually transpire (e.g., Costanza 1996; De Leo et al. 2001; Woodward and Bishop 1997).

Part of the reason that such disputes arise is because the models embody some very questionable assumptions. Some are specific to Nordhaus (e.g., Gundermann 2002, p. 154). But others are the result of two more general kinds of difficulty.

The first is practical. There are severe informational problems involved in any reliable cost-benefit analysis for climate change. In particular, over the timescale relevant for climate change, "society is bound to be radically transformed in ways which are utterly unpredictable to us now," and these changes will themselves be affected by climate (Broome 1992, p. 10; see also Jamieson 1992, pp. 288–89). Hence, Broome, for example, argues that fine-grained cost-benefit analyses are simply not possible for climate change.

The second kind of difficulty, of more interest to ethicists perhaps, is there are some basic philosophical problems inherent in the methods of conventional economic analysis. Here let me mention just two prominent examples.

One concerns the standard economic treatments of intergenerational issues. Economists typically employ a social discount rate (SDR) of 2–10 percent for future costs (Lomborg uses

5 percent; Nordhaus 3–6 percent). But this raises two serious concerns. The first is that, for the short- to medium-term effects of climate change (say, over ten to fifty years), model results can be extremely sensitive to the rate chosen. For example, Shultz and Kasting claim that the choice of SDR makes the rest of the climate change model largely irrelevant in Nordhaus's model, and variations in the SDR make a huge difference to model results more generally (Schultz and Kasting 1997, cited by Gundermann 2002, p. 147). The other concern is that, when the SDR is positive, all but the most catastrophic costs disappear after a number of decades, and even these become minimal over very long time periods. This has serious consequences for the intergenerational ethics of climate change. As John Broome puts it: "It is people who are now children and people who are not yet born who will reap most of the benefits of any project that mitigates the effects of global warming. Most of the benefits of such a project will therefore be ignored by the consumer-price method of project evaluation. It follows that this method is quite useless for assessing such long-term projects. This is my main reason for rejecting it [for climate change]" (Broome 1992, p. 72).

The second philosophical problem inherent in conventional economic analysis is that it cannot adequately capture all of the relevant costs and benefits. The obvious cases here are costs to non-humans (such as animals, plants, species, and eco-systems) and noneconomic costs to humans, such as aesthetic costs (Sagoff 1998; Schmidtz 2001). But there is also concern that conventional economic analysis cannot adequately take into account costs with special features, such as irreversible and nonsubstitutable damages, that are especially associated with climate change (Shogren and Toman 2000; Costanza 1996).

We can conclude, then, that there are strong reasons to be skeptical about Lomborg's cost argument in particular and about the reliability of fine-grained economic analyses of climate change more generally. Still, John Broome argues that two things can be said with some confidence: first, the specific effects of climate change "are very uncertain," where (as argued in the previous section) "this by itself has important consequences for the work that needs to be done," and, second, these effects "will certainly be long lived, almost certainly large, probably bad, and possibly disastrous" (Broome 1992, p. 12). To these claims we might add that at 2 percent of world production, the estimated costs of stabilizing emissions do not seem obviously prohibitive.

2. The Adaptation Argument

We can now turn to the more general argument that, instead of reducing emissions, we should pursue a policy of trying to adapt to the effects of climate change. The first thing to note about this argument is that adaptation measures will clearly need to be part of any sensible climate policy, because we are already committed to some warming due to past emissions, and almost all of the proposed abatement strategies envisage that overall global emissions will continue to rise for at least the next few decades, committing us to even more. Hence, the choice cannot be seen as being one between abatement and adaptation, since advocates of abatement generally support a combination of strategies. The real issue is rather whether adaptation should be our only strategy, so that abatement is ignored (Jamieson, forthcoming).

If this is the proposal, several points can be made about it. First, we should beware of making the case for adaptation a self-fulfilling prophesy. For example, it is true that the existing capital stock in the United States made it difficult for America to meet its original Kyoto target for 2008–12. But it is also true that a significant amount of this capital was invested after the United States committed itself to stabilizing emissions at the Rio Earth Summit of 1992. Furthermore, matters will only get worse. The Bush administration's current energy plan calls for the building of 1,300 new power plants in the next twenty years, boosting supply (and thereby emissions) by more than 30 percent.

Second, the comparison between abatement and adaptation costs looks straightforward but is not. In particular, we have to bear in mind the different kinds of economic costs at stake in each case. On the one hand, suppose we allow global warming to continue unchecked. What will we be adapting to? Chances are, we will experience both a range of general gradual climatic changes and an increase in severe weather and climate events. On the other hand, if we go for abatement, we will also be adapting, but this time to increases in tax rates on (or decreases in permits for) carbon emissions. But there is a world of difference between these kinds of adaptation: in the first case, we would be dealing with sudden, unpredictable, large-scale impacts which descend at random on particular individuals, communities, regions, and industries and visit them with pure, unrecoverable costs, whereas, in the second, we would be addressing gradual, predictable, incremental impacts, phased in so as to make adaptation easier. Surely, adaptation in the second kind of case is, other things being equal, preferable to the first.

Third, any reasonable abatement strategy would need to be phased in gradually, and it is well documented that many economically beneficial energy savings could be introduced immediately, using existing technologies. These facts suggest that the adaptation argument is largely irrelevant to what to do now. For the first steps that need to be taken would be economically beneficial, not costly. Yet opponents of action on climate change do not want to do even this much.

V. RISK MANAGEMENT AND THE PRECAUTIONARY PRINCIPLE

The risk assessment process . . . is as much policy and politics as it is science. A typical risk assessment relies on at least 50 different assumptions about exposure, dose-response, and relationships between animals and humans. The modeling of uncertainty also depends on assumptions. Two risk assessments conducted on the same problem can vary widely in results.

RAFFENSBERGER AND TICKNER, 1999, P. 2

Serious as they are, these largely technical worries about conventional economic analysis are not the only reasons to be wary of any economic solution to the climate change problem. For some writers suggest that exclusive reliance on economic analysis would be problematic even if all of the numbers were in, since the climate problem is ultimately one of values, not efficiency: as Dale Jamieson puts it, its "fundamental questions" concern "how we ought to live, what kinds of societies we want, and how we should relate to nature and other forms of life" (Jamieson 1992, p. 290).

But the problem may not be just that climate change raises issues of value. It may also show that our existing values are insufficient to the task. Jamieson, for example, offers the following argument. First, he asserts that our present values evolved relatively recently, in "low-population-density and low-technology societies, with seemingly unlimited access to land and other resources." Then he claims that these values include as a central component an account of responsibility which "presupposes that harms and their causes are individual, that they can be readily identified, and that they are local in time and space." Third, he argues that problems such as climate change fit none of these criteria. Hence, he concludes, a new value system is needed (Jamieson 1992, pp. 291–92).

How then should we proceed? Some authors advocate a rethinking of our basic moral practices. For example, Jamieson claims that we must switch our focus away from approaches (such as those of contemporary economics) which concentrate on "calculating probable outcomes" and instead foster and develop a set of "twenty-first century virtues," including "humility, courage, . . . moderation," "simplicity and conservatism" (Jamieson 1992, p. 294).

Other climate change theorists, however, are less radical. For example, Henry Shue employs the traditional notions of a "No Harm Principle" and rights to physical security (Shue 1999*a*, p. 43). He points out that even in the absence of certainty about the exact impacts of climate change, there is a real moral problem posed by subjecting future generations to the risk of severe harms. This implies a motive for action in spite of the scientific and economic uncertainties. Similarly, many policy makers appeal to the "precautionary principle," which is now popular in international law and politics and receives one of its canonical statements in the 1992 United Nations Framework Convention on Climate Change (1992). The exact formulation of the precautionary principle is controversial; but one standard version is the Wingspread Statement, which reads: "When an activity raises threats of harm to

human health or the environment, precautionary measures should be taken even if some cause and effect relationships are not fully established scientifically" (Wingspread Statement 1998).

Both no harm principles and the precautionary principle, are, however, controversial. No harm principles are often criticized for being either obscure or else overly conservative when taken literally; and the precautionary principle generates similar objections: its critics say that it is vacuous, extreme, and irrational. Still, I would argue that, at least in the case of the precautionary principle, many of these initial objections can be overcome (Gardiner 2004*a*). In particular, a core use of the precautionary principle can be captured by restricting its application to those situations which satisfy John Rawls's criteria for the application of a maximum principle: the parties lack, or have good reason to doubt, relevant probability information; they care little for potential gains; and they face unacceptable outcomes (Rawls 1999, p. 134). And this core use escapes the initial, standard objections.

More importantly for current purposes, I would also claim that a reasonable case can be made that climate change satisfies the conditions for the core precautionary principle (Gardiner 2004*a*). First, many of the predicted outcomes from climate change seem severe, and some are catastrophic. Hence, there are grounds for saying there are unacceptable outcomes. Second, as we have seen, for gradual change, either the probabilities of significant damage from climate change are high or else we do not know the probabilities; and for abrupt change the probabilities are unknown. Finally, given widespread endorsement of the view that stabilizing emissions would impose a cost of "only" 2 percent of world production, one might claim that we care little about the potential gains—at least relative to the possibly catastrophic costs.

There is reason to believe, then, that the endorsement by many policy makers of some form of precautionary or no harm approach is reasonable for climate change. But exactly which "precautionary measures" should be taken? One obvious first step is that those changes in present energy consumption which would have short-term, as well as long-term, economic benefits should be made immediately. In addition, we should begin acting on low-cost emissions-saving measures as soon as possible. Beyond that, it is difficult to say exactly how we should strike a balance between the needs of the present and those of the future. Clearly, this is an area where further thought is urgently needed.

Still, it is perhaps worthwhile closing this section with one, speculative, opinion about how we should direct our efforts. By focusing on the possibility of extreme events, and considering the available science, Brian O'Neill and Michael Oppenheimer suggest in a recent article in *Science* that "taking a precautionary approach because of the very large uncertainties, a limit of 2 C above 1990 global average temperature is justified to protect [the West Antarctic Ice Sheet]. To avert shutdown of the [Thermohaline circulation], we define a limit of 3 C warming over 100 years" (O'Neill and Oppenheimer 2002). It is not clear how robust these assertions are. Still, they suggest a reasonable starting point for discussion. For, on the assumption that these outcomes are unacceptable, and given the IPCC projections of a warming of between 1.4 and 5.8°C over the century, both claims appear to justify significant immediate action on greenhouse gas stabilization.

VI. RESPONSIBILITY FOR THE PAST

I'll tell you one thing I'm not going to do is I'm not going to let the United States carry the burden for cleaning up the world's air, like the Kyoto Treaty would have done. China and India were exempted from that treaty. I think we need to be more even-handed.

GEORGE W. BUSH, QUOTED BY
SINGER 2002, P. 30

Even in an emergency one pawns the jewellery before selling the blankets. . . . Whatever justice may positively require, it does not permit that poor nations be told to sell their blankets [compromise their development strategies] in order that the rich nations keep their jewellery [continue their unsustainable lifestyles].

SHUE, 1992, P. 397; QUOTED BY
GRUBB 1995, P. 478

To demand that [the developing countries] act first is patently unfair and would not even warrant serious debate were it not the position of a superpower.

HARRIS, 2003

Suppose, then, that action on climate change is morally required. Whose responsibility is it? The core ethical issue concerning global warming is that of how to allocate the costs and benefits of greenhouse gas emissions and abatement. On this issue, there is a surprising convergence of philosophical writers on the subject: they are virtually unanimous in their conclusion that the developed countries should take the lead role in bearing the costs of climate change, while the less developed countries should be allowed to increase emissions for the foreseeable future.

Still, agreement on the fact of responsibility masks some notable differences about its justification, form, and extent; so it is worth assessing the competing accounts in more detail. The first issue to be considered is that of "backward-looking considerations." The facts are that developed countries are responsible for a very large percentage of historical emissions, whereas the costs likely to be imposed by those emissions are expected to be disproportionately visited on the poorer countries (IPCC 1995, p. 94). This suggests two approaches. First, one might invoke historical principles of justice that require that one "clean up one's own mess." This suggests that the industrialized countries should bear the costs imposed by their past emissions. Second, one might characterize the earth's capacity to absorb man-made emissions of carbon dioxide as a common resource, or sink (Traxler 2002, p. 120), and claim that, since this capacity is limited, a question of justice arises in how its use should be allocated (Singer 2002, pp. 31–32). On this approach, the obvious argument to be made is that the developed countries have largely exhausted the capacity in the process of industrializing and so have, in effect, denied other countries the opportunity to use "their shares." On this view, justice seems to require that the developed countries compensate the less developed for this overuse.

It is worth observing two facts about these two approaches. First, they are distinct. On the one hand, the historical principle requires compensation for damage inflicted by one party on another and does not presume that there is a common resource; on the other, the sink consideration crucially relies on the presence of a common resource and does not presume that any (further) damage is caused to the disenfranchised beyond their being deprived of an opportunity for use. Second, they are compatible. One could maintain that a party deprived of its share of a common resource ought to be compensated both for that and for the fact that material harm has been inflicted upon it as a direct result of the deprivation.

Offhand, the backward-looking considerations seem weighty. However, many writers suggest that in practice they should be ignored. One justification that is offered is that, until comparatively recently, the developed countries were ignorant of the effects of their emissions on the climate and so should not be held accountable for past emissions (or at least those prior to 1990, when the IPCC issued its first report). This consideration seems to me far from decisive, because it is not clear how far the ignorance defense extends. On the one hand, in the case of the historical principle, if the harm inflicted on the world's poor is severe, and if they lack the means to defend themselves against it, it seems odd to say that the rich nations have no obligation to assist, especially when they could do so relatively easily and are in such a position largely because of their previous causal role. On the other hand, in the case of the sink consideration, if you deprive me of my share of an important resource, perhaps one necessary to my very survival, it seems odd to say that you have no obligation to assist because you were ignorant of what you were doing at the time. This is especially so if your overuse both effectively denies me the means of extricating myself from the problem you have created and also further reduces the likelihood of fair outcomes on this and other issues (Shue 1992).

A second justification for ignoring past emissions is that taking the past into account is impractical. For example, Martino Traxler claims that any agreement which incorporates backward-looking considerations would require "a prior

international agreement on what constitutes international distributive justice and then an agreement on how to translate these considerations into practical allocations" and that, given that "such an agreement is [un]likely in our lifetime," insisting on it "would amount to putting off any implementation concerning climate change indefinitely" (Traxler 2002, p. 128). Furthermore, he asserts that climate change takes the form of a commons problem and so poses a significant problem of defection: "Each nation is (let us hope) genuinely concerned with this problem, but each nation is also aware that it is in its interest not to contribute or do its share, regardless of what other countries do.... In short, in the absence of the appropriate international coercive muscle, defection, however unjust it may be, is just too tempting" (Traxler 2002, p. 122).

Though rarely spelled out, such pragmatic concerns seem to influence a number of writers. Still, I am not convinced—at least by Traxler's arguments. For one thing, I do not see why a complete background understanding of international justice is required, especially just to get started. For another, I am not sure that defection is quite the problem, or at least has the implications, that Traxler suggests. In particular, Traxler's argument seems to go something like this: since there is no external coercive body, countries must be motivated not to defect from an agreement; but (rich) countries will be motivated to defect if they are asked to carry the costs of their past (mis)behavior; therefore, past behavior cannot be considered, otherwise (rich) countries will defect. But this reasoning is questionable, on several grounds. First, it seems likely that if past behavior is not considered, then the poor countries will defect. Since, in the long run, their cooperation is required, this would suggest that Traxler's proposal is at least as impractical as anyone else's. Second, it is not clear that no external coercive instruments exist. Trade and travel sanctions, for example, are a possibility and have precedents. Third, the need for such sanctions (and indeed, the problem of defection in general) is not brought on purely by including the issue of backward-looking considerations in negotiation, nor is it removed by their absence. So it seems arbitrary to disallow such considerations on this basis. Finally, Traxler's argument seems to assume (first) that the only truly urgent issue that needs to be addressed with respect to climate change is that of future emissions growth, and (second) that this issue is important enough that concerns about (i) the costs of climate change to which we are already committed, and (ii) the problem of inequity in the proceeds from those emissions (e.g., that the rich countries may have, in effect, stolen rights to develop from the poorer countries) can be completely ignored. But such claims seem controversial.

The arguments in favor of ignoring past emissions are then, unconvincing. Hence, contrary to many writers on this subject, I conclude that we should not ignore the presumption that past emissions pose an issue of justice which is both practically and theoretically important. Since this has the effect of increasing the obligations of the developed nations, it strengthens the case for saying that these countries bear a special responsibility for dealing with the climate change problem.

VII. ALLOCATING FUTURE EMISSIONS

The central argument for equal per capita rights is that the atmosphere is a global commons, whose use and preservation are essential to human well being.

BAER, 2002, P. 401

Much like self-defense may excuse the commission of an injury or even a murder, so their necessity for our subsistence may excuse our indispensable current emissions and the resulting future infliction of harm they cause.

TRAXLER, 2002, P. 107

Let us now turn to the issue of how to allocate future emissions. Here I cannot survey all the proposals that have been made; but I will consider four prominent suggestions.

1. Equal Per Capita Entitlements

The most obvious initial proposal is that some acceptable overall level of anthropogenic greenhouse emissions should be determined . . . , and

then that this should be divided equally among the world's population, to produce equal per capita entitlements to emissions. This proposal seems intuitive but would have a radical redistributive effect. Consider the following illustration. Singer points out that stabilizing carbon emissions at current levels would give a per capita rate of roughly one tonne per year. But actual emissions in the rich countries are substantially in excess of this: the United States is at more than 5 tonnes per capita (and rising); and Japan, Australia, and Western Europe are all in a range from 1.6 to 4.2 tonnes per capita (with most below 3). India and China, on the other hand, are significantly below their per capita allocation (at 0.29 and 0.76, respectively). Thus, Singer suggests (against the present President Bush's claim at the beginning of the previous section), an "even-handed approach" implies that India and China should be allowed increases in emissions, while the United States should take a massive cut (Singer 2002, pp. 39–40).

Two main concerns have been raised about the per capita proposal. The first is that it might encourage population growth, through giving countries an incentive to maximize their population in order to receive more emissions credits (Jamieson 2001, p. 301). But this concern is easily addressed: most proponents of a per capita entitlement propose indexing population figures for each country to a certain time. For example, Jamieson proposes a 1990 baseline (relevant due to the initial IPCC report), whereas Singer proposes 2050 (to avoid punishing countries with younger populations at present). The second concern is more serious. The per capita proposal does not take into account the fact that emissions may play very different roles in people's lives. In particular, some emissions are used to produce luxury items, whereas others are necessary for most people's survival.

2. Rights to Subsistence Emissions

This concern is the basis for the second proposal on how to allocate emissions rights. Henry Shue argues that people should have inalienable rights to the minimum emissions necessary to their survival or to some minimal quality of life.

This proposal has several implications. First, it suggests that there might be moral constraints on the limitation of emissions, so that establishing a global emissions ceiling will not be simply a matter for climatologists or even economists. If some emissions are deemed morally essential then they may have to be guaranteed even if this leads to an overall allocation above the scientific optimum. Traxler is explicit as to why this is the case. Even if subsistence emissions cause harm, they can be morally excusable because "they present their potential emitters with such a hard choice between avoiding a harm today or avoiding a harm in the future" that they are morally akin to self-defense. Second, the proposal suggests that actual emissions entitlements may not be equal for all individuals and may vary over time. For the benefits that can actually be drawn from a given quantity of green-house gas emissions vary with the existing technology, and the necessity of them depends on the available alternatives. But both vary by region, and will no doubt evolve in the future, partly in response to emissions regulation. Third, as Shue says, the guaranteed minimum principle does not imply that allocation of any remaining emissions rights above those necessary for subsistence must be made on a per capita basis. The guaranteed minimum view is distinct from a more robust egalitarian position which demands equality of a good at all levels of its consumption (Shue 1995a, pp. 387–88); hence, above the minimum some other criterion might be adopted.

The guaranteed minimum approach has considerable theoretical appeal. However, there are [two] reasons to be cautious about it. First, determining what counts as a "subsistence emission" is a difficult matter, both in theory and in practice. For example, Traxler defines subsistence emissions in terms of physiologically and socially necessary emissions but characterizes social necessity as "what a society needs or finds indispensable in order to survive" (Traxler 2002, p. 106). But this is problematic. For one thing, much depends on how societies define what they find "indispensable." (It is hard not to recall the first President Bush's comment, back in 1992, that "the American way of life is not up

for negotiation.") For another, and perhaps more importantly, there is something procedurally odd about the proposal. For it appears to envisage that the climate change problem can be resolved by appealing to some notion of social necessity that is independent of, and not open to, moral assessment. But this seems somehow backwards. After all, several influential writers argue that part of the challenge of climate change is the deep questions it raises about how we should live and what kinds of societies we ought to have (Jamieson 1992, p. 290; and IPCC 2001a, 1.4; questioned by Lomborg 2001, pp. 318–22).

Second, in practice, the guaranteed approach may not differ from the per capita principle, and yet may lack the practical advantages of that approach. On the first issue, given the foregoing point, it is hard to see individuals agreeing on an equal division of basic emissions entitlements that does anything less than exhaust the maximum permissible on other (climatological and intergenerational) grounds; and easy to see them being tempted to overshoot it. Furthermore, determining an adequate minimum may turn out to be almost the same task as (a) deciding what an appropriate ceiling would be and then (b) assigning per capita rights to the emissions it allows. For a would also require a view about what constitutes an acceptable form of life and how many emissions are necessary to sustain it. On the second issue, the subsistence emissions proposal carries political risks that the per capita proposal does not, or at least not to the same extent. For one thing, the claim that subsistence emissions are nonnegotiable seems problematic given the first point (above) that there is nothing to stop some people claiming that almost any emission is essential to their way of life. For another, the claim that nonsubsistence emissions need not be distributed equally may lead some in developed countries to argue that what is required to satisfy the subsistence constraint is extremely minimal and that emissions above that level should be either grandfathered or else distributed on other terms favorable to those with existing fossil-fuel intensive economies. But this would mean that developing countries might be denied the opportunity to develop, without any compensation.

3. Priority to the Least Well-Off

The third proposal I wish to consider offers a different justification for departing from the per capita principle: namely, that such a departure might maximally (or at least disproportionately) benefit the least well-off. The obvious version of this argument suggests, again, that the rich countries should carry the costs of dealing with global warming, and the LDCs should be offered generous economic assistance. But there are also less obvious versions, some of which may be attributable to some global warming skeptics.

The first is offered by Bjorn Lomborg. Lomborg claims that the climate change problem ultimately reduces to the question of whether to help poor inhabitants of the poor countries now or their richer descendents later. And he argues that the right answer is to help now, since the present poor are both poorer and more easily helped. Kyoto, he says, "will likely cost at least $150 billion a year, and possibly much more," whereas "just $70–80 billion a year could give all Third World inhabitants access to the basics like health, education, water and sanitation" (Lomborg 2001, p. 322).

But this argument is far from compelling. For one thing, it seems falsely to assume that helping the poor now and acting on climate change are mutually exclusive alternatives (Grubb 1995, p. 473, n. 25). For another, it seems to show a giant leap of political optimism. If their past record is anything to go by, the rich countries are even less likely to contribute large sums of money to help the world's poor directly than they are to do so to combat climate change (Singer 2002, pp. 26–27).

A second kind of priority argument may underlie the present President Bush's proposal of a "greenhouse gas intensity approach," which seeks to index emissions to economic activity. Bush has suggested reducing the amount of greenhouse gas per unit of U.S. GDP by 18 percent in ten years, saying "economic growth is the solution, not the problem" and "the United States wants to foster economic growth in the developing world, including the world's poorest nations" (Singer 2002, p. 43). Hence, he seems to appeal to a Rawlsian principle.

Peter Singer, however, claims that there are two serious problems with this argument. First, it faces a considerable burden of proof: it must show that U.S. economic activity not only makes the poor better off, but maximally so. Second, this burden cannot be met: not only do CIA figures show the United States "well above average in emissions per head it produces in proportion to per capita GDP," but "the vast majority of the goods and services that the US produces— 89 percent of them—are consumed in the US" (Singer 2002, pp. 44–45). This, Singer argues, strongly suggests that the world's poor would be better off if the majority of the economic activity the United States undertakes (with its current share of world emissions) occurred elsewhere.

4. Equalizing Marginal Costs

A final proposal superficially resembles the equal intensity principle but is advocated for very different reasons. Martino Traxler proposes a "fair chore division" which equalizes the marginal costs of those aiming to prevent climate change. Such a proposal, he claims, is politically expedient, in that it (*a*) provides each nation in the global commons with "no stronger reasons to defect from doing its (fair) share than it gives any other nation" and so (*b*) places "the most moral pressure possible on each nation to do its part" (Traxler 2002, p. 129).

Unfortunately, it is not clear that Traxler's proposal achieves the ends he sets for it. First, by itself, *a* does not seem a promising way to escape a traditional commons or prisoner's dilemma situation. What is crucial in such situations is the magnitude of the benefits of defecting relative to those of cooperating; whether the relative benefits are equally large for all players is of much less importance. Second, this implies that *b* must be the crucial claim, but *b* is also dubious in this context. For Traxler explicitly rules out backward-looking considerations on practical grounds. But this means ignoring the previous emissions of the rich countries, the extent to which those emissions have effectively denied the LDCs "their share" of fossil-fuel-based development in the future, and the damages which will be disproportionately visited on the LDCs because of those emissions. So, it is hard to see why the LDCs will experience "maximum moral pressure" to comply. Third, equal marginal costs approaches are puzzling for a more theoretical reason. In general, equality of marginal welfare approaches suffer from the intuitive defect that they take no account of the overall level of welfare of each individual. Hence, under certain conditions, they might license taking large amounts from the poor (if they are so badly off anyway that changes for the worse make little difference), while leaving the rich relatively untouched (if they are so used to a life of luxury that they suffer greatly from even small losses). Now, Traxler's own approach does not fall into this trap, but this is because he advocates that costs should be measured not in terms of preferences or economic performance but, rather, in terms of subsistence, near subsistence, and luxury emissions. Thus, his view is that the rich countries should have to give up all of their luxury emissions before anyone else need consider giving up subsistence and near-subsistence emissions. But this raises a new concern. For in practice this means that Traxler's equal burdens proposal actually demands massive action from the rich countries before the poor countries are required to do anything at all (if indeed they ever are). And however laudable, or indeed morally right, such a course of action might be, it is hard to see it as securing the politically stable agreement that Traxler craves, or, at least, it is hard to see it as more likely to do so than the alternatives. So, the equal marginal costs approach seems to undercut its own rationale.

VIII. WHAT HAS THE WORLD DONE? THE KYOTO DEAL

This has been a disgraceful performance. It is the single worst failure of political leadership that I have seen in my lifetime.

AL GORE, QUOTED BY
HOPGOOD 1998, P. 199

The system is made in America, and the Americans aren't part of it.

DAVID DONIGER

We have seen that there is a great deal of convergence on the issue of who has primary responsibility to act on climate change. The most defensible accounts of fairness and climate change suggest that the rich countries should bear the brunt, and perhaps even the entirety, of the costs. What, then, has the world done?

The current international effort to combat climate change has come in three main phases. The first came to fruition at the Rio Earth Summit of 1992. There, the countries of the world committed themselves to the Framework Convention on Climate Change (FCCC), which required "stabilization of greenhouse gas concentrations in the atmosphere at a level that would prevent dangerous anthropogenic interference with the climate system" and endorsed a principle of "common but differentiated responsibilities," according to which, the richer, industrialized nations (listed under "Annex I" in the agreement) would take the lead in cutting emissions, while the less developed countries would pursue their own development and take significant action only in the future. In line with the FCCC, many of the rich countries (including the United States, European Union, Japan, Canada, Australia, New Zealand, and Norway) announced that they would voluntarily stabilize their emissions at 1990 levels by 2000.

Unfortunately, it soon became clear that merely voluntary measures were ineffective. For, as it turned out, most of those who had made declarations did nothing meaningful to try to live up to them, and their emissions continued to rise without constraint. Thus, a second phase ensued. Meeting in Berlin in 1995, it was agreed that the parties should accept binding constraints on their emissions, and this was subsequently achieved in Japan in 1997, with the negotiation of the Kyoto Protocol. This agreement initially appeared to be a notable success, in that it required the Annex I countries to reduce emissions to roughly 5 percent below 1990 levels between 2008 and 2012. But it also contained two major compromises on the goal of limiting overall emissions, in that it allowed countries to count forests as sinks and to meet their commitments through buying unused capacity from others, through permit trading.

The promise of Kyoto turned out to be short lived. First, it proved so difficult to thrash out the details that a subsequent meeting, in the Hague in November 2000, broke down amid angry recriminations. Second, in March 2001, the Bush administration withdrew U.S. support, effectively killing the Kyoto agreement. Or so most people thought. For, as it turned out, the U.S. withdrawal did not cause immediate collapse. Instead, during the remainder of 2001, in meetings in Bonn and Marrakesh, a third phase began in which a full agreement was negotiated, with the European Union, Russia, and Japan playing prominent roles, and sent to participating governments for ratification. Many nations swiftly ratified, including the European Union, Japan, and Canada, so that, at the time of writing, the Kyoto Treaty needs only ratification by Russia to pass into international law.

On the surface, then, the effort to combat global climate change looks a little bruised, but still on track. But this appearance may be deceptive. For there is good reason to think that the Kyoto Treaty is deeply flawed, both in its substance and its background assumptions (Barrett 2003; Gardiner 2004*b*). Let us begin with two substantive criticisms.

The first is that Kyoto currently does very little to limit emissions. Initial projections suggested that the Bonn-Marrakesh agreement would reduce emissions for participants by roughly 2 percent on 1990 levels, down from the 5 percent initially envisaged by the original Kyoto agreement (Ott 2001). But recent research suggests that such large concessions were made in the period from Kyoto to Marrakesh that (*a*) even full compliance by its signatories would result in an overall increase in their emissions of 9 percent above 2000 levels by the end of the first commitment period; and (*b*) if present slow economic growth persists, this would actually match or exceed projected business-as-usual emissions (Babiker et al. 2002). Coupled with emissions growth in the LDCs, this means that there will be another substantial global increase by 2012. This is nothing short of astounding given that by then we will be "celebrating" twenty years since the Earth Summit (Gardiner 2004*b*).

It is worth pausing to consider potential objections to this criticism. Some would argue

that, even if it achieves very little, the current agreement is to be valued either procedurally (as a necessary first step), symbolically (for showing that some kind of agreement is possible), geopolitically (for showing that the rest of the world can act without the United States), or as simply the best that is possible under current conditions (Athanasiou and Baer 2001, 2002, p. 24). There is something to be said for these views. For the current Kyoto Protocol sets targets only for 2008–12, and these targets are intended as only the first of many rounds of abatement measures. Kyoto's enthusiasts anticipate that the level of cuts will be deepened and their coverage expanded (to include the developing countries) as subsequent targets for new periods are negotiated.

Nevertheless, I remain skeptical. This is partly due to the history of climate negotiations in general, and the current U.S. energy policy in particular; and partly because I do not think future generations will see reason to thank us for symbolism rather than action. But the main reason is that there are clear ways in which the world could have done better (Gardiner 2004*b*).

This leads us to the second substantive criticism of Kyoto: that it contains no effective compliance mechanism. This criticism arises because, although the Bonn-Marrakash agreement allows for reasonably serious punishments for those who fail to reach their targets, these punishments cannot be enforced. For the envisioned treaty has been set up so that countries have several ways to avoid being penalized. On the one hand, enforcement is not binding on any country that fails to ratify the amendment necessary to punish it (Barrett 2003, p. 386). On the other, the penalties take the form of more demanding targets in the next decade's commitment period—but parties can take this into account when negotiating their targets for that commitment period, and in any case a country is free to exit the treaty with one year's notice, three years after the treaty has entered into force for it (FCCC, article 25).

The compliance mechanisms for Kyoto are thus weak. Some would object to this, saying that they are as strong as is possible under current institutions. But I argue that this is both misleading and, to some extent, irrelevant. It is misleading because other agreements have more serious, external sanctions (e.g., the Montreal Protocol on ozone depletion allows for trade sanctions), and also because matters of compliance are notoriously difficult in international relations, leading some to suggest that it is only the easy, and comparatively trivial, agreements that get made. It is somewhat irrelevant because part of what is at stake with climate change is whether we have institutions capable of responding to such global and long-term threats (Gardiner 2004*b*).

Kyoto is also flawed in its background assumptions. Consider the following three examples. First, the agreement assumes a "two track" approach, whereby an acceptable deal on climate can be made without addressing the wider issue of international justice. But this, Shue argues, represents a compound injustice to the poor nations, whose bargaining power on climate change is reduced by existing injustice (Shue 1992, p. 373). Furthermore, this injustice appears to be manifest, in that the treaty directly addresses only the costs of preventing future climate change and only indirectly (and minimally) addresses the costs of coping with climate change to which we are already committed (Shue 1992, p. 384). Second, the Bonn-Marrakesh deal eschews enforcement mechanisms external to the climate change issue, such as trade sanctions. Given the apparent fragility of such a commitment on the part of the participant countries, this is probably disastrous. Third, Kyoto takes as its priority the issue of cost-effectiveness. As several authors point out, this tends to shift the focus of negotiations away from the important ethical issues and (paradoxically) to tend to make the agreement less, rather than more, practical.

Why is Kyoto such a failure? The reasons are no doubt complex and include the political role of energy interests, confusion about scientific uncertainties and economic costs, and the inadequacies of the international system. But two further factors have also been emphasized in the literature. So, I will just mention them in closing. The first is the role of the United States, which, with 4 percent of the world's population, emits roughly 25 percent of global greenhouse gases. From the early stages, and on the most important issues, the United States effectively molded the agreement to its will, persistently objecting when other countries tried to make it stronger. But then it abandoned the treaty, seemingly repudiating even those parts on which it had previously agreed. This behavior has been heavily criticized for being seriously unethical (e.g., Brown 2002; Harris 2000*a*). Indeed, Singer even goes so far as to suggest that it is so unethical that the moral case for economic sanctions against the United States (and other countries which have refused to act on climate change) is stronger than it was for apartheid South Africa, since the South African regime, horrible as it was, harmed only its own citizens, whereas the United States harms citizens of other countries.

The second reason behind Kyoto's failure is its intergenerational aspect. Most analyses describe the climate change problem in intragenerational, game theoretic terms, as a prisoner's dilemma (Barrett 2003, p. 368; Danielson 1993, pp. 95–96; Soroos 1997, pp. 260–61) or battle-of-the-sexes problem (Waldron 1990). But I have argued that the more important dimension of climate change may be its intergenerational aspect (Gardiner 2001). Roughly speaking, the point is this. Climate change is caused primarily by fossil fuel use. Burning fossil fuels has two main consequences: on the one hand, it produces substantial benefits through the production of energy; on the other, it exposes humanity to the risk of large, and perhaps catastrophic, costs from climate change. But these costs and benefits accrue to different groups: the benefits arise primarily in the short to medium term and so are received by the present generation, but the costs fall largely in the long term, on future generations. This suggests a worrying scenario. For one thing, so long as high energy use is (or is perceived to be) strongly connected to self-interest, the present generation will have strong egoistic reasons to ignore the worst aspects of climate change. For another, this problem is iterated: it arises anew for each subsequent generation as it gains the power to decide whether or not to act. This suggests that the global warming problem has a seriously tragic structure. I have argued that it is this background fact that most readily explains the Kyoto debacle (Gardiner 2004*b*).

IX. CONCLUSION

This article has been intended as something of a primer. Its aim is to encourage and facilitate wider engagement by ethicists with the issue of global climate change. At the outset, I offered some general reasons why philosophers should be more interested in climate change. In closing, I would like to offer one more. I have suggested that climate change poses some difficult ethical and philosophical problems. Partly as a consequence of this, the public and political debate surrounding climate change is often simplistic, misleading, and awash with conceptual confusion. Moral philosophers should see this as a call to arms. Philosophical clarity is urgently needed. Given the importance of the problem, let us hope that the call is answered quickly.

✍ REFERENCES

Adler, Matthew D., and Posner, Eric A., eds. 2001. *Cost-Benefit Analysis: Legal, Economic and Philosophical Perspectives.* Chicago: University of Chicago Press.

Agarwal, Anil, and Narain, Sunita. 1991. *Global Warning in an Unequal World: A Case of Environmental Colonialism.* New Delhi: Centre for Science and Environment.

Agarwal, Anil; Narain, Sunita; and Sharma, Anju, eds. 1999. *Global Environmental Negotiations.* Vol. 1, *Green Politics.* New Delhi: Centre for Science and Environment.

Albin, Cecilia. 2001. *Justice and Fairness in International Negotiation.* Cambridge: Cambridge University Press.

Alley, Richard. 2000. *The Two Mile Time Machine: Ice Cores, Abrupt Climate Change, and Our Future.* Princeton, N.J.: Princeton University Press.

Athanasiou, Tom, and Baer, Paul. 2001. Climate Change after Marrakesh: Should Environmentalists Still Support Kyoto? Earthscape Update, December, http://www.earthscape.org/p1/att02/att02.html.

Athanasiou, Tom, and Baer, Paul. 2002. *Dead Heat: Global Justice and Global Warming.* New York: Seven Stories Press.

Babiker, Mustapha H.; Jacoby, Henry D.; Reilly, John M.; and Reiner, David M. 2002. The Evolution of a Climate Regime: Kyoto to Marrakech and Beyond. *Environmental Science and Policy* 5:195–206.

Baer, Paul. 2002. Equity, Greenhouse Gas Emissions, and Global Common Resources. In *Climate Change Policy: A Survey*, ed. Stephen H. Schneider, Armin Rosencranz, and John O. Niles, pp. 393–408. Washington, D.C.: Island Press.

Barrett, Scott. 1990. The Problem of Global Environmental Protection. *Oxford Review of Economic Policy* 6:68–79.

Barrett, Scott. 1998. The Political Economy of the Kyoto Protocol. *Oxford Review of Economic Policy* 14:20–39.

Barrett, Scott. 2003. *Environment and Statecraft.* Oxford: Oxford University Press.

Backerman, Wilfred, and Pasek, Joanna. 1995. The Equitable International Allocation of Tradable Carbon Emission Permits. *Global Environmental Change* 5:405–13.

Beckerman, Wilfred, and Pasek, Joanna. 2001. *Justice, Posterity and the Environment.* Oxford: Oxford University Press .

Broecker, Wallace S. 1997. Thermohaline Circulation, the Achilles' Heel of Our Climate System: Will Man-Made CO_2, Upset the Current Balance? *Science* 278 (November 28):1582–88.

Broome, John. 1992. *Counting the Cost of Global Warming.* Isle of Harris, UK: White Horse Press.

Broome, John. 1994. Discounting the Future. *Philosophy & Public Affairs* 23:128–56. Reprinted in *Ethics Out of Economics*, ed. John Broome, pp. 44–67. Cambridge: Cambridge University Press, 1999. References are to the latter version.

Brown, Donald. 2002. *American Heat: Ethical Problems with the United States' Response to Global Warming.* Lanham, Md.: Rowman & Littlefield.

Chang, Ruth, ed. 1997. *Incommensurability, Incomparability and Practical Reason.* Cambridge, Mass.: Harvard University Press .

Clover, Charles. 2001. Pollution Deal Leaves US Cold. *Daily Telegraph*, July 24.

Committee on the Science of Climate Change. 2001. *Climate Change Science: An Analysis of Some Key Questions.* Washington, D.C.: National Academy Press.

Costanza, Robert. 1996. Review of *Managing the Commons: The Economics of Climate Change*, by William D. Nordhaus. *Environment and Development Economics* 1:381–84.

Coward, Harold, and Hurka, Thomas, eds. 1993. *Ethics and Climate Change: The Greenhouse Effect.* Waterloo: Wilfred Laurier Press.

Danielson, Peter. 1993. Personal Responsibility. In Coward and Hurka 1993, pp. 81–98.

De Leo, Giulio; Rizzi, L.; Caizzi, A.; and Gatto, M. 2001. The Economic Benefits of the Kyoto Protocol. *Nature* 413:478–79.

Desombre, Elizabeth R. 2004. Global Warming: More Common Than Tragic. *Ethics and International Affairs* 18:41–46.

Dickson, Bob; Yashayaev, Igor; Meincke, Jens; Turrell, Bill; Dye, Stephen; and Holfort, Jurgen. 2002. Rapid Freshening of the Deep North Atlantic Ocean over the Past Four Decades. *Nature* 416 (April 25): 832–37.

Dimitrov, R. 2003. Knowledge, Power and Interests in Environmental Regime Formation. *International Studies Quarterly* 47:123–50.

Dubgaard, Alex. 2002. Sustainability, Discounting, and the Precautionary Principle. In *Sceptical Questions and Sustainable Answers*, by Danish Ecological Council, pp. 196–202. Copenhagen: Danish Ecological Council.

Earth Negotiations Bulletin. 2003. *COP-9 Final.* International Institute for Sustainable Development. Available at http://www.iisd.ca/linkages/climate/cop9.

Estrada-Oyuela, Raul A. 2002. Equity and Climate Change. In Pinguelli-Rosa and Munasinghe 2002, pp. 36–46.

Francis, Leslie Pickering. 2003. Global Systemic Problems and Interconnected Duties. *Environmental Ethics* 25:115–28.

Gagosian, Robert. 2003. Abrupt Climate Change: Should We Be Worried? Woods Hole Oceanographic Institute. Available at http://www.whoi.edu/nstitutes/occi/hottopics_climatechange.html.

Gardiner, Stephen M. 2001. The Real Tragedy of the Commons. *Philosophy & Public Affairs* 30: 387–416.

Gardiner, Stephen M. 2003. The Pure Intergenerational Problem. *Monist* 86:481–500.

Gardiner, Stephen M. 2004 *a*. A Core Precautionary Principle. *International Journal of Global Environmental Problems: Special Issue on the Precautionary Principle*, vol. 5, no. 2 (in press).

Gardiner, Stephen M. 2004b. The Global Warming Tragedy and the Dangerous Illusion of the Kyoto Protocol. *Ethics and International Affairs* 18:23–39.

Green, Michael. 2002. Institutional Responsibility for Global Problems. *Philosophical Topics* 30:1–28.

Grubb, Michael. 1995. Seeking Fair Weather: Ethics and the International Debate on Climate Change. *International Affairs* 71:463–96.

Grubb, Michael; Brewer, Tom; Muller, Benito; Drexhage, John; Hamilton, Kirsty; Sugiyama, Taishi; and Aiba, Takao, eds. 2003. *A Strategic Assessment of the Kyoto-Marrakesh System: Synthesis Report.* Sustainable Development Programme Briefing Paper 6. London: Royal Institute of International Affairs. Available at http://www.rifa.org.

Grubb, Michael, with Vroljik, Christian, and Brack, Duncan. 1999. *The Kyoto Protocol: A Guide and Assessment.* London: Royal Institute of International Affairs.

Grubler, A., and Fujii, Y.1991. Inter-generational and Spatial Equity Issues of Carbon Accounts. *Energy* 16:1397–1416.

Gundermann, Jesper. 2002. Discourse in the Greenhouse. In *Sceptical Questions and Sustainable Answers*, by Danish Ecological Council, pp. 139–64. Copenhagen: Danish Ecological Council.

Haller, Stephen, F. 2002. *Apacalypse Soon? Wagering on Warnings of Global Catastrophe.* Montreal: McGill-Queens.

Hansen, Bog; Turrell, William R.; and Osterhus, Svein. 2001. Decreasing Overflow from the Nordic Seas into the Atlantic Ocean through the Faroe Bank Channel since 1950. *Nature* 411 (June 21): 927–30.

Harding, Luke. 2002. Just So Much Hot Air. *Guardian,* October 31.

Harris, Paul, ed. 2000*a*. *Climate Change and American Foreign Policy.* New York: St. Martin's.

Harris, Paul. 2000*b*. International Norms of Responsibility and US Climate Change Policy. In Harris 2000*a*, pp. 225–40.

Harris, Paul. 2001. *International Equity and Global Environmental Politics.* Aldershot, UK: Ashgate.

Harris, Paul, 2003. Fairness, Responsibility, and Climate Change. *Ethics and International Affairs* 17:149–56.

Hayes, Peter, and Smith, Kirk, eds. 1993. *The Global Greenhouse Regime: Who Pays?* London: Earthscan.

Heavenrich, Robert, and Hellman, Karl. 2000. Light-Duty Automotive Technology Trends 1975 through 2000. EPA420-S-00-003. Available at http://ww.epa.gov/otaq/cert/mpg/fetrends/s00003.pdf.

Hirsch, Tim. 2003. Climate Talks End without Result. *BBC News,* October 3. Available at http://www.news.bbc.co.uk/1/hi/sci/tech/3163030.stm.

Holden, Barry, ed. 1996. *The Ethical Dimensions of Climate Change.* Basingstoke, UK: Macmillan.

Holden, Barry. 2002. *Democracy and Global Warming.* London: Continuum.

Hood, Robert. 2003. Global Warming. In *A Companion to Applied Ethics*, ed. R. G. Frey and Christopher Wellman, pp. 674–84. Oxford: Blackwell.

Hopgood, Stephen. 1998. *American Foreign Policy and the Power of the State.* Oxford: Oxford University Press.

Houghton, John. 1997. *Global Warming: The Complete Briefing.* 2d ed.Cambridge: Cambridge University Press.

IPCC (Intergovernmental Panel on Climate Change). 1995. *Climate Change 1995: Economic and Social Dimensions of Climate Change.* Cambridge: Cambridge University Press.

IPCC. 2001*a*. *Climate Change 2001: Mitigation.* Cambridge: Cambridge University Press. Available at http://www.ipcc.ch.

IPCC. 2001*b*. *Climate Change 2001: The Science of Climate Change.*Cambridge: Cambridge University Press. Available at http://www.ipcc.ch.

IPCC. 2001*c*. *Climate Change 2001: Synthesis Report.* University Press Cambridge: Cambridge. Available at http://www.ipcc.ch.

Jamieson, Dale. 1990. *Managing the Future: Public Policy, Scientific Uncertainty, and Global Warming.* In *Upstream/Downstream Essays in Environmental Ethics*, ed. D. Scherer, pp. 67–89. Philadelphia: Temple University Press.

Jamieson, Dale. 1991. The Epistemology of Climate Change: Some Morals for Managers. Society and *Natural Resources* 4:319–29.

Jamieson, Dale. 1992. Ethics, Public Policy and Global Warming. *Science, Technology and Human Values* 17:139–53. Reprinted in Dale Jamieson, *Morality's Progress.* Oxford: Oxford University Press, 2003. References are to the later version.

Jamieson, Dale. 1996. Ethics and Intentional Climate Change. *Climatic Change* 33:323–36.

Jamieson, Dale. 1998. Global Responsibilities: Ethics, Public Health and Global Environmental Change. *Indiana Journal of Global Legal Studies* 5:99–119.

Jamieson, Dale. 2001. Climate Change and Global Environmental Justice. In *Changing the Atmosphere: Expert Knowledge and Global Environmental Governance*, ed. P. Edwards and C. Miller, pp. 287–307. Cambridge, Mass.: MIT Press.

Jamieson, Dale. Forthcoming. Adaptation or Mitigation. In an as yet untitled volume to be edited by Walter Sinnott-Armstrong.

Johansen, Bruce. 2002. *The Global Warming Desk Reference.* Westport, Conn.: Greenwood.

Kettle, Martin, and Brown, Paul. 2001. US Stands Defiant Despite Isolation in Climate Debate. *Guardian*, July 24.

Lee, Jennifer. 2003. GOP Changes Environmental Message. *Seattle Times*, March 2.

Lomborg, Bjorn. 2001. Global Warming. In *The Sceptical Environmentalist*, by Bjorn Lomborg, pp. 258–324. Cambridge: Cambridge University Press.

Mabey, Nick; Hall, Stephen; Smith, Claire; and Gupta, Sujata. 1997. *Argument in the Greenhouse; The International Economics of Controlling Global Warming.* London: Routledge.

MacIlwain, Colin. 2000. Global-Warming Sceptics Left Out in the Cold. *Nature* 403 (January 20), p. 233.

Manson, Neil A. 2002. Formulating the Precautionary Principle. *Environmental Ethics* 24:263–74.

McKibben, Bill. 2001. Some Like It Hot: Bush in the Greenhouse. *New York Review of Books*, July 5.

Michaels, Patrick, and Balling, Robert, Jr. 2000. *The Satanic Gases: Clearing the Air about Global Warming.* Washington, D.C.: Cato Institute.

Moellendorf, Darrell. 2002. *Cosmopolitan Justice.* Boulder, Colo.: Westview.

Myers, Stephen Lee, and Revkin, Andrew C. 2003. Russia to Reject Pact on Climate, Putin Aide Says. *New York Times*, December 3.

Neumayer, Eric. 2000. In Defence of Historical Accountability for Greenhouse Gas Emissions. *Ecological Economics* 33:185–92.

Nicholls, N.; Gruza, G. V.; Jouzel, J.; Karl, T. R.; Ogallo, L. A.; and Parker, D. E. 1996. Observed Climate Variability and Change. In *Climate Change 1995: The Science of Climate Change*, ed. J. T. Houghton, L. G. M. Filho, B. A. Callander, N. Harris, A. Kattenberg, and K. Maskell, pp. 133–92. Cambridge: Cambridge University Press.

O'Neill, Brian C., and Oppenheimer, Michael. 2002. Dangerous Climate Impacts and the Kyoto Protocol. *Science* 296 (June 14): 1971–72.

O'Riordan, T.; Cameron, J.; and Jordan, A., eds. 2001. *Reinterpreting the Precautionary Principle.* London: Cameron & May.

Ott, Hermann. 2001. Climate Policy after the Marrakesh Accords: From Legislation to Implementation. Available at http://ww.wupperinst.org/-/download/Ott-after-marrakesh.pdf. Published as *Global Climate: Yearbook of International Law.* Oxford: Oxford University Press.

Ozonoff, David. 1999. The Precautionary Approach as a Screening Device. In Raffensberger and Tickner 1999, pp. 100–105.

Page, Edward. 1999. Intergenerational Justice and Climate Change. *Political Studies* 47:53–66.

Parfit, Derek. 1985. *Reasons and Person.* Oxford: Oxford University Press.

Parfit, Derek. 1997. Equality and Priority. *Ratio* 10:202–21.

Paterson, Matthew. 1996. *Global Warming and Global Politics.* London: Routledge.

Paterson, Matthew. 2001. Principles of Justice in the Context of Global Climate Change. In *International Relations and Global Climate Change*, ed. Urs Luterbacher and Detlef Sprinz, pp. 119–26. Cambridge, Mass.: MIT Press.

Pearce, David. 1993. *Economic Values and the Natural World.* London: Earthscan.

Pew Center on Global Climate Change. 2003. *COP 9 Milan.* Available through http://www.pewclimate.org.

Pinguelli-Rosa, Luiz, and Munasinghe, Mohan, eds.2002. *Ethics, Equity and International Negotiations on Climate Change.* UK: Edward Elgar Cheltenham,.

Pohl, Otto. 2003. US Left Out of Emissions Trading. *New York Times*, April 10.

Prestowitz, Clyde. 2003. Don't Pester Europe on Genetically Modified Food. *New York Times*, January 25.

Raffensberger, Carolyn. 1999. Uses of the Precautionary Principle in International Treaties and Agreements. Available at http://www.biotech-info .net/treaties_and_agreements.html.

Raffensberger, Carolyn, and Tickner, Joel, eds. 1999. Protecting Public Health and the Environment: Implementing the Precautionary Principle. Washington, D.C.: Island Press.

Rawls, John. 1999. *A Theory of Justice.* Rev. ed. Cambridge, Mass.: Harvard University Press.

Reilly, John; Stone, Peter H.; Forest, Chris E.; Webster, Mort D.; Jacoby, Henry D.; and Prinn, Ronald G. 2001. Climate Change: Uncertainty and Climate Change Assessments. *Science* 293:430–33.

Revkin, Andrew. 2001*a*. Deals Break Impasse on Global Warming Treaty. *New York Times*, November 11.

Revkin, Andrew. 2001*b*. Warming Threat. *New York Times*, June 12.

Revkin, Andrew. 2002. Climate Talks Will Shift Focus from Emissions. *New York Times*, October 23.

Sagoff, Mark. 1988. *The Economy of the Earth.* Cambridge: Cambridge University Press.

Santer, B., et al. 2003. Influence of Satellite Data Uncertainties on the Detection of Externally Forced Climate Change. *Science* 300 (May 23): 1280–84.

Schelling, Thomas. 1997. The Cost of Combating Global Warming: Facing the Tradeoffs. *Foreign Affairs* 76:8–14.

Schmidtz, David. 2001. A Place for Cost-Benefit Analysis. *Noûs* 11, suppl.: 148–71.

Schultz, Peter, and Kasting, James.1997. Optimal Reductions in CO_2 Emissions. Energy Policy 25:491–500.

Sen, Amartya. 1980. Equality of What? In *Tanner Lectures on Human Values*, ed. S. M. McMurrin, pp. 195–220. Salt Lake City: University of Utah Press.

Shogren, Jason, and Toman, Michael. 2000. Climate Change Policy. Dicussion Paper 00–22, Resources for the Future, Washington, D.C., May 14–25, available at http://www.rff.org.

Shue, Henry. 1992. The Unavoidability of Justice. In *The International Politics of the Environment*, ed. Andrew Hurrell and Benedict Kingsbury, pp. 373–97. Oxford: Oxford University Press.

Shue, Henry. 1993. Subsistence Emissions and Luxury Emissions. *Law and Policy* 15:39–59.

Shue, Henry. 1994. After You: May Action by the Rich Be Contingent Upon Action by the Poor? *Indiana Journal of Global Legal Studies* 1:343–65.

Shue, Henry, 1995*a*. Avoidable Necessity: Global Warming, International Fairness and Alternative Energy. In *Theory and Practice, NOMOS XXXVII*, ed. Ian Shapiro and Judith Wagner DeCew, pp. 239–64. New York: New York University Press.

Shue, Henry, 1995*b*. Equity in an International Agreement on Climate Change. In *Equity and Social Considerations Related to Climate Change*, ed. R. S. Odingo, A. L. Alusa, F. Mugo, J. K. Njihia, and A. Heidenreich, pp. 385–92. Nairobi: ICIPE Science Press.

Shue, Henry, 1996. Environmental Change and the Varieties of Justice. *In Earthly Goods: Environmental Change and Social Justice,* ed. Fen Osler Hampson and Judith Reppy, pp. 9–29. Ithaca, N.Y.: Cornell University Press.

Shue, Henry. 1999*a*. Bequeathing Hazards: Security Rights and Property Rights of Future Humans. In *Global Environmental Economics: Equity and* *the Limits to Markets,* ed. M. Dore and T. Mount, pp. 38–53. Oxford: Blackwell.

Shue, Henry, 1999*b*. Global Environment and International Inequality. *International Affairs* 75: 531–45.

Shue, Henry. 2001. Climate. In *A Companion to Environmental Philosophy,* ed. Dale Jamieson, pp. 449–59. Oxford: Blackwell.

Shue, Henry. In press. A Legacy of Danger: The Kyoto Protocol and Future Generations. In *Globalization and Equality,* ed. Keith Horton and Haig Patapan. London: Routledge.

Singer, Peter. 2002. One Atmosphere. In *One World: The Ethics of Globalization,* by Peter Singer, chap. 2. New Haven, Conn.: Yale University Press.

Soroos, Marvin S.1997. *The Endangered Atmosphere: Preserving a Global Commons.*Columbia: University of South Carolina Press.

Soule, Edward. 2000. Assessing the Precautionary Principle. *Public Affairs Quarterly* 14:309–28.

Toman, Michael. 2001. *Climate Change Economics and Policy.* Washington, D.C.: Resources for the Future, 2001.

Traxler, Martino. 2002. Fair Chore Division for Climate Change. *Social Theory and Practice* 28:101–34.

United Nations Environment Program. 1999. *Climate Change Information Kit.* Available at http://www.unep.ch.iuc.

United Nations Framework Convention on Climate Change. 1992. *Framework Convention on Climate Change.* Available at http://www.unfccc.int.

United Nations Framework Convention on Climate Change. 2002. *Report of the Conference of the Parties on Its Seventh Session, Held at Marrakesh from 29 October to 10 November 2001.* In vol. 3 of pt. 2, Action Taken by the Conference of the Parties, of the Addendum.

U.S. Environmental Protection Agency (EPA). 2003. Information accessed at http://www.fueleconomy.gov.

U.S. National Academy of Sciences. Committee on the Science of Climate Change. 2001. Climate Change Science: An Analysis of Some Key Questions. Washington, D.C.: National Academies Press.

U.S. National Research Council, Committee on Abrupt Climate Change. 2002. *Abrupt Climate Change: Inevitable Surprise.* Washington, D.C.: National Academies Press.

Victor, David. 2001. *The Collapse of the Kyoto Protocol and the Struggle to Slow Global Warming.* Princeton, N.J.: Princeton University Press.

Waldron, Jeremy. 1990. Who Is to Stop Polluting? Different Kinds of Free-Rider Problem. In *Ethical Guidelines for Global Bargains.* Program on Ethics and Public Life. Ithaca, N.Y.: Cornell University.

Wesley, E., and Peterson, F. 1999. The Ethics of Burden-Sharing in the Global Greenhouse. *Journal of Agricultural and Environmental Ethics* 11:167–96.

Wingspread Statement. 1998. Available at http://www.gdrc.org/u-gov/precaution-3.html.

Woodward, Richard, and Bishop, Richard. 1997. How to Decide When Experts Disagree: Uncertainty-Based Choice Rules in Environmental Policy. *Land Economics* 73:492–507.

🦠 STUDY QUESTIONS

1. Some people argue that we should not act until there is more scientific certainty about climate change. How does Gardiner address this argument?

2. Is Lomborg correct in saying that mitigation is economically and ethically unwarranted?

3. Should the industrialized nations be excused from moral responsibility for their past emissions because of their ignorance of the possibility of climate change?

4. What four proposals for allocating future emissions does Gardiner consider? Which is the most plausible one? Why?

5. Why does Gardiner believe that the Kyoto Protocol is a failure? Do you think he is correct? Why, or why not?

✄ FOR FURTHER READING

Gore, Al. *An Inconvenient Truth: The Planetary Emergency of Global Warming and What We Can Do About It*. Rodale Press, 2006.

Intergovernmental Panel on Climate Change (IPCC), http://www.ipcc.ch/.

Michaels, Patrick J. *Meltdown: The Predictable Distortion of Global Warming by Scientists, Politicians, and the Media*. Cato Institute (November 25, 2004).

Pew Center on Global Climate Change, http://www.pewclimate.org/.

Pittock, A. Barrie. *Climate Change: Turning Up the Heat*. Earthscan Press, 2006.

Weart, Spencer. *The Discovery of Global Warming*. Harvard University Press, 2003.

CHAPTER TWELVE

Economics and the Environment

ALTHOUGH POLITICAL LEADERS, ETHICISTS, and socially concerned citizens have become increasingly aware of growing global environmental degradation, mainstream economics has taken relatively little note of this problem. Yet economics lies at the core of our malaise. Agricultural and industrial production, energy consumption, and pollution create enormous environmental stress. The question is whether mainstream economics has the resources to deal with these growing concerns or whether we need a whole new understanding of economics. This question is the subject of the present chapter. Let us examine each of the following terms—*economics, ethics,* and *environment*—in order to understand their relationship to one another.

Economics is concerned with the production, distribution, and consumption of goods and services. It has to do with the allocation of scarce resources in a way that maximizes efficiency—that is, material social well-being. Economics arose out of a type of moral philosophy, classical utilitarianism, which stipulates that acts are morally right if and only if they maximize social welfare. Classical economics stipulates that a policy is economically right if and only if it maximizes material social welfare. But mainstream capitalist economics is also *libertarian,* calling for *laissez-faire* policies. People should be completely free to make market exchanges as they see fit. Government should not interfere with market transactions unless force or fraud is occurring. The theory, going back to Adam Smith (1723–1790), is that an *invisible hand* guides individual self-interested transactions in such a way that they actually result in utilitarian outcomes. "Every individual intends only his own gain, and he is in this, as in so many other cases, led by an invisible hand to promote an end which was no part of his intention." This is almost too good to be true—it's OK to act selfishly, for it is the best way to promote universal welfare!

Mainstream economics claims to be a *science,* a pure neutral description of how the market, led by supply and demand, works. It is free from value commitments or moral prescriptions. But this is a myth. It presupposes a powerful ideology—that selfish behavior is good, that material growth is always good, and that the former leads inexorably by an invisible hand to the latter. It teaches us that poverty and the suffering of those who lose out in market competition are the lesser of evils—the price we must pay for growth and freedom. Whether or not or to what extent these claims are true, the point is that neoclassical economics is filled to the brim with values.

Ethics, as we saw in the introduction to this book, is the study of right and wrong action, of good and evil. There are many moral theories, some deontological, others consequentialist (such as classical utilitarianism), and others combinations of the two types. Depending on what ethical theory you hold, a given economic policy may or may not be morally right. The prescriptions of an economic policy and those of a moral theory may conflict. A particular allocation of resources may be economically good but morally bad, or economically wrong but morally right. For example, classical economics may approve a system that results in the rich getting richer and the poor, simply through market mechanisms, becoming so poor that they suffer terribly and even starve—whereas many ethical theories would condemn this state of affairs as grossly unjust and immoral. What is economically sound may not be morally so and, vice versa, what is morally sound may not be economically so.

Now add the third term, *environment.* This idea further complicates an already complicated relationship. There are several problems with treating environmental concerns from the perspective of classical economics. They all have to do with the economic notion of cost–benefit analysis (CBA) and how it affects decisions regarding optional courses of action.

In our first reading, John Stuart Mill challenges the doctrine of unlimited economic growth, arguing for a steady-state model of economic and social life.

In our second reading, William Rees criticizes the materialist model of economics and argues that a fundamental change in society's perceptions is a prerequisite for environmental harmony and sustainable development. He points out that the United Nations' "World Commission on Environment and Development" (1987) study is flawed because it lacks an innovative paradigm for economic-environmental cooperation, which treats the environment as capital.

In out third reading, Herman Daly develops some of Mill's ideas further.

In our fourth reading, Mark Sagoff examines the relevance of an economic model to environmental concerns. An economic model based on cost–benefit analysis is rooted in the utilitarian idea that all values are reducible to personal preferences and how much people would be willing to spend for a good. But sometimes we judge things to be good independent of our personal preferences. The Kantian model, which treats people as ends in themselves rather than placeholders for pleasure, conflicts with the economic model, which asserts that justice should override utilitarian-economic considerations. For example, even if keeping African Americans separate and unequal would yield a higher utility than integration with white Americans, integration is more just and should be chosen. Similarly, questions of pollution and the preservation of the wilderness may not adequately be decided on a standard economic model.

In our fifth reading, David Schmidtz discusses the uses and abuses of cost–benefit analysis for environmental policy decisions. He distinguishes between narrow CBA and one that gives a full account of the costs, endorsing only the latter. He defends CBA against critics like Rees and Sagoff. Examining various objections to this standard, she contends that the method, though limited, is fine. Paraphrasing Shakespeare, we might say, "The fault, dear readers, is not with the science but with ourselves, that we are underlings who use it badly."

65   In Defense of Steady-State Economics

JOHN STUART MILL

A biographical sketch of John Stuart Mill appears before Reading 15. In this essay on steady-state economics, Mill challenges the notion that more economic growth, including more resource use, is equivalent to prosperity and welfare. On the contrary, we must restrain consumption and population growth in favor of quality of life—rather than quantity of consumption.

§ 1. [STATIONARY STATE OF WEALTH AND POPULATION IS DREADED AND DEPRECATED BY WRITERS]

The preceding chapters comprise the general theory of the economical progress of society, in the sense in which those terms are commonly understood; the progress of capital, of population, and of the productive arts. But in contemplating any progressive movement, not in its nature unlimited, the mind is not satisfied with merely tracing the laws of the movement; it cannot but ask the further question, to what goal? Towards what ultimate point is society tending by its industrial progress? When the progress ceases, in what condition are we to expect that it will leave mankind?

It must always have been seen, more or less distinctly, by political economists, that the increase of wealth is not boundless: that at the end of what they term the progressive state lies the stationary state, that all progress in wealth is but a postponement of this, and that each step in advance is an approach to it. We have now been led to recognise that this ultimate goal is at all times near enough to be fully in view; that we are always on the verge of it, and that if we have not reached it long ago, it is because the goal itself flies before us. The richest and most prosperous countries would very soon attain the stationary state, if no further improvements were made in the productive arts, and if there were a suspension of the overflow of capital from those countries into the uncultivated or ill-cultivated regions of the earth.

This impossibility of ultimately avoiding the stationary state—this irresistible necessity that the stream of human industry should finally spread itself out into an apparently stagnant sea—must have been, to the political economists of the last two generations, an unpleasing and discouraging prospect; for the tone and tendency of their speculations goes completely to identify all that is economically desirable with the progressive state, and with that alone. With Mr. M'Culloch, for example, prosperity does not mean a large production and a good distribution of wealth, but a rapid increase of it; his test of prosperity is high profits; and as the tendency of that very increase of wealth, which he calls prosperity, is towards low profits, economical progress, according to him, must tend to the extinction of prosperity. Adam Smith always assumes that the condition of the mass of the people, though it may not be positively distressed, must be pinched and stinted in a stationary condition of wealth, and can only be satisfactory in a progressive state. The doctrine that, to however distant a time incessant struggling may put off our doom, the progress of society must "end in shallows and in miseries," far from being, as many people still believe, a wicked invention of Mr. Malthus, was either expressly or tacitly affirmed by his

Reprinted from J. S. Mill, *Principles of Political Economy*, New York: D. Appleton: 1884. Notes edited.

most distinguished predecessors, and can only be successfully combated on his principles. Before attention had been directed to the principle of population as the active force in determining the remuneration of labour, the increase of mankind was virtually treated as a constant quantity; it was, at all events, assumed that in the natural and normal state of human affairs population must constantly increase, from which it followed that a constant increase of the means of support was essential to the physical comfort of the mass of mankind. The publication of Mr. Malthus' Essay is the era from which better views of this subject must be dated; and notwithstanding the acknowledged errors of his first edition, few writers have done more than himself, in the subsequent editions, to promote these juster and more hopeful anticipations.

Even in a progressive state of capital, in old countries, a conscientious or prudential restraint on population is indispensable, to prevent the increase of numbers from outstripping the increase of capital, and the condition of the classes who are at the bottom of society from being deteriorated. Where there is not, in the people, or in some very large proportion of them, a resolute resistance to this deterioration— a determination to preserve an established standard of comfort—the condition of the poorest class sinks, even in a progressive state, to the lowest point which they will consent to endure. The same determination would be equally effectual to keep up their condition in the stationary state, and would be quite as likely to exist. Indeed, even now, the countries in which the greatest prudence is manifested in the regulating of population, are often those in which capital increases least rapidly. Where there is an indefinite prospect of employment for increased numbers, there is apt to appear less necessity for prudential restraint. If it were evident that a new hand could not obtain employment but by displacing, or succeeding to, one already employed, the combined influences of prudence and public opinion might in some measure be relied on for restricting the coming generation within the numbers necessary for replacing the present.

§ 2. [BUT THE STATIONARY STATE IS NOT IN ITSELF UNDESIRABLE]

I cannot, therefore, regard the stationary state of capital and wealth with the unaffected aversion so generally manifested towards it by political economists of the old school. I am inclined to believe that it would be, on the whole, a very considerable improvement on our present condition. I confess I am not charmed with the ideal of life held out by those who think that the normal state of human beings is that of struggling to get on; that the trampling, crushing, elbowing, and treading on each other's heels, which form the existing type of social life, are the most desirable lot of human kind, or anything but the disagreeable symptoms of one of the phases of industrial progress. It may be a necessary stage in the progress of civilization, and those European nations which have hitherto been so fortunate as to be preserved from it, may have it yet to undergo. It is an incident of growth, not a mark of decline, for it is not necessarily destructive of the higher aspirations and the heroic virtues; as America, in her great civil war, has proved to the world, both by her conduct as a people and by numerous splendid individual examples, and as England, it is to be hoped, would also prove, on an equally trying and exciting occasion. But it is not a kind of social perfection which philanthropists to come will feel any very eager desire to assist in realizing. Most fitting, indeed, is it, that while riches are power, and to grow as rich as possible the universal object of ambition, the path to its attainment should be open to all, without favour or partiality. But the best state for human nature is that in which, while no one is poor, no one desires to be richer, nor has any reason to fear being thrust back, by the efforts of others to push themselves forward.

That the energies of mankind should be kept in employment by the struggle for riches, as they were formerly by the struggle of war, until the better minds succeed in educating the others into better things, is undoubtedly more desirable than that they should rust and stagnate. While minds are coarse they require coarse stimuli, and let them have them. In the meantime, those who do not accept the present very early stage of human improvement as its ultimate type, may be excused for being comparatively indifferent to the kind of economical progress which excites the congratulations of ordinary politicians; the mere increase of production and accumulation. For the safety of national independence it is essential that a country should not fall much behind its neighbours in these things. But in themselves they are of little importance, so long as either the increase of population or anything else prevents the mass of the people from reaping any part of the benefit of them. I know not why it should be matter of congratulation that persons who are already richer than any one needs to be, should have doubled their means of consuming things which give little or no pleasure except as representative of wealth; or that numbers of individuals should pass over, every year, from the middle classes into a richer class, or from the class of the occupied rich to that of the unoccupied. It is only in the backward countries of the world that increased production is still an important object: in those most advanced, what is economically needed is a better distribution, of which one indispensable means is a stricter restraint on population. Levelling institutions, either of a just or of an unjust kind, cannot alone accomplish it; they may lower the heights of society, but they cannot, of themselves, permanently raise the depths.

On the other hand, we may suppose this better distribution of property attained, by the joint effect of the prudence and frugality of individuals, and of a system of legislation favouring equality of fortunes, so far as is consistent with the just claim of the individual to the fruits, whether great or small, of his or her own industry. We may suppose, for instance (according to the suggestion thrown out in a former chapter), a limitation of the sum which any one person may acquire by gift or inheritance, to the amount sufficient to constitute a moderate independence. Under this twofold influence, society would exhibit these leading features: a well-paid and affluent body of labourers; no enormous fortunes, except what were earned and accumulated during a single lifetime; but a much larger body of persons than at present,

not only exempt from the coarser toils, but with sufficient leisure, both physical and mental, from mechanical details, to cultivate freely the graces of life, and afford examples of them to the classes less favourably circumstanced for their growth. This condition of society, so greatly preferable to the present, is not only perfectly compatible with the stationary state, but, it would seem, more naturally allied with that state than with any other.

There is room in the world, no doubt, and even in old countries, for a great increase of population, supposing the arts of life to go on improving, and capital to increase. But even if innocuous, I confess I see very little reason for desiring it. The density of population necessary to enable mankind to obtain, in the greatest degree, all the advantages both of cooperation and of social intercourse, has, in all the most populous countries, been attained. A population may be too crowded, though all be amply supplied with food and raiment. It is not good for man to be kept perforce at all times in the presence of his species. A world from which solitude is extirpated, is a very poor ideal. Solitude, in the sense of being often alone, is essential to any depth of meditation or of character; and solitude in the presence of natural beauty and grandeur, is the cradle of thoughts and aspirations which are not only good for the individual, but which society could ill do without. Nor is there much satisfaction in contemplating the world with nothing left to the spontaneous activity of nature; with every rood of land brought into cultivation, which is capable of growing food for human beings; every flowery waste or natural pasture ploughed up, all quadrupeds or birds which are not domesticated for man's use exterminated as his rivals for food, every hedgerow or superfluous tree rooted out, and scarcely a place left where a wild shrub or flower could grow without being eradicated as a weed in the name of improved agriculture. If the earth must lose that great portion of its pleasantness which it owes to things that the unlimited increase of wealth and population would extirpate from it, for the mere purpose of enabling it to support a larger, but not a better or a happier population, I sincerely hope, for the sake of posterity, that they will be content to be stationary, long before necessity compels them to it.

It is scarcely necessary to remark that a stationary condition of capital and population implies no stationary state of human improvement. There would be as much scope as ever for all kinds of mental culture, and moral and social progress; as much room for improving the Art of Living, and much more likelihood of its being improved, when minds ceased to be engrossed by the art of getting on. Even the industrial arts might be as earnestly and as successfully cultivated, with this sole difference, that instead of serving no purpose but the increase of wealth, industrial improvements would produce their legitimate effect, that of abridging labour. Hitherto it is questionable if all the mechanical inventions yet made have lightened the day's toil of any human being. They have enabled a greater population to live the same life of drudgery and imprisonment, and an increased number of manufacturers and others to make fortunes. They have increased the comforts of the middle classes. But they have not yet begun to effect those great changes in human destiny, which it is in their nature and in their futurity to accomplish. Only when, in addition to just institutions, the increase of mankind shall be under the deliberate guidance of judicious foresight, can the conquests made from the powers of nature by the intellect and energy of scientific discoverers, become the common property of the species, and the means of improving and elevating the universal lot.

✎ STUDY QUESTIONS

1. Mill asks toward what ultimate goal our society is tending. What does he mean by this? Toward what goal ought it to be moving? How does he answer these questions? How would you answer them?
2. What is Mill's idea of the *stationary state*? Is it a good thing? Does it imply a stagnant society? Explain your answer.
3. What does Mill think about population growth? Do you agree?
4. What is Mill's attitude toward increased material wealth?

66   Sustainable Development: Economic Myths and Global Realities

WILLIAM E. REES

William Rees is a bioecologist who teaches the ecological basis for planning and economic development at the University of British Columbia's School of Community and Regional Planning in Canada.

Rees responds to the 1987 United Nations' "World Commission on Environment and Development" report, calling for a global view of sustainable development that is both economically sound and environmentally progressive. He points out that the problem with this report is that it accepts the standard model of economics, which is fundamentally materialist. Rees argues that a new model of economics is needed if we are to do justice to environmental values. We must realize that the environment is capital, which is nonrenewable. Then we must learn to live off the interest, not depleting the capital, but holding it in perpetuity.

Reprinted from *Trumpeter* (Vol. 5.4, Fall 1988) by permission. Notes deleted.

INTRODUCTION

This paper develops one perspective on prospects for a sustainable future in Canada and the rest of the developed world. It is inspired by the recent publication of Our Common Future, the report of the United Nations' "World Commission on Environment and Development." . . . The UN study has stimulated an unprecedented level of public debate on environment and development-related matters, wherever it is available, much of which focuses on the intriguingly hopeful concept of "sustainable development."

Before addressing sustainable development directly, I would like to say a few things about Western society's perceptions of "the way things are" respecting people, development, and the environment. The following reasons for doing so also provide the premises of the paper.

1. While we think we act from factual knowledge, much individual action and government policy on development and environment is based on unconscious belief, on what Stafford Beer (1981) might call our "shared illusions";
2. This collective perception of reality is the real problem. Our culturally "shared illusions" stand in the way of sustainable development;
3. It follows that a fundamental change in society's perceptions and attitudes is a prerequisite for environmental harmony.

Let us be clear that by "perception," I am not referring to the garden variety beliefs and opinions that are amenable to change with the next edition of the National News or the Globe and Mail. Rather, I mean the unconscious "facts" and unquestioned assumptions out of which we more or less automatically react in the conduct of our day-to-day affairs. These culturally-transmitted perceptions shape our social relationships, our political systems, and the nature of economic enterprise. In short, I am talking about the deep-rooted beliefs and perceptions that constitute society's common philosophy and worldview. (The academically inclined may prefer the term "cultural paradigm.")

Whatever name we give it, it is this shared experience of reality that determines where we are "coming from" as a society. Since it also influences where we are going, it is worth some reflection here.

SCIENTIFIC MATERIALISM: SHALLOW SOIL FOR SUSTAINABLE DEVELOPMENT

The worldview that presently dominates is rooted in 19th century scientific materialism. . . . Building on the experimental "natural philosophy" of the previous 200 years, the late 1880's saw the deep entrenchment of scientific rationality and its companion, social utilitarianism, as the primary beacons of human progress.

Descartes had set the stage in the 17th Century with his division of reality into the separate and independent realms of mind and matter. This "Cartesian" division encouraged people to see themselves as separate and distinct from a physical reality "out there," and provided the perceptual framework for all subsequent scientific inquiry. But it was Bacon who gave modern science its raison d'etre by arguing that knowledge gained through science should be put to work. "From this perspective, knowledge is regarded not as an end but as a means, expressed and applied in technology, by which humans assume power over the material world." . . .

The resultant flowering of science and technology made possible the industrial revolution and unprecedented levels of material production. Not surprisingly, scientific method became associated with a glowing material future, while traditional thinking and values were scorned as obsolete and reactionary. Indeed, science came to be equated with the only true knowledge. "Facts" that have no authority of science behind them, are written off "as having no epistemological status at all." . . . The scientific worldview had succeeded in separating material knowledge from values, and asserted the primacy of the former over the latter. . . .

This materialistic rational empiricism remains the dominant paradigm of Western society. To judge from economic behavior, we see the external world, the biosphere, mainly as a warehouse to be plundered in satisfaction of the material needs and wants of humankind. Certainly, too, reductionist science remains our only acceptable analytic mode. Society's prevailing ecological myth sees "the environment" in terms of isolated, individual resources or, at best, as a mechanical construction, whose component parts are bendable to human will and purpose.

Even the organization of governments reflects this analytic perspective. Environmental management is institutionally segregated into Departments of Fisheries, Forests and Land, Water, Energy and Mines, etc., with little regard to interdependent properties of the whole. Ironically, this often leaves our federal and provincial Departments of Environment with little to do!

THE ASSUMPTIONS OF ECONOMICS

Modern economics springs from similar conceptual roots. The founders of the neoclassical school, impressed with the spectacular successes of Newtonian physics, strove to create economics as a sister science, "the mechanics of utility and self-interest." ... The major consequences of this mechanical analogue is a traditional view of economic process as "a self-sustaining circular flow between production and consumption within a completely closed system." By this perception, "everything . . . turns out to be just a pendulum movement. One business 'cycle' follows another.... If events alter the supply and demand propensities, the economic world returns to its previous position as soon as these events fade out." In short, "complete reversibility is the general rule, just as in mechanics...."

An important corollary of this equilibrium model is that mainstream economics essentially ignores the self-evident, continuous exchange of material resources (resources and waste disposal), and the unidirectional flow of free energy, between the economic process and the biophysical environment.

A second corollary of equilibrium theory is that continuous growth becomes theoretically possible.... Indeed, latter day economists seem to believe "not only in the possibility of continuous material growth, but in its axiomatic

necessity." ... This "growmania" ... "has given rise to an immense literature in which exponential growth is taken as the normal state of affairs." ... Meanwhile, any damage to environmental processes caused by this explosive human activity is assumed to be inconsequential or reversible.

That growth is entrenched as the measure of progress is evident from a glance at the business pages of any daily newspaper. The annual percent increase in gross national product (GNP) is still taken as every nation's primary indicator of national health. Rates of under 3% are considered sluggish, and most politicians and economic planners do not feel at ease until real growth in GNP tops 4% per annum. While such rates may seem modest, even a 4% increase implies a doubling of economic activity in a mere 17 years!

With its fixation on growth, the new conservatism of such countries as the US, Britain, and Canada increasingly demands that people accept the rigorous discipline of the marketplace as the primary wellspring of values and social well-being. Meanwhile, businessmen and technocrats have become the heroes of the new age and prominent role models for youth. The competitive ethic provides the accepted standard for individual self worth, with success measured in terms of conspicuous consumption and the accumulation of personal property. In some circles it is fashionable to be both socially unconcerned and aggressively oblivious to environmental destruction. While individual rights are loudly proclaimed, there is telling silence over matters of social responsibility.

It is noteworthy in this context, that capitalist states depend on the increasing size of the national economic pie to ensure that the poor receive enough of the national wealth to survive. Indeed, it is not exaggerating to say that economic growth is the major instrument of social policy. By sustaining hope for improvement, it relieves the pressure for policies aimed at more equitable distribution of wealth.

THE ECOLOGICAL REALITY

There are two ecological problems with common economic expectations. First, the expanding economic system is inextricably linked to the biosphere. Every economy draws on the physical environment for non-renewable resources and on ecosystems for renewable resources, and all the products of economic activity (i.e., both the waste products of the manufacturing process and the final consumer goods) are eventually discharged back into the biosphere as waste.

The ultimate regulator of this activity, and one that modern economic theory essentially ignores, the second law of thermodynamics (the entropy law): **In any closed isolated system, available energy and matter are continuously and irrevocably degraded to the unavailable state.**... The effect of this law is to declare that all so-called economic "production" is really "consumption"!

Since modern economies are partially dependent on stocks of non-renewable material and energy resources, the Second Law declares that they necessarily consume and degrade the very resources which sustains them. The substitution of one depleting resource for another can only be a stopgap on the road to scarcity. Even resource recycling has a net negative impact on remaining stocks of available energy and material. In short, much economic activity contributes to a constant increase in global net entropy (disorder), through the continuous dissipation of free energy and matter. Contrary to the assumptions of neoclassical theory, there is no equilibrium of any sort in the material relationship between industrial economies and the environment.

This means that the growth of many national economies (e.g., Japan, the US) can be sustained only by continuous resource imports from elsewhere, and only in the short run. The global economy, for all practical purposes, is a closed system, a reality that is little affected by shuffling resources around (world trade). Thus, contrary to the implicit assumptions of neo-classical economics, **sustainable development based on prevailing patterns of consumptive resource use is not even theoretically conceivable.**

The second ecological difficulty with the growth-dependent economy stems from the functional dynamics of ecosystems themselves. Ecosystems, like economic systems, depend on fixed stocks of material resources. However, the material resources of ecosystems are constantly

being transformed and recycled throughout the system via food-webs at the local level, and biogeochemical cycles on a global scale. In addition, evolution and succession in Nature tend toward greater order and resilience.

The material cycles and developmental trends of ecosystems thus appear at first glance to defy the thermodynamic law. **Ecosystems seem to be inherently self-sustaining and self-organizing, and therefore to contribute to a reduction in global net entropy.** This is possible only because ecosystems, unlike economic systems, are driven by an external source of free energy, the sun. Through photosynthesis, the steady stream of solar energy sustains essentially all biological activity and makes possible the diversity of life on Earth.

Material recycling, the self-renewing property of ecosystems, is therefore the source of all renewable resources used by the human economy. Moreover, since the flow of solar radiation is constant, steady, and reliable, **resource production from the ecological sector is potentially sustainable over any time scale relevant to humankind.**

But only potentially. Even ecological productivity is ultimately limited, in part, by the rate of energy input (the "solar flux") itself. Ecosystems therefore do not grow indefinitely. Unlike our present economy, which expands through intrinsic positive feedback, ecosystems are held in "steady-state" or dynamic equilibrium, regulated by limiting factors and negative feedback.

Why is this significant? First, human beings and their economies are now a dominant component of all the world's major ecosystems. Since these economies are growing and the ecosystems within which they are embedded are not, the consumption of ecological resources everywhere threatens to exceed sustainable rates of biological production. Second, overexploitation is exacerbated by pollution, which impairs the remaining productivity of ecosystems. (Recent reports that acid rain may be reducing rates of tree growth by as much as 25% in parts of eastern Canada serve as a timely example.) In short, modern industrial economies both directly undermine the potential for sustainable development through over-harvesting, and indirectly compromise future production through residuals discharge. It takes no special genius to realize that such trends are unsustainable.

The point of all this is not to argue for abandonment of scientific rationality or even the growth paradigm. Science, technology, and the human ingenuity to use them, are among the key factors required for sustainable development. However, I do want to stress that our current worldview, however successful in the past, is a dangerously shallow perception of present reality. In fact, the foregoing analysis shows many of its basic assumptions to be wrong. While this was of little consequence when the scale of human activity was limited, it is at the heart of the environment-development conundrum today. Only when we admit this possibility will the development question shift from: how to promote growth, to: how to achieve sustainability.

SUSTAINABLE DEVELOPMENT: CAN WE GET THERE FROM HERE?

According to the World Commission on Environment and Development, **sustainable development is development that meets the needs of the present without compromising the ability of future generations to meet their own needs**. There is nothing very threatening—or substantial here. However, Our Common Future goes on to define needs as the "essential needs of the world's poor, to which overriding priority should be given." It also recognized the "limitations imposed by the state of technology and social organization on the environment's ability to meet those needs." . . . These latter considerations raise painful questions for modern society.

To expand on the issues involved, let us define sustainable development as **any form of positive change which does not erode the ecological, social, or political systems upon which society is dependent.** Planning for sustainable development must therefore explicitly acknowledge ecological limits on the economy, and to be politically viable, have the full understanding, support, and involvement of the people affected. This in turn suggests the need for political and planning processes that are informed, open, and fair.

Social equity will inevitably become a central consideration. The World Commission reported that the 26% of the world's population living in developed countries consumes 80–86% of nonrenewable resources and up to 34–53% of food products. . . . Emerging ecological and social constraints suggest that reducing the present gap in standards of living between the rich and poor (between and within nations) may well require that the rich reduce both present consumption and future expectations so that the poor may enjoy a fairer share of the world's resources.

Ecologically and socially concerned citizens accept such notions as self-evident, but the more profound implications of sustainable development seem invisible to the mainstream worldview. For example, Canada was the first nation to respond with its own policy initiative to the work of the World Commission. The National Task Force on Environment and Economy was established in October 1986 to initiate dialogue and recommend action on environment-economy integration in Canada. Its subsequent report . . . is regarded by government and industry as a milestone document, but with suspicion by environmentalists and other critics.

Stepping to the right of the World Commission, the Task Force defined sustainable development as "development which ensures that the utilization of resources and the environment today does not damage prospects for their use by future generations." Its report goes on to state that at the core of the concept is the requirement "that current practices should not diminish the possibility of maintaining or improving living standards in the future." Also: "Sustainable development does not require the preservation of the current stock of natural resources or any particular mix of . . . assets." Nor does it place "artificial" limits on economic growth, provided that such growth is "economically and environmentally sustainable." . . .

This definition is self-contradictory and thus difficult to interpret rationally. First, as previously emphasized, the present generation cannot use any nonrenewable energy or material resource (e.g., oil, natural gas, phosphate ore) without eliminating the prospect for its use by future generations. Thus, the main part of the definition is simply invalid. Second, the Task Force is reluctant to admit the possibility that living standards for some may have to be reduced that others might live at all. It avoids this issue entirely. Third, and consistent with the foregoing, the Task Force clings to the growth ethic, implying that an expanding economy is the preferred, if not the only solution, to social inequity. Fourth, the Task Force disallows the possibility that the preservation of certain "mixes" of ecological resource systems may well be essential to sustainability.

In the final analysis, then, the Task Force definition of sustainable development could be used to defend practically any pattern of economic activity, including the status quo (which, one suspects, was the general idea).

To be fair, the Task Force does provide numerous recommendations for improved economic planning and environmental assessment; for demonstration projects in sustainable development; for more research into ecological problems; for better government-industry cooperation in the integration of environment and economy, etc. However, in failing to recognize its own epistemological assumptions, the Task Force was constrained from stretching beyond such commonplace adjustments.

One problem is that the Task Force report (and, to a lesser extent, **Our Common Future**) was written from within the materialist growth paradigm. This paradigm is the ecological equivalent of rose-coloured glasses. With our vision pleasantly impaired, we will always ask first that Nature continue to meet our growing demands; it is literally beyond imagining that we should seriously adapt to Nature's constraints.

Now do not get me wrong. There may well be a grand idea in the Task Force that is struggling to get out. But the fact there is a struggle is my central point. The idea we need cannot be born of the prevailing worldview; it is missing too many essential elements. If we are serious about sustainable development, we cannot get there from here, at least not directly. We have to start from a different paradigm.

TOWARD A NEW PARADIGM

I would like now to sketch some of the errant elements I believe are central to any ecologically sound approach to sustainable development. To promote understanding, I will use a metaphor drawn from the current paradigm and a model we all know, capital investment.

Environment as Capital

In the simplest case, if you have money to invest and manage it wisely, you expect your capital to grow. Indeed, the objective of this form of "development" is to accumulate capital (money, equipment, physical plant), to be better off after making your investment than before. Certainly no one sets out to deliberately lose his/her financial shirt.

Try now to conceive various living species and ecosystems processes as forms of capital. It is easy to think of species we harvest this way, since we all know that a given stock of fish, trees, or cattle is capable of generating variable rates of return (growth and reproduction) depending on the goals and skills of management. But we are much less aware of the valuable hidden services performed by ecosystems' processes mainly because they are performed so well. One example would be the inherent capacity of local ecosystems and the biosphere to absorb, neutralize, and recycle organic and nutrient wastes. These are free services that we might otherwise have to pay for, and as such can be considered as a return on our "investment" in the ecological capital doing the chore.

Clearly, any human activity dependent on the consumptive use of ecological resources (forestry, fisheries, agriculture, waste disposal, urban sprawl onto agricultural land) cannot be sustained indefinitely if it consumes not only the annual production from that resource (the "interest"), but also cuts into the capital base. In this simple truth lies the essence of our environmental crisis. We have not only been living off our ecological interest but also consuming the capital, and the rate at which we are doing so is increasing year by year. This is the inevitable consequence of exponential growth. Some examples:

1. Most major world fisheries peaked far short of their potential productivity in the early

1970's, and many, including B.C. salmon and Atlantic cod, are in a continuing state of decline from over-fishing and habitat destruction.

2. Historic forestry practices in B.C. have greatly reduced the last major temperate rain-forest, and our present "economic" clearcut methods leave an ecological disaster of denuded slopes and eroded soils. Meanwhile, tropical forests, habitat to half the world's species, have been reduced by 40%, and are being cut at the rate of 10–20 million hectares (ha.) (1–2%) per year;

3. The prairie soils of the North American breadbasket have lost half their organic content and natural nutrients under mechanized agriculture. Soil erosion from cultivated land typically claims 22 metric tons/ha./year, about ten times the rate of soil building...;

4. Abetted by deforestation, over-grazing, and inappropriate land use, the world's deserts claim an additional 21 million ha. of previously habitable land/year;

5. Acid rain is sterilizing thousands of lakes, destroying fisheries, and threatening forest and agricultural productivity in much of the Northern hemisphere;

6. Carbon dioxide production from the burning of fossil fuels and destruction of forests has long exceeded the capacity of the oceans and terrestrial plants to absorb the excess. Atmo-spheric CO_2 has risen 25% in the industrial age and is expected to double from preindustrial levels in the next century, contributing significantly to the greenhouse effect and potentially disastrous global warming.

Admittedly, interpreting such trends is difficult and their ultimate significance controversial. However, viewed in the same light as rising standards of living, the decline of the biosphere provides a novel perspective on the origins of our unprecedented wealth. These intersecting curves reveal that since the beginning of the steam age, we have been busily converting ecological capital into financial and material capital.

This means that much of our wealth is illusion. We have simply drawn down one account (the biosphere) to add to another (the bank). It might even be argued that we have been collectively impoverished in the process. Much

potentially renewable environmental capital has been permanently converted into machinery, plant, and possessions that will eventually wear out and have to be replaced (at the cost of additional resources—that irritating Second Law again!).

To put it another way, we have long been enjoying a free ride for which we now have to ante up. Forest products and food are undervalued in the marketplace to the extent the prices we pay do not include the costs of resource maintenance. Our paychecks and corporate profits are excessive to the extent that the resource base which produced them has been run down. That new CD player and the family's second car represent capital that was not plowed back into agriculture, soils management, and waste control. In simplest terms, the "good life" for some humans has been subsidized at the expense of all other life, and ultimately of our children and their descendants.

Living on the Interest

This suggests that for the foreseeable future, sustainable development is only possible if we are willing to live on the interest of our remaining ecological endowment. Fortunately, this is still generous enough, and with careful husbanding it should be possible to restore and even build up our capital base.

Success in this endeavor will obviously require a rewrite of the prevailing environmental myth and humankind's role in the scheme of things. To begin, the new eco-paradigm must dissolve our separateness and reunite humankind with the biosphere.

Let us be clear that while better environmental management may be an essential interim step, we are not merely talking about tougher environmental regulation or improved impact assessment. History has shown that restrictive measures to control inappropriate activities are simply inadequate. This is because regulation must be imposed to protect some social value that is perceived as secondary if not inimical to the interests of the regulatee. Corporations oriented to maximizing profits do not voluntarily incur the costs of pollution control. Moreover, if the general interests of society (or at least the politician) are more closely associated with profit than environment, regulations are not enthusiastically enforced.

True sustainable development cannot be forced. Rather, it is the natural product of a society that "comes from" a profound sense of being in, and of, the natural world. As noted at the outset, sustainable development requires a shift in fundamental social attitudes and values, a change in worldview. People must acquire in their bones a sense that violation of the biosphere is violation of self.

From this perspective, it would be psychologically and socially unconscionable for anyone to advance a development or resource management proposal whose long-term effect would be to reduce our ecological capital. Just as today, no sane person sets out purposely to go financially bankrupt, no one would dream of launching an ecologically bankrupt scheme. On the contrary, development would be planned and implemented, without force or coercion, in ways that would maintain or increase the renewable resource base. "Return on investment" would acquire a double meaning. Both ecological and financial criteria have to be satisfied in the cost/benefit calculus.

Think for the moment how different things would be today had enhancing our ecological capital been taken for granted as the guiding principle of resource development in British Columbia for the last 100 years. There would be no concerns that sawmills in the interior may run out of timber; no fight between loggers and conservationists over the last uncut valley in the southern half of the province; South Moresby would have been declared a National Park long ago; commercial and sport fishermen would not be locked in a bitter dispute over declining shares of a diminishing resource (and the costly salmon-enhancement program would not have been necessary). It might have cost more along the way, but paradoxically, we would be richer today.

To ears conditioned by the hard-nosed rhetoric of modern business and politics, this softer path to development will sound utterly ridiculous, vaguely threatening, or merely irrelevant. But remember, from within in the current paradigm, it is difficult to recognize any vision not supported by conventional values and assumptions. The orthodox mind can only deny the evidence and insist the Earth is flat.

This is a critical point. To acknowledge it is to admit the possibility of an alternative vision and future. With self-awareness, comes the realization that there is nothing fixed or sacred about our present way of being. Materialist society, its Rambo economics, and even the compulsive consumers of the "me" generation, are all creations of malleable culture, not of any physical law. **We made them up.** If they are no longer adapted to the changing reality, we can remake them ourselves, in an image that is.

While re-education will be a long and difficult process, it may have unexpected rewards. Human beings are multidimensional creatures, at once aggressively competitive and socially cooperative. But Western society plays up the former, while suppressing the latter; a perverted liberalism idolizes the individual, while Conservative economics deprives him/her of the community necessary to make him/her whole. The new paradigm may enable us to restore the balance in a rediscovery of self. At the least, our new consciousness should catalyze a shift in emphasis from the quantitative to the qualitative, from the material to the tangible, from growth to development, in the lives of people and communities.

The eco-paradigm is an inherently cooperative one. It springs from a felt responsibility to the whole planet and can only be expressed through socio-political effort at all levels of social organization. Although there must be leadership, no region, province, or nation can go it alone for long.

Sustainable development thus gives new meaning to McLuhan's "global village." The media that made it possible may finally have a message that makes it worthwhile. We are engaged in no less an enterprise than restoring the habitat for all of humankind, and this will require no less than total commitment and unity of purpose.

Listen for a collective sigh of relief, the arms race, which we never could afford, which consumes so much of our ecological capital, can only be seen as a perverse anachronism when viewed from the eco-paradigm. Giving up on war would free no less than 6% of gross world product for the sustainable redevelopment of the planet!

Now, of course, I am really staring off to ecotopia. It simply cannot happen, right? Perhaps, but if you cannot share this vision, take a long look from where you stand and ponder the alternative.

✎ STUDY QUESTIONS

1. Does Rees make a good case that traditional economics is materialistic and hence unable to deal with the kinds of concerns raised by environmental consciousness?

2. How might a proponent of standard economics respond to Rees's thesis that we must treat the environment as capital?

67 Consumption: The Economics of Value Added and the Ethics of Value Distributed

HERMAN E. DALY

Herman E. Daly is senior research scholar at the University of Maryland, School of Public Affairs. From 1988 to 1994 he was senior economist at the World Bank.

In this essay Daly argues that we are overconsuming Earth's resources, so that even if we distribute resources fairly, we are still doomed. Even if a ship distributes goods justly, it will sink it if takes on too many goods. Likewise, if we are to obtain a sustainable lifestyle, we must constrain our consumption and pollution. Daly begins with Mill's theory of steady state economics and applies it to our current crisis.

INTRODUCTION

The total of resource consumption (throughput), by which the economic subsystem lives off the containing ecosystem, is limited—because the ecosystem that both supplies the throughput and absorbs its waste products is itself limited. The earth-ecosystem is finite, nonexpanding, materially closed, and while open to the flow of solar energy, that flow is also nonexpanding and finite. Historically these limits were not generally binding, because the subsystem was small relative to the total system. The world was "empty." But

now it is "full," and the limits are more and more binding—not necessarily like brick walls, but more like stretched rubber bands.

John Stuart Mill (1857) foresaw the problem of moving from an empty to a full world and stated it clearly:

> Nor is there much satisfaction in contemplating the world with nothing left to the spontaneous activity of nature; with every rood of land brought into cultivation, which is capable of growing food for human beings; every flowery waste or natural pasture plowed up, all quadrupeds or birds which are not domesticated for man's use exterminated

From "Consumption: The Economics of Value Added and the Ethics of Value Distributed," In *The Business of Consumption*, ed. Laura Westra and Patricia H. Werhane (Rowman & Littlefield, 1999), pp. 17–30. Reprinted by permission.

as his rivals for food, every hedgerow or superfluous tree rooted out, and scarcely a place left where a wild shrub or flower could grow without being eradicated as a weed in the name of improved agriculture. If the earth must lose that great portion of its pleasantness which it owes to things that the unlimited increase of wealth and population would extirpate from it, for the mere purpose of enabling it to support a larger, but not a happier or better population, I sincerely hope, for the sake of posterity, that they will be content to be stationary, long before necessity compels them to it.[1]

The total flow of resource consumption is the product of population times per capita consumption. Many people have for a long time urged the wisdom of limiting population growth—few have recognized the need to limit consumption growth. In the face of so much poverty in the world it seems "immoral" to some to even talk about limiting consumption. But populations of cars, buildings, TVs, refrigerators, livestock, and yes, even of trees, fish, wolves, and giant pandas, all have in common with the population of human bodies that they take up space and require a throughput for their production, maintenance, and disposal. Nevertheless, some think the solution to human population growth lies in increasing the growth of populations of all the commodities whose services we consume. The "demographic transition" will automatically stop population growth only if per capita consumption grows fast enough. Arguing that one term of a product will stop growing if only the other term grows faster is not very reassuring if it is the product of the two terms that is limited. Will the average Indian's consumption have to rise to that of the average Swede before Indian fertility falls to the Swedish level? Can the eroding and crowded country of India support that many cars, power plants, buildings, and so on?

Never fear, the same people who brought you the demographic transition are now bringing you the Information Reformation, a.k.a. the "dematerialized economy." McDonald's will introduce the "infoburger," consisting of a thick patty of information between two slices of silicon, thin as communion wafers so as to emphasize the symbolic and spiritual nature of consumption. We can also dematerialize human beings by breeding smaller people—after all, if we were half the size there could be twice as many of us—indeed we would have to dematerialize people if we were to subsist on the dematerialized GNP! We can certainly eat lower on the food chain, but we cannot eat recipes. The Information Reformation, like the demographic transition before it, expands a germ of truth into a whale of a fantasy.

While all countries must worry about both population and per capita consumption, it is evident that the South needs to focus more on population, and the North more on per capita consumption. This fact will likely play a major role in all North-South treaties and discussions. Why should the South control its population if the resources saved thereby are merely gobbled up by Northern overconsumption? Why should the North control its overconsumption if the saved resources will merely allow a larger number of poor people to subsist at the same level of misery? Without for a minute minimizing the necessity of population control, it is nevertheless incumbent on the North to get serious about consumption control. Toward this end, a reconsideration of the meaning of consumption is offered below.

CONSUMPTION AND VALUE ADDED

When we speak of consumption, what is it that we think of as being consumed? Alfred Marshall reminded us of the laws of conservation of matter/energy and the consequent impossibility of consuming the material building blocks of commodities:

> Man cannot create material things—his efforts and sacrifices result in changing the form or arrangement of matter to adapt it better for the satisfaction of his wants—as his production of material products is really nothing more than a rearrangement of matter which gives it new utilities, so his consumption of them is nothing more than a disarrangement of matter which destroys its utilities.[2]

What we destroy or consume in consumption is the improbable arrangement of those building blocks, arrangements that give utility for humans, arrangements that were, according to Marshall, made by humans for human purposes. This utility added to matter/energy by human action is not production in the sense of creation of matter/energy, which is just as impossible as destruction by consumption. Useful structure is added to matter/energy (natural resource flows) by the agency of labor and capital stocks. The value of this useful structure imparted by labor and capital is what economists call "value added." This value added is what is "consumed," that is, used up in consumption. New value needs to be added again by the agency of labor and capital before it can be consumed again. That to which value is being added is the flow of natural resources, conceived ultimately as the indestructible building blocks of nature. The value consumed by humans is, in this view, no greater than the value added by humans—consumption plus savings equals national income—which in turn is equal to the sum of all value added. In the standard economist's vision we consume only that value which we added in the first place. And then we add it again, and consume it again, and so on. This vision is formalized in the famous diagram of the isolated circular flow of value between firms (production) and households (consumption), found in the initial pages of every economics textbook.

For all the focus on value added one would think that there would be some discussion of *that to which value is being added*. But modern economists say no more about it than Marshall. It is just "matter," and its properties are not very interesting. In fact, they are becoming ever less interesting to economists as science uncovers their basic uniformity. As Barnett and Morse put it: "Advances in fundamental science have made it possible to take advantage of the uniformity of matter/energy—a uniformity that makes it feasible, without preassignable limit, to escape the quantitative constraints imposed by the character of the earth's crust."[3]

That to which value is being added are merely homogeneous, indestructible building blocks—atoms in the original sense—of which there is no conceivable scarcity. That to which value is added is therefore inert, undifferentiated, interchangeable, and superabundant—very dull stuff indeed, compared to the value-adding agents of labor with all its human capacities, and capital that embodies the marvels of human knowledge. It is not surprising that value added is the centerpiece of economic accounting, and that the presumably passive stuff to which value is added has received minimal attention.[4]

CONSUMPTION AND PHYSICAL TRANSFORMATION

The vision sketched above, that of Marshall, of Barnett and Morse, and of all textbooks founded on the circular flow of value added, is entirely consistent with the first law of thermodynamics. Matter/energy is not produced or consumed, only transformed. But this vision embodies an astonishing oversight—it completely ignores the second law of thermodynamics.[5] Matter is arranged in production, disarranged in consumption, rearranged in production, and so on. The second law tells us that all this rearranging and recycling of material building blocks takes energy, that energy itself is not recycled, and that on each cycle some of the material building blocks are dissipated beyond recall. It remains true that we do not consume matter/energy, but we do consume (irrevocably use up) the *capacity to rearrange* matter/energy. Contrary to the implication of Barnett and Morse, matter/energy is not at all uniform in the quality most relevant to economics—namely, its capacity to receive and hold the rearrangements dictated by human purpose, the capacity to receive the imprint of human knowledge, the capacity to embody value added. The capacity of matter/energy to embody value added is not uniform, and it wears out and must be replenished. It is not totally passive. If the economic system is to keep going it cannot be an isolated circular flow. It must be an open system, receiving matter and energy from outside to make up for that which is dissipated to the outside. What is outside? The environment. What is the environment? It is a complex ecosystem that is finite, nonexpanding and materially closed, while open to a nonexpanding flow of solar energy.

Seeing the economy as an open subsystem forces us to realize that consumption is not only disarrangement within the subsystem but involves disarrangements in the rest of the system, the environment. Taking matter/energy from the larger system, adding value to it, using up the added value, and returning the waste clearly alters the environment. The matter/energy we return is not the same as the matter/energy we take in. If it were, we could simply use it again and again in a closed circular flow. Common observation tells us, and the entropy law confirms, that waste matter/energy is qualitatively different from raw materials. Low-entropy matter/energy comes in, high-entropy matter/energy goes out, just as in an organism's metabolism. We irrevocably use up not only the value we added by rearrangement, but also the pre-existing arrangement originally imparted by nature, as well as the very energetic capacity to further arrange, also provided by nature. We not only consume the value we add to matter, *but also the value that was added by nature before we imported it into the economic subsystem,* and that was necessary for it to be considered a resource in the first place. Capacity to rearrange used up value within the subsystem can be restored by importing low-entropy matter/energy from the larger system and exporting high-entropy matter/energy back to it. But the rates of import and export, determined largely by the scale of the subsystem, must be consistent with the complex workings of the parent system, the ecosystem. The scale of the subsystem matters.

From this perspective value is still being added to resources by the agents of labor and capital. But that to which value is added are not inert, indifferent, uniform building blocks or atoms. Value is added to that matter/energy which is most capable of receiving and embodying the value being added to it. That receptivity might be thought of as "value added by nature." Carbon atoms scattered in the atmosphere can receive value added only with the enormous expenditure of energy and other materials. Carbon atoms structured in a tree can be rearranged much more easily. Concentrated copper ore can hold value added; atoms of copper at average crustal abundance cannot. Energy concentrated in a lump of coal can help us add value to matter; energy at equilibrium temperature in the ocean or atmosphere cannot. The more work done by nature, the more concentrated and receptive the

resource is to having value added to it, the less capital and labor will have to be expended in rearranging it to better suit our purposes. If all value added is the result of labor and capital, then the total value that they jointly added should be distributed between them. But if nature also adds value, then there is a source other than labor and capital that has no obvious claimant in distribution. Who should get it? The ethical principle that value should go to whoever added it is no longer sufficient, unless nature is personified and somehow considered a claimant.

From a utility or demand perspective value added by nature ought to be valued equally with value added by labor and capital. But from the supply or cost side it is not, because value added by humans has a real cost of disutility of labor and an opportunity cost of both labor and capital use. We tend to treat natural value added as a subsidy, a free gift of nature. The greater the natural subsidy, the less the cost of labor and capital (value added) needed for further arrangement. The less the humanly added value, the lower the price, and the more rapid the use. Oil from East Texas was a much greater net energy subsidy from nature to the economy than is offshore Alaskan oil. But its price was much lower precisely because it required less value added by labor and capital. The larger the natural subsidy, the less we value it, and the less attention we pay to the ethical issue of how to distribute nature's value added.

Thanks in part to this natural subsidy the economy has grown relative to the total ecosystem to such an extent that the basic pattern of scarcity has changed. It used to be that adding value was limited by the supply of agents of transformation, labor, and capital. Now, value added is limited more by the availability of resources subsidized by nature to the point that they can receive value added. Mere knowledge means nothing to the economy until it becomes incarnate in physical structures. Low-entropy matter/energy is the restricted gate through which knowledge is incorporated in matter and becomes manmade capital. No low-entropy matter/energy, no capital—regardless of knowledge. Of course, new knowledge may include discovery of new low-entropy resources, and new methods of transforming them to better serve human needs. New knowledge may also discover new limits, and new impossibility theorems.

The physical growth of the subsystem is the transformation of natural capital into manmade capital. A tree is cut and turned into a table. We gain the service of the table; we lose the service of the tree. In a relatively empty world (small economic subsystem, ecosystem relatively empty of human beings and their artifacts) the service lost from fewer trees was nil, and the service gained from more tables was significant. In today's relatively full world fewer trees mean loss of significant services, and more tables are not so important if most households already have several tables, as in much of the world they do. Of course continued population growth will keep the demand for tables up, and we will incur ever greater sacrifices of natural services by cutting more and more trees, as long as population keeps growing. The size or scale of the economic subsystem is best thought of as per capita consumption times population (which of course is the same as total consumption). The point is that there is both a cost and a benefit to increasing the scale of the subsystem (total consumption). The benefit is economic services gained (more tables); the cost is ecosystem services sacrificed (fewer trees to sequester CO_2, provide wildlife habitat, erosion control, local cooling, etc.). As scale increases, marginal costs tend to rise; marginal benefits tend to fall. Equality of marginal costs and benefits defines the optimal scale, beyond which further growth would be anti-economic.

As we come to an optimal or mature scale, production is no longer for growth but for maintenance. A mature economy, like a mature ecosystem, shifts from a regime of growth efficiency (maximize P/B, or production per unit of biomass stock) to a regime of maintenance efficiency (maximize the reciprocal, B/P, or the amount of biomass stock maintained per unit of new production). Production is the maintenance cost of the stock and should be minimized. As K. Boulding argued almost fifty years ago,

> Any discovery which renders consumption less necessary to the pursuit of living is as much an economic gain as a discovery which improves our skills of production. Production—by which we

mean the exact opposite of consumption, namely the creation of valuable things—is only necessary in order to replace the stock pile into which consumption continually gnaws.[6]

CONSUMPTION AND WELFARE

The theoretical existence of an optimal scale of the economic subsystem is clear in principle. What remain vague are the measures of the value of services, especially of natural capital but also of manmade capital. But if economic policy is anything it is the art of dialectically reasoning with vague quantities in the support of prudent actions. We can have reasons for believing that an optimum scale exists, and that we are either above it or below it, without knowing exactly where it is. For policy purposes a judgment about which side of the optimum we are on is what is critical. Reasons are offered below for believing that we (both the United States and the world as a whole) have overshot the optimal scale—that is, that the marginal benefits of growth are less than commonly thought; that the marginal costs are greater than commonly thought; and that the marginal costs are on the whole greater than the marginal benefits.

Welfare is not a function of consumption flows, but of capital stocks. We cannot ride to town on the maintenance costs, the depletion and replacement flow of an automobile, but only in a complete automobile, a member of the current stock of automobiles. Once again Boulding got it right fifty years ago:

> I shall argue that it is the capital stock from which we derive satisfactions, not from the addition to it (production) or the subtractions from it (consumption): that consumption, far from being a desideratum, is a deplorable property of the capital stock which necessitates the equally deplorable activities of production: and that the objective of economic policy should not be to maximize consumption or production, but rather to minimize it, i.e., to enable us to maintain our capital stock with as little consumption or production as possible.[7]

Our empirical measures of the value of natural capital services (enjoyed or sacrificed) are virtually nonexistent. Even the concept barely exists in standard economic theory because the natural functions of source and sink have been considered free goods, as was reasonable when the world was relatively empty. But now the world is relatively full. Also, contrary to what many think, we have only piecemeal measures of the value of services of manmade capital. Our national income accounts overwhelmingly measure throughput, not service of capital stock. Furthermore, the throughput is valued by market prices that are based on marginal utility and consequently omit consumer surplus, by far the larger part of welfare. Also, diminishing marginal utility is ignored—a dollar used to satisfy basic needs counts the same as a dollar used to satisfy velleities. Yet diminishing marginal utility is the keystone of economic theory. National income has many well-known defects as an index of welfare—it adds up the utilities of different people, which is not allowed in standard economic theory; ignores the value of leisure, of household work, of working conditions, of security, and so on. The point is that even if we were able to construct accounts for valuing natural capital services that were *as good as* our accounts for valuing manmade capital services, we still would not have accomplished much because the latter has itself only been done to a very limited extent. And it is universally acknowledged that it is much harder to evaluate natural capital than manmade capital.

The quest for empirical measures always requires some sacrifice of conceptual purity, but so many sacrifices have been made in standard national income accounting that the number no longer bears any relationship to welfare. Indeed, what is worse, welfare was not even the concept that the statisticians were, for the most part, aiming to approximate. Politicians made that interpretation after the fact, and economists acquiesced in it because it enhanced their political importance. It is better to reason via correct welfare-related concepts to the theoretical existence of an optimal scale, and then figure out by dead reckoning from the North Star and familiar landmarks which side of the optimum we are on, than to rely on a statistical compass whose needle we know is not magnetized.

What then are our common sense, dead reckoning judgments about whether we are at, below,

or above the optimal scale? I suggest we are beyond the optimal scale. To show that we have exceeded the optimum it is *not* necessary to show that growth is physically impossible, nor that it has catastrophic costs, nor that it would have negative or zero marginal benefit, even if free. It is only necessary to show that marginal costs are greater than marginal benefits. It is quite logical and reasonable to argue that on the whole, up to the present time, the total benefits of growth have been greater than the total costs, and yet to hold that growth should cease because at the margin costs have now begun to outweigh benefits. Economists, of all people, surely understand this! They apply this logic to the micro level every day. Why it is not applied at the macro level has never been explained.[8]

What "dead reckoning judgments" can we make about the marginal benefits of growth in manmade capital? (Note that benefits from qualitative *development* are not in question, just those from quantitative *growth*.) For rich, full countries the marginal utility of extra growth is surely low. Great sums of money have to be spent on advertising to cajole people into buying more. As we have become goods-rich we have become time-poor. In rich countries people die more from stress and overconsumption than from starvation. Relative, rather than absolute, income seems to be the main determinant of self-evaluated welfare, and growth is powerless to increase everyone's relative income. The effect of aggregate growth on welfare in rich countries is therefore largely self-canceling.

What about the poor? An increase in wealth from subsistence to middle-class comforts surely increases welfare, if all other things are equal. Should these high marginal utility uses by the poor be paid for by cutting low marginal utility luxury consumption of the rich, or by converting more natural capital into manmade capital? The rich favor the latter, and perhaps the poor do also because they want to emulate the rich, and because they doubt the political likelihood of redistribution or imposed limits to the takeover of natural capital. Inequality is converted into pressure for growth.

However, the growth that often results from the pressure of inequality usually does not go to the poor. Consider for a moment what, exactly, is growing in a growth economy. It is the reinvested surplus that grows in the first instance. Who controls the surplus? Not the poor. They get only the trickle down from growth, and their relative position is more likely to worsen than to improve as a result of growth. This is especially so in light of the far more rapid rate of population growth of the poor than of the rich (due to greater natural increase and frequently to greater immigration as well). A large and growing supply of labor will keep wages from ever rising and thereby also keep profits up.

What are the marginal costs of further growth? How serious are the ecosystem services lost as a result of transformation of more natural into manmade capital? Here one can recite the by-now-familiar litany of CO_2 buildup, biodiversity loss, stratospheric ozone depletion, acid rain, topsoil depletion, aquifer depletion, chemical pollution—in sum, an overall reduction of the capacity of the earth to support life. Loss of natural capital is not deducted from GNP in calculating NNP. Only the value added in the process of transforming the natural capital into manmade capital is counted. A large part of our GNP is regrettably necessary defensive expenditure that we are forced to make to protect ourselves from the unwanted side effects of increasing production and consumption—for example, extra health care resulting from tobacco and alcohol consumption, chemical and radioactive poisoning, cleanup costs of oil spills, longer commuting times, and so on. Defensive expenditures should be subtracted as an intermediate cost of the goods whose production or consumption imposed these regrettably necessary activities. But instead we add them, and politicians, along with their academic magicians and media jesters, rejoice in the improvement.

Add to these considerations the corrosive effects of economic growth on community and on moral standards. Capital and labor mobility rip communities apart in the name of growth. Furthermore, an economy that must grow must also sell. It is easier to sell in a community with low standards—if anything goes, then nearly anything will sell, no matter how tawdry or shoddy. Common prudence is now referred to negatively as "sales resistance." We have plenty of landmarks to suggest that the marginal costs of growth are very high. Even a dead reckoning comparison of the low marginal benefits with the high marginal costs should be enough to convince us that it is time to redirect our economy away from growth and toward development.[9] As a North Star, we may occasionally check our course by the principle that if we are reducing the long-run capacity of earth to support life, then we have overshot the optimum.

CONCLUSION

Consumption is the disarrangement of matter, the using up of value added that inevitably occurs when we use goods. We consume not only value added by human agents of labor and capital, but also value previously added by nature. We are consuming value added, converting raw materials into waste, depicting and polluting, faster than nature can absorb the pollutants and regenerate the resources. Consumption, that is the transformation of natural capital into manmade capital and then ultimately into waste, leads to the basic question of what is the optimal extent of this transformation. What is the optimal scale of the economic subsystem, the scale beyond which further conversion of natural into manmade capital costs us more (in terms of natural capital services lost) than it benefits us (in terms of manmade capital services gained). Growing beyond the optimum is by definition anti-economic. Currently growth is anti-economic, as indicated by our dead reckoning considerations about marginal costs and benefits of growth. The future path of progress therefore is not growth, but development. Individual nations, not the globe, will control consumption by limiting both population and per capita consumption. Different national strategies for limiting consumption cannot coexist in an integrated world economy dominated by free trade, free capital mobility, and free migration. The use of tariffs and a general backing away from global integration toward relative self-sufficiency will likely be necessary.[10]

What are the consequences of the issues here discussed for North/South cooperation in economic development and in sharing the global economic pie? Consider two views.

(a) The traditional value-added view of income would lead one to reject the very notion of a global pie of income to be divided justly or unjustly among nations. There is no global pie—there are only a lot of separate national tarts that some statistician has stupidly aggregated into an abstract pie. The separate tarts are the products of value added by the labor and capital of the nations that produced them, and nothing more. If nation A is asked to share some of its large tart with nation B who baked a small tart, the appeal should be made to nation A's generosity, and not to any notion of distributive justice, much less exploitation.

If you believe that all value comes from labor and capital, and that nature contributes only a material substratum that is nondestructible and superabundant, and hence valueless, then this is a quite reasonable view. Is your country poor? Well, just add more value by your own labor and capital. You already have your own labor, and you can accumulate your own capital, or borrow it at interest from abroad. There are no limits from nature. Stop whining and get busy—and shut up about this imaginary pie. This view is common among neoclassical economists. And given its presuppositions it is reasonable. In fact it is a corollary to John Locke's justification of private property—to claim something as one's property requires that one has mixed one's labor with the materials of which it is made and added value to it.

(b) The alternative view of the ecological economist, that nature too adds value, also rejects the imaginary global pie. But it looks more carefully at the tarts that different peoples have baked. Is the tart really only the product of the cook's labor and the kitchen's capital that alone add value to random, substitutable, and superabundant atoms? Certainly not. To bake a tart you need more than just atoms—you need flour, sugar, butter, and apples. Before that you need wheat, sugar cane, milk, and apple trees. And before that you need gene pools for wheat, sugar cane, cows, and apples, with some minimal degree of diversity, and soil whose fertility is maintained by all sorts of worms, microbes, and minerals, and sunlight without too much ultraviolet, and rainfall that is not too acidic, and

catchment areas to keep that rain from eroding topsoil, and predictable seasonal temperatures regulated by the mix of gases in the atmosphere, and so on. In other words, we need nature or "natural capital" and the flow of natural resources and natural services that it renders—a whole lot more than indestructible building blocks! Our dowry of natural capital is more or less given and is not the product of human labor and capital. Parts of that dowry are highly systemic and indivisible among nations. And the part that is divisible was divided by natural, not economic, processes.

This distinction is why I want to shift attention from traditional value added to "that to which value is added." While one may argue that value added by labor and capital rightly belongs to the laborer and the capitalist (let them fight over how to divide it), one cannot distribute nature's value added so easily, especially the systemic life support services of global natural capital that transcend national boundaries. In this latter sense there really is a global pie, and the demands for justice regarding its division and stewardship cannot be subsumed under the traditional notion that value belongs to whoever added it. Nature's value added was not added by labor or capital—it is a gift. To whom was it given?

NOTES

1. John Stuart Mill, *Principles of Political Economy* (London: John W. Parker, 1857).
2. Alfred Marshall, *Principles of Economics* (New York: Macmillan, 1961), 63–64.
3. Harold Barnett and Chandler Morse, *Scarcity and Growth* (Baltimore: Johns Hopkins University Press, 1963).
4. H. Daly and J. Cobb, *For the Common Good* (Boston: Beacon Press, 1994), chap. 10.
5. E. P. Odum, "The Strategy of Ecosystem Development," *Science* (April 1969): 262–70.
6. Kenneth Boulding, "The Consumption Concept in Economic Theory," *American Economic Review* (May 1945): 2.
7. Kenneth Boulding, "Income or Welfare?" *Review of Economic Studies* 17 (1949): 79.
8. Reasoning in terms of broad aggregates has its limitations. Converting natural into manmade capital embraces both the extravagant conversion

of tropical hardwoods into toothpicks, and the frugal conversion of pine trees into shelters for the homeless. The point is not that all conversions of natural into manmade capital simultaneously cease being worthwhile, but rather that ever fewer remain worthwhile as growth continues.

9. Statistical evidence, beyond "dead reckoning," that we have reached this point in the United States is provided by the Index of Sustainable Economic Welfare, which since the early 1980s has declined slightly even as GNP has continued to increase. See appendix in Daly and Cobb, *For the Common Good*; see also Clifford W. Cobb and John B. Cobb Jr., *The Green National Product: A Proposed Index of Sustainable Economic Welfare* (Lanham, Md.: University Press of America, 1994), and Manfred Max-Neef, "Economic Growth and Quality of Life: A Threshold Hypothesis," *Ecological Economics* 15 (1995): 115–18.

10. Daly and Cobb, *For the Common Good*, chap. 11.

STUDY QUESTIONS

1. Explain how Daly applies the laws of energy to our ecological situation. What does he mean when he says once Earth was relatively empty, now it is relatively full?

2. What does Daly say about the relationship between pollution growth, consumption, and just distribution of resources? Do you agree?

68   At the Shrine of Our Lady of Fàtima, or Why Political Questions Are Not All Economic

MARK SAGOFF

Mark Sagoff is a research scholar at the Center for Philosophy and Public Policy, University of Maryland, College Park, and the author of several works on economic and social issues, including *The Economy of the Earth: Philosophy, Law and the Environment* (1988).

Sagoff examines and rejects the standard economic notion that the cost–benefit analysis is always the proper method for deciding social and environmental issues. Contrasting utilitarian with Kantian views of the human situation, he argues that the Kantian perspective, which treats humans as ends in themselves, should override utilitarian cost–benefit assessments. Sometimes efficiency should be sacrificed for principle.

Lewiston, New York, a well-to-do community near Buffalo, is the site of the Lake Ontario Ordnance Works, where the federal government, years ago, disposed of the residues of the Manhattan Project. These radioactive wastes are buried but are not forgotten by the residents, who say that when the wind is southerly radon gas blows through the town. Several parents at a recent conference I attended there described their terror on learning that cases of leukemia had been found among area children They feared for their own lives as well. At the other sides of the table, officials from New York State and from local corporations replied that these fears were ungrounded. People who smoke, they said, take greater risks than people who live close to waste disposal sites. One speaker talked in terms of "rational methodologies of

Source: *Arizona Law Review*, Vol. 23, pp. 1283–1298. Copyright © 1981 by the Arizona Board of Regents. Reprinted by permission. Notes deleted.

decisionmaking." This aggravated the parents' rage and frustration.

The speaker suggested that the townspeople, were they to make their decision in a free market, would choose to live near the hazardous waste facility, if they knew the scientific facts. He told me later they were irrational—he said, "neurotic"—because they refused to recognize or act upon their own interests. The residents of Lewiston were unimpressed with his analysis of their "willingness to pay" to avoid this risk or that. They did not see what risk-benefit analysis had to do with the issues they raised.

If you take the Military Highway (as I did) from Buffalo to Lewiston, you will pass through a formidable wasteland. Landfills stretch in all directions, where enormous trucks—tiny in that landscape—incessantly deposit sludge which great bulldozers, like yellow ants, then push into the ground. These machines are the only signs of life, for in the miasma that hangs in the air, no birds, not even scavengers, are seen. Along colossal power lines which crisscross this dismal land, the dynamos at Niagara send electric power south, where factories have fled, leaving their remains to decay. To drive along this road is to feel, oddly, the mystery and awe one experiences in the presence of so much power and decadence.

Henry Adams had a similar response to the dynamos on display at the Paris Exposition of 1900. To him "the dynamo became a symbol of infinity." To Adams, the dynamo functioned as the modern equivalent of the Virgin, that is, as the center and focus of power. "Before the end, one began to pray to it; inherited instinct taught the natural expression of man before silent and infinite force."

Adams asks in his essay "The Dynamo and the Virgin" how the products of modern industrial civilization will compare with those of the religious culture of the Middle Ages. If he could see the landfills and hazardous waste facilities bordering the power stations and honeymoon hotels of Niagara Falls he would know the answer. He would understand what happens when efficiency replaces infinity as the central conception of value. The dynamos at Niagara will not produce another Mont-Saint-Michel.

"All the steam in the world," Adams wrote, "could not, like the Virgin, build Chartres."

At the Shrine of Our Lady of Fàtima, on a plateau north of the Military Highway, a larger than life sculpture of Mary looks into the chemical air. The original of this shrine stands in central Portugal, where in May, 1917, three children said they saw a Lady, brighter than the sun, raised on a cloud in an evergreen tree. Five months later, on a wet and chilly October day, the Lady again appeared, this time before a large crowd. Some who were skeptical did not see the miracle. Others in the crowd reported, however, that "the sun appeared and seemed to tremble, rotate violently and fall, dancing over the heads of the throng...."

The Shrine was empty when I visited it. The cult of Our Lady of Fàtima, I imagine, has only a few devotees. The cult of Pareto optimality, however, has many. Where some people see only environmental devastation, its devotees perceive efficiency, utility, and maximization of wealth. They see the satisfaction of wants. They envision the good life. As I looked over the smudged and ruined terrain I tried to share that vision. I hope that Our Lady of Fàtima, worker of miracles, might serve, at least for the moment, as the Patroness of cost-benefit analysis. I thought of all the wants and needs that are satisfied in a landscape of honeymoon cottages, commercial strips, and dumps for hazardous waste. I saw the miracle of efficiency. The prospect, however, looked only darker in that light.

I

This essay concerns the economic decisions we make about the environment. It also concerns our political decisions about the environment. Some people have suggested that ideally these should be the same, that all environmental problems are problems in distribution. According to this view there is an environmental problem only when some resource is not allocated in equitable and efficient ways.

This approach to environmental policy is pitched entirely at the level of the consumer. It is his or her values that count, and the measure of these values is the individual's willingness to pay. The problem of justice or fairness in society becomes, then, the problem of distributing goods and services so that more people get more of what they want to buy. A condo on the beach. A snowmobile for the mountains. A tank full of gas. A day of labor. The only values we have, on this view, are those which a market can price.

How much do you value open space, a stand of trees, an "unspoiled" landscape? Fifty dollars? A hundred? A thousand? This is one way to measure value. You could compare the amount consumers would pay for a townhouse or coal or a landfill and the amount they would pay to preserve an area in its "natural" state. If users would pay more for the land with the house, the coal mine, or the landfill, than without—less construction and other costs of development—then the efficient thing to do is to improve the land and thus increase its value. That is why we have so many tract developments. And pizza stands. And gas stations. And strip mines. And landfills. How much did you spend last year to preserve open space? How much for pizza and gas? "In principle, the ultimate measure of environmental quality," as one basic text assures us, "is the value people place on these . . . services or their *willingness to pay.*"

Willingness to pay. What is wrong with that? The rub is this: not all of us think of ourselves simply as *consumers.* Many of us regard ourselves *as citizens* as well. We act as consumers to get what we want *for ourselves.* We act as citizens to achieve what we think is right or best *for the community.* The question arises, then, whether what we want for ourselves individually as consumers is consistent with the goals we would set for ourselves collectively as citizens. Would I vote for the sort of things I shop for? Are my preferences as a consumer consistent with my judgments as a citizen?

They are not. I am schizophrenic. Last year, I fixed a couple of tickets and was happy to do so since I saved fifty dollars. Yet, at election time, I helped to vote the corrupt judge out of office. I speed on the highway; yet I want the police to enforce laws against speeding. I used to buy mixers in returnable bottles—but who can bother to return them? I buy only disposables now, but,

to soothe my conscience, I urge my state senator to outlaw one-way containers. I love my car; I hate the bus. Yet I vote for candidates who promise to tax gasoline to pay for public transportation. I send my dues to the Sierra Club to protect areas in Alaska I shall never visit. And I support the work of the American League to Abolish Capital Punishment although, personally, I have nothing to gain one way or the other. (When I hang, I will hang myself.) And of course I applaud the Endangered Species Act, although I have no earthly use for the Colorado squawfish or the Indiana bat. I support almost any political cause that I think will defeat my consumer interests. This is because I have contempt for—although I act upon—those interests. I have an "Ecology Now" sticker on a car that leaks oil everywhere it's parked.

The distinction between consumer and citizen preferences has long vexed the theory of public finance. Should the public economy serve the same goals as the household economy? May it serve, instead, goals emerging from our association as citizens? The question asks if we may collectively strive for and achieve only those items we individually compete for and consume. Should we aspire, instead, to public goals we may legislate as a nation?

The problem, insofar as it concerns public finance, is stated as follows by R. A. Musgrave, who reports a conversation he had with Gerhard Colm.

> He [Colm] holds that the individual voter dealing with political issues has a frame of reference quite distinct from that which underlies his allocation of income as a consumer. In the latter situation the voter acts as a private individual determined by self-interest and deals with his personal wants; in the former, he acts as a political being guided by his image of a good society. The two, Colm holds, are different things.

Are these two different things? Stephen Marglin suggests that they are. He writes:

> The preferences that govern one's unilateral market actions no longer govern his actions when the form of reference is shifted from the market to the political arena. The Economic Man and the Citizen are for all intents and purposes two

different individuals. It is not a question, therefore, of rejecting individual...preference maps; it is, rather, that market and political preference maps are inconsistent.

Marglin observes that if this is true, social choices optimal under one set of preferences will not be optimal under another. What, then, is the meaning of "optimality"? He notices that if we take a person's true preferences to be those expressed in the market, we may, then, neglect or reject the preferences that person reveals in advocating a political cause or position. "One might argue on welfare grounds," Marglin speculates, "for authoritarian rejection of individuals' politically revealed preferences in favor of their market revealed preferences!"

II

On February 19, 1981, President Reagan published Executive Order 12,291 requiring all administrative agencies and departments to support every new major regulation with a cost-benefit analysis establishing that the benefits of the regulation to society outweigh its costs. The Order directs the Office of Management and Budget (OMB) to review every such regulation on the basis of the adequacy of the cost-benefit analysis supporting it. This is a departure from tradition. Traditionally, regulations have been reviewed not by OMB but by the courts on the basis of their relation not to cost-benefit analysis but to authorizing legislation.

A month earlier, in January 1981, the Supreme Court heard lawyers for the American Textile Manufacturers Institute argue against a proposed Occupational Safety and Health Administration (OSHA) regulation which would have severely restricted the acceptable levels of cotton dust in textile plants. The lawyers for industry argued that the benefits of the regulation would not equal the costs. The lawyers for the government contended that the law required the tough standard. OSHA, acting consistently with Executive Order 12,291, asked the Court not to decide the cotton dust case, in order to give the agency time to complete the cost-benefit analysis required by the textile industry. The Court

declined to accept OSHA's request and handed down its opinion on June 17, 1981.

The Supreme Court, in a 5–3 decision, found that the actions of regulatory agencies which conform to the OSHA law need not be supported by cost-benefit analysis. In addition, the Court asserted that Congress in writing a statute, rather than the agencies in applying it, has the primary responsibility for balancing benefits and costs. The Court said:

> When Congress passed the Occupational Health and Safety Act in 1970, it chose to place preeminent value on assuring employees a safe and healthful working environment, limited only by the feasibility of achieving such an environment. We must measure the validity of the Secretary's actions against the requirements of that Act.

The opinion upheld the finding of the Appeals Court that "Congress itself struck the balance between costs and benefits in the mandate to the agency."

The Appeals Court opinion in *American Textile Manufacturers* vs. *Donovan* supports the principle that legislatures are not necessarily bound to a particular conception of regulatory policy. Agencies that apply the law, therefore, may not need to justify on cost-benefit grounds the standards they set. These standards may conflict with the goal of efficiency and still express our political will as a nation. That is, they may reflect not the personal choices of self-interested individuals, but the collective judgments we make on historical, cultural, aesthetic, moral, and ideological grounds.

The appeal of the Reagan Administration to cost-benefit analysis, however, may arise more from political than economic considerations. The intention, seen in the most favorable light, may not be to replace political or ideological goals with economic ones but to make economic goals more apparent in regulation. This is not to say that Congress should function to reveal a collective willingness-to-pay just as markets reveal an individual willingness-to-pay. It is to suggest that Congress should do more to balance economic with ideological, aesthetic, and moral goals. To think that environmental or worker safety policy can be based exclusively on aspiration for a "natural" and "safe" world is as foolish as to hold that environmental law can be reduced to cost-benefit accounting. The more we move to one extreme, as I found in Lewiston, the more likely we are to hear from the other.

III

The labor unions won an important political victory when Congress passed the Occupational Safety and Health Act of 1970. That Act, among other things, severely restricts worker exposure to toxic substances. It instructs the Secretary of Labor to set "the standard which most adequately assures, to the extent feasible...that no employee will suffer material impairment of health or functional capacity even if such employee has regular exposure to the hazard-for the period of his working life."

Pursuant to this law, the Secretary of Labor, in 1977, reduced from ten to one part per million (ppm) the permissible ambient exposure level for benzene, a carcinogenic for which no safe threshold is known. The American Petroleum Institute thereupon challenged the new standard in court. It argued, with much evidence in its favor, that the benefits (to workers) of the one ppm standard did not equal the costs (to industry). The standard, therefore, did not appear to be a rational response to a market failure in that it did not strike an efficient balance between the interests of workers in safety and the interests of industry and consumers in keeping prices down.

The Secretary of Labor defended the tough safety standard on the ground that the law demanded it. An efficient standard might have required safety until it cost industry more to prevent a risk than it cost workers to accept it. Had Congress adopted this vision of public policy—one which can be found in many economic texts—it would have treated workers not as ends-in-themselves but as means for the production of overall utility. And this, as the Secretary saw it, was what Congress refused to do.

The United States Court of Appeals for the Fifth Circuit agreed with the American Petroleum Institute and invalidated the one ppm benzene standard. On July 2, 1980, the Supreme Court affirmed remanding the benzene standard back to OSHA for revision. The narrowly based Supreme Court decision was divided over the role economic considerations should play in judicial review. Justice Marshall, joined in dissent by three other justices, argued that the court had undone on the basis of its own theory of regulatory policy an act of Congress inconsistent with that theory. He concluded that the plurality decision of the Court "requires the American worker to return to the political arena to win a victory that he won before in 1970."

To reject cost-benefit analysis, as Justice Marshall would, as a basis for public policy making is not necessarily to reject cost-effectiveness analysis, which is an altogether different thing. *"Cost-benefit analysis,"* one commentator points out, "is used by the decision maker to establish societal goals as well as the means for achieving these goals, whereas *cost-effectiveness analysis* only compares alternative means for achieving 'given' goals." Justice Marshall's dissent objects to those who would make efficiency the goal of public policy. It does not necessarily object to those who would accomplish as efficiently as possible the goals Congress sets.

IV

When efficiency is the criterion of public safety and health one tends to conceive of social relations on the model of a market, ignoring competing visions of what we as a society should be like. Yet it is obvious that there are competing conceptions of how we should relate to one another. There are some who believe, on principle, that worker safety and environmental quality ought to be protected only insofar as the benefits of protection balance the costs. On the other hand, people argue, also on principle, that neither worker safety nor environmental quality should be treated merely as a commodity, to be traded at the margin for other commodities, but should be valued for its own sake. The conflict between these two principles is logical or moral, to be resolved by argument or debate. The question whether cost-benefit analysis should play a decisive role in policymaking is not to be decided by cost-benefit analysis. A contradiction between principles—between contending visions of the good society—cannot be settled by asking how much partisans are willing to pay for their beliefs.

The role of the *legislator,* the political role, may be more important to the individual than the role of *consumer.* The person, in other words, is not to be treated as merely a bundle of preferences to be juggled in cost-benefit analyses. The individual is to be respected as an advocate of ideas which are to be judged in relation to the reasons for them. If health and environmental statutes reflect a vision of society as something other than a market by requiring protections beyond what are efficient, then this may express not legislative ineptitude but legislative responsiveness to public values. To deny this vision because it is economically inefficient is simply to replace it with another vision. It is to insist that the ideas of the citizen be sacrificed to the psychology of the consumer.

We hear on all sides that government is routinized, mechanical, entrenched, and bureaucratized; the jargon alone is enough to dissuade the most mettlesome meddler. Who can make a difference? It is plain that for many of us the idea of a national political community has an abstract and suppositious quality. We have only our private conceptions of the good, if no way exists to arrive at a public one. This is only to note the continuation, in our time, of the trend Benjamin Constant described in the essay, *De La Liberte des Anciens Comparee a Celle des Modernes.* Constant observes that the modern world, as opposed to the ancient, emphasizes civil over political liberties, the rights of privacy and property over those of community and participation. "Lost in the multitude," Constant writes, "the individual rarely perceives the influence that he exercises," and, therefore, must be content with "the peaceful enjoyment of private independence." The individual asks only to be protected by laws common to all in his pursuit of his own self-interest. The citizen has been replaced by the consumer; the tradition of Rousseau has been supplanted by that of Locke and Mill.

Nowhere are the rights of the moderns, particularly the rights of privacy and property, less helpful than in the area of the natural environment. Here the values we wish to protect—cultural, historical, aesthetic, and moral—are

public values; they depend not so much upon what each person wants individually as upon what he or she believes we stand for collectively. We refuse to regard worker health and safety as commodities; we regulate hazards as a matter of right. Likewise, we refuse to treat environmental resources simply as public goods in the economist's sense. Instead, we prevent significant deterioration of air quality not only as a matter of individual self-interest but also as a matter of collective self-respect. How shall we balance efficiency against moral, cultural, and aesthetic values in policy for the workplace and the environment? No better way has been devised to do this than by legislative debate ending in a vote. This is not the same thing as a cost-benefit analysis terminating in a bottom line.

V

It is the characteristic of cost-benefit analysis that it treats all value judgments other than those made on its behalf as nothing but statements of preference, attitude, or emotion, insofar as they are value judgments. The cost-benefit analyst regards as true the judgment that we should maximize efficiency or wealth. The analyst believes that this view can be backed by reasons; the analyst does not regard it as a preference or want for which he or she must be willing to pay. The cost-benefit analyst, however, tends to treat all other normative views and recommendations as if they were nothing but subjective reports of mental states. The analyst supposes in all such cases that "this is right" and "this is what we ought to do" are equivalent to "I want this" and "this is what I prefer." Value judgments are beyond criticism if, indeed, they are nothing but expressions of personal preference; they are incorrigible since every person is in the best position to know what he or she wants. All valuation, according to this approach, happens *in foro interno,* debate *in foro publico* has no point. On this approach, the reasons that people give for their views, unless these people are welfare economists, do not count; what counts is how much they are willing to pay to satisfy their wants. Those who are willing to pay the most, for all intents and purposes, have the right view; theirs is the more informed opinion, the better aesthetic judgment, and the deeper moral insight.

The assumption that valuation is subjective, that judgments of good and evil are nothing but expressions of desire and aversion, is not unique to economic theory. There are psychotherapists—Carl Rogers is an example—who likewise deny the objectivity or cognitivity of valuation. For Rogers, there is only one criterion of worth: it lies in "the subjective world of the individual. Only he knows it fully." The therapist shows his or her client that a "value system is not necessarily something imposed from without, but is something experienced." Therapy succeeds when the client "perceives himself in such a way that no self-experience can be discriminated as more or less worthy of positive self-regard than any other...." The client then "tends to place the basis of standards within himself, recognizing that the 'goodness' or 'badness' of any experience or perceptual object is not something inherent in that object, but is a value placed in it by himself."

Rogers points out that "some clients make strenuous efforts to have the therapist exercise the valuing function, so as to provide them with guides for action." The therapist, however, "consistently keeps the locus of evaluation with the client." As long as the therapist refuses to "exercise the valuing function" and as long as he or she practices an "unconditional positive regard" for all the affective states of the client, then the therapist remains neutral among the client's values or "sensory and visceral experiences." The role of the therapist is legitimate, Rogers suggests, because of this value neutrality. The therapist accepts all felt preferences as valid and imposes none on the client.

Economists likewise argue that their role as policymakers is legitimate because they are neutral among competing values in the client society. The political economist, according to James Buchanan, "is or should be ethically neutral: the indicated results are influenced by his own value scale only insofar as this reflects his membership in a larger group." The economist might be most confident of the impartiality of his or her policy recommendations if he or she could derive them formally or mathematically from individual preferences. If theoretical difficulties make such

a social welfare function impossible, however, the next best thing, to preserve neutrality, is to let markets function to transform individual preference orderings into a collective ordering of social states. The analyst is able then to base policy on preferences that exist in society and are not necessarily his own.

Economists have used this impartial approach to offer solutions to many outstanding social problems, for example, the controversy over abortion. An economist argues that "there is an optimal number of abortions, just as there is an optimal level of pollution, or purity.... Those who oppose abortion could eliminate it entirely, if their intensity of feeling were so strong as to lead to payments that were greater at the margin than the price anyone would pay to have an abortion." Likewise economists, in order to determine whether the war in Vietnam was justified, have estimated the willingness to pay of those who demonstrated against it. Likewise it should be possible, following the same line of reasoning, to decide whether Creationism should be taught in the public schools, whether black and white people should be segregated, whether the death penalty should be enforced, and whether the square root of six is three. All of these questions depend upon how much people are willing to pay for their subjective preferences or wants—or none of them do. This is the beauty of cost-benefit analysis: no matter how relevant or irrelevant, wise or stupid, informed or uninformed, responsible or silly, defensible or indefensible wants may be, the analyst is able to derive a policy from them—a policy which is legitimate because, in theory, it treats all of these preferences as equally valid and good.

VI

Consider, by way of contrast, a Kantian conception of value. The individual, for Kant, is a judge of values, not a mere haver of wants, and the individual judges not for himself or herself merely, but as a member of a relevant community or group. The central idea in a Kantian approach to ethics is that some values are more reasonable than others and therefore have a better claim upon the assent of members of the community as such. The world of obligation, like the world of mathematics or the world of empirical fact, is intersubjective, it is public not private, so that objective standards of argument and criticism apply. Kant recognizes that values, like beliefs, are subjective states of mind, but he points out that like beliefs they have an objective content as well; therefore they are either correct or mistaken. Thus Kant discusses valuation in the context not of psychology but of cognition. He believes that a person who makes a value judgment—or a policy recommendation—claims to know what is *right* and not just what is *preferred*. A value judgment is like an empirical or theoretical judgment in that it claims to be *true*, not merely to be *felt*.

We have, then, two approaches to public policy before us. The first, the approach associated with normative versions of welfare economics, asserts that the only policy recommendation that can or need be defended on objective grounds is efficiency or wealth-maximization. Every policy decision after that depends only on the preponderance of feeling or preference, as expressed in willingness to pay. The Kantian approach, on the other hand, assumes that many policy recommendations other than that one may be justified or refuted on objective grounds. It would concede that the approach of welfare economics applies adequately to some questions, e.g., those which ordinary consumer markets typically settle. How many yo-yos should be produced as compared to how many frisbees? Shall pens have black ink or blue? Matters such as these are so trivial it is plain that markets should handle them. It does not follow, however, that we should adopt a market or quasi-market approach to every public question.

A market or quasi-market approach to arithmetic, for example, is plainly inadequate. No matter how much people are willing to pay, three will never be the square root of six. Similarly, segregation is a national curse and the fact that we are willing to pay for it does not make it better but only makes us worse. Similarly, the case for abortion must stand on the merits; it cannot be priced at the margin. Similarly, the war in Vietnam was a moral debacle and this can be determined without shadow-pricing the

willingness to pay of those who demonstrated against it. Similarly, we do not decide to execute murderers by asking how much bleeding hearts are willing to pay to see a person pardoned and how much hard hearts are willing to pay to see him hanged. Our failures to make the right decisions in these matters are failures in arithmetic, failures in wisdom, failures in taste, failures in morality—but not market failures. There are no relevant markets to have failed. What separates these questions from those for which markets are appropriate is this. They involve matters of knowledge, wisdom, morality, and taste that admit of better or worse, right or wrong, true or false—and these concepts differ from that of economic optimality. Surely environmental questions—the protection of wilderness, habitats, water, land, and air as well as policy toward environmental safety and health—involve moral and aesthetic principles and not just economic ones. This is consistent, of course, with cost-effectiveness and with a sensible recognition of economic constraints.

The neutrality of the economist, like the neutrality of Rogers' therapist, is legitimate if private preferences or subjective wants are the only values in question. A person should be left free to choose the color of his or her necktie or necklace—but we cannot justify a theory of public policy or private therapy on that basis. If the patient seeks moral advice or tries to find reasons to justify a choice, the therapist, according to Rogers' model, would remind him or her to trust his visceral and sensory experiences. The result of this is to deny the individual status as a cognitive being capable of responding intelligently to reasons; it reduces him or her to a bundle of affective states. What Rogers' therapist does to the patient the cost-benefit analyst does to society as a whole. The analyst is neutral among our "values"—having first imposed a theory of what value is. This is a theory that is impartial among values and for that reason fails to treat the persons who have them with respect or concern. It does not treat them even as persons but only as locations at which wants may be found. And thus we may conclude that the neutrality of economics is not a basis for its legitimacy. We recognize it as an indifference toward value—an indifference so deep, so studied, and so assured that at first one hesitates to call it by its right name.

VII

The residents of Lewiston at the conference I attended demanded to know the truth about the dangers that confronted them and the reasons for these dangers. They wanted to be convinced that the sacrifice asked of them was legitimate even if it served interests other than their own. One official from a large chemical company dumping wastes in the area told them, in reply, that corporations were people and that people could talk to people about their feelings, interests, and needs. This sent a shiver through the audience. Like Joseph K. in *The Trial*, the residents of Lewiston asked for an explanation, justice, and truth, and they were told that their wants would be taken care of. They demanded to know the reasons for what was continually happening to them. They were given a personalized response instead.

This response, that corporations are "just people serving people" is consistent with a particular view of power. This is the view that identified power with the ability to get what one wants as an individual, that is, to satisfy one's personal preferences. When people in official positions in corporations or in the government put aside their personal interests, it would follow that they put aside their power as well. Their neutrality then justifies them in directing the resources of society in ways they determine to be best. This managerial role serves not their own interests but those of their clients. Cost-benefit analysis may be seen as a pervasive form of this paternalism. Behind this paternalism, as William Simon observes of the lawyer-client relationship, lies a theory of value that tends to personalize power. "It resists understanding power as a product of class, property, or institutions and collapses power into the personal needs and dispositions of the individuals who command and obey." Once the economist, the therapist, the lawyer, or the manager abjures his own interests and acts wholly on behalf of client individuals, he appears to have no power of his own and thus justifiably manipulates and controls everything. "From this perspective it becomes difficult to distinguish the powerful from the powerless. In every case, both the exercise of power and submission to it are portrayed as a matter of personal accommodation and adjustment."

The key to the personal interest or emotive theory of value, as one commentator has rightly said, "is the fact that emotivism entails the obliteration of any genuine distinction between manipulative and non-manipulative social relations." The reason is that once the effective self is made the source of all value, the public self cannot participate in the exercise of power. As Philip Reiff remarks, "the public world is constituted as one vast stranger who appears at inconvenient times and makes demands viewed as purely external and therefore with no power to elicit a moral response." There is no way to distinguish tyranny from the legitimate authority that public values and public law create.

"At the rate of progress since 1900," Henry Adams speculates in his *Education*, "every American who lived into the year 2000 would know how to control unlimited power." Adams thought that the Dynamo would organize and release as much energy as the Virgin. Yet in the 1980s, the citizens of Lewiston, surrounded by dynamos, high tension lines, and nuclear wastes, are powerless. They do not know how to criticize power, resist power, or justify—power—for to do so depends on making distinctions between good and evil, right and wrong, innocence and guilt, justice and injustice, truth and lies. These distinctions cannot be made out and have no significance within an emotive or psychological theory of value. To adopt this theory is to imagine society as a market in which individuals trade voluntarily and without coercion. No individual, no belief, no faith has authority over them. To have power to act as a nation, however, we must be able to act, at least at times, on a public philosophy, conviction, or faith. We cannot replace with economic analysis the moral function of public law. The antinomianism [*antinomian*—the rejection of law and morality] of cost-benefit analysis is not enough.

✂ STUDY QUESTIONS

1. Do you agree with Sagoff in his distinction between the person as *consumer* and *citizen*? Should there be a radical divide ("schizophrenia") between our economic selves and our moral-political selves?

2. Sagoff seems to hold that not all values are subjective, but some are objectively true or better. What arguments can you think of for both views of values?

3. How is the psychotherapeutic model (Carl Rogers offers an example) similar to the economic model

of value preferences? Do you agree with Sagoff that psychotherapists leave out something important? What?

4. Can the standard economic analysis incorporate Sagoff's criticism, arguing that the moral-legislative aspects can be taken into account in assessing the total cost-benefits? Or is there a fundamental cleavage between these two ways of viewing things?

69   On the Value and Limits of Cost-Benefit Analysis

DAVID SCHMIDTZ

David Schmidtz is Professor of Philosophy and Joint Professor of Economics at the University of Arizona and is the author of several works in environmental ethics and ethical theory in general. In this essay Schmidtz examines the proper use of cost-benefit analysis (CBA) as well as its limitations. He distinguishes narrow CBA from full-cost CBA and applies such analysis to environmental concerns.

What next? We are forever making decisions. Typically, when unsure, we weigh pros and cons. Occasionally, we make the weighing explicit, listing pros and cons and assigning numerical weights. What could be wrong with that? In fact, things sometimes go terribly wrong. This paper considers what cost-benefit analysis can do, and also what it cannot.

WHAT IS CBA, AND WHAT IS IT FOR?

Here is an example of how things go wrong. Ontario Hydro is a Canadian government-owned utility company (a Crown Corporation, on a par with Canada Post). Ten years ago, Ontario Hydro was expecting to become a hugely

profitable provider of electricity to consumers all over the continent. At that time, Ontario circulated a report explaining how it planned to meet projected demand. Of interest to us is the report's admission that, "The analysis conducted in the development of the Demand/Supply Plans includes those costs which are borne directly by Hydro. It is these costs which can properly be included in Hydro's rates. Costs and benefits for the Ontario community, beyond these direct costs, are not factored into the cost comparisons." Why not? Because "even if desirable, these costs are difficult to estimate in monetary terms given the diffuse nature of the impacts and wide variety of effects." The costs that Ontario Hydro proposed to take into account "include the social and environmental costs incurred by Hydro but do not include social

David Schmidtz, "A Place for Cost-Benefit Analysis," *Philosophical Issues* 11 (2001): 148–71. Reprinted with permission of the author.

and environmental costs external to Hydro. This reflects normal business practice. In Hydro's judgment, including additional costs and benefits on an equitable basis would be impracticable."[1]

It is amazing that people would defend such a patently unethical stance by describing it as "normal business practice." Sadly, though, appealing to "normal business practice" is itself normal business practice, and Ontario Hydro is not especially guilty in that regard. Indeed, it is notable that Ontario Hydro was not duplicitous, since it did, after all, express its policy bluntly and publicly. Those who wrote the report evidently had no idea that what they were saying was wrong.

Environmentalists have their own "normal business practices," though, and it is too easy to condemn organizations like Ontario Hydro without thinking things through. Many critics of cost-benefit analysis (henceforth CBA) seem driven by a gut feeling that CBA is heartless. They think that, in denouncing CBA, they are taking a stand against heartlessness. This is unfortunate. The fact is, weighing a proposal's costs and benefits does not make you a bad person. What makes you a bad person is *ignoring* costs—the costs you impose on others.

The problem with Ontario Hydro arose, not when Ontario Hydro took costs and benefits into account, but rather when it decided *not* to do so. The problem in general terms is a problem of *external* costs. External costs are costs that decision makers ignore, leaving them to be paid by someone else. Ontario Hydro makes a decision that has certain costs. Some of the costs will fall not on Ontario Hydro but on innocent bystanders; following normal business practice, Ontario Hydro seems to say, "That's not our problem."

Decision makers naturally are tempted to ignore external costs. It is only human. Almost everyone does the same sort of thing in one context or another. Every time you leave an empty popcorn box in a theater rather than dispose of it properly, you are doing the same sort of thing as the person who dumps industrial waste in the river rather than dispose of it properly. Every time you drive a car, you are risking other people's lives, and you probably have never wasted a minute feeling guilty about it.

(And just like you, industrial polluters defend themselves by saying, "But everybody does it!") It is not only bad people who ignore the costs they impose on others. Part of the problem is simple laziness, when we think no one is watching. Another part of the problem is the normal human desire to conform, even when "normal practice" is unconscionable.

IS CBA ANTI-ENVIRONMENTALIST?

CBA comes in many variations, and there are many that no ethicist would defend. Needless to say, no ethicist would defend conventional CBA, that is, CBA in the narrowly focused way that Ontario Hydro used it at the end of the 1980s. All sides agree: there can be no general justification for foisting external costs on innocent bystanders. Any controversy concerns whether there exists some other form of CBA that can, in general, be justified.

Those with expertise in accounting are trained to draw fine-grained distinctions between different variations on the basic theme of conventional CBA. Full Cost Accounting, for example, refers to an attempt to carry out CBA in such a way as to take *all* known costs, external as well as internal, into account.[2] From here on, except where otherwise noted, when I speak of CBA, I will be referring to cost-benefit analysis with Full Cost Accounting. As E. J. Mishan's influential text defines it, "in cost-benefit analysis we are concerned with the economy as a whole, with the welfare of a defined society, and not any smaller part of it."[3]

Understood in this way, CBA is not merely an accounting method. It is a commitment to take responsibility for the consequences of one's actions. That is why, historically, environmentalists were among the most vocal *advocates* of CBA as a vehicle for making industries and governments answerable for the full cost of their decisions. It can work. Indeed, there has been an interesting further development in the case of Ontario Hydro. Perhaps having learned something about environmental ethics, Ontario Hydro changed its stance in 1993 and now trumpets its use of Full Cost Accounting methods.[4]

Under what general circumstances, then, should we want policy makers to employ CBA? Two answers come to mind: first, when one group pays the cost of a piece of legislation while another group gets the benefit; second, and more generally, whenever decision makers have an incentive not to take full costs into account. Where benefits of political decisions are concentrated while costs are dispersed, special interest groups can push through favorable policies even when costs to the population at large outweigh benefits.[5] To contain the proliferation of such unconscionable policies, we might require that policies be justified by the lights of a proper CBA. Requiring decision makers to provide a CBA, which is then made available for public scrutiny, is one way of trying to teach decision makers to take environmental costs into account. We do not want upstream people ignoring costs they foist on downstream people.[6] We want social and cultural and legal arrangements that encourage people to be aware of the full environmental cost, and also the full human cost, of what they do.

The most fundamental argument in favor of CBA has to do with CBA's role as a means of introducing accountability into decisions that affect whole communities. Think about it. If a business pollutes, would it be wrong to insist that the business should be paying the true full cost of its operation? As a mechanism for holding decision makers publicly accountable for external costs, CBA has the potential to constrain activities that are not worthwhile when external costs are taken into account. Accordingly, the National Policy Act of 1969 required CBA of all environment-related federal projects. To that extent, CBA is a friend of the environment. Or at least, it seemed that way at one time.

The tables seemingly have been turning, though. Throughout the 1970s, the Council on Wage and Price Stability and the Office of Management and Budget pressured the Environmental Protection Agency to pay more attention to the costs of complying with standards the EPA was trying to impose on industry. Finally, in 1981, President Reagan issued an Executive Order requiring government agencies to justify new regulations by submitting a formal CBA (of which an environmental impact statement would be only one part)

to the Office of Management and Budget. Why? Why force agencies to perform CBA of their regulatory proposals? The point, very generally, was to force agencies to take into account costs they otherwise would have preferred to ignore. The Reagan administration reputedly felt some regulations were being pushed through by environmental zealots who did not care what their proposals cost in human terms. Accordingly, the Executive Order mandating CBA was perceived as having an anti-environmental thrust. Perhaps partly because of that bit of recent history, current environmentalist opinion remains, on the whole, anti-CBA. The following sections consider some of the main reasons (some cogent, some not) for distrusting CBA.

IS CBA ANTHROPOCENTRIC?

Is it only the interests of human persons that can be taken into account in a CBA? If so, then isn't CBA essentially anthropocentric? The answer is no. CBA as construed here is partly an accounting procedure, and partly a way of organizing public debate. In no way is it a substitute for philosophical debate. Animal liberationists who think full costs must (by definition?) include pain suffered by animals, for example, must argue for that point in philosophical debate with those who think otherwise. If CBA presupposed one or the other position, thereby pre-empting philosophical debate, that would be a flaw.

DOES CBA PRESUPPOSE UTILITARIAN MORAL THEORY?

Utilitarian moral theory holds roughly that X is right if and only if X maximizes utility, where maximizing utility is a matter of producing the best possible balance of benefits over costs. It may seem obvious that CBA presupposes the truth of utilitarian moral theory. In fact, it does not. CBA is a way of organizing a public forum expressing respect for persons; persons present at the meeting and other persons as well, on whose behalf those present can speak (citizens of faraway countries, future generations, etc.). For that matter, those present at the forum will speak not only on behalf of other persons but on behalf of whatever they care about: animals, trees, canyons, historic sites, and so on.

The forum therefore is defensible on utilitarian grounds, but it does not depend on utilitarian moral theory, for this sort of CBA could and probably should be advocated by deontologists.[7] A conventional CBA that ignored external costs would be endorsed neither by deontologists nor utilitarians, but CBA with Full Cost Accounting, defended in a public forum, could be endorsed by either.[8]

DOES CBA TELL US TO SACRIFICE THE ONE FOR THE SAKE OF THE MANY?

We can imagine advocates of CBA jumping to the conclusion that policies are justified whenever benefits exceed costs. That would be a mistake. We need to be more circumspect than that. When benefits exceed costs, the conclusion should be that the policy has passed one crucial test and therefore further discussion is warranted. On the other hand, when a proposal *fails* the test of CBA, when costs exceed benefits, the implication is more decisive, namely that further discussion is not warranted. If enacting a certain proposal would help some people and hurt others, then showing that winners are gaining more than losers are losing counts for something, but it is not decisive. One must then argue that the gain is so great for some people that it justifies imposing a loss on other people. In contrast, to show that losers are losing more than winners are gaining should pretty much end the conversation. Failing CBA is a fairly reliable test of when something is wrong.[9] Passing CBA, however, is not a reliable test of when something is right.

Consider the following case.[10]

> HOSPITAL: Five patients lie on operating tables about to die for lack of suitable organ donors. A UPS delivery person just walked into the office. She is a suitable organ donor for all five patients. If you kidnap her and harvest her organs, you will be saving five and killing one.

Suppose we perform CBA in that case, and it yields the conclusion that, well, five is more than one. Would that imply that taking the delivery person's life is permissible? Required, even? No. Of course, we could quibble about how the calculation works out, but that would miss the fundamental point, which is that when we are talking about killing people, costs and benefits are not the only issue. CBA offers us guidance when our objective is to promote the best possible balance of costs and benefits, but not all situations call on us to maximize what is valuable. Promoting value is not always the best way of respecting it. There are times when morality calls on us not to maximize value but simply to respect it.

I argued that CBA does not presume the truth of utilitarian moral theory. Now it may seem that what I call CBA presumes that utilitarian moral theory is false! On the contrary, even from a broadly utilitarian perspective, we do not want ordinary citizens to have a license to kill whenever they think they can do a lot of good in the process. Some institutions have their utility precisely by *prohibiting* decisions based on utilitarian calculation. Hospitals, for example, cannot serve their purpose if they are a menace to innocent bystanders. Hospitals cannot serve their purpose unless people can trust hospitals to treat people as rights-bearers. Respecting people's rights is part of what helps make it safe to visit hospitals. And making it safe to visit the hospital is a prerequisite of hospitals functioning properly. Accordingly, we cannot justify cutting up one patient to save five simply by saying five is more than one. Sometimes, numbers do not count. It is good policy to forbid killing, requiring ordinary citizens to respect human rights, period.

Therefore, there are limits to the legitimate scope of CBA, and must be, even from a utilitarian perspective. Consider the case of *Peeveyhouse vs. Garland Coal.*[11] Having completed a strip-mining operation on the Peeveyhouse property, Garland Coal refused to honor its contractual promise to restore the land to its original condition. The restored land would have been worth only $300 and it would have cost $29,000 to restore it. Still, Peeveyhouse wanted the land restored and Garland Coal had promised to do it.

Incredibly, the Oklahoma court awarded Peevey house only the $300, judging that Garland Coal could not be held financially liable for a restoration when such restoration would not be cost-effective. The Court's verdict generally is regarded as utterly mistaken, though, and one way of understanding the mistake is to see it as a case of failing to understand the limits of CBA's legitimate scope. We live in a society where hospitals cannot take organs without consent. We live in a society where Garland Coal normally would have to honor its contract with Peeveyhouse. Thus, we know where we stand. We need not be perpetually preparing to prove before a tribunal that strip-mining our land or harvesting our internal organs without consent is not cost-effective. Instead, we have a right simply to say no. In giving us moral space that we govern by right, our laws limit the energy we have to waste: trying to influence public regulators, fighting to keep what belongs to us, fighting to gain what belongs to others. In treating us as rights-bearers, our laws enable us simply to decline proposals that would benefit others at our expense.

Crucially, our being able to say no teaches people to search for ways of making progress that benefit everyone. CBA in its simplest form allows some to be sacrificed for the sake of the greater good of others, and therefore CBA in its simplest form is morally problematic. In contrast, CBA as a framework for public discussion, in a regime that treats people as rights-bearers, creates at least some pressure to craft proposals that promise benefits for all.

Again, part of the message to take away from these discussions is that the proper purpose of CBA is not to show when a taking is permissible. If we see CBA as indicating when takings are permissible, we will have a problem, because breaking contracts, or taking things from people (including their lives) whenever the benefit is worth the cost is not a way of respecting people. But if we treat CBA as a *constraint* on takings, ruling out inefficient takings without licensing efficient takings, then it is not disrespectful.

Therefore, it would be a mistake to see CBA as an *alternative* to treating people as ends in themselves. On the contrary, when CBA is working properly, and in particular when treated not as a seal of approval for good proposals but rather as a means of filtering out bad proposals, CBA becomes a way of preventing people from treating each other as mere means. The point is to stop people from foisting the costs of their policies on innocent people without consent. In other words, requiring people to offer an accounting of the true costs and benefits of their operations is a way of holding them publicly accountable for failing to treat fellow citizens as ends in themselves. CBA will not filter out every proposal that ought to be filtered out, but it will help to filter out many of the most flagrantly disrespectful proposals, and that is its proper purpose.

MUST CBA TREAT ALL VALUES AS MERE COMMODITIES?

As Mark Sagoff nicely expresses the point, "There are some who believe on principle that worker safety and environmental quality ought to be protected only insofar as the benefits of protection balance the costs. On the other hand, people argue—also on principle—that neither worker safety nor environmental quality should be treated as a commodity to be traded at the margin for other commodities, but rather each should be valued for its own sake."[12] The second argument, though, presents a false dichotomy. CBA is perfectly compatible with the idea that worker safety and environmental quality ought to be valued for their own sake.

To see why, imagine a certain recycling process is risky to the workers involved. The process improves environmental quality, but inevitably workers risk getting their hands caught in the machines, and so on. Notice: although we treat both environmental quality and worker safety as ends in themselves, we still have to weigh the operation's costs and benefits. Is recycling's environmental benefit worth the risk? It is a good question, and we would be missing the point if we tried to answer it by saying environmental quality is valued for its own sake.

Nor must we imagine cases of different values (worker safety and environmental quality) coming into conflict. The need for CBA can arise even when environmental quality is the sole value at stake. For example, suppose the recycling process in question saves paper (and therefore trees), but saving trees comes at a cost of all the water and electricity used in the process; gasoline is used by trucks that collect the paper from recycling bins, and so on. Therefore, the very recycling process that reduces pollution and natural resource consumption in some respects also increases pollution and natural resource consumption in other respects. In this case, our reason to do CBA is precisely that we care about environmental quality. (If maintaining a politically correct environmentalist appearance were our only concern, we would not worry about it.)

Again, it would be beside the point to talk about environmental quality being valued for its own sake. In a nutshell, we sometimes find ourselves in situations of conflicting values, where the values at stake are really important. Critics of CBA sometimes seem to say, when values at stake are really important, that is when we should *not* think hard about the costs and benefits of resolving the conflict in one way rather than another. They seem to have things backwards.

Sagoff asserts, "It is the characteristic of cost-benefit analysis that it treats all value judgments other than those made on its behalf as nothing but statements of preference, attitude, or emotion."[13] There are several things going on in this passage. I will mention three. First, the words "other than those made on its behalf" are a jest at the pseudo-scientific posturing of radical subjectivists, and the jest is on target. Second, Sagoff is insinuating that it is a mistake simply to assume that all values are reducible to costs and benefits, and here too, Sagoff is on target. On the one hand, it is an economist's job to go as far as possible in treating values as preferences, and within economics narrowly construed, the reductionist bias serves a purpose. On the other hand, when we look at values in more philosophical terms, we cannot treat all values as mere preferences, as if attaching value to honesty were on a par with attaching value to chocolate. Accordingly, there is a problem with jumping from economic to philosophical discussions without stopping to remind ourselves that what is taken for granted in one kind of discussion cannot be taken for granted in the other.

The third thing Sagoff is saying is that CBA characteristically treats all values as mere preferences.

Now, if Sagoff means to say CBA *typically* does so, he may be right. But if Sagoff were saying CBA *necessarily* does so, he would be mistaken. CBA is about weighing costs and benefits. It does not presume everything is either a cost or a benefit. We have to decide which values can be treated as mere preferences, costs, or benefits, and which have to be treated separately, as falling outside the scope of CBA. CBA itself does not make that decision for us. It is true by definition that to care about X is to have a preference regarding X, but we can care about X without thinking X is merely a preference. CBA assumes nothing about the nature of values, other than that they sometimes come into conflict and that no matter what we do, we will in effect be trading them off against each other. It does not assume trading off values is unproblematic; it assumes only that we sometimes have no choice.

"Recycling" is a politically correct word, to be sure, but does that mean we should support any operation that uses the word in its title, even if the operation is environmentally catastrophic? Or should we instead stop to think about the operation's costs and benefits? Contra Sagoff, if we stop to think, that does not mean we are treating environmental quality as a mere "preference, attitude, or emotion." Stopping to think can be a way of showing respect.

CAN CBA HANDLE QUALITATIVE VALUES?

Steven Kelman says CBA presupposes the desirability of being able to express all values as dollar values. However, as Kelman correctly notes, converting values to dollars can be a problem. It can distort the true nature of the values at stake. On the other hand, it would be a mistake to think CBA *requires* us to represent every value as a dollar value. For example, Kelman and Sagoff surely would agree that if we care about Atlantic Green Turtles and do a CBA of alternative ways of protecting them, nothing in that process even suggests we have reduced the value of turtles to dollars.

We can do CBA with respect to different values; we can accept conflicts of value that prevent definitive answers. Kelman is right that something is gained when we genuinely and fairly can reduce all values to dollar values, because if we can do that, then there will be a "bottom line." We can simply tally up values, and it will be clear what CBA recommends. Often, though, trying to force the process to yield an unambiguously numerical bottom line would be to chase a mirage. If the art museum is about to close and I have one last chance to see either my beloved Vermeer or my beloved Seurat, but there is no time to see both, then I must make a choice. The interesting point is that, even when I know precisely what the costs and benefits will be of seeing the Vermeer versus seeing the Seurat, that does not entail that there will be an unambiguous bottom line. Normally, people do not attach numbers to their values. You never hear people saying, "Well, according to my calculations, the Vermeer experience is seven percent more valuable than the Seurat experience, so clearly Vermeer is the way to go." Nor do we hear, "Although I'm more in the mood for Seurat, the rational choice is the Vermeer, since appraisers say the Vermer is worth more money." The latter thought would be irrelevant when the values at issue concern my own appreciation of the paintings' intrinsic merits as paintings rather than the paintings' value as instruments for raising cash. In cases like that, the bottom line will be qualitative rather than quantitative. No matter how accurately I appraise the instrinsic merits of the paintings, my appraisals will still be qualitative.

An object's *intrinsic* value is the value it has in and of itself, beyond any value it has as a means to further ends. Note that an object's having intrinsic value does not imply that the object is priceless. There is such a thing as limited intrinsic value. A painting can have an intrinsic value that is real without being infinite, or even particularly large. The value I would get from selling it is its instrumental value to me. The value it has to me in and of itself, simply because it is a beautiful painting, is its intrinsic value to me.[14] Both values are real, but one is instrumental and the other is intrinsic. Neither is necessarily large.

A related point: it would be better if Kelman had not said, "selling a thing for money demonstrates that it was valued only instrumentally."[15] Suppose I sell a painting. The money I receive from the sale is the painting's instrumental value to me, but does my decision to sell imply that the painting had no intrinsic value? No. Suppose I love the painting, but I need to raise a large sum of money to save my life, so I sell the painting. What this implies is not that the painting has zero intrinsic value but rather that the instrumental value of selling it outweighs the intrinsic value of keeping it, in that circumstance.

More generally, we sometimes put dollar values on things even when their value to us is essentially different from the value of dollars. Incommensurability of different values is not generally an insurmountable obstacle to CBA. Still, there often is no point in trying to convert a qualitative balancing into something that *looks* like a precise quantitative calculation and thus *looks* scientific but in fact remains the same qualitative balancing, only now its qualitative nature is disguised by the attaching of made-up numbers.

Policy decisions can be like that. We can make up numbers when assessing the value of a public library we could build on land that otherwise will remain a public park. Maybe the numbers will mean something, maybe not. More often, even when we can accurately predict a policy's true costs and benefits, that does not entail that there will be any bottom line from which we simply read off what to do. When competing values cannot be reduced to a common measure without distortion, that makes it harder to know the bottom line. It may even mean there is no unitary bottom line to be known. Sometimes the bottom line is simply that one precious and irreplaceable thing is gained while another precious and irreplaceable thing is lost. Even so, that does not mean there is a problem with the very idea of taking costs and benefits into account. It just means we should not assume too much about what kind of bottom line we can expect to see.[16]

Ontario Hydro (since its reorganization), and the City of Vancouver Planning Department, to name two examples, say that in striving to provide a Full Cost Accounting, they try not to ignore vague nonmonetized costs, even though in practice such sensitivity means their bottom line will reflect not (or not only) numerical inputs so much as their version of informed common sense.[17] Consider an analogy. A computer program can play chess by algorithm. Human chess players cannot. Human chess players need creativity, experience, alertness to unintended consequences, and other skills and virtues that are not algorithmic. People who formulate policy need similar skills and virtues, and interpersonal skills as well. Employing CBA cannot change that.

SOME THINGS ARE PRICELESS. SO WHAT?

Critics of CBA think they capture the moral high ground when they say some things are beyond price. They miss the point. Even if Atlantic Green Turtles are a priceless world heritage, we still have to decide how to save them. We still need to look at costs and benefits of trying to protect them in one way rather than another, for two reasons. First, we need to know whether a certain approach will be effective, given available resources. Dollar for dollar, an effective way of protecting them is better than an ineffective way. Second, we need to know whether the cost of saving them involves sacrificing something else we consider equally priceless.

If baby Jessica has fallen into an abandoned well in Midland, Texas and it will cost nine million dollars to rescue her, is it worth the cost? It seems somehow wrong even to ask the question; after all, it is only money. But it is not wrong. If it would cost nine million dollars to save Jessica's life, what would the nine million dollars otherwise have purchased? Could it have been sent to Africa where it might have saved nine thousand lives? Consider an even more expensive case. If a public utility company in Pennsylvania (in the wake of a frivolous lawsuit blaming its high-voltage power lines for a child's leukemia) calculates that burying its power lines underground will cost two billion dollars, in the process maybe preventing one or two deaths from leukemia, is it only money? If the two billion dollars could have been sent to Africa where it might have saved two million lives, is it obvious we should *not* stop to think about it?

Critics like to say not all values are economic values. They are right, but no values whatsoever are purely economic values in that sense. Even money itself is never only money. In a small town in Texas in 1987, a lot of money was spent to save a baby's life—money that took several lifetimes to produce. It was not only money. It did after all save a baby's life. It also gave a community a chance to show the world what it stands for. These are not trivial things. Neither are many of the other things on which nine million dollars could have been spent.

There are things so valuable to us that we think of them as beyond price. Some economists might disagree, but it is, after all, a fact. What does this fact imply? When we have no choice but to make tradeoffs, should we ignore items we consider priceless, or should we take them into account?[18] The hard fact is, priceless values sometimes come into conflict. When that happens, and when we try rationally to weigh our options, we are in effect putting a price on that which is priceless. In that case, CBA is not the problem. It is a response to the problem. The world has handed us a painful choice, and trying rationally to weigh our options is our way of trying to cope with it.

Note in passing that although critics often speak of incommensurable values, incommensurability is not quite the issue, strictly speaking. Consider the central dilemma of the novel, *Sophie's Choice*.[19] Sopie's two children are about to be executed by a concentration camp commander. The commander says he will kill both children unless Sophie picks one to be killed, in which case the commander will spare the other one. Now, to Sophie, both children are beyond price. She does not value one more than the other. In some sense, she values each of them more than anything. Nevertheless, she does in the end pick one for execution, thereby saving the other one's life. The point is, although her values were incommensurate, she was still able to rank them in a situation where failing to rank them would have meant losing both. The values were incommensu*rate*, but not incommensu*rable*. To Sophie, both children were beyond price, but when forced to put a price on them, she could.

Of course, the decision broke her heart. As the sadistic commander foresaw, the process of ranking her previously incommensurate values was psychologically devastating. At some level, commensuration is *always* possible, but there are times when something (our innocence, perhaps) is lost in the process of making values commensurate. Perhaps that explains why some critics want to reject CBA; they see it as a mechanism for ranking values that should not be ranked. Unfortunately, although we can hope people like Sophie will never need to rank their children and can instead go on thinking of each child as having infinite value, and although we can wish we never had to choose between worker safety and environmental quality, or between different aspects of environmental quality, the real world sometimes requires tradeoffs.

DOES CBA WORK?

When individuals engage in CBA, they typically are asking themselves how much they should be willing to pay. That is an obvious and legitimate question because they are, after all, constrained by their budget. In contrast, legislators ask themselves how much they are willing to make *other* people pay, and that is a problem. In that case, paying has become an external cost, and it is no surprise if legislators seem rather cavalier about how much they are making other people pay. I said earlier that if the analysis shows that losers are losing more than winners are gaining, that should pretty much end the conversation. Unfortunately, in the real world, the conversation does not always stop there. When a program's benefits are concentrated within influential constituencies, legislators conceal how costly the program is to taxpayers at large. Similarly, owners of dogs that bark all night ignore the costs they impose on neighbors. Again, it is not because people are evil. They are only human. Situations where we are not fully accountable—where we have the option of not paying the full cost of our decisions—tend not to bring out the best in us. CBA with Full Cost Accounting is one way of trying to introduce accountability.

In theory, then, CBA is a way of organizing agenda for public debates that respect all persons, and valuable nonpersons, too. How does it work in practice? An effective resolution to hold decision makers and policy makers accountable for all costs would, in theory, make for a cleaner, safer, more prosperous society. The prospect of a public accounting can make corporations and governments rethink what they owe to the environment, and in Ontario Hydro's case, it seems to have done exactly that. Still, there is much corruption in the world and nothing like CBA will ever put an end to it. As with any other accounting method, the quality of the output typically will be only as good as the quality of the inputs. The valuations we supply as inputs drive the results, so how to avoid biased valuations? Biased inputs generate biased outputs. CBA, then, has the potential to be a smokescreen for the real action that takes place before numbers get added.

Can anything guarantee that the process of CBA will not itself be subject to the same political piracy that CBA was supposed to limit? Probably not. As I said earlier, the verdict in *Peeveyhouse* generally is regarded as mistaken. What I did not mention is that, as Andrew Morriss notes, "Shortly after the *Peeveyhouse* decision, a corruption investigation uncovered more than thirty years of routine of bribery of several of the court's members."[20] CBA per se does not correct for corrupted inputs. Neither does CBA stop people from applying CBA to cases in which CBA has no legitimate role. However, if the process is public, with affected parties having a chance to protest when their interests are ignored, public scrutiny will have some tendency to correct for biased inputs. It also will encourage planners to supply inputs that can survive scrutiny in the first place. If the process is public, people can step forward to scrutinize not only valuations, but also the list of options, suggesting possibilities that planners may have concealed or overlooked.

Even if we know the costs and benefits of any particular factor, that does not guarantee that we have considered everything. In the real world, we must acknowledge that for any actual calculation we perform, there could be some cost or benefit or risk we have overlooked. What can we do to avoid overlooking what in retrospect will become painfully obvious? Although it is no guarantee, the best thing I can think of is to open the process to public scrutiny.

Kelman says CBA presumes we should spare no cost in enabling policy makers to make decisions in accordance with CBA. Kelman is right to critical of such a presumption, for CBA is itself an activity with costs and benefits. The activity of analyzing costs and benefits is not always warranted on cost-benefit grounds. It can be a waste of time. Therefore CBA on its own grounds ought to be able to recognize that there is a limit to CBA's legitimate scope. Decisions have to be made about what options are worth considering in cost-benefit terms. When we bring people together to scrutinize a proposal, we risk starting a fight over how to distribute costs and benefits. We take people who otherwise might peacefully mind their own business, and we teach them to think of each other as political adversaries. Not all problems can be solved by community policy. Often enough, neighbors are perfectly capable of quietly working things out among themselves, and often enough it is best simply to let them.

MUST CBA MEASURE VALUATIONS IN TERMS OF WILLINGNESS TO PAY?

Suppose we want to assess the costs and benefits of building a library on land that otherwise would remain a public park. How are we supposed to measure costs and benefits? Must we look into people's souls to see how much they really want the library? What alternative do we have? What if we asked people how much they are willing to pay to have the library, and compared that to what they say they are willing to pay to keep the park? Would that be a reasonable way of ascertaining how much they care?

CBA often is depicted as requiring us to measure a good's value by asking how much people would pay for it. Such a requirement is indeed problematic. One problem: willingness to pay is a function not only of perceived values but also of resources available for bidding on those values. Poorer people show up as less willing to pay even

if, in some other sense, they value the good as much.

Is there anything we could do to make it legitimate to use willingness to pay as a surrogate for value in some other sense? Perhaps. Part of the problem, to judge from the literature, is that surveys designed to measure willingness to pay do not in fact take willingness to pay seriously. What they ask subjects to declare is not willingness to pay but *hypothetical* willingness to pay. The idea is, we justify building a waste treatment plant in a poorer neighborhood when we *judge* that poorer people would not pay as much as richer people would to have the plant built elsewhere. Critics call this environmental racism (because minorities tend to live in poorer neighborhoods). Whatever we call it, it looks preposterous.

Is there an alternative that would be more respectful of neighborhoods that provide the most likely building sites? Suppose we initially choose the site by random lottery, and suppose that by luck of the draw, Beverly Hills is selected as the site of the new waste treatment plant. Suppose we then ask Beverly Hill's rich residents what they are willing to pay to site the plant elsewhere. Suppose they say they jointly would pay ten million dollars to locate the plant elsewhere. Suppose we then announce that the people of Beverly Hills are actually, not just hypothetically, offering ten million to any neighborhood willing to make room for a waste treatment facility that otherwise will be built in Beverly Hills. Suppose one of the poorer neighborhoods votes to accept the bid. Would that be more respectful? Or instead, suppose no one accepts the Beverly Hills offer, and therefore the plant is built in Beverly Hills. Is there anything wrong with richer residents moving out, selling their houses to poorer people willing to live near the plant in order to live in better houses than they otherwise could afford? If sitting a waste treatment plant drives down property values so that poorer people can afford to live in Beverly Hills, while rich people take their money elsewhere, is that a problem?

Note that even a random lottery will produce nonrandom results. No matter where the waste treatment facility is built, people who can afford to move away from waste treatment plants tend to be richer than the people who cannot. Home buyers who move in, accepting the nuisance in order to have a nicer house at a lower price, will tend to be poorer than buyers who opt to pay higher prices to live farther from the nuisance. One thing will never change: waste treatment facilities will tend to be found in poorer neighborhoods. Not even putting them all in Beverly Hills could ever change that.

Oddly, activists in effect are agitating for plants to be sited as far as possible from people who work in them, since siting waste treatment facilities within walking distance of the homes of people who might want the jobs they provide is classified as environmental racism. Perhaps the question of how far people have to commute is not important; normally, though, environmentalists urge us to pay more attention to such issues. In any case, if a waste treatment plant must be in a populated area, neighbors will be affected. Someone will have to pay, and no accounting tool is to blame for that.

Critics presume the process of siting waste treatment facilities will *not* be conducted in a respectful manner. They presume politicians will site waste treatment facilities not in response to actual negotiations with communities but rather in response to calculations about what will minimize adverse effects on campaign contributions and ultimately on reelection bids. The critics may be right.[21] If that is how it actually works, then politicians are asking the wrong question, morally speaking. In that case, no accounting method can yield the right answer. Under those circumstances, the point of subjecting the decision to public scrutiny is to lead (possibly racist) politicians not to recalculate answers so much as to start asking the right questions.

MUST FUTURE GENERATIONS BE DISCOUNTED?

In financial markets, a dollar acquired today is worth more than a dollar we will acquire in a year. The dollar acquired today can be put to work immediately. At worst, it can be put in the bank, and thus be worth perhaps $1.05 in a year. Therefore, if you ask me how much I would pay today to be given a dollar a year

from now, I certainly would not pay as much as a dollar. I would pay something less, perhaps about ninety-five cents. Properly valued, then, the future dollar sells at a discount. Therefore, there is nothing irrational about borrowing against the future to get a profitable project off the ground, even though the cost of borrowing a thousand dollars now will be more than a thousand dollars later.

But here is the catch. There is nothing wrong with taking out a loan, so long as we *pay it back*. But there is something obviously wrong with taking out a loan we have no intention of repaying. In other words, discounting is one thing when the cost of raising capital is internalized; it is something else when we borrow against *someone else's* future rather than our own. We have no right to discount the price that *others* will have to pay for our projects. We have no right to discount externalities. *Redistributive* discounting is objectionable: morally, economically, and sometimes ecologically as well.

Some critics worry about the moral status of the discounting they think CBA presupposes. Thus, Peter Wenz says, "Absurdities arise when the current worth of future human lives is discounted, as CBA requires of all values that will be realized only in the future."[22] As an example of such an absurdity, Wenz goes on to calculate that at a five percent discount rate, "a human life today is worth four human lives that will not be realized for 28.8 years, eight lives that are 43.2 years in the future, and so on."[23] Obviously, Wenz is right: that would be absurd.[24] So, why think CBA requires that life's value, or any other value, be discounted? Some economists say it does not, and few (none that I know) would discount the value of lives in the way Wenz says they must.[25] There are economists who go so far as to claim a proper analysis requires that values *not* be discounted.[26] In any case, if we undertake a CBA, we must decide whether to introduce a discount rate. CBA will not make the decision for us. We also must decide whether to discount all considerations or only some. For example, we must decide whether to discount a life in the same way we discount the financial cost of *saving* a life (say, by building safer highways). To philosophers, the decision appears clear-cut: human lives are not commodities, although things we use to save lives typically are.

The thing about affluent people, and the reason why environmentalists are correct (not merely politically correct) to worry about poverty, is that affluent people can afford to be more future-oriented, that is, to operate with lower discount rates. The task, then, is twofold: first, to teach people to see their future as depending on resources they are in a position to preserve, conserve, or degrade, and, second, to put them in a position where they can afford to be future-oriented.

CONCLUSIONS

What can you do with a CBA? You can draw conclusions like this: "We conducted CBA, taking the following costs and benefits into account. The proposal before us appears to pass inspection by the lights of such analysis. We therefore recommend further discussion. Or where the proposal does not pass inspection, where the losers would lose more than the winners would gain, we recommend that the proposal be rejected. In either case, we could be wrong. First, there may be costs or benefits we have not anticipated. Second, even known costs and benefits are often impossible to quantify precisely; therefore, our numbers must be viewed with caution. Third, when used in support of a given proposal, CBA need not be decisive, for there are other grounds upon which policies can be prohibited, favorable CBA notwithstanding. Nevertheless, until someone either identifies additional costs or benefits for us to consider, or else informs us that the proposal violates a treaty (for example) that created rights and obligations that render costs and benefits moot, all we can do is go with our best understanding of the information before us. Barring new information, proceeding in accordance with the result of this CBA appears to be the best we can do."

I talked about doing CBA with Full Cost Accounting, but no mechanical procedure can be guaranteed to take all costs into account. For any mechanical procedure we devise, there will be situations where that procedure overlooks something important. This is not a reason to reject the very idea of CBA, though. Rather, it is a reason to be wary of the desire to make decisions in a mechanical way. We cannot wait for someone to devise the perfect procedure, guaranteed to give everything its proper weight. Whatever procedures we devise for making decisions as individuals or as a community, we need to exercise judgment. At some point we draw the line, make a decision, and get on with our lives, realizing that any real-world decision procedure inevitably will be of limited value. It will not be perfect. It never will be beyond question.

CBA with Full Cost Accounting is only one form of CBA. Many other forms of CBA are indefensible, and no ethicist would defend them. We do well not to conflate different forms of CBA, though, and we do well not to demonize the general idea of weighing costs and benefits. CBA is an important response to a real problem. However, it is not magic. There is a limit to what it can do. CBA is a way of organizing information. It can be a forum for eliciting further information. It can be a forum for correcting biased information. It can be a forum for giving affected parties a voice in community decision making, thereby leading to better understanding of, and greater acceptance of, the tradeoffs involved in running a community. CBA can be all of these good things, but it is not necessarily so. CBA can constrain a system's tendency to invite abuse, such as the environmental racism just discussed, but CBA is prone to the same abuse that infects the system as a whole. It is no panacea. It is an antidote to abuse that is itself subject to abuse.

CBA is not inherently biased, but if inputs are biased, then so will be the outputs, generally speaking. However, although the method does not inherently correct for biased inputs, if the process is conducted publicly, so that people can publicly challenge suppliers of biased inputs, there will be some tendency for the process to correct for biased inputs as well. We can hope there will be adequate opportunity for those with minority viewpoints to challenge mainstream biases, but we cannot guarantee it. The most we can say is that CBA done in public view helps to give democracies a fighting chance to operate as democracies are supposed to operate.

NOTES

1. Demand/Supply Report of the Ontario Hydro Commission, as quoted in Michael McDonald, J. T. Stevenson, and Wesley Craig, *Finding a Balance of Values: An Ethical Assessment of Ontario Hydro's Demand/Supply Plan*, Report to Aboriginal Research Coalition of Ontario (1992) pp. 33–34.

2. In speaking to different people, I find that the terms are not quite standardized. What I have in mind when I speak of Full Cost Accounting is what some people call Multiple Accounts Analysis or Life Cycle Analysis. They might reserve the term "Full Cost Accounting" to refer to a kind of CBA that considers all costs, but only in terms of their impact on current stakeholders. Whatever term we use, though, suffice it to say I have in mind a kind of CBA that does not deliberately ignore any cost whatever, including costs imposed on future generations.

3. E. J. Mishan, *Elements of Cost-Benefit Analysis*, 2nd ed. (London George Allen & Unwin, 1976), p. 11.

4. I do not know whether Ontario Hydro's change of heart was partly in response to the 1992 *Ethical Assessment* of McDonald, Stevenson, and Craig, cited above.

5. And if everyone belongs to one interest group or another, that does not mean we all break even in the final accounting. It is as if a hundred of us sat in a circle, and the government went round the circle collecting a penny from each, then favoring one of us with a fifty cent windfall. After repeating the process a hundred times, we are each a dollar poorer, fifty cents richer, and happy. So David Friedman describes the game in *The Machinery of Freedom* (LaSalle: Open Court Publishing, 1989).

6. This is the illuminating central metaphor used by Don Scherer in *Upstream/Downstream: Issues in Environmental Ethics*, edited by Donald Scherer (Philadelphia: Temple University Press, 1990).

7. In modern moral theory, deontology often is thought of as the main theoretical alternative to utilitarianism. Generally and roughly, deontology is the theory that X is right if and only if X expresses respect for all persons as ends in themselves, and treats no one as a mere means.

8. Kristin Shrader-Frechette offers different arguments for a similar conclusion in "A Defense of Risk-Cost-Benefit Analysis," *Environmental Ethics: Readings in Theory and Application*, edited by Louis Pojman, 2nd ed. (Belmont: Wadsworth, 1998), 507–14.

9. Steven Kelman argues that there are cases in which an action is right even though its costs exceed its benefits. Kelman has in mind actions that involve keeping a promise or speaking out against injustice, cases in which there something wrong with the very idea of asking about costs and benefits. In such cases, the balance of costs and benefits normally is not decisive because we should not have been asking about costs and benefits in the first place. All of that is compatible with my claim that, in cases where costs and benefits *should* be taken into account, determining that the losers are losing more than the winners are gaining should be considered a conversation stopper.

10. For a classic discussion of this case, see Judith Jarvis Thomson, "Killing, Letting Die, and the Trolley Problem," *Monist* 59 (1976), 204–17.

11. For a discussion of what the case shows about relative merits of statutory versus common law, see Andrew Morriss, "Lessons for Environmental Law from the American Codification Debate," *The Common Law and the Environment*, edited by Roger Meiners and Andrew Morriss (Lanham: Rowman & Littlefield, 2000) 130–57, here p. 144.

12. Mark Sagoff, "At the Shrine of Our Lady of Fatima, or Why Political Questions Are Not All Economic," *Arizona Law Review* 23 (1981) 1283–98, here 1288–89.

13. Sagoff, p. 1290–91.

14. There is also a debate over whether there is a kind of intrinsic value that does not presuppose the existence of a valuer. We often speak of persons as having a value as ends in themselves, independently of any value attributed to them by other valuers. The question is whether trees, for example, also can in this sense be ends in themselves. The purpose of the "Last Man Argument" in environmental ethics is to set the stage for discussion of this latter question.

15. Editors' note: Kelman authorized us to delete this phrase from the version of the paper to be reprinted in this volume.

16. See also Charles Lindblom, "The Science of Muddling Through," *Foundations of Administrative Law*, edited by Peter Schuck (New York: Oxford University Press, 1994), 104–10.

17. "Full Cost Accounting For Decision Making At Ontario Hydro: A Case Study," prepared by ICF Incorporated for the Environmental Protection Agency; "Visions, Tools, and Targets:

Environmentally Sustainable Development Guidelines For Southeast False Creek, "prepared by Sheltair Inc. For the City of Vancouver, 1998.

18. Hargrove notes that quantitative analysis may be inappropriate when dealing with intrinsic values. See Eugene C. Hargrove, *Foundations of Environmental Ethics* (Denton: Environmental Ethics Books, 1989), p. 211. Fair enough, but quantitative analysis often is inappropriate with purely instrumental values too. Not all instrumental values are reducible to monetary values. For example, seat belts are of purely instrumental value, yet when the car hits the ditch and begins to roll over, no amount of money would be a reasonable substitute for having our seat belts fastened.

19. William Styron, *Sophie's Choice* (New York: Random House, 1979).

20. Morriss, p. 144.

21. See Robert Bullard, *Dumping In Dixie: Race, Class, and Environmental Quality* (Boulder: Westview Press, 1990).

22. Peter Wenz, "Democracy and Environmental Change," *Ethics and Environmental Responsibility*, edited by Nigel Dower (Aldershot: Avebury, 1989) 91–109, here p. 100.

23. Wenz, p. 100.

24. Actually, it looks economically problematic as well. If we suppose a zero inflation rate, than a dollar in the future is not worth less than a dollar today. It is worth exactly one dollar. That does not change when we introduce the possibility of earning interest. The possibility of interest means only that it is better to get the dollar earlier because we then can earn additional interest. If lives are like dollars in that respect, then the implication is not that a life later is worth less than a life now. Rather, the implication is very roughly that, just as it would be better to have an extra year's interest, it would be better to have an extra year of life. (That is, if I were going to be given a second life, and if I knew my second life would end in the year 2150, I would pay to have that life begin in 2110 rather than 2130. For analogous reasons, the dollar that began to collect interest in 2110 rather than 2130 would sell at a premium.)

25. For a typically circumspect discussion, see J. E. Stiglitz, "The Rate of Discount for Benefit-Cost Analysis and the Theory of the Second Best," *Cost-Benefit Analysis*, edited by Richard Layard and Stephen Glaister (Cambridge: Cambridge University Press, 1994) 116–59.

26. See Tayler Cowen, "Consequentialism Implies a Zero Rate of Discount," in Peter Laslett and James Fishkin, editors, *Philosophy, Politics, and Society*, sixth series (New Haven: Yale University Press, 1992), 162–68.

STUDY QUESTIONS

1. Examine Schmidtz's analysis of cost-benefit analysis. Discuss the case of Ontario Hydro. How does Schmidtz think a moral use of CBA should work? Do you agree?

2. Define cost-benefit analysis. How does it work? What are its limits and benefits?

3. Is cost-benefit analysis anthropocentric?

4. Is cost-benefit analysis a utilitarian instrument? Of can it be incorporated within a deontological framework? What does Schmidtz think about this? What do you think?

5. Does CBA treat all values as commodities or preferences? Explain Schmitz's view and your view.

FOR FURTHER READING

Brown, Lester. *State of the World 1999*. New York: Norton, 1999.

Buchholz, Rogene. *Principles of Environmental Management: The Greening of Business*. Englewood Cliffs, NJ: Prentice Hall, 1993.

Clark, W. C. *Sustainable Development of the Biosphere*. Cambridge: Cambridge University Press, 1986.

Daly, Herman E., and John B. Cobb, Jr. *For the Common Good: Redirecting the Economy Toward Community, the Environment, and a Sustainable Future*. Boston: Beacon Press, 1989.

Dreyfus, S. E. "Formal Models vs. Human Situational Understanding: Inherent Limitations on the Modelling of Business Expertise," *Technology and People* 1 (1982).

Plumwood, Val, and Richard Routley, "World Rainforest Destruction—The Social and Economic Factors," *Ecologist* 12, no. 1 (January–February 1982).

Sagoff, Mark. *The Economy of the Earth.* Cambridge: Cambridge University Press, 1988.

Sayer, K. M., and K. E. Goodpaster, eds. *Ethics and Problems of the 21st Century.* Notre Dame, IN: University of Notre Dame Press, 1979.

Shrader-Frechette, Kristin. *Science, Policy, Ethics, and Economic Methodology.* Boston: Reidel, 1985.

Shrader-Frechette, Kristin, and E. McCoy. *Method in Ecology.* New York: Cambridge University Press, 1993.

Scientific American. "Managing the Earth," Special Issue, 26, no. 3 (September 1989).

Timberlake, Lloyd. *Only One Earth: Living for the Future.* New York: Sterling, 1987.

Tokar, Michael. *The Green Alternative: Creating an Alternative Future.* San Pedro, CA: R & E Miles, 1988.

Environmental Justice

ENVIRONMENTAL JUSTICE BEGINS with the observed fact that certain groups of people bear a disproportionate burden of environmental problems. That is, polluting factories, lead in water pipes, filthy air, polluted water, toxic soil, etc, are more likely to be found in places where people have less control over decision making—typically, minorities and the poor. There is an active debate as to whether this observed distribution of pollution is due to race or economic class. There is ample evidence that much of the inequitable distribution of pollutants is due to race, but there are also plenty of examples of poor nonminorities having more contact with pollutants than the richer folks.

In 1987, the original study by the United Church of Christ argued that the observed patterns amounted to 'environmental racism.' Although today the term 'environmental justice' is more commonly used so as to broaden the scope of the problem (the Environmental Protection Agency, for instance, has an office of Environmental Justice, not Environmental Racism), the fact that race is a factor is critically important. The United States and many other countries tolerate what is essentially discrimination on the basis of poverty, but they have enacted legislation to combat discrimination on the basis of race. Thus, inasmuch as environmental racism exists, it not only falls afoul of our moral sensibilities but also intersects with civil rights legislation. This merger of environmental concerns with concepts of race and class is arguably the single largest expansion of the environmental movement, ever.

Why? Environmentalism was previously a movement of the middle and upper classes, of people who had sufficient education and leisure time to understand and enjoy nature and what was happening to it. The movement consisted of people whose jobs did not depend on a polluting factory or logging a forest. Thus, in a sense, a split occurred within the left: the old school left, the socialist labor left (the left of Franklin Roosevelt), which sought to put people to work, and the environmentalists who sought to save nature.

This new movement of environmental justice or environmental racism is crossing that gap for the first time. The poor and disenfranchised of all types now have something in common with environmentalists, for it is they—the poor and disenfranchised—who bear the greatest burden of environmental degradation.

70 Overcoming Racism in Environmental Decision Making

ROBERT D. BULLARD

Robert Bullard is professor of sociology and Director of the Environmental Justice Resource Center at Clark Atlanta University. He is arguably the most visible leader of the environmental justice movement.

Despite the recent attempts by federal agencies to reduce environmental and health threats in the United States, inequities persist.[1] If a community is poor or inhabited largely by people of color, there is a good chance that it receives less protection than a community that is affluent or white.[2] This situation is a result of the country's environmental policies, most of which "distribute the costs in a regressive pattern while providing disproportionate benefits for the educated and wealthy."[3] Even the Environmental Protection Agency (EPA) was not designed to address environmental policies and practices that result in unfair outcomes. The agency has yet to conduct a single piece of disparate impact research using primary data. In fact, the current environmental protection paradigm has institutionalized unequal enforcement; traded human health for profit; placed the burden of proof on the "victims" rather than on the polluting industry; legitimated human exposure to harmful substances; promoted "risky" technologies such as incinerators; exploited the vulnerability of economically and politically disenfranchised communities; subsidized ecological destruction; created an industry around risk assessment; delayed cleanup actions; and failed to develop pollution prevention as the overarching and dominant strategy. As a result, low-income and minority communities continue to bear greater health and environmental burdens, while the more affluent and whites receive the bulk of the benefits.[4]

The geographic distribution of both minorities and the poor has been found to be highly correlated to the distribution of air pollution; municipal landfills and incinerators; abandoned toxic waste dumps; lead poisoning in children; and contaminated fish consumption.[5] Virtually all studies of exposure to outdoor air pollution have found significant differences in exposure by income and race. Moreover, the race correlation is even stronger than the class correlation.[6] The National Wildlife Federation recently reviewed some 64 studies of environmental disparities; in all but one, disparities were found by either race or income, and disparities by race were more numerous than those by income. When race and income were compared for significance, race proved to be the more important factor in 22 out of 30 tests.[7] And researchers at Argonne National Laboratory recently found that

In 1990, 437 of the 3,109 counties and independent cities failed to meet at least one of the EPA ambient air quality standards....57 percent of whites, 65 percent of African-Americans, and 80 percent of Hispanics live in 437 counties with substandard air quality. Out of the whole population, a total of 33 percent of whiles, 50 percent of African-Americans, and 60 percent of Hispanics live in the 136 counties in which two or more air pollutants exceed standards. The percentage living in the 29 counties designated as nonattainment areas for three or more pollutants are 12 percent of whites, 20 percent of African-Americans, and 31 percent of Hispanics.[8]

The public health community has very little information on the magnitude of many air pollution-related health problems. For example,

Reprinted from *Environment*, May 1994, by permission.

scientists are at a loss to explain the rising number of deaths from asthma in recent years. However, it is known that persons suffering from asthma are particularly sensitive to the effects of carbon monoxide, sulfur dioxide, particulate matter, ozone, and oxides of nitrogen.[9]

Current environmental decision making operates at the juncture of science, technology, economics, politics, special interests, and ethics and mirrors the larger social milieu where discrimination is institutionalized. Unequal environmental protection undermines three basic types of equity: procedural, geographic, and social.

PROCEDURAL EQUITY

Procedural equity refers to fairness—that is, to the extent that governing rules, regulations, evaluation criteria, and enforcement are applied in a nondiscriminatory way. Unequal protection results from nonscientific and undemocratic decisions, such as exclusionary practices, conflicts of interest, public hearings held in remote locations and at inconvenient times, and use of only English to communicate with and conduct hearings for non-English-speaking communities.

A 1992 study by staff writers from the *National Law Journal* uncovered glaring inequities in the way EPA enforces its Superfund laws:

> There is a racial divide in the way the U.S. government cleans up toxic waste sites and punishes polluters. White communities see faster action, better results and stiffer penalties than communities where blacks, Hispanics and other minorities live. This unequal protection often occurs whether the community is wealthy or poor.[10]

After examining census data, civil court dockets, and EPA's own record of performance at 1,177 Superfund toxic waste sites, the authors of the *National Law Journal* report revealed the following:

- Penalties applied under hazardous waste laws at sites having the greatest white population were 500 percent higher than penalties at sites with the greatest minority population. Penalties averaged out at $335,566 at sites in white areas but just $55,318 at sites in minority areas.

- The disparity in penalties applied under the toxic waste law correlates with race alone, not income. The average penalty in areas with the lowest median income is $113,491—3 percent more than the average penalty in areas with the highest median income.

- For all the federal environmental laws aimed at protecting citizens from air, water, and waste pollution, penalties for noncompliance were 46 percent higher in white communities than in minority communities.

- Under the Superfund cleanup program, abandoned hazardous waste sites in minority areas take 20 percent longer to be placed on the National Priority List than do those in white areas.

- In more than half of the 10 autonomous regions that administer EPA programs around the country, action on cleanup at Superfund sites begins from 12 to 42 percent later at minority sites than at white sites.

- For minority sites, EPA chooses "containment," the capping or walling off of a hazardous waste dump site, 7 percent more frequently than the cleanup method preferred under the law: permanent "treatment" to eliminate the waste or rid it of its toxins. For white sites, EPA orders permanent treatment 22 percent more often than containment.[11]

These findings suggest that unequal environmental protection is placing communities of color at risk. The National Law Journal study supplements the findings of several earlier studies and reinforces what grassroots activists have been saying all along.... Not only are people of color differentially affected by industrial pollution but they can expect different treatment from the government.[12]

GEOGRAPHIC EQUITY

Geographic equity refers to the location and spatial configuration of communities and their proximity to environmental hazards and locally unwanted land uses (LULUs), such as landfills, incinerators, sewage treatment plants, lead smelters, refineries, and other noxious facilities. Hazardous waste incinerators are not randomly scattered across the landscape. Communities with hazardous waste incinerators generally have large minority populations, low incomes, and low property values.[13]

A 1990 Greenpeace report, Playing with Fire, found that communities with existing incinerators have 89 percent more people of color than the national average; communities where incinerators are proposed for construction have minority populations that are 60 percent higher than the national average; the average income in communities with existing incinerators is 15 percent lower than the national average; property values in communities that host incinerators are 38 percent lower than the national average; and average property values are 35 percent lower in communities where incinerators have been proposed.[14]

The industrial encroachment into Chicago's Southside neighborhoods is a classic example of geographic inequity. Chicago is the nation's third largest city and one of the most racially segregated cities in the country. More than 92 percent of the city's 1.1 million African-American residents live in racially segregated areas. The Altgeld Gardens housing project, located on the city's southeast side, is one of these segregated enclaves. The neighborhood is home to 150,000 residents, of whom 70 percent are African-American and 11 percent are Latino.

Altgeld Gardens is encircled by municipal and hazardous waste landfills, toxic waste incinerators, grain elevators, sewage treatment facilities, smelters, steel mills, and a host of other polluting industries.[15] Because of its location, Hazel Johnson, a community organizer in the neighborhood, has dubbed the area a "toxic doughnut." There are 50 active or closed commercial hazardous waste landfills; 100 factories, including 7 chemical plants and 5 steel mills; and 103 abandoned toxic waste dumps.[16]

Currently, health and risk assessment data collected by the state of Illinois and EPA for facility permitting have failed to take into account the cumulative and synergistic effects of having so many "layers" of poisons in one community. Altgeld Gardens residents wonder when the government will declare a moratorium on permitting any new noxious facilities in their neighborhood and when the existing problems will be cleaned up. All of the polluting industries imperil the health of nearby residents and should be factored into future facility-permitting decisions.

In the Los Angeles air basin, 71 percent of African-Americans and 50 percent of Latinos live in areas with the most polluted air, whereas only 34 percent of whites live in highly polluted areas.[17] The "dirtiest" zip code in California (90058) is sandwiched between South-Central Los Angeles and East Los Angeles.[18] The one-square mile area is saturated with abandoned toxic waste sites, freeways, smokestacks, and waste-water pipes from polluting industries. Some 18 industrial firms in 1989 discharged more than 33 million pounds of waste chemicals into the environment.

Unequal protection may result from land-use decisions that determine the location of residential amenities and disamenities. Unincorporated communities of poor African-Americans suffer a "triple" vulnerability to noxious facility siting.[19] For example, Wallace, Louisiana, a small unincorporated African-American community located on the Mississippi River, was rezoned from residential to industrial use by the mostly white officials of St. John the Baptist Parish to allow construction of a Formosa Plastics Corporation plant. The company's plants have been major sources of pollution in Baton Rouge, Louisiana; Point Comfort, Texas; Delaware City, Delaware; and its home country of Taiwan.[20] Wallace residents have filed a lawsuit challenging the rezoning action as racially motivated.

Environmental justice advocates have sought to persuade federal, state, and local governments to adopt policies that address distributive impacts, concentration, enforcement, and compliance concerns. Some states have tried to use a "fair share" approach to come closer to geographic equity. In 1990, New York City adopted a fair share legislative model designed to ensure that every borough and every community within each borough bears its fair share of noxious facilities. Public hearings have begun to address risk burdens in New York City's boroughs.

Testimony at a hearing on environmental disparities in the Bronx points to concerns raised by African-Americans and Puerto Ricans who see their neighborhoods threatened by garbage transfer stations, salvage yards, and recycling centers:

> On the Hunts Point peninsula alone there are at least thirty private transfer stations, a large-scale Department of Environmental Protection (DEP) sewage treatment plant and a sludge de watering facility, two Department of Sanitation (DOS) marine transfer stations, a citywide private regulated medical waste incinerator, a proposed DOS resource recovery facility and three proposed DEP sludge processing facilities. That all of the facilities listed above are located immediately adjacent to the Hunts Point Food Center, the biggest wholesale food and meat distribution facility of its kind in the United States, and the largest source of employment in the South Bronx, is disconcerting. A policy whereby low-income and minority communities have become the "dumping grounds" for unwanted land uses, works to create an environment of disincentives to community-based development initiatives. It also undermines existing businesses.[21]

Some communities form a special case for environmental justice. For example, Native American reservations are geographic entities but are also quasi-sovereign nations. Because of less stringent environmental regulations than those at the state and federal levels, Native American reservations from New York to California have become prime targets for risky technologies.[22] Indian nations do not fall under state jurisdiction. Similarly, reservations have been described as the "lands the feds forgot."[23] More than 100 industries, ranging from solid waste landfills to hazardous waste incinerators and nuclear waste storage facilities, have targeted reservations.[24]

SOCIAL EQUITY

Social equity refers to the role of sociological factors, such as race, ethnicity, class, culture, lifestyles, and political power, in environmental decision making. Poor people and people of color often work in the most dangerous jobs and live in the most polluted neighborhoods, and their children are exposed to all kinds of environmental toxins on the playgrounds and in their homes and schools.

Some government actions have created and exacerbated environmental inequity. More stringent environmental regulations have driven noxious facilities to follow the path of least resistance toward poor, overburdened communities. Governments have even funded studies that justify targeting economically disenfranchised communities for noxious facilities. Cerrell Associates, Inc., a Los Angeles-based consulting firm, advised the state of California on facility siting and concluded that "ideally...officials and companies should look for lower socioeconomic neighborhoods that are also in a heavy industrial area with little, if any, commercial activity."[25]

The first state-of-the-art solid waste incinerator slated to be built in Los Angeles was proposed for the South-Central Los Angeles neighborhood. The city-sponsored project was defeated by local residents.[26] The two permits granted by the California Department of Health Services for state-of-the-art toxic waste incinerators were proposed for mostly Latino communities: Vernon, near East Los Angeles, and Kettleman City, a farm worker community in the agriculturally rich Central Valley. Kettleman City has 1,200 residents, of which 95 percent are Latino. It is home to the largest hazardous waste incinerator west of the Mississippi River. The Vernon proposal was defeated, but the Kettleman City proposal is still pending.

PRINCIPLES OF ENVIRONMENTAL JUSTICE

To end unequal environmental protection, governments should adopt five principles of environmental justice: guaranteeing the right to environmental protection, preventing harm before it occurs, shifting the burden of proof to the polluters, obviating proof of intent to discriminate, and redressing existing inequities.

The Right to Protection

Every individual has a right to be protected from environmental degradation. Protecting this right will require enacting a federal "fair environmental protection act." The act could be modeled after the various federal civil rights acts that have promoted nondiscrimination—with the ultimate goal of achieving "zero tolerance"—in such areas as housing, education, and employment. The act ought to address both the intended and unintended effects of public policies and industrial practices that have a disparate impact on racial and ethnic minorities and other vulnerable groups. The precedents for this framework are the Civil Rights Act of 1964, which attempted to address both de jure and de facto school segregation, the Fair Housing Act of 1968, the same act as amended in 1988, and the Voting Rights Act of 1965.

For the first time in the agency's 23-year history, EPA's Office of Civil Rights has begun investigating charges of environmental discrimination under Title VI of the 1964 Civil Rights Act. The cases involve waste facility siting disputes in Michigan, Alabama, Mississippi, and Louisiana. Similarly, in September 1993, the U.S. Civil Rights Commission issued a report entitled *The Battle for Environmental Justice in Louisiana: Government, Industry, and the People.* This report confirmed what most people who live in "Cancer Alley"—the 85-mile stretch along the Mississippi River from Baton Rouge to New Orleans—already knew: African-American communities along the Mississippi River bear disproportionate health burdens from industrial pollution.[27]

A number of bills have been introduced into Congress that address some aspect of environmental justice:

- The "Environmental Justice Act of 1993" (H.R. 2105) would provide the federal government with the statistical documentation and ranking of the top 100 "environmental high impact areas" that warrant attention.
- The "Environmental Equal Rights Act of 1993" (H.R. 1924) seeks to amend the Solid Waste Act and would prevent waste facilities from being sited in "environmentally disadvantaged communities."
- The "Environmental Health Equity Information Act of 1993" (H.R. 1925) seeks to amend the Comprehensive Environmental Response, Compensation, and Liability Act of 1990 (CERCLA) to require the Agency

for Toxic Substances and Disease Registry to collect and maintain information on the race, age, gender, ethnic origin, income level, and educational level of persons living in communities adjacent to toxic substance contamination.
- The "Waste Export and Import Prohibition Act" (H.R. 3706) would ban waste exports as of I July 1994 to countries that are not members of the Organization for Economic Cooperation and Development (OECD); the bill would also ban waste exports to and imports from OECD countries as of 1 January 1999.

The states are also beginning to address environmental justice concerns. Arkansas and Louisiana were the first two to enact environmental justice laws. Virginia has passed a legislative resolution on environmental justice. California, Georgia, New York, North Carolina, and South Carolina have pending legislation to address environmental disparities.

Environmental justice groups have succeeded in getting President Clinton to act on the problem of unequal environmental protection, an issue that has been buried for more than three decades. On 11 February 1994, Clinton signed an executive order entitled "Federal Actions to Address Environmental Justice in Minority Populations and Low-Income Populations." This new executive order reinforces what has been law since the passage of the 1964 Civil Rights Act, which prohibits discriminatory practices in programs receiving federal financial assistance.

The executive order also refocuses attention on the National Environmental Policy Act of 1970 (NEPA), which established national policy goals for the protection, maintenance, and enhancement of the environment. The express goal of NEPA is to ensure for all U.S. citizens a safe, healthful, productive, and aesthetically and culturally pleasing environment. NEPA requires federal agencies to prepare detailed statements on the environmental effects of proposed federal actions significantly affecting the quality of human health. Environmental impact statements prepared under NEPA have routinely down-played the social impacts of federal projects on racial and ethnic minorities and low-income groups.

Under the new executive order, federal agencies and other institutions that receive federal monies have a year to implement an environmental justice strategy. For these strategies to be effective, agencies must move away from the "DAD" (decide, announce, and defend) modus operandi. EPA cannot address all of the environmental injustices alone but must work in concert with other stakeholders, such as state and local governments and private industry. A new inter-agency approach might include the following:

- Grassroots environmental justice groups and their networks must become full partners, not silent or junior partners, in planning the implementation of the new executive order.
- An advisory commission should include representatives of environmental justice, civil rights, legal, labor, and public health groups, as well as the relevant governmental agencies, to advise on the implementation of the executive order.
- State and regional education, training, and outreach forums and workshops on implementing the executive order should be organized.
- The executive order should become part of the agenda of national conferences and meetings of elected officials, civil rights and environmental groups, public health and medical groups, educators, and other professional organizations.

The executive order comes at an important juncture in this nation's history: Few communities are willing to welcome LULUs or to become dumping grounds for other people's garbage, toxic waste, or industrial pollution. In the real world, however, if a community happens to be poor and inhabited by persons of color, it is likely to suffer from a "double whammy" of unequal protection and elevated health threats. This is unjust and illegal.

The civil rights and environmental laws of the land must be enforced even if it means the loss of a few jobs. This argument was a sound one in the 1860s, when the 13th Amendment to the Constitution, which freed the slaves in the United States, was passed over the opposition of pro-slavery advocates who posited that the new law would create unemployment (slaves had a zero unemployment rate), drive up wages, and inflict undue hardship on the plantation economy.

Prevention of Harm

Prevention, the elimination of the threat before harm occurs, should be the preferred strategy of governments. For example, to solve the lead problem, the primary focus should be shifted from treating children who have been poisoned to eliminating the threat by removing lead from houses.

Overwhelming scientific evidence exists on the ill effects of lead on the human body. However, very little action has been taken to rid the nation's housing of lead even though lead poisoning is a preventable disease tagged the "number one environmental health threat to children."[28]

Lead began to be phased out of gasoline in the 1970s. It is ironic that the "regulations were initially developed to protect the newly developed catalytic converter in automobiles, a pollution-control device that happens to be rendered inoperative by lead, rather than to safeguard human health."[29] In 1971, a child was not considered "at risk" unless he or she had 40 micrograms of lead per deciliter of blood (μg/dl). Since that time, the amount of lead that is considered safe has continually dropped. In 1991, the U.S. Public Health Service changed the official definition of an unsafe level to 10 μg/dl. Even at that level, a child's IQ can be slightly diminished and physical growth stunted.

Lead poisoning is correlated with both income and race. In 1988, the Agency for Toxic Substances and Disease Registry found that, among families earning less than $6,000, 68 percent of African-American children had lead poisoning, as opposed to 36 percent of white children.[30] In families with incomes exceeding $15,000, more than 38 percent of African-American children suffered from lead poisoning, compared with 12 percent of white children. Thus, even when differences in income are taken into account, middle-class African-American children are three times more likely to be poisoned with lead than are their middle-class white counterparts.

A 1990 report by the Environmental Defense Fund estimated that, under the 1991 standard of 10 μg/dl, 96 percent of African-American children and 80 percent of white children of poor families who live in inner cities have unsafe amounts of lead in their blood—amounts sufficient to reduce IQ somewhat, harm hearing, reduce the ability to concentrate, and stunt physical growth.[31] Even in families with annual incomes greater than $15,000, 85 percent of urban African-American children have unsafe lead levels, compared to 47 percent of white children.

In the spring of 1991, the Bush administration announced an ambitious program to reduce lead exposure of children, including widespread testing of homes, certification of those who remove lead from homes, and medical treatment for affected children. Six months later, the Centers for Disease Control announced that the administration "does not see this as a necessary federal role to legislate or regulate the cleanup of lead poisoning, to require that homes be tested, to require home owners to disclose results once they are known, or to establish standards for those who test or clean up lead hazards."[32]

According to the *New York Times,* the National Association of Realtors pressured President Bush to drop his lead initiative because they feared that forcing homeowners to eliminate lead hazards would add from $5,000 to $10,000 to the price of those homes, further harming a real estate market already devastated by the aftershocks of Reaganomics.[33] The public debate has pitted real estate and housing interests against public health interests. Right now, the housing interests appear to be winning.

For more than two decades, Congress and the nation's medical and public health establishments have waffled, procrastinated, and shuffled papers while the lead problem steadily grows worse. During the years of President Reagan's "benign neglect," funding dropped very low. Even in the best years, when funding has risen

to as much as $50 million per year, it has never reached levels that would make a real dent in the problem.

Much could be done to protect at-risk populations if the current laws were enforced. For example, a lead smelter operated for 50 years in a predominately African-American West Dallas neighborhood, where it caused extreme health problems for nearby residents. Dallas officials were informed as early as 1972 that lead from three lead smelters was finding its way into the bloodstreams of children who lived in two mostly African-American and Latino neighborhoods: West Dallas and East Oak Cliff.[34]

Living near the RSR and Dixie Metals smelters was associated with a 36-percent increase in childhood blood lead levels. The city was urged to restrict the emissions of lead into the atmosphere and to undertake a large screening program to determine the extent of the public health problem. The city failed to take immediate action to protect the residents who lived near the smelters.

In 1980, EPA, informed about possible health risks associated with the Dallas lead smelters, commissioned another lead-screening study. This study confirmed what was already known a decade earlier: Children living near the Dallas smelters were likely to have greater lead concentrations in their blood than children who did not live near the smelters.[35]

The city only took action after the local newspapers published a series of headline-grabbing stories in 1983 on the "potentially dangerous" lead levels discovered by EPA researchers in 1981.[36] The articles triggered widespread concern, public outrage, several class-action lawsuits, and legal action by the Texas attorney general.

Although EPA was armed with a wealth of scientific data on the West Dallas lead problem, the agency chose to play politics with the community by scrapping a voluntary plan offered by RSR to clean up the "hot spots" in the neighborhood. John Hernandez, EPA's deputy administrator, blocked the cleanup and called for yet another round of tests to be designed by the Centers for Disease Control with EPA and the Dallas Health Department. The results of the new study were released in February 1983. Again, this study established the smelter as the source of elevated lead levels in West Dallas children.[37] Hernandez's delay of cleanup actions in West Dallas was tantamount to waiting for a body count.[38]

After years of delay, the West Dallas plaintiffs negotiated an out-of-court settlement worth more than $45 million. The lawsuit was settled in June 1983 as RSR agreed to pay for cleaning up the soil in West Dallas, a blood-testing program for children and pregnant women, and the installation of new antipollution equipment. The settlement was made on behalf of 370 children— almost all of whom were poor, black residents of the West Dallas public housing project—and 40 property owners. The agreement was one of the largest community lead-contamination settlements ever awarded in the United States.[39] The settlement, however, did not require the smelter to close. Moreover, the pollution equipment for the smelter was never installed.

In May 1984, however, the Dallas Board of Adjustments, a city agency responsible for monitoring land-use violations, asked the city attorney to close the smelter permanently for violating the city's zoning code. The lead smelter had operated in the mostly African-American West Dallas neighborhood for 50 years without having the necessary use permits. Just four months later, the West Dallas smelter was permanently closed. After repeated health citations, fines, and citizens' complaints against the smelter, one has to question the city's lax enforcement of health and land-use regulations in African-American and Latino neighborhoods.

The smelter is now closed. Although an initial cleanup was carried out in 1984, the lead problem has not gone away.[40] On 31 December 1991, EPA crews began a cleanup of the West Dallas neighborhood. It is estimated that the crews will remove between 30,000 and 40,000 cubic yards of lead-contaminated soil from several West Dallas sites, including school property and about 140 private homes. The project will cost EPA from $3 million to $4 million. The lead content of the soil collected from dump sites in the neighborhood ranged from 8,060 to 21,000 parts per million.[41] Under federal standards, levels of 500 to 1,000 parts per million are considered hazardous. In April 1993, the entire West Dallas neighborhood was declared a Superfund site.

There have been a few other signs related to the lead issue that suggest a consensus on environmental justice is growing among coalitions of environmental, social justice, and civil libertarian groups. The Natural Resources Defense Council, the National Association for the Advancement of Colored People Legal Defense and Education Fund, the American Civil Liberties Union, and the Legal Aid Society of Alameda County joined forces and won an out-of-court settlement worth between $15 million and $20 million for a blood-testing program in California. The lawsuit (*Matthews v. Coye*) arose because the state of California was not performing the federally mandated testing of some 557,000 poor children who receive Medicaid. This historic agreement will likely trigger similar actions in other states that have failed to perform federally mandated screening.[42]

Lead screening is important but it is not the solution. New government-mandated lead abatement initiatives are needed. The nation needs a "Lead Superfund" cleanup program. Public health should not be sacrificed even in a sluggish housing market. Surely, if termite inspections (required in both booming and sluggish housing markets) can be mandated to protect individual home investment, a lead free home can be mandated to protect human health. Ultimately, the lead debate—public health (who is affected) versus property rights (who pays for cleanup)—is a value conflict that will not be resolved by the scientific community.

Shift the Burden of Proof

Under the current system, individuals who challenge polluters must prove that they have been harmed, discriminated against, or disproportionately affected. Few poor or minority communities have the resources to hire the lawyers, expert witnesses, and doctors needed to sustain such a challenge. Thus, the burden of proof must be shifted to the polluters who do harm, discriminate, or do not give equal protection to minorities and other overburdened classes.

Environmental justice would require the entities that are applying for operating permits for landfills, incinerators, smelters, refineries, and chemical plants, for example, to prove that their operations are not harmful to human health, will not disproportionately affect minorities or the poor, and are nondiscriminatory.

A case in point is Louisiana Energy Services' proposal to build the nation's first privately owned uranium enrichment plant. The proposed plant would handle about 17 percent of the estimated U.S. requirement for enrichment services in the year 2000. Clearly, the burden of proof should be on Louisiana Energy Services, the state government, and the Nuclear Regulatory Commission to demonstrate that local residents' rights would not be violated in permitting the plant. At present, the burden of proof is on local residents to demonstrate that their health would be endangered and their community adversely affected by the plant.

According to the Nuclear Regulatory Commission's 1993 draft environmental impact statement, the proposed site for the facility is Claiborne Parish, Louisiana, which has a per-capita income of only $5,800 per year—just 45 percent of the national average.[43] The enrichment plant would be just one-quarter mile from the almost wholly African-American community of Center Springs, founded in 1910, and one and one-quarter miles from Forest Grove, which was founded by freed slaves. However, the draft statement describes the socioeconomic and community characteristics of Homer, a town that is five miles from the proposed site and whose population is more than 50 percent white, rather than those of Center Springs or Forest Grove. As far as the draft is concerned, the communities of Center Springs and Forest Grove do not exist; they are invisible.

The racial composition of Claiborne Parish is 53.43 percent white, 46.09 percent African-American, 0.16 percent American Indian, 0.07 percent Asian, 0.23 percent Hispanic, and 0.01 percent "other."[44] Thus, the parish's percentage population of African-Americans is nearly four times greater than that of the nation and nearly two and one-half times greater than that of Louisiana. (African-Americans composed 12 percent of the U.S. population and 29 percent of Louisiana's population in 1990.)

Clearly, Claiborne Parish's current residents would receive fewer of the plant's potential benefits—high-paying jobs, home construction, and an increased tax base—than would those who moved into the area or commuted to it to work at the facility. An increasing number of migrants will take jobs at the higher end of the skill and pay scale. These workers are expected to buy homes outside of the parish. Residents of Claiborne Parish, on the other hand, are likely to get the jobs at the lower end of the skill and pay scale.[45]

Ultimately, the plant's social costs would be borne by nearby residents, while the benefits would be more dispersed. The potential social costs include increased noise and traffic, threats to public safety and to mental and physical health, and LULUs.

The case of Richmond, California, provides more evidence of the need to shift the burden of proof. A 1989 study, *Richmond at Risk*, found that the African-American residents of this city bear the brunt of toxic releases in Contra Costa County and the San Francisco Bay area.[46] At least 38 industrial sites in and around the city store up to 94 million pounds of 45 different chemicals, including ammonia, chlorine, hydrogen fluoride, and nitric acid. However, the burden of proof is on Richmond residents to show that they are harmed by nearby toxic releases.

On 26 July 1993, sulfur trioxide escaped from the General Chemical plant in Richmond, where people of color make up a majority of the residents. More than 20,000 citizens were sent to the hospital. A September 1993 report by the Bay Area Air Quality Management District confirmed that "the operation was conducted in a negligent manner without due regard to the potential consequences of a miscalculation or equipment malfunction, and without required permits from the District."[47]

When Richmond residents protested the planned expansion of a Chevron refinery, they were asked to prove that they had been harmed by Chevron's operation. Recently, public pressure has induced Chevron to set aside $4.2 million to establish a new health clinic and help the surrounding community.

A third case involves conditions surrounding the 1,900 *maquiladoras,* assembly plants operated by U.S., Japanese, and other countries' companies along the 2,000-mile U.S.-Mexican border.[48]

A 1983 agreement between the United States and Mexico requires U.S. companies in Mexico to export their waste products to the United States, and plants must notify EPA when they are doing so. However, a 1986 survey of 772 maquiladoras revealed that only 20 of the plants informed EPA when they were exporting waste to the United States, even though 86 percent of the plants used toxic chemicals in their manufacturing processes. And in 1989, only 10 waste shipment notices were filed with EPA.[49]

Much of the waste from the maquiladoras is illegally dumped in sewers, ditches, and the desert. All along the Rio Grande, plants dump toxic wastes into the river, from which 95 percent of the region's residents get their drinking water. In the border cities of Brownsville, Texas, and Matamoros, Mexico, the rate of anencephaly—being born without a brain—is four times the U.S. national average.[50] Affected families have filed lawsuits against 88 of the area's 100 maquiladoras for exposing the community to xylene, a cleaning solvent that can cause brain hemorrhages and lung and kidney damage. However, as usual, the burden of proof rests with the victims. Unfortunately, Mexico's environmental regulatory agency is understaffed and ill-equipped to enforce the country's environmental laws adequately.

Obviate Proof of Intent

Laws must allow disparate impact and statistical weight—as opposed to "intent"—to infer discrimination because proving intentional or purposeful discrimination in a court of law is next to impossible. The first lawsuit to charge environmental discrimination in the placement of a waste facility, *Bean v. Southwestern Waste*, was filed in 1979. The case involved residents of Houston's Northwood Manor, a suburban, middle-class neighborhood of homeowners, and Browning-Ferris Industries, a private disposal company based in Houston.

More than 83 percent of the residents in the subdivision owned their single-family, detached homes. Thus, the Northwood Manor neighborhood was an unlikely candidate for a municipal landfill except that, in 1978, it was more than 82 percent black. An earlier attempt had been made to locate a municipal landfill in the same general area in 1970, when the subdivision and local school district had a majority white population. The 1970 landfill proposal was killed by the Harris County Board of Supervisors as being an incompatible land use; the site was deemed to be too close to a residential area and a neighborhood school. In 1978, however, the controversial sanitary landfill was built only 1,400 feet from a high school, football stadium, track field, and the North Forest Independent School District's administration building.[51] Because Houston has been and continues to be highly segregated, few Houstonians are unaware of where the African-American neighborhoods end and the white ones begin. In 1970, for example, more than 90 percent of the city's African-American residents lived in mostly black areas. By 1980, 82 percent of Houston's African-American population lived in mostly black areas.[52]

Houston is the only major U.S. city without zoning. In 1992, the city council voted to institute zoning, but the measure was defeated at the polls in 1993. The city's African-American neighborhoods have paid a high price for the city's unrestrained growth and lack of a zoning policy. Black Houston was allowed to become the dumping ground for the city's garbage. In every case, the racial composition of Houston's African-American neighborhoods had been established before the waste facilities were sited.[53]

From the early 1920s through the late 1970s, all five of the city-owned sanitary landfills and six out of eight of Houston's municipal solid waste incinerators were located in mostly African-American neighborhoods.[54] The other two incinerator sites were located in a Latino neighborhood and a white neighborhood. One of the oldest waste sites in Houston was located in Freedmen's Town, an African-American neighborhood settled by former slaves in the 1860s. The site has since been built over with a charity hospital and a low-income public housing project.

Private industry took its lead from the siting pattern established by the city government. From 1970 to 1978, three of the four privately owned landfills used to dispose of Houston's garbage were located in mostly African-American neighborhoods. The fourth privately owned landfill, which was sited in 1971, was located in the mostly white Chattwood subdivision. A residential park or "buffer zone" separates the white neighborhood from the landfill. Both government and industry responded to white neighborhood associations and their NIMBY (not in my backyard) organizations by siting LULUs according to the PIBBY (place in blacks' backyards) strategy.[55]

The statistical evidence in *Bean v. Southwestern Waste* overwhelmingly supported the disproportionate impact argument. Overall, 14 of the 17 (82 percent) solid waste facilities used to dispose of Houston's garbage were located in mostly African-American neighborhoods. Considering that Houston's African-American residents comprised only 28 percent of the city's total population, they clearly were forced to bear a disproportionate burden of the city's solid waste facilities.[56] However, the federal judge ruled against the plaintiffs on the grounds that "purposeful discrimination" was not demonstrated.

Although the Northwood Manor residents lost their lawsuit, they did influence the way the Houston city government and the state of Texas addressed race and waste facility siting. Acting under intense pressure from the African-American community, the Houston city council passed a resolution in 1980 that prohibited city-owned trucks from dumping at the controversial landfill. In 1981, the Houston city council passed an ordinance restricting the construction of solid waste disposal sites near public facilities such as schools. And the Texas Department of Health updated its requirements of landfill permit applicants to include detailed land use, economic, and sociodemographic data on areas where they proposed to site landfills. Black Houstonians had sent a clear signal to the Texas Department of Health, the city of Houston, and private disposal companies that they would fight any future attempts to place waste disposal facilities in their neighborhoods.

Since *Bean v. Southwestern Waste,* not a single landfill or incinerator has been sited in an African-American neighborhood in Houston. Not until nearly a decade after that suit did environmental discrimination resurface in the courts. A number of recent cases have challenged siting decisions using the environmental discrimination argument: *East Bibb Twiggs Neighborhood Association v.*

Macon-Bibb County Planning & Zoning Commission (1989), *Bordeaux Action Committee v. Metro Government of Nashville* (1990), *R.I.S.E. v. Kay* (1991), and *El Pueblo para El Aire y Agua Limpio v. County of Kings* (1991). Unfortunately, these legal challenges are also confronted with the test of demonstrating "purposeful" discrimination.

Redress Inequities

Disproportionate impacts must be redressed by targeting action and resources. Resources should be spent where environmental and health problems are greatest, as determined by some ranking scheme—but one not limited to risk assessment. EPA already has geographic targeting that involves selecting a physical area, often a naturally defined area such as a watershed; assessing the condition of the natural resources and range of environmental threats, including risks to public health; formulating and implementing integrated, holistic strategies for restoring or protecting living resources and their habitats within that area; and evaluating the progress of those strategies toward their objectives.[57]

Relying solely on proof of a cause-and-effect relationship as defined by traditional epidemiology disguises the exploitative way the polluting industries have operated in some communities and condones a passive acceptance of the status quo.[58] Because it is difficult to establish causation, polluting industries have the upper hand. They can always hide behind "science" and demand "proof" that their activities are harmful to humans or the environment.

A 1992 EPA report, *Securing Our Legacy,* described the agency's geographic initiatives as "protecting what we love."[59] The strategy emphasizes "pollution prevention, multimedia enforcement, research into causes and cures of environmental stress, stopping habitat loss, education, and constituency building."[60] Examples of geographic initiatives under way include the Chesapeake Bay, Great Lakes, Gulf of Mexico, and Mexican Border programs.

Such targeting should channel resources to the hot spots, communities that are burdened with more than their fair share of environmental problems. For example, EPA's Region VI has developed geographic information system and comparative risk methodologies to evaluate environmental equity concerns in the region. The methodology combines susceptibility factors, such as age, pregnancy, race, income, pre-existing disease, and lifestyle, with chemical release data from the Toxic Release Inventory and monitoring information; state health department vital statistics data; and geographic and demographic data—especially from areas around hazardous waste sites—for its regional equity assessment.

Region VI's 1992 Gulf Coast Toxics Initiatives project is an outgrowth of its equity assessment. The project targets facilities on the Texas and Louisiana coast, a "sensitive...ecoregion where most of the releases in the five-state region occur."[61] Inspectors will spend 38 percent of their time in this "multimedia enforcement effort."[62] It is not clear how this percentage was determined, but, for the project to move beyond the "first-step" phase and begin addressing real inequities, most of its resources (not just inspectors) must be channeled to the areas where most of the problems occur.

A 1993 EPA study of Toxic Release Inventory data from Louisiana's petrochemical corridor found that "populations within two miles of facilities releasing 90% of total industrial corridor air releases feature a higher proportion of minorities than the state average; facilities releasing 88% have a higher proportion than the Industrial Corridor parishes' average.[63]

To no one's surprise, communities in Corpus Christi, neighborhoods that run along the Houston Ship Channel and petrochemical corridor, and many unincorporated communities along the 85-mile stretch of the Mississippi River from Baton Rouge to New Orleans ranked at or near the top in terms of pollution discharges in EPA Region VI's Gulf Coast Toxics Initiatives equity assessment. It is very likely that similar rankings would be achieved using the environmental justice framework. However, the question that remains is one of resource allocation—the level of resources that Region VI will channel into solving the pollution problem in communities that have a disproportionately large share of poor people, working-class people, and people of color.

Health concerns raised by Louisiana's residents and grassroots activists in such communities as Alsen, St. Gabriel, Geismer, Morrisonville, and Lions—all of which are located in close proximity to polluting industries—have not been adequately addressed by local parish supervisors, state environmental and health officials, or the federal and regional offices of EPA.[64]

A few contaminated African-American communities in southeast Louisiana have been bought out or are in the process of being bought out by industries under their "good neighbor" programs. Moving people away from the health threat is only a partial solution, however, as long as damage to the environment continues. For example, Dow Chemical, the state's largest chemical plant, is buying out residents of mostly African-American Morrisonville.[65] The communities of Sun Rise and Reveilletown, which were founded by freed slaves, have already been bought out.

Many of the community buy-out settlements are sealed. The secret nature of the agreements limits public scrutiny, community comparisons, and disclosure of harm or potential harm. Few of the recent settlement agreements allow for health monitoring or surveillance of affected residents once they are dispersed.[66] Some settlements have even required the "victims" to sign waivers that preclude them from bringing any further lawsuits against the polluting industry.

A FRAMEWORK FOR ENVIRONMENTAL JUSTICE

The solution to unequal protection lies in the realm of environmental justice for all people. No community—rich or poor, black or white—should be allowed to become a "sacrifice zone." The lessons from the civil rights struggles around housing, employment, education, and public accommodations over the past four decades suggest that environmental justice requires a legislative foundation. It is not enough to demonstrate the existence of unjust and unfair conditions; the practices that cause the conditions must be made illegal.

The five principles already described—the right to protection, prevention of harm, shifting the burden of proof, obviating proof of intent to discriminate, and targeting resources to redress inequities—constitute a framework for environmental justice. The framework incorporates a legislative strategy, modeled after landmark civil rights mandates, that would make environmental discrimination illegal and costly.

Although enforcing current laws in a nondiscriminatory way would help, a new legislative initiative is needed. Unequal protection must be attacked via a federal "fair environmental protection act" that redefines protection as a right rather than a privilege. Legislative initiatives must also be directed at states because many of the decisions and problems lie with state actions.

Noxious facility siting and cleanup decisions involve very little science and a lot of politics. Institutional discrimination exists in every social arena, including environmental decision making. Burdens and benefits are not randomly distributed. Reliance solely on "objective" science for environmental decision making—in a world shaped largely by power politics and special interests—often masks institutional racism. For example, the assignment of "acceptable" risk and use of "averages" often result from value judgments that serve to legitimate existing inequities. A national environmental justice framework that incorporates the five principles presented above is needed to begin addressing environmental inequities that result from procedural, geographic, and societal imbalances.

The antidiscrimination and enforcement measures called for here are no more regressive than the initiatives undertaken to eliminate slavery and segregation in the United States. Opponents argued at the time that such actions would hurt the slaves by creating unemployment and destroying black institutions, such as businesses and schools. Similar arguments were made in opposition to sanctions against the racist system of apartheid in South Africa. But people of color who live in environmental sacrifice zones"—from migrant farm workers who are exposed to deadly pesticides to the parents of inner-city children threatened by lead poisoning—will welcome any new approaches that will reduce environmental disparities and eliminate the threats to their families' health.

NOTES

1. U.S. Environmental Protection Agency, *Environmental Equity: Reducing Risk for All Communities* (Washington, D.C., 1992); and K. Sexton and Y. Banks Anderson, eds., "Equity in Environmental Health: Research Issues and Needs," *Toxicology and Industrial Health* 9 (September/October 1993).

2. R. D. Bullard, "Solid Waste Sites and the Black Houston Community," *Sociological Inquiry* 53, nos. 2 and 3 (1983): 273–88; idem, *Invisible Houston: The Black Experience in Boom and Bust* (College Station, Tex.: Texas A&M University Press, 1987); idem, *Dumping in Dixie: Race, Class, and Environmental Quality* (Boulder, Colo.: Westview Press, 1990); idem, *Confronting Environmental Racism: Voices from the Grassroots* (Boston, Mass.: South End Press, forth); D. Russell, "Environmental Racism," *Amicus Journal* 11, no. 2 (1989): 22–32; M. Lavelle and M. Coyle, "Unequal Protection," *National Law Journal,* 21 September 1992, 1–2; R. Austin and M. Schill, "Black, Brown, Poor, and Poisoned: Minority Grassroots Environmentalism and the Quest for Eco-Justice," *Kansas Journal of Law and Public Policy* 1 (1991): 69–82; R. Godsil, "Remedying Environmental Racism," *Michigan Law Review* 90 (1991): 394–427; and B. Bryant and P. Mohai, eds., *Race and the Incidence of Environmental Hazards: A Time for Discourse* (Boulder, Colo.: Westview Press, 1992).

3. R. B. Stewart, "Paradoxes of Liberty, Integrity, and Fraternity: The Collective Nature of Environmental Quality and Judicial Review of Administration Action," *Environmental Law* 7, no. 3 (1977): 474–76; M. A. Freeman, "The Distribution of Environmental Quality," in A. V. Kneese and B. F. Bower, eds., *Environmental Quality Analysis* (Baltimore, Md.: Johns Hopkins University Press for Resources for the Future, 1972); W. J. Kruvant, "People, Energy, and Pollution," in D. K. Newman and D. Day, eds., *American Energy Consumer* (Cambridge, Mass.: Ballinger, 1975), 125–67; and L. Gianessi, H. M. Peskin, and E. Wolff, "The Distributional Effects of Uniform Air Pollution Policy in the U.S.," *Quarterly Journal of Economics* 56, no. 1 (1979): 281–301.

4. Freeman, note 3 above; Kruvant, note 3 above; Bullard, 1983 and 1990, note 2 above; P. Asch and J. J. Seneca, "Some Evidence on the Distribution of Air Quality," *Land Economics* 54, no. 3 (1978): 278–97; United Church of Christ Commission for Racial Justice, *Toxic Wastes and Race in the United States: A National Study of the Racial and Socioeconomic*

Characteristics of Communities with Hazardous Waste Sites (New York: United Church of Christ, 1987); Russell, note 2 above; R. D. Bullard and B. H. Wright, "Environmentalism and the Politics of Equity; Emergent Trends in the Black Community," *Mid-American Review of Sociology* 12, no. 2 (1987): 21–37; idem, "The Quest for Environmental Equity: Mobilizing the African American Community for Social Change," *Society and Natural Resources* 3, no. 4 (1990): 301–11; M. Gelobter, "The Distribution of Air Pollution by Income and Race" (paper presented at the Second Symposium on Social Science in Resource management, Urbana, Ill., June 1988); R. D. Bullard and J. R. Feagin, "Racism and the City," in M. Gottdiene, and C. V. Pickvance, eds., *Urban Life in Transition* (Newbury Park, Calif.: Sage, 1991), 55–76; R. D. Bullard, "Urban Infrastructure: Social, Environmental, and Health Risks to African Americans," in B. J. Tidwell, ed., *The State of Black America 1992* (New York: National Urban League, 1992), 183–96; P. Ong and E. Blumenberg, "Race and Environmentalism" (paper prepared for the Graduate School of Architecture and Urban Planning, University of California at Los Angeles, 14 March 1990); and B. H. Wright and R. D. Bullard, "Hazards in the Workplace and Black Health," *National Journal of Sociology* 4, no. 1 (1990): 45–62.

5. Freeman, note 3 above; Gianessi, Peskin, and Wolff, note 3 above; Gelobter, note 4 above; D. R. Wernette and L. A. Nieves, "Breathing Polluted Air," *EPA Journal* 18, no. 1 (1992): 16–17; Bullard, 1983, 1987, and 1990, note 2 above; R. D. Bullard, "Environmental Racism," *Environmental Protection* 2 (June 1991): 25–26; L. A. Nieves, "Not in Whose Backyard? Minority Population Concentrations and Noxious Facility Sites" (paper presented at the Annual Meeting of the American Association for the Advancement of Science, Chicago, 9 February 1992); United Church of Christ, note 4 above; Agency for Toxic Substances and Disease Registry, *The Nature and Extent of Lead Poisoning in Children in the United States: A Report to Congress* (Atlanta, Ga. U.S. Department of Health and Human Services, 1988); K. Florini et al., *Legacy of Lead: America's Continuing Epidemic of Childhood Lead Poisoning* (Washington, D.C.: Environmental Defense Fund, 1990); and P. West, J. M. Fly, F. Larkin, and P. Marans, "Minority Anglers and Toxic Fish Consumption: Evidence of the State-Wide Survey of Michigan," in B. Bryant and P. Mohai, eds., *The Proceedings of the Michigan Conference on Race and the Incidence of Environmental Hazards* (Ann Arbor, Mich.: University of Michigan School of Natural Resources, 1990), 108–22.

6. Gelobter, note 4 above; and M. Gelobter, "Toward a Model of Environmental Discrimination," in Bryant and Mohai, eds., note 5 above, pages 87–107.

7. B. Goldman, *Not Just Prosperity: Achieving Sustainability with Environmental Justice* (Washington, D.C.: National Wildlife Federation Corporate Conservation Council, 1994), 8.

8. Wernette and Nieves, note 5 above, pages 16–17.

9. H. P. Mak, P. Johnson, H. Abbey, and R. C. Talamo, "Prevalence of Asthma and Health Service Utilization of Asthmatic Children in an Inner City," *Journal of Allergy and Clinical Immunology* 70 (1982): 367–72; I. F. Goldstein and A. L. Weinstein, "Air Pollution and Asthma: Effects of Exposure to Short-Term Sulfur Dioxide Peaks," *Environmental Research* 40 (1986): 332–45; J. Schwartz et al., "Predictors of Asthma and Persistent Wheeze in a National Sample of Children in the United States," *American Review of Respiratory Disease* 142 (1990): 555–62; U.S. Environmental Protection Agency, note I above; and E. Mann, L.A.'s *Lethal Air: New Strategies for Policy, Organizing and Action* (Los Angeles: Labor/Community Strategy Center, 1991).

10. Lavelle and Coyle, note 2 above, pages 1–2.

11. Ibid., 2.

12. Bullard, 1983 and 1990, note 2 above; Gelobter, note 4 above; and United Church of Christ, note 4 above.

13. Bullard, 1983 and 1990, note 2 above; P. Costner and J. Thornton, *Playing with Fire* (Washington, D.C.: Greenpeace, 1990); and United Church of Christ, note 4 above.

14. Costner and Thornton, note 13 above.

15. M. H. Brown, *The Toxic Cloud: The Poisoning of America's Air* (New York: Harper and Row, 1987); and J. Summerhays, *Estimation and Evaluation of Cancer Risks Attributable lo Air Pollution in Southeast Chicago* (Washington, D.C.: U.S. Environmental Protection Agency, 1989).

16. *Greenpeace Magazine,* "Home Street, USA: Living with Pollution," October/November/December 1991, 8–13.

17. Mann, note 9 above; and Ong and Blumenberg, note 4 above.

18. Mann, note 9 above; and J. Kay, "Fighting Toxic Racism: L.A.'s Minority Neighborhood Is the 'Dirtiest' in the State," *San Francisco Examiner,* 7 April 199 1, Al.

19. Bullard, 1990, note 2 above.

20. K. C. Colquette and E. A. Henry Robertson, "Environmental Racism: The Causes, Consequences, and Commendations," *Tulane Environmental Law Journal* 5, no. 1 (1991): 153–207.

21. F. Ferrer, "Testimony by the Office of Bronx Borough President," in *Proceedings from the Public Hearing on Minorities and the Environment: An Exploration into the Effects of Environmental Policies, Practices, and Conditions on Minority and Low-Income Communities* (Bronx, N.Y.: Bronx Planning Office, 20 September 1991).

22. B. Angel, *The Toxic Threat to Indian Lands: A Greenpeace Report* (San Francisco, Calif.; Greenpeace, 1992); and J. Kay, "Indian Lands Targeted for Waste Disposal Sites," *San Francisco Examiner,* 10 April 1991, Al.

23. M. Ambler, "The Lands the Feds Forgot," *Sierra,* May/June 1989, 44.

24. Angel, note 22 above; C. Beasley, "Of Poverty and Pollution: Deadly Threat on Native Lands," *Buzzworm* 2, no. 5 (1990): 39–45; and R. Tomsho, "Dumping Grounds: Indian Tribes Contend with Some of the Worst of America's Pollution," *Wall Street Journal,* 29 November 1990, A1.

25. Cerrell Associates, Inc., *Political Difficulties Facing Waste-to-Energy Conversion Plant Siting* (Los Angeles: California Waste Management Board, 1984).

26. L. Blumberg and R. Gottlieb, *War on Waste: Can America Win Its Battle with Garbage?* (Washington, D.C.: Island Press, 1989).

27. U.S. Commission on Civil Rights, *The Battle for Environmental Justice in Louisiana: Government, Industry, and the People* (Kansas City, Mo., 1993).

28. Agency for Toxic Substances and Disease Registry, note 5 above.

29. P. Reich, *The Hour of Lead* (Washington, D.C.: Environmental Defense Fund, 1992).

30. Agency for Toxic Substances and Disease Registry, note 5 above.

31. Florini et al., note 5 above.

32. P. J. Hilts, "White House Shuns Key Role in Lead Exposure," *New York Times,* 24 August 1991, 14.

33. Ibid.

34. Dallas Alliance Environmental Task Force, *Alliance Final Report* (Dallas, Tex.: Dallas Alliance, 1983).

35. J. Lash, K. Gillman, and D. Sheridan, *A Season of Spoils: The Reagan Administration's Attack on the Environment* (New York: Pantheon Books, 1984), 131–39.

36. D. W. Nauss, "EPA Official: Dallas Lead Study Misleading," *Dallas Times Herald,* 20 March 1983, 1; idem, "The People vs. the Lead Smelter," *Dallas Times Herald,* 17 July 1983, 18; B. Lodge, "EPA Official Faults Dallas Lead Smelter," *Dallas Morning News,* 20 March 1983, A1; and Lash, Gillman, and Sheridan, note 35 above.

37. U.S. Environmental Protection Agency Region VI, *Report of the Dallas Area Lead Assessment Study* (Dallas, Tex., 1983).

38. Lash, Gillman, and Sheridan, note 35 above.

39. Bullard, 1990, note 2 above.

40. S. Scott and R. L. Loftis, "'Slag Sites' Health Risks Still Unclear," *Dallas Morning News,* 23 July 1991, A1.

41. Ibid.

42. B. L. Lee, "Environmental Litigation on Behalf of Poor, Minority Children: Matthews v. Coye: A Case Study" (paper presented at the Annual Meeting of the American Association for the Advancement of Science, Chicago, 9 February 1992).

43. Nuclear Regulatory Commission, *Draft Environmental Impact Statement for the Construction and Operation of Claiborne Enrichment Center, Homer, Louisiana* (Washington, D.C., 1993), 3108.

44. See U.S. Census Bureau, *1990 Census of Population General Population Characteristics—Louisiana* (Washington, D.C.: U.S. Government Printing Office, May 1992).

45. Nuclear Regulatory Commission, note 43 above, pages 4–38.

46. Citizens for a Better Environment, *Richmond at Risk* (San Francisco, Calif., 1992).

47. Bay Area Air Quality Management District, *General Chemical Incident of July 26, 1993* (San Francisco, Calif., 15 September 1993), 1.

48. R. Sanchez, "Health and Environmental Risks of the Maquiladora in Mexicali," *Natural Resources Journal* 30 (Winter 1990): 16386.

49. Center for Investigative Reporting, *Global Dumping Grounds: The International Traffic in Hazardous Waste* (Washington, D.C.: Seven Locks Press, 1989), 59.

50. Working Group on Canada-Mexico Free Trade, "Que Pasa? A Canada-Mexico 'Free' Trade Deal," *New Solutions: A Journal of Environmental and Occupational Health Policy* 2 (1991): 10–25.

51. Bullard, 198 3, note 2 above.

52. Bullard, 1987, note 2 above.

53. Bullard, 1983, 1987, and 1990, note 2 above. The unit of analysis for the Houston waste study was the neighborhood, not the census tract. The concept of neighborhood predates census tract geography, which became available only in 1950.

Neighborhood studies date back nearly a century. Neighborhood as used here is defined as "a social/spatial unit of social organization . . . larger than a household and smaller than a city." See A. Hunter, "Urban Neighborhoods: Its Analytical and Social Contexts," *Urban Affairs Quarterly* 14 (1979): 270. The neighborhood is part of a city's geography, a place defined by specific physical boundaries and block groups. Similarly, the black neighborhood is a "highly diversified set of inter-related structures and aggregates of people who are held together by forces of white oppression and racism." See J. E. Blackwell, *The Black Community: Diversity and Unity* (New York: Harper & Row, 1985), xiii.

54. Bullard, 1983, 1987, and 1990, note 2 above.
55. Ibid.
56. Ibid.
57. U.S. Environmental Protection Agency, *Strategies and Framework for the Future: Final Report* (Washington, D.C., 1992), 12.
58. K. S. Shrader-Frechette, *Risk and Rationality: Philosophical Foundations for Populist Reform* (Berkeley, Calif.: University of California Press, 1992), 98.

59. U.S. Environmental Protection Agency, "Geographic Initiatives: Protecting What We Love," *Securing Our Legacy: An EPA Progress Report 1989–1991* (Washington, D.C., 1992), 32.
60. Ibid.
61. U.S. Environmental Protection Agency, note 1 above, vol. 2, Supporting Documents, page 60.
62. Ibid.
63. U.S. Environmental Protection Agency, *Toxic Release Inventory & Emission Reduction 1987–1990 in the Lower Mississippi River Industrial Corridor* (Washington, D.C., 1993), 25.
64. Bullard, 1990, note 2 above; C. Beasley, "Of Pollution and Poverty: Keeping Watch in Cancer Alley," *Buzzworm* 2, no. 4 (1990): 3945; and S. Lewis, B. Keating, and D. Russell, *Inconclusive by Design: Waste, Fraud, and Abuse in Federal Environmental Health Research* (Boston, Mass.: National Toxics Campaign, 1992).
65. J. O'Byrne, "The Death of a Town," *Times Picayune*, 20 February 1991, A1.
66. Bullard, 1990, note 2 above; J. O'Byrne and M. Schleifstein, "Invisible Poisons," *Times Picayune*, 18 February 1991, A1; and Lewis, Keating, and Russell, note 64 above.

STUDY QUESTIONS

1. Bullard argues that "unequal environmental protection undermines three basic types of equity: procedural, geographic, and social." Discuss each of these.
2. Bullard advocates the adoption of five principles to increase (or ensure) environmental justice. Discuss three of them in depth.

3. Discuss the following question: Is the disproportionate distribution of pollutants more due to racial discrimination or to economic class inequalities?

71   The Earth Charter: From Global Ethics to International Law Instrument

INTRODUCTION BY LAURA WESTRA

Laura Westra was, until her retirement, a professor of philosophy at the University of Windsor. A leading environmentalist, she also served as the secretary of the International Society for Environmental Ethics. She is the author of *An Environmental Proposal for Ethics: The Principle of Integrity* (1994); co-editor of *Faces of Environmental Racism* (1995); *Perspectives on Ecological Integrity* (1995); *The Greeks and the Environment* (1997), and *Technology and Values* (1997). She has published more than sixty articles and chapters in books and journals.

This introduction was commissioned for the fourth edition of this book and appeared there in print for the first time.

In 1972 the nations that were gathered at Stockholm agreed that environmental protection should be added to the core agenda of the United Nations, together with "peace, human rights, and equitable social and economic development" (Rockefeller, 2002:xi). This belief was emphasized and supported by many at the 1992 Earth Summit at Rio de Janeiro. In 1994, the Earth Charter Initiative worked to develop a document that would start by accepting the complete interdependence of humanity with global natural systems and that would involve all countries and nationalities from both the North and the South. As Rockefeller explained it,

> The product of a decade long, world-wide cross-cultural dialogue on shared values, the Earth Charter reflects an effort to build on and further develop the ethical visions in the Stockholm Declaration (1972), the World Charter for Nature (1982), the Rio Declaration (1992), and a variety of non-governmental covenants and declarations (Rockefeller, 2002:xii).

The Earth Charter is an "ethical vision," but it is also a compendium and re-working of soft law. In addition, the International Draft Covenant of Environment and Development (2000 revision) is presently under consideration at the United Nations, and its wording is being reviewed by a UN committee to ensure that the main principles of the Earth Charter are preserved within it. After the committee's work has been completed and the Covenant manifests as much as possible of the spirit, if not the letter, of the Earth Charter in its articles, the United Nations will ensure that it is presented for ratification to all states, as it proposes to bridge the sectors of environment and development.

The Covenant is thus intended to regulate "relations between humankind and nature" (UN Secretary-General's report) and to create "an agreed single set of fundamental principles like a code of conduct...which may guide states, intergovernmental organization and individuals" (Covenant, p. 14).

Turning now to specific provisions of the Covenant, both Objectives and Fundamental Principles repeat and support the main concerns of the Earth Charter, although the Covenant is much less detailed than the Charter, as well as less specific, thus manifesting, even in draft form, many of the same problems of vagueness and lack of prescriptive specificity of most international covenants, no matter what the topic.

This vagueness is not the result of chance: Through negotiations most international agreements are negotiated "down" from their original intent. Blocs and alliances fostered by the most powerful countries are intended to ensure that business-as-usual will prevail in the interest of those countries and that the regulatory regime under consideration does not cause too many impediments to affluent Western economies. Although the work on the Charter was done by non-governmental organizations (NGOs) and by citizens from countries all over the world, vagueness is not a problem. Consequently the Charter speaks with a strong voice, indicting harmful practices and explicitly defending life and the intrinsic value of both natural systems and processes, as well as biodiversity. It is vital to ensure that the major principles of the Earth Charter are thus preserved in the Covenant, especially those that emphasize the important connection between human health and human rights (Westra, 2000) and the interface between human rights and "ecological rights" (Taylor, 1998). The Earth Charter, Principle 2 says:

> 2: Care for the community of life with understanding, compassion and love, and
> 2(a): Accept that with the right to own, manage, and use natural resources comes the duty to prevent environmental harm and to protect the rights of people.

The connection between environmental harm and human rights is rendered explicit. In addition, Principle 6(c),

> Ensure that decision making addresses the cumulative, long-term, indirect, long distance, and global consequences of human activities

ensures that the connection between environmental harms and human activities and practices is spelled out.

In contrast, the Covenant's Articles 4, 5, 6, and 7 state only the following:

Article 4: Interdependent Values—Peace, development, environmental protection and respect for human rights and fundamental freedoms are interdependent.

Article 5: Intergenerational Equity—The freedom of action of each generation in regard to the environment is qualified by the needs of future generations.

Article 6: Prevention—Protection of the environment is best achieved by preventing environmental harm, rather than by attempting to remedy or compensate such harm.

Article 7: Precaution—Lack of scientific certainty is no reason to postpone action to avoid potentially irreversible harm to the environment.

Some of the key concepts are preserved, but the question of long-term, long-distance, and cumulative harms resulting from human activities is not addressed, nor are duties as well as rights emphasized. Human health itself is not even mentioned, yet a number of high-level, UN-sponsored World Health Organization (WHO) meetings on environment and health, with conferences in Frankfurt (1989) and Helsinki (1994), culminated in a "Declaration of the Third Ministerial Conference on Environment and Health" (London, 1999), which clearly connected environmental harms to human health and thereby to human rights.

It is both wrong and illogical to exclude the important scientific findings of the WHO in regard to human health in general, and in relation to environmental conditions specifically, from any document that is aimed at preventing environmental harm and promoting sustainability. The spurious separation between "environment" and "humankind" militates against Articles 4 and 5 of the Draft Covenant and against the main principles that animate the Earth Charter:

1: Respect Earth and life in all its diversity. and 1(a): Recognize that all beings are interdependent and every form of life has value regardless of its worth to human beings.

Hence the respect for human beings cannot be separated from respect for their habitat, one that they have in common with the rest of life. It is clear that if this connection is emphasized and made explicit, grave consequences would follow for present practices and institutions. For example, when the activities of tobacco companies were fully disclosed and the consequences of those activities were eventually scientifically documented, many business and institutional practices were severely curtailed because such rights as freedom of expression were pitted against public rights to health and *life*.

When linkages between climate-induced disasters, temperature extremes, and soil erosion that leads to desertification and famine are openly acknowledged, then state-supported but unsafe business practices and, in general, *a status quo* that gives privileges to trade over life will be brought into question. The changes required will be drastic for both institutional practices and the law, because not one industrial enterprise (e.g., tobacco companies) but all of them will have to admit their responsibility.

This Draft Covenant represents a "bridge" of sorts between the failure to protect that is so clear in most other international environmental instruments and the universal obligations that best define environmental duties. Insofar as the Draft Covenant will add the connections and the emphases that I propose and will not allow signatories to further water down and erode the underlying normative message of the Earth Charter, it may well become one of the first international legal instruments committed to the joint protection of humankind and its habitat.

It is significant that the development of the Earth Charter principles demonstrates the "bottom-up" globalization referred to earlier. From a substantive point of view, even more significant is the connection that many of its principles have with public health and hence with human rights; that emphasis helps to connect the Earth Charter to some of the strongest and most accepted international law instruments based on universal human rights, thus giving rise to universal rather than contractual obligations. Hence when the Earth Charter becomes part of an international covenant, the covenant will embody both aspects of cosmopolitanism.

The Earth Charter, as a cosmopolitan moral perspective, includes respect for the preconditions of life—a recognition of the interconnectedness of all life. It emphasizes a respect for communities and peoples that is basic to global ethics. It is a declaration of fundamental principles for creating a just, sustainable, and peaceful society in the twenty-first century.

BIBLIOGRAPHY

Rockefeller, Steven. 2002. "Foreword" to *Just Integrity,* Peter Miller and Laura Westra, eds. Lanham, MD: Rowman & Littlefield, xi–xiv.

Soskolne, Colin, and Bertollini, Roberto. 1999. *Ecological Integrity and Sustainable Development: Cornerstones of Public Health.* (www.euro.who.int/document/gch/globaleco/ecorep5.pdf)

Taylor, Prudence. 1998. "From Environmental to Ecological Human Rights: A New Dynamic in International Law?" *The Georgetown Int'l. Envtl. Law Review,* Vol. 1. 10:309.

Westra, Laura. 2000. "Institutionalized Environmental Violence and Human Rights" in *Ecological Integrity: Integrating Environment, Conservation and Health,* David Pimentel, Laura Westra, and Reed Noss, eds., Washington, DC: Island Press, pp. 279–294.

WHO European Centre for Environment and Health. 2000. "Annex B: Declaration of the Third Ministerial Conference on Environmental and Health" (signed in London on June 18, 1999), pp. 323–334.

THE EARTH CHARTER

PREAMBLE

We stand at a critical moment in Earth's history, a time when humanity must choose its future. As the world becomes increasingly interdependent and fragile, the future at once holds great peril and great promise. To move forward we must recognize that in the midst of a magnificent diversity of cultures and life forms we are one human family and one Earth community with a common destiny. We must join together to bring forth a sustainable global society founded on respect for nature, universal human rights, economic justice, and a culture of peace. Towards this end, it is imperative that we, the peoples of Earth, declare our responsibility to one another, to the greater community of life, and to future generations.

Earth, Our Home

Humanity is part of a vast evolving universe. Earth, our home, is alive with a unique community of life. The forces of nature make existence a demanding and uncertain adventure, but Earth has provided the conditions essential to life's evolution. The resilience of the community of life and the well-being of humanity depend upon preserving a healthy biosphere with all its ecological systems, a rich variety of plants and animals, fertile soils, pure waters, and clean air. The global environment with its finite resources is a common concern of all peoples. The protection of Earth's vitality, diversity, and beauty is a sacred trust.

The Global Situation

The dominant patterns of production and consumption are causing environmental devastation, the depletion of resources, and a massive extinction of species. Communities are being undermined. The benefits of development are not shared equitably and the gap between rich and poor is widening. Injustice, poverty, ignorance, and violent conflict are widespread and the cause of great suffering. An unprecedented rise in human population has overburdened ecological and social systems. The foundations of global security are threatened. These trends are perilous—but not inevitable.

The Challenges Ahead

The choice is ours: form a global partnership to care for Earth and one another or risk the destruction of ourselves and the diversity of life. Fundamental changes are needed in our values, institutions, and ways of living. We must realize that when basic needs have been met, human development is primarily about being more, not having more. We have the knowledge and technology to provide for all and to reduce our impacts on the environment. The emergence of a global civil society is creating new opportunities to build a democratic and humane world. Our environmental, economic, political, social, and spiritual challenges are interconnected, and together we can forge inclusive solutions.

Universal Responsibility

To realize these aspirations, we must decide to live with a sense of universal responsibility, identifying ourselves with the whole Earth community as well as our local communities. We are at once citizens of different nations and of one world in which the local and global are linked. Everyone shares responsibility for the present and future well-being of the human family and the larger living world. The spirit of human solidarity and kinship with all life is strengthened when we live with reverence for the mystery of being, gratitude for the gift of life, and humility regarding the human place in nature.

We urgently need a shared vision of basic values to provide an ethical foundation for the emerging world community. Therefore, together in hope we affirm the following interdependent principles for a sustainable way of life as a common standard by which the conduct of all individuals, organizations, businesses, governments, and transnational institutions is to be guided and assessed.

PRINCIPLES

I. Respect and Care for the Community of Life

1. Respect Earth and life in all its diversity.
   a. Recognize that all beings are interdependent and every form of life has value regardless of its worth to human beings.
   b. Affirm faith in the inherent dignity of all human beings and in the intellectual, artistic, ethical, and spiritual potential of humanity.
2. Care for the community of life with understanding, compassion, and love.
   a. Accept that with the right to own, manage, and use natural resources comes the duty to prevent environmental harm and to protect the rights of people.
   b. Affirm that with increased freedom, knowledge, and power comes increased responsibility to promote the common good.
3. Build democratic societies that are just, participatory, sustainable, and peaceful.
   a. Ensure that communities at all levels guarantee human rights and fundamental freedoms and provide everyone an opportunity to realize his or her full potential.
   b. Promote social and economic justice, enabling all to achieve a secure and meaningful livelihood that is ecologically responsible.
4. Secure Earth's bounty and beauty for present and future generations.
   a. Recognize that the freedom of action of each generation is qualified by the needs of future generations.
   b. Transmit to future generations values, traditions, and institutions that support the long-term flourishing of Earth's human and ecological communities.

In order to fulfill these four broad commitments, it is necessary to:

II. Ecological Integrity

5. Protect and restore the integrity of Earth's ecological systems, with special concern for biological diversity and the natural processes that sustain life.
   a. Adopt at all levels sustainable development plans and regulations that make environmental conservation and rehabilitation integral to all development initiatives.

b. Establish and safeguard viable nature and biosphere reserves, including wild lands and marine areas, to protect Earth's life support systems, maintain biodiversity, and preserve our natural heritage.

c. Promote the recovery of endangered species and ecosystems.

d. Control and eradicate non-native or genetically modified organisms harmful to native species and the environment, and prevent introduction of such harmful organisms.

e. Manage the use of renewable resources such as water, soil, forest products, and marine life in ways that do not exceed rates of regeneration and that protect the health of ecosystems.

f. Manage the extraction and use of non-renewable resources such as minerals and fossil fuels in ways that minimize depletion and cause no serious environmental damage.

6. Prevent harm as the best method of environmental protection and, when knowledge is limited, apply a precautionary approach.

a. Take action to avoid the possibility of serious or irreversible environmental harm even when scientific knowledge is incomplete or inconclusive.

b. Place the burden of proof on those who argue that a proposed activity will not cause significant harm, and make the responsible parties liable for environmental harm.

c. Ensure that decision making addresses the cumulative, long-term, indirect, long distance, and global consequences of human activities.

d. Prevent pollution of any part of the environment and allow no build-up of radioactive, toxic, or other hazardous substances.

e. Avoid military activities damaging to the environment.

7. Adopt patterns of production, consumption, and reproduction that safeguard Earth's regenerative capacities, human rights, and community well-being.

a. Reduce, reuse, and recycle the materials used in production and consumption systems, and ensure that residual waste can be assimilated by ecological systems.

b. Act with restraint and efficiency when using energy, and rely increasingly on renewable energy sources such as solar and wind.

c. Promote the development, adoption, and equitable transfer of environmentally sound technologies.

d. Internalize the full environmental and social costs of goods and services in the selling price, and enable consumers to identify products that meet the highest social and environmental standards.

e. Ensure universal access to health care that fosters reproductive health and responsible reproduction.

f. Adopt lifestyles that emphasize the quality of life and material sufficiency in a finite world.

8. Advance the study of ecological sustainability and promote the open exchange and wide application of the knowledge acquired.

a. Support international scientific and technical cooperation on sustainability, with special attention to the needs of developing nations.

b. Recognize and preserve the traditional knowledge and spiritual wisdom in all cultures that contribute to environmental protection and human well-being.

c. Ensure that information of vital importance to human health and environmental protection, including genetic information, remains available in the public domain.

III. Social and Economic Justice

9. Eradicate poverty as an ethical, social, and environmental imperative.

a. Guarantee the right to potable water, clean air, food security, uncontaminated soil, shelter, and safe sanitation, allocating the national and international resources required.

b. Empower every human being with the education and resources to secure a sustainable livelihood, and provide social security and safety nets for those who are unable to support themselves.

c. Recognize the ignored, protect the vulnerable, serve those who suffer, and enable them to develop their capacities and to pursue their aspirations.

10. Ensure that economic activities and institutions at all levels promote human development in an equitable and sustainable manner.

a. Promote the equitable distribution of wealth within nations and among nations.

b. Enhance the intellectual, financial, technical, and social resources of developing nations, and relieve them of onerous international debt.

c. Ensure that all trade supports sustainable resource use, environmental protection, and progressive labor standards.

d. Require multinational corporations and international financial organizations to act transparently in the public good, and hold them accountable for the consequences of their activities.

11. Affirm gender equality and equity as prerequisites to sustainable development and ensure universal access to education, health care, and economic opportunity.

a. Secure the human rights of women and girls and end all violence against them.

b. Promote the active participation of women in all aspects of economic, political, civil, social, and cultural life as full and equal partners, decision makers, leaders, and beneficiaries.

c. Strengthen families and ensure the safety and loving nurture of all family members.

12. Uphold the right of all, without discrimination, to a natural and social environment supportive of human dignity, bodily health, and spiritual well-being, with special attention to the rights of indigenous peoples and minorities.

a. Eliminate discrimination in all its forms, such as that based on race, color, sex, sexual orientation, religion, language, and national, ethnic or social origin.

b. Affirm the right of indigenous peoples to their spirituality, knowledge, lands and resources and to their related practice of sustainable livelihoods.

c. Honor and support the young people of our communities, enabling them to fulfill their essential role in creating sustainable societies.

d. Protect and restore outstanding places of cultural and spiritual significance.

IV. Democracy, Nonviolence, and Peace

13. Strengthen democratic institutions at all levels, and provide transparency and accountability in governance, inclusive participation in decision making, and access to justice.

a. Uphold the right of everyone to receive clear and timely information on environmental matters and all development plans and activities which are likely to affect them or in which they have an interest.

b. Support local, regional and global civil society, and promote the meaningful participation of all interested individuals and organizations in decision making.

c. Protect the rights to freedom of opinion expression, peaceful assembly, association, and dissent.

d. Institute effective and efficient access to administrative and independent judicial procedures, including remedies and redress for environmental harm and the threat of such harm.

e. Eliminate corruption in all public and private institutions.

f. Strengthen local communities, enabling them to care for their environments, and assign environmental responsibilities to the levels of government where they can be carried out most effectively.

14. Integrate into formal education and life-long learning the knowledge, values, and skills needed for a sustainable way of life.

a. Provide all, especially children and youth, with educational opportunities that empower them to contribute actively to sustainable development.

b. Promote the contribution of the arts and humanities as well as the sciences in sustainability education.

c. Enhance the role of the mass media in raising awareness of ecological and social challenges.

d. Recognize the importance of moral and spiritual education for sustainable living.

15. Treat all living beings with respect and consideration.

a. Prevent cruelty to animals kept in human societies and protect them from suffering.

b. Protect wild animals from methods of hunting, trapping, and fishing that cause extreme, prolonged, or avoidable suffering.

c. Avoid or eliminate to the full extent possible the taking or destruction of non-targeted species.

16. Promote a culture of tolerance, nonviolence, and peace.

a. Encourage and support mutual understanding, solidarity, and cooperation among all peoples and within and among nations.

b. Implement comprehensive strategies to prevent violent conflict and use collaborative problem solving to manage and resolve environmental conflicts and other disputes.

c. Demilitarize national security systems to the level of a non-provocative defense posture, and convert military resources to peaceful purposes, including ecological restorations.

d. Eliminate nuclear, biological, and toxic weapons and other weapons of mass destruction.

e. Ensure that the use of orbital and outer space supports environmental protection and peace.

f. Recognize that peace is the wholeness created by right relationships with oneself, other persons, other cultures, other life, Earth, and the larger whole of which all are a part.

THE WAY FORWARD

As never before in history, common destiny beckons us to see a new beginning. Such renewal is the promise of these Earth Charter Principles. To fulfill this promise, we must commit ourselves to adopt and promote the values and objectives of the Charter.

This requires a change of mind and heart. It requires a new sense of global interdependence and universal responsibility. We must imaginatively develop and apply the vision of a sustainable way of life locally, nationally, regionally, and globally. Our cultural diversity is a precious heritage and different cultures will find their own distinctive ways to realize the vision. We must deepen and expand the global dialogue that generated the Earth Charter, for we have much to learn from the ongoing collaborative search for truth and wisdom.

Life often involves tensions between important values. This can mean difficult choices. However, we must find ways to harmonize diversity with unity, the exercise of freedom with the common good, short-term objectives with long-term goals. Every individual, family, organization, and community has a vital role to play. The arts, sciences, religions, educational institutions, media, businesses, nongovernmental organizations, and governments are all called to offer creative leadership. The partnership of government, civil society, and business is essential for effective governance.

In order to build a sustainable global community, the nations of the world must renew their commitment to the United Nations, fulfill their obligations under existing international agreements, and support the implementation of Earth Charter principles with an international legally binding instrument on environment and development.

Let ours be a time remembered for the awakening of a new reverence for life, the firm resolve to achieve sustainability, the quickening of the struggle for justice and peace, and the joyful celebration of life.

72   Just Garbage: The Problem of Environmental Racism

PETER S. WENZ

Peter S. Wenz is professor of philosophy at the University of Illinois at Springfield and the author of several works in environmental ethics, including his books *Environmental Justice* (1988), *Nature's Keeper* (1996), and *Environmental Ethics for Everyone* (2000).

In this essay, Wenz argues that it is unjust for poor people, whether or not they are predominantly minorities, to be exposed disproportionately to pollution and other locally undesirable land uses (LULUs). He proposes a system whereby all communities must earn equal pollution points that cannot be bought and sold on the market. This would prevent rich people from buying their way out of exposure to environmental degradation and influence decision makers (who come mostly from economically advantaged groups) to reduce overall pollution to protect themselves and their families.

Environmental racism is evident in practices that expose racial minorities in the United States, and people of color around the world, to disproportionate shares of environmental hazards. These include toxic chemicals in factories, toxic herbicides and pesticides in agriculture, radiation from uranium mining, lead from paint on older buildings, toxic wastes illegally dumped, and toxic waster legally stored. In this chapter, which concentrates on issues of toxic waste, both illegally dumped and legally stored, I will examine the justness of current practices as well as the arguments commonly given in their defense. I will then propose an alternative practice that is consistent with prevailing principles of justice.

A DEFENSE OF CURRENT PRACTICES

Defenders often claim that because economic, not racial, considerations account for disproportionate impacts of nonwhites, current practices are neither racist nor morally objectionable. Their reasoning recalls the Doctrine of Double Effect. According to that doctrine, an effect whose production is usually blameworthy becomes blameless when it is incidental to, although predictably conjoined with, the production of another effect whose production is morally justified. The classic case concerns a pregnant woman with uterine cancer. A common, acceptable treatment for uterine cancer is hysterectomy. This will predictably end the pregnancy, as would an abortion. However, Roman Catholic scholars who usually consider abortion blameworthy consider it blameless in this context because it is merely incidental to hysterectomy, which is morally justified to treat uterine cancer. The hysterectomy would be performed in the absence of pregnancy, so the abortion effect is produced neither as an end-in-itself, nor as a means to reach the desired end, which is the cure of cancer.

Defenders of practices that disproportionately disadvantage nonwhites seem to claim, in keeping with the Doctrine of Double Effect, that racial effects are blameless because they are sought neither as ends-in-themselves nor as means to reach a desired goal. They are merely predictable side effects of economic and political practices that disproportionately expose poor people to toxic substances. The argument is that burial of toxic wastes, and other locally undesirable land uses

Reprinted with permission from *Faces of Environmental Racism* by Laura Westra and Peter S. Wentz (Lanham, MD: Rowman & Littlefield, 1995). Notes edited.

(LULUs), lower property values. People who can afford to move elsewhere do so. They are replaced by buyers (or renters) who are predominately poor and cannot afford housing in more desirable areas. Law professor Vicki Been puts it this way: "As long as the market allows the existing distribution of wealth to allocate goods and services, it would be surprising indeed if, over the long run, LULUs did not impose a disproportionate burden upon the poor." People of color are disproportionately burdened due primarily to poverty, not racism.[1] This defense against charges of racism is important in the American context because racial discrimination is illegal in the United States in circumstances where economic discrimination is permitted.[2] Thus, legal remedies to disproportionate exposure of nonwhites to toxic wastes are available if racism is the cause, but not if people of color are exposed merely because they are poor.

There is strong evidence against claims of racial neutrality. Professor Been acknowledges that even if there is no racism in the process of siting LULUs, racism plays at least some part in the disproportionate exposure of African Americans to them. She cites evidence that "racial discrimination in the sale and rental of housing relegates people of color (especially African Americans) to the least desirable neighborhoods, regardless of their income level."[3]

Without acknowledging for a moment, then, that racism plays no part in the disproportionate exposure of nonwhites to toxic waste, I will ignore this issue to display a weakness in the argument that justice is served when economic discrimination alone is influential. I claim that even if the only discrimination is economic, justice requires redress and significant alteration of current practices. Recourse to the Doctrine of Double Effect presupposes that the primary effect, with which a second effect is incidentally conjoined, is morally justifiable. In the classic case, abortion is justified only because hysterectomy is justified as treatment for uterine cancer. I argue that disproportionate impacts on poor people violate principles of distributive justice, and so are not morally justifiable in the first place. Thus, current practices disproportionately exposing nonwhites to toxic substances are not

justifiable even if incidental to the exposure of poor people.

Alternate practices that comply with acceptable principles of distributive justice are suggested below. They would largely solve problems of environmental racism (disproportionate impacts on nonwhites) while ameliorating the injustice of disproportionately exposing poor people to toxic hazards. They would also discourage production of toxic substances, thereby reducing humanity's negative impact on the environment.

THE PRINCIPLE OF COMMENSURATE BURDENS AND BENEFIT

We usually assume that, other things being equal, those who derive benefits should sustain commensurate burdens. We typically associate the burden of work with the benefit of receiving money, and the burdens of monetary payment and tort liability with the benefits of ownership.

There are many exceptions. For example, people can inherit money without working, and be given ownership without purchase. Another exception, which dissociates the benefit of ownership from the burden of tort liability, is the use of tax money to protect the public from hazards associated with private property, as in Superfund legislation. Again, the benefit of money is dissociated from the burden of work when governments support people who are unemployed.

The fact that these exceptions require justification, however, indicates an abiding assumption that people who derive benefits should shoulder commensurate burdens. The ability to inherit without work is justified as a benefit owed to those who wish to bequeath their wealth (which someone in the line of inheritance is assumed to have shouldered burdens to acquire). The same reasoning applies to gifts.

Using tax money (public money) to protect the public from dangerous private property is justified as encouraging private industry and commerce, which are supposed to increase public wealth. The system also protects victims in case private owners become bankrupt as, for example, in Times Beach, Missouri, where the government bought homes made worthless due to dioxin pollution. The company responsible for the pollution was bankrupt.

Tax money is used to help people who are out of work to help them find a job, improve their credentials, or feed their children. This promotes economic growth and equal opportunity. These exceptions prove the rule by the fact that justification for any deviation from the commensuration of benefits and burdens is considered necessary.

Further indication of an abiding belief that benefits and burdens should be commensurate is grumbling that, for example, many professional athletes and corporate executives are overpaid. Although the athletes and executives shoulder the burden of work, the complaint is that their benefits are disproportionate to their burdens. People on welfare are sometimes criticized for receiving even modest amounts of taxpayer money without shouldering the burdens of work, hence recurrent calls for "welfare reform." Even though these calls are often justified as means to reducing government budget deficits, the moral issue is more basic than the economic. Welfare expenditures are minor compared to other programs, and alternatives that require poor people to work are often more expensive than welfare as we know it.

The principle of commensuration between benefits and burdens is not the only moral principle governing distributive justice, and may not be the most important, but it is basic. Practices can be justified by showing them to conform, all things considered, to this principle. Thus, there is no move to "reform" the receipt of moderate pay for ordinary work, because it exemplifies the principle. On the other hand, practices that do not conform are liable to attack and require alternate justification, as we have seen in the cases of inheritance, gifts, Superfund legislation, and welfare.

Applying the principle of commensuration between burdens and benefits to the issue at hand yields the following: In the absence of countervailing considerations, the burdens of ill health associated with toxic hazards should be related to benefits derived from processes and products that create these hazards.

TOXIC HAZARDS AND CONSUMERISM

In order to assess, in light of the principle of commensuration between benefits and burdens, the justice of current distributions of toxic hazards, the benefits of their generation must be considered. Toxic wastes result from many manufacturing processes, including those for a host of common items and materials, such as paint, solvents, plastics, and most petrochemical-based materials. These materials surround us in the paint on our homes, in our refrigerator containers, in our clothing, in our plumbing, in our garbage pails, and elsewhere.

Toxins are released into the environment in greater quantities now than ever before because we now have a consumer-oriented society where the acquisition, use, and disposal of individually owned items is greatly desired. We associate the numerical dollar value of the items at our disposal with our "standard of living," and assume that a higher standard is conducive to, if not identical with, a better life. So toxic wastes needing disposal are produced as by-products of the general pursuit of what our society defines as valuable, that is, the consumption of material goods.

Our economy requires increasing consumer demand to keep people working (to produce what is demanded). This is why there is concern each Christmas season, for example, that shoppers may not buy enough. If demand is insufficient, people may be put out of work. Demand must increase, not merely hold steady, because commercial competition improves labor efficiency in manufacture (and now in the service sector as well), so fewer workers can produce desired items. More items must be desired to forestall labor efficiency-induced unemployment, which is grave in a society where people depend primarily on wages to secure life's necessities.

Demand is kept high largely by convincing people that their lives require improvement, which consumer purchases will effect. When improvements are seen as needed, not merely desired, people purchase more readily. So our culture encourages economic expansion by blurring the distinction between wants and needs.

One way the distinction is blurred is through promotion of worry. If one feels insecure without the desired item or service, and so worries about life without it, then its provision is easily seen as a need. Commercials, and other shapers of social expectations, keep people worried by adjusting downward toward the trivial what people are expected to worry about. People worry about the provision of food, clothing, and housing without much inducement. When these basic needs are satisfied, however, attention shifts to indoor plumbing, for example, then to stylish indoor plumbing. The process continues with need for a second or third bathroom, a kitchen disposal, and a refrigerator attached to the plumbing so that ice is made automatically in the freezer, and cold water can be obtained without even opening the refrigerator door. The same kind of progression results in cars with CD players, cellular phones, and automatic readouts of average fuel consumption per mile.

Abraham Maslow was not accurately describing people in our society when he claimed that after physiological, safety, love, and (self-) esteem needs are met, people work toward self-actualization, becoming increasingly their own unique selves by fully developing their talents. Maslow's Hierarchy of Needs describes people in our society less than Wenz's Lowerarchy of Worry. When one source of worry is put to rest by an appropriate purchase, some matter less inherently or obviously worrisome takes its place as the focus of concern. Such worry-substitution must be amenable to indefinite repetition in order to motivate purchases needed to keep the economy growing without inherent limit. If commercial society is supported by consumer demand, it is worry all the way down. Toxic wastes are produced in this context.

People tend to worry about ill health and early death without much inducement. These concerns are heightened in a society dependent upon the production of worry, so expenditure on health care consumes an increasing percentage of the gross domestic product. As knowledge of health impairment due to toxic substances increases, people are decreasingly tolerant of risks associated with their proximity. Thus, the same mindset of worry that elicits production that generates toxic wastes, exacerbates reaction to their proximity. The result is a desire for their placement elsewhere, hence the NIMBY syndrome—Not In My Back Yard. On this account, NIMBYism is not aberrantly selfish behavior, but integral to the cultural value system required for great volumes of toxic waste to be generated in the first place.

Combined with the principle of Commensurate Burdens and Benefits, that value system indicates who should suffer the burden of proximity to toxic wastes. Other things being equal, those who benefit most from the production of waste should shoulder the greatest share of burdens associated with its disposal. In our society, consumption of goods is valued highly and constitutes the principal benefit associated with the generation of toxic wastes. Such consumption is generally correlated with income and wealth. So other things being equal, justice requires that people's proximity to toxic wastes be related positively to their income and wealth. This is exactly opposite to the predominant tendency in our society, where poor people are more proximate to toxic wastes dumped illegally and stored legally.

REJECTED THEORIES OF JUSTICE

Proponents of some theories of distributive justice may claim that current practices are justified. In this section I will explore such claims.

A widely held view of justice is that all people deserve to have their interests given equal weight. John Rawls's popular thought experiment in which people choose principles of justice while ignorant of their personal identities dramatizes the importance of equal consideration of interests. Even selfish people behind the "veil of ignorance" in Rawls's "original position" would choose to accord equal consideration to everyone's interests because, they reason, they may themselves be the victims of any inequality. Equal consideration is a basic moral premise lacking serious challenge in our culture, so it is presupposed in what follows. Disagreement centers on application of the principle.

LIBERTARIANISM

Libertarians claim that each individual has an equal right to be free of interference from other people. All burdens imposed by other people are unjustified unless part of, or consequent upon, agreement by the party being burdened. So no individual who has not consented should be burdened by burial of toxic wastes (or the emission of air pollutants, or the use of agricultural pesticides, etc.) that may increase risks of disease, disablement, or death. Discussing the effects of air pollution, libertarian Murray Rothbard writes, "The remedy is simply to enjoin anyone from injecting pollutants into the air, and thereby invading the rights of persons and property. Period."[4] Libertarians John Hospers and Tibor R. Machan seem to endorse Rothbard's position.[5]

The problem is that implementation of this theory is impractical and unjust in the context of our civilization. Industrial life as we know it inevitably includes production of pollutants and toxic substances that threaten human life and health. It is impractical to secure the agreement of every individual to the placement, whether on land, in the air, or in water, of every chemical that may adversely affect the life or health of the individuals in question. After being duly informed of the hazard, someone potentially affected is bound to object, making the placement illegitimate by libertarian criteria.

In effect, libertarians give veto power to each individual over the continuation of industrial society. This seems a poor way to accord equal consideration to everyone's interests because the interest in physical safety of any one individual is allowed to override all other interests of all other individuals in the continuation of modern life. Whether or not such life is worth pursuing, it seems unjust to put the decision for everyone in the hands of any one person.

UTILITARIANISM

Utilitarians consider the interests of all individuals equally, and advocate pursuing courses of action that promise to produce results containing the greatest (net) sum of good. However, irrespective of how "good" is defined, problems with utilitarian accounts of justice are many and notorious.

Utilitarianism suffers in part because its direct interest is exclusively in the sum total of good, and in the future. Since the sum of good is all that counts in utilitarianism, there is no guarantee that the good of some will not be sacrificed for the greater good of others. Famous people could receive (justifiably according to utilitarians) particularly harsh sentences for criminal activity to effect general deterrence. Even when fame results from honest pursuits, a famous felon's sentence is likely to attract more attention than sentences in other cases of similar criminal activity. Because potential criminals are more likely to respond to sentences in such cases, harsh punishment is justified for utilitarian reasons on grounds that are unrelated to the crime.

Utilitarianism suffers in cases like this not only from its exclusive attention to the sum total of good, but also from its exclusive preoccupation with future consequences, which makes the relevance of past conduct indirect. This affects not only retribution, but also reciprocity and gratitude, which utilitarians endorse only to produce the greatest sum of future benefits. The direct relevance of past agreements and benefits, which common sense assumes, disappears in utilitarianism. So does direct application of the principle of Commensurate Burdens and Benefits.

The merits of the utilitarian rejection of common sense morality need not be assessed, however, because utilitarianism seems impossible to put into practice. Utilitarian support for any particular conclusion is undermined by the inability of anyone actually to perform the kinds of calculations that utilitarians profess to use. Whether the good is identified with happiness or preference-satisfaction, the two leading contenders at the moment, utilitarians announce the conclusions of their calculations without ever being able to show the calculation itself.

When I was in school, math teachers suspected that students who could never show their work were copying answers from other students. I suspect similarly that utilitarians, whose "calculations" often support conclusions that others reach by recourse to principles of gratitude, retributive justice, commensuration between burdens and benefits, and so forth, reach conclusions on grounds of intuitions influenced predominantly by these very principles.

Utilitarians may claim that, contrary to superficial appearances, these principles are themselves supported by utilitarian calculations. But, again, no one has produced a relevant calculation. Some principles seem *prima facie* opposed to utilitarianism, such as the one prescribing special solicitude of parents for their own children. It would seem that in cold climates more good would be produced if people bought winter coats for needy children, instead of special dress coats and ski attire for their own children. But utilitarians defend the principle of special parental concern. They declare this principle consistent with utilitarianism by appeal to entirely untested, unsubstantiated assumptions about counterfactuals. It is a kind of "Just So" story that explains how good is maximized by adherence to current standards. There is no calculation at all.

Another indication that utilitarians cannot perform the calculations they profess to rely upon concerns principles whose worth are in genuine dispute. Utilitarians offer no calculations that help to settle the matter. For example, many people wonder today whether or not patriotism is a worthy moral principle. Detailed utilitarian calculations play no part in the discussion.

These are some of the reasons why utilitarianism provides no help to those deciding whether or not disproportionate exposure of poor people to toxic wastes is just.

Free Market Approach

Toxic wastes, a burden, could be placed where residents accept them in return for monetary payment, a benefit. Since market transactions often satisfactorily commensurate burdens and benefits, this approach may seem to honor the principle of commensuration between burdens and benefits.

Unlike many market transactions, however, whole communities, acting as corporate bodies, would have to contract with those seeking to bury wastes. Otherwise, any single individual in the community could veto the transaction,

resulting in the impasse attending libertarian approaches.[6] Communities could receive money to improve such public facilities as schools, parks, and hospitals, in addition to obtaining tax revenues and jobs that result ordinarily from business expansion.

The major problem with this free market approach is that it fails to accord equal consideration to everyone's interests. Where basic or vital goods and services are at issue, we usually think equal consideration of interests requires ameliorating inequalities of distribution that markets tend to produce. For example, one reason, although not the only reason, for public education is to provide every child with the basic intellectual tools necessary for success in our society. A purely free market approach, by contrast, would result in excellent education for children of wealthy parents and little or no education for children of the nation's poorest residents. Opportunities for children of poor parents would be so inferior that we would say the children's interests had not been given equal consideration.

The reasoning is similar where vital goods are concerned. The United States has the Medicaid program for poor people to supplement market transactions in health care precisely because equal consideration of interests requires that everyone be given access to health care. The 1994 health care debate in the United States was, ostensibly, about how to achieve universal coverage, not about whether or not justice required such coverage. With the exception of South Africa, every other industrialized country already has universal coverage for health care. Where vital needs are concerned, markets are supplemented or avoided in order to give equal consideration to everyone's interests.

Another example concerns military service in time of war. The United States employed conscription during the Civil War, both world wars, the Korean War, and the war in Vietnam. When the national interest requires placing many people in mortal danger, it is considered just that exposure be largely unrelated to income and market transactions.

The United States does not currently provide genuine equality in education or health care, nor did universal conscription (of males) put all men at equal risk in time of war. In all three areas, advantage accrues to those with greater income and wealth. (During the Civil War, paying for a substitute was legal in many cases.) Imperfection in practice, however, should not obscure general agreement in theory that justice requires equal consideration of interests, and that such equal consideration requires rejecting purely free market approaches where basic or vital needs are concerned.

Toxic substances affect basic and vital interests. Lead, arsenic, and cadmium in the vicinity of children's homes can result in mental retardation of the children.[7] Navaho teens exposed to radiation from uranium mine tailings have seventeen times the national average of reproductive organ cancer.[8] Environmental Protection Agency (EPA) officials estimate that toxic air pollution in areas of South Chicago increases cancer risks one hundred to one thousand times.[9] Pollution from Otis Air Force base in Massachusetts is associated with alarming increases in cancer rates.[10] Non-Hodgkin's Lymphoma is related to living near stone, clay, and glass industry facilities, and leukemia is related to living near chemical and petroleum plants.[11] In general, cancer rates are higher in the United States near industries that use toxic substances and discard them nearby.[12]

In sum, the placement of toxic wastes affects basic and vital interests just as do education, health care, and wartime military service. Exemption from market decisions is required to avoid unjust impositions on the poor, and to respect people's interests equally. A child dying of cancer receives little benefit from the community's new swimming pool.

COST-BENEFIT ANALYSIS (CBA)

CBA is an economist's version of utilitarianism, where the sum to be maximized is society's wealth, as measured in monetary units, instead of happiness or preference satisfaction. Society's wealth is computed by noting (and estimating where necessary) what people are willing to pay for goods and services. The more people are willing to pay for what exists in society, the better off society is, according to CBA.

CBA will characteristically require placement of toxic wastes near poor people. Such placement usually lowers land values (what people are willing to pay for property). Land that is already cheap, where poor people live, will not lose as much value as land that is currently expensive, where wealthier people live, so a smaller loss of social wealth attends placement of toxic wastes near poor people. This is just the opposite of what the Principle of Commensurate Burdens and Benefits requires.

The use of CBA also violates equal consideration of interests, operating much like free market approaches. Where a vital concern is at issue, equal consideration of interests requires that people be considered irrespective of income. The placement of toxic wastes affects vital interests. Yet CBA would have poor people exposed disproportionately to such wastes.[13]

In sum, libertarianism, utilitarianism, free market distribution, and cost-benefit analysis are inadequate principles and methodologies to guide the just distribution of toxic wastes.

LULU POINTS

An approach that avoids these difficulties assigns points to different types of locally undesirable land uses (LULUs) and requires that all communities earn LULU points.[14] In keeping with the Principle of Commensurate Benefits and Burdens, wealthy communities would be required to earn more LULU points than poorer ones. Communities would be identified by currently existing political divisions, such as villages, towns, city wards, cities, and counties.

Toxic waste dumps are only one kind of LULU. Others include prisons, half-way houses, municipal waste sites, low-income housing, and power plants, whether nuclear or coal fired. A large deposit of extremely toxic waste, for example, may be assigned twenty points when properly buried but fifty points when illegally dumped. A much smaller deposit of properly buried toxic waste may be assigned only ten points, as may a coal-fired power plant. A nuclear power plant may be assigned twenty-five points, while municipal waste sites are only five points, and one hundred units of low-income housing are eight points.

These numbers are only speculations. Points would be assigned by considering probable effects of different LULUs on basic needs, and responses to questionnaires investigating people's levels of discomfort with LULUs of various sorts. Once numbers are assigned, the total number of LULU points to be distributed in a given time period could be calculated by considering planned development and needs for prisons, power plants, low-income housing, and so on. One could also calculate points for a community's already existing LULUs. Communities could then be required to host LULUs in proportion to their income or wealth, with new allocation of LULUs (and associated points) correcting for currently existing deviations from the rules of proportionality.

Wherever significant differences of wealth or income exist between two areas, these areas should be considered part of different communities if there is any political division between them. Thus, a county with rich and poor areas would not be considered a single community for purposes of locating LULUs. Instead, villages or towns may be so considered. A city with rich and poor areas may similarly be reduced to its wards. The purpose of segregating areas of different income or wealth from one another is to permit the imposition of greater LULU burdens on wealthier communities. When wealthy and poor areas are considered as one larger community, there is the danger that the community will earn its LULU points by placing hazardous waste near its poorer members. This possibility is reduced when only relatively wealthy people live in a smaller community that must earn LULU points.

PRACTICAL IMPLICATIONS

Political strategy is beyond the scope of this . . . , so I will refrain from commenting on problems and prospects for securing passage and implementation of the foregoing proposal. I maintain that the proposal is just. In a society where injustice is common, it is no surprise that proposals for rectifications meet stiff resistance.

Were the LULU points proposal implemented, environmental racism would be reduced enormously. To the extent that poor people exposed to environmental hazards are members of racial minorities, relieving the poor of disproportionate exposure would also relieve people of color.

This is not to say that environmental racism would be ended completely. Implementation of the proposal requires judgment in particular cases. Until racism is itself ended, such judgment will predictably be exercised at times to the disadvantage of minority populations. However, because most people of color currently burdened by environmental racism are relatively poor, implementing the proposal would remove 80 to 90 percent of the effects of environmental racism. While efforts to end racism at all levels should continue, reducing the burdens of racism is generally advantageous to people of color. Such reductions are especially worthy when integral to policies that improve distributive justice generally.

Besides improving distributive justice and reducing the burdens of environmental racism, implementing the LULU points proposal would benefit life on earth generally by reducing the generation of toxic hazards. When people of wealth, who exercise control of manufacturing processes, marketing campaigns, and media coverage, are themselves threatened disproportionately by toxic hazards, the culture will evolve quickly to find their production largely unnecessary. It will be discovered, for example, that many plastic items can be made of wood, just as it was discovered in the late 1980s that the production of many ozone-destroying chemicals is unnecessary. Similarly, necessity being the mother of invention, it was discovered during World War II that many women could work in factories. When certain interests are threatened, the impossible does not even take longer.

The above approach to environmental injustice should, of course, be applied internationally and intranationally within all countries. The same considerations of justice condemn universally, all other things being equal, exposing poor people to vital dangers whose generation predominantly benefits the rich. This implies that rich countries should not ship their toxic wastes to poor countries. Since many poorer countries, such as those in Africa, are inhabited primarily by nonwhites, prohibiting shipments of toxic wastes to them would reduce significantly worldwide environmental racism. A prohibition on such shipments would also discourage production of dangerous wastes, as it would require people in rich countries to live with whatever dangers they create. If the principle of LULU points were applied in all countries, including poor ones, elites in those countries would lose interest in earning foreign currency credits through importation of waste, as they would be disproportionately exposed to imported toxins.

In sum, we could reduce environmental injustice considerably through a general program of distributive justice concerning environmental hazards. Pollution would not thereby be eliminated, since to live is to pollute. But such a program would motivate significant reduction in the generation of toxic wastes, and help the poor, especially people of color, as well as the environment.

NOTES

1. Vicki Been, "Market Forces, Not Racist Practices, May Affect the Siting of Locally Undesirable Land Uses," in *At Issue: Environmental Justice,* ed. by Jonathan Petrikin (San Diego, Calif.: Greenhaven Press, 1995), 41.
2. See *San Antonio Independent School District v. Rodriguez,* 411 R.S. 1 (1973) and *Village of Arlington Heights v. Metropolitan Housing Development Corporation,* 429 U.S. 252 (1977).
3. Been, 41.
4. Murray Rothbard, "The Great Ecology Issue," *The Individualist* 21, no. 2 (February 1970): 5.
5. See Peter S. Wenz, *Environmental Justice* (Albany, N.Y.: State University of New York Press, 1988), 65–67 and associated endnotes.
6. Christopher Boerner and Thomas Lambert, "Environmental Justice Can Be Achieved Through Negotiated Compensation," in *At Issue: Environmental Justice.*
7. F. Diaz-Barriga et al., "Arsenic and Cadmium Exposure in Children Living Near to Both Zinc and Copper Smelters," summarized in *Archives of Environmental Health* 46, no. 2 (March/April 1991): 119.
8. Dick Russell, "Environmental Racism," *Amicus Journal* (Spring 1989): 22–32, 34.
9. Marianne Lavelle, "The Minorities Equation," *National Law Journal* 21 (September 1992): 3.
10. Christopher Hallowell, "Water Crisis on the Cape," *Audubon* (July/August 1991): 65–74, especially 66 and 70.
11. Athena Linos et al., "Leukemia and Non-Hodgkin's Lymphoma and Residential Proximity to Industrial Plants," *Archives of Environmental Health* 46, no. 2 (March/April 1991): 70–74.
12. L. W. Pickle et al., *Atlas of Cancer Mortality among Whites:* 1950–1980, HHS publication #(NIH) 87–2900 (Washington, D.C.: U.S. Department of Health and Human Services, Government Printing Office: 1987).
13. Wenz, 216–18.
14. The idea of LULU points comes to me from Frank J. Popper, "LULUs and Their Blockage," in *Confronting Regional Challenges: Approaches to LULUs, Growth, and Other Vexing Governance Problems,* ed. by Joseph DiMento and Le Roy Graymer (Los Angeles, Calif.: Lincoln Institute of Land Policy, 1991), 13–27, especially 24.

✿ STUDY QUESTIONS

1. If, as Wenz suggests, cost should not determine where toxic sites are located, what should the criterion be?
2. Wenz suggests that in general those who derive benefits from public policy should be the same ones who sustain the burdens associated with that policy. If you apply that principle to such social practices as nuclear power, industrial pollution, wilderness preservation, and the growth of agribusiness, what is the result?
3. What does Wenz mean by LULU points? Do you find his proposal reasonable? Practical?
4. Can you develop a response to Wenz's rejection of free market theories of justice?
5. Would it be just for an impoverished community to accept toxic waste for pay? Should poor communities be free to accept a disproportionate burden for compensation?

73   Deceiving the Third World: The Myth of Catching-Up Development

MARIA MIES

Maria Mies is professor of sociology in the Fachachhochscchule in Cologne and an environmental activist.

In this essay she challenges the idea that economic growth is the way for the poorer, southern countries to catch up with the richer, northern countries. Mies puts forth a case that the catch-up policy is both impossible and undesirable.

Virtually all development strategies are based on the explicit or implicit assumption that the model of "the good life" is that prevailing in the affluent societies of the North: the USA, Europe and Japan. The question of how the poor in the North, those in the countries of the South, and peasants and women worldwide may attain this "good life" is usually answered in terms of what, since Rostow, can be called the "catching-up development" path. This means that by following the same path of industrialization, technological progress and capital accumulation taken by Europe and the USA and Japan the same goal can be reached. These affluent countries and classes, the dominant sex—the men—the dominant urban centres and lifestyles are then perceived as the realized utopia of liberalism, a utopia still to be attained by those who apparently still lag behind. Undoubtedly the industrialized countries' affluence is the source of great fascination to all who are unable to share in it. The so-called "socialist" countries' explicit aim was to catch up, and even to overtake capitalism. After the breakdown of socialism in Eastern Europe, particularly East Germany, the aim is now to quickly catch up with the lifestyle of the so-called market economies, the prototype of which is seen in the USA or West Germany.

A brief look at the history of the underdeveloped countries and regions of the South but also at present day East Europe and East Germany can

teach us that this catching-up development path is a myth: nowhere has it led to the desired goal.

This myth is based on an evolutionary, linear understanding of history. In this concept of history the peak of the evolution has already been reached by some, namely, men generally, white men in particular, industrial countries, urbanites. The "others"—women, brown and black people, "underdeveloped" countries, peasants—will also reach this peak with a little more effort, more education, more "development." Technological progress is seen as the driving force of this evolutionary process. It is usually ignored that, even in the early 1970s, the catching-up development theory was criticized by a number of writers. Andre Gunder Frank, Samir Amin, Johan Galtung, and many others have shown that the poverty of the underdeveloped nations is not as a result of "natural" lagging behind but the direct consequence of the overdevelopment of the rich industrial countries who exploit the so-called periphery in Africa, South America and Asia. In the course of this colonial history, which continues today, these areas were progressively underdeveloped and made dependent on the so-called metropolis. The relationship between these overdeveloped centres or metropoles and the underdeveloped peripheries is a colonial one. Today, a similar colonial relationship exists between Man and Nature, between men and women, between urban and rural areas. We have called

Maria Mies and Vandana Shiva. *Ecofeminism*. London: Zed Books, 1993. Reprinted with permission. Notes deleted.

these the colonies of White Man. In order to maintain such relationships force and violence are always essential.

But the emotional and cognitive acceptance of the colonized is also necessary to stabilize such relationships. This means that not only the colonizers but also the colonized must accept the lifestyle of "those on top" as the only model of the good life. This process of acceptance of the values, lifestyle and standard of living of "those on top" is invariably accompanied by a devaluation of one's own: one's own culture, work, technology, lifestyle and often also philosophy of life and social institutions. In the beginning this devaluation is often violently enforced by the colonizers and then reinforced by propaganda, educational programmes, a change of laws, and economic dependency, for example, through the debt trap. Finally, this devaluation is often accepted and internalized by the colonized as the "natural" state of affairs. One of the most difficult problems for the colonized (countries, women, peasants) is to develop their own identity after a process of formal decolonization—identity no longer based on the model of the colonizer as the image of the true human being; a problem addressed by Fanon, Memmi, Freire, and Blaise. To survive, wrote Memmi, the colonized must oppress the colonization. But to become a true human being he/she, him/herself, must oppress the colonized which, within themselves, they have become. This means that he/she must overcome the fascination exerted by the colonizer and his lifestyle and re-evaluate what he/she is and does.

To promote the elimination of the colonizers from within the colonized, it is useful to look more closely at the catching-up development myth.

It may be argued that those who have so far paid the price for development also look up to those at the top as their model of the future, as their concrete utopia; that this is a kind of universal law. But if we also consider the price nature had to pay for this model, a price that now increasingly affects people in the affluent societies too, it may be asked why do not these people question this myth? Because even in the North, the paradigm of unlimited growth of science and technology, goods and services—of capital—and GNP have led to an increasing deterioration in the environment, and subsequently the quality of life.

DIVIDE AND RULE: MODERN INDUSTRIAL SOCIETY'S SECRET

Most people in the affluent societies live in a kind of schizophrenic or "double-think" state. They are aware of the disasters of Bhopal and Chernobyl, of the "greenhouse" effect, the destruction of the ozone layer, the gradual poisoning of ground-water, rivers and seas by fertilizers, pesticides, herbicides, as well as industrial waste, and that they themselves increasingly suffer the effects of air pollution, allergies, stress and noise, and the health risks due to industrially produced food. They also know that responsibility for these negative impacts on their quality of life lies in their own lifestyles and an economic system based on constant growth. And yet (except for very few) they fail to act on this knowledge by modifying their lifestyles.

One reason for this collective schizophrenia is the North's stubborn hope, even belief, that they can have their cake and eat it: ever more products from the chemical industry *and* clean air and water, more and more cars and no "greenhouse" effect; an ever increasing output of commodities, more fast- and processed-foods, more fancy packaging, more exotic, imported food *and* enjoy good health and solve the waste problem.

Most people expect science and technology to provide a solution to these dilemmas, rather than taking steps to limit their own consumption and production patterns. It is not yet fully realized that a high material living standard militates against a genuinely good quality of life, especially if problems of ecological destruction are clearly understood.

The belief, however, that a high material living standard is tantamount to a good or high quality of life is the ideological support essential to uphold and legitimize the constant growth and accumulation model of modern industrial society. Unless the masses of people accept this the system cannot last and function. This equation is the real ideological-political hegemony that overlies everyday life. No political party in the industrialized countries of the North dares question this schizophrenic equation, because they fear it would affect their election prospects.

We have already shown that this double-think is based on assumptions that there are no limits to our planet's resources, no limits to technological progress, no limits to space, to growth. But as, in fact, we inhabit a limited world, this limitlessness is mythical and can be upheld only by colonial divisions: between centres and peripheries, men and women, urban and rural areas, modern industrial societies of the North and "backward," "traditional," "underdeveloped" societies of the South. The relationship between these parts is hierarchical not egalitarian, and characterized by exploitation, oppression and dominance.

The economic reason for these colonial structures is, above all, the *externalization of costs* from the space and time horizon of those who profit from these divisions. The economic, social and ecological costs of constant growth in the industrialized countries have been and are shifted to the colonized countries of the South, to those countries'environment and their peoples. Only by dividing the international workforce into workers in the colonized peripheries and workers in the industrialized centres and by maintaining these relations of dominance even after formal decolonization, is it possible for industrial countries' workers to be paid wages ten times and more higher than those paid to workers in the South.

Much of the social costs of the reproduction of the labour force within industrial societies is externalized *within* those societies themselves. This is facilitated through the patriarchal-capitalist sexual division of labour whereby women's household labour is defined as non-productive or as non-work and hence not remunerated. Women are defined as housewives and their work is omitted from GNP calculations. Women can therefore be called the internal colony of this system.

The ecological costs of the industrial production of chemical fertilizers, pesticides, atomic energy, and of cars and other commodities, and the waste and damage for which they are responsible during both the production and the consumption process, are being inflicted on nature. They manifest themselves as air-, water-, soil-pollution and poisoning that will not only affect the present, but all future generations. This applies particularly to the long-term effects of modern high technology: atomic industry, genetic engineering, computer technology and their synergic effects which nobody can either predict or control. Thus, both nature and the future have been colonized for the short-term profit motives of affluent societies and classes.

The relationship between colonized and colonizer is based not on any measure of partnership but rather on the latter's coercion and violence in its dealings with the former. This relationship is in fact the secret of unlimited growth in the centres of accumulation. If externalization of all the costs of industrial production were not possible, if they had to be borne by the industrialized countries themselves, that is if they were internalized, an immediate end to unlimited growth would be inevitable.

CATCHING-UP IMPOSSIBLE AND UNDESIRABLE

The logic of this accumulation model, based on exploitation and colonizing divisions, implies that anything like "catching-up development" is impossible for the colonies, for all colonies. This is because just as one colony may, after much effort, attain what was considered the ultimate in "development," the industrial centres themselves have already "progressed" to a yet more "modern" stage of development; "development" here meaning technological progress. What today was the TV is tomorrow the colour TV, the day after the computer, then the ever more modern version of the "computer generation" and even later artificial intelligence machines and so forth. This catching-up policy of the colonies is therefore always a lost game. Because the very progress of the colonizers is based on the existence and the exploitation of those colonies.

These implications are usually ignored when development strategies are discussed. The aim, it is usually stated, is not a reduction in the industrialized societies' living standards but rather that all the "underdeveloped" should be enabled to attain the same level of affluence as in those societies. This sounds fine and corresponds to the values of the bourgeois revolutions: equality for all! But that such a demand is not only a logical, but also a material impossibility is ignored. The impossibility of this demand is obvious if one considers the ecological consequences of the universalization of the prevailing production system and lifestyle in the North's affluent industrial societies to everyone now living and for some further 30 years on this planet. If, for example, we note that the six per cent of the world's population who live in the USA annually consume 30 per cent of all the fossil energy produced, then, obviously, it is impossible for the rest of the world's population, of which about 80 per cent live in the poor countries of the South, to consume energy on the same scale.

According to Trainer, those living in the USA, Europe and Japan, consume three-quarters of the world's energy production. "If present world energy production were to be shared equally, Americans would have to get by on only one-fifth of the per capita amount they presently consume." Or, put differently, world population may be estimated at eleven billion people after the year 2050; if of these eleven billion people the per capita energy consumption was similar to that of Americans in the mid-1970s, conventional oil resources would be exhausted in 34–74 years; similar estimations are made for other resources.

But even if the world's resource base was unlimited it can be estimated that it would be around 500 years before the poor countries reached the living standard prevailing in the industrialized North; and then only if these countries abandoned the model of permanent economic growth, which constitutes the core of their economic philosophy. It is impossible for the South to "catch-up" with this model, not only because of the limits and inequitable consumption of the resource base, but above all, because this growth model is based on a colonial world order in which the gap between the two poles is increasing, especially as far as economic development is concerned.

These examples show that catching-up development is not possible for all. In my opinion, the powers that dominate today's world economy are aware of this, the managers of the transnational corporations, the World Bank, the IMF, the banks and governments of the club of the rich countries; and in fact they do not really want this universalization, because it would end their growth model. Tacitly, they accept that the colonial structure of the so-called market economy is maintained worldwide. This structure, however, is masked by such euphemisms as "North-South relations," "sustainable development," "threshold-countries" and so on which suggest that all poor countries can and will reach the same living standard as that of the affluent countries.

Yet, if one tries to disregard considerations of equity and of ecological concerns it may be asked if this model of the good life, pursued by the societies in the North, this paradigm of "catching-up development" has at least made people in the North happy. Has it fulfilled its promises there? Has it at least made women and children there more equal, more free, more happy? Has their quality of life improved while the GDP grew?

We read daily about an increase in homelessness and of poverty, particularly of women and children, of rising criminality in the big cities, of growing drug, and other addictions, including the addiction to shopping. Depression and suicides are on the increase in many of the affluent societies, and direct violence against women and children seems to be growing—both public and domestic violence as well as sexual abuse; the media are full of reports of all forms of violence. Additionally the urban centres are suffocating from motor vehicle exhaust emissions; there is barely any open space left in which to walk and breathe, the cities and highways are choked with cars Whenever possible people try to escape from these urban centres to seek relief in the countryside or in the poor South. If, as is commonly asserted, city-dwellers' quality of life is so high, why do they not spend their vacations in the cities?

It has been found that in the USA today the quality of life is lower than it was ten years ago.

There seems to be an inverse relationship between GDP and the quality of life; the more GDP grows, the more the quality of life deteriorates. For example: growing market forces have led to the fact that food, which so far was still prepared in the home is now increasingly bought from fast-food restaurants; preparing food has become a service, a commodity. If more and more people buy this commodity the GDP grows. But what also grows at the same time is the erosion of community, the isolation and loneliness of individuals, the indifference and atomization of the society. As Polanyi remarked, market forces destroy communities. Here, too, the processes are characterized by polarizations: the higher the GDP the lower the quality of life.

But "catching-up development" not only entails immaterial psychic and social costs and risks, which beset even the privileged in the rich countries and classes. With the growing number of ecological catastrophes—some man-made like the Gulf War or Chernobyl—material life also deteriorates in the rich centres of the world. The affluent society is one society which in the midst of plenty of commodities lacks the fundamental necessities of life: clean air, pure water, healthy food, space, time and quiet. What was experienced by mothers of small children after Chernobyl is now experienced by mothers in Kuwait. All the money of oil-rich Kuwait cannot buy people sunlight, fresh air, or pure water. This scarcity of basic common necessities for survival affects the poor and the rich, but with greater impact on the poor.

In short, the prevailing world market system, oriented towards unending growth and profit, cannot be maintained unless it can exploit external and internal colonies: nature, women and other people, but it also needs people as consumers who never say: "IT IS ENOUGH." The consumer model of the rich countries is not generalizable worldwide, neither is it desirable for the minority of the world's population who live in the affluent societies. Moreover, it will lead increasingly to wars to secure ever-scarcer resources; the Gulf War was in large part about the control of oil resources in that region. If we want to avoid such wars in the future the only alternative is a deliberate and drastic change in lifestyle, a reduction of consumption and a radical change in the North's consumer patterns and a decisive and broad-based movement towards energy conservation. . . .

These facts are widely known, but the myth of catching-up development is still largely the basis of development policies of the governments of the North and the South, as well as the ex-socialist countries. A TV discussion in which three heads of state participated—Robert Mugabe of Zimbabwe, Vaclav Havel of the CSFR, and Richard von Weizsacker, President of the then FRG—is a clear illustration of this. The discussion took place after a showing of the film *The March,* which depicted millions of starving Africans trying to enter rich Europe. The President of the FRG said quite clearly that the consumption patterns of the 20 per cent of the world's population who live in the affluent societies of the industrialized North are using 80 per cent of the world's resources, and that these consumption patterns would, in the long run, destroy the natural foundations of life—worldwide. When, however, he was asked, if it was not then correct to criticize and relinquish the North's consumption patterns and to warn the South against imitating the North he replied that it would be wrong to preach to people about reducing consumption. Moreover, people in the South had the right to the same living standard as those in the North. The only solution was to distribute more of "our" wealth, through development aid, to the poor in the South, to enable them to "catch-up." He did not mention that this wealth originated as a result of the North's plundering of the colonies, as has been noted.

The President of socialist Zimbabwe was even more explicit. He said that people in the South wanted as many cars, refrigerators, TV sets, computers, videos and the same standard of living as the people in the North; that this was the aim of his politics of development. Neither he nor von Weizsacker asked whether this policy of universalizing the North's consumption patterns through a catching-up strategy was materially feasible. They also failed to question the ecological consequences of such a policy. As elected heads of state they dared not tell the truth, namely that the lifestyle of the rich in the North cannot be universalized, and that it should be ended in these countries in order to uphold the values of an egalitarian world.

Despite these insights, however, the catching-up development myth remains intact in the erstwhile socialist countries of the East. Developments in East Germany, Poland and the ex-Soviet Union clearly demonstrate the resilience of this myth; but also the disaster that follows when the true nature of the "free" market economy becomes apparent. People in East Germany, the erstwhile GDR, were anxious to participate in the consumer model of capitalist FRG and, by voting for the destruction of their own state and the unification of Germany, hoped to become "equal." Political democracy, they were told, was the key to affluence. But they now realize, that in spite of political democracy and that they live in the same nation state as the West Germans, they are *de facto* treated as a cheap labour pool or a colony for West German capital, which is interested in expanding its market to the East but hesitates to invest there because the unification of Germany means that the East German workers will demand the same wages as their counterparts in West Germany. Where, then, is the incentive to go East? Less than a year after the unification, people in East Germany were already disappointed and depressed: unemployment had risen rapidly; the economy had virtually broken down; but no benefits had accrued from the new market system. According to the politicians, however, a period of common effort will be rewarded by catching-up with the West Germans. And, inevitably, the women in East Germany are worst affected by these processes. They who formerly had a participation rate of 90 per cent in the labour force are the first to lose their jobs, and more rapidly than men; they form the bulk of the unemployed. Simultaneously, they are losing whatever benefits the socialist state had provided for them: creches, a liberal abortion law, job security as mothers, time off for child-care, and so on.

But due to their disappointment with the socialist system people do not, yet, understand that this is the normal functioning of capitalism; that it needs colonies for its expansionism, that even democracy and formal equality do not result automatically in an equal standard of living or equal economic rewards.

In East Germany, the anger and the disappointment about what people call their betrayal by West German politicians, particularly Chancellor Kohl, has been converted into hostility towards other minorities, ethnic and racial minorities, foreign workers, other East Europeans, all of whom wanted to enter the "European House" and sit at the table of the rich.

In other parts of the world the collapse of the catching-up development myth leads to waves of fundamentalism and nationalism directed against religious, ethnic, racial, "others" within and outside their own territory. The main target of both nationalism and fundamentalism, and communalism, is women, because religious, ethnic and cultural identity are always based on a patriarchy, a patriarchal image of women, or rather control over "our" women, which, as we know from many examples, almost always amounts to more violence against women, more inequality for women. Moreover, the collapse of the myth of catching-up development results in a further militarization of men. Practically all the new nationalisms and fundamentalisms have led to virtual civil war in which young, militarized men play the key role. As unacceptable as equals by the rich men's club and unable to share their lifestyle they can only show their manhood—as it is understood in a patriarchal world—by shouldering a machine-gun.

The myth of catching-up development, therefore, eventually leads to further destruction of the environment, further exploitation of the "Third World," further violence against women and further militarization of men.

DOES CATCHING-UP DEVELOPMENT LIBERATE WOMEN?

. . . But more specifically let us ask why, for women, the catching-up development path even in the affluent societies of the industrialized North, is and will remain an illusion.

1. The promises of freedom, equality, self-determination of the individual, the great values of the French Revolution, proclaimed as universal rights and hence also meant for women, are betrayed for many women because all these rights

depend on the possession of property, and of money. Freedom is the freedom of those who possess money. Equality is the equality of money. Self-determination is the freedom of choice in the supermarket. This freedom, equality, self-determination is always dependent on those who control the money/property. And in the industrialized societies and nations they are mostly the husbands or the capitalists' state. This at least is the relationship between men and women that is protected by law; the man as breadwinner, the woman as housewife.

Self-determination and freedom are *de facto* limited for women, not only because they themselves are treated as commodities but also because, even if they possess money, they have no say in what is to be offered as commodities on the market. Their own desires and needs are constantly manipulated by those whose aim is to sell more and more goods. Ultimately, women are also persuaded that they want what the market offers.

2. This freedom, equality and self-determination, which depend on the possession of money, on purchasing power, cannot be extended to all women in the world. In Europe or the USA the system may be able to fulfil some of women's demand for equity with men, as far as income and jobs are concerned (or wages for housework, or a guaranteed minimum income), but only as long as it can continue the unrestricted exploitation of women as producers and consumers in the colonies. It cannot guarantee to *all* women worldwide the same standard of living as that of middle-class women in the USA or Europe. Only while women in Asia, Africa or Latin America can be forced to work for much lower wages than those in the affluent societies—and this is made possible through the debt trap—can enough capital be accumulated in the rich countries so that even unemployed women are guaranteed a minimum income, but all unemployed women in the world cannot expect this. Within a world system based on exploitation, "some are more equal than others."

3. This, however, also means that with such a structure there is no real material base for international women's solidarity. Because the core of individual freedom, equality, self-determination, linked to money and property, is the *self-interest*

of the individual and not altruism or solidarity; these interests will always compete with the self-interests of others. Within an exploitative structure interests will necessarily be antagonistic. It may be in the interest of Third World women, working in the garment industry for export, to get higher wages, or even wages equivalent to those paid in the industrialized countries; but if they actually received these wages then the working-class woman in the North could hardly afford to buy those garments, or buy as many of them as she does now. In her interest the price of these garments must remain low. Hence the interests of these two sets of women who are linked through the world market are antagonistic. If we do not want to abandon the aim of international solidarity and equality we must abandon the materialistic and self-centred approach to fighting only for our own interests. The interests' approach must be replaced by an ethical one.

4. To apply the principle of self-interest to the ecological problem leads to intensified ecological degradation and destruction in other parts of the world. This became evident after Chernobyl, when many women in Germany, desperate to know what to feed to their babies demanded the importation of unpolluted food from the Third World. One example of this is the poisoning of mothers' milk in the affluent countries by DDT and other toxic substances as a result of the heavy use of fertilizers, pesticides and insecticides in industrialized agriculture. Rachel Carson had already warned that poisoning the soil would eventually have its effect on people's food, particularly mothers' milk; now that this has happened many women in the North are alarmed. Some time ago a woman phoned me and said that in Germany it was no longer safe to breastfeed a baby for longer than three months; mothers' milk was poisoned. As a solution she suggested starting a project in South India for the production of safe and wholesome baby food. There, on the dry and arid Deccan Plateau, a special millet grows, called *ragi*. It needs little water and no fertilizer and is poor people's cheap subsistence food. This millet contains all the nutrients an infant needs. The woman suggested that ragi should be processed and canned as baby food and exported to Germany. This, she said, would

solve the problem of desperate mothers whose breast milk is poisoned and give the poor in South India a new source of money income. It would contribute to their development!

I tried to explain that if ragi, the subsistence food of the poor, entered the world market and became an export commodity it would no longer be available for the poor; its price would soar and that, provided the project worked, pesticides and other chemicals would soon be used to produce more ragi for the market in the North. But ragi production, she answered, would have to be controlled by people who would guarantee it was not polluted. This amounts to a new version of eco-colonialism. When I asked her, why as an alternative, she would not rather campaign in Germany for a change in the industrialized agriculture, for a ban

on the use of pesticides, she said that this would take too much time, that the poisoning of mothers' milk was an emergency situation. In her anxiety and concerned only with the interests of mothers in Germany she was willing to sacrifice the interests of poor women in South India. Or rather she thought that these conflicting interests could be made compatible by an exchange of money. She did not realize that this money would never suffice to buy the same healthy food for South Indian women's infants that they now had free of cost.

This example clearly shows that the myth of catching-up development, based on the belief of the miraculous workings of the market, particularly the world market, in fact leads to antagonistic interests even of mothers, who want only to give their infants unpolluted food.

&o STUDY QUESTIONS

1. Explain why Mies thinks the catch-up policy is a myth—both impossible and undesirable to obtain.
2. Evaluate the strength of Mies' arguments. Why are catch-up policies ill-conceived? Is it morally wrong

for poor countries to seek a higher standard of living?

3. What is Mies' alternative to catch-up policies? Do you agree with her? Explain your answer.

74   Environmental Risks, Rights, and the Failure of Liberal Democracy: Some Possible Remedies

LAURA WESTRA

A brief biography of Laura Westra appears at the beginning of Reading 71.
   In this article, Westra argues that democracies are failing to come to grips with environmental degradation. Traditional interpretations of rights, especially those of Judith Jarvis Thomson, fail to recognize the legitimate right not to be put at undue risk. Westra argues that this right can be defended and that political leaders must go beyond democracy in enforcing it. A rational risk response may require political activity that is revolutionary.

If you only have procedural democracy in a society that's exhibiting internal environmental stress and already has cleavages, say, ethnic cleavages, then procedural democracy will tend to aggravate these *problems and produce societal discord, rather than social concord.*

THOMAS HOMER-DIXON, 1996

DEMOCRACY IS NOT ENOUGH

The list of environmental assaults on the physical integrity of ecosystems and, through them, on our physical integrity and capacities occurs equally in affluent countries of North America and Western Europe and in developing ones of Southeast Asia. The global distribution of the threats, from remote islands in the Pacific Ocean (Colborn, Dumanoski, and Myers 1996) to "pristine" areas in the Arctic (Colborn 1996; Nikiforuk, 1996), demonstrate that geographic and political boundaries are not capable of containing and limiting environmental degradation and disintegrity. A careful study of the "hot spots" and locations where the worst hazards persist, shows that they are equally global in distribution. We cannot separate democracies from—say—military regimes and other nondemocratic states on the basis of the spread and severity of the environmental threats to which their citizens are exposed.

The "toxic doughnut" area in Chicago is a persistent threat to the life and health of residents (Gaylord and Bell 1995), although it is located in a country that prides itself on its status as the "land of the free" and that routinely allows its leaders and politicians to praise its democratic institutions, in contrast with other undesirable forms of government the world over. Equally hazardous, Royal Dutch Shell Oil's operation in Ogoniland, Nigeria, uses the dictatorship of General Sani Abbacha and his military clique to enforce the acceptance of extreme health hazards on its citizens. Of course, those who oppose these hazardous corporate activities in Nigeria are brutally and violently repressed or murdered, while the Chicago residents are not.

The U.S. residents, primarily minorities in most large cities (Westra and Wenz 1995; Bullard 1994), are not imprisoned or executed, and the army is not sent in to restrain and eliminate their protests. In some sense, their plight is therefore "better": They only suffer the physical harms imposed upon them by others, and their life and health are slowly, insidiously attacked and diminished. They only suffer from "ecoviolence"; they are not imprisoned and executed if they protest, as they might have been in Nigeria. But, in some sense, their plight is even worse. Ostensibly possessed of civil rights, basic education, access to information, and constitutional guarantees about freedom of choice, life, and the pursuit of happiness, they are manipulated instead to contribute willingly (but unknowingly) to their own plight. Aggressive advertising and marketing techniques render the products of modern technology not only extremely desirable but also "necessary" as things everyone should have—"free choices," though their corporate sponsors and originators employ "trade secret" and other hard-won rules and regulations to protect themselves while keeping citizens in the dark about the effects and consequences of their choices.

At the same time, public relation (PR) departments work steadily so that questions about the risks and harms imposed, and whether they are and should be truly offset by the so-called benefits available, are raised as rarely as possible. Further, as David Korten shows, two other severe problems arise in connection with the pursuit of economic gain through techno-corporate activities. The first is a clear attack on democracy, as independent PR firms are hired at great cost to generate "public movements" and campaigns, with the double aim of "selling" their ideas and preparing the public to accept and actively pursue certain products and services. The second problem is that legislative modifications, regulations, or deregulations favorable to business, are also sought.

The result of these activities is that "free democratic choices" are neither truly free nor truly democratic. Korten (1995) cites Washington journalist William Greider:

> [The corporations']...tremendous financial resources, the diversity of their interests, the squads of talented professionals—all these assets and some others—are now relentlessly focused on the politics of governing. This new institutional reality is the centerpiece in the breakdown of contemporary democracy. Corporations exist to pursue their own profit maximization, not the collective aspirations of the Society.

The problem is embedded in democracy in two senses:

1. Corporations are taken to be fictitious legal persons (French 1984) and are free to pursue their aims unless it can be proven (in the legal

sense) that some citizen or citizens are directly harmed by their chosen activities. Further, there is no overarching conception of "the good" for all that can be contrasted with *their* perception of the good, which is economic rather than intellectual or spiritual.

2. Moreover, because there is no "good" to guide public policy, aside from aggregate choices and preferences, and because the latter can be and in fact often is routinely manipulated and underinformed, the myth of "one man/one vote" remains a vague ideal, not a reality.

The justification often proposed to counterbalance these negative impacts centers on the "economic advantages" provided by multinational corporate giants. But, as we indicated in the Chicago example, the economic advantage is not evenly distributed or fairly apportioned among rich and poor: Moreover, if we shift to the global scene, even economic advances depend on "relative" rather than on "absolute" income. The Bruntlandt commission proposed a "3% global increase in per capita income." That would translate into a first-year per-capita increase (in U.S. dollars) of $633 for the United States and, among others, $3.60 for Ethiopia. After 10 years, the respective figures would be $7,257 for the United States and $41 for Ethiopia: a vast advantage for the "haves" over the "have nots." Korten (1995) adds, "This advantage becomes a life-and-death issue in a resource-scarce world in which the rich and the poor are locked in mortal competition for a depleting resource base" (see also Homer-Dixon 1994).

Objections may be raised about such polarized descriptions of corporate activities. For instance, David Crocker believes that "demonizing" corporations is philosophically fallacious and practically incorrect because many corporations are "good" and seek to support and implement the common good in their activities (Crocker, personal communication, 1996). This objection, however, is open to a counterobjection. The main point at issue is not that this or that corporation is "bad" and needs to be stopped, but that Western democracies and their institutions appear to have no mechanism

available, at this time, to protect the public from hazards and harms, many of which are—in part—self-inflicted under conditions of public misinformation and manipulation.

In this case, to say that there is no need to institute radical changes and to implement a system of criminal charges against the corporate risk imposers is like saying that, because many of us are generally decent people who do not view physical assaults and murder as acceptable activities, there is no need for strong laws and sanctions about these crimes. Leaving the choice to either engage in harmful activities or not, within the ambit of the present loose regulative structures and unrealistic legal criteria (Brown and Lemons 1995), to corporate goodwill of individual firms is to support tacitly the status quo, thereby becoming accomplices to the crimes perpetrated.

So far, this work has addressed the operation of legitimate business, registered, licensed and—to some extent—regulated. This sort of business is global in scope, but even licenses and regulations tend to lose their force when they reach national borders. And what about business that is neither regulated, licensed, nor even *known* as such to any nation or state? The "shadow economy," as Ed Ayres (1996) terms it, represents an additional pervasive global threat. We used to think of some of those "business" activities or of their concomitant effects as "externalities" and think of others as "anomalies." Ayres says:

> These are untaxed, unregulated, unsanctioned and—often—unseen. Most of them are things we've heard about but only fleetingly; we think of them as anomalies, rather than as serious or systemic threats to our mainframe institutions. They range from black markets in illicit drugs, cheap weapons, endangered wildlife, toxic waste, or ozone-depleting chemicals, to grey markets in unlisted securities or unapproved treatment for cancer.

Activities that fall under the heading of "shadow economy" include subsistence agricultural workers and those in other "unregistered occupations"—illegal industries, but also the work of "unlocated populations" such as migrants and refugees; it also includes "nonlocated activity" such as that arising from "electronic exchanges." Ayres (1996) lists the "three largest industries in the world" as (1) the military ($800 billion), (2) illicit drugs ($500 billion), and (3) oil ($450 billion). All three have a "shadow" side (1 and 3) or are entirely illegitimate (2). All three are among the most hazardous activities in the world because, aside from the individual hazards they involve or represent, they are in *principle* beyond the control of society in various ways.

The solution Ayres proposes might be the right one for all forms of techno-corporate enterprise. Neither national nor international databases carry accurate information about the shadow economy, hence, in the face of global threats, Ayres suggests that the "old geopolitical maps" are obsolete. Because borders no longer function as they were intended to do, because they have become impotent to contain benign and hazardous activities alike, the present maps should be superimposed with a "new kind of map"is, with "maps illuminating the kinds of phenomena that now count most: the watersheds, bioregions, climatic zones and migratory routes that are essential to the security of all future economies" (Ayres 1996).

For both the legitimate and the shadow economy, it is necessary to understand the essential nature of ecological and climate functions and related global threats. It is equally necessary for all of us to understand the natural functions of natural systems and the relation between the products we buy and these systems.

For these reasons, I propose a reexamination of environmental risks and harms from the standpoint of the ethics of integrity (Westra 1994a). I will argue that a proliferation of individual and aggregate rights is undesirable from the environmental point of view (and this has been argued here as well, in support of limits for corporate rights). Still, the right to life, health, and personal physical integrity appear to be primary and worthy of strong support. Moreover, the latter is necessarily embedded in ecosystem integrity, as Holmes Rolston argues (Rolston 1996; Westra 1995a).

In the next section, I consider some examples of the recent literature on the topic of risks and harms, in order to place the integrity argument in context.

RISKS AND HARMS; RIGHTS AND CONSENT

In her book *The Realm of Rights,* Judith Jarvis Thomson (1990) argues that "we do not have a claim against *merely being put at risk of harm*" and that we ought to reject what she terms the "risk thesis"—that is, the thesis that "we have claims against others that they not impose risks of harm on us." In contrast, Anthony Ellis (1995) argues that the risk thesis can be defended despite Thomson's condemnation. I will argue that his position is essentially correct and that Thomson's difficulties in drawing the line between risk and harm, for instance, is no sound reason to reject the thesis, particularly in the face of diffuse global threats, which prompted the recent acceptance of a "precautionary principle" (Brown and Lemons 1995). I will also argue that, although democracy is taken to be the form of government that is the best supporter and defender of human rights, it is precisely the unquestioned acceptance of the primacy of democratic institutions that presents the major obstacle to the prevention of public harms, particularly environmentally induced risks to public health.

Hence, the problematic interface between rights, democratic institutions, and health risks needs to be reexamined because the public interest in this respect may not be best supported by democratic choices without further controls. I will propose an argument based on an analogy with biomedical ethics and the moral and legal status of "quarantines" in response to disease-engendered public health threats. If, contrary to Thomson's opinion, *we* have the right not to be "put at risk of harm," then we need to find the best way of reaching public-policy decisions that will ensure our rights will not be infringed. Notwithstanding the close links between civil rights and democracy, on both practical and theoretical grounds, democratic practices appear insufficient to protect us from endangerment caused by the reckless practices of individuals and corporate citizens. Throughout this discussion and for the purposes of this work, *liberal democracy* and *democracy* will refer to the form of democracy we can observe implemented in North America and in Western European nations. I will not enter into the debate about the various ideological variants present in the constitutions and institutions of democratic states, because my argument is concerned with the real consequences of democracy as it is practiced in North America and Western Europe.

Environmental risks and *environmental harms* in this section will be compared to such "harms" as exposure to contagious diseases. The environmental harms considered will be those that impose threats of grave physical injury to human health: They are the *indirect* counterparts of the *direct* harms arising from exposure to contagious diseases. The environmental threats considered will be those that seriously affect life-support systems that we depend on in various ways. For example, even a noncatastrophic event like the elimination of earthworms and other biomass in the soils at an agricultural location may be a contributing factor to hazardous floods, particularly in conjunction with climatic changes. The latter are also fostered and magnified by environmental degradation (e.g., ozone-layer and deforestation problems). Although at times local environmental hazards may be contained so that the functioning of the system or the human health in the area wherein they occur, may not be affected, the onus to prove that this is the case should be on the would-be polluter. In general, the repeated occurrences of seemingly small and localized threats lead to system failure and global health threats.

It may seem that precise comparison with health threats may not be possible. But one might argue that a combination of infectious diseases, malnutrition, some organ malfunction, and the lack of local hygiene, when occurring jointly to someone in a developing country, may also render the combination a lethal threat, despite the fact that each problem might be curable or open to some solution in itself. Hence, for the environmental threats that pose, singly or jointly, an indirect but severe threat to our health, the analogy with health-care issues seems an apt one from several standpoints:

1. The magnitude and gravity of the threats
2. The lack of specific intentions to harm on the part of those who endanger us
3. The lack of intention to inflict harm on specific individuals
4. The necessity to restrain individual freedoms (on the part of risk imposers), although neither "punishment" nor "retribution" may be appropriate conceptual categories to define the restraints imposed
5. The lack of precise proofs of either direct "guilt" or even of specific "harm" inflicted.

These difficulties are common to environmentally induced harms as well as health endangerments, despite the many differences between the two fields.

Finally, I will argue against the common assumption that consent to certain institutionally approved practices and corporate activities entails the consent to all possible "side effects," including consent to be put at risk of harm. Even though we might derive some individual and collective benefits from those activities, it can be argued that consent to be harmed cannot be given, on moral grounds.

Risks, Harms, and Consent

From a moral (Kantian) point of view, we can argue against consent to harm, as long as *harm* is understood in the physical sense, not simply in the sense of being wronged or not getting one's due (Simmons 1979). But the claim that somehow embracing the lifestyle existing in affluent countries entails giving "tacit consent" to the bad consequences accompanying that way of life needs to be examined from the standpoint of political theory as well. Tacit consent, in the context of one's political obligation to governmental institutions, may not be assumed simply because we are silent or because we do not protest.

A. John Simmons (1979) argues that, although "consent is called tacit when it is given by remaining silent and inactive ...," it must be expressed "by the failure to do certain things" when a certain response is *required* to signify disagreement. Unless this sequence characterizes it, the "tacit consent" may simply represent "(1) a failure to grasp the nature of the situation, (2) a lack of understanding of proper procedures, or (3) a misunderstanding about how long one has to decide whether or not to dissent" (Simmons 1979).

Another possibility may be that a simple failure of communications has occurred. Thus, the conditions needed to establish the presence of tacit consent eliminate the possibility of simple, nonspecific voting in favor of some political institutions, without the particularity required for explicit consent to the hazardous practices in question. After citing the problems inherent in John Locke's position on this question, Simmons (1979) adds "calling consent 'tacit' on my account, specifies its mode of expression, not its lack of expression." Locke, Simmons argues, was confused about "acts of enjoyment" in one's country, such as enjoying public highways, police protection, and the like as "signs of consent" instead. Because of this confusion, Locke believed that one gave tacit consent to one's government simply because one used (and enjoyed) a country's amenities. If the same argument is applied here—that is, that enjoying some features of a system implies tacit consent for the system *in toto,* in all its activities including hazardous ones—then those who argue that by enjoying certain features of our modern, Western, technological lifestyle, we thereby give consent to any and all "side effects" that ensue might have a good point. However, they do not because this position is as "confused" as that of Locke's, Simmons (1979) argues.

Moreover, there are certain things to which we cannot consent in our social and political life. Enslavement is a clear example. Humans are created free and only acquire the obligation of a nation's citizen through consent (explicit). But, although consent is a powerful tool in general, its power does not extend to relinquishing one's "inalienable" rights, such as the right to life or to freedom itself: The right to self-defense cannot be abdicated. Thomas Hobbes (1958) says, "A man cannot lay down the right of resisting them

that assault him by force to take away his life." Simmons (1979) says that Kant argues for a similar position as well:

> Kant holds that "no contract could put a man into the class of domestic animals which we use at will for any kind of service"; that is because "every man has inalienable rights which he cannot give up even if he would."

Kant holds human life to have infinite value, and he believes that humans cannot affect (or permit others to affect) their physical integrity for any advantage or any other consideration. Hence, it may be argued that the human rights representing and supporting these inalienable human goods—such as life, freedom, and physical integrity—cannot be transferred or set aside, even if *explicit (tacit)* consent were present. In this case, there is a solid historical and theoretical basis for the somewhat novel position I have advanced in support of criminalizing those activities that represent an attack on our physical being.

To be sure, it is permissible and not immoral to trade off some of our freedom in exchange for wages, provided that respect for our humanity is present in the transaction, or for a great common ideal (say, the defense of our common freedom from enslavement), or to engage in warfare, that is, in a potentially lethal activity (in our country's defense). Not all cases are so clear-cut that they evidently fall either in one camp (of permissible activities) or in the other (of activities that represent an immoral trade-off) as some, or perhaps even all workplace activities normally entail at least some risk of harm. Even a philosophy professor who must drive her car, or walk to her teaching institution, exposes herself to some risk of traffic mishaps. If she were to remain at home and teach from her house, those risks would be avoided. But inactivity and a sedentary lifestyle are at least as hazardous to one's health as well.

We must keep in mind that the public-health threats considered here, whether they are directly posed by environmental conditions or indirectly caused by circumstances due to environmental disintegrity and degradation, are the sort of severe threats epidemiologists document (McMichael 1995); they are not the occasional or possible chance happenings one may encounter in the circumstances outlined in the previous paragraph. The health threats I have in mind are of three kinds:

1. Threats that seriously impair our natural capabilities (e.g., changes in our normal reproductive, intellectual, emotional, or immune systems).
2. Threats that pose an imminent danger of death to individuals or groups.
3. Threats that include long-term, delayed, and mutagenic effects: Like the reproductive effects in item 1, there are threats to *our species*, as well as to the affected individuals.

The effects named under these three headings have an undeniable negative impact on our rights, both human and legal, and we consider these further below in order to understand why the risk thesis should be rejected.

Risks, Harms, and Rights

W. N. Hohfeld (1923) described four forms of legal rights: (1) claim rights, (2) rights as privilege or liberty, (3) rights as power, and (4) rights as immunity. It is primarily the last form that concerns us, although where immunity rights are present, claim rights or liberty rights, for instance, may be present as well.

Hohfeld's discussion is primarily intended to clarify the meaning and scope of various judicial terms in common use and their relation to one another in order to understand the "deeper unity" present in the law: "In short the deeper the analysis, the greater becomes one's perception of fundamental unity and harmony in the law" (Hohfeld 1923). When we turn to his discussion of "immunities," both the cases and the examples he cites show that the concept may not be the most appropriate for our purpose. In a section on "Immunities and Disabilities," he says:

> A right is one's affirmative claim against another, and a privilege is one's freedom from the right or claim of another. Similarly, a power is one's affirmative "control" over a given legal relation as against another, whereas an *immunity* [my italics] is one's freedom from the legal power or

"control" of another, as regards some legal relation (Hohfeld 1923).

As an example of immunity, Hohfeld cites "exemption from taxation" as a better and more accurate term than "privilege." Hence, the meaning he proposes appears somewhat different from a concept used to refer to the right to the freedom from bodily harm. A better way to introduce the sort of "right" appropriate to our argument may be one of the personal rights, that is, the "rights of bodily safety and freedom." Hohfeld adds that it is "the duty of all of us not to interfere with our neighbors' lawful freedom." This is one of the primitive rights; it may also be termed "the right not to be interfered with" (Hohfeld 1923).

Thomson accepts the Hohfeldian framework, which includes the correlativity between rights and duties, but she rejects the risk thesis, as stated at the outset. She may base her rejection on the problem of "thresholds" and question the limits of both probability and gravity of harms as factors of the risk thesis (DeCew 1995). As Thomson rightly argues, it is problematic to identify *the* harm in many cases. She offers an example. A log left on a highway may well present a risk of harm to someone, but we have no certainty that a harm will happen to someone and no information about the possible gravity of such a harm. We can begin here to note the parallel between the example she offers of a log left on a highway (Thomson 1990; Ellis 1995), and that of risky environmental exposures or changes. She notes that we cannot be sure of several points, and that affects our acceptance of the risk thesis. These uncertainties are primarily (1) who is likely to be passing by and tripping over the log and (2) the precise harm such person or persons may incur, since these may range from very minor to quite grave depending on circumstances. We might envision icy road conditions and an elderly "tripper" or, at the other extreme, a clear, empty roadway and an athletic young person who would quickly get up with little or no harm.

In the case of environmental harms, we need not specify or prove that process X producing substance Y has actually harmed someone, before claiming that corporation Z (by engaging in process X) is liable, through Y, for the harm produced, if we accept the risk thesis. This represents the major current problem for those who are harmed: The required "proof" of harm is often unavailable, unclear, or delayed. The problems of environmental harm lie in (1) science's lack of predictive capacities; (2) the synergistic and cumulative effects of other contributory causes to the harm; (3) the lack of sustained research to sufficiently support item 2; (4) the accelerated introduction of substances, products, and processes, which further reduces the availability of research (as in item 3); (5) the difficulty of establishing clear thresholds, in the face of items 1–3; (6) the existence of harms, the effects of which develop and manifest themselves slowly over time (e.g., cancers). And this list, lengthy as it is, may only represent a partial list addressing only presently acknowledged problems (Shrader-Frechette 1991; T. Colborn et al. 1996).

However, both Ellis and Thomson agree on one issue: If an agreed-on threshold of harm is reached, then the risk violates a right. The difficulties listed above (1–6) show clearly how hard it is to draw a precise dividing line between a risk of harm that is plausible or probable and one that is not. Separating a minor harm from a significant one is equally difficult. It is also hard to indicate who specifically is "put at risk." In fact, from an environmental point of view, the level of harm inflicted may vary. For instance, a fetus, pregnant women, and older people may all encounter a greater risk than adult males from exposure to the same substance(s). It is equally impossible to specify who precisely may be at risk because some environmental hazards cause harms far from the location from where they occurred.

An example of the latter can be found in some of the recent cholera pandemics. Rita Colwell (1996) showed the connection between environmental degradation (engendered by such practices as deforestation, for instance), global climatic changes, ocean warming, the extraordinary growth of plankton in the oceans, and the way the latter fosters the spread of the *E. coli* bacterium from one continent to the other: "Cholera offers an excellent example of how greater understanding of environmental factors allows us to understand the disease better, not only its virulence but . . . its transmission and epidemiology." In this case, it would not be possible to point to *one* perpetrator, at *one* location, much less to designate specific persons as victims. Anthony Ellis (1995) argues one aspect of these issues, in response to Thomson:

> It is merely that it is indeterminate who is put at risk. If this simply means that it is hard, perhaps impossible, to find out who is put at risk, this is true, but irrelevant. If I illegitimately drop a bomb on a city, and it is impossible to determine whom, exactly, I killed, this does not imply that I did not violate anyone's rights; I violated the rights of all those I killed, whoever they may have been.

Other conceptual problems may include the following: (1) Too many people may have claims against those who impose risks; (2) the risk exposure may not actually cause harm (i.e., I dropped the bomb, but everyone was safe in an air shelter); (3) such a thesis may commit us to "absurd consequences"—for example, the consequence that "every time you drive your automobile you violate the rights of all those whom you put at risk, no matter how small the risk" (Ellis 1995). Finally, Ellis adds, we could reject such objections as the last one, by saying that "permission, in a democratic society, has been obtained in advance."

This, of course, is the crux of the problem, from the point of view of environmental hazards. Does living in a democracy, even in a Western industrialized country, with the lifestyle common to our society, mean giving *implicit* consent to risk exposure, or to the abandonment of our rights to security from harm? It does not mean giving tacit consent, as shown in our earlier discussion. Most arguments against tacit consent also show that some rights may not be relinquished, not to one's legitimate government (except in special cases, such as self-defense on behalf of one's own country, for instance; or perhaps to save another's life through a kidney donation). It is certainly immoral and impermissible to do so for economic advancement, even for one's own economic benefit. Implausible though such a thesis may be, Ellis raises it as a question, and it is often implicit and assumed in business ethics literature (Friedman 1993), with the common understanding of many who take for granted that "hazards" (unspecified) are the price one pays for technologic advances and, in general, for modern progress (Mesthene 1990; Winner 1977).

RISKS, RIGHTS, AND DEMOCRACY

John Rawls (1993) has argued that a "law of peoples" can be drawn from his theory of justice, and that a "social contract doctrine is universal in its reach." He also argued that both are not only compatible with but also dependent on a doctrine of human rights because these represent an integral part of a society's "common good conception of justice." The law in such societies must "at least uphold such basic rights as the right to life and security, to personal property, and elements of the rule of law ..." (Rawls 1993). For our purpose, the most important element mentioned here is the "right to life and security." The Canadian Charter of Rights refers to this as "the right to life and the security of persons." According to Rawls, it might seem that both human and civil rights could be supported and in fact identified with the practices and the ideals of democratic institutions. Yet in Western democracies as well as in less developed countries, it does not appear that environmental hazards and risks have been controlled or eliminated on the basis of general human rights to freedom from harm.

It is important to understand why this is so, and a good place to start is by considering a situation where democracy, civil rights, and due process are invoked in order to demonstrate the "right" way to deal with the hazards of technology transfers to third world countries. After listing statistics about deaths related to a chemical industry's operation and marketing, Kristin Shrader-Frechette (1991) argues that corporations "have an obligation to guarantee equal protection from risk across national boundaries" rather than employ what she terms the "isolationist strategy." Corporations cannot restrict their moral and legal restraints to the activities they practice in the country of origin. Yet Shrader-

Frechette admits that, "indeed, a rational risk response may require political activity that is nothing less than revolutionary." But at this time, both those in developing countries and those in minority communities in Western democracies are treated in ways that infringe their rights: Both are often "isolated" from moral consideration (Westra 1995a).

The problem is that there is no proof of intent to harm on the part of corporations or other institutions involved in these practices. In fact, if questioned, they may respond with several arguments in support of their activities. These are (1) the "social progress argument," (2) the "countervailing benefit argument," (3) "the consent argument," and (4) the "reasonable-possibility argument" (Shrader-Frechette 1991). But (1) only works if we accept the subordination of individual and group rights to some (unproven) consequentialist "good" such as "progress," a doubtful notion as it stands because of the gravity of its side effects. The next argument (2) is problematic as well: Even benefits ought not to be promoted at any cost. Shrader-Frechette (1991) says, "The argument is that a bloody loaf of bread is sometimes better than no loaf at all, that a dangerous job is preferable to no job, and that food riddled with pesticides banned is better than no food at all."

This argument is hard to defend even on utilitarian grounds, and it is impossible to support on Kantian grounds and from the standpoint of human rights. The "consent argument" (3) has been discussed and will be discussed in detail in the next section. For now, it is sufficient to note that the "free, informed consent" to which corporations appeal in defense of their limited responsibility is seldom, if ever, available from those who are "financially strapped and poorly educated." The final argument (4) suggests that risks and harms imposed are not preventable without "heroic" commitments that cannot in fairness be demanded of any corporation. But if there are human rights such as the right to the nonimposition of cancer (Gewirth 1983), then it is not heroism that is required but the simple adherence to morality.

So far, only physical, quantifiable harms have been discussed, without even envisaging the possibility of "social" or "group harms" (Simon 1995). The implication of this discussion? It is necessary though not sufficient to introduce democratic procedures and due process, globally, in order to attempt to prevent the unjust imposition of harms on the vulnerable and the disempowered. Rawls (1993) also argues for the extension of constructivist principles for justice as fairness, for "the basic structure of a closed and self-contained democratic society," to extend the ideal of justice and human rights through a "law of people." His starting point is the democratic, liberal society where he supports the "egalitarian features of the fair value of political liberties, of fair equality of opportunity, and of the difference principle." On the basis of this extension, he indicates the existence of respect for human rights and views it as a *condition* for admitting any country or national state to participate in the "law of nations." These are viewed as bedrock of any conception of justice, extended, as it were, from the starting point of appropriate basic principles within a self-contained democracy. I now turn to an examination of the real import of democracy when we consider risks and harms.

Democracy entails that collective decisions be based on open acceptance of certain choices and preferences over others and that these choices be reached through majority votes. But even in the countries where democratic systems are in power, it appears that the system is powerless to prevent the infringement of human rights through the imposition of harms to human life and health, at least through environmental means. Why does this happen? First, it is clear that democracy tends to further "the interests of the majority at the expense of the minority" (Gilbert 1995). Second, and even harder to address, is the fact that in the face of global hazards that affect everyone on Earth, there are still limits to the reach of democratic powers. For instance, in border issues that often give rise to violent conflicts, democracy is powerless because citizens on either side of the disputed border can only vote within the limits of their national area (Gilbert 1995; Westra 1994a). Further, the immense power of Western multinational corporations,

which represent the source of many of these hazards, is not subject to democratic decision making, either in their country of origin or in the (less developed) host countries (Westra 1994b; Korten 1995; Donaldson 1993).

Hence, self-contained democracies are not sufficient to mitigate these risks, and it seems urgent to establish respect and accept a risk thesis that would serve to link more clearly the existence of hazardous products and practices and the clear duties of all not to infringe upon the rights to "life and security of persons," through a "law of peoples" (Rawls 1993). This would help not only those who belong to the same community and are part of the same democratic nation but also all those who might be affected by these risks anywhere else.

Yet it is unclear just how democratic systems, even if globally implemented, would help solve the problem. Now it may make sense to say that a minority who lost out on its *political* choice must, under a democracy's rule, learn to live with its loss since it occurred through fair means and a fair opportunity to change the situation exists for the future. But it would be much harder to say that all those whose preference was not on the winning side must be equally stoic in the face of unchosen, unconsented, and uncompensated harms, which a majority chose to impose upon them (Westra 1995a). As Gewirth (1983) would argue, the imposition of grave harms cannot be supported on moral grounds because it constitutes a gross infringement of human rights.

Hence, we can drive a wedge between democratic political systems and the absolute support of human rights through a reconsideration of the imposition of risks and harms. Rex Martin discusses the relation between democracy and rights in the *System of Rights* (1993), and he argues that civil rights should have priority status: "In sum, the priority of civil rights holds over aggregative considerations insofar as those considerations concern policies for civil rights directly, or concern such rights in relation to other social policy matters." Martin's argument is that, in a system of rights, "External checks over and beyond those afforded by the representative principle are required to keep majority rule from mischief. . . . " Martin (1993) admits, " . . . representative democracy has some tendencies to the same abuse (as 'class-interested majority rule'), and therefore needs additional controls."

The example we considered earlier—of hazardous technology transfers to impoverished, uninformed, and unconsenting third world people—showed a case where the input of moral theories, utilities rights, and justice was deemed necessary to redress the injustices perpetrated because of the lack of due process and democratic procedures in those countries (Shrader-Frechette 1991). But the question now is not whether the consideration of these moral theories is necessary but whether the input of democracy is *sufficient* to ensure the presence of those moral considerations, especially the primacy of individual and group rights. The main problems with democracy seem to arise in connection with consent to the risk of harm. Should a majority have the right to consent, through their vote, to practices and activities that might impose the risk of harm upon defeated minorities? And even if we should answer this question in the affirmative, does anybody—whether in a majority or minority position within a democracy—have the right to consent even to their own harm? Both these questions need to be discussed. Speaking of environmental justice, Wigley and Shrader-Frechette (1995) say, "The doctrine of free informed consent, an important part of the traditional American value system, likewise provides a foundation for environmental justice." In this context, they proceed to analyze the concept of informed consent in the context of biomedical ethics, noting that the concept has not been used in either environmental or technological ethics. The following four criteria are suggested to indicate the presence of informed consent: " . . . The risk imposers must disclose full information about the threat; potential victims must be competent to evaluate it; they must understand the danger; and they must voluntarily accept it" (Wigley and Shrader-Frechette 1995).

In the light of our earlier discussion of democratic choices and of the lack of precision in both scientific information about specific harmful effects and of the possible geographic spread of risks, several other questions may be raised. One question might be: How and from whom should consent be sought? Another problem might be: Even if we could circumscribe a specific area where all inhabitants could be polled on such a question, the provided information may not be sufficient to guarantee that the four criteria are met, as Franz Ingelfinger, for instance, argues in "Informed (but Uneducated) Consent" (1991). The doctrine of informed consent in the biomedical setting is intended to be directed at the interaction between health-care provider and one patient or, at most, a group of patients. Hence, the consent criteria cannot be readily applied to great numbers of people from whom the risk imposers are separated by geographic location, language, cultural background, and the like.

But in that case, the imposition of wide-ranging environmental risks and harms does not fit the informed-consent model because it is more like experimentation on unconsenting subjects, contrary to the Nuremberg Code (1948). The problem is that often grave environmental hazards are, by their very nature, impossible to contain.

So far, I have argued that, unless we deal with such specifics as environmental justice at a certain location, for instance, the consent criteria cannot properly be applied. But even this argument assumes that, at least in theory and in principle, people can consent to harms, provided that they are free to choose, fully informed, and that they understand the full extent of the harm to which they are exposed. But this belief is not beyond critique. For instance, we *can* object on Kantian grounds to this assumption. Moral action implies universalizability and reversibility, and it precludes the use of any autonomous person as means to anyone's ends, even their own. Hence, as it would be impermissible, on Kantian grounds, to commit suicide even for our own "good" (e.g., for the cessation of terminal, excruciating pain); so too, it would be impermissible to accept trade-offs, such as consent to cancer risks, to obtain a hazardous job. Hence, it can be argued that

> The Categorical Imperative is formulated in such a way that consent can never be relevant in informing us of what our duties to others are. Thus one is precluded from even entertaining the notion that consent would be a defeasibility condition of the Categorical Imperative (Barnes 1996).

Although Kant's position that suicide is immoral is controversial, it is undoubtedly and clearly his position. Kant is somewhat closer to the present-day thought on not using any part of ourselves as means, even for a personally desired end. Kant is quite explicit on this point: We *cannot* consent to sales or trade-offs that would turn autonomous humans into slaves, for instance, or that might foster the exchange of bodily parts for money (Kant 1979). Hence, we can conclude that consent to harms is based on weak arguments both from the standpoint of political theory and from that of Kant's moral doctrine.

Moreover, it can also be claimed that, in general, utilitarian arguments should be considered only *after* human rights and justice principles. In that case, if consent to harm is not possible in principle, or if it is questionable even if obtained, then the introduction of truly democratic conditions and due process will not be sufficient to mitigate, let alone justify, the wide-ranging imposition of risks and harms on large numbers of unspecified persons, through environmental means. In sum, I have argued that we should accept, as Ellis suggests, the risk thesis Thomson rejects, as necessary because it can be argued that—although not all rights are primary—the right to life and freedom from harm is primary among them.

In contrast, the usually accepted connection between primary human rights and democracy can be shown to be less strong than it is generally thought to be. In that case, our next problem is: How are we to prevent harms, and to restrain risk imposers when even the "best," most enlightened form of governance (i.e., democracy) may not be sufficient to accomplish the goal? To attempt an answer, we will return to biomedical ethics and the moral and legal categories used to remedy the possible spread of infectious diseases.

RISK, RIGHTS AND CONSENT: A LESSON FROM THE "WHITE DEATH"

I have noted that biomedical ethics may not offer the best analogy for questions of consent arising from environmental and technological hazards. We could not ensure "full disclosure," reach everyone who might be at risk, and communicate clearly and understandably the extent and gravity of the harm; moreover, neither risk imposers nor risk assessors could predict accurately the probability and gravity of the harms. Yet uncertainties—endemic to scientific discourse involving a large range of variables, added to the impredictability about location, gravity of exposure, and other specifics—ought not to force us to reject with Thomson, the risk thesis.

And if we hold fast to both (1) the primacy of rights—especially the right to life and to freedom from harm—and (2) the risk thesis itself, then we need to seek another avenue to ensure that rights be protected, given the failure of present democratic institutions to guarantee appropriate restraints to risk imposers. The resurgence of many infectious diseases, assumed to have been conquered and eliminated (e.g., tuberculosis), for instance, may indicate a possible avenue for public policy. Tuberculosis is making a comeback in North America and in other parts of the world; it is now resistant to most antibiotics, harder than ever to control because of population density and other modern conditions, and therefore brings with it threats of the "white death." Tuberculosis is highly contagious and requires very little contact to spread, unlike, for instance, sexually transmitted diseases like AIDS. It is sufficient to sit next to an infected person, to breathe the same air, to be infected. Tuberculosis is curable, but it requires a lengthy course of treatment. Many people who want to get well decide to abandon the treatment when the worst symptoms subside, despite the fact that they are still highly contagious (Davis 1995). If these persons are not prepared to persevere with their treatment and yet want to continue to lead a normal life, interacting with others, they are "endangering" not only their close associates but also the general public.

The question is what to do when the disease, its course, treatment, and hazards are fully explained to contagious persons and they understand yet refuse to comply with either treatment or restraints. Some action must be taken in defense of the public interest and the public safety.

As in the case of contagious childhood diseases, what is necessary is the use of "quarantines" and other forms of involuntary restraints and treatment. The starting point is the realization that tuberculosis is a threat to public health "*par excellence*" (Davis 1995). As far as I know, however, only New York City has clear-cut legislation in this regard (at least at this time). The following course of action is supported by this new legislation:

> The City Department of Public Health may order a person removed to a hospital or detained for treatment there only if two conditions are met. First, the Department must have found the tuberculosis to be active and without treatment likely to be transmitted to others.... Second, the Department must have found the subject of the order unable or unwilling to undergo less restrictive treatment (Davis 1995).

The above requirements are based on "epidemiological or clinical evidence, X-rays or laboratory tests," and the final decision to commit rests with the courts in a way parallel to that designed to ensure commitment for mental illness (Davis 1995). Note that, in order to restrain the liberty of risk imposers in this context, it is not necessary to "prove" they have harmed someone in a court of law; it is sufficient to demonstrate that they and their activities are hazardous and potentially harmful to the public. Depending on the response of the infectious person to requests to be treated, the interests of public health may be served by "civil confinement for treatment," which in turn may be justified as preventing harm to the public through "reckless endangerment" (Davis 1995). In fact, jail could justifiably be used to stop the endangerment for anyone who might resist the suggested "civil confinement for treatment."

How can this situation help us conceptualize the problem of imposing restraints on those endangering the public through environmentally hazardous practices? First, we need to note that some public threats cannot be controlled through democratic institutions, that is, through *voluntary* public choices. One may counter that even the imposition of forced restraints is embedded in a general system of individual rights and democratic institutions. That is, of course, correct. But it is important to understand that rights to life and health are primary and should be put ahead of other choices and preferences. This perspective allows us to view environmental endangerment as something that needs to be controlled directly and even by coercive means, rather than something that is simply to be limited only by cost-benefit analyses or by a counting of heads and a weighing of preferences. To explain detention in medical cases, Davis (1995) says, "The alternative to detention is the moral equivalent of letting someone, without adequate justification, walk crowded streets with a large bomb that could go off at any moment."

In the "white death" threats, we are not sure of the gravity of the harm imposed; we cannot anticipate just who is at risk from the infected person with any certainty; we cannot be sure of precise numbers of potentially affected persons; we have information about risks and harms, but we cannot present a specific infected person or persons as "proof," to justify placing the risk imposer under criminal restraints. The reason and the only reason we can offer for imposing criminal restraints or civil restraints is reckless endangerment, without being able to point to one or many persons who might have been harmed.

In fact, it is in order *not* to have "victims" that we are justified in invoking civil and criminal restraints. Contrast this preventive approach with that of corporate bodies who expose persons in their immediate vicinity of their hazardous operations to risks of harms but who *demand* not proof of endangerment but clear proof of *actual harm* before they are even prepared to compensate, let alone to consider discontinuing their hazardous activities.

Much more could be said about this topic, and it is fair to say that there are disanalogies as well as analogies between cases in biomedical ethics, allowing justification for restraints in cases of reckless endangerment, and the imposition of environmental risks and harms. Perhaps the most problematic difference is that, while one person's "restraints" will only affect her life (and provide a much greater benefit in the process), restraints of corporate activities on a grand scale might have grave repercussions for all stake-holders, not only the corporation subject to restraints. Nevertheless, it seems that there are enough parallels to make a reasonable case for considering seriously the approach I suggest, for all others employed so far appear to have met with scant success.

THE GOOD AND THE COMMUNITY: LAWS RESTRAINING CHOICE

The argument I have proposed essentially contrasts individualism with communitarianism. But the latter is viewed as a special case: the case of a community of life, whereby each individual's personal integrity and the ecological integrity of her habitat are so completely intertwined that no question can be raised about whether the value of integrity in each case is intrinsic or instrumental. Rolston (1996) makes this point eloquently in his philosophical analysis of "biological immunity":

> The organismic integrity protected by immunity has to fit into an ecosystemic integrity. An organism without a habitat is soon extinct. The immune system is zealously defending the self, but all the while the ecosystem in which this self lives is the fundamental unit of development and survival. There are no immune organisms, period; there are only immune organisms-in-ecosystems.

From the perspective of immunity, our strong individual rights to life and self-defense can easily be extended to our habitat, in line with Rolston's proposed definition of our organisms as "organisms-in-ecosystems." Hence, to invoke stronger, changed laws appears entirely defensible on grounds of self-defense. These laws must replace laws that place economically driven, unintended harms, slowly unfolding over time, in a separate category so that only clear, quickly evident and intended harms are deemed to be

criminal. Attacks on our bodily integrity and our genetic capacities are also crimes; they might be defined as attacks on our capacities as a small c, embedded in the capital C, or the capacities of ecological integrity. In my previous work, the collaborative definition of integrity used the letter C to represent the undiminished capacities of an ecosystem in its unmanipulated state, following its natural evolutionary trajectory, free, as much as possible, from human interference or stress.

To better understand the sort of crime described in these "attacks," we may invoke the difference between premeditated murder and manslaughter. It seems intuitively true to say that pain and suffering aside, no one has the right to remove someone else's organs for their own purposes, no matter how "good" the perpetrators may perceive their purpose to be. It would seem equally intuitively true to add that it is equally impermissible to intrusively interfere with the natural functions of these organs. When the damage caused is more than damage to one individual but it becomes, as in the cases researched by Theo Colborn (Colborn et al. 1996), damage to reproductive capacities, to the next generations, hence to humanity in general, it becomes a case of attempted genocide, deserving even more than the punishment of the laws of the perpetrators' country: It requires that they be accountable to and punished by a world tribunal.

Surely, if there is a good that is not in doubt, it is the right we have to our own physical and intellectual capacities undiminished by others. This common good is neither based on the preferences of one culture or another, nor limited to any relative viewpoint, as it is compatible with a great variety of cultural "goods" and ideals. Hence, I propose our undiminished capacities c, as a basic good that permits with varying degrees of appropriateness a number of societal coercive actions, parallel to those needed to support the ecological integrity it requires to thrive C. This "good" may also be compatible with moral theories such as the Kantian respect for autonomously chosen ends and the Rawlsian emphasis on fairness and the difference principle. These possible connections need to be examined in some detail.

What does Rawls (1975) say about the good? His understanding may raise problems:

> That we have one conception of the good rather than another is not relevant from a moral standpoint. In acquiring it we are influenced by the same sort of contingencies that leads us to rule out a knowledge of our sex and class.

The defense of life through individual and systemic integrity may not be in conflict with a variety of conceptions of the good. But the wholesale acceptance of the possibility of any and all such "conceptions of the good" may well conflict with the spirit of the principle of integrity, in the same sense that utilitarianism also does. Michael Sandel (1982) examines the "status of the good" in Rawls. He argues:

> For Rawls, utilitarianism goes wrong not in conceiving the good as the satisfaction of arbitrarily given desires, undifferentiated as to worth—for justice as fairness shares in this, but only in being indifferent to the way these consummations are spread across individuals.

Although Rawls, in Sandel's estimation, departs from utilitarianism, the remaining connection with "the satisfaction of arbitrarily given desires" is—at best—compatible with the primacy of life, as the necessary prerequisite to the existence of "desires." But it is not compatible with the nonnegotiable status of the principle of integrity (PI). Some may argue, for instance, that the desire to accept a trade-off between diminished health, life span or genetic capacities, and economic advantage, if well understood, is legitimate for a society. Some may also argue that this is precisely what is happening in affluent democracies at this time; hence, only the *distributive* aspect of this "contract" should be scrutinized from the standpoint of morality, not its existence.

In contrast, the PI takes a strongly Kantian position in not permitting such trade-offs, whether or not they are fairly distributed across society. The basis of the principle of integrity is the value of integrity, which encompasses the infinite value of all life, of life-support systems, and of individual and systemic capacities, now and into the future. This excludes the possibility of legitimate trade-offs and places those concerns at the forefront of both morality and public policy. The primacy and the centrality of this value explains the emphasis on the need for national laws and for global regulative mechanisms to protect it as an absolute, rather than treating it as one value among many, subject to public choice or majoritarian preferences.

The holistic perspective is absolutely vital here: Life-support systems cannot be protected in piecemeal fashion. When hazards travel between continents, not only countries, clearly national policies will be insufficient. Global regulations and tight global security will also be required to prevent the present techno-hazard transfer between North American and Western European countries and Southeast Asian ones and into economically depressed minority areas in the affluent countries. An interesting parallel may be found in recent improvement in Canadian legislation directed at serial criminals of a special kind: the sexual predators.

One of the most horrible cases in Canada (1988–1994) saw Paul Bernardo and his wife Karla Homolka involved in terrible crimes over a lengthy period because of Bernardo's change of venue during his "career" as a rapist, torturer, and murderer. He was eventually found guilty of a series of viciously sadistic rapes in a Toronto suburb, which earned him the title of "Scarborough rapist." The DNA evidence that eventually implicated him, however, was neglected at one location when he moved to another, on the west side of Toronto, to St. Catharines, Ontario, about 50 kilometers away. There he met and married Homolka in a storybook wedding where the young, attractive couple, both blonde and blue-eyed, appeared to be the epitome of "nice" middle-class Canadians. But when Homolka's 15-year-old sister died under suspicious circumstances at their parents' home on Christmas Eve (with Karla and Bernardo in attendance) and two other schoolgirls 14 and 15 years old were eventually abducted, with only their remains found weeks later, it should have been clear that the Scarborough's rapist's career was not over. Because different police forces in different areas were involved in the investigations, the connection was not made in time to prevent at least the last two grisly murders.

Eventually, tapes recording the horror of the girls' sexual assaults and torture were discovered, and the wife, a full participant and assistant in the crimes and the abductions, testified against the husband (*The Globe and Mail* 1995). The similarity between the case of sexual predators, now the subject of a commissioned inquiry, and the hazardous practices described earlier in this essay is that both are cases of system failure. This can obviously occur even when the crimes committed are already in the criminal code as such; and even such cases cannot be easily stopped because of failures in coordination. We also need to take very seriously the crimes of ecoviolence that are not even properly treated as such now because they can lead to serial recurrences, with almost complete impunity to the perpetrators. According to Justice Archie Campbell, Head of the Commission reporting on serial predators, from 1988 to 1994, the name of Bernardo and a series of similar crimes kept "coming up." But lacking an investigative body capable of and charged with coordinating the findings of various jurisdictions, Bernardo was able to "throw investigations off stride by the simple act of moving from one police jurisdiction to another." Judge Campbell wrote, "When Bernardo stopped stalking, raping and killing in Toronto and started stalking, raping and killing in St. Catharines and Burlington, he might as well have moved to another country for a fresh start" (I. Ross, *The Globe and Mail* 1996).

Justice Campbell's remarks bring to mind the legal corporate practices that are taken for granted: Corporations simply close down one operation and move out to another location, often in a less developed country, which they perceive as less demanding in their environmental regulations. Perhaps the corporation has been charged and fined for repeated environmental infractions. Unfortunately for all of us, the move does not herald an increased environmental concern or a newly found respect for human life and its habitat. The move is most often followed by practices indicating the same disregard for human and ecological safety that led to the original problems.

As long as the charges are viewed as creating economic externalities only (and moving and reorganizing expenses are tax-deductible), the immorality becomes institutionalized, simply another way of doing business. Even repeated offenses, in different venues, cause little discomfort unless the public becomes aware of the infractions through some spectacular accident; and even then, there is no extradition for noncriminal cases. Like sexual predators, corporate predators can simply move and resume the activities that forced the move with little or no fear of retribution.

If even in criminal cases (short of murder, perhaps) it is far too easy to inflict great harm repeatedly on an unprotected public, then the move to criminalize hazardous practices, as a first step, appears inevitable. Like serial predators, corporations gain confidence and ability through repeated, almost routine moves. Unlike the average predator, they possess large resources that can be mobilized and utilized in defense of their goals. Hence, it is vital to recognize that good personal or corporate morality and conscience must be encouraged and supported through laws that will force those who lack such virtues to comply.

Therefore, to affirm the urgent need for strict global regulations for the protection of public life, health, and integrity is not to commit the hasty generalization of tarring all corporations, good and bad, with the same brush. It is intended to recognize the primacy of individual and ecological integrity and to attempt to coordinate and institutionalize principles and ideals that are already, for the most part, present in global regulations and in national and international laws. In essence it is to recognize the role of a holistic perceptive in public decision making (Brown 1995).

❧ REFERENCES

Ayres, E. "The Expanding Shadow Economy," *Worldwatch*, (July/August 1996): 11–23.

Barnes, C. "Consent Theory: Can One Consent to Be Harmed?" Unpublished paper, presented at the University of Windsor, 1996.

Brown, D., and J. Lemons, eds.1995. *Sustainable Development: Science Ethics and Public Policy*. Dordrecht, The Netherlands: Kluwer, 1995.

Bullard, R. *Dumping in Dixie*. Boulder, CO: Westview Press, 1994.

Colborn, Theo. "Plenary Address" to the International Association of Great Lakes Researchers, Erindale College, Toronto, May 27, 1996.

Colborn, Theo, Dianne Dumanoski, and John Peterson Myers. *Our Stolen Future.* New York: Dutton, 1996.

Colwell, Rita. "Global Change: Emerging Diseases and New Epidemics." President's Lecture, American Association for the Advancement of Science (AMSIE '96), February 1996.

Davis, M. "Arresting the White Death: Involuntary Patients, Public Health, and Medical Ethics." Paper presented at the central meeting of the American Philosophical Association, April 1995.

DeCew, J. "Rights and Risks." Comments on A. Ellis's "Risks and Rights." Unpublished paper. 1995.

Donaldson, Thomas. "Moral Minimums for Multinations." In *Ethical Issues in Business,* edited by T. Donaldson and P. Werhane. Englewood Cliffs, NJ: Prentice Hall, 1993, 58–75.

Ellis, Anthony. "Risks and Rights." Paper presented at the central meeting of the American Philosophical Association, April 1995.

French, P. A. *Collective and Corporate Responsibility.* New York: Columbia University Press, 1984.

Friedman, Milton. "The Social Responsibility of Business Is to Increase Its Profits." In *Ethical Issues in Business,* edited by T. Donaldson and P. Werhane. Englewood Cliffs, NJ: Prentice Hall, 1993, 249–254.

Gaylord, C., and E. Bell, "Environmental Justice: A National Priority." In *Faces of Environmental Racism,* edited by L. Westra and P. Wenz. Lanham, MD: Rowman & Littlefield, 1995.

Gewirth, A. "Human Rights and the Prevention of Cancer." In *Human Rights.* Chicago: University of Chicago Press, 1983, 181–217.

Gilbert, Paul. *Terrorism, Security and Nationality.* London: Routledge, 1995.

Hobbes, Thomas. *Leviathan.* New York: Bobbs-Merrill, 1958.

Hohfeld, W. N. *Fundamental Legal Conceptions.* New Haven, CT: Yale University Press, 1923.

Homer-Dixon, Thomas. "On the Threshold: Environmental Changes as Causes of Acute Conflict." *International Security* 16, no. 2 (Fall 1991): 76–116.

Homer-Dixon, Thomas. "Environmental Scarcity and Violent Conflict: Evidence from Cases." *International Security* 19, No. 1 (Summer 1994): 5–40.

Homer-Dixon, Thomas, in Hurst, Lyda, "The Global Guru," *The Toronto Star,* July 20, 1996, "Insight," pp C1 and C5.

Ingelfinger, Franz L. "Informed (but Uneducated) Consent." In *Biomedical Ethics,* edited by J. Zembaty and T. Mappes. eds., 1991, 220–221.

Kant, Immanuel. *The Metaphysical Elements of Justice.* New York: Bobbs-Merrill, 1965.

Kant, Immanuel. *On the Old Saw.* Philadelphia: University of Pennsylvania Press, 1974.

Kant, Immanuel. *Lectures on Ethics,* translated by Louis Infield. Indianapolis: Hackett, 1979, pp. 116–126 ("Duties to Oneself"); and pp. 157–160 ("Duties towards the Body Itself").

Korten, David. *When Corporations Rule the World.* West Hartford, CT: Kumarian Press, Berret Koehler Publishers, 1995.

Martin, Rex. *A System of Rights.* New York: Clarendon Press/Oxford University Press, 1993.

McMichael, Anthony J. *Planetary Overload.* Cambridge, UK: Cambridge University Press, 1995.

Mesthene, Emmanuel G. "The Role of Technology in Society." In *Technology and the Future,* 5th ed., edited by A. Teich. New York: St. Martin's Press, 1990, pp. 77–99.

Nikiforuk, A. "Arctic Pollution: Poisons for a Pristine Land." *The Globe and Mail* (July 20, 1996), D8.

Rawls, J. "From Fairness to Goodness." *Philosophical Review,* 1984 (1975): 536–554.

Rawls, J. "The Law of Peoples." In *On Human Rights.* New York: Basic Books/HarperCollins, 1993, pp. 41–82.

Rolston, Holmes, III. "Immunity in Natural History." In *Perspectives in Biology and Medicine* 39, no. 3 (Spring 1996): 353–372.

Sandel, Michael. *Liberalism and the Limits of Justice.* Cambridge, MA: Cambridge University Press, 1982.

Shrader-Frechette, K. *Risk and Rationality.* Berkeley, CA: University of California Press, 1991.

Simmons, A. John. *Moral Principles and Political Obligations.* Englewood Cliffs, NJ: Princeton University Press, 1979.

Simon, Thomas. "Group Harm." *Journal of Social Philosophy* 26, no. 3 (Winter 1995): 123–139.

Thomson, J. J. *The Realm of Rights.* Cambridge, MA: Harvard University Press, 1990.

Westra, L. *An Environmental Proposal for Ethics: The Principle of Integrity.* Lanham MD: Rowman & Littlefield, 1994a.

Westra, L. "Risky Business: Corporate Responsibility and Hazardous Products." *Business Ethics Quarterly* 4, no. 1, (1994b): 97–110.

Westra, L. "Ecosystem Integrity and Sustainability: The Foundational Value of the Wild." In *Perspectives on Ecological Integrity,* edited by L. Westra and J. Lemons. Dordrecht, The Netherlands: Kluwer, 1995a, pp. 12–33.

Westra, L. "Integrity, Health and Sustainability: Environmentalism Without Racism." In *The Science of the Total Environment.* Oxford, UK: Elsevier, for the World Health Organization, 1996.

Wigley, D., and Shrader-Frechette, K. "Consent, Equity and Environmental Justice: A Louisiana Case Study." In *Faces of Environmental Racism,* edited by L. Westra and P. Wenz. 1995. *The Faces of Environmental Racism: The Global Equity Issues,* Lanham, MD: Rowman & Littlefield, 1995, pp. 135–162.

Winner, Langdon. *Autonomous Technology.* Cambridge, MA: MIT Press, 1977.

STUDY QUESTIONS

1. Is Westra correct about the failure of democracies to deal with environmental degradation and risk?
2. Are there natural rights? What are they? Do we have a right against others that they not impose risks of harm on us, as Westra argues? Or is Thomson correct in rejecting such a right?
3. Is Westra's solution threatening to democracy itself?

FOR FURTHER READING

Bullard, Robert, *Confronting Environmental Racism.* Cambridge, MA: South End Press, 1993.

Serba, James P., ed., *Earth Ethics.* Englewood Cliffs, NJ: Prentice Hall, 1995.

Wenz, Peter S., *Environmental Justice.* Albany, NY: SUNY Press, 1988.

Westra, Laura. *An Environmental Proposal for Ethics.* Lanham, MD: Rowman & Littlefield, 1994.

Westra, Laura and Peter S. Wenz, eds., *Faces of Environmental Racism.* Lanham, MD: Rowman & Littlefield, 1995.

From Dysfunctional to Sustainable Society

IF WE ARE TO SURVIVE as a society, we will have to change our lifestyles. We may be forced to do this due to the depletion of scarce resources—such as fossil fuels, topsoil, and clean air—to changing climatic conditions and weather patterns caused by the greenhouse effect or to severe population overcrowding. In the worst case, a nuclear war or other catastrophe would be the catalyst for drastic change. It would be better to change our lifestyles gradually through a process of making peace with our environment by revealing the kinds of processes that are leading us toward a tragic end. In Chapter 12 we looked at the economic dimension of environmentalism. In this chapter, we want to look at the environmental situation from the perspective of our lifestyles and general practices.

We begin with a selection from Vice President Al Gore's book *The Earth in Balance* (1992). Gore argues that our tradition contains the resources to solve our ecological crisis. He criticizes radical ecologists, such as deep ecologists (see Chapter 3), but tries to incorporate some of their criticisms within the mainstream of American religious-philosophical tradition, correcting some alleged misinterpretations of it. Gore's essay deserves to be seriously debated, not simply because he occupied an influential position in government but because it is based on the general values of the Judeo-Christian tradition, which are the values of the majority of North and South Americans and Europeans for whom his work is primarily intended.

In our second reading, Alan Thein Durning's "An Ecological Critique of Global Advertising," we have an insightful analysis of the global pressures to create consumerism through subtle and skillful marketing skills. Advertising, as one of its proponents put it, is to make everyone unhappy until they buy the product in question. Is your hair too thin, your nose too short? Advertising offers you hope! "It preys on the weaknesses of its host. It creates an insatiable hunger. And it leads to debilitating overconsumption. In the biological realm, things of that nature are called parasites." Advertising is the global parasite of our time! Durning argues that this parasite threatens the lifeblood of our world.

Louis Pojman's essay offers a case for bicycling. Automobiles and trucks cause immense environmental stress, so less harmful modes of transportation must be adopted. Among these is that undervalued, wonder source of amazing power, the bicycle. The article, "The Challenge of the Future," outlines suggestions for extending ecological consciousness to the city and to the whole world.

In the next reading, Todd Saunders applies ecological concepts to community design.

"Strategic Monkeywrenching" by Dave Foreman advocates selective, nonviolent ecosabotage aimed at saving the wilderness, followed by Michael Martin's ethical analysis of such behavior.

In the final article of the book, "A Vision of a Sustainable World," Lester Brown, Christopher Flavin, and Sandra Postel of the Worldwatch Institute ask you to consider their vision of the task of building a sustainable world over the next forty years. It should provoke discussion as well as challenge us to work harder toward a sustainable society.

75 Dysfunctional Society

AL GORE

Al Gore was Vice President of the United States from 1992 to 2000 and the Democratic candidate who lost to the Republican candidate George W. Bush in the closest, most controversial presidential election in the history of the United States. A leading proponent of environmental concerns, in 1992 he published his book *Earth in the Balance*, from which the current selection is taken. More recently he produced a popular movie about global warming, *An Inconvenient Truth*. After criticizing deep ecology (see Chapter 3) for being anti-humanistic, Gore attempts to identify our present social and environmental malaise via the metaphor of the dysfunctional family.

At the heart of every human society is a web of stories that attempt to answer our most basic questions: Who are we, and why are we here? But as the destructive pattern of our relationship to the natural world becomes increasingly clear, we begin to wonder if our old stories still make sense and sometimes have gone so far as to devise entirely new stories about the meaning and purpose of human civilization.

One increasingly prominent group known as Deep Ecologists makes what I believe is the deep mistake of defining our relationship to the earth using the metaphor of disease. According to this story, we humans play the role of pathogens, a kind of virus giving the earth a rash and a fever, threatening the planet's vital life functions. Deep Ecologists assign our species the role of a global cancer, spreading uncontrollably, metastasizing in our cities and taking for our own nourishment and expansion the resources needed by the planet to maintain its health. Alternatively, the Deep Ecology story considers human civilization a kind of planetary HIV virus, giving the earth a "Gaian" form of AIDS, rendering it incapable of maintaining its resistance and immunity to our many insults to its health and equilibrium. Global warming is, in this metaphor, the fever that accompanies a victim's desperate effort to fight the invading virus whose waste products have begun to contaminate the normal metabolic processes of its host organism. As the virus rapidly multiplies, the sufferer's fever signals the beginning of the "body's" struggle to mobilize antigens that will attack the invading pathogens in order to destroy them and save the host.

The obvious problem with this metaphor is that it defines human beings as inherently and contagiously destructive, the deadly carriers of a plague upon the earth. And the internal logic of the metaphor points toward only one possible cure: eliminate people from the face of the earth. As Mike Roselle, one of the leaders of Earth First!, a group espousing Deep Ecology, has said, "You hear about the death of nature and it's true, but nature will be able to reconstitute itself once the top of the food chain is lopped off—meaning us."

Some of those who adopt this story as their controlling metaphor are actually advocating a kind of war on the human race as a means of protecting the planet. They assume the role of antigens, to slow the spread of the disease, give the earth time to gather its forces to fight off and, if necessary, eliminate the intruders. In the words of Dave Foreman, a cofounder of Earth First!, "It's time for a warrior society to rise up out of the earth and throw itself in front of the juggernaut of destruction, to be antibodies against the human pox that's ravaging this precious, beautiful planet." (Some Deep Ecologists, it should be added, are more thoughtful.)

Beyond its moral unacceptability, another problem with this metaphor is its inability to explain—in a way that is either accurate or believable—who we are and how we can create solutions for the crisis it describes. Ironically, just as René Descartes, Francis Bacon, and the other architects of the scientific revolution defined human beings as disembodied intellects separate from the physical world, Arne Naess, the Norwegian philosopher who coined the term Deep Ecology in 1973, and many Deep Ecologists of today seem to define human beings as an alien presence on the earth. In a modern version of the Cartesian dénouement of a philosophical divorce between human beings and the earth, Deep Ecologists idealize a condition in which there is no connection between the two, but they arrive at their conclusion by means of a story that is curiously opposite to that of Descartes. Instead of seeing people as creatures of abstract thought relating to the earth only through logic and theory, the Deep Ecologists make the opposite mistake, of defining the relationship between human beings and the earth almost solely in physical terms—as if we were nothing more than humanoid bodies genetically programmed to play out our bubonic destiny, having no intellect or free will with which to understand and change the script we are following.

The Cartesian approach to the human story allows us to believe that we are separate from the earth, entitled to view it as nothing more than an inanimate collection of resources that we can exploit however we like; and this fundamental misperception has led us to our current crisis. But if the new story of the Deep Ecologists is dangerously wrong, it does at least provoke an essential question: What new story can explain the relationship between human civilization and the earth—and how we have come to a moment of such crisis? One part of the answer is clear: our new story must describe and foster the basis for a natural and healthy relationship between human beings and the earth. The old story of God's covenant with both the earth and humankind, and its assignment to human beings of the role of good stewards and faithful servants, was—before it was misinterpreted and twisted in the service of the Cartesian world view—a powerful, noble, and just explanation of who we are in relation to God's earth. What we need today is a fresh telling of our story with the distortions removed.

But a new story cannot be told until we understand how this crisis between human beings and the earth developed and how it can be resolved. To achieve such an understanding, we must consider the full implications of the Cartesian model of the disembodied intellect.

Feelings represent the essential link between mind and body or, to put it another way, the link between our intellect and the physical world. Because modern civilization assumes a profound separation between the two, we have found it necessary to create an elaborate set of cultural rules designed to encourage the fullest expression of thought while simultaneously stifling the expression of feelings and emotions.

Many of these cultural rules are now finally being recognized as badly out of balance with what we are learning about the foundations of human nature. One such foundation is, of course, the brain, which is layered with our evolutionary heritage. Between the most basic and primitive part of our brain, responsible for bodily functions and instinct, and the last major structure within the brain to evolve, the part responsible for abstract thought and known as the neocortex, is the huge portion of our brain that governs emotion, called the limbic system. In a very real sense, the idea that human beings can function as disembodied intellects translates into the absurd notion that the functions of the neocortex are the only workings of our brains that matter.

Yet abstract thought is but one dimension of awareness. Our feelings and emotions, our sensations, our awareness of our own bodies and of nature—all these are indispensable to the way we experience life, mentally and physically. To define the essence of who we are in terms that correspond with the analytical activity of the neocortex is to create an intolerable dilemma: How can we concentrate purely on abstract thinking when the rest of our brain floods our awareness with feelings, emotions, and instincts?

Insisting on the supremacy of the neocortex exacts a high price, because the unnatural task of a disembodied mind is to somehow ignore the intense psychic pain that comes from the constant nagging awareness of what is missing: the experience of living in one's body as a fully integrated physical and mental being. Life confronts everyone with personal or circumstantial problems, of course, and there are many varieties of psychic pain from which we wish to escape. But the cleavage between mind and body, intellect and nature, has created a kind of psychic pain at the very root of the modern mind, making it harder for anyone who is suffering from other psychological wounds to be healed.

Indeed, it is not unreasonable to suppose that members of a civilization that allows or encourages this cleavage will be relatively more vulnerable to those mental disorders characterized by a skewed relationship between thinking and feeling. This notion may seem improbable, since we are not used to looking for the cause of psychological problems in the broad patterns of modern civilization. But it is quite common for epidemiologists to trace the cause of physical disorders to patterns adopted by societies that place extra stress on especially vulnerable individuals. Consider, for example, how the pattern of modern civilization almost certainly explains the epidemic level of high blood pressure in those countries—like the United States—that have a diet very high in sodium. Although the precise causal relationship is still a mystery, epidemiologists conclude that the nearly ubiquitous tendency of modern civilization to add lots of salt to the food supply is responsible for a very high background level of hypertension. In the remaining pre-industrial cultures where the food supply is not processed and sodium consumption is low, hypertension is virtually unknown, and is considered normal for an elderly man's blood pressure to be the same as that of an infant. In our society, we assume that it is natural for blood pressure to increase with age.

Resolving high blood pressure is much easier than resolving deep psychological conflicts, however. Most people respond to psychic pain the way they respond to any pain: rather than confront its source, they recoil from it, looking immediately for ways to escape or ignore it. One of the most effective strategies for ignoring psychic pain is to distract oneself from it, to do something so pleasurable or intense or otherwise absorbing that the pain is forgotten. As a temporary strategy, this kind of distraction isn't necessarily destructive, but dependence on it over the long term becomes dangerous and, finally, some sort of addiction. Indeed, it can be argued that every addiction is caused by an intense and continuing need for distraction from psychic pain. Addiction is distraction.

We are used to thinking of addiction in terms of drugs or alcohol. But new studies of addiction have deepened our understanding of the problem, and now we know that people can become addicted to many different patterns of behavior—such as gambling compulsively or working obsessively or even watching television constantly—that distract them from having to experience directly whatever they are trying to avoid. Anyone who is unusually fearful of something—intimacy, failure, loneliness—is potentially vulnerable to addiction, because psychic pain causes a feverish hunger for distraction.

The cleavage in the modern world between mind and body, man and nature, has created a new kind of addiction: I believe that our civilization is, in effect, addicted to the consumption of the earth itself. This addictive relationship distracts us from the pain of what we have lost: a direct experience of our connection to the vividness, vibrancy, and aliveness of the rest of the natural world. The froth and frenzy of industrial civilization mask our deep loneliness for that communion with the world that can lift our spirits and fill our senses with the richness and immediacy of life itself.

We may pretend not to notice the emptiness we feel, but its effects may be seen in the unnatural volatility with which we react to those things we touch. I can best illustrate this point with a metaphor drawn from electrical engineering. A machine using lots of electrical energy must be grounded to the earth in order to stabilize the flow of electricity through the machine and to prevent a volatile current from jumping to whatever might touch it. A machine that is not grounded poses a serious threat; similarly, a person who is not "grounded" in body as well as mind, in feelings as well as thoughts, can pose a threat to whatever he or she touches. We tend to think of the powerful currents of creative energy circulating through every one of us as benign, but they can be volatile and dangerous if not properly grounded. This is especially true of those suffering from a serious addiction. No longer grounded to the deeper meaning of their lives, addicts are like someone who cannot release a 600-volt cable because the electric current is just too strong: they hold tightly to their addiction even as the life force courses out of their veins.

In a similar way, our civilization is holding ever more tightly to its habit of consuming larger and larger quantities every year of coal, oil, fresh air and water, trees, topsoil, and the thousand other substances we rip from the crust of the earth, transforming them into not just the sustenance and shelter we need but much more that we don't need: huge quantities of pollution, products for which we spend billions on advertising to convince ourselves we want, massive surpluses of products that depress prices while the products themselves go to waste, and diversions and distractions of every kind. We seem increasingly eager to lose ourselves in the forms of culture, society, technology, the media, and the rituals of production and consumption, but the price we pay is the loss of our spiritual lives.

Evidence of this spiritual loss abounds. Mental illness in its many forms is at epidemic levels, especially among children. The three leading causes of death among adolescents are drug- and alcohol-related accidents, suicide, and homicide. Shopping is now recognized as a recreational activity. The accumulation of material goods is at an all-time high, but so is the number of people who feel an emptiness in their lives.

Industrial civilization's great engines of distraction still seduce us with a promise of fulfillment. Our new power to work our will upon the world can bring with it a sudden rush of exhilaration, not unlike the momentary "rush" experienced by drug addicts when a drug injected into their bloodstream triggers changes in the chemistry of the brain. But that exhilaration is fleeting; it is not true fulfillment. And the metaphor of drug addiction applies in another way too. Over time, a drug user needs a progressively larger dose to produce an equivalent level of exhilaration; similarly, our civilization seems to require an ever-increasing level of consumption. But why do we assume that it's natural and normal for our per capita consumption of most natural resources to increase every year? Do we need higher levels of consumption to achieve the same distracting effect once produced by a small amount of consumption? In our public debates about efforts to acquire a new and awesome power through science, technology, or industry, are we sometimes less interested in a careful balancing of the pros and cons than in the great thrill to accompany the first use of the new enhancement of human power over the earth?

The false promise at the core of addiction is the possibility of experiencing the vividness and immediacy of real life without having to face the fear and pain that are also part of it. Our industrial civilization makes us a similar promise:

the pursuit of happiness and comfort is paramount, and the consumption of an endless stream of shiny new products is encouraged as the best way to succeed in that pursuit. The glittering promise of easy fulfillment is so seductive that we become willing, even relieved, to forget what we really feel and abandon the search for authentic purpose and meaning in our lives.

But the promise is always false because the hunger for authenticity remains. In a healthy, balanced life, the noisy chatter of our discourse with the artificial world of our creation may distract us from the deeper rhythms of life, but it does not interrupt them. In the pathology of addiction, this dialogue becomes more than a noisy diversion; as their lives move further out of balance, addicts invest increasing amounts of energy in their relationship to the objects of their addiction. And once addicts focus on false communion with substitutes for life, the rhythm of their dull and deadening routine becomes increasingly incompatible, discordant, and dissonant with the natural harmony entrains the music of life. As the dissonance grows more violent and the clashes more frequent, peaks of disharmony become manifest in successive crises, each one more destructive than the last.

The disharmony in our relationship to the earth, which stems in part from our addiction to a pattern of consuming ever-larger quantities of the resources of the earth, is now manifest in successive crises, each marking a more destructive clash between our civilization and the natural world: whereas all threats to the environment used to be local and regional, several are now strategic. The loss of one and a half acres of rain forest every second, the sudden, thousand-fold acceleration of the natural extinction rate for living species, the ozone hole above Antarctica and the thinning of the ozone layer at all latitudes, the possible destruction of the climate balance that makes our earth livable—all these suggest the increasingly violent collision between human civilization and the natural world.

Many people seem to be largely oblivious of this collision and the addictive nature of our unhealthy relationship to the earth. But education is a cure for those who lack knowledge; much more worrisome are those who will not

acknowledge these destructive patterns. Indeed, many political, business, and intellectual leaders deny the existence of any such patterns in aggressive and dismissive tones. They serve as "enablers," removing inconvenient obstacles and helping to ensure that the addictive behavior continues.

The psychological mechanism of denial is complex, but again addiction serves as a model. Denial is the strategy used by those who wish to believe that they can continue their addicted lives with no ill effects for themselves or others. Alcoholics, for example, aggressively dismiss suggestions that their relationship to alcohol is wreaking havoc in their lives; repeated automobile crashes involving the same drunk driver are explained away in an alcoholic's mind as isolated accidents, each with a separate, unrelated cause.

Thus the essence of denial is the inner need of addicts not to allow themselves to perceive a connection between their addictive behavior and its destructive consequences. This need to deny is often very powerful. If addicts recognize their addiction, they might be forced to become aware of the feelings and thoughts from which they so desperately need distraction; abandoning their addiction altogether would threaten them with the loss of their principal shield against the fear of confronting whatever they are urgently trying to hold at bay.

Some theorists argue that what many addicts are trying to hold at bay is a profound sense of powerlessness. Addicts often display an obsessive need for absolute control over those few things that satisfy their craving. This need derives from, and is inversely proportional to, the sense of helplessness they feel toward the real world—whose spontaneity and resistance to their efforts at control are threatening beyond their capacity to endure.

It is important to recognize that this psychological drama takes place at the border of conscious awareness. Indeed, it is precisely that border which is being defended against the insistent intrusions of reality. Meanwhile, the dishonesty required to ensure that reality doesn't breach the ramparts often assumes such proportions that friends find it hard to believe that addicts don't know what they are doing to themselves and those around them. But the inauthenticity of addicts is, in one sense, easy to explain: they are so obsessed with the need to satisfy their craving that they subordinate all other values to it. Since a true understanding of their behavior might prove inhibiting, they insist they have no problem.

We are insensitive to our destructive impact on the earth for much the same reason, and we consequently have a similar and very powerful need for denial. Denial can take frightening and bizarre forms. For example, in southern California in 1991, the worsening five-year drought led some homeowners to actually spray-paint their dead lawns green, just as some undertakers apply cosmetics to make a corpse look natural to viewers who are emotionally vulnerable to the realization of death. As Joseph Conrad said in *The Heart of Darkness,* "The conquest of the earth is not a pretty thing when you look into it too much." But we are addicted to that conquest, and so we deny it is ugly and destructive. We elaborately justify what we are doing while turning a blind eye to the consequences. We are hostile to the messengers who warn us that we have to change, suspecting them of subversive intent and accusing them of harboring some hidden agenda—Marxism, or statism, or anarchism. ("Killing the messenger," in fact, is a well-established form of denial.) We see no relationship between the increasingly dangerous crises we are causing in the natural world; they are all accidents with separate, distinct causes. Those dead lawns, for example—could they be related to the fast-burning fires that made thousands homeless late in 1991? No matter; we are certain that we can adapt to whatever damage is done, even though the increasingly frequent manifestations of catastrophe are beginning to resemble what the humorist A. Whitney Brown describes as "a nature hike through the Book of Revelations."

The bulwark of denial isn't always impenetrable, however. In the advanced stages of addiction, when the destructive nature of the pattern becomes so overwhelmingly obvious that addicts find it increasingly difficult to ignore the need for change, a sense of resignation sets in. The addiction has by then so thoroughly defined the pattern of their lives that there seems to be no way out. Similarly, some people are finding it increasingly difficult to deny the destructive nature of our relationship to the earth, yet the response is not action but resignation. It's too late, we think; there's no way out.

But that way spells disaster, and recovery is possible. With addiction, an essential element in recovery is a willingness on the part of addicts to honestly confront the real pain they have sought to avoid. Rather than distracting their inner awareness through behavior, addicts must learn to face their pain—feel it, think it, absorb it, own it. Only then can they begin to deal honestly with it instead of running away.

So too our relationship to the earth may never be healed until we are willing to stop denying the destructive nature of the current pattern. Our seemingly compulsive need to control the natural world may have derived from a feeling of helplessness in the face of our deep and ancient fear of "Nature red in tooth and claw," but this compulsion has driven us to the edge of disaster, for we have become so successful at controlling nature that we have lost our connection to it. And we must also recognize that a new fear is now deepening our addiction: even as we revel in our success at controlling nature, we have become increasingly frightened of the consequences, and that fear only drives us to ride this destructive cycle harder and faster.

What I have called our addictive pattern of behavior is only part of the story, however, because it cannot explain the full complexity and ferocity of our assault on the earth. Nor does it explain how so many thinking and caring people can unwittingly cooperate in doing such enormous damage to the global environment and how they can continue to live by the same set of false assumptions about what their civilization is actually doing and why. Clearly, the problem involves more than the way each of us as an individual relates to the earth. It involves something that has gone terribly wrong in the way we collectively determine our mutual relationship to the earth.

A metaphor can be a valuable aid to understanding, and several metaphors have helped me understand what is wrong with the way we relate to the earth. One that has proved especially illuminating comes out of a relatively new theory about ailing families; a synthesis by psychologists and sociologists of research in addiction theory, family therapy, and systems analysis, this theory attempts to explain the workings of what has come to be called the dysfunctional family.

The idea of the dysfunctional family was first developed by theorists such as R. D. Laing, Virginia Satir, Gregory Bateson, Milton Erickson, Murray Bowen, Nathan Ackerman, and Alice Miller, and more recently it has been refined and brought to a popular audience by writers like John Bradshaw. The problem they have all sought to explain is how families made up of well-meaning, seemingly normal individuals can engender destructive relationships among themselves, driving individual family members as well as their family system into crisis.

According to the theory of dysfunctionality, unwritten rules governing how to raise children and purporting to determine what it means to be a human being are passed down from one generation of a family to the next. The modern version of these rules was shaped by the same philosophical world view that led to the scientific and technological revolution: it defines human beings as primarily intellectual entities detached from the physical world. And this definition led in turn to an assumption that feelings and emotions should be suppressed and subordinated to pure thought.

One consequence of this scientific view was a changed understanding of God. Once it became clear that science—instead of divine provenance—might explain many of nature's mysteries, it seemed safe to assume that the creator, having set the natural world in motion within discernible and predictable patterns, was somewhat removed and detached from the world, out there above us looking down. Perhaps as a consequence, the perception of families changed too. Families came to be seen as Ptolemaic systems, with the father as the patriarch and source of authority and all the other family members orbiting around him. This change had a dramatic effect on children. Before the scientific era, children almost certainly found it easier to locate and understand their place in the world because they could define themselves in relation both to their parents and to a God who was clearly present in nature.

With these two firm points of reference, children were less likely to lose their direction in life. But with God receding from the natural world to an abstract place, the patriarchal figure in the family (almost always the father) effectively became God's viceroy, entitled to exercise godlike authority when enforcing the family's rules. As some fathers inevitably began to insist on being the sole source of authority, their children became confused about their own roles in a family system that was severely stressed by the demands of the dominant, all-powerful father.

Fathers were accorded godlike authority to enforce the rules, and, as Bradshaw and others argue, one of the most basic rules that emerged is that the rules themselves cannot be questioned. One of the ways dysfunctional families enforce adherence to the rules and foster the psychic numbness on which they depend is by teaching the separation between mind and body and suppressing the feelings and emotions that might otherwise undermine the rules. Similarly, one of the ways our civilization secures adherence to its rules is by teaching the separation of people from the natural world and suppressing the emotions that might allow us to feel the absence of our connection to the earth.

The rules of both perpetuate the separation of thought from feeling and require full acceptance of the shared, unspoken lies that all agree to live. Both encourage people that it is normal not to know their feelings and to feel helpless when it comes to any thought of challenging or attempting to change the assumptions and rules upon which the divorce from feeling is based. As a result, these rules frequently encouraged psychological dramas and role playing. Rules that are simultaneously unreasonable and immune to questioning can perpetuate disorders like addiction, child abuse, and some forms of depression. This is the paradigm of the dysfunctional family.

It is not uncommon for one member of a dysfunctional family to exhibit symptoms of a serious psychological disorder that will be found, upon scrutiny, to be the outward manifestation of a pattern of dysfunctionality that includes the entire family. In order to heal the patient, therapists concentrate not on the pathology of the individual but on the web of family relationships—and the unwritten rules and understandings that guide his approach to those relationships.

For example, it has long been known that the vast majority of child abusers were themselves abused as children. In analyzing this phenomenon, theorists have found the blueprint for an archetypal intergenerational pattern: the child who is a victim remembers the intensity of the experience with his body but suppresses the memory of the pain in his mind. In a vain effort to resolve his deep confusion about what happened, he is driven to repeat or "recapitulate" the drama in which a powerful older person abuses a powerless child, only this time he plays the abuser's role.

To take a more subtle example, discussed in Alice Miller's seminal work on dysfunctionality, *The Drama of the Gifted Child,* children in some families are deprived of the unconditional love essential for normal development and made to feel that something inside them is missing. Consequently these children develop a low opinion of themselves and begin to look constantly to others for the approval and validation they so desperately need. The new term "codependency" describes the reliance on another for validation and positive feelings about oneself. The energy fueling this insatiable search continues into adulthood, frequently causing addictive behavior and an approach to relationships that might be described, in the words of the popular song, as "looking for love in all the wrong places." Sadly but almost inevitably, when they themselves have children, they find in the emotional hunger of their own infant a source of intense and undiluted attention that they use to satisfy their still insatiable desire for validation and approval, in a pattern that emphasizes taking rather than giving love. In the process, they neglect to give their own child the unconditional love the child needs to feel emotionally whole and complete. The child therefore develops the same sense that something is missing inside and seeks it in the faces and emotions of others, often insatiably. Thus the cycle continues.

The theory of how families become dysfunctional usually does not require identifying any particular family member as bad or as someone intent upon consciously harming the others. Rather, it is usually the learned pattern of family rules that represents the real source of the pain and tragedy the family members experience in each generation. As a diagnosis, dysfunctionality offers a powerful source of hope, because it identifies the roots of the problems in relationships rather than in individuals, in a shared way of thinking based on inherited assumptions rather than a shared human nature based on inherited destiny. It is therefore subject to healing and transformation.

That's the good news. The bad news is that many dysfunctional rules internalized during infancy and early childhood are extremely difficult to displace. Human evolution, of course, is responsible for our very long period of childhood, during much of which we are almost completely dependent on our parents. As Ashley Montagu first pointed out decades ago, evolution encouraged the development of larger and larger human brains, but our origins in the primate family placed a limit on the ability of the birth canal to accommodate babies with ever-larger heads. Nature's solution was to encourage an extremely long period of dependence on the nurturing parent during infancy and childhood, allowing both mind and body to continue developing in an almost gestational way long after birth. But as a result of this long period of social and psychological development, children are extremely vulnerable to both good and bad influences, and in a dysfunctional family, that means they will absorb and integrate the dysfunctional rules and warped assumptions about life that are being transmitted by the parents. And since much of what parents transmit are the lessons learned during their own childhood, these rules can persist through many generations.

Every culture is like a huge extended family, and perhaps nothing more determines a culture's distinct character than the rules and assumptions about life. In the modern culture of the West, the assumptions about life we are taught as infants are heavily influenced by our Cartesian world view—namely, that human beings should be separate from the earth, just as the mind should be separate from the body, and that nature is to be subdued, just as feelings are to be suppressed. To a greater or lesser degree, these rules are conveyed to all of us, and they have powerful effects on our perception of who we are.

The model of the dysfunctional family has a direct bearing on our ways of thinking about the environment. But this model also helps describe how we have managed to create such a profound and dangerous crisis in our relationship to the environment, why this crisis is not due to our inherently evil or pathogenic qualities, and how we can heal this relationship. As the use of this metaphor suggests, however, the environmental crisis is now so serious that I believe our civilization must be considered in some basic way dysfunctional.

Like the rules of a dysfunctional family, the unwritten rules that govern our relationship to the environment have been passed down from one generation to the next since the time of Descartes, Bacon, and the other pioneers of the scientific revolution some 375 years ago. We have absorbed these rules and lived by them for centuries without seriously questioning them. As in a dysfunctional family, one of the rules in a dysfunctional civilization is that you don't question the rules.

There is a powerful psychological reason that the rules go unquestioned in a dysfunctional family. Infants or developing children are so completely dependent that they cannot afford even to think there is something wrong with the parent, even if the rules do not feel right or make sense. Since children cannot bear to identify the all-powerful parent as the source of dysfunctionality, they assume that the problem is within themselves. This is the crucial moment when the inner psychological wound is inflicted—and it is a self-inflicted wound, a fundamental loss of faith by the children in themselves. The pain of that wound often lasts an entire lifetime, and the emptiness and alienation that result can give rise to enormous amounts of psychological energy, expended during the critical period when the psyche is formed in an insatiable search for what, sadly, can never be found: unconditional love and acceptance.

Just as children cannot reject their parents, each new generation in our civilization now feels utterly dependent on the civilization itself. The food on the supermarket shelves, the water in the faucets in our homes, the shelter and

sustenance, the clothing and purposeful work, our entertainment, even our identity—all these our civilization provides, and we dare not even think about separating ourselves from such beneficence.

To carry the metaphor further: just as children blame themselves as the cause of the family's dysfunction in their relationship with it, so we quietly internalize the blame for our civilization's failure to provide a feeling of community and a shared sense of purpose in life. Many who feel their lives have no meaning and feel an inexplicable emptiness and alienation simply assume that they themselves are to blame, and that something is wrong with them.

Ironically, it is our very separation from the physical world that creates much of this pain, and it is because we are taught to live so separately from nature that we feel so utterly dependent upon our civilization, which has seemingly taken nature's place in meeting all our needs. Just as the children in a dysfunctional family experience pain when their parent leads them to believe that something important is missing from their psyches, we surely experience a painful loss when we are led to believe that the connection to the natural world that is part of our birthright as a species is something unnatural, something to be rejected as a rite of passage into the civilized world. As a result, we internalize the pain of our lost sense of connection to the natural world, we consume the earth and its resources as a way to distract ourselves from the pain, and we search insatiably for artificial substitutes to replace the experience of communion with the world that has been taken from us.

Children in dysfunctional families who feel shame often construct a false self through which they relate to others. This false self can be quite elaborate as the children constantly refine the impression it makes on others by carefully gauging their reactions, to make the inauthentic appear authentic. Similarly, we have constructed in our civilization a false world of plastic flowers and Astro Turf, air conditioning and fluorescent lights, windows that don't open and background music that never stops, days when we don't know whether it has rained or not, nights when the sky never stops glowing, Walkman and Watchman, entertainment cocoons, frozen food for the microwave oven, sleepy hearts jump-started with caffeine, alcohol, drugs, and illusions.

In our frenzied destruction of the natural world and our apparent obsession with inauthentic substitutes for direct experience with real life, we are playing out a script passed on to us by our forebears. However, just as the unwritten rules in a dysfunctional family create and maintain a conspiracy of silence about the rules themselves, even as the family is driven toward successive crises, many of the unwritten rules of our dysfunctional civilization encourage silent acquiescence in our patterns of destructive behavior toward the natural world.

The idea of a dysfunctional civilization is by no means merely a theoretical construct. In this terrible century, after all, we have witnessed some especially malignant examples of dysfunctional civilization: the totalitarian societies of Nazi Germany under Hitler, fascist Italy under Mussolini, Soviet communism under Stalin and his heirs, and the Chinese communism of Mao Zedong and Deng Xaoping, as well as many less infamous versions of the same phenomenon. Indeed, only recently the world community mobilized a coalition of armies to face down the Baathist totalitarianism of Iraq under Saddam Hussein.

Each of these dysfunctional societies has lacked the internal validation that can only come from the freely expressed consent of the governed. Each has demonstrated an insatiable need to thrust itself and its political philosophy onto neighboring societies. Each has been oriented toward expansion through the forceful takeover of other countries. Moreover, each has fostered in its society a seamless web of shared assumptions that most people know are false but that no one dares to question. These societies reflect in macrocosm the pathology of dysfunctionality as it has been observed in families. A developing child in a dysfunctional family searches his parent's face for signals that he is whole and all is right with the world; when he finds no such approval, he begins to feel that something is wrong inside. And because he doubts his worth and authenticity, he begins controlling his inner experience—smothering spontaneity, masking emotion, diverting creativity into robotic routine, and distracting an awareness

of all he is missing with an unconvincing replica of what he might have been. Similarly, when the leadership in a totalitarian society dares to look in the faces of its people for signals of what they really feel, it is seldom reassured that all is right with the world. On the contrary, the leadership begins to fear that something is wrong because its people do not—cannot—freely express the consent of the governed. They stare back, trancelike, their vacant sullenness suggesting the uneasiness and apprehension that is so pervasive among oppressed populations everywhere. Denied validation in the countenance of its citizens, the totalitarian leadership feels no choice but to try to expand, out of an insatiable ambition to find—by imposing itself on others—conclusive evidence of its inner value.

Typically, the totalitarian expansion begins with the takeover of a weak and relatively defenseless neighboring society. Hoping that this initial conquest will satiate the aggressor, other societies frequently mute their response, some because they fear they might be the next targets, others because they are sure they will not be. But if the totalitarian society is deeply dysfunctional, it will not be satisfied for long and will continue to feel a need to expand. Alas, this horrifying pattern is all too familiar: totalitarian expansions have directly caused the deaths of more than 100 million human beings in this century.

The phenomenon of modern totalitarianism is, of course, extremely complex and involves political, economic, and historical factors unique to each of its incarnations. But whatever its specific causes, the psychology of totalitarianism has always been characterized by a fear of disorientation within and a search for legitimacy without. The pathology of expansion so evident in modern totalitarian societies results from this dysfunctional pattern, and the sense of wholeness they seek cannot be restored as long as they refuse to confront the dishonesty, fear, and violence eating away at the heart of their national identity.

The unprecedented assault on the natural world by our global civilization is also extremely complex, and many of its causes are related specifically to the geographic and historical context of its many points of attack. But in psychological terms, our rapid and aggressive expansion into what remains of the wildness of the earth represents an effort to plunder from outside civilization what we cannot find inside. Our insatiable drive to rummage deep beneath the surface of the earth, remove all of the coal, petroleum, and other fossil fuels we can find, then burn them as quickly as they are found—in the process filling the atmosphere with carbon dioxide and other pollutants—is a willful expansion of our dysfunctional civilization into vulnerable parts of the natural world. And the destruction by industrial civilization of most of the rain forests and old-growth forests is a particularly frightening example of our aggressive expansion beyond proper boundaries, an insatiable drive to find outside solutions to problems arising from a dysfunctional pattern within.

Ironically, Ethiopia, the first victim of modern totalitarian expansion, has also been an early victim of the dysfunctional pattern that has led to our assault on the natural world. At the end of World War II, after the Italian fascists had been forced out, 40 percent of Ethiopia's land was covered with, and protected by, trees. Less than a half century later, after decades marked by the most rapid population growth in the world, a relentless search for fuelwood, overgrazing, and the export of wood to pay interest on debts, *less than 1 percent* of Ethiopia is covered by trees. First, much of the topsoil washed away; then the droughts came—and stayed. The millions who have starved to death are, in a real sense, victims of our dysfunctional civilization's expansionist tendencies.

In studying the prospects for halting our destructive expansion, one is almost awestruck by our relentless and seemingly compulsive drive to dominate every part of the earth. Always, the unmet needs of civilization fuel the engine of aggression; never can these needs be truly satisfied. The invaded area is laid waste, its natural productivity is eviscerated, its resources are looted and quickly consumed—and all this destruction merely stokes our appetite for still more.

The weakest and most helpless members of the dysfunctional family become the victims of abuse at the hands of those responsible for providing nurture. In a similar fashion, we systematically abuse the most vulnerable and least defended areas of the natural world: the wetlands, the rain forests, the oceans. We also abuse other members of the human family, especially those who cannot speak for themselves. We tolerate the theft of land from indigenous peoples, the exploitation of areas inhabited by the poorest populations, and—worst of all—the violation of the rights of those who will come after us. As we strip-mine the earth at a completely unsustainable rate, we are making it impossible for our children's children to have a standard of living even remotely similar to ours.

In philosophical terms, the future is, after all, a vulnerable and developing present, and unsustainable development is therefore what might be called a form of "future abuse." Like a parent violating the personal boundaries of a vulnerable child, we violate the temporal boundaries of our rightful place in the chain of human generations. After all, the men and women of every generation must share the same earth—the only earth we have—and so we also share a responsibility to ensure that what one generation calls the future will be able to mature safely into what another generation will call the present. We are now, in effect, corruptly imposing our own dysfunctional design and discordant rhythms on future generations, and these persistent burdens will be terribly difficult to carry.

Police officers, doctors, and psychologists who deal with the victims of child sexual abuse often wonder how any adult—especially a parent—could commit such a crime. How could anyone be deaf to the screams, blind to the grief, and numb to the pain their actions cause? The answer, we now know, is that a kind of psychic numbness, induced by the adults' own adaptation to the dysfunctional pattern in which they were themselves raised as children, serves to anesthetize their conscience and awareness in order to facilitate their compulsive repetition of the crime that was visited upon them.

Just as the members of a dysfunctional family emotionally anesthetize themselves against the pain they would otherwise feel, our dysfunctional civilization has developed a numbness that prevents us from feeling the pain of our alienation from our world. Both the dysfunctional family and our dysfunctional civilization abhor direct contact with the full and honest experience of life. Both keep individuals in a seamless web of abstract, unfeeling thought, focused always on others, what others are assumed to be experiencing and what others might say or do to provide the wholeness and validation so desperately sought.

But there is a way out. A pattern of dysfunctionality need not persist indefinitely, and the key to change is the harsh light of truth. Just as an addict can confront his addiction, just as a dysfunctional family can confront the unwritten rules that govern their lives, our civilization can change—must change—by confronting the unwritten rules that are driving us to destroy the earth. And, as

Alice Miller and other experts have shown, the act of mourning the original loss while fully and consciously feeling the pain it has caused can heal the wound and free the victim from further enslavement. Likewise, if the global environment crisis is rooted in the dysfunctional pattern of our civilization's relationship to the natural world, confronting and fully understanding that pattern, and recognizing its destructive impact on the environment and on us, is the first step toward mourning what we have lost, healing the damage we have done to the earth and to our civilization, and coming to terms with the new story of what it means to be a steward of the earth.

✂ STUDY QUESTIONS

1. What is Gore's main message? How does he illustrate it? Has he made his case? Explain your responses.

2. What is Gore's criticism of deep ecology (refer to "Deep Ecology" in Chapter 3)? What does he offer in its place?

76   An Ecological Critique of Global Advertising

ALAN THEIN DURNING

Alan Thein Durning is a senior researcher at Worldwatch Institute in Washington, D.C., and the author of *How Much Is Enough? The Consumer Society and the Future of the Earth*. In this essay, he argues that advertising promotes consumerism, which creates artificial needs in such a way as to undermine a sustainable society. While Durning does not condemn the idea of advertising itself, as a means of providing useful information, he argues that today's Madison Avenue experts have gone far beyond the limits of that function and instead are promoting a dangerous false consciousness.

Last January a single message was broadcast simultaneously in every inhabited part of the globe. The message was not "love thy neighbor" or "thou shalt not kill." It was "Drink Coke."

This first global advertisement was, on the face of it, simply a piece of technical showmanship—an inevitable one, considering the pace of change in telecommunications. On a symbolic

level, however, it was something more. It was a neat encapsulation of the main trend in human communications worldwide: commercialization.

For better or for worse, almost all of humanity's 5.5 billion individuals, divided among 6,000 distinct cultures, are now soaking in the same gentle bath of advertising. The unctuous voices of the marketplace are insinuating themselves into ever

Reprinted from *Worldwatch*, Vol. 6.3 (May—June, 1993) by permission of the Worldwatch Institute.

more remote quarters of the globe and ever more private realms of human life.

Advertising has become one of the world's premier cultural forces. Almost every living person knew the word "Coke," for example, long before the global ad. Two years ago, the trade journal *Adweek* published a two-page spread depicting Hitler, Lenin, Napoleon, and a Coke bottle. "Only one," read the caption, "launched a campaign that conquered the world. How did Coke succeed when history's most ambitious leaders failed? By choosing the right weapon. Advertising."

Aside from the arrogance of that statement, what is disturbing about it is its truth. Owing to skillful and persistent marketing, Coke is sold in virtually every place people live. Go to the end of a rural road on any Third World continent, walk a day up a donkey trail to a hardscrabble village, and ask for a Coke. Odds are you'll get one. This state of affairs—development workers call it "Coca-Colonization"—means that Coke's secret formula has probably reached more villages and slums than has clean drinking water or oral rehydration formula.

The point here is not to single out Coca-Cola—others would have circum-advertised the globe soon if the soft drink empire hadn't—but rather to question whether advertising has outgrown its legitimate role in human affairs. Advertisers maintain that their craft, far from being too widely practiced, is just beginning to achieve its destiny: to stimulate business growth, create jobs, and to unify humanity by eroding the ancient hatreds that divide us and joining us together in the universal fellowship of a Coke.

But from the perspective of the Earth's long-term health, the advertising industry looks somewhat different. Stripped to its essentials, contemporary advertising has three salient characteristics. It preys on the weaknesses of its host. It creates an insatiable hunger. And it leads to debilitating over-consumption. In the biological realm, things of that nature are called parasites.

If that rather pointed metaphor is apt, we are left with the sticky problem doctors face in treating any parasite: finding a medicine and a dosage that will kill the worm without poisoning the patient. How can we restrain the excesses of advertising without resorting to poisonous state censorship or curtailing the flow of information in society? Actions that are too heavy-handed, for example, could bankrupt the free—but advertising—dependent—press.

THE MANUFACTURE OF NEEDS

The purpose of advertising, according to orthodox economic theory, is to provide us with information about the goods and services offered in the marketplace. Without that stream of information we consumers won't make informed choices, and Adam Smith's invisible hand will be not only invisible but also blind. We won't know when a better frozen dinner comes along, nor will we know where to get the best deal on a new car.

The contents of marketing messages themselves, however, show the simplemindedness of that explanation. Classified ads and yellow page telephone directories would suffice if advertising were only about telling people who already want something where to get it and what it costs. Rather, advertising is intended to expand the pool of desires, awakening wants that would lie dormant otherwise—or, as critics say, manufacturing wants that would not otherwise exist.

Entire industries have manufactured a need for themselves. Writes one advertising executive, ads can serve "to make [people] self-conscious about matter of course things such as enlarged nose pores [and] bad breath." Historically, advertisers have especially targeted women, playing on personal insecurities and self-doubt by projecting impossible ideals of feminine beauty.

As B. Earl Puckett, then head of the department store chain Allied Stores Corporation, put it 40 years ago, "It is our job to make women unhappy with what they have." Thus for those born with short, skinny eyelashes, the message mongers offer hope. For those whose hair is too straight, or too curly, or grows in the wrong places, for those whose skin is too dark or too light, for those whose body weight is distributed in anything but this year's fashion, advertising assures that synthetic salvation is close at hand.

Ads are stitched together from the eternal cravings of the human psyche. Their ingredients are images of sexual virility, eternal youth, social belonging, individual freedom, and existential fulfillment. Advertisers sell not artifacts but life-styles, attitudes, and fantasies, hitching their wares to the infinite yearnings of the soul.

They also exploit the desire individuals in mass societies feel to define a distinctive identity. Peter Kim, director of research and consumer behavior for the advertising agency J. Walter Thompson, says the role of brands in consumer society is "much akin to the role of myth in tra-ditional societies. Choosing a brand becomes a way for one group of consumers to differentiate themselves from another."

Advertisers are extraordinarily sophisticated in the pursuit of these ends. The most finely wrought ads are masterpieces—combining stunning imag-ery, bracing speed, and compelling language to touch our innermost fears and fancies. Prime-time television commercials in the industrial countries pack more suggestion into a minute than anything previously devised.

From an anthropological perspective, ads are among the supreme creations of this era, standing in relation to our technological, consumer cul-ture as the pyramids did to the ancients and the Gothic cathedrals to the medievals. Those struc-tures embodied faith in the transcendent, acted out a quest for immortality, and manifested hier-archical social rankings. Advertisements, like our age, are mercurial, hedonistic, image-laden, and fashion-driven; they glorify the individual, ideal-ize consumption as the route to personal fulfill-ment, and affirm technological progress as the motive force of destiny.

ADVERTISING AND THE EARTH

Of course, advertising is not the only force to pro-mote consumption in today's world. That point is amply evident in the recent history of Eastern Europe. There, where most advertising was illegal under the communist regimes of the past, popular desires for the Western consumer lifestyle were pervasive—indeed, they were among the forces that overthrew socialism. Communism had failed to deliver the goods.

Other forces driving the earth-threatening consumption levels of the world's affluent soci-eties include everything from human nature's acquisitive streak to the erosion of informal, neighborhood sharing networks that has accom-panied the rising mobility of our time. They include social pressures to keep up with the Joneses, the proliferation of "convenience" goods to meet the time-crunch created by rising working hours, national economic policies that favor consumption over savings and raw materials production over efficiency and recycling, and the prevailing trend in urban design—away from compact, human-scale cities toward anonymous, auto-scale mall and sprawl.

All these things—plus the weight of sheer pur-chasing power—define one of the world's most pressing environmental challenges: to trim resource consumption in industrial countries. Citi-zens of these nations typically consume 10 times as much energy as their developing country counter-parts, along with 10 times the timber, 13 times the iron and steel, 14 times the paper, 18 times the synthetic chemicals, and 19 times the aluminum.

The consumer societies take the lion's share of the output of the world's mines, logging opera-tions, petroleum refineries, metal smelters, paper mills, and other high-impact industrial plants. These enterprises, in turn, account for a dispropor-tionate share of the resource depletion, environ-mental pollution, and habitat degradation that humans have caused worldwide. A world full of consumer societies is an ecological impossibility.

And even if advertising is not the sole force driving up consumption, it is an important one. It is a powerful champion of the consumer life-style, and is spreading its influence widely.

COMMERCIALIZING THE GLOBE

"Fifty years ago," wrote philosopher Ivan Illich in 1977, "most of the words an American heard were personally spoken to him as an individual, or to someone standing nearby." That certainly isn't true today. Most of the words an American—or a citizen of any industrial country—hears are sales pitches broadcast over the airwaves to us as members of a mass market. The text we read, the images we see, and the public places we visit are all dominated by commercial messages.

Take the example of commercial television, long the premier advertising medium. Aside from sleeping and working, watching television is the leading activity in most consumer societies, from the United States and the United Kingdom to Japan and Singapore.

Commercial TV is advancing around the world, and everywhere it has proved exceptionally effective at stimulating buying urges. As Anthony J. F. Reilly, chief executive of the food conglomerate H. J. Heinz, told *Fortune* magazine, "Once television is there, people of whatever shade, culture, or origin want roughly the same things." Harnessed as an educational tool, TV can be powerful and effective, as in India and Africa, where lessons are beamed to teacher-less villages. But the overwhelming trend in broadcasting almost everywhere is commercialization.

In 1985, the International Advertising Association rhapsodized: "The magical marketing tool of television has been bound with the chains of laws and regulations in much of the world, and it has not been free to exercise more than a tiny fraction of its potential as a conduit of the consumer information and economic stimulation provided by advertising. Those chains are at last being chiseled off."

During the 1980s, governments deregulated or privatized television programming in most of Western Europe. Public broadcasting monopolies splintered in Belgium, France, Italy, Germany, Norway, Portugal, Spain, and Switzerland—allowing advertising on a scale previously witnessed only in the United States. As the European Community became both a single market and a common broadcasting region this year, advertising time on European TV became a hot commodity, providing access to the region's 330 million consumers and $4 trillion of disposable income.

Meanwhile, commercial television is quickly spreading outside the industrial countries. In India, declares Gurcharan Das, chairman of Procter & Gamble India, "an advertiser can reach 200 million people every night" through television. India has gone from 3 million TVs in 1983 to more than 14 million today. Latin America has built or imported 60 million sets, almost one per family, since the early 1950s. All told, perhaps half the world's people have access to commercial television broadcasts.

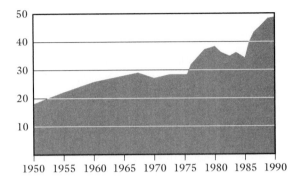

FIGURE 1 World Advertising Expenditures, Per Capita, 1950–90
Source: International Advertising Association.

The commercialization of television is just one part of the general expansion of advertising worldwide, an expansion that includes magazines and newspapers, billboards and displays, catalogs, and other media. The overall growth stands out starkly in historical trends.

Total global advertising expenditures multiplied nearly sevenfold from 1950 to 1990; they grew one-third faster than the world economy and three times faster than world population. They rose—in real, inflation-adjusted terms—from $39 billion in 1950 to $256 billion in 1990. (For comparison, the gross national product of India, the world's second most populous state, was just $253 billion that year.) In 1950, advertisers spent $16 for each person on the planet, in 1970 they spent $27, and in 1990, $48 (see Figure 1).

Americans are the most advertised-to people on Earth. U.S. marketers account for nearly half of the world's ad budget, according to the International Advertising Association in New York, spending $468 per American in 1991. Among the industrial countries, Japan is second in the advertising league, dedicating more than $300 per citizen to sales pitches each year. Western Europe is close behind. A typical European is the target of more than $200 worth of ads a year. The latest boom is underway in Eastern Europe, a region that John Lindquist of the Boston Consulting Group calls "an advertising executive's dream—people actually remember advertisements."

Advertising is growing fast in developing countries as well, though it remains small scale by Western standards. South Korea's advertising industry grew 35 to 40 percent annually in the late 1980s, and yearly ad billings in India jumped fivefold in the 1980s, surpassing one dollar per person for the first time.

AD-ING LIFE

The sheer magnitude of the advertising barrage in consumer societies has some ironic results. For one thing, the clamor for people's attention means relatively few advertisements stick. Typical Americans are exposed to some 3,000 commercial messages a day, according to *Business Week*. Amid such a din, who notices what any one ad says?

To lend their messages greater influence, marketers are forced to deliver ever higher quality pitches—and to seek new places to make them. They are constantly on the lookout for new routes into people's consciousness.

With the advent of the remote control, the mute button, and the video cassette recorder during the 1980s, people could easily avoid TV commercials, and advertisers had to seek out consumers elsewhere. Expanding on the traditional print and broadcast media, advertisers began piping messages into classrooms and doctors' offices, weaving them into the plots of feature films, posting them on chair-lift poles, printing them on postage stamps and board games, stitching them on Boy Scout merit badges and professional athletes' jerseys, mounting them in bathroom stalls, and playing them back between rings on public phones.

Marketers hired telephone solicitors, both human and computerized, to call people directly in their homes. They commissioned essays from well-known authors, packaged them between full-page ads fore and aft, and mailed them to opinion leaders to polish the sponsors' images. And they created ad-packed television programming for use at airports, bus stops, subway stations, exercise clubs, ski resorts, and supermarket checkout lines.

This creeping commercialization of life has a certain inevitability to it. As the novelty of each medium wears off, advertisers invent another one, relentlessly expanding the share of our collective attention span that they occupy with sales spiels.

Next, they will meet us at the mall, follow us to the dinner table, and shine down on us from the heavens. In shopping centers, they have begun erecting wall-sized video screens to heighten the frenzy of the shopping experience. Food engineers are turning the food supply into an advertising medium. The Viskase company of Chicago prints edible ad slogans on hot dogs, and Eggverts International is using a similar technique to advertise on thousands of eggs in Israel. Lighting engineers are hard at work on featherweight ways to turn blimps into giant airborne neon signs, and, demonstrating that not even the sky is the limit, Coca-Cola convinced orbiting Soviet cosmonauts to sip their soda on camera a couple of years ago.

The main outcome of this deadening commercialization is to sell not particular products, but consumerism itself. The implicit message of all advertising is the idea that there is a product to solve each of life's problems. Every commercial teaches that existence would be satisfying and complete if only we bought the right things. As religious historian Robert Bellah put it, "That happiness is to be attained through limitless material acquisition is denied by every religion and philosophy known to humankind, but is preached incessantly by every American television set."

GET 'EM WHILE THEY'RE YOUNG

The commercialization of space and time has been accompanied by the commercialization of youth. Marketers are increasingly targeting the young. One specialist in marketing to children told the *Wall Street Journal*, "Even two-year-olds are concerned about their brand of clothes, and by the age of six are full-out consumers." American children and teenagers sit through about three hours of television commercials each week—20,000 ads a year, translating to 360,000 by the time they graduate from high school.

The children's market in the United States is so valuable—topping $75 billion in 1990—that American companies spent $500 million marketing to kids in 1990, five times more than they spent a decade earlier. They started cartoons centered around toys and began direct-mail marketing to youngsters enrolled in their company-sponsored "clubs."

Such saturation advertising has allowed some firms to stake huge claims in the children's market. Mattel vice president Meryl Friedman brags, "Mattel has achieved a stunning 95 percent penetration with Barbie [dolls] among girls 3 to 11 in the United States."

Predictably, major retailers have opened Barbie departments to compete for the loyalty of doll-doting future consumers, and marketers pay premium prices to employ the dolls as an advertising medium. Barbies come equipped with Reebok shoes and Benetton clothes.

MADISON AVENUE'S PAPER TRAIL

Advertising's main ecological danger may be the consumption it inspires, but it also consumes heavily itself. Advertisers use a substantial share of the world's paper, particularly its heavily-processed high-quality paper. Paper production involves not only forest damage but also large energy inputs and pollution outputs.

Ads pack the daily mail: 14 billion glossy, difficult-to-recycle mail-order catalogs plus 38 billion other assorted ads clog the post office each year in the United States. Most of those items go straight into the trash—including 98 percent of advertising letters sent in direct-mail campaigns, according to the marketing journal *American Demographics.*

Ads fill periodicals: most American magazines reserve 60 percent of their pages for advertising, and some devote far more. *Bride's* was so proud of its February/March 1990 edition that it submitted the issue to the *Guinness Book of World Records* and boasted in *Advertising Age,* "The Biggest Magazine in History.... It contains 1,040 pages—including 798 advertising pages."

Newspapers are no different; in the United States, they typically contain 65 percent, up from 40 percent half a century ago. Every year, Canada cuts 42,000 acres of its primeval forests—an area the size of the District of Columbia—just to provide American dailies with newsprint on which to run advertisements.

For big and immediate paper savings, newspapers could shift classified advertising—and

telephone companies their directories—onto pay-per-use electronic data bases accessible through phone lines. Still, advertising remains heavy in nonclassified sections of newspapers. Trim out all the ads and most of the text would fit in a single section.

The problem in reducing the scale of advertising in the print media is that the financial viability of newspapers and magazines is linked to the number of advertising pages they sell. In the past two years of economic recession, for example, advertising pages have been harder to sell, and many periodicals have been forced to publish fewer articles. That is not good for the flow of information in democratic societies. To get less-commercialized information sources, subscribers may have to accept higher prices, as have the readers of *Ms.,* which dropped advertising three years ago.

THE INDUSTRY OF NEEDS

The needs industry—advertising—defends itself, ultimately, by claiming that advertising, whatever its social and cultural demerits, is an indispensable component of a healthy economy. As one Madison Avenue axiom counsels, "A terrible thing happens when you don't advertise: Nothing." Advertising, in this view, isn't the trim on the industrial economy, it's the fuel. Take out the ads, and the economy sputters to a halt; put in more ads, and the economy zooms. More ads equal more wants, more wants make more spending, and more spending makes more jobs.

Some promoters even call for governments to foster more advertising. The American Advertising Federation took out a full page in *Time* magazine last March to write, "Dear Mr. President...We respectfully remind you of advertising's role as an engine of economic growth. It raises capital, creates jobs, and spurs production.... It increases government revenues since jobs produce taxable income, and greater sales increase sales taxes...Incentives to advertise are incentives for growth."

The validity of such claims is dubious, of course, but they cut to the heart of a critical issue. Even if advertising does promote growth, the question remains as to what kind of growth. Growth in numbers of second mortgages and third cars and fourth televisions may increase the money flowing around the economy without making us one bit happier. If much advertising is an exercise in generating dissatisfaction so that people will spend more and work harder, the entire process appears morally questionable. Several generations ago, Catholic theologian John Ryan dubbed this treadmill "squirrel cage progress."

Many of the areas in which the world needs growth most desperately—environmental literacy, racial and sexual equality, and political participation, for example—are not the stuff of advertising campaigns. "Civilization, in the real sense of the term," advised Gandhi, "consists not in the multiplication, but in the deliberate and voluntary reduction of wants."

RE-CHANNELING ADVERTISING

What legitimate role is there for advertising, then? In a sustainable society, how much advertising would there be?

None! say some, as E. F. Schumacher commented in 1979: "What is the great bulk of advertising other than the stimulation of greed, envy and avarice...at least three of the seven deadly sins?" More succinctly, reader Charlotte Burrowes of Penacook, New Hampshire, wrote to *Worldwatch* a year ago, "There'll be a special hell for advertisers."

In fairness, though, some advertising does provide useful information about products and services. The task for democratic societies struggling to restore balance between themselves and their ecosystems is to decide how much advertising to tolerate, and while respecting the rights of individuals to speak their minds, to place appropriate limits on marketing.

The precise limits cannot yet be identified, but it may help define the issue to consider whether there are spaces that should be free of advertising. Churches? Schools? Hospitals? Funeral homes? Parks? Homes? Work places? Books? Public libraries? Public swimming pools? Public buildings? Public buses? Public streets? Mail boxes? Newspapers? Television broadcasts? What about times of day, days of the week, and times of life? Early morning? Sundays? Childhood?

Restraining the excesses of marketers and limiting commercials to their legitimate role of informing consumers would require fundamental reforms in the industry, changes that will not come about without a well-organized grassroots movement. The advertising industry is a formidable foe on the march around the world, and advertisers are masters at the slippery art of public relations. Madison Avenue can buy the best talents available to counter and circumvent reformers' campaigns, unless those campaigns are carefully focused and begin with the industry's vulnerabilities.

Advertising's Achilles heel is its willingness to push products demonstrably dangerous to human health, and this is the area where activists have been most successful and best organized. Tobacco ads are or soon will be banished from television throughout the Western democracies, and alcohol commercials are under attack as never before.

Another ready target for advertising reform activists is the assault that marketers make on children. Public sentiment runs strongly against marketing campaigns that prey on youngsters. Action for Children's Television, a citizens' group based in Boston, won a victory in late 1990 when the U.S. Congress limited television commercials aimed at children. The same year, public interest organizations in the European Community pushed through standards for European television that will put strict limits on some types of ads.

The Australian Consumers' Association is attacking junk food ads, calling for a ban or tough restrictions on hawking unhealthful fare to youngsters. Of food ads aired during children's television programs, the association's research shows that 80 percent are for high-fat, high-salt, excessively packaged snacks. The American Academy of Pediatrics is similarly concerned. Noting the high proportion of advertisements for products that violate nutrition guidelines, the organization is urging Congress to ban food ads that target the young.

Alternatively, consumers could take aim at trumped-up corporate environmental claims. Since 1989, marketers have been painting their products "green" in an attempt to defuse citizen anger at corporate ecological transgressions. In

1990, for example, the oil company Texaco offered Americans "free" tree seedlings to plant for the good of the environment; to qualify, a customer had to buy eight or more gallons of gasoline. Unmentioned in the marketing literature was the fact that it takes a typical tree about four years to store as much carbon dioxide as is released in refining and burning eight gallons of fuel, and that most tree seedlings planted by amateurs promptly die.

In the United States, one fourth of all new household products introduced in 1990 advertised themselves as "ozone-friendly," "biodegradable," "recyclable," "compostable," or something similar—claims that half of all Americans recognize as "gimmickry." Environmentalists in the Netherlands and France have attempted to cut away such misinformation by introducing a 12-point environmental advertising code in their national legislatures. Ten state attorneys general are pushing for similar national standards in the United States. Meanwhile, official and unofficial organizations throughout Europe, North America, and Japan have initiated "green labeling" programs, aiming to steer consumers to environmentally preferable products.

Efforts to restrict advertising of tobacco and alcohol, to curtail advertising to children, and to regulate environmental claims of marketers are parts of a broader agenda. The nonprofit Center for the Study of Commercialism in Washington, D.C., is calling for an end to brand-name plugs in feature films, for schools to declare themselves advertising-free zones, and for revision of the tax code so that money spent on advertising is taxable.

Just as the expanding reach of advertising is not going unchallenged, small networks of citizens everywhere are beginning to confront commercial television. In Vancouver, British Columbia, English teacher Michael Maser gets secondary students to study television production

so they will be able to recognize techniques used to manipulate viewers' sentiments. Millions of young people could benefit from such a course, considering how many products are pitched to them on TV. Along the same lines as Maser's teaching, the Center for Media and Values in Los Angeles has been promoting media literacy since 1989, by furnishing parents throughout North America with tips on teaching their children to watch with a critical eye.

More boldly, some attempt to fight fire with fire. The Vancouver-based Media Foundation is building a movement aimed at using the same cleverness and humor evident in much commercial advertising to promote sustainable ends. Local groups raise funds to show the group's products on commercial television and in commercial magazines. TV spots have run in California, Ontario, and a half-dozen other states and provinces. Their "Tube Head" series of ads tell viewers to shut off the set. In one magazine ad, above a photo of a dark, sleek sports car, a caption purrs, "At this price, it will surely take your breath away." And below: "$250,000." In fine print, it explains, "U.S. sticker price based on individual share of social costs associated with automobiles in U.S. over average car life of 10 years. Does not include... oil spills at sea and on land; acid rain from auto emissions... environmental and health costs from global warming."

The premier spot in the Media Foundation's "High on the Hog" campaign shows a gigantic animated pig frolicking on a map of North America while a narrator intones: "Five percent of the people in the world consume *one-third* of the planet's resources.... Those people are us." The pig belches.

Imagine a message like *that* broadcast simultaneously to every inhabited part of the globe!

STUDY QUESTIONS

1. Do you agree with Durning that advertising poses a dangerous threat to society? Provide illustrations from your experience to support your views on the matter.

2. How, according to Durning, is advertising like a parasite? Do you agree with him?

3. How can we ensure that advertising serves good purposes rather than environmentally bad purposes? Could the cure for advertising be worse than the parasite itself?

77   The Challenge of the Future: Private Property, the City, the Globe, and a Sustainable Society

LOUIS P. POJMAN

Louis P. Pojman was professor of philosophy at the United States Military Academy at West Point and the editor of this volume. He is the author of numerous books and articles. In this essay Pojman argues that we cannot rest content with saving the wilderness; we must also apply environmental ethics to city life. He outlines a theory of a global sustainable society and suggests some examples of working toward that goal.

Much of this book has been about the wilderness or natural habitats, as though the cities were anti-environmental. I want to correct this impression, focusing on sustainable city life. Then, I will bring together many of the themes in this anthology, pointing toward a universal environmental ethic and law that requires regulation by an international body. Finally, I want briefly to suggest some practical things we all can do to live responsibly toward the environment. First, I turn to the matter of the uses of private property.

1. PRIVATE PROPERTY AND ENVIRONMENTAL ETHICS

"Nor shall private property be taken for public use without just compensation." (From the Fifth Amendment of the Constitution of the United States of America, commonly known as the *Taking Clause*)

In January 1986 David Lucas purchased two beachfront lots on South Carolina's Isle of Palm for $975,000, planning to build a house on one lot and sell the other lot to a home builder. In 1988 the state subsequently passed the Beach-front Management Act, which prohibited building in the area, arguing that the proposed building projects would harm the dunes and hence were a nuisance. Lucas brought the case

to a local court, which awarded him $1.2 million in compensation. However, the South Carolina Supreme Court reversed the decision, citing a rule that where property is taken to prevent public harm, no compensation is required. Lucas appealed to the U.S. Supreme Court, which heard his arguments on March 2, 1992. Justice John Scalia wrote the Court's decision, which reversed the South Carolina Supreme Court decision, remanding the case back to the court to produce an equitable settlement. A strong component in majority decision was the *Taking Clause* of the Fifth Amendment (quoted above). Justice Scalia also quoted from Justice Oliver Wendell Holmes's exposition in *Pennsylvania Coal Co. v. Mahon* (1922) that "while property may be regulated to a certain extent, if regulation goes too far it will be recognized as a taking." And if it is a taking, then compensation is required. Justice Scalia conceded that the operative phrase "if regulation goes too far" was vague and relative to custom, but in *Agins v. Tiburon* the Court explained that a regulation goes "too far" if it "denies an owner [all] economically viable use of his land." Justice Scalia thought that this was occurring in Lucas's case.

Justice Harry Blackmun wrote a spirited minority dissent in which he defended the South Carolina Supreme Court's decision because it rested "on two premises that until

---

This essay is adapted from Louis P. Pojman, *Global Environmental Ethics* (McGraw-Hill, 2000).

today were unassailable—that the State has the power to prevent any use of property it finds to be harmful to its citizens, and that a state statute is entitled to a presumption of constitutionality."

> If the state legislature is correct that the prohibition on building in front of the setback line prevents serious harm, then, under this Court's prior cases, the Act is constitutional. "Long ago it was recognized that all property in this country is held under the implied obligation that the owner's use of it shall not be injurious to the community, and the Takings Clause did not transform that principle to one that requires compensation whenever the State asserts its power to enforce it." (*Keystone Bituminous Coal Assn. v. DeBenedictis*). The Court consistently has upheld regulations imposed to arrest a significant threat to the common welfare, whatever their economic effect on the owner.[1]

Blackmun's argument rests on the same reasoning as zoning laws (e.g., prohibiting pornography from being sold openly in stores or taverns from being opened in certain residential communities). Just because I buy a piece of land with the intention of building a liquor store on it does not automatically mean that I'm entitled to compensation when a zoning law rules out my endeavor. However, if no law exists and I start to build my liquor store, then, if the state zones against liquor stores, I am entitled to compensation. The fact that Lucas had not actually started to construct his buildings before the law was passed seems to weigh against compensation. On the other hand, the state should probably offer to buy the property from him at a fair price. Or perhaps an environmental organization should purchase Lucas's land at a fair price.

But the larger issues are (1) whether the state has the right to prohibit what it considers harmful use of the land and (2) whether it has to compensate anyone when it prohibits ecological degradation from occurring on the land. If land is valuable for the common good and posterity, environmentalists argue, we are doing harm by depleting its quality. The ramifications of this idea are far reaching. Many artificial lakes and reservoirs in the Southwest are used mainly for recreation and cover precious bottomland with good topsoil. We are running out of good topsoil. So should we prohibit interest groups from constructing these artificial lakes? Dammed-up lakes also affect the natural environment in deleterious ways. Should this reason be good enough to prohibit their construction? Even if the land is privately owned? Golf courses often take up similarly good land and typically require enormous quantities of water and fertilizer, the latter of which seeps into the underground water supply. Should we prevent private country clubs from creating golf courses? What about highways and parking lots and shopping malls that are constructed on land that will one day be needed for farming and whose waste seeps into the underground water supply? And should owners be compensated for the restrictions we put upon them? Similarly, suppose I want to fill in wetlands I own in order to construct a shopping mall. The courts have ruled that the state may forbid me from filling in these wetlands because wetlands provide natural habitats for wildlife, help reduce flooding by slowing the runoff of heavy rains, and promote the cycling of nutrients. Should the state be made to compensate me for not filling in the wetlands? This would be very costly and probably strain the state's coffers.

Taking the environment seriously certainly limits our freedom to do what we want with land. Private property no longer has the same meaning. Until recently we thought that the owner had virtually absolute control of his or her private property, absolute discretion in what uses he or she saw fit for the land—just as long as no one else was being harmed. But if environmentalists are right, there is no absolute right to do what you want with your land. Rather, we have to extend the notion of harm to include future use—even to future people. Joseph Sax calls such protections of nature "public rights" because their infringement need not harm any identifiable person, but whose harm may be diffuse and affect future people or existing people in the future. We now have to say that property rights have been severely constricted because the land is precious, a common good that must remain in good condition for future use in perpetuity. We are not absolute owners of the land, but stewards of it.

This thinking is not new. Suppose a pharmaceutical company, at great cost, produces a powerful drug that it believes will be a cure for some malady, but then it turns out that the drug has unanticipated harmful side effects. The company has no claim to compensation from the state, which has prohibited the use of the drug, but must swallow the loss itself. Similarly, when we discover that a use of the land, hitherto thought to be benign, is harmful, the state has a right to prohibit such use without having to compensate the owner. Or take the fact that refrigerators and air conditioners used chlorofluorocarbons (CFCs). In our ignorance we thought that such use was benign. Now we have evidence that CFCs are depleting the ozone layer, causing cancer. Aren't we within our rights to pass legislation demanding that a substitute be found for harmful CFCs? Just because they were allowed in a previous time of ignorance is no reason for thinking that the companies should now be compensated for being required to stop using such chemicals.[2] Whether the state should help in the research and development of substitutes is another matter. Perhaps it should.

Environmental considerations seem to require that we amend our understanding of *land* property rights. Once thought to be absolute—as long as we were not directly using our property to unjustly harm others—we now see that some uses of land, formerly thought benign, may well harm others, including those who will live after us. Or, if not harm them directly, at least prohibit them from using the land for optimal purposes (e.g., if I fill in the wetlands, species may be lost and we may be unable to restore them to their original state). We must see the land not as our inalienable, absolute property, but as an entrustment—that is, a stewardship model must replace the ownership model. The land is on loan to us to use and develop as long as we do not make it significantly worse.

The Wise Use Movement

I hope the preceding discussion sounds rational, even commonsensical to you. One might say that what environmentalists are advocating is wise use of the land, as well as the wilderness, the forests, and the waterways. Unfortunately,

words are cheap and names misleading. Alas, anti-environmentalists have coopted the good phrase "wise use" to defeat many of the programs necessary to maintain and preserve the environment. In 1979 Ron Arnold wrote a series of articles for *Logging Management* in which he called for a coalition to counter the environmental movement. Alan Gottlieb followed up on his call and together they organized what has become known as the Wise Use Movement, a phrase borrowed from Teddy Roosevelt's chief of the Forestry Service, Gifford Pinchot. It has become an umbrella organization for more than 200 organizations dedicated to fight environmentalist agenda—e.g., from promoting the cutting of old growths in national forests, removing protection from endangered species, allowing private development of public lands and strip mining, to mandating compensation for any *takings* by the government—when they are taken for environmental causes.

I regard the Wise Use Movement as a fearful reaction to the radical changes that are occurring in our understanding of humanity's relationship to its environment. It is hard to change old ways of thinking, and sometimes environmentalists are not patient, understanding, or ready to negotiate with those who haven't developed a sufficiently progressive attitude toward nature. Indeed, some environmentalists seem fanatical, resorting to eco-sabotage (see Reading 80). Although the Wise Use Movement must be exposed and resisted, more work probably needs to be done to find intermediate solutions for those who stand to lose their jobs, investments, and property as we pursue the quest for ecological wholeness.[3]

Let me now turn to another difficult issue on which more work needs to be done.

2. THE CITY

In 1800 about 2% of the world's population lived in urban areas; by 1900 the figure had doubled to 4%; in 1950 it had reached 30%. Since 1950 the number has jumped from 750 million to 2.64 billion—projected to reach 3.3 billion by 2005. In 1975 about one-third of the world's population lived in cities. In 1997, 2.64 billion people, or

46% of the world's population, lived in cities and, according to UN estimates, that figure will soon reach 53.7%. The projection is that almost two-thirds of humanity will live in cities by 2015. The 61 million people being added to cities each year come mainly through rural to urban migration. The most dramatic shifts are taking place in the developing nations, where urban population growth is 3.5% per annum, as opposed to 1% in the more developed nations. In 1800 about 6% of the U.S. population lived in cities. By 1900 the figure was 40%, and by 1997 it was 75%. Until a few generations ago most Americans lived on farms, produced their own food and clothes, educated their children at home, and lived a simple life, far from urban problems of overcrowding and crime. They rode horses and fished in nearby streams and rivers.

The number of urban areas is also increasing. In 1800 London was the only city with more than one million people. Today 326 cities have more than one million people, and 14 are megacities, urban areas with populations of more than 10 million. Tokyo is currently the most populous city with 27 million people in its densely populated urban area, about one-quarter of Japan's entire population. Lagos, Nigeria, growing at a rate of 5.4%, has increased from 10.3 million people in 1995 to more than 13.5 million in 2001, heading toward 25 million by 2015.

Our founding fathers were committed to small town, rural America. The first antiurban tract, *Notes on the State of Virginia* (1781), written by Thomas Jefferson, deplored urbanity as being opposed to good government.

> The mobs of the great cities add just as much to the support of pure government as sores do to the strength of the human body.[4]

In a letter to Benjamin Rush, Jefferson wrote, "I view great cities as pestilential to the morals, the health and the liberties of man."[5] He envisioned the simple living, citizen farmer, uncorrupted by urban luxury and sophistication, as the ideal democrat, the morally righteous man who had a stake in good government and who had no need for the unnecessary frills of urban society.

Nineteenth-century Americans shared Jefferson's faith in the farmer. Essayist Ralph Waldo Emerson thought that only farmers created wealth and that all trade depended on their endeavors. He shared Jefferson's views on the moral superiority of farmers:

> The uncorrupted behavior which we admire in animals and in young children belongs to [the farmer], to the hunter, the sailor—the man who lives in the presence of Nature. Cities force growth and make men talkative and entertaining, but they make them artificial.[6]

Similar sentiments are found in the writings of Plato (in Book II of the *Republic*), Henry Thoreau, Herman Melville, Nathaniel Hawthorne, and Edgar Allan Poe, who compared the city to a sewer of evil and wickedness. William James (1842–1910) deplored the "hollowness" and "brutality" of large cities and advocated their decentralization. James's colleague at Harvard, Josiah Royce (1855–1916), offered three criticisms of urbanity. (1) Cities were so overwhelmed with large numbers of alienated and unassimilated people that the essential fabric of society was stretched to the breaking point; (2) the centralization of culture produced mass conformity and intellectual stagnation; and (3) cities promoted the "spirit of the mob," which is the enemy of individualism and liberty.

These criticisms, though debatable, have continued throughout the twentieth century and seem likely to trouble us as we enter into the twenty-first century. Counterculture critic Ted Roszak sums up the present criticism—cities are decadent.

> . . . the problem posed by the city as an imperialistic cultural force that carries the disease of colossalism in its most virulent form. . . . At the same time, the city is a compendium of our society's ecological bad habits. It is the most incorrigible of wasters and polluters; its economic style is the major burden weighing upon the planetary environment. Of all the hypertrophic institutions our society has inflicted upon both the person and the planet, the industrial city is the most oppressive.[7]

The case against cities goes like this: Cities are parasites on the agricultural base located in the country. They take in resources—water from the mountains, food from the farms, oil from other nations, coffee and tea and other products from the developing countries. Although they take advantage of concentrated labor and produce important goods and services, which rural areas are unable to do, they also create expensive luxury items, which no one really needs and which may actually weaken society's moral fiber—like indulgent department stores for the rich, neon light districts, the compressed trees called the Sunday *New York Times,* and energy-inefficient buildings—and they typically are filled with vehicles which pollute the atmosphere. Advertising creates false consciousness and a craving for the spoils of splendor. The city is often a cesspool of pollution, a sewer of vice, violence, crime, corruption, poor schools, poverty, unemployment, high taxes, suffering, and alienation. Typically dense with the anonymous homeless, panhandlers, muggers, and drug addicts, pungent with the smell of decay, the ugly sights of gaudy graffiti and garish advertisements, and the noise of boomboxes, garbage trucks, and ambulances, the urban ulcer ubiquitously bombards our senses and crowds out our thoughts, alienating us from our selves. The barrage of sensory stimulation overwhelms us, suffocating the inner voice within, so that we become alienated individuals in the lonely crowd. A common, superficial media culture informs our ideas and dictates our tastes and fashions. These unnatural conditions close people off from the realities of the wilderness and agriculture—children and some adults actually suppose that food naturally comes wrapped in clean cellophane packages. Sheltered from the killings, from the blood and stench of the slaughterhouse, from the screams of the cattle and sheep and pigs, from the chickens *tortured* by our modern death chambers, the people of the city live in ignorance—not blissful ignorance, however, for decadence, disease, and death haunt their lives and render all too many of them meaningless.

Yet cities offer civilization:[8] culture and convenience, commerce and industry, employment and job-training, business headquarters and research centers, libraries and universities, music and theater, and a wide range of diverse ideas and attitudes. Its standards of sanitation and health care are usually better than those in rural areas. For the prosperous, city life can be liberating. The concentration of people, wealth, culture, and business offers enormous opportunities for those equipped to take advantage of them.

Cities like Minneapolis, Minnesota; Vancouver, Canada; and Melbourne, Australia—with their public parks, lakes, walking trails, bicycle paths, open spaces, low crime rates, and children's playgrounds—stand out as models for the future. Every home in Minneapolis is within six blocks of green spaces. Melbourne reduced land taxes to attract the middle class to its environs, restricted the height of buildings to 131 feet (about 12 stories), and successfully renovated the decrepit structures of its inner city. Some 50,000 people now live in the central business district, a fivefold increase from a decade ago. But only time will tell what difference the recent addition of a mammoth casino will make.[9]

In 1993, Cajamarca, Peru, one of the poorest communities in the world, was racked by disease, unemployment, and water problems. Its infant mortality rate of 94.7 per 1,000 live births was 82% higher than the Peruvian national average. The Kilish River, a source of drinking water for the poor, had been contaminated by mining operations and untreated sewage. Overgrazing in nearby rural areas and clear-cutting of forests for fuel had caused severe soil erosion, exacerbating flooding problems and contributing to a depressed economy. In 1993 nongovernmental organizations (NGOs), in cooperation with businesses and local unions, organized communities in the urban and nearby rural areas into 76 "minor population centers," each with its own mayor and council. This dramatic decentralization of government power enabled the people to deal with local issues while communicating with an area-wide, overarching authority. Together they set up carpentry schools, an efficient water delivery system, refuse collection, health services, and park improvements. In the rural areas outside the city they terraced the steep hillsides and put into operation a plan to reduce mining pollution.[10]

In 1980 an NGO developed the Orangi Pilot Project (OPP) in the poverty-stricken, ethnically diverse city of Karachi, Pakistan. The residents were organized into groups of 20 to 40 families living along the same lane and taught to use appropriate technology to construct low-cost sanitation facilities. After this four-year project was successful, OPP developed basic health and family planning programs, including immunization programs for children. Next it created a credit program to fund loans for small family enterprises, a low-cost housing upgrade program, a program to assist in improving educational facilities, a women's work center program, and a rural development program. Each house received a sanitary latrine. The Karachi government contributed to the construction costs of health and sanitation facilities, but by simplifying design and standardizing parts, these costs were greatly reduced, in some cases to as low as one-fifth of similar improvements elsewhere in the city. Within a decade 95% of the children were being immunized, 44% of the families were practicing birth control, epidemic disease was under control, and hygiene and nutrition had improved. Infant mortality fell from 130 per 1,000 live births in 1982 to 37 in 1991. Through the work center women learned to stitch clothing, enabling them to do piecework bound for international export at higher wages than they had ever earned, thus contributing to the overall wealth of the community.[11]

Such examples of sustainable urbanization, often in conjunction with nearby rural development, are impressive and offer models of a better future, but success stories are still too few and far between. Accessible clean water, sanitation systems, decentralized government, local empowerment to men and women, education, job training, and inexpensive basic health care—all seem necessary but not sufficient for sustainable city life. A moral consciousness must exist to energize and synthesize a community. People must believe in environmental goals and commit themselves to them.

The evils of cities, mentioned earlier, tend to compete with and even outweigh these possible environmental virtues, causing many people to fear urban existence, treating the city as a nice place to visit but a bad place to live. Because most of us want the benefits of city life, the question is, How can we restructure our cities so that they are environmentally sustainable centers of human flourishing?

This is the big question, and in answer I can only point to some attempts that have been made. We need to solve this problem. When we visit cities, we see children growing up without trees to climb or rivers in which to swim. In their place are urban jungles where skyscrapers replace redwoods on the near horizon. Comparing that with my own edge-of-the-town, semi-rural upbringing, where I spent summers playing barefoot in the woods, swimming in ponds and rivers, sadness overcomes me because urban children are missing these simple joys. I see children who are over-socialized, programmed from the nursery school to the university, never feeling the call of the wild or imbibing the wide open spaces of the prairie or the flow of the river, captives of too much repressive civilization, their watches mechanically dictating their schedules from their earliest years.

There are too many people in the cities. Every week one million people are added to these urban centers. Poor people are lured from the countryside of other countries by the promise of a better life, only to add to the malaise of urban poverty. Cities are densely populated, and the friction of our encounters ruffles our nerves and leaves us yearning for clean open spaces, for freedom of movement. We need more parks in our cities—much on the European model—and fewer cars and trucks. New York City, with its ban on motor vehicles in Central Park on weekends, has taken a step in the right direction. The ban should be extended to the other five days of the week and to other parts of our cities, because motor vehicles are the main air polluters in New York City and elsewhere. Affordable public transportation should replace cars wherever feasible. Recycling of aluminum cans, glass, and paper is cumbersome but is an environmental necessity. We must make it both natural and economical.

People in cities need more places to plant trees and gardens where they can grow flowers and vegetables. Tall buildings should not dominate the skyline, but smaller ones that allow the light to shine on its inhabitants. Political decentralization is necessary in order to afford people a greater opportunity to participate in the political process. An efficient government, a streamlined court system, and a sense of fairness must bind people to each other—promoting the commonweal. But this sense of a common life and a common cause is difficult to create, especially when politicians and intellectuals emphasize differences rather than commonality, where ethnic and cultural diversity are allowed to divide people. Neither a nation, nor a city divided against itself, can long survive, let alone flourish, and a political structure that allows unjust discrimination will sink in the quicksand of the swamps of exaggerated racial identity, ethnicity, and hate. Diversity may be enriching and has a legitimate placediversity of ideas—as long as people adhere to a common core morality, an agreed-upon political process that brings us together as a moral community— *e pluribus unum.* But where we do approach that common culture—in TV programs and films, for example—it is often shallow and amoral.

Because we prize freedom so much and depend on an unplanned free market economy to such a remarkable degree, it is difficult to solve these seemingly intractable environmental and social problems. Capitalism, our economic system, is like a powerful machine that is under no one's control, satisfying short-term wants and offering wealth, but threatening to uproot our traditions and all those spiritual bonds that tie us together. The truth is that we are not dealing with it successfully; we are allowing it to proceed unchecked in a manner dangerous to our future—as the rich get richer and the poor get prison.

Environmentalists have focused virtually all of their attention on the wilderness, on pristine nature. But in doing so, they may have missed something equally important, the urban environment. The challenge of the twenty-first century will be not only to preserve the wilderness but also to reinvigorate our urban centers with simple dignity and natural beauty.

3. GLOBALISM: ONE WORLD, ONE ETHIC

In the last section we saw that part of the solution to urban crises lay in decentralized authority combined with a supporting, enlightened government.

Reducing the locus of power to the smallest possible group, down to the individual, makes sense, because each individual or small group is a better authority on where the shoe pinches than a distant bureaucracy is. On the other hand, individuals and communities often lack resources to lift themselves from poverty or environmental degradation without help, so an overarching umbrella authority is necessary to distribute goods and services. Moreover, there is the problem of the tragedy of the commons to contend with, which leads to the necessity of an overarching regulatory system. My business or community or country is likely to reason that it is in our interest to use CFCs (or burn fossil fuels) because the benefits we reap are solely ours, whereas we share the harms, a depleted ozone layer (or enhanced greenhouse effect), with others. But if everyone thinks this way, the ozone layer is likely to be destroyed and everyone will suffer a cataclysmic global disaster. Similarly, with regard to emitting greenhouse gases, if we all act in our perceived immediate interest, we are bound to reap total and global ruin. Thus it is in all our interests to give up some of our autonomy and accept "mutually agreed-upon, mutually coercive regulations" which, if followed by the majority, will result in mutual benefit. Recently, I was in North Carolina and heard about the problem of disposing of pig waste (a pig, I was told, discharges an enormous amount of waste—five times the amount of an average human). The sanitation facilities were inadequate, and pig waste was seeping into the water supply in parts of the state, but the state government was reluctant to force the pig industry to invest in better waste disposal systems lest it move out of North Carolina to a state with more relaxed regulations. The solution in such cases is for a federal standard, nationally enforced. Similarly, I was told that Switzerland had imposed strict safety regulations on the pig industry. The result? All pig industries have moved out of Switzerland to less demanding countries. The Swiss still eat the same amount of pork but pay more for it. The solution is obvious: For the health of all people, we should have an international regulatory commission monitoring and enforcing safety standards.

Many of our most intractable environmental problems are international in nature. Radiation from Chernobyl was experienced as far west as Sweden and Switzerland; air pollution from Poland's factories drifts to neighboring countries; greenhouse gases effect climate patterns all over the globe; the depletion of the ozone layer affects the health of people in many nations; and we all will suffer from the loss of biodiversity. Rivers and underground water tables—aquifers—do not respect national boundaries, so that if country A depletes its water table, country B, frugal though it may be, will also experience a loss of water. The recent conferences on the environment in Stockholm (1972), Rio de Janeiro (1992), and Kyoto, Japan (December 1997), fragmented and seemingly fraught with controversy and national self-interest though they were, are a fledgling step in the right direction. At least, we're talking with each other about global environmental degradation and solutions to that degradation, seeking to work out a set of universal rights from which global environmental law will arise. Principles 7 and 8 of the Rio Declaration put the matter this way:

> Principle 7: States shall cooperate in a spirit of global partnership to conserve, protect and restore the health and integrity of the Earth's ecosystem. In view of the different contributions to global environmental degradation, States have common but differentiated responsibilities. The developed countries acknowledge the responsibility that they bear in the international pursuit of sustainable development in view of the pressures their societies place on the global environment and of the technologies and financial resources they command.

> Principle 8: To achieve sustainable development and a higher quality of life for all people, States should reduce and eliminate unsustainable patterns of production and consumption and promote appropriate demographic policies.

Other principles call for compensation of victims of pollution (13), a prohibition of reallocation of toxic substances to poorer countries (14), the internalization of the environmental costs of pollution (16), and the ecological protection of weaker countries from oppression and domination by the wealthier corporations and nations (23). The Charter of the United Nations will be the "appropriate means" for resolving "all their environmental disputes."[12]

As international body, such as the United Nations, will be needed to regulate and enforce these environmental laws. This will not be easy for nationalists to swallow, but we are gradually moving toward universal government to complement and qualify national autonomy. The world is shrinking. Already, several multinational corporations are among the wealthiest bodies in the world, richer than most nations.[13] Even as the capitalist economy has became global, the regulation of the environment must become more global. The road to an enforceable global environmental law will be fraught with obstacles, but in the end we must realize our common humanity, a common objective morality, and a common commitment to ecological wholeness and sustainable living.

4. WORKING FOR A SUSTAINABLE SOCIETY

On May 14, 1998, Marjory Stoneman Douglas died at the age of 108. The author of many short stories, novels, and works of nonfiction, she is best known for her influential 1947 call to arms, *The Everglades: River of Grass*, a natural and political history of the wetlands of southern Florida. Mrs. Douglas protested against the poor land management that was imperiling the Everglades' ecosystem, opposed state and local policies that encouraged overdevelopment, and led the campaign to have the central core of the Everglades preserved as a national park. The Everglades has shrunk from more than 4,000 square miles to less than half that size, the result of over-drainage, urban sprawl, and pollution from government-supported sugar cane and diary farming. Many environmentalists believe that its fate is still in doubt. Regarding the apathy of the people of South Florida to the plight of the Everglades, Mrs. Douglas said, "They could not get it through their heads that they had produced some of the worst conditions themselves, by their lack of cooperation, their selfishness, their mutual distrust and their willful refusal to consider the truth of the whole situation." Unless people act responsibly "over-drainage will go on ... and the soil will shrink and burn and be wasted and destroyed, in a continuing ruin." In 1969 she helped to found Friends of the Everglades, a conservation organization that now has 5,000 members. Joe Podgor, the former executive director, called her "the giant on whose shoulders we all stand." In 1990, on her 100th birthday—blind, hearing impaired, and frail—she continued to speak out against those who plundered the Everglades. Roderick J. Jude, a longtime leader of the Florida chapter of the Sierra Club, said, "The Everglades wouldn't be there for us to continue to save if not for her work through the years." Finally, in 1996, after decades of struggle, the voters of Florida approved a constitutional amendment for cleaning up of the Everglades. In 1997, hoping to rescue the endangered ecosystem from polluted run-off from the sugar cane industry, the Clinton administration and the state of Florida agreed to buy more than 50,000 acres of sugar cane fields on the outskirts of the Everglades National Park. In 1993 President Clinton awarded her the Presidential Medal of Freedom and said, "Long before there was an Earth Day, Mrs. Douglas was a passionate steward of our nation's natural resources, and particularly her Florida Everglades."[14]

Marjory Douglas deserves to be ranked with Henry Thoreau, John Muir, President Theodore Roosevelt, Aldo Leopold, Herman Daly, Rachel Carson, Chico Mendes, and Lois Gibbs—all mentioned earlier in this work—as one of the friends of the Earth, people, who by their integrity, courage, and commitment, made important contributions toward preserving and promoting ecological well-being. They all attest to the fact that citizens can make a difference in making this a better world. These are our present-day heroes, our much needed role models for simple living, local acting, and global thinking.

The fate of the Earth is still in doubt. Many questions about the state of the environment remain. Good and honest people can differ on their reading of the evidence regarding the best energy policy, the best ways to limit pollution, the prognosis of the greenhouse effect, the implications of population growth, and so forth. Some

of you, reading this book, will opt for radical action to save the planet, others for a more conservative policy, and still other for mixed strategies. We live in a democracy, which is sometimes dull and sluggish in promoting the common good, but which affords opportunity for open debate about these important and difficult environmental issues. But although the democratic processes are often painfully slow, they seem the most moral—or least dangerous—processes at our disposal. Those who become impatient with these processes may engage in nonviolent protest to get their point across, but certainly, if history has taught us anything, it is that violence—whether it be perpetrated in the name of the Palestinian cause on the West Bank or that of Catholic freedom in Northern Ireland, and including eco-sabotage—is counterproductive. Violence begets more violence, destroying even the good that exists. Concerned citizens, then, must engage in a peaceful political process, working for a raised consciousness about environmental concerns in the public domain. We must also live out our ecological philosophy because, to a remarkable degree, the personal is the political. Your actions speak louder than your words.

UNITED STATES: THE BIGGEST CONSUMER IN THE WORLD

In one lifetime (70 years) each person in the United States consumes and wastes:

Resource Consumption	Waste
623 tons of fossil fuel	840 tons of agricultural waste
613 tons of sand, gravel & stone	823 tons of garbage & industrial waste
26 million gallons of water	7 million gallons of polluted water
21,000 gallons of gasoline	70 tons of air pollution
50 tons of food	19,250 bottles
48 tons of wood	7 automobiles
19 tons of paper	

Each person in the United States uses 70 times as much energy as a Bangladeshi,

50 times as much as a Malagasy, and 20 times as much as a Costa Rican.

Because we typically live longer, the effect of each of us is further multiplied. In a year each person in the United States uses 300 times as much energy as a Malian; over a lifetime the total is 500 times as much.

Even if all such effects as the clearing of forests and burning of grasslands are factored in and attributed to poor people, those who live in the poor parts of the world are typically responsible for the annual release of one-tenth of a ton of carbon each, whereas the average for residents of the Western nations is 3.5 tons. The richest one-tenth of those in the United States annually emit 11 tons of carbon apiece.

Much has been accomplished since the 1960s, but much has yet to be done. On the plus side, a growing number of citizens have become conscious of environmental concerns, as the membership in environmental organizations such as the Sierra Club, the Wilderness Society, the Nature Conservancy, and others indicates. The celebration of Earth Day each April 22 since 1990 represents a heightened awareness of the environmental crisis. Many school systems, such as those of Wisconsin, incorporate environmental education into the curriculum. In the United States we've seen the passing of the Federal Water Pollution Control Act; the Clean Air Act; the Wilderness Act, setting aside or protecting several ecosystems; the Endangered Species Act, protecting species from harm; and the Toxic Substance Control Act, requiring the screening of new substances before they are widely used. These and the recent international conferences on environmental concerns, such as global warming and biodiversity, already discussed, are steps in the right direction.

On the negative side, the greenhouse effect is getting worse; carbon dioxide in the atmosphere has increased from 280 ppm at the beginning of the Industrial Revolution to 360 ppm, and it threatens to reach 500 ppm by the middle of the twenty-first century.[15] The great glaciers on Antarctica are breaking up, and climate patterns may be changing dangerously. The ozone layer continues to be depleted, and acid rain and other pollutants continue their destructive effect on lakes and forests.

The world's rivers and underground aquifers are increasingly polluted, and rich topsoil continues to be eroded. The destruction of the rain forests and the forests everywhere continues at a menacing pace. The future of the Earth is in jeopardy.

The Earth's population, which has passed 6.4 billion, continues to grow exponentially. People in the developing countries seek to increase their living standards and consumption in a manner similar to those of the developed countries, depleting resources and producing enormous pollution. Add to this the fact that we're losing much of our topsoil and our food production is declining. In 1981 Julian Simon, in his book *The Ultimate Resource*, showed how global food production had continued to rise, and thus become cheaper, for several decades. He wrote, "The obvious implication of this historical trend toward cheaper food—a trend that probably extends back to the beginning of agriculture—is that real prices for food will continue to drop.... It is a fact that portends more drops in price and even less scarcity in the future."[16]

A few years later, however, the sharp growth rates in food production began to level off. Now the gains in grain production are coming in smaller increments, too small to keep pace with the world's population growth. Bill McKibben points out that "The world reaped its largest harvest of grain per capita in 1984; since then the amount of corn and wheat and rice per person has fallen by six percent. Grain stockpiles have shrunk to less than two month's supply."[17]

Why Recycle Paper?

1. To save forests: Recycling one ton of office paper saves seventeen trees.
2. To save energy: It takes 60% less energy to manufacture paper from recycled stock than from virgin materials. Every ton of recycled paper saves 4,200 kilowatts of energy, enough to meet the energy needs of at least 4,000 people.
3. To save water: Making paper from recycled paper stock uses 15% less water than making paper "from scratch." Recycling one ton of paper saves 7,000 gallons of water, enough to supply the daily water needs of almost 30 households.

4. To reduce garbage overload: Every ton of paper not landfilled saves 3 cubit yards of landfill space.

What can we do? If the thoughts set forth in this work have any validity, we can and ought to live more simply. We in the West must lower our consumption levels and reduce the pollution we cause, at the same time encouraging people everywhere to deal with exponential population growth and resource consumption. We can use less and more efficient electricity, recycle paper, plastics, glass and metal, use fluorescent lights, incline toward a vegetarian diet, walk and cycle for short distances, and use public transportation wherever possible, instead of using cars. We can keep in good physical condition and decrease energy use by walking up stairs instead of using elevators. Instead of turning up the thermostat, put on an extra sweater. Wherever possible, we should install solar panels in our buildings. We can strive to make our cities more environmentally wholesome and, at the same time, promote organic farming and local gardens. We can increase our appreciation of the wilderness and spend time camping and hiking, observing wildlife, and appreciating the beauty and stillness of forests and canyonlands. We can join and support an environmental organization that best identifies our values and concerns. We can support political leaders who promote environmental integrity. We can share our ideas and vision of a better world with others, encouraging them to join the environmental movement for a better world. We can become informed citizens and then educate the media, newspapers, radio, and television personnel to the significance of environmental concerns. Our hope is in the young. If we can instill an environmental consciousness in the children, in our homes, churches, and schools, we may be able to save our global home—our planet.

In sum: Live simply so that others may simply live.

NOTES

1. *Lucas v. South Carolina Coastal Council* (Blackmun, J. dissenting).
2. I am indebted for this illustration to Gary Varner, "The Eclipse of Land as Private Property" in *Ethics and Environmental Policy*, eds. F. Ferre and P. Hartel (Athens, GA: The University of Georgia Press, 1994). Varner's article contains a helpful discussion of these matters.
3. For a good discussion of the "Wise Use Movement" see Lisa Newton and Catherine Dillingham, *Watersheds 2* (Wadsworth, 1997), Ch. 10.
4. Thomas Jefferson, *Notes on the State of Virginia* (New York: Harper & Row, 1964), 158.
5. Thomas Jefferson, *Works of Thomas Jefferson*, Vol. 4, ed. P. Ford (New York: Putnam, 1905), 146–7.
6. Ralph Waldo Emerson, *Society and Solitude* (Boston: Houghton Mifflin, 1883), 148.
7. Theodore Roszak, *Person/Planet* (London: Gollancz, 1979), pp. 253–4.
8. *Webster's Dictionary* defines *civilization* as "(1) a relatively high level of culture and technological development; specifically, the stage of cultural development at which writing and the keeping of written records is attained; (2) refinement of thought; (3) a situation of urban comforts.
9. "Cities at Work" by Brendan I. Koerner, *U.S. News & World Report*, June 8, 1998.
10. "Cities Take Action: Local Environmental Initiatives" by Jeb Brugmann, *World Resources: The Urban Environment 1996–97* (New York: Oxford University Press, 1996), pp. 128–9.
11. "The Orangi Pilot Project, Karachi, Pakistan," by Akhtar Badshah, *World Resources: The Urban Environment 1996–97* (New York: Oxford University Press, 1996), pp. 132–3.
12. *The Rio Declaration*, approved by the United Nations Conference on Environment and Development (Rio de Janeiro, Brazil, June 3–14, 1992) and later endorsed by the 47th session of the United Nations General Assembly on December 22, 1992. Reprinted in L. Pojman, ed. *Environmental Ethics*, 3rd ed. (Wadsworth, 2001).
13. For a good discussion of the coming global economy, see William Greider, *One World, Ready or Not* (New York: Simon & Schuster, 1997).
14. "Marjory Douglas, Champion of Everglades, Dies at 108," *New York Times*, May 15, 1998, p. A23.
15. "Climate Is an Angry Beast, and We Are Poking It with Sticks" (Wallace Broecker in McKibben, "A Special Moment in History," *Atlantic Monthly*, May 1998, p. 70).
16. Julian Simon, *The Ultimate Resource* (Princeton University Press, 1981).
17. Bill McKibben, "A Special Moment in History," *Atlantic Monthly*, May 1998, p. 62.

🐝 STUDY QUESTIONS

1. What should be done in cases like the one of David Lucas's property rights? Was the Supreme Court wrong in stating that he was entitled to compensation? Could such a policy bankrupt governments?
2. Why are cities crucial to environmental ethics? Do you agree that a major challenge of the twenty-first century will be to produce sustainable cities? Explain your answer.
3. What are the most important features in a sustainable city?
4. Assess the argument that the development of a global environmental ethic requires international environmental law. Will we need a global regulating body to enforce such law? Or is there a more effective way of dealing with environmental problems? Explain your answer.
5. What else can be done to produce a sustainable society?
6. What can you do to promote environmental well-being?
7. Imagine an ideal ecologically sustainable country. What would it look like?

78   Ecology and Community Design

TODD SAUNDERS

Todd Saunders is an ecological designer who has worked on ecologically based projects with Gaia Architects throughout Europe, including Bergen, Norway. In this essay he explores the idea of participation in ecological community design, aiming at an environmentally sound community with energy efficiency, recycling, and a balance with nature. In his study he examines five European communities that are trying to be models of ecological efficiency and offers guidelines for creating such communities.

LESSONS FROM NORTHERN EUROPEAN ECOLOGICAL COMMUNITIES

In many ways, ecology and community design are in contradiction. Most designs for development inevitably require the destruction of natural ecologies. Consequently, designers often face the paradox that sometimes the most ecologically desirable decision is not to build at all.... There are solutions to this paradox. Designers can create communities that have less impact on the natural environment and are practical alternatives to conventional community design.

Unfortunately, in North America, architectural and planning theorists, not practitioners, develop most ecology and community design concepts. While these works confirm the need for an alternative approach to design, the solutions put forward often are highly theoretical, and do not address practical concerns. Although many architects and planners profess an interest in both ecology and community design, there are virtually no contemporary built examples of "ecological communities" in North America.

Northern Europe, in contrast, supports a long tradition and ever-expanding practice of ecological community design, with a large palette

Reprinted from Todd Saunders, "*Ecology and Design,*" in *Eco-City Dimensions: Healthy Communities, Healthy Planet*, ed. Mark Roseland, 1997. Used by permission of New Society Publishers.

of academic and practical research to draw upon. In 1994, I spent four months visiting 15 ecological communities in northern Europe. I examined five in detail—Ecolonia, in Alphen aan der Rijn, The Netherlands; Lebensgarten, near Steyerberg, Germany; Frasenweg, in Kassel, Germany; Vallersund Gård, Norway; and Järna, Sweden—seeking to identify the guiding principles and main lessons we can learn from northern European ecological communities.

WHAT ARE ECOLOGICAL COMMUNITIES?

"Ecological community" is not a common term in the field of architecture and planning, and as such requires some definition. Ecological communities share similar principles with concepts created by other researchers, which include Green Cities..., Ecological Villages..., Sustainable Communities..., Eco-cities..., and Green Communities.... I chose ecological community as a generic term since all definitions available have common features. These researchers and designers of ecological communities, who look for new ways to integrate artificial environments with natural environments, study human settlements as ecosystems. Viewed as ecosystems, human settlements should be energy efficient, produce little waste, and be self-reliant—much the same as ecosystems appearing in nature.

In accordance with the authors mentioned, and through my own personal experience, I suggest that an ecological community exists if it: 1) applies renewable energy technologies—such as solar energy, combined heat and power schemes, or wind-generated electricity rather than fossil-fuel-related energy supplies; 2) uses alternative sewage and waste water treatment systems; 3) strives to work in conjunction with natural surroundings without disrupting natural features (e.g., soils, water, natural vegetation, and habitat); 4) attempts to function like ecosystems to conserve natural resources, to be self-regulating, and to produce little waste. Furthermore, people living in ecological communities practice recycling and waste recovery as a way of life. In sum, ecological communities are designed to imitate the efficiency in nature, where there is a balance of inputs and outputs of energies, products, and waste. And, ideally, the surplus of these materials is still valuable to the community.

On the basis of my observations and the literature of built ecological communities in northern Europe, I offer ten main recommendations for community designers and others wishing to translate ecological community theory into practice. While these recommendations should help participants to avoid common mistakes on similar projects, they are not definitive. Each community will have its own specific ecosystem and its own set of residents.

1. *Monitor Input and Output of Community Resources* In their efforts to integrate artificial environments with natural environments, ecological community researchers and designers study human settlements as ecosystems, which should be energy efficient and self-reliant and produce little waste. Herbert Girardet, for example, considers a community to be ecological when it adopts a circular metabolism (Figure 1), whereby outputs of the system are equal to the inputs, thus only affecting a small area (1992). Conventional communities have a linear metabolism (Figure 2) where input has no relationship with output: the community takes what it needs with no consideration to consequences.

Attaining the goal of an ecological community is easier when residents understand the input and output of resources. Monitoring is therefore an important educational tool that enables residents to learn how their homes and community are connected to a much larger system. In the five communities I examined in detail, residents are generally aware of the amount of waste materials, energy, and resources they create, produce, and utilize. They can point to areas of the community that need improvement or help establish a circular metabolism.

Residents at Vallersund Gård monitor the amount of energy produced and utilized by the community's windmill. Residents at Järna are aware of the amount and quality of effluent being treated by their biological wastewater

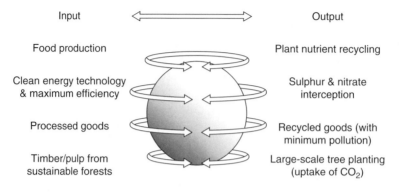

FIGURE 1 Circular Metabolism—Ecological Communities

Adapted from Herbert Girardet, *The Gaia Atlas of Cities: New Directions for Sustainable Urban Living* (New York: Doubleday/Anchor Books, 1992.)

treatment ponds. They avoid flushing plastic and other artificial objects down the toilet because they have seen and learned the consequences of these actions. All the communities in this study know the estimated amount of solid waste produced by and leaving the community. As well, most of the communities monitor their water consumption levels, and know when and how they reduce their water consumption. Through an understanding of these figures residents can take action to lessen environmental impacts and save money spent on excess water, energy, and waste handling.

Knowing the numbers for resource inputs and outputs is also crucial for change of political and public opinion. Awareness of energy savings, waste reduction, and water conservation equips residents with facts that prove the viability of their ecological community. For example, residents at the Frasenweg project reduced solid waste by 50 per cent, and were then able to convince authorities to reduce waste collection fees by the same percentage. Basically, the numbers make it easier for the public and politicians to visualize the efficiency of ecological communities.

2. *Involve the Community* Community involvement in the design and development of ecological communities is crucial, yet it is difficult to measure the quantitative and qualitative benefits. Community groups provide insight into local ecological and social opportunities and constraints that might otherwise be overlooked by architects and designers. Residents can offer first-hand

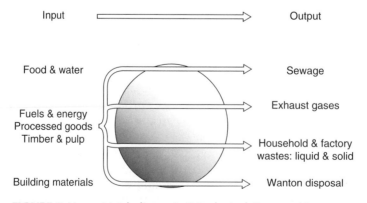

FIGURE 2 Linear Metabolism—Anti-Ecological Communities

Adapted from Herbert Girardet, *The Gaia Atlas of Cities: New Directions for Sustainable Urban Living* (New York: Doubleday/Anchor Books, 1992.)

solutions rather than acting as obstacles to the design of the community. In addition, residents can enhance community support for ecological concerns, and use their position as a mechanism for influencing continued environmental stewardship and motivation in the community.

In almost all the communities studied, residents have been and continue to be involved in major decisions concerning the design, management, or construction process. As a consequence, they understand their local environment. The community can create a design they are comfortable with, and change the design as their needs evolve. Because it is rooted in this understanding, the overall design reflects the needs of the community instead of preconceived design solutions imposed by outsiders.

Since the communities are able to make design, management, and construction decisions, residents respect and conserve the local environment because they have a vested interest in ecological protection. Topics of ecology are no longer abstract, but directly connected to the results of the decision-making process. With community involvement, designs are more likely to correspond to local ecological needs. Without community involvement, sustained environmental protection is unlikely (Agarwal and Narain 1989).

3. *Employ Alternative Housing Arrangements* The ecological communities studied consider the single-family detached house as anti-ecological. As a result they explore other housing forms. In the northern European ecological communities, the dominant housing includes multi-family and cooperative housing arrangements. Cooperative housing is particularly conducive to many environmental community technologies (for example, combined heat and power schemes and windmills) that would require excessive amounts of energy and capital if used for single-detached houses. Residents of cooperative housing share appliances, tools, and automobiles to minimize consumption levels. As well, residents can share maintenance activities, which reduces expenses and may increase leisure time.

Because of their higher densities, cooperative housing, cluster housing, and similar forms reduce urban sprawl as well as car dependency.

Higher densities encourage pedestrian and bicycle traffic, make public transit more efficient, allow shorter travel distances to community facilities, including schools, and lower costs for services such as waste and snow removal. Tighter arrangements of housing leave more land for gardening and play areas, and for the natural treatment of wastewater and storm water. The reduced built-over space facilitates conservation of environmentally sensitive areas that may otherwise be consumed by inefficient land uses. And, along with these contributions to efficiency and environmental protection, higher density housing forms frequently increase the availability of affordable housing.

4. *Design for the Pedestrian* A community designed for the pedestrian helps conserve the surrounding environment. All the northern European communities I visited have been designed for the pedestrian, while the automobile received a lesser priority. Close comparison of these communities' site plans with those of conventional communities confirms that ecological communities devote much less land to the automobile in every case.

With fewer roads in the community, more areas can come into use for children. Streets for pedestrians become active places for meeting residents in the community. And less parking space and fewer roads make it possible to increase space for housing, parkland, and natural habitats.

While living without an automobile is almost impossible in contemporary society, residents of the northern European ecological communities attempt to reduce auto dependency and use the car as a tool. The communities studied have used various methods to reduce car dependency. All the communities have access to public transportation. In addition, the residents of Steyerberg, Germany, Vallersund Gård, Norway, and Järna, Sweden, share their cars. They reserve the designated automobiles in advance, and group all of their chores into one or two days a week, to reduce unnecessary auto trips. The booking system caters to carpooling as well.

Residents of Frasenweg in Kassel, Germany, own their cars independently, but the cars stay outside the community in a carport at the entrance. The result for Frasenweg is an auto-free community. The design of Ecolonia, The Netherlands, controls and slows traffic. The designer, Lucien Kroll, employs the Dutch *woonerf* (living yard) in which the design of the road slows traffic to ten to 15 kilometres per hour. The *woonerf* includes changes such as speedbumps and signs at the entrance reminding drivers that they are entering a controlled traffic zone.

5. *Incorporate Natural Areas into the Community* Many of the northern European ecological communities include natural areas within their boundaries, protect them from disturbance during construction, and minimize other human interference. The presence of these natural areas allows people to experience, observe, and understand the cyclic processes of nature. In turn, this understanding can foster a greater appreciation of natural areas that is not possible in the biologically sterile landscapes of conventional communities. The absence of nature lessens people's perception and appreciation of natural processes and can lead to the loss of sensual perceptions, loss of orientation, and loss of identification (Hahn and Simonis 1991). The presence of nature can, however, achieve the opposite.

In conventional communities, designers often place natural areas at the edges of the community far from where most people live. The resulting travel distance limits the number of times a person can experience a natural area, wastes energy in the form of gasoline, and often leaves people without access to an automobile at a loss. Furthermore, Hough warns that the absence of nature can put environmentalists at a disadvantage. He argues that the perception of human settlements as separate from nature has long been a central problem for the environmental movement and for environmental thinking (Hough 1990).

6. *Use Experimental Projects to Induce Gradual Change of Opinion* Many of the communities in this study are experimental and recognize that standardized solutions outlined by government agencies cannot fulfill the needs and desires for those with a commitment to ecological living.... Residents and designers of ecological communities suggest that experimental projects

induce learning, encourage innovative thinking, and provide flexible opportunities to test new ideas. The general public understands models, especially working ones, better than concepts. As well, a built example is influential because lessons from experimentation can be employed and improved for future projects, thus contributing to the evolution of good design.

In a Canadian study involving extensive field research and interviews, William Perks and David Van Vliet found that experimental projects are considered essential if ecologically responsible community designs are to win acceptance from design professionals, public officials, citizens, and the private sector (Perks and Van Vliet 1993). They report that experimental projects provide real examples that persuade public and local authorities of the richness of ecologically sensitive living environments, and help create new housing markets as developers begin to show more interest in ecological communities....

7. *Change the Role of the Community Designer* It is becoming evident that environmental issues must become the primary responsibility for the architecture and community design profession, starting now and continuing into the future. A major difficulty, however, is that many of the solutions to environmental problems add to the numerous tasks a designer has to deal with in everyday practice. The need to assimilate so much more information before making any positive changes can easily seem overwhelming.

One response is an integrated team approach to ecological community design. Mark Alden-Branch notes that many projects are now being managed by designers who "assemble and lead teams of experts, including urban designers, material consultants, waste consultants, and others."... Similarly, John Turner calls for "professional enablement" where the designer can bring together specialized skills for the community to capitalize on.... In this manner the designer's outside knowledge can be combined with the community's insider knowledge to create a community that best suits all needs and desires.

Other designers believe that solving problems on a much smaller or intimate scale and assuming

an active role in the design and construction process will make the greatest difference. Many of the
designers of the northern European ecological
communities (including Declan and Margrit Ken-
nedy in Lebensgarten, Germany; Gernot Minke
and Doris and Manfred Hegger in Kassel, Germany; and Erik Asmussen in Järna, Sweden) have
submerged themselves in community design by
becoming residents. They argue that when the
design and construction processes are separated,
too many good design intentions are ignored or
never implemented.

Designers commonly avoid the site because if
they overlook mistakes they are often held
accountable for the problems that arise. The
designers living in the ecological communities
studied cannot avoid the site. Since the project
is their home, they have a vested interest in conserving the local ecosystems and educating other
residents. During site construction, designers are
able to meet frequently to discuss the preservation of the site. These designers are then able to
minimize the damages more easily and set precedents for others to follow. It is evident to these
designers that the organization of, and their
involvement in, the building process is the secret
to minimizing negative effects on the natural
environment.

8. *Plan in Stages and for the Long Term*
Many of the ecological communities in northern
Europe have adopted a comfortable pace of
development consisting of a series of stages to
be implemented over the years. The designers
and residents believe that over exertion contributes to an exhaustion of physical, emotional,
and financial resources. They also believe that
moving too slowly causes them to become overly
theoretical without accomplishing anything of
significance. Most have set flexible time limits to
meet their objective of eventually establishing a
fully ecological community.

It is often frustrating for designers to plan for
the long term. Designers concerned about the
future may want to rush their visions quickly
into reality so they can test their ideas. For the
community, however, the process of design and
construction is perhaps more important than
the final product.

During the design and construction process
people build a sense of community and develop
relationships. Developing in a series of stages
allows residents to revisit their initial design
assumptions and intentions. They can change
the community plan to adapt to their increased
understanding of the local ecologies, their evolving community identity, and their appreciation of
the lessons gained in the initial stages. The result
is a community design that more closely fits the
needs and desires of the residents.

9. *Share Information*   Many ecological communities have a multitude of factors in common.
Designers planning to create ecological communities may not want to reinvent the wheel, given
the increasing amount of research and practice
concerning ecological community design available. The problem, however, is that this information is scattered and hard to obtain.

Setting up organizations to disseminate
information can speed up the process of development and help communities avoid mistakes
that may have already been made by other communities. By spreading information across a
greater area, these organizations can help alternative design ideas permeate into mainstream
design practices. It is surprising how effective
information exchange can be for the success of
an idea.

Among the communities I visited, many
associate themselves with a larger organization.
Lebensgarten, Germany, is a member of Éko-
dorf—Informationen (Ecological Villages/Com-
munities—Information), an organization that
publishes a magazine every two months on matters pertaining to ecological communities around
Europe. Vallersund Gård in Norway belongs to
the Camphill Trust for the care of mentally challenged adults, which has five other communities
in Norway and upwards of 80 communities in
more than 18 countries around the world.

As well, many of the northern European countries have ecological community organizations to
assist the development of more ecological communities. Norway and Sweden have the Eco-com-
munity Programs and Denmark has its Green
Community Projects started in 1986, 1990, and
1989 respectively. They all aim to develop

strategies for participating ecological communities, and to serve as examples for other communities.

Such organizations can provide a forum where communities with similar interests learn from each other's successes as well as the inevitable failures. Institutional methods can be transferred from one community to another. Perhaps most importantly, the communities can benefit from shared support, especially in times of need. Central organizations can also represent smaller communities on a much larger scale, protect their interests, and extend their influence....

10. *Maintain a Balance* This final lesson combines all the observations above. Designers can misconceive ecological communities as single-purpose exercises and approach their task with, for example, only alternative energy systems or some other ecological feature in mind, neglecting such important aspects as community, economics, and lifestyle. Such single-purpose thinking has led the modern architecture and planning movement to create many problems. Eivor Bucht...suggests that many ecological communities in Scandinavia may unfortunately suffer the same result because their design was not approached in a holistic manner:

> there are many more examples of negative consequences of such a one-sided ecological design. The problem is that certain ecological criteria are allowed to dominate design and deprive it of the basic principle of good urban planning and design, comprehensive thinking. Therefore I view all ecological architecture and ecological design with scepticism.

Ecology can undoubtedly become the cornerstone of the community, but ecological responsibility is by no means a single remedy for success. Too much devotion to ecological issues may lead to neglect of the very residents who are needed for the persistence of the community. While the ecological factors are crucial, so is the human aspect, which was the reason why the community was constructed in the first place.

CONCLUSIONS

There are two conclusions I consider essential for the transition of the concept of ecological community design from theory into practice. These final points may help bridge the gap between the subjects of ecology and community design. First, in order for ecological communities to make an impact on current environmental problems, these communities must be able to transfer to existing urban areas, in addition to rural areas. Cities can be seen as a salvation for solving ecological and community design issues, but have been viewed by the public as anti-ecological. This conclusion, it may be argued, is not surprising. The literature is filled with examples proving that cities can easily adopt stronger ecological principles.... They argue that the city best represents the relationship between the artificial and the natural environments, and is the place where humans consume large amounts of resources, invent new technologies, affect popular culture, and constitute the largest segment of the world's present and future populations. The actions of cities have implications well beyond their own bioregions. As well, in the city it is possible to live without an automobile, thus minimizing the environmental problems associated with the automobile. For these reasons alone, the city presents the most appropriate place to begin solving current environmental problems.

In northern European countries, particularly Denmark and Germany, more and more of the ecological projects are now in cities. Designers devise efforts to restructure existing urban environments. Under the title urban ecologists, these people assist grassroots organizations and governments in changing the living environments and environmental values of city dwellers. Projects include retro-fitting buildings with environmental technologies, lobbying for more efficient transport systems, implementing waste management programs, and converting grey areas to green spaces. In Germany, these actions have been cunningly called "gentle urban renewal." The urban ecologists have found that their activities have increased community morale, reduced waste costs, created local jobs, and improved the vitality of the respective communities.

Second, the residents and designers of these ecological communities have accomplished a revival of real and practical solutions, that acts as springboards for elaborations of design ideas for the future. A return to rigorous studies that bridge the gap between theory and practice is desperately needed. The residents of these communities have discovered that by applying practical solutions, they are understanding more about themselves and their environment. When compared with conventional communities—not with perfection or the utopian dream—ecological communities and what they represent can provide designers with potential development alternatives.

In short, it is the combination of the principles of ecological communities that is decisive in the creation of viable ecological communities. Establishing well-rounded ecological communities that integrate all aspects of design is not just desirable, it is also clearly possible. The experience of the northern European ecological communities proves that it is practical and attractive to support a number of interests all in one design.

☙ STUDY QUESTIONS

1. According to Todd Saunders, why do ecology and design seem contradictory?
2. Discuss what Saunders means by ecological community.

3. Discuss the recommendations Saunders makes in planning ecological communities. What are the prospects of creating ecological communities in North America?

79   Pedaling Power: Sustainable Transportation

LOUIS P. POJMAN

A biographical sketch of Louis Pojman appears with Reading 77. In this essay, Pojman presents a case for making the bicycle the main instrument for short-distance travel, arguing that it is both far more energy efficient and healthier than the automobile.

Imagine that we invented a mighty Convenience Machine that would make our lives wonderfully more enjoyable and enable us to reach more of our goals. Unfortunately, using the machine would cost us about 50,000 lives per year, about as many casualties as 8 years of the war in Vietnam. Would you use the machine? Should we allow it to be sold on the market?

When I have posed this question to audiences, there is virtually universal agreement that we should not, for no amount of comfort equals the value of a single life.

The question then becomes, Why don't those who treat human life as sacred stop driving cars? The Convenience Machine in our thought

experiment is the motor vehicle. Each year about 50,000 people lose their lives in automobile accidents in the United States and about 250,000 worldwide, more than those killed by the atomic bombs in Hiroshima and Nagasaki in 1945. Since the introduction of the automobile in the United States 100 years ago, about 3 million people have been killed, more than in all the battlefields in all our wars.

The automobile provides us with enormous freedom and power. It makes us mobile and allows us to cover long distances in relatively small amounts of time. In moderation, the automobile is or could be a good thing, but we have become overdependent on it and have misused it.

This essay was written for the first edition of this work.

We have turned what could be a wonderful servant into a tyrannical idol, as the religion of Car Worship with its new urban cathedral, the multistoried parking lot, reeks with the incense of greed, waste, and deleterious exhaust fumes.

Here are some facts.

1. Our economy is overdependent on the motor vehicle. One-sixth of every dollar and one-sixth of every nonfarm job are related to the motor vehicle. It accounts for 20% of our GNP and an annual average of $300 to 500 billion in government subsidies, more than $1,000 per person above the direct costs to car users. The motor vehicle accounts for 63% of our oil use ($43 billion is spent to import oil each year, one-fourth of our national trade deficit).

2. The motor vehicle in the United States is the largest source of urban smog, accounting for 50% of air pollution, 13% of greenhouse gases, and 13% of chlorofluorocarbons (CFCs), thus contributing to the greenhouse effect and the breakdown of the ozone layer. Urban residents in cities throughout the world incur eye, nose, and throat irritation; asthma; headaches; heart attacks; cancer; and emphysema due to car-produced smog. Fuel emissions cause about 30,000 deaths annually in the United States.

3. Cars and trucks clog our highways and streets, causing traffic jams, which in turn greatly increase stress and produce hypertension, ulcers, and nervous disorders—sometimes leading to violence and murder. Further, these jams cause employees to arrive late to work. Government agencies estimate that over $100 billion is lost each year due to traffic jams. Each day 5 million vehicles crowd the Los Angeles freeways, contributing to the 100,000 hours per day that are wasted in traffic jams in that city. One-third of the city's land is given over to automobile-related roads, parking lots, and gas stations (half of downtown LA). Estimates are that the average American commuter spends 2 years of his or her life in traffic jams. In 1907 the average speed of a horse-drawn carriage through the streets of Manhattan was 11.5 mph. Today, a vehicle averaging the power of some 300 horses does the same mile at a pace of 5 mph. At present 38.4 million acres nationwide are given to roads and parking lots (that's the size of the state of Georgia).

Mass transit is both cleaner and more energy efficient. Ironically, in the early part of this century the United States had an effective public transportation system in most of its cities. Trolleys and street cars were used by 20 million riders in 1920, and Los Angeles had one of the best systems in the country. In the 1940s the National City Lines—a holding company formed by General Motors, Firestone Tire, Standard Oil, and Phillips Petroleum—bought up the privately owned streetcar systems in 100 major cities. The old systems were systematically dismantled and replaced with buses, and the use of cars was promoted. Gradually, the bus companies were allowed to fail in many of these cities, creating an increased demand for cars. The courts found the companies guilty of conspiracy to eliminate about 90% of the country's light-rail system and fined the corporate executive officers $1 each and each company $5,000. By that time, GM alone had made $25 million in additional bus and car sales.[1]

Mass transit systems need to be increased throughout the world; but for short trips, another mode of transportation is called for: the bicycle. It is an inexpensive alternative to automobile transport, thirty to forty times cheaper (when gas and maintenance are included—my two bikes, which are over 10 years old and with which I commute to work daily, each cost about $100 plus a combined total of about $500 in maintenance over a ten-year period). The material used to construct one mid-sized American car can construct 100 bicycles. In China and India the bicycle is becoming the preferred mode of transportation, and in some cities in the Netherlands between 40 and 50% of all trips are made by bike. In the United States the use of bicycles as a means of transportation has increased in the past few years, from less than 1% to 2%.

The bicycle is the most thermodynamically efficient mode of transportation ever invented, using less energy per mile than any other mode, including walking. The energy available from

TABLE 1 Energy Intensity of Selected Transport Modes, U.S., 1984

Mode	Calories/Passenger Mile
Bicycling	35
Walking	100
Transit rail	885
Transit bus	920
Automobile, single occupant	1860

Sources: President's Council on Physical Fitness and Sports, Washington, D.C., private communication, June 23, 1988; Mary C. Holcomb et al., *Transportation Energy Data Book: Edition 9* (Oakridge, Tenn.: Oak Ridge National Laboratory, 1987).

eating an ear of corn will get you 3½ miles, and there's less noise and no distilling or refining problem! The bicycle uses 35 calories per passenger mile; walking, 100; rail transport, 885; and the automobile, 1860 (53 times more than the bicycle! See Table 1).

Pedal power creates no air pollution, nor oil spills or climatic change. It cuts down on stress, and provides a good source of exercise, so that employees arrive at work more refreshed and healthier than those imprisoned in traffic jams. In urban areas bicycles move at the same average speed as cars, and sometimes faster. In fact, police in Seattle frequently use bikes to catch car thieves.

Of course, biking can be dangerous too, especially when using the same roads as powerful cars and trucks (90% of bicycle accidents involve collision with a car or truck). Still, bikes are far safer than cars. Although bikes outnumber cars throughout the world by 2 to 1, only 2% of traffic fatalities involve bicycles. But a cyclist should take precautions, wear a helmet, and use a rearview mirror attached to the handlebar or helmet.

Cities like Davis and Palo Alto, California, have extensive bike paths, and St. Paul, Minnesota, is currently in the process of building a 17-mile bicycle freeway. The Netherlands has more than 9,000 miles of bicycle paths, and Japan provides not only bicycle paths but large bicycle garages at train stations, thus combining public transportation with bicycle use.[2] By shifting to nonmotorized transportation, countries could save millions of dollars of fuel costs. A Worldwatch researcher estimates, "If 10% of Americans who commute by car switched to bike-and-ride, more than $1.3 billion could be shaved off the U.S. oil import bill."[3] A 1983 study of American commuters showed that turning to the bicycle could save each 150 gallons of gas per year.

In 1969 a group of University of Minnesota students dragged an automobile engine into downtown Minneapolis. "As a small crowd gathered, the students dropped the motor into a grave, covered it with dirt, and solemnly declared an end to the tyranny of the internal combustion engine over the lungs and lives of civilized people. As traffic rushed past on nearby streets, a young minister read the eulogy:

Ashes to ashes, dust to dust,
For the sake of mankind, iron to rust."[4]

Perhaps the university students' actions were overly dramatic and premature. The internal combustion engine is not likely to die a natural death in the near future. Hopefully, however, a less polluting, electrical car is on the horizon. But for several reasons—economic, health, and land use—the bicycle combined with increased public transportation should replace the automobile as the preferred mode of transportation in the United States and throughout the world. As author and cyclist James McGurn writes, "The bicycle is the vehicle of a new mentality. It quietly challenges a system of values which condones dependency, wastage, inequality of mobility, and daily carnage.... There is every reason why cycling should be helped to enjoy another Golden Age."[5]

The time has come to dethrone the automobile as the American vehicular idol, our destructive Convenience Machine, and to replace it with ecologically sounder modes of transportation, with the person-powered, two-wheeled vehicle as the centerpiece.

NOTES

1. G. Tyler Miller, *Living in the Environment*, 7th ed. (Belmont, CA: Wadsworth, 1992), p. 239. This is a good source for information on this issue.
2. Recently, I read that the City of Amsterdam, clogged with traffic, created a large wind tunnel, wherein people on bikes are blown at high speed from the suburbs into the central city.
3. Marcia Lowe, "Pedaling into the Future," in *World Watch Reader*, ed. Lester Brown (Washington, D.C.: Norton, 1991). I have used Lowe's research in this article.
4. Ed Ayers, "Breaking Away," *Worldwatch* (Vol. 6.1, Jan.–Feb. 1993). Ayers points out that the sprocket chain-driven bicycle and the gas-fueled combustion engine car were both invented in the same year, 1885, but the history of the two vehicles has been one wherein the bigger gadget has pushed the smaller off the road. Might makes Right—or at least, Right of Way.
5. Quoted in Marcia Lowe's *The Bicycle: Vehicle for a Small Planet* (Washington, D.C.: Worldwatch Institute, 1989), p. 46.

STUDY QUESTIONS

1. How feasible is a switch from automobiles to bicycles? Do you see any problems with the analysis in this article?

2. Would switching to electric cars and more efficient mass transit be more realistic ways to make progress in transportation?

80   Ecosabotage and Civil Disobedience

MICHAEL MARTIN

Michael Martin is emeritus professor of philosophy at Boston University. Here he asks if ecosabotage (sabotaging the mechanisms of environmental destruction, but causing no physical harm to humans) can be considered a form of civil disobedience. The question is important for legal reasons, because currently ecosabotage is essentially considered a form of terrorism. In fact, ecosabotage is often called ecoterrorism.

I define ecosabotage and relate this definition to several well-known analyses of civil disobedience. I show that ecosabotage cannot be reduced to a form of civil disobedience unless the definition of civil disobedience is expanded.

I suggest that ecosabotage and civil disobedience are special cases of the more general concept of conscientious wrongdoing. Although ecosabotage cannot be considered a form of civil disobedience on the basis of the standard analysis of this concept, the civil disobedience literature can provide important insights into the justification of ecosabotage. First, traditional appeals to a higher law in justifying ecosabotage are no more successful than they are in justifying civil disobedience. Second, utilitarian justifications of ecosabotage are promising. At present there is no a priori reason to suppose that some acts of ecosabotage could not be justified on utilitarian grounds, although such ecosaboteurs as Dave Foreman have not provided a full justification of its use in concrete cases.

INTRODUCTION

The recent arrest by the FBI of Dave Foreman, founder of the radical environmental group Earth First!, for conspiracy to sabotage two nuclear power plants and a facility that manufactures triggers for nuclear bombs[1] raises anew the issue of the morality of breaking the law for ethical purposes. In this paper I explore a number of analytic and moral questions connected with what has been called ecosabotage: sabotage for the purpose of ecological protection. What is ecosabotage? Is it a form of civil disobedience? Can it be morally justified? Have advocates of ecosabotage such as Foreman in fact provided an ethically acceptable justification for what they sometimes advocate? Although ecosabotage has received wide coverage in popular magazines[2] and other periodicals,[3] these important and difficult questions have been in large part neglected by environmental ethicists.[4]

ECOSABOTAGE DEFINED

Sabotage in the name of environmental protection not only has occurred in real life but has also been detailed in field guides and in fiction. In their book *Ecodefense: A Field Guide to Monkey Wrenching*, Dave Foreman and Bill Haywood describe a number of techniques that can be used to stop, or at least slow down, the destruction of the environment by lumber companies, land developers, and similar organizations.[5] These include how to spike trees with nails in

order to break saw blades, use cutting torches on power lines, puncture tires of road construction equipment, disable bulldozers, and burn billboards Edward Abbey's novel, *The Monkey Wrench Gang*, which influenced the leaders of Earth First!,[6] tells the story of a small group of environmental activists in the southwestern United States who, among other things, blow up railroad bridges, destroy construction machinery, and pull up survey stakes to frustrate land development and road construction.[7] Field guides and fictional accounts aside, environmental activists such as Margaret K. Millet, Mark L. Davis, and Marc A. Baker have reportedly actually tried to cut down a tower that carries power to pump water to the Central Arizona Project, a massive irrigation canal, Earth First! cofounder Howie Wolke is reported to have spent six months in jail for pulling up survey stakes that marked a road into a site where an oil well was being drilled,[8] Paul Watson, leader of the radical environment group the Sea Shepherds has claimed responsibility for sinking two of Iceland's four whaling ships by opening key valves in the ships,[9] and the Sea Shepherds also reportedly sank two Spanish whalers and one Cypriot whaling ship by attaching mines to the hulls.[10]

Can this great variety of acts of ecosabotage be subsumed under one definition? Perhaps, but the construction of such a definition is not easy. I approach the analytic task by first considering some of the elements that such a definition must include. First, any definition of ecosabotage must distinguish it from legal protests concerning environmental issues. Clearly this cannot be done merely in terms of the goals of the two kinds of activities, since an act of ecosabotage and a lawful ecological demonstration can have the same long-range goal, viz., the protection of the environment. Second, a definition of ecosabotage must distinguish it from sabotage for nonecological purposes, for example, wartime sabotage. This distinction cannot be made on purely behavioral grounds, since externally considered, some wartime sabotage might be indistinguishable from ecosabotage. For example, sabotaging a nuclear munitions plant might be either an act of wartime sabotage or an act of ecosabotage depending on what the act is supposed to achieve. Third, the definition must not restrict ecosabotage to the destruction of property. Even some acts of wartime sabotage do not involve this, for example, the removal of essential parts of machinery in a munitions factory. In ecosabotage, the removal of survey stakes from road construction sites might more appropriately be called obstruction rather the destruction.[11] Fourth, ecosabotage should be distinguished from the typical acts of civil disobedience that have been adapted by environmental organizations such as Greenpeace.[12] Fifth, ecosabotage must be distinguished from vandalism, the destruction of property or other mischief that is motivated by malice or spite.

It is also important to recognize that an adequate definition of ecosabotage must be as ethically neutral as possible—that is, the moral justification of ecosabotage must not be built into its definition. In other words, the question of what ecosabotage *means* must be separated as much as possible from the question of whether ecosabotage is *morally justified*. To be sure, these two questions are difficult to separate when, for example, it is unclear whether some critera are relevant to the definitional or the moral issues. For example, it could be argued that part of the definition of ecosabotage is that it does not aim at harming human beings or other animal forms. On the other hand, it could be maintained that this is not part of the definition of ecosabotage and that an act of ecosabotage that aims at harming human or animal forms is simply not morally justified. An adequate definition of ecosabotage must decide such issues in a principled way.

Taking these elements into account, I suggest the following definition:

> Person *P*'s act *A* is an act of ecosabotage iff (if and only if) (1) in doing *A*, *P* has as *P*'s aim to stop, frustrate, or slow down some process or act that *P* believes will harm or damage the environment, (2) *P*'s act *A* is motivated by a sense of religious or moral concern, (3) *A* is illegal, and (4) *A* is not a public act.

Condition (1) seems essential if ecosabotage is to be distinguished from other forms of sabotage.

Condition (2) also appears essential because it distinguishes ecosabotage from vandalism. Foreman, for example, argues that destroying the technology that is polluting the Earth is a moral responsibility. He also goes so far as to claim that "it's a form of worship toward the Earth. It's really a very spiritual thing to go out and do."[13] These remarks suggest that ecosaboteurs can be motivated by religious as well as moral considerations. Thus, we need not claim that an act of ecosabotage *must* be morally motivated, for it can be religiously inspired. Condition (3) also seems essential for any definition of ecosabotage. Without it, a private act of prayer aimed at petitioning the deity to stop the destruction of the environment would be an act of ecosabotage because such an act would otherwise meet conditions (1), (2), and (4). Condition (4) is the most controversial condition in the definition, for it is certainly not clear that it needs to be part of the definition and the vagueness of ordinary language makes it uncertain whether it should be a necessary condition for the correct application of the term.[14] However, I see no other way to distinguish a typical act of civil disobedience used by environmental activists, for example, placing one's body in front of road construction equipment, from an act of ecosabotage, such as pulling up survey stakes. As I have already noted, the crucial difference between these two acts is not that the latter destroys property and the former does not. The difference can best be seen when one compares the typical acts of civil disobedience practiced by organizations such as Greenpeace and the acts of ecosabotage that are allegedly practiced by members of Earth First!.[15] In a typical Greenpeace action, arrests are expected. Indeed, Greenpeace activists may want to be arrested as a way of advertising their cause. This is not to say that Greenpeace always publicizes its plans in advance. Surprise is essential for some of its actions. Nevertheless, once an action is completed—once the entrance to the incinerator is blocked or the whalers are frustrated—Greenpeace activists do not try to escape; they stay and accept their arrest, hoping that it will be reported in the media. On the other hand, an act of ecosabotage is done in secret. Even when ecosaboteurs do not destroy property but merely disturb operations, they do not intend to be caught. Indeed, part of Foreman and Haywood's field guide to monkey wrenching is devoted to instructing potential ecosaboteurs on how not to get arrested.[16] This is not to say that if ecosaboteurs are caught, they will not use their own arrests to their own advantage in the media, but getting caught is not typically part of their plan.

This definition is value neutral in the sense that it does not assume that act A is either religiously or morally justified or unjustified. Although it can be assumed that the ecosaboteur *believes* that his or her act is justified either morally or religiously, the ecosaboteur could be mistaken. Moreover, the definition is neutral about whether A is effective or not in stopping, frustrating, or slowing down some process that is believed to be damaging the environment. The ecosaboteur believes that the act will be effective, but, again, he or she could be mistaken.

I have chosen not to include the condition that P believes that A will not injure any human beings or living things in the *definition* of ecosabotage. To be sure, ecosaboteurs typically maintain that they intend no such injury. Foreman is reported to have said that his philosophy "is nonviolent because it is directed toward inanimate machinery."[17] Paul Watson, the leader of the Sea Shepherds, waited until after the crew had left to sink the Icelandic whaling ships. Doc Sarvis, the philosophical spokesperson for "the monkey wrench gang" in Abbey's novel, is also opposed to violence against human beings. However, it is doubtful that this condition should be part of the definition of ecosabotage. Consider the analogous case of wartime sabotage. A worker who, in order to help the enemy, intentionally caused damage to a munitions plant although he or she knew other workers would be injured, would not for that reason alone have failed to perform an act of sabotage. On analogy with this example, I am inclined to maintain that although considerations of intentional noninjury to human beings or other animals are relevant in determining the morality of an act of ecosabotage, they are irrelevant when we are simply considering whether some act is or is not one of ecosabotage.

ECOSABOTAGE AND CIVIL DISOBEDIENCE

Is ecosabotage as defined above a type of civil disobedience? On the standard account of civil disobedience, the answer seems to be "No." Consider these typical definitions of civil disobedience taken from discussions of the topic by leading contemporary philosophical theorists.[18] According to Hugo Bedau, an act A is an act of civil disobedience iff A is illegal, done publicly, nonviolently and conscientiously with the intent to frustrate (one of) the laws, policies or decisions of the government.[19] According to Jeffrie Murphy, an act A is an act of civil disobedience iff (i) there is some law L according to which A is illegal, (ii) L is believed by the agent to be immoral or unconstitutional or irreligious or ideologically objectionable, and (iii) this belief motivates or explains A.[20] According to Christian Bay, an act is an act of civil disobedience iff A is an act or process of public defiance of a law or policy enforced by established government authorities insofar as the action is premeditated, understood by the actor(s) to be illegal or contested legally, carried out and persisted in for limited public ends and by way of carefully chosen and limited means.[21] Finally, according to Carl Cohen, an act A is an act of civil disobedience iff A is an act of protest, deliberately unlawful, and conscientiously and publicly performed.[22]

On three of these definitions, an act of ecosabotage is clearly not an act of civil disobedience. For Bedau, Bay, and Cohen, it is a necessary condition of civil disobedience that it be publicly performed. Ecosabotage, however, by the definition proposed above is not publicly performed. In addition, Bedau's definition rules out many acts of ecosabotage as acts of civil disobedience by requiring that an act of civil disobedience be nonviolent. Furthermore, Bedau's and Bay's definitions rule out many acts of ecosabotage as acts of civil disobedience because acts of ecosabotage are often aimed at frustrating the actions or policies of private companies and not the government.

Murphy's definition does not seem to apply to the typical act of ecosabotage for a different reason. An ecosaboteur who breaks some law L by destroying construction equipment probably does not object on either moral or constitutional or religious grounds to the law L insofar as it states that it is illegal to knowingly destroy someone else's property. What he or she objects to is the use to which the construction equipment is being put. Murphy, however, in a footnote qualifies his definition by saying that "the agent may have no objection to L per se but may violate L because he views it as symbolic for or instrumentally involved with some other law L' ... to which he does object. In my view, such a person (Thoreau for example) is also to be regarded as civilly disobedient."[23] Taken by itself this seems to allow a typical act of ecosabotage to be an act of civil disobedience because, for example, the ecosaboteur objects to some law L' that allows the timber company to clear-cut the forest. Law L, the law that the ecosaboteur is breaking, is in some sense "instrumentally involved with L'." However, later on in the same footnote Murphy adds: "What is most important is that motives of this sort be distinguished from the typical criminal motive: self-interest. We do not think of a criminal act as a *public* act of *protest:* but these features *do* typically characterize acts of civil disobedience."[24] If we take this qualification seriously, then ecosabotage is not civil disobedience for it is certainly not a *public* act of protest. In the end, then, these four definitions of civil disobedience exclude ecosabotage because of the requirement that acts of civil disobedience must be done publicly.

Some general category is surely needed that includes both morally and religiously motivated illegal acts whether they are done publicly or not. One could accomplish this by expanding the concept of civil disobedience to include nonpublic acts. This, in fact, is the approach taken by Howard Zinn when he defines an act of civil disobedience "broadly" as a deliberate violation of the law for a vital social purpose.[25] Interestingly enough, from the standpoint of ordinary usage, Zinn's definition seems be more correct than the others so far considered. Certainly people who ran the underground railroad before the Civil War were said to have engaged in acts of civil disobedience, but these acts were not publicly performed.[26] In accordance with Zinn's definition, an act of ecosabotage *could* be an act of

civil disobedience on the grounds that by definition ecosaboteurs are motivated by a sense of religious or moral duty and that a least some ecosaboteurs do deliberately violate the law for a vital social, i.e., moral purpose. However, it is unclear if all acts of ecosabotage fall under Zinn's definition. Would an ecosaboteur who pulled up survey stakes or destroyed construction equipment because of a mystical-religious feeling of unity with nature be described as breaking the law for a vital *social* purpose?

I suggest taking a different approach. Let us allow that civil disobedience must be public, or at least that it must be done for a social purpose, and introduce the concept of *conscientious wrongdoing* to cover either public *or* nonpublic law breaking for either religious *or* moral purposes. In this context, we can then specify that an act A is an act of conscientious wrongdoing iff it is an act of breaking a law for some moral or religious purpose. In this way, acts of civil disobedience on both the standard account and Zinn's expanded version as well as acts of ecosabotage can be considered special cases of conscientious wrongdoing.

CAN ECOSABOTAGE BE GIVEN A CONSEQUENTIALIST JUSTIFICATION?

As I have just shown, without an expanded analysis of civil disobedience, ecosabotage cannot be viewed as a form of civil disobedience. Nevertheless, the civil disobedience literature can still provide insight into ecosabotage's possible justification. Most theorists of civil disobedience maintain that because acts of civil disobedience break the law and conflict with accepted modes of social conduct, they require some special justification to overcome what seems to be their prima facie wrongness. The same could be said about acts of ecosabotage.

If one follows this line of argument, the burden of justification is clearly on the civil disobedient person or the ecosaboteur. This burden is thought to be especially difficult to meet in a democracy because when laws are made by the people's representatives, they seem to have a legitimate claim to the obedience of all citizens. Yet this claim is never absolute. Democratic processes do not work perfectly: unjust and evil laws can be enacted; shortsighted and destructive policies can be pursued; it can either be impossible or can take too much time to change laws by lawful means. Thus, concerned citizens may sometimes legitimately entertain illegal means of changing the status quo and educating and arousing their fellow citizens. Before they become civil disobedients or ecosaboteurs, however, they need to have a clear rational justification for their actions.[27]

Carl Cohen, in his comprehensive study of civil disobedience, reports that historically there have been two basic ways to justify civil disobedience: the appeal to higher law and the appeal to teleological or consequentialist considerations.[28] Although both approaches are relevant to the justification of ecosabotage, I focus on the consequentialist justification in detail in this eassay.[29] This emphasis is in no way intended to suggest, however, that there are no limits to consequentialist justification.[30]

As Cohen maintains, a consequentialist justification need not be restricted to a specific calculus of goods or evils:

> It simply indicates that the justification will rely upon some intelligent weighing of consequences of the disobedient act. The protester here argues, in effect, that his particular disobedience of a particular law, at a particular time, under given circumstances, . . . is likely to lead in the long run to a better or more just society than would his compliance, under those circumstances, with the law in question.[31]

According to Cohen, the disobedient person appeals to two sorts of factors to justify his or her actions: moral principles that specify the goal of the disobedient act and factual considerations that specify the means to achieving this goal. The goals of the disobedient act, Cohen argues, are usually not in question but are shared by the vast majority of the citizens of the community. In the rare cases that they are not in harmony with the community, their justification "is almost certain to fail."[32] On the other hand, the means of achieving the goals are controversial and their justification involves a delicate and often inconclusive balancing of conflicting considerations. The person who is contemplating a disobedient act must consider the *background* of the case at hand and ask questions such as: "How serious is the injustice whose remedy is the aim of disobedient protest? How pressing is the need for that remedy?- Have extraordinary but lawful means—assemblies of protests, letter-writing campaigns, etc.—been given full trial?"[33] The potentially disobedient person must also consider the *negative* effects of the disobedience and ask questions such as:

> How great is the expense incurred by the community as a consequence of the disobedience? . . . Is any violence entailed or threatened by the disobedient act? And if so, to property or to persons? . . . Has a bad example been set, a spirit of defiance or hooliganism been encouraged? Has respect for law been decreased in the community, or the fundamental order to society disturbed?[34]

Finally, the potential disobedient must estimate the *positive* results from the contemplated action and ask questions such as: how much influence will the disobedient act have in accomplishing change? Will it bring significant pressure to bear on legislatures that can bring about change? Can it attract public attention to some wrong or evil? Will the public put pressure on lawmakers? Or will the action of the disobedient be misunderstood and cause resentment? Will there be a backlash against the protesters?

These considerations are surely relevant to any consequentialist justification of acts of ecosabotage. Further, there seems to be no reason why a successful justification could not be given for at least some such acts. On a general level, the environmental goal of the public seems to be very similar to the goal of the ecosaboteurs: saving the environment from destruction and pollution. Recent polls indicate that the public is extremely concerned about environmental problems and is willing to go far in affording it protection.[35] Whether the more specific goals of radical environmental groups would be approved by the public is less clear: for example, Earth First!'s goal of saving the grizzly bears or the Sea Shepherds' goal of saving the whales. Nevertheless, it is not implausible to suppose that most people are sympathetic with these specific goals to some degree.

Whether members of environmental groups who use ecosabotage can justify their means in relation to the goal of saving the environment is, of course, the crucial issue. Unless strong general arguments can be raised against *any* use of ecosabotage, the justification of each proposed act of ecosabotage must be decided individually. A consideration of some of the most obvious general arguments against ecosabotage suggests that such arguments are in fact weak and cannot therefore be used to undermine all ecosabotage.

First, it may be objected that ecosabotage is beyond the pale of moral legitimacy because it involves violence. However, since there is no plausible general argument against the use of violence in civil disobedience, it hardly seems likely that ecosabotage can be faulted simply on this ground. Even Thoreau[36] and Gandhi[37] allowed that violence is sometimes an appropriate action and history points to cases in which violence in civil disobedience has had a beneficial effect. As Zinn points out:

> Violent labor struggles of the 1930's brought significant gains for labor. Not until Negro demonstrations resulted in violence did the national government begin to work seriously on civil rights legislation. No public statement on race relations has had as much impact as the Kerner Commission report, the direct result of outbreaks of violence in the ghettos.[38]

In any case, the distinction between violence against people and violence against property that both Zinn[39] and Cohen[40] stress in the context of justifying civil disobedience is relevant here. Violence directed against property is much less difficult to justify than violence against people.[41] Zinn has emphasized that violence in the context of civil disobedience should "be guarded, limited, aimed carefully at the source of injustice."[42] Advocates of ecosabotage in Earth First! say that violence should be directed only against property: they advocate destroying only equipment and facilities that are themselves used to destroy, deface, and pollute the environment.[43] Ecosaboteurs in the Sea Shepards also attempt

to limit and focus their violence: they wreck equipment that is used to destroy whales.

A second possible objection to ecosabotage is that it erodes respect for the law, thus deteriorating the social fabric of civilized society. However, as a general argument against ecosabotage, this has no greater weight than it does against traditional civil disobedience. As Cohen notes, the allegation that civil disobedience erodes the social fabric is "essentially factual, not philosophical, but the facts are exceedingly complex and difficult to determine accurately.... The evidence available from the American experience of the 1950s and 1960s does not seem to support the allegation."[44] The same counterargument applies to ecosabotage. To be sure, there is a great amount of disrespect for the law in our country and in the world: murder, massacre, terrorism, rape, governmental corruption, and white collar crimes are rife. But it is pure conjecture to suppose that ecosabotage with its carefully circumscribed scope and targets has contributed or will significantly contribute to this disrespect.

In any case, one might argue that respect for the law is not the highest value. As Cohen points out: "It is possible, of course, that the wrong against which the civil disobedient protests is more serious than the alleged deleterious consequence to the social fabric."[45] Foreman and others would surely argue that what they are fighting for is more important than respect for the law. Indeed, they might maintain that respect for the law will be of little importance in a world with polluted air and water, devoid of natural wildernesses, and depleted of most of its natural variety. This value assessment is controversial, but it is not obviously wrong or absurd.

One important difference between civil disobedience and ecosabotage provides the basis for another objection. It could be argued that although civil disobedients disobey the law on one level, they show respect for it on another level by acting publicly—thus inviting arrest—and by accepting the result of the punishment. Ecosaboteurs, on the other hand, show their contempt for the law by acting secretly, thus attempting to avoid arrest and punishment. Although the standard accounts of civil disobedience that require publicly performed acts would not allow secret acts to be acts of civil disobedience, these same accounts provide a rationale for such secret acts. As Cohen argues in defense of the operation that helped runaway slaves escape to Canada, "To continue this practice in the interests of other, later runaways, it was essential for the managers of the underground railways to conceal their repeated violations of the fugitive slave laws. Concealment in such cases is a pressing tactical need, stemming from concern for the welfare of specific human beings, not from shame or remorse for the disobedient conduct."[46] Surely the same sort of argument could be used to defend ecosaboteurs: to continue protecting the environment, they must conceal their identity.[47] Concealment in such cases is a pressing tactical need, stemming from concern for the welfare of the environment, not from shame or remorse for unlawful conduct. There is no *a priori* reason to suppose that ecosaboteurs have less personal integrity than the managers of the underground railroad or that they consider their cause less morally significant than the managers of the underground railway considered theirs.

There are, of course, other general arguments that can be used against ecosabotage, but because they parallel the general ones that have been raised against civil disobedience and can be answered in a similar way, we need not consider them here.[48]

HAVE ADVOCATES OF ECOSABOTAGE SUCCESSFULLY JUSTIFIED ECOSABOTAGE?

One might reasonably conclude from the above that although ecosabotage can be morally justified on consequentialist grounds in some contexts and although there are no general arguments standing in the way of such justification, the case for particular acts of ecosabotage has yet to be made. Although it is beyond the scope of this paper to provide such a justification, I consider critically how in fact advocates of ecosabotage such as Foreman have attempted to justify ecosabotage. In some cases where there is a gap in the justification, I fill in what I believe is a reasonable extrapolation or reconstruction of

what a rational ecosaboteur might say. I show that the rationales given by advocates of ecosabotage follow in outline the sort of argument that, according to Cohen, a consequentialist justification of civil disobedience should take.

In a consequentialist justification, the moral goals of the civil disobedient are usually shared by the community. When they are not, they are likely to fail to persuade the community and not succeed politically. I have argued above that the general goals of ecosabotage are probably shared by most members of the community and that even the particular ones may be. However, Foreman explicitly interprets these goals in a nonanthropocentric way. Advocating the environmental philosophy of deep ecology, he argues:

> Deep ecology says that *every* living thing in the ecosystem has intrinsic worth and a nature-given right to be there. The grizzly bear, for example, has a right to exist for its *own* sake—not just for material or entertainment value to human beings. Wilderness has a right to exist for its *own* sake, and for the sake of the diversity of life-forms it shelters; we shouldn't have to justify the existence of the wilderness area by saying, "Well, it protects the watershed, and it's a nice place to backpack and hunt, and its pretty.... Furthermore, deep ecology goes beyond the individual and says that it's the *species* that's important. And more important yet is the *community of species* that makes up a given biosystem. And ultimately, our concern should be with the community of *communities*—the ecosystem.[49]

Whether Foreman's biocentrism and holism is philosophically justified, we cannot decide here.[50] But what does seem likely is that these points of view are not widely shared by the vast majority of the moral community and would be considered by the majority of the community to be rather eccentric. Given his biocentric and holistic interpretation of the goals of Earth First!, therefore, the means as well as the goals of the organization become controversial. As Cohen points out: "Even if the community is wrong [about the goals], and the eccentrics right, deliberate disobedient pursuit of their special objectives, as long as they are in the moral minority, is not likely to advance the protesters' goals and not likely to be defensible on utilitarian grounds."[51] However, the ecosaboteur need not pursue what the moral community will perceive as eccentric goals. There are good anthropocentric reasons why natural diversity should be preserved,[52] why tropical forest should be safeguarded,[53] why whales should be saved,[54] and so on.

According to Cohen, a civil disobedient must consider the background of the case at hand and evaluate both the importance of the goals and whether legal means have been given a fair trial. Foreman's statement certainly suggests that he advocates deliberating on the background of acts of ecosabotage very carefully and has considered the importance of the goals of ecosabotage and legal alternatives to it. Thus, he maintains:

> Species are going under everday. Old-growth forests are disappearing. Overgrazing continues to ruin our western public lands. Off-road vehicles are cutting up the countryside everywhere. Poisons are continually and increasingly being injected into the environment. Rain forests are being clear-cut. In short, the environment is *losing*...everywhere. And to try to fight such an essential battle with less than every weapon we have available to us is foolish and, in the long run, suicidal.[55]

One need not just take Foreman's word for this bleak picture of environmental devastation. Many environmentalists have painted a similar picture, albeit in more scholarly and less colorful tones.[56]

But are there not legal means of stopping the destruction? Foreman at one time certainly thought there were. At the beginning of his environmental career he was a Washington lobbyist for the conventional environmental group, the Wilderness Society. However, personal experience quickly led to his disillusionment with the effectiveness of such groups in bringing about change and stopping the devastation.[57] Now as a member of Earth First! he has had personal experience of illegal actions being effective. He cites one example in which the legal action of the Sierra Club, a conventional environmental organization, failed to stop the destruction of a wilderness while Earth First!'s blockage of road construction by civil disobedience provided enough public awareness to be successful.[58]

One wonders, of course, if Foreman's experience is typical and if he has reported the facts accurately. Are there cases not mentioned by Foreman where legal means have succeeded and where illegal ones have not? To give a more adequate justification, one would have to consider in a systematic way a wider range of cases than Foreman considers in which legal and illegal methods have been tried in order to see their relative effectiveness. His anecdotal evidence at most makes a prima facie case that illegal means are sometimes more effective than legal means for affording environmental protection.[59]

Cohen also suggests that in any utilitarian justification of civil disobedience it is important to consider the possible negative consequences of one's action. Foreman gives evidence of having done this. When asked whether monkey wrenching—his term for ecosabotage—is counterproductive to the environmental cause and serves only to make environmentalists look bad, Foreman had this to say:

> On the surface, this argument seems worth considering. But the fact is, there's *already* an awful lot of monkey wrenching going on, and such a backlash hasn't come about. The Forest Service tries to keep it quiet, industry tries to keep it quiet, and I think that there has even been an effort in the media to downplay the extent and effectiveness of monkey wrenching in America today.... It's easy to be cowed into compromising and being overly moderate by the charge that you are going to cause a negative reaction, going to tarnish the whole environmental movement. But in my opinion, the *argument itself* is a more fearsome anti-environmental weapon than any actual backlash could ever hope to be, because it keeps many of us from using all the tools we have available to slow down the destruction.[60]

Again independent evidence for a negative reaction should be sought. For example, do Greenpeace's door-to-door canvassers find it harder than a few years ago to obtain contributions because of the negative publicity occasioned by Earth First!? Do polls show that the public is becoming less sympathetic to environmental causes than it was before news of ecosabotage? Until evidence such as this is obtained we will not know if ecosabotage is having a negative impact. But Foreman is certainly justified in remaining skeptical about the purported negative impact until such evidence is produced.

Another possible negative consequence of ecosabotage is the unintentional injury to human beings. This problem is considered to be especially worrisome in the case of tree spiking. The main danger is that a saw blade can break and cause injury to the saw operator or to other people involved in the milling process. Ecosaboteurs respond to this problem in at least three different ways. Some tree spikers mark the trees they have spiked. For example, it is reported that after Mike Roselle, a member of Earth First!, spiked trees in Cathedral Forest, he painted a large *S* on them.[61] Thus, the recommended procedure is the notification of all parties who would be involved in cutting and milling trees. Consequently, only those who defied the warning were in jeopardy.[62] Other spikers, however, try to keep their spikes from being detected,[63] arguing that automation places most mill operators in control booths out of danger.[64] Although this might be true, it would not protect the sawyers cutting down the tree. The chain on the sawyer's chain saw can break upon hitting a spike, whip back into the sawyer and cause serious injuries. Moreover, some ecosaboteurs may argue that although they should take care not to injure people, "nothing is more dangerous to the long-term health of the people of this planet than the large-scale destruction of the environment, and we have to stop that."[65] Consequently, any potential danger to the mill workers must be weighed against the greater danger to the world's population through environmental damage.

Whether these answers are completely adequate is a difficult issue that we cannot pursue here.[66]

Cohen also maintains that a potential civil disobedient must estimate the positive results from the contemplated action. Does ecosabotage have positive results? For example, does it accomplish the goal of slowing or stopping the destruction of the environment? Foreman says:

> I'm convinced that monkey wrenching can be one of the most effective ways of protecting our few remaining wild places. If a sufficient number of sincere individuals and small groups around the country were to launch a serious campaign of strategic monkey wrenching—a totally defensive effort to halt the continued destruction of wilderness—it

would in fact cause the retreat of industrial civilization from millions of acres of wildlands.

> For example, if a logging company knows that the trees are going to be consistently spiked with large nails—which plays hell with expensive saw blades at the mills—or that roads will be repeatedly blocked by having rocks dumped onto them, it quickly becomes impractical to try to maintain a profitable operation . . . so industrialization will retreat, leaving more land for the grizzly bear, for elk, for old-growth forests. . . .

> For these reasons, along with the fact that conventional efforts to save the environment *are not working,* I believe that monkey wrenching is probably the single most effective thing that can be done to save natural diversity.[67]

It is important to notice that in this quotation Foreman argues only that ecosabotage *could* work, not that it *has* worked or *will* work. However, Foreman does cite actual cases in which conventional civil disobedience methods, for example, blockage of a road by human beings, have been successful in getting public sympathy and attention. An ecosaboteur might argue by analogy: because conventional methods of civil disobedience have worked, it is likely that methods of ecosabotage will work as well. However, this analogy is far from perfect. Human beings blocking a road may make good press and create favorable publicity whereas tree spiking and rock dumping may not. Foreman's argument, in any case, is not based on the favorable publicity that monkey wrenching will cause. He maintains that ecosabotage will make it economically unfeasible for industry to continue to destroy the wilderness. In principle, this may be true. But does the use of ecosabotage in fact work in this way? Until evidence is cited of industrialization *actually* retreating, "leaving more land for the grizzly bear, for elk, for old-growth forest" as a result of tree spiking and other acts of ecosabotage, one should leave as an open question whether ecosabotage is justified in terms of Cohen's utilitarian model of justification.

It is also important to note that in the passage just cited Foreman argues that ecosabotage can be effective if "a sufficient number" of individuals and groups engage in it. If it is not successful now, Foreman might argue, it is because not enough people are trained and devoted ecosaboteurs. This may or may not be true, but a similar argument could be invoked by environmentalists who are opposed to ecosabotage. After all, it might be argued, if enough people marched on Washington, wrote letters to their government representatives, and performed public acts of conscientious wrongdoing, that is, engaged in conventional civil disobedience, it would "cause the retreat of industrial civilization from millions of acres of wildlands." The number of people needed is unclear. But it is plausible to suppose that public outrage would have to be extensive—as, for example, it ultimately was in relation to the Vietnam War—to have the sort of impact that Foreman desires.

Foreman argues simultaneously that ecosabotage is already widespread, but that its presence is being covered up by government, industry, and the media, that the environment is losing, and that a sufficient number of ecosaboteurs would save the environment. Although there is no inconsistency in these remarks, they do raise the question of just how much more ecosabotage would have to occur to prevent the environment from losing and to save the environment from destruction. In response, it might argued that the number of ecosaboteurs that would be necessary for making a significant impact on environmental protection is several orders of magnitude less than the number of legal protesters, letter writers, public acts of civil disobedience, and so on that would produce the same impact. For this reason at least, it may be said, ecosabotage is to be recommended over conventional strategies. On the other hand, the training and dedication that is involved in leading the life of an ecosaboteur would surely limit the number of potential candidates. Indeed, it is not clear that there are enough potential ecosaboteurs to make the difference that Foreman wants. Furthermore, in view of probable arrests it would seem that their ranks would have to be constantly replenished. There are then indirect considerations suggesting that ecosabotage is not likely in practice to have the impact that Foreman anticipates in theory.

Although Foreman does not cite evidence that ecosabotage actually works, a very recent article by C.M. does.[68] C.M. maintains that

monkey wrenching is probably costing the government and industry about 20 to 25 million dollars per year in terms of damaged equipment, lost time, and legislative and law enforcement expenses. "This represents money industry is not able to use to deforest public lands, sink oil wells in the backcountry, invest in more destructive equipment, influence politicians with campaign contribution..."[69] Even if corporations pass on these costs to their customers, according to C.M., monkey wrenching will cause the price of wood products to increase and thus indirectly decrease their consumption.

C.M. supplements this theoretical argument by citing actual cases in which ecosabotage has worked. For example, C.M. claims that there have been two cases in which the Forest Service withdrew timber sales after learning that trees were spiked. Moreover, C.M. argues that the firebombing of a $250,000 wood chipper in Hawaii, which "was grinding rainforest into fuel for sugar mills (without a permit and in violation of a court order)," left the company bankrupt. Finally, he or she argues that the controversial nature of ecosabotage has publicity value by taking "seemingly obscure environmental issues out the dark of scientific calculations into the limelight of individual passion and commitment."[70]

C.M.'s arguments for ecosabotage, nevertheless, are not enough to justify its use on utilitarian grounds. For this, C.M. would also have to show that typical acts of civil disobedience, that is, public acts of conscientious wrongdoing, were ineffective, for surely these are more desirable otherwise on utilitarian grounds than acts of ecosabotage if only because they are less likely to be interpreted as showing contempt for the law. In general, nonpublic acts of conscientious wrongdoing can be justified only when public nonviolent acts of conscientious wrongdoing cannot be utilized. Presumably there was no public way to help runaway slaves.[71] In the case of ecosabotage, however, public illegal means seem to be available. Road construction can be halted, for example, by lying down in front of the equipment, as well as by monkey wrenching the engines that run the equipment; trees can be protected by climbing them as well as by spiking. These nonviolent acts of conscientious wrongdoing also cost the government and industry a large amount of money, and have publicity value. In order to make their case, ecosaboteurs must show that public nonviolent acts of conscientious wrongdoing cannot work *and* that acts of ecosabotage can. To my knowledge they have not done so.[72]

CONCLUSION

In this paper I have defined ecosabotage and related this definition to several well-known analyses of civil disobedience. The comparison shows that ecosabotage cannot be assimilated to civil disobedience unless one expands the definition of the latter. The standard analyses of civil disobedience simply exclude it. I have suggested that ecosabotage and civil disobedience be considered special cases of the more general concept of conscientious wrongdoing. I have argued that although ecosabotage cannot be considered a form of civil disobedience on the standard analysis of this concept, the civil disobedience literature can provide important insights into the justification of ecosabotage.

Although other types of justification are possible, only a consequentialist one was considered in this paper. At present, there is no reason to suppose that some acts of ecosabotage could not be justified on consequentialist grounds, but I have concluded that advocates of ecosabotage such as Dave Foreman have not provided a full consequentialist justification of its use in concrete cases.

Evidence has been cited by C.M. showing that it does actually work in practice, but evidence is lacking that acts of civil disobedience would not be preferable. Nevertheless, Foreman and other advocates of ecosaboteurs such as C.M. have come further along in giving an adequate consequentialist justification of ecosabotage than is often realized and they have also met many of the objections against its use.

NOTES

1. Jim Robbins, "For Environmentalist, Illegal Acts are Acts of Love," *Boston Globe*, 2 June 1989, p. 3.
2. See for example, John J. Berger, "Tree Shakers," *Omni* 9 (1987): 20–22; Jamie Malanowski, "Monkey-Wrenching Around," *The Nation*, 2 May 1987, pp. 568–70; Joe Kane, "Mother Nature's Army," *Esquire*, February 1987, pp. 98–106.
3. J. A. Savage, "Radical Environmentalists: Sabotage in the Name of Ecology," *Business and Society Review 56–59* (Summer 1986): 35–37; David Peterson, "The Plowboy Interview: Dave Foreman: No Compromise in Defense of Mother Earth," *Mother Earth, News,* January–February 1985, pp. 16–22.
4. Two notable exceptions are Eugene C. Hargrove, "Ecological Sabotage: Pranks or Terrorism?" *Environmental Ethics* 4 (1982): 291–92, and Roderick Nash, *The Rights of Nature: A History of Environmental Ethics* (Madison: University of Wisconsin Press, 1989), pp. 189–98.
5. Dave Foreman and Bill Haywood, eds., *Ecodefense: A Field Guide to Monkeywrenching*, 2d ed. (Tucson, Arizona: A Ned Ludd Book, 1987).
6. See Kane, "Mother Nature's Army," p. 100.
7. Edward Abbey, *The Monkey Wrench Gang* (New York: Avon Books, 1975).
8. Robbins, "For Environmentalists, Illegal Acts are Acts of Love," p. 3.
9. *New York Times,* 10 November 1986, p. A1; November 13, p. A21. Cited by Sissela Bok, *A Strategy for Peace* (New York: Pantheon Press, 1989), pp. 179–80, n. 12.
10. *New York Times,* 10 November 1986, p. A10. Cited by Bok, *A Strategy for Peace*, pp. 179–80, n. 12.
11. The point here is not whether the parts of the machinery or the survey stakes are property, but that no property needs to be destroyed. Of course, survey stakes might be destroyed by being burned, but this need not happen in order for an act of ecosabotage to occur. One might, of course, argue that a survey itself is a type of property, because it costs money to construct, and that pulling up the stakes destroys it, because it costs money to do the survey again. Nevertheless, in this broad sense of property, acts of civil disobedience, e.g., sit-ins and blockades, also destroy property in this sense because they cost money. On grounds of clarity I do not use property in this broad sense.
12. See Jan Knippers Black, "Greenpeace: The Ecological Warriors," *USA Today.* November 1986, pp. 26–29; Michael Harwood, "Daredevils for the Environment," *New York Times Magazine*, 2 October 1988, pp. 72–75.
13. Robbins, "For Environmentalist, Illegal Acts are Acts of Love," p. 3.

14. It may be objected that this definition has a mistaken implication, namely, that a public act cannot be an act of ecosabotage. Suppose that as members of the road construction crew watch in amazement an environmental activist disables a bulldozer in order to prevent road construction and suppose this act was motivated by a moral concern for the environment. Surely, it may be said, this would be a case of ecosabotage. However, the concept of sabotage is vague and in some cases people's linguistic intutions may differ over what is a correct application of the term. I personally would hesitate to call this an act of sabotage. At the very least, most people would agree that it is a marginal or borderline case. My definition can be understood as an *explication* of the concept of ecosabotage—that is, as an attempt to reconstruct the meaning of ecosabotage by eliminating vagueness and thus exclude certain borderline cases. For an account of explication see Michael Martin, *Concepts of Science Education* (Glenview, Ill.: Scott, Foresman and Company, 1972), pp. 77–79.

15. It should be noted that Earth First! does not *officially* advocate ecosabotage, but unlike Greenpeace it does not reject it.

16. Foreman and Haywood, *Ecodefense*, chap. 9.

17. Robbins, "For Environmentalist, Illegal Acts are Acts of Love," p. 3; see also Dave Foreman, "Strategic Monkeywrenching," in Foreman and Haywood, *Ecodefense*, p. 14.

18. It should be noted that except for Bedau's, these definitions do not include nonviolence as part of the *meaning* of civil disobedience. However, one should recall that nonviolent methods have been a crucial part of civil disobedience practice from Gandhi to King. See Gene Sharp, *The Politics of Nonviolent Action*, part 3, *The Dynamics of Nonviolent Action* (Boston: Porter Sargent Publisher, 1973), p. 608. Nevertheless, it is doubtful that nonviolent methods should be built into the meaning of civil disobedience. One may imagine circumstances in which a person honestly believes that he or she is justified in using violence to make his or her protest effective. To say that such a person's act could not be an act of civil disobedience seems arbitrary. See Carl Cohen, *Civil Disobedience: Conscience. Tactics, and the Law* (New York: Columbia University Press, 1971), pp. 22–36.

19. H. A. Bedau, "On Civil Disobedience," *Journal of Philosophy*, 53 (1961): 661. Quoted in Hugo Adam Bedau, ed., *Civil Disobedience: Theory and Practice* (New York: Pegasus, 1969), p. 218.

20. Jeffrie Murphy, "Introduction," *Civil Disobedience and Violence*, ed. Jeffrie Murphy (Belmont, Calif.: Wadsworth Publishing Co., 1971), p. 1.

21. Christian Bay, "Civil Disobedience: Prerequisite for Democracy in Mass Society," in *Civil Disobedience and Violence*, p. 76.

22. Cohen, *Civil Disobedience*, p. 39.

23. Murphy, "Introduction," *Civil Disobedience and Violence*, p. 1, n. 1.

24. Ibid.

25. Howard Zinn, "A Fallacy on Law and Order: That Disobedience must be Absolutely Nonviolent," in *Civil Disobedience and Violence*, p. 103.

26. See Cohen, *Civil Disobedience*, p. 18, who claims that such examples constitute "a marginal category."

27. In order to apply this argument to ecosabotage in the United States, certain assumptions must be made that might well be challenged. For example, it must be assumed that the laws that facilitate environmental destruction are democratically established and that it is prima facie wrong to disobey a democraticall established law.

28. Cohen, *Civil Disobedience*, chap. 5.

29. According to Cohen, civil disobedients have often attempted to justify their conduct by appeals to a law higher than human law. This higher law justification has taken two major forms: an appeal to commands of God that are revealed to human beings in the Bible or other allegedly divinely inspired works or an appeal to nontheological higher laws that are discerned by the light of natural reason. There are three serious problems with both types of justifications. First, there seems to be no objective way to decide what these higher laws are. Second, principles of higher law are usually stated vaguely and abstractly. Consequently, it seems impossible to reach any objective decision on how they apply to concrete cases. Third, such justification would at best justify *direct* civil disobedience, that is, the breaking of a law that is itself morally objectionable in terms of higher law principles. But many acts of civil disobedience are indirect—that is, the civil disobedient disobeys some law that he or she has no objection to because the disobedience is a means to eliminate some serious injustice in a related area. It could be argued that these same problems are found in any attempt to justify ecosabotage by appeal to higher law principles. However, Cohen is mistaken in limiting nonconsequentialist justifications of civil disobedience to the higher law tradition. A complete account of nonconsequentialist justifications of

civil disobedience would also have to take into account deontological theories of justification ranging from Kant to Rawls.

30. For a review of some recent literature see Hugo Bedau, "The Limits of Utilitarianism and Beyond," *Ethics* 95 (1985): 333–41. For a standard criticism of utilitarianism see William Frankena, *Ethics,* 2d ed. (Englewood Cliffs: Prentice-Hall, 1973), chap. 3. See also G. E. Moore, *Principia Ethica* (Cambridge: Cambridge University Press, 1903), chap. 5, secs. 91–93.

31. Cohen, *Civil Disobedience,* p. 120. If Cohen means that the goal must be shared by the vast majority to be *morally* justified, he is mistaken. I do not interpret him in this way, however. It is correct, nevertheless, that unless the goal is shared by the majority, the civil disobedient will not be practically successful—that is, the disobedient will have failed to justify his or her action to the community, and thus the disobedient will not be politically effective.

32. Ibid., p. 123.

33. Ibid., p. 125.

34. Ibid., pp. 125–26.

35. A recent national opinion survey indicates that eighty percent of Americans agree with the following statement: "Protecting the environment is so important that requirements and standards cannot be too high, and continuing environmental improvement must be made regardless of cost." Cited by Martin and Kathleen Feldstein. "In Defense of Pollution," *Boston Globe,* 1 August 1989, p. 24.

36. Thoreau defended John Brown in "A Plea for Captain John Brown," delivered in Concord and Boston a month before his execution. See Zinn, "A Fallacy on Law and Order," p. 105.

37. Gandhi wrote in *Young India,* "No rules can tell us how this disobedience may be done and by whom, when and where, nor can they tell us which laws foster in truth. It is only experience that can guide us." And "I do believe that where there is only a choice between cowardice and violence I would advise violence." See Zinn, "A Fallacy on Law and Order," p. 105.

38. Zinn, "A Fallacy on Law and Order," p. 110.

39. Ibid., p. 108.

40. Cohen, *Civil Disobedience,* p. 125.

41. Hargrove calls our attention to the fact that our society is "dedicated to the protection of property (including construction equipment and bridges)." See Hargrove, "Ecological Sabotage," p. 291. Even so there is a clear moral distinction to be drawn between violence against people and violence against property.

42. Zinn, "A Fallacy on Law and Order," p. 109.

43. See Foreman, "Strategic Monkeywrenching," *Ecodefense,* p. 15.

44. Cohen, *Civil Disobedience,* pp. 150–51.

45. Ibid., p. 150.

46. Ibid., pp. 19–20. On Cohen's own definition the managers of underground railways did not perform acts of civil disobedience. Cohen (p. 39) defines civil disobedience in terms of acts that are publicly performed.

47. T. O. Hellenbach, "The Future of Monkeywrenching," in Foreman and Haywood, *Ecodefense,* p. 19.

48. See Cohen, *Civil Disobedience,* chap. 6.

49. Peterson, "The Plowboy Interview," p. 18.

50. For a recent critique of these points of view see Bryan G. Norton, *Why Preserve Natural Variety?* (Princeton: Princeton University Press, 1989), chaps. 8 and 9.

51. Cohen, *Civil* Disobedience, p. 123.

52. See Norton, *Why Preserve Natural Variety?* Chap. 11.

53. Norman Myers, *The Primary Source: Tropical Forests and Our Future* (New York: W. W. Norton & Company, 1985), chaps. 10–15.

54. Peter M. Dora, "Cataceans: A Litany of Cain," *People, Penguins, and Plastic Tree,* ed. Donald VanDeVeer and Christine Pierce (Belmont, Calif.: Wadsworth Publishing Co., 1986), pp. 127–34.

55. Peterson, "The Plowboy Interview," p. 22; see also Foreman, "Strategic Monkeywrenching," *Ecodefense,* pp. 10–14.

56. See, for example, Lester R. Brown, Christopher Flavin, and Sandra Postel, "A World at Risk," *The State of the World: 1989,* ed. L. Brown et al. (New York: W. W. Norton & Company, 1989), pp. 3–20; Myers, *The Primary Source,* chaps. 5–9; Norman Myers, "The Sinking Ark," *People, Penguins, and Plastic Tree,* pp. 111–119.

57. Kane, "Mother Nature's Army," p. 100.

58. Peterson, "The Plowboy Interview," p. 19. It should be noted that this was not an act of ecosabotage.

59. However, the independent evidence provided by the effectiveness of the illegal actions of Greenpeace in protecting whales and seals confirms Foreman's contention. See Black, "Greenpeace: The Ecological Warriors," p. 29.

60. Peterson, "The Plowboy Interview," pp. 21–22.

61. Kane, "Mother Nature's Army," p. 980.

62. Savage, "Radical Environmentalists," p. 35.

63. See Foreman and Haywood, *Ecodefense*, pp. 24–51.
64. Malanowski, "Monkey-Wrenching Around," p. 569. But whether all employees of the mills, for example, the head rig offbearers who guide the logs, are safe is another question.
65. Ibid.
66. It should be noted that according to defenders of ecosabotage there has never been a documented case of anyone being seriously injured from its practice. See C.M., "An Appraisal of Monkeywrenching." *Earth First!*, 2 February 1990.
67. Peterson, "The Plowboy Interview," p. 21.
68. See C.M., "An Appraisal of Monkeywrenching." According to *Earth First!* C.M. "is a widely published writer and scholar whose career dictates anonymity."
69. Ibid.
70. Ibid.
71. See Lester Rhodes, "Carrying on a Venerable Tradition," *Earth First!*, 2 February 1990. Rhodes compares ecosaboteurs to those who ran the underground railroad.
72. To be sure, Foreman has argued that monkey wrenching should not be used when there is a non-violent civil disobedience action such as blockages taking place. But what must be shown is that blockages and the like cannot bring about the same results as ecosabotage. See Foreman, "Strategic Monkeywrenching," *Ecodefense*, p. 15.

✏ STUDY QUESTIONS

1. What are the different kinds of ecosabotage? Which of them should be called ecoterrorism, and which should not? Explain.

2. Summarize and criticize Martin's conclusion concerning the permissibility of ecosabotage.

81   Strategic Monkeywrenching

DAVE FOREMAN

Dave Foreman is the founder of Earth First!, an activist environmental organization that advocates "monkeywrenching." *Monkeywrenching* is the name coined for the destruction of machines or property that are used to destroy the natural world. It includes wrecking heavy equipment like bulldozers; hammering spikes into trees, which will later damage saw blades; and punching holes into whaling ships.

... Only one hundred and fifty years ago, the Great Plains were a vast, waving sea of grass stretching from the Chihuahuan Desert of Mexico to the boreal forest of Canada, from the oak-hickory forests of the Ozarks to the Rocky Mountains. Bison blanketed the plains—it has been estimated that 60 million of the huge, shaggy beasts moved across the grass. Great herds of pronghorn and elk also filled this Pleistocene landscape. Packs of wolves and numerous grizzly bears followed the immense herds.

One hundred and fifty years ago, John James Audubon estimated that there were several *billion* birds in a flock of passenger pigeons that flew past him for several days on the Ohio River. It has been said that a squirrel could travel from the Atlantic seaboard to the Mississippi River without touching the ground, so dense was the deciduous forest of the East.

At the time of the Lewis and Clark Expedition, an estimated 100,000 grizzlies roamed the western half of what is now the United States.

From *Ecodefense: A Field Guide to Monkeywrenching*, by Dave Foreman (Tucson, AZ: Ned Ludd, 1987), pp. 10–17.

The howl of the wolf was ubiquitous. The condor dominated the sky from the Pacific Coast to the Great Plains. Salmon and sturgeon filled the rivers. Ocelots, jaguars, margay cats and jaguarundis roamed the Texas brush and Southwestern deserts and mesas. Bighorn sheep in great numbers ranged the mountains of the Rockies, Great Basin, Southwest and Pacific Coast. Ivory-billed woodpeckers and Carolina parakeets filled the steamy forests of the Deep South. The land was alive.

East of the Mississippi, giant tulip poplars, chestnuts, oaks, hickories and other trees formed the most diverse temperate deciduous forest in the world. On the Pacific Coast, redwood, hemlock, Douglas fir, spruce, cedar, fir and pine formed the grandest forest on Earth.

In the space of a few generations we have laid waste to paradise. The tall grass prairie has been transformed into a corn factory where wildlife means the exotic pheasant. The short grass prairie is a grid of carefully fenced cow pastures and wheat fields. The passenger pigeon is no more. The last died in the Cincinnati Zoo in 1914. The endless forests of the East are tame woodlots. The only virgin deciduous forest there is in tiny museum pieces of hundreds of acres. Six hundred grizzlies remain, and they are going fast. There are only three condors left in the wild and they are scheduled for capture and imprisonment in the Los Angeles Zoo. Except in northern Minnesota and Isle Royale, wolves are known merely as scattered individuals drifting across the Canadian and Mexican borders (a pack has recently formed in Glacier National Park). Four percent of the peerless Redwood Forest remains and the monumental old growth forest cathedrals of Oregon are all but gone. The tropical cats have been shot and poisoned from our southwestern borderlands. The subtropical Eden of Florida has been transformed into hotels and citrus orchards. Domestic cattle have grazed bare and radically altered the composition of the grassland communities of the West, displacing elk, moose, bighorn sheep and pronghorn and leading to the virtual extermination of grizzly, wolf, cougar, bobcat and other "varmints." Dams choke the rivers and streams of the land.

Nonetheless, wildness and natural diversity remain. There are a few scattered grasslands ungrazed, stretches of free-flowing river undammed and undiverted, thousand-year-old forests, Eastern woodlands growing back to forest and reclaiming past roads, grizzlies and wolves and lions and wolverines and bighorn and moose roaming the backcountry; hundreds of square miles that have never known the imprint of a tire, the bite of a drill, the rip of a 'dozer, the cut of a saw, the smell of gasoline.

These are the places that hold North America together, that contain the genetic information of life, that represent sanity in a whirlwind of madness.

In January of 1979, the Forest Service announced the results of RARE II [its Roadless Area Review and Evaluation]: of the 80 million acres of undeveloped lands on the National Forests, only 15 million acres were recommended for protection against logging, road building and other "developments." In the big tree state of Oregon, for example, only 370,000 acres were proposed for Wilderness protection out of 4.5 million acres of roadless, uncut forest lands. Of the areas nationally slated for protection, most were too high, too dry, too cold, too steep to offer much in the way of "resources" to the loggers, miners and grazers. Those roadless areas with critical old growth forest values were allocated for the sawmill. Important grizzly habitat in the Northern Rockies was tossed to the oil industry and the loggers. Off-road-vehicle fanatics and the landed gentry of the livestock industry won out in the Southwest and Great Basin. . . .

The BLM [Bureau of Land Management] wilderness review has been a similar process of attrition. It is unlikely that more than 9 million acres will be recommended for Wilderness out of the 60 million with which the review began. Again, it is the more spectacular but biologically less rich areas that will be proposed for protection.

During 1984, Congress passed legislation designating minimal National Forest Wilderness acreages for most states (generally only slightly larger than the pitiful RARE II recommendations and concentrating on "rocks and ice" instead of crucial forested lands). In the next few years, similar picayune legislation for National Forest Wilderness in the remaining states and for BLM Wilderness will probably be enacted. The other roadless areas will be eliminated from consideration. National Forest Management Plans emphasizing industrial logging, grazing, mineral and energy development, road building, and motorized recreation will be implemented. Conventional means of protecting these millions of acres of wild country will largely dissipate. Judicial and administrative appeals for their protection will be closed off. Congress will turn a deaf ear to requests for additional Wildernesses so soon after disposing of the thorny issue. The effectiveness of conventional political lobbying by conservation groups to protect endangered wild lands will evaporate. And in half a decade, the saw, "dozer" and drill will devastate most of what is unprotected. The battle for wilderness will be over. Perhaps 3% of the United States will be more or less protected and it will be open season on the rest. Unless…

Many of the projects that will destroy roadless areas are economically marginal. It is costly for the Forest Service, BLM, timber companies, oil companies, mining companies and others to scratch out the "resources" in these last wild areas. It is expensive to maintain the necessary infrastructure of roads for the exploitation of wild lands. The cost of repairs, the hassle, the delay, the down-time may just be too much for the bureaucrats and exploiters to accept if there is a widely-dispersed, unorganized, *strategic* movement of resistance across the land.

It is time for women and men, individually and in small groups, to act heroically and admittedly illegally in defense of the wild, to put a monkeywrench into the gears of the machine destroying natural diversity. This strategic monkeywrenching can be safe, it can be easy, it can be fun, and—most importantly—it can be effective in stopping timber cutting, road building, overgrazing, oil and gas exploration, mining, dam building, powerline construction, off-road-vehicle use, trapping, ski area development and other forms of destruction of the wilderness, as well as cancerous suburban sprawl.

But it must be strategic, it must be thoughtful, it must be deliberate in order to succeed. Such a campaign of resistance would follow these principles:

Monkeywrenching Is Non-Violent

Monkeywrenching is non-violent resistance to the destruction of natural diversity and wilderness. It is not directed toward harming human beings or other forms of life. It is aimed at inanimate machines and tools. Care is always taken to minimize any possible threat to other people (and to the monkeywrenchers themselves).

Monkeywrenching Is Not Organized

There can be no central direction or organization to monkeywrenching. Any type of network would invite infiltration, *agents provocateurs* and repression. It is truly individual action. Because of this, communication among monkeywrenchers is difficult and dangerous. Anonymous discussion through this book and its future editions, and through the Dear Ned Ludd section of the *Earth First! Journal*, seems to be the safest avenue of communication to refine techniques, security procedures and strategy.

Monkeywrenching Is Individual

Monkeywrenching is done by individuals or very small groups of people who have known each other for years. There is trust and a good working relationship in such groups. The more people involved, the greater are the dangers of infiltration or a loose mouth. Earth defenders avoid working with people they haven't known for a long time, those who can't keep their mouths closed, and those with grandiose or violent ideas (they may be police agents or dangerous crackpots).

Monkeywrenching Is Targeted

Ecodefenders pick their targets. Mindless, erratic vandalism is counterproductive. Monkeywrenchers know that they do not stop a specific logging sale by destroying any piece of logging equipment which they come across. They make sure it belongs to the proper culprit. They ask themselves what is the most vulnerable point of a wilderness-destroying project and strike there. Senseless vandalism leads to loss of popular sympathy.

Monkeywrenching Is Timely

There is a proper time and place for monkey-wrenching. There are also times when monkey-wrenching may be counterproductive. Monkeywrenchers generally should not act when there is a non-violent civil disobedience action (a blockade, etc.) taking place against the opposed project. Monkeywrenching may cloud the issue of direct action and the blockaders could be blamed for the ecotage and be put in danger from the work crew or police. Blockades and monkeywrenching usually do not mix. Monkeywrenching may also not be appropriate when delicate political negotiations are taking place for the protection of a certain area. There are, of course, exceptions to this rule. The Earth warrior always thinks: Will monkeywrenching help or hinder the protection of this place?

Monkeywrenching Is Dispersed

Monkeywrenching is a wide-spread movement across the United States. Government agencies and wilderness despoilers from Maine to Hawaii know that their destruction of natural diversity may be met with resistance. Nation-wide monkeywrenching is what will hasten overall industrial retreat from wild areas.

Monkeywrenching Is Diverse

All kinds of people in all kinds of situations can be monkeywrenchers. Some pick a large area of wild country, declare it wilderness in their own minds, and resist any intrusion against it. Others specialize against logging or ORV's [off-road vehicles] in a variety of areas. Certain monkeywrenchers may target a specific project, such as a giant powerline, construction of a road, or an oil operation. Some operate in their backyards, others lie low at home and plan their ecotage a thousand miles away. Some are loners, others operate in small groups.

Monkeywrenching Is Fun

Although it is serious and potentially dangerous activity, monkeywrenching is also fun. There is a rush of excitement, a sense of accomplishment, and unparalleled camaraderie from creeping about in the night resisting those "alien forces from Houston, Tokyo, Washington, DC, and the Pentagon." As Ed Abbey says, "Enjoy, shipmates, enjoy."

Monkeywrenching Is Not Revolutionary

It does *not* aim to overthrow any social, political or economic system. It is merely non-violent self-defense of the wild. It is aimed at keeping industrial "civilization" out of natural areas and causing its retreat from areas that should be wild. It is not major industrial sabotage. Explosives, firearms and other dangerous tools are usually avoided. They invite greater scrutiny from law enforcement agencies, repression and loss of public support. (The Direct Action group in Canada is a good example of what monkeywrenching is *not*.) Even Republicans monkeywrench.

Monkeywrenching Is Simple

The simplest possible tool is used. The safest tactic is employed. Except when necessary, elaborate commando operations are avoided. The most effective means for stopping the destruction of the wild are generally the simplest: spiking trees and spiking roads. There are obviously times when more detailed and complicated operations are called for. But the monkeywrencher thinks: What is the simplest way to do this?

Monkeywrenching Is Deliberate and Ethical

Monkeywrenching is not something to do cavalierly. Monkeywrenchers are very conscious of the gravity of what they do. They are deliberate about taking such a serious step. They are thoughtful. Monkeywrenchers, although non-violent—are warriors. They are exposing themselves to possible arrest or injury. It is not a casual or flippant affair. They keep a pure heart and mind about it. They remember that they are engaged in the most moral of all actions: protecting life, defending the Earth.

A movement based on these principles could protect millions of acres of wilderness more stringently than any Congressional act, could insure the propagation of the grizzly and other threatened life forms better than an army of game wardens, and could lead to the retreat of industrial civilization from large areas of forest, mountain, desert, plain, seashore, swamp, tundra and woodland that are better suited to the maintenance of natural diversity than to the production of raw materials for overconsumptive technological human society.

If loggers know that a timber sale is spiked, they won't bid on the timber. If a Forest Supervisor knows that a road will be continually destroyed, he won't try to build it. If seismographers know that they will be constantly harassed in an area, they'll go elsewhere. If ORVers know that they'll get flat tires miles from nowhere, they won't drive in such areas.

John Muir said that if it ever came to a war between the races, he would side with the bears. That day has arrived.

STUDY QUESTIONS

1. What is the significance of the widespread destruction of the wilderness and animals described in the first part of Foreman's essay?
2. Why, according to Foreman, is monkeywrenching necessary for saving the environment?
3. What are the principles of monkeywrenching? Evaluate them.

82   A Vision of a Sustainable World

LESTER BROWN, CHRISTOPHER FLAVIN, AND SANDRA POSTEL

Lester Brown is the founder and past president of the Worldwatch Institute in Washington, D.C., an institute concerned with global environmental issues. Christopher Flavin and Sandra Postel are vice presidents for research at the Worldwatch Institute. In this essay, Brown and his associates project forty years into the future and predict the kind of global lifestyles and economic practices that will be present in a sustainable world.

On April 22nd, 1990, millions of people around the world celebrated Earth Day. Marking the twentieth anniversary of the original Earth Day, this event came at a time when public concern about the environmental fate of the planet had soared to unprecedented heights.

Threats such as climate change and ozone depletion underscore the fact that ecological degradation has reached global proportions. Meanwhile, the increasing severity and spread of more localized problems—including soil erosion, deforestation, water scarcity, toxic contamination, and air pollution—are already beginning to slow economic and social progress in much of the world.

Governments, development agencies, and people the world over have begun to grasp the need to reverse this broad-based deterioration of the environment. But, the result so far is a flurry of fragmented activity—a new pollution law here, a larger environment staff there—that lacks any coherent sense of what, ultimately, we are trying to achieve.

Building an environmentally stable future requires some vision of what it would look like.

Reprinted from *The Worldwatch Reader,* ed. Lester R. Brown (New York: Norton, 1991), by permission.

If not coal and oil to power society, then what? If forests are no longer to be cleared to grow food, then how is a larger population to be fed? If a throwaway culture leads inevitably to pollution and resource depletion, how can we satisfy our material needs?

In sum, if the present path is so obviously unsound, what picture of the future can we use to guide our actions toward a global community that can endure?

A sustainable society is one that satisfies its needs without jeopardizing the prospects of future generations. Unfortunately, no models of sustainability exist today. Most developing nations have for the past several decades aspired to the automobile-centered, fossil-fuel-driven economies of the industrial West. From the regional problems of air pollution to the global threat of climate change, though, it is clear that these societies are far from durable; indeed, they are rapidly bringing about their own demise.

Describing the shape of a sustainable society is a risky proposition. Ideas and technologies we can't now foresee obviously will influence society's future course. Yet, just as any technology of flight must abide by the basic principles of aerodynamics, so must a lasting society satisfy some elementary criteria. With that understanding and the experience garnered in recent decades, it is possible to create a vision of a society quite different from, indeed preferable to, today's.

Time to get the world on a sustainable path is rapidly running out. We believe that if humanity achieves sustainability, it will do so within the next 40 years. If we have not succeeded by then, environmental deterioration and economic decline will be feeding on each other, pulling us down toward social decay and political upheaval. At such a point, reclaiming any hope of a sustainable future might be impossible. Our vision, therefore, looks to the year 2030, a time closer to the present than is World War II.

Whether Earth Day 2030 turns out to be a day to celebrate lasting achievements or to lament missed opportunities is largely up to each one of us as individuals, for, in the end, it is individual values that drive social change. Progress toward sustainability thus hinges on a collective deepening of our sense of responsibility to the earth and to our offspring. Without a reevaluation of our personal aspirations and motivations, we will never achieve an environmentally sound global community.

BEGIN WITH THE BASICS

In attempting to sketch the outlines of a sustainable society, we need to make some basic assumptions. First, our vision of the future assumes only existing technologies and foreseeable improvements in them. This clearly is a conservative assumption: 40 years ago, for example, some renewable energy technologies on which we base our model didn't even exist.

Second, the world economy of 2030 will not be powered by coal, oil, and natural gas. It is now well accepted that continuing heavy reliance on fossil fuels will cause catastrophic changes in climate. The most recent scientific evidence suggests that stabilizing the climate depends on eventually cutting annual global carbon emissions to some 2 billion tons per year, about one-third the current level. Taking population growth into account, the world in 2030 will therefore have per-capita carbon emissions about one-eighth the level found in Western Europe today.

The choice then becomes whether to make solar or nuclear power the centerpiece of energy systems. We believe nuclear power will be rejected because of its long list of economic, social, and environmental liabilities. The nuclear industry has been in decline for over a decade. Safety concerns and the failure to develop permanent storage for nuclear waste have disenchanted many citizens.

It is possible scientists could develop new nuclear technologies that are more economical and less accident-prone. Yet, this would not solve the waste dilemma. Nor would it prevent the use of nuclear energy as a stepping stone to developing nuclear weapons. Trying to stop this in a plutonium-based economy with thousands of operating plants would require a degree of control incompatible with democratic political systems. Societies are likely to opt instead for diverse, solar-based systems.

The third major assumption is about population size. Current United Nations projections have the world headed for nearly nine billion people by 2030. This figure implies a doubling or tripling of the populations of Ethiopia, India, Nigeria, and scores of other countries where human numbers are already overtaxing natural support systems. But such growth is inconceivable. Either these societies will move quickly to encourage smaller families and bring birthrates down, or rising death rates from hunger and malnutrition will check population growth.

The humane path to sustainability by the year 2030 therefore requires a dramatic drop in birthrates. As of 1990, 13 European countries had stable or declining populations; by 2030, most countries are likely to be in that category. We assume a population 40 years from now of at most eight billion that will be either essentially stable or declining slowly toward a number the earth can comfortably support.

DAWN OF A SOLAR AGE

In many ways, the solar age today is where the coal age was when the steam engine was invented in the eighteenth century. At that time, coal was used to heat homes and smelt iron ore, but the notion of using coal-fired steam engines to power factories or transportation systems was just emerging. Only a short time later, the first railroad started running and fossil fuels began to transform the world economy.

Many technologies have been developed that allow us to harness the renewable energy of the sun effectively, but so far these devices are only in limited use. By 2030 they will be widespread and much improved. The pool of energy these technologies can tap is immense: The annual influx of accessible renewable resources in the United States is estimated at 250 times the country's current energy needs.

The mix of energy sources will reflect the climate and natural resources of particular regions. Northern Europe, for example, is likely to rely heavily on wind and hydropower. Northern Africa and the Middle East may instead use direct sunlight. Japan and the Philippines will tap their abundant geothermal energy. Southeast Asian countries will be powered largely by wood and

agricultural wastes, along with sunshine. Some nations—Norway and Brazil, for example— already obtain more than half of their energy from renewables.

By 2030, solar panels will heat most residential water around the world. A typical urban landscape may have thousands of collectors sprouting from rooftops, much as television antennas do today. Electricity will come via transmission lines from solar thermal plants located in desert regions of the United States, North Africa, and central Asia. This technology uses mirrored troughs to focus sunlight onto oil-filled tubes that convey heat to a turbine and generator that then produce electricity. An 80-megawatt solar thermal plant built in the desert east of Los Angeles in 1989 converted an extraordinary 22 percent of incoming sunlight into electricity—at a third less than the cost of power from new nuclear plants.

Power will also come from photovoltaic solar cells, a semiconductor technology that converts sunlight directly into electricity. Currently, photovoltaic systems are less efficient than and four times as expensive as solar thermal power, but by 2030 their cost will be competitive. Photovoltaics will be a highly decentralized energy source found atop residential homes as well as adjacent to farms and factories.

Using this technology, homeowners throughout the world may become producers as well as consumers of electricity. Indeed, photovoltaic shingles have already been developed that turn roofing material into a power source. As costs continue to decline, many homes are apt to get their electricity from photovoltaics; in sunny regions residents will sell any surplus to the utility company.

Wind power, an indirect form of solar energy generated by the sun's differential heating of the atmosphere, is already close to being cost competitive with new coal-fired power plants. Engineers are confident they can soon unveil improved wind turbines that are economical not just in California's blustery mountain passes, where they are now commonplace, but in vast stretches of the U.S. northern plains and many other areas. Forty years from now the United States could be deriving 10 to 20 percent of its electricity from the wind.

Small-scale hydro projects are likely to be a significant source of electricity, particularly in the Third World, where the undeveloped potential is greatest. As of 1990 hydro power supplied nearly one-fifth of the world's electricity. By 2030 that share should be much higher, although the massive dams favored by governments and international lending agencies in the late-twentieth century will represent a declining proportion of the total hydro capacity.

Living plants provide another means of capturing solar energy. Through photosynthesis, they convert sunlight into biomass that can be burned or converted to liquid fuels such as ethanol. Today, wood provides 12 percent of the world's energy, chiefly in the form of firewood and charcoal in developing countries. Its use will surely expand during the next 40 years, although resource constraints will not permit it to replace all of the vast quantities of petroleum in use today.

Geothermal energy taps the huge reservoir of heat that lies beneath the earth's surface, making it the only renewable source that does not rely on sunlight. Continuing advances will allow engineers to use previously unexploitable, lower-temperature reservoirs that are hundreds of times as abundant as those in use today. Virtually all Pacific Rim countries, as well as those along East Africa's Great Rift and the Mediterranean Sea, will draw on geothermal resources.

Nations in what now is called the Third World face the immense challenge of continuing to develop their economies without massive use of fossil fuels. One option is to rely on biomass energy in current quantities but to step up replanting efforts and to burn the biomass much more efficiently, using gasifiers and other devices. Another is to turn directly to the sun, which the Third World has in abundance. Solar ovens for cooking, solar collectors for hot water, and photovoltaics for electricity could satisfy most energy needs.

In both industrial and developing nations, energy production inevitably will be much more decentralized; this will break up the utilities and huge natural gas, coal, and oil industries that have been a dominant part of the economic scene in the late-twentieth century. Indeed, a world energy system based on the highly efficient use of renewable resources will be less vulnerable to disruption and more conducive to market economies.

EFFICIENT IN ALL SENSES

Getting total global carbon emissions down to 2 billion tons a year will require vast improvements in energy efficiency. Fortunately, many of the technologies to accomplish this feat already exist and are cost-effective. No technical breakthroughs are needed to double automobile fuel economy, triple the efficiency of lighting systems, or cut typical home heating requirements by 75 percent.

Automobiles in 2030 are apt to get at least 100 miles per gallon of fuel, four times the current average for new cars. A hint of what such vehicles may be like is seen in the Volvo LCP 2000, a prototype automobile. It is an aerodynamic four-passenger car that weighs half as much as today's models. Moreover, it has a highly efficient and clean-burning diesel engine. With the addition of a continuously variable transmission and a flywheel energy storage device, this vehicle will get 90 miles to the gallon

Forty years from now, Thomas Edison's revolutionary incandescent light bulbs may be found only in museums—replaced by an array of new lighting systems, including halogen and sodium lights. The most important new light source may be compact fluorescent bulbs that use 18 watts rather than 75 to produce the same amount of light.

In 2030, homes are likely to be weather-tight and highly insulated; this will greatly reduce the need for heating and cooling. Some superinsulated homes in the Canadian province of Saskatchewan are already so tightly built that it doesn't pay to install a furnace. Homes of this kind use one-third as much energy as do modern Swedish homes, or one-tenth the U.S. average. Inside, people will have appliances that are on average three to four times as efficient as those in use today.

Improving energy efficiency will not noticeably change lifestyles or economic systems. A highly efficient refrigerator or light bulb provides the same service as an inefficient one—just more economically. Gains in energy efficiency alone, however, will not reduce fossil-fuel related carbon emissions by the needed amount. Additional steps to limit the use of fossil fuels are likely to reshape cities, transportation systems, and industrial patterns and foster a society that is more efficient in all senses.

By the year 2030, a much more diverse set of transportation options will exist. The typical European or Japanese city today has already taken one step toward this future. Highly developed rail and bus systems move people efficiently between home and work: In Tokyo only 15 percent of commuters drive cars to the office. The cities of 2030 are apt to be crisscrossed by inexpensive street-level light rail systems that allow people to move quickly between neighborhoods.

Automobiles will undoubtedly still be in use four decades from now, but their numbers will be fewer and their role smaller. Within cities, only electric or clean hydrogen-powered vehicles are likely to be permitted, and most of these will be highly efficient "city cars." The energy to run them may well come from solar power plants. Families might rent efficient larger vehicles for vacations.

The bicycle will also play a major role in getting people about, as it already does in much of Asia as well as in some industrial-country towns and cities—in Amsterdam and Davis, California, bike-path networks encourage widespread pedaling. There are already twice as many bikes as cars worldwide. In the bicycle-centered transport system of 2030, the ratio could easily be 10 to 1.

Forty years from now, people will live closer to their jobs, and much socializing and shopping will be done by bike rather than in a 1-ton automobile. Computerized delivery services may allow people to shop from home—consuming less time as well as less energy. Telecommunications will substitute for travel as well. In addition, a world that allows only 2 billion tons of carbon emissions cannot be trucking vast quantities of food and other items thousands of miles; this is apt to encourage more decentralization of agriculture and allow local produce suppliers to flourish.

The automobile-based modern world is now only about 40 years old, but with its damaging air pollution and traffic congestion it hardly represents the pinnacle of human social evolution. Although a world where cars play a minor role may be hard to imagine, our grandparents would have had just as hard a time visualizing today's world of traffic jams and smog-filled cities.

NOTHING TO WASTE

In the sustainable, efficient economy of 2030, waste reduction and recycling industries will have largely replaced the garbage collection and disposal companies of today. The throwaway society that emerged during the late-twentieth century uses so much energy, emits so much carbon, and generates so much air pollution, acid rain, water pollution, toxic waste, and rubbish that it is strangling itself. Rooted as it is in planned obsolescence and appeals to convenience, it will be seen by historians as an aberration.

A hierarchy of options will guide materials policy in the year 2030. The first priority, of course, will be to avoid using any nonessential item. Second will be to reuse a product directly—for example, refilling a glass beverage container. The third will be to recycle the material to form a new product. Fourth, the material can be burned to extract whatever energy it contains, as long as this can be done safely. The option of last resort will be disposal in a landfill.

In the sustainable economy of 2030, the principal source of materials for industry will be recycled goods. Most of the raw material for the aluminum mill will come from the local scrap collection center, not from the bauxite mine. The steel mills of the future will feed on worn-out automobiles, household appliances, and industrial equipment. Paper and paper products will be produced at recycling mills, in which paper will move through a series of uses, from high-quality bond to newsprint and, eventually, to cardboard boxes. Industries will turn to virgin raw materials only to replace any losses in use and recycling.

The effect on air and water quality will be obvious. For example, steel produced from scrap reduces air pollution by 85 percent, cuts water pollution by 76 percent, and eliminates mining wastes altogether. Making paper from recycled material reduces pollutants entering the air by 74 percent and the water by 35 percent. It also reduces pressures on forests in direct proportion to the amount recycled.

The economic reasons for such careful husbanding of materials will by 2030 seem quite obvious. Just 5 percent as much energy is needed to recycle aluminum as to produce it from bauxite ore. For steel produced entirely from scrap, the saving amounts to roughly two-thirds. Newsprint from recycled paper takes 25 to 60 percent less energy to make than that from wood pulp. Recycling glass saves up to a third of the energy embodied in the original product.

Societies in 2030 may also have decided to replace multi-sized and -shaped beverage containers with a set of standardized ones made of durable glass that can be reused many times. These could be used for fruit juices, beer, milk, and soda pop.

One of the cornerstones of a sustainable society will likely be its elimination of waste flows at the source. Industry will have restructured manufacturing processes to slash wastes by a third or more from 1990 levels. Food packaging, which in 1986 cost American consumers more than American farmers earned selling their crops, will have been streamlined. Food items buried in three or four layers of packaging will be a distant memory.

As recycling reaches its full potential over the next 40 years, households will begin to compost yard wastes rather than put them out for curbside pickup. A lost art in many communities now, composting will experience a revival. Garbage flows will be reduced by one-fifth or more and gardeners will have a rich source of humus.

In addition to recycling and reusing metal, glass, and paper, a sustainable society must also recycle nutrients. In nature, one organism's waste is another's sustenance. In cities, however, human sewage has become a troublesome source of water pollution. Properly treated to prevent the spread of disease and to remove contaminants, sewage will be systematically returned to the land in vegetable-growing greenbelts around cities, much as is done in Shanghai and other Asian cities today.

Other cities will probably find it more efficient to follow Calcutta's example and use treated human sewage to fertilize aquacultural operations. A steady flow of nutrients from human waste can help nourish aquatic life, that in turn is consumed by fish.

HOW TO FEED EIGHT BILLION

Imagine trying to meet the food, fuel, and timber needs of eight billion people—nearly three billion more than the current world population—with 960 billion fewer tons of topsoil (more than twice the amount on all U.S. cropland) and one billion fewer acres of trees (an area more than half the size of the continental United States).

That, in a nutshell, will be the predicament faced by society in 2030 if current rates of soil erosion and deforestation continue unaltered for the next 40 years. It is a fate that can only be avoided through major changes in land use.

Of necessity, societies in 2030 will be using the land intensively; the needs of a population more than half again as large as today's cannot be met otherwise. But, unlike the present, tomorrow's land-use patterns would be abiding by basic principles of biological stability: nutrient retention, carbon balance, soil protection, water conservation, and preservation of species diversity. Harvests will rarely exceed sustainable yields.

Meeting food needs will pose monumental challenges, as some simple numbers illustrate. By 2030, assuming cropland area expands by 5 percent between now and then and that population grows to eight billion, cropland per person will have dropped to a third less than we have in today's inadequately fed world. Virtually all of Asia, and especially China, will be struggling to feed its people from a far more meager base of per-capital cropland area.

In light of these constraints, the rural landscapes of 2030 are likely to exhibit greater diversity than they do now. Variations in soils, slope, climate, and water availability will require different patterns and strains of crops grown in different ways to maximize sustainable output. For example, farmers may adopt numerous forms of agroforestry—the combined production of crops and trees—to provide food, biomass, and fodder, while also adding nutrients to soils and controlling water runoff.

Also, successfully adapting to changed climates resulting from greenhouse warming, as well as to water scarcity and other resource constraints, may lead scientists to draw on a much broader base of crop varieties. For example, a greater area will be devoted to salt-tolerant and drought-resistant crops.

Efforts to arrest desertification, now claiming 15 million acres each year, may by 2030 have transformed the gullied highlands of Ethiopia and other degraded areas into productive terrain. Much of the sloping land rapidly losing topsoil will be terraced and protected by shrubs or nitrogen-fixing trees planted along the contour.

Halting desertification also depends on eliminating overgrazing. The global livestock herd in 2030 is likely to be much smaller than today's three billion. It seems inevitable that adequately nourishing a world population 60 percent larger than today's will preclude feeding a third of the global grain harvest to livestock and poultry, as is currently the case. As meat becomes more expensive, the diets of the affluent will move down the food chain to greater consumption of grains and vegetables; this will also prolong lifespans.

A HEALTHY RESPECT FOR FORESTS

Forests and woodlands will be valued more highly and for many more reasons in 2030 than is the case today. The planet's mantle of trees, already a third smaller than in preagricultural times and shrinking by more than 27 million acres per year now, will be stable or expanding as a result of serious efforts to slow deforestation and to replant vast areas.

Long before 2030, the clearing of most tropical forests will have ceased. Since most of the nutrients in these ecosystems are held in the leaves and biomass of the vegetation rather than in the soil, only activities that preserve the forest canopy are sustainable. While it is impossible to say how much virgin tropical forest would remain in 2030 if sustainability is achieved, certainly the rate of deforestation will have had to slow dramatically by the end of this decade. Soon thereafter it will come to a halt.

Efforts to identify and protect unique parcels of forest will probably have led to a widely dispersed network of preserves. But a large portion of tropical forests still standing in 2030 will be exploited in a variety of benign ways by people living in and around them. Hundreds of "extractive reserves" will exist, areas in which local people harvest rubber, resins, nuts, fruits, medicines, and other forest products.

Efforts to alleviate the fuel-wood crisis in developing countries, to reduce flooding and landslides in hilly regions, and to slow the buildup of carbon dioxide may spur the planting of an additional 500 million acres or so of trees. Many of these plantings will be on private farms as part of agroforestry systems, but plantations may also have an expanded role. Cities and villages will turn to managed woodlands on their outskirts to contribute fuel for heating, cooking, and electricity. This wood will substitute for some portion of coal and oil use and, since harvested on a sustained-yield basis, will make no net contribution of carbon dioxide to the atmosphere.

Restoring and stabilizing the biological resource base by 2030 depends on a pattern of land ownership and use far more equitable than today's. Much of the degradation now occurring stems from the heavily skewed distribution of land that, along with population growth, pushes poor people into ever more marginal environments. Stewardship requires that people have plots large enough to sustain their families without abusing the land, access to means of using the land productively, and the right to pass it on to their children.

No matter what technologies come along, the biochemical process of photosynthesis, carried out by green plants, will remain the basis for meeting many human needs, and its efficiency can only be marginally improved. Given that humanity already appropriates an estimated 40 percent of the earth's annual photosynthetic product on land, the urgency of slowing the growth in human numbers is obvious. The sooner societies stabilize their populations, the greater will be their opportunities for achieving equitable and stable patterns of land use that can meet their needs indefinitely.

ECONOMIC PROGRESS IN A NEW LIGHT

The fundamental changes that are needed in energy, forestry, agriculture, and other physical systems cannot occur without corresponding shifts in social, economic, and moral character. During the transition to sustainability, political leaders and citizens alike will be forced to reevaluate their goals and aspirations and to adjust to a new set of principles that have at their core the welfare of future generations.

Shifts in employment will be among the most visible as the transition gets underway. Moving from fossil fuels to a diverse set of renewable energy sources, extracting fewer materials from the earth and recycling more, and revamping farming and forestry practices will greatly expand opportunities in new areas. Job losses in coal mining, auto production, and metals prospecting will be offset by gains in the manufacture and sale of photovoltaic solar cells, wind turbines, bicycles, mass-transit equipment, and a host of technologies for recycling materials.

Since planned obsolescence will itself be obsolete in a sustainable society, a far greater share of workers will be employed in repair, maintenance, and recycling activities than in the extraction of virgin materials and production of new goods.

Wind prospectors, energy efficiency auditors, and solar architects will be among the professions booming from the shift to a highly efficient, renewable energy economy. Numbering in the hundreds of thousands today, jobs in these fields may collectively total in the millions worldwide within a few decades. Opportunities in forestry will expand markedly.

As the transition to a more environmentally sensitive economy progresses, sustainability will gradually eclipse growth as the focus of economic policymaking. Over the next few decades, government policies will encourage investments that promote stability and endurance at the expense of those that simply expand short-term production.

As a yardstick of progress, the gross national product (GNP) will be seen as a bankrupt indicator. By measuring flows of goods and services, GNP undervalues the qualities a sustainable society strives for, such as durability and resource protection; and overvalues planned obsolescence and waste. The pollution caused by a coal-burning power plant, for instance, raises GNP by requiring expenditures on lung disease treatment and the purchase of a scrubber to control emis-sions. Yet society would be far better off if power were generated in ways that did not pollute the air in the first place.

National military budgets in a sustainable world will be a small fraction of what they are today. Moreover, sustainability cannot be achieved without a massive shift of resources from military endeavors into energy efficiency, soil conservation, tree planting, family planning, and other needed development activities. Rather than maintaining large defense establishments, governments may come to rely on a strengthened U.N. peacekeeping force.

A NEW SET OF VALUES

Movement toward a lasting society cannot occur without a transformation of individual priorities and values. Throughout the ages, philosophers and religious leaders have denounced materialism as a path to human fulfillment. Yet societies across the ideological spectrum have persisted in equating quality of life with increased consumption.

Because of the strain on resources it creates, materialism simply cannot survive the transition to a sustainable world. As public understanding of the need to adopt simpler and less consumptive lifestyles spreads, it will become unfashionable to own fancy new cars and clothes and the latest electronic devices. The potential benefits of unleashing the human energy now devoted to producing, advertising, buying, consuming, and discarding material goods are enormous.

As the amassing of personal and national wealth becomes less of a goal, the gap between haves and have nots will gradually close; this will eliminate many societal tensions. Ideological differences may fade as well, as nations adopt sustainability as a common cause, and as they come to recognize that achieving it requires a shared set of values that includes democratic principles, freedom to innovate, respect for human rights, and acceptance of diversity. With the cooperative tasks involved in repairing the earth so many and so large, the idea of waging war could become an anachronism.

The task of building a sustainable society is an enormous one that will take decades rather than years. Indeed, it is an undertaking that will easily absorb the energies that during the past 40 years have been devoted to the Cold War. The reward in the year 2030 could be an Earth Day with something to celebrate: the achievement of a society in balance with the resources that support it, instead of one that destroys the underpinnings of its future.

STUDY QUESTIONS

1. Evaluate the proposals set forth by Brown and his associates. Are they unduly optimistic about the future? Or are their predictions unrealistic? With which individual aspects do you agree or disagree? Explain your answer.

2. What do you think the world will be like in the year 2030? Set forth your vision and compare it with Brown and company.

FOR FURTHER READING

Berry, Wendell. *The Unsettling of America*. San Francisco: Sierra Club Books, 1986.

Brown, Lester. *State of the World 1993*. New York: Norton, 1993.

Clark, W. C. *Sustainable Development of the Biosphere*. Cambridge: Cambridge University Press, 1986.

Commoner, Barry. *Making Peace with the Planet*. New York: Pantheon Books, 1990.

Daly, Herman E., and John B. Cobb, Jr. *For the Common Good: Redirecting the Economy Toward Community, the Environment, and a Sustainable Future*. Boston: Beacon Press, 1989.

Dobson, Andrew, ed., *The Green Reader: Essays Toward a Sustainable Society*. San Francisco: Mercury House, 1991.

Goldsmith, Edward. *The Way: An Ecological World-View*. Boston: Sambala, 1993.

Kay, Jane Holz. *Asphalt Nation: How the Automobile Took over America and How We Can Take it Back*. New York: Crown Publishers, 1997.

Pojman, Louis P. *Global Environmental Ethics*. Mountain View, CA: Mayfield, 2000.

Revkin, Andrew. *The Burning Season*. Boston: Houghton Mifflin, 1990.

Sagoff, Mark. *The Economy of the Earth*. Cambridge: Cambridge University Press, 1988.

Sayer, K. M., and K. E. Goodpaster, eds. *Ethics and Problems of the 21st Century*. Notre Dame, IN: University of Notre Dame Press, 1979.

Scientific American. "Managing the Earth." Special Issue, 26, no. 3 (September 1989).

Shrader-Frechette, Kristin. *Science, Policy, Ethics, and Economic Methodology*. Boston: Reidel, 1985.

Timberlake, Lloyd. *Only One Earth: Living for the Future*. New York: Sterling, 1987.

Tokar, Michael. *The Green Alternative: Creating an Alternative Future*. San Pedro, CA: R & E Miles, 1988.

Westra, Laura. *The Principle of Integrity: An Environmental Proposal for Ethics*. Lanham, MD: Rowman & Littlefield, 1994.

Young, John E. *Discarding the Throwaway Society*. Washington, D.C.: Worldwatch Paper 101, 1991.